INTRODUCING PHILOSOPHY

A Text with Integrated Readings

Fifth Edition

Robert C. Solomon

University of Texas at Austin

Under the general editorship of
Robert J. Fogelin
Dartmouth College

Harcourt Brace College Publishers

Fort Worth   Philadelphia   San Diego   New York   Orlando   Austin   San Antonio
Toronto   Montreal   London   Sydney   Tokyo

Editor-in-Chief Ted Buchholz
Acquisitions Editor David Tatom
Developmental Editor Phoebe Woolbright Culp
Senior Project Editor Cliff Crouch
Production Manager J. Montgomery Shaw
Book Designers Serena Barnett Manning, Bill Brammer

Library of Congress Cataloging-in-Publication Data

Solomon, Robert C.
    Introducing philosophy : a text with integrated readings / Robert
C. Solomon. — 5th ed.
        p.   cm.
    Includes bibliographical references and index.
    ISBN 0-15-500376-3 (pbk.)
    1. Philosophy—Introductions.   I. Title.
BD21.S55   1992   92-53791
100—dc20   CIP

On the cover: Sarah Canright, *Israfel* (detail), 1986

Special acknowledgments of copyright ownership and of permission to reproduce works (or excerpts thereof) included in this volume follow the index and constitute an extension of this page.

Address editorial correspondence to: 301 Commerce Street, Suite 3700
                                        Fort Worth, Texas 76102
            Address orders to: 6277 Sea Harbor Drive
                                 Orlando, Florida 32887
                                 1-800-782-4479, or 1-800-433-0001 (in Florida)

Printed in the United States of America
3 4 5 6 7 8 9 0 1 2 016 9 8 7 6 5 4 3 2

For Vita P. Solomon
She brought me into life
and taught me it was art.

CONTENTS IN BRIEF

PREFACE

Introducing Philosophy: A Text with Integrated Readings presupposes no background in the subject and no special abilities. Intended primarily as a textbook for a one- or two-semester introductory course, the book provides not so much a course in itself as the materials for a course from which instructors and students can focus on a variety of problems and perspectives. The point of this text is to present students with alternatives on every issue and let them arrive at their own individual conclusions. These conclusions should be based on arguments in class and with friends or classmates, as well as on the discussions in this book. The assumption here is that the purpose of philosophy is to encourage everyone to think for himself or herself and that no single source of arguments or information can take the place of personal dialogues and discussions. A textbook is ultimately a sourcebook; everything in it is to be taken as a cause for further argument, not as a final statement of results. This text does not attempt to sway students toward any particular philosophical positions but rather presents basic philosophical problems and powerful philosophical arguments to enable students to think for themselves. That is what philosophy is about — thinking for oneself on basic issues.

This book derives from twenty years of teaching in very different schools in various states and cities. It is based on the belief that philosophy is a genuinely exciting subject, accessible not only to specialists and a few gifted undergraduate majors but to everyone. Everyone is a philosopher, whether enrolled in a philosophy course or not. Most of us are concerned with the same basic problems and use the same essential arguments. The difference is that someone who has studied philosophy has the advantage of having encountered stronger and more varied arguments than might have been available otherwise. In this book the views of the major philosophers of the past twenty-five hundred years are used to give students these various arguments. This approach has the advantage of offering introductory students the opportunity of having direct contact with substantial readings from significant works in the history of philosophy, but without the unreasonable demand that they confront these often difficult works in full and without commentary or editing, as they would in the originals or in most anthologies. This book is not, however, a historical introduction as such but rather an introduction to the *problems* of philosophy and the various ways in which they have been answered. The history of philosophy thus serves to illuminate these problems and replies, not the other way around.

Although the language of philosophy often is specialized and sometimes difficult, this book is as free of jargon and special terminology as is possible.

Where necessary, the most important and widely used philosophical terms are carefully introduced within the text and also summarized in glossaries at the end of each chapter. At the end of the book are brief biographies of the philosophers discussed in the text. Although the book deals principally with the philosophers' ideas rather than with their lives, it nevertheless is valuable to have the student learn their place in history.

Responses to the first four editions of *Introducing Philosophy* have been both gratifying and helpful in the preparation of this revision for a new generation of students. In this fifth edition, I have continued to edit the readings for clarity, develop the commentary and add new selections, but the most dramatic changes in the new edition are the addition and integration of the latest in feminist and "multicultural" material. This has affected virtually every chapter. The organization of the book remains mainly the same, and the new readings and commentary have been added within the existing structure. I have made every effort to integrate this material into the chapters and not present feminist and multicultural authors and texts as marginal afterthoughts; but, at the same time, I have made every effort to allow the instructor to give a traditional (strictly Western) course and skip over new material if he or she chooses to do so. The format of this book has been designed with this in mind.

In Chapter 1, I have supplemented the material on the pre-Socratic Greeks with some more or less contemporary discussions from that same remarkable period in history, when philosophy began not only in the Eastern Mediterranean but in India and China as well. In Chapter 2, I have added to the existing material on European rationalism a contrasting treatment of substance in non-Western philosophy. In Chapter 3, I have added some material on feminism, Indian epistemology, and skepticism. I have rewritten Chapter 4 to emphasize the problem of relativism. I have added some material on African philosophy, an excerpt from Schopenhauer (who was deeply influenced by Eastern philosophy), and a well-known essay by Richard Rorty. I have rewritten Chapter 6 to emphasize the great variety of world religions, giving more attention to non-Western religions and more attention to Islam. I have combined and rewritten Chapters 7 and 8 to expand the discussion of selfhood and bring in more material from other cultures and philosophical traditions. Chapters 9 through 12 have been rewritten to include feminist and non-Western concerns with freedom, ethics, justice, and art. I have tried to make these important additions without violating the philosophy sequences established in the earlier four editions. The following section will make clear the various possibilities for using *Introducing Philosophy* as a beginning philosophy textbook.

FOR THE INSTRUCTOR: HOW TO USE THIS BOOK

Introducing Philosophy is written for a complete course, and the chapters build on one another in logical sequence. But the book is also flexible, and each chapter has been written as an independent unit so that it is possible to use the text in a variety of ways and for a variety of courses. Within each chapter, too, various sections can be selected for shorter discussion. For example, some instructors may want to use only the first sections of Chapter 6 ("Religion") or only a few key sections from Chapter 7 ("Self") and 9 ("Freedom"). Some may want to emphasize the new multicultural material. Others may choose to skip over it.

A full course might include the Introduction and all eleven chapters, but this may be a heavy load for an average one-term course. At the other extreme, a short course (for example, a summer term or a class that meets only once a week, a quarter system, or a class that prefers to treat a few central issues in detail) might use only half the chapters. The following outlines are suggestions for a variety of uses of the book adapted to different lengths and kinds of classes:

>   Maximum course (one very full term):
>   Introduction, Chapters 1–11.
>   Minimum course (summer, part-time, quarter):
>   Introduction, Chapters 1, 3, 6, 8, and 7; possibly 9.
>   Two-term course:
>   First term: Introduction, Chapter 1–6;
>   Second term: Introduction, Chapters 7–11.
>   Average course (14–16 week term; chapters in parentheses are optional):
>   Introduction, Chapters 1, (2), 3, (4), 6, 7, 8, (9), (10), (11).
>   Ethics and Religion course:
>   Introduction, Chapters 6, 7, 9, (10), (11).
>   Metaphysics and Epistemology course:
>   Introduction, Chapters 1, 2, 3, 4, (5), (6), (7), 8.

Chapters 4 and 5 are the most difficult and thus may be the first deleted by some classes. Other classes may prefer to begin with either Chapter 6 ("Religion") or Chapter 9 ("Ethics") and reorder the sequence of chapters. Chapter 2 (which discusses the metaphysics of Descartes, Spinoza, and Leibniz) also may be deleted for many shorter courses. Therefore, the basic course—tailored to the average one-term, 14–16 week class meeting three times a week—would be:

>   Introduction, Chapters 1, 3, 6, 7, 8, 9.

The remaining chapters can be added as time and interest permit.

In this edition, I have used alphabetic letters to designate sections and subsections with the chapters. Because some of the most important chapters (e.g., "Knowledge," "Self," "Freedom," "Ethics") are quite long and involved, many instructors prefer to assign just this or that set of sections, rather than an entire chapter. The lettering of sections should make such scheduling much easier. For instance, in Chapter 4 some instructors may prefer to deal only with the standard four theories of truth and dispense with the material on European philosophy (Kant and after) in the sections that follow. Others may prefer to delete the theories of truth in Chapter 3 and launch right into Kant following the discussion of Hume. So too, some instructors may prefer to deal with the arguments concerning God's existence but dispense with the problem of evil; some may want to talk only about the basic problem of freedom versus determinism without subjecting students to the (comparative) subtleties and intrigue of the variations of "soft determinism." Other instructors may want to teach a brief history of ethics (Aristotle, Hume, Kant, Mill) without treating such general topics as ethical relativism or such technical concerns as those of metaethics. I am confident that this edition makes all of this much easier to do.

FOR THE STUDENT: *DOING* PHILOSOPHY

Your attempt to develop your own thoughts – to "do" philosophy as well as to read what others have done – is central to any study of philosophy. Philosophy, more than any other field, is not so much a subject as it is *a way of thinking*, one that can be appreciated fully only by joining in. While reading each section, therefore, do not hesitate to put down the book at any time and do your own thinking and writing. When reading about metaphysics, for example, think about how you would develop your own view of reality and how you would answer the questions raised by the first philosophers of ancient Greece or the Orient. When confronted by an argument, consider how you might argue for – or against – the same position. When facing an idea that seems very foreign to you, try to put it in your own terms and understand the vision that lies behind it. And when facing a problem, always be certain that you make the attempt to answer it for yourself as well as to read through the answers offered by earlier thinkers. In philosophy, unlike physics or biology, your own answer may be just as legitimate as those given by the philosophers of the past, and there may be equally interesting answers from different traditions. That is what makes philosophy so difficult to learn at first, but it is also what makes it so personally valuable and enjoyable.

WRITING PHILOSOPHY

With the foregoing in mind, it should be obvious why *talking* about philosophy with friends and classmates, raising questions and objections in class, and *writing* down ideas are so very important. Articulation reinforces comprehension, and arguing against objections broadens understanding. Writing papers in philosophy is a particularly important part of any philosophy course, and there are certain general guidelines to keep in mind:

1. Philosophy is concerned with *problems*, so always begin your essay with a leading *question*. "Thinking about" some philosophical issue can be fun, but too easily loses direction and purpose. For instance, thinking about "freedom" involves too much territory, far too many different problems and perspectives. Asking such questions as "Is freedom of action compatible with scientific determinism?" or "Can there be freedom in a socialist state?" gives your thinking a specific orientation and way of proceeding.

2. Be clear about the difficulties you face in tackling the question. Are the terms of the question clear? (It is not necessary to "define terms" at the start of your essay. Indeed, defining the key term might be the basic and most difficult conclusion you reach.) Also, it is often a poor idea to consult a dictionary (even a good one) as a way of clarifying your question. Dictionaries are not written by philosphers and generally reflect popular usage – which may include just such philosophical misunderstandings as you are attempting to correct.

3. Make clear what you are arguing. Don't force the reader (your professor) to guess where you are going. When you are clear about the ques-

tion you ask, it will help you clarify the answer you intend giving, and vice versa. In fact, you may well change your mind—both about the question and the answer—several times while you are writing (the real danger of attempting a one-draft-the-night-before approach to essay writing.)

4. *Argue* your case. Show clearly why you hold the position you do. The most frequent criticism of student papers is, "This is your assertion; where is the argument?"

5. Anticipate objections to your position and to your arguments, and take the offensive against rival positions. If you don't know what your position is opposed to, it is doubtful you are clear about what your own position is. If you can't imagine how anyone could possibly disagree with you, you probably haven't thought through your position thoroughly and carefully.

6. Don't be afraid to be yourself, to be humorous, or charming, or sincere, or personal. The most powerful philosophical writings—those that have endured for centuries—often reflect the author's deepest concerns and attitudes toward life. However, remember that no philosophical writing can be *just* humorous, or charming, or sincere, or personal. What makes it philosophy is that it involves general concerns and careful arguments, and that it attempts to prove an important point and answer one of the age-old questions.

ACKNOWLEDGMENTS

This book and its four previous editions have been made possible through the encouragement and help of many people, most importantly the several thousand introductory students I have had the pleasure of meeting and teaching over the past decade. For the original edition, I thank Susan Zaleski for her very special insights and criticism of the manuscript in its early stages; and Robert Fogelin, John McDermott, George Cronk, and Roland D. Zimany, for their encouragement and helpful suggestions. And I thank Terry Boswell, Lisa Erlich, David Blumenfeld, Paul Woodruff, Harry O'Hara, Stephanie Lewis, and Barbara Barratt, for their time and good advice. Revisions for the second edition were suggested by Paul Woodruff, Billy Joe Lucas, and Cheshire Calhoun. I benefited in the third edition from advice given by Peter Hutcheson, Richard Palmer, Norman Thomas, Greta Reed, Edward Johnson, Paul Woodruff, Don Branson, Hoke Robinson, Robert Fogelin, Meredith Michaels, Bruce Paternoster, and Maxine Morphis. I owe a special debt of gratitude to Bruce Ballard, both for his editorial suggestions and for his extensive help with the third-edition manuscript. And in the fourth edition, I was grateful for the constructive suggestions of Jeffery Coombs, Timothy Owen Davis, Conrad Gromada, Gregory Landini, Dan Bonevac, Paul Woodruff, Steven Phillips, Kathleen Higgins and Kristy Bartlett.

For this fifth edition, I owe a very special debt of gratitude to Janet Sepasi, who once again has combined her philosophical knowledge and enthusiasm, her talent for teaching and research, and her sensitivity to both students and the philosophical literature of other cultures to help me produce this improved textbook. I am also thankful for good advice from Marilyn Frye (Michigan State University), Jonathan Westphal (University of Hawaii), David J. Paul (Western Michigan University), Edward Johnson (University of New Orleans), Fred Tabor (Whatcom Community College), and Brian Kutin (Parkland Community College). Thanks also go to Clancy Martin for the index. Again I thank Steve Phillips for his continuing help in my understanding of Indian texts and philosophy.

At Harcourt Brace Jovanovich, my editors — David Tatom, Phoebe Woolbright Culp, and Cliff Crouch — have earned my appreciation for their work to give this edition its own distinctive character. Also deserving recognition are production manager Monty Shaw and designers Bill Brammer and Serena Barnett Manning. But I also want above all to once again thank my first philosophy teachers — Robert Hanson, Doris Yokum, Elizabeth Flower, James Ross, and C.G. Hempel — who provided me with the models and the materials for an ideal introductory philosophy course, and the many students who still continue to make the teaching of philosophy one of the more satisfying professions in a not easily satisfying world.

R.C.S.

CONTENTS

Introduction: Philosophy

The unexamined life is not worth living.

SOCRATES

A. SOCRATES

He was not the first philosopher, but he was, and is still, the ideal of philosophers. Once assured by the oracle at Delphi that he was the wisest man in Athens, Socrates (470–399 B.C.) borrowed his view of life from the inscription at Delphi, "Know Thyself." Mixing humility with arrogance, he boasted that his superiority lay in his awareness of his own ignorance, and he spent the rest of his life making fools of the self-proclaimed "wise men" of Athens.

In the opinion of Socrates and other critics of the time, the government of Athens was corrupt and notoriously bumbling, in marked contrast to the "Golden Age" of Pericles a few years before. Philosophical arguments had become all cleverness and demagoguery, rhetorical tricks to win arguments and legal cases; political ambition replaced justice and the search for the good life. Socrates believed that the people of Athens held their principles glibly, like banners at a football game, but rarely lived up to them and even more rarely examined them. Against this, he developed a technique of asking seemingly innocent questions, trapping his audience in their own confusions and hypocrisies, exploding the pretensions of his times. And against their easy certainties, he taught that "the unexamined life is not worth living." He referred to himself as a "gadfly" (an obnoxious insect with a painful bite), keeping his fellow citizens from ever becoming as smug and self-righteous as they would like to have been. Accordingly, he made many enemies and was satirized by Aristophanes in his play *The Clouds*.

◆ from *The Clouds,* by Aristophanes

STUDENT OF SOCRATES: Socrates asked Chaerephon how many of its own feet a flea could jump—one had bitten Chaerephon's brow and then jumped to Socrates' head.
STREPSIADES: And how did he measure the jump?
STUDENT: Most ingeniously. He melted wax, caught the flea, dipped its feet, and the hardened wax made Persian slippers. Unfastening these, he found their size.
STREPSIADES: Royal Zeus! What an acute intellect!
STUDENT: But yesterday a high thought was lost through a lizard.
STREPSIADES: How so? Tell me.
STUDENT: As he gaped up at the moon, investigating her paths and turnings, from off the roof a lizard befouled him.[1]

In the play, Aristophanes made Socrates and his students look utterly ridiculous, and the Athenian public enjoyed Aristophanes' sarcasm as a mild form of vengeance for Socrates' constant criticisms. Aristophanes' "clouds" refer to that confusion which we mean when we talk to someone "having his head in the clouds." Aristophanes probably expressed the general public opinion when he described Socrates as "shiftless" and merely a master at verbal trickery.

Socrates' students, however, virtually worshiped him. They described him as "the bravest, most wise and most upright man of our times" and perceived him as a martyr for the truth in a corrupted society. The price of his criticism was not merely the satire of the playwrights. Because he had been such a continual nuisance, the government arranged to have Socrates brought to trial for "corrupting the youth of Athens" and being an "atheist." And for these trumped-up "crimes," Socrates was condemned to death. But at his trial, he once again became a gadfly to those who condemned him.

◆ from *The Apology,* by Plato

There are many other reasons for my not being angry with you for convicting me, gentlemen of the jury, and what happened was not unexpected. I am much more surprised at the number of votes cast on each side, for I did not think the decision would be by so few votes but by a great many. As it is, a switch of only thirty votes would have acquitted me. I think myself that I have been cleared on Meletus' charges, and it is clear to all that, if Anytus and Lycon

[1] Aristophanes, *The Clouds,* in *The Complete Plays of Aristophanes,* trans. Moses Hadas (New York: Bantam, 1962).

had not joined him in accusing me, he would have been fined a thousand drachmas for not receiving a fifth of the votes.

He assesses the penalty at death. So be it. What counter-assessment should I propose to you, gentlemen of the jury? Clearly it should be a penalty I deserve, and what do I deserve to suffer or to pay because I have deliberately not led a quiet life but have neglected what occupies most people: wealth, household affairs, the position of general or public orator or the other offices, the political clubs and factions that exist in the city? I thought myself too honest to survive if I occupied myself with those things. I did not follow that path that would have made me of no use either to you or to myself, but I went to each of you privately and conferred upon him what I say is the greatest benefit, by persuading him not to care for any of his belongings before caring that he himself should be as good and as wise as possible, not to care for the city's possessions more than for the city itself, and to care for other things in the same way. What do I deserve for being such a man? Some good, gentlemen of the jury, if I must truly make an assessment according to my deserts, and something suitable.

Socrates here suggests that the state should give him a pension rather than a punishment, for being a public benefactor and urging his students to be virtuous.

It is for the sake of a short time, gentlemen of the jury, that you will acquire the reputation and the guilt, in the eyes of those who want to denigrate the city, of having killed Socrates, a wise man, for they will say that I am wise even if I am not. If you had waited but a little while, this would have happened of its own accord. You see my age, that I am already advanced in years and close to death. I am saying this not to all of you but to those who condemned me to death, and to these same jurors I say: Perhaps you think that I was convicted for lack of such words as might have convinced you, if I thought I should say or do all I could to avoid my sentence. Far from it. I was convicted because I lacked not words but boldness and shamelessness and the willingness to say to you what you would most gladly have heard from me, lamentations and tears and my saying and doing many things that I say are unworthy of me but that you are accustomed to hear from others. I did not think then that the danger I ran should make me do anything mean, nor do I now regret the nature of my defense. I would much rather die after this kind of defense than live after making the other kind. Neither I nor any other man should, on trial or in war, contrive to avoid death at any cost. Indeed it is often obvious in battle that one could escape death by throwing away one's weapons and by turning to supplicate one's pursuers, and there are many ways to avoid death in every kind of danger if one will venture to do or say anything to avoid it. It is not difficult to avoid death, gentlemen of the jury, it is much more difficult to avoid wickedness, for it runs faster than death. Slow and elderly as I am, I have been caught by the slower pursuer, whereas my accusers, being clever and sharp, have been caught by the quicker, wickedness. I leave you now, condemned to death by you, but they are condemned by truth to wickedness and injustice. So I maintain my assessment, and they maintain theirs. This perhaps had to happen, and I think it is as it should be.

Now I want to prophesy to those who convicted me, for I am at the point when men prophesy most, when they are about to die. I say gentlemen, to those who voted to kill me, that vengeance will come upon you immediately after my death, a vengeance much harder to bear than that which you took in killing me. You did this in the belief that you would avoid giving an account of your life, but I maintain that quite the opposite will happen to you. There will be more people to test you, whom I now held back, but you did not notice it. They will be more difficult to deal with as they will be younger and you will resent them more. You are wrong if you believe that by killing people you will prevent anyone from reproaching you for not living in the right way. To escape such tests is neither possible nor good, but it is best and easiest not to discredit others but to prepare oneself to be as good as possible. With this prophecy to you who convicted me, I part from you.[2]

In prison, he was given the opportunity to escape. He refused it. He had always taught that "the really important thing is not to live, but to live well." And to "live well" meant, along with the more enjoyable things in life, to live according to your principles. When his friend Crito tried to persuade him otherwise, Socrates responded in this manner:

◆ from *The Crito*, by Plato

SOCRATES: My good Crito, why should we care so much for what the majority think? The most reasonable people, to whom one should pay more attention, will believe that things were done as they were done.

CRITO: You see, Socrates, that one must also pay attention to the opinion of the majority. Your present situation makes clear that the majority can inflict not the least but pretty well the greatest evils if one is slandered among them.

SOCRATES: Would that the majority could inflict the greatest evils, for they would then be capable of the greatest good, and that would be fine, but now they cannot do either. They cannot make a man either wise or foolish, but they inflict things haphazardly.

---

[2]Plato, *The Apology,* in *The Trial and Death of Socrates,* 2nd ed., trans. G. M. A. Grube (Indianapolis, IN: Hackett, 1974).

CRITO: That may be so. But tell me this, Socrates, are you anticipating that I and your other friends would have trouble with the
informers if you escape from here, as having stolen you away,
and that we should be compelled to lose all our property or pay
heavy fines and suffer other punishment besides? If you have
any such fear, forget it. We would be justified in running this risk
to save you, and worse, if necessary. Do follow my advice, and
do not act differently.

SOCRATES: I do have these things in mind, Crito, and also many
others.

CRITO: Have no such fear. It is not much money that some people require to save you and get you out of here.

. . . .

Besides, Socrates, I do not think that what you are doing is
right, to give up your life when you can save it, and to hasten
your fate as your enemies would hasten it, and indeed have hastened it in their wish to destroy you.

. . . .

SOCRATES: My dear Crito, your eagerness is worth much if it
should have some right aim; if not, then the greater your
keenness the more difficult it is to deal with. We must therefore
examine whether we should act in this way or not, as not only
now but at all times I am the kind of man who listens only to the
argument that on reflection seems best to me. I cannot, now that
this fate has come upon me, discard the arguments I used; they
seem to me much the same. I value and respect the same
principles as before, and if we have no better arguments to bring
up at this moment, be sure that I shall not agree with you, not
even if the power of the majority were to frighten us with more
bogeys, as if we were children, with threats of incarcerations and
executions and confiscation of property. How should we examine this matter most reasonably? Would it be by taking up first
your argument about the opinions of men, whether it is sound in
every case that one should pay attention to some opinions, but
not to others? Or was that well-spoken before the necessity to
die came upon me, but now it is clear that this was said in vain
for the sake of argument, that it was in truth play and nonsense?
I am eager to examine together with you, Crito, whether this argument will appear in any way different to me in my present
circumstances, or whether it remains the same, whether we are
to abandon it or believe it. It was said on every occasion that one
should greatly value some opinions, but not others. Does that
seem to you a sound statement?

. . . .

Examine the following statement in turn as to whether it stays
the same or not, that the most important thing is not life, but the
good life.

CRITO: It stays the same.

SOCRATES: And that the good life, the beautiful life, and the just life are the same; does that still hold, or not?

CRITO: It does hold.

SOCRATES: As we have agreed so far, we must examine next whether it is right for me to try to get out of here when the Athenians have not acquitted me. If it is seen to be right, we will try to do so; if it is not, we will abandon the idea. As for those questions you raise about money, reputation, the upbringing of children, Crito, those considerations in truth belong to those people who easily put men to death and would bring them to life again if they could, without thinking; I mean the majority of men. For us, however, since our argument leads to this, the only valid consideration, as we were saying just now, is whether we should be acting rightly in giving money and gratitude to those who will lead me out of here, and ourselves helping with the escape, or whether in truth we shall do wrong in doing all this. If it appears that we shall be acting unjustly, then we have no need at all to take into account whether we shall have to die, if we stay here and keep quiet, or suffer in another way, rather than do wrong.

CRITO: I think you put that beautifully, Socrates, but see what we should do.

SOCRATES: Let us examine the question together, my dear friend, and if you can make any objection while I am speaking, make it and I will listen to you, but if you have no objection to make, my dear Crito, then stop now from saying the same thing so often, that I must leave here against the will of the Athenians. I think it important to persuade you before I act, and not to act against your wishes. . . .

SOCRATES: Then . . . I ask you: when one has come to an agreement that is just with someone, should one fulfill it or cheat on it?

CRITO: One should fulfill it.

SOCRATES: See what follows from this: If we leave here without the city's permission, are we injuring people whom we should least injure? And are we sticking to a just agreement, or not?

CRITO: I cannot answer your question, Socrates, I do not know.

SOCRATES: Look at it this way. If, as we were planning to run away from here, or whatever one should call it, the laws and the state came and confronted us and asked: "Tell me, Socrates, what are you intending to do? Do you not by this action you are attempting intend to destroy us, the laws, and indeed the whole city, as far as you are concerned? Or do you think it possible for a city not to be destroyed if the verdicts of its courts have no force but are nullified and set at naught by private individuals?" What shall we answer to this and other such arguments? For many things could be said, especially by an orator on behalf of this law we are destroying, which orders that the judgments of the courts shall be carried out. Shall we say in answer, "The city wronged me, and its decision was not right." Shall we say that, or what?

CRITO: Yes, by Zeus, Socrates, that is our answer.

SOCRATES: Then what if the laws said, "Was that the agreement between us, Socrates, or was it to respect the judgments that the city came to?" And if we wondered at their words, they would perhaps add: "Socrates, do not wonder at what we say but answer, since you are accustomed to proceed by question and answer. Come now, what accusation do you bring against us and the city, that you should try to destroy us? Did we not, first, bring you to birth, and was it not through us that your father married your mother and begat you? Tell us, do you find anything to criticize in those of us who are concerned with marriage?" And I would say that I do not criticize them. "Or in those of us concerned with the nurture of babies and the education that you too received? Were those assigned to that subject not right to instruct your father to educate you in the arts and in physical culture?" And I would say that they were right. "Very well," they would continue, "and after you were born and nurtured and educated, could you, in the first place, deny that you are our offspring and servant, both you and your forefathers? If that is so, do you think that we are on an equal footing as regards the right, and that whatever we do to you it is right for you to do to us? You were not on an equal footing with your father as regards the right, nor with your master if you had one, so as to retaliate for anything they did to you, to revile them if they reviled you, to beat them if they beat you, and so with many other things. Do you think you have this right to retaliation against your country and its laws? That if we undertake to destroy you and think it right to do so, you can undertake to destroy us, as far as you can, in return? And will you say that you are right to do so, you who truly care for virtue? Is your wisdom such as not to realize that your country is to be honoured more than your mother, your father, and all your ancestors, that it is more to be revered and more sacred, and that it counts for more among the gods and sensible men, that you must worship it, yield to it and placate its anger more than your father's? You must either persuade it or obey its orders, and endure in silence whatever it instructs you to endure, whether blows or bonds, and if it leads you into war to be wounded or killed, you must obey. To do so is right, and one must not give way or retreat or leave one's post, but both in war and in courts and everywhere else, one must obey the commands of one's city and country, or persuade it as to the nature of justice. It is impious to bring violence to bear against your mother or father, it is much more so to use it against your country." What shall we say in reply, Crito, that the laws speak the truth, or not?

CRITO: I think they do.

SOCRATES: "Reflect now, Socrates," the laws might say, "that if what we say is true, you are not treating us rightly by planning to do what you are planning.

· · · · · · · · · ·

"So decisively did you choose us and agree to be a citizen under us. Also, you have had children in this city, thus showing that it was congenial to you. Then at your trial you could have assessed your penalty at exile if you wished, and you are now attempting to do against the city's wishes what you could then have done with her consent. Then you prided yourself that you did not resent death, but you chose, as you said, death in preference to exile. Now, however, those words do not make you ashamed, and you pay no heed to us, the laws, as you plan to destroy us, and you act like the meanest type of slave by trying to run away, contrary to your undertakings and your agreement to live as a citizen under us. First then, answer us on this very point, whether we speak the truth when we say that you agreed, not only in words but by your deeds, to live in accordance with us." What are we to say to that, Crito? Must we not agree?

CRITO: We must, Socrates.

SOCRATES: "Surely," they might say, "you are breaking the undertakings and agreements that you made with us without compulsion or deceit, and under no pressure of time for deliberation. You have had seventy years during which you could have gone away if you did not like us, and if you thought our agreements unjust. You did not choose to go to Sparta or to Crete, which you are always saying are well governed, nor to any other city, Greek or foreign. You have been away from Athens less than the lame or the blind or other handicapped people. It is clear that the city has been outstandingly more congenial to you than to other Athenians, and so have we, the laws, for what city can please if its laws do not? Will you then not now stick to our agreements? You will, Socrates, if we can persuade you, and not make yourself a laughingstock by leaving the city.

"Be persuaded by us who have brought you up, Socrates. Do not value either your children or your life or anything else more than goodness, in order that you may have all this as your defense before the rulers there. If you do this deed, you will not think it better or more just or more pious, nor will any one of your friends, nor will it be better for you when you arrive yonder. As it is, you depart, if you depart, after being wronged not by us, the laws, but by men; but if you depart after shamefully returning wrong for wrong and injury for injury, after breaking your agreement and contract with us, after injuring those you should injure least—yourself, your friends, your country and us—we shall be angry with you while you are still alive, and our brothers, the laws of the underworld, will not receive [you] kindly, knowing that you tried to destroy us as far as you could. Do not let Crito persuade you, rather than we, to do what he says."

· · · · · · · · · ·

CRITO: I have nothing to say, Socrates.

> SOCRATES: Let it be then, Crito, and let us act in this way, since this is the way the god is leading us.[3]

Socrates believed that the good of his "soul" was far more important than the transient pleasures of life. Accordingly, he preferred to die for his ideas than live as a hypocrite. An idea worth living for may be an idea worth dying for as well.

> And while he was saying this, he was holding the cup, and then drained it calmly and easily. Most of us had been able to hold back our tears reasonably well up till then, but when we saw him drinking it and after he drank it, we could hold them back no longer; my own tears came in floods against my will. So I covered my face. I was weeping for myself—not for him, but for my misfortune in being deprived of such a comrade. Even before me, Crito was unable to restrain his tears and got up. Apollodorus had not ceased from weeping before, and at this moment his noisy tears and anger made everybody present break down, except Socrates, "What is this," he said, "you strange fellows. It is mainly for this reason that I sent the women away, to avoid such unseemliness, for I am told one should die in good omened silence. So keep quiet and control yourselves."
>   . . . .
> Such was the end of our comrade, Echecrates, a man who, we would say, was of all those we have known the best, and also the wisest and the most upright.[4]

Is there anything that you believe so passionately that you would die for it? Is there anything that you believe so passionately that it really makes your life worth living? For most people, now as always, life is rather a matter of "getting by." One of the more popular phrases of self-praise these days is "I'm a survivor." But, ironically, a person who is not willing to die for anything (for example, his or her own freedom) is thereby more vulnerable to threats and corruption. To be willing to die—as Socrates was—is to have a considerable advantage over someone for whom "life is everything."

If you look closely at your life, not only at your proclaimed ideals and principles but your desires and ambitions as well, do the facts of your life add up to its best intentions? Or are you too just drifting with the times, dissatisfied with ultimately meaningless jobs and mindless joyless entertainments, concerned with the price of gasoline and some stupidity

[3]Plato, *The Crito,* in *The Trial and Death of Socrates,* 2nd ed., trans. G. M. A. Grube (Indianapolis, IN: Hackett, 1974).
[4]Plato, *The Phaedo,* in *The Trial and Death of Socrates,* 2nd ed., trans. G. M. A. Grube (Indianapolis, IN: Hackett, 1974).

of the government, the petty competitions of school and society, the hassles of chores and assignments, car troubles and occasional social embarrassments, interrupted only by all too rare and too quickly passing pleasures and distractions? What we learn from Socrates is how to rise above all of this. Not that we should give up worldly pleasures—good food and fun, sex, sports, and entertainment—and put our heads in the "clouds"; but we should see them in perspective, and examine for ourselves that jungle of confused reactions and conditioned responses that we have unthinkingly inherited from our parents and borrowed from our peers. The point is not to give up what we have learned or to turn against our "culture." Rather, the lesson to be learned from Socrates is that thinking about our lives and clarifying our ideals can turn it from a dreary series of tasks and distractions into a self-conscious adventure, one even worth dying for and certainly worth living for. It is a special kind of abstract thinking, rising above petty concerns and transforming our existence into a bold experiment in living. This special kind of thinking is called—philosophy.

> SOCRATES: Do you agree, or not, that when we say that a man has a passion for something, we shall say that he desires that whole kind of thing, not just one part of it and not the other?
> GLAUCON: Yes, the whole of it.
> SOCRATES: The lover of wisdom, we shall say, has a passion for wisdom, not for this kind of wisdom and not that, but for every kind of wisdom?
> GLAUCON: True.
> SOCRATES: As for one who is choosy about what he learns, especially if he is young and cannot yet give a reasoned account of what is useful and what is not, we shall not call him a lover of learning or a philosopher, just as we shall not say that a man who is difficult about his food is hungry or has an appetite for food. We shall not call him a lover of food but a bad feeder.
> GLAUCON: And we should be right.
> SOCRATES: But we shall rightly call a philosopher the man who is easily willing to learn every kind of knowledge, gladly turns to learning things, and is unsatiable in this respect. Is that not so?[5]

B. WHAT IS PHILOSOPHY?

Philosophy is not like any other academic subject; rather it is a critical approach to all subjects, the comprehensive vision within which all other subjects are contained. Philosophy is a style of life, a life of ideas or the life of reason, which a person like Socrates lives all of the time, which

[5]Plato, *The Republic*, Bk. V, trans. G. M. A. Grube (Indianapolis, IN: Hackett, 1974).

many of us live only a few hours a week. It is thinking, about everything and anything. But mainly, it is living thoughtfully. Aristotle, the student of Plato, who was the student of Socrates, called this "contemplative" or philosophical life the ideal life for humankind. He did not mean, however, that one should sit and think all of the time without doing anything. Aristotle, like the other Greek philosophers, was not one to abstain from pleasure or from political and social involvement for the sake of isolated thinking. Philosophy need not, as commonly believed, put our heads in the clouds, out of touch with everyday reality. Quite to the contrary, philosophy takes our heads out of the clouds, enlarging our view of ourselves and our knowledge of the world, allowing us to break out of prejudices and harmful habits that we have held since we were too young or too naive to know better. Philosophy puts our lives and our beliefs in perspective, by enabling us to see afresh the ways in which we view the world, to see what we assume, what we infer, and what we know for certain. It also allows us to appreciate *other* views of the world. It encourages us to see the consequences of our views and sometimes their hopeless inconsistencies. It allows us to see the justification (or lack of it) for our most treasured beliefs, and to separate what we will continue to believe with confidence from what we should consider doubtful or reject. It allows us the option of considering alternatives. Philosophy gives us the intellectual strength to defend what we do and what we believe to others and to ourselves. It forces us to be clear about the limits as well as the warrants for our acts and beliefs. And, consequently, it gives us the intellectual strength to understand, tolerate, and even sympathize with and adopt views very different from our own.

Philosophy is first and foremost a discipline that teaches us how to articulate, hold, and defend beliefs that, perhaps, we have always held, but without having spelled them out and argued for them. For example, suppose you have been brought up in a deeply religious home; you have been taught respect for God and church, but you have never had to learn to justify or argue for your beliefs. You know that, although there are people who would disagree with you, your belief is a righteous and necessary one, but you have never had to explain this to anyone, nor have you ever tried to explain it to yourself. But now you enter college and immediately you are confronted by fellow students, some of whom you consider close friends and admire in many ways, who are vocally antireligious. Others accept very different doctrines and beliefs, and vociferously defend these. Your first reactions may be almost physical; you feel weak, flushed, and anxious. You refuse to listen, and if you respond at all, it is with a tinge of hysteria. You may get into fights as well as arguments. You feel as if some foundation of your life, one of its main supports, is slipping away. But slowly you gain some confidence; you begin to listen. You give yourself enough distance so that you will consider arguments about religion in just the same way you would consider arguments about some scientific or political dispute. You ask yourself *why* they don't believe. Are their arguments persuasive, their reasons *good* reasons? You begin asking yourself how you came to believe in your religion in the first place, and you may well come up with the answer (many freshmen do) that you were "conditioned" by your parents and by society in general. Consequently, you may, perhaps for a time, perhaps for a lifetime, question or reject the ideas you had once "naturally" accepted. Or you may reaffirm your faith with new commitment, determined that, whatever the source, your beliefs are right. But after further consideration and argument, perhaps with some new religious experience, you come to see both sides of the arguments. For the first time, you can weigh their merits and demerits against each other without defensively holding onto one and attacking the other. You may remain a believer; you may become an atheist or an agnostic (a person who admits not knowing whether there is a God or not). You may choose to convert to another faith. Or you may adopt a position in which you give all religions (and nonreligion) equal weight, continuing to believe but not insisting that your belief is the only correct one or that you are necessarily a superior person because of it. But whatever you decide, your position will no longer be naive and unthinking. You know the arguments, both for and against. You know how to defend yourself. And, most importantly, you have confidence that your position is secure, that you have considered its objections, and that you have mastered its strengths. So it is with all philosophical problems and positions. Philosophy does not pull us away from our lives; it clarifies them. It secures them on intellectual ground in place of the fragile supports provided by inherited prejudices, fragments of parental advice, and mindless slogans borrowed from television commercials.

"Philosophy" sounds like a new and mysterious discipline, unlike anything you have ever encountered. But the basic ideas of philosophy are familiar to all of us, even if we have not yet formally confronted the problems. In this sense, we are all philosophers already. Watch yourself in a crisis, or listen to yourself in an argument with a friend. Notice how quickly abstract concepts like "freedom," "mankind," "self-identity," "nature" and "natural," "relative," "reality," "illusion," and "truth" enter our thoughts and our conversations. Notice how certain basic philosophical principles—whether conservative or radical, pragmatic or idealistic, confident or skeptical, pedestrian or heroic—enter into our arguments and our thinking as well as our actions. We all have some opinions about God, about morality and its principles, about the nature of man and the nature of the universe. But because we haven't questioned them, they are merely the **assumptions** of our thinking. We believe many things without having thought about them, merely assuming them, sometimes without evidence or good reasons. What the study of philosophy does for us is to make our ideas explicit, to give us the means of defending our presuppositions, and to make alternative suppositions available to us as well. Where once we merely assumed a point of view, passively and for lack of alternatives, we now can argue for it with confidence, knowing that our acceptance is active and critical, systematic rather than merely a collection of borrowed beliefs (who knows from where). To be **critical** means to examine carefully and cautiously, willing, if necessary, to change one's own beliefs. It does not need to be nasty or destructive. There is "constructive criticism" as well. And to "argue" does not mean "to have a fight"; an **argument** may simply be the justification of our beliefs.

So what is philosophy? Literally, from the Greek *(philein, sophia)*, it is "the love of wisdom."[6] It is an attitude of critical and systematic thoughtfulness rather than a particular subject matter. This makes matters very difficult for the beginner, who would like a definition of philosophy of the same kind received when he or she began biology, as "the study of living organisms." But the nature of philosophy is itself among the most bitter disputes in philosophy. Many philosophers say that it is a science, in fact, the "Queen of the Sciences," the womb in which physics, chemistry, mathematics, astronomy, biology, and psychology began their development before being born into their own distinguished worlds and separate university departments. And insofar as one says that philosophy is the road to reality and that the goal of philosophy is truth, that would seem to make it the ultimate science as well.

But it has also been argued, as far back as Socrates, that the main business of philosophy is a matter of definitions—finding clear meanings for such important ideas as truth, justice, wisdom, knowledge, and happiness. Accordingly, many philosophers have taken advantage of the sophisticated tools of modern logic and linguistics in their attempts to find such definitions. Other philosophers, however, would insist that philosophy is rather closer to morality and religion, its purpose to give meaning to our lives and lead us down "the right path" to "the good life." Still others insist that philosophy is an art, the art of criticism and argumentation as well as the art of conceptual system building. So considered, philosophy may be akin to storytelling or mythology. Some philosophers place strong emphasis upon proof and argument; others place their trust in intuition and insight. Some philosophers reduce all philosophizing to the study of experience; other philosophers take it as a matter of principle not to trust experience. Also, some philosophers insist on being practical, in fact, insist that there are no other considerations but practicality; and then there are others who insist on the purity of the life of ideas, divorced from any practical considerations.

---

[6]The word was invented by Pythagoras (whom we shall meet in the next chapter). When he was asked if he was already a wise man, he answered, "No, I am not wise, but I am a *lover* of wisdom."

But philosophy cannot, without distortion, be reduced to any one of these preferences. All enter into that constantly redefined critical and creative life of ideas that Socrates was willing to die for. In fact, Socrates himself insisted that it is the seeking of wisdom that is the essence of philosophy and that anyone who is sure that he or she has wisdom already is undoubtedly wrong. In *The Apology,* for example, he makes this famous disclaimer:

◆ from *The Apology,* by Plato

The effect of these investigations of mine, gentlemen, has been to arouse against me a great deal of hostility, and hostility of a particularly bitter and persistent kind, which has resulted in various malicious suggestions, including the description of me as a professor of wisdom. This is due to the fact that whenever I succeed in disproving another person's claim to wisdom in a given subject, the bystanders assume that I know everything about that subject myself. But the truth of the matter, gentlemen, is pretty certainly this: that real wisdom is the property of God, and this oracle is his way of telling us that human wisdom has little or no value. It seems to me that he is not referring literally to Socrates, but has merely taken my name as an example, as if he would say to us "The wisest of you men is he who has realized, like Socrates, that in respect of wisdom he is really worthless."

That is why I still go about seeking and searching in obedience to the divine command, if I think that anyone is wise, whether citizen or stranger; and when I think that any person is not wise, I try to help the cause of God by proving that he is not. This occupation has kept me too busy to do much either in politics or in my own affairs; in fact, my service to God has reduced me to extreme poverty.[7]

Here is the true start of Western philosophy. But in Chinese philosophy, too, we find a similar message in the *Tao Te Ching:*

◆ from *Tao Te Ching,* by Lao Tsu

My mind is that of a fool—how blank and how muddled. Vulgar people have clear ideas. They see clear-cut distinctions. I alone make no distinctions. They all have a purpose. I drift like a high

---

[7]Plato, *The Last Days of Socrates,* trans. Hugh Tredennick (Harmondsworth, Middlesex: Penguin, 1954).

wind and the ocean. They are alert and smart. I am uncouth and rustic.

The highest good is like water. Water is good; it benefits all things and does not compete with them. It dwells in lowly places that all disdain. This is why it is so near to the Way.

· · · · · · · · · ·

The best rulers are those with a shadowy presence to the people. Next comes the ruler they love and praise. Next comes one they fear. The next are those they despise.

Therefore the sage says: I take no action and the people of themselves are transformed. I engage in no activities and the people of themselves become prosperous.

Act without action. Do without ado.

Therefore the sage never strives for the great.

C. A MODERN APPROACH TO PHILOSOPHY

The orientation to philosophy in this book is, inevitably, essentially a modern Western approach in which criticism plays a predominant role. Historically, modern European philosophy has its origins in the rise of science and technology. (As we shall see, philosophy and science both emerged in ancient Greece and Asia Minor and, about the same time, in South and East Asia.) We should understand science, however, not just as a particular discipline or subject matter, but rather as a state of mind, a way of looking at the world. In the European tradition, this means that the world is understandable and every event in the world is explainable. It sees the universe as *rational*—operating according to universal laws. And it sees the human mind as rational too—in the sense that it can grasp and formulate these laws for itself. European philosophy and science also put enormous emphasis on the mind of the individual.

Though science is essentially a team effort, requiring the labor and thinking of thousands of men and women, the great breakthroughs in science have often been the insights of one man or woman alone. The most famous modern example of this individual genius is the British philosopher-scientist Isaac Newton. In the eyes of his contemporaries and followers, he single-mindedly mastered the laws of the universe, while sitting (so the story goes) under an apple tree. The ideal of modern Western philosophy is, in a phrase, *thinking for yourself*. That is, philosophy is thinking for yourself about basic questions—about life, knowledge, religion, and what to do with yourself. It is *using* the rationality built into your brain to comprehend the rationality (or lack of it) in the world around you. In some cultures, however, the emphasis lies on the group or community, and thinking for yourself is not as important as maintaining group harmony and cohesiveness. In India and China, for example, it is the elusiveness of scientific knowledge that defines much of philosophy. And in many of these traditions enlightenment rather than scientific knowledge is the main goal of philosophy.

In Western tradition, the central demand of modern philosophy is *the autonomy of the individual person.* This means that each of us must be credited with the ability to ascertain what is true and what is right, through our own thinking and experience, without just depending upon outside authority: parents, teachers, popes, kings, or a majority of peers. Whether you believe in God must be decided by you, by appeal to your own reason and arguments that you can formulate and examine by yourself. Whether you accept a scientific theory, a doctor's diagnosis, a newspaper's version of the news, or the legitimacy of a new law are also matters to be decided by you on the basis of evidence, principles that you can accept, and arguments that you acknowledge as valid. This stress on individual autonomy stands at the very foundation of contemporary Western thought. We might say that it is our most basic assumption. (Accordingly, we shall have to examine it as well; but the obvious place to begin is to assume that we are—each of us—capable of carrying out the reflection and criticism that philosophy demands of us.)

Historically, the position of individual autonomy can be found most famously in Socrates, who went against the popular opinions of his day and, consequently, sacrificed his life for the "Laws" and principles he believed to be right. It also appears in many medieval philosophers, some of whom also faced grave danger in their partial rejection or questioning of the "authority" of the church. It can also be found in those philosophers who, like the Buddha, struck out from established society to find a new way. The stress on individual autonomy comes to dominate Western thinking in that intellectually brilliant period of history called "the Enlightenment," sometimes called "the Age of Reason," which began in the late seventeenth century and continued through the French Revolution (1789). It appeared in different countries with varying speed and intensity, but ultimately it influenced the thinking of Europe, from England and France to Spain and Russia, and became the ideology of young America, which used Enlightenment doctrines in the formulation of a "Declaration of Independence," a war for its own autonomy, and a new government established on Enlightenment principles. Those principles were, whatever the variations from one country or party to another, the autonomy of the individual and each person's right to choose and to speak his[8] own religious, political, moral, and philosophical beliefs, to "pursue happiness" in his own way, and to lead the life that he, as a reasonable person, sees as right.

If these principles have often been abused, creating confusion and sometimes anarchy, encouraging ruthlessness in politics and strife in a

[8]Not, at that point in history, *hers* as well. The concept of a woman's autonomy and right to choose is a late nineteenth-century idea that has only recently become accepted.

mixed society, they are principles that can be challenged only with great difficulty and a sense of imminent danger. Once the individual's right or the ability to decide such matters for himself or herself is denied, who shall decide? Society no longer agrees on any single unambiguous set of instructions from the Scriptures. Everyone in power is no longer trusted. Mankind is rightfully suspicious of those who attack the individual, because it is not known what else they have in mind. Whatever the abuses, and whatever political, social, or economic systems might be required to support it, philosophical autonomy is the starting point. Even in the most authority-minded societies, autonomy and the ability to think beyond prescribed limits, remain essential. (Think of the students in Tiananmen Square.)

The metaphor of enlightenment is common to many cultures. The comparison of clear thinking with illumination is to be found in ancient, Christian, and Eastern thought as well as in comic-book symbolism and modern philosophy. The seventeenth-century French philosopher René Descartes was one of the founders of the Enlightenment, and was particularly fond of the "illumination" metaphor. He is generally recognized as the father of modern philosophy. Like Socrates two thousand years before him, Descartes believed that each person was capable of ascertaining what beliefs were true and what actions were right. But whereas Socrates searched for the truth through dialogue and discussion, Descartes searched in the solitude of his own thinking. With considerable risk to his safety, he challenged the authority of the French government and the Catholic Church. He insisted that he would accept as true only those ideas that were demonstrably true to him. Against what he considered were obscure teachings of the church and often opaque commands of his government, Descartes insisted upon "clear and distinct ideas" and arguments based upon "the light of reason." The modern philosophy of individual autonomy began with Descartes. As a matter of fact, his results were quite conservative. He retained much of his medieval teachings: he continued to believe in God and the church, and he made it his first "moral maxim" to "obey the laws and customs of my country." His challenge to authority was rather his method, which signified one of the greatest revolutions in Western thought. From Descartes on, the ultimate authority was to be found in man's own thinking and experience, nowhere else.

None of this is meant to deny authority as such. Appeals are still made to authority, but authorities are never to be taken as absolutes. For example, none of us would particularly like to go out and establish on our own the figures of the 1990 census of the U.S. population. But it is up to the individual whether or not to accept the official "authoritative" figures, to question, if necessary, the integrity or motivation of the authorities, and to appeal, if necessary, to alternative sources of information.

For anyone beginning to study philosophy today, Descartes is a pivotal figure. His method is both easy to follow and very much in accord with our own independent temperaments. Descartes proceeded by means of logical arguments, giving his readers a long monologue of presentations and proofs of his philosophical doubts and beliefs. Like Socrates before him, Descartes used his philosophy to cut through the clouds of prejudice and unreliable opinions. He was concerned with their truth, no matter how many people already believed them—or how few. Descartes' arguments were his tools for finding this truth and distinguishing it from falsehood and mere opinion.

Philosophy has always been concerned with truth and mankind's knowledge of reality. Not coincidentally, Descartes' new philosophy developed in the age of Galileo and the rise of modern science. In ancient Greece, the origins of philosophy and the birth of Greek science were one and the same. The truth, however, is not always what most people believe at any given time. (Most people once believed that the earth was flat, for example.) But, at the same time that they simply refuse to accept "common sense," philosophers try not to say things that common sense finds absurd. For example, a philosopher who denied that anyone existed besides himself would clearly be absurd. So too, the philosopher who argued that he knew that nobody ever knows anything.

Accordingly, two of the most important challenges in the philosopher's search for truth are (1) skepticism and (2) paradox. In **skepticism,** the philosopher finds himself or herself unable to justify what every sane person knows to be the case; for example, that we are not merely dreaming all of the time. In Eastern as well as Western philosophy, skepticism has provided a valuable probe for our everyday presumptions of knowledge, and it sometimes becomes a philosophy in its own right. In a **paradox,** an absurd conclusion seems to result from perfectly acceptable ways of thinking. For example, there is the familiar paradox of Epimenides the Cretan, who claimed that "all Cretans are liars." (That sounds reasonable enough.) But . . . if what he said was true, then he was lying and what he said, accordingly, was false. But how can the same statement be both true and false? What Epimenides said was true only if it was false at the same time. That is a paradox. And whenever a philosophical argument ends in paradox, we can be sure that something has gone wrong. Again, in both East and West, philosophers have always been intrigued by paradoxes, and have often been prompted by them to strike out in bold new directions in search of a resolution.

Skepticism begins with *doubt.* The philosopher considers the possibility that something that everyone believes is possibly mistaken. Some doubt is a healthy sign of intellectual autonomy, but excessive doubting becomes skepticism, which is no longer healthy. It has its obvious dangers: If you doubt whether you are ever awake or not, you might well do things that wouldn't have serious consequences in a dream but would be fatal in real life (jumping out of a plane, for example). Philosophers who have doubts about the most ordinary and seemingly unquestionable beliefs are called *skeptics*. For example, there was the Chinese philosopher who, when he once dreamed that he was a butterfly, started wondering whether he really were a butterfly—dreaming that he was a philosopher. But however challenging skeptics may be as philosophers, in practice their skepticism is impossible. Accordingly, one of the main drives in philosophy has been to refute the skeptic and return philosophy to common sense (to prove, for example, that we are *not* dreaming all of the time). Opposed to skepticism is an ancient philosophical ideal, the ideal of **certainty,** the ability to prove beyond a doubt that what we believe is true. Socrates and Descartes, in their very different ways, tried to provide precisely this certainty for the most important beliefs, and thus refute the skeptics of their own times.

In Western philosophy, the precision of mathematics has long served as an ideal of knowledge. In mathematics, we believe, we can be **certain.** For Descartes, certainty is the **criterion,** that is, the test according to which beliefs are to be evaluated. But do we ever find such certainty? It seems that we do, at least in one discipline Descartes suggested—in mathematics. Who can doubt that two plus two equals four, or that the interior angles of a triangle total 180°? Using mathematics as his model, Descartes (and many generations of philosophers following him) attempted to apply a similar method in philosophy. First, he had to find, as in Euclidean geometry, a small set of "first principles" or **axioms** that were obvious or **self-evident.** They had to be assumed without proof or be so fundamental that they seemed not to allow any proof. These would serve as premises or starting points for the *arguments* that would take a person from the self-evident axioms to other principles that might not be self-evident at all. But if they could be deduced from other principles that were already certain, like the theorems of geometry, then they would share the certainty of the principles from which they have been derived.

Descartes was a scientist and a mathematician as well as a philosopher. With that in mind, we can understand his *Discourse on Method.* Descartes set out four basic rules that would define philosophy for many years:

◆ **from *Discourse on Method,*
by René Descartes**

The first of these was to accept nothing as true which I did not clearly recognise to be so; that is to say, carefully to avoid precipitation and prejudice in judgments, and to accept in them nothing more than what was presented to my mind so clearly and distinctly that I could have no occasion to doubt it.

The second was to divide up each of the difficulties which I examined into as many parts as possible, and as seemed requisite in order that it might be resolved in the best manner possible.

The third was to carry on my reflections in due order, commencing with objects that were the most simple and easy to understand, in order to rise little by little, or by degrees, to knowledge of the most complex, assuming an order, even if a fictitious one, among those which do not follow a natural sequence relatively to one another.

The last was in all cases to make enumerations so complete and reviews so general that I should be certain of having omitted nothing.[9]

One might say that the essence of these rules is to be cautious and to think for oneself. The premises, upon which all else depends, must be utterly beyond doubt, "perfectly certain," otherwise all else is futile. The test or criterion of such a premise is that it be "a clear and distinct idea," self-evident, and "springing from the light of reason alone."

We shall see much more of Descartes in the following chapters. In Chapter 3, we shall see that Descartes' technique for assuring the certainty of his premises will be what he called the method of doubt (or *methodological doubt*). In order to make sure that he did not accept any principle too quickly ("too precipitously") before being convinced of its "perfect certainty," he resolved to doubt every belief until he could prove it true beyond question, and to show that the very act of doubting this belief led to an intolerable paradox. The point of this kind of argument is not to become a skeptic, but, quite the contrary, to find those premises that even the skeptic cannot doubt. And from those premises, Descartes and many generations of philosophers following him have attempted and will attempt to prove that we do indeed know what we think we know. Like Socrates, Descartes begins by questioning what no one but a philosopher would doubt and ends up changing the way we think about ourselves and our knowledge for several centuries. And in other cultures too, entire societies have been dramatically altered by philosophers who challenged what seemed to be obvious; sometimes they challenged reality itself.

D. A BRIEF INTRODUCTION TO LOGIC

Descartes' strategy, and the technique of many philosophers, is to present arguments for what they believe. In Plato's *Crito*, Socrates and Crito offer arguments for their views, and Socrates wins because his

---

[9]René Descartes, *Discourse on Method*, in *The Philosophical Works of Descartes*, trans. Elizabeth S. Haldane and G. R. T. Ross (Cambridge: Cambridge University Press, 1911).

arguments are better. An argument is a verbal attempt to get other people to accept a belief or opinion by providing reasons why they should accept it. We usually think of an argument as a confrontation between two people. When they try to convince each other, they usually resort to certain verbal means and it is with these means that a philosopher is concerned. Of course, there are other ways of getting people to agree with you—tricks, bribes, brainwashing, and threats of physical force. But the use of arguments is the most durable and trustworthy, as well as the most respectable, way of getting others to agree. Freedom of speech is the cornerstone of democracy (and the bane of totalitarianism) just because of our faith in the ability of arguments to determine the best among competing opinions. On the other hand, one should not think of an argument as a political weapon whose purpose is to shut down conversation or put other people and their opinions on the defensive. It is always reasonable to ask for arguments, but it may not be reasonable to push a person for arguments that he or she cannot provide. To fail to argue for a position is not necessarily to give up on it, and to refute the arguments for a position is not necessarily to reject the position.

You don't have to be arguing with anyone in particular in order to construct an argument. Editorials in newspapers, for example, argue for a position, but not necessarily against anyone. But whether your argument is a letter to a magazine, in which you are trying to convince the entire American population of your views, or a personal letter, in which you are trying to convince a friend not to do something foolhardy, the main point of argument is to demonstrate or establish a point of view. A scientist describing an experiment tries to demonstrate to other scientists the truth of his or her theory. A politician tries to demonstrate to his or her constituency the need for higher taxes. A philosopher tries to demonstrate to us the value of a certain view of life, a certain view of reality, a certain view of ourselves. In each case, these people try to give as many reasons as possible why other people should accept their view of things; in short, they use arguments to persuade others.

Argument involves at least two components: **logic** and **rhetoric.** Logic concerns those reasons that should hold for anyone, anywhere, without appealing to personal feelings, sympathies, or prejudices. Rhetoric, on the other hand, does involve such personal appeals. Personal charm may be part of rhetoric, in a writer as well as in a public speaker. Jokes may be part of rhetoric. Personal pleas are effective rhetorical tools; so is trying to be sympathetic to readers, or playing off their fears. None of these personal tactics are part of logic, however. Logic is impersonal, and for this reason logic may be less flamboyant and personally exciting; but it has the advantage of being applicable to everyone. A logical argument goes beyond rhetorical appeal. But it is important to understand that logic and rhetoric virtually always function together. Although it is possible to be persuasive through pure rhetoric without being at all logical, such efforts often disappear as soon as readers have had a chance to think again about how they have been persuaded. One can also be logical without attention to rhetoric, but such arguments will be dry and unattractive, even if they do convince anyone who would take the time to read them. However, logic and rhetoric in combination can be very persuasive and are rarely separable in any great work of philosophy. In all of the readings in this book, you will notice the combination of impersonal logic and personal appeal, all aimed at getting the reader to agree with the author's point of view.

There are good arguments and there are bad arguments. Just as the success of a logically inadequate argument may depend upon the passing mood of a reader or the fact that he or she has not yet heard the other side, so a good argument must survive passing moods, reflection, and criticism. This requires good logic as well as effective rhetoric, and so it is important to master the basic rules of argument, as well as to be aware of the all too common pitfalls that lie in wait for those who ignore the rules. Knowing these rules and warnings will not only help you avoid what are called **fallacies**—it will also allow you to criticize effectively other people's arguments as well. Have you ever heard someone say, "Well, there's something wrong with that argument, but I'm not sure what it is"? Knowing a little logic may help you see clearly what is wrong with an argument.

Standard logic textbooks emphasize two primary forms of logical argument:

1) **Deductive arguments** reason from one statement to another by means of accepted logical rules; anyone who accepts the premises is bound logically to accept the conclusion.

2) **Inductive arguments** infer one statement from another, but it is possible for the conclusion to be false even if all of the premises are true. The most familiar example of an inductive argument is a **generalization** from a set of particular observations to a general statement called a "hypothesis."

1.   Deductive Arguments

A deductive argument is **valid** when it correctly conforms to the rules of deduction. Some examples of the most familiar rules are:

1) It was either Phyllis or Fred. (It was Phyllis *or* it was Fred.)
   It wasn't Phyllis.
   Therefore it was Fred.

2) Both Tom and Jerry went to the circus last night. (Tom went to the circus last night *and* Jerry went to the circus last night.)
   Therefore Tom went to the circus last night.

3) *If* Carol did that all by herself, *then* she's courageous.

Carol did it all by herself.
Therefore Carol is courageous.

It is important to emphasize that whether or not an argument is valid depends only on the form of the argument. A valid argument—one in the correct form—can still have a conclusion that is false. Consider:

4) If Carol did that all by herself, then elephants can fly.
Carol did it all by herself.
Therefore elephants can fly.

Notice that example 4 is identical in form to example 3. The conclusion is patently false, but the argument is still valid.

But what good is a deductive argument if its conclusion can be false? The answer is that if the initial statements are true, then the truth of the conclusion is guaranteed. The initial statements are called **premises,** and if the premises are true, then the conclusion must be true if the argument form is valid. It is important to remember that a deductive argument cannot prove its own premises. To be effective, you must be sure of the premises before beginning the deductive argument. Thus the following argument, although it is valid, is an appallingly bad argument.

5) If someone argues for socialized medicine, then he or she is a communist.
Communists want to kill people.
Therefore if someone is for socialized medicine, he or she wants to kill people.

This argument has the valid form:

5') If p then q.
If q then r.
Therefore if p then r.

But although the argument is valid, its premises are not true, and therefore they provide no guarantee that the conclusion is true. A valid argument guarantees the truth of the conclusion only if the premises are true. Therefore, in using or evaluating any deductive argument, you must always ask yourself two things:

a) Are the premises true?
b) Is the argument valid?

If the answer to both of these is yes, then the argument is said to be **sound.**

An argument in an essay may not appear exactly in the form provided by the rules of deduction. This does not mean that the argument is invalid. In example 5, the second premise, "Communists want to kill people," must be restated in "If . . . then . . ." form. In fact, straightforward copying of the rules of deduction in an essay makes boring reading, so arguments usually must be restated in order to fit these forms exactly. When you are writing an argument, it is necessary to pay attention both to the validity of the argument and to the degree of interest with which it is stated. Sometimes it is permissible to leave out one of the premises, if it is so obvious to every reader that actually stating it would seem absurd. For example,

> 6) Men can't give birth.
> Therefore Robert can't give birth.

The missing premise, of course, is

> Robert is a man.

But it would be unnecessary in most contexts to say this. When using deductive arguments effectively, rhetorical considerations are important too.

One of the best-known forms of deductive reasoning is called the **syllogism.** It refers to one kind in particular: deductive arguments, with two premises and a conclusion, usually involving membership in groups, and using the terms *all, some,* and *none.* The best-known example is

> 7) All men are mortal.
> Socrates is a man.
> Therefore, Socrates is mortal.

The first statement, "All men are mortal," is called the *major premise;* the second statement, "Socrates is a man," is called the *minor premise.* The final statement, following from the other two, is the *conclusion* and is generally preceded by the word "therefore." In this example, the words "men" and "man" are called the *middle term,* the word "mortal" is called the *predicate,* and the name "Socrates" is called the *subject.* The middle term serves to link the subject and the predicate, both of which are joined in the conclusion. The form of this syllogism is

> 7') All A's are B's.
> C is an A.
> Therefore C is a B.

Any nouns can be substituted for the A, B, and C in this deductive form. For example,

> 8) All cows are pigeons.
> George Washington is a cow.
> Therefore George Washington is a pigeon.

Argument 8 is valid, although its conclusion is false. The reason, of course, is that the premises are false. Again, a valid argument does not guarantee a true conclusion unless the premises are true. So always be certain that you have adequately defended the premises before beginning your deduction.

Valid arguments sometimes proceed from negative premises as well as positive assertions. For example,

9) No woman has ever been president.
Eleanor Roosevelt was a woman.
Therefore Eleanor Roosevelt was not president.

The form is

9') No A's are B's.
C is an A.
Therefore C is not a B.

Another common argument is

10) Some elephants weigh more than two thousand pounds.
Elephants are animals.
Therefore some animals weigh more than two thousand pounds.

The form, with a little rephrasing, is

10') Some A's are B's. (Some elephants are more than two thousand pounds in weight.)
All A's are C's. (All elephants are animals. The "all" is implicit.)
Therefore, some C's are B's. (Some animals are more than two thousand pounds in weight.)

Not all deductive arguments are syllogisms in this traditional sense. For example, the following is a valid deductive argument, but not a syllogism:

11) Jones is an idiot, and he (Jones) is also the luckiest man alive.
Therefore Jones is an idiot.

The form of this argument is

11') p and q.
Therefore p.

In the discussion that follows, therefore, we will talk about deductive arguments in general and not worry whether they are properly to be called "syllogisms" or not.

It is impossible in this introduction to list all of the correct forms of deduction. We will, however, describe some of the most dangerous *fallacies*, mistakes in deductive form. The following example is one, for it looks dangerously like example 10':

12) Some elephants are domesticated.

> Some camels are domesticated.
> Therefore some elephants are camels.

This form,

> 12') Some A's are B's.
> Some C's are B's.
> Therefore some A's are C's.

is **invalid** (not valid), and is thus a fallacy. This fallacy often appears in political arguments, for example,

> 13) We all know that some influential Republicans are corrupt.
> And we all know that at least some Communists are corrupt.
> Therefore we know that at least some Republicans are Communists.

When stated so simply, the fallacy is obvious. But when this argument is spread through a long-winded speech, such fallacies are often accepted as valid arguments. Using the logician's symbolic forms to analyze a complex speech or essay will often make clear the validity or invalidity of an argument.

Another common fallacy closely resembles the deductive form in example 3):

> 14) If this antidote works then the patient will live.
> The patient lived.
> Therefore the antidote works.

This looks valid at first glance, but it is not. The patient may have recovered on his or her own, proving nothing about the antidote. The form of this argument is

> 14') If p then q.
> q.
> Therefore p.

The correct deductive form of example 3 was

> If p then q.
> p.
> Therefore q.

Be particularly careful of the difference between these two.

"If . . . then . . ." statements are often used in another pair of arguments, one valid, one invalid. The valid one is

> 15) If this antidote works then the patient will live.
> The patient didn't live.
> Therefore the antidote did not work.

The form is

15′) If p then q.
   Not q.
   Therefore not p.

This is valid, although one might insist on adding an explicit qualification to the first premise. The qualification is, "for nothing else whatever can save the patient," since one might argue that something else, perhaps a miracle, might save the patient rather than the antidote. Notice that this qualification doesn't save the invalid argument in example 14, however, nor does it save the invalid argument in the following example:

16) If this antidote doesn't work, then the patient will die.
   The antidote works.
   Therefore the patient won't die.

Again, the patient might very well die of other causes, despite the antidote. The form,

16′) If p then q.
   Not p.
   Therefore not q.

is invalid.

Most valid and invalid deductive argument forms are a matter of common sense. What makes fallacies so common is not ignorance of logic so often as sloppy thinking or writing, or talking faster than one can organize thoughts in valid form. Most important, therefore, be careful in thinking and writing. And yet, even the greatest philosophers commit fallacies, and you will see some of them.

2. Inductive Arguments

In deduction, the conclusion never states more than the premises. (It is often said that the conclusion is already "contained in" the premises.) In an inductive argument, the conclusion *always* states more than the premises. It is, therefore, a less certain form of argument, but that does not mean that it is any less important. Many of the premises in deductive arguments will come from inductive ones, and most of our knowledge and almost all of science depends upon induction. Induction takes various forms and defies rigid characterization. One general form of an inductive argument is

Every A we have observed is a B.
Therefore every A is a B.

The argument, in other words, is from an observed set of things to an entire class of things, for example, from

> 17) Every crow we have observed in the past twenty years is black.

to

> All crows are black.

But induction, unlike deduction, does not guarantee the truth of the conclusion, even if we know that the observations are all correct. So the conclusion of example 17 should properly read

> It is probable that all crows are black.

This tentative conclusion is called a **hypothesis.** A hypothesis is an educated guess on the basis of the evidence collected thus far. It is always possible, when we are using induction, that a new piece of evidence will turn up that will refute the hypothesis. This new piece of evidence is called a **counter-example.** Inductive arguments must always be ready for such counter-examples; it must be admitted that no inductive argument guarantees certainty. There is always the possibility that a counter-example will be found, or that a better hypothesis will be formulated. This is not to say, however, that we should not accept such arguments. Human beings have observed millions of rabbits, and never has a rabbit weighed more than two thousand pounds. This does not mean that it is impossible to find a two-thousand-pound rabbit, but neither does it mean that we should therefore hesitate to believe that no rabbits weigh over two thousand pounds. Induction is never certain, but, on the basis of the evidence, we can nevertheless agree on the best hypothesis. It is worth noting, however, that some philosophers, following David Hume (see Chapter 3), have claimed that induction is without rational justification, no matter how undeniably useful it may be.

There are good (sound) and bad **(unsound)** inductive arguments. The most familiar reason why an inductive argument may be called unsound is generalization on the basis of too few examples. For instance, the following is clearly unsound:

> 18) Every American president from the state of Pennsylvania has been a Democrat.
> Therefore we can suppose that every American president from the state of Pennsylvania will be a Democrat.

There has only been one president from Pennsylvania, and the intricacies of politics are clearly such that the next president from Pennsylvania could as likely be a Republican as a Democrat. Similarly,

> 19) The driver of every Italian bus we rode had a beard.
> Therefore all Italian bus drivers have beards.

is unsound. Although the sampling involves more than one example, this is still not sufficient to make a sound inductive generalization. How many examples are required? It varies with the case. If a chemist, conducting an experiment, adds chemical g to chemical h and gets j, that in itself will probably warrant a hypothesis that

$$g + h \rightarrow j,$$

although this hypothesis, like all hypotheses, will have to be tested by further experiments and observations. (Deductions, on the contrary, do not have to be tested, assuming the truth of their premises.) A chemist can usually assume that one set of pure chemicals will react like any other set of the same chemicals. But when the hypothesis is about people, generalizations should be made with extreme caution, especially when writing about such a sensitive subject as "national character." For example, "Italians are . . . ," "Russians tend to be . . . ," "Americans are too . . ." require extreme care. But caution does not mean that it is impossible to write about such subjects. It has often been done brilliantly, and you might even agree that a person who refuses to see the general differences between different peoples and societies is even more foolish than someone who generalizes too quickly and carelessly. But all generalizations (even this one) must be made with care for the context and the subject matter.

A different kind of inductive unsoundness comes from generalizing to a hypothesis that goes too far beyond what the evidence will support. For example,

20) Every graduate we know of from Delmonico High School is an excellent athlete.
Therefore we can suppose that the physical education teachers there must be very good.

The problem here is not too small a sampling; in fact, we might even look at *every* graduate of Delmonico High School. The problem is that this kind of evidence isn't sufficient to prove anything about the teachers. The students might come from athletic homes. Or the food in the student cafeteria might be loaded with extra vitamins and protein. Or the students may enjoy playing sports outside of school, even though their gym classes are badly taught. It is important to be sure that the hypothesis you defend is supported by the right kind of evidence. In this case, we need evidence about the physical education teachers, not just about the students.

Not every inductive argument proceeds from evidence to a generalization. For example, detectives use inductive arguments in moving from the evidence to the indictment of a particular individual. (What Sherlock Holmes refers to as his "powers of deduction" is in fact his remarkable ability with induction.) It is worth noting that not every philosopher thinks that induction is so important for knowledge. For example, the contemporary British philosopher Karl Popper believes that the logic of science (and police investigations) proceeds not by way of induction but by way of the *disconfirmation* of proposed hypotheses with counter-examples. In other words, knowledge proceeds from hypothesis to hypothesis, not from evidence to hypothesis by way of induction. But whatever one thinks of the justifiability of induction and its importance, it is essential not to think of induction as occurring in a vacuum. Inductive reasoning always goes on against a background of other hypotheses, theories, and scientific viewpoints as well as an abundance of other evidence that is taken for granted, built into the hypothesis itself or, perhaps, ignored as irrelevant, undependable, or unimportant. Because of its formality, deduction can deal with isolated arguments. But induction, even when subjected to the formal rigors of probability theory, can never be so understood out of context. Background conditions and the state of knowledge at the moment are always in some sense presupposed. Because of this informal (if not chaotic) complexity, induction is just as much a matter of insight as logic.

A very different kind of problem arises for induction when the hypothesis is *self-confirming.* A self-confirming hypothesis creates its own confirmation or, alternatively, blocks all possible counter-examples from the start. Two familiar examples: a policeman (in uniform) tries to evaluate the driving patterns of the cars that pass him, making sure that they all drive at the legal speed. Of course they do! But the same sort of self-confirmation often goes on in subtle ways in science, for example, where the equipment itself is designed to present precisely the evidence it is supposed to be looking for. The other example is the paranoid, who advances the hypothesis that "they're all out to get me." And, given that way of looking at the world, indeed they are. Not only does the paranoid systematically interpret other people's behavior in a hostile way, he also behaves in such a way that people really do become wary of him, if not hostile to him. But again, this extreme case has thousands of more everyday instances; persons who feel friendless may easily work on a mild version of the paranoid hypothesis and confirm their own thesis. A person who entertains the hypothesis that "all people are basically selfish" will have little trouble finding what he or she is looking for, and, within that investigation, some selfish motive can always be found (for example, "in order not to feel guilty") for even the most generous and unselfish behavior. (We might note that there are also *self-defeating* hypotheses; the policeman may hypothesize that everyone breaks the law and goes out, in uniform, to catch them, thereby undermining his own hypothesis.)

3.   *Argument by Analogy*

A form of inductive argument that is sometimes objected to unfairly is *argument by analogy.* An argument by analogy defends the similarity between some aspect of two things on the basis of their similarity in other respects. For example, a politician defends the need for more efficient government and fewer unnecessary jobs on the basis of an argument by analogy between government and business. A government is like a business, the politician argues. It has a certain product to turn out, namely, services to the people, and receives a certain income from the sale of that product, namely, taxes. It employs a certain number of people, whose job it is to turn out that product and who are paid with that income. Their business is to produce the product as cheaply but as well as possible, to keep the cost down, and make a profit in order to be able to offer new and better services. Thus, the politician argues, the more efficiently it is run and the fewer unnecessary employees it must support, the better a government will be.

Such an argument is valuable in getting people to see similarities and in clarifying complex and confusing issues. The danger, and the reason why many logicians reject arguments by analogy altogether, is that no two things are similar in every respect. (Otherwise, they would be the same.) And just because two things are similar in certain respects, it doesn't follow that they will be similar in others. But this objection is too strong. If two things are similar in several respects, it is at least plausible to suggest that they will be similar in others. For example, running the government is like running a business. Both involve managing an organization. Both require skill in handling money. The success of both depends on the quality of the products and services they produce. Therefore, the way to handle the city transportation problem is to ask which plan will give the most service for the least money.

Arguments by analogy may employ both deductive and inductive arguments; insofar as A (government) is like B (a business) deductions appropriate in discussing A will be appropriate in discussing B as well. And if A and B are similar in so many ways, then it is inductively plausible that they will be similar in other ways too. So arguments by analogy are at least a valuable form of reasoning, if not always a reliable form of proof. It is important, however, to pay careful attention to each particular analogy, to make sure that the two things compared are significantly similar and, most importantly, that the aspect that is argued about is significantly similar in both cases. Arguments by analogy are extremely valuable, but they must always be used with care. In traditional Western philosophy, analogies and metaphors play an enormous but often unappreciated role in the great philosophical classics. The assumption, or at least the expectation, is that these analogies and metaphors can be recast in terms of deductive and inductive arguments. But not all philosophical traditions make this assumption. In Chinese philosophy, for example, analogical reasoning is far more central to philosophical disputation than deductive arguments. And in many folk philosophies around the world, the use of myth and metaphor has not yet been replaced—and probably cannot be replaced—by the standard logics of Western reasoning.

The three kinds of arguments discussed above—deductive, inductive, and argument by analogy—are attempts to defend a view or an opinion. But part of almost every argument is an attack on alternative views and opinions. In general, someone else's position can be attacked by asking the following questions:

a) What is he or she arguing? Is the position clear?

b) What are the arguments? Are they deductive? Inductive? Or by analogy?

　If deductive:

　　What are the premises and are they all true?

　　Are the deductive arguments valid?

　If the answer to either of these questions is no, a good counter-argument exists to show that the adversary has not given us a reason for accepting his or her view.

　If inductive:

　　Is there enough evidence to support the hypothesis?

　　Does the evidence support the hypothesis?

　　Is the hypothesis sufficiently clear?

　　Is this the best hypothesis to explain the evidence?

　If the answer to any of these is no, a good counter-argument exists to show that the adversary has not defended his or her general claim.

　If argument by analogy:

　　Are the things compared similar?

　　Are the things similar in the particular respect in question?

　If the answer to either of these is no, a good argument exists to show that the opponent's analogy is not a good one.

c) Does the conclusion mean what the opponent says it means?

4.　*Argument by Counter-Example*

Whenever anyone makes a general claim, it is possible to attack with an example that seems to go against the claim. This is a *counter-example*. We mentioned counter-examples with respect to inductive generalizations. A counter-example that refutes an hypothesis, such as "here is an *a* that is not *b*," will always give trouble to someone who argues that "all *a*'s are *b*'s." For example, if a bigot says, "All people from Poland are naturally unintelligent," the single counter-example of Copernicus, a Pole, is sufficient to undermine that claim. Counter-examples may also work in the face of deductively defended claims, however. Consider a common philosophical argument (which we shall discuss in Chapter 9):

21) All events in nature are determined by physical forces (gravity, chemistry, electromagnetic forces, and so on).
All human actions are events in nature.
Therefore all human actions are determined by physical forces.

This syllogism is a valid argument, of the form,

21′) All A's are B's.
All C's are A's.
Therefore all C's are B's.

One way to attack this valid argument, even if you don't see any reasons to reject the premises as such, is to use the method of counter-examples: "Look. I decided to come to this college of my own free will. I thought about it for a few days, and I remember the exact moment when I made my decision, while eating pizza at Harry's restaurant. Now I made that decision. It wasn't caused in me by physical forces. Therefore, I reject your conclusion."

What has happened here is this: On the one hand, if we accept the premises as true and the argument as valid, it would seem that we have to accept the conclusion. But what the counter-example does in this case is force the person who has argued the syllogism to clarify what is meant by "determined by physical forces" in both the premise and the conclusion. Does this mean only that *some* forces must be present? If so, the argument is not nearly so interesting as we thought, for everyone will admit that when a person makes a decision there is an electrical charge or a chemical change in the brain. Does it mean rather that there are *only* physical causes present, in which case "free will" is indeed excluded? But what then of the counter-example (your college decision)? The burden of proof is on the person who argued the syllogism; he or she is forced to explain how it seems that you made a decision of your own free will when in fact there is no such thing as free will. You can see how this philosophical argument could become very complicated, but we only want to make a simple point. A single, well-placed counter-example can open up a whole new discussion, even when it might seem as if the matter had already been settled.

A general comment is necessary here. It might seem to you as if arguments are conclusive, one way or the other. In fact, this is almost never the case. An argument can be convincing and persuasive, but there is always room for further argument if someone is stubborn or persistent enough. A good counter-example can always be explained away, and even a large number of counter-examples might be explained away. What ultimately sinks a bad hypothesis or general claim is the weight of the extra explanations it needs. For example, someone argues that there are Martians currently living on the earth. You point out that no one has ever seen a Martian. Your opponent explains this away by suggesting that the

Martians are invisible to the human eye. You argue that the atmosphere of the earth would not support Martian life. Your opponent argues that they are a different form of life, different from any that we can understand. You ask your opponent what these Martians do, and how we might come to test his or her view. He or she says that the Martians don't want us to know that they are here, so that they are careful not to do anything that would let us discover their presence. At this point, you will probably walk away in disgust. You have not silenced your opponent. In fact, he or she might go on inventing new ways out of your arguments forever. But, at a certain point, your opponent's explanations will have become so complicated and based on so much dubious knowledge that you and everyone else will be completely justified in ignoring him or her. The point of argument, remember, is to persuade. Absolute proof is impossible. But this means too that persuading some people is also impossible. There are limits to argument—at least, practical limits.

5.   *Reductio ad Absurdum*

One last argument deserves mention. It is usually called by its Latin name, **reductio ad absurdum,** and is a form of deductive argument. It is, however, an "indirect" argument. It consists of taking your opponent's view and showing that it has intolerable or contradictory consequences. For example, someone argues that one can never know whether minds exist other than one's own. You counter by pointing out that the very act of arguing this (with you) contradicts his point. He replies, no doubt, that he can't *know* that you exist. You show that he cannot even know that *he* exists. What you have done is reduce your opponent's view to absurdity, showing that it leads to consequences that no one could accept, in this case, the idea that he cannot have self-knowledge at all. A *reductio ad absurdum* argument, like a good counter-example, is often an excellent way of forcing other people to clarify their positions and explain more carefully exactly what they mean to argue.

6.   *The Worst Kinds of Fallacies*

No brief survey of logic would be adequate without identifying other fallacies, more general than those we discussed previously under deductive arguments. Whatever kind of arguments you employ, be careful that you *never* use the following:

MERE ASSERTION   The fact that you accept a position is not sufficient for anyone else to believe it. Stating your view is not an argument for it, and unless you are just answering a public opinion survey, every opinion always deserves a supporting argument. There are statements, of course, that everyone would accept at face value, and you need not argue those.

But that does not mean that they cannot be argued, for even the most obvious facts of common sense must be argued when challenged—this is what much of philosophy is about.

BEGGING THE QUESTION   Another fallacy is something that looks like an argument but simply accepts as a premise what is supposed to be argued for as a conclusion. For example, suppose you are arguing that one ought to be a Christian and your reason is that the Bible tells you so. This may, in fact, be conclusive for you, but if you are trying to convince someone who doesn't believe in Christ, he or she will probably not believe what the Bible says either. As an argument for becoming a Christian, therefore, referring to the Bible begs the question. Question begging often consists of a reworded conclusion, as in "this book will improve your grades because it will help you to do better in your courses."

VICIOUS CIRCLE   Begging the question is similar to another error, which is often called arguing in a "vicious circle." Consider a more elaborate version of the above fallacy. A person claims to know God exists because she has had a religious vision. Asked how she knows that the vision was religious rather than just the effect of something she ate, she replies that such an elaborate and powerful experience could not have been caused by anyone or anything but God. Asked how she knows this, she replies that God Himself told her—in the vision. Or, "he must be guilty because of the look on his face." "How do you know that he looks guilty rather than frightened or sad?" "Because he's the one who did it, that's why!" If you argue *A* because of *B*, and *B* because of *C*, but then *C* because of *A*, you have argued in a vicious circle. It is vicious because, as in begging the question, you have assumed just what you want to prove. But the following is worth remembering: Ultimately, all positions may come full circle, depending upon certain beliefs that can be defended only if you accept the rest of a great many beliefs. Debates between religious people and atheists are often like this, or arguments between free-marketeers and Marxists, where many hours of argument show quite clearly that each person accepts a large system of beliefs, all of which depend on the others. Some logicians call this a "virtuous circle," but this does not mean that there are no vicious circles. A virtuous circle is the development of an entire world-view, and it requires a great deal of thinking and organizing. Vicious circles, like begging the question, are usually shortcuts to nowhere that result from careless thinking.

IRRELEVANCIES   You have seen people who argue a point by arguing everything else, throwing up charts of statistics and complaining about the state of the universe and telling jokes; everything but getting to the point. This may be a technique of wearing out your opponent; it is not a way of persuading him or her to agree with you. No matter how brilliant an argument may be, it is no good to you unless it is relevant to the point you want to defend.

Ad Hominem Arguments   The most distasteful kind of irrelevancy is an attack on your opponent personally instead of arguing against his or her position. It may well be that the person you are arguing against is a liar, a sloppy dresser, bald and ugly, too young to vote or too old to work, but the only question is whether what he or she says is to be accepted. Harping on the appearance, reputation, manners, intelligence, friends, or possessions of your opponent may sometimes give your readers insight into why he or she holds a certain position, but it does not prove or disprove the position itself. As insight into an opponent's motives, personal considerations may, in small doses, be appropriate. But more than a very small dose is usually offensive, and it will usually weigh more against you than against your opponent. Whenever possible, avoid this kind of argument completely. It usually indicates that you don't have any good arguments yourself.

Unclear or Shifting Conclusions   One of the most frustrating arguments to read is an argument that has a vague conclusion or that shifts conclusions with every paragraph. If something is worth defending at all, it is worth stating clearly and sticking with it. If you argue that drug users should be punished, but aren't clear whether you mean people who traffic in heroin or people who take aspirin, you are not worth listening to. If you say that you mean illegal drug offenders, don't argue that drugs are bad for your body, since this is equally true for both legal and illegal drugs. If you say that you mean amphetamine users, then don't switch to talking about the illegality of drugs when someone explains to you the several medical uses of amphetamines. Know what you are arguing, or your arguments will have no point.

Changing Meanings   It is easy to miss a fallacy when the words seem to form a valid argument. For example, consider this:

> People are free as long as they can think for themselves.
> Prisoners in jail are free to think for themselves.
> Therefore, prisoners in jail are free.

This paradoxical conclusion is due to the ambiguity of "free," first used to refer to a kind of mental freedom, second to physical freedom. An interesting example is the argument often attributed to the famous British philosopher John Stuart Mill: "Whatever people desire, that is what is desirable." But notice that this argument plays with an ambiguity in language. Not everything that is in fact desired should be desired (for example, alcohol by alcoholics), so the argument is invalid. Be careful that the key terms in your argument keep the same meaning throughout.

DISTRACTION   Another familiar form of fallacy is the "red herring," the sometimes long-winded pursuit of an argument leading nowhere—except away from the point at issue. For example, in the middle of an argument about the relation between the mind and the brain, a neurologist may well enjoy telling you, in impressive detail, any number of odd facts about neurology, about brain operations he has performed, about silly theories that neurology-ignorant philosophers have defended in the past. But if these do not bear on the issue at hand, they are only pleasant ways of spending the afternoon, not steps to settling a difference of opinion. Distraction is a fallacy that is especially advantageous when the time for argument is limited. (For this reason, it is particularly prevalent in the classroom.)

PSEUDO-QUESTIONS   Sometimes fallacious reasoning begins with the very question being asked. For example, some philosophers have argued that asking such questions as "how is the mind related to the body?" or "could God create a mountain so heavy that even He could not move it?" are pseudo-questions; that is, they look like real questions—even profound questions—but are ultimately unanswerable because they are based on some hidden piece of nonsense. (In these two cases, it has been suggested that there is no legitimate distinction between mind and body, and therefore any question about how they are "related" is pointless; the second question presumes that God is "omnipotent" in the sense that He can do the logically impossible, which is absurd.) Pseudo-questions, like distractions, lead us down a lengthy path going nowhere, except that, with pseudo-questions, we start from nowhere too.

DUBIOUS AUTHORITY   We mentioned earlier that modern philosophy is based on the assumption that we have a right—and sometimes a duty—to question authority. And yet, most of our knowledge and opinions are based on appeals to authorities—whether scientists or "the people" are particularly wise or not. It would be extremely foolish, if not fatal, not to so appeal to authorities, especially in a world that has grown so technologically and socially complicated. We ask an economist what will happen if interest rates fall. We ask Miss Manners which fork to use for the salad. The fallacy of dubious authority arises when we ask the *wrong* person, when we appeal to an expert who is not in fact an expert in the area of concern. For example, when physicians are asked questions about nuclear policy, or physicists are asked questions about high school education, their expertise in one field does not necessarily transfer to the other. Appealing to opinions in books and newspapers depends on the authority of the authors and the publications in question. What is in print is not necessarily authoritative.

SLIPPERY SLOPE   Metaphors often pervade arguments. One of the more common metaphors is the "slippery slope," the greased incline which, once trod, inevitably carries us to the bottom. (In politics, it is sometimes called "the chilling effect" or "the domino theory.") For example, it is argued that any interference with free speech whatsoever, even forbidding someone to scream "fire" in a crowded auditorium, will sooner or later lead to the eradication of free speech of every kind, including informed, responsible political discussion. But is it the case that, by attacking an extreme instance, we thereby endanger an entire institution? Sometimes, this may be so. But more often than not, the slippery slope metaphor leads us to think that there is such inevitability when in fact there is no such thing.

ATTACKING A STRAW MAN   Real opponents with real arguments and objections are sometimes difficult to refute, and so the easy way out is to attack an unreal opponent with easily refutable arguments and objections. This unreal fellow is called "a straw man," and he provides us with the extra advantage of not fighting back. For example, a writer of religion attacks those who have suggested that Mohammed never existed, when in fact his opponents have only questioned a particular interpretation of his claim to divinity. A writer discussing the mind-body problem lampoons those who believe that there is *no* possible connection between the mind and the body—a position that has been argued by virtually no one.

PITY (AND OTHER EMOTIONAL APPEALS)   Some forms of fallacy appeal to the better parts of us, even as they challenge our fragile logical abilities. The appeal to pity has always been such an argument. Photographs of suffering people may well be an incentive to social action, but the connection between our pity—which is an undeniable virtue—and the social action in question is not yet an argument. The appeal to pity—and all appeals to emotion—have a perfectly legitimate place in philosophical argument, but such appeals are not yet themselves arguments for any particular position. An orator may make us angry, but what we are to do about the problem must be the product of further argument.

APPEAL TO FORCE   Physical might never makes philosophical right. Sometimes a person can be intimidated, but he or she is not thus refuted. Sometimes one has to back up a philosophical conviction with force, but it is never the force that justifies the conviction.

INAPPROPRIATE ARGUMENTS   The last fallacy we will mention has to do with choice of methods. To insist on deductive arguments when there are powerful inductive arguments against you is a fallacy too—not a fallacious argument, perhaps, but a mistake in logic all the same. For example, if you are arguing deductively that there cannot be any torture going on in a certain country, since Mr. Q rules the country and Mr. Q is a good man (where the implicit premise is that "good men don't allow torture in their country"), you had better be willing to give up the argument when dozens of trustworthy eyewitnesses publicly describe the tortures they have seen or experienced. To continue with your deduction in the face of such information is foolish. This may not tell you where your argument has gone wrong: Perhaps Mr. Q is not such a good man. Or perhaps he has been overpowered. Or perhaps good men can't prevent torture if they aren't told about it. But in any case, the argument must now be given up.

The same may be true the other way around. Certain abstract questions seem to be answerable only by deduction. When arguing about religious questions, for example, looking for evidence upon which to build an inductive argument may be foolish. What is at stake are your basic concepts of religion and their implications. Evidence, in the sense of looking around for pertinent facts, may be irrelevant. Very abstract questions often require deductive arguments only.

To be caught in one of these fallacies is almost always embarrassing and damaging to your overall argument. If you have a case to make, then make it in the most powerfully persuasive way. An intelligent combination of deductive and inductive arguments, coupled with analogies and proper criticisms of alternative positions, is the most effective persuasion available. If you think your opinions are important, then they deserve nothing less than the best supporting arguments you can put together.

As you proceed with your course, you will have the opportunity to use many of these logical forms, not only on the great philosophers of the past but on your own thinking as well. You will find that philosophical criticism is a powerful tool in the arguments you have with your friends and the debates you carry on, whatever the topic. Most importantly, philosophy is a valuable aid to getting together your own thoughts about things, about the problems of philosophy that you will encounter in this book, and about "life in general."

But then again, why should we assume that the truth is all that coherent or logical? As Ralph Waldo Emerson once wrote:

A foolish consistency is the hobgoblin of little minds, adored by lit-tle statesmen and philosophers and divines. With consistency a great soul has simply nothing to do. He may as well concern him-self with his shadow on the wall. Speak what you think now in hard words and to-morrow speak what to-morrow thinks in hard words again, though it contradict every thing you said to-day.—"Ah, so you shall be sure to be misunderstood."—Is it so bad then to be misunderstood? Pythagoras was misunderstood, and Socrates, and Jesus, and Luther, and Copernicus, and Galileo, and Newton, and every pure and wise spirit that ever took flesh. To be great is to be misunderstood.[10]

GLOSSARY

abstract   being overly general, not concrete, independent of particular concerns or objects. For example, a philosopher may attempt to ascertain the nature of justice without particular reference to any concrete practical case.

***ad hominem* argument**   an argument against the person instead of the position; for example, attacking a philosopher's living habits instead of asking whether or not his theories are true.

argument   process of reasoning from one claim to another. An argument may, but need not, be directed against an explicit alternative. A philosophical argument does not require an opponent or a disagreement.

assertion   a statement or declaration, taking a position. *Mere* assertion, when presented as an argument, is a fallacy; arguments consist not only of assertions but of reasons for them as well.

assumption   a principle taken for granted, without argument or proof.

autonomy   intellectual independence and freedom from authority; the presumed ability to determine the acceptability of one's own beliefs and actions.

axiom   a principle that is generally accepted from the beginning and so may be used without further debate as a starting point of argument.

begging the question   Merely restating as the conclusion of an argument one of its premises. For example, "Why do oysters give me indigestion? Because they upset my stomach."

Cartesianism   concerning Descartes. In particular, concerning his philosophical method. (Descartes' followers are generally called "Cartesians" and their method "Cartesianism.") The Cartesian method is essentially a deductive method, as in geometry, starting with self-evident axioms and deducing the rest.

certainty   beyond doubt. But it is important to insist that certainty in the philosophical sense is more than the common psychological use of certain ("feeling certain"). One can feel certain and yet be wrong or foolish. One can be certain, in this philosophical sense, only if one can prove that the matter is beyond doubt, that no reasons for doubt could be raised.

coherence   logical connection. A statement by a witness in a courtroom coheres with other testimony and evidence when it fits in and follows from that other testimony and evidence. To say that a philosophy must be

---

[10]Ralph Waldo Emerson, "Self Reliance" (New York, Wise, 1929) pp. 143–144.

coherent is to say that its various principles must fit together in an orderly and logically agreeable fashion.

consistent fitting together in an orderly logical way. Two principles are consistent if they do not contradict each other. A philosophy is consistent if none of its principles contradict each other.

contradiction logical relation of two principles in which the truth of one requires the falsity of the other. A witness's statement in court contradicts other testimony if both statements cannot be true.

counter-example an example that contradicts a generalization, such as "all elephants have tusks." A counter-example would be an elephant without tusks.

criterion the test or standard according to which a judgment or an evaluation can be made. For example, a test for a substance being an acid is that it turns litmus paper red.

critical thinking so as to be mindful of mistakes in reasoning; to be critical is not necessarily to be unpleasant.

declarative sentence a sentence in which one takes a position, states a fact, asserts a proposition.

deduction (deductive argument) a process of reasoning from one principle to another by means of accepted rules of inference. In a deductive argument, a conclusion follows necessarily from the premises, and so if you are certain of the premises, you can be certain of the conclusion, too.

dialectic argument through dialogue, disagreement, and successive revisions, out of which comes agreement.

doubt lack of certainty; lack of reasons to believe and perhaps having reasons not to believe. It is important to distinguish doubt in this philosophical sense from doubt in the ordinary psychological sense. Mere personal uncertainty or distrust is not sufficient; there must be a demonstrable reason for doubt, that is, reasons for not accepting the beliefs in question.

Enlightenment an important cultural and philosophical movement in the eighteenth century in Europe defined by a new confidence in human reason and individual autonomy. Some of the major figures of this movement were René Descartes, the metaphysician Baron Henri d'Holbach, the political philosopher Jean-Jacques Rousseau, and the political reformer-writer Voltaire in France. In Great Britain, Enlightenment philosophers were John Locke and David Hume; in Germany, Immanuel Kant.

fallacy an apparently persuasive argument which is really an error in reasoning, an unsound or invalid argument.

first principles those axioms and assumptions from which a philosophy begins. These must be solid and indisputable principles; they need not be those principles that one happens to first believe.

formal logic a branch of logic that is concerned with the principles of reasoning as such, in which the relationships between symbols are studied and not their interpretation.

generalization usually, a proposition about all of a group or set of things on the basis of a limited acquaintance with some of its members. In logic, however, a generalization may be universal ("all x's are y's") or existential ("there are some x's that are y's").

hypothesis   a provisional conclusion, accepted as most probable in the light of the known facts, or tentatively adopted as a basis for analysis.

implication   one statement logically follows from another. Statements imply one another: We infer one from the other.

incoherent   not fitting together in an orderly or logically agreeable fashion. Using fancy jargon that has no precise meaning may be a source of incoherence. So is a mere list of random beliefs, without any order or logic to hold them together. (They may even contradict each other as well.) An incoherent philosophy may be insightful and true in parts, but because it never coheres into a single system, it may well appear to be nonsense, or simply a jumble of words and phrases. In other cases, an incoherent philosophy may be one that makes no sense, whose terms are utter gibberish or whose principles are mere ramblings without intelligible connection or interpretation. (Opposite of coherent.)

inconsistent   not compatible; contradictory. One might also say that a person's actions are inconsistent with his or her principles. People as well as other principles can be inconsistent with a principle.

inductive argument   a process of reasoning in which the characteristics of an entire class or set of things is inferred on the basis of an acquaintance with some of its members. In an inductive argument, although the conclusion is supported by the premises, it does not follow necessarily from the premises and its truth is not guaranteed by them.

inference   reasoning from one set of principles to another, as in an argument. Deductive inference is but a single kind of inference.

invalid   not correctly following agreed-upon rules of inference in an argument. Always applied to arguments, not to statements. (Opposite of valid.)

logic   the study of the rules of valid inference and "rational argument." In general, a sense of order.

method   (sometimes, **methodology**) approach and strategy for resolving philosophical problems. For example, the appeal to experience, the appeal to divine revelation, the insistence upon mathematical logic, confidence in reason or trust in authority: all of these are aspects of philosophical methodology.

method of doubt   (or **methodological doubt**) Descartes' technique for discovering those principles of which we can be "perfectly certain"; namely, doubt everything, until you discover those principles that cannot be doubted.

paradox   a self-contradictory conclusion drawn from seemingly acceptable premises. For example, suppose you try to help all and only those people who do not help themselves. That sounds reasonable enough. But then, do you help yourself? If you do help everyone, then you would also help yourself. But if you don't help yourself, then you aren't helping all who don't help themselves. This is a paradox.

predicate   that which is asserted or denied of a thing, which refers to a property of things. Some familiar predicates would be "is red," "is an animal."

premise   the principle or one of those principles upon which an argument is based. The starting point of an argument.

presupposition   a principle that is assumed as a precondition for whatever else one believes, which itself may remain unexamined and uncriticized throughout the argument. For example, a lawyer presupposes that the court aims at justice and has some idea what is just. It is the philosopher, not the lawyer, who challenges those claims.

proof   in a deductive argument, a proof is a sequence of steps, each according to an acceptable rule of inference, to the conclusion to be proved.

proposition   an assertion that is either true or false.

reason   the ability to think abstractly, to form arguments and make inferences. Sometimes referred to as a "faculty" of the human mind (a leftover from eighteenth-century philosophy). More specialized meanings will be discussed in later chapters.

reasons   explanations, justifications, evidence, or some other basis for accepting a proposition.

reductio ad absurdum   a form of argument in which one refutes a statement by showing that it leads to self-contradiction or an otherwise intolerable conclusion.

reflection   to think about something, to "put it in perspective." We often do this with our beliefs and our emotions. For example, "This morning I was furious at you, but after reflecting on it at lunch, I decided that it was nothing to be angry about." One might say that philosophy is reflection about life and knowledge in general.

rhetoric   the persuasive use of language to convince other people to accept your beliefs.

rule of inference   a generally accepted principle according to which one may infer one statement from another. (We have not yet said anything about the nature of these "generally acceptable" rules; for now, we have simply presupposed that some such rules are acceptable to everyone; for example, "if *either* A is true *or* B is true, but we know that B is false, then we can conclude that A is true.")

self-contradictory   a contradiction within one and the same statement or set of statements. What I say may contradict what you say; but what I say might also contradict something else that I said, in which case I am being self-contradictory. Moreover, in a few strange cases, my own statement may be self-contradictory; for example, "I do not exist."

self-evident   obvious without proof or argument; for Descartes, a "clear and distinct idea," one about which there could be no doubt and it is obvious that there could be no doubt.

skepticism   a philosophical belief that knowledge is not possible, that doubt will not be overcome by any valid arguments. A philosopher who holds this belief is called a skeptic. Again, skepticism is not mere personal doubt; it requires systematic doubt with reasons for that doubt.

sound   an argument whose premises are true and that is valid.

syllogism   a three-line deductive argument; the best-known examples are those arguments of this form:

> All P's are Q's. (Major premise)
> S is a P. (Minor premise)
> _____
> *Therefore* S is a Q. (Conclusion)

The major premise asserts something about the predicate of the conclusion (in this case, Q). The minor premise asserts something about the subject of the conclusion (in this case, S).

system   an orderly formulation of principles (together with reasons, implications, evidence, methods, and presuppositions) that is comprehensive, consistent, and coherent and in which the various principles are interconnected as tightly as possible by logical implications.

trivial   obvious and not worth saying.

unsound   an argument whose premises are false or that is invalid.

valid   an argument that correctly follows agreed-upon rules of inference. Always applies to arguments, not statements.

vicious circle   use of two propositions or arguments to support one another with no other support. For example, "He must be guilty because he's got such a guilty look on his face. . . . Well, I can tell it's a guilty look because he's the one who is guilty."

◆ *BIBLIOGRAPHY AND FURTHER READING* ◆

A large number of alternative views of philosophy are available in Charles I. Bontempo and S. Jack Odell, eds., *The Owl of Minerva* (New York: McGraw-Hill, 1975). The trial, imprisonment, and death of Socrates are recounted by Plato in the dialogues *Apology, Crito,* and *Phaedo* in *The Last Days of Socrates,* trans. Hugh Tredennick (London: Penguin, 1954). An excellent account of Socrates' life is A. E. Taylor, *Socrates* (New York: Doubleday, Anchor, 1959). The best single book on the Enlightenment is Peter Gay, *The Enlightenment: An Interpretation* (New York: Vintage, 1966); a simpler discussion is Robert Anchor, *The Enlightenment Tradition* (New York: Harper & Row, 1967); and a philosophical anthology of the period is Isaiah Berlin, *The Age of Enlightenment* (New York: Mentor, 1955). Two standard introductions to logic are W. Salmon, *Logic* (Englewood Cliffs, NJ: Prentice-Hall, 1963) and I. Copi, *Introduction to Logic* (New York: Macmillan, 1961). A more original approach is R. D. Bradley and N. Schwartz, *Possible Worlds* (Indianapolis, IN: Hackett, 1979).

INTRODUCING PHILOSOPHY

PART
ONE

Knowing the World, and Beyond

1

REALITY: ANCIENT VIEWS

It must be that what can be spoken and thought is:
for it is possible for it to be,
and it is not possible for what is nothing to be.

PARMENIDES

A. "THE WAY THE WORLD REALLY IS"

Because it was a Greek who coined the term *philosophy* and in Greece where philosophy was first practiced as a formal discipline, philosophers today generally refer to the first Greek thinkers as the first "philosophers." Philosophy in this sense is said to begin with a seemingly odd claim made by the Greek philosopher Thales on the coast of Turkey sometime around 580 B.C. He suggested that the source of everything was water. The earth floats upon water, and it and all things on it are made of water. Aristotle later called his theory "childish," but he also acknowledged that his was the "oldest view that has been transmitted to us" (in his essay "On the Heavens"). In his *Metaphysics,* Aristotle went on to consider Thales' view in some detail:

> Most of the first philosophers thought that principles in the form of matter were the only principles of all things. For they say that the element and first principle of the things that exist is that from which they all are and from which they first come into being and into which they are finally destroyed, its substance remaining and its properties changing. . . . There must be some nature—either one or more than one—from which the other things come into being, it being preserved. But as to the number and form of this sort of principle, they do not all agree. Thales, the founder of this kind of philosophy, says that it is water (that is why he declares that the earth rests on water). He perhaps came to acquire this belief from

seeing that the nourishment of everything is moist and that heat itself comes from this and lives by this (for that from which anything
comes into being is its first principle)—he came to his belief both
for this reason and because the seeds of everything have a moist
nature, and water is the natural principle of moist things.[1]

So too, the commentator Simplicius suggested that "Thales was the first
to introduce the study of nature to the Greeks." His seemingly simple
claim, that the world rests on water, was in fact one of the most
remarkable claims of the ancient world, not because it is so implausible
(as his own students pointed out to him) but because it was one of the
first recorded attempts to describe "the way the world really is," beyond
all appearances and day-to-day opinions. Accordingly, Thales' theory
marks the beginning of Western science as well as philosophy. He was the
first Greek thinker to break with common sense and religion and offer
a general theory about the ultimate nature of reality. In place of
mythological accounts of nature and human behavior in terms of divine
agencies (gods, goddesses, and spirits), he and other thinkers of the
period provided explanations in terms of laws and abstract generalizations. Knowledge became an end in itself, one of the noblest pursuits of
humanity.

B. THE FIRST PHILOSOPHERS: THE "TURNING POINT OF CIVILIZATION"

We are all aware that the way the world really is may not correspond
to our everyday views of the world, the way it seems to be. For example,
we casually talk of "sunrises" and "sunsets," and surely it does seem as
if the sun goes "up" and "down," while we and our earth stay in place. It
took several thousand years for people in general to recognize that,
despite appearances, our earth actually moves around the sun. We now
accept that without question, even if there is little in our everyday
experience to support it. Similarly, consider the chair on which you are
sitting: Does it seem to you that it is composed mostly of empty space and
tiny electrically charged colorless particles whirling about at fantastic
speeds? Of course not, but modern science has taught you that "solid"
objects are indeed made up of just such spaces and particles. The world
is not as it seems. And the beginnings of both philosophy and science
were the first attempts of men and women to see beyond their "common
sense" views of things and try to find the reality behind them.

Although the pre-Socratic Greeks were the first thinkers to call
themselves "philosophers," we can look back from our modern vantage
point to many ancient traditions we might want to call "philosophical,"

[1] Aristotle, *Metaphysics* 983b6–11, pp. 17–27.

in the sense that they looked beyond ordinary experience for an understanding of "reality." The ancient philosophers did not have the advantage of either our scientific sophistication or a long history of philosophical thinking to give them support. Yet, there were lots of new and profoundly thoughtful opinions offered by the ancients about reality, whatever the differences in the ways different thinkers from different places thought about the world. The first investigations into the ultimate nature of reality, among which we include Thales' account, appeared in the middle of the first millennium B.C. Quite amazingly, several world-shattering views about reality appeared independently in different areas of the world during the same period. The twentieth-century philosopher Karl Jaspers described this as the "Axial Period"—the turning point of civilization.

◆**from the "Axial Period,"
by Karl Jaspers**

It would seem that this axis of history is to be found in the pe-riod around 500 B.C., in the spiritual process that occurred between 800 and 200 B.C. It is there that we meet with the most deep-cut dividing line in history. Man, as we know him today, came into being. For short we may style this the "Axial Period."

CHARACTERIZATION OF THE AXIAL PERIOD

The most extraordinary events are concentrated in this period. Confucius and Lao-tse were living in China, all the directions of Chinese philosophy came into being, including those of Mo-ti, Chuang-tse, Lieh-tsu, and a host of others; India produced the Upanishads and Buddha, and, like China, ran the whole gamut of philosophical possibilities down to skepticism, to materialism, sophism and nihilism; in Iran Zarathustra taught the challenging view of the world as a struggle between good and evil; in Palestine the prophets made their appearance, from Elijah, by way of Isa-iah and Jeremiah, to Deutero-Isaiah; Greece witnessed the appear-ance of Homer, of the philosophers—Parmenides, Heraclitus, and Plato—of the tragedians, of Thucydides, and of Archimedes. Every-thing that is merely intimated by these names developed during these few centuries almost simultaneously in China, India, and the Occident without any one of these knowing of the others.

What is new about this age, in all three of these worlds, is that man becomes aware of Being as a whole, of himself and his limita-tions. He experiences the terrible nature of the world and his own impotence. He asks radical questions. Face to face with the void he strives for liberation and redemption. By consciously recognizing his limits he sets himself the highest goals. He experiences unconditionality in the depth of selfhood and in the clarity of transcendence.

This took place in reflection. . . .

In this age were born the fundamental categories within which we still think today, and the beginnings of the world religions, by which human beings still live, were created. The step into universality was taken in every sense.

As a result of this process, hitherto unconsciously accepted ideas, customs, and conditions were subjected to examination, questioned, and liquidated. Everything was swept into the vortex. Insofar as the traditional substance still possessed vitality and actuality, its manifestations were illuminated and thereby transmuted.

The *Mythical Age*, with its tranquility and self-evidence, was at an end. . . .

For the first time *philosophers* appeared. Human beings dared to rely on themselves as individuals. Hermits and wandering thinkers in China, ascetics in India, philosophers in Greece, and prophets in Israel all belong together, however much they may differ from each other in their beliefs, the contents of their thought, and their inner dispositions. Man proved capable of confronting inwardly the entire universe. He discovered within himself the origin from which to raise himself above his own self and the world.

In *speculative thought* he lifts himself up toward Being itself.[2]

What is this "Being"? What is the way the world really is? How do you answer that question? Very likely you will appeal to the authority of modern science, and that is probably a reasonable beginning. But you know that the "science" of one generation is seen as the superstitions of another. (Once people believed that the earth was flat.) And you have probably, at least once in your school career, caught one of the "authorities"—perhaps a teacher, perhaps even a noted scientist—in a mistake. Can we simply accept what scientists tell us without question, any more than Descartes could accept the teachings of his teachers without question? Have you ever examined the evidence for the theory that the earth goes around the sun? If not, why should you believe it? Or, to take a very different example, scientists are generally agreed that some version of Darwin's theory of evolution is true. Does that mean that you have to believe it? Many people do not, because it seems to contradict the story of creation in the Bible. And so you have to decide which to believe. Even within science there are always disagreements and debates. There are different theories to answer the same questions, and you have to decide. Which are you to believe?

Your view of reality is influenced by modern science but it is also

[2]From Karl Jaspers: *Basic Philosophical Writings—Selections.* Edited, translated, and with introductions by Edith Ehrlich, Leonard H. Ehrlich, and George B. Pepper. (Athens, OH: Ohio University Press), pp. 382–87.

influenced by twenty-five hundred years of philosophy, even if you've never studied it before. We can say, with some confidence, that we know much more about the world than the ancient philosophers. But we must not be too confident. Not only are there still many scientific problems unsolved, there are and always will be conflicting views of how we are to see our world in more general terms. How much faith should we have in religion? How much should we see the world as a world of people and how much as a world of physical objects? How much should we accept "common sense" (which changes all the time) and how much should we indulge in scientific and philosophical speculation (which changes all the time also)?

1.   The Ionian Naturalists

Thales' approach was somewhat different from that of the thinkers of other early traditions; he is rightly credited with being the first in the line of philosophers of which Socrates was the culmination (called the "pre-Socratics"). Thales' answer, that ultimate reality is water, should not surprise nearly so much as the fact that he attempted such a theory at all. Indeed, we should be impressed by the fact that he even asked "what is the world really like?" because as far as we know, no one had attempted to ask such a question in such a way before him.

Thales was not willing to accept the opinions and mythologies that had been handed down for generations. He insisted, instead, on observing the world for himself, on thinking out his own answer, and on discussing it with his friends and neighbors, many of whom, no doubt, thought that he was slightly peculiar. (It is also said, however, that his cosmic speculations helped him to make a fortune in the olive oil business. No doubt his neighbors respected that.)

Thales was the first of a group of philosophers—or rather, the first of several groups of philosophers—scattered around the various Greek islands and the coasts of Asia Minor, or Ionia, who lived in the sixth and fifth centuries B.C., just before the time of Socrates. Accordingly, they are called Ionians, one group of the pre-Socratics. Their opinions varied greatly. Among them they developed a wide range of systematic views of the universe and the ultimate nature of reality. Unlike Socrates and most later philosophers, they were not very concerned with questions of method. They went straight to the heart of the question, to the nature of the universe itself. And some of them, as we shall see, came strikingly close to our modern scientific conceptions.

The idea that everything was water did not satisfy Thales' friends and students. They appreciated his attempt to find the "One Reality," but they thought that it must be something else. Thales' first student, named Anaximander, argued against his teacher that some things, for example, the dry, dusty cliffs of Asia Minor, could not possibly be made of water, which was naturally wet and never dry. Anaximander was the first recorded student to talk back to his teacher (which in philosophy, unlike most other subjects, is considered a virtue rather than a discourtesy). Thales had made the first gigantic step, rejecting the "obvious" answers of common sense and trying to find out "the way the world really is." But notice that Thales' answer to that question still appeals to a common-sense ingredient, water, which is so familiar to us. And Thales' defense of his thesis also depended on some very common-sensical claims: for example, the idea that if you dig deep enough into the earth, you will eventually hit water.

Once Thales had made the break with common sense and said that the way the world really is need not be at all like the way it seems to us, it was no longer necessary to suppose that reality was anything like our experiences. Anaximander, consequently, argued that ultimate reality could not be composed of any of the then-known elements—earth, air, fire, or water—since these were each so different from the others. They might be mixed together, as when earth and water are mixed to make mud or clay, but it made no sense to suppose that any of them might really be made up of any of the others. So Anaximander suggested that the ultimate nature of reality was something else—let us simply call it "primordial stuff"—that is not like anything we could ever experience.

The word Anaximander actually used was the *apeiron,* which is sometimes translated as "the indefinite" or "the unlimited." The *apeiron,* or "primordial stuff," was a chaos, or void which yielded the variety of things in the world. This notion of "stuff" was a second major step in philosophy and science. Today, we feel comfortable with the idea that things are made of "stuff" (atoms and molecules) that we never experience in everyday life. But in the ancient world, this suggestion must have seemed extremely exciting.

Anaximander's student, Anaximenes, thought his teacher's notion of "stuff" was too mysterious, but he also rejected Thales' theory and replaced it with the idea that air is the basic "stuff." Just as our soul, which is air, integrates us, so breath and air surround the whole cosmos. Air makes up the other elements and the various things of the world by becoming thicker and thinner. (Think of steam condensing to form water, and then ice.) Anaximenes thus introduced the idea that changes in the quantity of basic elements can produce changes in quality as well—a key principle of modern science.

2. Monism, Materialism, and Immaterial "Stuff"

The attempt to reduce all of the varied things in the world to one kind of thing as Thales and his students did with water, air, and *apeiron,* is called **monism.** It is the search for ultimate reality, which might be very different from the appearance of everyday life, that has motivated philosophy and science for twenty-five hundred years. So the debate began: Was the world really made of water? Perhaps, thought Thales' students, it is some other kind of "stuff." Today, the debate continues: Is everything made up of matter, or energy, or matter-energy? Are there basic particles that cannot be reduced to anything else? Scientists once thought that atoms were such particles; then they discovered electrons, protons, and neutrons that made up atoms. And since then, they have discovered dozens of other particles, and today they are debating a mysterious particle called a quark, which physicists now think may provide the ultimate answer to Thales' ancient question. But notice that all of these views are strictly physical. That is, they are concerned about basic questions of what we now call physics and chemistry, concerned about the material "stuff" of which all things are composed. This was true of Thales; and it is still true of modern "quark" theorists. Accordingly, the philosophies of all of these thinkers can be called **materialism,** the view that reality is ultimately composed of some kind of material "stuff." (In this context, "materialism" does not mean concern about the material things in life—money, cars, jewelry, or getting a new garbage disposal every year.)

If you think like a physical scientist, the idea that the universe is made up of some kind of material "stuff" sounds very plausible. In fact, you might wonder, what else could it be made of? Consider this: There are some things in the universe that could not plausibly be made of material "stuff." For example, what about your thoughts and feelings? Are they simply bits of matter, or are they composed of some entirely different kind of "stuff," perhaps some kind of mental or spiritual "stuff"? Some early philosophers, particularly to the east of Greece, claimed that reality was not made of just physical elements, like water, air, or even the *apeiron*, but rather that reality was inherently spiritual. Many of these thinkers claimed that the primordial "stuff" was divine, or godly. We will see that in Greece as well, the pre-Socratic philosopher, Heraclitus, was already groping for a conception of an immaterial "stuff," something which was not material, but rather spiritual or nonphysical. ("Immaterial," in a philosophical context, does not mean "unimportant.")

3.   The Upanishads

While the Ionian Naturalists were pursuing their proto-scientific inquiries in Greece, sages in India were developing their own doctrines about the nature of reality, which were essentially religious. The earliest articulation of the concept of God appears in the ancient Indian Vedic literature, especially in the appendages called **Upanishads,** "secret doctrines," from which later Eastern religious and spiritual notions efflorescenced. In addition to the innumerable sects and divisions of religious practice and belief traditionally termed Hindu or Buddhist, such lesser-known Indic religions as Jainism and even Sikhism owe a conceptual debt to the early Upanishads.

A passage from one of the oldest Upanishads (*c.* 800 B.C.) relates to the spiritual aspiration that sets the tone for much Upanishadic teaching (whom or what is invoked in this entreaty is not clear):

> From non-being *(asat)* to true being *(sat)* lead me.
> From darkness to light lead me.
> From death to immortality lead me.[3]

The "seeking" expressed in the early Upanishads centers on **Brahma** (usually anglicized as **"Brahman"**), somehow considered the secret both of ourselves and of the universe. The Upanishadic notion of Brahma is a seeking of a Unity underlying all individual selves and things—and the "Emptiness" and absolutist notions of much Buddhist thought as well. Buddhism's view of the supremely real as "Emptiness" or "Openness" is discussed in the following two ancient passages.

> An ocean, a single seer without duality becomes he whose world [of vision] is *brahma.* This is his supreme attainment. This is his highest fulfillment. This is his best world. This is his supreme bliss. Other creatures subsist on a small bit of this bliss.

This "Absolute" is considered to have a peculiar "logic," or "nature," unlike that of everyday, finite, physical things.

> Not moving the One is swifter than the mind. The gods do not reach That running [always] before. . . . That moves; That moves not. It is far, and It is near. It is within all this; It indeed is outside all this. He who experiences all things in the Self and the Self in all things thereupon does not fear.
>
> Om. That is the Full. This is the Full. From the Full, the Full proceeds. Taking away the Full of the Full, it is just the Full that remains.

The next passage illustrates doctrines that some have called "pantheism," an identification of God and Nature. Whether it illustrates pantheism or not, it reveals a doctrine of divine immanence, of divine *indwelling* in all things, and a deism—the Inner Controller though indwelling everywhere is thought to be in some sense "other" than the things, and selves, in which it indwells.

> Who standing in the earth is other than the earth, whom the earth knows not, whose body the earth is, who within controls the

[3]This passage and the following four passages are taken from *Brhadāranyaka* 1.3.28, *Brhadāranyaka* 4.3.32, *Īśā Upaniṣad* 4–6, *Brhadāranyaka* 5.1.1, *Brhadāranyaka* 3.7.3–3.7.23 passim, *Chāndogya* 6.11, and *Katha* 1.25–27, 2.11–12, and 2.20–23. Unless noted otherwise, all passages were translated by Stephen Phillips.

earth, that is this, the Self, the Inner Controller, the Immortal. Who standing in the waters is other than the waters, whom the waters know not, whose body the waters are, that is this, the Self, the Inner Controller. . . . Who standing in the wind is other than the wind, whom the wind knows not, whose body the wind is, who within controls the wind, that is this, the Self, the Inner Controller, the Immortal. . . . Who standing in all beings is other than all beings, whom all beings know not, whose body all beings are, that is this, the Self, the Inner Controller, the Immortal. . . . Who standing in the eye is other than the eye, whom the eye knows not, whose body the eye is, who within controls the eye, that is this, the Self, the Inner Controller, the Immortal. Who standing in the ear is other than the ear, whom the ear knows not, whose body the ear is, that is this, the Self, the Inner Controller, the Immortal. . . . Who standing in the understanding is other than the understanding, whom the understanding knows not, whose body the understanding is, who within controls the understanding, that is this, the Self, the Inner Controller, the Immortal. . . . Who standing in the seed of generation is other than the seed of generation, whom the seed of generation knows not, whose body the seed of generation is, that is this, the Self, the Inner Controller, the Immortal. Unseen, the seer, unheard, the hearer, unthought, the thinker, unknown, the knower; there is no other seer than this, no other hearer than this, no other thinker than this, no other knower than this. That is this, the Self, the Inner Controller, the Immortal; valueless is anything other.

The first passage above—one that is quoted repeatedly over centuries of commentary and discussion—illustrates a "spiritually monist" view that has enjoyed substantial prominence in India, a view that finds the "self" (or "*ātmā*") as the key to life and reality. Their spiritualism made the Upanishads recognize the small worth of worldly desires and attachments in the light of inevitable death and, to be sure, the possibility of an extraordinary knowledge, or experience, that is thought to carry us beyond this great fear.

"Were someone to hack the root of this large tree, dear child, it would bleed but live; were someone to hack its trunk, it would bleed but live; were someone to hack its tops, it would bleed but live. Pervaded by the living self (*ātmā*), it stands continually drinking and exulting. If life were to leave one branch, then that branch would dry up; if a second, then that would dry up; a third, then that would dry up; if the whole, then the whole would dry up. Just in this way indeed, dear child," he [Śvetaketu's teacher] said, "understand: this endowed most surely with life dies; life does not die. That which is this, this is the most subtle, everything here has that as its soul (*ātmā*). That is the reality; that is the self (*ātmā*);

you are that O Śvetaketu." "Please, sir, instruct me even further."
"Alright, dear one," he said. . . .

[Yama, "Death":] "Whatever desires, (even) the most difficult to
win in the world of mortals, have them all at your demand. Delightful females with chariots, with music—none like these may be won
by mortal men—be entertained by them, O Naciketas, given by
me. Do not inquire into dying." [Naciketas:] Existing only until tomorrow are such desires of a mortal, and, O Bringer-of-the-end,
they wear away the splendor and vigor of every sense and power
one has. Even all that is alive is of small worth indeed. Yours alone
are the chariots; yours the dancing and the singing. A person is
not to be satisfied with wealth. Are we to have wealth once we have
seen you? But the boon that I wish to choose is this (answer this
question): 'Will we continue to exist while you rule?'" . . . [Death:]
Having seen in your grasp, O Naciketas, the fulfillment of desire
and the foundation of the world and an infinity of power, of
self-will, and the safe shore of fearlessness, and great fame sung far
and wide, you wisely let it all go. A person who is wise and steadfast, discerning the God through spiritual discipline and
study—the one that is difficult to experience, who has plunged
deep into the hidden and is established in the secret place, standing in the cavern, the ancient—leaves joy and sorrow behind. . . .
Subtler than the subtle, grander than the grand, the self is set in
the secret heart of the creature. One who is without self-will experiences this (and becomes) free of sorrow; through his clearness
and purity towards material things [or, "through the grace of the
Creator"4], one experiences the self's greatness and breadth. Seated
he travels far; lying down he goes everywhere. Who other than I is
fit to know this God, the one that has both maddening pleasure
and freedom from maddening pleasure? The wise person, recognizing the bodiless in bodies, the settled in things unsettled, the great
and pervasive self *(ātmā),* does not grieve nor suffer. This the self
is not to be won by eloquent instruction, nor by intelligence, nor by
much study. Just that person whom this chooses, by such a person is this to be won; to such a person this the self reveals, uncov-
ers its very own form and body. . . .

4.   *Zarathustra*

In the sixth century B.C., a Persian reformer named Zarathustra
broke away from the Indic peoples who were the progenitors of the
Upanishads. He preached a **monotheism** over and against the early
Indian polytheism. Zarathustra claimed that his god—called **Ahura
Mazda**—was not just spiritual or divine nature, but a creator, the one
origin of all that existed. Ahura Mazda was a personal and all-good
god, who created all natural things. Thus, Zarathustra and the religion

---

4The Sanskrit text is ambiguous between these two meanings; the first suggests Buddhist
  doctrines, the alternative suggests Hindu theism.

he began (called Zoroastrianism) was extremely influential on the later monotheistic religions of Christianity, Judaism, and Islam.

Zarathustra was the first to recognize and formulate a doctrine regarding the existence and origin of good and evil in the universe. Ahura Mazda, the One Lord, created first among all things two twin spirits, lower sorts of divinities. The character of the first, called **Spenta Mainyush,** drew him and everything which followed him to goodness and good acts. The character of the other, called **Angra Mainyush,** led him and everything in his service to do evil. The twins are described in this passage from the *Gathas,* (the original portion of the **Zend Avesta,** the scripture of Zoroastrianism).

> Thus are the primeval spirits who as a pair (combining their oppo-
> site strivings), and (yet each) independent in his action, have been
> famed (of old). (They are) a better thing, they two, and a worse,
> as to thought, word, and as to deed. And between these two let the
> wisely acting choose right. (*Yasna,* XLV:2)[5]

Although Angra Mainyush and Spenta Mainyush are born with natural tendencies toward evil and good, respectively, they choose quite freely to express it in action. Thus, while Ahura Mazda is responsible for the creation of everything, still Angra Mainyush is responsible for unleashing evil, whose forms are deceit, destructiveness, and death.

The natural world, according to Zoroastrianism, is always spiritually endowed and is set against itself like two armies, in an eternal battle between good and evil. Everything that exists freely chooses its alliance in accordance with its tendencies. Human beings, however, are free and conscious decision-makers, and so have more choice about their moral alliances than do other creatures.

It followed that all natural entities were things either to be worshiped or reviled. Fire, which represented the "Beneficient Immortal" spirit, **Asha** or "Righteousness," was especially to be worshiped, as the best of the "good creation." In fact, in their own time, Zoroastrians were referred to as "Fire Worshipers."

In the following passage, also from the *Gathas,* Ahura Mazda despairs for his creation, should Asha find no good guardian for it.

> Upon this the creator of the Kine (the holy herds) asked of
> Righteousness: How (was) thy guardian for the Kine (appointed) by
> thee when, as having power (over all her fate), ye made

---

[5] All passages from the Yasna are taken from the Zend-Avesta, Part III, trans. L. H. Mills; part of the series. *The Sacred Books of the East,* ed. F. Max Muller (Westport, CT: Greenwood Press, 1972 (Oxford, 1887). All passages from the Yashts are taken from Zend-Avesta, Part II, trans. James Darmesteter; part of the series, *The Sacred Books of the East,* ed. F. Max Muller (Motilal Banarsidass: Delhi, 1965 (Oxford, 1883).

her? . . . Whom did ye select as her (life's) master who might hurl
back the fury of the wicked?

    Asha: . . . (Great was our perplexity); a chieftain who was capable
of smiting back (their fury), and who was himself without hate (was
not to be obtained by us).

Zarathustra freely takes initiative on behalf of the herd. Recognizing
his worthiness, God names Zarathustra its guardian. Zarathustra, then,
takes a profoundly spiritual perspective on the question of the underlying nature of reality.

    Although Zoroastrianism originally had no full-blown notion of
"immaterial stuff," or thought, as the essential nature of reality,
Zarathustra's Ahura Mazda is an immortal, conscious, entity which
creates from thought, and it is the human's ability to think, according to
Zarathustra, which gives humankind its unique moral capacity. In
addition, Zoroastrianism had a notion of eternity—of which our time
here on earth is only a part. At the end of our time, so it was claimed, the
evil creation would be eternally vanquished. In both these notions, as
well as in its conception of morality, Zoroastrianism achieved a level of
abstraction which was fully "philosophical" in a modern sense.

5.   Heraclitus

Back in Greece, another pre-Socratic philosopher of the same period,
named Heraclitus, quite independently defended the idea that Fire was
the fundamental "stuff" of reality. For Heraclitus, however, "Fire" seemed
to connote both the "natural element" it was for the Ionians, and a
"spiritual power." Heraclitus' philosophy was cryptically expressed, and
his contemporaries and commentators did not understand him very
well, calling him such things as "riddler." Indeed, Heraclitus seems to have
been a very cynical person, hardly interested in sharing his thoughts with
others. Nonetheless, Heraclitus' profound and provocative claims have
been an inspiration to many philosophers since, especially during the
nineteenth century.

    Although Heraclitus claimed that everything in the world was a mani-
festation of Fire, he did not understand Fire as an eternal and unchanging origin. Quite the opposite; he claimed that everything that exists is
fleeting and changeable. Fire was the element that best explained, or at
least represented, the constant flux which Heraclitus claimed underlay
nature. "It is in changing that things find repose,"[23][6] he stated, indicat-
ing that the only thing in the world which is constant is change. "You
cannot step into the same river, for other waters are continually flowing

---

[6]This and all following fragments of Heraclitus are either from *Heraclitus*, translated by
  Philip Wheelright (Princeton: Atheneum, 1959), or were translated by Paul Woodruff
  (used by permission of Mr. Woodruff).

on,"[21] he claimed. The fact that we refer to "the" river at all, however, shows that something is constant—the very change and flow itself.

"This world that is the same for all," one fragment of his work reads, ". . . ever was and is and shall be ever-living Fire that kindles in regular measures and goes out by regular measures."[B 30] This Fire, or on the other hand, the fluxuating flow of the river, itself seems to have measure, a rhythm, underlying it. Although the world never stops changing, the measure with which it does so can be understood. So, Heraclitus claimed, our ever-changing reality has a *form* which remains the same—which he called the *Logos*. The *Logos* is the deeper "nature" behind natural, changing things, but you cannot see it, or hear it, or touch it. Thus, "nature loves to hide"[17] beneath the constant flux of the ordinary world we perceive.

Heraclitus' doctrines were provocative, confusing, and sometimes maddening, as the following fragments indicate:

"People do not understand how that which is at variance with itself agrees with itself."[117]

"Listen . . . not to me, but to the *Logos*."[118]

6. Democritus, Atoms, and Pluralism

Not all materialists thought that there was only one ultimate component of reality. A number of philosophers appeared in the ancient world who believed in **pluralism,** that is, that more than one basic "stuff" made up the universe. The best known of the pluralists was Democritus, who suggested that the universe was made up of tiny bits of "stuff" that he called *atoms*. These combined together to form the many different things and qualities of the world. (The soul, he suggested, consists of smooth, round, unusually mobile atoms, disposed through-out the body.) Other pluralists stressed the idea that these different bits of "stuff" were very different in kind as well, so that the bits of "stuff" that composed water, for example, would be very different from that which composed fire. You can appreciate how modern these concepts are, given our current ideas in chemistry and physics. These ancient Greek issues and answers have not become obsolete; they have changed and become more refined. Some have been more in favor at one time and others at other times. But they are still very much with us.

7. Animism

These ancient attempts to find out the way the world really is should not be thought of as clumsy attempts to find out the things that modern scientists now know. All the theories of "stuff" were indeed the precursors of modern physics and chemistry. But you can already see that these philosophers were also concerned with what we would call the mental and the spiritual aspects of the world. Even the most materialistic among them, for example, Thales, did not believe that the basic matter of the universe was cold and lifeless "stuff." All of these philosophers believed that the universe itself, as well as everything in it, was alive in at least some limited way. That is, they all believed in **animism,** the doctrine that everything, volcanoes and stones as well as elephants and flowers, are living things. Furthermore, animism has not disappeared because of the advances of science, though in certain periods (like our own) it has been treated less favorably than in others. But even in the nineteenth century, when physics and chemistry were making some of their most spectacular advances, animism was an extremely popular doctrine, even among scientists. And a great many people today still accept a modified version of it. So don't think that the problems discussed by these ancient philosophers have been solved by science or simply gone away. The place of mind and spirit in a world of matter and energy is still among our basic problems. The ancient search for the way the world really is is still very much with us.

8.   Pythagoras

Another Greek pre-Socratic philosopher, Pythagoras, also attempted to defend a view of the world that did not depend upon the usual kinds of material "stuff." He believed, however, that numbers were the real nature of things, and he taught his students to worship the mathematical order of the universe. He was particularly inspired by new Greek discoveries in music and harmony, and he saw the universe itself as a grand *harmony.* (The term, "the music of the spheres," was part of his teachings.) Unlike the other pre-Socratic Greek philosophers we have met, Pythagoras was much more of a religious figure. He was a mystic and the leader of a powerful underground cult that believed in reincarnation and the **immortality** of the soul which he understood as that part of man which is capable of abstract thought, such as mathematics. In accordance with his religion, he gave the mind and the soul a much more prominent place in his view of the world than did other pre-Socratic philosophers.

Despite the sometimes mysterious views of Pythagoras and his cult, he is still recognized as one of the most important thinkers of the ancient world. With Heraclitus, he was one of the first Greeks to defend a view of reality that depended more on logic and thought than purely material "stuff." (The "Pythagorean theorem" that students learn in high school is named after him.) It was his discovery and proof.

9.   Confucius

In its earliest form in China, the concern with thinking was embedded in the study of human action. A Chinese thinker of the sixth century B.C., **Confucius,** explicitly figured thinking as our fundamental nature. He was concerned essentially for the human good, which he described as "gentlemanly," and he and his followers set the norms for Chinese society for millennia afterwards.

Confucius and his followers claimed that human beings were divided within themselves; that the muddle of human passions, ambitions, and confused loyalties distracted people from their moral duty. Through conscious and attentive adherence to propriety, they claimed, human beings could overcome their "personal selves" and achieve a goodness which was "impersonal." This impersonal life—the life of propriety—however, was a person's more "real" way of living. Through thinking, a person gained a sense of "self" as a Good Man. To "think," in the Confucian sense, was to become a different, better, person; and Confucius believed that few if any men were capable of such profound thought, as these passages from the *Analects* (Confucius' collected sayings) attest:

> The Master [Confucius] said, [in response to the saying] 'He who learns, but does not think, is lost', 'He who thinks but does not learn, is in grave danger.' (XI:5)

> The Master said, I have never yet seen anyone whose desire to build up his moral power was as strong as sexual desire. (IX:17)

> The Master said, I have never yet seen a man who was truly stead-fast. Someone answered, 'Shen Ch'eng'. The Master said, Ch'eng! He is at the mercy of his desires. How can he be called steadfast? (V:10)[7]

Confucian "thinking" was more like a consciousness, or attention, which the Good Man fixed upon his "inner self"—which was figured in the Confucian writings as in his heart or his stomach, not in his head. Thus, the thinking of the "gentleman" did not so much involve contemplation as unerring attention to duty, where "duty" was understood essentially as social propriety. The Confucian "doctrine of the mean"—not to be confused with Aristotle's doctrine of the same name, about which we learn below—directed that the "gentleman" always avoid extremity. "Moderation in all things" was the way of propriety. Thus, Confucius' dicta were often concerned with delineating proper dress, proper diet, proper manner, proper government, and proper respect for the examples set by the "Good Men" of past ages. This inner truth, attention to which led one always to act with propriety, was called the "Way" (or, **Tao**) of Goodness.

> Wealth and rank are what every man desires; but if they can only be retained to the detriment of the Way he possesses, he must

[7]From *The Analects of Confucius*, translated and annotated by Arthur Waley (New York: Vintage, 1938).

relinquish them. . . . The gentleman who ever parts company with goodness does not fulfill that name. Never for a moment does a gentleman quit the way of Goodness. (IV:5)

Music and ritual were vastly important to Confucius. Harmony represented, for him, not only the unity that could be achieved in music, but also that between the inner person and his exterior self, which was distracted by so many concerns. For Confucius, propriety and singleness of spirit were practical, not merely contemplative, activities; but they pointed, at least in the realm of human affairs, to a path between oneness and dispersion, inner reality and exterior appearance.

. . .[B]oth small matters and great depend upon it [harmony]. If things go amiss, he who knows the harmony will be able to attune them. But if harmony itself is not modulated by ritual, things will go amiss. (I:12)

10.   Lao Tsu, or, the Poets of the Tao Te Ching

In China during Confucius' own lifetime, or so the story goes, a religious mystic named Lao Tsu espoused a doctrine that rebelled against the powerful Chinese dynasty and the ancient heroes whom Confucius revered. This radical doctrine, which developed into the religion, Taoism, also rejected the Confucian faith in ritual, or the exterior expression of moral goodness. More likely, the poems which are attributed to Lao Tsu, called the poems of the *Tao Te Ching* (or, "Way of Life"), were composed by several authors who shared Confucius' frustration with unethical behavior and political corruption, but responded in a radically different way. They were mystic recluses who claimed that there was a nature of reality, called the **Tao,** or "Way," which they understood quite differently from Confucius. They claimed that the *Tao* could not be taught or understood through discourse or rules, nor mimicked through the constancy of gentlemanly conduct. Rather, they claimed, the *Tao* could be known only through direct acquaintance with it. The seeker after the *Tao* could only be prepared for its revelation to him through meditation, not ever through ritual. Thus, the poets of the *Tao Te Ching* shared Confucius' primarily practical and moral focus, including the impersonality of goodness. They believed, however, that "impersonal goodness" could be neither sought nor expressed in any visible, speakable, observable way. They claimed the *Tao* was "ineffable," and could not be known through words or thought.

From I:
   Existence is beyond the power of words
   To define:

Terms may be used
But are none of them absolute.[8]

From 18:
When people lost sight of the way to live
Came codes of love and harmony,
Learning came, charity came,
Hypocrisy took charge;. . .

Thus, these mystics were monists. They believed that the nature of reality is one, and that this One is, in a sense, living or conscious. But they did not go the way of the scientific and animistic doctrines of Greece. The poets of the *Tao Te Ching* claimed that the One, living reality, is fully beyond the visible, sensible world of our ordinary experience. It was certainly not one of the physical elements, nor could it be known by way of the rules set down by our ancestors.

From 14:
What we look for beyond seeing
And call the unseen
Listen for beyond hearing,
And call the unheard,
Grasp for beyond reaching
And call the withheld,
Merge beyond understanding
In a oneness. . . .

From 33:
Knowledge studies others,
Wisdom is self-known; . . .

From 57:
A realm is governed by ordinary acts,
A battle is governed by extraordinary acts,
The world is governed by no acts at all.

11. Buddha

Buddhism's historical founder, Siddhārtha Gautama of the Śākya clan, was born a prince in India (or perhaps what is now southern Nepal) near the year 560 B.C.E. The **Buddha** (the Sanskrit term *buddha* means literally "the awakened one") did not write anything himself. Records of his teachings and sermons apparently were kept by his disciples.

Through the centuries—first in India and then in almost every Asian country east of India—Buddhist doctrines and practices evolved; in each culture and epoch in which Buddhism prospered, local customs and

[8]From *The Way of Life: An American Version*, trans. Witter Bynner (New York: The John Day Co., 1944).

indigenous religious beliefs were assimilated, giving the religion a unique form.

As a young prince, the Buddha-to-be led a life of pleasure and enjoyment. His father, fearing the prophecy that his son would become a religious mendicant, tried to protect him from the sight of anything unpleasant or evil. However, one day the young prince journeyed some distance from the royal enclave and encountered first a diseased person, then a wrinkled and decrepit old man, and then a corpse. Inquiring about each of these and being told that all persons are subject to such infirmities, the prince renounced his life of enjoyments and vowed to search tirelessly for the origin and cause of these evils—and for the power to root them up. Buddha's experience of enlightenment did not occur immediately, however; he has to try various paths before arriving at the "Middle Way," a way of life he later proclaimed to his disciples. Eventually, after a long ordeal of meditation under a Bodhi tree, Buddha achieved the *summum bonum, "nibbana"* (the Sanskrit *"nirvāna"*), an extinction of evil at its roots. The remainder of his life, Buddha spent traveling and preaching—helping others to reach this supreme good.

Among the most important of Buddha's teachings are the **Four Noble Truths:**

1) All is suffering (and transitory).
2) The root of suffering is desire, attachment, and personal clinging.
3) There is a way to eliminate desire, and thereby eliminate suffering, namely *nibbana.*
4) The way to this supreme good is The Eightfold Noble Path: right thought, right resolve, right speech, right conduct, right livelihood, right effort, right mindfulness, and right concentration or meditation.

Other important doctrines proclaimed by Buddha include the "wheel of becoming," which shows the connectedness between life, craving, rebirth (rebirth seems never to have been doubted by the Buddha), and the causal interdependence of all things, their insubstantiality, and phenomenal nature as mere groups of "qualities," and similarly the insubstantiality of the self or soul—there is "no soul" according to the Buddha.[9] Although each of these doctrines and others received much thought and elaboration in later years, it is the practice-doctrines' emphases on meditation and compassion that underpin the main themes of the Buddha. What follows is one of the most famous of the many hundreds of sermons and discourses attributed to the Buddha.

[9]Some of these doctrines clearly have forerunners in the Upanishads; it is noteworthy that the Buddha upholds certain lines of continuity between his and previous spiritual preceptors' teachings. Others are distinctively Buddhist, in particular the "insubstantiality" doctrines.

◆the "Fire-Sermon," attributed to the Buddha

Then the Blessed One, having dwelt in Uruvelā as long as He wished, proceeded on his wanderings in the direction of Gayā Head, accompanied by a great congregation of priests, a thousand in number, who had all of them aforetime been monks with matted hair. And there in Gayā, on Gayā Head, The Blessed One dwelt, together with the thousand priests.

And there The Blessed One addressed the priests:

"All things, O priests, are on fire. And what, O priests, are all these things which are on fire?

"The eye, O priests, is on fire; forms are on fire; eye-consciousness is on fire; impressions received by the eye are on fire; and whatever sensation, pleasant, unpleasant, or indifferent, originates in dependence on impressions received by the eye, that also is on fire.

"And with what are these on fire?

"With the fire of passion, say I, with the fire of hatred, with the fire of infatuation; with birth, old age, death, sorrow, lamentation, misery, grief, and despair are they on fire.

"The ear is on fire; sounds are on fire; . . . the nose is on fire; odors are on fire; . . . the tongue is on fire; tastes are on fire; . . . the body is on fire; things tangible are on fire; . . . the mind is on fire; ideas are on fire; . . . mind-consciousness is on fire; impressions received by the mind are on fire; and whatever sensation, pleasant, unpleasant, or indifferent, originates in dependence on impressions received by the mind, that also is on fire.

"And with what are these on fire?

"With the fire of passion, say I, with the fire of hatred, with the fire of infatuation; with birth, old age, death, sorrow, lamentation, misery, grief, and despair are they on fire.

"Perceiving this, O priests, the learned and noble discipline conceives an aversion for the eye, conceives an aversion for forms, conceives an aversion for eye-consciousness, conceives an aversion for the impressions received by the eye; and whatever sensation, pleasant, unpleasant, or indifferent, originates in dependence on impressions received by the eye, for that also he conceives an aversion. Conceives an aversion for the ear, conceives an aversion for sounds, . . . conceives an aversion for the nose, conceives an aversion for odors, . . . conceives an aversion for the tongue, conceives an aversion for tastes, . . . conceives an aversion for the body, conceives an aversion for things tangible, . . . conceives an aversion for the mind, conceives an aversion for ideas, conceives an aversion for mind-consciousness, conceives an aversion for the impressions received by the mind; and whatever sensation, pleasant, unpleasant, or indifferent, originates in dependence on impressions received by the mind, for this also he conceives an aversion. And in conceiving this aversion, he becomes divested of passion, and by

the absence of passion he becomes free, and when he is free
he becomes aware that he is free; and he knows that rebirth is
exhausted, that he has lived the holy life, that he has done
what it behooved him to do, and that he is no more for this
world."

Now while this exposition was being delivered, the minds of the
thousand priests become free from attachment and delivered from
the depravities.

Here Endeth the Fire-Sermon.[10]

12.   The Appearance/Reality Distinction

All of the thinkers we have considered so far, whatever their differing
views and outlooks, have espoused an underlying reality which is
different from the way the world appears in one's ordinary experiences.
Many, as you will recall, claimed that this underlying reality was One;
others claimed that it was diverse and changing. In Greece, the profound
discrepancy between the way the world seems and the way it really must
be grew wider and wider. The problem has come to be called, not
surprisingly, the "appearance/reality distinction."

For Thales, water was the eternal and unchanging element, although
the forms it took might be very different and change constantly. For
Democritus, atoms were unchanging and indestructible, although the
things they combined to compose might change and be destroyed.

Heraclitus' *Logos* and Pythagoras' notion of the immortal "soul" were
right on the edge of an investigation into how the world can be both
one and many, both changing and stable. Because he believed that the
nature of reality was fire-like, Heraclitus appreciated the importance of
change, as in the flickering of a flame. But he insisted that the *logos*,
or logic, underlay the constant changes in the world. We shall see that
the presupposition that reality cannot change, however much things
seem to change, will remain one of the most important beliefs in
Western culture. (In Christianity, for example, the eternal and unchanging nature of God and the human soul are built upon the same
philosophical foundation.)

None of the early thinkers, however, offered an explanation as to why
the world should appear so differently to people than their philosophical
investigations led them to believe it really was. Nor did these thinkers
present any convincing argument that this should be so. The conflict
finally came to a head, and the argument was finally offered. The
philosopher who brought it out most clearly was a pre-Socratic Greek,
Parmenides.

[10]From the Mahā-Vagga, trans. Henry Clark Warren, *Buddhism in Translations* (Boston:
Harvard, 1896); reprinted (New York: Atheneum, 1973), pp. 351–53.

13. Parmenides

Parmenides was an accomplished mathematician who thought far more of the eternal certainties of arithmetic than he did the transient things of everyday experience. He too was a monist and believed in a single reality, "the One." Because he shared the assumption that reality must be eternal and unchanging, he came to an astonishing conclusion: This world, the world of our experience, cannot be real! Our world is constantly changing: Objects are created and destroyed; organisms live and die; people grow old, change their appearance, and move from place to place. And so this world, with all its changes, could not be the real world, nor could we ever know the real world, since we are as inconstant and changing as the other things of our experience. We are, at best, living in a kind of illusion, not in reality at all!

Parmenides gave us what is sometimes postulated to be the first full-scale philosophical argument:[11]

> (The goddess addresses the young philosopher) Come, I will tell you—and you, take the story when you have heard it—about the only routes there are for seeking to know: One says *is* and that there is no not being; this is the path of Persuasion (for she goes the way of Truth). The other says *is not,* and that not being is right. This I point out to you is an utterly ignorant footway. For you could not either get to know that which is not (for it is not attainable) or point to it.
> . . . because the same thing is for knowing (or "thinking about") that is for being.
> It is right that what is for saying and knowing should *be,* for it can *be;* but nothing can *not be.*
> . . . what is is unborn and imperishable, a whole of a single kind, unshakable and not incomplete. It neither was nor will be, because it is now, all of it together, one cohesive. For what birth will you seek for it? From what would it have grown? I will not let you say or think that it came from what is not. For "is not" cannot be said or thought.

The argument is: What really is cannot have come to be, for there is nothing outside of reality (what really is) that could have been its source. It is an argument that is the source of much of Western metaphysics. Naturally, no two scholars agree about what it means. But all agree on the main point: that philosophers should be interested only in *what is* in the fullest sense, and not in what is not, or in what sometimes is and sometimes is not. This means that philosophers should not be interested in anything that changes. The weather in Austin is cold one day, and not

[11]Parmenides, *Fragments* (B 2; B 3; B 6, 11 1–2; B 8, 11 3–9), trans. Paul Woodruff (with permission of Mr. Woodruff).

cold the next. Because it sometimes *is not* cold, it is not a proper subject for the pure philosopher. What is, according to Parmenides, is *unchanging and eternal.*

A simple way to understand the root of this argument is this: We cannot put nonexistent apples in a sack or nonexistent dollars in our wallet. By the same token, Parmenides assumes, we cannot put things that do not exist in our mind; we can only truly think about or know things that *are.* Moreover, only one kind of thought really contains knowledge of the thing we are thinking about. Suppose we are thinking about beer. It is no use thinking about all the things beer is not—like wine and orange juice. Really thinking about beer is thinking about what beer really is.

Since thinking about change involves thinking about things that are not always the same, it involves thinking, in a sense, about things that are not (as the weather is not cold today). But this, according to the Parmenides assumption, is impossible: We can only think about what is.

Since Thales, the main achievement of philosophy had been to break away from common sense and ordinary experience in order to find out the way the world really is. But now we can see how far away from common sense and ordinary experience this breaking away can lead us. In Parmenides' philosophy, if the results of his logic are incompatible with common sense and ordinary experience, so much the worse for common sense and ordinary experience. The followers of Parmenides, particularly the mathematician Zeno, carried these bizarre conclusions even further. Zeno argued, by means of a series of famous paradoxes, that all motion and change is nothing but an illusion.

14.   The Sophists

The following generation of philosophers, who called themselves **sophists** (who have ever since given "sophistry" a bad name because of their rhetorical debating tricks), went even further. They argued that there is no reality, and even if there were, we couldn't know anything about it anyway. (So argued the sophist Gorgias.) And the teaching of Protagoras, another sophist, is still well known today; he said, "Man is the measure of all things," which means that there is no reality except for what we take to be reality. We shall later see that the sophists, despite their bad reputation, anticipated many of the most important philosophical concerns of the twentieth century. In particular, they stressed *practical* questions rather than abstract questions, and thus anticipated our own American *pragmatists.* And, in suggesting that truth is *relative* to people, they anticipated the much-disputed question of *relativism*, the idea that truth might be different at different times for different people. Wandering around the countryside, giving lessons in debating and rhetoric, the sophists used the accomplishments of the earlier philosophers to ridicule philosophy and make fools of practically everyone. That is, until they met Socrates, whose arguments against them changed the course of philosophy and Western thought in general.

15. Metaphysics

These various theories about the way the world really is have a proper name. They are called metaphysical doctrines, and the attempt to develop such doctrines, in which we have been taking part for these past pages, is called **metaphysics.** The business of metaphysics is to ask and attempt to answer the most basic questions about the universe, its composition and the "stuff" of which it is composed, the rule of man and mind, and the nature of the immaterial aspects of the universe as well as its physical nature. But now that we are about to discuss metaphysics in its maturity, with Plato and Aristotle, let us also give "stuff" its proper name. It is called (first by Aristotle) **substance.** Accordingly, metaphysics, the study of "the way the world really is," begins with the answers to a series of questions about substance and how it is manifested in particular things (such as people and trees).

1) How many substances are there? (Monism vs. pluralism.)
2) What are they? (Water, air, fire, numbers, something unknown, minds, spirit, atoms?)
3) How are individual things composed? (And how do we tell them apart, identify them, reidentify them?)
4) How do different things and (if there is more than one) different substances interact?
5) How did substance come into being? (Created by God? Or has it always been there?)
6) Are substances "in" space and time? Are space and time substances? (If not, what are they?)

The first four questions are usually referred to as **ontology,** the study of being as such. The last questions are referred to as **cosmology,** the study of the universe. (For the pre-Socratics, these were the same.) Cosmological questions are necessarily shared between philosophers, physicists, and astonomers, and it is impossible for us to give them more than a cursory review within a strictly philosophical book. Ontology, on the other hand, is still considered by many philosophers to be the heart of metaphysics. Therefore, this chapter will be primarily concerned with ontology.

(Ontology and cosmology are not all there is to metaphysics. A further set of problems must be singled out because it is of particular personal importance to us. [The division follows that of the great German metaphysician Immanuel Kant, whom we shall meet in later chapters.] Kant summarized this second set of problems with the abbreviation

"God, Freedom, and Immortality," problems that "the human mind will never give up." The existence of God is both an ontological problem [God has been identified as the "substance of the universe"] and a cosmological problem [God as creator; God as eternal]. But the existence and nature of God quite obviously deserve separate study, however intricately bound up they may be with other ontological and cosmological problems. [We shall provide this separate study in Chapter 6.] The problem of the existence of the human soul is often tied to religious questions, particularly in the Christian tradition [which is the context Kant intended]. But it is more than this: We shall see how Plato used the concept of an immortal soul to explain our ability to know eternal truths. In a more secular and transient context, there is the metaphysical problem of the relationship between mind and body [Chapter 8]. Finally, the question of metaphysical freedom [the only one of these questions not deeply considered by any of the Greek philosophers] needs to be examined in detail before we can move on to any more "practical" questions involving human action [Chapter 9].)

C. TWO KINDS OF METAPHYSICS: PLATO AND ARISTOTLE

The term *metaphysics* is relatively new (from about 70 B.C. or so), but it is generally agreed that the first great systematic metaphysicians were Plato (428–348 B.C.) and Aristotle (384–322 B.C.). Plato had been a student of Socrates and his most faithful recorder. (Almost all that we have of Socrates' teachings comes to us through Plato.) Yet Socrates was a moralist, not a metaphysician, and most of the metaphysical doctrines that Plato discusses using Socrates as his mouthpiece are probably Plato's own. Aristotle never tried to be a faithful disciple of Plato, and he became his teacher's harshest and most famous critic. It has been said of each of them that the history of philosophy is nothing more than a series of footnotes to their brilliant dialogues and treatises of twenty-four hundred years ago.

Metaphysics is what Aristotle called "first philosophy," the investigation of "Being as Being," or ultimate reality. What does it mean for something to exist? What is it for something to change? What makes one thing like another? Sometimes these questions, or at least the answers to these questions, are presupposed in our everyday thinking, whether we actually think about them or not. For example, we "naturally" believe that a tree continues to exist when we aren't looking at it. But why do we believe this? Even when such questions are the creations of philosophers, they outline views of the world that nonphilosophers share with them. The problem is, as we shall see, that people disagree violently about these issues, even from one generation to the next (for example, from Plato to Aristotle). And what seems to be clear and obvious to one philosopher will seem obscure, merely metaphorical, or downright paradoxical to another. But as we watch the warring history of metaphysics, we too should be humbled by it, for it cannot be that all of those geniuses got it wrong while we now have it right. We too, whether explicitly or not, have metaphysical views, and we too may have to be ready to give them up as we think more about them and face further arguments.

With Plato and Aristotle, metaphysics becomes a cautious consuming enterprise, producing monumental systems of many volumes that require a lifetime of study to master. All we can do here is present a thumbnail sketch, with some brief selections of Plato's metaphysics and a very brief introduction to Aristotle's philosophy, which seems, at first glance, to be primarily a refutation of Plato. But like so many philosophers who seem to be attacking each other from completely opposed viewpoints, Plato and Aristotle have much in common. Both attempted to resolve the problems they inherited from the pre-Socratics: to find the ultimate substance of the universe, to understand what was eternal and unchanging, to understand change, and to show that the universe as a whole is intelligible to human understanding. Plato, following Parmenides and the other pre-Socratics who trusted their reason more than common sense, gave reason a grander position in human life and in the universe in general than it had ever received before. Aristotle, although he too defended reason, insisted that philosophy return to common sense and have a respect for ordinary opinion, which many of the Greek philosophers seemed to have lost. But whatever their differences, it is the shared grandeur of their enterprise that should impress us most about Plato and Aristotle. Between them, they established what we today call "philosophy." And between them, they also laid the intellectual foundations for Christian theology. St. Augustine, for example, was very much a Platonist, and St. Thomas Aquinas was thoroughly indebted to Aristotle.

1. Plato

The most important single feature of Plato's philosophy is his theory of **Forms.** (The Greek word is *Eidos.*) Plato's Forms are sometimes referred to as **Ideas,** but Plato does not mean "ideas" in a person's mind, but rather *ideal forms* or perfect examples—the perfect circle or perfect beauty. To avoid confusion, we shall not use the word "Ideas," but only "Forms."

Forms are the ultimate reality. Things change, people grow old and die, but Forms are eternal and unchanging. Thus Plato could agree with Heraclitus that the world of our experience is constantly changing; but he could also agree with Parmenides, who insisted that the real world, the eternal and unchanging world, was not the same as the world of our experience. According to Plato, it was a *world of Forms*, a world of eternal truths. There were, in other words, two worlds: (1) the world in which we live, a world of constant change or a *world of Becoming*, and (2) a world of Forms, an unchanging world, the real world or the *world of Being*. We can see here Plato's close connection with Parmenides, holding that ultimate reality (the Forms) must be changeless and eternal. Furthermore, also in accordance with Parmenides, it is only such changeless and eternal things that truly can be known. Our only access to this latter world, the real world, is through our reason, our capacity for intellectual thought. Plato's "two-worlds" view was to have a direct and obvious influence on Christian theology. It would also affect philosophers, mathematicians, mystics, poets, and romantics of all kinds until the present day. But in his own time it had a more immediate importance; it allowed him to reconcile Heraclitus and Parmenides, to resolve the problems of the pre-Socratics, and to finally give ideas their proper place in human thought.

Plato thought of the Forms as having the special features of *what is* according to Parmenides. The most exciting Form for Plato was the Form of beauty. Plato thought a person could get to know beauty by falling in love in the right way, and by realizing that the excitement of love is really aimed not at the personality of the person loved but at the link between that person and eternal beauty:

> You see, the man who has been thus far educated in matters of Love, who has beheld beautiful things in the right order and correctly, is coming now to the goal of Loving: he will suddenly catch sight of something wonderfully beautiful in its nature; that is the reason for all his earlier labors: First, it always *is,* and neither comes to be nor passes away, neither waxes nor wanes. Second, it is not beautiful this way and ugly that way, nor beautiful at one time and ugly at another; nor beautiful in relation to one thing and ugly in relation to another; nor is it beautiful here but ugly there. Nor will he perceive the beautiful in an image, like a face, or hands or some other part of a body. Nor will he find it in a theory or in any scientific understanding. It is not anywhere in another thing, as in an animal, or in earth, or in heaven, or in anything else.
>
> But itself by itself with itself, it is always one in Form; and all the other beautiful things share in that Form, in such a way that when those others come to be or pass away, the Form does not become the least bit smaller or greater, nor suffers any change.[12]

[12]Plato, *The Symposium,* trans. Paul Woodruff and Alexander Nehamas (Indianapolis, IN: Hackett, 1989).

For Plato, it is the world of Forms, the world of being, that is real. But this is not to say (as Parmenides had argued) that the world we live in, the world of becoming, is unreal. It is, however, less than real, not an illusion, but without those qualities of eternity and necessity that are the marks of true reality. This might seem like a verbal trick; it is not. The idea of a hierarchy of realities was already familiar in religions that antedated Plato's philosophy by centuries. And we still use such notions in our own thinking, comparing, for example, the world of film and novels to "the real world," or the dreary humdrum of working-day life to "really living." But the best illustration of Plato's two-worlds view is his own, which he offers us in a parable called the Myth of the Cave.

It is a parable about bringing people from the less real to the really real. Indeed, one of the most striking features of Plato's philosophy (and much of Greek philosophy in general) is its emphasis on the *love* of wisdom, the irresistibility of reality; and what is too easily lost in translation is the very erotic imagery Plato uses to describe our passion for the truth. The Myth of the Cave not only illustrates two kinds of knowledge, two kinds of worlds; it is also a parable about human timidity, the difficulties we have in facing the truth, and our resistance to the dazzling light of truth itself.

◆**from *The Republic*,**
by Plato

SOCRATES: Imagine men to be living in an underground cave-like dwelling place, which has a way up to the light along its whole width, but the entrance is a long way up. The men have been there from childhood, with their neck and legs in fetters, so that they remain in the same place and can only see ahead of them, as their bonds prevent them turning their heads. Light is provided by a fire burning some way behind them, and on a higher ground, there is a path across the cave and along this a low wall has been built, like the screen at a puppet show in front of the performers who show their puppets above it.

GLAUCON: I see it.

SOCRATES: See then also men carrying along that wall, so that they overtop it, all kinds of artifacts, statues of men, reproductions of other animals in stone or wood fashioned in all sorts of ways, and, as is likely, some of the carriers are talking while others are silent.

GLAUCON: This is a strange picture, and strange prisoners.

SOCRATES: They are like us, I said. Do you think, in the first place, that such men could see anything of themselves and each other except the shadows which the fire casts upon the wall of the cave in front of them?

GLAUCON: How could they, if they have to keep their heads still throughout life?

SOCRATES: And is not the same true of the objects carried along the wall?

GLAUCON: Quite.

SOCRATES: If they could converse with one another, do you not think that they would consider these shadows to be the real things?

GLAUCON: Necessarily.

SOCRATES: What if their prison had an echo which reached them from in front of them? Whenever one of the carriers passing behind the wall spoke, would they not think that it was the shadow passing in front of them which was talking? Do you agree?

GLAUCON: By Zeus, I do.

SOCRATES: Altogether then, I said, such men would believe the truth to be nothing else than the shadows of the artifacts?

GLAUCON: They must believe that.

SOCRATES: Consider then what deliverance from their bonds and the curing of their ignorance would be if something like this naturally happened to them. Whenever one of them was freed, had to stand up suddenly, turn his head, walk, and look up toward the light, doing all that would give him pain, the flash of the fire would make it impossible for him to see the objects of which he had earlier seen the shadows. What do you think he would say if he was told that what he saw was foolishness, that he was now somewhat closer to reality and turned to things that existed more fully, that he saw more correctly? If one then pointed to each of the objects passing by, asked him what each was, and forced him to answer, do you not think he would be at a loss and believe that the things which he saw earlier were truer than the things now pointed out to him?

GLAUCON: Much truer.

SOCRATES: If one then compelled him to look at the fire itself, his eyes would hurt, he would turn round and flee toward those things which he could see, and think that they were in fact clearer than those now shown to him.

GLAUCON: Quite so.

SOCRATES: And if one were to drag him thence by force up the rough and steep path, and did not let him go before he was dragged into the sunlight, would he not be in physical pain and angry as he was dragged along? When he came into the light, with the sunlight filling his eyes, he would not be able to see a single one of the things which are now said to be true.

GLAUCON: Not at once, certainly.

SOCRATES: I think he would need time to get adjusted before he could see things in the world above; at first he would see shadows most easily, then reflections of men and other things in water, then the things themselves. After this he would see objects

in the sky and the sky itself more easily at night, the light of the
stars and the moon more easily than the sun and the light of the
sun during the day.

GLAUCON: Of course.

SOCRATES: Then, at last, he would be able to see the sun, not
images of it in water or in some alien place, but the sun itself
in its own place, and be able to contemplate it.

GLAUCON: That must be so.

SOCRATES: After this he would reflect that it is the sun which
provides the seasons and the years, which governs everything
in the visible world, and is also in some way the cause of those
other things which he used to see.

GLAUCON: Clearly that would be the next stage.

SOCRATES: What then? As he reminds himself of his first dwelling place, of the wisdom there and of his fellow prisoners, would
he not reckon himself happy for the change, and pity them?

GLAUCON: Surely.

SOCRATES: And if the men below had praise and honours from
each other, and prizes for the man who saw most clearly the
shadows that passed before them, and who could best remember which usually came earlier and which later, and which came
together and thus could most ably prophesy the future, do you
think our man would desire those rewards and envy those who
were honoured and held power among the prisoners, or would
he feel, as Homer put it, that he certainly wished to be "serf to
another man without possessions upon the earth"[13] and go
through any suffering, rather than share their opinions and live
as they do?

GLAUCON: Quite so, I think he would rather suffer anything.

SOCRATES: Reflect on this too. If this man went down into the
cave again and sat down in the same seat, would his eyes not
be filled with darkness, coming suddenly out of the sunlight?

GLAUCON: They certainly would.

SOCRATES: And if he had to contend again with those who had
remained prisoners in recognizing those shadows while his sight
was affected and his eyes had not settled down—and the time
for this adjustment would not be short—would he not be
ridiculed? Would it not be said that he had returned from his
upward journey with his eyesight spoiled, and that it was not
worthwhile even to attempt to travel upward? As for the man
who tried to free them and lead them upward, if they would
somehow lay their hands on him and kill him, they would do so.

GLAUCON: They certainly would.

SOCRATES: This whole image, my dear Glaucon, must be related
to what we said before. The realm of the visible should be compared to the prison dwelling, and the fire inside it to the power

[13]*The Odyssey* 11, 489–90, where Achilles says to Odysseus, on the latter's visit to the
underworld, that he would rather be a servant to a poor man on earth than king among
the dead [transl. note].

of the sun. If you interpret the upward journey and the contemplation of things above as the upward journey of the soul to the intelligible realm, you will grasp what I surmise since you were keen to hear it. Whether it is true or not only the god knows, but this is how I see it, namely that in the intelligible world the Form of the Good is the last to be seen, and with difficulty; when seen it must be reckoned to be for all the cause of all that is right and beautiful, to have produced in the visible world both the light and the fount of light, while in the intelligible world it is itself that which produces and controls truth and intelligence, and he who is to act intelligently in public or in private must see it.

GLAUCON: I share your thought as far as I am able.

SOCRATES: Come then, share with me this thought also: do not be surprised that those who have reached this point are unwilling to occupy themselves with human affairs, and that their souls are always pressing upward to spend their time there, for this is natural if things are as our parable indicates.

GLAUCON: That is very likely.

SOCRATES: Further, do you think it at all surprising that anyone coming to the evils of human life from the contemplation of the divine behaves awkwardly and appears very ridiculous while his eyes are still dazzled and before he is sufficiently adjusted to the darkness around him, if he is compelled to contend in court or some other place about the shadows of justice or the objects of which they are shadows, and to carry through the contest about these in the way these things are understood by those who have never seen Justice itself?

GLAUCON: That is not surprising at all.

SOCRATES: Anyone with intelligence would remember that the eyes may be confused in two ways and from two causes, coming from light into darkness as well as from darkness into light. Realizing that the same applies to the soul, whenever he sees a soul disturbed and unable to see something, he will not laugh mindlessly but will consider whether it has come from a brighter life and is dimmed because unadjusted, or has come from greater ignorance into greater light and is filled with a brighter dazzlement. The former he would declare happy in its life and experience, the latter he would pity, and if he should wish to laugh at it, his laughter would be less ridiculous than if he laughed at the soul that has come from the light above.

GLAUCON: What you say is very reasonable.

SOCRATES: We must then, if these things are true, think something like this about them, namely that education is not what some declare it to be; they say that knowledge is not present in the soul and that they put it in, like putting sight into blind eyes.

GLAUCON: They surely say that.

SOCRATES: Our present argument shows that the capacity to learn and the organ with which to do so are present in every person's soul. It is as if it were not possible to turn the eye from darkness to light without turning the whole body; so one must turn one's whole soul from the world of becoming until it can endure to contemplate reality, and the brightest of realities, which we say is the Good.

GLAUCON: Yes.

SOCRATES: Education then is the art of doing this very thing, this turning around, the knowledge of how the soul can most easily and most effectively be turned around; it is not the art of putting the capacity of sight into the soul; the soul possesses that already but it is not turned the right way or looking where it should. This is what education has to deal with.

GLAUCON: That seems likely.[14]

Our world is like a set of shadows of the real world; that does not make it an illusion, but it does make it a mere imitation of the bright originals. Notice, too, the savior-like role of the philosopher that Plato is setting up here. (His famous argument that philosophers should be kings, and kings philosophers, is included here too.) Like Pythagoras, Plato believed that knowledge of pure Forms, knowledge of the world of "Being," is a person's only hope for salvation and the "good life."

Socrates had taught his students, Plato among them, that the truth, if we can know it at all, must be in us. Plato (using his teacher as his literary spokesman) gives this revelation a new twist. It begins with a puzzle. How is it possible to learn anything? If we don't already know it, how will we recognize it when we find it? And if we already do know it, it makes no sense to say that we "learn it." Now this puzzle sounds like nonsense if we think only of examples such as "what is the beer consumption rate in Omaha, Nebraska?" To answer such questions, obviously we can't simply "look into ourselves"; we have to go out into the world and get information. But Plato insists that he is after much bigger game than "information"; he wants Knowledge (with a capital K), knowledge of reality, to which we have access only through thinking. That world, unlike the world of change and "information" in which we live, is characterized by the fact that everything in it is eternal and necessary. In this eternal world, reality is not discoverable merely through observation and experience. For example, consider the simple truth, $2 + 2 = 4$; it never changes, no experience is necessary to know it; it is one of those eternal truths that deserves its place in Plato's world of Being.

Perhaps the best way to understand Plato's exciting but somewhat mysterious notion of the Forms is to think of them in terms of *definitions*. The Forms are what different things of the same kind have in common and what make them things of the same kind. For example, two horses have in common the Form horse, and you recognize a horse, Plato would say, because of its Form. Suppose that you've never seen a

[14]Plato, *The Republic*, Bk. VII, trans. G. M. A. Grube (Indianapolis, IN: Hackett, 1974).

horse before. Is it possible for you to know what a horse is? The answer is, "of course." It is enough that you have learned what a horse is (from pictures or descriptions) even if you've never seen one. But how is such learning possible? According to Plato, it is possible because we know a definition and thus recognize the Form of a horse, like the ideal Form of a triangle, and with it we are able to know what a horse is, even if we have never seen one, and we recognize horses when we do see them. In Plato's terms, we can recognize all horses, no matter what their age, shape, color, or peculiarities, just because they "participate" in the Form horse. And for Plato, the Form horse has even more reality than particular, flesh-and-blood horses.

The concept of Form allows Plato to explain what it is that one comes to understand when one learns that two or more things are of the same kind. But for Plato the notion of Form serves another purpose as well. In addition to what we know about things from experience, we also know some things independent of experience, and we know these things with certainty (the same certainty Descartes sought in our introduction). For example, we know that every horse is an animal. We know that not simply because every horse that we have seen has turned out to be an animal, but because we know, apart from any particular experiences with horses, that the very Form horse includes the Form animal. (In our times, we would say that the meaning of the English word "horse" already includes the concept of "being an animal"; accordingly, philosophers refer to this kind of truth as **conceptual truth.** But this term was not available to Plato.)

Definitions are essential because, without them, it is difficult to know exactly what one is talking about. But this quest for definitions should not be confused with the high school debating technique of asking your opponent to "define [your] terms." Rather, a definition is the *conclusion* of a philosophical argument—and very hard to come by. In his dialogue *The Meno,* Plato has Socrates push for a definition of "virtue"; his arguments here are a good illustration of the Socratic pursuit of the Forms as definitions.

◆**from *The Meno,*
by Plato**

MENO: Can you tell me, Socrates, can virtue be taught? Or is it
   not teachable but the result of practice, or is it neither of these,
   but men possess it by nature or in some other way?
SOCRATES: Before now, Meno, Thessalians had a high reputation
   among the Greeks and were admired for their horsemanship
   and their wealth, but now, it seems to me, they are also admired
   for their wisdom, not least the fellow citizens of your friend Aris-

tippus of Larissa. The responsibility for this reputation of yours lies with Gorgias, for when he came to your city he found that the leading Aleuadae, your lover Aristippus among them, loved him for his wisdom, and so did the other leading Thessalians. In particular, he accustomed you to give a bold and grand answer to any question you may be asked, as experts are likely to do. Indeed, he himself was ready to answer any Greek who wished to question him, and every question was answered. But here in Athens, my dear Meno, the opposite is the case, as if there were a dearth of wisdom, and wisdom seems to have departed hence to go to you. If then you want to ask one of us that sort of question, everyone will laugh and say: "Good stranger, you must think me happy indeed if you think I know whether virtue can be taught or how it comes to be; I am so far from knowing whether virtue can be taught or not that I do not even have any knowledge of what virtue itself is."

I myself, Meno, am as poor as my fellow citizens in this matter, and I blame myself for my complete ignorance about virtue. If I do not know what something is, how could I know what qualities it possesses? Or do you think that someone who does not know at all who Meno is could know whether he is good-looking or rich or well-born, or the opposite of these? Do you think that is possible?

MENO: I do not; but, Socrates, do you really not know what virtue is? Are we to report this to the folk back home about you?

SOCRATES: Not only that, my friend, but also that, as I believe, I have never yet met anyone else who did know.

MENO: How so? Did you not meet Gorgias when he was here?

SOCRATES: I did.

MENO: Did you then not think that he knew?

SOCRATES: I do not altogether remember, Meno, so that I cannot tell you now what I thought then. Perhaps he does know; you know what he used to say, so you remind me of what he said. You tell me yourself, if you are willing, for surely you share his views.—I do.

Let us leave Gorgias out of it, since he is not here. But, Meno, by the gods, what do you yourself say that virtue is? Speak and do not begrudge us, so that I may have spoken a most unfortunate untruth when I said that I had never met anyone who knew, if you and Gorgias are shown to know.

MENO: It is not hard to tell you, Socrates. First, if you want the virtue of a man, it is easy to say that a man's virtue consists of being able to manage public affairs and in so doing to benefit his friends and harm his enemies and to be careful that no harm comes to himself; if you want the virtue of a woman, it is not difficult to describe: she must manage the home well, preserve its possessions, and be submissive to her husband; the virtue of child, whether male or female, is different again, and so is that of an elderly man, if you want that, or if you want that of a free

> man or a slave. And there are very many other virtues, so that
> one is not at a loss to say what virtue is. There is virtue for every
> action and every age, for every task of ours and every one of
> us—and Socrates, the same is true for wickedness.
> SOCRATES: I seem to be in great luck, Meno; while I am looking
> for one virtue, I have found you to have a whole swarm of them.
> But, Meno, to follow up the image of swarms, if I were asking
> you what is the nature of bees, and you said that they are many
> and of all kinds, what would you answer if I asked you: "Do you
> mean that they are many and varied and different from one
> another in so far as they are bees? Or are they no different in
> that regard, but in some other respect, in their beauty, for exam-
> ple, or their size or in some other such way?" Tell me, what
> would you answer if thus questioned?
> MENO: I would say that they do not differ from one another in
> being bees.
> SOCRATES: If I went on to say: "Tell me, what is this very thing,
> Meno, in which they are all the same and do not differ from one
> another?" Would you be able to tell me?
> MENO: I would.[15]

Meno continues to try to satisfy Socrates with a definition of virtue, but
every time he either contradicts himself or argues in a circle. So how does
one know a definition? The answer, according to Plato, is that we
recognize the Forms. We know what a horse is because we recognize the
Form of a horse. We recognize that $2 + 2 = 4$ because we know the
Forms. But how do we *know* the Forms? If we do not and cannot learn
of them from experience (the changing world of Becoming in everyday
life), then how do we know them at all? The answer, according to Plato,
is that they already are "in us."

The second principle of Plato's metaphysics, our bridge between the
two worlds, is the immortality and immateriality of the human soul. Our
souls contain knowledge of the world of Being that is already in us at
birth. Such knowledge and ideas are called **innate.** Experience only
triggers them off and allows us to "remember" them. Here is the
extravagant answer to Plato's puzzle, "How is it possible to learn a truth
about the world of Being?" The answer is: We already "know" it; it's just
a matter of recalling it. Consider his famous illustration of this second
doctrine in *The Meno:*

> MENO: How will you look for it, Socrates, when you do not know
> at all what it is? How will you aim to search for something you
> do not know at all? If you should meet with it, how will you
> know that this is the thing that you did not know?

---

[15]Plato, *The Meno,* trans. G. M. A. Grube (Indianapolis, IN: Hackett, 1976). The subsequent
quotation from Plato also was translated by Grube.

SOCRATES: I know what you want to say, Meno. Do you realize what a debater's argument you are bringing up, that a man cannot search either for what he knows or for what he does not know? He cannot search for what he knows—since he knows it, there is no need to search—nor for what he does not know, for he does not know what to look for.

MENO: Does that argument not seem sound to you, Socrates?

SOCRATES: Not to me.

MENO: Can you tell me why?

SOCRATES: I can. I have heard wise men and women talk about divine matters. . . .

MENO: What did they say?

SOCRATES: What was, I thought, both true and beautiful.

MENO: What was it, and who were they?

SOCRATES: The speakers were among the priests and priestesses whose care it is to be able to give an account of their practices. Pindar too says it, and many others of the divine among our poets. What they say is this; see whether you think they speak the truth: They say that the human soul is immortal; at times it comes to an end, which they call dying, at times it is reborn, but it is never destroyed, and one must therefore live one's life as piously as possible:

> Persephone will return to the sun above in the ninth year the souls of those from whom she will exact punishment for old miseries, and from these come noble kings, mighty in strength and greatest in wisdom, and for the rest of time men will call them sacred heroes.

As the soul is immortal, has been born often and has seen all things here and in the underworld, there is nothing which it has not learned; so it is in no way surprising that it can recollect the things it knew before, both about virtue and other things. As the whole of nature is akin, and the soul has learned everything, nothing prevents a man, after recalling one thing only—a process men call learning—discovering everything else for himself, if he is brave and does not tire of the search, for searching and learning are, as a whole, recollection. We must, therefore, not believe that debater's argument, for it would make us idle, and fainthearted men like to hear it, whereas my argument makes them energetic and keen on the search. I trust that this is true, and I want to inquire along with you into the nature of virtue.

MENO: Yes, Socrates, but how do you mean that we do not learn, but that what we call learning is recollection? Can you teach me that this is so?

SOCRATES: As I said just now, Meno, you are a rascal. You now ask me if I can teach you, when I say there is no teaching but recollection, in order to show me up at once as contradicting myself.

MENO: No, by Zeus, Socrates, that was not my intention when I spoke, but just a habit. If you can somehow show me that things are as you say, please do so.

At this dramatic point in the dialogue, Socrates calls over an illiterate, uneducated slave-boy, and with minimal instructions leads him to discover an elementary geometrical proof. What is crucial is that Socrates does not tell the boy the answer but "draws it out of him." But then the question becomes, where was this answer "in him," and how did he recognize it? After the demonstration, Socrates draws his conclusions:

SOCRATES: What do you think, Meno? Has he, in his answers, expressed any opinion that was not his own?
MENO: No, they were all his own.
SOCRATES: And yet, as we said, he did not know a short time ago?
MENO: That is true.
SOCRATES: So these opinions were in him, were they not?
MENO: Yes.
SOCRATES: So the man who does not know has within himself true opinions about the things that he does not know?
MENO: So it appears.
SOCRATES: These opinions have now just been stirred up like a dream, but if he were repeatedly asked these same questions in various ways, you know that in the end his knowledge about these things would be as accurate as anyone's.
MENO: It is likely.
SOCRATES: And he will know it without having been taught but only questioned, and find the knowledge within himself?
MENO: Yes.
SOCRATES: And is not finding knowledge within oneself recollection?
MENO: Certainly.
SOCRATES: Must he not either have at some time acquired the knowledge he now possesses, or else have always possessed it?
MENO: Yes.
SOCRATES: If he always had it, he would always have known. If he acquired it, he cannot have done so in his present life. Or has someone taught him geometry? For he will perform in the same way about all geometry, and all other knowledge. Has someone taught him everything? You should know, especially as he has been born and brought up in your house.
MENO: But I know that no one has taught him.
SOCRATES: Yet he has these opinions, or doesn't he?
MENO: That seems indisputable, Socrates.
SOCRATES: If he has not acquired them in his present life, is it not clear that he had them and had learned them at some other time?

MENO: It seems so.

SOCRATES: Then that was the time when he was not a human being?

MENO: Yes.

SOCRATES: If then, during the time he exists and is not a human being he will have true opinions which, when stirred by questioning, become knowledge, will not his soul have learned during all time? For it is clear that during all time he exists either as a man or not.

MENO: So it seems.

SOCRATES: Then if the truth about reality is always in our soul, the soul would be immortal so that you should always confidently try to seek out and recollect what you do not know at present—that is, what you do not recollect?

MENO: Somehow, Socrates, I think that what you say is right.

SOCRATES: I think so too, Meno.[16]

The doctrine of the immortality of the soul was not original with Plato, of course. The ancient Egyptians had believed in it many centuries before the first Greek philosophers, and Pythagoras had taught it to his students. But Plato's doctrine had more than religious significance; it was his answer to the skeptics and our bridge to the eternal world of Being. Of course, as a student of Socrates, he also appreciated the advantages of believing in an afterlife. Socrates could face death so calmly, he told his students, just because he believed in life after death. But for Plato it signified something more; it provided us with knowledge in this life as well as continued existence in another.

Plato's doctrines of the world of Being and the immortality of the soul introduce a clearly immaterialist conception of reality, as opposed to all of the more or less materialist conceptions we have encountered so far (the world as "stuff"). Even Pythagoras' numbers and Heraclitus' *logos* had their materialistic foundations, for neither philosopher was willing to grant these things independent existence, independent, that is, of the material things of this world. The things of Plato's world of Being can exist apart from them.

What is in this "other world," this world of Being? We have already met one of its inhabitants: the simple truth, $2 + 2 = 4$. Its inhabitants are Forms. Consider the following familiar example: You are asked by your geometry teacher to prove that the internal angles of a triangle total 180°. Simple enough. You remember how: You extend the base of the triangle, draw a line parallel to the base through the apex, and then proceed with your proof. But now, how do you know that you have not only shown that the internal angles of *this* triangle total 180°? As a matter of fact, it is pretty obvious that what you have drawn isn't even a triangle; the sides sag, one of the angles is broken, and the lines are fat (after all, a real line

---

[16]Plato, *The Meno*, trans. G. M. A. Grube (Indianapolis, IN: Hackett, 1976).

has no width at all). But yet you claim to have proved something about all triangles. Well, it is clear that you needn't do the proof even twice, much less an infinite number of times, to make your claim. How come? Because, you will answer, what you have been working with is not this particular poorly drawn triangle in your notebook but an ideal triangle, the form of all and any triangles. And there it is—Plato's Form of a triangle. It is not identical to any particular triangle. (How could it be, for it would have to be acute, isosceles, right, and nonright all at the same time!) It is their ideal Form, which each particular triangle approximates, that has its own existence in the world of Being. Plato says that every triangle that we can draw participates in the ideal Form and that it is only through reason, not through observation of particular triangles, that we come into contact with these ideal Forms.

To know a Platonic Form is not just to "see" something. It is to fall in love with it; in fact, it is to fall madly in love. And so Socrates, in nearly all of Plato's dialogues, repeats the claim that a philosopher is a kind of lover. Indeed, he says that to know the Forms is to want to reproduce, to propagate, to teach everyone else to see them and to love them too. The Myth of the Cave, and the metaphor of the Sun and shadows, have two sides. The first is that the changing world of our everyday experience is only a shadow, an imitation of reality. But the second side is that the world of our everyday experience is also an image of the divine and ultimate reality, and so in the things of everyday life we get at least a glimpse of perfection.

Among the Forms are those ideals of human perfection which we should not only recognize but try to realize here in the world of Becoming: Wisdom, Justice, Beauty, and Goodness. To these ideals of perfection each of us aspires, and it is the definition of these ideals that is the task of every philosopher. His or her job (Socrates' main task in all of Plato's dialogues) is to sort out the common confusions about such vital matters. The business of the philosopher, in short, is to make others recognize eternal Forms and make it possible to achieve that heroic wisdom to which Plato's teacher, Socrates, had devoted his life.

I hope that you can appreciate, even from this brief sketch, the power of the metaphysical doctrines Plato has developed. You may also be aware of some of their difficulties. Most importantly, the gap between our world and the real world makes us exceedingly uncomfortable; none of us likes to think of ourselves living merely in the shadows. (And Plato himself warns, "wouldn't the prisoners who had never been released . . . laugh at him and even . . . kill" the philosopher who thus instructs them?) The connection between the world of Being and our own world of Becoming is not at all clear. Plato does say that the things of this latter world "participate" in the Forms of the former, but one thing that we shall have to learn right away in philosophy (and in every other discipline) is that the words that pretend to be explanations are often only cosmetic cover-ups. It looks as if we have a theory when in fact we have only a word. This is particularly true of Plato's word "participates" *(methexis)*, and he himself raises serious doubts about it in his later dialogues. But the real attack comes, as it should come in philosophy, from his own students, and in particular, from one, perhaps the greatest of them all, Aristotle.

2. Aristotle

Aristotle claimed that he did not understand Plato's concept of "participation." (When a philosopher claims "not to understand" something, it means that he is pushing for a better account of it, that he is not at all satisfied so far. Aristotle probably understood Plato as well as anybody ever has.) Aristotle's objection was, essentially, that Plato had failed to explain the relationship between the Forms and particular things, and that the word "participation" was no more than "a mere empty phrase and a poetic metaphor."[17] Furthermore, Plato's emphasis on the Forms made it impossible to appreciate the full reality of particular things, and the eternal permanence of the Forms made them useless for understanding how particular things could change. Indeed, the question "how do things change?" becomes the central theme of Aristotle's philosophy.

Aristotle also wanted to determine the nature of reality. But Plato had argued that reality was something other than the world of our experience. Aristotle, a practical man of the earth, a great biologist, physicist, and worldly tutor to Alexander the Great, would have none of this. This world, our world, is reality. He agreed with Plato that knowledge must be universal and concerned with what things have in common, but he rejected Plato's idea that these common universal ingredients—the Forms of things—could be separated from particular things. But this meant that Aristotle also rejected Plato's separation of the human soul from the body, and Aristotle, unlike Plato, saw human beings entirely as creatures of nature, "rational animals"—but still animals. Metaphysics, for Aristotle, was not the study of another world, recollected in our eternal souls; metaphysics was simply the study of nature *(physis)*, and, as importantly, the study of ourselves. Accordingly, he brought metaphysics "back home." But it must not be thought that he made it any simpler. The beginning student of Aristotle—as well as the trained scholar—will attest to the fact that he is among the most difficult authors in philosophy.

> There is a branch of knowledge that studies being *qua* being, and the attributes that belong to it in virtue of its own nature. Now this is not the same as any of the so-called special sciences, since none of these enquires universally about being *qua* being. They cut off

[17]Aristotle, *Metaphysics*, trans. W. D. Ross (Oxford: Oxford University Press, 1924).

some part of it and study the attributes of this part—that is what the mathematical sciences do, for instance. But since we are seeking the first principles, the highest causes, it is of being *qua* being that we must grasp the first causes.[18]

The study of being *qua* being is metaphysics, which Aristotle was the first to isolate from other branches of philosophy. It is, first of all, the study of the different ways the word *be* can be used. This leads Aristotle to his famous theory of categories:

There are several senses in which a thing may be said to "be." In one sense the "being" meant is "what a thing is" or a "this," while in another sense it means a quality or a quantity or one of the other things that are predicted as these are. While "being" has all these senses, the primary type of being is obviously the "what," which indicates the substance of the thing. For when we say of what quality something is, we say that it is good or bad, not that it is six feet long or that it is a man; but when we say *what* it is, we do not say "white" or "hot" or "six feet long," but "a man" or "a god." All *other* things are said to be because they are quantities of that which *is* in this primary sense, or qualities of it, or in some other way characteristics of it . . ."[19]

The primary use of "be" is to tell us what something *really is*, what it is in an unqualified sense: We are, in this sense, a certain individual human being. We are also a certain number of inches tall; but that fact is secondary, it is something *about* us, which could change without changing what we *are*, first and foremost, and belongs to the category of *quantity*. We may also be pale or dark; that fact also is secondary, and belongs to the category of *quality*. The primary category is that of *substance*. "Substance," as Aristotle defines it, is "that which stands alone." In other words, "substance" is *independent* being. You would exist, for instance, even if you didn't have hair. But *your* hair could not exist without you, and so is not a substance. Substances are the basic elements in Aristotle's metaphysics. A horse, a tree, and a butterfly are substances.

Tables and chairs are not primary beings for Aristotle, because he thinks of primary beings as having their own natures. Something made by a human being, such as a table, can only exist *along with* human beings. It cannot move or fulfill its nature—in this case, holding our foot—by itself. Our nature is what we will do if nothing stops us. A human being grows up and leads a human life, if nothing stops him; that's his nature. But a wooden table will inevitably rot if no one stops it, since that is the nature of the wood it is made of. Wood has a nature, tables do not.

[18]Aristotle, *Metaphysics* T.1.1003a21.
[19]Aristotle, *Metaphysics* Z.1.1028a10.

For that reason, Aristotle treats artifacts (things we make) as having a lower level of being than we do ourselves.

> Some people think that the nature and real being *[ousia]* of a natural object is the primary material in it (material in itself unformed)—in a bed it would be the wood, in a statue the bronze. It is an indication of this, according to Antiphon, that if you bury a bed, and the rotting wood becomes able to send up a shoot, what comes up will not be a bed, but wood—suggesting that the arrangement in accordance with the rules of the art belongs only incidentally, and that the reality—what the thing really is—is what actually persists through all those changes.[20]

> But there is another way of speaking, according to which the nature of a thing is its shape or form as given in its definition . . . and this rather than its matter is a thing's nature. For (i) each thing is called whatever it is, when it is that thing actually rather than just potentially [the wood or the seed, the matter, *is* not a table or a lettuce—though it may have the potentiality of being one—until it has actually been put together or has actually germinated and grown]. Further, (ii) men come to be from men, but not beds from beds. That is precisely why people say that the nature of a bed is not the shape but the wood; if it sprouts it is not a bed but wood that comes up. But if this shows that the wood is nature, form too is nature; for men come to be from men.[21]

The doctrines of Aristotle's metaphysics sound as simple as they could be. This world, the world of our experience, is reality; there is no other world. The ultimate things of reality, which he calls substances, are individual things—men, horses, trees, and butterflies. Change is real and much of reality is subject to change. Forms are real, but cannot exist separately from the particular substances whose forms they are. This is not as radical a departure from Plato as it may seem. Aristotle did believe that the highest level of reality was not subject to change. Gods, the heavens, and even the forms of biological species were changeless in his system. Aristotle did not believe in any form of evolution.

For Aristotle, the primary substances are individual things; secondary substances (less real than individuals) are what he called the "species" and the "genus" to which a thing belongs. To return to our equestrian example, this particular horse, for Aristotle, is the primary substance. The species, "horse," and the even broader genus, "animal," are less real than the horse itself. Aristotle, like Plato, has a hierarchy of reality. But he turns Plato's hierarchy upside down. Plato holds that the more abstract things are the more real; Aristotle argues that the more concrete

---

[20]Aristotle, *Physics* II.1.193a9.
[21]Aristotle, *Physics* II.1.193.

things, individuals, are the more real. For Aristotle, as in common sense, the more tangible things are considered to be the most real things.

What is a substance? Aristotle spends many pages giving a number of definitions, enough to keep the philosophers of the Middle Ages busy for a thousand years sorting them out. For our purposes, it will be enough to mention three different descriptions of substance, each of which is important for Aristotle and for later philosophy. The first characterization of substance is presented in terms of grammar. Aristotle says, "a substance is that which is neither predictable of a subject nor present in a subject; for instance, the individual man or horse."[22] More simply, a substance is the thing referred to by a noun, which is the subject of a sentence; for example, "the man is . . ." or "Socrates is . . ." or "the horse is. . . ." (This characterization would have been less confusing in Greek.) A more ontological way of saying this, but unfortunately very confusing too, is to say that a substance is independent of anything else. (We shall see how important this becomes in the modern metaphysics of Spinoza and Leibniz.) Other things might depend upon a substance, but a substance does not depend upon them. This is an awkward way of saying, perhaps, that the color of a horse could not exist without the horse; indeed, nothing could be true of a horse if it did not exist.

A second way of characterizing substance is to say that substance is what underlies all of the properties and changes in something. In this sense, you can say that you are the same person (that is, the same substance) that you were ten years ago, despite the fact that you are, quite obviously, very different in a great many ways. (Aristotle says, "Substance, while remaining the same, is capable of admitting contrary properties.") Combining these two characterizations, we can say that a substance is whatever is most basic to reality, like the pre-Socratic philosophers' notion of "stuff." It is the concrete individual thing, which remains constant despite the fact that it changes and has different properties at different times. You are the same person before and after you've gotten a haircut, tried on a new suit of clothes, or had your appendix removed.

The third characterization of substance requires the introduction of another new term, which became a central concern of philosophers before this century. A substance can be defined in terms of what is *essential*. An **essence** (or an **essential property**) is that aspect of an individual that identifies it as a particular individual. For example, it is part of the essence of being Socrates that he is a human being, that he lived in the fourth century B.C., and that he was wise. Anything that does not have these properties could not possibly be Socrates. There are other properties that Socrates has, of course; for example, the fact that he had a wart on his nose. But this is not an essential property. (Aristotle calls

[22]Aristotle, *Categories*, trans. J. L. Ackrill (Oxford: Oxford University Press, 1963).

it an *accident* or an *accidental property*.) Socrates still would have been Socrates without it. But Socrates could not have been a centipede, for it is part of his essence to be human.

A substance is a combination of form and matter. Aristotle's "form" is roughly the same as Plato's Form, except that for Aristotle, it does not exist apart from the individual things that have it; it is always *informing* some matter. Matter is a discovery of Aristotle's. It is, basically, what things are made out of; it is what is given shape and structure by the form. The matter of a boat is wood; its form is the design that the boatbuilder realized in the wood. (Notice that "form" is written with a small *f* here, although Aristotle uses the same word as Plato, *eidos*. His word for the matter is *hylē*.)

This enabled Aristotle to explain change. Earlier philosophers, he thought, believed only in matter that by itself would stay the same. Plato believed only in Forms that are eternally unchanging. But Aristotle believed in things that *combined* matter and form in a variety of ways. Substantial change, the "coming to be and passing away" of a substance, takes place when matter is given a new form.

With both concepts available, Aristotle thinks he can avoid the mistakes of his predecessors, especially the mistake of Parmenides, which he blames on inexperience:

> The first people to philosophise about the nature and truth of things got side-tracked and driven off course by inexperience. They said that nothing comes to be or passes away, because whatever comes to be must do so either from what is, or from what is not—and neither of these is possible. For what *is* cannot come to be, since it is already; and nothing can come to be from what is *not*, since there must [in all change and coming into being] be something underlying.[23]

The essence of a thing cannot change (or it would no longer be the same thing), and it is of little metaphysical importance if accidents change. So what does change?

Form and matter, Aristotle says, cannot exist separately, but they can be *distinguished* everywhere in nature. The best examples can be found in human craftsmanship. One can take a lump of clay, for example, and make it into a bowl of any number of shapes. Or one can take a piece of silver and make it into a fork, a spoon, a bracelet, or a couple of rings. The clay or the silver is the matter; the shape and the function define the form. Aristotle also says that the matter itself can be analyzed in terms of form and matter. The matter of the clay and the silver would be the basic elements—earth, air, fire, and water. The form would be the shape and proportion these elements assume to make clay or silver. Indeed,

[23] Aristotle, *Physics* I.8.191a24.

Aristotle even holds that the basic elements themselves can be analyzed in terms of more primitive matter—hotness, coldness, dryness, and wetness—which combine to give the form of the elements. It is the form of things that we can know and explain, according to Aristotle, never the matter. Thus, we can *talk* about form and matter separately, and so *understand* change. His predecessor, he thought, mistook the way we talk about reality for the way it is. The form, *by itself,* can never change, nor can the matter, but the way they combine can change. By changing their form, caterpillars turn into butterflies and seeds into fruits and flowers. Thus, Aristotle explains both change and stability.

You may already anticipate certain troubles that will plague later philosophers. How much can we change a person, for example, and still have him or her be the same? Provide a haircut? a college education? a ten-year jail sentence? a sex-change operation? But before we worry about such problems, let us appreciate the importance of this notion of essence in Aristotle's philosophy. With it, he can do everything that Plato wanted to do with his special notion of Forms, but without invoking anything otherworldly. According to Aristotle, we can know that Socrates is a man, for instance, just because the essence of Socrates includes the property of being a man. We can know that a horse is an animal because the essence of being a horse includes the property of being an animal. In Plato, a conceptual truth of this kind was a truth about eternal Forms; for Aristotle, it is the form that changes, and a conceptual truth is rather a statement about essences.

In Chapter 2, we shall see why the two concepts of substance and essence are so important to later philosophy. But for now, let us turn to a much more exciting aspect of Aristotle's philosophy, his cosmology. It has inspired literally thousands of great thinkers, notably St. Thomas Aquinas, who used Aristotle's metaphysics to build one of the great theological systems of Christianity.

To understand Aristotle's cosmology, we have to begin with a notion that is extremely foreign to people today; it is that the universe as a whole, and all things in it, have a purpose, a goal. The Greek word for "purpose" or "goal" is *telos,* and Aristotle's view is called **teleology.** Teleology can be directly contrasted with our modern scientific view of reality, which is primarily a *causal* view. Teleology explains something by looking for its purpose, goal, or end; causal explanations seek to understand *how* something came about, not *why* it came about. If you were asked why a frog has a heart, for example, the teleological answer would be "in order to keep it alive, by pumping the blood through its body." The causal answer, on the other hand, would be an explanation of the genetics, the evolutionary process, the development of the frog. If you were asked why a plant turns its leaves towards the sunlight, the teleological answer would be "in order to face the sun." The causal explanation, instead, would refer you to the fact that the cells grow faster on one side of the stem and that certain light-sensitive chemicals do such-and-such, and so on. In modern science, a causal answer is always preferable, and if a teleological answer is allowed at all it is always with the qualification that either there is an underlying causal explanation, or we do not yet have (but someday will have) an adequate causal explanation. In Aristotle's metaphysics, on the other hand, one does not have an explanation at all unless one knows what purpose a thing or an event serves. "Nature does nothing in vain" is the motto of the teleologist.[24]

Aristotle believed that every substance, every individual thing whether human, animal, vegetable, or mineral, had its own nature, its own internal principles, certain tendencies that were part of its essence. This was, for example, the basis of his famous theory of falling objects: Every object has its "place," and if that object is moved, it will return to its rightful place on its own power. That means that any object of sufficient size, whose place is on (or under) the ground, will fall toward the earth immediately if it is lifted into the air. And larger objects, which are not slowed down by the air's resistance, will fall faster than smaller ones. Indeed, this seemed so inherently reasonable to Aristotle and everyone around him that it never occurred to them to test it under experimental conditions. But gravitation, which Newton would not discover for another two millennia, is essentially a causal concept. Aristotle's explanation was a teleological one, which the Greeks found far more convincing. Moreover, even if they had had the equipment for a test, which they did not, the Greeks still might not have believed the answer. Aristotle could not understand how causation could possibly operate at a distance. Thus, Aristotle thought that the cause of an object falling had to be in the object and not in the earth.

A reader who begins Aristotle may be initially confused by his use of the word *cause (aition)* to include not only what we have been calling causal explanation but teleological accounts as well. In fact, Aristotle lists four different kinds of **cause,** all of which together explain why a thing is as it is at any given time. The first of these is the matter that makes it up, the *material cause,* the silver in the spoon or the flesh and blood that make up our bodies. The second is the principle or law by which it is made, the *formal cause,* the architect's blueprint or the craftsman's model. The third is what we would call "the cause," which Aristotle calls the *efficient cause,* the person or event that actually makes something happen, by doing something—pushing a button, causing an explosion, calling the person in charge. Fourth, there is the purpose of the thing, its *final cause,* its *telos.* Now notice that Aristotle's four causes are better suited for explaining human activities than giving what we would call scientific explanations about things that happen in nature. But this is

---

[24]Aristotle rejected a theory of natural selection argued by Empedocles twenty-three hundred years before Darwin because it was not a teleological theory.

indeed Aristotle's paradigm, and he even says in *Physics*,[25] "If purpose is present in art, it must also be present in nature." It is the final cause that provides us with the most important explanation.

We can understand this without any difficulty when we are explaining human activities. We want to know, first of all, what purpose a person has in doing something. But when it comes to nature, we do not generally ask about purpose, but are more likely to ask about (efficient) causes. We might ask of an animal, what purpose is served by a long neck, or certain features in its feet, or some kind of fur, but we are less likely to ask that of a plant and would find such a question unintelligible with reference to rocks, clouds, and stars. Aristotle and his fellow Greeks would not find this unintelligible at all. Indeed, he believed (and thousands of scientists followed him until the seventeenth century) that everything that existed had to be accounted for in terms of its inner purposes and the overall purpose it served in nature. Thus a magnet literally "attracts" little pieces of metal, and the stars really do have a purpose in their heavenly wanderings. And not only do all the things and creatures of the universe have their purposes, but the universe itself has its purpose too. Indeed, it is this ultimate purpose of the universe that gives all the particular things their significance. Indeed, for Aristotle, the idea that the universe as a whole might *not* have a purpose would have been absurd. And one of his most famous arguments is aimed at showing why there must be an ultimate purpose, a "first (Final) cause," or what he calls, "the prime mover."

> Moreover, it is obvious that there is some first principle, and that the causes of things are not infinitely many either in a direct sequence or in kind. For the material generation of one thing from another cannot go on in an infinite progression (e.g. flesh from earth, earth from air, air from fire, and so on without a stop); nor can the source of motion (e.g. man be moved by air, air by the sun, the sun by Strife, with no limit to the series). In the same way neither can the Final Cause [that is, purposes] recede to infinity— walking having health for its object, and health happiness, and happiness something else: one thing always being done for the sake of another. And it is just the same with the Formal Cause [that is, the essence]. For in the case of all intermediate terms of a series which are contained between a first and last term, the prior term is necessarily the cause of those which follow it; because if we had to say which of the three is the cause, we should say "the first." At any rate it is not the last term, because what comes at the end is not the cause of anything. Neither, again, is the intermediate term, which is only the cause of one (and it makes no difference whether there is one intermediate term or several, nor whether they are infinite or limited in number). But of series which are infinite in

[25]Aristotle, *Physics*, trans. W. D. Ross (Oxford: Oxford University Press, 1936).

this way, and in general of the infinite, all the parts are equally intermediate, down to the present moment. Thus if there is no first term, there is no cause at all.[26]

The argument, simply stated, is that teleological explanations cannot go on forever, or what philosophers sometimes call an **infinite regress.** For Aristotle, if *x* exists for the purpose of *y* and *y* exists for the purpose of *z,* there must be some ultimate purpose that will explain them all. A similar argument can be made with regard to efficient causes, that if *p* makes *q* happen and *r* makes *p* happen and so on, there must be an end to the "and so on," and so too with the material cause and the formal cause. But the most exciting aspect of this infinite regress argument is the idea that the universe itself must have a purpose, a Final cause, a "prime mover" that Aristotle characterizes as "pure thought, thinking about itself." It is an obscure but intriguing idea, which was taken up by Christian theology as an apt characterization of the Christian God (see Chapter 6). But Aristotle's prime mover has few of the characteristics of the Judeo-Christian-Islamic God; he (it) did not create the universe and has no special concern for man. The prime mover is more of a metaphysical necessity than a proper object of worship. But it is not too far-fetched to say that Aristotle, like most of the Greeks, viewed the universe as something like a cosmic organism, with an ultimate purpose, whose ultimate goal was thinking itself.

We can appreciate how this cosmology would become a source of inspiration for a great many philosophers, poets, and religious people. In more recent centuries, for example, it was used as a welcome alternative to the "nuts and bolts" materialism of modern Newtonian science (as we shall see in Leibniz). Tied to the technical details of Aristotle's ontology is an extremely imaginative cosmology; the picture of a purposeful universe, developing according to its own goals and principles. It is a fascinating picture and still an attractive alternative to the lifeless picture of the physical universe that is so central to our modern scientific outlook.

D. TWO IMPORTANT ASSUMPTIONS

We have just reviewed the two greatest metaphysical theories in the history of human thought. With Plato, humanity first began to appreciate the extent to which its world was structured by abstract Forms. With Aristotle, people began to realize the significance of language in structuring that world. But despite their intimate connections, Plato and Aristotle offer us very different **paradigms** (that is, ideal examples) of the

[26]Aristotle, *Metaphysics*, trans. Hugh Tredennick (Cambridge, MA: Harvard University Press, 1933).

nature of metaphysics. In Plato there is the leap into the realm of pure Forms, the thrill of esoteric argument, and the elegance of the proofs against common sense. In Aristotle, there is always the anchor of common sense and everyday experience, the cautious and piecemeal analysis of the concepts we use every day in talking about our world, in Aristotle's view, the only world. In an important sense, the history of philosophy is the interplay of these two paradigms. And philosophy is still very much involved in a debate between the two.

Before we skip two millennia to modern times, it is important that we make explicit two assumptions or presuppositions that have been generally accepted until very recently. These were assumed by the pre-Socratics from the very start of their venture; they were accepted by Plato and Aristotle and would be presupposed by most medieval and modern philosophers as well. Those assumptions are:

1) The world is intelligible. Every attempt to understand the world presupposes that the world can be understood, and understood by us. Another way of stating this is to say that all metaphysics assumes that our thought is adequate to understanding the world, or at least, to understanding the limits of our understanding (as, for example, in our attempts to understand God). It is this faith in thought as a guide to reality that Heraclitus was groping for with his *logos*, a first crude approximation of the doctrine that "thought" is a dependable guide to "Being." Plato assumed that thought could discover the world of Being. Aristotle, who didn't accept Plato's two-worlds view, nevertheless accepted Plato's confidence that an examination of the language we speak will allow us to discover truths about reality. So too, metaphysicians from Thales to Alfred North Whitehead in our own century have made the same assumption: Language and thought are more or less accurate vehicles for representing and recognizing reality, and that reality is thereby intelligible to us.

It is only very recently that this assumption has been seriously questioned. Without this assumption an embarrassing doubt arises. Why should we suppose that what we describe as the way the world really is is anything more than an autobiographical account of the only way that we can describe it? Perhaps our view of the world is determined by the structures and limitations of the language we learned from our parents and peers? Moreover, how can we even know that reality has any "structure" at all, apart from those structures that we impose upon it with our language? For example, could it not be that the distinctions Aristotle applies to reality are nothing other than a reflection of the structure of the Greek language? And could not the necessary truths we discover about reality be nothing other than the conceptual truths that are built right into the meanings of our words? Here the skeptic is armed with a particularly powerful set of arguments. If we give up the assumption that our language mirrors reality, then we must face the skeptic and we can never be assured of having a grasp of "the way the world really is" at all. For this reason, most philosophers have always felt compelled to hold on to this important assumption. Descartes, for example, though he tried to doubt everything, never for a second doubted the trustworthiness of his own language. But today, such leading scientist-philosophers as Albert Einstein have insisted that the intelligibility of the universe is itself a problem, a problem surmounted only by faith.

2) It is usually assumed that all statements about reality in metaphysics are **necessary truths.** Several times we have mentioned the fact that metaphysical claims are not simple statements about "the way the world really is" but actually claims about "the way the world *must* be." Every statement in metaphysics, in other words, must be taken as if the reality it described had to be that way, according to some rational principle or reason. This is what Descartes required of his "first principles." He demanded that they be "perfectly certain," and he insisted throughout his philosophy that the only truths really worth the honorific title of "knowledge" were those that could be known beyond all possible doubt. In Plato, we saw that necessary truth was the earmark of reality, eternal and unchanging. And in Aristotle, although the matter becomes more subtle, it is clear that he considered all of his principles—even his principles of natural science—as matters of necessity. This emphasis on necessity is of tremendous importance. We shall devote two later chapters to it (Chapters 4 and 5).

SUMMARY AND CONCLUSION

Metaphysics is the study of ultimate reality, the attempt to find out the way the world really is. The first recognized metaphysical theory in Western philosophy is Thales' suggestion that everything is ultimately made of water. After Thales, a number of schools of metaphysics suggested alternative theories, all of them depending on the speculative powers of human reason and diverging in various and important ways from "common sense." But these thinkers were not only the first significant Western philosophers; they were also the first theoretical scientists, anticipating in many ways some of the most sophisticated theories of contemporary physics, astronomy, and chemistry.

The first turning point in Western metaphysics came with Socrates, although Socrates himself was more interested in moral issues than in metaphysics as such. Socrates' student, Plato, and his student in turn, Aristotle, became the first great systematic metaphysicians, and philosophy ever since has been deeply indebted to them. Plato introduced an elaborate theory in which ultimate reality consisted of Forms, in contrast to the particular and changing things of everyday life. To support this "two-worlds" theory of Forms versus individual things, he offered a theory of learning, a "theory of recollection," in which he argued that the human soul is immortal and that each of us already knows, in some sense, what we appear to learn in our lives. Aristotle argues instead that only individual things deserve the ultimate claim to reality, for these individual things are the primary substances. Since Aristotle, metaphysicians have typically used the term *substance* as the name of the basic entities that compose reality.

GLOSSARY

Ahura Mazda   the God of Zoroastrianism.

Angra Mainyush   the evil spirit of Zoroastrianism.

Analects   one of the major works of Confucius.

animism   the view that things (or, at the extreme, all things) are alive. It may also be the view that the universe as a whole is one gigantic organism.

Becoming   (In Plato) the "world of Becoming" is the changing world of our daily experience, in which things and people come into being and pass away.

Being   (In Plato) the "world of Being" is the realm of eternal Forms, in which nothing ever changes. It is, for him, reality, and, in general, Being is used by philosophers to refer to whatever they consider ultimately real (substance, God).

Bhagavadgita (Gita)   the "Song of God" of ancient Hinduism; the epic poem of Krishna, the Hindu God.

Buddha   "the awakened one"; the historical founder of Buddhism.

cause   that which brings something about. Philosophers usually add, "as a matter of necessity." In Aristotle, "cause" means something like "reason," and he distinguishes four different kinds of "causes" of a change: (1) the *formal* cause, the principle or essential idea according to which a change comes about (think of a blueprint for a building, or the plans for a project); (2) the *material* cause, the matter that undergoes the change (think of the raw materials for building a house—lumber, bricks, cement); (3) the *efficient* cause, that which initiates the change (the construction workers and their tools); (4) the *final* cause, or the purpose of the change (to build a place where Socrates and his family can live, for example).

conceptual truth   a statement that is true and that we can see to be true by virtue of the meanings of the words (or we should say, the "concepts") that compose it. For example, "a horse is an animal" is a conceptual truth because anyone who speaks English and knows the meaning of the words "horse" and "animal" knows that such a statement must be true. (We shall discuss such statements in greater detail in Chapters 4 and 5.) In Plato, a conceptual truth is a truth about Forms. In Aristotle, a conceptual truth is a matter of describing the essence of a thing. (See *Form, essence.*)

cosmology the study of the universe in its entirety (from the Greek word for "universe"—*cosmos*).

dharma in Hinduism, righteousness, the way of the good.

essence the necessary or defining characteristics or properties of a thing. "That which makes a thing what it is," in other words, those features which one must list in a definition or uniquely identifying description. (For example, the fact that Socrates is a man is part of his essence, the fact that he never smoked on Saturdays is not.)

Form (In Plato) an independently existing entity in the world of Being, which determines the nature of the particular things of this world. In Aristotle, forms have no independent existence.

Four Noble Truths among the most important teachings of the Buddha: All is suffering, the need to eliminate desire, the way to eliminate desire, and the right path to the good.

Idea In Plato, a Form.

immaterialism the metaphysical view that accepts the existence of nonspatial, nonsensory entities such as numbers, minds, and ideas. The weak version asserts merely that there are such entities. The strong version asserts that there are *only* such entities (that is, there are no physical objects).

immortality the idea that the soul survives death (and, in some belief systems, precedes birth).

ineffable impossible of expression in words.

infinite regress a sequence going back endlessly. For example, "A is caused by B, and B by C, and C by D . . . and so on to infinity." Aristotle believed such a regress to be an intellectual absurdity.

innate ideas knowledge that is "programmed" into us from birth and need not be learned. Experience may be necessary to "trigger off" such ideas, but they are already "in" all of us. In Plato, the theory of innate ideas is part of a general theory of the immortality of the soul.

karma in Hinduism, the tendency of any course of action to be repeated; the limitation of one's own free will by one's own habits.

Krishna in Hinduism, God incarnate.

materialism the metaphysical view that only physical matter and its properties exist. Such intangible entities as numbers, minds, and ideas are really properties of physical bodies. To talk about energy, for example, is, in a way, to talk about physical potential; to talk about minds is, as a kind of shorthand, to talk about behavior; to talk about ideas is, in a misleading way, to talk about the various structures and interrelationships between objects. Numbers have no existence of their own but only represent sets of sets of objects (the set of all sets of eight things is the number eight, for example). Materialism has always been a powerful world-view in modern scientific culture. It was also the most common view among the pre-Socratic philosophers.

metaphysics most simply, the study of the most basic (or "first") principles. Traditionally, the study of ultimate reality, or "Being as such." Popularly, any kind of very abstract or obscure thinking. Most philosophers today would define metaphysics as the study of the most general concepts of science and human life, for example, "reality," "existence," "freedom," "God," "soul," "action," "mind." In general, we can divide metaphysics into: ontology, cosmology, and an ill-defined set of problems concerning God and the immortality of the human soul. (See *ontology, cosmology,* and Chapters 7–10.)

monism   the metaphysical view that there is ultimately only one substance, that all reality is one. Less strictly, it may be applied to philosophers who believe in only one kind of substance.

monotheism   belief in one God.

mysticism   the belief that immediate, intuitive knowledge of God is possible, and the attempt to achieve it.

naturalism   the belief that ultimate reality is a natural property.

necessary truth   a statement which could not possibly be false under any conceivable circumstances; for instance, "2 + 2 = 4." (See Chapters 4 and 5.)

ontology   the study of being. That is, that part of metaphysics that asks such questions as, "What is there?" "What is it for something to exist?" "What is an individual thing?" "How do things interact?" Traditionally, these questions were formulated as questions about substance (see page 71). Today, much of ontology is part of logic and linguistics and is the study of the concepts we use to discuss such matters. Sometimes ontology is used as a synonym for metaphysics, but usually the latter is the broader discipline.

pantheism   belief that everything is divine, or that God is in everything.

paradigm   an ideal example. Philosophers often talk about "a paradigm such-and-such" or "a paradigm case of. . . ." For example, "a paradigm case of willpower is my getting up early on Sunday morning."

participation   Plato's obscure and unexplained relationship between the things of this world and the Forms of which they are manifestations. He tells us that individual things "participate" in their Forms.

pluralism   the metaphysical view that there are many distinct substances in the universe, and, perhaps, many different kinds of substances as well.

polytheism   belief in many gods.

prime mover   in Aristotle the "cause-of-itself," the first cause, which (Who) initiates all changes but is not itself (Himself) affected by anything prior. Aristotle believes there must be a prime mover if we are to avoid an infinite regress, which he considers an absurdity. Aristotle also refers to the prime mover as "God," and medieval philosophers (for example, St. Thomas Aquinas) have developed these views into Christian theology.

property   properties are generally distinguished from the substances in which they "inhere" by pointing to the fact that a property cannot exist without being a property of something; for example, there can be any number of red things but no redness that exists independently. (Many philosophers have challenged this idea, but this problem, which is called the "problem of universals," will not be discussed in this introductory course.)

reason   in our introduction, we defined "reason" as simply "the ability to think abstractly." In metaphysics, however, it often has a more controversial meaning, namely, that human ability to go beyond experience to determine, through thought alone, what reality is really like.

sophists ancient Greek philosophers and teachers who believed that no reality exists except for what we take to be reality.

Spenta Mainyush the good spirit of Zoroastrianism.

substance the essential reality of a thing or things that underlies the various properties and changes of properties. Its most common definitions: "that which is independent and can exist by itself," and "the essence of a thing which does not and cannot change." In traditional metaphysics, substance is the same as "ultimate reality," and the study of substance is that branch of metaphysics that studies reality, namely, ontology. (See *essence, ontology.*)

Tao the "Way"; in Confucianism, the "way" to be a gentleman, for example, following the rituals; in Taoism, the underlying and ineffable "way" of nature or reality.

teleology (teleological) the belief that all phenomena have a purpose, end, or goal (from the Greek *telos*, meaning "purpose"). Aristotle's metaphysics is a teleology, which means that he believes that the universe itself—and consequently everything in it—operates for purposes and can be explained according to goals.

Upanishads the "secret doctrines" that form the basis of Hinduism and Buddhism.

Zend Avesta the scripture of Zoroastrianism.

Zoroastrianism the religion of ancient Persia.

◆ *BIBLIOGRAPHY AND FURTHER READING* ◆

General surveys of ancient Greek philosophy can be found in J. Burnet, *Early Greek Philosophy* (London: Black, 1958) and W. K. C. Guthrie, *The Greek Philosophers: From Thales to Aristotle* (New York: Harper & Row, 1960). The most important texts from the pre-Socratics are in G. S. Kirk and J. E. Raven, *The Presocratic Philosophers* (Cambridge: Cambridge University Press, 1957). Plato's dialogues are collected in *Plato, Dialogues,* 4th ed., trans. Benjamin Jowett (Oxford: Oxford University Press, 1953); a helpful survey of his work is A. E. Taylor, *Plato: The Man and His Work* (New York: Dial, 1936). Aristotle's works are collected in R. McKeon, ed., *The Basic Works of Aristotle* (New York: Random House, 1941). An excellent survey of all Aristotle's works is W. D. Ross, *Aristotle* (New York: Meridian, 1959). Brief surveys of the pre-Socratics, Socrates, Plato, and Aristotle are D. J. O'Connor, ed., *A Critical History of Western Philosophy* (New York: Free Press, 1964) and P. Edwards, ed., *The Encyclopedia of Philosophy* (New York: Macmillan, 1967). General introductions to metaphysics are Richard Taylor, *Metaphysics* (Englewood Cliffs, NJ: Prentice-Hall, 1963) and D. F. Pears, ed., *The Nature of Metaphysics* (London: Macmillan, 1957). An exciting history of metaphysics is A. Lovejoy, *The Great Chain of Being* (Cambridge, MA: Harvard University Press, 1936). An excellent collection of sources from non-Western cultures is Bonevac, Boon and Phillips, eds., *Beyond the Western Tradition* (Mountain View, CA: Mayfield, 1992).

2

REALITY: A FEW MODERN VIEWS

The greatest good is the knowledge of the union which the mind has with the whole nature.

BENEDICTUS DE SPINOZA

The best way to learn modern metaphysics is to study the works of the great philosophers. We can also study the problems of ontology and cosmology as separate subjects, but then what is lost is the most striking aspect of metaphysics—the sense of system that ties these separate problems together and distinguishes the great metaphysicians from lesser philosophical technicians. It is within the scope of such all-encompassing systems or world-views that these problems are unified into a matter of deep intellectual and cultural concern.

Throughout the Middle Ages, philosophers and theologians developed elaborate systems of metaphysics, many of them derived directly or indirectly from the thoughts and theories of Plato and Aristotle. Inherent in all such systems was the confidence that the world is ultimately intelligible, and that the truths that reason can discern about reality are not only true, but necessarily true. Throughout this rich millennium of philosophy (from the later days of the Roman Empire through the Renaissance and Reformation), philosophy and theology in Europe became pretty much a single subject, until the rise of the "new" science in the sixteenth and seventeenth centuries. At that time a series of revolutions took place that justify a discussion about the beginning of the "modern" era of philosophy. What distinguished these revolutions was not a separation from religion and theology (most of these philosophers were pious theists whose God played a central role in their thinking), but rather a new boldness of thought, often in contradiction with church authority and strikingly original in its form. The father of these revolutions was René Descartes (whom we met earlier in our introduction), whose philosophy represented a radically new turn in some very old ways of metaphysical thinking. (We should remind ourselves that no thinker, however bold or brilliant, carries off a revolution all alone. Generations paved the way for Descartes' revolution.)

Descartes' metaphysical system was an amalgam of the latest theories in science and mathematics (some of which he discovered), established theology, and the new science of psychology. The method itself (discussed briefly in the introduction) was based on the model of mathematical proof, starting with premises that were self-evident and arguing deductively to conclusions that were therefore equally certain. We consider Descartes' contributions to knowledge—and the famous arguments beginning with his *Cogito* ("I think, therefore I am")—in the following chapter. Here we consider Descartes' equally famous metaphysical model of the world, one which has set the stage for much of philosophy ever since. (The basic idea that mind and body are distinct is still referred to as "Cartesian dualism.") Next we look at Descartes' two most famous and brilliant followers, who developed elaborate metaphysical systems quite different from—and in opposition to—his own. The first is a Jewish philosopher, excommunicated for his heresies, who lived his life in poverty on the outskirts of Amsterdam. He is Benedictus[1] de Spinoza (1632–1677). The second is his slightly younger contemporary, Gottfried Wilhelm von Leibniz (1646–1716), Germany's first, great, modern philosopher. Together, they present us with the best possible lesson in modern Western metaphysics. We then turn to the East to meet Sadra, a metaphysician of Islam.

A. RENÉ DESCARTES

Modern metaphysics begins with Descartes, his insistence upon perfect certainty and mathematical deduction as the legitimate methodology. But methodology aside, metaphysics is a continuous enterprise from the Greeks through medieval philosophy, with Descartes its direct heir. We should not be surprised, for example, to find that the central concept of Descartes' metaphysics is *substance*, and that his definition of it (and the term itself) comes straight from Aristotle: "a thing existing in such a manner that it has need of no other thing in order to exist." (Both Spinoza and Leibniz follow Descartes in taking substance as their central concept, and they follow him also in their method. The three philosophers are usually grouped together as a single school of thought called *Rationalism*.)

Descartes' metaphysics can be understood best in terms of a monumental historical conflict between the "new" science (developed by Galileo and others) and the established authority of the Roman Catholic

[1] Born Baruch, he changed his name after he was excommunicated from the Jewish faith.

Church. Descartes, like many of the most important philosophers to follow him, was both an enthusiast of the new science—in fact he was an important contributor to both science and its mathematical foundations—and a religious man. He could not tolerate the idea that science should replace the orderly, meaningful world-view of Christianity with a Godless, amoral universe of mere "matter in motion." Neither could Descartes ever agree that science should reduce human existence—in particular, the thinking self—to another mere machine. (It is often noted that Descartes did think that animals were mere machines: What we too generously attribute to them by way of learning and responding to the environment is in fact nothing but a mechanical adjustment.) Accordingly, his metaphysics divides the world into three sorts of "substances": God; the mind, or self; and physical, material being. The latter two sorts of substances are, of course, created by and dependent on God. Indeed, Descartes begins all his studies with a proof of the existence of the world (and one's knowledge of it) that rests on the presumption of God's goodness. Because God is rational and good, we can trust (within limits) our own limited knowledge of the world. (We examine some of these proofs and arguments in the following chapter.) But because the world (of minds and matter) depends on God, there is no danger that science should leave us with a Godless, meaningless, mechanical universe. In Aristotelian terms, the ultimate causes in the universe are "final" (or purposive) causes, not "efficient" (or mechanical) causes. The physical world is God's creation; and though it must be understood by science according to causal mechanisms, it is, nevertheless, within the domain of God's providence.

Within the domain of nature there are two (sorts of) substances, mind and body. Because these are substances, they are utterly distinct and independent. One immediate advantage of this "Cartesian dualism" is that the science of mind and the science of physical bodies (like theology and science) do not and cannot contradict one another. There is a science of the self and a science of physics, and there is no reason to suppose that science will deny the freedom of the self anymore than there is reason to fear that science will ultimately conflict with theology. What is true of physical bodies is not what is true of minds, and vice versa. Bodies may be wholly constrained by the laws of physics, but minds are free.

What is **substance,** according to Descartes?

◆ On Substance, by René Descartes

PRINCIPLE LI

What substance is, and that it is a name which we cannot attribute in the same sense to God and to His creatures.

As regards these matters which we consider as being things or modes of things, it is necessary that we should examine them here one by one. By substance, we can understand nothing else than a thing which so exists that it needs no other thing in order to exist. And in fact only one single substance can be understood which clearly needs nothing else, namely, God. We perceive that all other things can exist only by the help of the concourse of God. That is why the word substance does not pertain *univoce* to God and to other things, as they say in the Schools, that is, no common signification for this appellation which will apply equally to God and to them can be distinctly understood.[2]

PRINCIPLE LII

That it may be attributed univocally to the soul and to body, and how we know substance.

Created substances, however, whether corporeal or thinking, may be conceived under this common concept; for they are things which need only the concurrence of God in order to exist. But yet substance cannot be first discovered merely from the fact that it is a thing that exists, for that fact alone is not observed by us. We may, however, easily discover it by means of any one of its attributes because it is a common notion that nothing is possessed of no attributes, properties, or qualities. For this reason, when we perceive any attribute, we therefore conclude that some existing thing or substance to which it may be attributed, is necessarily present.

PRINCIPLE LIII

That each substance has a principal attribute, and that the attribute of the mind is thought, while that of body is extension.

But although any one attribute is sufficient to give us a knowledge of substance, there is always one principal property of substance which constitutes its nature and essence, and on which all the others depend. Thus extension in length, breadth and depth, constitutes the nature of corporeal substance; and thought constitutes the nature of thinking substance. For all else that may be attributed to body presupposes extension, and is but a mode of this extended thing; as everything that we find in mind is but so many diverse forms of thinking. Thus, for example, we cannot conceive figure but as an extended thing, nor movement but as in an extended space; so imagination, feeling, and will, only exist in a thinking thing. But, on the other hand, we can conceive extension without figure or action, and thinking without imagination or

[2]René Descartes, *Principles of Philosophy*, in *The Philosophical Works of Descartes*, eds. E. Haldane and G. R. T. Ross (Cambridge: Cambridge University Press, 1911). All subsequent Cartesian Principles are from this edition.

sensation, and so on with the rest; as is quite clear to anyone who attends to the matter.

This is to say, following Aristotle, everything is either a substance or an attribute of substance, and a substance (as opposed to an attribute) can be thought of independently and can exist independently. Strictly speaking, this is true only of God. But we can also so define physical and mental substances. What defines physical substance, Descartes tells us, is its *extension in space*. Mind, by contrast, is unextended; that is, a thought does not have (in the sense that a wooden box has) a location in the physical dimensions of space.

PRINCIPLE LIV

That the nature of body consists . . . in . . . extension alone.

The nature of matter or of body in its universal aspect, does not consist in its being hard, or heavy, or coloured, or one that affects our senses in some other way, but solely in the fact that it is a substance extended in length, breadth and depth. . . . If, whenever we moved our hands in some direction, all the bodies in that part retreated with the same velocity as our hands approached them, we should never feel hardness; and yet we have no reason to believe that the bodies which recede in this way would on this account lose what makes them bodies. It follows from this that the nature of body does not consist in hardness. The same reason shows us that weight, colour, and all the other qualities of the kind that is perceived in corporeal matter, may be taken from it, it remaining meanwhile entire: it thus follows that the nature of body depends on none of these.

PRINCIPLE XIII

What external place is . . .

The words place and space signify nothing different from the body which is said to be in a place, and merely designate its magnitude, figure, and situation as regards other bodies. . . . For example, if we consider a man seated at the stern of a vessel when it is carried out to sea, he may be said to be in one place if we regard the parts of the vessel . . . : and yet he will be found continually to change his position, if regard be paid to the neighbouring shores. . . . But if at length we are persuaded that there are no points in the universe that are really immovable, as will presently be shown to be probable, we shall conclude that there is nothing that has a permanent place except in so far as it is fixed by our thought.

Physical nature is ruled by mechanical, causal laws; mental substance (the mind, the self) is defined by its freedom.

PRINCIPLE XXXIX

That freedom of the will is self-evident.

Finally it is so evident that we are possessed of a free will that can give or withhold its assent, that this may be counted as one of the first and most ordinary notions that are found innately in us. We had before a very clear proof of this, for at the same time as we tried to doubt all things and even supposed that He who created us employed His unlimited powers in deceiving us in every way, we perceived in ourselves a liberty such that we were able to abstain from believing what was not perfectly certain and indubitable. But that of which we could not doubt at such a time is as self-evident and clear as anything we can ever know.

However, this raises a serious philosophical-theological question, one that had been raised centuries before by St. Augustine. (We discuss this in detail in Chapter 6 [section D].) That is: How can we be free if in fact God has infinite knowledge of all that will be and has ordained our futures in advance? Descartes gives us a somewhat ambiguous answer:

PRINCIPLE XL

That we likewise know certainly that everything is pre-ordained of God.

But because that which we have already learnt about God proves to us that His power is so immense that it would be a crime for us to think ourselves ever capable of doing anything which He had not already pre-ordained, we should soon be involved in great difficulties if we undertook to make His pre-ordinances harmonise with the freedom of our will, and if we tried to comprehend them both at one time.

PRINCIPLE XLI

How the freedom of the will may be reconciled with Divine pre-ordination.

Instead of this, we shall have no trouble at all if we recollect that our thought is finite, and that the omnipotence of God, whereby He has not only known from all eternity that which is or can be, but also willed and pre-ordained it, is infinite. In this way we may have intelligence enough to come clearly and distinctly to know that this power is in God, but not enough to comprehend how He leaves the free action of man indeterminate; and, on the other hand, we are so conscious of the liberty and indifference which exists in us, that there is nothing that we comprehend more clearly and perfectly. For it would be absurd to doubt that of which we inwardly experience and perceive as existing within ourselves, just because we do not comprehend a matter which from its nature we know to be incomprehensible.

But the mind not only "wills"; it also understands. We perceive the world and come to know its objects. But since the physical world and the mind are two distinct substances, how can there be a link between the two? The answer is that we have *ideas*, which are states of mind but nevertheless represent objects in the world that are their causes. However, this raises a number of ancient and more modern problems. Descartes, like Plato and Aristotle, has far more faith in reason and its favorite methods (e.g., mathematics) than he does in perception and the information gleaned from the senses. The senses can fool us, and we tend to rush to judgment prematurely on the basis of sensory experience. For instance:

> When I feel pain in my foot, my knowledge of physics teaches me that this sensation is communicated by means of nerves dispersed through the foot, which, being extended like cords from there to the brain, when they are contracted in the foot, at the same time contract the inmost portions of the brain which is their extremity and place of origin, and then excite a certain movement which nature has established in order to cause the mind to be affected by a sensation of pain represented as existing in the foot. But because these nerves must pass through the tibia, the thigh, the loins, the back and the neck, in order to reach from the leg to the brain, it may happen that although their extremities which are in the foot are not affected, but only certain ones of their intervening parts, this action will excite the same movement in the brain that might have been excited there by a hurt received in the foot, in consequence of which the mind will necessarily feel in the foot the same pain as if it had received a hurt. And the same holds good of all the other perceptions of our senses. . . .
>
> From this it is quite clear that, notwithstanding the supreme goodness of God, the nature of man, inasmuch as it is composed of mind and body, cannot be otherwise than sometimes a source of deception.[3]

But there is another source of ideas in addition to those caused in us by perception. There are also *innate* ideas, those implanted in us by God. Because of innate ideas we can know certain propositions to be true *for certain* (e.g., the propositions of geometry, as Plato also had argued). It is because of innate ideas that we are able to *reason* and, in particular, to do philosophy, to know God, to know universal truths. But even here a dramatic difference must be noted between Descartes and his ancient

[3]Descartes, *Meditations*, pp. 196–98.

predecessors. Plato and Aristotle would have claimed to know reality itself (whether this consisted of Forms or essences). But Descartes ultimately claims that we know only the ideas. There is always that gap between the mind and the world that the ancients never allowed and never entertained. Thus the doctrine of innate ideas might be said to play an even more essential role in Descartes' philosophy than in Plato's. Nevertheless, in his time Descartes was accused by the Roman Catholic Church of overreaching our claim to knowledge: His claim that the human mind has access to the truth through innate ideas was still a challenge to the church's claim to being the sole authority in all ultimate matters.

The most difficult problem facing Descartes' philosophy, however, was the relationship between the various substances. How could God create a substance if that so-called substance were then dependent on God? For example, how could one substance interact with another as physical objects must do if they are to cause in us a perception? In general, how do the mind and the body interact, as surely they must, on Descartes' account? By definition substances are distinct and independent; interaction would seem to be interdependence, and not logically possible. These are the questions that most bothered Spinoza and Leibniz—the questions that would define much of philosophy for years to come.

At first glance, the problems of modern metaphysics appear to be the same that faced the pre-Socratics: How many substances are there? What are they? How are individuals distinguished? How do different things (or substances) interact? How does substance come into being? Is there a beginning to the universe? But two momentous changes in the intervening centuries forced modern philosophers to deal with problems that had barely even occurred to Greek philosophers.

The long and powerful hold of Christianity had given immaterialism (including the immortality of the human soul and the existence of a spiritual God) a status it had only rarely enjoyed in materialistic Greece. Accordingly, few philosophers held to the ancient view that only material "stuff" existed, that is, the view we call materialism. It was now obligatory for any philosopher to account for those mysterious immaterial entities, minds. And, of course, God. Descartes' metaphysics, for example, began by acknowledging two kinds of "created substances," one physical, one mental. And then there was one (and only one) "uncreated substance"—God. Other philosophers, Leibniz for one, went so far as to argue that there were only immaterial substances. Such a position is now called **idealism.** In modern philosophy, materialism ("it's all matter, never mind") and idealism ("it's all in the mind, no matter") have been fighting it out for three centuries. Idealism typically carries with it a religious conviction, for the concept of mind and the concept of spirit are never far apart. (In German, for example, they are the same word, *Geist.*) Materialism, on the other hand, usually draws its power from the remarkable advancements in the sciences, and here we find our second momentous change.

With the rise of modern science, it became the generally accepted view that the universe was a giant machine, perhaps set up by God, but in any case a well-coordinated and predictable mechanism. Isaac Newton's discovery of the causal laws of motion and gravity only brought to a climax a scientific world-view that had been in the making for centuries. And though ancient animism was still alive and belief in God and spirituality was still virtually universal, the modern mechanical view of reality was an absolutely unavoidable consideration for any metaphysician.

Both Spinoza and Leibniz fully appreciated this modern scientific view, although they interpreted it very differently. They were both religious men. (Spinoza, ironically, was branded an atheist and his philosophy banned from most of Europe.) They both accepted Descartes' "rationalist," deductive method and both developed their thinking along the lines of a geometrical system. They both began by considering the concept of substance. Yet Spinoza emerged as a monist, Leibniz as a pluralist. In viewing their impressive systems of thought, it is important to keep in mind the long history we have quickly reviewed, the powerful influences of Christianity and science and, most importantly, the various metaphysical problems to which we were introduced in the preceding chapter.

B. BENEDICTUS DE SPINOZA

Spinoza's *Ethics* is one of the few modern works that is accepted as an unqualified classic by virtually everyone in philosophy. It is the author's only major work. Spinoza was an avid political reformer, particularly on the issue of religious toleration, and even in liberal Amsterdam that made him a dangerous person to know. The following work, which, as you will see, is much more than a study in "ethics," was his most forceful contribution to the issue of tolerance. Spinoza introduced a shockingly radical reinterpretation of God and his relation to the universe. He also gave an equally shocking theory of our roles in the universe. So while you are attempting to comprehend these difficult statements and proofs about "substance," keep your mind open for the dramatic changes in the way Spinoza teaches us to look at our world and for his radical rethinking of Judaism.

Spinoza begins with a set of definitions:

◆from *Ethics,*
by **Benedictus**
de Spinoza

DEFINITIONS

    I. By that which is *self-caused,* I mean that of which the essence involves existence, or that of which the nature is only conceivable as existent.
    II. A thing is called *finite after its kind,* when it can be limited by another thing of the same nature; for instance, a body is called finite because we always conceive another greater body. So, also, a thought is limited by another thought, but a body is not limited by thought, nor a thought by body.
    III. By *substance,* I mean that which is in itself, and is conceived through itself: in other words, that of which a conception can be formed independently of any other conception.
    IV. By *attribute,* I mean that which the intellect perceives as constituting the essence of substance.
    V. By *mode,* I mean the modifications of substance, or that which exists in, and is conceived through, something other than itself.
    VI. By *God,* I mean a being absolutely infinite—that is, a substance consisting in infinite attributes, in which each expresses eternal and infinite essentiality.
    VII. That thing is called free, which exists solely by the necessity of its own nature, and of which the action is determined by itself alone. On the other hand, that thing is necessary, or rather constrained, which is determined by something external to itself to a fixed and definite method of existence or action.
    VIII. By *eternity,* I mean existence itself, in so far as it is conceived necessarily to follow solely from the definition of that which is eternal.[4]

    These definitions sound much more forbidding than they really are. Notice first how many of these terms and definitions are familiar to us from Aristotle: for example, the definition of substance as the basic "stuff" that has various properties but is dependent only on itself and can be thought of without thinking of anything else. **Attributes** and **modes,** on the other hand, are properties: attributes consist of essential characteristics of a substance; modes are modifications of attributes. (For example, having a body is an attribute of substance; being blond and blue-eyed are merely modes.) The **cause-of-itself** is like Aristotle's prime mover, but with some very important differences. Spinoza's

---

[4]Benedictus de Spinoza, *Ethics,* in *The Rationalists,* trans. R. H. M. Elwes (New York: Doubleday, 1960). All subsequent quotations from Spinoza are from this edition of *Ethics.*

"mover" turns out to be identical to the universe, and Spinoza's "God" is much more than "thought thinking itself," as in Aristotle. But the basic starting point of the entire system, as summarized in these definitions and axioms, is the Aristotelian notion of substance. Like the ancient metaphysicians, Spinoza insists that whatever really exists, exists eternally (Definition VIII, above). But that also means—there can be no Creation and no Creator!

As in geometry, the definitions are followed by a set of *axioms*, that is, principles that are so obvious that they need no defense. In plane geometry, such an axiom would be "the shortest distance between two points is a straight line." Spinoza's axioms may not seem quite so obvious at first glance, partly because of the unfamiliarity of his metaphysical terminology.

AXIOMS

I. Everything which exists, exists either in itself or in something else.

II. That which cannot be conceived through anything else must be conceived through itself.

III. From a given definite cause an effect necessarily follows, and, on the other hand, if no definite cause be granted, it is impossible that an effect can follow.

IV. The knowledge of an effect depends on and involves the knowledge of a cause.

V. Things which have nothing in common cannot be understood, the one by means of the other; the conception of one does not involve the conception of the other.

VI. A true idea must correspond with its ideate or object.

VII. If a thing can be conceived as non-existing, its essence does not involve existence.

You can see that the axioms follow approximately the same sequence as the definitions, and the axioms in most cases are based on the definitions, although they do not strictly follow from them. For example, Axiom 1, like Definition 1, concerns the idea that everything has an explanation. Definition 1, although stated in terms of "cause" ("self-caused"), concerns that which must exist if it can just be thought of. Axiom 1 says that everything must either be explainable through itself (that is, "self-caused") or through something else.

Similarly, Definition 2 uses a technical term ("finite after its kind") to talk about things that can be explained only by reference to something greater, while Axiom 2 says that anything that cannot be so explained must be explained simply in terms of itself ("self-caused" again). Axioms 3 and 4 outline the basic principles of cause and effect; that is, that a cause makes its effect happen necessarily, and without the cause, there would be no effect, and that the knowledge of the effect depends on knowing the cause. (These principles have had a long and important history in both metaphysics and theories of science and knowledge. They will play a key role in Spinoza's theory of determinism [the idea that everything happens necessarily because of its causes] and in "deterministic" theories generally. These will be discussed in Chapter 9 in detail.) Axioms 5–7 return to the central theme of explanation begun in Axioms 1 and 2; Axiom 5 insists that one thing can be explained in terms of another only if they have "something in common." Thus you explain one physical event in terms of another physical event (since they have in common certain physical properties). Axiom 6 repeats the important assumption we made explicit at the end of Chapter 1, namely, that our ideas are capable of grasping reality. (This axiom also states a seemingly innocent theory of truth, often called "the correspondence theory of truth," which says that "a true idea corresponds with some actual fact [*ideate* or *object*] in the world." This is discussed in Chapter 4.) Axiom 7 returns to the idea of "essence involving existence," in other words, that which is self-caused, or substance or God. Axiom 7 is stated negatively, however, and says that if we can think of something as not existing (for example, we can imagine what it would be like to live in a world without freeways, or without stars, or even without other people) then "its essence does not involve existence." That is, existing is not one of its essential characteristics and it is not "self-caused."

The general theme of the axioms, therefore, is that everything has an explanation for its existence, either by reference to something else or because it is "self-caused" or self-explanatory, that is, its "essence involves its existence" or it is entirely "in itself and conceived through itself." This last phrase is from the definition of "substance" (Def. 3), so you can see how, even in his axioms and definitions, Spinoza is setting up his main thesis, that there can only be one substance.

Starting with these definitions and axioms, which he takes to be unobjectionable, Spinoza begins the "proofs" of his "propositions," which follow like the theorems of Euclidean geometry from the definitions of terms such as "line," "point," and "parallel." Again, these look forbidding, but their philosophical relevance should be clear.

PROPOSITIONS

PROP. I. *Substance is by nature prior to its modifications.*
Proof.—This is clear from Deff. iii. and v.
PROP. II. *Two substances, whose attributes are different, have nothing in common.*
Proof.—Also evident from Def. iii. For each must exist in itself, and be conceived through itself; in other words, the conception of one does not imply the conception of the other.

PROP. III. *Things which have nothing in common cannot be one the cause of the other.*

Proof.—If they have nothing in common, it follows that one cannot be apprehended by means of the other (Ax. v.), and, therefore, one cannot be the cause of the other (Ax. iv.). *Q.E.D.* [Latin, *quod erat demonstrandum,* a phrase used in traditional logic meaning "thus it is proven."]

PROP. IV. *Two or more distinct things are distinguished one from the other either by the difference of the attributes of the substances, or by the difference of their modifications.*

Proof.—Everything which exists, exists either in itself or in something else (Ax. i.),—that is (by Deff. iii. and v.), nothing is granted in addition to the understanding, except substance and its modifications. Nothing is, therefore, given besides the understanding, by which several things may be distinguished one from the other, except the substances, or, in other words (see Ax. iv.), their attributes and modifications. *Q.E.D.*

PROP. V. *There cannot exist in the universe two or more substances having the same nature or attribute.*

Proof.—If several distinct substances be granted, they must be distinguished one from the other, either by the difference of their attributes, or by the difference of their modifications (Prop. iv.). If only by the difference of their attributes, it will be granted that there cannot be more than one with an identical attribute. If by the difference of their modifications—as substance is naturally prior to its modifications (Prop. i.),—it follows that setting the modifications aside, and considering substance in itself, that is truly, (Deff. iii. and vi.), there cannot be conceived one substance different from another,—that is (by Prop. iv.), there cannot be granted several substances, but one substance only. *Q.E.D.*

PROP. VI. *One substance cannot be produced by another substance.*

Proof.—It is impossible that there should be in the universe two substances with an identical attribute, *i.e.,* which have anything common to them both (Prop. ii.), and, therefore (Prop. iii.), one cannot be the cause of another, neither can one be produced by the other. *Q.E.D.*

Corollary.—Hence it follows that a substance cannot be produced by anything external to itself. For in the universe nothing is granted, save substances and their modifications (as appears from Ax. i. and Deff. iii. and v.). Now (by the last Prop.) substance cannot be produced by another substance, therefore it cannot be produced by anything external to itself. *Q.E.D.* This is shown still more readily by the absurdity of the contradictory. For, if substance be produced by an external cause, the knowledge of it would depend on the knowledge of its cause (Ax. iv.), and (by Def. iii.) it would itself not be substance.

So far, the main point is quite simple: if there is more than one substance, the substances could have no possible relation to each other. Therefore, by a kind of *reductio ad absurdum* argument, there can only be one substance. In the propositions that follow (and especially the note to Prop. VIII), this is demonstrated again:

PROP. VII. *Existence belongs to the nature of substance.*

Proof.—Substance cannot be produced by anything external (Corollary, Prop. vi.), it must, therefore, be its own cause—that is, its essence necessarily involves existence, or existence belongs to its nature.

PROP. VIII. *Every substance is necessarily infinite.*

Proof.—There can only be one substance with an identical attribute, and existence follows from its nature (Prop. vii.); its nature, therefore, involves existence, either as finite or infinite. It does not exist as finite, for (by Def. ii.) it would then be limited by something else of the same kind, which would also necessarily exist (Prop. vii.); and there would be two substances with an identical attribute, which is absurd (Prop. v.). It therefore exists as infinite. *Q.E.D.*

Note.—No doubt it will be difficult for those who think about things loosely, and have not been accustomed to know them by their primary causes, to comprehend the demonstration of Prop. vii.: for such persons make no distinction between the modifications of substances and the substances themselves, and are ignorant of the manner in which things are produced; hence they attribute to substances the beginning which they observe in natural objects. Those who are ignorant of true causes, make complete confusion—think that trees might talk just as well as men—that men might be formed from stones as well as from seed; and imagine that any form might be changed into any other. So, also, those who confuse the two natures, divine and human, readily attribute human passions to the deity, especially so long as they do not know how passions originate in the mind. But, if people would consider the nature of substance, they would have no doubt about the truth of Prop. vii. In fact, this proposition would be a universal axiom, and accounted a truism. For, by substance, would be understood that which is in itself, and is conceived through itself—that is, something of which the conception requires not the conception of anything else; whereas modifications exist in something external to themselves, and a conception of them is formed by means of a conception of the thing in which they exist. Therefore, we may have true ideas of non-existent modifications; for, although they may have no *actual* existence apart from the conceiving intellect, yet their essence is so involved in something external to themselves that they may through it be conceived. Whereas the only truth substances can have, external to the intellect, must consist in their existence, because they are conceived through themselves. Therefore, for a person to say that he has a clear and distinct—that is, a true—idea of a substance, but that he is not sure whether such substance exists, would be the same as if he said that he had a true idea, but was not sure whether or not it was false (a little consideration will make this plain); or if anyone affirmed that substance is created, it would be the same as saying that a false idea was true—in short, the height of absurdity. It must, then, necessarily be admitted that the existence of substance as its essence is an eternal truth. And we can hence conclude by another process of reasoning—that there is but one such substance.

This last phrase summarizes the key doctrine of the entire *Ethics*, that there can be but one substance. The argument in this note, which insists that the essence of substance includes its existence, was a very popular argument throughout the Middle Ages. It means, quite simply, that if you can even imagine something whose essence includes existence, then you know that thing necessarily exists. In a further digression (but it is the digressions that often contain the most philosophy), Spinoza adopts Aristotle's insistence (see p. 93) that everything (or every event) must have its cause:

There is necessarily for each individual existent thing a cause why it should exist.
This cause of existence must either be contained in the nature and definition of the thing defined, or must be postulated apart from such definition.

Such an assertion gives Aristotle the basis for his "prime mover" argument. But Spinoza, unlike Aristotle, has no qualms about the idea of an "infinite regress"; and so, in his view, the universe extends back in time forever, has always existed, and at no time ever came into existence.

What then follows is the working-out of the notion that there is one substance:

PROP. IX. *The more reality or being a thing has, the greater the number of its attributes* (Def. iv.).
PROP. X. *Each particular attribute of the one substance must be conceived through itself.*
Proof.—An attribute is that which the intellect perceives of substance, as constituting its essence (Def. iv.), and, therefore, must be conceived through itself (Def. iii.). *Q.E.D.*

Spinoza goes on to explain that, although we might think of different attributes separately (for example, think of minds and bodies as totally different from each other), we must not conclude that they are different substances. They are rather separate properties of one and the same substance. He then concludes that:

> Consequently it is abundantly clear, that an absolutely infinite being must necessarily be defined as consisting in infinite attributes, each of which expresses a certain eternal and infinite essence.
>
> If anyone now ask, by what sign shall he be able to distinguish different substances, let him read the following propositions, which show that there is but one substance in the universe, and that it is absolutely infinite, wherefore such a sign would be sought for in vain.

Now this looks complicated, but we can appreciate its straightforward significance by looking at it through our earlier questions in ontology and cosmology (p. 71): first, how many substances does Spinoza say that there are (and must be)? Only one—he is a monist, like the earliest pre-Socratics. Descartes, Spinoza's immediate predecessor, had argued that there are three kinds of substance: bodies, minds, and God. Spinoza, however, argues that the very definition of substance makes it necessary that there be only one substance, and that bodies and minds are attributes of this one substance, not substances themselves.

So the answer to our second ontological question, "what kind of substances?" is "one infinite substance," the full nature of which we cannot know. But at least we know two of its properties, namely body and mind. Now notice that this gets around a problem that will plague Descartes (see Chapter 7): How can different substances, which by definition are independent, interact with one another (our fourth question)? If mind and body are separate substances, then how can they come together to form a person? For Spinoza, since there is only one substance, this problem does not arise. With regard to our third question, "how do we distinguish different things (attributes, bodies, and minds)?" Spinoza's answer is fantastic; there is ultimately only one body, namely the physical universe, and one mind, namely all of the thinking in the universe (which in turn are different attributes of the one substance). This means that distinctions between our bodies ("my" body and "your" body) and between our bodies and the rest of the physical universe are ultimately unwarranted, a humanistic pretension that has no basis in reality. But even more surprising is the idea that there is but a single mind, and that our individual minds are somehow only "part of it" (that is, particular modes) but not individual minds at all! Your pride in your "individuality," therefore, has no foundation in reality. You are only a part of that one cosmic substance, the universe.

But the universe is also God. Here is where the innocent-looking obscurity of Spinoza's system becomes the heresy that was banned throughout Europe. By Proposition X, Spinoza has proved that God, substance, and the cause-of-itself are all identical. In the next few propositions, he proves that God necessarily exists (we shall see similar proofs in Chapter 6). Then, Proposition XIV: *"Besides God, no substance can be granted or conceived."* This means that God and the universe are one and the same. This position, called *pantheism* (literally, "everything is God"), was considered sacrilege, even in liberal Amsterdam. It means, against all traditional Judeo-Christian teachings, that God has no existence independent of the universe and that He therefore cannot be its Creator. Look again at the explanation to Definition VIII and then at Proposition XV and those that follow:

> PROP. XV. *Whatsoever is, is in God, and without God nothing can be, or be conceived.*
> PROP. XVI. *From the necessity of the divine nature must follow an infinite number of things in infinite ways—that is, all things which can fall within the sphere of infinite intellect.*
> PROP. XVII. *God acts solely by the laws of his own nature, and is not constrained by anyone.*
> PROP. XVIII. *God is the indwelling and not the transient cause of all things.*
> PROP. XIX. *God, and all the attributes of God, are eternal.*
> PROP. XX. *The existence of God and his essence are one and the same.*
> PROP. XXI. *All things which follow from the absolute nature of any attribute of God must always exist and be infinite, or, in other words, are eternal and infinite through the said attribute.*
> PROP. XXII. *Whatever follows from any attribute of God, in so far as it is modified by a modification, which exists necessarily and as infinite, through the said attribute, must also exist necessarily and as infinite.*
> PROP. XXIII. *Every mode which exists both necessarily and as infinite must necessarily follow either from the absolute nature of some attribute of God, or from an attribute modified by a modification which exists necessarily and as infinite.*
> PROP. XXIV. *The essence of things produced by God does not involve existence.*
> PROP. XXV. *God is the efficient cause not only of the existence of things, but also of their essence.*

Yes, Spinoza believes in God. But God is nothing other than the universe. He has few of the characteristics traditionally attributed to Him and worshiped in Him. For example, Spinoza goes on to argue, on the basis of what he has said already, that God has no will, that He doesn't do anything, and ultimately, He doesn't care about anything either, including humanity. Here is a scientific world-view that is so unrelenting that even Newton himself would be shocked by it. This does not mean that Spinoza is a materialist; quite to the contrary, the importance of his constant insistence upon "the infinite attributes of God," of which we are capable of knowing only two (could you imagine what some of the others might be like?) is to say that God has not only physical existence but (at least) mental existence as well.

But where the scientific outlook becomes most dramatic is in Spinoza's defense of the doctrine we shall call **determinism,** the thesis that every event in the universe necessarily occurs as the result of its cause. The ultimate cause is God, which is to say, the universe itself. Once again, the terms come from Aristotle, but it is therefore important to insist that Spinoza does not believe—with either Aristotle or Christendom—that the universe has any purpose whatsoever. Nor does he believe that the universe or God has any beginning or end, thus answering our two sets of cosmological questions with a single necessary truth, once again, derived directly from the definition of substance.

The ultimate meaning of Spinoza's arguments for determinism is that no action, whether of man or God, is ever free. Everything in the universe, according to Spinoza, is exactly as it must be; the universe couldn't be any other way. Nothing is so pointless as struggling against a universe in which everything, including our own natures and actions, is already determined.

PROP. XXVI. *A thing which is conditioned to act in a particular manner has necessarily been thus conditioned by God; and that which has not been conditioned by God cannot condition itself to act.*

PROP. XXVII. *A thing, which has been conditioned by God to act in a particular way, cannot render itself unconditioned.*

PROP. XXVIII. *Every individual thing, or everything which is finite and has a conditioned existence, cannot exist or be conditioned to act, unless it be conditioned for existence and action by a cause other than itself, which also is finite and has a conditioned existence; and likewise this cause cannot in its turn exist or be conditioned to act, unless it be conditioned for existence and action by another cause, which also is finite and has a conditioned existence, and so on to infinity.*

PROP. XXIX. *Nothing in the universe is contingent, but all things are conditioned to exist and operate in a particular manner by the necessity of the divine nature.*[5]

PROP. XXX. *Intellect, in function finite, or in function infinite, must comprehend the attributes of God and the modifications of God, and nothing else.*

PROP. XXXI. *The intellect in function, whether finite or infinite, as will, desire, love, & c., should be referred to passive nature and not to active nature.*

[5]We are all determined by the nature of God or the universe. But then, here is a problem: Are we not then compelled to struggle, and can't help doing so? If so, what is the point of Spinoza's urging us not to?

> PROP. XXXII. *Will cannot be called a free cause, but only a necessary cause.*
> PROP. XXXIII. *Things could not have been brought into being by God in any manner or in any order different from that which has in fact obtained. [God is determined too.]*
> PROP. XXXIV. *God's power is identical with his essence.*
> PROP. XXXV. *Whatsoever we conceive to be in the power of God, necessarily exists.*
> PROP. XXXVI. *There is no cause from whose nature some effect does not follow.*

Part II of the *Ethics* discusses "the Nature and Origin of the Mind." It begins with a further set of definitions and axioms, most importantly, the definition of body as "extended thing," that is, extended in space (which Spinoza got directly from Descartes and the medieval philosophers) and idea, "the mental conception which is formed by the mind as a thinking thing." Mind, unlike body, is defined as **unextended** (that is, it has no spatial dimensions). It is in this part that Spinoza argues those surprising doctrines that we have already summarized: Mind and body are each one of an infinite number of attributes of God, not substance themselves (as they were for Descartes), and our individual minds are really indistinguishable modifications of the one Great Mind of the One Substance. And Spinoza joins with all of his metaphysical colleagues in insisting that "the order and connection of ideas is the same as the order and connection of things" (Prop. VII). Here again is Spinoza's affirmation of his confidence in thought to grasp reality. (Remember Heraclitus, "thought is Being.")

The upshot of Part II, and the subject that dominates the *Ethics* for the remaining three Parts, is Spinoza's determinism.

> PROP. XLVIII. *In the mind there is no absolute or free will; but the mind is determined to wish this or that by a cause, which has been determined by another cause, and this last by another cause, and so on to infinity.*

Spinoza has none of Aristotle's fears of an "infinite regress," and if he believes in a "cause-of-itself" that is not the same as a "first cause," for there is no such thing. We shall talk more about this "free will and determinism" problem in Chapter 8; but it is worth noting, as a way of summing up, Spinoza's drastic answer to the problem. As an unyielding determinist, he rejects every attempt to save some space for freedom of human action. But he assures us that we can, with heroic effort (Prop. XLVII), understand the nature of this determinism, and accept it gracefully. The folly is in the fighting, he tells us. The remainder of the *Ethics* is given over to the attempt to draw out the logical consequences of this stoic conclusion.

Part III is a long argument against emotions and what we would call "emotional involvement" as the needless cause of suffering and vice. Against them, Spinoza argues the virtues of human reason, which penetrates the useless involvements of the emotions and allows us to understand the causes of our actions and feelings. And to understand an emotion, Spinoza believes, is to change and eliminate it. For example, to understand why one is angry, according to Spinoza, is sufficient to let us get rid of our anger. To realize that we are unable to change, according to Spinoza, is the only freedom we can really be said to have.

What you have just seen is modern metaphysics at its most brilliant. The geometrical method, however, is no longer fashionable, and much of Spinoza's language is, to us, antiquated and unnatural. But the intricacies of his system, the way he ties so many different ideas together, the answers he gave to ancient philosophical problems, and the boldness with which he sets out a new vision of the universe, have made Spinoza's philosophy widely appreciated despite his difficult style. What you are about to read, though, is no less astonishing, no less brilliant, and its author no less remarkable a genius. The work from which these excerpts come is a very short work (of about ninety paragraphs) written by Leibniz, who begins with much the same concepts and definitions as Spinoza, but ends up with a wholly different metaphysical system. (Leibniz and Spinoza met several times and discussed these issues. But Leibniz found Spinoza's opinions too shocking and acquaintanceship with him too dangerous.)

C. GOTTFRIED WILHELM VON LEIBNIZ

Leibniz begins with the same technical notion of substance, but from it he weaves an entirely different but equally fantastic picture of the universe. Where Spinoza's universe was mechanical and wholly dependent upon causes, Leibniz's universe is very much alive, and everything happens for a purpose (as in Aristotle's ancient teleology). The guiding principle of Leibniz's philosophy is called "The Principle of Sufficient Reason," which says, simply, that there must be a reason for everything. Even God, on this account, cannot act capriciously but must have a reason for whatever He has created. We shall see that this principle is among the most important guidelines to Leibniz's philosophy. From it, he develops a radical alternative to Isaac Newton's physics and a spectacularly optimistic view that, because God acts according to this principle, this world that He created must be "the best of all possible worlds."

Where Spinoza argues that there can be at most one substance, Leibniz argues that there are many. He calls them **monads.** Every monad is different from every other, and God (who is something of a supermonad and the only "uncreated monad") has created them all. The work presented here, accordingly, is called the *Monadology* ("the study of monads"), written in 1714. It is a very condensed summary of Leibniz's metaphysics:

◆ **from *Monadology*,**
by Gottfried Wilhelm von Leibniz

1. The Monad, of which we will speak here, is nothing else than a simple substance, which goes to make up composites; by simple, we mean without parts.
2. There must be simple substances because there are composites; for a composite is nothing else than a collection or *aggregatum* of simple substances.[6]

A simple substance is one that cannot be divided. The argument is curious: any "composite" is obviously divisible. That means that every composite must be "composed" of some simple substances that make it up. (There is a hidden infinite regress argument here: If there weren't ultimately simple substances, then we could go on dividing things forever.) But if the simple substances were extended in space, then they too would be further divisible, for anything that has length, for example, no matter how small, can be cut in two (at least in theory). Therefore, Leibniz concludes, these basic simple substances or monads must be immaterial and have no extension. They can have neither parts, nor extension, nor divisibility:

3. Now, where there are no constituent parts there is possible neither extension, nor form, nor divisibility. These Monads are the true Atoms of nature, and, in fact, the Elements of things.

Here, in Leibniz's first three propositions, are the answers to our first two ontological questions: "How many substances are there?" Many. This answer makes Leibniz a pluralist. "What kind of substances are they?" Simple and immaterial substances, which makes Leibniz an *immaterialist.* (Don't be misled by the term "atoms": we are used to thinking of atoms as the smallest material substances, but Leibniz's atoms are *im*material.) And now, in three more propositions, Leibniz answers our first cosmological question: "Are these substances eternal, or do they come into being at some time? How do they come into being? And are they destructible?":

[6]Gottfried W. von Leibniz, *Monadology,* in *The Rationalists,* trans. George Montgomery (New York: Doubleday, 1960). All subsequent quotations from Leibniz are from this edition of *Monadology.*

4. Their dissolution, therefore, is not to be feared and there is no way conceivable by which a simple substance can perish through natural means.

5. For the same reason there is no way conceivable by which a simple substance might, through natural means, come into existence, since it cannot be formed by composition.

6. We may say then, that the existence of Monads can begin or end only all at once, that is to say, the Monad can begin only through creation and end only through annihilation. Composites, however, begin or end gradually.

Spinoza had argued that the one substance could neither be created nor destroyed; it had neither beginning nor end. Leibniz's substances, or "monads," can be created or destroyed, but not by any "natural" means. They can be created or destroyed only "all at once." Anticipating later propositions, we can guess that Leibniz will have God (who is something of a supermonad) create them. But notice that compounds of monads, for example, "material objects," can be created and destroyed "naturally."

Now our third question, "How do we distinguish different substances or monads?":

8. Still Monads must have some qualities, otherwise they would not even be existences. And if simple substances did not differ at all in their qualities, there would be no means of perceiving any change in things. Whatever is in a composite can come into it only through its simple elements and the Monads, if they were without qualities, since they do not differ at all in quantity, would be indistinguishable one from another. For instance, if we imagine *a plenum* or completely filled space, where each part receives only the equivalent of its own previous motion, one state of things would not be distinguishable from another.

9. Each Monad, indeed, must be different from every other. For there are never in nature two beings which are exactly alike, and in which it is not possible to find a difference either internal or based on an intrinsic property.

Only God could actually know everything about every monad in order to compare and contrast them. But even God can distinguish different monads only because they in fact have differences between them. This leads Leibniz to suggest one of his most controversial principles, the so-called "Principle of the Identity of Indiscernibles": no two monads can have the same properties (Prop. 9). Why is this? According to the "Principle of Sufficient Reason" (Prop. 32) nothing can be without good reason. Even God, therefore, would have no good reason for duplicating any monad. If two monads were identical, Leibnitz argues, God could have no reason for putting one in one place and the other in another place, or for creating them both in the first place. Therefore, no two monads could be exactly alike. A strange kind of argument, but very much at the heart of Leibniz's philosophy, as we shall see later.

How does a monad, which is by definition "simple," alter or combine with other monads to form the changing and familiar universe of our experience? (Here you should be reminded of the similar problems that faced the ancient pre-Socratics and Plato.) Here is our fourth question, and the most difficult Leibniz has to answer: "How do substances interact?" By definition, monads cannot literally "interact." And so Leibniz's answer is extremely speculative and imaginative:

> 7. There is also no way of explaining how a Monad can be al-
> tered or changed in its inner being by any other created thing,
> since there is no possibility of transposition within it, nor can we
> conceive of any internal movement which can be produced,
> directed, increased or diminished there within the substance, such
> as can take place in the case of composites where a change can
> occur among the parts. The Monads have no windows through
> which anything may come in or go out.

The problem is that different substances, by definition, are independent and cannot, therefore, have anything to do with one another. Descartes, as we shall see in Chapter 7, had a terrible time getting together his two substances of mind and body. Spinoza, as a monist, solved the problem in the simplest possible way; since there is only one substance, no question of "interaction" is applicable. But Leibniz is a pluralist; there are many substances. They cannot interact as such. They cannot even perceive each other in the usual sense. They "have no windows," in his peculiar but now famous expression; "nothing can come in or go out." And unlike the ancient (and modern) materialist atomists, Leibniz cannot have his monads simply combine and recombine to form new compounds in any usual sense. They cannot, in Leibniz's words, "be altered or changed in [their] inner being by any other created thing." So, how do monads change? They must have all changes already created (by God) within themselves.

Remember the animism that was so prevalent in the ancient Greek philosophers. For them, the phenomenon of life was the model for metaphysics. The idea of Newtonian mechanics would have been incomprehensible to them. Leibniz, we may now say, was vehemently anti-Newton. He was, we may also say, one of the outstanding modern animists. A monad is as different as can be from a Newtonian material atom; a monad is alive, and its changes come from within, never from without. (Except, that is, for its initial creation.) Think of a monad as a living being, "programmed" (to use a modern word) with all of the information and experiences it needs to develop in a certain way, like an acorn developing into an oak tree. Thus the changes in the monad are all internal, programmed by God at the creation. Now keep in mind that a monad is immaterial, and so its "growth" cannot be thought of as a development in the physical world. The growth too, therefore, must be internal, and the apparent interaction between monads must really be changes in the perceptions of the monads themselves.

10. I assume it as admitted that every created being, and consequently the created Monad, is subject to change, and indeed that this change is continuous in each.

11. It follows from what has just been said, that the natural changes of the Monad come from an internal principle, because an external cause can have no influence upon its inner being.

12. Now besides this principle of change there must also be in the Monad a manifoldness which changes. This manifoldness constitutes, so to speak, the specific nature and the variety of the simple substances.

13. This manifoldness must involve a multiplicity in the unity or in that which is simple. For since every natural change takes place by degrees, there must be something which changes and something which remains unchanged, and consequently there must be in the simple substance a plurality of conditions and relations, even though it has no parts.

14. The passing condition which involves and represents a multiplicity in the unity, or in the simple substance, is nothing else than what is called Perception. This should be carefully distinguished from Consciousness.

Leibniz argues here that what we are really describing when we talk about a squirrel climbing a particular tree at a particular moment in time, is ourselves. The perception of the squirrel is a permanent part of one unchanging monad—our perception as a whole. The apparent differences between parts of a monad are really changes in perception. Leibniz is arguing that the sense in which material things seem to exist in space is as different perceptions or experiences of a perceiving monad. What is ultimately real, therefore, is the perceiving monad. Perceptions change, within each monad, to create the appearance of a moving and changing material world. Notice that Leibniz carefully distinguishes "Perception" from what he calls "Consciousness." Perception is experience, in general, and is present, in some degree, in every monad. Consciousness, on the other hand, is a very special kind of experience, reflective and articulate, and is to be found only in a few monads. (It is worth noting that, with this distinction, Leibniz precociously introduces the concept of "the unconscious" into German philosophy two hundred years before Freud.)

15. The action of the internal principle which brings about the change or the passing from one perception to another may be

called Appetition. It is true that the desire is not always able to attain to the whole of the perception which it strives for, but it always attains a portion of it and reaches new perceptions.

16. We, ourselves, experience a multiplicity in a simple substance, when we find that the most trifling thought of which we are conscious involves a variety in the object. Therefore all those who acknowledge that the soul is a simple substance ought to grant this multiplicity in the Monad. . . .

17. It must be confessed, however, that Perception, and that which depends upon it, are inexplicable by mechanical causes, that is to say, by figures and motions. Supposing that there were a machine whose structure produced thought, sensation, and perception, we could conceive of it as increased in size with the same proportions until one was able to enter into its interior, as he would into a mill. Now, on going into it he would find only pieces working upon one another, but never would he find anything to explain Perception.

Here is the attack on Newton's more materialist view of the universe. Such a view, Leibniz complains, cannot account for experience (perception), in other words, the immaterial aspects of the universe.

It is accordingly in the simple substance, and not in the composite nor in a machine that the Perception is to be sought. Furthermore, there is nothing besides perceptions and their changes to be found in the simple substance. And it is in these alone that all the internal activities of the simple substance can consist.

18. All simple substances or created Monads may be called Entelechies, because they have in themselves a certain perfection. There is in them a sufficiency which makes them the source of their internal activities, and renders them, so to speak, incorporeal Automations. [In other words, every monad is alive, to a certain extent.]

19. If we wish to designate as soul everything which has perceptions and desires in the general sense that I have just explained, all simple substances or created Monads could be called souls. But since feeling is something more than a mere perception I think that the general name of Monad or Entelechy should suffice for simple substances which have only perception, while we may reserve the term Soul for those whose perception is more distinct and is accompanied by memory. [Again, Leibniz insists that "Perception" is most primitive and is common to all monads.]

20. We experience in ourselves a state where we remember nothing and where we have no distinct perception, as in periods of fainting, or when we are overcome by a profound, dreamless sleep. In such a state the soul does not sensibly differ at all from a simple Monad. As this state, however, is not perman-

ent and the soul can recover from it, the soul is something more.

21. Nevertheless it does not follow at all that the simple substance is in such a state without perception. This is so because of the reasons given above; for it cannot perish, nor on the other hand would it exist without some affection and the affection is nothing else than its perception. When, however, there are a great number of weak perceptions where nothing stands out distinctively, we are stunned; as when one turns around and around in the same direction, a dizziness comes on, which makes him swoon and makes him able to distinguish nothing. Among animals, death can occasion this state for quite a period.[!]

22. Every present state of a simple substance is a natural consequence of its preceding state, in such a way that its present is pregnant with its future. [Here is Leibniz's version of the thesis that one cause necessarily follows another.]

23. Therefore, since on awakening after a period of unconsciousness we become conscious of our perceptions, we must, without having been conscious of them, have had perceptions immediately before; for one perception can come in a natural way only from another perception, just as a motion can come in a natural way only from a motion.

24. It is evident from this that if we were to have nothing distinctive, or so to speak prominent, and of a higher flavor in our perceptions, we should be in a continual state of stupor. This is the condition of Monads which are wholly bare.

25. We see that nature has given to animals heightened perceptions, having provided them with organs which collect numerous rays of light or numerous waves of air and thus make them more effective in their combination. Something similar to this takes place in the case of smell, in that of taste and of touch, and perhaps in many other senses which are unknown to us.

· · · · · · · · ·

29. It is the knowledge of eternal and necessary truths that distinguishes us from mere animals and gives us reason and the sciences, thus raising us to a knowledge of ourselves and of God. This is what is called in us the Rational Soul or the Mind.

30. It is also through the knowledge of necessary truths and through abstractions from them that we come to perform Reflective Acts, which cause us to think of what is called the I, and to decide that this or that is within us. It is thus, that in thinking upon ourselves we think of *being,* of *substance,* of the *simple* and *composite,* of a *material* thing and of *God* himself, conceiving that what is limited in us is in him without limits. These Reflective Acts furnish the principal objects of our reasonings.

The answer to our fourth question is, "Monads don't interact." Each is locked into itself, and contains within itself its own view of the universe as a whole.

56. Now this interconnection, relationship, or this adaptation of all things to each particular one, and of each one to all the rest, brings it about that every simple substance has relations which express all the others and that it is consequently a perpetual living mirror of the universe.

57. And as the same city regarded from different sides appears entirely different, and is, as it were multiplied respectively, so, because of the infinite number of simple substances, there are a similar infinite number of universes which are, nevertheless, only the aspects of a single one as seen from the special point of view of each monad.

But, of course, the perspective of any one monad is extremely one-sided and confused.

60. Besides, in what has just been seen can be seen the *a priori* reasons why things cannot be otherwise than they are. It is because God, in ordering the whole, has had regard to every part and in particular to each monad; and since the Monad is by its very nature *representative,* nothing can limit it to represent merely a part of things. It is nevertheless true that this representation is, as regards the details of the whole universe, only a confused representation, and is distinct only as regards a small part of them, that is to say, as regards those things which are nearest or greatest in relation to each Monad. If the representation were distinct as to the details of the entire universe, each Monad would be a Deity. It is not in the object represented that the Monads are limited, but in the modifications of their knowledge of the object. In a confused way they reach out to infinity or to the whole, but are limited and differentiated in the degree of their distinct perceptions.

Now Leibniz has an alternative to Newton: bodies (composite monads) only seem to interact; in fact, it all happens within each monad, programmed and created by God in "pre-established harmony."

61. In this respect composites are like simple substances, for all space is filled up; therefore, all matter is connected. And in a plenum or filled space every movement has an effect upon bodies in proportion to this distance, so that not only is every body affected by those which are in contact with it and responds in some way to whatever happens to them, but also by means of them the body responds to those bodies adjoining them, and their intercommunication reaches to any distance whatsoever. Consequently every body responds to all that happens in the universe, so that he who saw all could read in each one what is happening everywhere, and even what has happened and what will happen.

62. Thus although each created Monad represents the whole universe, it represents more distinctly the body which specially per-

tains to it and of which it constitutes the entelechy. And as this body expresses all the universe through the interconnection of all matter in the plenum, the soul also represents the whole universe in representing this body, which belongs to it in a particular way.

Every monad develops as a reflection of the development of all the other monads in the universe as well. If, for example, we are watching a squirrel climb around a tree, Leibniz's view is that the reality of the squirrel climbing around the tree is actually our perception of this. But you can see that this alone is not sufficient; we might simply dream or hallucinate this view, and it would then not be "real" at all. The difference between the dream and the reality is the changes in the other monads, for instance, the monads that constitute the squirrel, and any other observers of the same scene, including God. Reality is composed of the totality of all monads, each perceiving from its own perspective (although God, Leibniz insists, perceives from all perspectives at once). The "pre-established harmony" guarantees that all of these views from all of these perspectives are in agreement, so that our view of the squirrel, for example, is matched by the squirrel's view of us.

This view of the pre-established harmony between monads allows Leibniz to give a surprising answer to our fourth question, "How do different substances interact?" By definition, substances cannot interact as such. But they can seem to interact if their perceptions are coordinated. Thus, the collision of two billiard balls is in fact a harmony of perceptions about the collision of two billiard balls. Two people fighting is in fact a harmony of perceptions by each of the two people (and anyone else who is watching) about those two people fighting. This answer may seem to be extreme, but given Leibniz's conception of the universe as composed of a great number of immaterial substances, it is an answer that is necessary for his philosophy to be consistent. It is an answer that is also necessary, however, to enable him to reject Newton's cosmology, which he and many of his contemporaries found even more extreme and difficult to understand than Leibniz's own strange view of interaction.

The last of our initial set of questions about substance and our second cosmological question is, "Are space and time themselves substances?" According to Leibniz, the answer to this question is an emphatic no. It is on this question that Leibniz makes his sharpest break with Newton's physics. Are monads "in" space? Leibniz would have said no. But he also seems to give the surprising answer that not only are monads not "in" space (since they are immaterial) they are, strictly speaking, not "in" time either. The monad does not change in time, but rather, time is in the monad. That is, time is a relation between experiences of the monad. It is not something independent. These views of space and time are intimately tied to Leibniz's analysis of the only seeming "interaction" between monads. Both are rejections of Newton's theory, and an attempt to offer an alternative.

To our way of thinking, Leibniz's views seem bizarre, compared to the almost common-sense character of Newton's theory. Newton had argued that the universe was the motion of (material) atoms in empty space, acting against each other according to the laws of motion, force, and gravity that he had so elegantly formulated. But Newton's theories, which seem almost quaintly obvious to us now, contained what most people of his and Leibniz's time—including Newton himself—considered to be manifest absurdities. One, relating to our fourth ontological question, was the idea of **action-at-a-distance,** the idea that one object could affect another although the two were not even in contact. (For example, the idea that the moon and the earth have gravitational attraction for each other.) Thus Leibniz's conception of windowless monads, each seeming to interact with others but in fact only developing within itself, would have seemed to his contemporaries no more absurd than Newton's view of causality. Leibniz didn't need causality; he had his "pre-established harmony." Newton, meanwhile, had a great deal of trouble reconciling his mechanistic theories with the traditional ideas of God and Creation, which he continued to hold for the rest of his life.

The most famous disagreement between Leibniz and Newton concerns the nature of space and time, a topic that is still being debated because of the impact of Einstein's theory of relativity at the beginning of this century. Newton's mechanical theory seemed to presuppose the existence of some permanent container, namely space, in which the material atoms of his theory could mutually attract and bounce against each other. This container, which could exist independently of its contents, is called **absolute space.** In itself, this sounds entirely reasonable; we talk about things "moving in space" and "taking up space." But then, can we also talk about the entire universe being "in" space, the way a basketball can be said to be "in" the basket? This idea has some absurd consequences that led Leibniz and many of his contemporaries to reject it. The idea that space could exist apart from all things in it, perhaps even entirely empty (or what many philosophers called the **void**), would mean that it makes sense to talk about movement or location in space even when there isn't anything in space, not even points and rulers with which to measure distances or dimensions. Bertrand Russell, one of Leibniz's most famous followers, pointed out the absurdity of this idea by asking, "if space is absolute, then wouldn't it make sense to suggest that the universe might have doubled in size last night?" But what would it mean to say that the universe has gotten larger? An elephant or a planet or even a galaxy can get larger, but only in comparison to some measuring stick and a frame of reference. It is only by such comparisons that such "size" talk makes sense. But to say that the universe doubles in size is to say that our measuring stick, and we ourselves, double in size also. So all comparisons remain the same. Similarly, what would it mean to say that the universe in its entirety moved one foot to the left? All of the one-foot measurements are in the universe. There is no way to talk about the universe itself moving. On the basis of such considerations, Leibniz rejected Newton's idea of absolute space as absurd. In its place, he insisted that space is relative, that is, relative to measurements and things that are measured. There is no absolute space; there is only space relative to the various positions of the monads, that is, to observers.

The same is true of time. Newton believed in **absolute time** also, time as existing apart from anything happening "in" it. But the same consequences follow this initially reasonable idea. If time is absolute, it seems to make sense to ask, "when did the universe begin?" (In fact, astronomers are again asking this question.) But what could this "when" refer to? It can't refer to any measurement in the universe (clocks, the age of rocks or stars) for it is the universe itself that is being measured. And, there aren't any measures of time outside of the universe. Consequently, Leibniz rejected absolute time along with absolute space. Both are relative to the monads and have no possible existence of their own. This means, among other things, that there could be no void or empty space, nor could there be any sense of time in which literally nothing happened. Space and time, according to Leibniz, are relative to our own perceptions.

Now I said many pages ago that such cosmological issues were never the domain of philosophy alone, and you are well aware that current physics and astronomy are still very much involved with these questions. Both alternatives, from Newton and from Leibniz, are still very much alive. Scientists do indeed still talk about the beginning of the universe, and with awesome sophistication; and of course they also talk in strictly relativistic terms, like Leibniz, but now à la Einstein. To delve into these issues any further, therefore, we should have to leave eighteenth-century metaphysics and move into twentieth-century physics. What is often relevant to these philosophical debates are the new and sometimes strange experimental findings that are always emerging from the sciences. Recently, for example, experiments with the speed of light have brought about startling changes in our views of space and time. One consequence of this changed view is the idea that we cannot talk intelligibly about two events happening "at the same time" if they are a sufficiently great distance apart, say several billion light years. The discovery of radiation from outer space and the expansion of galaxies has raised old issues about creation in a new way: whether the universe was created all at once and then started to expand and change (the "big-bang theory") or whether there is continuous creation going on even now (the "steady-state theory"). Because of recent theories in science, philosophers are now willing to say things that would have seemed like utter nonsense to both Newton and Leibniz—for example, that "space is curved."

These are not issues to be settled by scientists alone, however; it is philosophical theories that give structure and meaning to the scientific experiments. But neither can philosophers simply cut themselves off from science and pretend that they can solve these problems "just in their heads." At the outer reaches of science, you will find philosophy, just as, at the beginnings of philosophy, you will find the unanswered problems of science.

In an earlier chapter, we stressed the importance of a basic assumption of all metaphysics, that the universe is intelligible. In Leibniz's philosophy, this assumption is presented as one of the basic presuppositions of all thinking; he calls it,

> 32. . . . *the Principle of Sufficient Reason,* in virtue of which we believe that no fact can be real and no statement true unless it has a sufficient reason why it should be thus and not otherwise. Most frequently, however, these reasons cannot be known to us.

They can, however, be known to God, who knows everything. It is on the basis of this principle, for example, that Leibniz defends the claim he made in Proposition 9, that two monads can never be identical ("the identity of indiscernibles"). The reasoning is this: Since God is the supremely rational Being (monad), He must have a reason for all that He does. But Leibniz also argues (Prop. 58) that God must have created the universe "with the greatest possible variety together with the greatest order that may be." Here is the reason why God would not have created any two monads alike. But the Principle of Sufficient Reason has a further implication; it also serves as a principle of divine ethics. Among the various possible worlds (that is, among the infinitely many ways in which the world might have been), God chooses the most perfect, that is, "the best of all possible worlds." Here is the doctrine of cosmic optimism that Voltaire so brilliantly lampooned in his novel *Candide.* But Leibniz took this concept of "the best of all possible worlds" very seriously. In the next century, it was to provide a foundation for much of the optimism of the Enlightenment. And in Leibniz's own metaphysics, it provides the concluding propositions of *Monadology,* a joyous optimism that creates as close to a "happy ending" as one can expect to find in a serious philosophical treatise.

> 85. Whence it is easy to conclude that the totality of all spirits must compose the city of God, that is to say, the most perfect state that is possible under the most perfect monarch.
>
> · · · · · · · · · ·
>
> 90. Finally, under this perfect government, there will be no good action unrewarded and no evil action unpunished; everything must turn out for the well-being of the good; that is to say, of those who

are not disaffected in this great state, who, after having done their duty, trust in Providence and who love and imitate, as is meet, the Author of all Good, delighting in the contemplation of his perfections according to the nature of that genuine, pure love which finds pleasure in the happiness of those who are loved. It is for this reason that wise and virtuous persons work in behalf of everything which seems conformable to presumptive or antecedent will of God, and are, nevertheless, content with what God actually brings to pass through his secret, consequent and determining will, recognizing that if we were able to understand sufficiently well the order of the universe, we should find that it surpasses all the desires of the wisest of us, and that it is impossible to render it better than it is, not only for all in general, but also for each one of us in particular, provided that we have the proper attachment for the author of all, not only as the Architect and the efficient cause of our being [our Creator] but also as our Lord and the Final Cause [purpose of our existence] who ought to be the whole goal of our will, and who alone can make us happy.

This theological "happy ending" is not an afterthought for Leibniz; it is the heart of his philosophy. Like his older contemporary Spinoza, his involvement in metaphysics is ultimately a very personal concern for religion and for his own view of himself and his place in the world. From this perspective, it is revealing to see the vast differences between the two philosophers. Spinoza's view of humanity is extremely anti-individualistic, and each individual is wholly submerged in the concept of the one substance. In Leibniz, however, his pluralism reinforces the view that each individual is a world in himself or herself, and his idealism places an emphasis on mind and thought that is in sharp contrast with Spinoza's balance between thought and body (although many critics have charged Spinoza with emphasizing body to an alarming degree). Spinoza's determinism and his view that ultimately we can do nothing but understand is surely a gloomy view compared to Leibniz's happy confidence that this is the "best of all possible worlds." And, of course, Spinoza's heretical view of God as the one substance (sometimes called *pantheism*) is very different from Leibniz's more traditional and pious view.

Of equal importance, however, are the more technical issues that are raised by Leibniz and Spinoza, for these have preoccupied scientists and metaphysicians alike for over two centuries. The nature of ultimate reality ("substance") and the nature of space and time are still unresolved questions. These questions are still the subject of some of the most current investigations in science and philosophy. And many of the current answers are modeled after those of Spinoza and Leibniz. In addition to the content of their theories, the methods of Spinoza and Leibniz also continue to dominate much of modern philosophy. Leibniz's logic, for example, is considered by many modern logicians, Bertrand Russell for one, to be one of the most important advances in modern thinking.

Our concern in this chapter has been to study the best modern examples of a metaphysical system. For this purpose, Spinoza's *Ethics* and Leibniz's *Monadology* serve excellently. But now that we have investigated these two systems and come to appreciate their admirable intelligence as well as some of their obscurities, it is necessary to end on a note of doubt. We have seen two of the most brilliant minds in the history of philosophy begin with the same basic concept, "substance," and use similar methods of deduction to arrive at wholly different views of reality. How could they disagree so radically? And, thinking of ourselves, how are we to decide which of them to agree with? How can we defend one system against the other? Since the systems flatly contradict each other on several points (for example, whether there is only one or whether there are many substances), we cannot logically agree with both of them. Thus the question arises, how can one prove a metaphysical theory? How can we know the way the world really is? Or, more skeptically, can we know the way the world really is?

D. SADR AL-DIN SHIRAZI (MULLA SADRA)

Sadr al-Din Shirazi (approx. 1571–1641), called "Mulla Sadra," was a modern Islamic philosopher of tremendous depth and influence. His name is not as well known in the West as other, medieval, Islamic thinkers. That may perhaps be because Sadra was a theologian, and in the West philosophers have tended to associate theology primarily with the Middle Ages and to study modern thought in a secular context. (That may seem strange to you, after reading Descartes, Spinoza, and Leibniz, who are deeply concerned with theological questions about the nature of God and our relationship to Him. Nonetheless, their metaphysics can be understood separately from their religious beliefs.) In the Islamic world, however, theology remained the center of all philosophical investigations; in some countries this is still the case even today.

Sadra shares the moderns' concerns about "substance" and our knowledge of it. His unique and thoroughly Islamic solutions to those problems, however, make him an interesting contrast to the other thinkers we have discussed in this chapter.

Sadra's work is famously complex and intricate. This is due in part to his magnificent integration of a very wide range of philosophical traditions into a coherent picture of the universe. His synthesis of seemingly opposing schools has been compared to that of the eighteenth-century German philosopher Immanual Kant, whom we will meet in later chapters. It is important to know a little bit about these different traditions in order to follow Sadra's reasoning. On each question that he considers, Sadra may bring to bear one or any combination of the following:

Qur'anic passages. The Qur'an is the Muslim scripture. Sadra often weaves passages from the holy book right into his text in order to lend scriptural authority to his claims, and in order to clarify what he believes is its true interpretation.

Hadith. The *hadiths* are the recorded sayings of the prophet Mohammed of Islam. His sayings, recorded by his disciples, are a sort of addendum to the Qur'an. Mulla Sadra was a *Shi'ite* Muslim, which means that he believed in the authority of the *Imams* in addition to that of Mohammed. The Imams were the descendants of Mohammed through his sister, Fatimah, and Shi'ite Muslims believed that they inherited the true understanding of Islam. The Shi'ites recognized a whole additional set of the Imams' *hadiths,* and some of Sadra's quotations are chosen from these.

The kalam. As in Christianity and Judaism, early Islam had theologians who decided religious questions and interpreted scripture for their religious community. Early on, some theologians were looked upon as authorities on Islamic law, and their method of interpreting scripture, called the "kalam" method, was established as a tradition and precedent for the Muslim community. Because the kalam is so integral to Islamic life, it is important that Sadra be clear about his position regarding it, although in many places he is critical of it.

The "peripatetics." This is just a fancy word for "Aristotelians." Many Islamic thinkers, like other Western theologians, followed Aristotle on many questions. The most famous of the Islamic Aristotelians is ibn-Sina (or Avicenna). Sadra often compares or contrasts his view to that of ibn-Sina or of other "peripatetics."

The Illuminationists and Sufis. Another school of Islamic theology—*Illuminationism*—combined Platonic metaphysics with Islamic mysticism—**Sufism.** The Sufis, like most mystics of any faith, believed that it was possible to have an immediate knowledge of God. Illuminationism gave a philosophical explanation for how this immediate knowledge was possible. Obviously, this required a very different metaphysics from that of Aristotle. Mulla Sadra is very strongly influenced by both Sufism and Illuminationism. His main Sufi influence is ibn-Arabi. Illuminationism was founded by Yahia Suhrawardi in Persia in the late Middle Ages, and Suhrawardi was also a formative influence on Mulla Sadra's thought.

Mulla Sadra, like Suhrawardi and ibn-Arabi, tried to integrate Platonism with Islamic mysticism. However, Sadra also took on the challenge of integrating as well the "Western" categories and discursive technique. Sadra claimed—and quite effectively demonstrated, as we will see—that discursive reasoning, revelation, and mystical illumination are consonant with each other and mutually dependent. He claimed that the hidden, "true" meaning of the *hadiths* corresponded with the immediate knowledge of God achieved by the prepared soul of the mystic. Both revelation and illumination, Sadra claimed, were fully rational in their content and so could be rationally argued and demonstrated. His method, then, combined literary, or symbolic, interpretation of scripture with the logic of the ancient Greeks and the defense of mystical experience. In the "Concluding Testament" to the work excerpted below, Sadra gives both an argument and a beautiful example of this integrative style:

> Know that to attain the true inner divine knowledge one must follow a *proof* or "unveiling" by immediate vision, just as He—May He be exalted!—said *Say: "Bring your proof, if you are among those who speak truthfully!"* (2:111); and He—May He be exalted!—said: *Whoever calls upon another god together with God has no proof for that* (23:117).[7] This *proof* is a Light that God casts on the Heart of the man of true faith, a Light that illuminates his inner vision so that he "sees things as they really are," as it was stated in the prayer of the Prophet—May God's blessings and peace be with him!—for himself and the elect among his community and his close disciples: "O my God, cause us to see things as they really are!"
>
> Know, too, that those questions concerning which the commonality of the philosophers have disagreed with the prophets—May God bless them!—are not matters that can easily be grasped and attained; nor can they be acquired by rejecting our rational, logical intellects, with their (intrinsic) measures and their contemplative activities of learning and investigating. If this were so, then there would never have been any disagreement (with the prophets) concerning these questions on the part of those intelligent men who were busy all their lives using the tool of thought and reflection to acquire a (true) conception of things; those (philosophers) would never have fallen into error in these questions and there would have been no need for the sending of the prophets (if these metaphysical realities were so easy to grasp). So it should be known that these questions can only be comprehended by taking over Lights from the Lamp-niche of Prophecy, and by earnestly seeking Them. For these are the Secrets which are the true inner meaning of Discipleship and Sainthood.
>
> Therefore you must completely free the Heart (from any attachments to the body) and totally purify the innermost self. You must be rigorously detached from created being, and (devote yourself to) repeated intimate communion with the Truly Real, in spiritual

[7]The passages in italics are from the Qur'an, or Islamic scripture. In parentheses are their chapter and verse citations. This and all following passages are from *The Wisdom of the Throne: An Introduction to the Philosophy of Mulla Sadra*, trans. by James Winston Morris (Princeton: Princeton University Press, 1981).

retreat. And you must shun the carnal desires, the various forms of the will to dominate, and the other animal ends (which follow from our bodily condition), by means of a pure and untroubled inner intention and sincere faith. In this way your action will itself become your reward, and your knowledge will be precisely the same as your attaining the Goal of your aspiration, so that when *the dark covering is removed* (50:22) and the veil is lifted (from your heart and inner vision), you will be standing in the Presence of the Lord of Lords—just as you already were in your *innermost heart* (2:269; etc.).

Sadra's most famous work is the *al-Hikma al-Muta'ālīya fi al-Asfār al-'Arba'a al-'Aqliya (The Transcendent Wisdom of the Four Noetic Journeys)*. "Noetic" means "of divine knowledge." So, we can see that Sadra is thinking of the knower or philosopher as "journeying" through stages until he or she achieves a knowledge which brings him or her close to God. The *Asfār* (as it is known for short) gives very detailed explanations and arguments for Sadra's metaphysical doctrines. The work I have excerpted, *al-Hikma al-'Arshiya (The Wisdom of the Throne)*, is a more summary and somewhat more introductory work on similar themes.

The "Throne" in this title is the seat of God. Hence, the title designates the work as a description of that very knowledge which brings the knower close to God. Consequently, the work itself stands as an example or evidence of Sadra's Sufi premise that transcendent union with God, through knowledge, is possible. Sadra's metaphysics, then, investigates what Being and Knowledge must be like in order for the union of knower and known to be possible.

As we have seen already, Descartes, Leibniz, and even Spinoza were consumed by the problem of how to conceive existence such that the existence of both ideas and their objects—which seem so different from each other—could be understood intelligibly. Descartes claimed there are two radically different substances, Leibniz that there are fundamentally different kinds of monads, and Spinoza that there are two different modes of substance. These different metaphysical approaches all account for the difference between thinking and other kinds of existence. But they do not account for interactions between ideas and their objects. In other words, they do not explain very well how knowledge is possible. Consequently, the Western thinkers were enmeshed in problems of knowledge, sometimes irresolveably. Sadra, on the other hand, worked out a metaphysics that follows from the assumption that knowledge is possible. His metaphysics, therefore, contrasts very greatly with those of the other thinkers discussed in this chapter.

In the "Concluding Testament" quoted above, Sadra talks about "taking over the lights from the 'Lamp-niche' of Prophecy." Sadra took it from the Illuminationists that *light* was a perfect and intelligible example of the manifestation of existence in the universe. Existence, in its most pure and intense degree, is God. God manifests Himself, like light spilling out from its source, in lesser and lesser degrees of purity and intensity. Just as the source of light is at the same time both the origin and the actual content of the diffuse rays which spring from it, God is both the origin of the existence of all things, and their very content. God is the "Necessary Being" whose existence is simple and unmixed with any imperfection. This is where Sadra begins. He calls it the "First Place" of Illumination.

◆**from *The Wisdom of the Throne*,**
by Sadr al-Din Shirazi

PART I: FIRST PLACE OF ILLUMINATION, CONCERNING KNOWLEDGE OF
    GOD, OF HIS ATTRIBUTES, HIS NAMES, AND HIS SIGNS

It contains (the following) Principles:

§1. *Principle (deriving from) the divine Presence, concerning*
    the divisions of Being and the establishment of the Primary
    Being

That which exists is either the Reality of Being or something else. By the Reality of Being we mean That which is not mixed with anything but Being, whether a generality or a particularity, a limit or a bound, a quiddity [an essence], an imperfection, or a privation— and this is what is called the "Necessary Being." Therefore we say that if the Reality of Being did not exist, then nothing at all would exist. But the consequence (of this conditional statement) is self-evidently false; therefore its premise is likewise (false).

In his claim that necessary existence exists before any "quiddity" (a fancy word for "essence") or privation, Sadra was taking a strong stand on a long-disputed theological issue. Many hundred years before, ibn-Sina (one of the peripatetics) had made a distinction between *essence* and *existence*. The distinction was related to and inspired by Aristotle's distinction between form and matter, which we introduced in the last chapter. Each thing, claimed ibn-Sina, had its essence—its nature or kind—and its existence—what makes the essence real, its content of reality. For instance, a squirrel has an essence—call it, "this-squirrel-ness." But it also has existence—it *is* an *actual* squirrel, in which its "squirrelness" inheres and comes to be. Ibn-Sina had said that existence was more fundamental, or "prior" to, essences of things.

Suhrawardi had disagreed with ibn-Sina and claimed that essence was prior to existence. In other words, Suhrawardi claimed a thing's essence was its *truer* nature, a higher order of reality, than its existence, much like Plato's Forms were thought by Plato to be a higher order of reality than were the things which participated in them. Mulla Sadra, although he followed Suhrawardi on many issues, disagreed strongly on this important point.[8]

Sadra reasserted the priority of existence over essence. He claimed, however, against ibn-Sina and the peripatetics, that all existence is fundamentally One. This was Sadra's understanding of the concept of "God's Unity," which was a fundamental principle of Islam, proclaimed by the Qur'an. Each particular manifestation of God's existence, claimed Sadra, was a limitation (a "privation") upon it. His singular existence is limited at certain points in time and space and levels or degrees of intensity. These limits upon existence are the essences (or "quiddities") of things. Each thing, therefore, has its own distinct essence which makes it the particular thing it is. The essence, then, for Sadra, is *particular*, and it is in the thing, not in the mind of the perceiver. This is a very different meaning for "essence" from that which was held by earlier Islamic thinkers and by the Western philosophers discussed in this chapter.

For Sadra, the essences of things were *not* the same as the *ideas* of things which we have in the mind, and which we may *call* "essences." Our idea of "squirrelness" (i.e., "a little rodent with a fluffy tail, who eats nuts") is abstracted by our mind from the squirrels we see. But the essence of that squirrel—its own "this-squirrelness" is in that squirrel, and so is not fully apprehended by our general idea.

Essences, then, for Sadra, are the particular natures of particular things, which *cannot* exist separately from the things of which they are the essences. Neither can essences be *understood* fully in separation from the things of which they are essences.

In this way, Sadra offered a solution to the problem, mentioned above, that had plagued the Western metaphysicians—the problem of how ideas can represent existence. For Sadra, the apprehension of the idea of a thing by the mind falls short of the knowledge of that thing, and certainly falls short of full knowledge of existence. Yet it is possible, on Sadra's scheme, to have knowledge of existence, but only when the knower's *existence* actually *accesses the existence* of the thing known. In this way, Sadra establishes two levels of knowledge and existence (or rather of "knowledge-existence," since we can now see that Sadra is thinking of knowledge as existent in precisely the same way as is anything else). By gaining knowledge of the existence of a thing, the

[8]This is another way in which Sadra might be compared to Immanuel Kant. He is claiming here, as Kant did against St. Anselm, that "existence is not a predicate." See Chapter 6.

knower goes beyond the abstracted idea of it, and actually extends his or her own existence to it. The knower's very existence is broadened or intensified by knowledge of existence. He or she actually becomes more real.

By understanding knowledge this way, as a union of the knower and the known, Sadra avoids any kind of dualism or pluralism. Only existence exists. For Sadra there exist only different levels or limitations of existence, of which the things we call "essences" (i.e., our ideas) exist only at a very weak, obscure, and ephemeral level. When we, as thinkers, go beyond these ideas to an understanding of existence, we actually join with reality, become more real ourselves, and so become more *really* ourselves. This is the "transcendence" or "inner knowledge" or "Illumination" referred to in Sadra's titles.

Like Leibniz, Sadra claimed that God's existence is singular and simple. Nothing but God has as high an intensity or degree of existence as does God, who is whole and wholly existent. Therefore, no mind but God's may understand God fully. His existence is unlimited by *any* essence, and so cannot be comprehended in its entirety by the human mind. Through reflection and Sufi practice, however, human beings can join with God to the full extent that their essences allow. Since God is their origin and content, as He is for all things, this joining is really a *re*-unification. Through transcendent knowledge, human beings are able to return to their own true natures.

> As for showing the necessity (of the actual existence) of this Primary Being, this is because everything other than this Reality of Being is either a specific quiddity or a particular being, mixed with privation and imperfection. Now every quiddity other than Being (Itself) exists only through Being, not by itself. How (could it exist without Being)?! For if a quiddity were to be taken by itself, separate from being, that quiddity itself could not even "be" itself, to say nothing of its being existent. Because to affirm something (in this case, "being") of something else (in this case, a particular quiddity) already presupposes the establishment and being of that other thing. And that being—if it is anything other than the Reality of Being—is composed of Being *per se* (or "Being *qua* Being") and of some other particularity. But every particularity other than Being is (taken by itself) nonexistent or privative. Thus every compound (of a particular quiddity and Being) is posterior to the simplicity of Being and stands in need of Being.
>
> So privation (or "nonbeing") does not enter into the existence and actual occurrence of a thing, although it may enter into its definition and its concept. For to affirm any concept of something and to predicate it of that thing—whether (the concept be) a quiddity or some other attribute, and whether it be affirmed or denied of

something—always presupposes the being of that thing. Our discussion always comes back to Being: either there is an infinite regression (of predications and subjects) or one arrives in the end at an Absolute Being, unmixed with anything else.

Thus it has become evident that the Source of existence of everything that exists is this Pure Reality of Being, unmixed with anything other than Being. This Reality is not restricted by any definition, limitation, imperfection, contingent potentiality, or quiddity; nor is It mixed with any generality, whether of genus, species, or differentia, nor with any accident, whether specific or general. For Being is prior to all these descriptions that apply to quiddities, and That which has no quiddity other than Being is not bound by any generality or specificity. It has no specific difference and no particularity apart from Its own Essence (or Self); It has no form, nor has It any agent or end. On the contrary, It is Its own Form, and That which gives form to every thing, because It is the completion of the essence of every thing. And It is the completion of every thing because Its Essence is actualized in every respect.

No one can describe Him or reveal Him but He Himself, and there is no demonstration of Him but His own Essence (or Self). Therefore He gave witness through His Self to Himself and to the Unicity of His Self when He said: *God gives witness that there is no god but He* (3:18). For His Unity is not the particular unity that is found in an individual of a (particular) nature; nor is It the generic or specific unity that is found in any general notion or any quiddity. [221] Neither is It the conjunctive unity that is found when a number of things become assembled or unified into a single thing; nor is It the unity of contiguity found in quantities and measurable things. Nor, as you will learn, is It any of the other relative unities, such as unity by resemblance, homogeneity, analogy, correspondence, reduplication—although (certain) philosophers have allowed that—congruence, or any of the other kinds of unity that are not the True Unity. No, His Unity is other (than these relative ones), unknowable in Its innermost core, like His Essence—May He be exalted!—except that His Unity is the Source of all (these other) unities, just as His being is the Source of all (particular) beings. Hence *He has no second* (112:4).

Similarly, His unitary Knowledge is precisely the Reality of that Knowledge which is unmixed with any ignorance, so that It is Knowledge of all things in every respect. And the same can be said of all of His Attributes of Perfection (that is, Life, Power, Will, etc.—which are likewise One with His Essence and Being).

In the next section, Sadra offers a proof of the claim that the simple is the whole, and that compounds are more limited than simples. Notice the similarity to Leibniz with which Sadra begins, and how different are his reasoning and conclusions.

§2. *Principle (deriving from) the Throne (concerning the Simplicity of Being)*

All that which is Simple in Its essential Reality is, by virtue of Its (absolute) Unity, all things. It is deprived of none of those things, except for what is on the order of imperfections, privations, and contingencies.

(For example, taking any particular being "A," suppose) you say "A is not B": now if that with respect to which A is (itself A) were exactly the same as that with respect to which A is not-B, so that A in itself would of its very essence be the criterion for this negation—(if this were so), then the very essence of A would be something privative, such that everyone who intellected A would also intellect "not-B." But this consequence is (obviously) false, and its antecedent is also false. Thus it is established that (in any particular being "A") the substrate of "A-ness" is something essentially compound (of Being and a particular quiddity). And even according to the mind (that is, at the level of mental, conceptual being, the notion of "A-ness" is a compound composed) of the notion of something having being, by which A exists, and the notion of the privation of something, by which A is not B nor any of the other things that are negated of it.

Thus it is known that every thing of which something that has being may be negated is not absolutely Simple in its essential reality. And the converse is likewise true: all That which is Simple in Its essential Reality can have nothing that has being negated of It. Otherwise, It would not be Simple in Its essential Reality, but rather composed of two aspects: an aspect by which it is such (such as "A") and an aspect by which it is some other way (that is, not-B, not-C, and so on). So now it has been established that the Simple (Being) is all existent things with respect to their being and perfection, but not with respect to their privations and imperfections.

And by this it is established [222] that His Knowledge of all existent things is Simple Knowledge, and that their presence in Him is Simple in its essential Reality. For all things in Him are included in His Knowledge in a higher and more perfect way, since "knowledge" is (only) an expression for Being, on the condition that It be unmixed with matter.

So understand this, my beloved, and profit by it!

§3. *Principle (deriving from) the Source of Illumination (concerning the Uniqueness of the Necessary Being)*

The Necessary Being is "One and without partner" because He is Complete in Reality, Perfect in Essence, Infinite in Power and Intensity, and because—as you have learned—He is the Pure Reality of Being, unlimited and without bound. For if His Being had some limit or particularity in any respect, It would have to be limited and particularized by something other than Being; there would have to

be something with power over Him limiting, specifying, and circumscribing Him. But that is impossible. So there is no good and no
perfection of being that does not have its Source in Him and grow
out of Him.

Here is the proof of the affirmation of His Uniqueness. The Necessary Being cannot be multiple, because if that were so, it would
require postulating a being both necessary and yet circumscribed
in its being, as the second member of a pair. But then He (that is,
the "first" Necessary Being) could not encompass every being, since
there would turn out to be another being that did not belong to
Him and did not derive from or emanate from Him. In turn, this
would result in His having a privative aspect of impossibility or
contingency, so that He would have to be one of a pair and composite (of being and a particular restricted quiddity) like other contingent things, and therefore could not be included in that Reality of
Being which is unmixed with any limitation or with the privation
(implied by) this difference.

Thus it has been determined that *He has no second* (112:4) in
Being and that every perfection of being is a sprinkling of His Perfection, every good a glimmering from the radiant Light of His
Beauty. For He is the Source of Being, and everything else is subordinate to Him, dependent on Him for the substantiation of its
essence.

At this point, Sadra makes explicit his doctrine that the knower's
existence is the same as that of the thing known. This is the only sensical
way to construe existence, Sadra claims. If one says that knowledge
"exists" and that this apple "exists," one must be saying the same thing
about the apple and the knowledge. But for the knower to actually be
joined with the known, existence must be such that it can change, move,
extend itself across the limitations of essences. So it is, claims Sadra. In
other words, existence is prior to substances, and so substances can
change. This is Sadra's important doctrine of "trans-substantiation," or
of "substantial motion." We might imagine, then, that Sadra would argue
against the other modern thinkers in this chapter, that because of their
commitment to the static notion of substance, they cannot properly
understand existence or the possibility of knowledge. Unless substances
can change, and the substance of the knower can join with that of the
thing known, knowledge cannot be understood to exist in any way
similarly to other existents.

§10. *Principle (deriving from) the divine Throne (concerning the
unity of knower and known)*

Everything that is intelligible in its being is also actively intelligiz-
ing. Indeed, every form in perception—whether it be intelligible or
sensible—is unified in its being with that which perceives it.

The proof of this, emanating from God's Presence, is that every form of perception—even if it is sensible, for example—has some sort of separation from matter, so that its being in itself and its being sensible are really only one thing and do not differ at all. Thus one cannot suppose that the specific form might have a mode of being with respect to which it would not be sensible, because its very being is a being *in sensation*—quite different from the being of the heavens or earth or anything else which is in external (material being). For the being of those (material) things is not in sensation, and they are grasped by sense or by the intellect only in an accidental manner and in consequence of a form in sensation corresponding to them.

Now if [228] this is so, then we can say of that form in sensation, whose being is precisely the same as its being sensed, that its being could not possibly be separate from the being of the substance which senses it. For if it had its being and the substance sensing it had another (different) being, and they only subsequently became connected in the relation of that which senses and that which is sensed, then this would be like the case of a father and son, each with his own essence and being independent of their relationship—yet who could be intellected in no way other than through (their relation of) fatherhood and sonship. But something like this is impossible in the case we are considering. For this form in sensation is not such that one could ever conceive of its having a being with respect to which it would not be sensible, so that its essence in itself would not be sensible. It is not like the (example of the) man who is not a father by the being of his essence in itself, but who only becomes a father through the accidental occurrence of a state of relation which happens to the being of his essence.

No, the essence of the form existing in sensation is sensible by its very essence. Therefore its very being is sensible by essence—whether or not there exists in the world a sensing substance which is separate from it. Indeed, even if we completely ignored everything else (but this form in sensation) or supposed that there did not exist in the world any separate sensing substance—even in that condition and under that supposition this form would still be sensible in essence. For its essence is sensible for itself, so that its essence in itself is at once the thing sensed, that which senses, and that which is sensed. This is because one of the terms of the relation (between that which senses and that which is sensed), insofar as it is part of the relation, cannot be separated from its partner in their being, at any of the levels of (intensity of) that being. And the same rule holds for the status of the form in imagination or intellection with respect to its being identical with that which imagines or intelligizes.

One of the ancient philosophers (that is, Porphyry), in speaking of "the unification of the intelligible and that which intelligizes," probably intended the same (truth) we have just confirmed. Those who criticized his approach and attacked him concerning this unification of the intelligible and that which intelligizes—and these include most of the more recent philosophers—did not penetrate to the crux of his approach and failed to grasp it properly. For they did not arrive at its source, the proof of which depends on the denial of the unification of two (originally separate) things. (Their mistaken conception of this "unification" would require) that there should exist in actuality two things different in number, which subsequently became a single existent. But this is something which is undoubtedly impossible.

It is not impossible, though, that a single essence (that is, the soul) might become so perfected and increase so much in the strength of its essence and the intensity of its stage (of being) that it could become in its essence the basis of something for which it was not previously a basis, and the source of things that had not developed in it before. This is (not impossible) because of the great extent of (the soul's) field of being.

The soul's unification with the "Productive (or Active) Intellect" is nothing but its becoming in its essence an intellect actually productive of forms. For the Intellect cannot be many in number (like corporeal things). Rather, it has another, comprehensive Unity that is not like that numerical unity which applies generally to the particular individuals of a species. The Productive Intellect, at the same time as It produces (or "brings into actuality") these souls which are connected with bodies, is also an End of perfection, ordering them, and an intellective Form for them, encompassing them all. And these souls are like delicate and subtle threads radiating from It to the bodies, and then returning to It when the souls become perfected and immaterial (or "transcendent").

But the (complete) verification of these topics would require a detailed discussion that cannot be contained in this treatise.

The second part of the treatise, called the "Return," deals with the nature and effect of this transcendent knowledge. When the knower comes to the fullest possible knowledge allowed by his or her essence, he or she has actually perfected his or her existence. In other words, since the essence of the knower is "to know," the knower actually knows him or herself better as his or her knowledge increases and intensifies. Since knowledge, for Sadra, is a unification with the known object, the knower who has achieved his or her fullest possible knowledge *is* actually a fuller, more perfect, thing. This "perfect man" (which was the Sufi name for the mystic who achieved full unity with God), joins with God and achieves an eternal existence.

PART II: SECOND PLACE OF ILLUMINATION, CONCERNING KNOWLEDGE OF THE RETURN

A. First Illumination, concerning the inner knowledge of the soul

§1. *Principle (concerning the failure of earlier philosophers and the necessity of illumination in this area)*

Know that the inner knowledge of the soul is one of those extremely difficult (fields of) knowledge in which the philosophers—not to mention the mere dialecticians—were exceedingly neglectful, despite the length of their investigations, the power of their thought, and the frequency of their endeavors in this field. For this knowledge can only be acquired through illumination from the Lamp-niche of Prophecy and through following the lights of Revelation and Prophethood and the lanterns of the Book and the Tradition that has come down (to us) in the Path of our Imams, masters of guidance and infallibility, from their ancestor the Seal of the prophets—May the greatest of blessings and prayers of those who pray be upon him and upon the other prophets and messengers!

§2. Principle (concerning the levels of the soul)

The human soul has many levels and stations, from the beginning of its generation to the end of its goal; and it has certain essential states and modes of being. At first, in its state of connection (with the body) it is a corporeal substance. Then it gradually becomes more and more intensified and develops through the different stages of its natural constitution until it subsists by itself and moves from this world to the other world, and so *returns to its Lord* (89:27).

Thus the soul is originated in a corporeal (state), but endures in a spiritual (state). The first thing to be generated in its state (of connection with the body) is a corporeal power; next is a natural form; then the sensible soul with its levels; then the cognitive and recollective; and then the rational soul. Next, after the practical intellect, it acquires the theoretical intellect according to its various degrees, from the rank of the intellect in potency to that of the intellect in actuality and the Active Intellect—which is the same as that "Spirit" of the divine Command which is ascribed to God in His saying: *Say: "The Spirit is from my Lord's Command!"* (17:85). This last degree occurs only in a very small number of individuals of the human species. Moreover, (merely human) effort and labor do not suffice to acquire it, since a certain divine attraction is also necessary for its attainment, as it is mentioned in the Prophetic tradition: "A single attraction from God outbalances all the efforts of men and jinn."

§4. Principle (concerning the inner senses of the soul)

The soul in its essence has hearing, sight, smell, taste, and touch other than those which are ordinarily exposed. These (external senses) may become inoperative through disease, sleep, unconsciousness, chronic illness, or death, while those (inner) senses do not cease their activity.

The external senses are veils and coverings over these (inner powers proper to the soul), which are the root of those passing (external perceptions). In this, too, there is a secret.

§5. *Principle (concerning the true nature of vision)*

Vision does not occur through the emission of visual rays from the eye, as the mathematicians maintained. Nor is it caused by the impression of phantasms from the visible object on the crystalline membrane of the eye, as the natural philosophers held. Both of these views are untenable, for many reasons which have been mentioned in other (scientific) books.

It is likewise impossible that vision should occur through the soul's direct witnessing of a form external to the eye and subsisting in matter, which is the well-known position of the Illuminationist philosophers and has been approved by a group of more recent thinkers such as Alfarabi and Suhrawardi. We have mentioned the reasons for the falsity of this theory in our commentary on (Suhrawardi's) *Hikmat al-Ishrāq* ("The Philosophy of Illumination"). Among my objections is that what is in the external materials (of physical objects) is not the sort of thing that can be connected in essence with perception, nor can it be present immediately in perception and have being in consciousness. Another objection is that this connection (which they posited between the act of vision and an externally subsisting material form) cannot be, since the relation between what has no position (that is, the soul's act of vision) and something having material dimensions (that is, the "object" of vision, in their theory) is impossible except by means of something having position. So that even if one should suppose the validity (of their theory of vision) through an intermediary (between the soul and the material object of vision), the relation would not be one of illuminative knowledge, but rather a material and spatial one, since all the activities of material powers and everything which they undergo must be in a spatial location.

Rather, the truth about vision—as God has shown us by inspiration—is that after the fulfillment of certain specific conditions, with God's permission, there arise from the soul forms suspended (from their noetic archetypes), subsisting through the soul, present in the soul, and appearing in the world of the soul—not in this (material) world. Ordinarily, people are heedless of this and claim that perception is connected with these forms submerged in matter. But what we actually attain in the state of vision might most suitably be called an "illuminative relation," because both terms of the relation (that is, the soul and the form perceived) exist through a being that is luminous in essence. Indeed, you have already learned that the forms in perception all exist in another world.

Verily there is a message in this for a people who worship (their Lord)! (21:106).

§6. *Principle (concerning the substantiality of the world of soul)*

In man, the imaginal power is a substance transcending this world, that is, the world of physical beings and the motions and transformations of material things. We set forth decisive proofs about this matter in (our book) *al-Asfār al-Arba'a* ("The Four Journeys"). But this power is not (totally) separate from generated being, since in that case it would have to be (pure) Intellect and object of intellection.

Rather, its being is in another world, one that corresponds to this (physical) world in that it comprises heavens, elements, different species of plants, animals, and so on—only multiplied many times over (the things of) this world. Now everything that man perceives and sees directly by means of his imaginal faculty and his interior sense does not at all inhere in the body of the brain or in some power inhering in that area (as maintained by Avicenna and Galenic physiology); nor is it located in the bodies of the heavenly spheres or in a world separated from the soul, as some followers of the Illuminationist (philosophers) have maintained. Instead, it subsists in the soul—not like something inhering in something else, but rather like an act subsisting through its agent.

Now these forms present in the world of the soul may differ in manifestness and hiddenness, in intensity and weakness. The stronger and more substantial the power of this imaginal soul— (which is to say), the more it returns to its own essence and the less it is preoccupied with the distractions of this body and the use of the bodily powers of motion—the more manifestly will these forms appear in the soul and the stronger will be their being. For when these forms have become strengthened and intensified, there is no proportion between them and the things existing in this (physical) world so far as the intensity of their being, actualization, and certainty of effect. It is not true, as is vulgarly supposed, that these forms are mere phantom images without the regular effects of real being, as is the case with most dreams. For in sleep, too, the soul is usually preoccupied with the body.

The complete manifestation of these forms and the perfection of the power of their being occurs only after death. (This is true) to such a degree that compared to the forms man will see after death, the forms he sees in this world are like dreams. This is why the Commander of the truly faithful (the Imam Ali)—Peace be with him!—said: "Mankind are sleeping; when they die, they awaken." Then the Unseen becomes directly visible, and knowledge becomes immediate vision. In this is the secret of the "Return" and the resurrection of the body.

§7. *Principle (concerning the soul's relation to the body)*

The "soulhood of the soul" is not a relation accidentally occurring to its being, as the commonality of the philosophers claimed in likening its relation to the body to that of a ruler to his city or of a captain to his ship. No, the soulhood of the soul is nothing but its mode of being—not like the relation of ruler, captain, father, or anything else that has its own proper essence and only falls into relation with something else after already being in that essence. For one cannot conceive of the soul's having being—so long as it is soul (and not pure Intellect)—except for a being such that it is in connection with the body and utilizing the bodily powers, unless. . . .

Unless it should become transformed in its being and intensified in its substantialization to such a degree that it becomes independent in its own essence and able to dispense with its connection to the physical body. Then *he shall return to his people rejoicing* (84:9). *Or he shall be burned in a blazing Fire* (111:3).

Thus, Sadra, in positing the doctrine of transubstantiation, and in differently understanding knowledge than do his European contemporaries, offers some interesting solutions to some of the perennial problems of metaphysics.

SUMMARY AND CONCLUSION

In this chapter we have summarized the thought of some of the greatest metaphysical thinkers of modern times. In Europe, they begin from the concept of "substance" and attempt to use deduction as a method for proving the ultimate nature of reality. Sadra's mystical metaphysics begins with the fact of transcendent knowledge. Their answers are extremely different. Spinoza argues that there can only be one substance; Leibniz argues that there are many. For Spinoza, God is identical to the universe, to the one substance; for Leibniz, God is distinct from all other substances, which He created. For Spinoza, mind and body are but two of an infinite number of attributes of God, the only two that we can know; for Leibniz, all substances are ultimately immaterial. But beneath these technical concerns is a struggle by both philosophers to answer the most important problems of human existence: the nature of God and proper religion, the place of man and woman in the universe, and the role and foundations of science. In Islam, too, these questions received delicate and thorough attention, and however we wish to draw the line between West and East, we should remember that philosophy circles the globe, and that our Western tradition of metaphysics is not the only one extant.

GLOSSARY

absolute (space and time)   the view that space and time exist independently of objects and events "in" them, a view defended by Newton. In general, absolute, as used in philosophy, means independent and nonrelative, unqualified and all-inclusive.

action-at-a-distance   the idea that one object can have a causal effect on another from a distance, as in Newton's laws of gravitational attraction. Leibniz's rejection of this idea as "absurd" led him to develop a non-causal interpretation of the same phenomena.

animism   (see Glossary, Ch. 1)

attribute   in Spinoza, an essential property of God; for example, having a physical nature, having thoughts. In general, an attribute is a property (as in Aristotle).

best of all possible worlds   Leibniz's view that God demands a perfect universe and makes it "the best possible," all things considered.

cause-of-itself *(causa sui)*   that which explains its own existence, often said of God. It also follows from the usual definitions of substance.

determinism   the view that every event in the universe is dependent upon other events, which are its causes. On this view, all human actions and decisions, even those which we would normally describe as "free" and "undetermined," are totally dependent on prior events that cause them. (This problem will be examined in Ch. 8.)

divine pre-ordination   God's knowledge of and power over all that will happen, including our own future actions.

extended   having spatial dimensions. Philosophers (for example, Descartes, Leibniz, and Spinoza) often define bodies as "extended," minds and ideas as "unextended."

extended (substance)   physical matter in space and time, material objects.

freedom of the will   actions undetermined by external causes, including the power of God (though how God can leave us this "indeterminacy" in spite of God's power and knowledge over us is and must be incomprehensible to us).

idealism   the metaphysical view that only minds and their ideas exist.

Identity of Indiscernibles   a principle of Leibniz's philosophy according to which no two things can possibly have all of the same properties, or be absolutely identical in all respects.

modes   in Spinoza, inessential properties or modifications of attributes.

monad   in Leibniz, the simple immaterial substances that are the ultimate constituents of all reality. God, the one uncreated monad, created all of the others as self-enclosed ("windowless"), predetermined entities.

Principle of Sufficient Reason   in Leibniz, the insistence that all events must have a justification and that ultimately all events must be justified by God's reasons. The principle is sometimes invoked to assert that everything must have some explanation, whether or not God is involved. (For example, scientists use such a principle in their work, as we shall see in the following chapter.)

pre-established harmony   the belief that the order of the universe is pre-arranged by God. In Leibniz, this view allows him an alternative to Newton's theory of causal relationships.

substance (in Descartes)   a thing which so exists that it needs no other thing in order to exist (God). Created substances need only the occurrence of God to exist.

unextended   not having spatial dimensions. Philosophers (for example, Descartes, Leibniz, and Spinoza) often define mind and ideas as unextended.
void   empty space.

◆ *BIBLIOGRAPHY AND FURTHER READING* ◆

Benedictus de Spinoza's *Ethics* is in *The Rationalists* (New York: Doubleday, 1960); an excellent account of Spinoza's philosophy is S. Hampshire, *Spinoza* (London: Penguin, 1951). A convenient collection of Gottfried W. von Leibniz's major works is Philip Wiener, ed., *Leibniz, Selections* (New York: Charles Scribner's Sons, 1951). Two recent studies of Leibniz are Ruth Saw, *Leibniz* (London: Penguin, 1954) and Hidé Ishiguro, *Leibniz's Philosophy of Logic and Language* (Ithaca, NY: Cornell University Press, 1972). An important but biased study is Bertrand Russell, *A Critical Exposition of the Philosophy of Leibniz* (London: George Allen and Unwin, 1937). To study more recent metaphysical systems, see A. Lovejoy, *The Great Chain of Being* (Cambridge, MA: Harvard University Press, 1936). Jacques Maritain, *A Preface to Metaphysics* (London: Sheed, 1948); Henri Bergson, *An Introduction to Metaphysics,* trans. T. E. Hulme (New York: Bobbs-Merrill, 1949); Martin Heidegger, *An Introduction to Metaphysics,* trans. Ralph Manheim (New Haven, CT: Yale University Press, 1959); and R. G. Collingwood, *An Essay on Metaphysics* (Oxford: Clarendon Press, 1940). On Islamic philosophy, see A. Hyman and J. Walsh, *Philosophy in the Middle Ages* (Indianapolis: Hackett, 1973).

3

KNOWLEDGE

Once upon a time, I, Chuang Tzu, dreamt I was a butterfly, fluttering hither and thither, to all intents and purposes a butterfly. I was conscious only of following my fancies as a butterfly, and was unconscious of my individuality as a man. Suddenly, I waked, and there I lay, myself again. Now I do not know whether I was then a man dreaming I was a butterfly, or whether I am now a butterfly dreaming I am a man.

CHUANG-TZU[1]

After an evening of heated but fruitless metaphysical debate with a number of his friends, the British physician John Locke turned to them and asked, "Shouldn't we first determine whether we are capable of answering such questions?" They agreed. Perhaps you are thinking much the same thing. These great metaphysical systems are surely monuments to human intelligence. But do they achieve what they are intended to? Do they tell us "the way the world really is?" Since each of the contending systems claims that it does, how can it be that they disagree? Which is right? And how can we decide?

In 1690 Locke took philosophy around a sharp turn, one that had been suggested by Descartes a half century before. But Descartes had broached the question, "What can we know?" only as a preface to his metaphysics. Locke, on the other hand, decided to put questions about reality on the shelf until he could develop an adequate theory of human knowledge. Accordingly, his great book is not primarily an inquiry into substance or reality or God or truth (although all of these enter in); it is *An Essay Concerning Human Understanding.* From metaphysics, the study of ultimate reality, we now turn to **epistemology**, the study of

---

[1] From Herbert A. Giles, translator, *Chuang-Tzu; Taoist Philosopher and Chinese Mystic.* London: George Allen and Unwin, 1961 [1889], p. 47.

human knowledge—how we get it, what it is, whether we have it, or why we don't.

Even before Plato, Parmenides had seen that between a false belief and knowledge of reality are many opinions and appearances of reality, which might be very different from the reality itself. Plato's "Myth of the Cave" is a graphic illustration of this distinction. Descartes, although he distrusted his senses and wasn't certain that they gave accurate representations of reality, at least could be certain of the appearances themselves—he could not be mistaken about them. And here is the problem that has defined epistemology, the seeming abyss between reality and mere appearance. Perhaps we know the appearances of things, but how can we know that we know the reality "behind" them?

Let us return for a moment to the central idea of traditional metaphysics, that of substance. Substance is that which underlies all of the various properties of a thing (or things); and it is the properties, never the substance itself, that are experienced by us. Now, presumably, there can be no properties unless they are properties of something. That seems to be a platitude. But yet, we cannot experience the nature of the substance itself. And here begins the embarrassment of metaphysics.

The problem was stated succinctly by the best-known British philosopher of this century, Bertrand Russell, in a little volume called *The Problems of Philosophy*. He says:

◆**from *The Problems
of Philosophy*,
by Bertrand Russell**

In daily life, we assume as certain many things which, on a closer scrutiny, are found to be so full of apparent contradications that only a great amount of thought enables us to know what it is that we really may believe. In the search for certainty, it is natural to begin with our present experiences, and in some sense, no doubt, knowledge is to be derived from them. But any statement as to what it is that our immediate experiences make us know is very likely to be wrong. It seems to me that I am now sitting in a chair, at a table of a certain shape, on which I see sheets of paper with writing or print. By turning my head I see out of the window buildings and clouds and the sun. I believe that the sun is about ninety-three million miles from the earth; that it is a hot globe many times bigger than the earth; that, owing to the earth's rotation, it rises every morning, and will continue to do so for an indefinite time in the future. I believe that, if any other normal person comes into my room, he will see the same chairs and tables and books and papers as I see, and that the table which I see is the same as the table which I feel pressing against my arm. All this seems to be so evident as to be hardly worth stating, except in answer to a man who doubts whether I know anything. Yet all this may be reasonably doubted, and all of it requires much careful discussion before we can be sure that we have stated it in a form that is wholly true.

To make our difficulties plain, let us concentrate attention on the table. To the eye it is oblong, brown and shiny, to the touch it is smooth and cool and hard; when I tap it, it gives out a wooden sound. Any one else who sees and feels and hears the table will agree with this description, so that it might seem as if no difficulty would arise; but as soon as we try to be more precise our troubles begin. Although I believe that the table is "really" of the same colour all over, the parts that reflect the light look much brighter than the other parts, and some parts look white because of reflected light. I know that, if I move, the parts that reflect the light will be different, so that the apparent distribution of colours on the table will change. It follows that if several people are looking at the table at the same moment, no two of them will see exactly the same distribution of colours, because no two can see it from exactly the same point of view, and any change in the point of view makes some change in the way the light is reflected.

For most practical purposes the differences are unimportant, but to the painter they are all-important: the painter has to unlearn the habit of thinking that things seem to have the colour which common sense says they "really" have, and to learn the habit of seeing things as they appear. Here we have already the beginning of one of the distinctions that cause most trouble in philosophy—the distinction between "appearance" and "reality," between what things seem to be and what they are. The painter wants to know what things seem to be, the practical man and the philosopher want to know what they are; but the philosopher's wish to know this is stronger than the practical man's, and is more troubled by knowledge as to the difficulties of answering the question.

To return to the table. It is evident from what we have found, that there is no colour which preeminently appears to be *the* colour of the table, or even of any one particular part of the table—it appears to be of different colours from different points of view, and there is no reason for regarding some of these as more really its colour than others. And we know that even from a given point of view the colour will seem different by artificial light, or to a colour-blind man, or to a man wearing blue spectacles, while in the dark there will be no colour at all, though to touch and hearing the table will be unchanged. This colour is not something which is inherent in the table, but something depending upon the table and the spectator and the way the light falls on the table. When, in ordinary life, we speak of *the* colour of the table, we only mean the sort of colour which it will seem to have to a normal spectator from an ordinary point of view under usual conditions of light. But the other colours which appear under other conditions have just as good a right to be considered real; and therefore, to avoid favouritism, we are compelled to deny that, in itself, the table has any one particular colour.

The same thing applies to the texture. With the naked eye one can see the grain, but otherwise the table looks smooth and even. If we looked at it through a microscope, we should see roughnesses and hills and valleys, and all sorts of differences that are imperceptible to the naked eye. Which of these is the "real" table? We are naturally tempted to say that what we see through the microscope is more real, but that in turn would be changed by a still more powerful microscope. If, then, we cannot trust what we see with the naked eye, why should we trust what we see through a microscope? Thus, again, the confidence in our sense with which we began deserts us.

The *shape* of the table is not better. We are all in the habit of judging as to the "real" shapes of things, and we do this so unreflectingly that we come to think we actually see the real shapes. But, in fact, as we all have to learn if we try to draw, a given thing looks different in shape from every different point of view. If our table is "really" rectangular, it will look, from almost all points of view, as if it had two acute angles and two obtuse angles. If opposite sides are parallel, they will look as if they converged to a point away from the spectator; if they are of equal length, they will look as if the nearer side were longer. All these things are not commonly noticed in looking at a table, because experience has taught us to construct the "real" shape from the apparent shape, and the "real" shape is what interests us as practical men. But the "real" shape is not what we see; it is something inferred from what we see. And what we see is constantly changing in shape as we move about the room; so that here again the senses seem not to give us the truth about the table itself, but only about the appearance of the table.

Similar difficulties arise when we consider the sense of touch. It is true that the table always gives us a sensation of hardness, and we feel that it resists pressure. But the sensation we obtain depends upon how hard we press the table and also upon what part of the body we press with; thus the various sensations due to various pressures or various parts of the body cannot be supposed to reveal *directly* any definite property of the table, but at most to be *signs* of some property, which *causes* all the sensations, but is not actually apparent in any of them. And the same applies still more obviously to the sounds which can be elicited by rapping the table.

Thus it becomes evident that the real table, if there is one, is not the same as what we immediately experience by sight or touch or hearing. The real table, if there is one, is not *immediately* known to us at all, but must be an inference from what is immediately known. Hence, two very difficult questions at once arise;

namely, (1) Is there a real table at all? (2) If so, what sort of object can it be?[2]

In these few pages, Russell succeeds in summarizing the problems that have dominated British philosophy since Locke's original epistemological studies. But why say "British philosophy"? Why should this problem have been more serious there than on the continent of Europe, where most of the great metaphysicians were working? Why should it have had more impact on Locke and his followers than on Descartes, Spinoza, Leibniz, and their latter-day followers? Because of a single profound difference, which has always created a general gap in understanding between British-American philosophy and European philosophy. Descartes, Spinoza, and Leibniz retained their faith in human reason's ability to give us knowledge of reality, despite the fact that reality was beyond our every possible experience. Because of their confidence in the powers of reason, they are usually called **rationalists**. And because it happens that all three were Europeans (Descartes was French; Spinoza, Dutch; and Leibniz, German), they are often called *continental rationalists*. The movement developed by John Locke, on the other hand, is generally called **empiricism**, because of its insistence upon the data of experience (or *empirical* data) as the source of all knowledge. (A **datum** [plural, *data*] is a bit of "given" information; modern empiricist philsophers sometimes talk of *sense-data*, that is, the information immediately given by the senses.) Also included in this group of empiricists are Bishop George Berkeley[3] and David Hume, whom we shall also meet in this chapter. And because they were all from Great Britain, they are often called *British empiricists*. (Berkeley was Irish; Hume, Scottish; Russell is generally considered a more contemporary member of this same movement.)

Although epistemology received a renewed attention and a new kind of treatment in the era after Descartes, the rift between the claims of rationalists and those of empiricists was not new. The basics of the debate were laid out by Plato, in his dialogue, *Theatetus*:

◆from the *Theatetus*, by Plato

Socrates: But the question you were asked, Theatetus, was not, what are the objects of knowledge, nor yet how many sorts of knowledge there are. We did not want to count them, but to find out what the thing itself—knowledge—is.
· · · · · · · · · ·

---

[2]Bertrand Russell, *The Problems of Philosophy* (Oxford: Oxford University Press, 1912).
[3]Bishop Berkeley traveled to America; Berkeley, California, is named after him.

> Perception, you say, is knowledge?
>
> Theatetus: Yes.
>
> Socrates: The account you give of the nature of knowledge is not, by any means, to be despised. It is the same that was given by Protagoras, though he stated it in a somewhat different way. He says, you will remember, that "man is the measure of all things—alike of the being of things that are and of the not-being of things that are not." No doubt you have read that.
>
> Theatetus: Yes, often.
>
> Socrates: He puts it in this sort of way, doesn't he, that any given thing is "is to me such as it appears to me and is to you such as it appears to you," you and I being men?
>
> Theatetus: Yes, that is how he puts it.
>
> Socrates: Well, what a wise man says is not likely to be nonsense. So let us follow his meaning. Sometimes, when the same wind is blowing, one of us feels chilly, the other does not, or one may feel slightly chilly, the other quite cold.
>
> Theatetus: Certainly.
>
> Socrates: Well, in that case are we to say that the wind in itself is cold or not cold? Or shall we agree with Protagoras that it is cold to the one who feels chilly and not to the other?
>
> · · · · · · · · · ·
>
> . . . [I]ndeed the doctrine is a remarkable one. It declares that nothing is *one* thing just by itself, nor can you rightly call it by one definite name, nor even say it is of any definite sort.

In this way, Socrates claims that the empiricist cannot have any knowledge at all. He defends the rationalist's claim earlier in the dialogue:

> Socrates: You do not suppose a man can understand the name of a thing when he does not know what the thing is?
>
> Theatetus: Certainly not.
>
> Socrates: Then, if he has no idea of knowledge, "knowledge about shoes" conveys nothing to him?
>
> Theatetus: No.
>
> Socrates: "Cobblery" in fact, or the name of any other art has no meaning for anyone who has no conception of knowledge.[4]

Russell, like Theatetus, associates knowledge with perception, or "sense-data." Thus, he had assumed that any notion of "substance" we might have must be *derived* from our perceptions. Socrates claimed that our varied perceptions can never give us a notion of substance. All we would be able to get out of a bunch of differing perceptions is a bunch of differing perceptions. Since we *have* a notion of substance, however, (in

[4]Translated by F. M. Cornford, reprinted in *The Collected Dialogues of Plato*, ed. Edith Hamilton and Huntington Cairnes, Bollingen series (Princeton: Princeton University Press, 1980), p. 61.

Russell's example, for instance, of a "table") we must have gotten it from something other than our perceptions. Knowledge, concludes Socrates, must be something other than perception. The continental rationalists in a sense, agreed with Socrates on this point and claimed that the nonperceptual source of knowledge must be "reason" itself. The British empiricists went the other way, claiming that there simply wasn't any other source of ideas other than perception. ("Perception" actually can mean both "sense-data" and "understanding." We mean the first sense here.)

So, how are we to know reality? By retaining confidence in our own powers of abstract reason? Or by appeal to experience, which carries with it the threat that we many never know reality beyond our experience at all? In the pages that follow, you will see one of the most vigorous and long-lasting dialogues in philosophy, not only between the rationalists and the empiricists but (as we saw in the juxtaposition of Spinoza and Leibniz in Chapter 2) between various rationalists and empiricists as well.

Is the choice between reason and experience a "false dilemma" (a kind of pseudo-question)? Among the issues in dispute are not only the emphasis and faith in reason versus experience but also the nature of reason and the nature of experience. What is an idea that can be known to be true by reason alone—a "truth of reason"? How can we infer from the nature of our private experience what the world "outside" is like? How do we even know that there *is* an "external" world? How is it possible to have "abstract" ideas, that is, ideas that are not simply based on the concrete particulars of experience, such as *this* dog, *this* table, *that* star over there to the left of the Big Dipper? How do we get the idea, for example, of "dog" in general, not this dog or that dog or big dog or little dog or Chihuahua or German Shepherd but just "dog," which includes all of them?

The question of *substance* comes up again and again; what is a substance? How do we know of substances? So does the notion of *cause*. Is an idea *caused* by an object of which it is the idea, or do we make the idea up, and so "cause" it ourselves? And, a more specific set of questions: What aspects of a thing are *in it*? What aspects of a thing are rather *in us*, that is, in the way we perceive it, in the mental apparatus that we use in our knowledge? But beneath the welter of questions and debates, there is a singular shared concern. All of the rationalists and empiricists are men of science who appreciate the advances of modern physics and its kindred disciplines, who think of knowledge as one of the highest human attributes, and who want to understand knowledge and its foundations as a way of justifying their faith in science. At the bottom of all of these disputes, in other words, is that basic admiration and concern for knowledge as such, and the question "how is this knowledge possible?" is itself an extension of that same admiration and concern.

A. THE RATIONALIST'S CONFIDENCE: DESCARTES

Let's return to the philosopher who began the modern emphasis on methodology, René Descartes. We have already mentioned his "method of doubt," but the goal of this method is not to defend the doubts but, quite to the contrary, to move from doubt to knowledge and certainty. Descartes' doubt is intended only to separate what is doubtful from what is not. He never doubted, nor did his followers, that he would be able to find beliefs about reality. These beliefs would be "clear and distinct" and "perfectly certain." (Spinoza refers to such ideas as "adequate ideas"; Leibniz calls them "truths of reason.") Once Descartes had found even one such belief, he could use it as a premise from which he could deduce all of his other beliefs about reality. And none of this depends upon the data of experience; it is entirely a process of reason, of examining the clarity of his beliefs and the logical connections between them.

Once again, it is important to remind ourselves that these problems and their sometimes radical complications and solutions do not appear in a vacuum. Descartes lived in the time of Galileo, and Galileo's new science is always in the background of Descartes' method of doubt. In undermining the traditional science of Aristotle and the Middle Ages, Galileo had raised the doubt that what we think that we see we might not really see at all. Colors, for example, seemed to be more in the minds of men and women than in the objects themselves. But if we could be mistaken about something so seemingly certain as the color of objects, Descartes reasons, could we not be mistaken about much else besides? Indeed, could we not be mistaken in our perceptions *in general*? For this reason Descartes appeals to reason rather than to experience (although, as we shall see, he dangerously calls reason into question as well). We might also add that, although he was a devout Catholic, Descartes could not help but be affected by Martin Luther's challenge to church authority, the century before. Thus the insistence of resolving these doubts for oneself, instead of appealing to established authority, was very much a part of the radical temperament of the time.

In six famous "meditations," Descartes begins with the resolve to doubt everything that he believes, that is, until he can find a first premise that is beyond doubt, from which he can then argue for the truth of other beliefs, which he can then use as premises to prove more beliefs, and so on. In the first meditation, he states his method of doubt and begins to eliminate all of those beliefs about which he could possibly be mistaken. He doubts his senses; could they not mislead him, as they do in an optical illusion or a hallucination? He examines his belief in God; could it be that his Jesuit teachers had been fooling him? He even doubts the existence of the world; is it not conceivable that he is merely dreaming? Here is the first of the meditations.

◆ **from "Meditation I,"
by René Descartes**

> OF THE THINGS WHICH MAY BE BROUGHT WITHIN THE SPHERE
> OF THE DOUBTFUL
>
>   It is now some years since I detected how many were the false beliefs that I had from my earliest youth admitted as true, and how doubtful was everything I had since constructed on this basis; and from that time I was convinced that I must once for all seriously undertake to rid myself of all the opinions which I had formerly accepted, and commence to build anew from the foundation, if I wanted to establish any firm and permanent structure in the sciences.

In order to "build anew" his system of beliefs and eliminate his false beliefs, Descartes resolves to doubt everything that he believes. But this does not mean that he has to list every belief he has; that might take forever. Instead, it is necessary only for him to examine those "first principles" upon which all of his other beliefs are based.

>   Now for this object it is not necessary that I should show that all of these are false—I shall perhaps never arrive at this end. But inasmuch as reason already persuades me that I ought no less carefully to withhold my assent from matters which are not entirely certain and indubitable than from those which appear to me manifestly to be false, if I am able to find in each one some reason to doubt, this will suffice to justify my rejecting the whole. And for that end it will not be requisite that I should examine each in particular, which would be an endless undertaking; for owing to the fact that the destruction of the foundations of necessity brings with it the downfall of the rest of the edifice, I shall only in the first place attack those principles upon which all my former opinions rested.

The first set of principles to be doubted is that "common-sense" set of beliefs that relies upon the senses—seeing, hearing, tasting, smelling, touching. Descartes argues that, despite our common-sense reliance on these, it is nevertheless possible that we could be deceived by our senses.

>   All that up to the present time I have accepted as most true and certain I have learned either from the senses or through the senses; but it is sometimes proved to me that these senses are de-

ceptive, and it is wiser not to trust entirely to any thing by which we have once been deceived.

But it may be that although the senses sometimes deceive us concerning things which are hardly perceptible, or very far away, there are yet many others to be met with as to which we cannot reasonably have any doubt, although we recognise them by their means. For example, there is the fact that I am here, seated by the fire, attired in a dressing gown, having this paper in my hands and other similar matters. And how could I deny that these hands and this body are mine, were it not perhaps that I compare myself to certain persons, devoid of sense, whose cerebella are so troubled and clouded by the violent vapours of black bile, that they constantly assure us that they think they are kings when they are really quite poor, or that they are clothed in purple when they are really without covering, or who imagine that they have an earthenware head or are nothing but pumpkins or are made of glass. But they are mad, and I should not be any the less insane were I to follow examples so extravagant.

Now Descartes makes one of his most famous philosophical moves: He wonders whether he could possibly be dreaming all of his experience; for in a dream, as we all know, it is possible that everything can still seem perfectly real, as if we were actually awake:

At the same time I must remember that I am a man, and that consequently I am in the habit of sleeping, and in my dreams representing to myself the same things or sometimes even less probable things, than do those who are insane in their waking moments. How often has it happened to me that in the night I dreamt that I found myself in this particular place, that I was dressed and seated near the fire, whilst in reality I was lying undressed in bed! At this moment it does indeed seem to me that it is with eyes awake that I am looking at this paper; that this head which I move is not asleep, that it is deliberately and of set purpose that I extend my hand and perceive it; what happens in sleep does not appear so clear nor so distinct as does all this. But in thinking over this I remind myself that on many occasions I have in sleep been deceived by similar illusions, and in dwelling carefully on this reflection I see so manifestly that there are no certain indications by which we may clearly distinguish wakefulness from sleep that I am lost in astonishment. And my astonishment is such that it is almost capable of persuading me that I now dream.

Thus Descartes has brought himself to the point where he doubts the existence of the whole of nature, even the existence of his own body. After all, one can dream that one's body has changed grotesquely, and on rare occasions it is even possible to dream that one leaves one's body altogether. So isn't it possible, according to this strict method of doubt, to wonder whether one does indeed have a body, just as it is possible to wonder how one knows of the existence of the "external world" in general?

But there is one sphere of knowledge that would seem to be immune even to Descartes' radical doubting—the principles of arithmetic and geometry:

> Arithmetic, Geometry and other sciences of that kind which only treat of things that are very simple and very general, without taking great trouble to ascertain whether they are actually existent or not, contain some measure of certainty and an element of the indubitable. For whether I am awake or asleep, two and three together always form five, and the square can never have more than four sides, and it does not seem possible that truths so clear and apparent can be suspected of any falsity [or uncertainty].

But these can be doubted, too. To do so, Descartes turns his attention to God, his Creator, and asks whether God might be able to deceive him even about these apparently certain principles:

> Nevertheless I have long had fixed in my mind the belief that an all-powerful God existed by whom I have been created such as I am. But how do I know that He has not brought it to pass that there is no earth, no heaven, no extended body, no magnitude, no place, and that nevertheless [I possess the perceptions of all these things and that] they seem to me to exist just exactly as I now see them? And, besides, as I sometimes imagine that others deceive themselves in the things which they think they know best, how do I know that I am not deceived every time that I add two and three, or count the sides of a square, or judge of things yet simpler, if anything simpler can be imagined? But possibly God has not desired that I should be thus deceived, for He is said to be supremely good. If, however, it is contrary to His goodness to have made me such that I constantly deceive myself, it would also appear to be contrary to His goodness to permit me to be sometimes deceived, and nevertheless I cannot doubt that He does permit this.

Descartes' argument, which he will use again later in his *Meditations*, is that God is good and would not deceive him. But suppose, just suppose, that God did not exist?

> There may indeed be those who would prefer to deny the existence of a God so powerful, rather than believe that all other things are uncertain. But let us not oppose them for the present, and grant that all that is here said of a God is a fable; nevertheless in whatever way they suppose that I have arrived at the state of being

that I have reached—whether they attribute it to fate or to accident, or make out that it is by a continual succession of antecedents, or by some other method—since to err and deceive oneself is a defect, it is clear that the greater will be the probability of my being so imperfect as to deceive myself ever, as is the Author to whom they assign my origin the less powerful. To these reasons I have certainly nothing to reply, but at the end I feel constrained to confess that there is nothing in all that I formerly believed to be true, of which I cannot in some measure doubt, and that not merely through want of thought or through levity, but for reasons which are very powerful and maturely considered; so that henceforth I ought not the less carefully to refrain from giving credence to these opinions than to that which is manifestly false, if I desire to arrive at any certainty [in the sciences].

To bring his method to its extreme conclusion, Descartes now introduces a drastic supposition, namely, that not a good God but an evil genius, a malicious demon, is constantly deceiving him, even about those things of which he seems to be most certain:

I shall then suppose, not that God who is supremely good and the fountain of truth, but some evil genius not less powerful than deceitful, has employed his whole energies in deceiving me; I shall consider that the heavens, the earth, colours, figures, sound, and all other external things are nought but the illusions and dreams of which this genius has availed himself in order to lay traps for my credulity; I shall consider myself as having no hands, no eyes, no flesh, no blood, nor any senses, yet falsely believing myself to possess all these things; I shall remain obstinately attached to this idea, and if by this means it is not in my power to arrive at the knowledge of any truth, I may at least do what is in my power [i.e., suspend my judgment], and with firm purpose avoid giving credence to any false thing, or being imposed upon by this arch deceiver, however powerful and deceptive he may be. But this task is a laborious one, and insensibly a certain lassitude leads me into the course of my ordinary life. And just as a captive who in sleep enjoys an imaginary liberty, when he begins to suspect that this liberty is but a dream, fears to awaken, and conspires with these agreeable illusions that the deception may be prolonged, so insensibly of my own accord I fall back into my former opinions, and I dread awakening from this slumber, lest the laborious wakefulness which would follow the tranquility of this repose should have to be spent not in daylight, but in the excessive darkness of the difficulties which have just been discussed.[5]

[5]Descartes, *Meditations on First Philosophy*, in *The Philosophical Works of Descartes*, trans. Elizabeth S. Haldane and G. R. T. Ross (Cambridge: Cambridge University Press, 1911). All subsequent "Meditatons" by Descartes are from this edition.

Descartes has taken his doubt as far as he can possibly go; he now doubts everything, until, that is, he finds the one principle that is beyond all doubt and perfectly certain. That principle is the fact of his own existence. That he cannot doubt, for if he doubts it, he still knows that he must exist to doubt. Thus, he can be certain of one thing, at least, that he himself exists. And from this first principle, Descartes proceeds, through the "Meditations" that follow, to reestablish his confidence in other things he believes as well—the existence of God, the existence of the "external world," and the existence of his own body.

Many philosophers have challenged the extremity of Descartes' method and have often objected that once you begin to doubt things so thoroughly, you wil never again be able to argue your way back to certainty. One way of making this objection is to ask, how can Descartes possibly get rid of an "evil genius" who is deceiving him about everything once he has introduced this possibility? Indeed, the supposition of an evil genius was so extreme that even Descartes, in the years that followed the publication and many disputes about his *Meditations*, insisted that no one should take his argument too seriously. But in the "Meditations" themselves he tried to show that we could indeed get rid of the evil genius. Having watched Descartes work his way into the depth of Plato's cave, let us now watch him work his way out again.

◆from "Meditation II," by Descartes

OF THE NATURE OF THE HUMAN MIND; AND THAT IT IS MORE EASILY KNOWN THAN THE BODY

The Meditation of yesterday filled my mind with so many doubts that it is no longer in my power to forget them. And yet I do not see in what manner I can resolve them; and, just as if I had all of a sudden fallen into very deep water, I am so disconcerted that I can neither make certain of setting my feet on the bottom, nor can I swim and so support myself on the surface. I shall nevertheless make an effort and follow anew the same path as that on which I yesterday entered, i.e. I shall proceed by setting aside all that in which the least doubt could be supposed to exist, just as if I had discovered that it was absolutely false; and I shall ever follow in this road until I have met with something which is certain, or at least, if I can do nothing else, until I have learned for certain that there is nothing in the world that is certain. Archimedes, in order that he might draw the terrestrial globe out of its place, and transport it elsewhere, demanded only that one point should be fixed and immovable; in the same way I shall have the right to conceive high hopes if I am happy enough to discover one thing only which is certain and indubitable.

I suppose, then, that all the things that I see are false; I persuade myself that nothing has ever existed of all that my fallacious memory represents to me. I consider that I possess no senses; I imagine that body, figure, extension, movement and place are but the fictions of my mind. What, then, can be esteemed as true? Perhaps nothing at all, unless that there is nothing in the world that is certain.

But how can I know there is not something different from those things that I have just considered, of which one cannot have the slightest doubt? Is there not some God, or some other being by whatever name we call it, who puts these reflections into my mind? That is not necessary, for is it not possible that I am capable of producing them myself? I myself, am I not at least something? But I have already denied that I had senses and body. Yet I hesitate, for what follows from that? Am I so dependent on body and senses that I cannot exist without these? But I was persuaded that there was nothing in all the world, that there was no heaven, no earth, that there were no minds, nor any bodies; was I not then likewise persuaded that I did not exist? Not at all; of a surety I myself did exist since I persuaded myself of something [or merely because I thought of something]. But there is some deceiver or other, very powerful and very cunning, who ever employs his ingenuity in deceiving me. Then without doubt I exist also if he deceives me, and let him deceive me as much as he will, he can never cause me to be nothing so long as I think that I am something. So that after having reflected well and carefully examined all things, we must come to the definite conclusion that this propostion: I am, I exist, is necessarily true each time that I pronounce it, or that I mentally conceive it.

Here it is, the one, certain truth that Descartes needs to start his argument. The more famous formulation of this truth, *cogito, ergo sum,* "I think, therefore I am," occurs in his earlier *Discourse on Method* (1637). (It may be worth pointing out that a similar argument appears in St. Augustine, over one thousand years earlier.)

But now that Descartes knows that he exists, what is he? His answer: "a thing which thinks."

But I do not yet know clearly enough what I am, I who am certain that I am; and hence I must be careful to see that I do not imprudently take some other object in place of myself, and thus that I do not go astray in respect of this knowledge that I hold to be the most certain and most evident of all that I have formerly learned. That is why I shall now consider anew what I believed myself to be before I embarked upon these last reflections; and of my former opinions I shall withdraw all that might even in a small degree be invalidated by the reasons which I have just brought forward, in order that there may be nothing at all left beyond what is absolutely certain and indubitable.

What then did I formerly believe myself to be? Undoubtedly I believed myself to be a man. But what is a man? Shall I say a reasonable animal? Certainly not; for then I should have to inquire what an animal is, and what is reasonable; and thus from a single question I should insensibly fall into an infinitude of others more difficult; and I should not wish to waste the little time and leisure remaining to me in trying to unravel subtleties like these. But I shall rather stop here to consider the thoughts which of themselves spring up in my mind, and which were not inspired by anything beyond my own nature alone when I applied myself to the consideration of my being. In the first place, then, I considered myself as having a face, hands, arms, and all that system of members composed of bones and flesh as seen in a corpse which I designated by the name of body. In addition to this I considered that I was nourished, that I walked, that I felt, and that I thought, and I referred all these actions to the soul: but I did not stop to consider what the soul was, or if I did stop, I imagined that it was something extremely rare and subtle like a wind, a flame, or an ether, which was spread throughout my grosser parts. As to body I had no manner of doubt about its nature, but thought I had a very clear knowledge of it; and if I had desired to explain it according to the notions that I had then formed of it, I should have described it thus: By the body I understand all that which can be defined by a certain figure: something which can be confined in a certain place, and which can fill a given space in such a way that every other body will be excluded from it; which can be perceived either by touch, or by sight, or by hearing, or by taste, or by smell: which can be moved in many ways not, in truth, by itself, but by something which is foreign to it, by which it is touched [and from which it receives impressions]: for to have the power of self-movement, as also of feeling or of thinking, I did not consider to appertain to the nature of body: on the contrary, I was rather astonished to find that faculties similar to them existed in some bodies.

But what am I, now that I suppose that there is a certain genius which is extremely powerful, and, if I may say so, malicious, who employs all his power in deceiving me? Can I affirm that I possess the least of all those things which I have just said pertain to the nature of body? I pause to consider, I revolve all these things in my mind, and I find none of which I can say that it pertains to me. It would be tedious to stop to enumerate them. Let us pass to the attributes of soul and see if there is any one which is in me? What of nutrition or walking [the first mentioned]? But if it is so that I have no body it is also true that I can neither walk nor take nourishment. Another attribute is sensation. But one cannot feel without body, and besides I have thought I perceived many things during sleep that I recognized in my waking moments as not having been experienced at all. What of thinking? I find here that thought is an attribute that belongs to me; it alone cannot be separated from me. I am, I exist, that is certain. But how often? Just when I think; for it might possibly be the case if I ceased entirely to think, that I should likewise cease altogether to exist. I do not now admit anything which is not necessarily true: to speak accurately I am not more than a thing which thinks, that is to say a mind or a soul, or an understanding, or a reason, which are terms whose significance was formerly unknown to me. I am, however, a real thing and really exist; but what thing? I have answered: a thing which thinks. . . . What is a thing which thinks? It is a thing which doubts, understands, [conceives], affirms, denies, wills, refuses, which also imagines and feels.

In other words, Descartes cannot know for certain that he has a body, much less a particular kind of body, since the evil genius could fool him about that. The only thing that the evil genius could not possibly fool him about is his own thinking, and therefore, the "I" that he knows to exist can only be a thinking "I", not a person or a man in the more usual sense. Later on, this will cause Descartes to raise a gigantic problem, namely, how to explain the connection between this thinking self and the body with which it is associated. But for now, we are more interested in the way he will use his discovery of a single, certain truth. (His discussion of the "mind-body" connection occurs in "Meditation VI," which we shall discuss in Chapter 7, pp. 442–444.)

Descartes has his premise, the fact of his own existence as a "thinking thing." What must follow, then is the use of this premise in an argument that will "prove" the beliefs he began by doubting: the existence of his own body, the existence of the "external" world, and the existence of God. And, finally, he must somehow get rid of his tentative supposition of the evil demon. But first, he raises once again the old metaphysical question of substance. In a famous example from "Meditation II" he argues:

Let us begin by considering the commonest matters, those which we believe to be the most distinctly comprehended, to wit, the bodies which we touch and see; not indeed bodies in general, for these general ideas are usually a little more confused, but let us consider one body in particular. Let us take, for example, this piece of wax: it has been taken quite freshly from the hive, and it has not yet lost the sweetness of the honey which it contains; it still retains somewhat of the odour of the flowers from which it has been culled; its colour, its figure, its size are apparent; it is hard, cold, easily handled, and if you strike it with the finger, it will emit a sound. Finally all the things which are requisite to cause us distinctly to recognize a body, are met with in it. But notice that while I speak and approach the fire what remained of the taste is exhaled, the smell evaporates, the colour alters, the figure is destroyed, the size increases, it becomes liquid, it heats, scarcely can one handle it, and when one strikes it, no sound is emitted. Does the same wax remain after this change? We must confess that it remains; none would judge otherwise. What then did I know so distinctly in this piece of wax? It could certainly be nothing of all that the senses brought to my notice, since all these things which fall under taste, smell, sight, touch and hearing, are found to be changed, and yet the same wax remains.

Perhaps it was what I now think, viz. that this wax was not that sweetness of honey, nor that agreeable scent of flowers, nor that particular whiteness, nor that figure, nor that sound, but simply a body which a little while before appeared to me as perceptible under these forms, and which is now perceptible under others. But what, precisely, is it that I imagine when I form such conceptions? Let us attentively consider this, and, abstracting from all that does not belong to the wax, let us see what remains. Certainly nothing remains excepting a certain extended thing which is flexible and movable. But what is the meaning of flexible and movable? Is it not that I imagine that this piece of wax being round is capable of becoming square and of passing from a square to a triangular figure? No, certainly it is not that, since I imagine it admits of an infinitude of similar changes, and I nevertheless do not know how to compass the infinitude of my imagination, and consequently this conception which I have of the wax is not brought about by the faculty of imagination. What now is this extension? Is it not also unknown? For it becomes greater when the wax is melted, greater when it is boiled, and greater still when the heat increases; and I should not conceive [clearly] according to truth what wax is, if I did not think that even this piece that we are considering is capable of receiving more variations in extension that I have ever imagined. We must then grant that I could not even understand through the imagination what this piece of wax is, and that it is my mind alone which perceives it. I say this piece of wax in particular, for as to wax in general it is yet clearer. But what is this piece of wax which cannot be understood excepting by the [understanding or] mind? It is certainly the same that I see, touch, imagine, and finally it is the same which I have always believed it to be from the beginning. But what must particularly be observed is that its perception is neither an act of vision, nor of touch, nor of imagination, and has never been such although it may have appeared formerly to be so, but only an intuition of the mind, which may be imperfect and confused as it was formerly, or clear and distinct as it is at present, according as my attention is more or less directed to the elements which are found in it, and of which it is composed.

This "intuition of mind" is the key to all rationalist thinking. Intuition is where the rationalist obtains his premises, from which he argues to all other conclusions. And the difference between the rationalist and the empiricist, at least in what they say that they are doing, is the rationalist's heavy reliance on nonempirical intuition. Both would agree on the legitimacy of the deductions that follow; it is the source of the premises that is in dispute. And intuition, according to the rationalists, has its source in reason alone. (Notice that "reason" refers not only to the activity of reasoning but to unreasoned intuitions and insights as well.) Accordingly it is this source of intuition that will be the center of the dispute rather than the actual arguments that Descartes then uses to "prove" his other beliefs. The strategy of Descartes' argument is as follows. First, there is the premise, which you have seen

I *exist* (as a thinking thing).

Then (in "Meditation III"), Descartes uses this premise to prove the existence of God. This is the second key move in the argument. (The first is the establishment of the premise, "I exist.") The argument itself is a version of two arguments called "the cosmological argument" and "the ontological argument for God's existence." We will discuss them in detail in Chapter 6 ("Religion") but the basic logic of both arguments is this: if a finite, dependent, and merely contingent being like myself can even think of an infinite, independent, and necessary being, then such a being must exist. The details of these arguments, however, are not so much the concern of epistemology or the theory of knowledge as they are of the special logical considerations necessary when talking about the Supreme Being. For now, therefore, let us simply grant Descartes his second step, with the promissory note that the proofs will be explained in the later chapter on the philosophy of religion. So, we have

I *exist* (as a thinking thing). (premise)
God exists (because I could not exist without Him).

Now we can say that, by His very nature (another intuition), God is good, in fact, perfectly good. And so, as Descartes says in "Meditation VI,"

◆**from "Meditation VI,"**
by Descartes

Since He has given me a very strong inclination to believe that these ideas (of trees, houses, etc.) arise from corporeal objects, I do not see how He could be vindicated from the charge of deceit, if in truth they proceeded from any other source, or were produced by other causes than corporeal things? (For example, by the evil demon, or in dreams.)

Therefore:

> *We cannot be deceived* [whether by the evil demon or whatever else].
>
>   . . . I cannot doubt but that there is in me a certain passive faculty of perception, that is, of receiving and taking knowledge of the ideas of sensible things; but this would be useless to me, if there did not also exist in me, or in some other thing, another active faculty capable of forming and producing those ideas. But this active faculty cannot be in me [in as far as I am but a thinking thing], seeing that it does not presuppose thought, and also that those ideas are frequently produced in my mind without my contributing to it in any way, and even frequently contrary to my will. This faculty must therefore exist in some substance different from me, in which all the objective reality of the ideas that are produced by this faculty is contained formally or eminently, as I before remarked: and this substance is either a body, that is to say, a corporeal nature in which is contained formally [and in effect] all that is objectively [and by representation] in those ideas; or it is God himself, or some other creature, of a rank superior to body, in which the same is contained eminently. But as God is no deceiver, it is manifest that he does not of himself and immediately communicate those ideas to me, nor even by the intervention of any creature in which their objective reality is not formally, but only eminently, contained. For as he has given me no faculty whereby I can discover this to be the case, but, on the contrary, a very strong inclination to believe that those ideas arise from corporeal objects, I do not see how he could be vindicated from the charge of deceit, if in truth they proceeded from any other source, or were produced by other causes than corporeal things: and accordingly it must be concluded, that corporeal objects exist. Nevertheless they are not perhaps exactly such as we perceive by the senses, for their comprehension by the senses is, in many instances, very obscure and confused; but it is at least necessary to admit that all which I clearly and distinctly conceive as in them, that is, generally speaking, all that is comprehended in the object of speculative geometry, really exists external to me.

The argument is not convincing, as Descartes' critics were quick to point out. Where does Descartes get his confidence in reason to begin with, such that he feels confident in his own abilities to prove God's existence? Descartes' answer is that we get that confidence from God Himself. But with this answer he has begged the question; that is, he has presumed the existence of God in order to get the confidence with which he then proves God's existence. (This circularity of argument is often called "the Cartesian Circle.") Another way of criticizing the same strategy is to say that, having once introduced the evil demon, Descartes has no way of getting rid of him, since that supposition undermines his confidence in his own reason just as thoroughly as his confidence in God bolsters it.

Our primary concern, however, is with Descartes' claim that certain beliefs are self-evident or "clear and distinct" on the basis of intuition and reason alone. These are beliefs that we don't have to learn—in fact, couldn't learn—from experience. It is not just Descartes' "I exist" premise that is such a belief; all of the rules of inference, which he uses in his arguments, are also beliefs of this kind. And, ultimately, his confidence in reason itself is one, too. But how does one defend these beliefs, for not every philosopher agrees with them. In particular, John Locke, in his disillusionment with metaphysics, begins his philosophy with an assault on the very idea of knowledge that is independent of experience. Thus he begins with an attack on the heart of the rationalist methodology.

B. CONCERNING HUMAN UNDERSTANDING: JOHN LOCKE

Regarding metaphysics, John Locke is reported to have commented to a friend, "you and I have had enough of this kind of fiddling." Against the sometimes fantastic claims of the metaphysicians, Locke sought a restoration of common sense.[6] Just as Aristotle had acted as a critic of Plato's extravagant two-worlds view, Locke acted as a corrective to the metaphysical enthusiasm of the medieval and modern worlds. He accepted Descartes' method of tentative skepticism, but he questioned his French predecessor's urge to metaphysics as well as his confidence in the insights of pure reason. He rejected the unsupportable "intuitions" that provided Descartes with his rules and his premises, and he turned instead to the data of experience as the ultimate source of all knowledge. He therefore rejected Descartes' exclusively deductive method and supplanted it with a method appropriate to generalizations from experience, or **induction**. In inductive reasoning, the conclusion always goes beyond the premises and therefore, unlike deductions, is always less certain than they are. (For example, from the observed fact that all the philosophy professors that you have met have been absent-minded [the premise] you conclude by **inductive generalization** that all philosophy professors are probably absent-minded.) Accordingly, Locke also modified Descartes' demand for "perfect certainty" and allowed for probability and "degrees of assent." But it must not be thought that

---

[6]British empiricism traditionally has considered itself the defender of "common sense" against the excesses of metaphysics. This was even true of Berkeley and Hume, who reached conclusions more outrageous than any metaphysician. And it is also true of Bertrand Russell and G. E. Moore in this century.

Locke therefore rejected reason as such. He still accepted the certainty of mathematical reasoning and the validity of deductive inferences; but he also expanded the concept of rationality to include inductive reasoning and probability as well as deduction and certainty.

Locke's *Essay Concerning Human Understanding* (1689) is built on a single premise, namely, that all our knowledge comes from experience. This means, in his view, that there cannot possibly be ideas that are prior to experience, ideas that are "born into" us, as suggested so vividly by Plato. In other words, Locke refuses to accept the notion of innate ideas, by which he means not only those ideas that are literally "born into us" but all ideas that are derived without appeal to experience. This includes, in his opinion, Descartes' "clear and distinct ideas," Spinoza's "adequate ideas" and Leibniz's "truths of reason."

◆from *An Essay Concerning Human Understanding,* by John Locke

1. *The way shown how we come by any knowledge, sufficient to prove it not innate.*—It is an established opinion among some men, that there are in the understanding certain innate principles; some primary notions, κοιναί έννοιαι, characters, as it were, stamped upon the mind of man which the soul receives in its very first being, and brings into the world with it. It would be sufficient to convince unprejudiced readers of the falseness of this supposition, if I should only show (as I hope I shall in the following parts of this discourse) how men, barely by the use of their natural faculties, may attain to all the knowledge they have, without the help of any innate impressions, and may arrive at certainty, without any such original notions or principles. . . .

2. *General Assent the great Argument.*—There is nothing more commonly taken for granted, than that there are certain principles, both speculative and practical (for they speak of both), universally agreed upon by all mankind, which therefore, they argue, must needs be constant impressions which the souls of men receive in their first beings, and which they bring into the world with them, as necessarily and really as they do any of their inherent faculties.

3. *Universal Consent proves nothing innate.*—This argument, drawn from universal consent, has this misfortune in it, that if it were true in matter of fact that there were certain truths wherein all mankind agreed, it would not prove them innate, if there can be any other way shown how men may come to that universal agreement in the things they do consent in, which I presume may be done.

4. *"What is, is," and "it is impossible for the same Thing to be and not to be," not universally assented to.*—But, which is worse, this argument of universal consent, which is made use of to prove innate principles, seems to me a demonstration that there are none such; because there are none to which all mankind give an universal assent. I shall begin with the speculative, and instance in those magnified principles of demonstration, "Whatsoever is, is" and "It is impossible for the same thing to be, and not to be"; which, of all others, I think, have the most allowed title to innate. These have so settled a reputation of maxims universally received that it will no doubt be thought strange if anyone should seem to question it. But yet I take liberty to say that these propositions are so far from having an universal assent that there are a great part of mankind to whom they are not so much as known.

5. *Not on the Mind naturally imprinted, because not known to Children, Idiots, &c.*—For, first, it is evident that all children and idiots have not the least apprehension or thought of them; and the want of that is enough to destroy that universal assent which must needs be the necessary concomitant of all innate truths: it seeming to me near a contradiction to say that there are truths imprinted on the soul which it perceives or understands not; imprinting, if it signify anything, being nothing else but the making certain truths to be perceived. For to imprint anything on the mind without the mind's perceiving it, seems to me hardly intelligible. If therefore children and idiots have souls, have minds, with those impressions upon them, they must unavoidably perceive them, and necessarily know and assent to these truths; which since they do not, it is evident that there are no such impressions. For if they are not notions naturally imprinted, how can they be innate, and if they are notions imprinted, how can they be unknown? To say a notion is imprinted on the mind, and yet at the same time to say that the mind is ignorant of it, and never yet took notice of it, is to make this impression nothing. No proposition can be said to be in the mind which it never yet knew, which it was never yet conscious of.[7]

The argument is straightforward; there is, in fact, no universal agreement regarding supposedly "innate" principles, and even if there were, that would not prove their "innateness." Rather, he argues:

Let us suppose the mind to be, as we say, a blank tablet (*tabula rasa*) of white paper, void of all characters, without any ideas; how comes it to be furnished? Whence comes it by that vast store, which the busy and boundless fancy of man has painted on it with

[7] John Locke, *An Essay Concerning Human Understanding*, ed. A. C. Fraser (Oxford: Clarendon Press, 1894). All subsequent quotations from Locke are from this edition.

almost endless variety? Whence has it all the materials of reason and knowledge? To this I answer in one word, from *experience*: in that all our knowledge is founded, and from that it ultimately derives itself.

It is this premise that Locke is concerned to defend and use, and his attack on innate ideas is by way of introduction. But Locke fails to succeed in proving that the human mind does not have inborn potentials and limitations, and more importantly, he fails to recognize that inference from experience might itself require principles that are not drawn from experience. In fact, Leibniz, one of the chief targets of Locke's attack, was not long in providing what we might call "the rationalist's reply." Turning Locke against himself, Leibniz argued that, by his own principles, he could not attack the concept of innate ideas.

◆Leibniz's Rebuttal, from *New Essays on the Human Understanding*, by Gottfried Wilhelm von Leibniz

. . . The question at issue is whether the soul in itself is entirely empty, like the tablet upon which nothing has yet been written (*tabula rasa*), as is the view of Aristotle and the author of the *Essay* (Locke), and whether all that is traced on it comes solely from the senses and from experience; or whether the soul contains originally the principles of various notions and doctrines which external objects merely awaken from time to time, as I believe, with Plato and even with the Schoolmen, and with all those who take in this sense the passage of St. Paul (Romans, 2:15) where he remarks that the law of God is written in the heart. . . . From this there arises another question, whether all truths depend on experience, that is to say, on induction and examples, or whether there are some that have some other basis. For if some events can be foreseen before any trial has been made of them, it is clear that we must here contribute something of our own. The senses, although necessary for all our actual knowledge, are not sufficient to give us the whole of it, since the senses never give anything except examples, that is to say, particular or individual truths. All examples which confirm a general truth, however numerous they may be, are not enough to establish the universal necessity of this same truth; for it does not follow that what has happened will happen again in the same way.

. . . It would seem that necessary truths, such as are found in pure mathematics, and especially in arithmetic and in geometry, must have principles the proof of which does not depend on examples, nor, consequently, on the testimony of the senses, although without the senses it would never have occurred to us to think of them. This ought to be well recognised; Euclid has so well understood it that he often demonstrates by reason what is obvious enough through experience and by sensible images. Logic also, together with metaphysics and ethics, one of which forms natural theology and the other natural jurisprudence, are full of such truths; and consequently their proof can only come from internal principles, which are called innate. It is true that we must not imagine that these eternal laws of the reason can be read in the soul as in an open book, as the edict of the praetor can be read in his *album* without difficulty or research; but it is enough that they can be discovered in us by dint of attention, for which opportunities are given by the senses. The success of experiments serves also as confirmation of the reason, very much as proofs serve in arithmetic for better avoiding error of reckoning when the reasoning is long. . . .

It seems that our able author claims that there is nothing potential in us and nothing even of which we are not at any time actually conscious; but he cannot mean this strictly, or his opinion would be too paradoxical; for acquired habits and the contents of our memory are not always consciously perceived and do not even always come to our aid at need, although we often easily bring them back to mind on some slight occasion which makes us remember them, just as we need only the beginning of a song to remember the song. Also he modifies his assertion in other places by saying that there is nothing in us of which we have not been at least formerly conscious. But besides the fact that no one can be sure by reason alone how far our past apperceptions, which we may have forgotten, may have gone, especially in view of the Platonic doctrine of reminiscence, which, mythical as it is, is not, in part at least, incompatible with bare reason; in addition to this, I say, why is it necessary that everything should be acquired by us through the perceptions of external things, and that nothing can be unearthed in ourselves? Is our soul, then, such a blank that, besides the images borrowed from without, it is nothing? . . . there are a thousand indications that lead us to think that there are at every moment numberless perceptions in us, but without apperception and without reflections; that is to say, changes in the soul itself of which we are not conscious, because the impressions are either too slight and too numerous, or too even, so that they have nothing sufficient to distinguish them one from the other; but, joined to others, they do not fail to produce their effect and to make themselves felt at least confusedly in the mass. . . .[8]

[8]Gottfried W. von Leibniz, *New Essays on the Human Understanding*, trans. A. G. Langley (La Salle, IL: Open Court, 1949).

Locke himself did not continue the debate; he was already convinced of his own position and had more urgent problems to worry about (the political chaos in London following the "Glorious Revolution" of 1688). But the debate continued in different forms. The rise of anthropology in the nineteenth century, with the discoveries of societies whose basic ideas were radically different from our own, seemed to support Locke's claim that no one will believe in innate universal principles if they "ever look beyond the smoke of their own chimneys." But in the nineteenth century a great many philosophers still argued for the existence of universal principles not learned through experience. (Immanuel Kant did this in a very powerful set of arguments that we will view in the next several chapters.) In the early twentieth century, opinion was in general accord with Locke, but recently it has taken another swing back to Leibniz, this time, ironically, supported by anthropology. A major movement in the social sciences, usually called structuralism (whose main proponent is Claude Lévi-Strauss in France), has argued that underneath the many superficial differences between very different societies there are certain basic "structures" that are universal and innate. And in America, the notion of innate ideas has appeared once again in the work of the well-known linguist Noam Chomsky. According to Chomsky, certain capacities for language are built into us from birth, and this allows him to explain not only the similarities of human thinking (which was the view that Locke attacked) but also the enormous capacity for learning different languages quickly. (The average three-year-old learns a language in six months.) The Locke-Leibniz debate is still very much alive.

C. THE EMPIRICIST THEORY OF KNOWLEDGE

The *tabula rasa* or "blank tablet" view of the mind is Locke's most famous epistemological concept. Leaving aside those special concerns that involve only "the relations between ideas" (as in mathematics, logic, and trivial conceptual truths such as "a horse is an animal"), all of our ideas are derived from experience. Epistemology (and philosophy in general) now became a kind of psychology (indeed, the two disciplines were not yet distinguished), a study of the history of our common experiences in order to discover where we get our ideas, particularly such ideas as substance, God, and our various conceptions of reality. In his theory, Locke uses three familiar terms: **sensation** (or what more modern empiricists call sense-data), **ideas** (not in the Platonic sense but simply "the immediate object of perception, thought, or understanding"), and **quality** (or what we have so far been calling property, for example, being red, being round, being heavy).

◆from the *Essay,* by Locke

1. Concerning the simple ideas of Sensation, it is to be considered—that whatsoever is so constituted in nature as to be able, by affecting our senses, to cause any perception in the mind, doth thereby produce in the understanding a simple idea; which, whatever be the external cause of it, when it comes to be taken notice of by our discerning faculty, it is by the mind looked on and considered there to be a real positive idea in the understanding, as much as any other whatsoever; though, perhaps, the cause of it be but a privation of the subject.

2. Thus the ideas of heat and cold, light and darkness, white and black, motion and rest, are equally clear and positive ideas in the mind; though perhaps, some of the causes which produce them are barely privations, in those subjects from whence our senses derive those ideas. These the understanding, in its view of them, considers all as distinct positive ideas, without taking notice of the causes that produce them: which is an inquiry not belonging to the idea, as it is in the understanding, but to the nature of the things existing without us. These are two very different things, and carefully to be distinguished; it being one thing to perceive and know the idea of white or black, and quite another to examine what kind of particles they must be, and how ranged in the superficies, to make any object appear white or black. . . .

7. To discover the nature of our *ideas* the better, and to discourse of them intelligibly, it will be convenient to distinguish them *as they are ideas or perceptions in our minds; and as they are modifications of matter in the bodies that cause such perceptions in us:* that so we may not think (as perhaps usually is done) that they are exactly the images and resemblances of something inherent in the subject; most of those of sensation being in the mind no more the likeness of something existing without us, than the names that stand for them are the likeness of our ideas, which yet upon hearing they are apt to excite in us.

8. Whatsoever the mind perceives *in itself*, or is the immediate object of perception, thought, or understanding, that I call *idea*; and the power to produce any idea in our mind, I call *quality* of the subject wherein that power is. Thus a snowball having the power to produce in us the ideas of white, cold, and round—the power to produce those ideas in us, as they are in the snowball, I call qualities; and as they are sensations or perceptions in our understanding, I call them ideas; which *ideas*, if I speak of sometimes as in the things themselves, I should be understood to mean those qualities in the objects which produce them in us.

Notice that the basis of Locke's theory is the "common sense" distinction between physical objects in the world and sensations and ideas in our minds. Accordingly, we may talk of the qualities or properties inherent in the objects in the world, such as size and shape, and the qualities or properties they merely appear to have, such as color or texture, but that do not exist independently of the objects' effects on our sense organs. Locke refers to those properties of the objects themselves as **primary qualities;** he calls those "properties" of the objects which we merely see them as having, **secondary qualities.**

PRIMARY QUALITIES:

Qualities thus considered in bodies are, *First,* such as are utterly inseparable from the body, in what state soever it be; and such as in all the alterations and changes it suffers, all the force can be used upon it, it constantly keeps; and such as sense constantly finds in every particle of matter which has bulk enough to be perceived; and the mind finds inseparable from every particle of matter, though less than to make itself singly be perceived by our senses: e.g. Take a grain of wheat, divide it into two parts; each part has still solidity, extension, figure, and mobility: divide it again, and it retains still the same qualities; and so divide it on, till the parts become insensible; they must retain still each of them all those qualities. For division (which is all that a mill, or pestle, or any other body, does upon another, in reducing it to insensible parts) can never take away either solidity, extension, figure, or mobility from any body, but only makes two or more distinct separate masses of matter, of that which was but one before; all which distinct masses, reckoned as so many distinct bodies; after division, make a certain number. These I call *original* or *primary qualities* of body, which I think we may observe to produce simple ideas in us, viz. solidity, extension, figure, motion or rest, and number.

· · · · · · · · · ·

SECONDARY QUALITIES:

Secondly, such qualities which in truth are nothing in the objects themselves but powers to produce various sensations in us by their primary qualities, i.e, by the bulk, figure, texture, and motion of their insensible parts, as colours, sounds, tastes, &c. These I call *secondary qualities*. To these might be added a *third* sort, which are allowed to be barely powers; though they are as much real qualities in the subject as those which I, to comply with the common way of speaking, call qualities, but for distinction, secondary qualities. For the power in fire to produce a new colour, or consistency, in *wax* or *clay*—by its primary qualities, is as much a quality in fire, as the power it has to produce in *me* a new idea or sensation of warmth or burning, which I felt not before—by the same primary qualities, viz. the bulk, texture, and motion of its insensible parts.

The question, then, is how physical objects cause us to have sensations and ideas. Locke's answer (which, like his theory as a whole, is very strongly influenced by the physical theories of his contemporary Isaac Newton) is, by impulse. This might not seem illuminating until you try to think of the Newtonian theory of force as a product of particles and masses in motion. And on this model, Locke develops what is now called his "Causal Theory of Perception." First, for the primary qualities:

> If then external objects be not united to our minds when they produce ideas therein; and yet we perceive these *original* qualities in such of them as singly fall under our senses, it is evident that some motion must be thence continued by our nerves, or animal spirits, by some parts of our bodies, to the brains or the seat of sensation, there to produce in our minds the particular ideas we have of them. And since the extension, figure, number, and motion of bodies of an observable bigness, may be perceived at a distance by the sight, it is evident some singly imperceptible bodies must come from them to the eyes, and thereby convey to the brain some motion; which produces these ideas which we have of them in us.

Then, for secondary qualities:

> After the same manner that the ideas of these original qualities are produced in us, we may conceive that the ideas of *secondary* qualities are also produced, viz. by the operation of insensible particles on our senses. For, it being manifest that there are bodies and good store of bodies, each whereof are so small, that we cannot by any of our senses discover either their bulk, figure, or motion—as is evident in those particles of the air and water, and others extremely smaller than those; perhaps as much smaller than the particles of air and water, as the particles of air and water are smaller than peas or hail-stones;—let us suppose at present that the different motions and figures, bulk and number, of such particles, affecting the several organs of our senses, produce in us those different sensations which we have from the colours and smells of bodies; e.g. that a violet, by the impulse of such insensible particles of matter, of peculiar figures and bulks, and in different degrees and modifications of their motions, causes the ideas of the blue colour, and sweet scent of that flower to be produced in our minds. It being no more impossible to conceive that God should annex such ideas to such motions, with which they have no similitude, than that he should annex the idea of pain to the motion of a piece of steel dividing our flesh, with which that idea hath no resemblance.
> What I have said concerning colours and smells may be understood also of tastes and sounds, and other the like sensible qualities; which, whatever reality we by mistake attribute to them,

are in truth nothing in the objects themselves, but powers to produce various sensations in us; and depend on those primary qualities, viz. bulk, figure, texture, and motion of parts [as I have said.]

Therefore:

> I think it easy to draw this observation—that the ideas of pri-
> mary qualities of bodies are resemblances of them, and their pat-
> terns do really exist in the bodies themselves, but the ideas pro-
> duced in us by these secondary qualities have no resemblance of
> them at all. There is nothing like our ideas, existing in the bodies
> themselves. They are, in the bodies we denominate from them, only
> a power to produce those sensations in us: and what is sweet, blue,
> or warm in idea, is but the certain bulk, figure, and motion of the
> insensible parts, in the bodies themselves, which we call so.
>
> Flame is denominated hot and light; snow, white and cold; and
> manna, white and sweet, from the ideas they produce in us. Which
> qualities are commonly thought to be the same in those bodies
> that those ideas are in us, the one the perfect resemblance of the
> other, as they are in a mirror, and it would by most men be judged
> very extravagant if one should say otherwise. And yet he that will
> consider that the same fire that, at one distance produces in us the
> sensation of warmth, does, at a nearer approach, produce in us
> the far different sensation of pain, ought to bethink himself what
> reason he has to say—that this idea of warmth, which was pro-
> duced in him by fire, is *actually in the fire;* and his idea of pain,
> which the same fire produced in him the same way, is *not* in the
> fire. Why are whiteness and coldness in snow, and pain not, when
> it produces the one and the other idea in us; and can do neither,
> but by the bulk, figure, number, and motion of its solid parts?
>
> The particular bulk, number, figure, and motion of the parts of
> fire or snow are really in them—whether any one's senses perceive
> them or no: and therefore they may be called *real* qualities, be-
> cause they really exist in those bodies. But light, heat, whiteness, or
> coldness, are no more really in them than sickness or pain is in
> manna. Take away the sensation of them; let not the eyes see light
> or colours, nor the ears hear sounds; let the palate not taste, nor
> the nose smell, and all colours, tastes, odours, and sounds, *as they
> are such particular ideas*, vanish and cease, and are reduced to
> their causes, i.e., bulk, figure, and motion of parts.

This is the basic empiricist theory as Locke had it. The logical
consequences of empiricism, as we shall see when we study Berkeley and
Hume, are not nearly so palatable. But how does the "causal theory of
perception" allow Locke to approach the traditional questions of
metaphysics? Significantly, the first two steps in the argument are
identical with those we traced in Descartes—one's own existence and the

existence of God—and Locke even includes the problematic notion of "intuition."

> 1. The knowledge of our own being we have by intuition. The existence of God, reason clearly makes known to us.

But then, the strict empiricist reemerges and insists.

> The knowledge of the existence of *any other thing* we can have only by *sensation*: for there being no necessary connexion of real existence with any *idea* a man hath in his memory; nor of any other existence but that of God with the existence of any particular man: no particular man can know the existence of any other being, but only when, by actual operating upon him, it makes itself perceived by him. For, the having the idea of anything in our mind, no more proves the existence of that thing, than the picture of a man evidences his being in the world, or the visions of a dream make thereby a true history.
>
> 2. It is therefore the *actual receiving* of ideas from without that gives us notice of the existence of other things, and makes us know, that something doth exist at that time without us, which causes that idea in us; though perhaps we neither know nor consider how it does it. For it takes not from the certainty of our senses, and the ideas we receive by them, that we know not the manner wherein they are produced: e.g. whilst I write this, I have, by the paper affecting my eyes, that idea produced in my mind, which, whatever object causes, I call *white*; by which I know that that quality or accident (i.e. whose appearance before my eyes always causes that idea) doth really exist, and hath a being without me. And of this, the greatest assurance I can possibly have, and to which my faculties can attain, is the testimony of my eyes, which are the proper and sole judges of this thing; whose testimony I have reason to rely on as so certain, that I can no more doubt, whilst I write this, that I see white and black, and that something really exists that causes that sensation in me, than that I write or move my hand; which is a certainty as great as human nature is capable of, concerning the existence of anything, but a man's self alone, and of God.

And here Locke asserts his alternative to the strict Cartesian limitation of knowledge to matters of certainty and deduction:

> 3. The notice we have by our senses of the existing of things without us, though it be not altogether so certain as our intuitive knowledge, or the deductions of our reason employed about the clear abstract ideas of our own minds; yet it is an assurance that deserves the name of *knowledge*. If we persuade ourselves that our

faculties act and inform us right concerning the existence of those objects that affect them, it cannot pass for an ill-grounded confidence: for I think nobody can, in earnest, be so sceptical as to be uncertain of the existence of those things which he sees and feels. At least, he that can doubt so far, (whatever he may have with his own thoughts,) will never have any controversy with me; since he can never be sure I say anything contrary to his own opinion. As to myself, I think God has given me assurance enough of the existence of things without me: since, by their different application, I can produce in myself both pleasure and pain, which is one great concernment of my present state. This is certain: the confidence that our faculties do not herein deceive us, is the greatest assurance we are capable of concerning the existence of material beings. For we cannot act anything but by our faculties; nor talk of knowledge itself, but by the help of those faculties which are fitted to apprehend even what knowledge is.

Experience has its own supports:

> . . . besides the assurance we have from our senses themselves, that they do not err in the information they give us of the existence of things without us, when they are affected by them, we are further confirmed in this assurance by other concurrent reasons:—
>
> 4. It is plain those perceptions are produced in us by exterior causes affecting our senses: because those that want the *organs* of any sense, never can have the ideas belonging to that sense produced in their minds. This is too evident to be doubted: and therefore we cannot but be assured that they come in by the organs of that sense, and no other way. The organs themselves, it is plain, do not produce them: for then the eyes of a man in the dark would produce colours, and his nose smell roses in the winter: but we see nobody gets the relish of a pineapple, till he goes to the Indies, where it is, and tastes it.
>
> 5. II. Because sometimes I find that *I cannot avoid having those ideas produced in my mind.* For though, when my eyes are shut, or windows fast, I can at pleasure recall to my mind the ideas of light, or the sun, which former sensations had lodged into my memory; so I can at pleasure lay by *that* idea, and take into my view that of the smell of a rose, or taste of sugar. But, if I turn my eyes at noon towards the sun, I cannot avoid the ideas which the light or sun then produces in me. So that there is a manifest difference between the ideas laid up in my memory, (over which, if they were there only, I should have constantly the same power to dispose of them and lay them by at pleasure,) and those which force themselves upon me, and I cannot avoid having. And therefore it must needs be some exterior cause, and the brisk acting of some objects without me, whose efficacy I cannot resist, that produces those ideas in my mind, whether I will or no. Besides,

there is nobody who doth not perceive the difference in himself between contemplating the sun, as he hath the idea of it in his memory, and actually looking upon it: of which two, his perception is so distinct, that few of his ideas are more distinguishable one from another. And therefore he hath certain knowledge that they are not *both* memory, or the actions of his mind, and fancies only within him; but that actual seeing hath a cause without.

6. III. Add to this, that many of those ideas are *produced in us with pain*, which afterwards we remember without the least offence. Thus, the pain of heat or cold, when the idea of it is revived in our minds, gives us no disturbance; which, when felt, was very troublesome; and is again, when actually repeated: which is occasioned by the disorder the external object causes in our bodies when applied to them: and we remember the pains of hunger, thirst, or the headache, without any pain at all; which would either never disturb us, or else constantly do it, as often as we thought of it, were there nothing more but ideas floating in our minds, and appearance entertaining our fancies, without the real existence of things affecting us from abroad. The same may be said of *pleasure*, accompanying several actual sensations. And though mathematical demonstration depends not upon sense, yet the examining them by diagrams gives great credit to the evidence of our sight, and seems to give it a certainty approaching to that of demonstration itself. For, it would be very strange, that a man should allow it for an undeniable truth, that two angles of a figure, which he measures by lines and angles of a diagram, should be bigger one than the other, and yet doubt of the existence of those lines and angles, which by looking on he makes use of to measure that by.

7. IV. Our *senses* in many cases *bear witness to the truth of each other's report*, concerning the existence of sensible things without us. He that *sees* a fire, may, if he doubt whether it be anything more than a bare fancy, feel it too; and be convinced, by putting his hand in it. Which certainly could never be put into such exquisite pain by a bare idea or phantom, unless that the pain be a fancy too: which yet he cannot, when the burn is well, by raising the idea of it, bring upon himself again.

Thus I see, whilst I write this, I can change the appearance of the paper; and by designing the letters, tell *beforehand* what new idea it shall exhibit the very next moment, by barely drawing my pen over it: which will neither appear (let me fancy as much as I will) if my hands stand still; or though I move my pen, if my eyes be shut: nor, when those characters are once made on the paper, can I choose afterwards but see them as they are; that is, have the ideas of such letters as I have made. Whence it is manifest, that they are not barely the sport and play of my own imagination, when I find that the characters that were made at the pleasure of my own thoughts, do not obey them; nor yet cease to be, whenever I shall fancy it, but continue to affect my senses constantly and regularly, according to the figures I made them. To which if we will add, that the sight of those shall, from another man, draw such sounds as I beforehand design they shall stand for, there will be little reason left to doubt that those words I write do really exist without me, when they cause a long series of regular sounds to affect my ears, which could not be the effect of my imagination nor could my memory retain them in that order.

8. But yet, if after all this any one will be so sceptical as to distrust his senses, and to affirm all that we see and hear, feel and taste, think and do, during our whole being, is but the series and deluding appearance of a long dream, whereof there is no reality; and therefore will question the existence of all things, or our knowledge of anything: I must desire him to consider, that, if all be a dream, then he doth but dream that he makes the question, and so it is not much matter that a waking man should answer him. But yet, if he pleases, he may dream that I make him this answer, that the certainty of things existing in *rerum natura* when we have the testimony of our senses for it is not only as great as our frame can attain to, but as our condition needs. For, our faculties being suited not to the full extent of being, nor to a perfect, clear, comprehensive knowledge of things free from all doubt and scruple; but to the preservation of us, in whom they are; and accommodated to the use of life: they serve to our purpose well enough, if they will but give us certain notice of those things, which are convenient or inconvenient to us. For he that sees a candle burning, and hath experimented the force of its flame by putting his finger in it, will little doubt that this is something existing without him, which does him harm, and puts him to great pain: which is assurance enough, when no man requires greater certainty to govern his actions by than what is as certain as his actions themselves. And if our dreamer pleases to try whether the glowing heat of a glass furnace be barely a wandering imagination in a drowsy man's fancy, by putting his hand into it, he may perhaps be wakened into a certainty greater than he could wish, that it is something more than bare imagination. So that this evidence is as great as we can desire, being as certain to us as our pleasure or pain, i.e., happiness or misery; beyond which we have no concernment, either of knowing or being. Such an assurance of the existence of things without us is sufficient to direct us in the attaining the good and avoiding the evil which is caused by them, which is the important concernment we have of being made acquainted with them.

9. In summary, then, when our senses do actually convey into our understanding any idea, we cannot but be satisfied that there doth something *at that time* really exist without us, which doth affect our senses, and by them give notice of itself to our apprehensive faculties, and actually produce that idea which we then perceive.

We are now ready to return to the traditional metaphysical notion of substance—that which underlies both the primary and the secondary qualities of a thing.

1. *Ideas of Substances, how made.*—The mind being, as I have declared, furnished with a great number of the simple ideas conveyed in by the senses, as they are found in exterior things, or by reflection on its own operations, takes notice, also, that a certain number of these simple ideas go constantly together; which being presumed to belong to one thing, and words being suited to common apprehensions, and made use of for quick dispatch, are called, so united in one subject, by one name; which, by inadvertency, we are apt afterward to talk of and consider as one simple idea, which indeed is a complication of many ideas together: because, as I have said, not imagining how these simple ideas can subsist by themselves, we accustom ourselves to suppose some substratum wherein they do subsist, and from which they do result; which therefore we call "substance."

2. *Our Ideas of Substance in general.*—So that if anyone will examine himself concerning his notion of pure substance in general, he will find he has no other idea of it at all, but only a supposition of he knows not what support of such qualities which are capable of producing simple ideas in us; which qualities are commonly called "accidents." If anyone should be asked, "What is the subject wherein colour or weight inheres?" he would have nothing to say but, "The solid extended parts." And if he were demanded, "what is it that solidity and extension inhere in?" he would not be in a much better case than the Indian . . . who, saying that the world was supported by a great elephant, was asked what the elephant rested on? to which his answer was, "a great tortoise"; but being again pressed to know what gave support to the broad-backed tortoise, replied—something, he knew not what. And thus here, as in all other cases where we use words without having clear and distinct ideas, we talk like children, who, being questioned what such a thing is which they know not, readily give this satisfactory answer, that it is something, which in truth signifies no more, when so used, either by children or men, but that they know not what; and that the thing they pretend to know and talk of is what they have no distinct idea of at all, and so are perfectly ignorant of it, and in the dark. The idea, then, we have, to which we give the general name "substance" being nothing but the supposed, but unknown, support of those qualities we find existing, which we imagine cannot subsist *sine re substante*, "without something to support them," we call that support *substantia*; which, according to the true import of the word, is, in plain English, "standing under," or "upholding."

. . . .

Hence, when we talk or think of any particular sort of corporeal substances, as horse, stone, &c., though the idea we have of either of them be but the complication or collection of those several simple ideas of sensible qualities which we used to find united in the thing called "horse" or "stone"; yet because we cannot conceive how they should subsist alone, nor one in another, we suppose

> them existing in, and supported by some common subject; which
> support we denote by the name "substance," though it be certain
> we have no clear or distinct idea of that thing we suppose a
> support.

Substance is "we know not what." Yet Locke hesitates to reject the
notions, for he cannot escape the suspicion that talk of "qualities" makes
no sense unless the qualities are the qualities of something. But this
suspicion is dispensable according to Locke's own principles. And so,
it turns out, is his central distinction between primary and secondary
qualities, as Bishop Berkeley is soon to point out. And the consequence of these simple, technical moves will be shocking, to say the
least.

D. COMMON SENSE UNDONE: BISHOP BERKELEY

Beginning from John Locke's common-sense philosophy, Bishop Berkeley developed the most provocative thesis in all philosophy. Berkeley's
thesis is called **subjective idealism.** It is the doctrine that there are no
material substances, no physical objects, only minds and ideas in mind.
(His concept of "idea" comes directly from Locke.) This surprising
position emerges directly from Locke's thesis by three simple steps.
First, it accepts the argument that we have no idea whatsoever what a
substance might be, and it agrees that all that we can ever know of a thing
are its sensible properties (or "qualities"). Second, it is shown that the
distinction between primary and secondary qualities cannot be, as Locke
had argued, a distinction between properties inherent in the objects
themselves as opposed to properties which the objects simply cause in
us. And third, once one has agreed that all knowledge of the world (except
for knowledge of one's own existence and of God) must be based upon
experience, the question becomes why we should ever think that there is
anything other than our experiences. Locke had argued that our
experiences were caused by the physical objects; but how could this
claim be justified by experience? Since we have no experience of either
the objects themselves or their causation, but only of their effects (that
is, the ideas they cause in us) a consistent empiricist must give up not
only the causal theory of perception but the notion of physical objects as
well.

   Berkeley is an exceptionally clear writer, and the following excerpts
from his *Treatise Concerning the Principles of Human Knowledge*
(1710) should not be difficult to understand:

◆ from *Treatise Concerning the Principles of Human Knowledge,* by Bishop George Berkeley

1. It is evident to anyone who takes a survey of the objects of human knowledge, that they are either ideas (1) actually imprinted on the senses, or else such as are (2) perceived by attending to the passions and operations of the mind, or lastly (3) ideas formed by help of memory and imagination, either compounding, dividing, or barely representing those originally perceived in the aforesaid ways. By sight I have the ideas of lights and colors, with their several degrees and variations. By touch I perceive hard and soft, heat and cold, motion and resistance, and of all these more and less either as to quantity or degree. Smelling furnishes me with odors, the palate with tastes, and hearing conveys sounds to the mind in all their variety of tone and composition. And as several of these are observed to accompany each other, they come to be marked by one name, and so to be reputed as one thing. Thus, for example, a certain color, taste, smell, figure, and consistence, having been observed to go together, are accounted one distinct thing, signified by the name "apple." Other collections of ideas constitute a stone, a tree, a book, and the like sensible things; which, as they are pleasing or disagreeable, excite the passions of love, hatred, joy, grief, and so forth.

2. But besides all that endless variety of ideas or objects of knowledge, there is likewise something which knows or perceives them, and exercises divers operations, as willing, imagining, remembering, about them. This perceiving, active being is what I call *mind, spirit, soul,* or *myself.* By which words I do not denote any one of my ideas, but a thing entirely distinct from them wherein they exist, or, which is the same thing, whereby they are perceived, for the existence of an idea consists in being perceived.

3. That neither our thoughts, nor passions, nor ideas formed by the imagination, exist without the mind, is what everybody will allow. And it seems no less evident that the various sensations or ideas imprinted on the sense, however blended or combined together (that is, whatever objects they compose), cannot exist otherwise than in a mind perceiving them. I think an intuitive knowledge may be obtained of this by anyone that shall attend to what is meant by the term "exist" when applied to sensible things. The table I write on I say exists—that is, I see and feel it; and if I were out of my study I should say it existed—meaning thereby that if I was in my study I might perceive it, or that some other spirit actually does perceive it. There was an odor, that is, it was smelt; there was a sound, that is, it was heard; a color or figure, and it was perceived by sight or touch. This is all that I can understand by these and the like expressions. For as to what is said of the ab-

solute existence of unthinking things without any relation to their being perceived, that seems perfectly unintelligible. Their *esse* is *percipi*,[9] nor is it possible they should have any existence out of the minds or thinking things which perceive them.

4. It is indeed an opinion strangely prevailing amongst men, that houses, mountains, rivers, and in a word all sensible objects, have an existence, natural or real, distinct from their being perceived by the understanding. But with how great an assurance and acquiescence so ever this principle may be entertained in the world, yet whoever shall find in his heart to call it in question may, if I mistake not, perceive it to involve a manifest contradiction. For what are the forementioned objects but the things we perceive by sense? And what do we perceive *besides our own ideas or sensations?* And is it not plainly repugnant that any one of these, or any combination of them, should exist unperceived?

This is Berkeley's central thesis—that "to be is to be perceived" (*esse est percipi*). In what follows, Berkeley argues that there is nothing other than these perceptions, or "ideas," and it is nonsense to suppose that there are things outside of the mind "like" our ideas—for "nothing is like an idea but another idea."

6. Some truths there are so near and obvious to the mind that a man need only open his eyes to see them. Such I take this important one to be, to wit, that all the choir of heaven and furniture of the earth, in a word all those bodies which compose the mighty frame of the world, have not any subsistence without a mind, that their *being* is to be perceived or known; that consequently so long as they are not actually perceived by me, or do not exist in my mind or that of any other created spirit, they must either have no existence at all, or else subsist in the mind of some Eternal Spirit; it being perfectly unintelligible, and involving all the absurdity of abstraction, to attribute to any single part of them an existence independent of a spirit. To be convinced of which, the reader need only reflect and try to separate in his own thoughts the *being* of a sensible thing from its *being perceived.*

7. From what has been said it follows there is not any other substance than *spirit*, or that which perceives. But for the fuller proof of this point, let it be considered the sensible qualities are color, figure, motion, smell, taste, etc.—that is, the ideas perceived by sense. Now, for an idea to exist in an unperceiving thing is a manifest contradiction, for to have an idea is all one as to perceive; that therefore wherein color, figure, and the like qualities exist must perceive them; hence it is clear there can be no unthinking substance or *substratum* of those ideas.

8. But, say you, though the ideas themselves do not exist without the mind, yet there may be things *like* them, whereof they are

[9]*To be is to be perceived.*

copies or resemblances, which things exist without the mind in an unthinking substance. I answer, an idea can be like nothing but an idea; a color or figure can be like nothing but another color or figure. If we look but never so little into our thoughts, we shall find it impossible for us to conceive a likeness except only between our ideas. Again, I ask whether those supposed originals or external things, of which our ideas are the pictures or representations, be themselves perceivable or no? If they are, then they are ideas and we have gained our point; but if you say they are not, I appeal to anyone whether it be sense to assert a color is like something which is invisible, hard or soft, like something which is intangible; and so of the rest.

At this point Berkeley takes up Locke's distinction between "primary and secondary qualities," and maintains that the arguments Locke put forward regarding the latter also can be applied to the former. Primary qualities too can be ideas only, and not properties of matter.

9. Some there are who make a distinction betwixt *primary* and *secondary* qualities. By the former they mean extension, figure, motion, rest, solidity or impenetrability, and number; by the latter they denote all other sensible qualities, as colors, sounds, tastes, and so forth. The ideas we have of these they acknowledge not to be the resemblances of anything existing without the mind, or unperceived, but they will have our ideas of the primary qualities to be patterns or images of things which exist without the mind, in an unthinking substance which they call *matter*. By *matter*, therefore, we are to understand an inert, senseless substance, in which extension, figure, and motion do actually subsist. But it is evident from what we have already shown, that extension, figure, and motion are only ideas existing in the mind, and that an idea can be like nothing but another idea, and that consequently neither they nor their archetypes can exist in an unperceiving substance. Hence, it is plain that the very notion of what is called *matter*, or *corporeal substance*, involves a contradiction in it.

10. They who assert that figure, motion, and the rest of the primary or original qualities do exist without the mind in unthinking substances, do at the same time acknowledge that color, sounds, heat, cold, and suchlike secondary qualities, do not; which they tell us are sensations existing in the mind alone, that depend on and are occasioned by the different size, texture, and motion of the minute particles of matter. This they take for an undoubted truth, which they can demonstrate beyond all exception. Now, if it be certain that those original qualities are inseparably united with the other sensible qualities, and not, even in thought, capable of being abstracted from them, it plainly follows that they exist only in the mind. But I desire anyone to reflect and try whether he can, by any abstraction of thought, conceive the extension and motion of

a body without all other possible sensible qualities. For my own part, I see evidently that it is not in my power to frame an idea of a body extended and moving, but I must withal give it some color or other sensible quality which is acknowledged to exist only in the mind. In short, extension, figure, and motion, abstracted from all other qualities, are inconceivable. Where therefore the other sensible qualities are, there must be these also, to wit, in the mind and nowhere else. . . .

14. I shall farther add that, after the same manner as modern philosophers prove certain sensible qualities to have no existence in matter, or without the mind, the same thing may be likewise proved of all other sensible qualities whatsoever. Thus, for instance, it is said that heat and cold are affections only of the mind, and not at all patterns of real beings, existing in the corporeal substances which excite them, for that the same body which appears cold to one hand seems warm to another. Now, why may we not as well argue that figure and extension are not patterns or resemblances of qualities existing in matter, because to the same eye at different stations, or eyes of a different texture at the same station, they appear various, and cannot therefor be the images of anything settled and determinate without the mind? Again, it is proved that sweetness is not really in the sapid thing, because the thing remaining unaltered the sweetness is changed into bitter, as in case of a fever or otherwise vitiated palate. Is it not as reasonable to say that motion is not without the mind, since if the succession of ideas in the mind become swifter, the motion, it is acknowledged, shall appear slower without any alteration in any external object?

15. In short, let anyone consider those arguments which are thought manifestly to prove that colors and taste exist only in the mind, and he shall find they may with equal force be brought to prove the same thing of extension, figure, and motion—though it must be confessed this method of arguing does not so much prove that there is no extension or color in an outward object, as that we do not know by sense which is the true extension or color of the object. But the arguments foregoing plainly show it to be impossible that any color or extension at all, or other sensible quality whatsoever, should exist in an unthinking subject without the mind, or in truth, that there should be any such thing as an outward object.

Must there be substances apart from the mind? Berkeley asks. It is true that we are somehow "affected," but it does not follow that there must be material objects. How would we know of any such objects?

18. But though it were possible that solid, figured, movable substances may exist without the mind, corresponding to the ideas we have of bodies, yet how is it possible for us to know this? Either

we must know it by sense or by reason. As for our senses, by them we have the knowledge only of our sensations, ideas, or those things that are immediately perceived by sense, call them what you will; but they do not inform us that things exist without the mind, or unperceived, like to those which are perceived. This the materialists[10] themselves acknowledge. It remains therefore that if we have any knowledge at all of external things, it must be by reason, inferring their existence from what is immediately perceived by sense. But what reason can induce us to believe the existence of bodies without the mind, from what we perceive, since the very patrons of matter themselves do not pretend there is any necessary connection betwixt them and our ideas? I say it is granted on all hands (and what happens in dreams, frenzies, and the like, puts it beyond dispute) that *it is possible we might be affected with all the ideas we have now, though there were no bodies existing without, resembling them.* Hence, it is evident the supposition of external bodies is not necessary for the producing our ideas; since it is granted they are produced sometimes, and might possibly be produced always in the same order we see them in at present, without their concurrence.

19. But, though we might possibly have all our sensations without them, yet perhaps it may be thought easier to conceive and explain the manner of their production by supposing external bodies in their likeness rather than otherwise; and so it might be at least probable there are such things as bodies that excite their ideas in our minds. But neither can this be said; for though we give the materialists their external bodies, they by their own confession are never the nearer knowing how our ideas are produced, since they own themselves unable to comprehend in what manner body can act upon spirit, or how it is possible it should imprint any idea in the mind. Hence it is evident the production of ideas or sensations in our minds can be no reason why we should suppose matter or corporeal substances, since that is acknowledged to remain equally inexplicable with or without this supposition. If therefore it were possible for bodies to exist without the mind, yet to hold they do so, must needs be a very precarious opinion; since it is to suppose, without any reason at all, that God has created innumerable things that are entirely useless, and serve to no manner of purpose.

20. In short, if there were external bodies, it is impossible we should ever come to know it; and if there were not, we might have the very same reasons to think there were that we have now. Suppose (what no one can deny possible) an intelligence without the help of external bodies, to be affected with the same train of sensations or ideas that you are, imprinted in the same order and with like vividness in his mind. I ask whether that intelligence hath

---

[10]Berkeley uses "materialists" to refer to those who believe in the existence of matter, not to those who believe in only matter, its usual meaning.

not all the reason to believe the existence of corporeal substances, represented by his ideas, and exciting them in his mind, that you can possibly have for believing the same thing? Of this there can be no question; which one consideration were enough to make any reasonable person suspect the strength of whatever argument he may think himself to have for the existence of bodies without the mind. . . .

23. But, say you, surely there is nothing easier than for me to imagine trees, for instance, in a park, or books existing in a closet, and nobody by to perceive them. I answer, you may so, there is no difficulty in it; but what is all this, I beseech you, more than framing in your mind certain ideas which you call books and trees, and the same time omitting to frame the idea of anyone that may perceive them? But do not you yourself perceive or think of them all the while? This therefore is nothing to the purpose; it only shews you have the power of imagining or forming ideas in your mind: but it doth not shew that you can conceive it possible the objects of your thought may exist without the mind. To make out this, it is necessary that you conceive them existing unconceived or unthought of, which is a manifest repugnancy. When we do our utmost to conceive the existence of external bodies, we are all the while only contemplating our own ideas.[11]

But what, then, can explain the fact that we cannot simply "think" things into existence by imagining them? And how can we say that a thing exists when no one is there to perceive it? ("If a tree falls in the forest, and there's no one there to hear it, does it make a sound?") It is here that God enters the picture as a matter of necessity.

29. But, whatever power I may have over my own thoughts, I find the ideas actually perceived by Sense have not a like dependence on my will. When in broad daylight I open my eyes, it is not in my power to choose whether I shall see or no, or to determine what particular objects shall present themselves to my view; and so likewise as to the hearing and other senses, the ideas imprinted on them are not creatures of my will. There is therefore some *other* Will or Spirit that produces them.

30. The ideas of Sense are more strong, lively, and distinct than those of the Imagination; they have likewise a steadiness, order, and coherence, and are not excited at random, as those which are the effects of human wills often are, but in a regular train or series—the admirable connexion whereof sufficiently testifies the wisdom and benevolence of its Author. Now the set rules or established methods wherein the Mind we depend on excites in us the ideas of sense, are called the *laws of nature*; and these we learn by experience, which teaches us that such and such ideas are

[11] George Berkeley, *Treatise Concerning the Principles of Human Knowledge* (New York: Bobbs-Merrill, 1957).

attended with such and such other ideas, in the ordinary course of things.

31. This gives us a sort of foresight which enables us to regulate our actions for the benefit of life. And without this we should be eternally at a loss; we could not know how to act anything that might procure us the least pleasure, or remove the least pain of sense. That food nourishes, sleep refreshes, and fire warms us; that to sow in the seedtime is the way to reap in the harvest; and in general that to obtain such or such ends, such or such means are conducive—all this we know, not by discovering any *necessary connexion* between our ideas, but only by the *observation* of the settled laws of nature, without which we should be all in uncertainty and confusion, and a grown man no more know how to manage himself in the affairs of life than an infant just born. . . .

33. The ideas imprinted on the senses by the Author of nature are called *real things*; and those excited in the imagination, being less regular, vivid, and constant, are more properly termed *ideas*, or *images* of *things*, which they copy and represent. But then our sensations, be they never so vivid and distinct, are nevertheless ideas, that is, they exist in the mind, or are perceived by it, as truly as the ideas of its own framing. The ideas of sense are allowed to have more reality in them, that is, to be more strong, orderly, and coherent than the creatures of the mind; but this is no argument that they exist without the mind. They are also less dependent on the spirit, or thinking substance which perceives them, in that they are excited by the will of another and more powerful spirit; yet still they are *ideas*, and certainly no idea, whether faint or strong, can exist otherwise than in a mind perceiving it.[12]

> There was a young man who said, "God
> Must think it exceedingly odd
>   If he finds that this tree
>   Continues to be
> When there's no one about in the Quad."

> REPLY

> Dear Sir:
>   Your astonishment's odd:
> I am always about in the Quad.
>   And that's why the tree
>   Will continue to be,
> Since observed by
>   *Yours faithfully,*
>   GOD.

[12]This final formulation, that the things of the world are nothing other than ideas in the mind of God, is the subject of a limerick by Ronald Knox, quoted for us by Bertrand Russell.

And finally, the defense against common sense:

> 38. But after all, say you, it sounds very harsh to say we eat and drink ideas, and are clothed with ideas. I acknowledge it does so; the word "idea" not being used in common discourse to signify the several combinations of sensible qualities which are called "things"; and it is certain that any expression which varies from the familiar use of language will seem harsh and ridiculous. But this doth not concern the truth of the proposition, which in other words is no more than to say, we are fed and clothed with those things which we perceive immediately by our senses.
>
> 39. If it be demanded why I make use of the word "idea," and do not rather in compliance with custom call them "thing"; I answer, I do it for two reasons—first, because the term "thing" in contradistinction to "idea," is generally supposed to denote somewhat existing without the mind; secondly, because "thing" hath a more comprehensive signification than "idea," including spirit or thinking things as well as ideas. Since therefore the objects of sense exist only in the mind, and are withal thoughtless and inactive, I chose to mark them by the word "idea," which implies those properties.[13]

Is this where Locke was leading us? If so, it looks as if the "new metaphysics" is every bit as fantastic as the old ones. But the controversial development of Locke's empiricism has still another step to go.

E. THE CONGENIAL SKEPTIC: DAVID HUME

It isn't very far from Berkeley's subjective idealism to David Hume's outrageous, but seemingly irrefutable, skepticism. Russell, writing about Hume two hundred years later (1945), says

> To refute him has been, ever since he wrote, a favorite pastime among metaphysicians. For my part, I find none of their refutations convincing; nevertheless, I cannot but hope that something less skeptical than Hume's system may be discoverable.

And

> Hume's skeptical conclusions . . . are equally difficult to refute and to accept. The result was a challenge to philosophers, which, in my opinion, has still not been adequately met.[14]

---

[13]Berkeley, *Treatise Concerning the Principles of Human Knowledge.*
[14]Bertrand Russell, *A History of Western Philosophy* (New York: Simon and Schuster, 1945).

There have been philosophers who have said—or feared—that Hume's skepticism is the last word in philosophy. But in any case, it is one of those positions that no philosophy student can avoid taking seriously.

Hume's *Treatise of Human Nature* (1739) was written when he was in his early twenties; his ambition was no less than to be the Isaac Newton of philosophy and psychology, following but outdoing John Locke. The book failed to attract much attention (he said "it fell stillborn from the press"), and Hume turned his attention to other matters, making himself famous as a historian. Later, in 1748, he wrote a more popular version of his earlier *Treatise*, which he called *An Enquiry Concerning Human Understanding*. It was extremely successful, and Hume became widely known as a "devil's advocate" during his lifetime, a position he generally enjoyed. Both the *Treatise* and the *Enquiry* are firmly committed to Locke's empiricist methodology, but where Locke was generous with doubtful ideas with no clear experiential basis (notably, substance and God), Hume was ruthless. In a famous threatening passage, he had bellowed

> When we run over libraries, persuaded of these [empiricist] principles, what havoc must we make? If we take in our hand any volume of divinity or school metaphysics, for instance, let us ask, Does it contain any abstract reasoning concerning quantity or number? No. Does it contain any experimental reasoning concerning matter of fact and existence? No, Commit it to the flames, for it can contain nothing but sophistry and illusion.[15]

In this unveiled threat to traditional metaphysics we can see in a glance Hume's formidable tactics—the insistence that every justifiable belief must be either a "relation of ideas," for example, a statement of mathematics, logic, or a trivial conceptual truth, or a "matter of fact," which can be confirmed by appeal to our experience. (This "either-or" is sometimes called "Hume's fork.") Of course, most of the modern philosophers we have discussed shared this insistence upon justifiability either by reason ("relation of ideas") or by experience. But it is only Hume who realizes the severity of this demand and the embarrassing number of our fundamental beliefs that do not allow justification either by reason or experience.

Like his empiricist predecessor, Hume insists that all knowledge begins with basic units of sensory experience. Hume's "impressions" (Locke's "sensations") are these basic units (what we would still call "sensations" or "sense-data").

---

[15]David Hume, *An Enquiry Concerning Human Understanding*, 2nd ed., ed. L. A. Selby-Bigge (Oxford: Oxford University Press, 1902). All subsequent quotations from Hume's *Enquiry* are from this edition unless otherwise noted.

◆ from *A Treatise of Human Nature*, by David Hume

All the perceptions of the human mind resolve themselves into two distinct kinds, which I shall call **impressions** and **ideas**. The difference betwixt these consists in the degrees of force and liveliness with which they strike upon the mind, and make their way into our thought or consciousness. Those perceptions, which enter with most force and violence, we may name *impressions*; and under this name I comprehend all our sensations, passions and emotions, as they make their first appearance in the soul. By *ideas* I mean the faint images of these in thinking and reasoning; such as, for instance, are all the perceptions excited by the present discourse, excepting only, those which arise from the sight and touch, and excepting the immediate pleasure or uneasiness it may occasion. I believe it will not be very necessary to employ many words in explaining this distinction. Every one of himself will readily perceive the difference betwixt feeling and thinking. The common degrees of these are easily distinguished; tho' it is not impossible but in particular instances they may very nearly approach to each other. Thus in sleep, in a fever, in madness, or in any very violent emotions of soul, our ideas may approach to our impressions: As on the other hand it sometimes happens, that our impressions are so faint and low, that we cannot distinguish them from our ideas. But notwithstanding this near resemblance in a few instances, they are in general so very different, that no-one can make a scruple to rank them under distinct heads, and assign to each a peculiar name to mark the difference.

There is another division of our perceptions, which it will be convenient to observe, and which extends itself both to our impressions and ideas. This division is into **simple** and **complex**. Simple perceptions or impressions and ideas are such as admit of no distinction nor separation. The complex are the contrary to these, and may be distinguished into parts. Tho' a particular colour, taste, and smell are qualities all united together in this apple, 'tis easy to perceive they are not the same, but are at least distinguishable from each other.

Having by these divisions given an order and arrangement to our objects, we may now apply ourselves to consider with the more accuracy their qualities and relations. The first circumstance, that strikes my eye, is the great resemblance betwixt our impressions and ideas in every other particular, except their degree of force and vivacity. The one seem to be in a manner the reflexion of the other; so that all the perceptions of the mind are double, and appear both as impressions and ideas. When I shut my eyes and think of my chamber, the ideas I form are exact representations of the impressions I felt, nor is there any circumstance of the one, which is not to be found in the other. In running over my other perceptions, I find still the same resemblance and representation. Ideas and impressions appear always to correspond to each other. This circumstance seems to me remarkable, and engages my attention for a moment.

Upon a more accurate survey I find I have been carried away too far by the first appearance, and that I must make use of the distinction of perceptions into *simple and complex*, to limit this general decision, *that all our ideas and impressions are resembling*. I observe, that many of our complex ideas never had impressions, that corresponded to them, and that many of our complex impressions never are exactly copied in ideas. I can imagine to myself such a city as the *New Jerusalem*, whose pavement is gold and walls are rubies, tho' I never saw any such. I have seen *Paris*; but shall I affirm I can form such an idea of that city, as will perfectly represent all its streets and houses in their real and just proportions?

I perceive, therefore, that tho' there is in general a great resemblance betwixt our *complex* impressions and ideas, yet the rule is not universally true, that they are exact copies of each other. We may next consider how the case stands with our *simple* perceptions. After the most accurate examination, of which I am capable, I venture to affirm, that the rule here holds without any exception, and that every simple idea has a simple impression, which resembles it; and every simple impression a correspondent idea. That idea of red, which we form in the dark, and that impression, which strikes our eyes in sun-shine, differ only in degree, not in nature. That the case is the same with all our simple impressions and ideas, 'tis impossible to prove by a particular enumeration of them. Every one may satisfy himself in this point by running over as many as he pleases. But if any one should deny this universal resemblance, I know of no way of convincing him, but by desiring him to show a simple impression that has not a correspondent idea, or a simple idea, that has not a correspondent impression. If he does not answer this challenge, as 'tis certain he cannot, we may from his silence and our own observation establish our conclusion.

Thus we find, that all simple ideas and impressions resemble each other; and as the complex are formed from them, we may affirm in general, that these two species of perception are exactly correspondent. Having discover'd this relation, which requires no farther examination, I am curious to find some other of their qualities. Let us consider how they stand with regard to their existence, and which of the impressions and ideas are causes, and which effects.

The *full* examination of this question is the subject of the present treatise; and therefore we shall here content ourselves with establishing one general proposition. *That all our simple ideas in their first appearance are deriv'd from simple impres-*

> sions, which are correspondent to them, and which they exactly
> represent.[16]

According to Hume, simple ideas are derived from simple impressions. A simple idea would be something like a red, round image; the
simple impression would be seeing a red, round image. More complex
ideas, for example, the idea of an apple, are complex arrangements and
associations of simple ideas. To justify a belief as knowledge, therefore,
we must break up its complex ideas into simple ideas and then find the
impressions upon which those ideas are based. If I claim to see an apple,
for example, I analyze my experience; my idea that there is an apple out
there depends upon my seeing several red, round images from different
angles, feeling something smooth, tasting something fruity and tart,
and so on. If I claim that there are objects of a certain kind (apples,
for example), I must identify the simple ideas and impressions upon
which my supposed knowledge is based. And if I make a metaphysical
claim, about the existence of God or substances, I must either be
preapproved to identify the ideas and impressions upon which such a
claim is based, or I must show that it is nothing other than a "relation of
ideas"; otherwise, the claim cannot be justified ("commit it to the
flames").

But, to the embarrassment of most metaphysical doctrines, they
cannot be defended by either of the methods allowed by Hume. They are,
by their very nature, about things beyond everyday experience (for
example, God, substance) and so are not based upon "impression"; nor
are they "relations of ideas" that can be demonstrated by a simple logical
or mathematical proof. Therefore, they cannot be justified. The problem,
however, is that the same argument extends far beyond the debatable
claims of metaphysics and undermines some of the beliefs that are most
essential to our everyday experiences as well.

In Hume's philosophy, three such beliefs in particular are singled out
for analysis. On the one hand, they are so fundamental to our daily
experience and common knowledge that no sane man or woman could
possibly doubt them; but, on the other hand, they are completely without
justification. As Hume argues, first, there is our idea of **causation** (or
causality), of one event bringing about or causing another event.

From this idea, which provides what Hume calls "the strongest
connections" of our experience and, elsewhere, "the cement of the
universe," we derive a most important principle, the **principle of
universal causation**, which states that every event has its cause (or
causes). It is evident that we invoke such a principle every time we explain
anything; for example, the car won't start. We search for the cause, but
everything seems to check out—the carburetor, the electrical system,

[16]David Hume, *A Treatise of Human Nature*, ed. L. A. Selby-Bigge (Oxford: Oxford
University Press, 1888).

and so on. Now we might search for hours without finding the cause, but there is one thing that we know for certain, and that is that there must be a cause somewhere—even if it is a very complex cause. What is not possible is that there be no cause. Presupposed in our everyday thinking is this principle, that every event has its cause. (You may recognize this principle as a version of Leibniz's Principle of Sufficient Reason, but substituting the more Newtonian notion of "cause" for the notion of "reason.")

Second, because of our presupposed belief in causation and its universal applicability, we are able to think beyond our immediate "ideas" and predict the future and explain the past. But to do so, we must also believe that our observations of the present will have some relevance in the future, that we can in fact draw valid inductive generalizations from our experience. Of course, we do so all of the time; for example, when I wake up at 6:00 in the morning, I expect the sun to rise within the hour. Why? Because it has always done so, because it is February 26th and the almanac says it will. In making every such prediction, we presuppose a **principle of induction,** that is, that the laws of nature that have always held in the past will continue to hold in the future. The principle of induction is sometimes summarized as "the future will be like the past," which is all right only so long as it is not taken too literally; for of course the future is never just like the past (you are now fifteen seconds older, for example, and have added a whole new expression to your knowledge, and, [unless you are eating while you read] lost a tiny bit of weight as well). But the laws of nature, at least, do not change from moment to moment.

And third, there is our belief in the "external world," that is, a physical or material world that exists independently of our impressions and ideas, which it presumably causes in us. Bishop Berkeley had already done Hume's work for him here. Hume, following Berkeley, also rejects all notions of substance as unintelligible, including even that minimal "we know not what" of John Locke. But where Berkeley turned the rejection of matter and substance into a metaphysics (namely, his subjective idealism) and used it to defend the existence of God, Hume rejects this idealist metaphysics as well and remains wholly skeptical, refusing to accept the existence of God. He remains firm in his insistence that our belief in the existence of anything is no different from "the idea of what we conceive to be existent."

We can see that these three basic beliefs are intimately tied together; the notion of cause supports the principle of induction,[17] and the causal theory of perception supports our belief in the "external world." Accordingly, Hume takes causation to be the central idea of all reason-

---

[17]Modern philosophers have given a great deal of attention to inductive inferences that are not based upon any obvious causes, for example, statistical probabilities (as in genetics or gambling).

ing,[18] that is, all attempts to connect separate ideas together in a single belief. Hume's arguments are both elegant and simple to follow. He refutes both the principle of universal causation and the principle of induction by showing that neither can be defended either as a "relation of ideas" or as a "matter of fact." He begins with a statement that all human knowledge must be one or the other, explains what he means by "relations of ideas" and "matters of fact," shows how it is that "cause and effect" are the basis of all reasoning, and then proceeds to show that such reasoning can be neither a relation of ideas nor a simple matter of fact.

◆from the *Enquiry*, by Hume

All the objects of human reason or enquiry may naturally be divided into two kinds, to wit, *Relations of Ideas*, and *Matters of Fact*. Of the first kind are the sciences of Geometry, Algebra, and Arithmetic; and in short, every affirmation which is either intuitively or demonstratively certain. *That the square of the hypothenuse is equal to the square of the two sides*, is a proposition which expresses a relation between these figures. *That three times five is equal to the half of thirty*, expresses a relation between these numbers. Propositions of this kind are discoverable by the mere operation of thought, without dependence on what is anywhere existent in the universe. Though there never were a circle or triangle in nature, the truths demonstrated by Euclid would for ever retain their certainty and evidence.

Matters of fact, which are the second objects of human reason, are not ascertained in the same manner; nor is our evidence of their truth, however great, of a like nature with the foregoing. The contrary of every matter of fact is still possible; because it can never imply a contradiction, and is conceived by the mind with the same facility and distinctness, as if ever so conformable to reality. *That the sun will not rise tomorrow* is no less intelligible a proposition, and implies no more contradiction than the affirmation, *that it will rise*. We should in vain, therefore, attempt to demonstrate its falsehood. Were it demonstratively false, it would imply a contradiction, and could never be distinctly conceived by the mind.

It may, therefore, be a subject worthy of curiosity, to enquire what is the nature of that evidence which assures us of any real existence and matter of fact, beyond the present testimony of our senses, or the records of our memory. This part of philosophy, it is observable, has been little cultivated, either by the ancients or moderns; and therefore our doubts and errors, in the prosecution

[18]It is important to remember that Hume, like Locke, models his philosophy-psychology after Newton's physics. So even if he rejects Locke's "causal theory of perception," the Newtonian model, in which causality is central, remains at the heart of his theories.

of so important an enquiry, may be the more excusable; while we march through such difficult paths without any guide or direction. They may even prove useful, by exciting curiosity, and destroying that implicit faith and security, which is the bane of all reasoning and free enquiry. The discovery of defects in the common philosophy, if any such there be, will not, I presume, be a discouragement, but rather an incitement, as is usual, to attempt something more full and satisfactory than has yet been proposed to the public.

All reasonings concerning matter of fact seem to be founded on the relations of *Cause and Effect*. By means of that relation alone we can go beyond the evidence of our memory and senses. If you were to ask a man, why he believes any matter of fact, which is absent; for instance, that his friend is in the country, or in France; he would give you a reason; and this reason would be some other fact; as a letter received from him, or the knowledge of his former resolutions and promises. A man finding a watch or any other machine in a desert island, would conclude that there had once been men in that island. All our reasonings concerning fact are of the same nature. And here it is constantly supposed that there is a connexion between the present fact and that which is inferred from it. Were there nothing to bind them together, the inference would be entirely precarious. The hearing of an articulate voice and rational discourse in the dark assures us of the presence of some person: Why? because these are the effects of the human make and fabric, and closely connected with it. If we anatomize all the other reasonings of this nature, we shall find that they are founded on the relation of cause and effect, and that this relation is either near or remote, direct or collateral. Heat and light are collateral effects of fire, and the one effect may justly be inferred from the other.

Hume's argument, which we shall see again and again, is that we explain our experiences and events by appeal to other experiences and events. If I burn my finger and wonder how, I look down and see that I have just placed my hand too near the stove-top burner. I explain that the heat of the burner is the cause and the burn is the effect of the hot burner. Indeed, we are perplexed whenever we cannot find some causal explanation, and the suggestion that there might not be one ("there was no cause; you just burned yourself, that's all") is all but unintelligible to us. But now, Hume asks, where do we get this knowledge of causes and effects?

If we would satisfy ourselves, therefore, concerning the nature of that evidence, which assures us of matters of fact, we must enquire how we arrive at the knowledge of cause and effect.

I shall venture to affirm, as a general proposition, which admits of no exception, that the knowledge of this relation is not, in any instance, attained by reasonings *a priori*; but arises entirely from experience, when we find that any particular objects are constantly conjoined with each other. Let an object be presented to a man of ever so strong natural reason and abilities; if that object be entirely new to him, he will not be able, by the most accurate examination of its sensible qualities, to discover any of its causes or effects. Adam, though his rational faculties be supposed, at the very first, entirely perfect, could not have inferred from the fluidity and transparency of water that it would suffocate him, or from the light and warmth of fire that it would consume him. No object ever discovers, by the qualities which appear to the senses, either the causes which produced it, or the effects which will arise from it; nor can our reason, unassisted by experience, ever draw any inference concerning real existence and matter of fact.

This proposition, *that causes and effects are discoverable, not by reason but by experience,* will readily be admitted with regard to such objects, as we remember to have once been altogether unknown to us; since we must be conscious of the utter inability, which we then lay under, of foretelling what would arise from them. Present two smooth pieces of marble to a man who has no tincture of natural philosophy; he will never discover that they will adhere together in such a manner as to require great force to separate them in a direct line, while they make so small a resistance to a lateral pressure. Such events, as bear little analogy to the common course of nature, are also readily confessed to be known only by experience; nor does any man imagine that the explosion of gunpowder, or the attraction of a lodestone, could ever be discovered by arguments *a priori.* In like manner, when an effect is supposed to depend upon an intricate machinery or secret structure of parts, we make no difficulty in attributing all our knowledge of it to experience. Who will assert that he can give the ultimate reason, why milk or bread is proper nourishment for a man, not for a lion or a tiger?

But the same truth may not appear, at first sight, to have the same evidence with regard to events, which have become familiar to us from our first appearance in the world, which bear a close analogy to the whole course of nature, and which are supposed to depend on the simple qualities of objects, without any secret structure of parts. We are apt to imagine that we could discover these effects by the mere operation of our reason, without experience. We fancy, that were we brought on a sudden into this world, we could at first have inferred that one Billiard-ball would communicate motion to another upon impulse; and that we needed not to have waited for the event, in order to pronounce with certainty concerning it. Such is the influence of custom, that, where it is strongest, it not only covers our natural ignorance, but even conceals itself, and seems not to take place, merely because it is found in the highest degree.

But to convince us that all the laws of nature, and all the operations of bodies without exception, are known only by experience, the following reflections may, perhaps, suffice. Were any object presented to us, and were we required to pronounce concerning the effect, which will result from it, without consulting past observation; after what manner, I beseech you, must the mind proceed in this operation? It must invent or imagine some event, which it ascribes to the object as its effect; and it is plain that this invention must be entirely arbitrary. The mind can never possibly find the effect in the supposed cause, by the most accurate scrutiny and examination. For the effect is totally different from the cause, and consequently can never be discovered in it. Motion in the second Billiard-ball is a quite distinct event from motion in the first; nor is there anything in the one to suggest the smallest hint of the other. A stone or piece of metal raised into the air, and left without any support, immediately falls: but to consider the matter *a priori*, is there anything we discover in this situation which can beget the idea of a downward, rather than an upward, or any other motion in the stone or metal?

And as the first imagination or invention of a particular effect, in all natural operations, is arbitrary, where we consult not experience; so must we also esteem the supposed tie or connexion between the cause and effect, which binds them together, and renders it impossible that any other effect could result from the operation of that cause. When I see, for instance, a Billiard-ball moving in a straight line towards another; even suppose motion in the second ball should by accident be suggested to me, as the result of their contact or impulse; may I not conceive, that a hundred different events might as well follow from that cause? May not both these balls remain at absolute rest? May not the first ball return in a straight line, or leap off from the second in any line or direction? All these suppositions are consistent and conceivable. Why then should we give the preference to one, which is no more consistent or conceivable than the rest? All our reasonings *a priori* will never be able to show us any foundations for this preference.

Hume's argument so far is that we do not know particular causes and effects through reason, but only through experience. Because you have seen it so many times, you know that a billiard ball moving toward and striking another billiard ball sets the second in motion on a predictable path. But if you had never seen anything like it before—perhaps if you were Adam or Eve (pool tables were not created until the eighth day of creation)—you would not have any idea what to expect. Both balls might stop dead. Both might explode. The second might start a lawsuit. Prediction of cause and effect, in other words, depends upon prior experience, and no amount of mere reasoning will suffice by itself.

In a word, then, every effect is a distinct event from its cause. It could not, therefore, be discovered in the cause, and the first invention or conception of it, *a priori*, must be entirely arbitrary. And even after it is suggested, the conjunction of it with the cause must appear equally arbitrary; since there are always many other effects, which, to reason, must seem fully as consistent and natural. In vain, therefore, should we pretend to determine any single event, or infer any cause or effect, without the assistance of observation and experience.

· · · · · · · · · ·

When we reason *a priori*, and consider merely any object or cause, as it appears to the mind, independent of all observation, it never could suggest to us the notion of any distinct object, such as its effect; much less, show us the inseparable and inviolable connexion between them. A man must be very sagacious who could discover by reasoning that crystal is the effect of heat, and ice of cold, without being previously acquainted with the operations of these qualities.

In this argument, we see Hume applying the first half of his "fork" to the idea of causation. The idea of cause and effect cannot be a relation of ideas because, no matter how closely we examine, for example, the idea of fire we will never discover the idea of its causing gunpowder to explode. Reasoning alone cannot reveal the causes or effects of particular events. At the outset of this argument, Hume also suggests that the idea of causation is not discoverable through perception either: Although we perceive many different qualities of fire, we never perceive its power to cause gunpowder to explode. Hume concludes that the idea of cause and effect must be derived from our experience of the constant conjunction of two events. We observe, for example, that every time we set a match to gunpowder it explodes; and because we expect the future to be like the past, we infer that the application of fire is the cause of the gunpowder's exploding. In short, our knowledge of causes is arrived at through induction from past experiences.

Hume's argument against induction, and in particular against the inductive principle that the future will be like the past, takes exactly the same form. Again he begins with his "fork" between "relations of ideas" and "matters of fact," and again he proves that one of the basic assumptions of all our thinking, the principle of induction, cannot be established either way:

But we have not yet attained any tolerable satisfaction with regard to the question first proposed. Each solution still gives rise to a new question as difficult as the foregoing, and leads us on to further enquiries. When it is asked, *What is the nature of all our reasonings concerning matter of fact?* the proper answer seems to be, that they are founded on the relation of cause and effect. When again it is asked, *What is the foundation of all our reasonings and conclusions concerning that relation?* it may be replied in one word, Experience. But if we still carry on our sifting humour, and ask, *What is the foundation of all conclusions from experience?* this implies a new question, which may be of more difficult solution and explication. Philosophers, that give themselves airs of superior wisdom and sufficiency, have a hard task when they encounter persons of inquisitive dispositions, who push them from every corner to which they retreat, and who are sure at last to bring them to some dangerous dilemma. The best expedient to prevent this confusion, is to be modest in our pretensions; and even to discover the difficulty ourselves before it is objected to us. By this means, we may make a kind of merit of our very ignorance.

I shall content myself, in this section, with an easy task, and shall pretend only to give a negative answer to the question here proposed. I say then, that, even after we have experience of the operations of cause and effect, our conclusions from that experience are *not* founded on reasoning, or any process of the understanding. This answer we must endeavour both to explain and to defend.

It must certainly be allowed, that nature has kept us at a great distance from all her secrets, and has afforded us only the knowledge of a few superficial qualities of objects; while she conceals from us those powers and principles on which the influence of those objects entirely depends. Our senses inform us of the colour, weight, and consistence of bread; but neither sense nor reason can ever inform us of those qualities which fit it for the nourishment and support of a human body. Sight or feeling conveys an idea of the actual motion of bodies; but as to that wonderful force or power, which would carry on a moving body for ever in a continued change of place, and which bodies never lose but by communicating it to others; of this we cannot form the most distant conception. But notwithstanding this ignorance of natural powers and principles, we always presume, when we see like sensible qualities, that they have like secret powers, and expect that effects, similar to those which we have experienced, will follow from them. If a body of like colour and consistence with that bread, which we have formerly eat, be presented to us, we make no scruple of repeating the experiment, and foresee, with certainty, like nourishment and support. Now this is a process of the mind or thought, of which I would willingly know the foundation. It is allowed on all hands that there is no known connexion between the sensible qualities and the secret powers; and consequently, that the mind is not led to form such a conclusion concerning their constant and regular conjunction, by anything which it knows of their nature. As to past *Experience*, it can be allowed to give *direct* and *certain* information of those precise objects only, and that precise period of time, which fell under its cognizance: but why this experience should be extended to future times, and to other objects, which for aught we know, may be only in appearance similar; this is the main question on which I would insist. The bread, which I formerly eat, nourished

me; that is, a body of such sensible qualities was, at that time, en-
dued with such secret powers: but does it follow, that other bread
must also nourish me at another time, and that like sensible qualities must always be attended with like secret powers? The consequence seems nowise necessary. At least, it must be acknowledged
that there is here a consequence drawn by the mind; that there is
a certain step taken; a process of thought, and an inference, which
wants to be explained. These two propositions are far from being
the same, *I have found that such an object has always been
attended with such an effect,* and *I foresee, that other objects,
which are, in appearance, similar, will be attended with similar
effects.*

The argument so far is just like the argument regarding cause and effect,
namely, that it is only from experience that we know the properties and
effects of things and events, that moving bodies cause others to move, for
instance, or that eating bread gives me nourishment. But now Hume
distinguishes two propositions: (1) I have recognized a certain cause-
and-effect relationship in my past experience and (2) I predict that a
similar cause-and-effect relationship will hold in the future also. The
reference is surely reasonable, Hume says, but again he forces us to say
why such an inference is reasonable, and he argues that we cannot do so.

I shall allow, if you please, that the one proposition may justly be
inferred from the other: I know, in fact, that it always is inferred.
But if you insist that the inference is made by a chain of reasoning,
I desire you to produce the reasoning. The connexion between
these propositions is not intuitive. There is required a medium,
which may enable the mind to draw such an inference, if indeed it
be drawn by reasoning and argument. What that medium is, I must
confess, passes my comprehension; and it is incumbent on those
to produce it, who assert that it really exists, and is the origin of all
our conclusions concerning matter of fact.

This negative argument must certainly, in process of time, become altogether convincing, if many penetrating and able philosophers shall turn their enquiries this way and no one be ever able to
discover any connecting proposition or intermediate step, which
supports the understanding in this conclusion. But as the question
is yet new, every reader may not trust so far to his own penetra-
tion, as to conclude, because an argument escapes his enquiry, that
therefore it does not really exist. For this reason it may be requisite to venture upon a more difficult task; and enumerating all the
branches of human knowledge, endeavour to show that none of
them can afford such an argument.

Here is "Hume's fork"; the division of all knowledge into reasoning about
relations of ideas (which he here calls "demonstrative") and reasoning

about matters of fact (which he here calls "moral"). He says that it is clear from the above arguments that no demonstrative reasoning is available to justify our predictions of the future. But then he goes on to argue that no reasoning about matters of fact—no appeal to experience—can justify our propensity to make predictions either. For in order to justify our belief that the future will resemble the past on the basis of our experience, we would in effect be arguing that we know that the future will be like the past because in the past the future has always been like the past, and this is "begging the question" and a "vicious circle" in which one defends a proposition by referring it back to itself. (Like asking a suspected liar, "Are you lying to me?") Therefore our propensity for predicting can't be justified by appealing to experience either, which leaves us without any justification at all.

All reasonings may be divided into two kinds, namely, demonstrative reasoning, or that concerning relations of ideas, and moral reasoning, or that concerning matter of fact and existence. That there are no demonstrative arguments in the case seems evident; since it implies no contradiction that the course of nature may change, and that an object, seemingly like those which we have experienced, may be attended with different or contrary effects. May I not clearly and distinctly conceive that a body, falling from the clouds, and which, in all other respects, resembles snow, has yet the taste of salt or feeling of fire? Is there any more intelligible proposition than to affirm, that all the trees will flourish in December and January, and decay in May and June? Now whatever is intelligible, and can be distinctly conceived, implies no contradiction, and can never be proved false by any demonstrative argument or abstract reasoning *a priori*.

If we be, therefore, engaged by arguments to put trust in past experience, and make it the standard of our future judgement, these arguments must be probable only, or such as regard matter of fact and real existence, according to the division above mentioned. But that there is no argument of this kind, must appear, if our explication of that species of reasoning be admitted as solid and satisfactory. We have said that all arguments concerning existence are founded on the relation of cause and effect; that our knowledge of that relation is derived entirely from experience; and that all our experimental conclusions proceed upon the supposition that the future will be conformable to the past. To endeavour, therefore, the proof of this last supposition by probable arguments, or arguments regarding existence, must be evidently going in a circle, and taking that for granted, which is the very point in question.

. . . When a man says, *I have found, in all past instances, such sensible qualities conjoined with such secret powers:* And when he says, *Similar sensible qualities will always be conjoined with similar secret powers,* he is not guilty of tautology, nor are these propositions in any respect the same. You say that the one proposition is an inference from the other. But you must confess that the inference is not intuitive; neither is it demonstrative: Of what nature is it, then? To say it is experimental, is begging the question. For all inferences from experience suppose, as their foundation, that the future will resemble the past, and that similar powers will be conjoined with similar sensible qualities. If there be any suspicion that the course of nature may change, and that the past may be no rule for the future, all experience becomes useless, and can give rise to no inference or conclusion. It is impossible, therefore, that any arguments from experience can prove this resemblance of the past to the future; since all these arguments are founded on the supposition of that resemblance. Let the source of things be allowed hitherto ever so regular; that alone, without some new argument or inference, proves not that, for the future, it will continue so. In vain do you pretend to have learned the nature of bodies from your past experience. Their secret nature, and consequently all their effects and influence may change, without any change in their sensible qualities. This happens sometimes, and with regard to some objects: Why may it not happen always, and with regard to all objects? What logic, what process of argument secures you against this position? My practice, you say, refutes my doubts. But you mistake the purport of my question. As an agent, I am quite satisfied in the point; but as a philosopher, who has some share of curiosity, I will not say scepticism, I want to learn the foundation of this inference. No reading, no enquiry has yet been able to remove my difficulty, or give me satisfaction in a matter of such importance. Can I do better than propose the difficulty to the public, even though, perhaps, I have small hopes of obtaining a solution? We shall at least, by this means, be sensible of our ignorance, if we do not augment our knowledge.

Hume's arguments against the principle of universal causation and the principle of induction are also arguments against rationalism in general. What he is saying is that reasoning alone, without information from experience, cannot tell us anything whatever about the world. Reasoning *a priori*, that is, thinking without any appeal to experience, is incapable of proving any of those theorems so important to the rationalists, such as the existence of substances, a God, and causes, as well as the conformity of future events to past ones. His arguments are at the same time skeptical ones, since he reasons that even an appeal to experience cannot prove the reality of any of these things.

What is the solution to these skeptical doubts? If we seek a justification or defense, there is none, according to Hume. But in everyday life, such philosophical doubts need have no effect at all, for though there is no justification of our beliefs, we can yet remain confident that at least there is an explanation for them.

Suppose a person, though endowed with the strongest faculties of reason and reflection, to be brought on a sudden into this world; he would, indeed, immediately observe a continual succession of objects and one event following another, but he would not be able to discover anything further. He would not at first, by any reasoning, be able to reach the idea of cause and effect, since the particular powers by which all natural operations are performed never appear to the senses; nor is it reasonable to conclude, merely because one event in one instance precedes another, that therefore the one is the cause, the other the effect. The conjunction may be arbitrary and casual. There may be no reason to infer the existence of one from the appearance of the other: and, in a word, such a person without more experience could never employ his conjecture or reasoning concerning any matter of fact or be assured of anything beyond what was immediately present to his memory or senses.

Suppose again that he has acquired more experience and has lived so long in the world as to have observed similar objects or events to be constantly conjoined together—what is the consequence of this experience? He immediately infers the existence of one object from the appearance of the other, yet he has not, by all his experience, acquired any idea or knowledge of the secret power by which the one object produces the other, nor is it by any process of reasoning he is engaged to draw this inference; but still he finds himself determined to draw it, and though he should be convinced that his understanding has no part in the operation, he would nevertheless continue in the same course of thinking. There is some other principle which determines him to form such a conclusion.

This principle is *custom* or *habit*. For wherever the repetition of any particular act or operation produces a propensity to renew the same act or operation without being impelled by any reasoning or process of the understanding, we always say that this propensity is the effect of *custom*. By employing that word we pretend not to have given the ultimate reason of such a propensity. We only point out a principle of human nature which is universally acknowledged, and which is well known by its effects. Perhaps we can push our inquiries no further or pretend to give the cause of this cause, but must rest contented with it as the ultimate principle which we can assign of all our conclusions from experience. It is sufficient satisfaction that we can go so far without repining at the narrowness of our faculties, because they will carry us no further. And it is certain we here advance a very intelligible proposition at least, if not a true one, when we assert that after the constant conjunction of two objects, heat and flame, for instance, weight and solidity, we are determined by custom alone to expect the one from the appearance of the other. This hypothesis seems even the only one which explains the difficulty why we draw from a thousand instances an inference which we are not able to draw from one instance that is in no respect different from them. Reason is incapable of any such variation. The conclusions which it draws from considering one circle are the same which it would form upon surveying all the circles in the universe. But no man, having seen only one body move after being impelled by another, could infer that every other body will move after a like impulse. All inferences from experience, therefore, are effects of custom, not of reasoning.

In other words, there is no "solution to these skeptical doubts," but, at most, what Hume calls "a skeptical solution." It means an end, not only to philosophy, but to all rational inquiry and all claims that we can know anything (even that the sun will rise tomorrow, or that there is a typewriter now in front of me). You might think that such conclusions would have driven Hume mad or caused him such confusion that he would have been incapable of coping with the most everyday chores. Yet we know that he was the most practical and jolliest sort of fellow. As a philosopher, he has been driven right up against the wall of Plato's Cave. But he remains unperturbed. In a famous passage at the end of the *Treatise*, he simply remarks:

Most fortunately it happens, that since reason is incapable of dispelling these clouds, nature herself suffices to that purpose, and cures me of this philosophical melancholy and delirium, either by relaxing this bent of mind, or by some avocation, and lively impression of my senses, which obliterate all these chimeras. I dine, I play a game of backgammon, I converse, and am merry with my friends; and when after three or four hours' amusement, I wou'd return to these speculations, they appear so cold, and strain'd, and ridiculous, that I cannot find in my heart to enter into them any farther.

Perhaps you too find "these speculations cold, strained and ridiculous." If so, however, this is not the time to run off to dinner and an evening of games and conversation. Something has gone very wrong. The empiricist attempt to restore common sense to philosophy has ended in the least commonsensical philosophy imaginable. A person who really believed that there might be no material world, or that the future will not resemble the past (and therefore, having been hit by a truck last week, steps into the street convinced that it will not happen again) would be crazy! How can our intellects be so out of joint with our experience? or our philosophy so far away from practical life? How serious is Hume's skepticism?

F. AN ANCIENT SKEPTIC: NĀGĀRJUNA

As we mentioned above, the epistemological questions raised by the modern rationalists and empiricists were not original to the modern era.

One ancient empiricist continued the philosophical effort that Hume abandoned. Nāgārjuna, an Indian Buddhist philosopher (probably a Mahayana Buddhist) of the late second century A.D.), *begins* his philosophy with a denial of our knowledge of causation. The very first verse (after the dedication) of his *Mādhyamaka-Kārikās* reads:

"No existents whatsoever are evident anywhere that are arisen from themselves, from another, from both, or from a non-cause."[19]

Thus, Nāgārjuna has a logic which includes four concepts of cause: self-causation, external causation, joint causation, and noncausation (or eternality). But there is no perception of anything being caused by any of them. In other words, Nāgārjuna claims, just as Hume does, that we have no impression of cause; indeed like Hume he says that without cause, we have no impression of "things" (or substances) at all.

In fact, Nāgārjuna denies the existence of substance entirely. And without the notion of substance, the question of the possibility of knowledge is very different than it was for the other thinkers at whom we have looked in this chapter. So far, the sense in which "knowledge" has been understood is as knowledge *of* whether and how a *thing* exists. When Hume proved to his satisfaction that we couldn't know the nature and existence of substances, he concluded that knowledge was impossible. Nāgārjuna, instead, pursues an epistemology in the absence of substance and causation. Where Hume says that we simply must, as is our custom, rely on the concept of cause, Nāgārjuna says we are bound, if we are dedicated empiricists, to change our custom.

> A condition of an effect that is either non-existent or existent is not proper. Of what non-existent [effect] is a condition? Of what use is a condition of the existent [effect]? (I:6)
>
> Since a thing that is existent or non-existent or both existent and non-existent is not produced, how pertinent in that context would a producing cause be? (I:7)

Thus, Nāgārjuna advocates pursuing a more "appropriate" logic, which he calls—after the Buddhist doctrine—an "analysis in terms of *emptiness (sūnyata).*" Such an analysis involves limiting our claims to what we can know, that is impressions.

> Seeing, hearing, smelling, tasting, touching, and mind are the six faculties. Their spheres consist of the object of seeing, etc. (III:1)
>
> Seeing does not perceive itself, its own form. How can that which does not perceive itself, see others? (III:2)

We have no knowledge and should make no claims, therefore, to the effect that we see, hear, taste, touch, smell, *or intellect* a substance. There

---

[19]All passages from the *Mādhyamaka-Kārikās* are from *Nāgārjuna: The Philosophy of the Middle,* trans. by David J. Kalupuhana (Albany: SUNY Press, 1986).

exist only instances of seeing-being seen, hearing-being heard, etc., even in the case of thinking-being thought.

> Seeing does not perceive (i.e., "know a thing"), nor does non-seeing perceive. One should admit that a seer is explained by [the analysis of] seeing itself. (III:5)

Thus, neither the seer nor the form seen are independent substances. Rather, they are "empty" of substance. Since our experience is ample evidence of the mutual dependence of sensation and sensed-form, Nāgārjuna felt that the burden of proof lay upon the believer in substance. Thus, his "emptiness" was not, as it was for Hume, a dark and threatening realization which demanded the end of his investigation, but rather, an opportunity for a wealth of valuable analyses of experience. The believer in substance, in a sense, has dug his own pit whether he is an empiricist or a rationalist, because all the evidence of experience is unavailable to him.

> When an analysis is made in terms of emptiness, whosoever were to address a refutation, all that is left unrefuted by him will be equal to what is yet to be proved. (IV:8)
> When an explanation in terms of emptiness is given, whosoever were to address a censure, all that is left uncensured by him will be equal to what is yet to be proved. (IV:9)

G. IS KNOWLEDGE MASCULINE? FEMINISM AND EPISTEMOLOGY

The example of Nāgārjuna shows that what counts for knowledge may differ from culture to culture. It seems that religious background, national ancestry, and other social distinctions may affect the epistemological project. (In the case of Nāgārjuna, for example, his access to the Buddhist concepts of "emptiness" and "nonself" gave him the opportunity to think about knowledge in different terms than were apparently available to the modern European rationalists and empiricists.) One important distinction which has recently come to epistemologists' attention is the difference between the sexes.

If one is an empiricist, goes one feminist claim, then if women can be shown to have different sense-experiences from men (which they surely do) then women must have a very different sort of knowledge. If one is a rationalist, and if women have a different "nature" or way of reasoning than do men, then one must admit that women have a very different sort of knowledge. Different interests and different backgrounds, perhaps, lead different people to set different criteria for knowledge.

To the extent that this is true, claims American philosopher Virginia Held, epistemology has been a masculine enterprise with a masculine conception of knowledge.

◆**from "Feminism and Epistemology,"
by Virginia Held**

Would the world seem entirely different if it were pictured, felt, described, studied, and thought about from the point of view of women? A great deal looks altogether different when we notice the realities of class brought to our attention by Marx and others. Not only do economic activity, government, law, and foreign policies take on a very different appearance. "Knowledge" itself can be seen as quite a different enterprise when subject to the scrutiny of the sociology of knowledge. When connections are drawn between intellectual enterprise and class interests, social sciences claiming to be "value-free" can be seen to lend support to a capitalist status quo, and we can recognize how normative theories presented as impartial can be used to mystify reality rather than to contribute to needed change.

Gender is an even more pervasive and fundamental aspect of reality than class. If feminists can succeed not only in making visible but also in keeping within our awareness the aspects of "mankind" that have been so obscured and misrepresented by taking the "human" to be the masculine, virtually all existing thought may be turned on its head. As Carolyn Hielbrun noted in a recent issue of *Academe* devoted to "Feminism and the Academy," a revolution is occurring that is as important as those that took place when the views of Copernicus, Darwin, and Freud changed so radically man's view of man. Some feminists think this latest revolution will be even more profound.

· · · · · · · · · ·

To whatever extent human interest colors knowledge, whether the extent is total, large, or only partial, feminists must insist that knowledge count the interests of women as of equal importance with those of men. It is difficult to see how men who would be consistent with their own claims that knowledge is more than propaganda could disagree.

The long-awaited collection of essays edited by Sandra Harding and Merrill B. Hintikka called *Discovering Reality* is the best and most comprehensive examination so far of the epistemological speculations of feminists. From a feminist standpoint, even the reliability of the physical sciences, and of all that has been thought to be most objective and immune to distortion, can be doubted. Perhaps our standard views of reality itself at its most fundamental are masculine views, and perhaps a feminist standpoint would give us a quite different understanding of even physical reality.

The usual metaphysical assumption made by the sciences is that there are entities which have properties. But, as Merrill B. Hintikka and Jaakko Hintikka point out, "studies seem to show that boys tend to bracket together objects (or pictures of objects) whose intrinsic characteristics are similar," whereas girls attach more weight to the "functional and relational characteristics of the entities to be compared. . . . " In sum, "women are generally more sensitive to, and likely to assign more importance to, relational characteristics (e.g., interdependencies) than males, and less likely to think in terms of independent discrete units. Conversely, males generally prefer what is separable and manipulatable. If we put a premium on the former features, we are likely to end up with one kind of cross-identification and one kind of ontology; if we follow the guidance of the latter considerations, we end up with a different one. . . ."

All this is heady stuff, and it needs to deal more than has been the case so far with the fact that continental and non-western approaches have often been based far more than the Anglo-American views with which we are most familiar on a relational and more holistic view of reality. Such continental and non-western views have usually been even more misogynous than have Anglo-American views, yet they seem epistemologically closer to what is now being suggested as a more characteristically feminine approach. One might continue the argument in some such way as the following: It would not be inconsistent for non-Anglo-American epistemological styles to be more "feminine" in the sense of incorporating more characteristically feminine ways of viewing reality, and yet to have led to more misogynous outcomes. For relative to relational and holistic views that ignore women, views that pay attention to discrete individuals represent progress; at least then individual women can recognize their own reality even if the reality of women as an entire category continues to be obscured. But then more relational and holistic views that do recognize women (along with other collectivities) may represent progress over those that can see only discrete entities and their properties. Developing such arguments, and explanations for the more relational and holistic thinking of continental and non-western approaches, remains work to be done rather than an obstacle to the views in question. And then questions concerning the implications for normative ethics and meta-ethics of such epistemological and metaphysical issues need to be considered.[20]

Evelyn Fox Keller, however, argues that our traditional model of scientific knowledge is broad enough to encompass feminist critiques, and ought to attend to them if it is to be intellectually honest.

[20]Virginia Held, "Feminism and Epistemology: Recent Work on the Connection Between Gender and Knowledge" in *Philosophy and Public Affairs* 14, no. 3 (1985):296.

◆from "Feminism and Science,"
by Evelyn Fox Keller

In recent years, a new critique of science has begun to emerge from a number of feminist writings. The lens of feminist politics brings into focus certain masculinist distortions of the scientific enterprise, creating, for those of us who are scientists, a political dilemma. Is there a conflict between our commitment to feminism and our commitment to science? As both a feminist and a scientist, I am more familiar than I might wish with the nervousness and defensiveness that such a potential conflict evokes. As scientists, we have very real difficulties in thinking about the kinds of issues that, as feminists, we have been raising. These difficulties may, however, ultimately be productive.

My purpose in the present essay is to explore the implications of recent feminist criticisms of science for the relationship between science and feminism. Do these criticisms imply conflict? If they do, how necessary is that conflict? I will argue that those elements of feminist criticism that seem to conflict most with at least conventional conceptions of science may, in fact, carry a liberating potential for science. It could therefore benefit scientists to attend closely to feminist criticism. I will suggest that we might even use feminist thought to illuminate and clarify part of the substructure of science (which may have been historically conditioned into distortion) in order to preserve the things that science has taught us, in order to be more objective.

· · · · · · · · · ·

These critiques, which maintain that a substantive effect on scientific theory results from the predominance of men in the field, are almost exclusively aimed at the "softer," even the "softest," sciences. Thus they can still be accommodated within the traditional framework by the simple argument that the critiques, if justified, merely reflect the fact that these subjects are not sufficiently scientific. Presumably, fair-minded (or scientifically minded) scientists can and should join forces with the feminists in attempting to identify the presence of bias—equally offensive, if for different reasons, to both scientists and feminists—in order to make these "soft" sciences more rigorous.

It is much more difficult to deal with the truly radical critique that attempts to locate androcentric bias even in the "hard" sciences, indeed in scientific ideology itself. This range of criticism takes us out of the liberal domain and requires us to question the very assumptions of objectivity and rationality that underlie the scientific enterprise. To challenge the truth and necessity of the conclusions of natural science on the grounds that they too reflect the judgment of men is to take the Galilean credo and turn it on its head. It is not true that "the conclusions of natural science are true and necessary, and the judgement of man has nothing to do with them"; it is the judgment of woman that they have nothing to do with.

The impetus behind this radical move is twofold. First, it is supported by the experience of feminist scholars in other fields of inquiry. Over and over, feminists have found it necessary, in seeking to reinstate women as agents and as subjects, to question the very canons of their fields. They have turned their attention, accordingly, to the operation of patriarchal bias on ever deeper levels of social structure, even of language and thought.

But the possibility of extending the feminist critique into the foundations of scientific thought is created by recent developments in the history and philosophy of science itself. As long as the course of scientific thought was judged to be exclusively determined by its own logical and empirical necessities, there could be no place for any signature, male or otherwise, in that system of knowledge. Furthermore, any suggestion of gender differences in our thinking about the world could argue only too readily for the further exclusion of women from science. But as the philosophical and historical inadequacies of the classical conception of science have become more evident, and as historians and sociologists have begun to identify the ways in which the development of scientific knowledge has been shaped by its particular social and political context, our understanding of science as a social process has grown. This understanding is a necessary prerequisite, both politically and intellectually, for a feminist theoretic in science.

Joining feminist thought to other social studies of science brings the promise of radically new insights, but it also adds to the existing intellectual danger a political threat. The intellectual danger resides in viewing science as pure social product; science then dissolves into ideology and objectivity loses all intrinsic meaning. In the resulting cultural relativism, any emancipatory function of modern science is negated, and the arbitration of truth recedes into the political domain. Against this background, the temptation arises for feminists to abandon their claim for representation in scientific culture and, in its place, to invite a return to a purely "female" subjectivity, leaving rationality and objectivity in the male domain, dismissed as products of a purely male consciousness.

Many authors have addressed the problems raised by total relativism; here I wish merely to mention some of the special problems added by its feminist variant. They are several. In important respects, feminist relativism is just the kind of radical move that transforms the political spectrum into a circle. By rejecting objectivity as a masculine ideal, it simultaneously lends its voice to an enemy chorus and dooms women to residing outside of the realpolitik modern culture; it exacerbates the very problem it wishes to solve. It also nullifies the radical potential of feminist criticism for our understanding of science. As I see it, the task of a feminist theoretic in science is twofold: to distinguish that which is parochial from that which is universal in the scientific impulse, reclaiming for women what has historically been denied to them; and to legitimate those elements of scientific culture that have been denied precisely because they are defined as female.

It is important to recognize that the framework inviting what might be called the nihilist retreat is in fact provided by the very ideology of objectivity we wish to escape. This is the ideology that asserts an opposition between (male) objectivity and (female) subjectivity and denies the possibility of mediation between the two. A first step, therefore, in extending the feminist critique to the foundations of scientific thought is to reconceptualize objectivity as a dialectical process so as to allow for the possibility of distinguishing the objective effort from the objectivist illusion. As Piaget reminds us:

> Objectivity consists in so fully realizing the countless intrusions of the self in everyday thought and the countless illusions which result—illusions of sense, language, point of view, value, etc.—that the preliminary step to every judgement is the effort to exclude the intrusive self. Realism, on the contrary, consists in ignoring the existence of self and thence regarding one's own perspective as immediately objective and absolute. Realism is thus anthropocentric illusion, finality—in short, all those illusions which teem in the history of science. So long as thought has not become conscious of self, it is a prey to perpetual confusions between objective and subjective, between the real and the ostensible.

In short, rather than abandon the quintessentially human effort to understand the world in rational terms, we need to refine that effort. To do this, we need to add to the familiar methods of rational and empirical inquiry the additional process of critical self-reflection. Following Piaget's injunction, we need "to become conscious of self." In this way, we can become conscious of the features of the scientific project that belie its claim to universality.[21]

SUMMARY AND CONCLUSION

Epistemology is the study of human knowledge—what we can know, how we can know it, and what we cannot know. In this sense, epistemology and metaphysics are complementary disciplines. Epistemology becomes the method of approach to the knowledge of the way the world really is. For some philosophers, for example, Descartes, this approach places its primary trust in reason; accordingly, they are called rationalists. For other philosophers, for example, Locke, the preferred approach is to

[21] Evelyn Fox Keller, "Feminism and Science" reprinted in *The Signs Reader*, ed. Elizabeth Abel and Emily K. Abel (Chicago: University of Chicago Press, 1983), 109–22.

trust the senses and experience; they are called empiricists. The problem for both the rationalists and the empiricists is to get beyond the mere appearance of things to the reality behind them. The rationalist tries to do this by appealing to intuition and certain principles from which he or she can deduce the way the world really is. The empiricist, on the other hand, appeals to his or her experiences, trying to find there evidence for the nature of reality. For both views, however, the danger is that their methods do not always seem to achieve as much as they would like. Rationalists disagree about which principles to start with and which intuitions to trust. Empiricists find that their own method of experience makes it impossible to say anything about what lies beyond experience. Thus Berkeley argues that only our ideas and the minds that have these ideas exist (including God), and Hume concludes that we can never know anything about reality, but only about our own associations of ideas. Epistemologists are still working on more satisfactory answers to the questions of knowledge, and still trying to defeat or defend once and for all the skeptical conclusions so brilliantly argued by Hume and other skeptics centuries ago. But some are turning to other traditions in an attempt to understand alternative approaches to knowledge and the limitations that may be built into our way of seeing the world. The differences between the sexes have also been added to our questions about knowledge. Do women and men know the world differently? How personal is knowledge—how relative to the individual and his or her cultural context and biology?

GLOSSARY

appearance   the way something seems to us, through our senses. Usually philosophers worry about something's being a mere appearance, such that it bears no faithful resemblance to the reality of which it is the appearance.

a priori (knowledge)   "before experience," or more accurately, independent of all experience. A priori knowledge is always necessary, for there can be no imaginable instances that would refute it and no intelligible doubting of it. One might come to know something a priori through experience (for example, you might find out that no parallel lines ever touch each other by drawing tens of thousands of parallel lines) but what is essential to a priori knowledge is that no such experience is needed. Knowledge is a priori if it can be proven independently of experience. The most obvious examples of a priori knowledge are analytic sentences, such as "a horse is an animal," and "if all men are mammals and Socrates is a man, then Socrates is a mammal."

association of ideas   a central idea of empiricist philosophy, according to which all knowledge is composed of separate ideas that are connected by their resemblance to one another (e.g., "this one looks exactly like that one"), by their contiguity in space and time (e.g., "every time I see this, I see that as well") and causality (e.g., "every time a thing of that sort happens it is followed by something of this sort"). (The three different "associations" here are Hume's.)

causation or causality   the relation of cause and effect, one event's bringing about another according to natural law. In Hume, (1) one event's following another necessarily (or so it seems to us); (2) one type of event regularly following another (see *association of ideas* above).

cause   that which produces an effect; an event (or state of affairs, object, act, or person) that brings about another event.

causal theory of perception   the view that our experience (our sensations and ideas) are the effects of physical objects acting upon our sense organs (which are thereby the causes).

cogito, ergo sum   or "I think, therefore I am" is Descartes' only principle that he finds "beyond doubt" and "perfectly certain." ("Think" here refers to any kind of idea or experience in the mind, not just what we would call "thinking.") It is the premise of his entire philosophy.

datum   Latin, literally, "what is given." (plural, *data*)

empiricism   the philosophy that demands that all knowledge, except for certain logical truths and principles of mathematics, comes from experience. British empiricism is often used to refer specifically to the three philosophers Locke, Berkeley, and Hume. It is still very much alive, however, and includes Bertrand Russell in our own century and a great many philosophers of the past forty years who have called themselves "logical empiricists" (better known as logical positivists).

emptiness   in Buddhism, in Nāgārjuna, being without substance: the proper understanding of being as without substance.

epistemology   the study of human knowledge, its nature, its sources, its justification.

explanation   an account—usually a causal account—of something; it is opposed to *justification*, which also defends. One can, for example, explain one's action (say, by claiming that he or she was drunk) without thereby justifying it, that is, showing it to be right. Hume ultimately explains our knowledge but does not justify it.

generalization from experience (*or* **inductive generalization)**   inference from observation, experience, and experiment to a generalization about all members of a certain class. For example, in a laboratory, a researcher finds that certain experiments on tobacco plants always have the same result. He or she generalizes, through induction, from experimental observations to a claim (or *hypothesis*) about all tobacco plants. But notice that this generalization is never certain (like the generalization in geometry from a proof of a theorem about this triangle to a theorem about all triangles). It might always turn out that there was a fluke in the experiment or that he/she chose a peculiar sample of plants.

Hume's fork   Hume's insistence that every belief be justified either as a "relation between ideas" or as a "matter of fact."

idea   in epistemology, almost any mental phenomenon (not, as in Plato, with existence independent of individual minds). The terminology varies slightly; Locke uses "idea" to refer to virtually any "mental content"; Hume reserves "idea" for those mental atoms that are derived by the mind from impressions.

impression   Hume's word for sensations or sense-data, that which is given to the mind through the senses.

induction; inductive reasoning; inductive generalization   induction is the process of inferring general conclusions (for example, "all swans are white") from a sufficiently large sample of particular observations ("this swan is white, that swan is white, and that one, and that one, and that one . . . "). It is usually contrasted with **deduction** (see Ch. 1), in that, while deductive reasoning guarantees that the conclusion shall be as certain as the premises, induction never gives us a conclusion as certain as the premises. Its conclusions are, at most, merely probable. ("There might always be some black swan somewhere"; and there are, in Western Australia). (See "A Brief Introduction to Logic," pp 20–40.)

innate ideas   literally, ideas that are "born into the mind." Locke's famous attack on such ideas took them to be literally ideas that all men share from birth. The rationalist philosophers he was supposedly attacking, however held a much more sophisticated notion; they did not believe that ideas were literally "born into us," but they did believe that we are born with certain "innate" capacities and dispositions, which will develop with proper education (and mental health). And these ideas, most importantly, can be defended or justified without appeal to any particular experiences or experiments. This is the claim that Locke ultimately rejected.

intuition   immediate knowledge, without the aid of reasoning or inference. It must be stressed, however, that intuition is often (even usually) argued to be a function of reason, and capable of rational insights even if they are, by their very nature, not defensible by any arguments.

justification   an attempt to defend a position or an act, to show that it is correct (or at least reasonable). (Cf. *explanation* above.)

masculinist   from the point of view of men's interests and advantage, as opposed to those of women.

perception   a kind of knowledge, sense experience.

primary qualities   in Locke, those properties ("qualities") that inhere in the object.

principle of induction   the belief that the laws of nature will continue to hold in the future as they have in the past. (Crudely, "the future will be like the past.")

principle of universal causation   the belief that every event has its cause (or causes). In scientific circles, it is usually added, "its sufficient natural cause," in order to eliminate the possibility of miracles and divine intervention (which are allowed in Leibniz's similar but broader Principle of Sufficient Reason).

probable   likely; or supported by the evidence (but not conclusively). The empiricist's middle step between the extremities of certainty and doubt. (Probability is the measure of how probable something is.)

quality   in Locke (and other authors), a property.

rationalism   the philosophy that is characterized by its confidence in reason, and intuition in particular, to know reality independently of experience. (See *reason* and *intuition*.) Continental rationalism is usually reserved for the three great European philosophers, Descartes, Spinoza, and Leibniz.

reason   in rationalism the faculty that allows us to know reality, through intuition. In empiricism, simply the ability to recognize certain principles that are "relations of ideas," for example, trivial truths ("a cat is an animal") and, more complicated, principles of arithmetic and geometry. Empiricists deny that reason allows us special insight into reality, however; it tells us only relations between ideas.

relations of ideas   in empiricism, knowledge that is restricted to the logical and conceptual connections between ideas, not to the correspondence of those ideas to experience or to reality.

secondary qualities   in Locke, those properties ("qualities") that are caused in us by objects, but do not inhere in the objects themselves (for example, color).

sensation   the experimental result of the stimulation of a sense organ, for example, *seeing* red, *hearing* a ringing noise, *smelling* something burning. The simplest of mental phenomena.

sense-data   that which is given to the senses, prior to any reasoning or organization on our part.

skepticism   the philosophical belief (or fear) that knowledge is not possible, and that no rational arguments will succeed in overcoming our doubts.

subjective idealism   the view that only ideas and mind exist, and that there are no substances, matter, or material objects. In particular, the philosophy of Bishop Berkeley.

substance   a "unit" of existence–a being; something which "stands by itself."

Sunyata   Buddhist term for emptiness; see *emptiness*.

tabula rasa   in Locke's philosophy, the "blank tablet" metaphor of the mind, in opposition to the doctrine that there are innate ideas. In other words, the mind is a "blank" at birth, and everything we know must be "stamped in" through experience.

◆ BIBLIOGRAPHY AND FURTHER READING ◆

Several studies of the various problems in René Descartes' epistemology are in Willis Doney, ed., *Descartes* (New York: Doubleday, Anchor, 1967). Gottfried W. von Leibniz's reply to John Locke is spelled out at length in Leibniz's *New Essays on Human Understanding,* trans. A. G. Langley (La Salle, IL: Open Court, 1949). Locke's *Essay Concerning Human Understanding* is published by Dover Publications (New York, 1959). Bishop Berkeley's *Treatise* is printed in full in T. E. Jessop. ed., *Berkeley, Philosophical Writings* (Austin, TX: University of Texas Press, 1953). Of special interest is Berkeley's *Three Dialogues Between Hylas and Philonous* (La Salle, IL: Open Court, 1935), in which the arguments of his *Treatise* are worked out in entertaining dialogue form. David Hume's *Treatise of Human Nature* is available, edited by L. A. Selby-Bigge (Oxford: Oxford University Press, 1888), but most beginners will find Hume's *Enquiry Concerning Human Understanding* (Oxford: Oxford University Press, 1902) much easier reading. Bertrand Russell, *Problems of Philosophy* (London: Oxford University Press,

1912) is an excellent introduction to the problems of epistemology and some of the problems of metaphysics. Two more modern epistemological studies are A. J. Ayer, *The Problem of Knowledge* (New York: St. Martin's Press, 1956) and Roderick Chisholm, *Theory of Knowledge* (Englewood Cliffs, NJ: Prentice-Hall, 1956). A modern series of studies is R. J. Swartz, ed., *Perceiving, Sensing, Knowing* (New York: Doubleday, Anchor, 1965). For a comprehensive anthology on epistemology, see E. Nagel and R. Brandt, eds., *Meaning and Knowledge* (New York: Harcourt Brace Jovanovich, 1965). A modern defense of skepticism is Peter Unger, *Ignorance* (London: Oxford University Press, 1975). On feminist theories of knowledge, see Ann Garry and Marilyn Pearsall, *Women, Knowledge and Reality* (Boston: Unwin Hyman, 1989). For a concise overview of Indian skepticism, see Stephen Phillips, "Indian Philosophy," in R. Solomon and K. Higgins, *From Africa to Zen* (Savage, Md.: Rowman and Littlefield, 1993).

CHAPTER

4

TRUTH AND RELATIVISM

Truth is the kind of error without which a certain species of life could not live.

FRIEDRICH NIETZSCHE

We turned from metaphysics to epistemology because we began to question our ability to know "the way the world really is." Hence, we thought we should first find out what we can know. But then after Hume, it seemed that not only were we incapable of doing metaphysics but we could not justify even the most ordinary and obvious principles of our everyday lives. If we can't even know with certainty that there is an "external" world, then how can we claim to know anything—except, perhaps, our own isolated and limited experiences? But then, what is the *truth*? Surely it cannot be solely a function of our ideas. If it is true that there is a bald-headed man in the governor's mansion, then there must *be* a bald-headed man in the governor's mansion, not just our impression or idea of him. Furthermore, if our knowledge of reality is colored by our ideas and "habits" of understanding and interpretation, could it be possible that reality will be different for different people, who have different ideas and different intellectual and perceptual habits? Did Aristotle and the ancient animists live in the same world as John Locke and modern scientists? Did Confucius share a world with Lao Tsu or the Buddha? Or were their ideas about the world so different that the worlds they lived in were different as well? Is there, in that case, any such thing as "the Truth"? Or does it make sense to say that what is true for one person might nevertheless be false for someone else?

The problem of truth has always been central to philosophy. In asking "what is reality *really* like?" the ancient philosophers were trying to ascertain the truth behind the appearances of reality. And some of them, such as Parmenides and Plato, quite clearly distinguished between the True World—or simply "the Truth"—and the world of our everyday

223

experiences. Descartes and Locke were both looking for the truth, but in different ways, and the difference in their approaches signified a difference in their sense of what the truth should be. But they both believed that there was such a thing as the Truth, that their preferred philosophical methods would get them the truth. It is with the skeptics—and Hume in particular—that this assurance has broken down.

The multiplicity of cultures and philosophies—and different *types* of philosophy—also throw open the question of truth. If different cultures and philosophies only disagree in their perspective and style, then despite their differences it may nonetheless be true that there is a truth that all of them describe, but they orient themselves to that truth in different ways. It is like the old Persian story about the several blind men fondling an elephant, one of whom claims that the beast is as big as a barrel, another that the elephant is more like a snake, two others that it is like a rope or an ivory sword. But in this familiar story it is obvious that the blind men could, by moving around the animal, come to agree.

The real problem arises if it turns out that our various perspectives and the language in which we describe them render us immobile, incapable of appreciating (except in the abstract) other orientations. It is as if we never experience reality itself—the thesis shared by various idealists and the skeptics alike—but know only our own interpretations. Or, to take a different metaphor, it is as if we were reading a book, a translation of an ancient text into English, which itself was translated from another ancient language, which was in turn translated from another ancient language, which was copied from some ancient scrolls which now no longer exist and, just possibly, never existed in the first place. Do other cultures share our world but just see it differently, or do they live in some sense in a different world? If so, as Nietzsche writes, there may be many kinds of "truth," and thus no truth at all (in his book, *The Will to Power*).

The view of the Truth as "out there," in the world, is the basis of both common sense and much of the history of philosophy. Even Bishop Berkeley, who argued that the world consists of ideas, insisted that these ideas were caused by God, Who is the Truth. But skepticism challenges God as Truth just as it challenges our assumption that most of what we know is the Truth. The idea that the Truth is outside of us becomes no longer a matter of common sense but the source of serious paradoxes. If it is outside of us, how will we ever know it? If it is not outside of us, is there anything at all to know?

What now comes into question are the very assumptions that have ruled metaphysics and common sense since the time of the first philosophers. First of all, there is Plato's "two-worlds" view: "the world of Being," which is the true world, and "the world of Becoming," the world of our daily experience that, though perhaps not unreal, is less real than the world of Being. Now, the actual model Plato uses (the real world as the world of Forms as over against our world as the world of material objects and change) has not been accepted by all modern philosophers, and it is certainly out of line with common sense. Many philosophers, of both East and West, *have* accepted the distinction between appearance and reality. The empiricists, for example, held precisely the reverse of Plato's view. According to modern empiricism, it is the material world that becomes the real world, and the world of ideas—our mental "ideas" and experiences—becomes the less real world. The problem, in Descartes, Locke, Hume, and Russell, is always how to know that our "ideas" or experiences in fact match up to the real world. The fact that Descartes is confident that he can know that his experiences "match up," while Hume believes that we can never know even if there is such a world, must not hide from us the "two-worlds" model that both of them presuppose: reality (if there is one) on the one side, our experience on the other. How do we move from experience to reality?

Second, we mentioned two assumptions in Chapter 2, common not only to Plato and Aristotle but to most modern thinkers as well, Spinoza and Leibniz, for example. They were: (1) faith in our language to capture the structures of reality and the idea that the world in itself is intelligible to us, and (2) the idea that all knowledge of reality (that is, metaphysical knowledge) must consist of necessary truths. The first assumption seems to presuppose the "two-worlds" model in some sense, because something (our language) can't be "faithful" unless it is faithful to something else, outside of itself (reality). But it also assumes that the language we (or the Greeks) use to express ourselves is also adequate to describe the world without distortion. Is that so obviously the case? For example, could the words we use to pick out individual objects in fact distort the truth for us, forcing certain things into categories not natural to them and making impossible the identification of other things for which we do not have a word? Does our language delude us by picking out objects at all? Are there objects (substances) at all? Are we substances? And could it be that different languages (English and ancient Greek, for example) actually interpret the world in different ways?

This last very difficult question—which raises the problem that many philosophers call **relativism**—is also a problem that infects the assumption that knowledge of reality consists of necessary truths. (We will discuss necessary truth in detail in Chapter 5.) Relativism is the thesis that truth varies from context to context; truth is *relative* to a language, a culture, a way of looking at the world. (But what, then, is "the world," if there are only so many ways of looking at it?) But to say that knowledge consists of necessary truths is to insist that knowledge *could not be mistaken*. But is this a fact about the world, or is it rather an inability on our part to see through the common assumptions that are, perhaps, built right into our language? How do we know that what we believe to be necessary—because of the structure of our language—is not just necessary for us, and not true of reality at all? So we have to ask, "Are we trapped inside our language? Is it impossible for us to know anything about reality that we have not ourselves imposed through language?"

Once again, the issue of multiculturalism crashes in on traditional Western philosophy with a vengeance. Could it be that the structure Western philosophers and scientists posit in the world is in fact a projection of their language and methods? Could it be that the emphasis on abstract theory is an oversimplification or even a distortion of the truth? African folk traditions, for example, explain the ways of the world in what we would call metaphorical or mythological language. Is it correct or fair to insist, as Western philosophers and scientists have for nearly three thousand years, that those folk traditions are false or misleading, rather than an equally but extremely different way of trying to express one of several possible visions of the world?

The assumption that knowledge consists of necessary truths has already begun to bother us, since Locke and his empiricist followers insisted that all of our knowledge of the world must consist of truths based upon experience, and since, by the very nature of inductive arguments from experience, we could not actually be certain of anything. Descartes had insisted that any belief worth the honorific title "knowledge" had to be certain ("perfectly certain," he said). But now, let us ask, wasn't he demanding a bit too much? In fact, much too much! Surely I have the right to say that I know that I'm not dreaming right now, even if it's true that I might be wrong. In other words, it is time to weaken our demands. Perhaps it will be enough if we believe what is **rational** to believe, even if it is not certain and even if it does not "match up" with some unexperienceable reality. You might even say, "perhaps it is not necessary to believe what is true," but notice that you would have already presupposed that what makes our belief true is some reality beyond our experience. It is just this notion of truth we must examine in this chapter.

A. WHAT IS TRUTH?

That familiar question was raised by Pontius Pilate as he dismissed Christ's case from his court. He was just a politician; he did not take the question seriously. Philosophers do. It is their business to find the truth, to expose fraudulent beliefs and superstitions, and to assure us that we can know, at least most of the time, what is true from what is false.

What indeed is truth? Should we say, as we have so far, that our beliefs are true if and only if they "match up" with reality? Or, in accordance with our present suspicions, should we not perhaps hold out for some different conception of "truth," one that does not place such emphasis on "matching up" and the separation of reality on the one hand from our beliefs and experiences on the other?

The proper philosophical name for this notion of "matching up" our beliefs and experiences with reality is the **correspondence theory of truth.** On the one hand, it is an obvious truism: for example, when I tell you "there is beer in the refrigerator," what I tell you is true if and only if there is in fact beer in the refrigerator. So obvious is this "correspondence" criterion of truth—that a belief or a statement is true if and only if it corresponds to the facts—that no one would have thought of calling it a "theory" at all until recently. In his *Metaphysics*, Aristotle dismissed the whole "problem of truth" in a single sentence: "To say of what is that it is not, or of what is not that it is, is false, while to say of what is that it is, or of what is not that it is not, is true." As long as philosophers (and everyone else) believed themselves unquestionably capable of knowing reality as such, this common-sense platitude was as appropriate for the investigations of metaphysics as it was for the daily task of checking to see whether there was beer in the refrigerator. But as empiricism and Hume's skepticism grew in persuasiveness and the confidence that we could know reality was thrown into question, the platitude became a problem.

For Descartes, the correspondence between our ideas and reality had to be demonstrated. Locke expressed his doubts; Berkeley rejected the "external world" altogether, leaving only God (and other minds like Berkeley's own); and Hume left us with the seemingly irrefutable argument that we could never know reality outside of us, or even if there was a reality to be known. Hume had given us a *reductio ad absurdum* argument; one of his premises—perhaps not an explicit one—has brought us to the absurdity of not being able to defend the most common-sense beliefs. But all of these philosophers presuppose the correspondence theory of truth, the idea that knowledge is the correspondence of our ideas to reality and that the only knowledge worthy of the name is our being certain of this correspondence. It is here that Kant returns to the beginnings of Hume's arguments, and everyone else's, and roots out the correspondence theory of truth as the implicit premise that is the cause of all the trouble.

Now it will probably seem odd to you to even question something so obviously "true" as the correspondence theory of truth. Of course, we cannot deny that "there is beer in the refrigerator" is true if and only if there is beer in the refrigerator. But let us note immediately that the correspondence theory is not so obviously adequate for all true statements. What does "two plus two equals four" correspond to that makes it true? One might suggest that it corresponds to all combinations in the world of two things (walnuts, elephants, acres, or apples) and two other things of the same kind. "Two plus two equals four" would still be true even if there were no such combinations in the universe. A tautology such as "either it is snowing or it is not snowing" does not correspond to anything; it "tells us nothing about the world." A conceptual truth such as "blue is a color" tells us only about the meanings of the words in our language. A rule of inference tells us how to think. But none of these "correspond" to anything. So, at most, we shall have to say that the correspondence theory is good as an account of empirical knowledge only! (This is the conclusion of most empiricists, including more contemporary "logical positivists.")

But there are more serious problems, even within the domain of empirical knowledge. Let's look again at the truism, " 'there's beer in the refrigerator' is true if and only if there is beer in the refrigerator." Let's ask, first of all, in what sense the noises you utter (the sounds, "there's beer . . . ") correspond to the fact that there is beer in the refrigerator. If you think of one thing corresponding to another, you might think of a map corresponding to the terrain it is a map of: smaller scale with many omissions, but at least it is the same shape, same proportions, and has representations of things in that terrain that you can recognize. But how do those sounds coming out of your mouth (which, now that you listen to them, might sound strange indeed) "correspond" to that six-pack of beer in the kitchen? Now you will say that it is not merely "the sounds" that correspond but rather what you are saying or meaning. And, of course, this is correct. But notice that what those words mean is not a matter of their use in this particular instance; they depend upon their role in a language (American English), which you happen to speak. (If you spoke only Eskimo and pronounced the same sounds, it would be a remarkable coincidence, but wouldn't mean anything.) And the "correspondence" between those words with their meanings and the fact that there is beer in the refrigerator depends not only on the whole American-English language and your knowledge of it but also on a set of conventions that both you and your friend must understand as referring to the beer in the refrigerator.

In class, for example, your teacher says, "there is beer in the refrigerator" as an example of an English sentence. But you do not get up and look for a refrigerator. You know that although your teacher has said the same words that you say to your friend when offering a beer he or she is not directly referring to anything. And the statement does not "correspond" to a fact that there is beer in the refrigerator. It is clear that what you've said (and the same is true of what you've thought) cannot correspond to anything by itself. In a sense, you might say that what corresponds to the fact that there is beer in the refrigerator when you offer your friend a beer is the whole of the English language, with all of its conventions and everything that you and your friend know that is relevant to the meaning of your statement in this particular case.

And from the other side of this "correspondence" matters are no less complicated. What is "the fact" that there is beer in the refrigerator?

Sounds like an easy question. The answer is—that there is beer in the refrigerator! But how do we pick out this fact, except by using our language to distinguish this fact from any number of others. Suppose, instead of saying anything, you were simply to point toward the refrigerator for your friend. Now, of course, knowing you, your friend knows what you mean. In this case, the pointing is shorthand for the statement, and presupposes it. But suppose your friend is a time-traveler from thirteenth-century China who had no idea what a refrigerator was, or a beer for that matter? Would he pick out the right "fact"? How would he know whether you were pointing to the kitchen, to the door of the refrigerator, or to its contents? Is the "beer" to be drunk or to be poured on one's feet? How do we even understand the pointing gesture? (When I point my finger toward the cat food, my cats smell my finger!) So, if it seems obvious to you that "the facts" are simply there, waiting to be corresponded to by our verbal or gestural pointing, think again. One distinguishes the facts of the world only by picking them out by language. The language then can't be said to "correspond" to the world, for it is language that "carves up" our world into those individually identifiable "facts."

This charge against the "correspondence theory" has been defended recently by the influential philosopher Donald Davidson. Ultimately, Davidson defends what he calls a "version" of the correspondence theory (which we discuss shortly under "the semantic theory of truth"). Davidson argues that the usual appeal of the correspondence theory to "the facts" is mistaken, for there can be no way of picking out particular facts without language. Without language, Davidson maintains, there could be but one fact, "The Great Fact," and this renders the correspondence theory useless. The following excerpt is from Davidson's *Truth and Interpretation*.

◆**from *Truth and Interpretation*,
by Donald Davidson**

A true statement is a statement that is true to the facts. This remark seems to embody the same sort of obvious and essential wisdom about truth as the following about motherhood: a mother is a person who is the mother of someone. The *property* of being a mother is explained by the *relation* between a woman and her child; similarly, the suggestion runs, the property of being true is to be explained by a relation between a statement and something else. Without prejudice to the question what the something else might be, or what word or phrase best expresses the relation (of being true to, corresponding to, picturing), I shall take the licence of calling any view of this kind a *correspondence theory* of truth.

Correspondence theories rest on what appears to be an ineluctable if simple idea, but they have not done well under examination. The chief difficulty is in finding a notion of fact that explains anything, that does not lapse, when spelled out, into the trivial or the empty. Recent discussion is thus mainly concerned with deciding whether some form of correspondence is true and trivial (". . . the theory of truth is a series of truisms") or, in so far as it is not confused, simply empty ("The correspondence theory requires, not purification, but elimination"[1]). Those who have discussed the semantic concept of truth in connection with correspondence theories have typically ruled the semantic concept either irrelevant or trivial.

· · · · · · · · · ·

I have said nothing about the purposes served in (non-philosophical) conversation by uttering sentences containing "true" and cognates. No doubt the idea that remarks containing the word "true" typically are used to express agreement, to emphasize conviction or authority, to save repetition, or to shift responsibility, would gain support if it could be shown that truth-words can always be eliminated without cognitive loss by application of a simple formula. Nevertheless, I would hold that theories about the extra-linguistic aims with which sentences are issued are logically independent of the question what they mean; and it is the latter with which I am concerned.

We have failed to find a satisfactory theory to back the thesis that attributions of truth to statements are redundant; but even if it could be shown that no such theory is possible, this would not suffice to establish the correspondence theory. So let us consider more directly the prospects for an account of truth in terms of correspondence.

It is facts correspondence to which is said to make statements true. It is natural, then, to turn to talk of facts for help. Not much can be learned from sentences like

(5) The statement that Thika is in Kenya corresponds to the facts.

or such variants as "It is a fact that Thika is in Kenya," "That Thika is in Kenya is a fact," and "Thika is in Kenya, and that's a fact." Whether or not we accept the view that correspondence to facts explains truth, (5) and its kin say no more than "The statement that Thika is in Kenya is true" (or "Is it true that . . . " or " . . . , and that's the truth," etc.). If (5) is to take on independent interest, it will be because we are able to give an account of facts and correspondence that does not circle back immediately to truth.

---

[1] J. L. Austin and P. F. Strawson, symposium on "Truth." The quoted remarks are from Austin and Strawson, respectively.

Such an account would enable us to make sense of sentences with this form:

(6) The statement that *p* corresponds to the fact that *q*.

The step to truth would be simple: a statement is true if there is a fact to which it corresponds: [(5) could be rewritten "The statement that Thika is in Kenya corresponds to a fact."]

When does (6) hold? Certainly when "*p*" and "*q*" are replaced by the same sentence; after that the difficulties set in. The statement that Naples is farther north than Red Bluff corresponds to the fact that Naples is further north than Red Bluff, but also, it would seem, to the fact that Red Bluff is farther south than Naples (perhaps these are the same fact). Also to the fact that Red Bluff is farther south than the largest Italian city within thirty miles of Ischia. When we reflect that Naples is the city that satisfies the following description: it is the largest city within thirty miles of Ischia, and such that London is in England, then we begin to suspect that if a statement corresponds to one fact, it corresponds to all. ("Corresponds to the *facts*" may be right in the end.)

• • • • • • • • • •

Since aside from matters of correspondence no way of distinguishing facts has been proposed, and this test fails to uncover a single difference, we may read the result of our argument as showing that there is exactly one fact. Descriptions like "the fact that there are stupas in Nepal," if they describe at all, describe the same thing: The Great Fact. No point remains in distinguishing among various names of The Great Fact when written after "corresponds to"; we may as well settle for the single phrase "corresponds to The Great Fact." This unalterable predicate carries with it a redundant whiff of ontology, but beyond this there is apparently no telling it apart from "is true."[2]

Now none of this is to say that your statement, "there's beer in the refrigerator" isn't true if and only if there is beer in the refrigerator. It is rather to say that this simple "correspondence" is possible only because of the enormous number of systematic assumptions we share within our language and about the world and about the way we refer to particular "facts" in the world by use of certain statements. In everyday life we don't have to think about such things. But in philosophy, they make us marvel at what complex and clever creatures we are. Bertrand Russell, certainly one of the smartest among us, spent forty years trying to make sense out of the "common sense" correspondence theory. He never did. He never succeeded in formulating an adequate defense of the idea that some single unit of language could "correspond" to discrete "facts" in the

[2]Donald Davidson, *Truth and Interpretation* (New York: Oxford University Press, 1984).

world. And today, most philosophers would agree, no matter what kind of method they follow, that the correspondence theory alone cannot make sense of the notion of truth. A statement means something only within a language, and a "fact" is "corresponded to" only after it has been picked out by language. And that means that truth can't be simple correspondence.

And so, the seemingly simple act of "saying what is true" turns out to be enormously complicated. And against the "correspondence theory of truth," there are three telling arguments:

1) It is, at best, limited. All cases of necessary truth, and perhaps some others, cannot be accounted for by it at all.
2) There is no such thing as a statement or a belief that by itself is capable of "corresponding" to anything.
3) There is no such thing as a "fact" that can be picked out independently of the language used to describe it.

Next time you say or think that there is beer in the refrigerator, you might marvel at the complex that has just come into action. That won't, unfortunately, guarantee that your statement or thought will be true. For despite all this sophisticated, intellectual apparatus we still occasionally forget to buy the beer.

B. THEORIES OF TRUTH

Now what? We find ourselves with some ill-defined complex in which our language and reality are tied together and mutually depend on each other. But what have we been leading up to, finally, is that we need something more than the naive common-sense "correspondence theory of truth," one which takes into account this complexity of interrelations. Three such theories have achieved prominence in this century, although all three of them were anticipated by Immanuel Kant, whom we shall meet later in this chapter. The three theories are:

1) The **coherence theory of truth:** which says that a statement or a belief is true if and only if it "coheres" or ties in with other statements and beliefs.
2) The **pragmatic theory of truth:** which says that a statement or a belief is true if and only if "it works," if it allows us to predict certain results, if it allows us to function effectively in everyday life, and if it encourages further inquiry or helps us lead better lives.
3) The **semantic theory of truth:** which says that a statement or a belief is true because the rules of our language set up a correspondence between certain statements and "the facts" that our

language picks out in the world. Superficially this theory looks like the correspondence theory, but it is very different. The correspondence theory accepts facts as "already there," independent of our language. The semantic theory explains this apparent correspondence by telling us that it is our language that sets it up in the first place.

1.   The Coherence Theory

The coherence theory of truth does not necessarily oppose the common-sense idea that true statements "correspond" to facts in the world, but it does shift the focus of the discussion away from this correspondence—if there is one—to the interdependence of the statements themselves. In other words, it seizes on the observation made above, in our discussion of the correspondence theory, that a simple statement of fact ("there's beer in the refrigerator") involves, in some sense, the whole English language. The words in that simple sentence would not mean much if they did not also have the same meaning in an unlimited number of other sentences, and their ability to refer to the world therefore depends on their role in a language.

Furthermore, when we try to ascertain the truth of a statement, how do we do it? By ascertaining the truth of other statements and arguing, deductively or inductively, for the consequent truth of this one. Thus the coherence theory places its emphasis on the ways in which we find out the truth, and it rightly points out that knowledge is not just a matter of establishing the truth of one statement after another; it is a matter of getting more and more statements to cohere in a unified body of knowledge. This coherence makes them true, whether or not there is some metaphysical sense in which they cohere because, in fact, they are true.

To represent the coherence theory, here is a selection from the American philosopher, Brand Blanshard.

◆On the Coherence Theory, by Brand Blanshard

To think is to seek understanding. And to seek understanding is an activity of mind that is marked off from all other activities by a highly distinctive aim. This aim . . . is to achieve systematic vision, so to apprehend what is now unknown to us as to relate it, and relate it necessarily, to what we know already.

But may it not be that what satisfies thought fails to conform to the real world? Where is the guarantee that when I have brought my ideas into the form my ideal requires, they should be

true? . . . In our long struggle with the relation of thought to reality
we saw that if thought and things are conceived as related only
externally, then knowledge is luck; there is no necessity whatever
that what satisfies intelligence should coincide with what really is.
It may do so, or it may not; on the principle that there are many
misses to one bull's-eye, it more probably does not. But if we get
rid of the misleading analogies through which this relation has
been conceived, of copy and original, stimulus and organism, lan-
tern and screen, and go to thought itself with the question what reference to an object means, we get a different and more hopeful
answer. To think of a thing is to get that thing itself in some degree
within the mind. To think of a color or an emotion is to have that
within us which if it *were developed and completed*, would
identify itself with the object. In short, if we accept its own report,
thought is related to reality as the partial to the perfect fulfillment
of a purpose. The more adequate its grasp the more nearly does
it approximate, the more fully does it realize in itself, the nature
and relations of its objects.

· · · · · · · · · ·

. . . We may look at the growth of knowledge, individual or social,
either as an attempt by our own minds to return to union with
things as they are in their ordered wholeness, or the affirmation
through our minds of the ordered whole itself. And if we take this
view, our notion of truth is marked out for us. Truth is the approximation of thought to reality. It is thought on its way home. Its
measure is the distance thought has travelled, under guidance of
its inner compass, toward that intelligible system which unites its
ultimate object with its ultimate end. Hence at any given time the
degree of truth in our experience as a whole is the degree of system
it has achieved. The degree of truth of a particular proposition is
to be judged in the first instance by its coherence with experience
as a whole, ultimately by its coherence with that further whole,
all-comprehensive and fully articulated, in which thought can come
to rest.[3]

The coherence theory of truth, according to Blanshard, begins with
the observation that we test the truth of a belief by seeing its implications
and other logically connected beliefs. But the theory is not confined to
this test. Truth itself, he insists, is nothing other than the interconnect-
edness of our various beliefs. The truth of a particular belief is nothing
other than how well it fits in with everything else we believe.

2.   The Pragmatic Theory

Pragmatism is the one major philosophical movement to originate
and remain more or less completely in America. The three philosophers

[3]Brand Blanshard, *The Nature of Thought* (New York: Macmillan, 1941).

most easily identified with this movement are Charles Peirce, William James, and John Dewey, all of them Americans (Peirce and James in Massachusetts, Dewey in Chicago and New York). We shall see more of pragmatism later in this chapter, but for now, what is important to us is the pragmatists' theory or theories of truth (for they did not entirely agree with one another). As one might expect, both from the name "pragmatism" and the characteristic American concern for what is "practical," a pragmatic theory of truths begins with a certain impatience for the abstractions and obscurities of traditional metaphysics and epistemology. In particular, the inadequacies of the correspondence theory of truth struck them not just as a philosophical dilemma, but a genuine source of scandal. How is it possible, they asked, that the traditional theories of truth ended up in skepticism?

Charles Peirce found the traditional discussions absurd just because they tried to conceive of truth without any concern or reference whatsoever to the practical circumstances in which we worry about the truth. Truth is not a relationship between sentences and the world, nor is it a complex relationship among sentences. Truth is the answer to questions that we ask, because we are uncertain, because we have doubts. The truth is what we all, eventually, agree upon. According to Peirce, "The opinion which is fated to be ultimately agreed to by all who investigate, is what we mean by the truth." The emphasis thus gets shifted from truth as a property of sentences and beliefs and their relationships to facts and each other to truth as a function of asking questions, carrying on investigations, and clearing up actual mysteries and disagreements. The test of truth is neither correspondence nor coherence but agreement, what in fact solves our problems and answers our inquiries.

Peirce was deeply concerned with the practices of scientific investigation, and his theory of truth was aimed primarily at questions of truth in science, where experimentation and observation should lead, eventually, to agreement on one hypothesis or theory or another. William James, on the other hand, had much broader interests in philosophy. While he was interested in science (and, indeed, was one of America's leading physicians and psychologists), he was also interested in the less scientific aspects of human life, in which truth was also a critical issue. For example, he wrote extensively on the topic of religious belief in which questions of experimentation and observation play virtually no role at all. (One of his best known essays is included in Chapter 6.)

Accordingly, James places very little emphasis on agreement as the test of truth. However appropriate this might be in science, it is surely not even plausible in the subject of religion. Instead, he stressed the advantages of a certain belief in life. By "practical," James meant the concrete, the effective, not that which leads to scientific agreement. Thus a religious belief can be said to be true, for example, according to its effects on us. Believing in a good, just God makes us optimistic and happy; believing that life is meaningless makes us miserable. Thus truth refers to what significance a belief has in our lives, not correspondence, coherence or, we can add, the limited success of scientific hypotheses and theories. Scientific truth still has its place in James' philosophy, of course. But that kind of truth is defined by the restricted context of an investigation; it should not be generalized as a concept of truth in all contexts. (It should be noted that Peirce so radically disagreed with James' generalization of his theory that he actually changed the name of his philosophy, from "pragmatism" to "pragmaticism," which he noted was a word "sufficiently ugly" to avoid popularization.)

John Dewey returned the pragmatic theory to its narrower focus. He did not restrict truth to scientific truth, but he did restrict it to *experiential* truth. But whereas James would include, for example, religious experience, Dewey insists that the only meaningful notion of "experience" must be limited to empirically verifiable matters. That eliminates questions of theology. And like Peirce, Dewey emphasizes the context of investigation, in particular, the intellectually painful experience of doubt. Like James and unlike Peirce, Dewey does not emphasize the notion of general agreement as the test of truth so much as he emphasizes its efficacy in ending doubts and closing an investigation. A police case, for example, comes to an end when "all the pieces fall into place." But that is not a matter of coherence so much as it is a matter of resolving doubts and "tying together loose ends," satisfying all of our questions and quieting critics and skeptics. A scientific hypothesis is said to be true when all attempts to falsify it have failed and every attempt to confirm it comes out successfully. Again, it is an end to the inquiry, a solution to the problem. Where traditional philosophy gets into trouble is in trying to understand "truth" in a vacuum, without reference to any inquiry or investigation, without any reference to the context in which truth makes a difference.

The following selections are from Charles Peirce, "How to Make Our Ideas Clear," and William James, *Pragmatism*.

◆**from "How to Make Our Ideas Clear," by Charles Peirce**

Let us now approach the subject of logic, and consider a conception which particularly concerns it, that of *reality*. Taking clearness in the sense of familiarity, no idea could be clearer than this. Every child uses it with perfect confidence, never dreaming that he does not understand it. As for clearness in its second grade, however, it would probably puzzle most men, even among those of a re-

flective turn of mind, to give an abstract definition of the real. Yet
such a definition may perhaps be reached by considering the
points of difference between reality and its opposite, fiction. A fig-
ment is a product of somebody's imagination; it has such characters as his thought impresses upon it. That those characters are independent of how you or I think is an external reality. There are,
however, phenomena within our own minds, dependent upon our
thought, which are at the same time real in the sense that we really
think them. But though their characters depend on how we think,
they do not depend on what we think those characters to be. Thus,
a dream has a real existence as a mental phenomenon, if somebody
has really dreamt it; that he dreamt so and so, does not depend
on what anybody thinks was dreamt, but is completely independent
of all opinions on the subject. On the other hand, considering, not
the fact of dreaming, but the thing dreamt, it retains its peculiarities by virtue of no other fact than that it was dreamt to possess
them. Thus we may define the real as that whose characters are independent of what anybody may think them to be.

But, however satisfactory such a definition may be found, it
would be a great mistake to suppose that it makes the idea of reality perfectly clear. Here, then, let us apply our rules. According to
them, reality, like every other quality, consists in the peculiar, sensible effects which things partaking of it produce. The only effect
which real things have is to cause belief, for all the sensations
which they excite emerge into consciousness in the form of beliefs.
The question, therefore, is, how is true belief (or belief in the real)
distinguished from false belief (or belief in fiction). Now, as we have
seen in the former paper, the ideas of truth and falsehood, in their
full development, appertain exclusively to the scientific method of
settling opinion. A person who arbitrarily chooses the propositions
which he will adopt can use the word truth only to emphasize the
expression of his determination to hold on to his choice. Of course,
the method of tenacity never prevailed exclusively; reason is too
natural to men for that. But in the literature of the Dark Ages we
find some fine examples of it. When Scotus Erigena is commenting
upon a poetical passage in which hellebore is spoken of as having
caused the death of Socrates, he does not hesitate to inform the inquiring reader that Helleborus and Socrates were two eminent
Greek philosophers, and that the latter having been overcome in
argument by the former took the matter to heart and died of it!
What sort of an idea of truth could a man have who could adopt
and teach, without the qualification of a "perhaps," an opinion
taken so entirely at random? The real spirit of Socrates, who I
hope would have been delighted to have been "overcome in argument," because he would have learned something by it, is in
curious contrast with the naïve idea of the glossist, for whom (as
for the "born missionary" of today) discussion would seem to have
been simply a struggle. When philosophy began to awake from its
long slumber, and before theology completely dominated it, the

practice seems to have been for each professor to seize upon any philosophical position he found unoccupied and which seemed a strong one, to intrench himself in it, and to sally forth from time to time to give battle to the others. Thus, even the scanty records we possess of those disputes enable us to make out a dozen or more opinions held by different teachers at one time concerning the questions of nominalism and realism. Read the opening part of the *Historia Calamitatum* of Abélard, who was certainly as philosophical as any of his contemporaries, and see the spirit ofcombat which it breathes. For him, the truth is simply his particular stronghold. When the method of authority prevailed, the truth meant little more than the Catholic faith. All the efforts of the scholastic doctors are directed toward harmonizing their faith in Aristotle and their faith in the Church, and one may search their ponderous folios through without finding an argument which goes any further. It is noticeable that where different faiths flourish side by side, renegades are looked upon with contempt even by the party whose belief they adopt; so completely has the idea of loyalty replaced that of truth-seeking. Since the time of Descartes, the defect in the conception of truth has been less apparent. Still, it will sometimes strike a scientific man that philosophers have been less intent on finding out what the facts are than on inquiring what belief is most in harmony with their system. It is hard to convince a follower of the *a priori* method by adducing facts; but show him that an opinion he is defending is inconsistent with what he has laid down elsewhere, and he will be very apt to retract it. These minds do not seem to believe that disputation is ever to cease; they seem to think that the opinion which is natural for one man is not so for another, and that belief will, consequently, never be settled. In contenting themselves with fixing their own opinions by a method which would lead another man to a different result, they betray their feeble hold of the conception of what truth is.

On the other hand, all the followers of science are fully persuaded that the processes of investigation, if only pushed far enough, will give one certain solution to each question to which they can be applied. One man may investigate the velocity of light by studying the transits of Venus and the aberration of the stars; another by the oppositions of Mars and the eclipses of Jupiter's satellites; a third by the method of Fizeau; a fourth by that of Foucault; a fifth by the motions of the curves of Lissajous; a sixth, a seventh, an eighth, and a ninth, may follow the different methods of comparing the measures of statical and dynamical electricity. They may at first obtain different results, but, as each perfects his method and his processes, the results will move steadily together toward a destined center. So with all scientific research. Different minds may set out with the most antagonistic views, but the progress of investigation carries them by a force outside of themselves to one and the same conclusion. This activity of thought by which we are carried, not where we wish, but to a foreordained goal, is like the operation of destiny. No modification of the point of view taken, no selection of other facts for study, no natural bent of mind even, can enable a man to escape the predestinate opinion. This great law is embodied in the conception of truth and reality. The opinion which is fated[4] to be ultimately agreed to by all who investigate is what we mean by the truth, and the object represented in this opinion is real. That is the way I would explain reality.

But it may be said that this view is directly opposed to the abstract definition which we have given of reality, inasmuch as it makes the characters of the real depend on what is ultimately thought about them. But the answer to this is that, on the one hand, reality is independent, not necessarily thought of in general, but only of what you or I or any finite number of men may think about it; and that, on the other hand, though the object of the final opinion depends on what that opinion is, yet what that opinion is does not depend on what you or I or any man thinks. Our perversity and that of others may indefinitely postpone the settlement of opinion; it might even conceivably cause an arbitrary proposition to be universally accepted as long as the human race should last. Yet even that would not change the nature of the belief, which alone could be the result of investigation carried sufficiently far; and if, after the extinction of our race, another should arise with faculties and disposition for investigation, that true opinion must be the one which they would ultimately come to. "Truth crushed to earth shall rise again," and the opinion which would finally result from investigation does not depend on how anybody may actually think. But the reality of that which is real does depend on the real fact that investigation is destined to lead, at last, if continued long enough, to a belief in it.[5]

◆ on the Pragmatic Theory, by William James

I fully expect to see the pragmatist view of truth run through the classic stages of a theories career. First, you know, a new theory is attacked as absurd; then it is admitted to be true, but obvious and insignificant; finally it is seen to be so important that its adversaries claim that they themselves discovered it. Our doctrine of truth is at present in the first of these three stages, with symptoms of the second stage having begun in certain quarters. . . . Truth, as any dictionary will tell you, is a property of certain of our ideas.

[4]Fate means merely that which is sure to come true, and cannot be avoided. It is a superstition to suppose that a certain sort of events are ever fated, and it is another to suppose that the word *fate* can never be freed from its superstitious taint. We are all fated to die.

[5]Charles S. Peirce, "How to Make Our Ideas Clear" in *Popular Science Monthly* (January 1878).

It means their "agreement," as falsity means their disagreement, with "reality." Pragmatism and intellectualists both accept this definition as a matter of course. They begin to quarrel only after the question is raised as to what may precisely be meant by the term "agreement," and what by the term "reality," when reality is taken as something for our ideas to agree with.

In answering these questions the pragmatists are more analytic and painstaking, the intellectualists more offhand and irreflective. The popular notion is that a true idea must copy its reality. Like other popular views, this one follows the analogy of the most usual experience. Our true ideas of sensible things do indeed copy them. Shut your eyes and think of yonder clock on the wall, and you get just such a true picture or copy of its dial. But your ideas of its "works" (unless you are a clock-maker) is much less of a copy, yet it passes muster, for it in no way clashes with the reality. Even though it should shrink to the mere word "works," that word still serves you truly; and when you speak of the "time-keeping function" of the clock, or of its spring's "elasticity," it is hard to see exactly what your ideas can copy.

You perceive that there is a problem here. Where our ideas cannot copy definitely their object, what does agreement with that object mean? Some idealists seem to say that they are true whenever they are what God means that we ought to think about that object. Other hold the copy-view all through, and speak as if our ideas possessed truth just in proportion as they approach to being copies of the Absolute's eternal way of thinking.

These views, you see, invite pragmatistic discussion. But the great assumption of the intellectualists is that truth means essentially an inert static relation. When you've got your true idea of anything, there's an end of the matter. You're in possession: you *know*; you have fulfilled your thinking destiny. You are where you ought to be mentally; you have obeyed your categorical imperative; and nothing more need follow on that climax of your rational destiny. Epistemologically you are in stable equilibrium.

Pragmatism, on the other hand, asks its usual question, "Grant an idea or belief to be true," it says, "what concrete difference will its being true make in any one's actual life? How will the truth be realized? What experiences will be different from those which would obtain if the belief were false? What, in short, is the truth's cash-value in experiential terms?"

The moment pragmatism asks this question, it sees the answer: *True ideas are those that we can assimilate, validate, corroborate and verify. False ideas are those that we can not.* That is the practical difference it makes to us to have true ideas; that therefore, is the meaning of truth, for it is all that truth is known as.

This thesis is what I have to defend. The truth of an idea is not a stagnant property inherent in it. Truth *happens* to an idea. It *becomes* true, is *made* true by events. Its verity *is* in fact an event, a process: the process namely of its verifying itself, its veri-*fication*. Its validity is the process of its valid*ation*.

But what do the words verification and validation themselves pragmatically mean? They again signify certain practical consequences of the verified and validated idea. It is hard to find any one phrase that characterizes these consequences better than the ordinary agreement-formula—just such consequences being what we have in mind whenever we say that our ideas "agree" with reality. They lead us, namely, through the acts and other ideas which they instigate, into or up to, or towards, other parts of experience with which we feel all the while—such feeling being among our potentialities—that the original ideas remain in agreement. The connexions and transitions come to us from point to point as being progressive, harmonious, satisfactory. This function of agreeable leading is what we mean by an idea's verification. Such an account is vague and it sounds at first quite trivial, but it has results which it will take the rest of my hour to explain.

Let me begin by reminding you of the fact that the possession of true thoughts means everywhere the possession of invaluable instruments of action; and that our duty to gain truth, so far from being a blank command from out of the blue, or a "stunt" self-imposed by our intellect, can account for itself by excellent practical reasons.

The importance to human life of having true beliefs about matters of fact is a thing too notorious. We live in a world of realities that can be infinitely useful or infinitely harmful. Ideas that tell us which of them to expect count as the true ideas in all this primary sphere of verification, and the pursuit of such ideas is a primary human duty. The possession of truth, so far from being here an end in itself, is only a preliminary means towards other vital satisfactions. If I am lost in the woods and starved, and find what looks like a cow-path, it is of the utmost importance that I should think of a human habitation at the end of it, for if I do so and follow it, I save myself. The true thought is useful here because the house which is its object is useful. The practical value of true ideas is thus primarily derived from the practical importance of their objects to us. Their objects are, indeed, not important at all times. I may on another occasion have no use for the house; and then my idea of it, however verifiable, will be practically irrelevant, and had better remain latent. Yet since almost any object may some day become temporarily important, the advantage of having a general stock of *extra* truths, of ideas that shall be true of merely possible situations, is obvious. We store such extra truths away in our memories, and with the overflow we fill our books of reference. Whenever such an extra truth becomes practically relevant to one of our emergencies, it passes from cold storage to do work in the world and our belief in it grows active. You can say of it then either that "it is useful because it is true" or that "it is true because it is useful." Both these phrases mean exactly the same thing, namely that here is an idea that gets fulfilled and can be verified. True is the name for whatever idea starts the verification-process, useful is the name for its completed function in experience. True ideas would never have been singled out as such, would never have acquired a class-name, least of all a name suggesting value, unless they had been useful from the outset in this way.

· · · · · · · · · ·

To "agree" in the widest sense with a reality *can only mean to be guided either straight up to it or into its surroundings, or to be put into such working touch with it as to handle either it or something connected with it better than if we disagreed.*

· · · · · · · · · ·

"The true," to put it very briefly, is only the expedient in the way of our thinking, just as "the right" is only the expedient way of our behaving.[6]

In other words, truth, according to the pragmatic theory, is what allows us to handle situations better, what is expedient, what "works." This includes, however, not isolated tasks (in which a "false" belief might occasionally work better) but the entire process of scientific verification, so that the truth of a belief depends not only on its workability on some particular occasion, but, as in the coherence theory, on its connection with scientific testing and the whole of our lives.

3.   The Semantic Theory

The semantic theory is most difficult of all, partly because of its misleading, superficial resemblance to the correspondence theory, but mainly because it has been a purely formal theory. That is, it is neutral regarding the other theories and the ordinary, "natural" languages (for example, English or French). In a sense, it is a theory that has been developing in many ways since the Kantian turn in philosophy. In its formal "semantic" version, however, it is generally credited to the American logician Alfred Tarski.

◆**from "The Semantic Theory of Truth," by Alfred Tarski**

. . . we must always relate the notion of truth, like that of a sentence, to a specific language; for it is obvious that the same expression which is a true sentence in one language can be false or meaningless in another.

[6]William James, *Pragmatism: A New Name for Some Old Ways of Thinking* (New York: Longmans, Green, 1907).

Let us start with a concrete example. Consider the sentence *"snow is white."* We ask the question under what conditions this sentence is true or false. It seems clear that if we base ourselves on the classical conception of truth, we shall say that the sentence is true if snow is white, and that it is false if snow is not white. Thus, if the definition of truth is to conform to our conception, it must imply the following equivalence:

> The sentence *"snow is white"* is true, if, and only if, snow is white.

We shall now generalize the procedure which we have applied above. Let us consider an arbitrary sentence; we shall replace it by the letter *"p."* We form the name of this sentence and we replace it by another letter, say *"X."* We ask now what is the logical relation between the two sentences *"X is true"* and *"p."* It is clear that from the point of view of our basic conception of truth these sentences are equivalent. In other words, the following equivalence holds:

> (T) X is true if, and only if, p.

We shall call any such equivalence (with *"p"* replaced by any sentence of the language to which the word *"true"* refers, and *"X"* replaced by a name of this sentence) an *"equivalence of the form (T)."*

Now at last we are able to put into a precise form the conditions under which we will consider the usage and the definition of the term *"true"* as adequate from the material point of view: we wish to use the term *"true"* in such a way that all equivalences of the form (T) can be asserted, and *we shall call a definition of truth "adequate" if all these equivalences follow from it.*

I should like to propose the name *"the semantic conception of truth"* for the conception of truth which has just been discussed.

Semantics is a discipline which, speaking loosely, *deals with certain relations between expressions of a language and the objects* (or "states of affairs") "referred to" by those expressions. As typical examples of semantic concepts we may mention the concepts of *designation, satisfaction,* and *definition* as these occur in the following examples:

> the expression *"the father of his country"* designates (denotes) *George Washington;*
> snow satisfies the sentential function (the condition) *"x is white";*
> The equation *"2 · x = 1"* defines (uniquely determines) the number ½

While the words *"designates," "satisfies,"* and *"defines"* express relations (between certain expressions and the object "referred to" by these expressions), the word *"true"* is of a different logical

nature: it expresses a property (or denotes a class) of certain expressions, viz., of sentences. However, it is easily seen that all the
formulations which were given earlier and which aimed at the
meaning of this word ("true") referred not only to sentences themselves, but also to objects "talked about" by these sentences, or
possibly to "states of affairs" described by them. . . . A definition of
truth can be obtained in a very simple way from that of another
semantic notion, namely, of the notion of *satisfaction*.[7]

Very simply explained, Tarski's semantic theory picks out a "class" of
"individuals" (objects, states of affairs, or "facts") and specifies, for every
sentence in the language, which individuals will or will not "satisfy" it,
that is, make it "true" or not. But since the logician must "set up" each
pair of sentences and individuals that will satisfy it, it is obvious that this
formula will work only for a relatively small number of basic sentences
with a manageable class of individuals. Here is the problem in extending
the theory to natural languages (such as American English), which have
a potentially infinite number of sentences and have to deal with an
indefinite number of individuals. (This extension is being attempted
today, however, by several leading philosophers, particularly Donald
Davidson.) But for our purposes, the theory comes to this: We must set
up the rules of satisfaction according to which our sentences become
true or false. "Correspondence" is not a relation for which we supply only
the appropriate sentences. In developing a language, we must also specify
the relation of the language to the world, and thus "set up" the world to
correspond to our language.

The semantic theory certainly resembles the correspondence theory.
(Some philosophers, such as Karl Popper, have insisted that it *is* a
version of the correspondence theory.) But in the development of the
semantic theory of truth, Tarski and his followers have avoided
traditional talk of "facts"; indeed facts are in disfavor. Instead, the
emphasis is on the semantic conception of "satisfaction" (and the related
notion of "reference"). *Something* outside of the language makes
statements true—that is, satisfies them, but the semantic theory, unlike
the traditional correspondence theory, does not insist or suggest that this
"something" consists of already discrete and complete units of reality.
The "something" too is defined through language by its stipulative role
in our statements. (It is an open question, for the semantic theory,
whether the same references, the same *somethings*, are available in
every language or whether reference and satisfaction are limited to particular languages; in other words, it is still being argued—vigorously—
whether or not the semantic theory leads to relativism.)

Taken individually, each of these theories has its opponents. We have

[7]Alfred Tarski, "The Semantic Theory of Truth," in *Philosophy and Phenomenological
Research* 4, no. 3 (March 1944).

attacked the correspondence theory sufficiently. Against the coherence theory, other philosophers have objected that a system of statements and beliefs can be "coherent" but yet not be true. For example, take a simple system of true beliefs and deny them all. They will still form a coherent system, but they will all be false. Similarly, we said in Chapter 1 that an argument can be valid (which makes it coherent) but yet have false premises and false conclusions.

Two opposed systems of statements and beliefs can be equally "coherent," but surely both cannot be true, for they claim opposite things about the world. (Think of the metaphysical systems of Spinoza and Leibniz.) So, truth must be more than mere coherence.

Against the pragmatic theory, philosophers have objected that a belief might "work" but not be true. Scientists have often made great headway with false hypotheses. Political demagogues have often obtained great power and even achieved positive results with lies. And false beliefs often make us happier than the truth. ("What you don't know won't hurt you" and "the truth hurts.") The reason some beliefs "work" better than others, it has been argued (for example, by Bertrand Russell), is that they are true. They are true, therefore, not because they "work," but they work because they are true to the facts.

And against the semantic theory, philosophers have objected that ultimately, it is still a restatement of the correspondence theory (" 'snow is white' is true if and only if snow is white"). Although the semantic theory is an improvement because it emphasizes the role of language in picking out the facts that make our statements true, it still leaves the nature of the "picking out" as obscure as ever. We are not in the position of a logician, who can make up his semantic models and languages at will. (Consider the following silly but profoundly philosophical joke: Eve says to Adam: "Let's call that one a hippopotamus." Adam: "Why 'hippopotamus'?" Eve: "Because it looks more like a hippopotamus than anything else we've seen so far.")

An adequate semantic theory of truth must be far more than merely formal. It must specify how such a theory would apply to natural (unformalized and open-ended) languages. Truth cannot be only formally defined. If the semantic theory is true, then translations between languages are impossible since the rules of satisfaction are unique to each language.

The debate between these theories continues, but the likeliest outcome is usually a combination of theories rather than the exclusive victory of any particular one. Each makes up for the deficiencies in the others. But one of the most important consequences of this debate, ironically, has been the loss of interest in the very concept of Truth (with a capital "T"). In everyday contexts, of course, philosophers, like everyone else, will talk about statements and beliefs being "true" and "false" on the basis of a primitive "correspondence" notion, that is, "correspondence to the facts." But philosophically, the power of the word "Truth" has always dwelled in its strong metaphysical linkage to "the way the world really is." And having given up on that grandiose conception of Truth, many philosophers are sometimes inclined to give up the word "truth" altogether. They concern themselves only with what we ordinarily mean when we say that a statement is "true."[8] Other philosophers, however, refuse to give up the traditional search for truth, and new and improved versions of the traditional and newer theories are still appearing.

C. KANT'S REVOLUTION

What, then, is truth? It seems that either it is "out there," independent of us but perhaps therefore unknowable, or else it is, in some sense, "in us"—in the language we speak or the practical concerns we bring to our inquiries. The correspondence and semantic theories of truth accept this dualism of language and world; the coherence and pragmatic theories challenge it but, however hesitantly, find themselves uneasy about denying correspondence altogether, and with it, "the real world." But there is another tradition—one of which the coherence theory and the pragmatic theory are partial heirs—in which this very distinction between language and world, between us and Truth, is rejected. The prime mover of this other tradition is the German philosopher Immanuel Kant.

Immanuel Kant is considered by a great many philosophers to be the greatest thinker since Plato and Aristotle. He stands at the beginning of almost every modern movement in philosophy in America and Europe, as an inspiration and as a kind of founder. Existentialism would not be possible without him; nor would phenomenology, pragmatism, or many of the varieties of linguistic philosophy that have dominated English and American philosophy for most of this century. He brings together the often opposed threads of rationalism and empiricism and weaves them into a single, monumental philosophical system, which he published primarily in three "critiques" (*The Critique of Pure Reason, The Critique of Practical Reason,* and *The Critique of Judgment*) in the last two decades of the eighteenth century. His writing is notoriously difficult, but it is possible for even a beginning philosophy student to appreciate the main theme of his self-proclaimed "revolution" in philosophy. It is, in one sense, a total reorientation of what we mean when we talk about the Truth.

Ever since the ancient Greeks, almost all philosophers had accepted the idea that there is a reality "out there," which we could come to know

[8] J. L. Austin, for example, begins an essay on "Truth" by declaring, "*In vino veritas,* ('in wine, truth') perhaps, but in a sober symposium, *verum* ('true')."

through reason, through experience, or perhaps which we could not come to know at all, according to a skeptic such as David Hume. The idea of an "external world" seemed innocent enough, until metaphysicians began to find that their contradictory views about this world could not be reconciled. This dilemma prompted John Locke to turn away from metaphysics and pay more attention to the way we acquire knowledge. The shift of attention to knowledge led Hume to argue that we couldn't even know that the sun would rise tomorrow, or that one billiard ball in fact causes the movement of another, or that there is indeed a world outside of our own ideas.

This skeptical conclusion seemed utterly absurd to Kant, who was, in his own words, "awakened from his dogmatic slumbers" by Hume. Kant had been a metaphysician (a follower of Leibniz), but reading Hume convinced him that there was a serious problem, not only for metaphysics, but for our claims to know the world at all. And Kant, who was also a scientist and an enthusiastic supporter of Isaac Newton and the new physics, saw that he had to refute Hume if he was going to keep claiming that scientists (and everyone else) could know anything at all. But the problem, as he diagnosed it, turned out to be the unquestioned idea that there was a distinction to be made between our beliefs and experience of the world, on the one hand, and the world itself, Reality or Truth, on the other.

What Kant suspected, and what many philosophers believe today, is that our "ideas"—our concepts and our language—do not just correspond to reality but in some sense "set up" the world, impose upon the world the structures we experience. We see material objects instead of just patterns of light and colors (as seen perhaps by a newborn baby), and this is our contribution to experience. We experience events in a cause-and-effect relationship, instead of as mere sequences of events, and this is not because of experience alone, but because we *make* our experience conform to causal rules. We expect certain events in the future on the basis of what we have experienced in the past; and this too is not mere habit, but a set of rules we impose necessarily on every experience. According to Kant, space and time do not exist "out there," independent of our experience; we impose the forms of three-dimensional space and one-dimensional time on our experience, and through these forms come to know the world. So too, Kant argues, all of our knowledge of the world is in part a product of the various forms and rules that we impose upon, or use to "set up," our experience. The word Kant uses for "set up" is "constitutes." A "constitution" sets up a government, provides it with its rules and structures. We **constitute** our own experience in the sense that we provide the rules and structures according to which we experience objects, as objects in space and time, as governed by the laws of nature and the relations of cause and effect. Kant writes, "the understanding does not derive its laws from, but prescribes them to, nature."

According to Kant's philosophy, reality has no existence that we can understand except as we constitute it through our basic concepts. Kant took these concepts—or what he called "categories"—to be the basic rules of the human mind as such, common to all peoples in all places at all times. Today, many philosophers would rather say that these concepts through which we constitute the world are part of a language, which raises the intriguing but controversial possibility that the world might be quite different for people who speak different languages. (Kant himself did not believe this.) Truth, in other words, is a function of our concepts. It is not correspondence; it is not mere coherence. And it is not just a matter of what "works" or satisfies our investigations. Kant's revolution rejects the very idea of an external Reality and instead looks to the concepts through which we "constitute" Reality. Thus there is no point to wondering whether our concepts match up to Reality, since there would be no Reality without our concepts. Our concepts not only cohere with each other; they "set up" a corresponding reality as well. And of course those concepts "work"—it is as if someone were to wonder how it is that a ceramic mold exactly fits a piece of jewelry, when the mold gave shape to the jewelry in the first place.

Previous philosophers had asked, "How can we know that our ideas correspond with the way the world really is?" Kant rejected that question. Instead, he asked, *"How do our ideas constitute the world?"* "What is the structure and what are the rules (the *concepts* or *categories*) of the human mind according to which we 'set up' our world, the world of our experience?"

The project of Kant's *Critique of Pure Reason* is to analyze and prove the necessity of these concepts, which we can know a priori—independently of all experience and with certainty, just because they are the rules within which all of our knowledge is possible. Think of it this way: you take a number of pieces of wood and a checkerboard and "set up" the game by making up rules about what can be moved where, how, and when. Then, within the game, you are free to make any number of moves, some brilliant, some stupid, but you are always bound by the rules that you yourself have "set up." And since you yourself have established these rules, it would be absurd to wonder whether or not they are "true."

Kant's revolution changed our conception of truth and, along with it, our conception of reality, our conception of knowledge, and, most importantly, our conception of ourselves. Truth is no longer correspondence between our ideas and reality, but our own system of rules (concepts or categories) by which we constitute our reality. Knowledge, accordingly, is no longer the comprehending of a reality beyond our experience, but knowledge of our experience. But this does not mean knowledge of experience, distinct from knowledge of objects, for the objects of our experience are all there is to reality. Moreover, in making this move, Kant gives the philosophers something which they thought they had lost, a renewed ideal of certainty, for, he argued, we can be certain of the rules of our own experience. Kant defended the necessity of the truths of arithmetic and geometry as those rules that have to do with the a priori forms of our intuitions of space and time. According to Kant's philosophy in general, reality is the world of our experience, as we constitute it through the concepts of our understanding. Therefore, we can know it with certainty, for truth, in general, is our own construction.

You might at first think that there is some trick here, as if Kant is saying, "Well, if we can't have knowledge in the hard sense, then I'll simply redefine the words *knowledge, reality,* and *truth*." But what he has done is to point to the difficulty of the picture that other philosophers had accepted; he has shown that what we normally mean by "truth," "knowledge," and "reality" is not an insatiable appeal to a world beyond our experience. My everyday statement, "there's beer in the refrigerator," is true, whatever any philosopher might say, if there is beer in the refrigerator—if I can go and look, see it, pick it up, open the can, and drink it. As for some beer beyond my experience that is the real beer, what kind of absurdity is that? Underneath Kant's spectacular pronouncements there is, once again, a return to common sense. This world, the one I stand in, touch, and see, is the real world. But what makes it real, according to Kant, is not just that I stand in, touch, and see it, but that I actively constitute it as the way it is, apply my own rules for understanding it, and structure it through my own experience.

In 1781 Kant already anticipated the three "theories of truth" that would become so powerful in the twentieth century. In his emphasis on our constitution of reality through interconnected rules and concepts, Kant anticipates the coherence theory of truth, which stresses precisely these interconnections. In his emphasis on the workability of these rules, he anticipates the pragmatic theory. And in his theory that it is our concepts and rules that "set up" reality, Kant anticipates Tarski's semantic theory. But what is of equal importance is that Kant does not endorse any single one of these theories, but embraces them all.

Kant gives us a general way of giving an account of all those truths that metaphysicians have always argued about. Using Kant's terminology, we can say they are forms of *synthetic* a priori knowledge. Such knowledge is, briefly characterized, knowledge of our own rules with which we (necessarily) constitute reality. If a truth is not true because of our experiences, nor is it true because of the grammar or meanings of the sentences of our language, how else could it be defended? This was Hume's dilemma, and with this two-test system of justification, he eliminated many of our most important beliefs as "unjustifiable," as neither "truths of reason" nor "matters of fact." But now, we have our third way: A belief can be true, necessarily true, if it is one of those rules that we impose to constitute our experience. Thus we saw that Kant defended the truths of arithmetic and geometry by showing that they were the "(a priori) forms of intuition," the ways in which we must experience our world. So too will he defend all of those truths that Hume had claimed to be unjustifiable.

The principle of universal causation is neither a generalization from experience nor an analytic truth, but rather a *rule* for "setting up" our world. And that rule is, "Always look for regular (or 'lawlike') connections between events, so that you can explain an event as an *effect* of previous events, and therefore predict future events as well." Like a rule in chess, this is not a move within the game but one of those rules that defines the game. So too with the principle of induction; it is neither based upon experience nor a trivial truth but a rule with which we govern all of our experience. And so too for our belief in the "external" or material world, which Berkeley and Hume found so problematic. Our experience alone will not tell us whether we are dreaming or not, and the idea of the material ("external") world is not a tautology or a conceptual truth. It too is one of the rules that we use to constitute our experience, namely, that we shall *always* interpret our experience of objects in space as external to us and as material or *substantial*. But notice, our metaphysical notion of substance is no longer that which is, by definition, outside of our experience. It is now part of the rules by which we set up our experience.

◆**from *Prolegomena***
to *Any Future Metaphysics*,
by Immanuel Kant

My purpose is to persuade all those who think metaphysics worth studying that it is absolutely necessary to pause a moment and, regarding all that has been done as though undone, to propose first the preliminary question, "Whether such a thing as metaphysics be even possible at all?"

If it be science, how is it that it cannot, like other sciences, obtain universal and lasting recognition? If not, how can it maintain its pretensions and keep the human mind in suspense with hopes never ceasing, yet never fulfilled? Whether then we demonstrate our knowledge or our ignorance in this field, we must come once and for all to a definite conclusion respecting the nature of this so-called science, which cannot possibly remain on its present footing. It seems almost ridiculous, while every other science is continually advancing, that in this, which pretends to be wisdom incarnate, for whose oracle everyone inquires, we should constantly move round the same spot, without gaining a single step. And so its votaries having melted away, we do not find men confident of their ability to shine in other sciences venturing their reputation here, where everybody, however ignorant in other matters, presumes to deliver a final verdict, because in this domain there is actually as yet no standard weight and measure to distinguish sound knowledge from shallow talk.

· · · · · · · · · ·

Hume started chiefly from a single but important concept in metaphysics, namely, that of the connection of cause and effect (including its derivatives force and action, and so on). He challenged reason, which pretends to have given birth to this concept of herself, to answer him by what right she thinks anything could be so constituted that if that thing be posited, something else also must necessarily be posited; for this is the meaning of the concept of cause. He demonstrated irrefutably that it was perfectly impossible for reason to think *a priori* and by means of concepts such a combination, for it implies necessity. We cannot at all see why, in consequence of the existence of one thing, another must necessarily exist or how the concept of such a combination can arise *a priori*. Hence he inferred that reason was altogether deluded with reference to this concept, which she erroneously considered as one of her own children, whereas in reality it was nothing but a bastard of imagination, impregnated by experience, which subsumed certain representations under the law of association and mistook a subjective necessity (habit) for an objective necessity arising from insight. Hence he inferred that reason had no power to think such combinations, even in general, because her concepts would then be purely fictitious and all her pretended *a priori* cognitions nothing but common experiences marked with a false stamp. In plain language, this means that there is not and cannot be any such thing as metaphysics at all.

· · · · · · · · · ·

I openly confess my recollection of David Hume was the very thing which many years ago first interrupted my dogmatic slumber and gave my investigations in the field of speculative philosophy a quite new direction. I was far from following him in the conclusions at which he arrived by regarding, not the whole of his problem, but a part, which by itself can give us no information. If we start from a well-founded, but undeveloped, thought which another has bequeathed to us, we may well hope by continued reflection to advance farther than the acute man to whom we owe the first spark of light.

I therefore first tried whether Hume's objection could not be put into a general form, and soon found that the concept of the connection of cause and effect was by no means the only concept by which the understanding thinks the connection of things *a priori*, but rather that metaphysics consists altogether of such concepts. I sought to ascertain their number; and when I had satisfactorily succeeded in this by starting from a single principle, I proceeded to the deduction of these concepts, which I was now certain were not derived from experience, as Hume had attempted to derive them, but sprang from the pure understanding. This deduction (which seemed impossible to my acute predecessor, which had never even occurred to anyone else, though no one had hesitated to use the concepts without investigating the basis of their objective validity) was the most difficult task which ever could have been undertaken in the service of metaphysics; and the worst was that metaphysics, such as it is, could not assist me in the least because this deduction alone can render metaphysics possible. But as soon as I had succeeded in solving Hume's problem, not merely in a particular case, but with respect to the whole faculty of pure reason, I could proceed safely, though slowly, to determine the whole sphere of pure reason completely and from universal principles, in its boundaries as well as in its contents. This was required for metaphysics in order to construct its system according to a safe plan.[9]

Kant gives us a way of resolving the age-old disputes of metaphysics—questions concerning reality as such. Since the claims of the metaphysicians are all synthetic a priori, Kant provides us with the following policy:

1. Those claims that are rules by which we must interpret our experience are true—necessarily true.
2. Those claims that contradict rules by which we must interpret our experience are false—necessarily false.
3. Those that are not rules by which we must interpret our experience are either analytic, contingently true, or contingently false.
4. Finally, those claims that cannot be decided by appeal to the rules of our experiences and make no difference to our experience one way or the other, are to be rejected as possible topics of knowledge.

The logical positivists in this century took this last part of Kant's policy as a program for a devastating attack on metaphysics in general. Although the logical positivists, as empiricists in the tradition of David Hume, did not accept much of Kant's theory, they wholeheartedly endorsed his rejection of claims that made no difference whatever to our experience. They said that any claim that makes no difference to our experience—that cannot be tested in any way—is meaningless.

Some of the metaphysician's claims will be upheld. For example, Kant saves Newton's (and Spinoza's) determinism in his rule of causality, thus rejecting Leibniz's "pre-established harmony" view as necessarily false. With some revisions, he accepts a large pat of Leibniz's view of space and time as relative, that is, relative to our experience. He saves the notion of substance because he says that one of the most important rules of our experience is that we see objects as substantial (that is, as "real"). But he

[9]Immanuel Kant, *Prolegomena to Any Future Metaphysics*, trans. Lewis White Beck (New York: Bobbs-Merrill, 1950).

does not accept the view that substance is something independent of human experience, for such a view, by definition, means that substance would be irrelevant to our experience. Nor does he accept the central dispute between Spinoza and Leibniz, whether there is but one substance or many, for no rule of our experience is concerned one way or another. It makes no difference to our experience. It is a metaphysician's game and not a possible topic for knowledge.

Kant's revolution is the elimination of "reality" and "truth" as external to ourselves. Since Kant, many philosophers no longer view human knowledge as the passive reception of sensations or intuitions. And, needless to say, the problems of philosophy have become radically changed.

Kant destroyed the old problems, resolved the old disputes, and answered Hume's skepticism, at least for a while. In rejecting the correspondence theory of truth and the idea of an "external" reality, he eliminated the basis of those problems, disputes, and doubts. But I expect that you can already see a new and even more virulent version of those problems, disputes, and doubts on the horizon. By denying us our anchor in reality, Kant launches philosophy in a bold new direction, and he creates the dilemma that still defines philosophy today: If we supply our own rules for experience, is there any uniquely correct way of describing the way the world is?

The basis of Kant's theory is that we supply the rules according to which we constitute our experience. Truth can be talked about only within our experience and according to those rules. But you can see what happens when we raise the following question: What about people (or creatures) who are very different from us? Will they use the same rules? Will they have the same experiences? And, if we do differ from them, who is "right"? Whose rules are "better"? Whose experience is "true"? You can see here the problems of the coherence theory of truth coming to haunt Kant's philosophy. Suppose there are two (or more) sets of rules, equally coherent? Can they both be "true"? And the problems of the semantic theory, too: What if there are different languages with different basic concepts or categories, constituting different "facts"? Are they all "true"? You can appreciate how easily the German Romantic philosophers who immediately followed Kant replaced his notion of "constitution" with the more exciting notion of "creation." We create our realities, they announced. We are all artists, building our worlds. And notice the words "realiti*es*" and "world*s*"; there is no longer confidence, much less a guarantee, that there is only one reality or one world.

Kant's most immediate follower, a German named Johann Gottlieb Fichte, used the pragmatic theory of truth to come to the same conclusion; the truth is, according to him, that which is most practical, most conducive to the good life, and the evaluation of different realities depends wholly on the practical consequences. (He said, in his most famous dictum: "The kind of philosophy a man chooses depends upon the kind of man he is.") With Kant's revolution, the Truth seems destined to be replaced by many truths.

But before we go on to explore these intriguing complications, let us make it clear that Kant himself never accepted a word of all this. According to him, there was still but one possible set of rules, and therefore only one way of constituting our experience, whoever we are, wherever we're from, and no matter what kind of conscious creature we happen to be. And this means: one world, one science, one reality, and one truth. Kant tries to prove this in the central section of his *Critique of Pure Reason*, in a formidable argument that he calls a "transcendental deduction."

Like so much philosophical jargon, Kant's term is easily explained, and is used often enough to make it worth explaining. You already know what a deduction is, an inference from one statement to another according to a set of rules of inference. In this case, Kant attempts to infer from various statements that we believe, the basic rules (concepts, categories) of human experience. And this is what "transcendental" means, the basic rules of human experience. But a transcendental deduction is not satisfied with simply deducing some such rules; it also proves that they are the *only* rules that we are able to use to constitute our experience. That is why it is so important to Kant. It allows him his revolution without its anarchist consequences.

The argument itself is enormously complicated and scholars who have studied it for half their lives still do not agree what it is or whether it is a valid argument. So, obviously, we won't try to summarize it for you here. What can and must be said is this, however: Kant believed that such a transcendental deduction would prove that, although it is we ourselves who supply the rules of our experience and determine what can be true for us, we don't have a choice in the matter. There still is only one truth for all of us.

Philosophers are still arguing whether any such transcendental argument (Kant's or not) might succeed. If one does, then people must, in their basic rules, all agree. (Of course, they will always disagree about particular matters; no two chess players make all the same moves.) But if there is no successful transcendental argument, then there need be no such universal agreement. It then makes sense to talk about different truths for different people. This, we may say, is the dominant battle of twentieth-century philosophy in America and in Europe. But obviously, it is not new to the twentieth century. Those who believe that there is only one set of rules and one truth are often called **absolutists** (though many philosophers find that name repulsive because it sounds so dogmatic). Others, who believe that there are different rules for different people and therefore different "truths," are called **relativists.** You have probably already figured out that Plato, Aristotle, and Descartes, for example, were absolutists, and that Protagoras and the Sophists were relativists. Kant was an absolutist. Most of his followers were relativists. (This is obscured by the confusing fact that many of them talked about "the Absolute" all the time. But, they were still relativists, and to avoid confusion, we shall not talk about "the Absolute" at all in this book.)

D. THE BATTLE IN EUROPE AFTER KANT: RELATIVISM AND ABSOLUTISM

The story of philosophy in Europe since Kant is largely the story of a war between relativism and absolutism, in which even the politics and arts of the times play a continuing role. The philosophers immediately following Kant, as we have already mentioned, pursued relativism with a relish, developing alternative systems of philosophy as fast as they could find publishers. The philosopher Friedrich Schelling, for example, produced about one system a year at the turn of the century. He became the best-known "Romantic" philosopher of a large group of "Romantic" intellectuals, poets, and critics throughout Europe who turned to the virtual worship of individual "genius" and competed for the most extravagant and creative views of the world. The virtually undisputed winner of this contest, however, was not Schelling but one of his schoolmates, Georg Wilhelm Friedrich Hegel.

1. Hegel

Hegel was in college (Tübingen Lutheran seminary) when the French revolution was raging just across the border. And he was just starting to put together his mature philosophy when Napoleon was attempting to take over all of Europe. This international turmoil helps us understand the global reach of Hegel's philosophy and his bold effort to proclaim an "absolute" position with reference to knowledge. Like many young German intellectuals in that exciting period, he was trying to get outside his provincial perspective and to understand the world from a larger, even a "divine" point of view. Accordingly, Hegel's theory of truth is part and parcel of his all-embracing system of thought.

Hegel begins by rejecting many key metaphors that have ruled modern philosophy, especially all the "correspondence" metaphors in which the world in itself (or "the Absolute") is on one side and our knowledge (beliefs, sentences, utterances) are on the other, separated by some distorting filter (our senses) or actively altered by the machinery of our understanding. In place of such metaphors (and the skepticism they inevitably engender), Hegel suggests a holistic world-view in which consciousness and the world are not separate but inseparably integrated. In traditional terms, this means that there is no world, no reality-in-itself apart from consciousness.

It also means that we must give up our view of consciousness and the self as self-enclosed and, in some sense, "inside" us. Indeed, Hegel also suggests that we give up the view that the self is essentially a feature of the individual: the self—or "Spirit"—is shared by all of us; or rather, in more Platonic language, we all "participate" in Spirit. Not surprisingly, Hegel was familiar with some Oriental thinkers and incorporated some Eastern views into his notion of truth. However, the truth, according to Hegel, "is the whole"—that is, the unity of all our consciousnesses and the world. This means that there is no saying (and no point in attempting to say) what the world might be apart from our conceptions of it. But neither is this to invite skepticism, for the world is nothing but the synthesis of all our possible conceptions of it.

Hegel, like Kant, is an idealist. He calls himself an "absolute idealist" (in contrast to Kant's "transcendental idealism"). This means, simply stated, that reality is the product of mind (not individual minds, of course)—the cosmic mind, "Spirit." Yet this opens the way for the most radical departure from Kant, who had argued at great length that there could be but one possible way of conceiving the world—that is, one a priori set of forms of intuition (space and time) and one set of categories (substance, causality, etc.). Hegel's predecessor (Kant's immediate successor) Fichte had already argued that there are at least two basically different ways of envisioning the world—the scientific, objective ("dogmatic") way and the practical, moral, activist ("idealist") way—and rather than being simply "right" or "wrong," Fichte had declared famously that "The philosophy a man chooses depends upon the kind of man that he is." Hegel goes a giant step further and provides a long series of possible conceptions of the world—or "forms of consciousness"—conceptions that are not divided into "practical" and "theoretical" but, Hegel tells us, all of which have both their practical and their theoretical aspects. (Once again Hegel rejects an age-old dichotomy.) Such views are not simply alternative options, as if we could each simply choose one or another (as Kierkegaard would argue some years later). The way we view the world is already determined by our place in history, our language, and our society. Nor is the variety of forms of consciousness a demonstration of the now-popular view that there is no "correct" way of knowing. The various forms of consciousness emerge one from another by way of improvement or by way of opposition (as, for example, scientific theories tend to follow one another), and (again, as in science) there is always the necessary sense that they are all moving toward some final end—the correct view. So, too, Hegel insists that all these different conceptions and ways of viewing the world are leading up to something—to a viewpoint that is not relative to any particular viewpoint or perspective. This is the standpoint he calls "absolute knowing."

This idea that the various forms of consciousness emerge one from another and lead us eventually to the absolute is perhaps Hegel's most exciting philosophical contribution to Western thinking. Virtually every other philosopher we have discussed, whether metaphysician or epistemologist, essentially offered us a static view of knowledge, a concept of the understanding that—except for education from childhood and the detailed knowledge gained by the sciences—did not change, did not grow, did not develop. Hegel provides philosophy (and humanity) with a historical perspective. Truth is not, as many philosophers had insisted ever since ancient times, what is. Truth develops, as the human mind develops. Truth is not being but becoming. Truth develops through conflict and confrontation, or what Hegel famously calls a **dialectic** (a term he borrowed from Kant but which goes back to the Greeks).

In an important sense, it is Hegel who discovers (or invents) the history of philosophy. Other philosophers had talked about their predecessors, of course. (Aristotle, for instance, provided us with much of what we know about the pre-Socratic philosophers.) But what Hegel suggests is that something more is to be gleaned than a mere sequence of refutations, additions, and improvements to thought; it is reality itself that is being converted. The history of philosophy, accordingly, is but one aspect of an incredible cosmic odyssey, a "phenomenology of spirit"—the development through time not only of consciousness but of reality too.

The selection that follows is from the Introduction of Hegel's 1807 masterpiece, *The Phenomenology of Spirit*. In this book, Hegel presents a dialectic of various forms of consciousness, from the most primitive sensory perception to the sophisticated views of the Enlightenment and "Revealed Religion" (Christianity), culminating in that final stage of "Absolute Knowing." In these paragraphs, Hegel rejects the traditional metaphors of epistemology and argues that skepticism should not be taken at all seriously. He then suggests the holistic form of his overall system. (There is more on Hegel's notion of "Spirit" in Chapter 7, pp. 562–563.)

◆**from *The Phenomenology of Spirit*,
by G. W. F. Hegel**

It is a natural assumption that in philosophy, before we start to deal with its proper subject-matter, *viz.* the actual cognition of what truly is, one must first of all come to an understanding about cognition, which is regarded either as the instrument to get hold of the Absolute, or as the medium through which one discovers it. A certain uneasiness seems justified, partly because there are different types of cognition, and one of them might be more appropriate than another for the attainment of this goal, so that we could make a bad choice of means; and partly because cognition is a faculty of a definite kind and scope, and thus, without a more precise definition of its nature and limits, we might grasp clouds of error instead of the heaven of truth. This feeling of uneasiness is surely bound to be transformed into the conviction that the whole project of securing for consciousness through cognition what exists in itself is absurd, and that there is a boundary between cognition and the Absolute that completely separates form. For, if cognition is the instrument for getting hold of absolute being, it is obvious that the use of an instrument on a thing certainly does not let it be what it is for itself, but rather sets out to reshape and alter it. If, on the other hand, cognition is not an instrument of our activity but a more or less passive medium through which the light of truth reaches us, then again we do not receive the truth as it is in itself, but only as it exists through and in this medium. Either way we employ a means which immediately brings about the opposite of its own end; or rather, what is really absurd is that we should make use of a means at all.

It would seem, to be sure, that this evil could be remedied through an acquaintance with the way in which the *instrument* works; for this would enable us to eliminate from the representation of the Absolute which we have gained through it whatever is due to the instrument, and thus get the truth in its purity. But this "improvement" would in fact only bring us back to where we were before. If we remove from a reshaped thing what the instrument has done to it, then the thing—here the Absolute—becomes for us exactly what it was before this (accordingly) superfluous effort. On the other hand, if the Absolute is supposed merely to be brought nearer to us through this instrument, without anything in it being altered, like a bird caught by a lime-twig, it would surely laugh our little ruse to scorn, if it were not with us, in and for itself, all along, and of its own volition. For a ruse is just what cognition would be in such a case, since it would, with its manifold exertions, be giving itself the air of doing something quite different from creating a merely immediate and therefore effortless relationship. Or, if by testing cognition, which we conceive of as a *medium*, we get to know the law of its refraction, it is again useless to subtract this from the end result. For it is not the refraction of the ray, but the ray itself whereby truth reaches us, that is cognition; and if this were removed, all that would be indicated would be a pure direction or a blank space.

Meanwhile, if the fear of falling into error sets up a mistrust of Science, which in the absence of such scruples gets on with the work itself, and actually cognizes something, it is hard to see why we should not turn round and mistrust this very mistrust. Should we not be concerned as to whether this fear of error is not just the error itself? Indeed, this fear takes something—a great deal in fact—for granted as truth, supporting its scruples and inferences on what is itself in need of prior scrutiny to see if it is true. To be specific, it takes for granted certain ideas about cognition as an *instrument* and as a *medium*, and assumes that there is a *difference between ourselves and this cognition*. Above all, it pre-supposes that the Absolute stands on one side and cognition on the other, independent and separated from it, and yet is something real; or in other words, it presupposes that cognition which, since it is excluded from the Absolute, is surely outside of the truth as well, is nevertheless true, an assumption whereby what calls itself fear of error reveals itself rather as fear of the truth.

This conclusion stems from the fact that the Absolute alone is true, or the truth alone is absolute.

· · · · · · · · · ·

Now, because it has only phenomenal knowledge for its object, this exposition seems not to be Science, free and self-moving in its own peculiar shape; yet from this standpoint it can be regarded as the path of the natural consciousness which presses forward to true knowledge; or as the way of the Soul which journeys through the series of its own configurations as though they were the sta-tions appointed for it by its own nature, so that it may purify itself for the life of the Spirit, and achieve finally, through a completed experience of life itself, the awareness of what it really is in itself.

Natural consciousness will show itself to be only the Notion of knowledge, or in other words, not to be real knowledge. But since it directly takes itself to be real knowledge, this path has a negative significance for it, and what is in fact the realization of the Notion, counts for it rather as the loss of its own self; for it does lose its truth on this path. The road can therefore be regarded as the path-way of *doubt*, or more precisely as the way of despair. For what happens on it is not what is ordinarily understood when the word "doubt" is used: shilly-shallying about this or that presumed truth, followed by a return to that truth again, after the doubt has been appropriately dispelled—so that at the end of the process the mat-ter is taken to be what it was in the first place. On the contrary, this path is the conscious insight into the untruth of phenomenal knowledge, for which the supreme reality is what is in truth only the unrealized Notion. Therefore this thoroughgoing scepticism is also not the scepticism with which an earnest zeal for truth and Science fancies it has prepared and equipped itself in their service: the *resolve*, in Science, not to give oneself over to the thoughts of others, upon mere authority, but to examine everything for oneself and follow only one's conviction, or better still, to produce every-thing oneself, and accept only one's deed as what is true.

The series of configurations which consciousness goes through along this road is, in reality, the detailed history of the *education* of consciousness itself to the standpoint of Science. That zealous re-solve represents this education simplistically as something directly over and done with in the making of the resolution; but the way of the Soul is the actual fulfillment of the resolution, in contrast to the untruth of that view. Now, following one's own conviction is, of-course, more than giving oneself over to authority; but changing an opinion accepted on authority into an opinion held out of personal conviction, does not necessarily alter the content of the opinion, or replace error with truth. The only difference between being caught up in a system of opinions and prejudices based on personal conviction, and being caught up in one based on the authority of others, lies in the added conceit that is innate in the former position. The scepticism that is directed against the whole range of phenomenal consciousness, on the other hand, renders the Spirit for the first time competent to examine what truth is. For it brings about a state of despair about all the so-called natural ideas, thoughts, and opinions, regardless of whether they are called one's own or someone else's, ideas with which the consciousness that sets about the examination (of truth) *straight away* is still filled and hampered, so that it is, in fact, incapable of carrying out what it wants to undertake.

The necessary progression and interconnection of the forms of the unreal consciousness will by itself bring to pass the *completion* of the series. To make this more intelligible, it may be remarked, in a preliminary and general way, that the exposition of the untrue consciousness in its untruth is not a merely *negative* procedure. The natural consciousness itself normally takes this one-sided view of it; and a knowledge which makes the one-sidedness its very essence is itself one of the patterns of incomplete consciousness which occurs on the road itself, and will manifest itself in due course. This is just the scepticism which only ever sees pure nothingness in its result and abstracts from the fact that this nothingness is specifically the nothingness of that *from which it results.* For it is only when it is taken as the result of that from which it emerges, that it is, in fact, the true result; in that case it is itself a *determinate* nothingness, one which has a *content.* The scepticism that ends up with the bare abstraction of nothingness or emptiness cannot get any further from there, but must wait to see whether something new comes along and what it is, in order to throw it too into the same empty abyss. But when, on the other hand, the result is conceived as it is in truth, namely, as a *determinate* negation, a new form has thereby immediately arisen, and in the negation the transition is made through which the progress through the complete series of forms comes about of itself.

· · · · · · · · · ·

This contradiction and its removal will become more definite if we call to mind the abstract determinations of truth and knowledge as they occur in consciousness. Consciousness simultaneously *distinguishes* itself from something, and at the same time *relates* itself to it, or, as it is said, this something exists *for* consciousness; and the determinate aspect of the *relating,* or of the *being* of something for a consciousness, is *knowing.* But we distinguish the being-for-another from *being-in-itself;* whatever is related to knowledge or knowing is also distinguished from it, and posited as existing outside of this relationship; this *being-in-itself* is called *truth*. Just what might be involved in these determinations is of no further concern to us here. Since our object is phenomenal knowledge, its determinations too will at first be taken directly as they present themselves; and they do present themselves very much as we have already apprehended them.

Now, if we inquire into the truth of knowledge, it seems that we are asking what knowledge is *in itself.* Yet in this inquiry knowledge is *our* object, something that exists *for us;* and the *in-itself* that would supposedly result from it would rather be the being of knowledge *for us.* What we asserted to be its essence would be not so much its truth but rather just our knowledge of it. The essence or criterion would lie within ourselves, and that which was to be compared with it and about which a decision would be reached through this comparison would not necessarily have to recognize the validity of such a standard.[10]

Starting from a clearly Kantian perspective, Hegel taught that we have to stop talking about "true" and "false" philosophies, and "true" and "false" religions, political systems, societies, scientific theories, and values. There are only different "forms of consciousness," some more sophisticated and perspicacious than others, but none wholly true (or false) to the exclusion of others. Hegel wholly endorsed the Kantian thesis that the world is nothing other than the way in which we constitute it.

Hegel's dialectic was essentially a dialectic of ideas, a series of confrontations of various forms of consciousness so that we could see how they all form an interlocking view of reality. But although philosophy and human history improve through time—eventually reaching a form of absolute knowledge and (Hegel hoped) world peace and universal freedom—the movement itself is by no means a smooth progression. It was often violent, both in the intellectual realm and in the flesh-and-blood world of human politics, which Hegel grimly referred to as "the slaughter-bench of history."

One of Hegel's most enthusiastic followers, a young student in Berlin named Karl Marx, thought that Hegel had the dialectic of history turned upside down. It is not ideas that determine world history, Marx argued, but rather the details of history—in particular the economic details—that determine the ideas, including the ideas of philosophers. From this notion of dialectic Marx developed his powerful and influential view of history as class conflict, replacing Hegel's abstract "forms of consciousness" with the day-to-day battles of wages, jobs, exploitation, and profits.[11]

[10]G. W. F. Hegel, *The Phenomenology of Spirit*, trans. A. V. Miller (New York: Oxford University Press, 1977).

[11]The familiar doctrine of Hegel's dialetic is often known only in terms of "thesis-antithesis-synthesis." In fact these categories are rarely used by either Hegel or Marx.

In what follows, Hegel presents an overview of his all-embracing notion of "spirit" (also called "the Idea"). Spirit, in one sense, is God, but the concept embraces all of humanity, all of history, and all of nature as well. The point of the argument is that the world itself *develops* and *changes*, and so the virtues and truths of one generation may well become inadequate to the next generation. Yet this is not relativism in the crude sense, such that a truth, for example, is only true for a particular person or people. First, truth is not, in this sense, subjective; it is to be found in the world and not just in the minds of individuals or groups. Second, and even more important, to say that a truth is inadequate from a later, probably more expansive, point of view is not to say that it "was true but is now false;" rather, it shows that we are slowly approaching an ever more adequate conception of the truth, a truth which, in the following selection, Hegel calls "Freedom." Freedom is God's purpose developing through history and humanity.

◆from *Reason in History*
("Introduction: Lectures on the Philosophy of History"),
by Hegel

THE IDEA AND THE INDIVIDUAL

The question of the *means* whereby Freedom develops itself into a world leads us directly to the phenomenon of history. Although Freedom as such is primarily an internal idea, the means it uses are the external phenomena which in history present themselves directly before our eyes. The first glance at history convinces us that the actions of men spring from their needs, their passions, their interests, their characters, and their talents. Indeed, it appears as if in this drama of activities these needs, passions, and interests are the sole springs of action and the main efficient cause. It is true that this drama involves also universal purposes, benevolence, or noble patriotism. But such virtues and aims are insignificant on the broad canvas of history. We may, perhaps, see the ideal of Reason actualized in those who adopt such aims and in the spheres of their influence; but their number is small in proportion to the mass of the human race and their influence accordingly limited. Passions, private aims, and the satisfaction of selfish desires are, on the contrary, tremendous springs of action. Their power lies in the fact that they respect none of the limitations which law and morality would impose on them; and that these natural impulses are closer to the core of human nature than the artificial and troublesome discipline that tends toward order, self-restraint, law, and morality.

When we contemplate this display of passions and the consequences of their violence, the unreason which is associated not only with them, but even—rather we might say *especially*—with *good* designs and righteous aims; when we see arising therefrom the evil, the vice, the ruin that has befallen the most flourishing kingdoms which the mind of man ever created, we can hardly avoid being filled with sorrow at this universal taint of corruption. And since this decay is not the work of mere nature, but of human will, our reflections may well lead us to a moral sadness, a revolt of the good will (spirit)—if indeed it has a place within us. Without rhetorical exaggeration, a simple, truthful account of the miseries that have overwhelmed the noblest of nations and polities and the finest exemplars of private virtue forms a most fearful picture and excites emotions of the profoundest and most hopeless sadness, counter-balanced by no consoling result. We can endure it and strengthen ourselves against it only by thinking that this is the way it had to be—it is fate; nothing can be done. And at last, out of the boredom with which this sorrowful reflection threatens us, we draw back into the vitality of the present, into our aims and interests of the moment; we retreat, in short, into the selfishness that stands on the quiet shore and thence enjoys in safety the distant spectacle of wreckage and confusion.

But in contemplating history as the slaughter-bench at which the happiness of peoples, the wisdom of states, and the virtue of individuals have been sacrificed, a question necessarily arises: To what principle, to what final purpose, have these monstrous sacrifices been offered?

From here one usually proceeds to the starting point of our investigation: the events which make up this picture of gloomy emotion and thoughtful reflection are only the means for realizing the essential destiny, the absolute and final purpose, or, what amounts to the same thing, the true result of world history. We have all along purposely eschewed that method of reflection which ascends from this scene of particulars to general principles. Besides, it is not in the interest of such sentimental reflections really to rise above these depressing emotions and to solve the mysteries of Providence presented in such contemplations. It is rather their nature to dwell melancholically on the empty and fruitless sublimities of their negative result. For this reason we return to our original point of view. What we shall have to say about it will also answer the questions put to us by this panorama of history.

The first thing we notice—something which has been stressed more than once before but which cannot be repeated too often, for it belongs to the central point of our inquiry—is the merely general and abstract nature of what we call principle, final purpose, destiny, or the nature and concept of Spirit. A principle, a law is something implicit, which as such, however true in itself, is not completely real (actual). Purposes, principles, and the like, are at first in our thoughts, our inner intention. They are not yet in reality. That which is in itself is a possibility, a faculty. It has not yet emerged out of its implicitness into existence. A second element must be added for it to become reality, namely, activity, actualization. The principle of this is the will, man's activity in general. It is only through this activity that the concept and its implicit ("being-in-themselves") determinations can be realized, actualized; for of themselves they have no immediate efficacy. The activity which puts them in operation and in existence is the need, the instinct, the inclination, and passion of man. When I have an idea I am greatly interested in transforming it into action, into actuality. In its realization through my participation I want to find my own satisfaction. A purpose for which I shall be active must in some way be my purpose; I must thereby satisfy my own desires, even though it may have ever so many aspects which do not concern me. This is the infinite right of the individual to find itself satisfied in its activity and labor. If men are to be interested in anything they must have "their heart" in it. Their feelings of self-importance must be satisfied. But here a misunderstanding must be avoided. To say that an individual "has an interest" in something is justly regarded as a reproach or blame; we imply that he seeks only his private advantage. Indeed, the blame implies not only his disregard of the common interest, but his taking advantage of it and even his sacrificing it to his own interest. Yet, he who is active for a cause is not simply "interested," but "interested *in it.*" Language faithfully expresses this distinction. Nothing therefore happens, nothing is accomplished, unless those concerned with an issue find their own satisfaction in it. They are particular individuals; they have their special needs, instincts, and interests. They have their own particular desires and volitions, their own insight and conviction, or at least their own attitude and opinion, once the aspirations to reflect, understand, and reason have been awakened. Therefore people demand that a cause for which they should be active accord with their ideas. And they expect their opinion—concerning its goodness, justice, advantage, profit—to be taken into account. This is of particular importance today when people are moved to support a cause not by faith in other people's authority, but rather on the basis of their own independent judgment and conviction.

We assert then that nothing has been accomplished without an interest on the part of those who brought it about. And if "interest" be called "passion"—because the whole individuality is concentrating all its desires and powers, with every fiber of volition, to the neglect of all other actual or possible interests and aims, on one object—we may then affirm without qualification that *nothing great in the world* has been accomplished without passion.

· · · · · · · · · ·

. . . [O]ne may indeed question whether those manifestations of vitality on the part of individuals and peoples in which they seek and satisfy their own purposes are, at the same time, the means and tools of a higher and broader purpose of which they know nothing, which they realize unconsciously. This purpose has been questioned, and in every variety of form denied, decried, and denounced as mere dreaming and "philosophy." On this point, however, I announced my view at the very outset, and asserted our hypothesis—which eventually will appear as the result of our investigation—namely, that Reason governs the world and has consequently governed its history. In relation to this Reason, which is universal and substantial, in and for itself, all else is subordinate, subservient, and the means for its actualization. Moreover, this Reason is immanent in historical existence and reaches its own perfection in and through this existence. The union of the abstract universal, existing in and for itself, with the particular or subjective, and the fact that this union alone constitutes truth are a matter of speculative philosophy which, in this general form, is treated in logic. But in its historical development [*the subjective side, consciousness, is not yet able to know what is*] the abstract final aim of history, the idea of Spirit, for it is then itself in process and incomplete. The idea of Spirit is not yet its distinct object of desire and interest. Thus desire is still unconscious of its purpose; yet it already exists in the particular purposes and realizes itself through them. The problem concerning the union of the general and the subjective may also be raised under the form of the union of freedom and necessity. We consider the immanent development of the Spirit, existing in and for itself, as necessary, while we refer to freedom the interests contained in men's conscious volitions.[12]

2. Schopenhauer

Arthur Schopenhauer claimed to be a faithful student of Kant. Indeed, he claimed to be the only faithful interpreter of what he took to be Kant's central idea, the distinction between the constituted world of our experience and an underlying reality which could be found in the realm of the Will. But Schopenhauer, who was one of the great eccentrics in the history of philosophy, gave Kant's philosophy a dramatic twist, encouraged by his readings of Eastern philosophy. In place of Kant's confidence in the truth of the world of our experience, Schopenhauer invokes the Buddhist conception of the "veil of Maya" and declares our experience of the world to be largely illusion. Meanwhile the Will, which Kant takes to be inherently rational, becomes an irrational, impersonal, inner force for Schopenhauer, exerting itself to no particular purpose within us. The most evident manifestation of the Will, in us and in all creatures, Schopenhauer suggests, is sexual desire, the often urgent and foolish

---

[12]G. W. F. Hegel, *Reason in History*, trans. Robert S. Hartman (New York: Bobbs-Merrill, 1953).

desire to reproduce ourselves, so that our offspring can reproduce themselves, and so on and so on, to no end whatever. Thus Schopenhauer, like the Buddha, stresses the futility of desire, and his whole philosophy is aimed at giving us some relief from the Will. (In our final chapter on aesthetics, "Beauty," we will see that Schopenhaeur invokes the power of art to give us this relief.) But the Will is ultimate reality, and within its purposeless striving dwell all of the peoples and all of the creatures of nature. The following selection is from Schopenhauer's great book, *The World as Will and Representation*:

◆from *The World as Will and Representation,* by Arthur Schopenhauer

The will, considered purely in itself, is devoid of knowledge, and is only a blind, irresistible cure, as we see it appear in inorganic and vegetable nature and in their laws, and also in the vegetative part of our own life. Through the addition of the world as representation, developed for its service, the will obtains knowledge of its own willing and what it wills, namely that this is nothing but this world, life, precisely as it exists. We have therefore called the phenomenal world the mirror, the objectivity, of the will; and as what the will wills is always life, just because this is nothing but the presentation of that willing for the representation, it is immaterial and a mere pleonasm if, instead of simply saying "the will," we say "the will-to-live."

As the will is the thing-in-itself, the inner content, the essence of the world, but life, the visible world, the phenomenon, is only the mirror of the will, this world will accompany the will as inseparably as a body is accompanied by its shadow; and if will exists, then life, the world, will exist. Therefore life is certain to the will-to-live, and as long as we are filled with the will-to-live we need not be apprehensive for our existence, even at the sight of death. It is true that we see the individual come into being and pass away; but the individual is only phenomenon, exists only for knowledge involved in the principle of sufficient reason, in the *principium individuationis*. Naturally, for this knowledge, the individual receives his life as a gift, rises out of nothing, and then suffers the loss of this gift through death, and returns to nothing. We, however, wish to consider life philosophically, that is to say, according to its Ideas, and then we shall find that neither the will, the thing-in-itself in all phenomena, nor the subject of knowing, the spectator of all phenomena, is in any way affected by birth and death. Birth and death belong only to the phenomenon of the will, and hence to life; and it is essential to this that is manifest itself in individuals that come into being and pass away, as fleeting phenomena, appearing in the form of time, of that which in itself knows no time, but must be manifested precisely in the way aforesaid in order to objectify its real nature. Birth and death belong equally to life, and hold the balance as mutual conditions of each other, or, if the expression be preferred, as poles of the whole phenomenon of life. The wisest of all mythologies, the Indian, expresses this by giving to the very god who symbolizes destruction and death (just as Brahma, the most sinful and lowest god of the Trimurti, symbolizes generation, origination, and Vishnu preservation), by giving, I say, to Shiva as an attribute not only the necklace of skulls, but also the lingam, that symbol of generation which appears as the counterpart of death. In this way it is intimated that generation and death are essential correlatives which reciprocally neutralize and eliminate each other. It was precisely the same sentiment that prompted the Greeks and Romans to adorn the costly sarcophagi, just as we still see them, with feasts, dances, marriages, hunts, fights between wild beasts, bacchanalia, that is with presentations of life's most powerful urge. This they present to us not only through such diversions and merriments, but even in sensual groups, to the point of showing us the sexual intercourse between satyrs and goats. The object was obviously to indicate with the greatest emphasis from the death of the mourned individual the immortal life of nature, and thus to intimate, although without abstract knowledge, that the whole of nature is the phenomenon, and also the fulfillment, of the will-to-live. The form of this phenomenon is time, space, and causality, and through these individuation, which requires that the individual must come into being and pass away. But this no more disturbs the will-to-live—the individual being only a particular example or specimen, so to speak, of the phenomenon of this will—than does the death of an individual injure the whole of nature. For it is not the individual that nature cares for, but only the species; and in all seriousness she urges the preservation of the species, since she provides for this so lavishly through the immense surplus of the seed and the great strength of the fructifying impulse. The individual, on the contrary, has no value for nature, and can have none, for infinite time, infinite space, and the infinite number of possible individuals therein are her kingdom. Therefore nature is always ready to let the individual fall, and the individual is accordingly not only exposed to destruction in a thousand ways from the most insignificant accidents, but is even destined for this and is led towards it by nature herself, from the moment that individual has served the maintenance of the species. In this way, nature quite openly expresses the great truth that only the Ideas, not individuals, have reality proper, in other words are a complete objectivity of the will. Now man is nature herself, and indeed nature at the highest grade of her self-consciousness, but nature is only the objectified will-to-live; the person who has grasped and retained this point of view may certainly and justly console himself for his own death and for that of his friends by looking back on the immortal life of nature, which he himself is.[13]

3.   *Nietzsche*

After Hegel, relativism became ever more sophisticated. In Marx, differences in philosophical world-views were explained in terms of different economic and social circumstances. The question was no longer "which view of the world is true?" but rather, "what circumstances would make a person believe that?" Hegel's rival Arthur Schopenhauer defended the radical idea that what we called reality was in fact an illusion; and a few years later, following Schopenhauer, a similar view was defended by the eccentric but brilliant iconclast, Friedrich Nietzsche. He too attacked the traditional notions of truth with a vengeance and argued that there could be as many equally "true" (or equally "false"—it doesn't matter) world-views as there were creative people and societies. He also urged that every person adopt for himself or herself as many different world-views as possible, at one time or another, as a matter of "experiment."

Like Schopenhauer, he considered all such views as dictated by the Will and not merely as knowledge as such, and, like Marx, he replaced the old question, "which view of the world is true?" with a question of circumstances. But Nietzsche was not interested in economic or social circumstances so much as psychological factors. And so he asked, "what kind of personality would need to believe that?" Truth is no longer even an issue. In fact, even rationality is starting to feel the threat of relativism. For, with Nietzsche, not only is truth out the window, but coherence and pragmatism are forced to take second place as well. What comes first? Excitement, adventure, heroism, creativity, and what Nietzsche generally calls "the will to power." Of course, one must still act rationally if one is to achieve these things, but thinking, in Nietzsche's view, plays at most a secondary role in our lives.

Nietzsche's view of truth was, to put it mildly, startling. His basic claim was a paradox: "truth is error." This can be interpreted in many different ways, and Nietzsche himself interprets and reinterprets it from many different perspectives—which is quite in line with his view of truth itself. "There are no facts," he tells us, "only interpretations." Elsewhere he tells us that there are only "perspectives," various ways of viewing the world and no ultimately correct (or incorrect) way. The very idea of "Truth," he writes, and the curious obsession with truth enjoyed by the scholars, is a kind of pathology, or at least a real curiousity, that requires examination. Why are we so enamored with the idea of "the Truth?" How

[13]Arthur Schopenhauer, *The World as Will and Representation*, pp. 275 *et supra*.

and why did philosophers ever get the idea that there is another world, more real and "better" than this one?

◆from various works, by Friedrich Nietzsche

Chemistry of concepts and sensations.—Almost all the problems of philosophy once again pose the same form of question as they did 2,000 years ago: how can something originate in its opposite, for example rationality in irrationality, the sentient in the dead, logic in illogic, disinterested contemplation in covetous desire, living for others in egoism, truth in errors? Metaphysical philosophy has hitherto surmounted this difficulty by denying that the one originates in the other and assuming for the more highly valued thing a miraculous source in the very kernel and being of the "thing in itself." Historical philosophy, on the other hand, which can no longer be separated from natural science, the youngest of all philosophical methods, has discovered in individual cases (and this will probably be the result in every case) that there are no opposites, except in the customary exaggeration of popular or metaphysical interpretations, and that a mistake in reasoning lies at the bottom of this antithesis: according to this explanation there exists, strictly speaking, neither an unegoistic action nor completely disinterested contemplation; both are only sublimations, in which the basic element seems almost to have dispersed and reveals itself only under the most painstaking observation. All we require, and what can be given us only now that the individual sciences have attained their present level, is a chemistry of the moral, religious, and aesthetic conceptions and sensations, likewise of all the agitations we experience within ourselves in cultural and social intercourse and indeed even when we are alone: what if this chemistry would end up by revealing that in this domain, too, the most glorious colors are derived from base, indeed from despised materials? Will there be many who desire to pursue such researches? Mankind likes to put questions of origin and beginnings out of its mind: must one not be almost inhuman to detect in oneself a contrary inclination?—

Metaphysical world.—It is true, there could be a metaphysical world; the absolute possibility of it is hardly to be disputed. We behold all things through the human head and cannot cut off this head; while the question nonetheless remains what of the world would still be there if one had cut it off. This is a purely scientific problem and one not very well calculated to bother people overmuch; but all that has hitherto made metaphysical assumptions *valuable, terrible, delightful* to them, all that has begotten these assumptions, is passion, error and self-deception; the worst of all methods of acquiring knowledge, not the best of all, have taught belief in them. When one has disclosed these methods as the foundation of all extant religions and metaphysical systems one has refuted them! Then that possibility still remains over; but one can do absolutely nothing with it, not to speak of letting happiness, salvation and life depend on the gossamer of such a possibility.— For one could assert nothing at all of the metaphysical world except that it was a being-other, an inaccessible, incomprehensible being-other; it would be a thing with negative qualities.—Even if the existence of such a world were never so well demonstrated, it is certain that knowledge of it would be the most useless of all knowledge: more useless even than knowledge of the chemical composition of water must be to the sailor in danger of shipwreck.[14]

· · · · · · · · · ·

Now, we praise and censure, however, only under this false presupposition that there are *identical* facts, that there exists a graduated order of *classes* of facts which corresponds to a graduated world-order: thus we *isolate*, not only the individual fact, but also again groups of supposedly identical facts (good, evil, sympathetic, envious actions, etc.)—in both cases erroneously.—The word and the concept are the most manifest ground for our belief in this isolation of groups of actions: we do not only *designate* things with them, we think originally that through them we grasp the *true* in things. Through words and concepts we are still continually misled into imagining things as simpler than they are, separate from one another, indivisible, each existing in and for itself. A philosophical mythology lies concealed in *language* which breaks out again every moment, however careful one may be otherwise. Belief in freedom of will—that is to say in *identical* facts and in *isolated* facts—has in language its constant evangelist and advocate.

Source of knowledge.—Throughout tremendous periods of time the intellect begot nothing but errors; some of them proved useful and preservative of the species: he who came upon them or inherited them fought his fight for himself and his posterity with greater good fortune. These articles of belief, which have been repeatedly handed down and have finally become almost a basic component of the human species, are for example the following: that there are enduring things, that there are identical things, that there are things, material, bodies, that a thing is what it appears to be, that our willing is free, that what is good for me is good in itself. Deniers and doubters of these propositions appeared only very late—truth, as the feeblest form of knowledge, appeared only

[14]Friedrich Nietzsche, *Human-All-Too-Human*, trans. R. J. Hollingdale in *The Nietzsche Reader* (New York: Penguin, 1977).

very late. It seemed one was incapable of living with truth, our organism was adapted to the opposite; all its higher functions, the
perceptions of the senses and every kind of sensation in general
worked in concert with those primevally incorporated fundamental
errors. More: those propositions became even within the domain
of knowledge the norms according to which one meted out "true"
and "untrue"—right into the remotest regions of pure logic. Thus
the *strength* of items of knowledge lies, not in their degree of truth,
but in their age, their incorporatedness, their character as a condition of life. Where life and knowledge seem to come into contradiction there is never any serious contest; doubt and denial here
count as madness. Those exceptions as thinkers, the Eleatics, who
nonetheless advanced and maintained the antithesis of these natural errors, believed it was possible to *live* this opposite, too: they
invented the sage as the man of unchangeability, impersonality, universality of perception, as one and at the same time all, with a
special capacity for that inverted knowledge; they held the belief
that their knowledge was at the same time the principle of *life*. [. . .]
The evolution of honesty and scepticism in greater refinement at
length rendered these people, too, impossible. [. . .] This more
refined honesty and scepticism everywhere had its origin when two
antithetical propositions seemed to be *applicable* to life because
both were compatible with those fundamental errors, when, that is
to say, there could be dispute as to the greater or less degree of
utility for life of these propositions; likewise wherever novel propositions, though not useful to life, were at any rate not harmful to
it, being expressions of an intellectual instinct for play, at the same
time innocent and happy, like all play. Gradually the human brain
was filled with such judgements and convictions; fermentation,
struggle and lust for power arose within this throng. Not only utility
and pleasure, every kind of drive took sides in the struggle over
"truth"; the intellectual struggle became an occupation, excitement,
profession, duty, dignity: knowledge and the striving after the true
finally ordered itself as a need among the other needs. From then
on not only belief and conviction, but examination, denial, mistrust, contradiction, too, were a *power*, all the "evil" instincts
were subordinated to knowledge and placed in its service and
acquired the lustre of the permitted, honoured, useful and finally
the eye and innocence of the *good*. Knowledge thus becomes a
piece of life itself and, as life, a perpetually increasing power: until
at last knowledge and those primeval fundamental errors come
into collision, both as life, both as power, both in the same man.
The thinker: this is now the being within whom the drive to truth
and those life-preservative errors fight their first fight, after which
the drive to truth, too, has proved itself a life-preservative power.
In comparison with the importance of this fight everything else
is a matter of indifference: the ultimate question as to the conditions of life is posed here, and the first attempt to answer this
question by experiment is made here. To what extent can truth

> endure incorporation?—that is the question, that is the exper-
> iment.[15]
>
> . . . .
>
> The falseness of a judgement is to us not necessarily an objection
> to a judgement [. . .] The question is to what extent it is life-advanc-
> ing, life-preserving, species-preserving, perhaps even species-
> breeding; and our fundamental tendency is to assert that the fals-
> est judgements (to which synthetic *a priori* judgements belong) are
> the most indispensable to us, that without granting as true the
> fictions of logic, without measuring reality against the purely in-
> vented world of the unconditional and self-identical, without a con-
> tinual falsification of the world by means of numbers, mankind
> could not live—that to renounce false judgements would be to re-
> nounce life, would be to deny life [. . .][16]

Although Nietzsche wrote in the last half of the nineteenth century, his
works were ignored until this century, when they made an enormous
impact (not all of it positive), first in Germany and, only recently, in
Europe and in the United States. Nietzsche's relativistic view of truth,
while very much at home with many current thinkers, was still quite alien
to the ideas of the nineteenth century, when thinkers—following Hegel or
Kant or natural science—were still trying to develop a unified and "true"
picture of the world. However, one of Nietzsche's German colleagues did
have an impact, just at the end of the last century, and though his
relativistic view of truth was not nearly so extreme as Nietzsche's, he
provoked extensive activity and comment. We speak of Wilhelm Dilthey.
The doctrine he promoted, which is still tremendously influential in both
Europe and the United States, is called **historicism**. Historicism is
Hegel's dialectic of forms of consciousness, pinned down to precise
social and historical periods. It is the thesis, simply, that truth and
rationality are relative to particular peoples at particular times in history
and that overall comparison of them, with the intention of finding out
which is "true," is totally mistaken. It is, obviously, a very strong relativist
doctrine, so strong and so influential that the absolutists in philosophy,
who had had much less publicity and success than the relativists for the
last century, started looking around for a champion. They found him in
the "phenomenologist" Edmund Husserl.

E. PHENOMENOLOGY

Phenomenology is a self-consciously "scientific" and "rigorous"
discipline, modeled after mathematics (as it was for Descartes and the

[15]Friedrich Nietzsche, *Gay Science*, trans. R. J. Hollingdale in *The Nietzsche Reader* (New
York: Penguin, 1977).
[16]Friedrich Nietzsche, *Beyond Good and Evil*, trans. R. J. Hollingdale in *The Nietzsche
Reader* (New York: Penguin, 1977).

ancient Greeks). Phenomenology is the study of the essential structures of the human mind, and because these are essential, they can be known to be true, universally and necessarily. Husserl was a new kind of rationalist, who believed that the truths of arithmetic and geometry are known—and known with certainty—by appeal to a certain kind of intuition, which he called "essential" intuition. Believing that such intuitions are adequate for arithmetic and geometry, Husserl turned his theory elsewhere, to philosophy in general. Husserl, as much as any philosopher of his time (the early twentieth century), was horrified by what he saw as rampant relativism. He saw it, in fact, not only as a crisis in philosophy but as "a crisis in European civilization." And so he turned his phenomonology to attack it. Turning against Dilthey, for example, he argued that:

> Historicism takes its position in the factual sphere of the empirical life of the spirit. To the extent that it posits this latter absolutely, without exactly naturalizing it (the specific sense of nature in particular lies far from historical thinking and in any event does not influence it by determining it in general), there arises a relativism that has a close affinity to naturalistic psychologism and runs into similar sceptical difficulties.
>   . . . In view of this constant change in scientific views we would actually have no right to speak of sciences as objectively valid unities instead of merely as cultural formations. It is easy to see that historicism, if consistently carried through, carries over into extreme sceptical subjectivism. The ideas of truth, theory, and science would then, like all ideas, lose their absolute validity. That an idea has validity would mean that it is a factual construction of spirit which is held as valid and which in its contingent validity determines thought. There would be no unqualifed validity, or validity-in-itself, which is what it is even if no one has achieved it and though no historical humanity will ever achieve it. Thus too there would then be no validity to the principle of contradiction nor to any logic, which latter is nevertheless still in full vigor in our time. The result, perhaps, will be that the logical principles of noncontradiction will be transformed into their opposites.[17]

Using both Kant's terminology and his absolutist intentions, Husserl attacked all forms of relativism and attempted to develop a *transcendental phenomenology*, in other words, a phenomenology that discovers the basic rules of all experience (just as he had discovered them for arithmetic and geometry before). And because these rules (or "ideal laws") were discovered to be essential, they were, Husserl concluded, the only rules possible. In Husserl as in Kant, the word *transcendental* means the basic and the only rules with which we "constitute" our world.

---

[17]Edmund Husserl, "Philosophy as Rigorous Science," in *Phenomenology and the Crisis of Philosophy*, trans. Quentin Lauer (New York: Harper & Row, 1965).

(Husserl used the notion of "constitution" also, with much the same meaning that Kant did.) But what is *phenomenology*? It is the study of human consciousness. These essential rules of experience, in other words, were to be found in consciousness, not in a mysterious Platonic "world of Being" nor simply in our language. Consciousness itself, with the objects of its own constitution, becomes our new anchor. (The following selection by Husserl—one of his clearest introductions to phenomenology—is from a series of lectures Husserl delivered in Paris, at the Sorbonne, in 1929. The readings may be supplemented by another Husserl section in Chapter 5, pp. 320–326.)

◆from *The 1929 Paris Lectures,* by Edmund Husserl

I am filled with joy at the opportunity to talk about the new phenomenology at this most venerable place of French learning, and for very special reasons. No philosopher of the past has affected the sense of phenomenology as decisively as René Descartes, France's greatest thinker. Phenomenology must honor him as its genuine patriarch. It must be said explicitly that the study of Descartes' *Meditations* has influenced directly the formation of the developing phenomenology and given it its present form, to such an extent that phenomenology might almost be called a new, a twentieth century, Cartesianism.

Under these circumstances I may have advance assurance of your interest, especially if I start with those themes in the *Meditationes de prima philosophia* which are timeless, and if through them I point out the transformations and new concepts which give birth to what is characteristic of the phenomenological method and its problems.

Every beginner in philosophy is familiar with the remarkable train of thought in the *Meditations*. Their goal, as we remember, is a complete reform of philosophy, including all the sciences, since the latter are merely dependent members of the one universal body of knowledge which is philosophy. Only through systematic unity can the sciences achieve genuine rationality, which, as they have developed so far, is missing. What is needed is a radical reconstruction which will *satisfy* the ideal of philosophy as being the *universal unity of knowledge* by means of a unitary and *absolutely rational foundation*. Descartes carries out the demand for reconstruction in terms of a subjectively oriented philosophy. This subjective turn is carried out in two steps.

First, anyone who seriously considers becoming a philosopher must once in his life withdraw into himself and then, from within attempt to destroy and rebuild all previous learning. Philosophy is the supremely personal affair of the one who philosophizes. It is the question of *his sapientia universalis*, the aspiration of *his* knowledge for the universal. In particular, the philosopher's quest is for truly scientific knowledge, knowledge for which he can assume—from the very beginning and in every subsequent step—complete responsibility by using *his* own absolutely self-evident justifications. I can become a genuine philosopher only by freely choosing to focus my life on this goal. Once I am thus committed and have accordingly chosen to begin with total poverty and destruction, my first problem is to discover an absolutely secure starting point and rules of procedure, when, in actual fact, I lack any support from the existing disciplines. Consequently, the Cartesian meditations must not be viewed as the private affair of the philosopher Descartes, but as the necessary prototype for the meditations of any beginning philosopher whatsoever.

When we now turn our attention to the content of the *Meditations*, a content which appears rather strange to us today, we notice immediately a *return to the philosophizing ego* in a second and deeper sense. It is the familiar and epoch-making return to the ego as subject of his pure *cogitationes*. It is the ego which, while it suspends all beliefs about the reality of the world on the grounds that these are not indubitable, discovers itself as the only apodictically certain being.

The ego is engaged, first of all, in philosophizing that is seriously solipsistic. He looks for apodictically certain and yet purely subjective procedures through which an objective external world can be deduced. Descartes does this in a well-known manner. He first infers both the existence and *veracitas* of God. Then, through their meditation, he deduces objective reality as a dualism of substances. In this way he reaches the objective ground of knowledge and the particular sciences themselves as well. All his inferences are based on immanent principles, *i.e.*, principles which are innate to the ego.

So much for Descartes. We now ask, is it really worthwhile to hunt critically for the eternal significance of these thoughts? Can these infuse life into our age?

Doubt is raised, in any event, by the fact that the positive sciences, for which the meditations were to have served as absolutely rational foundation, have paid so very little attention to them. Nonetheless, and despite the brilliant development experienced by the sciences over the last three centuries, they feel themselves today seriously limited by the obscurity of their foundations. But it scarcely occurs to them to refer to the Cartesian meditations for the reformulation of their foundations.

On the other hand, serious consideration must be given to the fact that the meditations constitute an altogether unique and epochal event in the history of philosophy, specifically because of their return to the *ego cogito*. As a matter of fact, Descartes inaugurates a completely new type of philosophy. Philosophy, with its style now changed altogether, experiences a radical conversion from naive objectivism to *transcendental subjectivism*. This subjectivism strives toward a pure end-form through efforts that are constantly renewed yet always remain unsatisfactory. Might it not be that this continuing tendency has eternal significance? Perhaps it is a vast task assigned to us by history itself invoking our collective cooperation.

The splintering of contemporary philosophy and its aimless activity make us pause. Must this situation not be traced back to the fact that the motivations from which Descartes' meditations emanate have lost their original vitality? Is it not true that the only fruitful renaissance is one which reawakens these meditations, not in order to accept them, but to reveal the profound truth in the radicalism of a return to the *ego cogito* with the eternal values that reside therein?

In any case, this is the path that led to transcendental phenomenology.

Let us now pursue this path together. In true Cartesian fashion, we will become philosophers meditating in a radical sense, with, of course, frequent and critical modification of the older Cartesian meditations. What were merely germinal in them must be freely developed here.

We thus begin, everyone for himself and in himself, with the decision to disregard all our present knowledge. We do not give up Descartes' guiding goal of an absolute foundation for knowledge. At the beginning, however, to presuppose even the possibility of that goal would be prejudice. We are satisfied to discover the goal and nature of science by submerging ourselves in scientific activity. It is the spirit of science to count nothing as really scientific which cannot be fully justified by the evidence. In other words, science demands proof *by reference to the things and facts themselves, as these are given in actual experience and intuition.* Thus guided, we, the beginning philosophers, make it a rule to judge only by the evidence. Also, the evidence itself must be subjected to critical verification, and that on the basis, of course, of further available evidence. Since from the beginning we have disregarded the sciences, we operate within our prescientific life, which is likewise filled with immediate and mediate evidences. This, and nothing else, is first given to us.

Herein arises our first question. Can we find evidence that is both immediate and apodictic? Can we find evidence that is primitive, in the sense that it must by necessity precede all other evidence?

As we mediate on this question one thing does, in fact, emerge as both prior to all evidence and as apodictic. It is the existence of the world. All science refers to the world, and, before that, our ordinary life already makes reference to it. *That the being of the world precedes everything is so obvious* that no one thinks to articulate it in a sentence. Our experience of the world is continuous, incessant, and unquestionable. But is it true that this experiential evidence, even though taken for granted, is really apodictic and primary to all other evidence? We will have to deny both. Is it not the case that occasionally something manifests itself as a sensory illusion? Has not the coherent and unified totality of our experience been at times debased as a mere dream? We will ignore Descartes' attempt to prove that, notwithstanding the fact of its being constantly experienced, the world's nonbeing can be conceived. His proof is carried out by a much too superficial criticism of sensory experience. We will keep this much: experiential evidence that is to serve as radical foundation for knowledge needs, above all, a critique of its validity and range. It cannot be accepted as apodictic without question and qualification. Therefore, merely to disregard all knowledge and to treat the sciences as prejudices is not enough. Even the experience of the world as the true universal ground of knowledge becomes an unacceptably naive belief. We can no longer accept the reality of the world as a fact to be taken for granted. *It is a hypothesis that needs verification.*

Does there remain a ground of being? Do we still have a basis for all judgments and evidences, a basis on which a universal philosophy can rest apodictically? Is not "world" the name for the totality of all that is? Might it not turn out that the world is not the truly ultimate basis for judgment, but instead that its existence presupposes a prior ground of being?

Here, specifically following Descartes, we make the great shift which, when properly carried out, leads to *transcendental subjectivity*. This is the shift to the *ego cogito*, as the apodictically certain and *last basis for judgment* upon which all radical philosophy must be grounded.

Let us consider: as radically meditating philosophers we now have neither knowledge that is valid for us nor a world that exists for us. We can no longer say that the world is real—a belief that is natural enough in our ordinary experience—; instead, it merely makes a claim to reality. This skepticism also applies to other selves, so that we rightly should not speak communicatively, that is, in the plural. Other people and animals are, of course, given to me only through sensory experience. Since I have questioned the validity of the latter I cannot avail myself of it here. With the loss of other minds I lose, of course, all forms of sociability and culture. In short, the entire concrete world ceases to have reality for me and becomes instead mere appearance. However, whatever may be the veracity of the claim to being made by phenomena, whether they represent reality or appearance, phenomena in themselves cannot be disregarded as mere "nothing." On the contrary, it is precisely the phenomena themselves which, without exception, render possible for me the very existence of both reality and appearance. Again, I may freely abstain from entertaining my belief about experience—which I did. This simply means that I refuse to assert the reality of the world. Nonetheless, we must be careful to realize that this epistemological abstention is still what it is: it includes the whole stream of experienced life and all its particulars, the appearances of objects, other people, cultural situations, etc. Nothing changes, except that I no longer accept the world simply as real; I no longer judge regarding the distinction between reality and appearance. I must similarly abstain from any of my other opinions, judgments, and valuations about the world, since these likewise assume the reality of the world. But for these, as for other phenomena, epistemological abstention does not mean their disappearance, at least not as pure phenomena.

This ubiquitous detachment from any point of view regarding the objective world we term the *phenomenological epoché*. It is the methodology through which I come to understand myself as that ego and life of consciousness in which and through which the entire objective world exists for me, and is for me precisely as it is. Everything in the world, all spatio-temporal being, exists for me because I experience it, because I perceive it, remember it, think of it in any way, judge it, value it, desire it, etc. It is well known that Descartes designates all this by the term *cogito*. For me the world is nothing other than what I am aware of and what appears valid in such *cogitationes*. *The whole meaning and reality of the world rests exclusively on such cogitationes.* My entire worldly life takes its course within these. I cannot live, experience, think, value, and act in any world which is not in some sense in me, and derives its meaning and truth from me. If I place myself above that entire life and if I abstain from any commitment about reality, specifically one which accepts the world as existing, and if I view that life exclusively as consciousness *of* the world, then I reveal myself as the pure ego with its pure stream of *cogitationes*.

I certainly do not discover myself as one item among others in the world, since I have altogether suspended judgment about the world. I am not the ego of an individual man. I am the ego in whose stream of consciousness the world itself—including myself as an object in it, a man who exists in the world—first acquires meaning and reality.

We have reached a dangerous point. It seems simple indeed to understand the pure ego with its *cogitationes* by following Descartes. And yet it is as if we were on the brink of a precipice, where the ability to step calmly and surely decides between philosophic life and philosophic death. Descartes was thoroughly sincere in his desire to be radical and presuppositionless. However, we know through recent researches—particularly the fine and penetrating work of Messrs. Gilson and Koyré—that a great deal of Scholasticism is hidden in Descartes' mediations as unarticulated prejudice. But this is not all. We must above all avoid the prejudices, hardly noticed by us, which derive from our emphasis on the mathmatically oriented natural sciences. These prejudices make it appear as if the phrase *ego cogito* refers to an apodictic and primitive axiom, one which, in conjunction with others to be derived from it, provides the foundation for a deductive and universal science, a science *ordine geometrico*. In relation to this we must under no circumstances take for granted that, with our apodictic and pure ego, we have salvaged a small corner of the world as the single indubitable fact about the world which can be utilized by the philosophizing ego. It is not true that all that now remains to be done is to infer the rest of the world through correct deductive procedures according to principles that are innate to the ego.

Unfortunately, Descartes commits this error, in the apparently insignificant yet fateful transformation of the ego to a *substantia cogitans*, to an independent human *animus*, which then becomes the point of departure for conclusions by means of the principle of causality. In short, this is the transformation which made Descartes the father of the rather absurd transcendental realism. We will keep aloof from all this if we remain true to radicalism in our self-examination and with it to the principle of pure intuition. We must regard nothing as veridical except the pure immediacy and givenness in the field of the *ego cogito* which the *epoché* has opened up to us. In other words, we must not make assertions about that which we do not ourselves *see*. In these matters Descartes was deficient. It so happens that he stands before the greatest of all discoveries—in a sense he has already made it—yet fails to see its true significance, that of transcendental subjectivity. He does not pass through the gateway that leads into genuine transcendental philosophy.

The independent *epoché* with regard to the nature of the world as it appears and is real to me—that is, "real" to the previous and natural point of view—discloses the greatest and most magnificent of all facts: I and my life remain—in my sense of reality—untouched by whichever way we decide the issue of whether the world is or is not. To say, in my natural existence, "I am, I think, I live," means that I am one human being among others in the world, that I am related to nature through my physical body, and that in this body my *cogitationes*, perceptions, memories, judgments, etc. are incorporated as psycho-physical facts. Conceived in this way, I, we, humans, and animals are subject-matter for the objective sciences, that is, for biology, anthropology, and zoology, and also for psychology. The life of the psyche, which is the subject-matter of all philosophy, is understood only as the psychic life in the world. The methodology of a purified Cartesianism demands of me, the one who philosophizes, the phenomenological *epoché*. This *epoché* eliminates as worldly facts from my field of judgment both the reality of the objective world in general and the sciences of the world. *Consequently, for me there exists no "I" and there are no psychic actions, that is, psychic phenomena in the psychological sense.* To myself I do not exist as a human being, ⟨nor⟩ do my *cogitationes* exist as components of a psycho-physical world. But through all this I have discovered my true self. I have discovered that I alone am the pure ego, with pure existence and pure capacities (for example, the obvious capacity to abstain from judging). Through this ego alone does *the being of the world*, and, for that matter, any being whatsoever, make sense *to me* and has possible validity. The world—whose conceivable non-being does not extinguish my pure being but rather presupposes it—is termed *transcendent*, whereas my pure being or my pure ego is termed *transcendental*. Through the phenomenological *epoché* the natural human ego, specifically my own, is reduced to the transcendental ego. This is the meaning of the phenomenological reduction.

Further steps are needed so that what has been developed up to this point can be adequately applied. What is the philosophic use of this transcendental ego? To be sure, for me, the one who philosophizes, it obviously precedes, in an epistemological sense, all objective reality. In a way, it is the basis for all objective knowledge, be it good or bad. But does the fact that the transcendental ego precedes and presupposes all objective knowledge mean also that it is an epistemological ground in the ordinary sense? The thought is tempting. All realistic theories are guilty of it. But the temptation to look in the transcendental subjectivity for premises guaranteeing the existence of the subjective world evanesces once we realize that all arguments, considered in themselves, exist already in transcendental subjectivity itself. Furthermore, all proofs for the world have their criteria set in the world just as it is given and justified in experience. However, these considerations must not be construed as a rejection of the great Cartesian idea that the ultimate basis for objective science and the reality of the objective world is to be sought in transcendental subjectivity. Otherwise— our criticisms aside—we would not be true to Descartes' method of meditation. However, the Cartesian discovery of the ego may perhaps open up a *new concept of foundation, namely, a transcendental foundation*.[18]

Husserl's battle, from beginning to end, was a battle against relativism, against all of those philosophies that held that there can be different equally true or equally rational world-views. And it must be said that his phenomenology, for all of its internal struggles, was immensely successful and still attracts the attention of a great many philosophers today. But phenomenology was not the solution to relativism. Husserl thought that phenomenology could be transcendental and prove that certain rules were basic and essential to all human thinking. But just as Kant opened the door to relativism with his view that we constitute our world, Husserl opened it wider with his view that a study of consciousness was the way to do philosophy. For were there not, his followers asked, many different forms of consciousness? (Thus returning to Hegel rather than Kant.) And phenomenology as it developed in France, rather than Germany, became the source of a new relativism, which is extremely fashionable today.

[18]Edmund Husserl, *The 1929 Paris Lectures*, trans. Peter Koestenbaum (Hague: Nijhoff, 1975).

F. HERMENEUTICS AND PRAGMATISM: RELATIVISM RECONSIDERED

Absolutism seems to deny the obvious fact that people are different and disagree, not only in superficial ways but in terms of their most basic beliefs. Relativism, on the other hand, seems to imply that we will never be able to understand one another—or find the truth—at all. One attempt to bridge the gap between dogmatic absolutism and solipsistic relativism is **hermeneutics.**

"Hermeneutics" is an old name for "interpretation," with an eye to getting at the Truth. For many centuries, this formidable word was applied exclusively to the interpretation of the Bible, with the aim of understanding the Word of God. Today, however, the term has a much broader meaning. It is often used in literary criticism to talk about the interpretation of texts—any text and not only the Bible. But it is now used in philosophy too to refer to the discipline of interpreting and understanding the world, which becomes, in effect, our text, and different cultures' views of the world, which may seem initially to be mutually incommensurable.

The modern father of hermeneutics is the German "historicist" Wilhelm Dilthey, whom we encountered in the previous section. Dilthey came to realize that the methods of the physical sciences were not very successful when applied to the "human sciences," in part because history played such enormous importance in human life. He also realized that there was a very real danger in the Kantian attempt to overcome traditional philosophical distinctions between appearance and reality, subjectivity, and objective truth. While his historicism lent itself to relativism, Dilthey himself was vehemently anti-relativist. The problem, he argued, was to develop a method for *understanding* human differences. But he believed that all of these were ultimately superficial and thus not incommensurable at all.

Contemporary hermeneutics is just this attempt to provide a way of understanding viewpoints other than our own. It is simply dogmatic to insist—as Kant and many other philosophers have insisted—that the structures of the human mind are everywhere the same and, consequently, that we all share a common basis of knowledge. But it is simple-minded, on the other hand, to insist that we are all different and have different truths, since there is at least enough overlap for us to understand that we do disagree. For example, the medievals saw God and the earth as the spiritual and spatial centers of the universe. How can a twentieth-century scientist understand them? Well, not just by dismissing their views as nonsense, nor can we sensibly say, "Well, they have their opinions and we have ours." Hermeneutics is just this attempt to step into someone else's shoes (but without taking off our own shoes first).

In this century, hermeneutics has been turned into a powerful style of philosophizing by the German metaphysician Martin Heidegger. It was Heidegger, in his monumental book *Being and Time* (1928), who suggested that life is like a text, and the purpose of our lives is to understand that text. Heidegger was a student of Husserl, and thus a phenomenologist. But in his hermeneutical phenomenology he tries to "uncover" the hidden meanings in our experience. He rejects the scientific tone of Husserl's phenomenology and prefers to talk about the structures of life itself, including our profound sense of history, which defines human life.

The most important proponent of hermeneutics, however, is a student of Heidegger, Hans Georg Gadamer. In fact, Gadamer is so wary of the fact that method—and not only the scientific method—may distort our understanding that he insists that hermeneutics must resist the temptation to become another method. It is rather the attempt to overcome methods, to dispense with the overemphasis on proofs and arguments and the quest for certainty and emphasize instead the shared understandings that we already have with one another. The substance of philosophy then becomes dialogue rather than individual phenomenology or abstract proofs. Interpretation thus becomes not an abstract function of the intellect but a process that permeates our every activity.

Gadamer's hermeneutics does not reject the notion of truth, but it does give up entirely the idea that there is a Truth wholly outside of us which we need a method (rationalism, empiricism, scientific psychology) to discover. Like the coherence theorist and the pragmatist, he gives up the idea of secure *foundations* for our knowledge—such as the raw experiences or "sense data" discussed by some empiricists, or the a priori principles defended by Kant. But where both the coherence theorist and the pragmatist tend to interpret truth as a function of the present—coherence of beliefs and workability, respectively—the hermeneuticist insists that truth must be understood *historically*, in terms of a *tradition*. Thus the philosophical tradition, ironically, has tended to ignore the importance of its own tradition and look for strictly eternal truths. Gadamer's hermeneutics hold rather that it is only within a tradition, and by looking at our tradition, that philosophical truth is possible at all. Does this mean that we must accept whatever our tradition may be, even if it is wrong? But what would it be, Gadamer asks, for a tradition to be wrong? We can criticize ourselves, of course, and that is just the point of hermeneutics. But does it mean that we must also justify ourselves and what we have always believed? "Do we need to justify," he asks rhetorically, "that which has always supported us?"

Does relativism mean that there can be no truth? Does relativism apply only to philosophical views, not to *real* theories? Could there be *really* different views of the world—and different worlds? But does it even make sense to talk about relative truth, that is, a truth that is only "true for" one person or group and not another?

If such a phrase even makes sense, it must mean that a statement is true for a person or group by virtue of the scheme or conceptual framework they employ; thus it is true for a certain society that the witchdoctor embodies the power of the devil, but true for another society that the powers of the so-called witchdoctor are nothing but the combination of natural pharmaceuticals plus the power of suggestion. But we must not fall into the radical trap of Protagoras and claim that "man is the measure of all things"—if we are to continue using the word *truth* at all. A statement or a belief cannot be true just by virtue of its being believed, in other words, if there is no possibility that a person or a group can believe what is false (or, not believe some statement that is nevertheless true). Furthermore, as in hermeneutics, it is essential that we do not close off the possibility that one truth might be under-standable—perhaps in different terms—by those who believe another, apparently contradictory truth. This would be to deny the possibility of cross-cultural communication—to cut people of different cultures off from each other completely.

Hermeneutics has had a recent resurgence in American philosophy, particularly in discussions of relativism and multiculturalism. In the following essay, the contemporary American philosopher, Richard Rorty, who claims a profound debt to hermeneutics, defends a vision of "solidarity"—which he contrasts with the traditional notion of "objec-tivity," which he associates with "pragmatism." His claim is that the pragmatic theory of truth which we outlined above is essentially the theory that truth has a moral standard—the solidarity of a community—rather than a metaphysical one—objectivity. In other words, he claims that pragmatism defines "truth" as "what it is morally best for our community to believe." And using this definition, he can claim that it is morally best for us to believe in pragmatism.

◆from "Solidarity or Objectivity?" by Richard Rorty

There are two principal ways in which reflective human beings try, by placing their lives in a larger context, to give sense to those lives. The first is by telling the story of their contribution to a commu-nity. This community may be the actual historical one in which they live, or another actual one, distant in time or place, or a quite imaginary one, consisting perhaps of a dozen heroes and heroines selected from history or fiction or both. The second way is to de-scribe themselves as standing in immediate relation to a nonhu-man reality. This relation is immediate in the sense that it does not derive from a relation between such a reality and their tribe, or their nation, or their imagined band of comrades. I shall say that stories of the former kind exemplify the desire for solidarity, and that stories of the latter kind exemplify the desire for objectivity. Insofar as a person is seeking solidarity, he or she does not ask about the relation between the practices of the chosen community and something outside that community. Insofar as he seeks objectivity, he distances himself from the actual persons around him not by thinking of himself as a member of some other real or imaginary group, but rather by attaching himself to something which can be described without reference to any particular human beings.

· · · · · · · · · ·

Those who wish to ground solidarity in objectivity—call them "realists"—have to construe truth as correspondence to reality. So they must construct a metaphysics which has room for a special relation between beliefs and objects which will differentiate true from false beliefs. They also must argue that there are procedures of justification of belief which are natural and not merely local. So they must construct an epistemology which has room for a kind of justification which is not merely social but natural, springing from human nature itself, and made possible by a link between that part of nature and the rest of nature. On their view, the various procedures which are thought of as providing rational justification by one or another culture may or may not really *be* rational. For to be truly rational, procedures of justification *must* lead to the truth, to correspondence to reality, to the intrinsic nature of things.

By contrast, those who wish to reduce objectivity to solidarity—call them "pragmatists"—do not require either a metaphysics or an epistemology. They view truth as, in William James' phrase, what it is good for *us* to believe. So they do not need an account of a relation between beliefs and objects called 'correspondence,' nor an account of human cognitive abilities which ensures that our species is capable of entering into that relation. They see the gap between truth and justification not as something to be bridged by isolating a natural and transcultural sort of rationality which can be used to criticize certain cultures and praise others, but simply as the gap between the actual good and the possible better. From a pragmatist point of view, to say that what is rational for us now to believe may not be *true*, is simply to say that somebody may come up with a better idea. It is to say that there is always room for improved belief, since new evidence, or new hypotheses, or a whole new vocabulary, may come along. For pragmatists, the desire for objectivity is not the desire to escape the limitations of one's community, but simply the desire for as much intersubjective agreement as possible, the desire to extend the reference of "us" as far as we can. Insofar as pragmatists make a distinction between knowledge and opinion, it is simply the distinction between topics on which such agreement is relatively easy to get and topics on which agreement is relatively hard to get.

"Relativism" is the traditional epithet applied to pragmatism by realists. Three different views are commonly referred to by this name. The first is the view that every belief is as good as every other. The second is the view that "true" is an equivocal term, having as many meanings as there are procedures of justification. The third is the view that there is nothing to be said about either truth or rationality apart from descriptions of the familiar procedures of justification which a given society—*ours*—uses in one or another area of inquiry. The pragmatist holds the ethnocentric third view. But he does not hold the self-refuting first view, nor the eccentric second view. He thinks that his views are better than the realists, but he does not think that his views correspond to the nature of things. He thinks that the very flexibility of the word "true"—the fact that it is merely an expression of commendation—insures its univocity. The term "true," on his account, means the same in all cultures, just as equally flexible terms like "here," "there," "good," "bad," "you," and "me" mean the same in all cultures. But the identity of meaning is, of course, compatible with diversity of reference, and with diversity of procedures for assigning the terms. So he feels free to use the term "true" as a general term of commendation in the same way as his realist opponent does—and in particular to use it to commend his own view.

However, it is not clear why "relativist" should be thought an appropriate term for the ethnocentric third view, the one which the pragmatist *does* hold. For the pragmatist is not holding a positive theory which says that something is relative to something else. He is, instead, making the purely *negative* point that we should drop the traditional distinction between knowledge and opinion, construed as the distinction between truth as correspondence to reality and truth as a commendatory term for well-justified beliefs. The reason that the realist calls this negative claim "relativistic" is that he cannot believe that anybody would seriously deny that truth has an intrinsic nature. So when the pragmatist says that there is nothing to be said about truth save that each of us will commend as true those beliefs which he or she finds good to believe, the realist is inclined to interpret this as one more positive theory about the nature of truth: a theory according to which truth is simply the contemporary opinion of a chosen individual or group. Such a theory would, of course, be self-refuting. But the pragmatist does not have a theory of truth, much less a relativistic one. As a partisan of solidarity, his account of the value of cooperative human inquiry has only an ethical base, not an epistemological or metaphysical one. Not having *any* epistemology, *a fortiori* he does not have a relativistic one.

. . . [T]he question is not about how to define words like "truth" or "rationality" or "knowledge" or "philosophy," but about what self-image our society should have of itself. The ritual invocation of the "need to avoid relativism" is most comprehensible as an expression of the need to preserve certain habits of contemporary

European life. These are the habits nurtured by the Enlightenment, and justified by it in terms of an appeal of Reason, conceived as a transcultural human ability to correspond to reality, a faculty whose possession and use is demonstrated by obedience to explicit criteria. So the real question about relativism is whether these same habits of intellectual, social, and political life can be justified by a conception of rationality as criterionless muddling through, and by a pragmatist conception of truth.

I think that the answer to this question is that the pragmatist cannot justify these habits without circularity, but then neither can the realist. The pragmatists' justification of toleration, free inquiry, and the quest for undistorted communication can only take the form of a comparison between societies which exemplify these habits and those which do not, leading up to the suggestion that nobody who has experienced both would prefer the latter. It is exemplified by Winston Churchill's defense of democracy as the worst form of government imaginable, except for all the others which have been tried so far.

· · · · · · · · · ·

My suggestion that the desire for objectivity is in part a disguised form of the fear of the death of our community echoes Nietzsche's charge that the philosophical tradition which stems from Plato is an attempt to avoid facing up to contingency, to escape from time and chance. Nietzsche thought that realism was to be condemned not only by arguments from its theoretical incoherence, the sort of argument we find in Putnam and Davidson, but also on practical, pragmatic grounds. Nietzsche thought that the test of human character was the ability to live with the thought that there was no convergence. He wanted us to be able to think of truth as:

> a mobile army of metaphors, metonyms, and anthromorphisms—in short a sum of human relations, which have been enhanced, transposed, and embellished poetically and rhetorically and which after long use seem firm, canonical, and obligatory to a people.

Nietzsche hoped that eventually there might be human beings who could and did think of truth in this way, but who still liked themselves, who saw themselves as *good* people for whom solidarity was *enough*.

I think that pragmatism's attack on the various structure-content distinctions which buttress the realist's notion of objectivity can best be seen as an attempt to let us think of truth in this Nietzschean way, as entirely a matter of solidarity. That is why I think we need to say, despite Putnam, that "there is only the dialogue," only *us*, and to throw out the last residues of the notion of "transcultural rationality." But this should not lead us to repudiate, as Nietzsche sometimes did, the elements in our movable host which embody the ideas of Socratic conversation, Christian fellowship, and Enlightenment science. Nietzsche ran together his diagnosis of philosophical realism as an expression of fear and resentment with his own resentful idiosyncratic idealizations of silence, solitude, and violence. Post-Nietzschean thinkers like Adorno and Heidegger and Foucault have run together Nietzsche's criticisms of the metaphysical tradition on the one hand with his criticisms of bourgeois civility, of Christian love, and of the nineteenth century's hope that science would make the world a better place to live, on the other. I do not think that there is any interesting connection between these two sets of criticisms. Pragmatism seems to me, as I have said, a philosophy of solidarity rather than of despair. From this point of view, Socrates' turn away from the gods, Christianity's turn from an Omnipotent Creator to the man who suffered on the Cross, and the Baconian turn from science as contemplation of eternal truth to science as instrument of social progress, can be seen as so many preparations for the act of social faith which is suggested by a Nietzschean view of truth.

The best argument we partisans of solidarity have against the realistic partisans of objectivity is Nietzsche's argument that the traditional Western metaphysico-epistemological way of firming up our habits simply isn't working anymore. It isn't doing its job. It has become as transparent a device as the postulation of deities who turn out, by a happy coincidence, to have chosen *us* as their people. So the pragmatist suggestion that we substitute a "merely" ethical foundation for our sense of community—or, better, that we think of our sense of community as having no foundation except shared hope and the trust created by such sharing—is put forward on practical grounds. It is *not* put forward as a corollary of a metaphysical claim that the objects in the world contain no intrinsically action-guiding properties, nor of an epistemological claim that we lack a faculty of moral sense, nor of a semantical claim that truth is reducible to justification.[19]

Rorty makes the point that our metaphysical theory of "truth" has political overtones. The belief that there is one, single, truth can lead to condescension and disrespect toward people who believe differently from oneself. Only, however, if the absolutist believes, in addition to his or her absolutism, that he or she or his or her culture is closer to that one truth than are others. Need the absolutist always think that the objective truth is his or her sole dominion? This seems to cut off the possibility of communication and learning between cultures.

Is "solidarity *enough*"? Below, Japanese philosopher Isamu Nagami looks phenomenologically at the communication between individuals and cultures, which he calls "inter-subjectivity," and suggests that neither "solidarity" nor "objectivity" is politically "enough."

---

[19]Richard Rorty, "Solidarity or Objectivity?" from *Consequences of Pragmatism: Essays 1972–1980* (Minneapolis: University of Minnesota Press, 1982).

◆**from "Cultural Gaps: Why Do We Misunderstand?"**
by Isamu Nagami

A well-known Japanese psychologist, Takeo Doi, expressed his
frustration and puzzlement with American ways of life in his book,
The Anatomy of Dependence:

> From time to time I began to feel an awkwardness arising from
> the difference between my ways of thinking and feeling and those
> of my hosts (That is Americans). For example, not long after my
> arrival in America I visited the house of someone to whom I have
> been introduced by a Japanese acquaintance, and was talking
> to him when he asked me, "Are you hungry? We have some ice
> cream if you'd like it." As I remember, I was rather hungry, but
> finding myself asked point-blank if I was hungry by someone
> whom I was visiting for the first time, I could not bring myself to
> admit it, and ended by denying the suggestion. I probably cher-
> ished a mild hope that he would press me again; but my host,
> disappointingly, said "I see" with no further ado, leaving me
> regretting that I had not replied more honestly. And I found my-
> self thinking that a Japanese would almost never ask a stranger
> unceremoniously if he was hungry, but would produce
> something to give him without asking.

Those who have lived in foreign countries have experienced more
or less the sort of cultural shock Doi expressed so well. These
kinds of intercultural experiences have led many thinkers to probe
into the core elements of culture for comparative study. In Japan,
for example, we find many popular writers who explain the difference between Japanese culture and that of the Western nations including the U.S.A. in terms of group orientation and individual
identity. The thesis for this type of argument is that while Japanese
behavior in general can be explained by orientation within the
group, Americans behave on the basis of individual freedom. There
is no doubt that this reveals a meaningful comparison between the
two cultures to those who have journalistic interests. But if we start
by inquiring into various modalities of the experiential world of
daily life in culture, we find we cannot follow the above approach
primarily for three reasons. 1) Those who accept the group versus
individual thesis tend to explain every cultural phenomenon in
terms of this and as a result they conceal many other rich possibilities which every culture may contain. 2) Certain features are common to all social worlds. In this respect every culture can share
a kind of symbolic common denominator through which we can
compare differences. Yet, this approach of contrast ignores the universality in human existence. 3) The very fact that people understand and describe different cultures reveals a kind of cultural
ethos in which their thinking is embedded. That is to say, their

ways of thinking are inescapably and necessarily cultural. This thought process is not self-critically oriented in the sense that it is not able to show its historico-cultural character and, therefore, tends to be ideological.

The most striking characteristic of these approaches is based on their inability to provide any critical perspective and at the same time on a sort of false legitimacy in our actual human life. Thus it is crucial for us to find another way to understand culture in its most sensible manners. In this respect, we would propose a method of phenomenological reflection, for phenomenology can reveal the various dimensions of human life which, I believe, symbolize culture and thereby can help us to overcome the aforementioned difficulties.

· · · · · · · · · ·

INTERSUBJECTIVITY, LANGUAGE AND TAKEN-FOR-GRANTEDNESS

When, for instance a boy and his mother see a cedar, she is most likely to call it a tree rather than a cedar. After a while if he happens to see an oak tree and asks her "What's that?" she will again call it a tree. At that time he might be very confused with that term simply because there is a difference between a cedar and an oak and yet they partake of the same name, tree. But gradually he realizes that the word or sound "tree" implies a certain group of characteristics which belong to the same category. It is clear that a word "tree" signifies an abstract expression in the sense that it represents certain characteristics and ignores others such as those that belong to the category "flower." In this respect, concreteness in common sense is not concrete in reality, but rather abstract. The reason why people mistake abstract expressions for concrete reality is due to the fact that they unconsciously accept the expressions as taken-for-granted, rooted in a specific-temporal world. Hence some concrete meanings in one culture are not concrete but very enigmatic, non-concrete expressions in another. In English, people distinguish tree from parts of tree which are used for architectural and other purposes, that is "wood." But in Japanese we don't do so. We express the idea of tree and wood both with one term, *Ki*. Yet, the dictionary usually describes *Ki* as having the same meaning as tree. Languages also differ in their built-in grammatical signals, that is in semantics, syntax and phonetics. In English people are very conscious of specifying the number of people involved in what they are discussing. But in Japanese the contrary is often true. Here we can see that the very nature of language through which we comprehend the world and understand ourselves inevitably involves us in the cultural context of language. Hence languages differ immensely from one another not only in pronunciation, vocabulary and grammar, but also in the way they recognize certain things and ignore others, thereby reflecting the society and culture they serve. Experience and language are reciprocal in the sense that human beings can experience outside reality only in terms of the meanings disclosed by language. Human beings are thrown into language worlds in which they learn to identify things as well as to understand reality. In this sense it is obvious that our ways of understanding and interpreting reality are already conditioned by the socially given knowledge.

If we accept that our knowledge is socially given, it seems that we are caught in the relativistic position of suggesting that there is no such thing as objectivity. Hence, we may ask a further question: How can we affirm something as an objective entity on which everybody can agree? In this question we again need to reflect on what I will call the intersubjective world which language as well as our everyday life thinking always presupposes. Situationally we unconsciously put ourselves as the center of spatio-temporal coordinates in the world. This means that I usually see the position I occupy as "here," distinguished from "there" taken by a fellow human being. Yet we can inter-change our positions freely, as if we can place ourselves in the other's situation. A saying such as "Do unto others as you would have them do unto you," implies this interchangeability. This interchangeability is possible because there is an intersubjectively acknowledged spatio-temporal world in which both s/he and I are embedded and therefore can exchange, as well as share, our positions in essentially the same fashion with essentially the same possibilities and consequences. The concept of intersubjectivity signifies this intersubjectively acknowledged spatio-temporal world. Each socio-cultural environment presupposes an intersubjective world which historically develops various conceptions of the world as symbolized in language. Those who have been living in American society share various typicalities as a horizon of familiarity and of unquestioned pre-experience. Through the use of these we can converse with one another and understand the objects of the world as the reality of the taken-for-granted. The meanings of words such as tree or flower are simply taken for granted and therefore are self-evident. In other words, we are speaking, acting and understanding within an intersubjective world in which we share our perspectives through knowledge gained by previous experience. The fact that I am able to express my thinking to a fellow human being already presupposes an intersubjective world in which both s/he and I are embedded and, therefore, s/he can share my thinking and I hers/his. This sharing is the very basis with which we can affirm objective reality for we are able to identify an entity within the same perspective. Understanding, hence, always presupposes a common social heritage of an intersubjective world with the participation of Mystery. It is in this intersubjectivity that we can understand our ways of perceiving outside reality as the objective one.

THE PROBLEM OF INTERSUBJECTIVITY

Up till this point in our discussion, intersubjectivity has not seemed to present a crucial problem to our cultural concerns.

However, when we consider cases in which there are two distinctive groups responding differently according to their own intersubjective worlds, the problem of intersubjectivity can be seen. In order to reveal this problem, let me follow Alfred Schutz's notion of "in-group" and "out-group." The in-group, as defined by Schutz, are those who accept the ready-made standardized scheme of a socio-cultural environment, that is, an intersubjective world as an unquestioned and an unquestionable system of knowledge. For them the system of knowledge in everyday life situation as manifested in language, tradition, habits and various social systems appears to have sufficient coherence, clarity and consistency. In contrast those who stand outside of that world are defined as the out-group. Members of the out-group sometimes feel that what is taken-for-granted by the in-group is actually an ambiguous and enigmatic reality since the out-group have not had any sharing experience with the in-group's historical traditions. Suppose, for instance, that an American who has never lived in any foreign country has to live in Japan, without first learning about the culture or studying the language, and to work at a Japanese factory in a Japanese style. Being astonished by the Japanese employee's daily singing of the company's song or quoting the company's slogan in a militaristic manner, s/he would as a result have considerable difficulty in understanding the Japanese way of life simply because s/he does not share his/her intersubjective world with that of the Japanese. The self-evidence of everyday life for the members of an in-group may not be self-evident for those of the out-group. It is this gap that creates misunderstandings.

I explained a sharing world of an in-group in distinction to that of out-groups. Actually this characterization does not really indicate the true meaning of sharing because the sharing world of an in-group eventually destroys the sharing world in the global sense. A sharing world of an in-group becomes a kind of confinement in which we tend to glorify ourselves as a sharing people, as exemplified in Germany and Japan during the Second World War. As long as we understand "sharing a world" in terms of in-group and out-group, we in a sense validate a dualism of the human condition in which in-group stands apart from out-group. This does not really signify the true meaning of sharing. To share various human concerns in the world means not to differentiate in-group from out-group, but to take part in every possible activity in the world. This participation can create a sort of "fusion of horizons" in which the differences between in-group and out-group eventually disappear, creating a new horizon of understanding which involves a broadening of the present horizon.

FUSION OF HORIZON: OPENNESS AND LISTENING

The encounter between in-group and out-group usually creates tension. How can we overcome this tension and at the same time attain a respectful understanding of each other, allowing every individual and every culture to their own dignity? Indeed this is an important question. Let us recall Gadamer's attempt to explain the encounter between text and interpreter in his *magnum opus*, *Truth and Method*, for his analysis is helpful in understanding the question of the encounter between in-group and out-group. He states:

> The concept of the 'horizon' suggests itself because it expresses the wide, superior vision that the person who is seeking to understand must have. To acquire a horizon means that one learns to look beyond what is close at hand—not in order to look away from it, but to see it better within a larger whole and in truer proportion.

"To acquire a horizon means that one learns to look beyond what is close at hand." What does that mean? It means that we need to learn to understand the out-group's own dignity enabling them to disclose their true nature. This requires from us an openness towards out-groups, a willingness to listen to what the members of out-groups would say. Earlier I discussed the example of the notions of tree and *Ki*; so long as we are caught up within the taken-for-grantedness of our notions in language, we will never be able to understand the real meanings of out-groups' expressions. But if we are able to admit that our understanding is historically conditioned and therefore to allow ourselves to be open to what an out-group says, then a new horizon between us may come into being in the sense that everybody will become able to realize the limitedness of both tree and *Ki* in a larger context. Openness and listening are keys to understanding other cultures as well as other human beings. It is true that an understanding of other cultures involves issues more complex than the difference between tree and *Ki*. Yet, if we lose a sense of listening and openness, there is no possibility for us to understand different cultures and people.

At present we are confronted by the nuclear crisis. This came about because we lost the attitude of listening to others, because we forgot that human beings are rooted in the common destiny of the world, because we manipulated others at our disposal, and because we lost the original meaning of the Biblical story about human beings on earth: human beings were created to bring to light and to protect the world in the context of relationships within which different people and things belong together with mutual dependency.

In the question of fusion of horizons between different cultures and people, language reveals very mysterious powers. Since every language is tied up to a particular historical setting, various languages differ from one another. Language is also the medium through which human beings are able to identify various historico-cultural phenomena in their settings. Hence, historico-cultural differences can be understood as differences among languages. In this regard, language always discloses particular characteristics of its own historico-cultural setting.

But how can we mediate these differences of language? Clearly it is also through language that differences can be fused or compared. In this respect, language discloses the universal dimension through which differences can be overcome. It is true that the English language is different from Japanese. But if English discloses totally different characteristics from Japanese, is it possible for any Japanese to understand the various meanings of English? The very fact that I can translate different English expressions into Japanese already presupposes that there are universally shared meanings between the two languages. Thus language discloses not only particular modes of being, but also the universal dimensions of our existence.

Language, furthermore, has the immanently transcending power by which I mean that language is able to overcome its own limited meaning in its historical condition. Here, paradoxically speaking, our fateful situation is not fateful when we reflect on, and open ourselves to, the fatefulness of our existence. When I say that the tree of the English language is different from the *Ki* of Japanese, I note that the meanings of tree and *Ki* are limited. Yet, in so pointing out, language can open much larger possibilities than those of tree and *Ki*. Because any society signifies linguistically its historical heritage in which human relationality dwells, human relationships, too, disclose particular modes of being as well as universality. Human relationality contains something common to all humanity. Everywhere we find language, cultural objects, playthings for children, family life through which human beings live and celebrate such great events of life as birth, initiation, marriage and death. These are given universally. Human beings are different and yet we share various dimensions of human existence as universally shared meanings. It is in this human sharing that we can appreciate and understand different people.

We cannot escape the "taken-for-grantedness" of our world. We are fatefully thrown into that world where we must find meanings for our existence. It is impossible for us to have meaningful dialogue with others if we do not take our language for granted. For example, it is impossible for us to bring our sick baby to a doctor if we do not take some medical knowledge for granted. In this regard "taken-for-grantedness" discloses appreciative human meanings in addition to its ideological dimensions. One of the fundamental mistakes utopian theorists often make is to assume that they themselves are the vanguard as they claim *a-priori* powers to transcend the ideological power of culture. But, in so doing, they themselves become ideological in the sense that they negate the ultimate human condition: human beings are historical beings who disclose a fateful as well as a transformative mode of life and thought. It seems to me that every human being at certain points has to share in the ideological power of existence. We are, in a sense, living within original sin. However, this does not mean that we cannot transcend various modes of ideological power in our respective cultures. We are living in a constant transformative process within the horizon of encounters between different people. If we are open and responsive to other people in dialogue, then Mystery can lead humans to learn to trust and find a way of reconciling the differences of culture and existence. This awareness opens up much richer possibilities of shaping various modes of our existence in more meaningful ways. The genuine work of education, it seems to me, is to provide and teach this dialogical-critical ability to human beings so that we can create and develop meaningful societies in a global sense.[20]

SUMMARY AND CONCLUSION

Philosophers have always seen their main business as the search for truth. But the notion of truth has itself become a problem, and several competing theories of truth have emerged. The traditional theory is the correspondence theory of truth, which claims that a belief (or statement) is true if it "matches up" or corresponds to the facts of reality. But there have been many arguments to show that this view is inadequate. Accordingly, philosophers have defended the coherence theory of truth, which says that a belief or statement is true if it is logically connected to other beliefs and statements; the pragmatic theory of truth, which says that a belief or statement is true if it helps us in practice with our work and our lives; and a semantic theory of truth, which says that truth is a function of our language as well as a question about the "facts" of the world.

Since the writings of Immanuel Kant, truth is sometimes discussed in terms of our "constitution" of reality, but this also tends to lead to "relativism," the view that there is no reality—no truth—independent of our consciousness and "constitution" of the world.

GLOSSARY

absolutism   the thesis that there is but one correct view of reality. Opposed to *relativism.*

analytic philosophy   the movement in twentieth-century philosophy, particularly in America and Britain, that focuses its primary attention on language and linguistic analysis. Also called "linguistic philosophy."

categories   Kant's word (borrowed from Aristotle) for those most basic and a priori concepts of human knowledge, for example, "causality," and "substance."

coherence theory of truth   a statement or a belief is true if and only if it

---

[20]Isamu Nagami, "Cultural Gaps: Why Do We Misunderstand?" from *Liberation Ethics: Essays in Religious and Social Ethics in Honor of Gibson Winter.* Edited by Charles Amjad-Ali and W. Alvin Pitcher. Center for Scientific Study of Religion, Chicago, 1985.

"coheres" with a system of statements or beliefs. A truth of mathematics is "true" because it forms part of the nexus in the complex of mathematical truths. A geometrical theorem is "true" because it can be proven from other theorems (axioms, definitions) of the geometrical system. A "factual" statement is "true" insofar as other "factual" statements, including general statements about experience that are logically relevant to the original statement, support it. Since we can never get "outside" our experience, the only sense in saying that a belief is true (according to this theory) is that it "coheres" with the rest of our experience.

constitute   to put together, "set up," or synthesize experience through categories or concepts. First used by Kant, later by Husserl.

correspondence theory of truth   a statement or belief is true if and only if it "corresponds" with "the facts." Even when restricting our attention to statements of fact, however, this commonsensical "theory" gets into trouble as soon as it tries to pick out what corresponds to what. How can we identify a "fact," for example, apart from the language we use to identify it? And what does it mean to say that a statement "corresponds" to a fact?

dialectic   a "logic" developed by Hegel in which different forms or philosophies are arranged according to increasing sophistication and scope. The "logic" is a development from one form, whose inadequacies are demonstrated, to another, which corrects these inadequacies, and so on. Marx borrows this "dialectic" and gives it a social interpretation. (The "logic" need not be anything like the form "thesis-antithesis-synthesis.")

essence or **essential intuition**   in Husserl, those ideal objects and laws that constitute necessary truths. The term *essence* is borrowed from Aristotle (and the medieval philosophers) and used in much the same way, except that Husserl's notion of essence is always tied to "intuition" and consciousness.

hermeneutics   the discipline of interpretation of texts. Broadly conceived (as by Heidegger, Gadamer) it is the "uncovering" of meanings in everyday life, the attempt to understand the signs and symbols of one's culture and tradition in juxtaposition with other cultures and traditions.

historicism   a philosophy that localizes truth and different views of reality to particular times, places, and peoples in history. It is generally linked to a very strong relativist thesis as well, that there is no truth apart from these various historical commitments.

phenomenology   a contemporary European philosophy, founded by the German-Czech philosopher Edmund Husserl, that begins with a "pure description of consciousness." Originally developed as an answer to certain questions of necessary truth in the foundations of arithmetic, it was later expanded to answer more general philosophical questions and, in the hands of its later practitioners, it became a "philosophy of man" as well as a theory of knowledge.

pragmatic theory of truth   a statement or a belief is true if and only if it "works," that is, if it allows us to predict certain results and function effectively in everyday life, and if it encourages further inquiry and helps us lead better lives.

pragmatism a distinctly American philosophical movement founded by Charles Sanders Peirce at the turn of this century and popularized by William James and John Dewey. Its central thesis is obvious in its name, that truth (etc.) is always to be determined by reference to practical (pragmatic) considerations. Only those metaphysical distinctions that make some difference in practice are worth considering. And the only ultimate defense of any belief is that "it works."

rational in accordance with the rules of effective thought: coherence, consistency, practicability, simplicity, comprehensiveness, looking at the evidence and weighing it carefully, not jumping to conclusions, etc. Rationality may not guarantee truth; all of the evidence and everything we believe may point to one conclusion, while later generations, who know things that we do not, may see that our conclusion was incorrect. Yet it would still be, for us, the rational conclusion. Rationality points to the manner of thinking rather than its ultimate conclusions. Philosophically, the stress on rationality takes the emphasis off reality and places it on our manner of philosophizing.

realism the thesis that reality exists in itself and it is independent of our consciousness of it.

relativism the thesis that there is no single correct view of reality, no single truth. Relativists often talk about the possibility of "different conceptual frameworks," "alternative lifestyles," and various "forms of consciousness." They are opposed, often violently, to realists and absolutists.

semantics the meanings of a sentence and its various components. Also, the study of those meanings. (So, we can talk about the semantics of a sentence, and we can talk about doing semantics.) "Merely semantic" is a nasty way of referring to conceptual truths, analytic sentences that are true just by virtue of meanings.

semantic theory of truth a formal theory, best known from the work of Alfred Tarski, that defines "true" in terms of a technical notion of *satisfaction*. According to the theory, every sentence in the language is either satisfied or not by a distinct class of individuals. This is adequate, however, only for artificially constructed languages. Generalizing the theory to natural language (for example, American English), we can say that the theory suggests that we (but not each of us personally) set up the rules according to which our sentences do or do not "correspond with the facts" of the world.

transcendental referring to the basic rules of human knowledge, usually with an absolutist suggestion that there can be but a single set of such basic rules. Thus Kant's "transcendental deduction" attempted to deduce the one possible set of basic rules for human understanding, and Husserl's transcendental phenomenology attempted to lay bare the one set of basic ("essential") laws of human consciousness. Contemporary philosophers sometimes talk about "the transcendental turn" in philosophy, in other words, the attempt to move beyond claims that might apply only to ourselves and our way of viewing things to the way that things must be viewed.

transcendental deduction Kant's elaborate attempt to prove that there is but one set of categories (basic rules or a priori concepts) that all rational creatures must use in constituting their experience.

◆ BIBLIOGRAPHY AND FURTHER READING ◆

Discussion and criticism of the various theories of truth can be found in Alan R. White, *Truth* (New York: Doubleday, Anchor, 1970). A discussion of Alfred Tarski's theory is in W. V. O. Quine, *Philosophy of Logic* (Englewood Cliffs, NJ: Prentice-Hall, 1970). Brand Blanshard's argument is developed in his *Nature of Thought* (New York: Macmillan, 1941). William James develops his pragmatic theory in his *Pragmatism: A New Name for Some Old Ways of Thinking* (New York: Longmans Green, 1907). Two brief but helpful introductions to Immanuel Kant's philosophy are J. Kemp, *The Philosophy of Kant* (London: Oxford University Press, 1968) and G. J. Warnock, "Kant," in *A Critical History of Western Philosophy*, ed. D. J. O'Connor (New York: Free Press, 1964). A short introduction to German idealism is R. Solomon, *Introducing the German Idealists* (Indianapolis, IN: Hackett, 1981). The best basic discussion of hermeneutics is David Hoy, *The Critical Circle* (Berkeley: University of California Press, 1978). A compendium of writings by Gadamer is *Philosophical Hermeneutics*, trans. Linge (Berkeley: University of California Press, 1976). *Relativism* is the subject of the essays collected by M. Kraucze and J. Meiland, eds. (Notre Dame, IN: University of Notre Dame Press, 1982). A controversial discussion of the whole problem of truth and its complications is Richard Rorty, *Philosophy and the Mirror of Nature* (Princeton: Princeton University Press, 1979).

5

NECESSITY

The limits of my language mean the limits of my world.

LUDWIG WITTGENSTEIN

Surely there are some things that we can know with certainty! Even Hume, for example, granted that some of our beliefs are beyond the range of his skeptical doubts, namely, those which he calls "relations of ideas," such as the basic principles of arithmetic. Nothing could make us doubt that two plus two equals four. Descartes may have suggested that it was possible that an evil demon was fooling him about even this; but what would it mean to be "fooled" about such matters? How could he have been wrong about that? Of course, he could always say that he might be wrong about two plus two equalling four, just as we could always say that two plus two equals five. But what could we possibly mean by that? We can understand what it would be like to be wrong about some factual belief, such as "there are no Chinese paratroopers in Cuba"; perhaps it even makes sense, however implausible, to suggest that we might be dreaming right now. But one can't even imagine, no matter how hard one tries, what it would be for "two plus two equals four" to be false.

Beliefs that we cannot even imagine being false and that lie beyond the range of all possible doubt and refutation are called **necessary truths.** In short, they must be true. Necessary truth is contrasted with **contingent truth,** which is a belief that is in fact true but might not have been. It is true, for example, that I am now wearing a sweater, but we can easily imagine what it would be for me not to wear one. That is a contingent truth. Necessary truths, because we cannot even imagine what it would be like for them to be false, are always "perfectly certain"; contingent truths, because we can always imagine that they might be false (and that we are possibly fooled or misled in believing them) are never "perfectly certain" but always merely probable. We can always think of some way, no matter how implausible, in which we might be wrong. (I might be dreaming that I'm wearing a sweater, for example.) But one cannot be mistaken about a necessary truth. (There is a curious but important exception to this distinction that is already familiar to you: Descartes' "I exist" is both necessary [it can't be intelligibly doubted] and contingent [since it is possible that he might not have existed].)

A partial distinction between necessary truth and contingent truth is this: Contingent truths are based upon experience and necessary truths are not. Accordingly, contingent truths allow for some further experience that would change our minds. We may be sure that there are no armadillos on the upper east side of Manhattan, but because that is a contingent truth, it is always possible that we shall see an armadillo crossing 86th Street, and thereby have to give up our belief.

Because of this essential link between contingent truths and experience, philosophers often refer to our knowledge of them as **empirical** knowledge. Necessary truths, on the other hand, are not based upon experience, and no possible experience—real or imagined—could change our minds about them. For this reason, philosophers talk about these truths as being prior to experience or **a priori** and knowledge of them is also considered to be a priori, in other words, to be knowledge that is independent of experience. It is important to stress that the word *prior* which means "before," does not mean "earlier in time." For example, it does not mean that we know a priori that "two plus two equals four" before we ever have experience of two things adding up with two other things to give us four things. It means rather that the justification of a priori knowledge does not depend on any possible experience. You cannot refute "two plus two equals four" through experience. But neither can you justify it through experience. You could spend a year adding up different pairs of things: walnuts, elephants, pieces of chalk, people, and scoops of ice cream. You would then have the general claim that "whenever I add two things to two things I get four things," but you would fail to prove the necessity of that truth.

There are philosophers, as we have seen, who do take a priori to mean literally "before"; that is, those philosophers who believe in innate ideas believe that we actually do have certain knowledge before we have any experience at all. We are born with it, and that would explain, if you accept this theory, how it is that a priori knowledge is possible. But it is important to emphasize that the belief in innate ideas is not essential to the notion of either necessary truth or a priori knowledge, and most philosophers talk about the latter without ever mentioning the former.

What then is the source of a priori knowledge? For those philosophers who believe in innate ideas, the answer is that we are born with it. But even this is not enough, for it is necessary to say how it is that we are born with such knowledge. Even if it is "stamped in our minds by God," as some philosophers have held, how do we recognize it? The traditional answer, for those who believe in innate ideas and for those who do not, is through reason. In fact, reason is traditionally defined (for example, by Plato, Aristotle, Spinoza, and Leibniz) as our ability to know necessary truths. But our account is circular; we are told that we can know necessary truths because of reason, but reason is defined as our ability to know necessary truths. So, in this chapter we must ask, what is this ability? How do we have it? How is a priori knowledge possible?

Although we shall be exclusively concerned with necessary and contingent truths, it is important to say that there is a similar distinction between necessary and contingent falsehoods. "Every triangle has at least five sides" is a necessary falsehood—it could not possibly be true. "There are no eagles in America," is a contingent falsehood—it is in fact false, but we can (too easily) imagine that it might be true.

We will divide our discussion of necessary truths into three parts:

1. *Analytic truths or logical truths:* these are, for example, trivial statements such as "either it is raining or it is not raining" and "a horse is an animal." Analytic truths can be known to be true by analyzing the form of the statement and the meanings of the words of the statement.

2. *Truths of arithmetic and geometry:* many philosophers, following Kant, have insisted that these are not analytic, that is, known to be true just because of the form of the statement or the meanings of its component terms. "413 plus 2785 = 3198," for example does not seem to be true because of the meanings of the terms, "413," "2785," etc., yet this would seem to be a necessary truth if anything is. The same would be true of "the internal angles of a triangle equal two right angles." Are these analytic, or something else?

3. *Truths of metaphysics:* these are the principles of metaphysics formulated by the great metaphysicians (Plato, Aristotle, Leibniz, Spinoza), which were claimed to be necessary truths. It has also been suggested that the principles Hume claimed could not be justified, the principle of universal causation and the principle of induction, are necessary truths, (You can guess that this category of necessary truths will be far more controversial than the first two.)

A. ANALYTIC TRUTHS

Consider the utterly trivial statement, "all bachelors are unmarried." Not very interesting, to be sure, but it is, obviously, a necessary truth. We can be perfectly certain that this statement is true, and we know in advance that no study of bachelors could possibly turn up an instance of one who was married. We cannot even imagine a situation in which this statement would be false, and there is no sense in wondering, "well, we've only looked at the bachelors in our neighborhood, what about the bachelors in southern California?" All we have to know to know that "all bachelors are unmarried" is the meaning of the English sentence, nothing else.

Now consider the contingent claim, "all bachelors are happy." Of course, in order to find out whether that is true or not you have to know the meanings of the words, but you cannot tell whether or not it is true just by looking at the words. This statement raises an empirical question. In order to know whether or not it is true you have to go interview bachelors. To falsify the claim that all bachelors are happy, you would have to find only one unhappy bachelor. But even if you never found one, you could never be perfectly certain of the truth of the claim. There might always be one unhappy bachelor, living in a cave off the coast of Madagascar. A contingent claim, therefore, is never perfectly certain. One can always at least imagine some circumstance that would prove it false, even if it seems, on the basis of the present evidence, to be true.

The example "all bachelors are unmarried" is an analytic truth. Its truth can be demonstrated just by referring to the meanings of the words in the sentence. This particular example is what we referred to in earlier chapters as a conceptual truth (such as, "a horse is an animal"). **Conceptual truths** are a special class of analytic truths. Aristotle discussed such truths in terms of essences. He would say that "the essence of a bachelor is to be unmarried." More modern philosophers would talk about concepts. They would say that "the concept 'bachelor' includes the concept of being unmarried." Today most philosophers would rather say that "bachelor means unmarried person." But these different formulations all point to the same fact, that conceptual truths are necessary truths because of the meaning of the words in the sentence.

Not all analytic truths are conceptual truths, however. Consider the statement, "either it is raining or it is not raining." Now obviously you don't have to look out the window to see whether this is true or not. It is true just because of the form of the sentence, which is *"P or not P."* Such sentences are called **tautologies.** They are true by virtue of the form of the sentence alone, and it doesn't matter what phrase you substitute for *P*. For example, you know that "either there are exactly 7,500 comets in our galaxy or there are not," even if you don't know anything about astronomy, or exactly what a "comet" or a "galaxy" is. (*"P or not P"* is called the **law of the excluded middle**—either a sentence or its denial must be true.)

Tautologies are not very interesting. They are the most boring and uninformative sentences in our language, but they are also very important. Every tautology gives us what we called (in the Introduction) a **rule of inference,** one of those basic rules that we use in all our thinking. (This is true even for people who claim "not to be logical" or actually attack logic.) According to these rules of inference we define the validity of our arguments. But here a problem arises. How can we defend a rule of inference itself? We cannot say that it is valid, since we have to use such rules in order to say that anything is valid. And we can't use a rule to prove itself. (That would be the same as appointing a magistrate to judge his or her own alleged corruption.) To answer this question, many philosophers appeal to **intuition** as a defense of fundamental rules of inference. Rationalists feel comfortable with this since they have confidence in reason to show us such basic truths through intuition. Empiricists tend to feel very uncomfortable, however, for they would rather these rules be based upon experience (but they are not) or that they be matters of reasoning (but this can't be either, since they are the foundation of all reasoning). So, empiricists try to find as small a set of basic rules as possible, from which they can derive all of the others. The problem then becomes, how do you defend that basic set of rules?

The most fundamental of these rules is called the **law of contradiction,** which says, a statement and its denial cannot both be true. For example, it cannot be true that it is raining and that it is not raining at the same place at the same time. This law has been used by many philosophers (for example, Leibniz and Hume) to define analytic truths in general. They say that a statement is analytic if when you deny it you get a contradiction. The recognition of the importance of this law, however, goes as far back as Aristotle, who worried about this law and what makes it true. After considerable thought, he concluded:

◆**from *Metaphysics*,
by Aristotle**

This is the most certain of all principles, for it is impossible for anyone to suppose that the same thing is and is not . . . then clearly it is impossible for the same man to suppose at the same time that the same thing is and is not; for the man who made this error would entertain two contrary opinions at the same time. Hence all men who ares demonstrating anything refer back to this as an ultimate belief; for it is by nature the starting-point of all the other axioms as well.

· · · · · · · · ·

Some, indeed, demand to have the law proved, but this is because they lack education; for it shows lack of education not to know of what we should require proof, and of what we should not. For it is quite impossible that everything should have a proof; the process would go on to infinity, so that even so there would be no proof. If on the other hand there are some things of which no proof need be sought, they cannot say what principle they think to be more self-evident. Even in the case of this law, however, we can demonstrate the impossibility of refutation, if only our opponent makes some statement. If he makes none, it is absurd to seek for an argument against one who has no arguments of his own about anything, in so far as he has none; for such a person, in so far as he is such, is really no better than a vegetable.[1]

Aristotle's answer is still accepted by most philosophers. This one principle, at least, cannot be defended except to say that it would be utterly absurd to deny it. Even if a philosopher will not accept the appeal to intuition in any other case, it seems that he must at least in this one.

There are many other kinds of analytic truths, but it would take a course in logic to adequately discuss them. But what they all have in common is that they are necessary truths that can be known simply by the analysis of the form of the sentence or the meanings of the words within the sentence. But will this account of analytic truths cover all cases of necessary truths? For example, will it work for the truths of arithmetic and geometry too?

B. THE TRUTHS OF ARITHMETIC AND GEOMETRY

Since ancient times, the principles of arithmetic and geometry have been considered necessary truths. The explanations of them varied, from religious laws of the cosmos (as in Pythagoras and many ancient cults of astrology) to Plato's theory of ideal forms. But this much has seemed obvious to almost everyone who has thought about the nature of these principles: No stretch of the imagination could describe a circumstance in which they would not be true. No matter how the world changed, and no matter what else people came to believe, two plus two would still equal four, and the principles of Euclidean geometry would still be true.

Think for a moment about the simple truth of arithmetic, "two plus two equals four." It is not the case that two things plus two things of the same kind always result in four things: two drops of ink added to two more drops of ink give you one big drop, not four. But this doesn't give us a counter-example to the laws of arithmetic, since the volume of the large drop would still have to equal the total volume of the two plus two smaller drops. Similarly, you can draw a triangle whose interior angles do not equal two right angles, as Euclid shows they must, by drawing the triangle on the curved surface of a globe. But this does not show that Euclid's principles, which are specifically concerned with figures drawn on a flat surface, could possibly be false. In general, people have believed that, even if there are apparent counter-examples to the truths of

[1]Aristotle, *Metaphysics*, Bk. IV, trans. Hugh Tredennick (Cambridge, MA: Harvard University Press, 1933).

arithmetic and geometry, those truths themselves are absolutely necessary and cannot be challenged.

The defense of this necessary truth, however, and all such truths of mathematics, Euclidean geometry, and arithmetic, does not simply appeal to the meaning of the words involved. The truth of "two plus two equals four" does not depend on replacing one synonym with another, as in "all bachelors are unmarried." The number four, for example, can be described in many ways, as "two plus two," as "one plus three," as "the number following three" or "the number preceding five," as "the number that is the first nonprime," and as "the square root of sixteen." This list could be extended indefinitely (for example, "one half of eight," "one third of twelve," "one fourth of sixteen"). Consequently, it is difficult to see how "two plus two equals four" is true just because the meaning of "four" is "two plus two." If the symbolic system that we call arithmetic makes its principles necessarily true by some system of interconnected definitions, they would have to be infinitely more complicated than any of the analytic truths we have seen thus far.

There is another consideration, however, that has often been argued as a reason for thinking that the truths of arithmetic and geometry cannot be merely analytic. The argument was originally formulated by Immanuel Kant. He pointed out, against Hume and his other predecessors who so glibly spoke of "relations of ideas" and "truths of reason," that the truths of arithmetic and geometry are not just abstract formulas that we accept as true because we accept the overall system of which they are a part. We also apply these principles to the world in concrete ways, to give us new knowledge of things. For example, we count things, "one, two, three . . ." and this means that our number system must be linked up with the world of experience as well as being a self-contained system of necessary truths. (Logicians refer to any logical system of abstract symbols as a **calculus;** a system that is applied to the world, such as arithmetic, is an *interpreted calculus.*) Analytic truths, as we have described them, do not tell us anything about the world; logical principles tell us how we reason, but they say nothing of what we reason about. Conceptual truths tell us something about the meanings of words, but (except for teaching young children the categories to which things belong, as for example, "a horse is an animal, but a tree is a plant") they too tell us nothing about the world itself. But arithmetic and geometry, it seems, give us new information that we did not have before. This is obviously true of the principles of physics and of "higher" mathematics. Perhaps it is also true of the simplest truths of arithmetic.

In elementary education, there are some problems that we learn to calculate, given the basic principles of arithmetic. "Long" division, for example, presupposes the simple truths of "short" division, multiplication, and subtraction. These simple truths, however, like the simple truths of multiplication, subtraction, and addition "tables," are not calculated but memorized. The important question, then, is whether these basic principles can themselves be proved or calculated, or whether they can only be memorized. How do we defend these basic truths? Can we only say, "by intuition"? Further, there are some evident truths of arithmetic that no mathematicians have ever been able to prove. There is now a general proof, developed only a few years ago by a contemporary logician named Jurt Gödel, which shows that there can never be a system of proofs that can succeed in proving all truths of arithmetic without proving some false claims as well. The same is true in Euclidean geometry. You may remember from high school that problematic theorem, that one and only one line can be drawn through a point parallel to a given line. It is obviously true, necessarily true, but no one can develop a valid proof for it.

1. The Empiricist Argument

The basic principles of arithmetic would seem to be necessary truths if anything is. But are they logical truths, true by virtue of their logical form? or conceptual truths, true by virtue of their symbolic meanings? It is here that the arguments about the nature of necessary truth become most violent and most brilliant. Once again, rationalists need not be particularly disturbed, for their confidence in reason allows them to agreeably accept the idea that certain nonanalytic truths may yet be necessary and known by intuition. For them, it is enough to say, along with Plato, Descartes, and Leibniz, that certain principles of mathematics are "self-evident," "intuitively obvious," or even "innate ideas." But for empiricists, who insist that all knowledge is based upon either experience or analytic sentences, the foundations of arithmetic prove to be an embarrassing problem. It is worth noting that all three traditional empiricists, Locke, Berkeley, and Hume, simply accepted the idea that the truths of arithmetic are "relations of ideas," without looking any further. Modern empiricists, however, have not been so negligent. The most famous of the British "logical positivists," A. J. Ayer, for example, states the empiricist problem in the following way:

◆**from *Language, Truth and Logic*, by A. J. Ayer**

Where the empiricist does encounter difficulty is in connection with the truths of formal logic and mathematics. For whereas a scientific generalization is readily admitted to be fallible, the truths of mathematics and logic appear to everyone to be necessary and certain. But if empiricism is correct no proposition which has a factual content can be necessary or certain. Accordingly the empiricist must deal with the truths of logic and mathematics in one of the two following ways: he must say either that they are not necessary truths, in which case he must account for the universal conviction that they are; or he must say that they have no factual content, and then he must explain how a proposition which is empty of all factual content can be true and useful and surprising.

If neither of these courses proves satisfactory, we shall be obliged to give way to rationalism. We shall be obliged to admit that there are some truths about the world which we can know independently of experience; that there are some properties which we can ascribe to all objects, even though we cannot conceivably observe that all objects have them. And we shall have to accept it as a mysterious inexplicable fact that our thought has this power to reveal to us authoritatively the nature of objects which we have never observed. . . . It is vital, therefore, for us to be able to show that one or other of the empiricist accounts of the propositions of logic and mathematics is correct. If we are successful in this, we shall have destroyed the foundations of rationalism. For the fundamental tenet of rationalism is that thought is an independent source of knowledge, and is moreover a more trustworthy source of knowledge than experience; indeed some rationalists have gone so far as to say that thought is the only source of knowledge. And the ground for this view is simply that the only necessary truths about the world which are known to us are known through thought and not through experience. So that if we can show either that the truths in question are not necessary or that they are not "truths about the world," we shall be taking away the support on which rationalism rests. We shall be making good the empiricist contention that there are no "truths of reason" which refer to matters of fact.[2]

The alternatives are few, but the variety of ways in which they have been developed is dazzling. One possibility is to simply deny what we have seemingly accepted as obvious all along, namely, the truths of arithmetic are necessary truths. The fact that they are not analytic does not therefore appear as a problem. They are rather, according to this empiricist position, well-confirmed matters of fact (and therefore not "relations of ideas" at all). John Stuart Mill, the most famous British philosopher of the nineteenth century, argued this position as follows:

◆ from *A System of Logic,* by John Stuart Mill

Why are mathematics by almost all philosophers, and (by some) even those branches of natural philosophy which, through the me-

---

[2]A. J. Ayer, *Language, Truth and Logic,* 2nd ed. (London: Victor Gollancz, 1936; rpt. New York: Dover, 1946).

dium of mathematics, have been converted into deductive sciences, considered to be independent of the evidence of experience and observation, and characterized as systems of Necessary Truth?

The answer I conceive to be, that this character of necessity, ascribed to the truths of mathematics, and (even with some reservations to be hereafter made) the peculiar certainty attributed to them, is an illusion; in order to sustain which, it is necessary to suppose that those truths relate to, and express the properties of, purely imaginary objects. It is acknowledged that the conclusions of geometry are deduced, partly at least, from the so-called Definitions, and that those definitions are assumed to be correct representations, as far as they go, of the objects with which geometry is conversant. Now we have pointed out that, from a definition as such, no proposition, unless it be one concerning the meaning of a word, can ever follow; and that what apparently follows from a definition, follows in reality from an implied assumption that there exists a real thing comformable thereto. This assumption, in the case of the definitions of geometry, is not strictly true: there exist no real things exactly conformable to the definitions. There exist no points without magnitude; no lines without breadth, nor perfectly straight; no circles with all their radii exactly equal, nor squares with all their angles perfectly right. It will perhaps be said that the assumption does not extend to the actual, but only to the possible, existence of such things. I answer that, according to any test we have of possibility, they are not even possible. Their existence, so far as we can form any judgment, would seem to be inconsistent with the physical constitution of our planet at least, if not of the universe. To get rid of this difficulty, and at the same time to save the credit of the supposed system of necessary truth, it is customary to say that the points, lines, circles, and squares which are the subjects of geometry, exist in our conceptions merely, and are part of our minds; which minds, by working on their own materials, construct an *a priori* science, the evidence of which is purely mental, and has nothing whatever to do with outward experience. By howsoever high authorities this doctrine may have been sanctioned, it appears to me psychologically incorrect. The points, lines, circles, and squares which any one has in his mind, are (I apprehend) simply copies of the points, lines, circles, and squares which he has known in his experience. Our idea of a point, I apprehend to be simply our idea of the *minimum visible*, the smallest portion of surface which we can see. A line, as defined by geometers, is wholly inconceivable. We can reason about a line as if it had no breadth; because we have a power, which is the foundation of all the control we can exercise over the operations of our minds; the power, when a perception is present to our senses, or a conception to our intellects, of *attending* to a part only of that perception or conception, instead of the whole. But we can not *conceive* a line without breadth; we can form no mental picture of such a line: all the lines which we have in our minds are lines possessing breadth.

If any one doubts this, we may refer him to his own experience. I much question if any one who fancies that he can conceive what is called a mathematical line, thinks so from the evidence of his consciousness: I suspect it is rather because he supposes that unless such a conception were possible, mathematics could not exist as a science: a supposition which there will be no difficulty in showing to be entirely groundless.

Since, then, neither in nature, nor in the human mind, do there exist any objects exactly corresponding to the definitions of geometry, while yet that science can not be supposed to be conversant about nonentities; nothing remains but to consider geometry as conversant with such lines, angles, and figures, as really exist; and the definitions, as they are called, must be regarded as some of our first and most obvious generalizations concerning those natural objects. The correctness of those generalizations, *as* generalizations, is without a flaw: the equality of all the radii of a circle is true of all circles, so far as it is true of any one: but it is not exactly true of any circle; it is only nearly true; so nearly that no error of any importance in practice will be incurred by feigning it to be exactly true. . . .

When, therefore, it is affirmed that the conclusions of geometry are necessary truths, the necessity consists in reality only in this, that they correctly follow from the suppositions from which they are deduced. Those suppositions are so far from being necessary, that they are not even true; they purposely depart, more or less widely, from the truth. The only sense in which necessity can be ascribed to the conclusions of any scientific investigation, is that of legitimately following from some assumption, which, by the conditions of the inquiry, is not to be questioned. In this relation, of course, the derivative truths of every deductive science must stand to the inductions, or assumptions, on which the science is founded, and which, whether true or untrue, certain or doubtful in themselves, are always supposed certain for the purposes of the particular science. . . .

From these considerations it would appear that Deductive or Demonstrative Sciences are all, without exception, Inductive Sciences; that their evidence is that of experience.

· · · · · · · · · ·

One theory attempts to solve the difficulty apparently inherent in the case, by representing the propositions of the science of numbers as merely verbal, and its processes as simple transformations of language, substitutions of one expression for another. The proposition, Two and one is equal to three, according to these writers, is not a truth, is not the assertion of a really existing fact, but a definition of the word three; a statement that mankind have agreed to use the name three as a sign exactly equivalent to two and one; to call by the former name whatever is called by the other more clumsy phrase. According to this doctrine, the longest process in algebra is but a succession of changes in terminology, by which equivalent expressions are substituted one for another; a series of translations of the same fact, from one into another language; though how, after such a series of translations, the fact itself comes out changed (as when we demonstrate a new geometrical theorem by algebra), they have not explained; and it is a difficulty which is fatal to their theory.

It must be acknowledged that there are peculiarities in the processes of arithmetic and algebra which render the theory in question very plausible, and have not unnaturally made those sciences the stronghold of Nominalism. The doctrine that we can discover facts, detect the hidden processes of nature, by an artful manipulation of language, is so contrary to common sense, that a person must have made some advances in philosophy to believe it: men fly to so paradoxical a belief to avoid, as they think, some even greater difficulty, which the vulgar do not see. What has led many to believe that reasoning is a mere verbal process is, that no other theory seemed reconcilable with the nature of the Science of Numbers. For we do not carry any ideas along with us when we use the symbols of arithmetic or of algebra. In a geometrical demonstration we have a mental diagram, if not one on paper; AB, AC, are present to our imagination as lines, intersecting other lines, forming an angle with one another, and the like, but not so *a* and *b*. These may represent lines or any other magnitudes, but those magnitudes are never thought of; nothing is realized in our imagination but *a* and *b*. The ideas which, on the particular occasion, they happen to represent, are banished from the mind during every intermediate part of the process, between the beginning, when the premises are translated from things into signs, and the end, when the conclusion is translated back from signs into things. Nothing, then, being in the reasoner's mind but the symbols, what can seem more inadmissible than to contend that the reasoning process has to do with any thing more?

Nevertheless, it will appear on consideration, that this apparently so decisive instance is no instance at all; that there is in every step of an arithmetical or algebraical calculation a real induction, a real inference of facts from facts; and that what disguises the induction is simply its comprehensive nature, and the consequent extreme generality of the language. All numbers must be numbers of something; there are no such things as numbers in the abstract. *Ten* must mean ten bodies, or ten sounds, or ten beatings of the pulse. But though numbers must be numbers of something, they may be numbers of any thing. Propositions, therefore, concerning numbers, have the remarkable peculiarity that they are propositions concerning all things whatever; all objects, all existences of every kind, known to our experience. All things possess quantity; consist of parts which can be numbered; and in that character possess all the properties which are called properties of numbers. That half of four is two, must be true whatever the word four represents, whether four hours, four miles, or four pounds weight. We need only conceive a thing divided into four equal parts (and all things may be conceived as so divided), to be able to predicate of it every property of the number four, that is, every arithmetical proposition in which the number four stands on one side of the equation.

· · · · · · · · · ·

There is another circumstance, which still more than that which we have now mentioned, gives plausibility to the notion that the propositions of arithmetic and algebra are merely verbal. That is, that when considered as propositions respecting Things, they all have the appearance of being identical propositions. The assertion, Two and one is equal to three, considered as an assertion respecting objects, as for instance, "Two pebbles and one pebble are equal to three pebbles," does not affirm equality between two collections of pebbles, but absolute identity. It affirms that if we put one pebble or two pebbles, those very pebbles are three. The objects, therefore, being the very same, and the mere assertion that "objects are themselves" being insignificant, it seems but natural to consider the proposition, Two and one is equal to three, as asserting mere identity of signification between the two names.

This, however, though it looks so plausible, will not bear examination. The expression "two pebbles and one pebble," and the expression "three pebbles," stand indeed for the same aggregation of objects, but they by no means stand for the same physical fact. They are names of the same objects, but of those objects in two different states: though they *de*note the same thing, their *con*notation is different. Three pebbles in two separate parcels, and three pebbles in one parcel, do not make the same impression on our senses; and the assertion that the very same pebbles may by an alteration of place and arrangement be made to produce either the one set of sensations or the other, though a very familiar proposition, is not an identical one. It is a truth known to us by early and constant experience: an inductive truth; and such truths are the foundation of the science of Number. The fundamental truths of that science all rest on the evidence of sense; they are proved by showing to our eyes and our fingers that any given number of objects—ten balls, for example—may by separation and re-arrangement exhibit to our senses all the different sets of numbers the sums of which is equal to ten. All the improved methods of teaching arithmetic to children proceed on a knowledge of this fact. All who wish to carry the child's *mind* along with them in learning arithmetic; all who wish to teach numbers, and not mere ciphers— now teach it through the evidence of the senses, in the manner we have described.

We may, if we please, call the proposition, "Three is two and one," a definition of the number three, and assert that arithmetic, as it has been asserted that geometry, is a science founded on definitions. But they are definitions in the geometrical sense, not the logical; asserting not the meaning of a term only, but along with it an observed matter of fact. The proposition, "A circle is a figure bounded by a line which has all its points equally distant from a point within it," is called the definition of a circle; but the proposition from which so many consequences follow, and which is really a first principle in geometry, is, that figures answering to this description exist. And thus we may call "Three is two and one" a definition of three; but the calculations which depend on that proposition do not follow from the definition itself, but from an arithmetical theorem presupposed in it, namely, that collections of objects exist, which while they impress the senses thus, ° ° °, may be separated into two parts thus, ° ° °. This proposition being granted, we term all such parcels Threes, after which the enunciation of the above-mentioned physical fact will serve also for a definition of the word Three.

The Science of Number is thus no exception to the conclusion we previously arrived at, that the processes even of deductive sciences are altogether deductive, and that their first principles are generalizations from experience.[3]

In this selection, John Stuart Mill challenges what has been one of the best established beliefs in the history of Western thought, the belief that arithmetical and geometrical truths are necessary and could not be otherwise. He argues that these truths, like all truths, are nothing other than generalizations from experience and that they differ only in the degree of confirmation, not in kind. He uses the Kantian argument that arithmetic is never simply abstract calculation, but also applicable to the world. And this means, according to Mill (but not according to Kant), that there must always be some inference from facts about the world. Numbers are never simply numbers, he argues, they are always numbers of something, and this means that the meaning of a number (for example, "four") always extends beyond the language of arithmetic alone. The truths of arithmetic and geometry, in other words, are just like the truths of science—generalizations about the world.

Most empiricists, however, have not taken Mill's alternative of arguing that these truths are not necessary. Like A. J. Ayer, they have generally agreed that the principles of arithmetic and geometry are indeed necessary truths, and therefore, they conclude, must be analytic. Mill refers to several such attempts in his own day. The problem, however, is to show how these truths are derivable either from principles of logic or from the meanings of arithmetical or geometrical terms. The attempt to derive arithmetic from logic was begun by the German Gottlob Frege, who attacked the defenders of Mill's empirical interpretation in his own

[3]John Stuart Mill, *A System of Logic*, 8th ed. (New York: Harper, 1874).

country. The project was fully developed in England by Bertrand Russell and Alfred North Whitehead in their *Principia Mathematica*. In what has been called the most brilliant single philosophical campaign in the twentieth century, they proved that the principles of arithmetic could be deduced from a small set of axioms (developed by an Italian mathematician named Giuseppe Peano), which could in turn be defined and defended in logical terms alone.

In what follows, the basic empiricist position is presented by the contemporary American philosopher C. G. Hempel. Hempel argues that mathematical truths are necessary and analytic, but he employs some of the very sophisticated logical machinery that had been developed by Peano, Frege, Russell, and Whitehead. He goes beyond Ayer in trying to show how mathematical truths can be derived from simpler logical rules, thus demonstrating their analyticity. He begins, however, by first attacking the rationalist's belief that mathematical truths are "self-evident" as well as Mill's belief that mathematics is a form of empirical knowledge. He then goes on to show how mathematical truths can be derived by logical inference from a limited number of axioms.

◆**from "On the Nature**
of Mathematical Truth,"
by C. G. Hempel

ARE THE PROPOSITIONS OF MATHEMATICS SELF-EVIDENT TRUTHS?

One of the several answers which have been given to our problem asserts that the truths of mathematics, in contradistinction to the hypotheses of empirical science, require neither factual evidence nor any other justification because they are "self-evident." This view, however, which ultimately relegates decisions as to mathematical truth to a feeling of self-evidence, encounters various difficulties. First of all, many mathematical theorems are so hard to establish that even to the specialist in the particular field they appear as anything but self-evident. Secondly, it is well known that some of the most interesting results of mathematics—especially in such fields as abstract set theory and topology—run counter to deeply ingrained intuitions and the customary kind of feeling of self-evidence. Thirdly, the existence of mathematical conjectures such as those of Goldbach and of Fermat, which are quite elementary in content and yet undecided up to this day, certainly shows that not all mathematical truths can be self-evident. And finally, even if self-evidence were attributed only to the basic postulates of mathematics, from which all other mathematical propositions can be deduced, it would be pertinent to remark that judgments as to what may be considered as self-evident are subjective; they may vary from person to person and certainly cannot constitute an adequate basis for decisions as to the objective validity of mathematical propositions.

IS MATHEMATICS THE MOST GENERAL EMPIRICAL SCIENCE?

According to another view, advocated especially by John Stuart Mill, mathematics is itself an empirical science which differs from the other branches such as astronomy, physics, chemistry, etc., mainly in two respects: its subject matter is more general than that of any other field of scientific research, and its propositions have been tested and confirmed to a greater extent than those of even the most firmly established sections of astronomy or physics. Indeed, according to this view, the degree to which the laws of mathematics have been borne out by the past experiences of mankind is so overwhelming that—unjustifiably—we have come to think of mathematical theorems as qualitatively different from the well-confirmed hypotheses or theories of other branches of science: we consider them as certain, while other theories are thought of as the best "very probable" or very highly confirmed.

But this view, too, is open to serious objections. From a hypothesis which is empirical in character—such as, for example, Newton's law of gravitation—it is possible to derive predictions to the effect that under certain specified conditions certain specified observable phenomena will occur. The actual occurrence of these phenomena constitutes confirming evidence, their nonoccurrence disconfirming evidence for the hypothesis. It follows in particular that an empirical hypothesis is theoretically disconfirmable; i.e., it is possible to indicate what kind of evidence, if actually encountered, would disconfirm the hypothesis. In the light of this remark, consider now a simple "hypothesis" from arithmetic: $3 + 2 = 5$. If this is actually an empirical generalization of past experiences, then it must be possible to state what kind of evidence would oblige us to concede the hypothesis was not generally true after all. If any disconfirming evidence for the given proposition can be thought of, the following illustration might well be typical of it: We place some microbes on a slide, putting down first three of them and then another two. Afterwards we count all the microbes to test whether in this instance 3 and 2 actually added up to 5. Suppose now that we counted 6 microbes altogether. Would we consider this as an empirical disconfirmation of the given proposition, or at least as a proof that it does not apply to microbes? Clearly not; rather, we would assume we had made a mistake in counting or that one of the microbes had split in two between the first and the second count. But under no circumstances could the phenomenon just described invalidate the arithmetical proposition in question; for the latter asserts nothing whatever about the behavior of microbes; it merely states that any set consisting of $3 + 2$ objects may also be said to consist of 5 objects. And this is so because the symbols "3 + 2" and "5" denote the same number: they are synonymous by virtue of the fact that the symbols "2," "3," "5," and "+" are *defined* (or tacitly understood) in such a way that the above identity holds as a consequence of the meaning attached to the concepts involved in it.

THE ANALYTIC CHARACTER OF MATHEMATICAL PROPOSITIONS

The statement that $3 + 2 = 5$, then, is true for similar reasons as, say, the assertion that no sexagenarian is 45 years of age. Both are true simply by virtue of definitions or of similar stipulations which determine the meaning of key terms involved. Statements of this kind share certain important characteristics: Their validation naturally requires no empirical evidence; they can be shown to be true by a mere analysis of the meaning attached to the terms which occur in them. In the language of logic, sentences of this kind are called analytic or true *a priori*, which is to indicate that their truth is logically independent of, or logically prior to, any experiential evidence. And while the statements of empirical science, which are synthetic and can be validated only *a posteriori*, are constantly subject to revision in the light of new evidence, the truth of an analytic statement can be established definitely, once and for all. However, this characteristic "theoretical certainty" of analytic propositions has to be paid for at a high price: An analytic statement conveys no factual information. Our statement about sexagenarians, for example, asserts nothing that could possibly conflict with any factual evidence: it has no factual implications, no empirical content; and it is precisely for this reason that the statement can be validated without recourse to empirical evidence.

Let us illustrate this view of the nature of mathematical propositions by reference to another, frequently cited, example of a mathematical—or rather logical—truth, namely the proposition that whenever $a = b$ and $b = c$ then $a = c$. On what grounds can this so-called "transitivity of identity" be asserted? Is it of an empirical nature and hence at least theoretically disconfirmable by empirical evidence? Suppose, for example, that a, b, c, are certain shades of green, and that as far as we can see, $a = b$ and $b = c$, but clearly $a \neq c$. This phenomenon actually occurs under certain conditions; do we consider it as disconfirming evidence for the proposition under consideration? Undoubtedly not; we would argue that if $a \neq c$, it is impossible that $a = b$ and also $b = c$; between the terms of at least one of these latter pairs, there must obtain a difference, though perhaps only a subliminal one. And we would dismiss the possibility of empirical disconfirmation, and indeed the idea that an empirical test should be relevant here, on the grounds that identity is a transitive relation by virtue of its definition or by virtue of the basic postulates governing it. Hence, the principle in question is true *a priori.*

· · · · · · · · · ·

. . . the following conclusion is obtained, which is also known as *the thesis of logicism concerning the nature of mathematics:*

Mathematics is a branch of logic. It can be derived from logic in the following sense:

a. All the concepts of mathematics, i.e., of arithmetic, algebra, and analysis, can be defined in terms of four concepts of pure logic.

b. All the theorems of mathematics can be deduced from those definitions by means of the principles of logic (including the axioms of infinity and choice).[4]

2. The Rationalist Response

What kinds of truths are the truths of arithmetic and geometry? We just watched various empiricists try to show that (1) the truths of mathematics are not necessary and not analytic and therefore not known a priori (Mill), and (2) they are necessary and analytic and therefore known a priori (Ayer, Hempel).

Against both of these empiricist views, the rationalist continues to insist that the truths of arithmetic and mathematics are neither empirical nor analytic, but matters of necessity in some other way. Traditionally, particularly in the philosophy of Descartes, this other way is through "intuition," the anathema of the empiricist. The empiricist does not trust the appeal to intuition, for, by its very nature, it cannot be defended either by rational argument or by appeal to ordinary experience.

The last two centuries have seen a great many rationalist attempts to work out the problematic notion of "intuition" and to display the viability of confidence in human reason. In this chapter we shall mention only two of them. One is by Immanuel Kant, the man whom most contemporary philosophers would call the greatest philosopher since Plato and Aristotle. The other, which emerged only in this century, is called **phenomenology.** It was invented by the German-Czech philosopher-mathematician Edmund Husserl, and it is a philosophy that has enormous influence in both Europe and the United States.

Of course, even the empiricist may be eventually forced back to intuition if there is no further justification of ultimate principles and "relations of ideas." But unlike the traditional rationalist, the empiricist believes that such intuition follows from our use of language or our

[4]C. G. Hempel, "On the Nature of Mathematical Truth," in *American Mathematical Monthly* 52 (1945).

adopting a certain logic. We can only intuit analytic truths. If the rationalist is right, we can also intuit truths that are necessary but not analytic. What kind of truth could this be?

KANT AND SYNTHETIC A PRIORI KNOWLEDGE   In historical terms, the discovery of a third alternative (a truth that is neither analytic nor empirical) precedes the empiricist attempts of the nineteenth and twentieth centuries (by Mill and later by Frege, Russell, Whitehead, Hempel, and Ayer). It was discovered by Kant in the 1770s as an answer to both the traditional rationalists and the empiricists. He found their theories all unacceptable. Both Leibniz and Hume, for example, had simply distinguished necessary from contingent truths, without further distinction. And we so far have done the same thing, only using more sophisticated terminology. But are all necessary truths analytic, known by analysis of the sentence alone? Or might there be some a priori knowledge of the world rather than just of language? The rationalist believes that there is, and Kant, a new kind of rationalist, shows what it would be.

It is one thing to say that knowledge is either *a priori* or *empirical*. It is quite another to say that sentences are either analytic or not analytic. The first distinguishes two kinds of knowledge; the second distinguishes two kinds of sentences. The term Kant used for "not analytic" is **synthetic;** so we have two sets of distinctions, a priori versus empirical and analytic versus synthetic.

We have been talking as if all a priori knowledge were based on analytic sentences. But then, we have also been talking as if only empirical knowledge could be stated in nontrivial or synthetic sentences: for example, "not all trees are green all year." But isn't it possible that there might be synthetic sentences whose truth can be known a priori? Kant thinks that there can be, and he calls such knowledge *synthetic a priori knowledge*. Arithmetic and geometry are his most important examples, but he also uses this notion of "the synthetic a priori" to provide a generally new conception of the problems and principles of philosophy.

So far, we haven't resolved anything. You remember (in our discussion of Plato's word "participation") that we insisted we must always be careful not to mistake a new word for an explanation, and, so far, that's all we have. The words "synthetic a priori," though very impressive, only tell us that the truths of arithmetic are neither analytic nor empirical. In other words, it is a restatement of the problem, which still remains. How does one justify synthetic a priori principles?

In what follows, Kant makes his distinctions between a priori and empirical (a posteriori) knowledge and between analytic and synthetic sentences (or "judgments"). Then he introduces the idea of synthetic a priori knowledge. And, finally, he gives us his radically new way of defending the truths of arithmetic and geometry.

◆from *The Critique of Pure Reason,* by Immanuel Kant

THE DISTINCTION BETWEEN PURE *(A PRIORI)* AND EMPIRICAL *(A POSTERIORI)* KNOWLEDGE

That all our knowledge begins with experience there can be no doubt. For how should the faculty of knowledge be called into activity, if not by objects which affect our senses, and which either produce representations by themselves, or rouse the activity of our understanding to compare, or connect, or to separate them, and thus to convert the raw material of our sensuous impressions into a knowledge of objects, which we call experience? In respect of time, therefore, no knowledge within us is antecedent to experience, but all knowledge begins with it.

But although all our knowledge begins with experience, it does not follow that it arises from experience. For it is quite possible that even our empirical experience is a compound of that which we receive through impressions, and of that which our own faculty of knowledge (incited only by sensuous impressions), supplies from itself, a supplement which we do not distinguish from that raw material, until long practice has roused our attention and rendered us capable of separating one from the other.

It is therefore a question which deserves at least closer investigation, and cannot be disposed of at first sight, whether there exists a knowledge independent of experience, and even of all impressions of the senses? Such *knowledge* is called *a priori,* and distinguished from *empirical* knowledge, which has its source *a posteriori,* that is, in experience.

The idea that our "faculty of knowledge supplies from itself a supplement" to our experience is the key to Kant's theory of necessity. A priori knowledge, according to Kant, is possessed by everyone everwhere at all times precisely because these are the rules that consciousness imposes upon every experience; indeed, these are the rules that make our experience possible. Kant will answer Hume's skepticism by insisting that our knowledge of necessary principle is knowledge of the workings of the mind itself.

The distinction between *analytic* and *synthetic* judgments is the key to Kant's argument. He defines an analytic judgment as one whose predicate is "contained" in the concept of the subject. His example is "all bodies are extended" (that is, take up space), since the idea of "taking up space" is already "contained in" the concept of a physical body. On the other hand, the judgment "all bodies are heavy" would not be analytic, but rather synthetic, since "the predicate is quite different from anything I think in the mere concept of body in general, and the addition of such a predicate therefore yields a synthetic judgment."

Judgments of experience, Kant tells us, are all synthetic. But not all synthetic judgments are merely empirical. Synthetic a priori judgments are not derived from experience but rather precede every experience, and these in turn provide all of those necessary truths that are not merely analytic, not merely tautologies and logical truths.

The most notorious deviation that Kant makes in his attempt to defend what other philosophers called "truths of reason" is his inclusion of the judgments of mathematics as synthetic, rather than "analytic." Here he disagrees with all the empiricists who preceded him and followed him, too. "All mathematical judgments, without exception, are synthetic." These are necessary and not derived from experience, but they are not mere tautologies or logical truths, and not, Kant thinks, reducible to, or derivable from, any set of merely logical principles.

> At first sight one might suppose indeed that the proposition
> $7 + 5 = 12$ is merely analytical, following, according to the princi-
> ple of contradiction, from the concept of a sum of 7 and 5. But,
> if we look more closely, we shall find that the concept of the sum of
> 7 and 5 contains nothing beyond the union of both sums into one,
> whereby nothing is told us as to what this single number may be
> which combines both. We by no means arrive at a concept of
> Twelve, by thinking that union of Seven and Five; and we may ana-
> lyse our concept of such a possible sum as long as we will, still we
> shall never discover it in the concept of Twelve. We must go beyond
> these concepts, and call in the assistance of the intuition corre-
> sponding to one of the two, for instance, our five fingers, or, as Seg-
> ner does in his arithmetic, five points, and so by degrees add the
> units of the Five, given in intuition, to the concept of the Seven. For
> I first take the number 7, and taking the intuituion of the fingers
> of my hand, in order to form with it the concept of the 5, I
> gradually add the units, which I before took together, to make up
> the number 5, by means of the image of my hand, to the number 7,
> and I thus see the number 12 arising before me. That 5 should be
> added to 7 was no doubt implied in my concept of a sum $7 + 5$,
> but not that that sum should be equal to 12. An arithmetical prop-
> osition is, therefore, always synthetical, which is seen more easily
> still by taking larger numbers, where we clearly perceive that, turn
> and twist our conceptions as we may, we could never, by means
> of the mere analysis of our concepts and without the help of intu-
> ition, arrive at the sum that is wanted.
>
> Nor is any proposition of pure geometry analytical. That the
> straight line between two points is the shortest, is a synthetical
> proposition. For my concept of *straight* contains nothing of magni-
> tude (quantity), but a quality only. The concept of the *shortest* is,
> therefore, purely adventitious, and cannot be deduced from the

concept of the straight line by any analysis whatsoever. The aid of intuition, therefore, must be called in, by which alone the synthesis is possible.

It is true that some few propositions, presupposed by the geometrician, are really analytical, and depend on the principle of contradiction: but then they serve only, like identical propositions, to form the chain of the method, and not as principles.[5]

Mathematics, according to Kant as well as the empiricists, is a product of human reason. However, he also argued that it is entirely synthetic; "how then," he asks, "is it possible for human reason to produce such knowledge entirely *a priori?*" His answer lies in the notion of "intuition"; mathematics (and geometry) are representations of the "pure forms of sensibility," in particular, our intuitions of space and time.

◆ from *Prolegomena to Any Future Metaphysics,* by Kant

. . . We find that all mathematical cognition has this peculiarity: it must first exhibit its concept in intuition and indeed *a priori;* therefore in an intuition which is not empirical but pure. Without this mathematics cannot take a single step; hence its judgments are always intuitive.

. . . In one way only can my intuition anticipate the actuality of the object, and be a cognition *a priori,* namely: *if my intuition contains nothing but the form of sensibility, antedating in my mind all the actual impressions through which I am affected by objects.*

. . . .

Now, the intuitions which pure mathematics lays at the foundation of all its cognitions and judgments which appear at once apodictic and necessary are space and time. For mathematics must first present all its concepts in intuition, and pure mathematics in pure intuition; that is, it must construct them. If it proceeded in any other way, it would be impossible to take a single step; for mathematics proceeds, not analytically by dissection of concepts, but synthetically, and if pure intuition be wanting there is nothing in which the matter for synthetical judgments *a priori* can be given. Geometry is based upon the pure intuition of space. Arithmetic achieves its concept of number by the successive addition of units in time, and pure mechanics cannot attain its concepts of motion without employing the representation of time. Both representations, however, are only intuitions; for if we omit from the empirical intuitions of bodies and their alterations (motion) everything empirical,

[5] Immanuel Kant, *The Critique of Pure Reason,* rev. 2nd ed., trans. Max Müller (London: Macmillan, 1927).

> that is, belonging to sensation, space and time still remain, which are therefore pure intuitions that lie *a priori* at the basis of the empirical.
>
> . . . .
>
> The problem of the present section is therefore solved. Pure mathematics, as synthetical cognition *a priori*, is possible only by referring to no other objects than those of the senses. At the basis of their empirical intuition lies a pure intuition (of space and of time) which is *a priori*, because the latter intuition is nothing but the mere form of sensibility, which precedes the actual appearance of the objects, since in fact it makes them possible. Yet this faculty of intuiting *a priori* affects not the matter of the phenomenon (that is, the sensation in it, for this constitutes that which is empirical), but its form, namely, space and time. . . . Consequently, the basis of mathematics actually is pure intuitions, which make its synthetical and apodictically valid propositions possible.[6]

Kant's solution to the problem of mathematical truth is colossal. He is defending the claim that the truths of arithmetic depend upon certain intuitions which can give us a priori knowledge. But, for Kant, these intuitions are nothing other that the forms of space and time, by which we organize our perceptual experiences; geometry is nothing other than a formalized set of descriptions about the way we must experience space, and the same is true of arithmetic and time. Now notice two things about this theory. First, in addition to explaining something about the nature of arithmetic and geometry, it also provides a middle way between Newton and Leibniz's theories of space and time, which we mentioned in Chapter 2 (pp. 121–134). In agreement with Newton, Kant says that space and time are absolute, but he also agrees with Leibniz that they don't exist outside of experience. But second, and much more important, here is an example of Kant's philosophical strategy, which is basic to carry out his revolution in philosophy. What he is saying, in effect, is that the necessary truths of arithmetic and geometry are true because they describe the *essential structures of the human mind*, in this case, the ways in which we are aware of space and time.

HUSSERL AND PHENOMENOLOGY   Husserl was also a rationalist. He began as a mathematician, and his first theory (and his first book) was a defense of the empiricist approach of John Stuart Mill. That is, he thought that the truths of arithmetic and geometry were simply well-confirmed empirical generalizations. An argument with Frege changed his mind, and he turned to the position that such truths must be what they seem to be, namely necessary. But he refused to accept the idea that they were

[6]Immanuel Kant, *Prolegomena to Any Future Metaphysics*, trans. Lewis White Beck (New York: Bobbs-Merrill, 1950).

also trivial analytic truths, true by linguistic convention or derivable from basic logical truths, the positions defended during his lifetime by Frege, Russell, and Whitehead. He held, like Kant before him, that such truths were synthetic a priori. And he held that these truths were known through a special kind of *intuition*. Husserl spent his life, and many tens of thousands of pages, trying to say precisely what this special kind of "intuition" amounted to.

The heart of Husserl's phenomenology is that there are two very different kinds of "experience": (1) ordinary "experience," which he calls "individual intuition," such as my present awareness that there are three bananas and two cats on my desk, and (2) a special kind of intuition, which Husserl calls *essential* (or, when he uses the Greek, *eidetic*) *intuition*. In this second kind of intuition, we do not see particular things but rather universal truths, or essences (the Greek here is *eidos*). Now this theory, and even its Greek terminology, ought to seem very familiar to you. From where? From Plato and Aristotle. Husserl is revising a very old theory, in which such things as numbers and triangles and the various truths of arithmetic and geometry are ideal objects and laws, like Plato's Forms. (The word Plato uses is also *Eidos*, and the title of Husserl's best-known work is *Ideas*.) But Husserl, unlike Plato, does not believe that these special entities have an existence independent of human consciousness. Here he shares Aristotle's criticisms of Plato. These essences, such as numbers and triangles and the laws of arithmetic and geometry, are "in consciousness," and *phenomenology* is the attempt to study consciousness in order to determine what these essences are.

What Husserl is doing, then, is giving an overall theory of the rationalist's important appeal to intuition. And how can we defend this appeal to intuition? Phenomenologists still don't agree on the defense of intuition. Well, at least this much is clear: We can reject a claim based on intuition if not everyone shares that intuition, since the most important characteristic of rational intuitions and essences is that everyone shares them. Properly described, everyone in the world will agree about a rational intuition. But here we recall Locke's argument, that even universal agreement among men would not prove that an idea was *necessarily* common to all men. And the phenomenologist must respond again to this old argument. You can see that these are still very much living issues, not formulated in more sophisticated language, but still much the same as they were when Leibniz and Locke debated them centuries ago.

Husserl is a notoriously difficult author, but it is important to include at least a sample of his work. What follows is from *Ideas* (Vol. I) and outlines his distinction between two kinds of intuition: "individual" (contingent and particular) and "essential" (necessary and universal).

◆**from *Ideas*,
by Edmund Husserl**

Individual Being of every kind is, to speak quite generally, *"accidental."* It is so-and-so, but essentially it could be other than it is. . . . But the import of this contingency, which is there called matter-of-factness, is limited in this respect that the contingency is correlative to a *necessity* which does not carry the mere actuality-status of a valid rule of connexion obtaining between temporo-spatia facts, but has the character of *essential necessity,* and therewith a relation to *essential universality.* Now when we stated that every fact could be "essentially" other than it is, we were already expressing thereby *that it belongs to the meaning of everything contingent that it should have essential being and therewith an Eidos to be apprehended in all its purity;* and this Eidos comes under *essential truths of varying degrees of universality.*

ESSENTIAL INSIGHT AND INDIVIDUAL INTUITION

At first "essence" indicated that which in the intimate self-being of an individual discloses to us *"what"* it is. But every such What can be "set out as Ideas." *Empirical or individual intuition* can be transformed into *essential insight* (ideation)—a possibility which is itself not to be understood as empirical but as essential possibility. The object of such insight is then the corresponding *pure* essence or *eidos,* whether it be the highest category or one of its specializations, right down to the fully "concrete."

Of whatever kind the individual intuition may be, whether adequate or not, it can pass off into essential intuition, and the latter, whether correspondingly adequate or not, has the character of a dator act. And this means that—

The essence (Eidos) is an object of a new type. Just as the datum of individual or empirical intuition is an individual object, so the datum of essential intuition is a pure essence.

Here we have not a mere superficial analogy, but a radical community of nature. *Essential insight is still intuition,* just as the eidetic object is still an object. . . . It is an intuition of a fundamentally *unique* and *novel* kind, namely in contrast to the types of intuition which belong as correlatives to the object-matters of other categories, and more specifically to intuition in the ordinary narrow sense, that is, individual intuition.

It lies undoubtedly in the intrinsic nature of essential intuition that it should rest on what is a chief factor of individual intuition, namely the striving for this, the visible presence of individual fact, though it does not, to be sure, presuppose any apprehension of the individual or any recognition of its reality. Consequently it is certain that no essential intuition is possible without the free possibility of directing one's glance to an individual *counterpart* and of shaping an illustration; just as contrariwise no individual intuition is possible without the free possibility of carrying out an act of ideation and therein directing one's glance upon the corresponding essence which exemplifies itself in something individually visible; but that does not alter the fact that *the two kinds of intuition differ in principle,* and in assertions of the kind we have just been making it is only the essential relations between them that declare themselves. Thus, to the essential differences of the intuitions correspond the essential relations between "existence" (here clearly in the sense of individual concrete being) and "essence," between *fact* and *eidos.*[7]

Husserl begins with the very old distinction, taken from Aristotle and medieval philosophers, between "essence" and "accident." An "accident," according to this usage, could possibly be other than it is, an essence could not. For example, it is possible that some particular triangle might have been drawn acute rather than isosceles, but it is not possible that it could have been drawn as a triangle with five angles. Having three angles is essential to being a triangle, being isosceles is not. This essence is what Husserl calls the *eidos,* and an *eidos,* within a certain description ("various degrees of universality") provides us with a necessary truth. Thus the *eidos* of this particular figure drawn as a triangle includes having three angles. Its *eidos* as a geometric figure, however, does not include having any particular number of angles, but it does require that it consist of lines on a plane. Husserl insists that the essence or *eidos* makes something "what" it is; in other words, it defines it as a certain kind of thing. The distinction between individual intuition and essential intuition is then a difference between (1) *particular* things, which might be different or might not exist at all, and (2) essence or *eidos,* which enables us to talk about a *kind* of thing (for example, centaurs or unicorns) even if they do not, never have, and never will, exist.

The most important claim of Husserl's argument is his insistence that the *eidos* is itself "an object of a new type." In other words, it is something which can be intuited itself, apart from particular examples of it. (In medieval philosophy and since, these entities which represent "kinds of things" are called "universals." The problems of necessary truth are sometimes called "the problem of universals.") A geometer can talk about the properties of a right triangle, for example, without using or thinking of any particular right triangle. He is talking about the type, about the *eidos.* And Husserl's central claim is that, through phenomenology, we learn to recognize the essence or *eidos* by special sorts of intuition. Such intuitions make necessary truths possible. In other words, where Kant insisted that the form of our intuitions (as space and time) makes the principles of arithmetic and geometry necessarily true,

---

[7]Edmund Husserl, *Ideas,* trans. W. R. Boyce-Gibson (New York: Collier, Macmillan, 1962).

Husserl says that it is the content of our intuitions that makes these principles true. That content is what he calls the *eidos* or essence. This is his way of developing the rationalist's belief that necessary truths can be known by intuition. It is also the basis of what he calls *phenomenology*.

◆**from "An Introduction to Phenomenology," by Husserl**

INTRODUCTION

The term "phenomenology" designates two things: a new kind of descriptive method which made a breakthrough in philosophy at the turn of the century, and an a priori science derived from it; a science which is intended to supply the basic instrument *(Organon)* for a rigorously scientific philosophy and, in its consequent application, to make possible a methodical reform of all the sciences. Together with this philosophical phenomenology, but not yet separated from it, however, there also came into being a new psychological discipline parallel to it in method and content: the a priori pure or "phenomenological" philosophy, which raises the reformational claim to being the basic methodological foundation on which alone a scientifically rigorous empirical philosophy can be established. An outline of this psychological phenomenology, standing nearer to our natural thinking, is well suited to serve as a preliminary step that will lead up to an understanding of philosophical phenomenology.

· · · · · · · · · ·

2. THE PURELY PSYCHICAL IN SELF-EXPERIENCE AND COMMUNITY EXPERIENCE. THE UNIVERSAL DESCRIPTION OF INTENTIONAL EXPERIENCES.

To establish and unfold this guiding idea, the first thing that is necessary is a clarification of what is peculiar to experience, and especially to the pure experience of the psychical—and specifically the purely psychical that experience reveals, which is to become the theme of a pure philosophy. It is natural and appropriate that precedence will be accorded to the most immediate types of experience, which in each case reveal to us our own psychic being.

Focusing our experiencing gaze on our own psychic life necessarily takes place as reflection, as a turning about of a glance which had previously been directed elsewhere. Every experience can be subject to such reflection, as can indeed every manner in which we occupy ourselves with any real or ideal objects—for instance, thinking, or in the modes of feeling and will, valuing and striving.

So when we are fully engaged in conscious activity, we focus exclusively on the specific things, thoughts, values, goals, or means involved, but not on the psychical experience as such, in which these
things are known *as* such. Only reflection reveals this to us.
Through reflection, instead of grasping simply the matter straight-
out—the values, goals, and instrumentalities—we grasp the corresponding subjective experiences in which we become "conscious"
of them, in which (in the broadest sense) they "appear." For this
reason, they are called "phenomena," and their most general essential character is to exist as the "consciousness-of" or "appearance-
of" the specific things, thoughts (judged states of affairs, grounds,
conclusions), plans, decisions, hopes, and so forth. This relatedness [of the appearing to the object of appearance] resides in the
meaning of all expressions in the vernacular languages which relate
to psychic experience—for instance, perception *of* something, recalling *of* something, thinking *of* something, hoping *for* something,
fearing something, striving *for* something, deciding on something,
and so on. If this realm of what we call "phenomena" proves to be
the possible field for a pure psychological discpline related exclusively to phenomena, we can understand the designation of it as
phenomenological psychology. The terminological expression, deriving from Scholasticism, for designating the basic character of being as consciousness, as consciousness of something, is *intentionality.* In unreflective holding of some object or other in consciousness, we are turned or directed towards it: our *"intentio"* goes out
towards it. The phenomenological reversal of our gaze shows that
this "being directed" *[Gerichtetsein]* is really an immanent essential feature of the respective experiences involved; they are "intentional" experiences.

3. THE SELF-CONTAINED FIELD OF THE PURELY PSYCHICAL—PHENOMENOLOGICAL REDUCTION AND TRUE INNER EXPERIENCE

The idea of a phenomenological psychology encompasses the
whole range of tasks arising out of the experience of self and the
experience of the other founded on it. But it is not yet clear
whether phenomenological experience, followed through in exclu-
siveness and consistency, really provides us with a kind of
closed-off field of being, out of which a science can grow which is
exclusively focused on it and completely free of everything psycho-
physical. Here [in fact] difficulties do exist, which have hidden from
psychologists the possibility of such a purely phenomenological
psychology even after Brentano's discovery of intentionality. They
are relevant already to the construction of a really pure self-experience, and therewith of a really pure psychic datum. A particular
method of access is required for the pure phenomenological field:
the method of "phenomenological reduction." This *method of "phe-*

nomenological reduction" is thus the foundational method of pure psychology and the presupposition of all its specifically theoretical methods. Ultimately the great difficulty rests on the way that already the self-experience of the psychologist is everywhere intertwined with external experience, with that of extrapsychical real things. The experienced "exterior" does not belong to one's intentional interiority, although certainly the experience itself belongs to it as experience—*of* the exterior. Exactly this same thing is true of every kind of awareness directed at something out there in the world. A consistent epoche of the phenomenologist is required, if he wishes to break through to his own consciousness as pure phenomenon or as the totality of his purely mental processes.

4. EIDETIC REDUCTION AND PHENOMENOLOGICAL PSYCHOLOGY AS AN EIDETIC SCIENCE

To what extent does the unity of the field of phenomenological experience assure the possibility of a psychology exclusively based on it, thus a pure phenomenological psychology? It does not automatically assure an empirically pure science of *facts* from which everything psychophysical is abstracted. But this situation is quite different with an a priori science. In it, every self-enclosed field of possible experience permits *eo ipso* the all-embracing transition from the factual to the essential form, the *eidos.* So here, too. If the phenomenological actual fact as such becomes irrelevant; if, rather, it serves only as an example and as the foundation for a free but intuitive variation of the factual mind and communities of minds *into* the a priori possible (thinkable) ones; and if now the theoretical eye directs itself to the necessarily enduring invariant in the variation; then there will arise with this systematic way of proceeding a realm of its own, of the "a priori." There emerges therewith the eidetically necessary typical form, the *eidos;* this *eidos* must manifest itself throughout all the potential forms of mental being in particular cases, must be present in all the synthetic combinations and self-enclosed wholes, if it is to be at all "thinkable," that is, intuitively conceivable. Phenomenological psychology in this manner undoubtedly must be established as an "eidetic phenomenology"; it is then exclusively directed toward the invariant essential forms. . . . If the phenomenological reduction contrived a means of access to the phenomenon of real and also potential inner experience, the method founded in it of "eidetic reduction" provides the means of access to the invariant essential structures of the total sphere of pure mental process.[8]

---

[8]Edmund Husserl, "An Introduction to Phenomenology," in F. Elliston and M. McCormick, eds., *Husserl: Shorter Works* (Notre Dame, IN: University of Notre Dame Press, 1981).

C. THE TRUTHS OF METAPHYSICS

Because the principles of metaphysics are so very basic to all human thought and experience, it has often been argued that they too, like the principles of logic and mathematics, must be necessary truths. As the foundation principles of all of our knowledge, they must have as much certainty as possible, just as a building must have the strongest foundations possible. Without such foundations, everything built on top will be rickety and uncertain. Furthermore, traditional rationalists have claimed that the way in which we come to understand these basic principles, namely, through reason, guarantees us precisely this certainty. The principles of reason, unlike principles drawn from experience, are by their very nature necessary truths.

The various principles of metaphysics advanced by Plato, Aristotle, Spinoza, and Leibniz were all supposed to be necessary truths by virtue of reason. Spinoza's argument that there can only be one substance, for instance, was based upon definitions and axioms that were necessarily true by virtue of reason and derived in the form of theorems (or "propositions") in much the same way that geometrical theorems are derived from the definitions and axioms of Euclidean geometry. The idea that there could be but one substance was not drawn from experience and was not intended to be merely a hypothesis or a viewpoint. It had to be true in exactly the same sense that the principles of arithmetic had to be true, as necessary truths.

But if Spinoza's principle is a necessary truth, then how is it possible that Leibniz, using a similar set of definitions and a similar deductive method, arrived at the very opposite conclusion, that there are many substances? He too claimed this as a necessary truth about the universe. But obviously these cannot both be true; either there is only one substance or there is more than one substance. There cannot be both only one and more than one. But this means (assuming that the systems of Spinoza and Leibniz are consistent within themselves) that either one of them is wrong and the other right, or else that they have each given us a view of the world without giving us necessary truths at all. Each is giving us a possible, not a necessary, principle, nothing more. How can one decide which of these great philosophers is correct? Or should we rather say that neither of them has in fact given us a necessary truth and that each has given us an elegant but only speculative idea about the way the world really is? Reason alone seems not to be enough.

The problem of justifying supposedly necessary truths of metaphysics arises even in those cases in which there is no such direct disagreement. The basic principles of our knowledge (for example, the principle of universal causation, which states that every event has its cause, or the principle of induction, which asserts that the future will be like the past) display the same problem of justification. The problem here is not so much whether or not we should accept these principles (although a few philosophers might reject them, as Leibniz rejects the first principle). We do in fact accept them and use them virtually every moment of our lives. The problem is showing that they are necessarily true and not merely habitual or useful to us. Yet is is clear, as David Hume argued, that such principles can be neither analytic ("relations of ideas") nor straightforward "matters of fact," since upon these principles all "matters of fact" are based. Because of this, Hume suggested that such principles were only matters of habit and custom, that we had become so accustomed to using these principles that we now assumed (wrongly) that they were necessary. But because they could not be defended either as principles of reason—as analytic truths or as principles like those of arithmetic and geometry—or as principles drawn from experience, they could not be justified at all. It is largely against Hume, therefore, that modern metaphysics has had to defend itself.

There is a sense in which the entire history of metaphysics, from Plato to the present day, revolves around the various attempts to establish metaphysical principles as necessary truths based on a foundation that is certain. Traditionally, confidence in reason itself, as divinely inspired and capable of grasping necessary truths, was sufficient to justify confidence in metaphysics. In modern times, this tradition is continued by many rationalists, but it has also been subjected to critical scrutiny and rejected by a great many empiricists and others. This critical scrutiny reaches its extremes with Hume, who dismisses not only the whole of traditional metaphysics and theology as "sophistry and illusion" but the basic principles of all human knowledge as unjustifiable as well. It is at this point in history that Kant steps into the picture, attempting to reestablish the traditional claims of metaphysicians to be able to provide necessary truths. This is not to say that he accepts all the suggestions of the metaphysicians in the past. It is clear that he prefers Leibniz to Spinoza on many issues, for example. Moreover, there are some metaphysical disputes, such as the dispute between Leibniz and Spinoza about whether there can be only one substance or more than one, which he dismisses as irresolvable and useless. There are still other metaphysical principles, for example, belief in God and in the immortality of the human soul, which he defends as necessary—but on practical grounds, not as necessary truths or necessary knowledge.

But at least some of the principles that Hume rejected as unjustifiable are defended by Kant in his unique way as synthetic a priori truths, truths that are neither analytic nor empirical (as Hume had also argued) but that are nevertheless necessary truths (which Hume had denied). Kant argued that these principles are, like the principles of arithmetic and geometry, basic to the structure of the human mind. What makes them necessarily true, therefore, is just the fact that they represent the only possible way in which we can conceive and perceive the world. Here is a third way of defending metaphysical claims that earlier philosophers had not anticipated. By showing that such principles as the principle of universal causation and the principle of induction are necessary for any human knowledge whatever, Kant succeeds in providing a new way of looking at metaphysics and a new way of defending its principles as necessary truths.

SUMMARY AND CONCLUSION

Do we know some things for certain, for example, the basic principles of logic and arithmetic and geometry? The answer isn't as sure as we would like. On the other hand, it is clear that we can't even imagine what it would be like for such necessary truths to be false or for us to be mistaken about them. But on the other hand, it is not clear how these truths can be justified. We can appeal to intuition, but can we absolutely trust our intuitions? We can deduce some of these truths from other truths, but then how do we justify the truths that act as premises? And then some philosophers (for example, Mill) argue that these are not necessary truths at all, but only well-confirmed generalizations from experience, which could possibly (but not likely) turn out to be false.

Although philosophers do not agree about how to justify the basic principles of logic and arithmetic and geometry, most would agree that they are the most certain principles of our knowledge. A much more difficult problem arises with the necessary truths of metaphysics, however. Everyone agrees that two plus two equals four, even if they don't agree about why they so confidently agree. But not everyone agrees that there is only one substance, or that God exists, or that human acts are free from causal determination. In this chapter, we have discussed the difficulties that are involved in defending even those necessary truths that we all agree about. In later chapters, we shall find it even more difficult to defend those claims that people don't agree about. Yet they would still argue that what they believe is necessarily true.

GLOSSARY

analytic (of a sentence or truth)   demonstrably true (and necessarily true) by virtue of the logical form or the meanings of the component words. The concept was introduced by Kant, who defined it in terms of a sentence (he called it a "judgment") in which the "predicate was contained in the subject" and "added nothing to it." For example, in "a horse is an animal," he would say that the concept of "horse" already includes the concept of being an amimal; we would say that "horse" means "an animal which . . ." and thus "is an animal" adds nothing to what we already know just from "horse." Kant also says that the *criterion* or test for analytic sentences (or *analyticity*) is the principle of contradiction; an analytic sentence is one whose denial yields a self-contradiction.

a posteriori (knowledge)   "after experience," or empirical. (See *empirical*.)

a priori (knowledge)   independent of all experience. A priori knowledge is always necessary, for there can be no imaginable instances that would refute it and no intelligible doubting of it. One might come to know something a priori through experience (for example, you might find out that no parallel lines ever touch each other by drawing tens of thousands of parallel lines) but what is essential to a priori knowledge is that no such experience is needed. Knowledge is a priori if it can be proven independently of experience. The most obvious examples of a priori knowledge are analytic sentences, such as "a horse is an animal" and "if all men are mammals and Socrates is a man, then Socrates is a mammal."

calculus   any logical system of abstract symbols, whether interpreted or not.

conceptual truth   an analytic sentence that is true by virtue of the meanings of its component words, or concepts. The example, "a horse is an animal," is a conceptual truth because part of the definition of the word *horse* is "an animal." "All sisters are females" is a conceptual truth because part of the meaning of "sister" is "female."

contingent (truth)   dependent on the facts; neither logically necessary nor logically impossible. A contingent state of affairs could have been otherwise. One test to see if a state of affairs is contingent is to see if it is conceivable that it could be other than it is. It is contingent, for example, that heavy objects fall toward the earth, since it is easily imaginable what it would be like if they did not. This is so even though, in another sense, we say that it is (physically) necessary that heavy objects fall. The philosophical terms *contingent* and *necessary* refer to logical possibility, not to the factual question whether a statement is true or not.

definition   a statement which gives the meaning of a word or phrase. Some definitions, called stipulative definitions, actually introduce the meaning of a word with rigor and distinct boundaries (for example, the logician's definition of "validity"). But, most of the time, a definition is an attempt to capture the not very exact ways in which we ordinarily use a word. In conceptual truths, we can say that they are true "by definition," that is, they are true by virtue of the meanings of the component words, for one word (the subject) contains another (the predicate) in its definition; for example, "a cow is an animal" and the definition of "cow" is "the female *animal* of the genus *Bos*."

eidos   (in Husserl), see *essence*.

empirical (knowledge)   derived from and to be defended by appeal to experience. Empirical knowledge can only be so derived and so defended (as opposed to a priori knowledge, which need not be).

essence   (in Husserl), an ideal object (for example, a number) or an ideal law (of arithmetic).

hypothesis   a provisional suggestion that must be confirmed (or falsified) through experience. Hypotheses are the bulwark of all empirical knowledge and the end point of all inductive reasoning.

intuition   immediate knowledge of the truth, without the aid of any reasoning and without appeal to experience. Intuition, as rational intuition (there are other kinds), is a central concern of the rationalist philosophers, who consider intuition one of the main functions of reason. But because of its very nature, intuition cannot be argued for, nor can it be defended by experience. Accordingly, many philosophers, especially empiricists, reject the notion of intuition and accept it only when absolutely unavoidable. In this century, Edmund Husserl has defended the appeal to intuition in his phenomenology.

law of contradiction   that basic rule of logic that demands that a sentence and its denial cannot both be true. "Not (*P* and not *P*)." This law is used by many philosophers (Kant, Leibniz, and Hume, for example) as a criterion for analyticity or analytic truth.

law of the excluded middle   that rule of logic that says that either a sentence or its denial must be true: "Either *P* or not *P*." In formal logic, this law, together with the law of contradiction, forms the basis of a great many arguments (for example, that form of *reductio ad absurdum* argument in which the consequences of one premise are shown to be absurd, and therefore its denial is accepted. Many logicians are now reconsidering this law, for it is becoming evident that not all sentences are either true or false. For example, consider Russell's famous example, "the King of France is bald" (when there is no king of France); is that true or false? It surely isn't true, but neither can it be false, for there is no king of France who is not bald. Or what of, "green ideas sleep furiously"? Many philosophers would say that these are neither true nor false, thus rejecting the law of the excluded middle.

logic   that part of philosophy which studies the rules of valid inference and (we now add) the rules of inductive generalization. It is also, however, the study of the form of sentences, their grammar or syntax, or logical form. More loosely, "logic" sometimes means simply "order."

logical truth   a sentence that can be shown to be true by virtue of its logical form alone (by virtue of the connectives, "and," "or," etc.).

logicism   the thesis that all necessary truths are reducible to logical or analytic truths.

matter of fact   (in Hume), an empirical claim, to be confirmed or falsified through experience.

necessary (truth)   cannot be otherwise and cannot be imagined to be otherwise. In philosophy, it is not enough that something be "necessary" according to physical laws (for example, the law of gravity), or "necessary" according to custom or habit (for example, the "necessity" of laws against rape, or the felt necessity of having a cigarette after dinner). Necessary allows for not even imaginary counter-examples; thus it is a necessary truth that two plus two equals four. Not only do we believe this with certainty and find ourselves incapable of intelligibly doubting it, but we cannot even suggest what it might be for it to be false, no matter how wild our imaginations.

necessity   in accordance with a necessary truth.

phenomenology   the philosophy of Edmund Husserl, a twentieth-century rationalism that defends appeals to intuition in the defense of necessary truths.

relation of ideas   in traditional empiricist philosophy, analytic truths, which can be demonstrated without appeal to experience. Arithmetic and geometry were taken to be paradigm examples of "relations of ideas."

rules of inference   those rules of logic according to which validity is defined. All such rules are analytic, but there is considerable disagreement whether all are so by virtue of their own logical form or whether some are so because they are derived from other, more basic rules. There is also the following question: given that these rules define correct logical form, how is it possible to say that they have correct logical form?

synonym   "meaning the same." Two words are synonymous if they are interchangeable in a sentence, without losing the meaning of the sentence. For example, "criminal" and "felon" are synonyms in most contexts. The test of a supposedly conceptual truth is to replace certain words with synonyms, and then see if its denial yields a self-contradiction. In other words, substituting synonyms turns a conceptual truth into an analytic truth. For example, "ferns are plants"; substituting for "fern" its synonym (or, in this case, also its definition) "a primitive plant that bears spores, etc." we have "a plant is a plant," whose denial is a contradiction ("a plant is not a plant") and thus is analytic.

synthetic (statement)   a noncontradictory proposition in which the predicate is not entailed by the subject, for example, "horses are generally obstinate." ("Synthetic" is opposed, in this sense, to "analytic.") A synthetic sentence cannot be shown to be true by appeal to the logical form or the meanings of the component words. Kant defined a "synthetic" sentence as one that "adds an idea to the subject which is not already contained in it." For example, "a horse is the source of a large income for some people" is a strictly synthetic sentence. No appeal to the meaning of "horse" will help you find out whether it is true or not, and its denial surely does not result in self-contradiction. But, according to Kant, it must not be concluded that all synthetic sentences can be shown to be true solely by appeal to experience. Some, he claimed, are known a priori.

synthetic a priori (knowledge)   knowledge that is necessary and known independently of experience (and thus a priori), but that does not derive its truth from the logic or meaning of sentences (thus synthetic). This is the focal concept of Kant's philosophy.

tautology   a trivial truth that is true by virtue of logical form alone and tells us nothing about the world. (Popularly, a bit of repetitive nonsense, for example, "a rose is a rose is a rose." Technically, [in logic] a sentence that can be shown to be true no matter what the truth or falsity of its component parts.)

truth of reason   in traditional rationalism, a belief that can be justified solely by appeal to intuition or deduction from premises based upon intuition. Arithmetic and geometry were, for the rationalists as for the empiricists, a paradigm case of such truths. They disagreed mainly on the scope of such truths, and the restrictions to be placed on the problematic appeal to intuition.

◆ *BIBLIOGRAPHY AND FURTHER READING* ◆

Two recent anthologies are Robert Sleigh, ed., *Necessary Truth* (Englewood Cliffs, NJ: Prentice-Hall, 1972) and L. W. Sumner and John Woods, *Necessary Truth: A Book of Readings* (New York: Random House, 1970). For a comprehensive anthology on the foundations of mathematics, see P. Benacerraf and H. Putnam, eds., *Philosophy of Mathematics* (Englewood Cliffs, NJ: Prentice-Hall, 1964). W. V. O. Quine's now-classic attack on the notion of "analytic truth" is in "Two Dogmas of Empiricism" in *From a Logical Point of View* (Cambridge, MA: Harvard University Press, 1953). An attempted rebuttal is by H. P. Grice and P. F. Strawson, "In Defense of Dogma," in *Philosophical Review 65* (1956). Selections in the chapter are developed at length in A. J. Ayer, *Language, Truth and Logic* (New York: Dover Publications, 1946); John Stuart Mill, *A System of Logic*, 8th ed. (New York: Harper, 1874); Edmund Husserl, *Ideas*, trans. W. R. Boyce-Gibson (New York: Macmillan, 1962); Immanuel Kant, *The Critique of Pure Reason*, trans. Norman Kemp-Smith (London: St. Martin's Press, 1933). Reasonably straightforward expositions of Husserl and Kant can be found in R. Schmitt, "Phenomenology," in *The Encyclopedia of Philosophy*, ed. P. Edwards (New York: Macmillan, 1967) and S. Körner, *Kant* (London: Penguin, 1955).

6

RELIGION

Now faith is the substance of things hoped for, the evidence of things not seen.

HEBREWS 11:1

The age-old efforts of metaphysicians to know the way the world really is have rarely been motivated by curiosity or the scientific spirit alone. Most often, metaphysics and philosophy in general have been motivated by religious devotion. The search for truth and the concern with what we can know and how we ought to behave have often been tied to the very personal concern about the nature of the divine and its relationship to us. For many thoughtful people, there is no more powerful an experience than religious experience, and they have no more important beliefs than their religious beliefs. Religion defines their lives, and their religious views define reality. Although the issues of religion are philosophically within the domain of metaphysics, epistemology, and ethics, its importance demands special attention. It involves experiences of a kind that are not common to other ontological and cosmological concerns. Religious beliefs involve emotions that are not relevant to the technical concerns with substance and science. And it is this emotional involvement in religion that has inspired some of the greatest art, the bloodiest wars, the kindest actions, and the most brilliant philosophy in history.

A. WHAT IS RELIGION?

We say that religion has an important role in the history of philosophy. But there have been many different religions. Some differ so drastically from one another that it is hard to say what they have in common. For instance, you might be inclined to cite "belief in God or gods" as a criterion for calling something a religion. But one of the biggest religious followings in the world—Buddhism—has no such concept. Or, you might cite as a criterion some sort of social organization, such as a prayer gathering. But there are many Christian Protestant sects who believe that religion is an entirely private affair, for which neither congregation nor priest are necessary.

Although we saw in Chapter 1 that many philosophical schools share their beginnings with religions, we would not necessarily want to call our Methodist minister a philosopher. Nor would we want to call our college teacher, who assigns the works of Maimonides (an important Jewish theologian), a rabbi. Although religion and philosophy are intimately linked, we hesitate to identify them. Central to both, however, is religious belief. A person who believes in a single, independent Being, God, who is the Creator of the universe, is a **theist,** a believer, whether Jewish, Catholic, Protestant, or Muslim. (To refuse to believe in God is to be an **atheist.** To admit one's ignorance, and simply accept the fact that one does not know and perhaps has no way of knowing whether there is such a being or not, is to be an **agnostic.** We will discuss some atheistic and agnostic claims, as well as several different religious traditions, later in this chapter.)

Before we investigate specific religious-philosophical debates, however, let us take a look at how some philosophers have answered two preliminary questions: (1) What is religion, in general, and (2) how does religion relate to and differ from philosophy? In a now famous symposium of thirty years ago, three British philosophers argued about just this problem. The three philosophers are Antony Flew, who pursued an argument derived from Hume; R. M. Hare (also following Hume), who argued that the attempt to explain the universe may not be the point of religion and that it doesn't matter if nothing could count against religious beliefs; and Basil Mitchell, who also argued that explanation is not primary to religion, but rather that the key ingredient must be "faith."

Flew's opening comments are a response to a famous article by the twentieth-century philosopher John Wisdom, a student of Ludwig Wittgenstein, in which Wisdom claims that the essential feature of religious belief is a certain "attitude" that the religious person has toward his or her surroundings, and that the gap between the religious "attitude" and that of the philosopher or scientist interested in explanation, is unbridgeable. All four, arguing entirely within a Christian context, assume that religious belief is a belief in God. On the assumption, however, that whatever belief—or faith— is, that it is essential to all activities we would want to call religious, their debate is helpful in establishing a general academic definition of religion.

◆ from "Gods,"
by John Wisdom

Two people return to their long neglected garden and find among the weeds a few of the old plants surprisingly vigorous. One says to the other "It must be that a gardener has been coming and doing something about these plants." Upon inquiry they find that no neighbor has ever seen anyone at work in their garden. The first man says to the other "He must have worked while people slept." The other says "No, someone would have heard him and besides, anybody who cared about the plants would have kept down these weeds." The first man says "Look at the way these are arranged. There is purpose and a feeling for beauty here. I believe that someone comes, someone invisible to mortal eyes. I believe that the more carefully we look the more we shall find confirmation of this." They examine the garden ever so carefully and sometimes they come on new things suggesting the contrary and even that a malicious person has been at work. Besides examining the garden carefully they also study what happens to gardens left without attention. Each learns all the other learns about this and about the garden. Consequently, when after all this, one says "I still believe a gardener comes" while the other says "I don't" their different words now reflect no difference as to what they have found in the garden, no difference as to what they would find in the garden if they looked further, and no difference about how fast untended gardens fall into disorder. At this stage, in this context, the gardener hypothesis has ceased to be experimental; the difference between one who accepts and one who rejects it is now not a matter of the one expecting something the other does not expect. What is the difference between them? The one says: "A gardener comes unseen and unheard. He is manifested only in his works with which we are all familiar." The other says "There is no gardener." And with this difference in what they say about the gardener goes a difference in how they feel toward the garden, in spite of the fact that neither expects anything of it which the other does not expect.

But is this the whole difference between them—that the one calls the garden by one name and feels one way toward it, while the other calls it by another name and feels in another way toward it? And if this is what the difference has become, then is it any longer appropriate to ask "Which is right?" or "Which is reasonable?"[1]

---

[1] John Wisdom, "Gods," in *Proceedings of the Aristotelian Society,* XLV (London: Harrison & Sons, 1944–45).

◆Antony Flew

Let us begin with a parable. It is a parable developed from a tale told by John Wisdom in his haunting and revelatory article "Gods." Once upon a time two explorers came upon a clearing in the jungle. In the clearing were growing many flowers and many weeds. One explorer says, "Some gardener must tend this plot." The other disagrees, "There is no gardener." So they pitch their tents and set a watch. No gardener is ever seen. "But perhaps he is an invisible gardener." So they set up a barbed-wire fence. They electrify it. They patrol with bloodhounds. (For they remember how H. G. Wells's *The Invisible Man* could be both smelt and touched though he could not be seen.) But no shrieks ever suggest that some intruder has received a shock. No movements of the wire ever betray an invisible climber. The bloodhounds never give cry. Yet still the Believer is not convinced. "But there is a gardener, invisible, intangible, insensible to electric shocks, a gardener who has no scent and makes no sound, a gardener who comes secretly to look after the garden which he loves." At last the Sceptic despairs, "But what remains of your original assertion? Just how does what you call an invisible, intangible, eternally elusive gardener differ from an imaginary gardener or even from no gardener at all?"

In this parable we can see how what starts as an assertion, that something exists or that there is some analogy between certain complexes of phenomena, may be reduced step by step to an altogether different status, to an expression perhaps of a "picture preference." The Sceptic says there is no gardener. The Believer says there is a gardener (but invisible, etc.). One man talks about sexual behaviour. Another man prefers to talk of Aphrodite (but knows there is not really a superhuman person additional to, and somehow responsible for, all sexual phenomena). The process of qualification may be checked at any point before the original assertion is completely withdrawn and something of that first assertion will remain (Tautology). Mr. Wells's invisible man could not, admittedly, be seen, but in all other respects he was a man like the rest of us. But though the process of qualification may be, and of course usually is, checked in time, it is not always judiciously so halted. Someone may dissipate his assertion completely without noticing that he has done so. A fine brash hypothesis may thus be killed by inches, the death by a thousand qualifications.

And in this, it seems to me, lies the peculiar danger, the endemic evil, of theological utterance. Take such utterances as "God has a plan," "God created the world," "God loves us as a father loves his children." They look at first sight very much like assertions, vast cosmological assertions. Of course, this is no sure sign that they either are, or are intended to be, assertions. But let us confine ourselves to the cases where those who utter such sentences intend them to express assertions. (Merely remarking parenthetically that those who intend or interpret such utterances as crypto-commands, expressions of wishes, disguised ejaculations, concealed ethics, or as anything else but assertions, are unlikely to succeed in making them either properly orthodox or practically effective.)

Now to assert that such and such is the case is necessarily equivalent to denying that such and such is not the case. Suppose then that we are in doubt as to what someone who gives vent to an utterance is asserting, or suppose that, more radically, we are sceptical as to whether he is really asserting anything at all, one way of trying to understand (or perhaps it will be to expose) his utterance is to attempt to find what he would regard as counting against, or as being incompatible with, its truth. For if the utterance is indeed an assertion, it will necessarily be equivalent to a denial of the negation of that assertion. And anything which would count against the asssertion, or which would induce the speaker to withdraw it and to admit that it had been mistaken, must be part of (or the whole of) the meaning of the negation of that assertion. And to know the meaning of the negation of an assertion, is as near as makes no matter, to know the meaning of that assertion. And if there is nothing which a putative assertion denies then there is nothing which it asserts either: and so it is not really an assertion. When the Sceptic in the parable asked the Believer, "Just how does what you call an invisible, intangible, eternally elusive gardener differ from an imaginary gardener or even from no gardener at all?" he was suggesting that the Believer's earlier statement had been so eroded by qualification that it was no longer an assertion at all.

Now it often seems to people who are not religious as if there was no conceivable event or series of events the occurrence of which would be admitted by sophisticated religious people to be a sufficient reason for conceding "there wasn't a God after all" or "God does not really love us then." Someone tells us that God loves us as a father loves his children. We are reassured. But then we see a child dying of inoperable cancer of the throat. His earthly father is driven frantic in his efforts to help, but his Heavenly Father reveals no obvious sign of concern. Some qualification is made—God's love is "not a merely human love" or it is "an unscrutable love," perhaps—and we realize that such sufferings are quite compatible with the truth of the assertion that "God loves us as a father (but, of course . . .)." We are reassured again. But then perhaps we ask: what is this assurance of God's (appropriately qualified) love worth, what is this apparent guarantee really a guarantee against? Just what would have to happen not merely (morally and wrongly) to tempt but also (logically and rightly) to entitle us to say "God does not love us" or even "God does not exist"? I therefore put to the succeeding symposiasts the simple central questions, "What would have to occur or to have occurred to constitute for you a disproof of the love of, or of the existence of, God?"

◆R. M. Hare

I wish to make it clear that I shall not try to defend Christianity in particular, but religion in general—not because I do not believe in Christianity, but because you cannot understand what Christianity is, until you have understood what religion is.

I must begin by confessing that, on the ground marked out by Flew, he seems to me to be completely victorious. I therefore shift my ground by relating another parable. A certain lunatic is convinced that all dons want to murder him. His friends introduce him to all the mildest and most respectable dons that they can find, and after each of them has retired, they say, "You see, he doesn't really want to murder you; he spoke to you in the most cordial manner; surely you are convinced now?" But the lunatic replies, "Yes, but that was only his diabolical cunning; he's really plotting against me the whole time, like the rest of them; I know it I tell you." However many kindly dons are produced, the reaction is still the same.

Now we say that such a person is deluded. But what is he deluded about? About the truth or falsity of an assertion? Let us apply Flew's test to him. There is no behaviour of dons that can be enacted which he will accept as counting against his theory; and therefore his theory, on this test, asserts nothing. But it does not follow that there is no difference between what he thinks about dons and what most of us think about them—otherwise we should not call him a lunatic and ourselves sane, and dons would have no reason to feel uneasy about his presence in Oxford.

Let us call that in which we differ from the lunatic, our respective *bliks*. He has an insane *blik* about dons; we have a sane one. It is important to realize that we have a sane one, not no *blik* at all; for there must be two sides to any argument—if he has a wrong *blik*, then those who are right about dons must have a right one. Flew has shown that a *blik* does not consist in an assertion or system of them; but nevertheless it is very important to have the right *blik*.

Let us try to imagine what it would be like to have different *bliks* about other things than dons. When I am driving my car, it sometimes occurs to me to wonder whether my movements of the steering-wheel will always continue to be followed by corresponding alterations in the direction of the car. I have never had a steering failure, though I have had skids, which must be similar. Moreover, I know enough about how the steering of my car is made, to know the sort of thing that would have to go wrong for the steering to fail—steel joints would have to part, or steel rods break, or something—but how do I know that this won't happen? The truth is, I don't know; I just have a *blik* about steel and its properties, so that normally I trust the steering of my car; but I find it not at all difficult to imagine what it would be like to lose this *blik* and acquire the opposite one. People would say I was silly about steel;

but there would be no mistaking the reality of the difference between our respective *bliks*— for example, I should never go in a
motorcar. Yet I should hesitate to say that the difference between
us was the difference between contradictory assertions. No amount
of safe arrivals or bench-tests will remove my *blik* and restore the
normal one; for my *blik* is compatible with any finite number of
such tests.

It was Hume who taught us that our whole commerce with the
world depends upon our *blik* about the world; and that difference
between *bliks* about the world cannot be settled by observation
of what happens in the world. That was why, having performed the
interesting experiment of doubting the ordinary man's *blik* about
the world, and showing that no proof could be given to make us
adopt one *blik* rather than another, he turned to backgammon to
take his mind off the problem. It seems, indeed, to be impossible
even to formulate as an assertion the normal *blik* about the world
which makes me put my confidence in the future reliability of steel
joints, in the continued ability of the road to support my car, and
not gape beneath it revealing nothing below; in the general non-
homicidal tendencies of dons; in my own continued well-being (in
some sense of that word that I may not now fully understand) if
I continue to do what is right according to my lights; in the general
likelihood of people like Hitler coming to a bad end. But perhaps
a formulation less inadequate than most is to be found in the
Psalms: "The earth is weak and all the inhabiters thereof: I bear up
the pillars of it."

The mistake of the position which Flew selects for attack is to regard this kind of talk as some sort of *explanation,* as scientists are
accustomed to use the word. As such, it would obviously be ludi-
crous. We no longer believe in God as an Atlas—*nous n'avons pas
besoin de cette hypothèse.* But it is nevertheless true to say that,
as Hume saw, without a *blik* there can be no explanation; for it
is by our *bliks* that we decide what is and what is not an explanation. Suppose we believe that everything that happened, happened
by pure chance. This would not of course be an assertion; for it
is compatible with anything happening or not happening, and so,
incidentally, is its contradictory. But if we had this belief, we should
not be able to explain or predict or plan anything. Thus, although
we should not be *asserting* anything different from those of a more
normal belief, there would be a great difference between us; and
this is the sort of difference that there is between those who really
believe in God and those who really disbelieve in him.

The word "really" is important, and may excite suspicion. I put it
in, because when people have had a good Christian upbringing, as
have most of those who now profess not to believe in any sort of religion, it is very hard to discover what they really believe. The reason why they find it so easy to think that they are not religious,
is that they have never got into the frame of mind of one who suffers from the doubts to which religion is the answer. Not for them

the terrors of the primitive jungle. Having abandoned some of the
more picturesque fringes of religion, they think that they have
abandoned the whole thing—whereas in fact they still have got, and
could not live without, a religion of comfortably substantial, albeit
highly sophisticated, kind, which differs from that of many "religious people" in little more than this, that "religious people" like to
sing Psalms about theirs—a very natural and proper thing to do.
But nevertheless there may be a big difference lying behind—the
difference between two people who, though side by side, are walking in different directions. I do not know in what direction Flew
is walking; perhaps he does not know either. But we have had
some examples recently of various ways in which one can walk
away from Christianity, and there are any number of possibilities.
After all, man has not changed biologically since primitive times;
it is his religion that has changed, and it can easily change again.
And if you do not think that such changes make a difference,
get acquainted with some Sikhs and some Mussulmans of the
same Punjabi stock; you will find them quite different sorts of
people.

There is an important difference between Flew's parable and my
own which we have not yet noticed. The explorers do not *mind*
about their garden; they discuss it with interest, but not with concern. But my lunatic, poor fellow, minds about dons; and I mind
about the steering of my car; it often has people in it that I care for.
It is because I mind very much about what goes on in the garden
in which I find myself, that I am unable to share the explorers'
detachment.

◆ Basil Mitchell

Flew's article is searching and perceptive, but there is, I think,
something odd about his conduct of the theologian's case. The
theologian surely would not deny that the fact of pain counts
against the assertion that God loves men. This very incompatibility
generates the most intractable of theological problems—the problem of evil. So the theologian *does* recognize the fact of pain as
counting against Christian doctrine. But it is true that he will not
allow it—or anything—to count decisively against it; for he is committed by his faith to trust in God. His attitude is not that of the
detached observer, but of the believer.

Perhaps this can be brought out by yet another parable. In time
of war in an occupied country, a member of the resistance meets
one night a stranger who deeply impresses him. They spend that
night together in conversation. The Stranger tells the partisan that
he himself is on the side of the resistance—indeed that he is in
command of it, and urges the partisan to have faith in him no matter what happens. The partisan is utterly convinced at that meet-

ing of the Stranger's sincerity and constancy and undertakes to trust him.

They never meet in conditions of intimacy again. But sometimes the Stranger is seen helping members of the resistance, and the partisan is grateful and says to his friends, "He is on our side."

Sometimes he is seen in the uniform of the police handing over patriots to the occupying power. On these occasions his friends murmur against him: but the partisan still says, "He is on our side." He still believes that, in spite of appearances, the Stranger did not deceive him. Sometimes he asks the Stranger for help and receives it. He is then thankful. Sometimes he asks and does not receive it. Then he says, "The Stranger knows best." Sometimes his friends, in exasperation, say "Well, what *would* he have to do for you to admit that you were wrong and that he is not on our side?" But the partisan refuses to answer. He will not consent to put the Stranger to the test. And sometimes his friends complain, "Well, if *that's* what you mean by his being on our side, the sooner he goes over to the other side the better."

The partisan of the parable does not allow anything to count decisively against the proposition "The Stranger is on our side." This is because he has committed himself to trust the Stranger. But he of course recognizes that the Stranger's ambiguous behaviour *does* count against what he believes about him. It is precisely this situation which constitutes the trial of his faith.

When the partisan asks for help and doesn't get it, what can he do? He can (a) conclude that the Stranger is not on our side or; (b) maintain that he is on our side, but that he has reasons for withholding help.

The first he will refuse to do. How long can he uphold the second position without its becoming just silly?

I don't think one can say in advance. It will depend on the nature of the impression created by the Stranger in the first place. It will depend, too, on the manner in which he takes the Stranger's behaviour. If he blandly dismisses it as of no consequence, as having no bearing upon his belief, it will be assumed that he is thoughtless or insane. And it quite obviously won't do for him to say easily, "Oh, when used of the Stranger the phrase 'is on our side' *means* ambiguous behaviour of his sort." In that case he would be like the religious man who says blandly of a terrible disaster "It is God's will." No, he will only be regarded as sane and reasonable in his belief, if he experiences in himself the full force of the conflict.

It is here that my parable differs from Hare's. The partisan admits that many things may and do count against his belief: whereas Hare's lunatic who has a *blik* about dons doesn't admit that anything counts against his *blik*. Nothing *can* count against *bliks*. Also the partisan has a reason for having in the first instance committed himself, viz, the character of the Stranger; whereas the lunatic has no reason for his *blik* about dons—because, of course, you can't have reasons for *bliks*.

This means that I agree with Flew that theological utterances must be assertions. The partisan is making an assertion when he says, "The Stranger is on our side."

Do I want to say that the partisan's belief about the Stranger is, in any sense, an explanation? I think I do. It explains and makes sense of the Stranger's behaviour: it helps to explain also the resistance movement in the context of which he appears. In each case it differs from the interpretation which the others put upon the same facts.

"God loves men" resembles "the Stranger is on our side" (and many other significant statements, e.g., historical ones) in not being conclusively falsifiable. They can both be treated in at least three different ways: (1) As provisional hypotheses to be discarded if experience tells against them; (2) As significant articles of faith; (3) As vacuous formulae (expressing, perhaps, a desire for reassurance) to which experience makes no difference and which make no difference to life.

The Christian, once he has committed himself, is precluded by his faith from taking up the first attitude: "Thou shalt not tempt the Lord thy God." He is in constant danger, as Flew has observed, of slipping into the third. But he need not; and, if he does, it is a failure in faith as well as in logic.

◆Antony Flew

The challenge, it will be remembered, ran like this. Some theological utterances seem to, and are intended to, provide explanations or express assertions. Now an assertion, to be an assertion at all, must claim that things stand thus and thus; *and not otherwise.* Similarly an explanation, to be an explanation at all, must explain why this particular thing occurs; *and not something else.* Those last clauses are crucial. And yet sophisticated religious people—or so it seemed to me—are apt to overlook this, and tend to refuse to allow, not merely that anything actually does occur, but that anything conceivably could occur, which would count against their theological assertions and explanations. But in so far as they do this their supposed explanations are actually bogus, and their seeming assertions are really vacuous.

Mitchell's response to this challenge is admirably direct, straightforward, and understanding. He agrees "that theological utterances must be assertions." He agrees that if they are to be assertions, there must be something that would count against their truth. He agrees, too, that believers are in constant danger of transforming their would-be assertions into "vacuous formulae." But he takes me to task for an oddity in my "conduct of the theologian's case. The theologian surely would not deny that the fact of pain counts against the assertion that God loves men. This very incompatibility

generates the most intractable of theological problems, the problem of evil." I think he is right. I should have made a distinction
between two very different ways of dealing with what looks like
evidence against the love of God: the way I stressed was the expedient of qualifying the original assertion; the way the theologian
usually takes, at first, is to admit that it looks bad but to insist
that there is—there must be—some explanation which will show
that, in spite of appearances, there really is a God who loves us.
His difficulty, it seems to me, is that he has given God attributes
which rule out all possible saving explanations. In Mitchell's parable of the Stranger it is easy for the believer to find plausible excuses for ambiguous behaviour: for the Stranger is a man. But
suppose the Stranger is God. We cannot say that he would like to
help but cannot: God is omnipotent. We cannot say that he would
help if he only knew: God is omniscient. We cannot say that he is
not responsible for the wickedness of others: God creates those
others. Indeed an omnipotent, omniscient God must be an accessory before (and during) the fact to every human misdeed; as well
as being responsible for every non-moral defect in the universe.
So, though I entirely concede that Mitchell was absolutely right
to insist against me that the theologian's first move is to look for
an *explanation,* I still think that in the end, if relentlessly pursued, he will have to resort to the avoiding action of *qualification.*
And there lies the danger of that death by a thousand qualifications, which would, I agree, constitute "a failure in faith as well as
in logic."

Hare's approach is fresh and bold. He confesses that "on the
ground marked out by Flew, he seems to me to be completely victorious." He therefore introduces the concept of *blik.* But while I
think that there is room for some such concept in philosophy, and
that philosophers should be grateful to Hare for his invention, I
nevertheless want to insist that any attempt to analyse Christian religious utterances as expressions or affirmations of a *blik* rather
than as (at least would-be) assertions about the cosmos is fundamentally misguided. *First,* because thus interpreted they would be
entirely unorthodox. If Hare's religion really is a *blik,* involving no
cosmological assertions about the nature and activities of a supposed personal creator, then surely he is not a Christian at all?
Second, because thus interpreted, they could scarcely do the job
they do. If they were not even intended as assertions then many religious activities would become fraudulent, or merely silly. If "You
ought *because* it is God's will" asserts no more than "You ought,"
then the person who prefers the former phraseology is not really
giving a reason, but a fraudulent substitute for one, a dialectical
dud cheque. . . . Religious utterances may indeed express false or
even bogus assertions: but I simply do not believe that they are not
both intended and interpreted to be or at any rate to presuppose
assertions, at least in the context of religious practice; whatever

shifts may be demanded, in another context, by the exigencies of theological apologetic.[2]

For Wisdom, Flew, Hare, and Mitchell, religious belief is basically defined in contrast to the scientific quest for causal explanation, with which they associate philosophy. Since the scientific revolution of the sixteenth to eighteenth centuries, many philosophers have tried to define religion and science in contrast to one another, and many have tried to cast their lots with science. But there is plenty of resistance to such a move. Many scientists are deeply religious people, and many religious thinkers accept the authority of science without compromising their religious faith. No less a scientist than Albert Einstein, for example, has argued that it is this religious awe and appreciation for the complex regularities of nature that has spawned the great efforts of science to understand it. Indeed, he says, science itself inspires a "cosmic religious feeling."

◆ on the Design of the Universe, by Albert Einstein

It is easy to see why the churches have always fought science and persecuted its devotees. On the other hand, I maintain that the cosmic religious feeling is the strongest and noblest motive for scientific research. Only those who realize the immense efforts and, above all, the devotion without which pioneer work in theoretical science cannot be achieved are able to grasp the strength of the emotion out of which alone such work, remote as it is from the immediate realities of life, can issue. What a deep conviction of the rationality of the universe and what a yearning to understand, were it but a feeble reflection of the mind revealed in this world, Kepler and Newton must have had to enable them to spend years of solitary labor in disentangling the principles of celestial mechanics! Those whose acquaintance with scientific research is derived chiefly from its practical results easily develop a completely false notion of the mentality of the men who, surrounded by a skeptical world, have shown the way to kindred spirits scattered wide through the world and the centuries. Only one who has devoted his life to similar ends can have a vivid realization of what has inspired these men and given them the strength to remain true to their purpose in spite of countless failures. It is cosmic religious feeling that gives a man such strength. A contemporary has said, not

[2] Antony Flew, R. M. Hare, and Basil Mitchell, "Theology and Falsification," *University* (1950–51), rpt. *New Essays in Philosophical Theology,* eds. A. Flew and A. MacIntyre (New York: Macmillan, 1955).

unjustly, that in this materialistic age of ours the serious scientific workers are the only profoundly religious people.[3]

Einstein's statement of scientific faith is particularly important in times when science and religion seem once again at each other's throats. Current controversies over "Creation" versus "evolution," for example, have made it seem as if science and religion are utterly irreconcilable, with completely opposed visions of the world. Consider in much the same vein some recent remarks by Cambridge physicist Stephen Hawking, who is at the forefront of new investigations into the origins of the universe. Although not a theist himself, Hawking suggests that the scientific and religious quests are compatible.

◆on God and the Universe, by Stephen Hawking

Hawking once told an interviewer that he wanted to know why the universe exists at all and why it is as it is. I quote that back to him and ask if his search has a religious component. "I suppose so. But I would have thought that everyone would want to know that." Is the search in competition with religion? "If one took that attitude," he replies, "then Newton"—a very religious man— "would not have discovered the law of gravity."

"The whole history of human thought has been to try to understand what the universe was like. I think you can do that without prejudice as to the idea that God exists. Even if God created the universe, we want to know what it is like." I start to ask a clarifying question, but he interrupts me. "One attitude would be that God set up the universe in a completely arbitrary way, with all that anyone can say about anything is that it is just the will of God. But in fact, the more we examine the universe, we find it is not arbitrary at all but obeys certain well-defined laws that operate in different areas. It seems very reasonable to suppose that there may be some unifying principles, so that all laws are part of some bigger law. So what we are trying to find out is whether there is some bigger law from which all other laws can be derived. I think you can ask that question whether or not you believe in God."

For some people, I remind him, the existence of God is a satisfactory answer to all the questions he is dealing with. "Yes, but it is certainly not to me. I don't think that it answers anything. Whether you say that God created the universe does not really make any difference. I would regard it as a very meaningless statement, unless you're going to attach some other attributes to God. I'm not sure that I believe anything else about God. If that is the only

---

[3]Albert Einstein, "Religion and Science," in *Ideas and Opinions,* trans. Sonia Bargmann (New York: Crown, 1954).

attribute, then it is an unnecessary concept, because it doesn't have any consequences."

Yet man does need to explain the Beginning, The First Cause. How did it all start—and what existed to make a start possible? Science has not achieved that explanation, and the theoretical physicists are still searching. "I have an idea that people would feel happier with the idea of a big bang than of a universe that existed forever and ever," says Hawking. "The big bang may not be very like Genesis, but at least you can regard it as a creation, and you can invoke God as the creator. But if you had a universe that existed forever, people might feel there was not much room for God. I was at a conference on cosmology at the Vatican last year, and the Roman Catholic Church seems to be very happy with the idea of the big bang."[4]

How might we try, then, to define the essence of religion without comparison to any other endeavor—as it is in itself? One philosopher who has recently tried to do just this is Keiji Nishitani, a Japanese philosopher conversant in both Christianity and Buddhism. Nishitani claims that the distinguishing feature of religion is the "personal/ impersonal," or in other words, the deeply personal recognition that each of us must give to the existence which we share with all other things in the universe. To step outside of ourselves, to consider the world from an impersonal perspective—called "personal nihility" by Nishitani—is an ironically intimate and unique activity. But it is a necessary one. Everyone, whether consciously or unconsciously, must engage in it at some point in his or her life.

◆from "What Is Religion?" by Keiji Nishitani

"What is religion?" we ask ourselves, or, looking at it the other way around, "What is the purpose of religion for us? Why do we need it?" Though the question about the need for religion may be a familiar one, it already contains a problem. In one sense, for the person who poses the question, religion does not seem to be something he needs. The fact that he asks the question at all amounts to an admission that religion has not yet become a necessity for him. In another sense, however, it is surely in the nature of religion to be necessary for just such a person. Wherever questioning individuals like this are to be found, the need for religion is there as well. In short, the relationship we have to religion is a contradictory one: those for whom religion is *not* a necessity are, for that reason, the very ones for whom religion *is* a necessity. There is no other thing of which the same can be said.

[4]From *The New York Times*, Jan. 23, 1983.

When asked, "Why do we need learning and the arts?" we might try to explain in reply that such things are necessary for the advancement of mankind, for human happiness, for the cultivation of the individual, and so forth. Yet even if we can say why we need such things, this does not imply that we cannot get along without them. Somehow life would still go on. Learning and the arts may be indispensable to living well, but they are not indispensable to living. In that sense, they can be considered a kind of luxury.

Food, on the other hand, is essential to life. Nobody would turn to somebody else and ask him why he eats. Well, maybe an angel or some other celestial being who has no need to eat might ask such questions, but men do not. Religion, to judge from current conditions in which many people are in fact getting along without it, is clearly not the kind of necessity that food is. Yet this does not mean that it is merely something we need to live *well*. Religion has to do with life itself. Whether the life we are living will end up in extinction or in the attainment of eternal life is a matter of the utmost importance for life itself. In no sense is religion to be called a luxury. Indeed, this is why religion is an indispensable necessity for those very people who fail to see the need for it. Herein lies the distinctive feature of religion that sets it apart from the mere life of "nature" and from culture. Therefore, to say that we need religion for example, for the sake of social order, or human welfare, or public morals is a mistake, or at least a confusion of priorities. Religion must not be considered from the viewpoint of its *utility*, any more than life should. A religion concerned primarily with its own utility bears witness to its own degeneration. One can ask about the utility of things like eating for the natural life, or of things like learning and the arts for culture. In fact, in such matters the question of utility should be of constant concern. Our ordinary mode of being is restricted to these levels of natural or cultural life. But it is in breaking through that ordinary mode of being and overturning it from the ground up, in pressing us back to the elemental source of life where life itself is seen as useless, that religion becomes something we need—a *must* for human life.

Two points should be noted from what has just been said. First, religion is at all times the individual affair of each individual. This sets it apart from things like culture, which, while related to the individual, do not need to concern each individual. Accordingly, we cannot understand what religion is from the outside. The religious quest alone is the key to understanding it; there is no other way. This is the most important point to be made regarding the essence of religion.

Second, from the standpoint of the essence of religion, it is a mistake to ask "What is the purpose of religion for us?" and one that clearly betrays an attitude of trying to understand religion apart from the religious quest. It is a question that must be broken through by another question coming from within the person who asks it. There is no other road that can lead to an understanding of what religion is and what purpose it serves. The counterquestion that achieves this breakthrough is one that asks, "For what purpose do I myself exist?" Of everything else we can ask its purpose for us, but not of religion. With regard to everything else we can make a *telos* of ourselves as individuals, as man, or as mankind, and evaluate those things in relation to our life and existence. We put ourselves as individuals/man/mankind at the center and weigh the significance of everything as the *contents* of our lives as individuals/man/mankind. But religion upsets the posture from which we think of ourselves as *telos* and center for all things. Instead, religion poses as a starting point the question: "For what purpose do I exist?"

We become aware of religion as a need, as a must for life, only at the level of life at which everything else loses its necessity and its utility. Why do we exist at all? Is not our very existence and human life ultimately meaningless? Or, if there is a meaning or significance to it all, where do we find it? When we come to doubt the meaning of our existence in this way, when we have become a question to ourselves, the religious quest awakens within us. These questions and the quest they give rise to show up when the mode of looking at and thinking about everything in terms of how it relates to *us* is broken through, where the mode of living that puts us at the center of everything is overturned. This is why the question of religion in the form, "Why do we need religion?" obscures the way to its own answer from the very start. It blocks our becoming a question to ourselves.

The point at which the ordinarily necessary things of life, including learning and the arts, all lose their necessity and utility is found at those times when death, nihility, or sin—or any of those situations that entail a fundamental negation of our life, existence, and ideals, that undermine the roothold of our existence and bring the meaning of life into question—become pressing personal problems for us. This can occur through an illness that brings one face-to-face with death, or through some turn of events that robs one of what had made life worth living. . . .

Nihility refers to that which renders meaningless the meaning of life. When we become a question to ourselves and when the problem of why we exist arises, this means that nihility has emerged from the ground of our existence and that our very existence has turned into a question mark. The appearance of this nihility signals nothing less than that one's awareness of self-existence has penetrated to an extraordinary depth.

Normally we proceed through life, on and on, with our eye fixed on something or other, always caught up with something within or without ourselves. It is these engagements that prevent the deepening of awareness. They block off the way to an opening up of that horizon on which nihility appears and self-being becomes a question. This is even the case with learning and the arts and the whole range of other cultural engagements. But when this horizon does open up at the bottom of those engagements that keep life moving continually on and on, something seems to halt and linger before us. This something is the meaninglessness that lies in wait at the bottom of those very engagements that bring meaning to life. This is the point at which that sense of nihility, that sense that "everything is the same" we find in Nietzsche and Dostoevski, brings the restless, forward-advancing pace of life to a halt and makes it take a step back. In the Zen phrase, it "turns the light to what is directly underfoot."

In the forward progress of everyday life, the ground beneath our feet always falls behind as we move steadily ahead; we overlook it. Taking a step back to shed light on what is underfoot of the self— "stepping back to come to the self," as another ancient Zen phrase has it—marks a conversion in life itself. This fundamental conversion in life is occasioned by the opening up of the horizon of nihility at the ground of life. It is nothing less than a conversion from the self-centered (or man-centered) mode of being, which always asks what *use* things have for us (or for man), to an attitude that asks for what *purpose* we ourselves (or man) exist. Only when we stand at this turning point does the question "What is religion?" really become our own. . . .

Man sneezes, God does not. When a man without faith sneezes, he encounters the nihility of the self because the existence of a creature that sneezes is constituted from the very first on a nihility. When a man of faith sneezes, he, too, encounters the nihility of the self because he believes himself to have been created by God *ex nihilo.* But if the believer stops short at that insight, he does not get beyond the standpoint of entertaining that sort of idea about God, of thinking about his impressions of God. This then brings him to the dilemma of transcendence and omnipotence in God: man sneezes and God cannot; therefore, man is capable of something that God is not.

The situation is different when viewed from an existential standpoint. Man was made by God in such a way that he *can* sneeze, and that is a display of divine omnipotence. Even when he sneezes, man does so within the omnipotence of God. There is no sneezing without it. Thus, from the existential standpoint, even in something so trivial as a sneeze man encounters the nihility of the self and at the same time the onmnipotence of God. Here divine omnipotence means that man encounters the separation of absolute negation and absolute affirmation of the self in the comings and goings, the ins and outs of daily life. It means that the self in its entirety, body and mind, is brought to the crossroads of life and death. In the words of Jesus:

> Do not fear those who kill the body, and after have no more that they can do. But I will warn you whom to fear: fear him who, after he has killed, has power to cast into hell; yes, I tell you,

fear him! Are not five sparrows sold for two pennies? And not one of them is forgotten before God. Why, even the hairs of your head are all numbered. [Luke 12:4–7]

Thus the omnipotence of God must be something that one can encounter at any time, listening to the radio, reading the paper, or chatting with a friend. Moreover, it must be something encountered as capable of destroying both body and soul, something that makes man fear and tremble and presses him to a decision. Without this sense of urgency, for all our talk about them, divine omnipotence and God himself, remain mere concepts. The omnipotence of God must be accepted as altogether near at hand, that is to say, present in the comings and goings, the ins and outs of daily life, bringing us to fear and trembling. Only then is it really accepted as a reality. . . .

When divine omnipotence is thus really accepted, the faith that drives out fear is also constituted as a reality:

Why, even the hairs of your head are all numbered. Fear not; you are of more value than many sparrows. And I tell you, every one who acknowledges me before men, the Son of man also will acknowledge before the angels of God; but he who denies me before men will be denied before the angels of God. [Luke 12:7–9]

We remarked earlier that faith as dying to self and living in God means letting oneself be driven by the *motif* of conversion contained within God himself (in his relationship to man) from absolute negation to absolute affirmation. There may be no need to repeat the point here, but, briefly put, it means that the *motif* of that conversion is actualized in the self which thereby appropriates it. . . .

As stated above, the incongruence between a world order dependent on divine omnipotence and the evil in human existence has long been a perplexing problem. Basically, though, it is no different from the problem contained in sneezing or listening to the radio. God does not sneeze, but he made some of his creatures so that they do. The omnipotence of God makes itself present in the sneezing of those creatures, and that primarily as an absolute negativity: as the grounding of all things in *nihilium* through creation. Similarly, God created man with the freedom to do evil. Even the evil acts of man, therefore, fall within the compass of that divine omnipotence that makes itself present in man's power to do evil and use that power. Here, too, it shows up primarily as an absolute negativity: divine wrath. But even this stems from the fact that man's ability to commit evil arises out of the nihility that lies at the ground of his existence by virtue of his having been created *ex nihilo*. And when man himself becomes the locus of nihility in his awareness of radical evil, as discussed above, when the conversion of faith becomes a reality, then salvation is realized even though man remains a sinner unable to rid himself of evil. Here divine omnipotence is realized as the absolute affirmation that permits evil even while persisting in its absolute negation. This absolute affirmation as negation directed at the evildoer is nothing other than the pardoning of evil in the man of faith. It is divine love. There is absolutely no evil in God, and yet evil falls absolutely within the compass of divine omnipotence.

In the problems of evil and sin, the relationship of God and man becomes *personal* in the original sense of the word. Christianity speaks of the punishment of man in the "first Adam" and his redemption through the "second Adam." Modern theologians, with their modern notions of personality, even assert a radical distinction between evil and sin, the latter only being possible in a "personal" relationship with God. But in a relationship grounded on absolute affirmation as absolute negation, an evil act and an involuntary reflex action like sneezing are the same. They both depend on the createdness of man, that is, on the nihility at the ground of his very being. And seen on that basis, even a personal relationship can be called impersonally personal (or personally impersonal) in the sense outlined above.[5]

Even if we accept some claim such as one of those offered above, about what religion is in itself, we would still have no answer to our second question; we would not have an explanation of the interrelationship between philosophy and religion. Where do they come together? Where do they part ways? Abu Hamid Mohammad ibn Mohammad al-Ghazali (1058–1111), a medieval Islamic philosopher and mystic, writing in a context where all philosophizing was religious, attempted in his *Deliverance From Error* to distinguish the different kinds of religious thinking. We find in the passage below a categorization of four disciplines which cover the spectrum along which religion and philosophy mix together and purify: theology, the study of the *Batin*, (or the message of the Qurán), philosophy, and mysticism. For al-Ghazali, each discipline plays a role in the Islamic community, but only mysticism gives the seeker genuine access to truth. Al-Ghazali compares these four disciplines and the differences between them to four approaches to drunkenness: there is the drunk (who is like the mystic), the philosopher (who knows what the term *drunkenness* means), the scientist (who knows the causes of drunkenness and is like the theologian), and the doctor (who understands drunkenness scientifically, but in order to cure it, who is like the *Batiniyah*).

[5] Keiji Nishitani, "What Is Religion?", from *Religion and Nothingness*, trans. Jan Van Bragt (Berkeley: University of California Press, 1982).

◆from *The Deliverance from Error,*
by Mohammad al-Ghazali

III. THE CLASSES OF SEEKERS

When God by His grace and abundant generosity cured me of this disease [skepticism], I came to regard the various seekers (*sc.* after truth) as comprising four groups:—

(1) the *Theologians (mutakallimūn),* who claim that they are the exponents of thought and intellectual speculation;
(2) the *Bātinīyah,* who consider that they, as the party of 'authoritative instruction' *(ta'līm),* alone derive truth from the infallible *imam;*
(3) the *Philosophers,* who regard themselves as the exponents of logic and demonstration;
(4) the *Sufis* or *Mystics,* who claim that they alone enter into the 'presence' (*sc.* of God), and possess vision and intuitive understanding.

I said within myself: 'The truth cannot lie outside these four classes. These are the people who tread the paths of the quest for truth. If the truth is not with them, no point remains in trying to apprehend the truth. There is certainly no point in trying to return to the level of the naive and derivative belief *(taqlīd)* once it has been left, since a condition of being at such a level is that one should not know one is there; when a man comes to know that, the glass of his naive beliefs is broken. This is a breakage which cannot be mended, a breakage not to be repaired by patching or by assembling of fragments. The glass must be melted once again in the furnace for a new start, and out of it another fresh vessel formed.'

I now hastened to follow out these four ways and investigate what these groups had achieved, commencing with the science of theology and then taking the way of philosophy, the 'authoritative instruction' of the Bātinīyah, and the way of mysticism, in that order.

I. THE SCIENCE OF THEOLOGY: ITS AIMS AND ACHIEVEMENTS

I commenced, then, with the science of Theology ('ilm al-kalām), and obtained a thorough grasp of it. I read the books of sound theologians and myself wrote some books on the subject. But it was a science, I found, which, though attaining its own aim, did not attain mine. Its aim was merely to preserve the creed of orthodoxy and to defend it against the deviations of heretics. . . .

This was of little use in the case of one who admitted nothing at all save logically necessary truths. Theology was not adequate to my case and was unable to cure the malady of which I complained. It is true that, when theology appeared as a recognized discipline and much effort had been expended in it over a considerable period of time, the theologians, becoming very earnest in their endeavours to defend orthodoxy by the study of what things really are, embarked on a study of substances and accidents with their nature and properties. But, since that was not the aim of their science, they did not deal with the question thoroughly in their thinking and consequently did not arrive at results sufficient to dispel universally the darkness of confusion due to the different views of men. I do not exclude the possibility that for others than myself these results have been sufficient; indeed, I do not doubt that this has been so for quite a number. But these results were mingled with naïve belief in certain matters which are not included among first principles.

My purpose here, however, is to describe my own case, not to disparage those who sought a remedy thereby, for the healing drugs vary with the disease. How often one sick man's medicine proves to be another's poison!

2. PHILOSOPHY

After I had done with theology I started on philosophy. I was convinced that a man cannot grasp what is defective in any of the sciences unless he has so complete a grasp of the science in question that he equals its most learned exponents in the appreciation of its fundamental principles, and even goes beyond and surpasses them, probing into some of the tangles and profundities which the very professors of science have neglected. Then and only then is it possible that what he has to assert about its defects is true.

So far as I could see none of the doctors of Islam have devoted thought and attention to philosophy. In their writings none of the theologians engaged in polemic against the philosophers, apart from obscure and scattered utterances so plainly erroneous and inconsistent that no person of ordinary intelligence would be likely to be deceived, far less one versed in the sciences.

I realized that to refute a system before understanding it and becoming acquainted with its depth is to act blindly. I therefore set out in all earnestness to acquire a knowledge of philosophy from books, by private study without the help of an instructor [. . . .]

Again, when a man has been bitten by a snake and needs the antidote, his being turns from it in loathing because he learns it is extracted from the snake, the source of the poison, and he requires to be shown the value of the antidote despite its source. Likewise, a poor man in need of money, who shrinks from receiving the gold taken out of the bag of the counterfeiter, ought to have it brought to his notice that his shrinking is pure ignorance and is the cause of his missing the benefit he seeks; he ought to be informed that the proximity between the counterfeit and the good coin does not make the good coin counterfeit nor the counterfeit good. In the same way

the proximity between truth and falsehood does not make truth
falsehood nor falsehood truth.

This much we wanted to say about the baneful and mischievous
influence of philosophy.

· · · · · · · · · ·

4. THE WAYS OF MYSTICISM

When I had finished with these sciences, I next turned with set
purpose to the method of mysticism (or Sufism). I knew that the
complete mystic 'way' includes both intellectual belief and practical
activity; the latter consists in getting rid of the obstacles in the self
and in stripping off its base characteristics and vicious morals, so
that the heart may attain to freedom from what is not God and
to constant recollection of Him.

The intellectual belief was easier to me than the practical activity.
I began to acquaint myself with their belief by reading their books,
such as *The Food of the Hearts* by Abū Tālib al-Makkī (God have
mercy upon him), the works of al-Hārith al-Muhāsibī, the various
anecdotes about al-Junayd, ash-Shiblī and Abū Yazīd al-Bistāmī
(may God sanctify their spirits), and other discourses of their leading men. I thus comprehended their fundamental teachings on the
intellectual side, and progressed, as far as is possible by study and
oral instruction, in the knowledge of mysticism. It became clear
to me, however, that what is most distinctive of mysticism is something which cannot be apprehended by study, but only by immediate experience (*dhawq*—literally 'tasting'), by ecstasy and by a
moral change. What a difference there is between *knowing* the definition of health and satiety, together with their causes and presuppositions, and *being* healthy and satisfied! What a difference between being acquainted with the definition of drunkenness—
namely, that it designates a state arising from the domination of the
seat of the intellect by vapours arising from the stomach—and being drunk! Indeed, the drunken man while in that condition does
not know the definition of drunkenness nor the scientific account
of it; he has not the very least scientific knowledge of it. The sober man, on the other hand, knows the definition of drunkenness
and its basis, yet he is not drunk in the very least. Again the
doctor, when he is himself ill, knows the definition and causes of
health and the remedies which restore it, and yet is lacking in
health. Similarly there is a difference between knowing the true nature and causes and conditions of the ascetic life and actually
leading such a life and forsaking the world.

I apprehended clearly that the mystics were men who had real
experiences, not men of words, and that I had already progressed
as far as was possible by way of intellectual apprehension. What
remained for me was not to be attained by oral instruction and
study but only by immediate experience and by walking in the
mystic way.

> Now from the sciences I had laboured at and the paths I had traversed in my investigation of the revelational and rational sciences (that is, presumably, theology and philosophy), there had come to me a sure faith in God most high, in prophethood (or revelation), and in the Last Day. These three credal principles were firmly rooted in my being, not through any carefully argued proofs, but by reason of various causes, coincidences and experiences which are not capable of being stated in detail.[6]

B. THE WESTERN RELIGIONS

Among the world religions, Judaism, Christianity, and Islam bear a special relationship to each other and to philosophy, in the sense of the tradition which derives from the Greeks. They might be called the "Abrahamic" religions, because all three trace their roots to Abraham of the Old Testament. Thus, the God worshiped in all three of these religions is the "God of Abraham, the God of Isaac, the God of Jacob." We might also call these the three "Western" religions, in that they all originate among peoples living west of the Indus River (one traditional dividing line between East and West).

Judaism, Christianity, and Islam are closely associated together and with the West for another reason, as well. The early religious thinking of all three was heavily influenced by the Greek philosophy of Plato and Aristotle. Although some other religions make use of Greek philosophy, its influence in other faiths does not approach the status it holds in Christian, Jewish, and Muslim thought.

Yet the God who appears in the Old Testament is not readily understood in either Platonic or Aristotelian terms. (You might look back at our discussions of Plato and Aristotle in earlier chapters and see if you can find anything akin to the Judeo-Christian God described there.) Therefore, early thinkers, particularly in the Middle Ages, had their work cut out for them in offering defenses of their beliefs, or in arriving at rational religious beliefs, using the Greeks as their model. The medieval philosophers' attempts to do so are among the most monumental of efforts in the history of philosophy, with some of the most provocative and widely influential results.

In many cases, philosophy played a crucial role in the conversions of individuals, and whole countries, to one of these religions. In others, philosophical disputes were the primary cause of sectarian secessions. In all cases, philosophical arguments were a vital ingredient in the development of the doctrines that have come down to us today.

The principal issues for all three of these great monotheisms, of

[6]From *Philosophy in the Middle Ages: The Christian, Islamic, and Jewish Traditions,* edited by Arthur Hyman and James J. Walsh (Indianapolis: Hackett, 1973, 1983).

course, are the existence and character of God. The God of Judaism, Christianity and Islam has many characteristics that must be identified for our understanding. Most importantly, it is generally believed that God is an independent being, the Creator of the universe, and distinct from the universe He created. It is generally agreed that God is the supremely rational and moral being with concern for human justice and human suffering. It is agreed that He is all-powerful **(omnipotent),** all-knowing **(omniscient),** and that He is everywhere at once **(omnipresent).** In the Old Testament, it is made evident that God has emotions; for example, we read of God as "a jealous God" and we hear of "the wrath of God." It is the attempt to understand the being who has these characteristics that defines Western theology and a great deal of Western metaphysics.

To insist that God is an independent being, the Creator of the universe but distinct from that universe, is of the utmost importance for Western religion. When people try to reinterpret God so that He is nothing other than some universal quality, as in "God is love," or "God is ultimate force," or "God is life," or "God is the universe," there is a very real possibility that God's existence as an independent being is being denied. One can say "God is love" as shorthand for "God loves us and wants us to love each other" without this danger. But if one believes that God simply is identical to people's loving one another, then it is evident that this belief is no different from that of a person who might not believe in God at all but just believes in love. Similarly, it is one thing to believe that God is a "force," among other things, who created the universe; but if you believe that God is nothing other than a force that created the universe, without consciousness or concern, then your belief does not differ from that of someone who also believes that some force created the universe but does not believe in God.

In Judaism, Christianity, and Islam, the independence of God from the universe He created is an all-important belief. Philosophers and theologians refer to this independence as the **transcendence** of God. (Don't confuse this word with the adjective "transcendental" we used in Chapter 4.) We say that God "transcends" the universe and mankind. We also say that He "transcends" all human experience. It is this notion of transcendence that raises an immediate epistemological problem. If God transcends our experience, how can we know that He exists at all? If He is outside of our every possible experience—if we cannot see, hear, or touch Him—what possible evidence can we have for His existence? And how would we have any way of knowing what He must be like?

In some ancient religions, gods and goddesses were very much like human beings. They were usually stronger and perhaps smarter. The Greek and Roman gods, for example, were like this. Although they were immortal, they often misbehaved and became jealous or furious at one another. Philosophers use the word **anthropomorphism** when they refer to the perception of gods more or less as human. It is quite natural, when people try to envision their deities, that they should endow them with those characteristics they understand best, human characteristics.

The God of Judaism, Christianity, and Islam is much less anthropomorphic than the gods and goddesses of ancient Greece and Rome. But it would be a mistake to deny that God is conceived in certain anthropomorphic ways as well. The God of the Hebrews frequently took their side in battle in the Old Testament, helping them to fell the walls of Jericho, keeping the sun still for extra hours, and holding apart the waters of the Red Sea. The God of the Old Testament has many human emotions: He becomes jealous or angry when His commands are not carried out, having people swallowed by whales and sometimes destroying whole cities. Even the notion that God is a loving God carries with it anthropomorphism. It is often said that these are mere approximations, based on the idea that we can never really know or understand what God is like. (For example, it is said that we cannot understand divine love and that we use our all-too-human conception of love as the only example we can find.) But it must also be said that such anthropomorphic projections are in no way an objection to belief in God; it is only to be expected that people will try to understand religion in those terms that they know best.

The scriptural emphasis on God's sense of justice and His concern for mankind also demonstrates anthropomorphic characteristics, even if it is true, as we are so often told, that God's conception of justice may be very different from our own. And these characteristics are so important that if a person does not believe that God is a merciful and concerned being with a strong sense of justice, then that person probably does not believe in God at all. (For example, Aristotle's "prime mover," despite the Western theologians' marvelous adaptation of the concept to their religions, is not on the face of it very much like the Judeo-Christian God.) Prayer is meaningful only on the assumption that God listens to us and understands us; faith is intelligible only on the assumption that God cares about us. Without these characteristics, God would not be a moral force in our lives.

Some sophisticated theists and theologians have tried to purge belief in God of all anthropomorphic characteristics, speaking, for example, only of "Being Itself" rather than the usual characterization of God as "Him." Still, although we might not actually believe that God, like Zeus, resembles some superhuman immortal being, it is clear that our traditional conception of God is far more anthropocentric than some theologians would no doubt prefer.

The Western religions' conception of God has been varied in so many ways that we can't even begin to consider them. The differences between the God of the Old Testament and the God of the New Testament have been often discussed. Then there are the obvious differences between the various sects of Judaism, Christianity, and Islam. And the differences between this God and other gods (Zeus, Krishna, Isis) are so enormous that traditional Christians, Jews, and Muslims would hesitate to call these "God" at all.

1. Can We Know That God Exists?

It is one thing to be taught that there is a God; it is another to believe in God for good reason, rationally, and to know what one believes. Of course, there have been many people who have insisted that belief in God is not a matter of rationality or knowledge at all but only of faith. But the turn to faith logically comes after attempts to know. So before we turn to examine other philosophical questions raised by religious belief, let us ask whether or not we can know that God exists.

The problem is a familiar one. Since God by definition transcends our experience, how can we have evidence for His existence? It is the same problem we faced with substance (for that reason God and substance are so intertwined in metaphysics, as for example in Spinoza). There are people who claim to have been direct witnesses to miracles or to have heard God's own voice. But, assuming that none of us is one of them, our problem remains: Should we believe their reports? Might they have been victims of imagination or hallucination? Is there any evidence in our experience that would allow us to know of God's existence? And if not, what reasons can we give for a belief in God?

In the long history of Western theology, three major sets of "proofs" have emerged as attempts to demonstrate God's existence. Each has received various formulations, and all are still being discussed today. They are called (1) the *ontological argument*, (2) the *cosmological argument*, and (3) the *teleological argument*.

THE ONTOLOGICAL ARGUMENT   This is the most difficult, for it is a purely logical proof; it attempts to argue from the idea of God to His necessary existence. Descartes used this argument in his *Meditations* to prove God's existence. Similar arguments were to be found in both Spinoza and Leibniz. But the man who is generally credited with the invention of the argument is an eleventh-century monk named St. Anselm. Because the argument depends wholly on the idea of God's existence, it is called *ontological.* Here is how Anselm presents it:

◆**the Ontological Argument,
by St. Anselm**

Some time ago, at the urgent request of some of my brethren, I published a brief work, as an example of meditation on the grounds of faith. I wrote it in the role of one who seeks, by silent reasoning with himself, to learn what he does not know. But when I reflected on this little book, and saw that it was put together as a long chain of arguments, I began to ask myself whether *one* argument might possibly be found, resting on no other argument for its proof, but sufficient in itself to prove that God truly exists, and that he is the supreme good, needing nothing outside himself, but needful for the being and well-being of all things. I often turned my earnest attention to this problem, and at times I believed that I could put my finger on what I was looking for, but at other times it completely escaped my mind's eye, until finally, in despair, I decided to give up searching for something that seemed impossible to find. But when I tried to put the whole question out of my mind, so as to avoid crowding out other matters, with which I might make some progress, by this useless preoccupation, then, despite my unwillingness and resistance, it began to force itself on me more persistently than ever. Then, one day, when I was worn out by my vigorous resistance to the obsession, the solution I had ceased to hope for presented itself to me, in the very turmoil of my thoughts, so that I enthusiastically embraced the idea which in my disquiet, I had spurned.

. . . .

GOD TRULY IS

And so, O Lord, since thou givest understanding to faith, give me to understanding—as far as thou knowest it to be good for me—that thou dost exist, as we believe, and that thou art what we believe thee to be. Now we believe that thou art a being than which none greater can be thought. Or can it be that there is no such being, since "the fool hath said in his heart, 'There is no God'"? But when this same fool hears what I am saying—"A being than which none greater can be thought"—he understands what he hears, and what he understands is in his understanding, even if he does not understand that it exists. For it is one thing for an object to be in the understanding, and another thing to understand that it exists. When a painter considers beforehand what he is going to paint, he has it in his understanding, but he does not suppose that what he has not yet painted already exists. But when he has painted it, he both has it in his understanding and understands that what he has now produced exists. Even the fool, then, must be convinced that a being than which none greater can be thought exists at least in his understanding, since when he hears this he understands it, and whatever is understood is in the understanding. But clearly that than which a greater cannot be thought cannot exist in the understanding alone. For if it is actually in the understanding alone, it can be thought of as existing also in reality, and this is greater. Therefore, if that than which a greater cannot be thought is in the understanding alone, this same thing than which a greater cannot be thought is that than which a greater can be thought. But obviously this is impossible. Without doubt, therefore, there exists, both in the understanding and in reality, something than which a greater cannot be thought.

GOD CANNOT BE THOUGHT OF AS NONEXISTENT

And certainly it exists so truly that it cannot be thought of as nonexistent. For something can be thought of as existing, which cannot be thought of as not existing, and this is greater than that which *can* be thought of as not existing. Thus, if that than which a greater cannot be thought can be thought of as not existing, this very thing than which a greater cannot be thought is *not* that than which a greater cannot be thought. But this is contradictory. So, then, there truly is a being than which a greater cannot be thought—so truly that it cannot even be thought of as not existing.

And *thou* art this being, O Lord our God. Thou so truly are, then, O Lord my God, that thou canst not even be thought of as not existing. And this is right. For if some mind could think of something better than thou, the creature would rise above the Creator and judge its Creator; but this is altogether absurd. And indeed, whatever is, except thyself alone, can be thought of as not existing. Thou alone, therefore, of all beings, has being in the truest and highest sense, since no other being so truly exists, and thus every other being has less being. Why, then, has "the fool said in his heart, 'There is no God,'" when it is so obvious to the rational mind that, of all beings, thou dost exist supremely? Why indeed, unless it is that he is a stupid fool?

HOW THE FOOL HAS SAID IN HIS HEART WHAT CANNOT BE THOUGHT

But how did he manage to say in his heart what he could not think? Or how is it that he was unable to think what he said in his heart? After all, to say in one's heart and to think are the same thing. Now if it is true—or, rather, since it is true—that he thought it, because he said it in his heart, but did not say it in his heart, since he could not think it, it is clear that something can be said in one's heart or thought in more than one way. For we think of a thing, in one sense, when we think of the word that signifies it, and in another sense, when we understand the very thing itself. Thus, in the first sense God can be thought of as nonexistent, but in the second sense this is quite impossible. For no one who understands what God is can think that God does not exist, even though he says these words in his heart—perhaps without any meaning, perhaps with some quite extraneous meaning. For God is that than which a greater cannot be thought, and whoever understands this rightly must understand that he exists in such a way that he cannot be nonexistent even in thought. He, therefore, who understands that God thus exists cannot think of him as nonexistent.

Thanks be to thee, good Lord, thanks be to thee, because I now understand by thy light what I formerly believed thy gift, so that even if I were to refuse to believe in thy existence, I could not fail to understand its truth.[7]

The logic of the argument is deceptively simple: the concept of "God" is defined, innocently enough, as "a being greater than which none can be thought." Then, Anselm asks, "which would be greater, a being who is merely thought, or a being who actually exists?" The answer, of course, is a being who actually exists. But since God is, by definition, the greatest being who can be thought, He must therefore exist. "God cannot be nonexistent even in thought." Anselm goes on to argue that the idea of an eternal being who either does not yet exist or no longer exists is self-contradictory, so that the very idea we have of such a being requires existence. It is worth noting that, while formulating the ontological argument, Anselm was also putting into place some of the final ingredients in the Christian conception of God, as not only a perfect or even the most perfect being but rather as the greatest (most perfect) *conceivable* being.

The argument has had a long, influential history, and logicians are still arguing about it. The argument was not seriously altered for five centuries, when Descartes took up Anselm's argument and gave it its modern formulation. In the seventeenth century, Descartes (in his *Meditations*) made explicit the presupposition of the argument, that existence is a property which, like color, shape, weight, and charm, a thing may either have or not have. Some properties, however, are essential to a thing: three angles are essential to a triangle, spots are essential to a Dalmatian. So too, Descartes suggests, perfection is essential to the most perfect being, and existence is a perfection. One can no more conceive of a most perfect being without existence than one can a triangle without three angles or a Dalmatian without spots.

◆the Ontological Argument, by René Descartes

But now, if just because I can draw the idea of something from my thought, it follows that all which I know clearly and distinctly as pertaining to this object does really belong to it, may I not derive from this an argument demonstrating the existence of God? It is certain that I no less find the idea of God, that is to say, the idea of a supremely perfect Being, in me, than that of any figure or number whatever it is; and I do not know any less clearly and distinctly that an [actual and] eternal existence pertains to this nature than

---

[7]St. Anselm, *Proslogion*, in *A Scholastic Miscellany*, Vol. 10, The Library of Christian Classics, ed. and trans. Eugene R. Fairweather (Philadelphia: Westminster Press, 1956).

I know that all that which I am able to demonstrate of some figure or number truly pertains to the nature of this figure or number, and therefore, although all that I concluded in the preceding Meditations were found to be false, the existence of God would pass with me as at least as certain as I have ever held the truths of mathematics (which concern only numbers and figures) to be.

This indeed is not at first manifest, since it would seem to present some appearance of being a sophism. For being accustomed in all other things to make a distinction between existence and essence, I easily persuade myself that the existence can be separated from the essence of God, and that we can thus conceive God as not actually existing. But, nevertheless, when I think of it with more attention, I clearly see that existence can no more be separated from the essence of God than can its having its three angles equal to two right angles be separated from the essence of a [rectilinear] triangle, or the idea of a mountain from the idea of a valley; and so there is not any less repugnance to our conceiving a God (that is, a Being supremely perfect) to whom existence is lacking (that is to say, to whom a certain perfection is lacking), than to conceive of a mountain which has no valley.

But although I cannot really conceive of a God without existence any more than a mountain without a valley, still from the fact that I conceive a mountain with a valley, it does not follow that there is such a mountain in the world; similarly although I conceive of God as possessing existence, it would seem that it does not follow that there is a God which exists; for my thought does not impose any necessity upon things, and just as I may imagine a winged horse, although no horse with wings exists, so I could perhaps attribute existence to God, although no God existed.

But a sophism is concealed in this objection; for from the fact that I cannot conceive a mountain without a valley, it does not follow that there is any mountain or any valley in existence, but only that the mountain and the valley, whether they exist or do not exist, cannot in any way be separated one from the other. While from the fact that I cannot conceive God without existence, it follows that existence is inseparable from Him, and hence that He really exists; not that my thought can bring this to pass, or impose any necessity on things, but, on the contrary, because the necessity which lies in the thing itself, i.e. the necessity of the existence of God determines me to think in this way. For it is not within my power to think of God without existence (that is of a supremely perfect Being devoid of a supreme perfection) though it is in my power to imagine a horse either with wings or without wings.

And we must not here object that it is in truth necessary for me to assert that God exists after having presupposed that He possesses every sort of perfection, since existence is one of these, but that as a matter of fact my original supposition was not necessary, just as it is not necessary to consider that all quadrilateral figures can be inscribed in the circle; for supposing I thought of this,

I should be constrained to admit that the rhombus might be inscribed in the circle since it is a quadrilateral figure, which, however, is manifestly false. Although it is not necessary that I should at any time entertain the notion of God, nevertheless whenever it happens that I think of a first and a sovereign Being, and, so to speak, derive the idea of Him from the storehouse of my mind, it is necessary that I should attribute to Him every sort of perfection, although I do not get so far as to enumerate them all, or to apply my mind to each one in particular. And this necessity suffices to make me conclude (after having recognised that existence is a perfection) that this first and sovereign Being really exists; just as though it is not necessary for me ever to imagine any triangle, yet, whenever I wish to consider a rectilinear figure composed only of three angles, it is absolutely essential that I should attribute to it all those properties which serve to bring about the conclusion that its three angles are not greater than two right angles, even although I may not then be considering this point in particular. But when I consider which figures are capable of being inscribed in the circle, it is in no way necessary that I should think that all quadrilateral figures are of this number; on the contrary, I cannot even pretend that this is the case, so long as I do not desire to accept anything which I cannot conceive clearly and distinctly. And in consequence there is a great difference between the false suppositions such as this, and the true ideas born within me, the first and principal of which is that of God. For really I discern in many ways that this idea is not something factitious, and depending solely on my thought, but that it is the image of a true and immutable nature; first of all, because I cannot conceive anything but God himself to whose essence existence [necessarily] pertains; in the second place because it is not possible for me to conceive two or more Gods in this same position; and, granted that there is one such God who now exists, I see clearly that it is necessary that He should have existed from all eternity and that He must exist eternally; and finally, because I know an infinitude of other properties in God, none of which I can either diminish or change.[8]

Descartes' version is

> I cannot conceive of a God without the property of existence.
> ("His existence cannot be separated from His essence.")
> Therefore, God exists.

and then he adds

> My conception of God is such that He has every sort of perfection.
> Existence is a perfection.
> Therefore, God necessarily exists.

[8] René Descartes, "Meditation IV," in *Meditations on First Philosophy*, in *The Philosophical Works of Descartes*, trans. Elizabeth S. Haldane and G. R. T. Ross [Cambridge: Cambridge University Press, 1911].

These arguments are valid as stated, but are they also sound? Consider the following argument, which has been proposed in the same form as the above arguments. Define a "grenlin" as "the greenest imaginable creature." Now, which is greener, a green creature that does exist, or one that does not? Obviously the one that exists. Therefore, at least one grenlin exists.

It is worth noting that this objection had been raised against Anselm too, by Gaunilo of Marmoutier, who suggested the existence of an island more perfect than any other, on the same grounds that it would be contradictory for the most perfect island not to exist. Anselm replied that the argument cannot be applied to islands (or grenlins) or anything else whose nonexistence is even conceivable. The question, then, is what it means for nonexistence to be conceivable, or for existence to be a necessary property of a thing.

Descartes faced a similar challenge to his formulation when a critic attacked his analogy with triangles and insisted that, while it may be true that *if* a triangle exists, then it must have three angles, it does not follow that triangles must exist, or that any in fact do exist. Descartes' answer is similar to Anselm's response to his critic: the essence of triangle does not include the perfection of existence, as God's surely does.

The ontological argument makes a special case for God, because He is the only "greatest conceivable" or "most perfect" being. Nevertheless, the argument has made many believers uneasy, and has been dismissed as a clever trick by nonbelievers. But, whatever our unease, the argument is clearly valid.

The argument is a straightforward syllogism of the "All men are mortal/Socrates is a man/Socrates is mortal" type, the only real (but significant) difference being that, while there can be any number of men, there can be only one God, one "most perfect" being. But what we have so far taken for granted in the above presentations of the argument is the presupposition that existence is a property, like a color or shape. One way of attacking the logic of the argument, even while accepting its validity, is to challenge this presupposition, and thus the soundness of the argument. Should we be allowed to write, in our second premise, "Ex"? In other words, is "exists" a predicate, like "barks" and "is green"? Or is it rather a quantifier, like "all" and "none" and "some" (which is, essentially, "there exists at least one . . . ")? The objection that "existence is not a predicate" was formulated against the ontological argument by Immanuel Kant.

The great philosopher Kant suggested that the problem lies in the central idea, shared by the ontological argument and the unacceptable arguments that follow the same form, that existence is one of the essential properties, that is, part of the definition of a thing. But existence, Kant argues, is not a property and cannot be part of a definition. In an often quoted passage of his *Critique of Pure Reason*, he argues:

◆against the Ontological Argument, by Immanuel Kant

I answer:—Even in introducing into the concept of a thing, which you wish to think in its possibility only, the concept of its existence, under whatever disguise it may be, you have been guilty of a contradiction. If you were allowed to do this, you would apparently have carried your point; but in reality you have achieved nothing, but have only committed a tautology. I simply ask you, whether the proposition, that *this* or *that thing* (which, whatever it may be, I grant you as possible) *exists*, is an analytical or a synthetical proposition? If the former, then by its existence you add nothing to your thought of the thing; but in that case, either the thought within you would be the thing itself, or you have presupposed existence, as belonging to possibility, and have according to your own showing deduced existence from internal possibility, which is nothing but a miserable tautology. The mere word *reality*, which in the concept of a thing sounds different from existence in the concept of the predicate, can make no difference. For if you call all accepting or positing (without determining what it is) reality, you have placed a thing, with all its predicates, within the concept of the subject, and accepted it as real, and you do nothing but repeat it in the predicate. If, on the contrary, you admit, as every sensible man must do, that every proposition involving existence is synthetical, how can you say that the predicate of existence does not admit of removal without contradiction, a distinguishing property which is peculiar to analytical propositions only, the very character of which depends on it?

I might have hoped to put an end to this subtle argumentation, without many words, and simply by an accurate definition of the concept of existence, if I had not seen that the illusion, in mistaking a logical predicate for a real one (that is the predicate which determines a thing), resists all correction. Everything can become a *logical predicate*, even the subject itself may be predicated of itself, because logic makes no account of any contents of concepts. *Determination*, however, is a predicate, added to the concept of the subject, and enlarging it, and it must not therefore be contained in it.

Being is evidently not a real predicate, or a concept of something that can be added to the concept of a thing. It is merely the admission of a thing, and of certain determinations in it. Logically, it is merely the copula of a judgment. The proposition, *God is almighty*, contains two concepts, each having its object, namely, God and almightiness. The small word *is*, is not an additional predicate, but only serves to put the predicate *in relation* to the subject. If, then, I take the subject (God) with all its predicates (including that of almightiness), and say, *God is*, or there is a God, I do not put a new predicate to the concept of God, but I only put the subject by itself, with all its predicates, in relation to my concept, as its object. Both must contain exactly the same kind of thing, and nothing can have been added to the concept, which expresses possibility only, by my thinking its object as simply given and saying it is. And thus the real does not contain more than the possible. A hundred real dollars do not contain a penny more than a hundred possible dollars. For as the latter signify the concept, the former the object and its position by itself, it is clear that, in case the former contained more than the latter, my concept would not express the whole object, and would not therefore be its adequate concept. In my financial position no doubt there exists more by one hundred real dollars, than by their concept only (that is their possibility), because in reality the object is not only contained analytically in my concept, but is added to my concept (which is a determination of my state), synthetically; but the conceived hundred dollars are not in the least increased through the existence which is outside my concept.[9]

What Kant is arguing is that the existence of a thing can never be merely a matter of logic. (This is what he means when he says that the proposition that a thing exists cannot be analytic.) "Existence" or "being," he argues, isn't a "real predicate" (though it is a grammatical predicate) because it does not tell us anything more about whatever is said to have existence or being. In other words, there is something odd about the statement, "this apple is red, round, ripe, and exists." What is odd is that "exists" does not give a characteristic of the apple but rather says that there is an apple with these characteristics. The proper characterization of God, therefore, includes the various characteristics we discussed earlier in this chapter, but it should not include, according to Kant, any characteristic that implies God's existence. It is one thing to say that God, if He exists, has such-and-such characteristics; it is something more to say that such a God exists. (This is what Kant means by his example about the one hundred real versus one hundred possible dollars; they both have exactly the same number of cents, but only the one hundred real dollars are worth anything.)

Many contemporary philosophers agree with Kant's argument, but many do not. Furthermore, contemporary logicians have developed versions of the ontological argument that can even dispense with this controversial notion of existence as a property. For example, with just the seemingly innocent premise "if God exists, then He necessarily exists," some logicians have recently argued according to the sophisticated rules of modern logic that the conclusion that "God exists" does follow. The premise is innocent because you can grant that "if God exists" without in any way admitting that God in fact exists. Charles Hartshorne, for

[9]Immanuel Kant, *The Critique of Pure Reason*, rev. 2nd ed., trans. Max Müller (London: Macmillan).

example, has argued that, if our concept of God is of a being who is eternal and self-existent then the question of God's existence cannot be a contingent matter but must be a matter of logical necessity (or impossibility). An existent being, but one which we can imagine not existing, could not be God, for, following Anselm, God is the being of whom it must be said (by definition) that nothing greater is conceivable. But instead of employing the objectionable presupposition—that existence is a predicate—Hartshorne's argument simply goes on to demonstrate that there is nothing self-contradictory in the concept of such a being, and therefore we must conclude that God necessarily exists. (The presupposition here is that either a most perfect being necessarily exists or he necessarily does not exist—what logicians call "the law of the excluded middle"; in other words, there are no other possibilities.)

Whether or not the argument succeeds in its classical form, it can be understood in another way, which clearly distinguishes it from all the absurd arguments that apparently have the same form. If you believe in God, then the argument might be taken in a very different way, not as a "proof" but as an attempt to articulate your belief. The theologian Karl Barth has argued that this is what Anselm's argument really tries to do, and as you read over his argument a second or third time it becomes clear that he is expressing his faith as much as he is offering a logical proof. In general, the "proofs" of God's existence have been such articulations and expressions as well as proper logical arguments. And even if they fail as proofs, they often succeed in this other, and perhaps more important function. Descartes' and Anselm's argument is, ultimately, that we cannot think about God and at the same time doubt His existence.

It is clear that, considered simply as a logical argument, the ontological argument does not have the power to convert nonbelievers into believers. Or if you are a believer, it is clear that an objection to the "proof" is not going to shake your faith in any way whatsoever. So the significance of the proof is ambiguous; as a logical exercise it is brilliant, as an expression of faith it may be edifying, but as an actual proof that God exists or as a means of converting atheists it seems to have no power at all.

THE COSMOLOGICAL ARGUMENT   The second "proof" of God's existence is a set of arguments that date back to Aristotle's argument for the prime mover. The basis of all these arguments is the intolerability if not the unthinkability of an infinite regress and the need for some ultimate explanation. Together they are called the **cosmological argument,** and their best-known formulation is by St. Thomas Aquinas as the first three of his "five ways" of proving God's existence.

◆the Cosmological Argument, by St. Thomas Aquinas

The first and more manifest way is the argument from motion. It is certain, and evident to our senses, that in the world some things are in motion. Now whatever is moved is moved by another, for nothing can be moved except it is in potentiality to that towards which it is moved whereas a thing moves inasmuch as it is in act. For motion is nothing else than the reduction of something from potentiality to actuality. But nothing can be reduced from potentiality to actuality, except by something in a state of actuality. Thus that which is actually hot, as fire, makes wood, which is potentially hot, to be actually hot, and thereby moves and changes it. Now it is not possible that the same thing should be at once in actuality and potentiality in the same respect, but only in different respects. For what is actually hot cannot simultaneously be potentially hot; but it is simultaneously potentially cold. It is therefore impossible that in the same respect and in the same way a thing should be both mover and moved, i.e., that it should move itself. Therefore, whatever is moved must be moved by another. If that by which it is moved be itself moved, then this also must needs be moved by another, and that by another again. But this cannot go on to infinity, because then there would be no first mover, and consequently, no other mover, seeing that subsequent movers move only inasmuch as they are moved by the first mover, as the staff moves only because it is moved by the hand. Therefore, it is necessary to arrive at a first mover, moved by no other; and this everyone understands to be God.

The second way is from the nature of efficient cause.[10] In the world of sensible things we find there is an order of efficient causes. There is no case known (neither is it, indeed, possible) in which a thing is found to be the efficient cause of itself; for so it would be prior to itself, which is impossible. Now in efficient causes it is not possible to go on to infinity, because in all efficient causes following in order, the first is the cause of the intermediate cause, and the intermediate is the cause of the ultimate cause, whether the intermediate cause be several, or one only. Now to take away the cause is to take away the effect. Therefore, if there be no first cause among efficient causes, there will be no ultimate, nor any intermediate cause. But if in efficient causes it is possible to go on to infinity, there will be no first efficient cause, neither will there be an ultimate effect, nor any intermediate efficient causes; all of which is plainly false. Therefore it is necessary to admit a first efficient cause, to which everyone gives the name of God.

The third way is taken from possibility and necessity, and runs

---

[10]An *efficient cause* is an event (or an agent) that brings something about. The term comes from Aristotle. See glossary to Chapter 1, "cause."

thus. We find in nature things that are possible to be and not to be, since they are found to be generated, and to be corrupted, and consequently, it is possible for them to be and not to be. But it is impossible for these always to exist, for that which can not-be at some time is not. Therefore, if everything can not-be, then at one time there was nothing in existence. Now if this were true, even now there would be nothing in existence, because that which does not exist begins to exist only through something already existing. Therefore, if at one time nothing was in existence, it would have been impossible for anything to have begun to exist; and thus even now nothing would be in existence—which is absurd. Therefore, not all beings are merely possible, but there must exist something the existence of which is necessary. But every necessary thing either has its necessity caused by another, or not. Now it is impossible to go on to infinity in necessary things which have their necessity caused by another, as has been already proved in regard to efficient causes. Therefore we cannot but admit the existence of some being having of itself its own necessity, and not receiving it from another, but rather causing in others their necessity. This all men speak of as God.

And in his "fourth way," Aquinas combines the form of cosmological argument with some of the ideas from the ontological argument:

The fourth way is taken from the gradation to be found in things. Among beings there are some more and some less good, true, noble, and the like. But *more* and *less* are predicated of different things according as they resemble in their different ways something which is the maximum, as a thing is said to be hotter according as it more nearly resembles that which is hottest; so that there is something which is truest, something best, something noblest, and, consequently, something which is most being, for those things that are greatest in truth are greatest in being, as it is written in [Aristotle's] *Metaphysics.* . . . Now the maximum in any genus is the cause of all in that genus, as fire, which is the maximum of heat, is the cause of all hot things, as is said in the same book. Therefore, there must also be something which is to all beings the cause of their being, goodness, and every other perfection; and this we call God.[11]

The cosmological argument, in all of these versions, is also both an attempt at "proof" and an expression of one's belief in God. Accordingly, it must be appreciated for its role in articulating the concept of God in traditional Christianity and evaluated as a logical argument. As a logical argument, there are two modern objections that seem to have consid-

[11]St. Thomas Aquinas, *Summa Theologica*, trans. Fathers of the English Dominican Province (New York: Benziger, Bruce & Glencoe, 1948).

erable weight. First, even if the argument is formally valid, it proves only that there is some "first mover" or "first cause" or "necessary being." it does not prove that this being has all of the other attributes that allow us to recognize God. (Aquinas' fourth "way," however, includes moral attributes of perfection as well.) Taken at face value, the first three versions of the cosmological argument are similar to Aristotle's argument for the "prime mover" (Chapter 1) except that Aquinas takes the "first cause" to be an "efficient" as well as "final" cause, that is, as the creator as well as the meaning of of the universe.

Furthermore, Aristotle (in his *Physics*) allows that there might be several prime movers, while Aquinas is clear that there can be only one. Nevertheless, one might accept the argument and believe only in a "first cause" and deny the existence of God. Or if it is accepted that there must be a first cause, why could the universe itself not be its own cause? In current physics, scientists would argue that this idea is just as plausible as the idea that there must have been something else that caused our universe to exist. And this leads us to the second objection, which would have been unthinkable to Aquinas (or Aristotle), but is generally accepted today. The idea of an "infinite regress," that the universe did not have a beginning but has always existed, seemed like an obvious absurdity until the last century. But now, even though scientists and mathematicians talk about the beginning of the universe and the relativity of time, they no longer consider an infinite regress as necessarily impossible. And without the idea that every infinite regress is an absurdity, the cosmological argument loses its main premise.

In fact, Aquinas admits that there is no valid argument against the claim that God and the universe existed for all eternity, but he has another argument to help him here. He says that the beginning of the universe required an *act*, which means that the universe could not have been the cause of itself. Furthermore, even if the universe existed eternally, it would still require a prime mover to keep it in motion. Therefore, he concludes, God must exist even if the infinite regress argument by itself does not prove this.

THE TELEOLOGICAL ARGUMENT   The third "proof" of God's existence is the one that is probably most familiar to you. It is usually called "the argument from design." Immanuel Kant called it the **teleological argument.** It is often the most universally appealing of the three arguments because it depends as much on our emotions and our sense of wonder as it does on logical principles. The classical form of the argument goes like this. Suppose you are walking across a deserted beach and come across a watch, lying in the sand. You immediately conclude, "people have been here." Why? Because it is highly unlikely that a mechanism as intricately designed as a watch might be thrown together by the chance forces of nature. A pebble on the beach might be curiously shaped, but anything approaching the complexity of a tool or a piece of sculpture, much less a complex mechanism, would strike us as proof of some intelligent being. Now, looking at the universe, it is easy to wonder at its complexity, the intricate workings of the heavens or even a single-celled organism and the grand variety and interconnection of all living things. And from this, one concludes that the universe as a whole must have been rationally designed.

One classic version of the teleological argument is St. Thomas Aquinas' "fifth way":

◆ the "Fifth Way," by St. Thomas Aquinas

The fifth way is taken from the governance of the world. We see that things which lack knowledge, such as natural bodies, act for an end, and this is evident from their acting always, or nearly always in the same way, so as to obtain the best result. Hence it is plain that they achieve their end, not fortuitously, but designedly. Now whatever lacks knowledge cannot move towards an end, unless it be directed by some being endowed with knowledge and intelligence; as the arrow is directed by the archer. Therefore some intelligent being exists by whom all natural things are directed to their end; and this being we call God.[12]

The argument is powerful psychologically, but it too has its problems. Like the earlier two arguments, it may prove much less about God than the theist needs to have proven. The God who has rationally designed the universe need not have the slightest concern for humankind, for example. He may well consider us just one of those little curiosities of evolution that, for a few thousand years, interfered with His other interests. But there are other problems peculiar to this argument. It is easily mocked, and Voltaire, who was around when the argument was most popular, parodied its logic in *Candide* (by suggesting that, among other things, it was marvelous that God gave us noses so that we can wear eyeglasses). About the same time, the German Enlightenment writer Georg Christoph Lichtenberg commented that it was clever of God to put holes in the cat's skin right where his eyes are. These nonsensical comments make an important point, however. The "design" in nature appears as such only to one who is already predisposed to believe in a designer. This is most powerfully presented by David Hume in his blasphemous (and therefore posthumous) *Dialogues on Natural Religion:*

[12] Aquinas, *Summa Theologica.*

◆an Imperfect Universe, by David Hume

In a word, Cleanthes, a man who follows your hypothesis is able, perhaps, to assert or conjecture that the universe sometime arose from something like design; but beyond that position he cannot ascertain one single circumstance and is left afterwards to fix every point of his theology by the utmost license of fancy and hypothesis. This world, for aught he knows, is very faulty and imperfect compared to a superior standard and was only the first rude essay of some infant deity who afterwards abandoned it, ashamed of his lame performance; it is the work only of some dependent, inferior deity and is the object of derision to his superiors; it is the production of old age and dotage in some superannuated deity and, ever since his death, has run on at adventures from the first impulse and active force which it received from him.[13]

Hume's argument is, quite simply, that this is not a perfect world, which means that the God who supposedly designed it cannot be perfect either. And one can even wonder whether a universe that has been so badly designed has been designed at all. But Cleanthes replies that he rejects both the suppositions and the tone of these sarcastic remarks and even insists that the argument that the universe is badly designed presupposes a designer. There are more powerful replies, however: that the world is in fact designed as well as it could possibly be, or else that it is a design that has not yet been fully realized and has not yet come to see full perfection.

The credibility of the argument from design has suffered enormously (but perhaps needlessly) from the shock of Darwin's theory of evolution. Accordingly, the Christian Church has combated the latter with all of the resources at its command. But the battle has been largely unnecessary and, if anything, has falsely overemphasized the conflict between science and religion, weakening the credibility of the church. For evolution need not deny the argument from design. It only changes the argument from the traditional idea that God created the universe all at once (though even in Genesis, He spread it out over several days) to the idea that He created it over a long period of time, using natural selection as one of His tools.

But the logic of evolution does undermine the appeal of the argument from design in a more subtle way. The power of the argument is, boiled down to essentials, "Isn't it marvelous that things are as they are!" But our "marvel" depends on our putting some premium on "the way things are." We place a high premium on "the way things are" because according to the laws of probability (or chance) the odds against this way are enormous. Now consider the following analogy: you are playing cards,

[13]David Hume, *Dialogues on Natural Religion*, ed. Norman Kemp Smith (Oxford: Oxford University Press, 1935).

stud poker, and the dealer gives you excellent hands twice in a row. You would be suspicious. The odds are against it. And, particularly if you lose both times, you will be certain that some "design" (namely, the dealer's) is behind it. But now, why would you not have the same suspicions given any two consecutive hands, for the odds are exactly the same against any combination of cards? (The odds against receiving any hand of the same five cards twice consecutively are 2.6 million to one.) The answer, of course, has nothing to do with the "likelihood" of getting one set of hands rather than another but with the significance you place on the one combination rather than the other. So too, with the argument from design.

Evolution has given the world many different "ways that things are" and will give it many more. The reason for our marveling at this particular "way that things are" is that we suppose that the odds against it are uniquely high. But they are not. They are equally high against every other possible "way that things are," and so this "way" seems to deserve no special explanation. This does not deny "design," of course; it only emphasizes the importance of a certain way of seeing the world, a way shared by science and nature-lovers as well as theists. Wittgenstein summed up this view toward the argument from design in a phrase: "What is remarkable is not how things are, but that they are at all." (This turns us back to the cosmological argument.)

C. RELIGION, MORALITY, AND EVIL

The three traditional forms of "proof" don't seem to be adequate as literal proofs. In order to accept any of them, it looks as if one has to *begin* by believing in God. Moreover, what each of them proves is not the existence of *God,* but at most the existence of something; something that is defined by its existence, something that is a first cause, or something that is an intelligent "designer." But a very different view of God is defended, for example, by Immanuel Kant. On this view, the most important attribute of the traditional Western God—the reason why men and women have worshiped Him, prayed to Him, feared Him, fought wars, and died for Him—is their belief in God's divine justice. Thus the most important attributes of God in Western religion are His moral qualities. Without them, our belief in God would be very different than it is.

According to this view, the importance of God in Western thought is His role as the source of our moral laws, as the judge of our actions and feelings, and as the sanction that stands behind those laws and judgments. The preceding "proofs" of God's existence are not wholly convincing, even if they are valid, just because they leave out this all-important moral aspect of belief in God. What distinguishes theists from atheists is not a matter of mere theory or argument ("a mere hypothesis," the French philosopher La Place called it), but a difference in lifestyle and confidence. The theist believes in a divine source of morality, in a judgment of one's actions that transcends everyday life, and the promise of reward (or threat of punishment) after death. The atheist also believes in morality, but not in divine morality, and he believes that all judgments of our actions and all rewards and punishments must take place in this life, or not at all. Accordingly, the question of God's existence has a distinctly moral dimension. Our conception of the human good depends on, as believers, our conception of God.

Immanuel Kant, after attempting to refute all three of the traditional arguments of God's existence, offered one of his own. He no longer tried to "prove" God's existence as such and even said that, strictly speaking, we could have no knowledge of God at all, since God, as transcendent, cannot be the object of any possible experience. So Kant, following a long tradition in Christianity, said that belief in God is a matter of faith. But this does not mean, as people so often take it to mean, that it is an irrational belief. Quite to the contrary, Kant insisted that it is the most rational belief of all. For without it, we would not have the anchor for our morality, nor would we have any reason to suppose that our good deeds would in fact be eventually rewarded or evil deeds punished. It was obvious to Kant, as it has been to every person with his or her eyes open since ancient times, that justice is not always delivered in this life. Innocent children are butchered in wars; evil men live grand lives well into old age. Therefore, according to Kant, it was rational to believe in God, rational to have faith, even if faith was not, strictly speaking, a matter of knowledge. It is, he says, a "Postulate of Practical Reason."

◆ on God and Morality, by Immanuel Kant

The moral law led, in the foregoing analysis, to a practical problem which is assigned solely by pure reason and without any concurrence of sensuous incentives. It is the problem of the completeness of the first and principal part of the highest good, viz., morality; since this problem can be solved only in eternity, it led to the postulate of immortality. The same law must also lead us to affirm the possibility of the second element of the highest good, i.e., happiness proportional to that morality; it must do so just as disinterestedly as heretofore, by a purely impartial reason. This it can do on the supposition of the existence of a cause adequate to this effect, i.e., it must postulate the existence of God as necessarily belonging to the possibility of the highest good (the object of our will which is necessarily connected with moral legislation of pure reason). We proceed to exhibit this connection in a convincing manner.

Happiness is the condition of a rational being in the world, in whose whole existence everything goes according to wish and will.

It thus rests on the harmony of nature with his entire end and with the essential determining ground of his will. But the moral law commands as a law of freedom through motives wholly independent of nature and of its harmony with our faculty of desire (as incentives). Still, the acting rational being in the world is not at the same time the cause of the world and of nature itself. Hence there is not the slightest ground in the moral law for a necessary connection between the morality and proportionate happiness of a being which belongs to the world as one of its parts and as thus dependent on it. Not being nature's cause, his will cannot by its own strength bring nature, as it touches on his happiness, into complete harmony with his practical principles. Nevertheless, in the practical task of pure reason, i.e., in the necessary endeavor after the highest good, such a connection is postulated as necessary: we *should* seek to further the highest good (which therefore must be at least possible). Therefore also the existence is postulated of a cause of the whole of nature, itself distinct from nature, which contains the ground of the exact coincidence of happiness with morality. This supreme cause, however, must contain the ground of the agreement of nature not merely with a law of the will of rational beings but with the idea of this law so far as they make it the supreme ground of determination of the will. Thus it contains the ground of the agreement of nature not merely with actions moral in their form but also with their morality as the motives to such actions, i.e., with their moral intention. Therefore, the highest good is possible in the world only on the supposition of a supreme cause of nature which has a causality corresponding to the moral intention. Now a being which is capable of actions by the idea of laws is an intelligence (a rational being), and the causality of such a being according to this idea of laws is his will. Therefore, the supreme cause of nature, in so far as it must be presupposed for the highest good, is a being which is the cause (and consequently the author) of nature through understanding and will, i.e., God. As a consequence, the postulate of the possibility of a highest derived good (the best world) is at the same time the postulate of the reality of a highest original good, namely, the existence of God. Now it was our duty to promote the highest good; and it is not merely our privilege but a necessity connected with duty as a requisite to presuppose the possibility of this highest good. This presupposition is made only under the condition of the existence of God, and this condition inseparably connects this supposition with duty. Therefore, it is morally necessary to assume the existence of God.[14]

The key to Kant's argument is the obvious fact that good deeds are not always rewarded in this life and evil deeds are often not punished. Why then, he asks, should a person be moral and do what is right? If we are

[14]Immanuel Kant, *Critique of Practical Reason*, trans. Lewis White Beck (New York: Bobbs-Merrill, 1956).

to rationally decide to be moral, therefore, we must also believe that happiness and morality will be in harmony (what Kant calls "the highest good"), that good people will be rewarded with happiness and evil people will be punished. But if this does not happen in this life, then we must believe that it happens in another life (". . . this problem can be solved only in eternity"). Further, we must believe in some ultimate source of justice, a divine judge who will weigh good against evil and make certain that eternal happiness and punishment are meted out fairly. This argument is at one and the same time a defense of the Christian belief in the immortality of the human soul and in God. It is necessary to believe in both, according to Kant, in order to sustain our willingness to be moral. "Therefore, it is morally necessary to assume the existence of God."

A similar position was argued more recently by the pragmatist William James. His position is a "pragmatic" one; that is, believing in God is "rational" insofar as it doesn't conflict with our other beliefs (for example, our beliefs in science, a matter that Kant stressed also) and if it tends to make us lead better lives. He argues:

◆from "The Will to Believe," by William James

Science says things are; morality says some things are better than other things; and religion says essentially two things.

First, she says that the best things are the more eternal things, the overlapping things, the things in the universe that throw the last stone, so to speak, and say the final word. "Perfection is eternal"—this phrase of Charles Secrétan seems a good way of putting this first affirmation of religion, an affirmation which obviously cannot yet be verified scientifically at all.

The second affirmation of religion is that we are better off even now if we believe her first affirmation to be true.

Now, let us consider what the logical elements of this situation are *in case the religious hypothesis in both its branches be really true.* (Of course, we must admit that possibility at the outset. If we are to discuss the question at all, it must involve a living option. If for any of you religion be a hypothesis that cannot, by any living possibility be true, then you need go no farther. I speak to the "saving remnant" alone.) So proceeding, we see, first, that religion offers itself as a *momentous* option. We are supposed to gain, even now, by our belief, and to lose by our nonbelief, a certain vital good. Secondly, religion is a *forced* option, so far as that good goes. We cannot escape the issue by remaining sceptical and waiting for more light, because, although we do avoid error in that way *if religion be untrue,* we lose the good, *if it be true,* just as certainly as if we positively chose to disbelieve. It is as if a man should hesitate indefinitely to ask a certain woman to marry him because he was not perfectly sure that she would prove an angel after he brought her home. Would he not cut himself off from that particular angel-possibility as decisively as if he went and married someone else? Scepticism, then, is not avoidance of option; it is option of a certain particular kind of risk. *Better risk loss of truth than chance of error*—that is your faith-vetoer's exact position. He is actively playing his stake as much as the believer is; he is backing the field against the religious hypothesis, just as the believer is backing the religious hypothesis against the field. To preach scepticism to us as a duty until "sufficient evidence" for religion be found, is tantamount therefore to telling us, when in presence of the religious hypothesis, that to yield to our fear of its being error is wiser and better than to yield to our hope that it may be true. It is not intellect against all passions, then; it is only intellect with one passion laying down its law. And by what, forsooth, is the supreme wisdom of this passion warranted? Dupery for dupery, what proof is there that dupery through hope is so much worse than dupery through fear? I, for one, can see no proof; and I simply refuse obedience to the scientist's command to imitate his kind of option, in a case where my own stake is important enough to give me the right to choose my own form of risk. If religion be true and the evidence for it be still insufficient, I do not wish, by putting your extinguisher upon my nature (which feels to me as if it had after all some business in this matter), to forfeit my sole chance in life of getting upon the winning side—that chance depending, of course, on my willingness to run the risk of acting as if my passional need of taking the world religiously might be prophetic and right.

All this is on the supposition that it really may be prophetic and right, and that, even to us who are discussing the matter, religion is a live hypothesis which may be true. Now, to most of us religion comes in a still further way that makes a veto on our active faith even more illogical. The more perfect and more eternal aspect of the universe is represented in our religions as having personal form. The universe is no longer a mere *It* to us, but a *Thou,* if we are religious; and any relation that may be possible from person to person might be possible here. For instance, although in one sense we are passive portions of the universe, in another we show a curious autonomy, as if we were small active centres on our own account. We feel, too, as if the appeal of religion to us were made to our own active good-will, as if evidence might be forever withheld from us unless we met the hypothesis half-way. To take a trivial illustration: just as a man who in a company of gentlemen made no advances, asked a warrant for every concession, and believed no one's word without proof, would cut himself off by such churlishness from all the social rewards that a more trusting spirit would earn—so here, one who should shut himself up in snarling logicality and try to make the gods extort his recognition willy-nilly, or not get it at all, might cut himself off forever from his only opportunity of making the gods' acquaintance. This feeling, forced on us we know not whence, that by obstinately believing that there are gods (although not to do so would be so easy both for our logic and our life) we are doing the universe the deepest service we can, seems part of the living essence of the religious hypothesis. If the hypothesis *were* true in all its parts, including this one, then pure intellectualism, with its veto on our making willing advances, would be an absurdity; and some participation of our sympathetic nature would be logically required. I, therefore, for one, cannot see my way to accepting the agnostic rules of truth-seeking, or willfully agree to keep my willing nature out of the game. I cannot do so for this plain reason, that *a rule of thinking which would absolutely prevent me from acknowledging certain kinds of truth if those kinds of truth were really there, would be an irrational rule.* That for me is the long and short of the formal logic of the situation, no matter what the kinds of truth might materially be.[15]

This "practical" argument for belief in God ruled philosophy from the time of Kant until the present century. It has its origins in a short but brilliant argument by the French philosopher Blaise Pascal. Pascal offered an argument that he called a wager, literally a bet about God. It isn't a proof of God's existence in any sense; in fact, one of its explicit terms is the fact that we can't know whether God exists or not. But then, he says, if God exists, and we believe in Him, we are entitled to an infinite reward. If He exists and we don't believe in Him, on the other hand, we are really in for it—eternal damnation. Even if He doesn't exist, we are still better off believing in God because of the qualities faith brings to life in us. In support of the decision to believe, Pascal asks:

> Now, what harm will befall you in taking this side? You will be faithful, honest, humble, grateful, generous, a sincere friend, truthful. Certainly you will not have those poisonous pleasures, glory and luxury; but will you not have others? I will tell you that you will thereby gain in this life, and that, at each step you take on this road, you will see so great certainty of gain, so much nothingness in what you risk, that you will at last recognize that you have wagered for something certain and infinite, for which you have given nothing.[16]

So, if we treat this as a betting situation, in which our option is simply to believe or not believe, our betting odds look like this:

[15]William James, "The Will to Believe," in *The Will to Believe and Other Essays in Popular Philosophy* (New York: Longmans, Green, 1896).
[16]Blaise Pascal, *Pensées,* #233 (New York: Modern Library, 1941).

"Pascal's Wager"

	AND GOD EXISTS	AND GOD DOESN'T EXIST
If we believe:	Eternal reward.	We've wasted a little piety but perhaps been better people.
If we don't believe:	Eternal damnation.	No reward, no punishment.

Looking at the odds as a betting person, it is obvious which option we ought to choose. The risk of eternal damnation overwhelms the promise of a few "poisonous" pleasures; and the promise of eternal reward is well worth the risk that we may be wrong, considering what is gained even in this life. The conclusion, then, on strictly practical grounds, is that we ought to believe in God.

All three of these arguments by Kant, James, and Pascal are based on the same all-important assumption that "God is just." On the basis of this assumption, they then argue that it is rational to believe in God, even if it is not possible to prove (or even know) that He exists. Accordingly, belief in God is a matter of faith, but this faith can be argued and justified as rational belief. Just because it is faith and not knowledge, it does not follow that it is "blind faith" or irrational, beyond argument or arbitrary. To insist that belief in God is a matter of faith, therefore, is not to say that it is beyond the reach of philosophy or rational consideration.

1.   The Problem of Evil

These "moral" arguments for believing in God are sound only as long as we accept the assumption that "God is just." There have been few sophisticated theists who have actually denied this, of course, but there have been a great many, particularly in modern times, who have worried about it considerably. The problem is called "the problem of evil." It can be stated very simply, but the solution, if you believe in God, is not simple at all. The problem is this: If God is all-powerful (omnipotent), all-knowing (omniscient), and just, then how is it possible that there is so much unearned suffering and unpunished wickedness in the world? Or simply, if God exists, how can the world be so full of evil? It cannot be that He does not know of these misfortunes, for He is all-knowing. Nor can it be that He is unable to do anything about them, for He is all-powerful. And if He is just and has concern for human beings, then He must care about protecting the innocent and punishing or preventing evil.

The problem of evil is a problem because few believers in any religion are willing to give up their faith in the power of nature or of its Creator, its innate goodness, or the belief that there is real justice in it. The clearest and most widely known characterization of the problem of evil for the religious belief is probably still the one found in the Biblical Book of Job, in which Job, deeply pious yet undeservedly suffering, struggles to keep his faith:

> Then his wife said to him, "Are you still unshaken in your integrity? Curse God and die!" But he answered, ". . . If we accept good from God, shall we not accept evil?" (2:9–10)

But eventually, Job asks God:

> "Why should the sufferer be born to see the light? Why is life given to men who find it so bitter?" (3:20)

The most common solution to the problem of evil is offered to Job by his friend Eliphaz:

> "Mischief does not grow out of the soil
> nor trouble spring from the earth;
> man is born to trouble,
> as surely as birds fly upwards." (Job 5:6, New English Bible)

In other words, Eliphaz suggests that man has been created by God with the kind of nature which brings with it its own creation of troubles.

This has often been the solution offered by philosophers and theologians to the problem of evil. There are several versions even of this solution (that human beings have "free will"). The version most influential in Christianity was offered by St. Augustine. In his youth, Augustine had come under the influence of a religion called Manichaeism, which was branded as heresy by all of the great monotheisms (including, at that time, the Persian religion, Zoroastrianism, about whose founder we studied in Chapter 1), precisely because of the explanation of evil which it espoused. The Manichaeans claimed that there were two equally powerful gods, one of which was good and one evil. The good god ruled the spirit and mind, and the evil god ruled the body. According to the Manichaeans, then, neither god was all-powerful and human beings were not free, but rather at the mercy of one or the other of the gods. Only at death, claimed the Manichaeans, when the soul is separated forever from the body, could human beings achieve real moral goodness.

Augustine abandoned Manichaeism and embraced Christianity. As a Christian, he wrote eloquently about the freedom of the will and the ability of human beings to observe the moral obligations to which God has commanded them.

◆from *Confessions,* by St. Augustine

But although I declared and firmly believed that you, our Lord God, the true God who made not only our souls but also our bodies and not only our souls and bodies but all things, living and inanimate, as well, although I believed that you were free from corruption or mutation or any degree of change, I still could not find a clear explanation, without complications, of the cause of evil. Whatever the cause might be, I saw that it was not to be found in any theory that would oblige me to believe that the immutable God was mutable. If I believed this, I should myself become a cause of evil, the very thing which I was trying to discover. So I continued the search with some sense of relief, because I was quite sure that the theories of the Manichees were wrong. I repudiated these people with all my heart, because I could see that while they were inquiring into the origin of evil they were full of evil themselves, since they preferred to think that yours was a substance that could suffer evil rather than that theirs was capable of committing it.

I was told that we do evil because we choose to do so of our own free will, and suffer it because your justice rightly demands that we should. I did my best to understand this, but I could not see it clearly. I tried to raise my mental perceptions out of the abyss which engulfed them, but I sank back into it once more. Again and again I tried, but always I sank back. One thing lifted me up into the light of your day. It was that I knew that I had a will, as surely as I knew that there was life in me. When I chose to do something or not to do it, I was quite certain that it was my own self, and not some other person, who made this act of will, so that I was on the point of understanding that herein lay the cause of my sin. If I did anything against my will, it seemed to me to be something which happened to me rather than something which I did, and I looked upon it not as a fault, but as a punishment. And because I thought of you as a just God, I admitted at once that your punishments were not unjust.

But then I would ask myself once more: "Who made me? Surely it was my God, who is not only good but Goodness itself. How, then, do I come to possess a will that can choose to do wrong and refuse to do good, thereby providing a just reason why I should be punished? Who put this will into me? Who sowed this seed of bitterness in me, when all that I am was made by my God, who is Sweetness itself? If it was the devil who put it there, who made the devil? If he was a good angel who became a devil because of his own wicked will, how did he come to possess the wicked will which made him a devil, when the Creator, who is entirely good, made him a good angel and nothing else?"

These thoughts swept me back again into the gulf where I was being stifled. But I did not sink as far as that hell of error where no one confesses to you his own guilt, choosing to believe that you suffer evil rather than that man does it.

· · · · · · · · · ·

"Where then is evil? What is its origin? How did it steal into the world? What is the root or stem from which it grew? Can it be that there simply is no evil? If so, why do we fear and guard against something which is not there? If our fear is unfounded, it is itself an evil, because it stabs and wrings our hearts for nothing. In fact the evil is all the greater if we are afraid when there is nothing to fear. Therefore, either there is evil and we fear it, or the fear itself is evil.

"Where then does evil come from, if God made all things and, because he is good, made them good too? It is true that he is the supreme Good, that he is himself a greater Good than these lesser goods which he created. But the Creator and all his creation are both good. Where then does evil come from?

"Can it be that there was something evil in the matter from which he made the universe? When he shaped this matter and fitted it to his purpose, did he leave in it some part which he did not convert to good? But why should he have done this? Are we to believe that, although he is omnipotent, he had not the power to convert the whole of this matter to good and change it so that no evil remained in it? Why, indeed, did he will to make anything of it at all? Why did he not instead, by this same omnipotence, destroy it utterly and entirely? Could it have existed against his will? If it had existed from eternity, why did he allow it to exist in that state through the infinite ages of the past and then, after so long a time, decide to make something of it? If he suddenly determined to act, would it not be more likely that he would use his almighty power to abolish this evil matter, so that nothing should exist besides himself, the total, true, supreme, and infinite Good? Or, if it was not good that a God who was good should not also create and establish something good, could he not have removed and annihilated the evil matter and replaced it with good, of which he could create all things? For he would not be omnipotent if he could not create something good without the help of matter which he had not created himself."

These were the thoughts which I turned over and over in my unhappy mind, and my anxiety was all the more galling for the fear that death might come before I had found the truth. But my heart clung firmly to the faith in Christ your Son, our Lord and Saviour, which it had received in the Catholic Church. There were many questions on which my beliefs were still indefinite and wavered from the strict rule of doctrine, yet my mind never relinquished the faith but drank it in more deeply day by day. . . .

12

It was made clear to me also that even those things which are subject to decay are good. If they were of the supreme order of goodness, they could not become corrupt; but neither could they become corrupt unless they were in some way good. For if they were supremely good, it would not be possible for them to be corrupted. On the other hand, if they were entirely without good, there would be nothing in them that could become corrupt. For corruption is harmful, but unless it diminished what is good, it could do no harm. The conclusion then must be either that corruption does no harm—which is not possible; or that everything which is corrupted is deprived of good—which is beyond doubt. But if they are deprived of all good, they will not exist at all. For if they still exist but can no longer be corrupted, they will be better than they were before, because they now continue their existence in an incorruptible state. But could anything be more preposterous than to say that things are made better by being deprived of all good?

So we must conclude that if things are deprived of all good, they cease altogether to be; and this means that as long as they are, they are good. Therefore, whatever is, is good; and evil, the origin of which I was trying to find, is not a substance, because if it were a substance, it would be good. For either it would be an incorruptible substance of the supreme order of goodness, or it would be a corruptible substance which would not be corruptible unless it were good. So it became obvious to me that all that you have made is good, and that there are no substances whatsoever that were not made by you. And because you did not make them all equal, each single thing is good and collectively they are very good, for our God made his whole creation *very good*.

13

For you evil does not exist, and not only for you but for the whole of your creation as well, because there is nothing outside it which could invade it and break down the order which you have imposed on it. Yet in the separate parts of your creation there are some things which we think of as evil because they are at variance with other things. But there are other things again with which they are in accord, and then they are good. In themselves, too, they are good. And all these things which are at variance with one another are in accord with the lower part of creation which we call the earth. The sky, which is cloudy and windy, suits the earth to which it belongs. So it would be wrong for me to wish that these earthly things did not exist, for even if I saw nothing but them, I might wish for something better, but still I ought to praise you for them alone. For all things *give praise to the Lord on earth, monsters of the sea and all its depths; fire and hail, snow and mist; and the storm-wind that executes his decree; all you mountains and hills, all you fruit trees and cedars; all you wild beasts and cattle, creeping things and birds that fly in air; all you kings and peoples of the world, all you that are princes and judges on earth; young men and maids, old men and boys together; let them all give praise to the Lord's name.* The heavens, too, ring with your praises, O God, for you are the god of us all. *Give praise to the Lord in heaven; praise him, all that dwells on high. Praise him, all you angels of his, praise him, all his armies. Praise him, sun and moon; praise him, every star that shines. Praise him, you highest heavens, you waters beyond the heavens. Let all these praise the Lord.* And since this is so, I no longer wished for a better world, because I was thinking of the whole of creation, and in the light of this clearer discernment I had come to see that though the higher things are better than the lower, the sum of all creation is better than the higher things alone.[17]

The problem arises once again, however, if we ask "how could God have given people free will, knowing—as He must have—that they would misuse it so badly?" Would everyone be much better off if we had a bit less "free will," or at least if we would have more desires to do good and fewer impulses to cause trouble and suffering?

There are several traditional responses to this. One is that God has allowed us moral latitude to provide a test of our virtue, for if we were all "naturally" good, there would be little question of good versus evil or salvation versus damnation. But it is open to question whether these distinctions are themselves desirable; wouldn't it have been better for humanity to have stayed in the Garden of Eden? Why did God have to create temptation, and what would have been lost from the world if Adam and Eve had been created with a bit more fortitude and obedience?

And then there is the familiar defense, "but doesn't the world need some evil, in order that we recognize the good?" But it isn't at all obvious that we need anything like the amount of evil and suffering we have in the world in order to recognize what is good. But even if we were to agree on this "free will" defense of the traditional conception of God as omnipotent, omniscient, and perfectly just, laying the blame for suffering to people's own choices, that would not solve the problem of evil. This is why we said that this line of "free will" defense is, at best, a partial solution. For not all human hardships and sufferings seem to be our own doing; much of the evil in the world does not seem to depend on human action in any way.

[17]St. Augustine, *Confessions*, Bk. VII, trans. R. S. Pine-Coffin (Harmondsworth, England: Penguin Books, 1961), pp. 136–49.

Even if we accept the claim that we cause evil through free choice, we still need to explain how the effects of our choices can seem so unrelated to the actions which are supposedly their cause. The Western religions' concept of "original sin" offers one such explanation, and it too finds its first expression in the Book of Job. When Job insists that he has done nothing to warrant his suffering, his friend Bildad suggests: "Inquire now of older generations and consider the experience of their fathers" (8:8), implying that the "sins of the fathers," the original sin of the whole human race, justifies Job's punishment. The punishment by God of any individual person, so goes the claim, is just, even though that particular individual did nothing to deserve it. Thus, God remains both Just and Good.

But this solution, rejected by Job himself, undermines our hopes that right action will be rewarded, and so again it belies the moral force which God is supposed to play in our lives. For if we were destined to suffer anyway for sins committed by others, then God would not appear to be just, and there would be little incentive for us to be faithful and follow God's commandments.

2.   Morality and Eastern Religions

The difficulties stemming from the "free will" solution to the problem of evil may be an indication to some that the Western religions' conceptions of God and of human nature are just not adequate. The Western religions characterize human beings as so limited in our understanding of God's justice that we can never predict the evil or good effects of our actions. But then how can we have any meaningful moral theory at all? Similarly, these religions claim that the wrongdoings we engage in during our short life here on earth are punished eternally by God, and our occasional good actions are rewarded eternally. The view that each and every human lifetime belongs to a unique eternal soul would seem to make all of God's rewards and punishments intrinsically unjust—way out of proportion to the insignificant actions which are supposedly their cause.

One interesting alternative to these conceptions of humans and God is offered by the Hindu religion, whose solution to the problem of evil is unique, in its use of the notion of "karma."

Hinduism is not actually a single religion. At best it is a family of religious beliefs and practices united, among other things, by a belief in the notion of social caste and a shared lineage from the Indic religions, such as Upanishadism, which we discussed in Chapter 1. There are no identifiable "core" Hindu *beliefs*—beyond a "reverence" for the Veda, though it is rarely read, and a participation in a social organization. Nevertheless, one may speak of "scriptures" and of ideas that over the centuries have been more at the center of Hindu culture than others. In general, a theistic world-view has more than any other dominated Hindu belief and guided religious practices. However, the Hindu conception of God is radically different from that shared by Judaism, Christianity, and Islam. The Hindu notion of human nature is also radically different from the Western notion. For most Hindus, human beings do have free will, but the free exercise of that will *changes* the human being. This is the doctrine of karma, which claims that any course of action that one undertakes creates a psychological tendency, or habit, to repeat it. One's free will thus becomes limited by one's own dispositions to action, or habits, dispositions that according to much ancient Indian thought continue even into a new birth. The inveterate smoker, for instance, is drawn to the taste of tobacco at a young age in her next incarnation.

Of all the many, many "scriptures" and sacred texts that over the centuries have moved the hearts of the faithful in India, the **Bhagavadgītā** (or "**Gītā**"), the "Song of God" (ca. 200 B.C.E.), clearly stands out as the most important. The *Gītā* is a small portion of a long epic poem. The central theme of the passages given below is the unique Hindu response to the "problem of evil". The warrior **Krishna** is the ruler of a neighboring state. Throughout most of the long poem Krishna is an ordinary person though an able, just, clever, and politically astute one. The key event of the entire epic is a battle over political succession. The political issues involved are complex; only one side of the warring family has a just claim. Five brothers are the principal representatives of the just family. (Although many noble and venerable sages and heroes fight against them.) Krishna joins the battle line as charioteer for the third of the five brothers, a champion archer named Arjuna. The *Gītā* is a dialogue between Krishna and Arjuna that occurs just minutes before the battle begins. In the dialogue, Krishna ceases to be a mere mortal and reveals Himself to Arjuna as God incarnate. So His advice to Arjuna, at least according to Hindu theists, is not simply the encouragement of a friend or the wise teachings of a guru; His words are the voice of God speaking to a human being in a time of personal moral crisis. Arjuna insists that it cannot be the morally right thing to do to fight and kill his kinsmen, teachers, friends, and loved ones who face him on the far side of the field of Kuruksetra.

"No good do I see in killing my own family in battle. I desire not victory, nor rule, nor pleasures, Krishna; what is power to us, enjoyments, or life, Govinda? Those who make rulership desirable for us, and enjoyments and pleasures, it is they that are arrayed in battle (against us), abandoning life and wealth. Teachers, fathers, sons, grandfathers, uncles, inlaws—these I do not wish to kill even if it means that I must die, Krishna—not even to rule the three worlds, why then for the earth?"[18]

---

[18]*Gita* 1.31b–35.

Despite the passion and sincerity of moral feeling that Arjuna expresses, Krishna insists that the right thing to do in the circumstances is to fight, to kill the opposing warriors, and to win the battle.

There are several dimensions to Krishna's explanation why fighting is the right course of action for Arjuna, and more commentary has been elicited by His response to Arjuna's plea for guidance than by any other comparably brief text, except perhaps the Torah and the Gospels. In the verses that follow (part of Krishna's reply), Krishna first explains the cosmic foundations of human action. Next He states His own motive as God for assuming mortal birth. Krishna goes on to talk again about human action and closes with a refrain recurring throughout the *Gītā*—injunctions about the practice of *yoga*, (i.e., spiritual "discipline"). Through such self-discipline in general—whether *karmayoga*, *jñānayoga*, or *bhaktiyoga* (the yoga of action, the yoga of knowledge and meditation, the yoga of love and devotion)—Krishna lays out the three "paths" by which one may live a spiritually transformed life.

[Krishna:] Without personal attachment undertake action, Arjuna, for just one purpose, for the purpose of sacrifice. From work undertaken for purposes other than sacrifice, this world is bound to the law of **karma.**[19] Having loosed forth creatures along with sacrifice, the Creator said of old, "With this may you bring forth fruit, let it be your horn-of-plenty.[20] Make the gods flourish with this and may the gods make you flourish. Mutually fostering one another, you will attain the supreme good. For made to flourish by sacrifice, the gods will give you the enjoyments you desire. One who not giving to them enjoys their gifts is nothing but a thief.". . . Know action to have its origin in the Absolute, Brahman, and Brahman to have its foundation in the Immutable. Therefore is the omnipresent Brahman established through all time in sacrifice. . . . Although I exist as the unborn, the imperishable self (*ātmā*), and although I exist as the Lord of beings, resorting to and controlling my own nature I come into (phenomenal) being by my own magical power of self-delimitation. Whenever there is a crisis of **dharma** [righteousness, the good, the cosmic direction], Arjuna, and a rising up of *adharma*, then I loose myself forth. For the protection of good people and for the destruction of evil-doers, for the establishment of *dharma*, I take birth age after age. . . . Just in the ways in which I am approached, so do I receive to my love. People on all sides follow the path that is mine, Arjuna. . . . Actions do not stain me; nor do I have desire for the fruits of works. The person who recognizes me as this way is himself not bound by dispositions of action. So knowing, very ancient seekers of liberation and enlightenment carried out works. Therefore simply do actions as were done of old by the ancients. What action is (and all its implications), and

[19]Ibid.
[20]Literally, "wish-fulfilling cow."

what inaction, even the seer-sages are confused on this score. To you I will explain that kind of action which when understood you will be free from the untoward and evil. . . . For action must be understood, and wrong action as well; inaction must be understood—deep, dark, and dense is the nature of action. Were one to see inaction in action and action in inaction, that person among mortals would be the one with wisdom, he, spiritually disciplined; would be the agent of all works. One whose instigations and undertakings are all free from the motive of personal desire, the wise see that person as the truly learned, as one whose personal dispositions have been burned up in the fire of knowledge. . . . Satisfied with whatever gain comes to him, passed beyond oppositions and dualities, untouched by jealousy, equal-minded and balanced in the face of both success and failure, such a person though he acts is not bound (by karmic dispositions). All dispositions dissolve and wash away when a person is free from attachment, "liberated," and has his mind firmly fixed in knowledge—acting in a spirit of sacrifice. . . . This world does not belong to one who fails to sacrifice, so how could the next, Arjuna? In this way, numerous diverse sacrifices are spread wide in the mouth of Brahman. Know them all as born in action. Thus knowing, you will be "liberated" and enlightened. The sacrifice that is knowledge, O you who are a great warrior, is superior to any sacrifice involving material things. All work and action in its entirety, Arjuna, culminates and is fulfilled in (spiritual) knowledge. . . . Even if of all sinners you are now the very worst evil-doer, once in the boat of knowledge you will safely cross over the crookedness of evil. As a fire kindled reduces its fuel to ashes, Arjuna, so the fire of knowledge makes ashes all *karma.* . . . In yoga, in "spiritual discipline," take your stand; son of Bharata, stand up and fight.[21]

Yet another approach to religion and the problem of evil is offered in Buddhism, whose Indian roots and spread throughout Asia was discussed in Chapter 1. In Buddhism, the problem of evil is avoided entirely, since Buddhism abandons any conception of an anthropomorphic God. Yet Buddhism retains a belief in moral obligation and in reason. The highest form of Buddhism confronts evil—or, rather, human suffering—by working to help others in need. The answer to "the problem of evil," in other words, is *compassion.* This is particularly true of the Northern, or Mahāyāna, doctrines. Against those Buddhists who encourage a course of spiritual discipline towards a solely personal end, the Mahāyāna argue that such an end is not the best and the highest. If we strive for our own personal salvation alone and if we intend to follow no career *("yāna")* helping others to the supreme good of *nirvāna,* we would belong to the "Hīnayāna," literally "a being with no career" (a term used by Mahāyānists in deprecation of such a "path"). Mahāyānists, "beings

[21]*Gītā* 3.9–12, 3.15, 4.6–8, 4.11, 4.14–19, 4.22–24, 4.31–33, 4.36–37, and 4.42b.

with wide and great careers," however, seek not only personal salvation but "deliverance of all sentient beings from suffering and ignorance." A follower of this "wide path" attempts to acquire the six moral, intellectual, and spiritual perfections *(pāramitā)* possessed by Siddhārtha Gautama who, in this conception, is less "the Buddha" than a *Bodhisattva*–one who has one foot in the bliss of *nirvāna,* so to say, but whose being is turned naturally through compassion toward achieving the welfare of all beings. Thus Mahāyāna is more world-affirming than "Hīnayāna," in that the development of individual perfections is the goal, not an extinction of individuality and personality in an other-worldly bliss. One does not aim at extinction of individual form; one needs individual form and body as a medium with which to help others.

The six personal perfections sought by Mahāyānists are liberality or charity, good moral character, patience or peace in the face of anger or desires, energy (energy to strive for the good), ability to maintain deep meditation, and, last, the most important, insight or wisdom *(prajñā)*.

Thus the natural world is in the Mahāyāna view not viewed as an evil place to be abandoned but as—could we only perceive it as such—the "Body of the Buddha," the *dharmakāya*. But even though nature comes to be viewed in such a positive way, Buddhist philosophy throughout the long history of Mahāyāna tends to be thoroughly "idealistic," and the answer to evil lies not in the world but in us.

3.   *The Problem of Evil and Shaken Faith*

Even the Hindu notion of karma and the Buddhist notion of compassion, however, fail to justify faith in the face of *indiscriminate* and awful acts of nature. There doesn't seem to be any religious world-view, at least any one which has a conception of goodness and morality, which can make random acts meaningful and sustain our faith without challenging our reason. During the Enlightenment, the European world found itself in a state of theological confusion because of a monstrous earthquake that killed thousands of people, including many children, in Lisbon, Portugal. And to make matters worse, the earthquake struck on a Sunday morning, just as people were in church worshiping, so that the pious people were more likely to be killed than the atheists who had drunk themselves to sleep on the beach. And today theists are forced to ask the same question after every such "natural" disaster: What could justify a punishment that killed innocent children and spared the guilty? Or what could justify a "test" in which people are killed just to see if they are still faithful? These sorts of occurrences incline us to believe nature is totally random, not governed by a good God at all.

No one, perhaps, has felt and written more incisively from within this tension than the pivotal French Enlightenment figure Pierre Bayle. With the Huguenot (French Protestants) persecution under Louis XIV, Bayle lost his teaching position (1681), was forced into exile in Holland and later suffered the loss of his brother, a Protestant cleric still in France. These losses, compounded with his expulsion from a Rotterdam teaching post (1693) for "sedition," put Bayle at the experiential center of the religious controversies racking his age. With all of his formidable scholarship, theological training, and personal losses, this "Christian Skeptic" brings the problem of evil to its absolute pitch in his article on the Paulicians in his *Historical and Critical Dictionary* (1697). In this selection from "Paulicians" (Armenian Manicheans), Bayle exposes the insufficiency of reason to resolve the dilemma using *any* sort of "free will" defense.

◆ on the Problem of Evil, by Pierre Bayle

Their fundamental doctrine was that of the two co-eternal principles which were independent one from another. This dogma inspires horror at first, and consequently it is strange that the Man-
ichean sect was able to deceive so many people. On the other hand,
it is so difficult to answer its objections concerning the origin of
evil that it is not astonishing that the hypothesis of the two principles, one good and the other evil, dazzled several ancient philosophers and found so many disciples in Christianity where the doctrine which teaches the enmity of the devils to the true God is
always accompanied by the doctrine which teaches the rebellion
and fall of one part of the good angels. . . . According to the Scripture there is only one principle of good, and nonetheless moral and
physical evil found their way into the human race. It is therefore
not against the nature of the good principle both to permit the introduction of moral evil and to punish crime, for it is not more evident that four and four are eight than it is evident that an event is
possible if it has happened. *Ab actu ad potentiam valet conse-
quentia* is one of the clearest and most incontestable axioms of all
metaphysics. Now here we find an invulnerable rampart, and that
is sufficient to insure the victory of the orthodox even though their
a priori reasons might be refuted. But is it true that they can be
refuted? I will answer, "Yes," for the way in which evil was introduced into the world under the dominion of a Supreme Being who
is infinitely good, all wise, and all powerful is not only inexplicable but even incomprehensible. Therefore, when we undertake to
explain why this Being permitted evil, we are confronted on every
side with objections which are more in accord with our natural
light of understanding and with our ideas of order than is our
explanation.

REASON IS INCAPABLE OF UNRAVELING THE QUESTION

If upon strictly unscriptual and rational grounds we undertake to ascertain the reasons for which sin entered into the world, we will find ourselves opposed by other reasons which have a greater appearance of truth and harmony and our ideas of order, no matter how good our own reasons might be. For example, if you say that God permitted sin in order to manifest His wisdom, which is more resplendent in the midst of the disorders which the evil of men produces every day than it would be in a state of innocence, you will be answered that one might as well compare the Godhead with a father who had let the legs of his children be broken in order to display before an entire city the skill which he has in setting bones; or with a monarch who would allow strife and seditions to spring up throughout his kingdom in order to acquire the glory of having put an end to them. The conduct of this father and of this monarch is so contrary to the clear and distinct ideas which we have of goodness and wisdom, and in general, of all the duties of a father and a king, that our reason cannot understand that God should act as they do. "But," you will say, "the ways of God are not our ways." I will say, "Go no further. Hold to this text of the Scripture (Isaiah 55:8) and make no further pretense to reasoning." Give up trying to tell us or convince us that without the fall of the first man the justice and mercy of God would have remained unknown, for we will answer you that there was nothing easier than to make known these two attributes to man. Nothing more than the idea of the sovereignly perfect Being makes known very clearly to sinful man that God possesses all of the virtues which are worthy in every way of an infinite nature. How much more then would this idea have made known to innocent man that God is infinitely just? Could it be that if man had remained innocent, God could not have punished anyone and therefore could not have exercised His justice? No, we cannot make this supposition, because if no one would have been worthy of punishment God could have exercised his attribute of justice perpetually by refraining from punishing anyone. Tell me what you think of two princes, one of which lets his subjects fall into abject wretchedness in order that he may deliver them after they have groaned in their misery for some time, and the other who preserves his subjects in a continual state of prosperity. Is not the latter better and more merciful than the first? Those who teach the Immaculate Conception of the Holy Virgin prove demonstratively that God shed forth upon her His mercy and redemptive grace more than upon other humans. But one does not have to be deeply versed in metaphysics to know, as does the veriest villager, that it is a greater goodness to prevent a man from falling into a ditch than to let him fall in it and then pull him out after an hour, and that it is better to keep a murderer from killing someone than to torture him on the rack for the murders that he has been permitted to commit. All of this warns us that we should not enter into dispute with the Manicheans without establishing first of all the dogma of "the elevation of faith and the abasement of reason."

THE DOCTRINE OF FREE AGENCY CANNOT ACCOUNT FOR THE PRESENCE
OF EVIL IN THE WORLD.

There are those who say that God permitted sin because He could not have prevented it without compromising the free agency of man, which was the best gift that He had given him. But they leave themselves open to many objections. The reason they give is fine enough and has a certain dazzling quality to it, and one even finds a certain grandeur in it; but even so, it can be opposed by reasons which are more within the reach of all men and founded more solidly upon common sense and our ideas of order.

Without having read the fine treatise of Seneca upon blessings, we know by the natural light of our intelligence that it is in the essence of a benefactor to refrain from giving any gift which he knows would be the ruin of the recipient. If this were not so, there would be no enemy so bitter that he would not heap gifts upon his adversary. We also know that it is the essence of a benefactor to go to any lengths to assure that his gifts will procure the happiness of the person whom he is honoring. If he could confer upon the recipient of his gifts the ability to use these gifts well and then refused to do so, we would say that he did not long retain the characteristics of a benefactor, and our opinion of him would not be any better if he could prevent his beneficiary from making ill-usage of his gifts and did not do so by curing him of all of his evil inclinations. These are ideas which are as well known to the common people as to the philosophers. I admit that one would not be obliged to prevent the ill-usage of a gift if the only way to do so were to break the arms and legs of its recipient, or to cast him into the bottom of a dungeon in irons, but in that case, it would be much better not to give the gift. However, if one could prevent an ill-usage of it by changing the disposition of the heart and in giving the recipient an inclination toward good, one should do it. Now this is what God could have done easily if He had willed it. . . .

IF HUMANS ACTED AS GOD IS SAID TO HAVE DONE,
THEY WOULD BE CONDEMNED.

There is no good mother who, having given permission to her daughters to go to a ball, would not revoke this permission if she were assured that they would there succumb to gallant enticings and part company with their virginity. Moreover, any mother who knowing most assuredly that this unfortunate event would infallibly take place and who would nonetheless let her daughters go to the ball after simply exhorting them to virtue and threatening them with disgrace if they returned home deflowered, would draw upon herself at least the merited condemnation of having loved neither her daughters nor chastity. No matter how hard she tried to justify her conduct by saying that she did not wish to infringe upon the liberty of her daughters, neither to show any lack of confidence in them, people would nonetheless answer her that her great circumspection was not called for and more befitted a spiteful step-dame than a mother. They would add that it would have been better to keep her daughters under her eye than to give them such a privilege of liberty or such marks of confidence so inappropriately.

This example shows the temerity of those who tell us that God permitted sin so as not to infringe upon the free agency of the first man. It is better to believe and be silent than to advance reasons which can be refuted by the examples which I have just given. . . .

FREE AGENCY WAS NOT A GOOD GIFT.

With these reasons it is easy to show that the free agency of the first man was not a good gift, since it was given to him inviolable in circumstances where he would use it for his own ruin, the ruin of the human race, the eternal damnation of the greater part of his descendants, and the introduction into the world of a dreadful deluge of moral and physical evils. We will never be able to understand how this gift could have been preserved in man because of God's goodness and because of His love of holiness. Again, those who say that there had to be free beings in order for God to be loved with a love freely chosen, feel in their conscience that this hypothesis does not satisfy the demands of reason, for when it is foreseen that these free beings will choose, not the love of good but the love of sin, it is easily seen that the intended purpose is frustrated, and thus it is not at all necessary to preserve free agency.

PROVIDENCE IS NOT EXONERATED BY DENYING DIVINE FOREKNOWLEDGE.

In addition, if you agree with those who come the closest to exonerating Providence and say that God did not foresee the fall of Adam, you gain very little. For He at least knew most certainly that the first man would run the risk of losing his innocence and introducing into the world all of the evils of pain and guilt which followed his revolt. Neither His goodness, His holiness, nor His wisdom could have permitted Him to run the risk of these events. Our reason convinces us most clearly that when a mother would let her daughters go to a ball knowing very certainly that they would run a great risk with respect to their honor, she would witness that she loved neither her daughters nor chastity. Furthermore, if we suppose that she has an infallible preservative against all temptations and does not give it to her daughters in sending them to the ball, we can be most assured that she is guilty and cares very little about the virginity of her daughters.

Let us carry this comparison a little further. Suppose that this mother herself went to the ball and happened to see through a window that one of her daughters was defending herself very feebly in some secluded corner against the pleadings of some young gallant. If she then saw that her daughter had only one step to take to acquiesce to the desires of the tempter and then did not rush to her aid to keep her from this pitfall, would we not justly say that she was acting as a cruel stepdame and that she would be capable of selling the honor of her own daughter?

· · · · · · · · · ·

Howsoever this be explained, it follows plainly, that God was willing that man should sin, and that he preferred this to the perpetual duration of innocence, which it was so easy for him to produce and ordain. Reconcile this if you can with the goodness he ought to have for his creatures, and the infinite love he ought to have for holiness.[22]

A popular response at this point is to refer to "God's mysterious ways" and to argue that we cannot possibly understand God's ultimate purposes. This is the eventual conclusion of the Book of Job. This response does succeed in answering the problem of evil, but only at considerable cost. In all of the arguments we have considered so far, and in most of the history of Western religion, belief in God, and belief in God's omnipotence, omniscience, and perfect justice, has been a matter of rational belief (whether this was considered a matter of knowledge or of faith). But with the reference to "God's mysterious ways," we mark a major breach with this rational tradition, and we admit that not only can we not know about God, but we cannot even understand or rationally argue these matters. In other words, the phrase "God's mysterious ways" solves the problem of evil only at the cost of ending discussion altogether.

D. REASON AND FAITH

Many philosophers and religious people do not object to this costly consequence. It is costly, they would argue, only to the interests of those who insist on arguing and rationalizing these religious matters; it need have no effect on religious belief itself. In the next section, we shall discuss some of these nonrational alternatives to the philosophy of religion. But it is first important to appreciate that there is a long history of efforts to demonstrate rationally the tenets of faith and to save a more or less traditional conception of God. The discrepancy between the claims of reason and the claims of faith was a particular concern for Islamic theologians, because of the role played by the prophet Mohammed in the Muslim faith. The Islamic scripture, the Qur'an, is believed by Muslims to be the actual word of God, or Allah, as revealed to

[22]From Pierre Bayle, "Paulicians," in *Historical and Critical Dictionary* (London: Harper, 1710).

Mohammed. Still, there were disputes after the prophet's death about the interpretation of scripture. How can the direct word of God be understood in different ways, some right and some wrong? How can mere human beings, uninformed by revelation, decide between competing interpretations? Islamic theology begins with these questions, which were understood as disputes between the authority of reason versus that of revelation in knowing the truth revealed by God.

The first Muslims to favor a rationalistic method in Qur'anic studies—called the Kalam—were the Mu't-Azilites, considered a heretical sect when they first began their school. Despite their radical method, however, the Mu'tazilites gained popularity. They were eventually challenged, however, and largely overshadowed, by the Ash'arites, who advocated applying rational method to Qur'anic interpretation, but only as an elucidation of the literal word of the Qur'an.

The Spanish Muslim, ibn-Rushd (called Averroës in the West) (1126–1198), is generally thought to be the culmination of Aristotelianism in Islamic theology. He advocated an Aristotelian metaphysics against the Platonism of earlier Islamic theologians. In the following passage, from *The Decisive Treatise Determining the Nature of the Connection Between Religion and Philosophy*, he claims that the pursuit of rational explanation is actually commanded by God. Somewhat ironically, but quite within the tradition set by the Ash'arites, ibn-Rushd justified his claim with scriptural authority.

◆ on the Philosophic Study of God, by ibn-Rushd

CHAPTER ONE. THE LAW MAKES PHILOSOPHIC STUDIES OBLIGATORY.

If teleological study of the world is philosophy, and if the Law commands such a study, then the Law commands philosophy.

We say: If the activity of 'philosophy' is nothing more than study of existing beings and reflection on them as indications of the Artisan, i.e. inasmuch as they are products of art (for beings only indicate the Artisan through our knowledge of the art in them, and the more perfect this knowledge is, the more perfect the knowledge of the Artisan becomes), and if the Law has encouraged and urged reflection on beings, then it is clear that what this name signifies is either obligatory or recommended by the Law.

The Law commands such a study.

That the Law summons to reflection on beings, and the pursuit of knowledge about them, by the intellect is clear from several verses of the Book of God, Blessed and Exalted, such as the saying of the Exalted, 'Reflect, you have vision' (Koran, LIX, 2): this is textual authority for the obligation to use intellectual reasoning, or a combination of intellectual and legal reasoning (VII, 185). Another example is His saying, 'Have they not studied the kingdom of the heavens and the earth, and whatever things God has created?': this is a text urging the study of the totality of beings. Again, God the Exalted has taught that one of those whom He singularly honoured by this knowledge was Abraham, peace on him, for the Exalted said (VI, 75), 'So we made Abraham see the kingdom of the heavens and the earth, that he might be' [and so on to the end of the verse]. The Exalted also said (LXXXVIII, 17–18), 'Do they not observe the camels, how they have been created, and the sky, how it has been raised up?' and He said (III, 191), 'and they give thought to the creation of the heavens and the earth', and so on in countless other verses.

This study must be conducted in the best manner, by demonstrative reasoning.

Since it has now been established that the Law has rendered obligatory the study of beings by the intellect, and reflection on them, and since reflection is nothing more than inference and drawing out of the unknown from the known, and since this is reasoning or at any rate done by reasoning, therefore we are under an obligation to carry on our study of beings by intellectual reasoning. It is further evident that this manner of study, to which the Law summons and urges, is the most perfect kind of study using the most perfect kind of reasoning; and this is the kind called 'demonstration.'

To master this instrument the religious thinker must make a preliminary study of logic, just as the lawyer must study legal reasoning. This is no more heretical in the one case than in the other. And logic must be learned from the ancient masters, regardless of the fact that they were not Muslims.

The Law, then, has urged us to have demonstrative knowledge of God the Exalted and all the beings of His creation. But it is preferable and even necessary for anyone, who wants to understand God the Exalted and the other beings demonstratively, to have first understood the kinds of demonstration and their conditions [of validity], and in what respects demonstrative reasoning differs from dialectical, rhetorical and fallacious reasoning. But this is not possible unless he has previously learned what reasoning as such is, and how many kinds it has, and which of them are valid and which invalid. This in turn is not possible unless he has previously learned the parts of reasoning, of which it is composed, i.e. the premises and their kinds. Therefore he who believes in the Law, and obeys its command to study beings, ought prior to his study to gain a knowledge of these things, which have the same place in theoretical studies as instruments have in practical activities.

For just as the lawyer infers from the Divine command to him to acquire knowledge of the legal categories that he is under obligation to know the various kinds of legal syllogisms, and which are valid and which invalid, in the same way he who would know

[God] ought to infer from the command to study beings that he is under obligation to acquire a knowledge of intellectual reasoning and its kinds. Indeed it is more fitting for him to do so, for if the lawyer infers from the saying of the Exalted, 'Reflect, you who have vision', the obligation to acquire a knowledge of legal reasoning, how much more fitting and proper that he who would know God should infer from it the obligation to acquire a knowledge of intellectual reasoning!

It cannot be objected: 'This kind of study of intellectual reasoning is a heretical innovation since it did not exist among the first believers.' For the study of legal reasoning and its kinds is also something which has been discovered since the first believers, yet it is not considered to be a heretical innovation. So the objector should believe the same about the study of intellectual reasoning. (For this there is a reason, which it is not the place to mention here.) But most [masters] of this religion support intellectual reasoning, except a small group of gross literalists, who can be refuted by [sacred] texts.[23]

There have been many other attempts to sustain a purely rational conception of the Judeo-Christian-Islamic God. Spinoza's **pantheism,** for example, is one of these many attempts to save belief in God while maintaining a rational picture of nature. More radical versions of pantheism deny that God is just and that He has any moral characteristics at all. In Spinoza's theory, however, which has often been compared to that of the Eastern religions, God is identical to the universe. He is not its creator. He is not a moral agent, so He has neither concern nor ability for the misfortunes and suffering of the world. He has no special concern for people and no concern for justice. If one defends an extreme determinism in which no one—not even God—has "free will," questions of moral responsibility, reward, and punishment become irrelevant, a matter of human vanity, nothing more.

This way of avoiding the problem of evil by advocating a more purely rational religious belief was quite common in the Enlightenment, that period of Western thought in which people were rebelling against medieval authority. The best example of this attitude was the French genius Voltaire. He was a vehement opponent of Christianity. ("I have heard enough how it took only twelve men to establish Christianity; I should like to prove that only one can destroy it.") But he wouldn't give up God, so he invented a new religion (that he in many ways borrowed from the English), which sheared the concept of God of all His moral attributes, thus avoiding the problem of evil by denying God His attribute of "justice." "It makes no more sense to say that God is just or unjust than it does to say that he is blue or green." For Voltaire, God was just a

[23]*op cit.* Hyman & Walsh, pp. 298–299.

"hypothesis," the creator who turned on the giant Newtonian machine but then left it to go on its own. This peculiarly truncated version of theism is usually called **deism.** It believes in God, but not much of one. It is essentially an appeal to the cosmological argument; and it is satisfied with a minimal deity, which stops far short of our traditional conception of God. Needless to say, Voltaire despised the "argument from design" with all of its hidden moralizing. The world is full of evil, Voltaire insisted, and there is no denying it. And since there is evil, there cannot be an all-powerful, all-knowing God who is also just. And there can be no appeal to His "mysterious ways." He has no "mysterious ways"; in fact, He has no "ways" at all. Thus Voltaire made his point against Leibniz and his "best of all possible worlds" hypothesis by imagining a whole book full of disasters and tragedies and evils of the most sadistic sort, all greeted rather foolishly by a Leibnizian character named Dr. Pangloss. The book was called *Candide,* and it remains one of the classics of Western literature.

The seeming irrationality of God's actions also haunted the great Russian novelist, Fyodor Dostoyevski, a devout Christian whose faith had been shaken many times, not least by the cruelty that he often witnessed (and of which he was occasionally the victim) in feudal Tsarist Russia. In his novel *The Brothers Karamazov,* he portrays a conversation between two of the three Karamazov brothers, Ivan—who like the author is wracked with doubts—and Alyosha—who has joined a monastery and aspires to be a true Christian. Ivan presents us with a vivid picure of how instances of patently unjust evil pit reason against faith, especially for someone who wants desperately to believe in God.

◆**from *The Brothers Karamazov,***
by Fyodor Dostoyevski

"It will reduce the scope of my argument to about a tenth of the total, but I still prefer to restrict myself to the subject of children. Not that that restriction is to my advantage. But, in the first place, it *is* possible to love children, at close quarters, even if they are dirty, even if they have ugly faces, although to me a child's face is never really ugly. In the second place, I also will not speak of adults at the moment, because, besides being disgusting and undeserving of love, they have something to compensate them for their suffering: they have eaten their apple of knowledge, they know about good and evil and are like gods themselves. And they keep eating the apple. But little children haven't eaten it. They're not yet guilty of anything. Do you like small children, Alyosha? I know you do and that you'll understand why I have chosen to speak exclusively of them. Well then, if they suffer here in this world, it's because they're paying for the sins of their fathers who ate the apple. But that is the reasoning of another world and it's incomprehensible to the human heart here on earth. No innocent should be made to suffer for another man's sins, especially innocents such as these!

· · · · · · · · · ·

"Do you understand this . . . my dear friend, my brother, you gentle novice who is so eager to spend his life in the service of God? Tell me, do you understand the purpose of this absurdity? Who needs it and why was it created? They say that man could not do without it on earth, for otherwise he would not be able to learn the difference between good and evil. But I say I'd rather not know about their damned good and evil than pay such a terrible price for it. I feel that all universal knowledge is not worth that child's tears when she was begging 'gentle Jesus' to help her! I'm not even talking about the suffering of adults: they, at least, have eaten their apple of knowledge, so the hell with them. But it's different when it comes to children. It seems I'm hurting you, Alyosha, my boy. You don't look very well. I won't go on if you don't want me to."

"Never mind. I want to suffer too," Alyosha mumbled.

"One more little sketch then, the last, and that only because it's a rather curious little story and a very typical one.

"Well, this happened early in our nineteenth century, during the darkest days of serfdom—and, by the way, long live our Tsar Alexander II, the Liberator of the People! Well then, at the turn of the century, there lived a retired general, a man with the highest connections, a big landowner, one of those, you know (although even at that time there were only a few such left), who, upon retiring from the service of their country, feel sure that they have earned the right of life and death over those subjected to them. Yes, there used to be such people then. This general lived on his estate, which had two thousand serfs. He strutted around, feeling immensely important, and bullying his lesser neighbors as if they were hangers-on and clowns obliged to amuse him. He had hundreds of hounds and just about as many kennel attendants, all dressed in special livery and every one of them mounted.

"It so happened that one day an eight-year-old boy, playing in the courtyard, threw a stone and inadvertently hit the General's favorite hound in the leg, injuring it. 'Why is my favorite hound limping?' the General demanded, and he was informed that the boy had hit it with a stone. 'So it was you,' the General said, looking the boy up and down. 'Lock him up.' They took the boy away from his mother and locked him up in the guardroom for the whole night. The next day, at dawn, the General rode out to the hunt in full dress, surrounded by his obsequious neighbors, hounds, kennel attendants, huntsmen, every one of them on horseback. All the serfs of the estate were summoned too, for their edification, and so was the boy's mother. They brought the boy out of the guardroom. It was a bleak, foggy, raw day—an ideal day for hunting. The General ordered the boy stripped naked. The boy was shivering. He seemed paralyzed with fear. He didn't dare utter a sound. 'Off with him now, chase him!' 'Hey, you, run, run!' a flunkey yelled, and the boy started to run. 'Sic 'im!' the General roared. The whole pack was set on the boy and the hounds tore him to pieces before his mother's eyes. I believe that, as a result of this, the General was later declared incompetent to administer his own estates without an appointed supervisory body. . . . But perhaps you could tell me what should have been done in this case? Perhaps he ought to have been shot, to satisfy the moral indignation that such an act arouses in us? Well, speak up, my boy, go on!"

"Yes, shot . . . " Alyosha murmured, raising his eyes to his brother with a strange, faint, twisted grin.

"Good!" Ivan cried with affected delight. "Now, if you say so, it really shows that . . . Ah, you little novice, so there is that devil lurking in your heart too, you wicked Alyosha Karamazov, you!"

"What I said was pretty stupid, but. . . ."

"Yes, that 'but' is just the thing!" Ivan cried. "I want you to know, novice, that absurdity is very much needed on this earth of ours. Indeed, the whole universe is founded on absurdity, and, perhaps, without absurdity there would be nothing at all. There are a few things we do know, after all."

· · · · · · · · · ·

Ivan remained silent for a moment and suddenly his face grew very sad.

"I want you to understand me," he said, "I spoke only of small children to make my point more obvious. I didn't mention the other human tears with which our earth is soaked from crust to core, because I was deliberately narrowing the subject. I'm nothing but a bug and I most humbly admit that it's quite beyond me why things are arranged the way they are. I suppose that men themselves are to blame for it: they were given a paradise on earth, but they wanted freedom and they stole fire from heaven, although they knew that it would bring them unhappiness. So there's no reason to be sorry for them. All that my puny, Euclidean, earthling's mind can grasp is that there is such a thing as suffering, that no one can be blamed for it, that quite uncomplicatedly cause precedes effect, that everything that flows finds its proper level—but then all that is just Euclidean gibberish, and, being aware of that fact, I cannot agree to live by it! What good does it to do me to know that no one is to blame, that every effect is determined by a cause, which itself is an effect of some other cause, and so on, and that, therefore, no one should ever be blamed for anything? For, even though I may know it, I still need retribution. Without it I'd rather destroy myself. And I must have that retribution not somewhere far off in infinity but here, on earth. I want to see it myself. I believe in justice and I want to see justice done with my own eyes; if I should be dead by that time, I want to be brought back to life, because the idea that, when justice finally does triumph, I won't even be there to witness it is too abhorrent to me. No, I want to see with my own eyes the lamb lie down with the lion and the resurrected victim rise and embrace his murderer. I want to be here when everyone understands why the world has been arranged the way it is. It is on that craving for understanding that all human religions are founded, so I am a believer. But then, what about the children? How will we ever account for their sufferings? For the hundredth time I repeat, there are many questions that could be asked, but I ask you only one—about the children—because I believe it conveys fully and clearly what I am trying to tell you. Listen, even if we assume that every person must suffer because his suffering is necessary to pay for eternal harmony, still do tell me, for God's sake, where the children come in. If the suffering of little children is needed to complete the sum total of suffering required to pay for the truth, I don't want that truth, and I declare in advance that all the truth in the world is not worth the price! And finally, I don't really want to see the mother of the little boy embrace the man who set the hounds on him to tear him apart! She won't be able to forgive him. If she wants to, she may forgive him for herself, for having caused her, the mother, infinite suffering. But she has no right to forgive him for her child torn to pieces. She may not forgive him, even if the child chooses to forgive him himself. And if I am right, if they cannot forgive, what harmony can there be? Is there one single creature in the whole world who could forgive or would have the right to do so? No, I want no part of any harmony; I don't want it, out of love for mankind. I prefer to remain with my unavenged suffering and my unappeased anger—*even if I happen to be wrong.* I feel, moreover, that such harmony is rather overpriced. We cannot afford to pay so much for a ticket. And so I hasten to return the ticket I've been sent. If I'm honest, it is my duty to return it as long as possible before the show. And that's just what I'm trying to do, Alyosha. It isn't that I reject God; I am simply returning Him most respectfully the ticket that would entitle me to a seat."

"That's rebellion," Alyosha said softly, lowering his eyes.

"Rebellion? I wish you hadn't used that word," Ivan said feelingly. "I don't believe it's possible to live in rebellion, and I want to live! Tell me yourself—I challenge you: let's assume that you were called upon to build the edifice of human destiny so that men would finally be happy and would find peace and tranquility. If you knew that, in order to attain this, you would have to torture just one single creature, let's say the little girl who beat her chest so desperately in the outhouse, and that on her unavenged tears you could build that edifice, would you agree to do it? Tell me and don't lie!"

"No, I would not," Alyosha said softly.[24]

[24]Fyodor Dostoyevski, *The Brothers Karamazov*, trans. Andrew R. MacAndrew (New York: Bantam, 1970).

The number of alternative religions during this intellectually creative period of European history was truly astounding. But virtually all had approximately the same purpose: to continue to believe in God, at least nominally, but to avoid the problem of evil by cutting out at least one of God's traditional attributes—in other words, to make it more *rational* to have faith. During this period Kant invented his "moral proof," attempting to plug up the problem of evil by postponing all judgments of justice until some indefinite future date. It was also during this period that many of the still-popular formulas, "God is the energy of the universe," "God is life," and "God is universal love," became influential and respectable. The problem with these moves is already familiar: It is not clear whether they are, as they seem, revisions of the concept of God or rather subtle denials of God's existence. Many people have doubts about their religion at one time or another, but very few are willing to jump immediately from theism to atheism (although people often jump from atheism to theism in a single "revelation"). Accordingly, people who are torn between religious belief on the one hand and arguments against such belief on the other often adopt an ambiguous intermediary position, holding onto the name of God explicitly but sometimes giving up much of the substance of their traditional belief. And just as this is an important crisis in individual lives, it is also a crisis in history. The Enlightenment was one such period in history. The outcome is by no means inevitably atheism; it might just as well be a renewed commitment to religion. But at least, such crises require rigorous thinking and a renewed attempt to understand and justify beliefs that were once taken for granted.

E. FAITH AND IRRATIONALITY

Whenever you can defend your belief rationally it is obviously desirable to do so. The move from rationality to irrationality in the defense of religion, therefore, is a serious step. Kant, who defended belief in God as a matter of faith, nevertheless defended this belief as rational. But there have always been religious people who have defended faith against reason, emphasizing the impossibility of rational justification and the irrelevance of the usual forms of understanding and knowledge where religion is concerned. In some cases, particularly in modern times, this step away from rationality may be a convenient escape from arguments and doubts that have become too overpowering. But it is not always, or even usually, taken for this reason. As we've seen, there has always been an enthusiastic movement within the sometimes overly formal confines of all the organized religions and dogmas to emphasize the experience of religious belief, called *mysticism*. Such experience may well be indescribable and incommunicable. (Philosophers would thereby say it is **ineffable.**) But it is precisely the fact that it defies description and contradicts our everyday rational beliefs that makes such experiences so important to those who have had them.

GOD AS EXPERIENCE   In earlier chapters, we discussed the rationalist notion of intuition, a special kind of experience that allows us to know some things for certain without argument and without abstraction from experience in the usual sense. According to the rationalists, we know the basic principles of logic and arithmetic in this way, and perhaps the basic principles of metaphysics as well. But when we introduced intuition, however, we emphasized that not everyone believed that intuition was part of rationality. In addition to rational insight, there may also be, according to most religious mystics, extra-rational or even irrational insight. Their epistemology is often ambiguous at this point. On the one hand, mystics want to deny the rational nature of their intuitions. But at the same time, they want to insist that what they experience is true. You can see how this will generate considerable confusion. When the mystic insists that his experience is true, he has made a claim that is on a par with the rationalist's claim (whether they agree or disagree in their conclusions). If they disagree, that is, if the mystic insists that there is a God (perhaps he has even "seen" Him) and the rationalist denies it, it should be obvious that there will be little room for constructive argument. The mystic considers the rationalist's arguments irrelevant; the rationalist considers the mystic obstinate and unwilling to argue rationally. At this point, assuming the discussion does not degenerate to name-calling and fisticuffs, the rationalist will probably storm out of the room in frustration and the mystic, like a Zen master, may just shrug his shoulders. In such a case, that is probably the most rational response for both of them.

The mystic need not argue that what he has experienced is true, however. He might insist only that what he has "seen" is extremely important to him personally. And if he does so, it is clear that he need have no disagreement whatsoever with the rationalist, either in conclusions or in methods. They are different, of course, but not at odds. This is rare, of course, since it is a rare person indeed who does not yield to the temptation to insist that his or her experience is the truth about reality as well. Or the mystic could argue, as the Islamic mystics (or *Sufis*) from al-Ghazalion have done, that rationalist and mystical experience lead to the same truths by different "paths." But whether the mystical experience is an intuition of the (more or less) traditional Judeo-Christian God, whether it is a vision of the Virgin or simply a "feeling of oneness with the universe," whether the experience is the result of twenty years of prayer and meditation or induced in an evening with peyote or mescaline, the philosophical question that follows is always one of interpretation. Without denying the reality of the experience, the question is always whether one ought to interpret the experience as the knowledge of reality. Is it just an experience? perhaps beautiful, worth repeating, even worth building your life around? It is very different to claim that the experience is true, a breakthrough in our normal perceptions (or, perhaps, our everyday illusions) to the reality behind them. This is not to say that the mystic must be wrong. It is only to say that, given the impossibility of argument, there is no way to decide the issue. Just because the mystic is "irrational" doesn't mean that he is wrong.

Following the Enlightenment, particularly in Germany, religion took a dramatic swing to the subjective. Attempts at rational defense were given up entirely. The German Romantic philosopher Friedrich Schlierma-cher insisted that religion was simply a matter of intense feelings of dependence, nothing more. (His contemporary, Hegel, wryly retorted that this would make a dog a better Christian than most of us.) Other philosophers turned to modernized mysticism, including very contemporary experiments with drug-induced experiences, in an attempt to save their religion from rational criticism. The American philosopher William James, for example, wrote about mysticism in his book *The Varieties of Religious Experience* and defended the idea that personal religious experience has a central place in religion and that mysticism is the root of such experience. He too insists that mystical experiences are essentially "ineffable," that is, impossible to describe to anyone else, and he compares this experience with the experience of listening to a symphony or being in love. But he also insists that mystical experiences provide us with knowledge, "states of insight into depths of truth unplumbed by the discursive intellect." And so James concludes that "the existence of mystical states absolutely overthrows the pretension of non-mystical states to be the sole and ultimate dictators of what we may believe." "The mystic," he writes, "is *invulnerable*, and must be left, whether we like it or not, in undisturbed enjoyment of his creed."[25]

THE LEAP OF FAITH   The best and most famous of all of these "new" Christians was an eccentric Danish philosopher, Søren Kierkegaard, who is often claimed as the father of both the "new" Christianity and that nonreligious philosophy called "existentialism." Kierkegaard was born into a society in which everyone was a Christian; they all believed the same dogmas, without thinking about them. They all went to the same (Lutheran) churches for Sunday services and Friday afternoon bingo games and enjoyed these social gatherings immensely. They were all entitled to call themselves "Christians" just by virtue of the fact that they had been born of certain parents, brought as children to certain churches, and continued to mouth certain doctrines that they didn't understand or care to understand in the slightest. What they all lacked

[25]William James, "The Varieties of Religious Experience," in *The Writings of William James*, ed. John J. McDermott (New York: Random House, 1967).

was passion. Their religion and they themselves, according to Kierke-gaard, were boring through and through. Whatever happened to the phrase "the fear of God in their hearts"? These people felt no "fear," just the security of a comfortable and self-righteous society and warm swill of beer in their bellies, he complained. And Kierkegaard, who had been brought up in an unusually devout Lutheran home, was disgusted with them. This isn't Christianity, he insisted, and the sophisticated disputes over doctrine and dogma had nothing more to do with being religious than the calculations of an accountant at tax time.

Accordingly, Kierkegaard offered his alternative—a new (in fact, very old) way of seeing oneself as a Christian. Rational argument was irrelevant. The doctrines of Christianity, he admitted, were absolutely absurd. But that didn't matter. In fact, it was the very absurdity of these beliefs that made the passion of Christianity possible. After all, if it were simply a matter of accepting some proposition, why should we feel anything? And "proofs" of God's existence, needless to say, were as irrelevant—in fact, offensive—as you could imagine. "Christianity is passion!" he insisted. "Religion is feeling and commitment." No talk of "truth"—unless you mean simply **subjective truth,** truth for me alone. No talk of "proof" and no talk of "rationality." There is simply, to use his most famous phrase, *the leap of faith,* across the borders of rationality and thinking to the passion-filled life of old-fashioned Christian fear and awe of God. "My only analogy is Socrates. My task is a Socratic task—to revise the conception of what it means to be a Christian."

Kierkegaard's move away from rationality is characterized as a rejection of "objectivity." Being a Christian, he says, is not a matter of "objective faith" (consisting of reason, doctrines, and "proofs") but of subjectivity, passion, and "inwardness."

◆ on Subjective Truth, by Søren Kierkegaard

. . . The objective faith, what does that mean? It means a sum of doctrinal propositions. But suppose Christianity were nothing of the kind; suppose on the contrary it were inwardness, and hence also the paradox, so as to thrust the individual away objectively, in order to obtain significance for the existing individual in the in-wardness of his existence, in order to place him as decisively as no judge can place an accused person, between time and eternity in time, between heaven and hell in the time of salvation. The objec-tive faith—it is as if Christianity also had been promulgated as a little system, if not quite so good as the Hegelian; it is as if Christ—aye, I speak without offense—it is as if Christ were a professor, and as if the Apostles had formed a little scientific society. Verily, if it was once difficult to become a Christian, now I believe it becomes increasingly difficult year by year, because it has now become so easy that the only ambition which stirs any competition is that of becoming a speculative philosopher. And yet the speculative philosopher is perhaps at the farthest possible remove from Christianity, and it is perhaps far preferable to be an offended individual who nevertheless sustains a relation to Christianity than a speculative philosopher who assumes to have understood it.

· · · · · · · · · ·

Suppose, on the other hand, that subjectivity is the truth, and that subjectivity is an existing subjectivity, then, if I may so express myself, Christianity fits perfectly into the picture. Subjectivity culminates in passion, Christianity is the paradox, paradox and passion are a mutual fit, and the paradox is altogether suited to one whose situation is, to be in the extremity of existence. Aye, never in all the world could there be found two lovers so wholly suited to one another as paradox and passion, and the strife between them is like the strife between lovers, when the dispute is about whether he first aroused her passion, or she his. And so it is here; the existing individual has by means of the paradox itself come to be placed in the extremity of existence. And what can be more splendid for lovers than that they are permitted a long time together without any alteration in the relationship between them, except that it becomes more intensive in inwardness?[26]

Religion is a confrontation with the unknown, not something knowable.

But what is this unknown something with which the Reason collides when inspired by its paradoxical passion, with the result of unsettling even man's knowledge of himself? It is the Unknown. It is not a human being, in so far as we know what man is; nor is it any other known thing. So let us call this unknown something: *the God.* It is nothing more than a name we assign to it. The idea of demonstrating that this unknown something (the God) exists, could scarcely suggest itself to the Reason. For if the God does not exist it would of course be impossible to prove it; and if he does exist it would be folly to attempt it. For at the very outset, in beginning my proof, I would have presupposed it, not as doubtful but as certain (a presupposition is never doubtful, for the very reason that it is a presupposition), since otherwise I would not begin, readily understanding that the whole would be impossible if he did not exist. But if when I speak of proving the God's existence I mean that I propose to prove that the Unknown, which exists, is the God, then I express myself unfortunately. For in that case I do not prove anything, least of all an existence, but merely develop the content of a conception. Generally speaking, it is a difficult matter to prove that anything exists; and what is still worse for the intrepid souls

[26]Søren Kierkegaard, *Concluding Unscientific Postscript*, trans. David F. Swenson and Walter Lowrie (Princeton, NJ: Princeton University Press, 1941).

who undertake the venture, the difficulty is such that fame scarcely awaits those who concern themselves with it. The entire demonstration always turns into something very different and becomes an additional development of the consequences that flow from my having assumed that the object in question exists. Thus I always reason from existence, not toward existence, whether I move in the sphere of palpable sensible fact or in the realm of thought. I do not for example prove that a stone exists, but that some existing thing is a stone. The procedure in a court of justice does not prove that a criminal exists, but that the accused, whose existence is given, is a criminal. Whether we call existence an *accessorium* [something predicated] or the eternal *prius* [first given or assumed], it is never subject to demonstration. Let us take ample time for consideration. We have no such reason for haste as have those who from concern for themselves or for the God or for some other thing, must make haste to get existence demonstrated. Under such circumstances there may indeed to need for haste, especially if the prover sincerely seeks to appreciate the danger that he himself, or the thing in question, may be nonexistent unless the proof is finished and does not surreptitiously entertain the thought that it exists whether he succeeds in proving it or not.

If it were proposed to prove Napoleon's existence from Napoleon's deeds, would it not be a most curious proceeding? His existence does indeed explain his deeds, but the deeds do not prove *his* existence, unless I have already understood the word "his" so as thereby to have assumed his existence. But Napoleon is only an individual, and in so far there exists no absolute relationship between him and his deeds; some other person might have performed the same deeds. Perhaps this is the reason why I cannot pass from the deeds to existence. If I call these deeds the deeds of Napoleon the proof becomes superfluous, since I have already named him; if I ignore this, I can never prove from the deeds that they are Napoleon's, but only in a purely ideal manner that such deeds are the deeds of a great general, and so forth. But between the God and his works there is an absolute relationship; God is not a name but a concept. Is this perhaps the reason that his *essentia involvit existentiam* [essence entails existence]? The works of God are such that only the God can perform them. Just so, but where then are the works of the God? The works from which I would deduce his existence are not directly and immediately given. The wisdom in nature, the goodness, the wisdom in the governance of the world—are all these manifest, perhaps, upon the very face of things? Are we not here confronted with the most terrible temptations to doubt, and is it not impossible finally to dispose of all those doubts? But from such an order of things I will surely not attempt to prove God's existence; and even if I began I would never finish, and would in addition have to live constantly in suspense, lest something so terrible should suddenly happen that my bit of proof would be demolished. From what works then do I propose to derive the proof? From the works as apprehended through an ideal interpretation, i.e., such as they do not immediately reveal themselves. But in that case it is not from the works that I make the proof; I merely develop the ideality I have presupposed, and because of my confidence in *this* I make so bold as to defy all objections, even those that have not yet been made. In beginning my proof I presuppose the ideal interpretation, and also that I will be successful in carrying it through; but what else is this but to presuppose that the God exists, so that I really begin by virtue of confidence in him?[27]

You can see how little Kierkegaard thinks of the ingenious "proofs" of God's existence, as well as all attempts to "know" Him. The point of religion, he says, is precisely not to know, but rather to feel. And it is the absurdity and the irrationality of Christian doctrines, he insists, that makes this rare intensity of feeling possible.

. . . The absurd is precisely by its objective repulsion the measure of the intensity of faith in inwardness. Suppose a man who wishes to acquire faith; let the comedy begin. He wishes to have faith, but he wishes also to safeguard himself by means of an objective inquiry and its approximation-process. What happens? With the help of the approximation-process the absurd becomes something different; it becomes probable, it becomes increasingly probable, it becomes extremely and emphatically probable. Now he is ready to believe it, and he ventures to claim for himself that he does not believe as shoemakers and tailors and simple folk believe, but only after long deliberation. Now he is ready to believe it; and lo, now it has become precisely impossible to believe it. Anything that is almost probable, or probable, or extremely and emphatically probable, is something he can almost know, or as good as know, or extremely and emphatically almost *know*—but it is impossible to *believe*. For the absurd is the object of faith, and the only object that can be believed.[28]

Christianity, Kierkegaard concludes, is suffering, the suffering that comes with the anticipation of our own death and our feeling of smallness and insignificance when we consider the eternal order of things. And for those who try to minimize this suffering through professional "understanding" and knowledge, Kierkegaard has little but sarcasm: "*The two ways.* One is to suffer; the other is to become a professor of the fact that another suffered."

[27]Søren Kierkegaard, *Philosophical Fragments,* trans. David Swenson (Princeton, NJ: Princeton University Press, 1936).
[28]Kierkegaard, *Concluding Unscientific Postscript.*

GOD AS ULTIMATE CONCERN   Following Kierkegaard, Christian "irrational-ism" changed the complexion of Western religion and gave faith a meaning that is not vulnerable to rational arguments. Recently Paul Tillich proposed an extremely powerful form of Christianity that also gives up the traditional view of God and moves the focus of the religion to purely personal concerns and commitments. These are our religion, and we don't need anything more.

◆the Ultimate Concern, by Paul Tillich

RELIGIOUS SYMBOLS

We have discussed the meaning of symbols generally because, as we said, man's ultimate concern must be expressed symbolically! One may ask: Why can it not be expressed directly and properly? If money, success, or the nation is someone's ultimate concern, can this not be said in a direct way without symbolic language? Is it not only in those cases in which the content of the ultimate concern is called "God" that we are in the realm of symbols? The answer is that everything which is a matter of unconditional concern is made into a god. If the nation is someone's ultimate concern, the name of the nation becomes a sacred name and the nation receives divine qualities which far surpass the reality of the being and functioning of the nation. The nation then stands for and symbolizes the true ultimate, but in an idolatrous way. Success as ultimate concern is not the natural desire of actualizing potentialities, but its readi-ness to sacrifice all other values of life for the sake of a position of power and social predominance. The anxiety about not being a success is an idolatrous form of the anxiety about divine condem-nation. Success is grace; lack of success, ultimate judgment. In this way concepts designating ordinary realities become idolatrous symbols of ultimate concern.

The reason for this transformation of concepts into symbols is the character of ultimacy and the nature of faith. That which is the true ultimate transcends the realm of finite reality infinitely. Therefore, no finite reality can express it directly and properly. Re-ligiously speaking, God transcends his own name. This is why the use of his name easily becomes an abuse or a blasphemy. Whatever we say about that which concerns us ultimately, whether or not we call it God, has a symbolic meaning. It points beyond itself while participating in that to which it points. In no other way can faith ex-press itself adequately. The language of faith is the language of symbols. If faith were what we have shown that it is not, such an assertion could not be made. But faith, understood as the state of being ultimately concerned, has no language other than symbols.

When saying this I always expect the question: Only a symbol? He who asks this question shows that he has not understood the difference between signs and symbols nor the power of symbolic language, which surpasses in quality and strength the power of any nonsymbolic language. One should never say "only a symbol," but one should say "not less than a symbol." With this in mind we can now describe the different kinds of symbols of faith.

The fundamental symbol of our ultimate concern is God. It is always present in any act of faith, even if the act of faith includes the denial of God. Where there is ultimate concern, God can be denied only in the name of God. One God can deny the other one. Ultimate concern cannot deny its own character as ultimate. Therefore, it affirms what is meant by the word "God." Atheism, consequently, can only mean the attempt to remove any ultimate concern—to remain unconcerned about the meaning of one's existence. Indifference toward the ultimate question is the only imaginable form of atheism. Whether it is possible is a problem which must remain unsolved at this point. In any case, he who denies God as matter of ultimate concern affirms God, because he affirms ultimacy in his concern. God is the fundamental symbol for what concerns us ultimately. Again, it would be completely wrong to ask: So God is nothing but a symbol? Because the next question has to be: A symbol for what? And then the answer would be: For God! God is symbol for God. This means that in the person of God we must distinguish two elements: the element of ultimacy, which is a matter of immediate experience and not symbolic in itself, and the element of concreteness, which is taken from our ordinary experience and symbolically applied to God. The man whose ultimate concern is a sacred tree has both the ultimacy of concern and the concreteness of the tree which symbolizes his relation to the ultimate. The man who adores Apollo is ultimately concerned, but not in an abstract way. His ultimate concern is symbolized in the divine figure of Apollo. The man who glorifies Jahweh, the God of the Old Testament, has both an ultimate concern and a concrete image of what concerns him ultimately. This is the meaning of the seemingly cryptic statement that God is the symbol of God. In this qualified sense God is the fundamental and universal content of faith.

It is obvious that such an understanding of the meaning of God makes the discussions about the existence or nonexistence of God meaningless. It is meaningless to question the ultimacy of an ultimate concern. This element in the idea of God is in itself certain. The symbolic expression of this element varies endlessly through the whole history of mankind. Here again it would be meaningless to ask whether one or another of the figures in which an ultimate concern is symbolized does "exist." If "existence" refers to something which can be found within the whole of reality, no divine being exists. The question is not this, but: Which of the innumerable symbols of faith is most adequate to the meaning of faith? In other words, which symbol of ultimacy expresses the ultimate without idolatrous elements? This is the problem, and not the so-called "existence of God"—which is in itself an impossible combination of words. God as the ultimate in man's ultimate concern is more certain than any other certainty, even that of oneself. God as symbolized in a divine figure is a matter of daring faith, of courage and risk.

God is the basic symbol of faith, but not the only one. All the qualities we attribute to him, power, love, justice, are taken from finite experiences and applied symbolically to that which is beyond finitude and infinity. If faith calls God "almighty," it uses the human experience of power in order to symbolize the content of its infinite concern, but it does not describe a highest being who can do as he pleases. So it is with all the other qualities and with all the actions, past, present, and future, which men attribute to God. They are symbols taken from our daily experience, and not information about what God did once upon a time or will do sometime in the future. Faith is not the belief in such stories, but it is the acceptance of symbols that express our ultimate concern in terms of divine actions.

Another group of symbols of faith are manifestations of the divine in things and events, in persons and communities, in words and documents. This whole realm of sacred objects is a treasure of symbols. Holy things are not holy in themselves, but they point beyond themselves to the source of all holiness, that which is of ultimate concern.[29]

Notice how far Tillich has moved from the traditional Judeo-Christian-Islamic conception of God. Yet he is still a theist and a Christian. But it is not clear that "God" means the same for Tillich as it does in the Old and New Testaments. God is a symbol of "ultimate concern." Nevertheless, is this God as Christians are supposed to think of Him? The belief in God is now expanded to represent the fact that one finds his or her life meaningful. Tillich says that this "makes the discussions about the existence or nonexistence of God meaningless." It also undercuts the Western idea that God is a single kind of being with the characteristics we discussed earlier, and brings Tillich's theism very close to the *general* idea of religion which Nishitani described in the passage we looked at earlier. God is whatever concerns us ultimately, whatever is most important in our lives. This is even true, Tillich says, when one denies the existence of God. "Where there is ultimate concern, God can be denied only in the name of God."

[29]Paul Tillich, *Dynamics of Faith* (New York: Harper & Row; London: George Allen and Unwin, 1957).

F. DOUBT

One can be an atheist and still be religious. A Zen Buddhist, for example, may be extremely religious, but he or she does not believe in God. One can be religious as a humanist—as a lover of humanity—and not believe in God. Religion, in general, is the sense that something, at least, is sacred. But, in the context of traditional Western religion, being an *atheist* means one thing in particular, not believing in God. For some, atheism is not merely an intellectual position, it is a tragedy. For others, it is simply the logical conclusion of contemporary rationality and a proper antidote for centuries of superstition. In the following two selections, we will see the difference between these views. The first is another selection from the Russian novelist Fyodor Dostoyevski, who found himself facing unwelcome and terrifying doubts abut Christianity. He reflects his despair in all of his works. His doubts began with the problem of evil but now develop to such a pitch that he begins to wonder whether the whole of Christianity has been nothing more than a sham, so much so that if Christ were to return as promised, He would be burned as a heretic.

Here again is Dostoyevski, from *The Brothers Karamazov:*

[Ivan to Alyosha] ". . . do you find acceptable the idea that those for whom you are building that edifice should gratefully receive a happiness that rests on the blood of a tortured child and, having received it, should continue to enjoy it eternally?"

"No, I do not find that acceptable," Alyosha said and his eyes suddenly flared up. "But a moment ago you asked whether there was in the world 'a single creature who could forgive.' Well, there is. And He can forgive everyone for everything, because He Himself gave His innocent blood for everyone's sins and for everyone's sake. You forgot to mention Him, although it is on Him that the edifice must be founded, it is to Him that they will sing, 'You were right, O Lord, for Your ways have now been revealed to us!'"

"You mean 'the one without sin' and His blood! No, Alyosha, I hadn't forgotten about Him. Indeed, I was wondering how long it would take you to bring Him into our discussion, because the people on your side usually make use of Him above all else in their arguments. You know—well, don't laugh now—about a year or so ago I composed a sort of poem and, if you're willing to waste, say, another ten minutes with me, I could recite it to you."

"You? You wrote a poem?"

"Why should an author forego even one listener, after all?" Ivan said with a grin. "So, are you willing to hear it?"

"I'm listening attentively."

"My poem is called 'The Grand Inquisitor.' It's a ridiculous piece really, but I'd like you to hear it."

THE GRAND INQUISITOR

"Fifteen centuries have passed since He promised to come in His glory, fifteen centuries since His prophet wrote, 'Behold, I come quickly.' 'Of that day and hour knoweth no man, neither the Son, but the Father,' as He Himself announced when He was still on earth. But men still wait for Him with the same faith, with the same love. Nay, with even greater faith, for fifteen centuries have passed without a sign from heaven to mankind.

". . . He decided to show Himself, if only for a moment, to His people, long-suffering, tormented, sinful people who loved Him with a childlike love. My story takes place in Spain, in Seville, during the grimmest days of the Inquisition, when throughout the country fires were burning endlessly to the greater glory of God and

> In autos-da-fé resplendent
> Wicked heretics were burned.

"Of course, this was not the coming in which He had promised to appear in all His heavenly glory at the end of time and which would be as sudden as a bolt of lightning cutting the sky from east to west. No, He wanted to come only for a moment to visit His children and He chose to appear where the fires were crackling under the heretics.

"In His infinite mercy He came among men in human form, just as He had walked among them fifteen centuries before. He came down to that sunbaked Southern city the day after nearly a hundred heretics had been burned all at once *ad majorem gloriam Dei,* in a resplendent auto-da-fé by the order of the Cardinal, the Grand Inquisitor, and in the presence of the King, the royal court, knights, beautiful ladies-in-waiting, and the entire population of Seville.

"He came unobserved and moved about silently but, strangely enough, those who say Him recognized Him at once. This might, perhaps, be the best part of my poem—I mean if I could explain what made them recognize Him. . . . People are drawn to Him by an irresistible force, they gather around Him, follow Him, and soon there is a crowd. He walks among them in silence, a gentle smile of infinite compassion on His lips. The sun of love burns in His heart; light, understanding, and spiritual power flow from His eyes and set people's hearts vibrating with love for Him. He holds His hands out to them, blesses them, and just from touching Him, or even His clothes, comes a healing power. An old man who has been blind from childhood suddenly cries out to Him: 'Cure me, O Lord, so that I may see You too!' And it is as if scales had fallen from his eyes, and the blind man sees Him. People weep and kiss the ground on which He walks. Children scatter flowers in His path and cry out to Him, 'Hosannah!' 'It is He, He Himself!' people keep saying. 'Who else could it be!' He stops on the steps of the cathedral of Seville at a moment when a small white coffin is carried into the church by weeping bearers. In it lies a girl of seven, the only daughter of a prominent man. She lies there amidst flowers. 'He will raise your child from the dead!' people shout to the weeping mother. The priest, who has come out of the cathedral to meet the procession, looks perplexed and frowns. But now the mother of the dead child throws herself at His feet, wailing, 'If it is truly You, give me back my child!' and she stretches out her hands to Him. The procession stops. They put the coffin down at His feet. He looks down with compassion, His lips form the words *'Talitha cumi'*—arise, maiden—and the maiden arises. The little girl sits up in her coffin, opens her little eyes, looks around in surprise, and smiles. She holds the white roses that had been placed in her hand when they had laid her in the coffin. There is confusion among the people, shouting and weeping. . . .

"Just at that moment, the Cardinal, the Grand Inquisitor himself, crosses the cathedral square. He is a man of almost ninety, tall and erect. His face is drawn, his eyes are sunken, but they still glow as though a spark smoldered in them. Oh, now he is not wearing his magnificent cardinal's robes in which he paraded before the crowds the day before, when they were burning the enemies of the Roman Church; no, today he is wearing just the coarse cassock of an ordinary monk. He is followed by his grisly assistants, his slaves, his 'holy guard.' He sees the crowd gathered, stops, and watches from a distance. He sees everything: the placing of the coffin at His feet and the girl rising from it. His face darkens. He knits his thick white brows; his eyes flash with an ominous fire. He points his finger and orders his guards to seize Him.

"The Grand Inquisitor's power is so great and the people are so submissive and tremblingly obedient to him that they immediately open up a passage for the guards. A death-like silence descends upon the square and in that silence the guards lay hands on Him and lead Him away.

"Then everyone in the crowd, to a man, prostrates himself before the Grand Inquisitor. The old man blesses them in silence and passes on.

"The guards take their prisoner to an old building of the Holy Inquisition and lock Him up there in a dark, narrow, vaulted prison cell. The day declines and is replaced by the stifling, black Southern night of Seville. The air is fragrant with laurel and lemon.

"Suddenly, in the complete darkness, the iron gate of the cell opens and there stands the Grand Inquisitor himself, holding a light in his hand. The old man enters the cell alone and, when he is inside, the door closes behind him. He stops and for a long time— one or even two minutes—he looks at Him. At last he sets the light down on the table and says: "You? Is it really You?' Receiving no answer, he continues in great haste:

"You need not answer me. Say nothing. I know only too well what You could tell me now. Besides, You have no right to add anything to what You said before. Why did You come here, to inter-

fere and make things difficult for us? For You came to interfere—
You know it. But shall I tell You what will happen tomorrow? Well,
I do not know who You really are, nor do I want to know whether
You are really He or just a likeness of Him, but no later than tomorrow I shall pronounce You the wickedest of all heretics and
sentence You to be burned at the stake, and the very people who
today were kissing Your feet will tomorrow, at a sign of my hand,
hasten to Your stake to rake the coals. Don't You know it? Oh yes,
I suppose You do,' he added, deeply immersed in thought, his eyes
fixed for a moment on his prisoner."

"And the prisoner—He just looks at him and says nothing?"

"Why, yes," Ivan laughed once more, "and that's as it should be
in any case. Besides, the old man himself reminds Him that He
may not add a single word to what He has said before. I might add
that this may be the most crucial feature of Roman Catholicism,
at least the way I see it. It's as if the Grand Inquisitor said to Him:
'You have transmitted all Your authority to the Pope and now he
wields it. As to You, You had better stay away or, at any rate, not
interfere with us for the time being.' They don't just say that, they
even have it in writing, at least the Jesuits have. I've read it myself
in the works of their theologians.

"'Do You think You have the right to reveal even a single mystery
of the world from which You come?' the Grand Inquisitor asks Him
and then answers himself: 'No, You do not, for You may not add
anything to what has been said before and You may not deprive
men of the freedom You defended so strongly when You were on
earth. Anything new that You might reveal to them now would en-
croach upon the freedom of their faith, for it would come to them
as a miracle, and fifteen centuries ago it was freely given faith that
was most important to You. Didn't You often tell them then that
You wanted to make them free. Well, then,' the old man adds with
a grin, 'so now You have seen *free* men. Yes, that business cost
us a great deal,' he continues, looking sternly at Him, 'but at last, in
Your name, we saw it through. For fifteen hundred years we were
pestered by that notion of freedom, but in the end we succeeded in
getting rid of it, and now we are rid of it for good. You don't believe
that we got rid of it, do You? You look at me so gently, and You do
not even consider me worthy of Your anger? I want You to know,
though, that on this very day men are convinced that they are freer
than they have ever been, although they themselves brought us
their freedom and put it meekly at our feet. This is what we have
achieved, but was it really what You wanted, was this the freedom
that You wanted to bring them?'"

"I'm afraid I'm lost again," Alyosha interrupted Ivan, "is he being
sarcastic? Is he laughing at Him?"

"He certainly is not. Indeed, he is claiming for himself and his
church the credit for having done away with freedom and having
thus given happiness to mankind.

"'It is only now,' he says, obviously thinking of the Inquisition,
'that it has become possible, for the first time, to think of men's

happiness. Man is a rebel by nature and how can a rebel be happy? You were warned;' he says to Him. 'There was no lack of warnings and signs, but You chose to ignore them. You spurned the only way that could have brought happiness to men. Fortunately, though, You allowed us to take over from You when You left. You made commitments to us, You sealed them with Your word, You gave us the right to loosen and to bind their shackles, and, of course, You cannot think of depriving us of that right now.'"

And then, the most troublesome doubt of all: Jesus leans over and kisses the Grand Inquisitor. Is this a sign that He is willing to forgive absolutely anyone? Or does it mean that God loves most those who rebel against Him?

Alyosha blurted out: "You don't really believe in God." He had the impression that his brother was looking at him sarcastically; he lowered his eyes and asked: "Does it have an ending, your poem, or is that how it ends?"

"Here's how I propose to end, it," Ivan said, continuing.

"The Grand Inquisitor falls silent and waits for some time for the prisoner to answer. The prisoner's silence has weighed on him. He has watched Him; He listened to him intently, looking gently into his eyes, and apparently unwilling to speak. The old man longs for Him to say something, however painful and terrifying. But instead, He suddenly goes over to the old man and kisses him gently on his old, bloodless lips. And that is His only answer. The old man is startled and shudders. The corners of his lips seem to quiver slightly. He walks to the door, opens it, and says to Him, 'Go now, and do not come back . . . ever. You must never, never come again!' And he lets the prisoner out into the dark streets of the city. The prisoner leaves."

"And what about the old man?"

"The kiss glows in his heart. . . . But the old man sticks to his old idea."

"And you too, you stick to it?" Alyosha cried out bitterly. Ivan laughed.

"You know what," he said. "it's all nonsense really, a meaningless poem by a scatter-brained student who's never written two lines of poetry in his life. Why must you take it so seriously?"[30]

Dostoyevski was torn by doubt; not so British logical positivist A. J. Ayer. In the cool and logical style of his positivism, Ayer dismantles religion like a piece of old machinery that has never worked correctly. Belief in God

[30]Fyodor Dostoyevski, *The Brothers Karamazov,* trans. Andrew R. MacAndrew (New York: Bantam, 1970).

is nonsense, he tells us. And so too is belief that God does not exist, and so too are doubts about whether He does or doesn't. In other words, Ayer says, the whole issue is *meaningless,* not a matter of proof or disproof, nor even of uncertainty.

◆ **"God" Is Meaningless,**
by A. J. Ayer

It is now generally admitted, at any rate by philosophers, that the existence of a being having the attributes which define the god of any non-animistic religion cannot be demonstratively proved. To see that this is so, we have only to ask ourselves what are the premises from which the existence of such a god could be deduced. If the conclusion that a god exists is to be demonstratively certain, then these premises must be certain; for, as the conclusion of a deductive argument is already contained in the premises, any uncertainty there may be about the truth of the premises is necessarily shared by it. But we know that no empirical proposition can ever be anything more than probable. It is only *a priori* propositions that are logically certain. But we cannot deduce the existence of a god from an *a priori* proposition. For we know that the reason why *a priori* propositions are certain is that they are tautologies. And from a set of tautologies nothing but a further tautology can be validly deduced. It follows that there is no possibility of demonstrating the existence of a god.

What is not so generally recognised is that there can be no way of proving that the existence of a god, such as the God of Christianity, is even probable. Yet this also is easily shown. For if the existence of such a god were probable, then the proposition that he existed would be an empirical hypothesis. And in that case it would be possible to deduce from it, and other empirical hypotheses, certain experiential propositions which were not deducible from those other hypotheses alone. But in fact this is not possible. It is sometimes claimed, indeed, that the existence of a certain sort of regularity in nature constitutes sufficient evidence for the existence of a god. But if the sentence "God exists" entails no more than that certain types of phenomena occur in certain sequences, then to assert the existence of a god will be simply equivalent to asserting that there is the requisite regularity in nature; and no religious man would admit that this was all he intended to assert in asserting the existence of a god. He would say that in talking about God, he was talking about a transcendent being who might be known through certain empirical manifestations, but certainly could not be defined in terms of those manifestations. But in that case, the term "god" is a metaphysical term. And if "god" is a metaphysical term, then it cannot be even probable that a god exists. For to say that "God exists" is to make a metaphysical utterance which cannot be either true or false. And by the same criterion, no sentence which purports to describe the nature of a transcendent god can possess any literal significance.

It is important not to confuse this view of religious assertions with the view that is adopted by atheists, or agnostics. For it is characteristic of an agnostic to hold that the existence of a god is a possibility in which there is no good reason either to believe or disbelieve; and it is characteristic of an atheist to hold that it is at least probable that no god exists. And our view that all utterances about the nature of God are nonsensical, so far from being identical with, or even lending any support to, either of these familiar contentions, is actually incompatible with them. For if the assertion that there is a god is nonsensical, then the atheist's assertion that there is no god is equally nonsensical, since it is only a significant proposition that can be significantly contradicted. As for the agnostic, although he refrains from saying either that there is or that there is not a god, he does not deny that the question whether a transcendent god exists is a genuine question. He does not deny that the two sentences "There is a transcendent god" and "There is no transcendent god" express propositions one of which is actually true and the other false. All he says is that we have no means of telling which of them is true, and therefore ought not to commit ourselves to either. But we have seen that the sentences in question do not express propositions at all. And this means that agnosticism is also ruled out.

Thus we offer the theist the same comfort as we gave to the moralist. His assertions cannot possibly be valid, but they cannot be invalid either. As he says nothing at all about the world, he cannot justly be accused of saying something false, or anything for which he has insufficient grounds. It is only when the theist claims that in asserting the existence of a transcendent god he is expressing a genuine proposition that we are entitled to disagree with him.

It is to be remarked that in cases where deities are identified with natural objects, assertions concerning them may be allowed to be significant. If, for example, a man tells me that the occurrence of thunder is alone both necessary and sufficient to establish the truth of the proposition that Jehovah is angry, we may conclude that, in his usage of words, the sentence, "Jehovah is angry" is equivalent to "It is thundering." But in sophisticated religions, though they may be to some extent based on men's awe of natural processes which they cannot sufficiently understand, the "person" who is supposed to control the empirical world is not himself located in it; he is held to be superior to the empirical world, and so outside it; and he is endowed with super-empirical attributes. But the notion of a person whose essential attributes are nonempirical is not an intelligible notion at all. We may have a word which is used as if it named this "person," but, unless the sentences in which it occurs express propositions which are empirically verifiable, it cannot be said to symbolise anything. And this is the case with regard to the word "god," in the usage in which it is intended to refer to a transcendent object. The mere existence of the noun is enough to foster the illusion that there is a real, or at any rate a possible entity corresponding to it. It is only when we inquire what God's attributes are that we discover that "God," in this usage, is not a genuine name.

It is common to find belief in a transcendent god conjoined with belief in an after-life. But, in the form which it usually takes, the content of this belief is not a genuine hypothesis. To say that men do not ever die, or that the state of death is merely a state of prolonged insensibility, is indeed to express a significant proposition, though all the available evidence goes to show that it is false. But to say that there is something imperceptible inside a man, which is his soul or his real self, and that it goes on living after he is dead, is to make a metaphysical assertion which has no more factual content than the assertion that there is a transcendent god.

It is worth mentioning that, according to the account which we have given of religious assertions, there is no logical ground for antagonism between religion and natural science. As far as the question of truth or falsehood is concerned, there is no opposition between the natural scientist and the theist who believes in a transcendent god. For since the religious utterances of the theist are not genuine propositions at all, they cannot stand in any logical relation to the propositions of science. Such antagonism as there is between religion and science appears to consist in the fact that science takes away one of the motives which make men religious. For it is acknowledged that one of the ultimate sources of religious feeling lies in the inability of men to determine their own destiny; and science tends to destroy the feeling of awe with which men regard an alien world, by making them believe that they can understand and anticipate the course of natural phenomena, and even to some extent control it. The fact that it has recently become fashionable for physicists themselves to be sympathetic towards religion is a point in favour of this hypothesis. For this sympathy towards religion marks the physicists' own lack of confidence in the validity of their hypotheses, which is a reaction on their part from the antireligious dogmatism of nineteenth-century scientists, and a natural outcome of the crisis through which physics has just passed.

It is not within the scope of this enquiry to enter more deeply into the cause of religious feeling, or to discuss the probability of the continuance of religious belief. We are concerned only to answer those questions which arise out of our discussion of the possibility of religious knowledge. The point which we wish to establish is that there cannot be any transcendent truths of religion. For the sentences which the theist uses to express such "truths" are not literally significant.

An interesting feature of this conclusion is that it accords with what many theists are accustomed to say themselves. For we are often told that the nature of God is a mystery which transcends the human understanding. But to say that something transcends the human understanding is to say that it is unintelligible. And what is unintelligible cannot significantly be described. Again, we are told that God is not an object of reason but an object of faith. This may be nothing more than an admission that the existence of God must be taken on trust, since it cannot be proved. But it may also be an assertion that God is the object of a purely mystical intuition, and cannot therefore be defined in terms which are intelligible to the reason. And I think there are many theists who would assert this. But if one allows that it is impossible to define God in intelligible terms, then one is allowing that it is impossible for a sentence both to be significant and to be about God. If a mystic admits that the object of his vision is something which cannot be described, then he must also admit that he is bound to talk nonsense when he describes it.

For his part, the mystic may protest that his intuition does reveal truths to him, even though he cannot explain to others what these truths are; and that we who do not possess this faculty of intuition can have no ground for denying that it is a cognitive faculty. For we can hardly maintain *a priori* that there are no ways of discovering true propositions except those which we ourselves employ. The answer is that we set no limit to the number of ways in which one may come to formulate a true proposition. We do not in any way deny that a synthetic truth may be discovered by purely intuitive methods as well as by the rational method of induction. But we do say that every synthetic proposition, however it may have been arrived at, must be subject to the test of actual experience. We do not deny *a priori* that the mystic is able to discover truths by his own special methods. We wait to hear what are the propositions which embody his discoveries, in order to see whether they are verified or confuted by our empirical observations. But the mystic, so far from producing propositions which are empirically verified, is unable to produce any intelligible propositions at all. And therefore we say that his intuition has not revealed to him any facts. It is no use his saying that he has apprehended facts but is unable to express them. For we know that if he really had acquired any information, he would be able to express it. He would be able to indicate in some way or other how the genuineness of his discovery might be empirically determined. The fact that he cannot reveal what he "knows," or even himself devise an empirical test to validate his "knowledge," shows that his state of mystical intuition is not a genuinely cognitive state. So that in describing his vision the mystic does not give us any information about the external world; he merely gives us indirect information about the condition of his own mind.

These considerations dispose of the argument from religious experience which many philosophers still regard as a valid argument in favour of the existence of a god. They say that it is logically possible for men to be immediately acquainted with God, as they are immediately acquainted with a sense content, and that there is no reason why one should be prepared to believe a man when he says that he is seeing a yellow patch, and refuse to believe him when he says that he is seeing God. The answer to this is that if the man who asserts that he is seeing God is merely asserting that he is experiencing a peculiar kind of sense-content, then we do not for a moment deny that his assertion may be true. But, ordinarily, the man who says that he is seeing God is saying not merely that he is experiencing a religious emotion, but also that there exists a transcendent being who is the object of his emotion; just as the man who says that he sees a yellow patch is ordinarily saying not merely that his visual sense-field contains a yellow sense-content, but also that there exists a yellow object to which the sense-content belongs. And it is not irrational to be prepared to believe a man when he asserts the existence of a yellow object, and to refuse to believe him when he asserts the existence of a transcendent god. For whereas the sentence "There exists here a yellow-coloured material thing" expresses a genuine synthetic proposition which could be empirically verified, the sentence "There exists a transcendent god" has, as we have seen, no literal significance.

We conclude, therefore, that the argument from religious experience is altogether fallacious. The fact that people have religious experiences is interesting from the psychological point of view, but it does not in any way imply that there is such a thing as religious knowledge, any more than our having moral experiences implies that there is such a thing as moral knowledge. The theist, like the moralist, may believe that his experiences are cognitive experiences, but, unless he can formulate his "knowledge" in propositions that are empirically verifiable, we may be sure that he is deceiving himself. It follows that those philosophers who fill their books with assertions that they intuitively "know" this or that moral or religious "truth" are merely providing material for the psycho-analyst. For no act of intuition can be said to reveal a truth about any matter of fact unless it issues in verifiable propositions. And all such propositions are to be incorporated in the system of empirical propositions which constitutes science.[31]

It is important to notice that neither of these positions is "atheist" in the literal sense—neither denies the existence of God as such. Dostoyevski's character Ivan speaks for his author in what might be called an extremely sentimental and traumatic agnosticism, filled with the doubts that arise from the problem of evil and from a general cynicism about humanity. "If there is not God," he worries, "then everything is permitted." But even if there is God, the Grand Inquisitor tells us, the purpose of religion has little to do with Him. It is instead an instrument

[31]A. J. Ayer, *Language, Truth and Logic,* 2nd ed. (New York: Dover, 1946).

of unfreedom and a way to keep people ignorant and hopeful. Ayer explicitly rejects atheism as well as theism, but he does this not as an agnostic (that is, one who does not know) but as a philosopher who claims that the very notion of "God" is ultimately meaningless. This too is atheism, if by that word we mean not believing in God. What Ayer rejects under that name is the assertion that something with certain characteristics that might exist does indeed exist. Ayer insists that there is no sense even in suggesting that God might exist. Notice the difference between Ayer and Tillich, however. For Ayer, the notion that it makes no sense to discuss the existence of God is an argument for atheism; for Tillich the same notion is an argument for theism.

G. THE ATTACK ON RELIGION: MARX, NIETZSCHE, AND FREUD

But even if religion is a matter of personal viewpoint, beyond rational argument and mere passion or "experience," this is not to say that it is immune from attack. The truth and falsity of religious doctrines may not be subject to rational scrutiny, but the motivation of religious thinking might be. Why do people turn to religion? Is it just for edification? or to give them hope? or as a rationalization for the lack of justice in this world? Or is it an escape, a kind of irresponsible reaction to a world we cannot cope with, perhaps a childish unwillingness to give up an illusion of security we ought to have outgrown in adolescence?

Karl Marx is often quoted for his incisive critique of religion. His point is simple, and he makes it powerfully. Humans invent religion to escape their intolerable social conditions. And once we see this, we should reject religion as an escape and turn instead to the correction of those conditions that make such an escape necessary.

> The basis of irreligious criticism is this: *man makes religion;* religion does not make man. Religion is indeed man's self-consciousness and self-awareness so long as he has not found himself or has lost himself again. But *man* is not an abstract being, squatting outside the world. Man is *the human world,* a state, society. This state, this society, produce religion which is an *inverted world consciousness,* because they are an *inverted world.* Religion is the general theory of this world, its encyclopedic compendium, its logic in popular form, its spiritual *point d'honneur,* its enthusiasm, its moral sanction, its solemn complement, its general basis of consolation and justification. It is *the fantastic realization* of the human being inasmuch as the *human being* possesses no true reality. The struggle against religion is, therefore, indirectly a struggle against *that world* whose spiritual *aroma* is religion.
> *Religious* suffering is at the same time an *expression* of real suf-

fering and a *protest* against real suffering. Religion is the sigh of the oppressed creature, the sentiment of a heartless world, and the soul of soulless conditions. It is the *opium* of the people.

The abolition of religion as the *illusory* happiness of men, is a demand for their *real* happiness. The call to abandon their illusions about their condition is a *call to abandon a condition which requires illusions*. The criticism of religion is, therefore, *the embryonic criticism of this vale of tears* of which religion is the halo.

Criticism has plucked the imaginary flowers from the chain, not in order that man shall bear the chain without caprice or consolation but so that he shall cast off the chain and pluck the living flower. The criticism of religion disillusions man so that he will think, act and fashion his reality as a man who has lost his illusions and regained his reason; so that he will revolve about himself as his own true sun. Religion is only the illusory sun about which man revolves so long as he does not revolve about himself.

· · · · · · · · · ·

It is clear that the arm of criticism cannot replace the criticism of arms. Material force can only be overthrown by material force; but theory itself becomes a material force when it has seized the masses. Theory is capable of seizing the masses when it demonstrates *ad hominem*, and it demonstrates *ad hominem* as soon as it becomes radical. To be radical is to grasp things by the root. But for man the root is man himself. What proves beyond doubt the radicalism of German theory, and thus its practical energy, is that it begins from the resolute *positive* abolition of religion. The criticism of religion ends with the doctrine that *man is the supreme being for man.* It ends, therefore, with the *categorical imperative to overthrow all those conditions* in which man is an abased, enslaved, abandoned, contemptible being—conditions which can hardly be better described than in the exclamation of the Frenchman on the occasion of a proposed tax upon dogs: "Wretched dogs! They want to treat you like men!"[32]

Fifty years later, Friedrich Nietzsche opened an even more blistering attack on religion in general, on Christianity in particular. Christianity is accused of being nothing other than rationalizations for impotence, an expression of everything that is most contemptible in human nature.

In the Jewish "Old Testament," the book of divine justice, there are men, things, and speeches in so grand a style that Greek and Indian literature have nothing to compare with it. One stands in awe and reverence before these tremendous remnants of what man once was, and sad thoughts come to one about ancient Asia and

---

[32]Karl Marx, *Critique of Hegel's Philosophy of Right,* in *Early Writings,* trans. T. Bottomore (New York: McGraw-Hill, 1963).

its jutting peninsula, Europe, which wants so definitely to signify, as against Asia, the "progress of man." Of course, those who are merely wretched tame domestic animals and know only the wants of domestic animals (like our cultivated people of today, including the Christians of "cultivated" Christianity) need neither be amazed nor even sorry when faced with these ruins: the taste for the Old Testament is a touchstone of "greatness" and "smallness." Perhaps they will even find the New Testament, the book of grace, more to their taste (it is full of the odor of the real, effeminate, stupid canter and petty soul). To have glued this New Testament, a kind of rococo of taste in every respect, to the Old Testament to form one book—the "Bible," *the* book—that is perhaps the greatest audacity and "sin against the spirit" which literary Europe has on its conscience.[33]

• • • • • • • • • •

Christianity should not be beautified and embellished: it has waged deadly war against this higher type of man; it has placed all the basic instincts of this type under the ban; and out of these instincts it has distilled evil and the Evil One: the strong man as the typically reprehensible man, the "reprobate." Christianity has sided with all that is weak and base, with all failures; it has made an ideal of what *contradicts* the instinct of the strong life to preserve itself; it has corrupted the reason even of those strongest in spirit . . . it has in fear of them bred the opposite type—the domestic animal, the herd animal, the sick human animal—the Christian.

As long as the priest is considered a *higher* type of man—this *professional* negator, slanderer, and poisoner of life—there is no answer to the question: what *is* truth? For truth has been stood on its head when the conscious advocate of nothingness and negation is accepted as the representative of "truth."

In Christianity neither morality nor religion has even a single point of contact with reality.

. . . This *world of pure fiction* is vastly inferior to the world of dreams insofar as the latter *mirrors* reality, whereas the former falsifies, devalues, and negates reality. . . . Who alone has good reason to lie his way out of reality? He who suffers from it.

• • • • • • • • • •

The Christian conception of God—God as god of the sick, God as a spider, God as spirit—is one of the most corrupt conceptions of the divine ever attained on earth. It may even represent the low-water mark in the descending development of divine types.

• • • • • • • • • •

This pitiful god of Christian monotono-theism! This hybrid product of decay, this mixture of zero, concept, and contradiction, in

---

[33]Friedrich Nietzsche, *Beyond Good and Evil*, trans. Walter Kaufmann (New York: Random House, 1966).

which all the instincts of decadence, all cowardices and weari-
nesses of the soul, find their sanction![34]

Not surprisingly, Nietzsche sees the decline of Christianity, and
religion in general, with great enthusiasm. It is Nietzsche who popularized the old Lutheran phrase, "God is dead," but with an antireligious
twist and a shout of delight that declared open war on all remaining
forms of religious "weaknesses."

> The most important of more recent events—that "God is dead,"
> that the belief in the Christian God has become unworthy of
> belief–already begins to cast its first shadows over Europe. To the
> few at least whose eye, whose *suspecting* glance, is strong enough
> and subtle enough for this drama, some sun seems to have set,
> some old, profound confidence seems to have changed into doubt:
> our old world must seem to them daily more darksome, distrust-
> ful, strange and "old." In the main, however, one may say that the
> event itself is far too great, too remote, too much beyond most peo-
> ple's power of apprehension, for one to suppose that so much as
> the report of it could have *reached* them; not to speak of many
> who already knew *what* had taken place, and what must all col-
> lapse now that this belief had been undermined—because so much
> was built upon it, so much rested on it, and had become one with
> it: for example, our entire European morality. This lengthy, vast
> and uninterrupted process of crumbling, destruction, ruin and
> overthrow which is now imminent: who has realised it sufficiently
> to-day to have to stand up as the teacher and herald of such a
> tremendous logic of terror, as the prophet of a period of gloom and
> eclipse, the like of which has probably never taken place on earth
> before? . . . Even we, the born riddle-readers, who wait as it were
> on the mountains posted 'twixt to-day and tomorrow, and engirt by
> their contradiction, we, the firstlings and premature children of
> the coming century, into whose sight especially the shadows which
> must forthwith envelop Europe *should* already have come–how it
> is that even we, without genuine sympathy for this period of gloom,
> contemplate its advent without any *personal solicitude* or *fear?*
> Are we still, perhaps, too much under the *immediate effects* of the
> event—and are these effects, especially as regards *ourselves,* per-
> haps the reverse of what was to be expected—not at all sad and de-
> pressing, but rather like a new and indescribable variety of light,
> happiness, relief, enlivenment, encouragement, and dawning
> day? . . . In fact, we philosophers and "free spirits" feel ourselves ir-
> radiated as by a new dawn by the report that the "old God is
> dead"; our hearts overflow with gratitude, astonishment, presenti-
> ment and expectation. At last the horizon seems open once more,
> granting even that it is not bright; our ships can at least put out to

[34]Friedrich Nietzsche, *The Antichrist,* in *The Portable Nietzsche,* ed. and trans. Walter
Kaufmann (New York: Viking, 1954).

sea in face of every danger; every hazard is again permitted to the discerner; the sea, *our* sea, again lies open before us; perhaps never before did such an "open sea" exist.—[35]

Finally, in our own century, the attack has been given a psychoanalytic foundation by Sigmund Freud, who also reduces the grand aspirations of religion to mere illusions, but, even worse, the illusions of an insecure child who has never properly grown up. In *The Future of an Illusion*, he says

> . . . if we turn our attention to the psychical origin of religious ideas. These, which are given out as teachings, are not precipitates of experience or end results of thinking: they are illusions, fulfilments of the oldest, strongest and most urgent wishes of mankind. The secret of their strength lies in the strength of those wishes. As we already know, the terrifying impression of helplessness in childhood aroused the need for protection–for protection through love–which was provided by the father; and the recognition that this helplessness lasts throughout life made it necessary to cling to the existence of a father, but this time a more powerful one. Thus the benevolent rule of a divine Providence allays our fear of the dangers of life; the establishment of a moral world-order ensures the fulfilment of the demands of justice, which have so often remained unfulfilled in human civilization; and the prolongation of earthly existence in a future life provides the local and temporal framework in which these wish-fulfilments shall take place. Answers to the riddles that tempt the curiosity of man, such as how the universe began or what the relation is between body and mind, are developed in conformity with the underlying assumptions of this system. It is an enormous relief to the individual psyche if the conflicts of its childhood arising from the father-complex—conflicts which it has never wholly overcome—are removed from it and brought to a solution which is universally accepted.
>
> When I say that these things are all illusions, I must define the meaning of the word. An illusion is not the same thing as an error; nor is it necessarily an error. Aristotle's belief that vermin are developed out of dung (a belief to which ignorant people still cling) was an error; so was the belief of a former generation of doctors that *tabes dorsalis* is the result of sexual excess. It would be incorrect to call these errors illusions. On the other hand, it was an illusion of Columbus's that he had discovered a new searoute to the Indies. The part played by his wish in this error is very clear. One may describe as an illusion the assertion made by certain nationalists that the Indo-Germanic race is the only one capable of civilization; or the belief, which was only destroyed by psycho-analysis,

---

[35]Friedrich Nietzsche, *The Joyful Wisdom*, trans. Thomas Common, in *The Complete Works of Friedrich Nietzsche*, Oscar Levy, General Editor (1909–11) (New York: Russell & Russell, 1964).

that children are creatures without sexuality. What is characteristic of illusions is that they are derived from human wishes. In this respect they come near to psychiatric delusions. But they differ from them, too, apart from the more complicated structure of delusions. In the case of delusions, we emphasize as essential their being in contradiction with reality. Illusions need not necessarily be false—that is to say, unrealizable or in contradiction of reality. . . . Thus we call a belief an illusion when a wish-fulfilment is a prominent factor in its motivation, and in doing so we disregard its relations to reality, just as the illusion itself sets no store by verification.[36]

In conclusion, Freud agrees with Marx and Nietzsche that the only proper concern of man is humanity. But is this necessarily an indictment of religion? Freud was fascinated by Jewish mysticism, and Nietzsche offered extravagant praise of Buddhism. Many Christians, Muslims, and Jews have used their religion as a metaphysical support for concerted social activism and humanism (as well as "holy" wars), and for many people religion is an emotional support without which they could not even function as human beings. The balance is precarious. No one can deny that there have been thousands of atrocities—to both spirit and body—in the name of religion. But neither has it been proved that such cruelty is necessary for religion nor that religion is as easily dispensable as some of its critics have suggested. (Even Nietzsche had his serious doubts.)

H. RELIGION AGAINST OPPRESSION

Although Marx, Nietzsche and Freud abhorred religion, one can be religious and still take their criticisms, both against religion and against society, to heart. In fact, a number of Christian social radicals do just that. Their movement started in the 1960s, when many such progressive movements began, and has built into a community of discourse—and action—around the world. This so-called "Christian Marxism," going by the locution "the theology of liberation," has been popular with some in Latin America, where the Catholic Church is strong among the populace and the political oppression in some countries is excruciating. The claims made by these radical Christians begin with the belief, discussed already, that God is first and foremost a moral force in human life. Since this is so, they claim, the church has an obligation to help fight for moral goods, like freedom and justice, wherever they are threatened. The following passages, the first by a philosophical leader in various political

---

[36]Sigmund Freud, *The Future of an Illusion*, ed. and trans. James Strachey (New York: Norton, 1961).

movements of the 1960s, the second by a Czechoslavakian freedom fighter, discuss the intersection of politics and religion. Marcuse was a member of the "Frankfurt School," a group of European philosophers, many of whom studied what they considered to be the repressive nature of modern society and advocated revolutionary changes to reshape it. Lochman is a veteran of the 1968 Soviet Communist invasion that crushed the "Prague Spring" freedom movement.

◆from "Marxism and the New Humanity," by Herbert Marcuse

This libertarian radicalism seems to link Marxism with a quite different western tradition. This would be not so much the liberal tradition (which still contains much of the repressive puritanism with which it was once connected), but the great radical heretic movements which, since the twelfth and thirteenth centuries, have become an essential element in the western tradition: libertarian trends in Christianity, libertarian humanism, Brothers of the Free Spirit, Edomites, and others.

While Marxian theory remains irreconcilable with Christian dogma and its institution, it finds an ally in those tendencies, goups, and individuals committed to the part of the Christian teaching that stands uncompromisingly against inhuman, exploitative power. In our times these radical religious tendencies have come to life in the priests and ministers who have joined the struggle against facism in all its forms, and those who have made common cause with the liberation movements in the Third World, especially in Latin America. They are part of the global anti-authoritarian movement against the self-perpetuating power structure, east and west, which is less and less interested in human progress. This anti-authoritarian character brings to life long-forgotten or reduced anarchist, heretic tendencies.

Even the bizarre, extreme forms which the student opposition assumes today must be taken very seriously. They express, it seems, the fact that the young militants have lost patience with the traditional forms of opposition which go on and on without really changing the essentials—which go on and on, still sustaining the ghettoes, still sustaining and even extending poverty and misery—which still go on while hundreds are daily killed, tortured, and burned in an immoral and illegal war. Whether we like it or not, this opposition exists.

This brings us full circle. There is indeed a force in this opposition with which religion and the churches should properly come to grips, because there is a strong moral element in it, a moral element which has for too long been neglected or overlooked. This moral element has now become a political force.[37]

[37]*Marxism and Radical Religion: Essays Toward A Revolutionary Humanism*, ed. John C. Raines and Thomas Dean (Philadelphia: Temple Univ. Press, 1970), pp. 9–25.

◆from "Marxism, Liberalism, and Religion," by Jan Lochman

THE RELIGIOUS PERSPECTIVE

In thinking of my own experience in Czechoslovakia in 1968, I do not hesitate to give a positive answer to this question. This is not just wishful thinking. This has been part of our fundamental living reality during these past few years. I refer to what was suggested earlier, the growing participation of religious people in the public life of society. The religious people (in our country, of course, predominantly Christians, because the Jewish population was liquidated by the Nazis) emerged not as outsiders of society but as insiders. The reasons for this lie deep, because the goal of democratic socialism in a sense corresponds, in our own conception, to the deepest insights of the biblical prophetic tradition. If we think of the vision of greater social justice as proclaimed by the Old Testament prophets, or again, if we think of the New Testament apostolic vision of the inalienable rights of every individual, then there is no doubt that the best insights of our own religious tradition point in the direction of a democratic socialism. So the involvement in the democratization of our society was for us not just a general trend into which we could be drawn from outside, but was very much our own necessary activity and task, and, in all modesty, our own contribution as well.

If the focus is narrowed to indicate in a few words the central and distinctive possible contribution of the religious tradition in this common goal of humanization, then one point especially which seems to be crucial should be emphasized. In my judgment, the basic contribution of the distinctively religious tradition toward the humanization of man's social life is an opening up of the perspective of hope. This is the classical religious perspective. It is well known that Immanuel Kant, when he tried to delineate the different areas of human life and culture, claimed quite justly that the basic sphere of religion is exactly this context of hope. *What can I hope for?* is the basic religious question of man. We know that today theology, both Roman Catholic and Protestant, seems to have learned from Kant. It emphasizes very strongly this basic perspective of hope.

This new emphasis is justified, for this perspective of hope is truly unique to the biblical heritage. If there was something really new in the biblical contribution to mankind, it was certainly an opening up of history as a meaningful process, a breaking-through of all mythological or, as they are sometimes called, "ontocratic" structures. By this are meant those models of thought which consider the universe as closed, sacred, established in itself. Here everything is a perfect *kosmos,* everything is preordained, everything has its place and must be accepted basically as a divine order. This model of thought prevailed in both ancient mythology

and philosophy. Biblical thought was utterly different. The basic
biblical perspective is the perspective of Exodus. It proclaims the
way out of captivity to preordained structures and established
orders. It opens new possibilities for responsible human initiative
in history.

Now if this is the basic vision of the biblical message (and in my
opinion it clearly is), then this biblical vision has some important
implications for the whole realm of politics. For there is one
constant danger in the political sphere: the danger of fatalism. Politics is conceived as purely a game of power-politics, the El Dorado
of the managers. The political structures are absolutized. Nation-
ally, the "principalities and powers" of the establishment dominate
the political scene. Internationally, the "big powers" divide their
"spheres of influence" and declare them untouchable. Any threat to
the "balance"—often arbitrarily defined—causes a power-political
nemesis. The only responsible political attitude is "realism," that is,
the cult of the given "law and order," of the status quo. Thus the
sphere of politics is theoretically interpreted by many political scientists and politicians, while it is managed practically as the sphere
of fate. In this atmosphere of "realism," responsible political quest
and action are very much limited. The mood of "realism" is not
far from the mood of fatalism.

It is exactly here that there might open a creative role for religion. But we must immediately qualify; certainly not for all religion.
Much of traditional religion only cemented the spirit of fatalism.
There is a religious tradition which is truly an "opiate of the
people": an attempt to interpret the religious vision in purely transcendental and spiritual terms and to separate it from all secular
implications in providing a purely "celestial" consolation. There
is also a religious tradition sanctifying the status quo: an identification with the authority of God of what is powerfully present in the
realm of political authority. And there is an outspoken religious
fatalism: an understanding of God's Providence in terms of
unchangeable destiny which must be accepted in an attitude of un-
questioning resignation.

Thus there were always priests of fate, of the establishment, and
of pious quietism. Yet there is also the biblical prophetic tradition,
and this is very different. Certainly, the biblical vision of the
Kingdom of God opens a dimension which is not simply "of this
world." It transcends the potentialities of the world of man, of what
can be achieved in history. It is the Kingdom of *God.* Yet this
"transcending" kingdom is seen precisely in its dynamic relationship to men in history. The biblical God does not encourage any
escapism. He is not an abstract transcendence, aloof from all secular concerns. On the contrary, he is the God involved in history,
opening new possibilities, the God of the open future. He is all this
in a concretely articulated way: his basic revelation in the Old
Testament is the Exodus—an event of liberation. His basic revelation in the New Testament is the way of Jesus of Nazareth: his

unconditional solidarity with men, particularly with those who are oppressed and poor. Thus, this is the way of his Kingdom, this is the way for man.

This vision opens new dimensions to human lives and action. It demythologizes the universe, which is no longer considered "sacred" and unchangeable, and it opens a perspective for meaningful commitment in history and society. This vision also opens a new perspective on man's understanding of himself. For biblical anthropology, man is neither a free angel nor a determined beast. Rather, the mystery of the human situation encompasses the knowledge that man has emerged from the earth. That means that he is limited, conditioned in all respects—psychologically, socially, culturally—while, at the same time, he knows that he is not just the sum total of those conditions. Man, created in the image of God, has a dimension of transcendence which is not simply to be identified with the horizon of man's social conditioning. From the biblical perspective, man is not just the sum total of human conditioning; rather, it is a part of his "condition of being human" to transcend his humanness as well, to have the limited possibility of steering and shaping his future, his destiny, by his action. Such action may be constructive or it may be destructive—the world depends on us as we depend on our world. In short, the biblical view of man as both mundane creature and as bearer of the image of God moves between two extremes: between an idealistic indeterminism (which claims that man is, so to say, just the free act, *actus purus*) and a materialistic determinism (which claims that man is simply the outcome of natural or social conditioning). Man in truth is neither an *actus purus* nor a determined product of nature and history. Man is, at one and the same time, conditioned, yet called to action and responsibility.

In the light of Exodus, in the light of God's involvement in the history of man in Jesus of Nazareth, the spell of fate is doubly broken. The world is demythologized. The "principalities and powers" do not have the ultimate keys of the world and of man. They are potent. The power-political element of the politician is to be taken very seriously. Moralism and idealism do not help. And yet, the politicians are not omnipotent. There is an open space and an open future for meaningful political work and action. So also, "reality" is not just what is given, the sum total of the determined conditions, the passive raw material for "the engineers of the future." Reality is also the challenge of the coming Kingdom of God, and man's response to that challenge in the search for greater freedom and justice.

To keep alive that spirit of challenge and to keep open that dimension of hope is a possible contribution of religious people to the world of politics today. Responsible politicians are not blind to that possibility. A word of John F. Kennedy to church leaders indicates this possibility: "Help me to create the climate in which bolder steps for a policy of peace and justice are possible again."

Indeed, this "climate" is of ultimate importance if politics is to become and to remain a meaningful human activity. The dimension of sober hope is very much needed in all societies, perhaps particularly in both the United States and Czechoslovakia. The problems of these societies are overwhelming. Responsible citizens are often frustrated. Here a religious perspective of hope as a call to persevere in the effort toward humanization may make its modest contribution. It reminds us that the forces of chaos and oppression cannot eventually prevail. The world is not left irrevocably in the hands of political managers and manipulators. So it should not be left to them by us. Certainly the world of man is also the world of tanks. Yet the world of tanks is not the whole world of man. They must be challenged.

Every one of us is asked to get involved. In the perspective of hope this involvement is never in vain. It is worth while not to give up, but instead to strive, despite all possible and real difficulties, toward a change of all those conditions under which man is an oppressed, enslaved, destitute, and despised being.[38]

SUMMARY AND CONCLUSION

Religion is one of the most important, and therefore one of the most controversial and sensitive, parts of our lives. It is therefore also one of the most important, controversial, and sensitive areas of philosophy. Initially, religion seems to be part of metaphysics, an examination of the way the world really is, and the answer of religion is that reality is, in a word, divine. But we have seen that religion is much more than a search for knowledge; it is also a search for meaning, for morality, for ultimate justice, and for a type of experience that is like no other. Philosophy of religion begins as a metaphysical discipline, attempting to define a supreme entity of a certain type (God) and to demonstrate His existence through rational arguments and proofs. But many philosophers and religious people deny that such a metaphysical approach is either possible or appropriate. Some philosophers deny that we can *know* God but insist that it is necessary to have faith. But while some philosophers interpret this faith as a form of rationality, others claim that it is strictly an emotional commitment beyond the domain of rational argument and understanding.

These various approaches to the philosophy of religion are all very much alive, and so too are the doubts that accompany each approach. Those who believe that we can know God are at odds with those who deny that we can know Him. Those who insist on faith disagree among themselves whether this faith can be or ought to be justified. There are

[38]*Marxism and Radical Religion: Essays Toward a Revolutionary Humanism*, ed. John C. Raines and Thomas Dean (Philadelphia: Temple Univ. Press, 1970).

those who want to believe in God but find that certain problems (for example, the problem of evil) make it difficult or impossible for them to do so. There are those who see belief in God as an outmoded belief, left over from the inadequate science and metaphysics of previous centuries. And there are those who attack religion as not only outmoded but as insidious, as a symptom of decadence, weakness, or immaturity. But in the face of these various doubts and attacks, the traditional religious beliefs of Judaism and Christianity continue to grow and to raise new questions. Religion is humanity's oldest philosophy, and it is still the most controversial area of philosophical concern.

GLOSSARY

Abrahamic religions   the Western monotheisms: Judaism, Christianity, and Islam (they all trace their roots from the prophet Abraham).

agnosticism   the refusal to believe either that God exists or that He does not exist, usually on the grounds that there can be no sufficient evidence for either belief.

anthropomorphic   human-like. An anthropomorphic conception of God ascribes human attributes to Him.

argument from design   see *teleological argument.*

atheism   the belief that there is no God. A person who believes that there is no God is an *atheist.*

Batin, Batinya   in Islamic mysticism, the "hidden truth" of the Qur'an, and those who know it or seek it.

Bhagavadgītā ("Gītā")   the "Song of God" of ancient Hinduism; the epic poem of Krishna, who is God incarnate.

Brahma ("Brahman")   precursor of God in Hindu theism; the idea of the One, the unity underlying all things.

Buddha   "the awakened one"; the historical founder of Buddhism.

cosmological argument   an argument (or set of arguments) that undertakes to "prove" that God exists on the basis of the idea that there must have been a first cause or an ultimate reason for the existence of the universe (the cosmos).

deism   a variation of the Judeo-Christian religion that was extremely popular in the science-minded eighteenth century. Deism holds that God must have existed to create the universe with all of its laws (and thereby usually accepts some form of the cosmological argument) but also holds that there is no justification for our belief that God has any special concern for man, any concern for justice, or any of those anthropomorphic attributes for which we worhip Him, pray to Him, and believe in biblical stories about Him.

dharma   in Hinduism, righteousness, the good.

faith   in the popular sense, believing in something for which you have inadequate evidence or little good reason. In theology, faith usually refers to the trust that a believer should have in God's ultimate grace and fairness. Sometimes, faith is defended as a rational belief in God (for example, in Kant). More often, faith is defended against rationality (as in Kierkegaard).

Four Noble Truths   among the most important teachings of the Buddha: "All is suffering (and transitory)," the need to eliminate desire, the way to eliminate desire, and the right path to the good.

God   in traditional Judeo-Christian theology, that being who created the universe and exists independently of it, who is all-powerful, all-knowing, everywhere at once, and concerned with justice and the ultimate welfare of humankind. When spelled with a small "g" the word refers to any supernatural being worthy of worship or at least extraordinary respect.

illusion   a false belief motivated by intense wishes. According to Marx, religion is an illusion that is intended to compensate for an intolerable social situation. According to Freud, religion is an illusion that attempts to hold onto our childhood desires for fatherly protection and security.

ineffable   indescribable.

karma   in Hinduism, the tendency of any course of action to be repeated; the limitation of one's free will by one's own habits and dispositions (even into the next life).

Krishna   in Hinduism, God incarnate.

mysticism   the belief that one can come to grasp certain fundamental religious truths (the existence of God, the oneness of the universe) through direct experience, but of a very special kind, different from ordinary understanding and often at odds with reason.

nihility   "the nothing," "nothingness."

omnipotent   all-powerful, usually said of God.

omnipresent   everywhere at once, usually said of God.

omniscient   all-knowing, usually said of God.

ontological argument   an argument (or set of arguments) that tries to "prove" the existence of God from the very concept of "God." For example, "God," by definition, is that being with all possible perfection; existence is a perfection; therefore, God exists.

pantheism   the belief that God is identical to the universe as a whole. Spinoza, for example, was a pantheist. Hinduism is a form of pantheism in that it includes a conception of the divine in all things, rather than as a separate Creator.

problem of evil   the dilemma that emerges from tryng to reconcile the belief that God is omnipotent, omniscient, and just with the suffering and evil in the world.

subjective truth   in Kierkegaard, the "truth" of strong feelings and commitment.

Sufism   Islamic mysticism.

teleological argument   (for God's existence) an argument that attempts to "prove" that God exists because of the intricacy and "design" of nature. It is sometimes called the "argument from design," since the basis of the argument is that, since the universe is evidently designed, it must have a designer. The analogy most often used is our inference from finding a complex mechanism on the beach (for example, a watch) that some intelligent being must have created it.

theism   belief in God.

Theology of Liberation   Christian Marxism; especially in Latin Ameria, the religiously motivated search for political freedoms.

transcendent   independent of. In the philosophy of religion, a *transcendent God* is one who is distinct and separate from the universe he created. This is contrasted with the concept of an immanent God, for example, in pantheism, where God is identical with his creation, or, to take a different example, in certain forms of humanism, in which God is identical with humankind. (Hegel argued such a thesis.)

◆ *BIBLIOGRAPHY AND FURTHER READING* ◆

Several good anthologies on the philosophy of religion are S. Cahn, ed., *Philosophy of Religion* (New York: Harper & Row, 1970); J. Hick, ed., *Faith and the Philosophers* (New York: St. Martin's Press, 1964); and N. Smart, ed., *Historical Selections in the Philosophy of Religion* (New York: Harper & Row, 1962). A general discussion of religious issues is J. Hick, *Faith and Knowledge,* 2nd ed. (Ithaca, NY: Cornell University Press, 1966). A good series of studies on the problem of evil is N. Pike, ed., *Good and Evil* (Englewood Cliffs, NJ: Prentice-Hall, 1964). David Hume's *Dialogues on Natural Religion* (New York: Bobbs-Merrill, 1963) makes excellent and provocative reading. A convenient collection of Søren Kierkegaard's writings is W. H. Auden, *The Living Thoughts of Kierkegaard* (Bloomington, IN: Indiana University Press, 1963). Two good studies of Kierkegaard are J. Collins, *The Mind of Kierkegaard* (Chicago: Regnery, 1953) and Louis Mackey, *Kierkegaard: A Kind of Poet* (Philadelphia: University of Pennsylvania Press, 1972). The selections from Karl Marx, Friedrich Nietzsche, and Sigmund Freud are developed in Karl Marx, *Early Writings,* trans. T. Bottomore (New York: McGraw-Hill, 1963); Friedrich Nietzsche, *The Antichrist* in *The Viking Portable Nietzsche,* trans. Walter Kaufmann (New York: Viking, 1959); and Sigmund Freud, *The Future of an Illusion,* trans. W. D. Robson-Scott (New York: Doubleday, Anchor, 1953). On medieval religions, see A. Hyman and J. Walsh, *Philosophy in the Middle Ages* (Indianapolis: Hackett, 1973). On Nishitani see, *Religion and Nothingness* (Berkeley: University of California Press) and D. T. Suzuki, *Zen Buddhism* (New York: Doubleday, 1956).

PART
TWO

Knowing Oneself, and Acting

7

SELF-IDENTITY, MIND, AND BODY

"I'm not myself today, you see," Alice said to the caterpillar.
"I don't see," said the caterpillar.

LEWIS CARROLL

"Just be yourself!" How often have you heard that? What is it to be a "self"? And what does it mean to be a particular self? In the abstract, these questions seem obscure. But in everything that we do, we adopt some conception of our identity, both as a person and as an individual, whether we are called upon to articulate it or not. As a student, you walk into a classroom with certain conceptions of your own abilities and intelligence, your status among other students, your role vis-á-vis the professor, some haunting memories, perhaps some embarrassment or a certain vanity about your looks, your clothes, your grades, or just your new pair of shoes.

If you had to identify yourself as an individual, describe what makes you you, how would you do it? What features are essential to being a person? What are essential to being the person you are and what features distinguish you from other persons? Think for a moment of yourself in an office, applying for a job or a scholarship for professional school or just filling out one of those dozens of forms that bombard you during the year. You dutifully fill in your birthdate, where you were born, your grades in school, your service in the army if any, awards you have received, arrests and other troubles, whether you're married or not, male or female, perhaps your race and religion. This list of facts about yourself would be one way of identifying "you." But at some point, I am sure you have felt that sense of absurdity and rebellion, "this isn't me!" or "this is all irrelevant!" What may seem more relevant to your self-identity are your political views, your tastes in art and music, your favorite books and movies, your loves and hates, habits and beliefs, or just the fact, perhaps, that you think your own thoughts. These more personal, or "internal," features as well as the "cold facts," or "external" features, about yourself are important for identifying you as an individual different from other individuals.

In one sense, your **self-identity** is the way you characterize yourself as an individual. The philosophical problem of self-identity is thus concerned in part with what these characterizing qualities are. Are they just concerned with status and roles among other people? Or is there something that can truly be called "your self," your "essence," or maybe even your soul, without reference to anyone else? Should we think of ourselves as individuals? Or should we instead view ourselves as mere components of a larger organism—society, mankind, or perhaps the world as a whole? How should we identify ourselves?

There is another sense in which we might talk about a person's self-identity. You may know someone who has experienced a religious conversion, or who has just undergone treatment for alcoholism; or perhaps you can think of someone you see again after a long time who says, "I'm not the same person." What does this mean? And how is it possible to say you are not the same person? When someone says, "I'm not the same person I was," he or she is pointing to the fact that some significant aspects of himself or herself have changed; this person has a new self-identity. And yet, in another sense, this is still the same person; the old identity and the new identity are both identities of the same person.

So we have a second sense of "self-identity." Here your self-identity is what makes you the same person over time. Thus, the second philosophical problem, which is the one that has most concerned philosophers, is how to identify an individual as the *same* individual over time. What is it about you without which you wouldn't be you? Presumably you would still be you if you changed your religious beliefs or tastes in music. But what if you had a sex-change operation? Or what if you completely lost your memory, all recollection of your family and friends? Or what if you physically disappeared altogether, remaining only a wispy consciousness, a spirit, or a ghost without a body? Would it then make sense to say that you are still you?

There is yet a third sense in which we talk about self-identity. What is it that *allows* us to be individual people at all? Interestingly, the fact of consciousness—of having thoughts and feelings—seems the most private and individual thing a person possesses, and yet is the very thing which we tend to believe *all* people possess. Whatever our attempts to answer the problems of self-identity, they begin with a single "fact," our own consciousness. We will see that this was the logical beginning for Descartes, who used the fact of his own consciousness as the starting point for his whole philosophy. It was true for Locke, as well, who argued that our identity is to be found in the continuity of our consciousness rather than in the continuity of our bodies. We will see that it was even used by Hume, who used his own consciousness as the basis of his denial that there is any such thing as the self!

Of course, these questions assume some metaphysical claims that can and have been questioned. Later in this chapter, we will look at some of these assumptions, and some criticisms of them. Is self-identity a matter of nature? Are we born with an identity? Or is it a matter of personal choice, or of environmental factors such as our upbringing or education? Must a person have only one "self," or might he or she in fact have several or many selves? Is there a "self" at all? Or is the self, as many Eastern philosophers have argued, an illusion? Should self-lessness be our ideal self-identity? Ought we even to conceive of ourselves as individuals? Or ought we instead think of ourselves as organic components of a larger community or society?

In this chapter, we shall explore a number of different questions and conceptions about self-identity. We will consider the question of what makes you *you*, both in the sense of what makes you a person, and in the sense of what makes you the particular person you are. Freud, the great nineteenth-century psychologist, once said that every man is in some ways like all other men, in some ways like some other men, and in some ways like no other man. Philosophers who investigate the problem of self-identity attempt to figure out exactly how and why this might be so. We will begin with an all-important and still influential tradition in philosophy, from Descartes and Locke to Hume and Kant, which focuses on self-consciousness as the sole key to personal identity.

A. CONSCIOUSNESS AND THE SELF: FROM DESCARTES TO KANT

Sometimes we act out our identities without being aware of it at all. At other times, particularly when we talk about ourselves or are placed in a situation where we are forced to "look at ourselves as others see us," we are very much aware—even painfully aware—of our identities. At such times we say we are **self-conscious.** In general, most modern philosophers and psychologists would argue that you can't have a concept of who you are unless you are also sometimes (not necessarily always) self-conscious. Conversely, you can't even be self-conscious unless you have some sense of identity, no matter how crude. The two concepts, in other words, go hand in hand and cannot be separated from each other.

Many philosophers have argued that not only is self-consciousness crucial to having a concept of one's own individuality, but it is also crucial for establishing that one is an enduring self, that is, the same person over time. Descartes is an example. Remember how he characterized himself:

> But what then am I? A thing which thinks. What is a thing which
> thinks? It is a thing which doubts, understands, affirms, denies,
> wills, refuses, which also imagines and feels.

And, he goes on to say, I am a thing with desires, who perceives light and
noise and feels heat. Clearly, Descartes' concept of "self" is of thought, or
consciousness—a human essence—which each person has and with
which each person identifies himself or herself. He also claims to show
by his method of doubt, that all of this might be so even if he were not
to have a body at all. Perhaps, he argues, I am fooled about my "having"
a body just as I might be fooled about all sorts of other things. Therefore,
he concludes, it is not my body that provides me with an identity or with
the self from which I begin my philosophy. It follows from this that the
particular aspects of my self—whether I am male or female, black or
white, tall or short, handsome or ugly, strong or weak—are associated
with my body only, and cannot be essential to my identity. My self-identity
is in my mind, in my thinking, doubting, feeling, perceiving, imagining,
and desiring. I am, essentially, "a thing which thinks."

1.   The Mind-Body Problem

It is important to appreciate the kind of step Descartes has taken here.
What he is saying is that self-identity depends on consciousness. Our
identity does not depend in any way on our body remaining the same, and
so human identity is different from the identity of anything else in the
world.

Descartes' metaphysics supported his conception of human identity.
He said that there are two different kinds of substances: mind or mental
substance, and body or physical substance. Accordingly, he is usually
called a *dualist* and the position, in general, that mind and body are
different substances is called **Cartesian dualism.**[1] You remember that
Descartes insisted that his identity was as a "thinking thing," in other
words, a mental substance. But now, what of his body?

◆**from "Meditation VI,"
by René Descartes**

... Therefore, just because I know certainly that I exist, and that
meanwhile I do not remark that any other thing necessarily
pertains to my nature or essence, excepting that I am a thinking
thing, I rightly conclude that my essence consists solely in the fact
that I am a thinking thing [or a substance whose whole essence

[1] Named after Descartes. As a matter of fact, Descartes believed there were three kinds of
substances, the third being God. But we need not worry about that third substance at this
point. For our purposes, he is simply a dualist.

or nature is to think]. And although possibly (or rather certainly, as I shall say in a moment) I possess a body with which I am very intimately conjoined, yet because, on the one side, I have a clear and distinct idea of myself inasmuch as I am only a thinking and unextended thing, and as, on the other, I possess a distinct idea of body, inasmuch as it is only an extended and unthinking thing, it is certain that this I [that is to say, my soul by which I am what I am], is entirely and absolutely distinct from my body, and can exist without it. . . .

We have seen that Descartes believed that he could intelligibly doubt the existence of his body but not of his mind. But what is so special about this body that, unlike other bodies (the chair in front of him, the body of the king), was so intimately connected to his mind? It moved when he willed it to move, it walked when he decided to walk, it wrote what he wanted to write.

Nor was I altogether wrong in likewise believing that that body which, by a special right, I called my own, pertained to me more properly and strictly than any of the others; for in truth, I could never be separated from it as from other bodies: I felt in it and on account of it all my appetites and affections, and in fine I was affected in its parts by pain and the titillation of pleasure, and not in the parts of the other bodies that were separated from it. But when I inquired into the reason why, from this I know not what sensation of pain, sadness of mind should follow, and why from the sensation of pleasure joy should arise, or why this indescribable twitching of the stomach, which I call hunger, should put me in mind of taking food, and the parchedness of the throat of drink, and so in other cases, I was unable to give any explanation, unless that I was so taught by nature; for there is assuredly no affinity, at least none that I am able to comprehend, between this irritation of the stomach and the desire of food, any more than between the perception of an object that causes pain and the consciousness of sadness which springs from the perception.

It matters not by what power this separation is made, in order to be compelled to judge them different; and, therefore, merely because I know with certitude that I exist, and because in the meantime, I do not observe that aught necessarily belongs to my nature or essence beyond my being a thinking thing, I rightly conclude that my essence consists only in my being a thinking thing [or a substance whose whole essence or nature is merely thinking]. And although I may, or rather, as I will shortly say, although I certainly do possess a body with which I am very closely conjoined; nevertheless, because, on the one hand, I have a clear and distinct idea of myself, in as far as I am only a thinking and unextended thing, and as, on the other hand, I possess a distinct idea of body, in as far as it is only an extended and unthinking thing, it is certain that I [that is, my mind, by which I am what I am] is entirely and truly distinct from my body, and may exist without it.[2]

Descartes' distinction between mind and body is integral to his religious conception of personal identity—namely, of an eternal individual soul. He makes this motivation explicit in the letter of dedication to *The Meditations.*

> And as to the soul: although many have regarded its nature as incapable of easy inquiry, and some have gone so far as to say that human reasoning convinces them that the soul dies with the body, and that the contrary is to be held on faith alone; nevertheless, because the Lateran Council under Leo X, in Session 8, condemned these people and explicitly enjoined Christian philosophers to refute their arguments and to use all their abilities to make the truth known, I too have not hesitated to go forward with this.[3]

Apparently, Descartes felt that the concept of an eternal soul could only be derived from a dualistic metaphysics, which completely distinguished mind and body as two different substances. But his strict dualism raises many difficult problems of its own. First, how can two different substances, particularly two such different kinds of substances, interact? We know what it is for two bodies to interact, but how can a body make contact with a mind, which seems so intangible and "ghostly"? How is consciousness connected to your body? You decide to raise your hand, and your hand goes up. You formulate an answer to your friend's question, and it comes out of your mouth. How does what takes place "in your mind" determine what happens with your body? A familiar image, borrowed from untold numbers of cartoons, is the little man (or woman) in your head, operating your body as a construction worker operates a giant steam shovel. But this is no answer at all. First, there is no little man. But even if there were, the same problem would then focus on him (or her). How does he or she move a body by making certain mental decisions? The same problem arises in the other direction, from body to mind. A friend steps on your toe—your physiology teacher can explain to you what happens—nerves are pinched and signals are sent through your central nervous system into that huge complex of fat cells called your brain. But then, at some point, there is something else, the feeling, the pain. How does this happen? How does

---

[2] René Descartes, "Meditation VI," in *Meditations on First Philosophy,* in *The Philosophical Works of Descartes,* trans. Elizabeth S. Haldane, and G. R. T. Ross (Cambridge: Cambridge University Press, 1911).

[3] René Descartes, "Letter of Dedication to the Dean and Doctors of the Faculty of Sacred Theology of Paris," in *Meditations on First Philosophy* trans. Donald A. Cress (Indianapolis: Hackett, 1979).

a feeling emerge from that complex and still unknown network of neurological reactions going on in your body?

You can see that this problem of mind-body interaction is no longer just a technical metaphysical problem having to do with the special notion of substance. But even if you don't want to talk of subtances at all, there is still the problem of explaining how your mind affects your body and how your body affects your mind. For whether or not you accept the special problems of the eighteenth-century metaphysicians, you have to admit that your mind is very different from your body. And that is the source of the trickiest of all modern philosophy problems, the "mind-body problem." How are mind and body related?

The human body, like any other physical body, can be described in terms of its size, weight, chemical composition, and movements in space. The workings of the human nervous system, although very complex and not yet adequately understood, can be described just like any other biological reaction, in terms of the changes in cell membranes and chemical reactions, the procession of chemoelectric nerve "impulses," and the computer-like network of different nerve components that are stimulated at any given time. The human brain can be seen as a complex machine, like a gooey computer. The human mind, however, is not to be characterized in any such spatial or chemical terms. The mind is not the same as the brain. It has no shape, no weight, and has the awkward property of being observable—in any particular case—by one and only one person. (Anyone can see my brain if they can get inside my skull.) We can understand how a body might interact with another body, even when the "forces" involved are hard to picture (for example, the gravitational attraction between two distant planets). But how does a body interact with something that has none of the crucial characteristics of a body? You might think of "energy" here, for energy would seem to have at least some of the intangible and "unextended" features of mind. It too, in a very limited sense, "has no size or weight." But energy is a function of physical bodies, force is a function of mass and acceleration. They are not, like our experiences, "private": a lightning bolt is observable to anyone who looks. And no one has ever claimed that descriptions of energy states, like descriptions of our ideas, are incorrigible. And while it has often been demonstrated (by Einstein) that energy and mass are interconvertible, any such "interconvertibility" of mind and matter is still at the highly speculative stage, limited to freak performances by a few isolated and now wholly dependable "psychics" and such. We may well talk about "mental energy," but it is far from clear what we mean. (And the fact that transcendental meditation gives us more of "whatever it is" only proves that we don't yet know what meditation is either.)

How can something so different as ideas and sensations interact with nervous systems and brain cells? Philosophers have proposed a number of solutions, all of them controversial and none of them yet satisfactory.

But even before we look at some of them, it is important to stress the following point: The "mind-body problem" is not simply a matter of how little we still know about the human nervous system. No matter how our knowledge develops, we will still be faced with that mysterious gap between the last known neurological occurrence and the experience. Right now we can trace our neural impulses only so far, and the "last known neurological occurrence" is not very far along. But even when we have complete "brain maps" and can say for every mental occurrence what is going on in the brain at the same time, the problem will still remain: How are the two related?[4]

The classic attempt to resolve the problem of dualism is by Descartes. The following selection is from his essay "The Passions of the Soul."

◆from "The Passions of the Soul," by Descartes

But in order to understand all these things more perfectly, we must know that the soul is really joined to the whole body, and that we cannot, properly speaking, say that it exists in any one of its parts to the exclusion of the others, because it is one and in some manner indivisible, owing to the disposition of its organs, which are so related to one another that when any one of them is removed, that renders the whole body defective; and because it is of a nature which has no relation to extension, nor dimensions, nor other properties of the matter of which the body is composed, but only to the whole conglomerate of its organs, as appears from the fact that we could not in any way conceive of the half or the third of a soul, nor of the space it occupies, and because it does not become smaller owing to the cutting off of some portion of the body, but separates itself from it entirely when the union of its assembled organs is dissolved.

It is likewise necessary to know that although the soul is joined to the whole body, there is yet in that a certain part in which it exercises its functions more particularly than in all the others; and it is usually believed that this part is the brain, or possibly the heart: the brain, because it is with it that the organs of sense are connected, and the heart because it is apparently in it that we experience the passions. But, in examining the matter with care, it seems as though I had clearly ascertained that the part of the body in which the soul exercises its functions immediately is in nowise the heart, nor the whole of the brain, but merely the most inward of all its parts, to wit, a certain very small gland which is situated

[4] Scientific research could show, although it is extremely unlikely, that the brain and our mind have very little to do with each other, that the presumed coordination between the two does not exist. It once was thought, for example, that the heart had to do with emotions (Aristotle and Descartes, for example). Science has proved them wrong. But science cannot do more than lay the ground for the problem. It cannot solve it.

in the middle of its substance and so suspended above the duct whereby the animal spirits in its anterior cavities have communication with those in the posterior, that the slightest movements which take place in it may alter very greatly the course of these spirits; and reciprocally that the smallest changes which occur in the course of the spirits may do much to change the movements of this gland.[5]

. . . .

Let us then conceive here that the soul has its principal seat in the little gland which exists in the middle of the brain, from whence it radiates forth through all the remainder of the body by means of the animal spirits, nerves, and even the blood, which, participating in the impressions of the spirits, can carry them by the arteries into all the members. And recollecting what has been said above about the machine of our body, i.e. that the little filaments of our nerves are so distributed in all its parts, that on the occasion of the diverse movements which are there excited by sensible objects, they open in diverse ways the pores of the brain, which causes the animal spirits contained in these cavities to enter in diverse ways into the muscles, by which means they are capable of being moved; and also that all the other causes which are capable of moving the spirits in diverse ways suffice to conduct them into diverse muscles; let us here add that the small gland which is the main seat of the soul is so suspended between the cavities which contain the spirits that it can be moved by them in as many different ways as there are sensible diversities in the object, but that it may also be moved in diverse ways by the soul, whose nature is such that it receives in itself as many diverse impressions, that is to say, that it possesses as many diverse perceptions as there are diverse moments in this gland. Reciprocally, likewise, the machine of the body is so formed that from the simple fact that this gland is diversely moved by the soul, or by such other cause, whatever it is, it thrusts the spirits which surround it toward the pores of the brain, which conduct them by the nerves into the muscles, by which means it causes them to move the limbs.[6]

The technical name given to this theory is **causal interactionism,** in other words, mental changes cause bodily changes and vice versa. Unlike his followers, Descartes did not take seriously the problem of separate substances or radically different changes causally affecting one another. He apparently felt satisfied, if not exactly comfortable, with such a causal account. He was vigorously attacked in this by most of his immediate

---

[5] The gland Descartes is referring to is what is now called the pineal gland, a small endocrine gland at the base of the brain. It had only recently been discovered in Descartes' time, and its functions are still not adequately understood. It is currently hypothesized that it controls mating cycles in higher animals and possibly any number of other activity cycles.

[6] René Descartes, "The Passions of the Soul," in *The Philosophical Works of Descartes.*

followers, including Spinoza, Leibniz, and many of the empiricists. "Different substances cannot interact," they insisted. Or, in more modern dress, they argued that only physical bodies can causally interact, not anything so different as physical bodies and minds. Yet one thing remains obvious. And that is that the familiar coordination of our mental activities and the movements of our bodies must be accounted for. And to do so, without bringing in causal interaction, required considerable ingenuity on the part of Descartes' critics.

Spinoza, seeing Descartes' troubles, insists that there is only one substance and that body and mind are but different "attributes" of that one substance. That avoids the metaphysical question, for there is no trouble about interaction within a substance. That still leaves a sizable problem, namely, how these two attributes are coordinated. That is a question Spinoza never answers. And Leibniz, attacking the same problem, finds it preferable to deny the reality of physical substance altogether. There are only mental substances, monads, each locked into its own experience. The extravagance of these two solutions should give you some idea of the difficulty of the problem.

We have already seen the two metaphysical alternatives that immediately followed Descartes. The first was formulated by Leibniz as part of his overall theory of monads. He insisted that there could be no causal interaction between monads, and specifically, there could be no sense made of the claim that mental substances interacted with anything that we call "physical bodies." So what could he suggest as an alternative? His answer to the problem was that God, who had created monads in the first place, had also "programmed" them in such a way that our mental activities and what we call our bodily activities are exactly coordinated. Leaving aside the rest of Leibniz's theory and looking just at the mind-body problem, we can restate his solution as a form of what is called **parallelism.** His "pre-established harmony" between monads can now be viewed as the somewhat strange theory that our mental lives and the movements of our bodies are exactly coordinated (so that I feel pain when you step on my toe and so that my hand goes up just when I "decide" that it should).

Yet there is no causal interaction between them whatsoever. It is like the sound and visual tracks of a movie film, moving along exactly parallel but never in fact interacting. (That is, the character who appears to be talking in the movie does not cause the sounds that you hear as if he or she were producing them. The sounds are actually produced separately and would continue even if the projector bulb burned out and the figure on the screen disappeared altogether.) Of course, to accept this theory you must also accept the considerable metaphysical and theological supports that it requires. If you don't believe in a God who could set up this complex system, there is absolutely no way of explaining the remarkable coordination of mind and body. And even if you do believe in God, you may well think that the mind-body problem requires some more plausible and secular solution.

Spinoza's theory need not be kept in the "one substance" metaphysics that he used to present it. In fact, much the same theory was defended only a few years ago by Bertrand Russell, without reference to the metaphysical notion of substance at all. Russell said, as Spinoza had said centuries before, that mind and body, mental events and physical changes, are different aspects of one and the same "something." For Spinoza, the "something" was "the one substance" and the aspects were what he called "attributes." Russell claimed only that our experiences and ideas were one aspect of some events or activities of which the various chemical reactions of the brain were another aspect. Accordingly, the theory has often been called the **dual aspect theory,** whether or not it is specifically addressed to the problem of substances and their attributes. Since we are now talking about two "aspects" of the same thing rather than two different things, the problem of interaction doesn't arise. But, as we complained before, this only hides the problem rather than solves it. What is this mysterious "something" of which mind and body are merely "aspects"? It is neither brain nor mind, so what could it be? By the nature of the case, we can't find out. And it leaves us with the equally embarrassing question, "How could one and the same thing have such different aspects?" You might say, "Well, a hot coal has both 'aspects' of being heavy and being hot." But that we can explain. What are we to say of a "something" that is neither brain nor mind but both?

Obviously, mind-body dualism has had many critics, both in the eighteenth century and afterward. In succeeding sections, we will consider some of the nineteenth- and twentieth-century attempts to solve the "mind-body problem." For now, we will look further at how the early moderns developed their theories of individual self-identity.

2.   The Enduring Self

Descartes' notion of himself as a "thinking thing" may be a good foundation for the notion of a soul separable from his body, but does it give an adequate notion of the individual self? A particular problem with Descartes' dualism is that our thoughts, unlike our bodies, seem to change radically from moment to moment, in a "stream of conscious-ness." Yet we don't think of our *identities* as changing so drastically or so fast as our thoughts. In fact, it seems just the opposite—that our "selves" stay the same over time while other features, such as our ideas, change. Of course, our bodies do not stay the same over time, either. Our hair grows, our skin gets wrinkly, we get sick, and so forth. So, we cannot explain the endurance of the self over time on the basis of our bodies alone. Yet, our minds change, if anything, more rapidly than our bodies. For Descartes, once again, the identification of himself with his mind supports a religious viewpoint. He claimed that his fleeting thoughts could not be brought together into a coherent, enduring, self, without the intervention of God. In "Meditation III" he states:

◆ from "Meditation III," by Descartes

. . . Because the entire period of one's life can be divided into countless parts, each of which in no way depends on the others, it does not follow from the fact that I existed a short while ago that I now ought to exist, unless some cause creates me once again, as it were, at this moment—that is to say, preserves me. For it is obvious to one who is cognizant of the nature of time that the same force and action is needed to preserve anything at all during the individual moments that it lasts as is needed to create that same thing anew—if it should happen not yet to exist. It is one of those things that is manifest by the light of nature that preservation differs from creation solely by virtue of a distinction of reason.

Therefore I ought now to ask myself whether I have some power through which I can bring it about that I myself, who now am, will also exist a little later? Because I am nothing but a thing that thinks—or at least because I am now dealing only with precisely that part of me that is a thing that thinks—if such a power were in me, then I would certainly be aware of it. But I observe that there is no such power; from this fact I know most evidently that I depend upon a being other than myself.

John Locke, like Descartes, sees self-consciousness as the key to self-identity. But unlike Descartes, he argues that this identity does not depend on our remaining the same thinking substance, that is, on our having the same soul. Indeed, in the course of our life our soul might be replaced with new souls just as in the course of a tree's growth its cells are replaced with new cells. What makes the tree the same tree is the fact that the same life is present in spite of changes in its physical structure; and what makes a person the same person is that the same *consciousness* and memories are present. Thus Locke differs from Descartes in distinguishing between the soul (a substance) and consciousness. It is our consciousness that we call our "self." In *An Essay Concerning Human Understanding*, Locke argues:

◆ on Personal Identity, by John Locke

To find wherein personal identity consists, we must consider what *person* stands for;—which, I think, is a thinking intelligent being, that has reason and reflection, and can consider itself as it-self, the same thinking thing, in different times and places; which it does only by that consciousness which is inseparable from think-ing, and as it seems to me, essential to it: it being impossible for any one to perceive without *perceiving* that he does perceive. When we see, hear, smell, taste, feel, meditate, or will anything, we know that we do so. Thus it is always as to our present sensations and perceptions: and by this every one is to himself that which he calls *self:*—it not being considered, in this case, whether the same self be continued in the same or divers substances. For, since con-sciousness always accompanies thinking, and it is that which makes every one to be what he calls self, and thereby distinguishes himself from all other thinking things, in this alone consists per-sonal identity, i.e. the sameness of a rational being: and as far as this consciousness can be extended backwards to any past action or thought, so far reaches the identity of that person; it is the same self now it was then; and it is by the same self with this present one that now reflects on it, that that action was done.

Consciousness makes personal Identity.—But it is further in-quired, whether it be the same identical substance. This few[7] would think they had reason to doubt of, if these perceptions, with their consciousness, always remained present in the mind, whereby the same thinking thing would be always consciously present, and, as would be thought, evidently the same to itself. But that which seems to make the difficulty is this, that this consciousness being interrupted always by forgetfulness, there being no moment of our lives wherein we have the whole train of all our past actions before our eyes in one view, but even the best memories losing the sight of one part whilst they are viewing another; and we sometimes, and that the greatest part of our lives, not reflecting on our past selves, being intent on our present thoughts, and in sound sleep having no thoughts at all, or at least none with that consciousness which remarks our waking thoughts,—I say, in all these cases, our con-sciousness being interrupted, and we losing the sight of our past selves, doubts are raised whether we are the same thinking thing, i.e. the same *substance* or no. Which, however reasonable or unreasonable, concerns not *personal* identity at all. The question being what makes the same person; and not whether it be the same identical substance, which always thinks in the same person, which, in this case, matters not at all: different substances, by the same consciousness (where they do partake in it) being united into one person, as well as different bodies by the same life are united into one animal, whose identity is preserved in that change of substances by the unity of one continued life. For, it being the same consciousness that makes a man be himself to himself, personal identity depends on that only, whether it be annexed solely to one individual substance, or can be continued in a succession of

[7]Locke refers here to Descartes.

several substances. For as far as any intelligent being *can* repeat the idea of any past action with the same consciousness it had of it at first, and with the same consciousness it has of any present action; so far it is the same personal self. For it is by the consciousness it has of its present thoughts and actions, that it is *self to itself* now, and so will be the same self, as far as the same consciousness can extend to actions past or to come; and would be by distance of time, or change of substance, no more two persons, than a man be two men by wearing other clothes to-day than he did yesterday, with a long or a short sleep between: the same consciousness uniting those distant actions into the same person, whatever substances contributed to their production.

Personal Identity in Change of Substance.—That this is so, we have some kind of evidence in our very bodies, all whose particles, whilst vitally united to this same thinking conscious self, so that *we feel* when they are touched, and are affected by, and conscious of good or harm that happens to them, are a part of ourselves; i.e. of our thinking conscious self. Thus, the limbs of his body are to every one a part of himself; he sympathizes and is concerned for them. Cut off a hand, and thereby separate it from that consciousness he had of its heat, cold, and other affections, and it is then no longer a part of that which is himself, any more than the remotest part of matter. Thus, we see the *substance* whereof personal self consisted at one time may be varied at another, without the change of personal identity; there being no question about the same person, though the limbs which but now were a part of it, be cut off.

· · · · · · · · · ·

If the same consciousness (which, as has been shown, is quite a different thing from the same numerical figure or motion in body) can be transferred from one thinking substance to another, it will be possible that two thinking substances may make but one person. For the same consciousness being preserved, whether in the same or different substances, the personal identity is preserved. Whether the same immaterial being, being conscious of the action of its past duration, may be wholly stripped of all the consciousness of its past existence, and lose it beyond the power of ever retrieving it again: and so as it were beginning a new account from a new period, have a consciousness that *cannot* reach beyond this new state. All those who hold pre-existence are evidently of this mind; since they allow the soul to have no remaining consciousness of what it did in the pre-existing state, either wholly separate from body, or informing any other body; and if they should not, it is plain experience would be against them. So that personal identity, reaching no further than consciousness reaches, a pre-existent spirit not having continued so many ages in a state of silence, must needs make different persons. Suppose a Christian Platonist or a Pythagorean should, upon God's having ended all his works of creation the seventh day, think his soul hath existed ever since; and should imagine it has revolved in several human bodies; as I once met with one, who was persuaded his had been the *soul* of Socrates (how reasonably I will not dispute; this I know, that in the post he filled, which was no inconsiderable one, he passed for a very rational man, and the press has shown that he wanted not parts of learning;)—would any one say, that he, being not conscious of any of Socrates' actions or thoughts, could be the same *person* with Socrates? Let any one reflect upon himself, and conclude that he has in himself an immaterial spirit, which is that which thinks in him, and, in the constant change of his body keeps him the same: and is that which he calls *himself.*

The body, as well as the soul, goes to the making of a Man.— And thus may we be able, without any difficulty, to conceive the same person at the resurrection, though in a body not exactly in make or parts the same which he had here,—the same consciousness going along with the soul that inhabits it. But yet the soul alone, in the change of bodies, would scarce to any one but to him that makes the soul the man, be enough to make the same man. For should the soul of a prince, carrying with it the consciousness of the prince's past life, enter and inform the body of a cobbler, as soon as deserted by his own soul, every one sees he would be the same *person* with the prince, accountable only for the prince's actions: but who would say it was the same *man?* The body too goes to the making the man, and would, I guess, to everybody determine the man in this case, wherein the soul, with all its princely thoughts about it, would not make another man: but he would be the same cobbler to every one besides himself. I know that, in the ordinary way of speaking, the same person, and the same man, stand for one and the same thing.

Consciousness alone unites actions into the same Person.—But though the same immaterial substance or soul does not alone, wherever it be, and in whatsoever state, make the same *man;* yet it is plain, consciousness, as far as ever it can be extended—should it be to ages past—unites existences and actions very remote in time into the same *person,* as well as it does the existences and actions of the immediately preceding moment: so that whatever has the consciousness of present and past actions, is the same person to whom they both belong. Had I the same consciousness that I saw the ark and Noah's flood, as that I saw an overflowing of the Thames last winter, or as that I write now, I could no more doubt that I who write this now, that saw the Thames overflowed last winter, and that viewed the flood at the general deluge, was the same *self,*—place that self in what *substance* you please—than that I who write this am the same *myself* now whilst I write (whether I consist of all the same substance, material or immaterial, or no) that I was yesterday. For as to this point of being the same self, it matters not whether this present self be made up of the same or other substances—I being as much concerned, and as justly accountable for any action that was done a thousand years since, appropriated to me now by this self-consciousness, as I am for what I did the last moment.

Self depends on Consciousness, not on Substance.—Self is that conscious thinking thing,—whatever substance made up of, (whether spiritual or material, simple or compounded, it matters not)—which is sensible or conscious of pleasure and pain, capable of happiness or misery, and so is concerned for itself, as far as that consciousness extends. Thus every one finds that, whilst comprehended under that consciousness, the little finger is as much a part of himself as what is most so. Upon separation of this little finger, should this consciousness go along with the little finger, and leave the rest of the body, it is evident the little finger would be the person, the same person; and self then would have nothing to do with the rest of the body. As in this case it is the consciousness that goes along with the substance, when one part is separate from another, which makes the same person, and constitutes this inseparable self: so it is in reference to substances remote in time. That with which the consciousness of this present thinking thing *can* join itself, makes the same person, and is one self with it, and with nothing else; and so attributes to itself, and owns all the actions of that thing, as its own, as far as that consciousness reaches, and no further.[8]

The main thesis of Locke's argument is this: Personal self-identity is based upon self-consciousness, in particular, upon memories about one's former experiences. In this, he argues, man is different from animals, whose identity (that is, "the same dog" or "the same horse") is based on the continuity of the body, just as you would say that you have had "the same car" for ten years even if almost every part except the chassis has been replaced during that time. The identity of a "person," that is, "personal" identity, depends on self-consciousness.

Locke's idea that memory is what constitutes self-identity is inspired by the distinctly Cartesian notion that a person's relationship to her own thoughts is unique. You cannot think my thoughts and I cannot think yours. Since memory is a species of thought, it follows that you cannot remember my experiences, nor I yours. For example, you may remember your first day of school. Because *you* are remembering that experience as one that happened to *you*, you are self-identical to the person who had the earlier experience. According to Locke, then, memory provides an infallible link between what we might call different "stages" of a person. Memory seems to guarantee the identity of the person who is now remembering with the person who was then having the experience.

While Locke's theory has the advantage over Descartes' of allowing us

[8]John Locke, *An Essay Concerning Human Understanding*, ed. A. C. Fraser (Oxford: Clarendon Press, 1894).

to understand self-identity in terms of consciousness without requiring that we posit the existence of a persisting immaterial soul, it is not without its own difficulties. First, much of what we experience, we later forget. Do you remember everything that has ever happened to you? Undoubtedly, the answer is no. Even a person who has a very good memory does not remember being born, learning to walk, or what he had for breakfast on June 3, 1972. Probably you have completely forgotten some fairly long stretches of your past. Does it follow that you did not exist during those stretches? According to Locke's theory, it is not clear that *you* did.

Second, our memories are not always accurate. Sometimes we remember things that never happened. For example, you might remember very clearly lending your copy of *Introducing Philosophy* to a friend, only to find later that you had, in fact, been using it as a doorstop. Even more disturbing, though fortunately less frequent, cases of inaccurate memory occur when a person sincerely remembers experiences which, in fact, happened, but didn't happen to him. There are people who now remember delivering the Gettysburg Address, discovering radium, or singing "I wanna hold your hand" with George, John, Paul, and Ringo at Carnegie Hall. What are we to say of the memories of the deluded and the deranged? They are not *genuine* memories, but are only *apparent* memories. Clearly, Locke did not intend merely apparent memories to count among those which guarantee identity. We must, then, find a way to distinguish between those cases in which a memory is genuine and those in which it is not. But to do this, it seems that we would have to say that the memories are in fact the correct memories *of that person.* If this is so, it would appear that the Memory Theory is circular.

A genuine memory, as opposed to a merely apparent one, is, of course, a memory of an experience the rememberer actually had. The person who is having the memory must be the one who had the experience. Now you can see that in distinguishing genuine from apparent memory, we have presupposed the existence of a persisting, self-identical person. That would be all very well were it not for the fact that the concept of self-identity is precisely what we are trying to explain. We cannot use the concept of memory to explain self-identity and then use the concept of self-identity to explain memory. Moreover, once we reflect on the nature of genuine memory, we can see that Locke was, indeed, putting the cart before the horse. When a person says, "I remember when I learned to ride my bike," the truth of his statement presupposes, rather than establishes, that he is self-identical to the little boy with the scabby knees.

Nevertheless, modern theories of personal identity have by and large appealed to some notion of memory, self-consciousness, or psychological continuity. It is worth mentioning that ancient philosophers, Aristotle for example, did not believe this and probably would not even have understood much of what Descartes and Locke were arguing about. For

Aristotle, self-identity was essentially bodily identity, without any particular reference to self-consciousness. But neither must it be thought that the modern thesis has been without its critics, in fact, its devastating critics.

Hume completely undercuts Descartes' and Locke's view of self-identity. Relying on his belief that any idea must be derived from an impression, Hume argues that when we are self-conscious we are only aware of fleeting thoughts, feelings, and perceptions; we do not have an impression of the self or a thinking substance. He concludes that the idea of the self is simply a fiction. Moreover, since we are never aware of any enduring self, we are never justified in claiming we are the same person we were a year or a minute ago.

◆ "There is No *Self,*" by David Hume

There are some philosophers, who imagine we are every moment intimately conscious of what we call our SELF, that we feel its existence and its continuance in existence and are certain, beyond the evidence of a demonstration, both of its perfect identity and simplicity. The strongest sensation, the most violent passion, say they, instead of distracting us from this view, only fix it the more intensely, and make us consider their influence on *self* either by their pain or pleasure. To attempt a farther proof of this were to weaken its evidence; since no proof can be deriv'd from any fact, of which we are so intimately conscious; nor is there any thing, of which we can be certain, if we doubt of this.

Unluckily all these positive assertions are contrary to that very experience, which is pleaded for them, nor have we any idea of *self*, after the manner it is here explain'd. For from what impression cou'd this idea be deriv'd? This question 'tis impossible to answer without a manifest contradiction, and absurdity; and yet 'tis a question, which must necessarily be answer'd, if we wou'd have the idea of self pass for clear and intelligible. It must be some one impression, that gives rise to every real idea. But self or person is not any one impression, but that to which our several impressions and ideas are suppos'd to have a reference. If any impression gives rise to the idea of self, that impression must continue invariably the same, thro' the whole course of our lives; since self is suppos'd to exist after that manner. But there is no impression constant and invariable. Pain and pleasure, grief and joy, passions and sensations succeed each other, and never all exist at the same time. It cannot, therefore, be from any of these impressions, or from any other, that the idea of self is deriv'd; and consequently there is no such idea.

But farther, what must become of all our particular perceptions upon this hypothesis? All these are different, and distinguishable, and separable from each other and may be separately consider'd, and may exist separately, and have no need of any thing to support their existence. After what manner, therefore, do they belong to self and how are they connected with it? For my part, when I enter most intimately into what I call *myself*, I always stumble on some particular perception or other, of heat or cold, light or shade, love or hatred, pain or pleasure. I never can catch *myself* at any time without a perception, and never can observe any thing but the perception. When my perceptions are remov'd for any time, as by sound sleep; so long am I insensible of myself, and may truly be said not to exist. And were all my perceptions remov'd by death, and cou'd I neither think, nor feel, nor see, nor love, nor hate after the dissolution of my body, I shou'd be entirely annihilated, nor do I conceive what is further requisite to make me a perfect non-entity. If any one upon serious and unprejudiced reflexion, thinks he has a different notion of *himself*, I must confess I can reason no longer with him. All I can allow him is, that he may be in the right as well as I, and that we are essentially different in this particular. He may, perhaps, perceive something simple and continu'd, which he calls *himself*; tho' I am certain there is no such principle in me.

But setting aside some metaphysicians of this kind, I may venture to affirm of the rest of mankind, that they are nothing but a bundle or collection of different perceptions, which succeed each other with an inconceivable rapidity, and are in a perpetual flux and movement. Our eyes cannot turn in their sockets without varying our perceptions. Our thought is still more variable than our sight; and all our other senses and faculties contribute to this change; nor is there any single power of the soul, which remains unalterably the same, perhaps for one moment. The mind is a kind of theatre, where several perceptions successively make their appearance; pass, repass, glide away, and mingle in an infinite variety of postures and situations. There is properly no *simplicity* in it at one time, nor *identity* in different; whatever natural propension we may have to imagine that simplicity and identity. The comparison of the theatre must not mislead us. They are the successive perceptions only, that constitute the mind: nor have we the most distant notion of the place, where these scenes are represented, or of the materials, of which it is compos'd.

What then gives us so great a propension to ascribe an identity to these successive perceptions, and to suppose ourselves possest of any invariable and uninterrupted existence thro' the whole course of our lives?[9]

To answer this question, Hume draws an analogy between the fictitious identity we ascribe to persons and the equally fictitious identity

---

[9]David Hume, *A Treatise of Human Nature*, ed. L. A. Selby-Bigge (Oxford: Oxford University Press, 1888).

we ascribe to things. Just as we can never find an impression of the self that will explain human identity, so we can never find an impression of an object or substance to explain the identity of plants, animals, and things. According to Hume, then, we are never justified in claiming that, for example, a tree we see now is the same tree we saw five years ago or even five minutes ago. The cells and parts of the tree are continuously being replaced so that at no time is it ever literally the same tree. But Hume's argument goes further than this; even if that were not so, we would still have no way of justifying our belief that this tree is the same one we saw some time ago, rather than another, reasonably similar to it, but yet different. How do we know, for example, that someone has not come along and replaced it with another?

The temptation to ascribe identity to things and persons, Hume thinks, arises in part from the spatiotemporal continuity of the thing; the tree is in the same place at different times. People, however, have the troublesome habit of moving around, going to Europe for the summer or college for the semester; we still see the continuity of his or her movement, receive postcards from the appropriate places at the appropriate times, and so we conclude that it is the same person. In addition to spatiotemporal continuity, we ordinarily rely on resemblance as a criterion of identity. We tolerate small changes, a haircut or a new scar, perhaps even a lost leg or a bit of plastic surgery. As long as there is a strong resemblance between two individuals, for example before and after a haircut, we think of them as the same. Only when there is a great change, as from Dr. Jekyll to Mr. Hyde, do we question the identity of the two individuals.

Hume, however, argues that spatiotemporal continuity and resemblance do not in fact guarantee identity:

> The identity, which we ascribe to the mind of man, is only a ficti-
> tious one, and of a like kind with that which we ascribe to vege-
> tables and animal bodies. It cannot, therefore, have a different ori-
> gin, but must proceed from a like operation of the imagination
> upon his objects.
>
> We have a distinct idea of an object, that remains invariable and
> uninterrupted thro' a suppos'd variation of time; and this idea we
> call that of *identity* or *sameness*. We have also a distinct idea of
> several different objects existing in succession, and connected
> together by a close relation; and this to an accurate view affords as
> perfect a notion of *diversity*, as if there was no manner of relation
> among the objects. But tho' these two ideas of identity, and a
> succession of related objects be in themselves perfectly distinct,
> and even contrary, yet 'tis certain, that in our common way of
> thinking they are generally confounded with each other. That action
> of the imagination, by which we consider the uninterrupted and
> invariable object, and that by which we reflect on the succession of

related objects, are almost the same to the feeling, nor is there much more effort to thought requir'd in the latter case than in the former. The relation facilitates the transition of the mind from one object to another, and renders its passage as smooth as if it contemplated one continu'd object. This resemblance is the cause of the confusion and mistake, and makes us substitute the notion of identity, instead of that of related objects.

Our last resource is to . . . boldly assert that these different related objects are in effect the same, however interrupted and variable. In order to justify to ourselves this absurdity, we often feign some new and unintelligible principle, that connects the objects together, and prevents their interruption or variation. Thus we feign the continu'd existence of the perceptions of our senses, to remove the interruption; and run into the notion of a *soul,* and *self,* and *substance,* to disguise the variation. But we may farther observe, that where we do not give rise to such a fiction, our propension to confound identity with relation is so great, that we are apt to imagine something unknown and mysterious connecting the parts, beside their relation; and this I take to be the case with regard to the identity we ascribe to plants and vegetables. And even when this does not take place, we still feel a propensity to confound these ideas, tho' we are not able fully to satisfy ourselves in that particular, nor find any thing invariable and uninterrupted to justify our notion of identity. . . .

Suppose any mass of matter, of which the parts are contiguous and connected, to be plac'd before us; 'tis plain we must attribute a perfect identity to this mass, provided all the parts continue uninterruptedly and invariably the same, whatever motion or change of place we may observe either in the whole or in any of the parts. But supposing some very *small* or *inconsiderable* part to be added to the mass, or subtracted from it; tho' this absolutely destroys the identity of the whole, strictly speaking; yet as we seldom think so accurately, we scruple not to pronounce a mass of matter the same, where we find so trivial an alteration. The passage of the thought from the object before the change to the object after it, is so smooth and easy, that we scarce perceive the transition, and are apt to imagine, that 'tis nothing but a continu'd survey, of the same object.[10]

Hume's argument is familiar to us from our discussion of empiricism in Chapter 3. All we perceive, he says, is a sequence of impressions, and nowhere do we encounter an impression either of a substance (an enduring object) or of the self. What right do we have, therefore, to identify the object of this impression with the object of another? What right do we have to identify the person we are now with someone in the past?

[10]Hume, *A Treatise of Human Nature.*

But Hume's argument that "I never can catch myself . . ." suffers from a peculiar but obvious form of self-contradiction. He can't even deny that there is a self without in some sense pointing to himself in order to do it. This point was not missed by Kant. Kant agrees with Hume that the enduring self is not to be found in self-consciousness. The enduring self is not an object of experience—Hume was right on this point and both Descartes and Locke were mistaken. In Kant's words, the enduring self is not empirical. It is transcendental.

By "transcendental" Kant means what is a necessary condition for the possibility of *any* experience. Kant saw that if there were a different self at each moment of consciousness, we would not be able to perceive anything. In order to experience an object, we must be able to combine our various impressions of it in a unified consciousness. Thus, if we do in fact experience objects, we must assume that we have a unified consciousness that combines these impressions into the perception of an object. Or, to take a different example, Hume talks of different sorts of relations of impressions, for example, succession. In order for an individual to perceive two impressions as successive, these impressions must have been perceived by the *same* consciousness.

The self of "I" for Kant, then, is the necessary logical subject of any thought, perception, feeling, and so on. It is not an object of experience but transcends and is presupposed by all experience.

Hume's error, as in other matters, was in confusing the supposed experience of self-consciousness with the transcendental rules with which we tie these various experiences together. Accordingly, Kant argues, Descartes and Locke are both correct in equating self-identity and self-consciousness, but it must not be thought that the self is therefore a "thing" (as Descartes said) that we find in experience.

According to Kant, the self is the activity of consciousness, in particular the activity of organizing our various experiences. Kant borrows Hume's argument, but he turns it toward the opposite conclusion: True, I never find a self "in" my experiences, but I can always find myself in that "I" that has the experience. Kant's "self," in other words, is the act of having experiences rather than anything that we experience itself. But for Kant this self is not merely the passive recipient of experiences, and here is where the notion of self as activity becomes all-important. The self is the activity of applying the rules by which we organize our experience. Moreover, Kant argues that one of the most basic rules of this activity is that the self organize its experience as its own experience. The rule is that we must always "synthesize" our various experiences into a unity, for we could not come to have any knowledge whatever of a scattering of various impressions and sensations without this synthesis. (Think, for example, of the slightly painful and generally meaningless sensations you have when someone sets off a camera flashbulb in your eyes.) This basic rule of synthesis allows Kant to say that not only is the self the activity that applies the various rules to experience but its existence as a unified self with a unified synthesis of experiences is itself a rule.

Kant gives this curious idea of the self as a rule a formidable name, "the transcendental unity of apperception." What is important in this concept is that the self for Kant is indeed essential to self-consciousness, but it is not "in" self-consciousness. Metaphorically, it is often said that it is "behind" self-consciousness, that is, it is the activity of bringing our various experiences together in accordance with the basic rules of our experience. Accordingly, Kant refers to this self as the **transcendental ego,** "transcendental" because, as we discussed in Chapter 5, it is basic and necessary for all possible human experience. The difference between Hume and Kant is sometimes illustrated in this way: Hume looks for the self among our experiences and doesn't find it. Kant agrees with Hume but argues that he looked in the wrong place. The self, Kant says, is the thread that ties together our various experiences. Accordingly, the self is not in the bundle of our experiences; it is rather the "transcendental" thread that holds them all together and is as real as any experience.

Kant returns to Descartes and challenges his main theses, even while agreeing with parts of them. First, while Descartes thought that we had to be self-conscious all the time, Kant insists that it is only necessary for "the 'I think' to be able to accompany all experiences." It is not necessary to be always conscious of our selves but only to be, at any point in our experience, capable of becoming self-conscious; we can turn our attention when we want to from whatever we are doing and watch ourselves doing what we are doing. This is an important point: our concern with self-consciousness is given impetus just because we are often not self-conscious. In fact, several philosophers (and many mystics) have argued that self-consciousness is bad, a useless thing, and should be avoided as much as possible. According to Descartes, this is not possible, for to exist at all as a human being is to exist self-consciously. According to Kant, on the other hand, to exist as a human being is "to be able" to be self-conscious.

Second, Kant objects to Descartes' belief that the thinking self is a thinking thing. He objects to this, first of all, because of his insistence (as a result of Hume's argument) that the self (or "transcendental ego") is not in our experience but rather "behind" it and responsible for it. More literally, he says that the self must be thought of as an activity. You can see what a radical move this is when you recall the traditional doctrine of the soul in Plato, in Christianity, and in much of modern thought. The soul, quite simply, is the self conceived of as a thing, an enduring thing that can survive the death of the body. By saying that the self is an activity,

Kant undermines (as Hume had intended to undermine) the traditional concept of soul.[11]

◆Against the Soul, by Immanuel Kant

Pure reason requires us to seek for every predicate of a thing its own subject, and for this subject, which is itself necessarily nothing but a predicate, its subject, and so on indefinitely (or as far as we can reach). But hence it follows that we must not hold anything at which we can arrive to be an ultimate subject.

Now we appear to have this substance in the consciousness of ourselves (in the thinking subject), and indeed in an immediate intuition; for all the predicates of an internal sense refer to the *ego*, as a subject, and I cannot conceive myself as the predicate of any other subject. Hence completeness in the reference of the given concepts as predicates to a subject—not merely an Idea, but an object—that is, the absolute subject itself, seems to be given in experience. But this expectation is disappointed. For the ego is not a concept, but only the indication of the object of the inner sense, so far as we know it by no further predicate. Consequently it cannot indeed be itself a predicate of any other thing; but just as little can it be a definite concept of an absolute subject, but is, as in all other cases, only the reference of the inner phenomena to their unknown subject. Yet this idea (which serves very well as a regulative principle totally to destroy all materialistic explanations of the internal phenomena of the soul) occasions by a very natural misunderstanding a very specious argument, which infers its nature from this supposed knowledge of the substance of our thinking being. This is specious so far as the knowledge of it falls quite without the complex of experience.

But though we may call this thinking self (the soul) "substance," as being the ultimate subject of thinking which cannot be further represented as the predicate of another thing, it remains quite empty and without significance if permanence—the quality which renders the concept of substances in experience fruitful—cannot be proved of it.

But permanence can never be proved of the concept of a substance as a thing in itself, but for the purposes of experience only.

If, therefore, from the concept of the soul as a substance we would infer its permanence, this can hold good as regards possible experience only, not of the soul as a thing in itself and beyond all possible experience. Life is the subjective condition of all our possi-

---

[11] It is worth mentioning that Kant held onto the Christian concept of soul; to do so, he defended it as a "postulate of practical reason," in other words, as a strictly moral claim, much as he had defended his belief in God. Later philosophers borrowed Kant's arguments to get rid of the concept of the soul altogether.

ble experience; consequently we can only infer the permanence of the soul in life, for the death of a man is the end of all experience which concerns the soul as an object of experience, except the contrary be proved—which is the very question in hand. The permanence of the soul can therefore only be proved (and no one cares to do that) during the life of man, but not, as we desire to do, after death. The reason for this is that the concept of substance, so far as it is to be considered necessarily with the concept of permanence, can be so combined only according to the principles of possible experience, and therefore for the purposes of experience only.[12]

Third, Kant argued that we need two very different conceptions of self. He saw that this conception of self as self-consciousness was not sufficient to do the whole job that philosophers had wanted it to do. One part of Descartes' enterprise was to find out what was essential to his existence, what could not be doubted and so could serve as a first premise for his *Meditations.* So too Locke and Hume had tried to find (though Locke did and Hume didn't) that self that defined us through our various changes, which identified Jekyll and Hyde and identifies us from year to year, day to day, and mood to mood. But the function of the self was also to serve as a way of identifying ourselves in distinction from other people and other things. Thus Descartes' concept of the self as a thinking thing was not sufficient to tell us what made one person different from another, and he found it necessary to supplement his concept of self with an account of how a person was composed of a self and a body in some special way.

Similarly, Locke distinguishes between personal identity and identity as a man (that is, as a biological example of the species Homo sapiens) and tells us that both are necessary for us to understand how one particular person is different from another particular person. We can now clearly see that the question of self-identity divides into two questions: (1) What is essential to being a self? and (2) What is essential to being a particular self? Kant's conception of self as that which has experiences, the transcendental self, only answers the first question. Nothing in the notion of transcendental self allows us to distinguish between different people and tell them apart. Accordingly, he identifies another "self" that he calls the **empirical ego,** which includes all of those

---

[12]Immanuel Kant, *Prolegomena to Any Future Metaphysics,* trans. Lewis White Beck (New York: Bobbs-Merrill, 1950). Ludwig Wittgenstein, for example, used a Kantian thesis to deny the existence of the subject altogether. In his *Tractatus Logico-Philosophicus,* he tells us: The thinking, presenting subject—there is no such thing. *In an important sense* there is no subject. The subject does not belong to the world, but is a limit of the world. There is [therefore] really a sense in which in philosophy we can talk non-psychologically of the I. The I occurs in philosophy through the fact that the "world is my world." The philosophical I is not the man, not the human body, or the human soul of which psychology treats, but the metaphysical subject, the limit—not a part of the world.

particular things about us that make us different people. Differences in our bodies, our looks, our size, our strength would be such differences. So too would our different personalities, our different thoughts and memories. It is the empirical self that identifies us as individual persons. The transcendental self makes us human.

These have been the answers to the philosophical problem of self-identity as it was posed by the early modern European philosophers. What is it that makes one "the same person" from moment to moment and year to year? What makes one an individual person at all? The spatiotemporal **continuity** of the body would seem to be a part of the answer. But philosophers since (and before) Descartes have seen quite clearly that this is never enough, that it is also self-consciousness that provides the key to self-identity. But this has not solved the problem.

B. ONE SELF? ANY SELF? QUESTIONING THE CONCEPT OF PERSONAL "ESSENCE"

So far, we have talked as if self-identity is something singular, a unified set of ideals and characteristics according to which one identifies himself or herself. But need we think of the "self" in this way?

In his novel *Steppenwolf,* Hermann Hesse presents a character whose "self" is something quite different. Hesse's Harry Haller is a *multiple* or *pluralistic* self, a collection of "selves," with no one of them "real" or "essential." Like many of us, he lives with the myth of "two selves," one human, rational, and well-behaved, the other beastly, wild and wolf-like. He is torn between the two. But, Hesse tells us, Harry's unhappiness is not, as he thinks, a result of his "war between the selves" at all but rather the result of an oversimplified notion of self. "The Steppenwolf is a fiction," writes Hesse, a "mythological simplification." The idea of two selves, one wolf, one man, is as old as the mind-body distinction, as the Christian division between the body and the soul—even older, in fact, dating back to Pythagoras and Plato. Hesse's argument is that this simple self is a strictly "bourgeois convention," a middle-class argument for the simplicity and unity of the self; indeed, Harry is unhappy because of the tension and complexity of only two selves: the "human" who has culture and cultivated thoughts and feelings and the "wolf" who is savage and cruel, the dark world of Freud's unconscious instincts and raw, untamed nature. Hesse argues:

◆**from *Steppenwolf,*
by Hermann Hesse**

Suppose that Harry tried to ascertain in any single moment of his life, any single act, what part the man had in it and what part the wolf, he would find himself at once in a dilemma, and his whole beautiful wolf theory would go to pieces. For there is not a single human being . . . not even the idiot, who is so conveniently simple that his being can be explained as the sum of two or three principal elements; and to explain so complex a man as Harry by the artless division into wolf and man is a hopelessly childish attempt. Harry consists of a hundred or a thousand selves, not of two. His life oscillates, as everyone's does, not merely between two poles, such as the body and the spirit, the saint and the sinner, but between thousand and thousands.

Why is it, Hesse asks, that we all seem to have this need to think of ourselves in such deceptive terms and regard the self as a single unit? Because, he suggests, we are deluded by an analogy; since each of us has but one body, it is assumed that each of us has a single soul too. From this analogy we assume that there must be one self within each body. But it is here that Hesse contrasts our view with the views of ancient India and notes with admiration that there is no trace of such a notion in the poems of the ancient Asiatics. He then offers us his own analogy:

Man is an onion made up of a hundred integuments, a texture made up of many threads. The ancient Asiatics knew this well enough, and in the Buddhist Yoga an exact technique was devised for unmasking the illusion of the personality. The human merry-go-round sees many changes: The illusion that cost India the efforts of thousands of years to unmask is the same illusion that the West has labored just as hard to maintain and strengthen.[13]

Hesse refers to Buddhist concepts of the self with praise. Although he remains entrenched in Western ideas as well, Hesse is already more than halfway to one of the ancient Eastern conceptions of self, which is essentially a denial of the self as we think of it. As we've seen in Chapter 1, the Buddhist says, "give up your self-identity," "give up your self-consciousness," and finally, "give up your self." This is a familiar refrain among many Eastern mystics. It may also be an ideal secular aspiration, however. For instance, the contemporary French philosopher and feminist Luce Irigeray claims that the unified, "essential" self is a limiting and oppressive notion, particularly when applied to women. In her book *The Sex Which Is Not One* she claims that the genuine and free identity of a woman is a multiplicity or plurality of characters. Note the deliberate play on words in her title: "the sex which is not one." With it, she implies a multiplicity of meanings: The female sex is not singular and unified; women are not unified together; the female is not *a sex* at all. With this last reading, we see that Irigeray is not only claiming that

[13]Hermann Hesse, *Steppenwolf*, trans. Basil Creighton and Rev. Joseph Mileck (New York: Holt, Rinehart and Winston, 1929).

a woman has multiple selves instead of a single body and a single soul, but also that all human beings, men included, may have multiple sexualities, multiple identities—that there may not be any natural masculinity or femininity at all in the plural "self" from which we sort them out. Thus, Irigeray is making a feminist criticism of all our social and sexual roles at the same time as she offers a theory of self-identity.

◆**from *The Sex Which Is Not One*, by Luce Irigeray**

. . . not knowing what she wants, ready for anything, even asking for more, so long as he will "take" her as his "object" when he seeks his own pleasure. Thus she will not say what she herself wants; moreover, she does not know, or no longer knows, what she wants. As Freud admits, the beginnings of the sexual life of a girl child are so "obscure," so "faded with time," that one would have to dig down very deep indeed to discover beneath the traces of this civilization, of this history, the vestiges of a more archaic civilization that might give some clue to woman's sexuality. That extremely ancient civilization would undoubtedly have a different alphabet, a different language . . . Woman's desire would not be expected to speak the same language as man's; woman's desire has doubtless been submerged by the logic that has dominated the West since the time of the Greeks.

· · · · · · · · · ·

"She" is indefinitely other in herself. This is doubtless why she is said to be whimsical, incomprehensible, agitated, capricious . . . not to mention her language, in which "she" sets off in all directions leaving "him" unable to discern the coherence of any meaning. Hers are contradictory words, somewhat mad from the standpoint of reason, inaudible for whoever listens to them with ready-made grids, with a fully elaborated code in hand. For in what she says, too, at least when she dares, woman is constantly touching herself. She steps ever so slightly aside from herself with a murmur, an exclamation, a whisper, a sentence left unfinished . . . When she returns, it is to set off again from elsewhere. From another point of pleasure, or of pain. One would have to listen with another ear, as if hearing *an "other meaning" always in the process of weaving itself, of embracing itself with words, but also of getting rid of words in order not to become fixed, congealed in them.* For if "she" says something, it is not, it is already no longer, identical with what she means. What she says is never identical with anything, moreover; rather, it is contiguous. *It touches (upon).* And when it strays too far from that proximity, she breaks off and starts over at "zero," her body-sex.

It is useless, then, to trap women in the exact definition of what they mean, to make them repeat (themselves) so that it will be clear; they are already elsewhere in that discursive machinery where you expected to surpise them. They have returned within themselves. Which must not be understood in the same way as within yourself. They do not have the interiority that you have, the one *you* perhaps suppose they have. Within themselves means *within the intimacy of that silent, multiple, diffuse touch.* And if you ask them insistently what they are thinking about, they can only reply: Nothing. Everything.

Thus what they desire is precisely nothing, and at the same time everything. Always something more and something else besides that *one*—sexual organ, for example—that you give them, attribute to them. Their desire is often interpreted, and feared, as a sort of insatiable hunger, a voracity that will swallow you whole. Whereas it really involves a different economy more than anything else, one that upsets the linearity of a project, undermines the goal-object of a desire, diffuses the polarization toward a single pleasure, disconcerts fidelity to a single discourse . . .

Must this multiplicity of female desire and female language be understood as shards, scattered remnants of a violated sexuality? A sexuality denied? The question has no simple answer. The rejection, the exclusion of a female imaginary certainly puts woman in the position of experiencing herself only fragmentarily, in the little-structured margins of a dominant ideology, as waste, or excess, what is left of a mirror invested by the (masculine) "subject" to reflect himself, to copy himself. Moreover, the role of "femininity" is prescribed by this masculine specula(riza)tion and corresponds scarcely at all to woman's desire, which may be recovered only in secret, in hiding, with anxiety and guilt.

But if the female imaginary were to deploy itself, if it could bring itself into play otherwise than as scraps, uncollected debris, would it represent itself, even so, in the form of *one* universe? Would it even be volume instead of surface? No.

. . . .

(Re-)discovering herself, for a woman, thus could only signify the possibility of sacrificing no one of her pleasures to another, of identifying herself with none of them in particular, *of never being simply one.* A sort of expanding universe to which no limits could be fixed and which would not be incoherence . . . nonetheless—nor that polymorphous perversion of the child in which the erogenous zones would lie waiting to be regrouped under the primacy of the phallus.

Woman always remains several, but she is kept from dispersion because the other is already within her and is autoerotically familiar to her. Which is not to say that she appropriates the other for herself, that she reduces it to her own property. Ownership and property are doubtless quite foreign to the feminine. At least sexually. But not *nearness.* Nearness so pronounced that it makes all discrimination of identity, and thus all forms of property, impossible.[14]

Irigeray is not the only feminist philosopher to criticize the notion of "self" which was assumed by Descartes and adopted by many of his successors. Many feminists are critical of the Cartesian notion "self" particularly because of the way the mind-body distinction is related to stereotypes of gender. Because our society has come to accept the "masculinity" of the mind and the "femininity" of the body, these feminists claim, the philosophical notion of the "self" as consciousness or mind incorporates sexism right into our notions of human nature.

In the following passage, Genevieve Lloyd, a contemporary feminist and philosopher, criticizes the mind-body distinction over its whole history from a feminist perspective.

◆ from "the Man of Reason," by Genevieve Lloyd

By the Man of Reason I mean the ideal of rationality associated with the rationalist philosophies of the seventeenth century. And, secondly, something more nebulous—the residue of that ideal in our contemporary consciousness, our inheritance from seventeenth century rationalism. This is, I think, a substantial component in what reason has come to be. But it is not, of course, the only component. In focusing on it to the exclusion of any other developments in the notion of reason since the seventeenth century, this paper inevitably presents an incomplete picture of reason, but one that does highlight, I think, some aspects of reason that are of considerable relevance to philosophical aspects of feminism.

The main feature of the Man of Reason that I am concerned to bring into focus is his maleness. This in itself, I think, is a matter of philosophical interest. More is involved here than the supposedly "neutral" sense of "man" to include women. We are all familiar with the fact that linguistic usage commonly fails to recognize that humanity comprises two sexes. But there is something deeper to the maleness of the Man of Reason; something more deeply engrained in consciousness. He is after all a creation of reflective consciousness. When the Man of Reason is extolled, philosophers are not talking about idealizations of human beings. They are talking about ideals of manhood.

What I want to do in this paper is to bring this undoubted maleness of the Man of Reason into clearer focus. There are, I think, reasons that belong in the history of philosophy for the association

[14]Luce Irigaray, "The Sex Which Is Not One," chapter 2 of *The Sex Which Is Not One* (Ithaca: Cornell University Press, 1985).

between reason and masculinity. Some parts of the history of philosophy can throw light here on a very confused and tension-ridden area of human experience. Past philosophical reflection has after all helped form our present thought structures. And the creature I am calling the Man of Reason embodies some of the fundamental ideals of our culture. Let us try then to bring him into sharper focus.

THE ASSOCIATION OF "MALE" WITH "RATIONAL"

The associations between "male" and "rational" and between "female" and "non-rational" have, of course, a very long history. The idea that the rational is somehow specially associated with masculinity goes back to the Greek founding fathers of rationality as we know it. Aristotle thought that woman was "as it were an impotent male, for it is through a certain incapacity that the female is female." This intrinsic female incapacity was a lack in the "principle of soul" and hence associated with an incapacity in respect of rationality. The claim is not of course that women do not have rationality, but they have it in an inferior, fainter way. They have rationality; they are distinguished from the animals by being rational. Yet they are not equal to men. They are somehow *lesser* men, lesser in respect of the all-important thing; rationality.

. . . .

REASON IN THE SEVENTEENTH CENTURY

One of the most striking things that happens to reason in the seventeenth century is the attempt to encapsulate it in a systematic method for attaining certainty. The paradigm of this approach to reason is Descartes's *Regulae,* the *Rules for the Direction of the Mind,* written in 1628. Here there emerges a new conception of what is involved in knowledge. The acquisition of knowledge is a matter of the systematic pursuit of an orderly method. The essence of the method is to break down all the complex operations involved in reasoning into their most basic constituents and to render the mind adept in performing these simple operations—intuition and deduction. Intuition is the undoubting conception of an unclouded and attentive mind which comes from the light of reason alone. This is the basis for Descartes's later influential doctrine of clear and distinct ideas. Deduction is the process by which we extend knowledge beyond intuitions by connecting them in series. These are the only mental operations Descartes will admit into his method; but the proper understanding and use of them will, he thinks, yield all that lies within the province of knowledge. Anything else is in fact an impediment to knowledge:

nothing can be added to the pure light of reason which does not in some way obscure it.

The method is universally applicable, regardless of any difference in subject matter:

> we must not fancy that one kind of knowledge is more obscure than another, since all knowledge is of the same nature throughout, and consists solely in combining what is self evident.

This universality of Cartesian method is emphasized in the *Discourse on Method*, published in 1637:

> provided only that we abstain from receiving anything as true which is not so, and always retain the order which is necessary in order to deduce the one conclusion from the other, there can be nothing so remote that we cannot reach to it, nor so recondite that we cannot discover it.

For Descartes, then, all knowledge consists in self-evident intuition and necessary deduction. We are to break down the complex and obscure into what is simple and self-evident, then combine the resultant units in an orderly manner. In order to know we must isolate the "simple natures," the objects of intuition, and "scrutinise them separately with steadfast mental gaze." We then combine them in chains of deductions. The whole of human knowledge consists in a distinct perception of the way in which these simple natures combine in order to build up other objects.

There is a deeper, metaphysical, dimension to the Cartesian treatment of reason. In the course of elaborating a method for attaining certain knowledge Descartes thinks he is uncovering the unity of all the sciences, the unity of knowledge. For him this is identical with the order of thought itself, with the very structure of the knowing mind. And this order of thought is taken as transparently reflecting the order of things. In the *Regulae* there is no gap between intuitions and the simple natures that are their objective correlates. In the later *Meditations* (1641) the possibility of radical doubt opens a gap between ideas and the material world, between the structure of the mind and the structure of the reality it attempts to know. But this gap is then closed by the existence of a veracious God. Introspection of the nature of thought in an individual mind ultimately yields access to universal reason, God given and God guaranteed, and hence to the structure of reality itself, conceived by Cartesian rationalism to be identical with that of the mind.

This isomorphism, between reason and reality, founded on a veracious God, gives reason a quasi-divine character. Reason is God imbued, the divine spark in man. This is the seventeenth century version of the treatment of man's rational faculty as reflecting the godhead, as that in virtue of which man is made in God's image.

Another feature of Descartes's treatment of reason that is crucial here is its connection with his antithesis between mind and matter. The basic units of Cartesian method are discrete, sharp edged and self-contained mental items. This becomes even more pronounced in his later works. The vehicles of knowledge are clear, precisely bordered mental states, sharply separated from one another:

> The distinct is that which is so precise and different from all other objects that it contains within itself nothing but what is clear.

And this discrete, delineated character of the units of knowledge is grounded in Descartes's distinction between mind and matter. The absolute certainty that accompanies clear and distinct ideas derives from their purely mental character. Intuition, as Descartes puts it, is free of the "fluctuating testimony of the senses" and the "blundering constructions of imagination." Cartesian method is essentially a matter of forming the "habit of distinguishing intellectual from corporeal matters." It is a matter of shedding the sensuous from thought.

The search for the "clear and distinct," the separating out of the emotional, the sensuous, the imaginative, now makes possible polarizations of previously existing contrasts—intellect versus the emotions; reason versus imagination; mind versus matter. We have seen that the claim that women are somehow lacking in respect of rationality, that they are more impulsive, more emotional, than men is by no means a seventeenth century innovation. But these contrasts were previously contrasts *within* the rational. What ought to be dominated by reason had not previously been so sharply delineated from the intellectual. The conjunction of Cartesian down-grading of the sensuous with the use of the mind-matter distinction to establish the discrete character of Cartesian ideas introduces possibilities of polarization that were not there before.

Another relevant factor here is that shedding the non-intellectual from our mental states is something that demands training. In earlier centuries too, of course, it was thought appropriate to give the education of women a different character from that of men. And it was possible to present this as justified by their being different in respect of rationality. But with the seventeenth century there is a new dimension. Women can now be excluded from training *in* reason, that is, from the acquisition of method. And since this training is explicitly a matter of learning to leave one's emotions, imagination, etc., out of account, there now emerges a new dimension to the idea that women are more emotional or more impulsive, etc., than men. If they are excluded from training in rationality, women are perforce *left* emotional, impulsive, fancy ridden. They are not trained out of the "blundering constructions of the imagination" to enter the rarified air of reason. So thought styles, that are in the seventeenth century sense pre-rational, can survive in women. This *makes* it true, in a way it need not have been before, that women are less rational than men.

Also, it now becomes possible, as it was not before, to have a reasoned basis for assigning the emotions, the imagination, the sensuous in general, to women as their special area of responsibility. The training of a Man of Reason does after all involve getting him to shed many of his normal characteristics. It can now be seen as woman's role to preserve for him the areas of warmth and sensuousness that training in reason demands that he himself transcend. A great deal happens of course between the time of Descartes and that of Rousseau. But we can see this theme, elaborated almost to the point of parody, in Rousseau's views on the education of women in *Emile,* which so outraged Mary Wollstonecraft in the *Vindication of the Rights of Women:*

> To be pleasing in his sight, to win his respect and love, to train him in childhood, to tend him in manhood, to counsel and console, to make his life pleasant and happy, these are the duties of woman for all time, and this is what she should be taught while she is young.

The contrast involved in the idea that man was made in God's image and woman was made to be a companion for man thus takes on a new dimension in the seventeenth century. We now have a separation of functions backed by a theory of mind. Given an already existing situation of sexual inequality, reason—the godlike, the spark of the divine in man—is assigned to the male. The emotions, the imagination, the sensuous are assigned to women. They are to provide comfort, relief, entertainment and solace for the austerity that being a Man of Reason demands. Something like this had of course been the case before. Different training was given to men and women to fit them for different life styles. But now the transcending of the sensuous can be seen as an end in itself. It is not in order to fit him for the heroic that the Man of Reason is to be trained out of his soft emotions and his sensuousness, but because that is precisely what it is to be rational. The division between reason and the non-rational can now be seen as reflexing and as being reenacted in the division between the sexes—in a way it was not before.

The stage is now set for the emergence of the Man of Reason as a male character ideal.[15]

Although these feminist criticisms are contemporary, there have long been criticism of the notion of the unified "self" in the Eastern religions, as Hesse noted. Around the world, in fact, mystic sects of all faiths have

---

[15] Genevieve Lloyd, "The Man of Reason," first published in *Metaphilosophy* 10, 1 (January 1979): 18–37; rpt. in *Women, Knowledge, and Reality: Explorations in Feminist Philosophy,* ed. Ann Garry and Marylin Pearsall (Boston: Unwin, Hyman, 1989).

tended toward a different conception of self-identity from that which has been dominant in Western philosophy. Of course, even these mystics admit that people have "personalities" and "egos" in some sense; most people most of the time think of "themselves." Some Eastern religions claim, however, that this vision of "ourselves" is a false image. It is just an illusion which one accepts out of moral weakness or backwardness. Thus, in these Eastern religions the multiple self or the non-self is an ideal understanding which can be achieved only with enlightenment.

An early Buddhist work, for instance, the *Dhammapada* (ca. 250 B.C.), contains several passages about this ideal.

◆from the *Dhammapada*

CHAPTER XII SELF

Let each man first direct himself to what is proper, then let him teach others; thus a wise man will not suffer.

If a man make himself as he teaches others to be, then, being himself well-subdued, he may subdue others; for one's own self is difficult to subdue.

Self is the lord of self, who else could be the lord? With self well-subdued, a man finds a lord such as few can find.

The evil done by one's self, born of one's self, begotten by one's self, crushes the foolish, as a diamond breaks even a precious stone. . . .

The foolish man who scorns the instruction of the saintly, of the elect [*ariya*], of the virtuous, and follows a false doctrine—he bears fruit to his own destruction, like the fruits of the *Katthaka* reed.

By one's self the evil is done, by one's self one suffers; by one's self evil is left undone; by one's self one is purified. The pure and the impure stand and fall by themselves; no one can purify another.

Let no one forget his own duty for the sake of another's, however great; let a man after he has discerned his own duty, be faithful to his duty.

All forms are unreal—he who knows and sees this is at peace though in a world of pain; this is the way that leads to purity.

He who does not rouse himself when it is time to rise, who, though young and strong, is full of sloth, whose will and thought are weak, that lazy and idle man never finds the way to wisdom.

Watching his speech, well-restrained in mind, let a man never commit any wrong with his body! Let a man but keep these three roads of action clear, and he will achieve the way which is taught by the wise.

Through zeal knowledge is gained, through lack of zeal knowledge is lost; let a man who knows this two-fold path of gain and loss thus place himself that knowledge may grow.

Cut down the whole forest of desires, not a tree only! Danger comes out of the forest of desires. When you have cut down both the forest of desires and its undergrowth, then, *bhikshus,* you will be rid of the forest and of desires!

So long as the desire of man toward women, even the smallest, is not destroyed, so long is his mind in bondage, as the calf that drinks milk is to its mother.

Cut out the love of self, like an autumn lotus with your hand! Cherish the road to peace. Nirvana has been shown by the Blessed One.[16]

The thirteenth poem of the *Tao Te Ching* touches on the same theme:

◆*Tao Te Ching,* **13:**

Favor and disfavor have been called equal worries,
Success and failure have been called equal ailments.
How can favor and disfavor be called equal worries?
Because winning favor burdens a man
With the fear of losing it.
How can success and failure be called equal ailments?
Because a man thinks of the personal body as self.
When he no longer thinks of the personal body as self,
Neither failure nor success can ail him.
One who knows his lot to be the lot of all other men
Is a safe man to guide them.
One who recognizes all men as members of his own body
Is a sound man to guard them.[17]

These Eastern examples are certainly not the only alternatives to the early modern European notion of the self accepted by Descartes. Islamic, Christian, and Jewish mystics in the West as well as other Eastern traditions also offered alternatives to this conception. There have always been challenges to the notion of a unified self.

C. EXISTENTIALISM: SELF-IDENTITY AND FREE CHOICE

The idea of a multiple, or non-self introduced a very important alternative to Western, essentially Judeo-Christian conceptions. In addi-

---

[16]From the *Dhammapada,* parts rpt. in E. A. Burtt, ed., *The Teachings of the Compassionate Buddha: Early Discourses, the Dhammapada, and Later Basic Writings* (New York: New American Library, 1955).

[17]From *The Way of Life According to Lao tzu: An American Version,* trans. Witter Bynner (New York: John Day, 1944).

tion to the concern for survival in Heaven or Hell, this Western conception is typically concerned with striving and ambition, status and planning for the future, "making something of yourself." Existentialism is one form of this conception. The American dream and the Protestant and capitalist ethics in general are another. But from the conception of non-self comes a very different picture—of unqualified acceptance of things as they are rather than struggling to change them, which involves a rejection of such notions as "status" and "making something of yourself."

Once again we must not confuse this rejection of traditional Western conceptions of the self with a rejection of the philosophical question of self-identity. "Who am I?" is as important a question for the mystic as it is for the Western philosopher. It is just that his answer to the question is radically different. Does it make sense to say that the one is more "correct" than the other? This too is part of the question of self-identity. Must there be a single "correct" answer for everyone? There is nothing necessary about this, or even desirable. The problem of self-identity, both in each individual case and as a general problem, is the problem of deciding which of the many possible characteristics (not necessarily one) should be chosen as our own standards for self-identity, and that choice is not just one that philosophers make, but one which each person makes at some point or points during his or her life.

A self-identity isn't simply a label you throw on yourself in the casual discussion of a philosophy class. It is a mask and a role that you wear in every social encounter (though perhaps slightly different masks and roles for significantly different encounters). It is the way you think of yourself and the standards by which you judge yourself in every moment of reflection and self-evaluation. It is the self-image you follow in every action, when you decide that one thing is "worth doing" more than another or when you decide how to act in a given circumstance. Because of it, you feel proud, guilty, ashamed, or delighted after you have done something. The problem of self-identity is not just a problem for philosophers; it is a problem we all face, either explicitly or implicitly, every self-conscious minute of our lives.

But, you might say, why make it sound as if there is any single notion or goal of a correct self-identity? The way in which a contemporary Chinese farmer will think of himself and judge himself is very different from that of a contemporary American college student. And a very handsome but stupendously dumb bully will surely have a very different conception of self-identity than an extremely intelligent and talented college mathematics major. This may not stop the medieval scholastic, for he will immediately declare all of that irrelevant, and insist that "before God" all of us are the same, and our identities are to be judged accordingly. And most of us, despite the glib relativism we usually defend, would insist on a category that transcends all such individual considerations; we call it "being a good person." Ultimately we would judge the dumb bully and the budding young artist according to the same criterion, and, in doing so, we would think that they should share the criterion "being a good person." Even where cultural differences would seem to demand entirely different conceptions of self-identity, we might still insist on applying the same criterion. For example, a South Sea Islander might well think of himself or herself in terms that would be wholly unacceptable to us, but we can always reduce any variance from our norms to mere "accidental differences," insisting that we are essentially the same. Of course people are different and think differently of themselves; but it does not follow that those differences are essential, nor does it follow that relativism is true. Ultimately when you say that all people are "essentially the same," then you believe that there are, indeed, universal criteria for self-identity and that the differences between people, though we need not deny them, are merely superficial.

One of the most powerful schools of contemporary thought, however, has been dedicated to the idea that self-identity, in every case, is a matter of individual choice. This school, which we have briefly met before, is **existentialism.** Its most powerful advocate is the French philosopher Jean-Paul Sartre. According to Sartre, there are no set standards for self-identity, either for individuals or for people in general. There is, he argues, no such thing as "human nature," and what we are—and what it means to be a human being—are always matters of decision. There is no correct choice; there are only choices, he claims. In a well-known essay from the late 1940s, he argues:

◆ on Existentialism, by Jean-Paul Sartre

What existentialists have in common is simply the fact that they believe that *existence* comes before *essence*—or, if you will, that we must begin from the subjective. What exactly do we mean by that?

If one considers an article of manufacture—as, for example, a book or paper-knife—one sees that it has been made by an artisan who had a conception of it; and he has paid attention, equally, to the conception of a paper-knife and to the pre-existent technique of production which is a part of that conception and is, at bottom, a formula. Thus the paper-knife is at the same time an article producible in a certain manner and one which, on the other hand, serves a definite purpose, for one cannot suppose that a man would produce a paper-knife without knowing what it was for. Let us say, then, of the paper-knife that its essence—that is to say the sum of the formulae and the qualities which made its production and its definition possible—precedes its existence. The presence of such-and-such a paper-knife or book is thus determined before my eyes. Here, then, we are viewing the world from a technical standpoint, and we say that production precedes existence.

When we think of God as the creator, we are thinking of him, most of the time, as a supernal artisan. Whatever doctrine we may be considering, whether it be a doctrine like that of Descartes, or of Leibniz himself, we always imply that the will follows, more or less, from the understanding or at least accompanies it, so that when God creates he knows precisely what he is creating. Thus, the conception of man in the mind of God is comparable to that of the paper-knife in the mind of the artisan: God makes man according to a procedure and a conception, exactly as the artisan manufactures a paper-knife, following a definition and a formula. Thus each individual man is the realisation of a certain conception which dwells in the divine understanding. In the philosophic atheism of the eighteenth century, the notion of God is suppressed, but not, for all that, the idea that essence is prior to existence; something of that idea we still find everywhere, in Diderot, in Voltaire and even in Kant. Man possesses a human nature; that "human nature," which is the conception of human being, is found in every man; which means that each man is a particular example of an universal conception, the conception of Man. In Kant, this universality goes so far that the wild man of the woods, man in the state of nature and the bourgeois are all contained in the same definition and have the same fundamental qualities. Here again, the essence of man precedes that historic existence which we confront in experience.

· · · · · · · · · ·

What do we mean by saying that existence precedes essence? We mean that man first of all exists, encounters himself, surges up in the world—and defines himself afterwards. If man as the existentialist sees him is not definable, it is because to begin with he is nothing. He will not be anything until later, and then he will be what he makes of himself. Thus, there is no human nature, because there is no God to have a conception of it. Man simply is. Not that he is simply what he conceives himself to be, but he is what he wills, and as he conceives himself after already existing—as he wills to be after that leap towards existence. Man is nothing else but that which he makes of himself. That is the first principle of existentialism. And this is what people call its "subjectivity," using the word as a reproach against us. But what do we mean to say by this, but that man is of a greater dignity than a stone or a table? For we mean to say that man primarily exists—that man is, before all else, something which propels itself towards a future and is aware that it is doing so. Man is, indeed, a project which possesses a subjective life, instead of being a kind of moss, or a fungus or a cauliflower. Before that projection of the self nothing exists; not even in the heaven of intelligence: man will only attain existence when he is what he purposes to be. Not, however, what he may wish to be. For what we usually understand by wishing or willing is a conscious decision taken—much more often than not—after we have made ourselves what we are. I may wish to join a party, to write a book or to marry—but in such a case what is usually called my will is probably a manifestation of a prior and more spontaneous decision. If, however, it is true that existence is prior to essence, man is responsible for what he is. Thus, the first effect of existentialism is that it puts every man in possession of himself as he is, and places the entire responsibility for his existence squarely upon his own shoulders. And, when we say that man is responsible for himself, we do not mean that he is responsible only for his own individuality, but that he is responsible for all men.

When we say that man chooses himself, we do mean that every one of us must choose himself; but by that we also mean that in choosing for himself he chooses for all men. For in effect, of all the actions a man may take in order to create himself as he wills to be, there is not one which is not creative, at the same time, of an image of man such as he believes he ought to be.[18]

But this existentialist doctrine of choice doesn't make the problem of self-identity any easier. In fact, it complicates it enormously. Earlier in this section, we began by asking whether the facts about a person are sufficient to determine his or her identity. And we said surely not all of them are necessary, some are more essential than others. But this isn't yet an answer to the question, for it may be that all the essential facts are still not sufficient to determine a person's identity.

According to the existentialist, this is made even more complex by the fact that a person chooses which facts are to be considered as essential. Are the facts alone ever sufficient to determine our identity? Sartre's answer, which he adapted from a German existentialist names Martin Heidegger, is "never!" The facts that are true of a person are always, at least so long as a person is alive, only indicative of what a person has been and done so far. In judging a person's identity, we must always consider more than the facts that are true of him or her (which Sartre and Heidegger collectively name, somewhat technically, a person's **facticity**); we must also consider their projections into the future, their ambitions, plans, intentions, hopes, and fantasies. (Sartre calls these considerations a person's **transcendence.** Notice that this is the third different way in which "transcendence" has been used, so be careful.) This way of viewing the person makes the question of self-identity impossibly complex, in fact, irresolvable. For example, consider Sartre's example of what he calls "bad faith" in one of his most important works, *Being and Nothingness* (1943).

Bad faith, quite simply, is refusing to accept yourself.[19] And this can

---

[18] Jean-Paul Sartre, *Existentialism As a Humanism,* trans. Philip Mairet (New York: Philosophical Library, 1949).

[19] This is, however, the main concept of *Being and Nothingness* and takes well over seven hundred pages to analyze correctly.

happen in two different ways. Either you can refuse to accept the facts and actions as relevant to your self-identity (for example, denying that your repeated cowardly behavior establishes your identity as a coward). Or you can go too far in the opposite direction, believing that your actions conclusively and unalterably establish your self-identity (for example, denying that you could ever alter your cowardly self-identity through an act of heroism).

◆ on Bad Faith, by Sartre

Let us take an example: A homosexual frequently has an intolerable feeling of guilt, and his whole existence is determined in relation to this feeling. One will readily foresee that he is in bad faith. In fact it frequently happens that this man, while recognizing his homosexual inclination, while avowing each and every particular misdeed which he has committed, refuses with all his strength to consider himself *"a homosexual."* His case is always "different," peculiar; there enters into it something of a game, of chance, of bad luck; the mistakes are all in the past; they are explained by a certain conception of the beautiful which women cannot satisfy; we should see in them the results of a restless search, rather than the manifestations of a deeply rooted tendency, *etc., etc.* Here is assuredly a man in bad faith who borders on the comic since, acknowledging all the facts which are imputed to him, he refuses to draw from them the conclusion which they impose. His friend, who is his most severe critic, becomes irritated with this duplicity. The critic asks only one thing—and perhaps then he will show himself indulgent: that the guilty one recognize himself as guilty, that the homosexual declare frankly—whether humbly or boastfully matters little—"I am a homosexual." We ask here: Who is in bad faith? The homosexual or the champion of sincerity?

The homosexual recognizes his faults, but he struggles with all his strength against the crushing view that his mistakes constitute for him a *destiny*. He does not wish to let himself be considered as a thing. He has an obscure but strong feeling that a homosexual is not a homosexual as this table is a table or as this red-haired man is red-haired. It seems to him that he has escaped from each mistake as soon as he has posited it and recognized it; he even feels that the psychic duration by itself cleanses him from each misdeed, constitutes for him an undetermined future, causes him to be born anew. Is he wrong? Does he not recognize in himself the peculiar, irreducible character of human reality? His attitude includes then an undeniable comprehension of truth. But at the same time he needs this perpetual rebirth, this constant escape in order to live; he must constantly put himself beyond reach in order to avoid the terrible judgment of collectivity. Thus he plays on the word *being.* He would be right actually if he understood the phrase, "I am not a homosexual" in the sense of "I am not what I am." That is, if he declared to himself, "To the extent that a pattern of conduct is defined as the conduct of a paederast and to the extent that I have adopted this conduct, I am a homosexual. But to the extent that human reality cannot be finally defined by patterns of conduct, I am not one." But instead he slides surreptitiously toward a different connotation of the word "being." He understands "not being" in the sense of "not-being-in-itself." He lays claim to "not being a homosexual" in the sense in which this table *is not* an inkwell. He is in bad faith.[20]

And then, Sartre lays bare the heart of his theory. Bad faith points to the most important single fact about personal self-identity—there isn't any. In somewhat paradoxical terminology, Sartre tells us, "one is what one is not, and one is not what one is." In other words, whatever the facts about you, you are always something more than those facts. The homosexual in Sartre's example *is* a homosexual to the extent that all his past actions and desires are those of a homosexual. He falls into bad faith by refusing to see that his past actions point to his having a self-identity as a homosexual. Yet at the same time, there is a genuine sense in which he is *not* a homosexual: In the future, he may radically alter his lifestyle. It would, then, also be bad faith were he to totally accept his self-identity as a homosexual, denying that he could be anything else. As long as a person is alive, he or she is identified by intentions, plans, dreams, and hopes as much as by what is already true by virtue of the facts. And given this complexity, the problem of deciding "who I am" takes on dramatic and extravagant complications. Consider the following scene from Sartre's famous play, *No Exit,* in which one of the characters (now dead and "living" in hell) tries to justify his image of himself as a hero, despite the facts of his life, which would indicate that he was a coward.

◆**from *No Exit,*
by Sartre**

GARCIN: They shot me.
ESTELLE: I know. Because you refused to fight. Well, why shouldn't you?
GARCIN: I—I didn't exactly refuse. [*In a far-away voice*] I must say he talks well, he makes out a good case against me, but he never says what I should have done instead. Should I have gone to the general and said: "General, I decline to fight"? A mug's game; they'd have promptly locked me up. But I wanted to show

---

[20] Jean-Paul Sartre, *Being and Nothingness,* trans. Hazel E. Barnes (New York: Philosophical Library, 1956).

my colors, my true colors, do you understand? I wasn't going to be silenced. [*To* ESTELLE] So I—I took the train. . . . They caught me at the frontier.

ESTELLE: Where were you trying to go?

GARCIN: To Mexico. I meant to launch a pacifist newspaper down there. [*A short silence.*] Well, why don't you speak?

ESTELLE: What could I say? You acted quite rightly, as you didn't want to fight. [GARCIN *makes a fretful gesture.*] But, darling, how on earth can I guess what you want me to answer?

INEZ: Can't you guess? Well, *I* can. He wants you to tell him that he bolted like a lion. For "bolt" he did, and that's what's biting him.

GARCIN: "Bolted," "went away"—we won't quarrel over words.

ESTELLE: But you *had* to run away. If you'd stayed they'd have sent you to jail, wouldn't they?

GARCIN: Of course. [*A pause.*] Well, Estelle, am I a coward?

ESTELLE: How can I say? Don't be so unreasonable, darling. I can't put myself in your skin. You must decide that for yourself.

GARCIN: [*wearily*]: I can't decide.

ESTELLE: Anyhow, you must remember. You must have had reasons for acting as you did.

GARCIN: I had.

ESTELLE: Well?

GARCIN: But were they the real reasons?

ESTELLE: You've a twisted mind, that's your trouble. Plaguing yourself over such trifles!

GARCIN: I'd thought it all out, and I wanted to make a stand. But was that my real motive?

INEZ: Exactly. That's the question. Was that your real motive? No doubt you argued it out with yourself, you weighed the pros and cons, you found good reasons for what you did. But fear and hatred and all the dirty little instincts one keeps dark—they're motives too. So carry on, Mr. Garcin, and try to be honest with yourself—for once.

GARCIN: Do I need you to tell me that? Day and night I paced my cell, from the window to the door, from the door to the window. I pried into my heart, I sleuthed myself like a detective. By the end of it I felt as if I'd given my whole life to introspection. But always I harked back to the one thing certain—that I had acted as I did, I'd taken that train to the frontier. But why? Why? Finally I thought: My death will settle it. If I face death courageously, I'll prove I am no coward.

INEZ: And how did you face death?

GARCIN: Miserably. Rottenly. [INEZ *laughs.*] Oh, it was only a physical lapse—that might happen to anyone; I'm not ashamed of it. Only everything's been left in suspense, forever. [*To* ESTELLE] Come here, Estelle. Look at me. I want to feel someone looking at me while they're talking about me on earth. . . . I like green eyes.

INEZ: Green eyes! Just hark to him! And you, Estelle, do you like cowards?

ESTELLE: If you knew how little I care! Coward or hero, it's all one—provided he kisses well.

GARCIN: There they are, slumped in their chairs, sucking at their cigars. Bored they look. Half-asleep. They're thinking: "Garcin's a coward." But only vaguely, dreamily. One's got to think of something. "That chap Garcin was a coward." That's what they've decided, those dear friends of mine. In six months' time they'll be saying: "Cowardly as that skunk Garcin." You're lucky, you two; no one on earth is giving you another thought. But I—I'm long in dying.

GARCIN: [*putting his hands on* (INEZ's) *shoulders*]: Listen! Each man has an aim in life, a leading motive; that's so, isn't it? Well, I didn't give a damn for wealth, or for love. I aimed at being a real man. A tough, as they say. I staked everything on the same horse. . . . Can one possibly be a coward when one's deliberately courted danger at every turn? And can one judge a life by a single action?

INEZ: Why not? For thirty years you dreamt you were a hero, and condoned a thousand petty lapses—because a hero, of course, can do no wrong. An easy method obviously. Then a day came when you were up against it, the red light of real danger—and you took the train to Mexico.

GARCIN: I "dreamt," you say. It was no dream. When I chose that hardest path, I made my choice deliberately. A man is what he wills himself to be.

INEZ: Prove it. Prove it was no dream. It's what one does, and nothing else, that shows the stuff one's made of.

GARCIN: I died too soon. I wasn't allowed time to—to do my deeds.

INEZ: One always dies too soon—or too late. And yet one's whole life is complete at that moment, with a line drawn neatly under it, ready for the summing up. You are—your life, and nothing else.[21]

D. MATERIALISM AND FUNCTIONALISM: SCIENTIFIC CHALLENGES TO THE NOTION OF "SELF"

So far, in looking at criticisms of the Cartesian conception of "self," we have focused on critics who wanted to expand the notion from a Cartesian dualism to a multiple, plural, or even infinite "self." But philosophical problems arise even if one accepts the Cartesian dualism. To see this, consider the following two bizarre but illuminating examples:

[21] Jean-Paul Sartre, *No Exit*, trans. Stuart Gilbert (New York: Vintage, 1948).

In the movie *All of Me,* the soul of a woman who has recently died (played by Lily Tomlin) winds up occupying the body of a male lawyer (played by Steve Martin). The resulting character, played by Martin, still looks, acts, and thinks like the Steve Martin character, but now also possesses the memories and personality traits of Lily Tomlin's original character. Who is this dual character?

For another example, consider someone—call him or her "Smith"—who, like a clone or like a multiple split personality, undergoes an exact copying procedure. Like a one-celled animal, he or she splits, head to toe, forming an exact duplicate of the original, same memories and personality, same habits, knowledge, likes and dislikes, skills, and so on. Which of the two is "Smith"? Does it make any sense to say that both are? Surely, that would violate the concept of the transcendental self. It would also violate common sense. But, given their exact similarity and common origin, could we really say that one of the two was "fake"?

These examples demonstrate some deep internal problems with both Cartesian dualism and with the unified "self." Many other problems have come to our attention from within the Cartesian tradition by way of progress within the sciences of medicine, neuropsychology, chemistry, and physics.

To consider the bizarre complications, here is Massachusetts philosopher Meredith Michaels, who has written extensively on the problem of personal identity:

◆ **"Personal Identity,"**
by Meredith Michaels

While they are illuminating, particularly in relation to one another, these traditional answers to the philosophical problem of self-identity raise as many questions as they answer. To see this, let us travel to a not very distant make-believe world.

One night, after a serious bout with the library, you and your best friend Wanda Bagg (or Walter, if you prefer) decide to indulge yourselves at the College Haven. Before you can stop her, Wanda steps out in front of a steamroller that happens to be moving down Main Street. Wanda is crushed. Witnessing the horror of the accident, you have a stroke. Fortunately, Dr. Hagendaas, the famous neurosurgeon who has been visiting the campus, is also on the way to the College Haven. Taking charge, he rushes you and Wanda to the Health Center, where he performs a "body transplant." He takes Wanda's brain, which miraculously escaped the impact of the steamroller, and puts it in the place of yours, which was, of course, severely damaged by the stroke. After several days, the following battle ensues: Wanda's parents claim that they are under no obligation to continue paying tuition. After all, Wanda was killed by a steamroller. Your parents claim that they are under no obligation to continue paying tuition. After all, you died of a stroke. It is clear, then, that a basic question is in need of an answer: who is the person lying in bed in the Health Center? Is it Wanda? Is it you? Is it someone else altogether? For the sake of discussion, let us call the person lying in the bed Schwanda. What reasons do we have for believing that Schwanda is Wanda? Given that one's self-consciousness, one's thoughts, beliefs and feelings are all mental phenomena, we might naturally conclude that a person goes wherever her brain goes (on the assumption that our mental characteristics are more likely "located" in the brain than in, say, our smallest left toe). Schwanda will remember having set off for the College Haven with you; she will remember receiving the college acceptance letter addressed: "Dear Wanda, We are happy to inform you that . . ."; she'll remember being hugged by Wanda's mother on the afternoon of her first day of school. That is, Schwanda will *believe* that she's Wanda.

Nevertheless, the fact that Schwanda believes herself to be Wanda does not in itself guarantee that she is. Do we have any basis for insisting that Schwanda is Wanda and not someone who is *deluded* into thinking that she's Wanda? How can we determine whether Schwanda's Wanda memories are genuine and not merely apparent? As we came to realize in our discussion of Locke's Memory Theory, it is not legitimate at this point to appeal to the self-identity of Schwanda and Wanda, since that is precisely what we're trying to determine. In other words, in attempting to establish that Schwanda's Wanda memories are genuine memories, we cannot argue that they are genuine on the grounds that Schwanda *is* Wanda.

Perhaps it is possible to stop short of circularity. Why couldn't we say that Schwanda's Wanda memories are genuine because the *brain* that is remembering is the same as the brain that had the original experiences. Thus, the experiences are preserved in the very organ that underwent them. Though there is an initial plausibility to this response, it fails to solve our problem. Suppose that Schwanda is Wanda—remembering the experience of learning to ride a bicycle. Though the brain in question is indeed the same, it is nonetheless clear to all of us that brains alone do not learn to ride bicycles. Nor, indeed, do brains alone remember having done so. *People* learn to ride bicycles and *people* remember having done so. And the question we are trying to answer is whether Schwanda (who is remembering) is the same person as Wanda (who did the bicycling). The appeal to the fact that the same brain is involved in each event does not provide us with a way out of the Lockean circle.

It is at this point that philosophers begin to reconsider the Aristotelian position, mentioned earlier, that self-identity is essentially *bodily* identity. If the Body Theory of Personal Identity is true, then the person lying in bed at the Health Center is you, deluded into believing that you are Wanda. That is, Schwanda is self-identical to you.

You might wonder, at this point, whether there are any positive reasons for endorsing the Body Theory, or whether it is simply a place to which one retreats only in defeat? The following case is designed to persuade you that there is at least *some* plausibility to the Body Theory. Suppose that an evil scientist, Dr. Nefarious, has selected you as his prime subject for a horrible experiment. You are dragged into his office. He says, "Tomorrow at 5:00, you will be subjected to the most terrible tortures. Your nails will be pulled out one by one. Rats will be caged around your head. Burning oil will drip slowly on your back. The remainder I leave as a surprise."

Are you worried about what will happen to you at 5:00 tomorrow? If you have any sense, you are. You think of the excruciating pain and suffering you will undergo and would surely do just about anything to avoid it.

But now, Dr. Nefarious says, "Tomorrow at 4:55, I will use my Dememorizer to erase your memory of this conversation." Are you still anxious about what is going to happen to you tomorrow at 5:00? Surely you are. After all the fact that you won't, between 4:55 and 5:00, be anticipating your torture doesn't entail that the torture itself will be any less painful. When you forget that your Calculus professor told the class there would be a test on Friday, you aren't thereby spared the experience of taking the test (in fact, in that case the experience is made worse by your not having had the opportunity to anticipate it).

Now, Dr. Nefarious says, "Tomorrow at 4:57, I will use my Dememorizer to erase *all* of your memories." Are you still anxious about what will happen tomorrow at 5:00? Isn't it natural to describe the situation as one in which you will undergo horrible torture, though you won't know who you are or why this is happening to you? *You* will still experience *your* fingernails being pulled out, *your* back being burned, *your* face being eaten up by rats. Surely, those experiences are ones you would like to avoid.

Finally, Dr. Nefarious says to you, "Tomorrow at 4:58, I am going to use my Rememorizer to implant in your brain all of Ronald Reagan's memories." Though this may not please you for personal or political reasons, the relevant question remains this: are you still worried about what is going to happen tomorrow at 5:00? Isn't it again perfectly natural to describe the situation as one in which you will undergo horrible torture, all the while believing that you are Ronald Reagan. Do you not *now* remain concerned that you will experience excruciating pain and intolerable suffering? Look at your fingernails while you consider your answer to this question.

What this story demonstrates is not the conclusive superiority of the Body Theory over the Memory (or Brain) Theory, but rather the importance of our bodies to our self-identity. This is something that tends to get lost in the traditional conceptions of personal identity. Furthermore, returning to the case of Schwanda, we can now see that it is not altogether preposterous to argue that Schwanda is indeed you, deluded into believing that she is Wanda. In other words, anyone who wishes to dismiss the possibility must also dismiss the possibility that the person who undergoes the torture is indeed you, deluded into believing that you are Ronald Reagan.

While it is true that we tend to identify ourselves with and by our thoughts, beliefs, inclinations and feelings, our discussion of the Body Theory should remind us that there are reasons for believing that our bodies are, at the very least, important to who we are. Some philosophers would argue that our bodies *are* who we are, that self-identity *is* bodily identity.

In considering these admittedly fanciful problem cases, we have seen that we lack a concept of self-identity that allows us to predict when we would or wouldn't persist through time. This might suggest to us that our concept of self-identity is not an all-or-nothing one, that, in fact, our concept is one which admits of degrees. If so, we are no longer talking about identity *per se,* which is an all-or-nothing concept, but rather about some other relation of psychological and physical connectedness. Nevertheless, we can now see first, that the answer to the question "Who ought to pay Schwanda's tuition?" will depend upon which theory of personal identity we are inclined to endorse and second, that the answer may not be as clear and unequivocal as we would like it to be.[22]

If the problem with our notion of "self" is dualism, then perhaps the answer is the rejection of dualism. Of course, we still have to account for the obvious facts of the case: that we feel something when certain things happen to our bodies, that we do something when we mentally decide to. But philosophers of recent years—and nearly all psychologists—have taken a dim view toward dualism in all of the above forms.

A first, still timid step toward eliminating dualism consists of minimizing, though not rejecting, the mental side of dualism. This theory is usually called **epiphenomenalism,** and William James was one of its best-known defenders. Epiphenomenalism allows for causal interaction, but only in one direction. Bodies and changes in bodies cause mental events. You might think of a boiler system or automobile engine equipped with various gauges to tell us how the machine is functioning at any given time. The machine works on, registering certain results on the attached gauges. But notice that the gauge is relatively unimportant to the working of the machine. In fact, the gauge can break and the machine can function for years. What is the significance of such a theory? Many philosophers and psychologists are interested primarily in the continuity of physical and physiological laws without the problematic

[22]This essay was written by Meredith Michaels for the third edition of *Introducing Philosophy.*

disruption of mysterious "mental causes." For them, such a theory allows them to concentrate wholly on the physical side of the matter and ignore "the mind" completely. If an objection is raised one can always insist: "Oh, I'm not denying that you feel something too." But this is an unimportant detail, a side-product, an epiphenomenon, that need not be taken all that seriously.

1.   Radical Behaviorism

Epiphenomenalism is a timid rejection of dualism. It doesn't actually reject dualism, but it minimizes one half the duality. Other forms of attack are not so timid. In psychology, it has long been accepted by many authors that all talk of "the mental" is a hopeless tangle of confusions that, by the nature of the case, cannot be resolved through any experiment whatsoever. (That is, only one person could observe the results of the experiment in any given case, and the very nature of a scientific experiment is that is must be observable by anyone.) Accordingly, many psychologists have followed the American theorist John Watson in practicing what they call **behaviorism.**

Today the best-known behaviorist is the late psychologist B. F. Skinner. Behaviorism, as a form of science, refuses to even consider any events that cannot be publicly witnessed. That immediately and logically excludes mental events. Behaviorism is primarily a scientific method and need not deny the existence of mental events. Most behaviorists, however, have gone beyond the method—which only says that they will not scientifically study such events—and have done a bit of metaphysics as well; they also deny that there can be any mental events. Watson, for example, goes so far as to suggest that belief in consciousness goes back to the ancient days of superstition and magic. He insists that any good behaviorist can catch the average undergraduate student in a mess of tongue-tied contradictions but concludes from this not that our concept of consciousness is complicated and confused but rather that there could not possibly be any such thing. His argument is self-consciously "scientific," the alternative to which is being a mere "savage and still believing in magic." His test is simply whether the soul (philosophers and psychologists often shift too easily between "soul" and "consciousness") can be experienced; "no one has ever touched a soul, or seen one in a test tube, or has in any other way come into relationship with it as he has with the other objects of his daily experience."[23] Thus Watson shifts from his view as a scientist, able to write about only what he can measure and observe, to a view as a metaphysician, insisting that there cannot be any such thing as consciousness and that no rational person should believe that there is.

[23] John Watson, *Behaviorism* (New York: Norton, 1930).

2.   Logical Behaviorism

Philosophers too have turned to behaviorism as a way of escaping the problems of Cartesian dualism. Oxford philosopher Gilbert Ryle, following some suggestions by Ludwig Wittgenstein, established a new form of behaviorism—*logical* behaviorism—in his book *The Concept of Mind* (1949). Its first chapter is appropriately called "Descartes' Myth." First he describes what he calls "the official doctrine":

◆ **"Descartes' Myth,"**
by Gilbert Ryle

There is a doctrine about the nature and place of minds which is so prevalent among theorists and even among laymen that it deserves to be described as the official theory. Most philosophers, psychologists and religious teachers subscribe, with minor reservations, to its main articles and, although they admit certain theoretical difficulties in it, they tend to assume that these can be overcome without serious modifications being made to the architecture of the theory. It will be argued here that the central principles of the doctrine are unsound and conflict with the whole body of what we know about minds when we are not speculating about them.

The official doctrine, which hails chiefly from Descartes, is something like this. With the doubtful exceptions of idiots and infants in arms every human being has both a body and a mind. Some would prefer to say that every human being has both a body and a mind. His body and his mind are ordinarily harnessed together, but after the death of the body his mind may continue to exist and function.

Human bodies are in space and are subject to the mechanical laws which govern all other bodies in space. Bodily processes and states can be inspected by external observers. So a man's bodily life is as much a public affair as are the lives of animals and reptiles and even as the careers of trees, crystals and plants.

But minds are not in space, nor are their operations subject to mechanical laws. The workings of one mind are not witnessable by other observers; its career is private. Only I can take direct cognisance of the states and processes of my own mind. A person therefore lives through two collateral histories, one consisting of what happens in and to his body, the other consisting of what happens in and to his mind. The first is public, the second private. The events in the first history are events in the physical world, those in the second are events in the mental world.

It has been disputed whether a person does or can directly monitor all or only some of the episodes of his own private history; but, according to the official doctrine, of at least some of these episodes he has direct and unchallengeable cognisance. In consciousness, self-consciousness and introspection he is directly and authentically apprised of the present states and operations of his mind. He may have great or small uncertainties about concurrent and adjacent episodes in the physical world, but he can have none about at least part of what is momentarily occupying his mind.

It is customary to express this bifurcation of his two lives and of his two worlds by saying that the things and events which belong to the physical world, including his own body, are external, while the workings of his own mind are internal. This antithesis of outer and inner is of course meant to be construed as a metaphor, since minds, not being in space, could not be described as being spatially inside anything else, or as having things going on spatially inside themselves. But relapses from this good intention are common and theorists are found speculating how stimuli, the physical sources of which are yards or miles outside a person's skin, can generate mental responses inside his skull, or how decisions framed inside his cranium can set going movements of his extremities.

Even when "inner" and "outer" are construed as metaphors, the problem how a person's mind and body influence one another is notoriously charged with theoretical difficulties. What the mind wills, the legs, arms and the tongue execute; what affects the ear and the eye has something to do with what the mind perceives; grimaces and smiles betray the mind's moods and bodily castigations lead, it is hoped, to moral improvement. But the actual transactions between the episodes of the private history and those of the public history remain mysterious, since by definition they can belong to neither series. They could not be reported among the happenings described in a person's autobiography of his inner life, but nor could they be reported among those described in someone else's biography of that person's overt career. They can be inspected neither by introspection nor by laboratory experiment. They are theoretical shuttlecocks which are forever being bandied from the physiologist back to the psychologist and from the psychologist back to the physiologist.

Underlying this partly metaphorical representation of the bifurcation of a person's two lives there is a seemingly more profound and philosophical assumption. It is assumed that there are two different kinds of existence or status. What exists or happens may have the status of physical existence, or it may have the status of mental existence. Somewhat as the faces of coins are either heads or tails, or somewhat as living creatures are either male or female, so, it is supposed, some existing is physical existing, other existing is mental existing. It is a necessary feature of what has physical existence that it is in space and time; it is a necessary feature of what has mental existence that it is in time but not in space. What has physical existence is composed of matter, or else is a function of matter; what has mental existence consists of consciousness, or else is a function of consciousness.

· · · · · · · · · ·

What sort of knowledge can be secured of the workings of a mind? On the one side, according to the official theory, a person has direct knowledge of the best imaginable kind of the workings of his own mind. Mental states and processes are (or are normally) conscious states and processes, and the consciousness which irradiates them can engender no illusions and leaves the door open for no doubts. A person's present thinkings, feelings and willings, his perceivings, rememberings and imaginings are intrinsically "phosphorescent"; their existence and their nature are inevitably betrayed to their owner. The inner life is a stream of consciousness of such a sort that it would be absurd to suggest that the mind whose life is that stream might be unaware of what is passing down it.

· · · · · · · · · ·

On the other side, one person has no direct access of any sort to the events of the inner life of another. He cannot do better than make problematic inferences from the observed behaviour of the other person's body to the states of mind which, by analogy from his own conduct, he supposes to be signalised by that behaviour. Direct access to the workings of a mind is the privilege of that mind itself; in default of such privileged access, the workings of one mind are inevitably occult to everyone else. For the supposed arguments from bodily movements similar to their own to mental workings similar to their own would lack any possibility of observational corroboration. Not unnaturally, therefore, an adherent of the official theory finds it difficult to resist this consequence of his premises, that he has no good reason to believe that there do exist minds other than his own. Even if he prefers to believe that to other human bodies there are harnessed minds not unlike his own, he cannot claim to be able to discover their individual characteristics, or the particular things that they undergo and do. Absolute solitude is on this showing the ineluctable destiny of the soul. Only our bodies can meet.

Then, in section 2, Ryle argues that the "official doctrine" is "absurd" and is based upon what he calls "a category mistake":

Such in outline is the official theory. I shall often speak of it with deliberate abusiveness, as "the dogma of the Ghost in the Machine." I hope to prove that it is entirely false, and false not in detail but in principle. It is not merely an assemblage of particular mistakes. It is one big mistake and a mistake of a special kind. It is, namely, a category-mistake. It represents the facts of mental life as if they belonged to one logical type of category (or range of types or categories), when they actually belong to another. The dogma is therefore a philosopher's myth. In attempting to explode the myth I shall probably be taken to be denying well-known facts about the mental life of human beings, and my plea that I aim to do nothing more than rectify the logic of mental-conduct concepts will probably be disallowed as mere subterfuge.

I must first indicate what is meant by the phrase "Category-mistake." This I do in a series of illustrations.

A foreigner visiting Oxford or Cambridge for the first time is shown a number of colleges, libraries, playing fields, museums, scientific departments and administrative offices. He then asks "But where is the university? I have seen where the members of the Colleges live, where the Registrar works, where the scientists experiment and the rest. But I have not yet seen the University in which reside and work the members of your University." It has then to be explained to him that the University is not another collateral institution, some ulterior counterpart to the colleges, laboratories and offices which he has seen. The University is just the way in which all that he has already seen is organized. When they are seen and when their coordination is understood, the University has been seen. His mistake lay in his innocent assumption that it was correct to speak of Christ Church, the Bodleian Library, the Ashmolean Museum *and* the University, to speak, that is, as if "the University" stood for an extra member of the class of which these other units are members. He was mistakenly allocating the University to the same category as that to which the other institutions belong. . . .

One more illustration. A foreigner watching his first game of cricket learns what are the functions of the bowlers, the batsmen, the fielders, the umpires and the scorers. He then says "But there is no one left on the field to contribute the famous element of team-spirit. I see who does the bowling, the batting and the wicket-keeping; but I do not see whose role it is to exercise *espirit de corps*." Once more, it would have to be explained that he was looking for the wrong type of thing. Team-spirit is not another cricketing-operation supplementary to all of the other special tasks. It is, roughly, the keenness with which each of the special tasks is performed, and performing a task keenly is not performing two tasks. Certainly exhibiting team-spirit is not the same thing as bowling or catching, but nor is it a third thing such that we can say that the bowler first bowls *and* then exhibits team-spirit or that a fielder is at a given moment *either* catching *or* displaying *espirit de corps.*

These illustrations of category-mistakes have a common feature which must be noticed. The mistakes were made by people who did not know how to wield the concepts *University* . . . and *team-spirit.* Their puzzles arose from inability to use certain items in the English vocabulary.[24]

---

[24]Gilbert Ryle, *The Concept of Mind* (New York: Barnes & Noble, 1949).

A *category mistake*, in general, is mistaking one *type* of thing for another. For example, it would be a category mistake to ask, "what color is the number 3?" The philosophically interesting mistakes, of course, are neither so obvious nor so silly as the above examples. They are mistakes made when we try to think abstractly. Most important are the category mistakes that philosophers make when they talk about "the mind":

> My destructive purpose is to show that a family of radical category-mistakes is the source of the double-life theory. The representation of a person as a ghost mysteriously ensconced in a machine derives from this argument. Because, as is true, a person's thinking, feeling and purposive doing cannot be described solely in the idioms of physics, chemistry and physiology, therefore they must be described in counterpart idioms. As the human body is a complex organised unit, so the human mind must be another complex organized unit, though one made of a different sort of stuff and with a different sort of structure. Or, again, as the human body, like any other parcel of matter, is a field of causes and effects, so the mind must be another field of causes and effects, though not (Heaven be praised) mechanical causes and effects.

This disastrous category mistake, which Ryle attributes primarily to Descartes, is thinking that "the mind" and its events are some strange and mysteriously private sort of *thing* behind our behavior, when, in fact, mind is the *pattern* of our behavior and not "behind" behavior at all.

> When two terms belong to the same category, it is proper to construct conjunctive propositions embodying them. Thus a purchaser may say that he bought a left-hand glove and a right-hand glove, but not that he bought a left-hand glove, a right-hand glove and a pair of gloves. "She came home in a flood of tears and a sedan-chair" is a well-known joke based on the absurdity of conjoining terms of different types. It would have been equally ridiculous to construct the disjunction "She came home either in a flood of tears or else in a sedan-chair." Now the dogma of the Ghost in the Machine does just this. It maintains that there exist both bodies and minds; that there occur physical processes and mental processes; that there are mechanical causes of corporeal movements and mental causes of corporeal movements. I shall argue that these and other analogous conjunctions are absurd; but, it must be noticed, the argument will not show that either of the illegitimately conjoined propositions is absurd in itself. I am not, for example, denying that there occur mental processes. Doing long division is a mental process and so is making a joke. But I am saying that the

phrase "there occur mental processes" does not mean the same sort of thing as "there occur physical processes," and, therefore, that it makes no sense to conjoin or disjoin the two.[25]

The key to Ryle's analysis is what he calls a disposition. A *disposition* is a tendency for something to happen given certain conditions. For example, we say that "if the lever is disturbed, the mousetrap will snap closed." The key is the *"if . . . then"* (or "hypothetical") form of the statement. Ryle explains this in the following way:

> There are at least two quite different senses in which an occurrence is said to be "explained"; and there are correspondingly at least two quite different senses in which we ask "why" it occurred and two quite different senses in which we say that it happened "because" so and so was the case. The first sense is the causal sense. To ask why the glass broke is to ask what caused it to break, and we explain, in this sense, the fracture of the glass when we report that a stone hit it. The "because" clause in the explanation reports an event, namely the event which stood to the fracture of the glass as cause to effect.
>
> But very frequently we look for and get explanations of occurrences in another sense of "explanation." We ask why the glass shivered when struck by the stone and we get the answer that it was because the glass was brittle. Now "brittle" is a dispositional adjective; that is to say, to describe the glass as brittle is to assert a general hypothetical proposition about the glass. So when we say that the glass broke when struck because it was brittle, the "because" clause does not report a happening or a cause; it states a law-like proposition. People commonly say of explanations of this second kind that they give the "reason" for the glass breaking when struck.
>
> How does the law-like general hypothetical proposition work? It says, roughly, that the glass, *if* sharply struck or twisted, etc. *would* not dissolve or stretch or evaporate but fly into fragments. The matter of fact that the glass did at a particular moment fly into fragments, when struck by a particular stone, is explained, in this sense of "explain," when the first happening, namely the impact of the stone, satisfies the protasis of the general hypothetical proposition, and when the second happening, namely the fragmentation of the glass, satisfies its apodosis.

He then applies this concept of disposition to his analysis of "mind." (This occupies him for most of his book.) The main idea is this: everything "mental" is really a disposition to behave in certain ways. Consider, for example, his brief analysis of acting from vanity:

[25]Ryle, *The Concept of Mind.*

> . . . The statement "he boasted from vanity" ought, on one view, to be construed as saying that "he boasted and the cause of his boasting was the occurrence in him of a particular feeling or impulse of vanity." On the other view, it is to be construed as saying "he boasted on meeting the stranger and his doing so satisfies the law-like proposition that whenever he finds a chance of securing the admiration and envy of others, he does whatever he thinks will produce this admiration and envy."

And then the general argument:

> . . . To say that a person knows something, or aspires to be something, is not to say that he is at a particular moment in process of doing or undergoing anything, but that he is able to do certain things, when the need arises, or that he is prone to do and feel certain things in situations of certain sorts.
>
> • • • • • • • • • •
>
> Abandonment of the two-worlds legend involves the abandonment of the idea that there is a locked door and a still to be discovered key. Those human actions and reactions, those spoken and unspoken utterances, those tones of voice, facial expressions and gestures, which have always been the data of all the other students of men, have, after all, been the right and the only manifestations to study. They and they alone have merited, but fortunately not received, the grandiose title "mental phenomena."[26]

Ryle's (and Wittgenstein's) logical behaviorism differs from the radical behaviorism of the psychologists in that it is not a theory about behavior and its causes so much as it is a theory about the language of mind, about the meaning of "mentalistic" terms such as "wants," "believes," "hurts," "loves," "feels," and "thinks." Ryle's basic thesis, stripped of his polemic against "the ghost in the machine," is that applying a mental term— attributing a mental property to a person—is logically equivalent to saying that the person will act in a certain way. The advantage of this is that it eliminates all mysterious things mental by translating the mental terminology into statements about behavior, not "inner events." Instead of thinking of love as "a feeling deep inside," for example, the logical behaviorist would say, unromantically perhaps, that "John loves Mary" means that John will be with Mary every chance he gets, he will buy her flowers if flowers are available, he will take her to the movies if she utters the stimulating words, "Let's go to the movies!" As you can see from this example, the number of acts and possible acts involved in the translation of a mentalistic term can be indefinitely large, since, in various circumstances and with various opportunities, a person in love might do almost anything. (The case is not so complicated, usually, with such

[26]Ryle, *The Concept of Mind.*

mental predicates as "is thirsty" and "has an itch.") But however complicated the translation from mental language to behavioral disposition, the problem of dualism does not arise. The causal interaction between mind and body has been reformulated as the causal connection between a physical state—a disposition to behave in certain ways—and the actual consequent behavior. Saying "he will marry her because he loves her" is therefore no more metaphysically problematic than saying "the glass will break because it is brittle."

There is a problem with all forms of behaviorism—both radical and logical. However tempting such a theory might be when we are studying other people at a distance, it seems utterly absurd when we try to think behavioristically while talking to a friend or listening to someone talk to us. And behaviorism becomes pure nonsense in one's own case, when we are trying to understand and talk about our own mental states. My pain is not the same as my behavior, and no matter how easy it may be for you to infer from my behavior that I am in pain, that is certainly not how *I* know that I am in pain, and it is not what I mean by my report, "I am in pain." Indeed, when I tell you "I am in pain," I am not predicting my behavior. I am telling you what I *feel*, quite apart from anything I might *do*. Whatever the logic of mental language, that undeniable feeling seems to remind us that behaviorism, however therapeutic in psychology and however powerful as an antidote to Cartesianism, cannot be the whole story. Watson's behaviorism helped correct an absurd amount of mentalistic theorizing about the behavior of animals ("the rat is trying to figure out how to get the door open"). So too, Ryle's behaviorism is a vital challenge to the too-easy supposition that our "minds" are ghostly containers filled with equally ghostly entities and processes. But as an alternative account of the mind, behaviorism inevitably bangs up against that ultimate mark of the mental, Descartes's "I think." There is no way you can think consistently that you never think or think that your thinking is nothing but your tendency to behave. As one of Watson's early critics commented, "What behaviorism shows is that psychologists do not always think very well, not that they don't think at all."

The rejection of dualism need not be a rejection of the mental side of the duality, although that is the obvious preference of most scientists. We have seen at least one philosopher, however, who escapes the problems of Cartesian dualism by rejecting the physical side of the problem. That is Bishop Berkeley, who quite clearly, in attacking Locke and defending his own "subjective idealism," provides a radical solution to the mind-body problem as well. His theory is that there are only minds and their ideas, no physical bodies. Therefore, there is no problem of interaction. He too (like Leibniz), however, needs God to hold his system together. But idealism has not been as rare an answer to the mind-body problem as you might think, although we see little of it nowadays. The religious idealists of the past century, in America as well as in England

and Europe, were so powerful that they virtually ruled philosophy for a number of decades.

3.   The Identity Theory

The most powerful and most plausible rejection of dualism, however, consists neither of denying consciousness nor of denying physical bodies. To deny dualism by denying mind or body strikes us as a bit simple-minded. There is a better way. Why not say that there are not two things at all, as there appear to be, but only one. In other words, mind and body, or more accurately, mental events and certain bodily events (presumably brain events) are identical. This theory, accordingly, is called the **identity theory,** and it once was one of the hottest controversies in American philosophy. You can see that it was anticipated, in a sense, by Spinoza and Russell with their dual aspect theory. But the identity theory, unlike the others, tries to tie itself as closely as possible with current scientific research, and although it is not a scientific theory itself, it will allow no such mysterious "something" such as we found in Spinoza and Russell. Accordingly, it is usually considered a form of materialism (although it does not deny the existence—only the ontological independence—of mental events).

The identity theory says that there are mental events, but they are identical to—the same thing as—certain physical events, that is, processes in the brain. Unlike behaviorism (radical or logical), the identity theory does not deny that mentalistic terms refer to something. The identity theory rather denies dualism by insisting that what mentalistic terms such as "wants," "believes," and "loves" refer to is not only some further unspecifiable mental state; it is also a neurological process that scientists, someday, will be able to specify precisely. Dualism is eliminated because there are no longer two things to interact; there is just a single event, a mental-neurological event, which can be described in either of two ways, in either of two quite different languages. One can (truthfully) say, "I have a headache" or, if one knows an extensive amount of neurology, one could just as well say, "such and such (the details are not for a philosophy book) is going on in my brain."

The following essay is one of the classic statements of the identity theory by Australian philosopher J. J. C. Smart:

◆ **"Sensations and Brain Processes,"**
by J. J. C. Smart

It seems to me that science is increasingly giving us a viewpoint whereby organisms are able to be seen as physico-chemical mechanisms: it seems that even the behavior of man himself will one day be explicable in mechanistic terms. There does seem to be, so far as science is concerned, nothing in the world but increasingly complex arrangements of physical constituents. All except for one place: in consciousness. That is, for a full description of what is going on in a man you would have to mention not only the physical processes in his tissue, glands, nervous system, and so forth, but also his states of consciousness: his visual, auditory, and tactual sensations, his aches and pains. That these should be *correlated* with brain processes does not help, for to say that they are *correlated* is to say that they are something "over and above." You cannot correlate something with itself. You correlate footprints with burglars, but not Bill Sikes the burglar with Bill Sikes the burglar. So sensations, states of consciousness, do seem to be the one sort of thing left outside the physicalist picture, and for various reasons I just cannot believe that this can be so. That everything should be explicable in terms of physics (together of course with descriptions of the ways in which the parts are put together—roughly, biology is to physics as radio-engineering is to electromagnetism) except the occurrence of sensations seems to me to be frankly unbelievable. Such sensations would be "nomological danglers," to use Feigl's expression. It is not often realized how odd would be the laws whereby these nomological danglers would dangle. It is sometimes asked, "Why can't there be psycho-physical laws which are of a novel sort, just as the laws of electricity and magnetism were novelties from the standpoint of Newtonian mechanics?" Certainly we are pretty sure in the future to come across new ultimate laws of a novel type, but I expect them to relate simple constituents: for example, whatever ultimate particles are then in vogue. I cannot believe that ultimate laws of nature could relate simple constituents to configurations consisting of perhaps billions of neurons (and goodness knows how many billion billions of ultimate particles) all put together for all the world as though their main purpose in life was to be a negative feedback mechanism of a complicated sort. Such ultimate laws would be like nothing so far known in science. They have a queer "smell" to them. I am just unable to believe in the nomological danglers themselves, or in the laws whereby they would dangle. If any philosophical arguments seemed to compel us to believe in such things, I would suspect a catch in the argument. In any case it is the object of this paper to show that there are no philosophical arguments which compel us to be dualists.

· · · · · · · · · ·

Why should sensations just be brain processes of a certain sort? There are, of course, well-known (as well as lesser-known) philosophical objections to the view that reports of sensations are reports of brain-processes, but I shall try to argue that these arguments are by no means as cogent as is commonly thought to be the case.

Let me first try to state more accurately the thesis that sensations are brain processes. It is not the thesis that, for example, "after-image" or "ache" means the same as "brain process of sort X" (where "X" is replaced by a description of a certain sort of brain process). It is that, in so far as "after-image" or "ache" is a report of a process, it is a report of a process that *happens to be* a brain process. It follows that the thesis does not claim that sensation statements can be *translated* into statements about brain processes. Nor does it claim that the logic of a sensation statement is the same as that of a brain-process statement. All it claims is that in so far as a sensation statement is a report of something, that something is in fact a brain process. Sensations are nothing over and above brain processes. Nations are nothing "over and above" citizens, but this does not prevent the logic of nation statements being very different from the logic of citizen statements, nor does it insure the translatability of nation statements into citizen statements. (I do not, however, wish to assert that the relation of sensation statements to brain-process statements is very like that of nation statements to citizen statements. Nations do not just *happen to be* nothing over and above citizens, for example. I bring in the "nations" example merely to make a negative point: that the fact that the logic of A-statements is different from that of B-statements does not insure that A's are anything over and above B's.)

Remarks on identity   When I say that a sensation is a brain process or that lightning is an electric discharge, I am using "is" in the sense of strict identity. (Just as in the—in this case necessary—proposition "7 is identical with the smallest prime number greater than 5.") When I say that a sensation is a brain process or that lightning is an electric discharge I do not mean just that the sensation is somehow spatially or temporally continuous with the brain process or that the lightning is just spatially or temporally continuous with the discharge. When on the other hand I say that the successful general is the same person as the small boy who stole the apples I mean only that the successful general I see before me is a time slice of the same four-dimensional object of which the small boy stealing apples is an earlier time slice. However, the four-dimensional object which has the general-I-see-before-me for its late time slice is identical in the strict sense with the four-dimensional object which has the small-boy-stealing-apples for an early time slice. I distinguish these two senses of "is identical with" because I wish to make it clear that the brain-process doctrine asserts identity in the *strict* sense.

I shall now discuss various possible objections to the view that the processes reported in sensation statements are in fact processes in the brain. Most of us have met some of these objections in our first year as philosophy students. All the more reason to take a good look at them. Others of the objections will be more recondite and subtle.

Objection 1   Any illiterate peasant can talk perfectly well about his after-images, or how things look or feel to him, or about his aches and pains, and yet he may know nothing whatever about neurophysiology. A man may, like Aristotle, believe that the brain is an organ for cooling the body without any impairment of his ability to make true statements about his sensations. Hence the things we are talking about when we describe our sensations cannot be processes in the brain.

Reply   You might as well say that a nation of slug-abeds, who never saw the morning star or knew of its existence, or who had never thought of the expression "the Morning Star," but who used the expression "the Evening Star" perfectly well, could not use this expression to refer to the same entity as we refer to (and describe as) "the Morning Star."

. . . .

In short, the *reply* to *Objection 1* is that there can be contingent statements of the form "A is identical with B," and a person may well know that something is an A without knowing that it is a B. An illiterate peasant might well be able to talk about his sensations without knowing about his brain processes, just as he can talk about lightning though he knows nothing of electricity. . . .

Objection 3   Even if *Objections 1* and *2* do not prove that sensations are something over and above brain-processes, they do prove that the qualities of sensations are something over and above the qualities of brain-processes. That is, it may be possible to get out of asserting the existence of irreducibly psychic processes, but not out of asserting the existence of irreducibly psychic *properties*. For suppose we identify the Morning Star with the Evening Star. Then there must be some properties which logically imply that of being the Morning Star, and quite distinct properties which entail that of being the Evening Star. Again, there must be some properties (for example, that of being a yellow flash) which are logically distinct from those in the physicalist story. . . .

Now how do I get over the objection that sensation can be identified with a brain process only if it has some phenomenal property, not possessed by brain processes, whereby one-half of the identification may be, so to speak, pinned down?

Reply   My suggestion is as follows. When a person says, "I see a yellowish-orange after-image," he is saying something like this: *"There is something going on which is like what is going on when* I have my eyes open, am awake, and there is an orange illuminated in good light in front of me, that is, when I really see an orange." (And there is no reason why a person should not say the same thing when he is having a veridical sense-datum, so long as we construe "like" in the last sentence in such a sense that something can be like itself.) Notice that the italicized words, namely "there is somthing going on which is like what is going on when," are all quasi-logical or topic-neutral words. This explains why the ancient Greek peasant's reports about his sensations can be neutral between dualistic metaphysics or my materialistic metaphysics. It explains how sensations can be brain-processes and yet how those who report them need know nothing about brain-processes. For he reports them only very abstractly as "something going on which is like what is goin on when. . . ." Similarly, a person may say "someone is in the room," thus reporting truly that the doctor is in the room, even though he has never heard of doctors. (There are not two people in the room: "someone" *and* the doctor.) This account of sensation statements also explains the singular elusiveness of "raw feels"—why no one seems to be able to pin any properties on them. Raw feels, in my view, are colorless for the very same reason that *something* is colorless. This does not mean that sensations do not have properties, for if they are brain-processes they certainly have properties. It only means that in speaking of them as being like or unlike one another we need not know or mention these properties.

This, then, is how I would reply to *Objection 3.* The strength of my reply depends on the possibility of our being able to report that one thing is like another withoug being able to state the respect in which it is like. I am not sure whether this is so or not, and that is why I regard *Objection 3* as the strongest with which I have to deal.

· · · · · · · · · ·

Objection 5   It would make sense to say of a molecular movement in the brain that it is swift or slow, straight or circular, but it makes no sense to say this of the experience of seeing something yellow.

Reply   So far we have not given sense to talk of experiences as swift or slow, straight or circular. But I am not claiming that "experience" and "brain-process" mean the same or even that they have the same logic. "Somebody" and "the doctor" do not have the same logic, but this does not lead us to suppose that talking about somebody telephoning is talking about someone over and above, say, the doctor. The ordinary man when he reports an experience is reporting that something is going on, but he leaves it open as to what sort of thing is going on, whether in a material solid medium, or perhaps in some sort of gaseous medium, or even perhaps in some sort of nonspatial medium (if this makes sense). All that I am saying is that "experience" and "brain-process" may in fact refer to the same thing, and if so we may easily adopt a convention (which is not a change in our present rules for the use of experience words but an addition to them) whereby it would make sense to talk of an experience in terms appropriate of physical processes.

Objection 6   Sensations are private, brain processes are *public.* If I sincerely say, "I see a yellowish-orange after-image" and I am not making a verbal mistake, then I cannot be wrong. But I can be wrong about a brain-process. The scientist looking into my brain might be having an illusion. Moreover, it makes sense to say that two or more people are observing the same brain-process but not that two or more people are reporting the same inner experience.

Reply   This shows that the language of introspective reports has a different logic from the language of material processes. It is obvious that until the brain-process theory is much improved and widely accepted there will be no *criteria* for saying, "Smith has an experience of such-and-such a sort" *except* Smith's introspective reports. So we have adopted a rule of language that (normally) what Smith says goes.

Objection 7   I can imagine myself turned to stone and yet having images, aches, pains, and so on.

Reply   I can imagine that the electrical theory of lightning is false, that lightning is some sort of purely optical phenomenon. I can imagine that lightning is not an electrical discharge. I can imagine that the Evening Star is not the Morning Star. But it is. All the objection shows is that "experience" and "brain-process" do not have the same meaning. It does not show that an experience is not in fact a brain process.[27]

As compatible as the identity theory may seem with contemporary science and as plausible as it may seem as a way of rejecting dualism without rejecting the obvious facts about feelings and thinking, the identity theory too runs up against its share of paradoxes. The idea that one thing (a brain event = a mental event) can be referred to and described in two different languages sounds plausible and impressive. But, in this case, the two languages are so very different that there is very good reason to suppose that the thing(s) they refer to is/are very different as well. To pursue this line of criticism, here is a reevaluation of the identity theory by the American philosopher Jerome Shaffer.

◆Against the Identity Theory, by Jerome Shaffer

. . . The sense of "identity" relevant here is that in which we say, for example, that the morning star is "identical" with the evening star. It is not that the expression "morning star" means the same as the expression "evening star"; on the contrary, these expressions mean something different. But the object referred to by the two expressions is one and the same; there is just one heavenly body, namely, Venus, which when seen in the morning is called the morning star and when seen in the evening is called the evening star. The morning star is identical with the evening star; they are one and the same object.[28]

[27]From J. J. C. Smart, "Sensations and Brain Processes," *Philosophical Review* 68 (1959), pp. 141–56.

[28]Both refer to the planet Venus, one as seen in the morning, the other at night. But it took many years for this identity to be discovered.

Of course, the identity of the mental with the physical is not exactly of this sort, since it is held to be simultaneous identity rather than the identity of a thing at one time with the same thing at a later time. To take a closer example, one can say that lightning is a particularly massive electrical discharge from one cloud to another or to the earth. Not that the word "lightning" *means* "a particularly massive electrical discharge. . ."; when Benjamin Franklin discovered that lightning was electrical, he did not make a discovery about the meaning of words. Nor when it was discovered that water was H_2O was a discovery made about the meanings of words; yet water is identical with H_2O.

In a similar fashion, the identity theorist can hold that thoughts, feelings, wishes, and the like are identical with physical states. Not "identical" in the sense that mentalistic terms are synonymous in meaning with physicalistic terms but "identical" in the sense that the actual events picked out by mentalistic terms are one and the same events as those picked out by physicalistic terms.

· · · · · · · · · ·

What are the advantages of the identity theory? As a form of materialism, it does not have to cope with a world which has in it both mental phenomena and physical phenomena, and it does not have to ponder how they might be related. There exist only the physical phenomena, although there do exist two different ways of talking about such phenomena: physicalistic terminology and, in at least some situations, mentalistic terminology. We have here a dualism of language, but not a dualism of entities, events or properties.

But do we have merely a dualism of languages and no other sort of dualism? In the case of Venus, we do indeed have only one object, but the expression "morning star" picks out one phase of that object's history, where it is in the mornings, and the expression "evening star" picks out another phase of the object's history, where it is in the evenings. If that object did not have these two distinct aspects, it would not have been a *discovery* that the morning star and the evening star were indeed one and the same body, and, further, there would be no point to the different ways of referring to it.

Now it would be admitted by identity theorists that physicalistic and mentalistic terms do not refer to different phases in the history of one and the same object. What sort of identity is intended? Let us turn to an allegedly closer analogy, that of the identity of lightning and a particular sort of electrical phenomenon. Yet here again we have two distinguishable aspects, the appearance to the naked eye on the one hand and the physical composition on the other. And this is also not the kind of identity which is plausible for mental and physical events. The appearance *to the naked eye* of a neurological event is utterly different from the experience of having a thought or a pain.

It is sometimes suggested that the physical aspect results from looking at a particular event "from the outside," whereas the mental results from looking at the same event "from the inside." When the brain surgeon observes my brain he is looking at it from the outside, whereas when I experience a mental event I am "looking" at my brain "from the inside."

Such an account gives us only a misleading analogy, rather than an accurate characterization of the relationship between the mental and the physical. The analogy suggests the difference between a man who knows his own house from the inside, in that he is free to move about within, seeing objects from different perspectives, touching them, etc., but can never get outside to see how it looks from there, and a man who cannot get inside and therefore knows only the outside appearance of the house, and perhaps what he can glimpse through the windows. But what does this have to do with the brain? Am I free to roam about inside my brain, observing what the brain surgeon may never see? Is not the "inner" aspect of my brain far more accessible to the brain surgeon than to me? He has the X rays, probes, electrodes, scalpels, and scissors for getting at the inside of my brain. If it is replied that this is only an analogy, not to be taken literally, then the question still remains how the mental and the physical are related. . . .

One of the leading identity theorists, J. J. C. Smart, holds that mentalistic discourse is simply a vaguer, more indefinite way of talking about what could be talked about more precisely by using physiological terms. If I report a red afterimage, I mean (roughly) that something is going on which is like what goes on when I really see a red patch. I do not actually *mean* that a particular sort of brain process is occurring, but when I say something is going on I refer (very vaguely, to be sure) to just that brain process. Thus the thing referred to in my report of an afterimage is a brain process. Hence there is no need to bring in any nonphysical features. Thus even the taint of dualism is avoided.

Does this ingenious attempt to evade dualistic implications stand up under philosophical scrutiny? I am inclined to think it will not. Let us return to the man reporting the red afterimage. He was aware of the occurrence of something or other, of some feature or other. Now it seems to me obvious that he was not necessarily aware of the state of his brain at that time (I doubt that most of us are ever aware of the state of our brain) nor, in general, necessarily aware of any physical features of his body at that time. He might, of course, have been incidentally aware of some physical feature but not insofar as he was aware of the red afterimage as such. Yet he was definitely aware of something, or else how could he have made that report? So he must have been aware of some nonphysical feature. That is the only way of explaining how he was aware of anything at all.

Of course, the thing that our reporter of the afterimage was aware of might well have had further features which he was *not* aware of, particularly, in this connection, physical features. I may be aware of certain features of an object without being aware of others. So it is not ruled out that the event our reporter is aware of might be an event with predominantly physical features—he just does not notice those. But he must be aware of some of its features, or else it would not be proper to say he was aware of *that* event. And if he is not aware of any physical features, he must be aware of something else. And that shows that we cannot get rid of those nonphysical features in the way that Smart suggests. . . .

· · · · · · · · · ·

Do mental events occur in the same place the corresponding physical events occur? This is also a very difficult question to answer, for two reasons. First our present ignorance of neurophysiology, especially concerning the brain and how it functions, allows us to say very little about the location of the relevant physical events. This much does seem likely: they are located in the brain. Much more than that we do not at present know, although as the time passes, we should learn much more. The second reason for our difficulty in telling if there is coexistence in space has to do with the location of mental events. Where do thoughts, feelings, and wishes occur? Do they occur in the brain? Suppose you suddenly have the thought that it is almost suppertime; where does that occur? The most sensible answer would be that it occurs wherever you are when you have that thought. If you are in the library when you have that thought, then the thought occurs in the library. But it would be utterly unnatural to ask where inside your body the thought occurred; in your foot, or your liver, or your heart, or your head? It is not that any one of these places is more likely than another. They are all wrong. Not because thoughts occur somewhere *else* within your body than your foot, liver, heart, or head—but because it *makes no sense at all* to locate the occurrence of a thought at some place within your body. We would not understand someone who pointed to a place in his body and claimed that it was *there* that his entertaining of a thought was located. Certainly, if one *looked* at that place, one would not *see* anything resembling a thought. If it were replied to this that pains can be located in the body without being seen there, then it should be pointed out that one *feels* the pain there but one hardly feels a thought in the body.

The fact that it makes no sense at all to speak of mental events as occurring at some point within the body has the result that the identity theory cannot be true. This is because the corresponding physical events do occur at some point within the body, and if those physical events are identical with mental events, then those mental events must occur at the same point within the body. But those mental events do not occur at any point within the body, because any statement to the effect that they occurred here, or there, would be senseless. Hence the mental events cannot meet the condition of coexistence in space, and therefore cannot be identical with physical events.

Our inability to give the location within the body of mental events is different from our inability to give the location of the corresponding physical events within the body. In the latter case, it is that we do not know enough about the body, particularly the brain. Some day, presumably, we will know enough to pin down pretty exactly the location of the relevant physical events. But in the case of mental events it is not simply that at present we are ignorant but that someday we may well know. What would it be like to discover the location of a thought in the brain? What kind of information would we need to be able to say that the thought occurred exactly *here?* If by X rays or some other means we were able to see every event which occurred in the brain, we would never get a glimpse of a thought. If, to resort to fantasy, we could so enlarge a brain or so shrink ourselves that we could wander freely through the brain, we would still never observe a thought. All we could ever observe in the brain would be the *physical* events which occur in it. If mental events had location in the brain, there should be some means of detecting them there. But of course there is none. The very idea of it is senseless.[29]

Shaffer disagrees with the identity theory, but both his presentation and his criticism of it are central to ongoing debate. In defending the identity theory, it is most important to stress that the identity of brain processes and thoughts is an empirical identity, that is, an identity that must be discovered through experiment and experience. It is not a logical identity, as if the two terms "brain process" and "thought" are synonymous. The latter suggestion is obviously false, and modern defenders of the identity theory are always emphasizing that future neurophysiological research will prove them right. Shaffer's criticism, however, is based on a principle that must be distinguished from the all-too-easy attack on the logical identity suggestion. The principle is that if two things are identical, then they must have all the same properties. But, Shaffer argues, no amount of research could possibly show that brain processes and thought have the same properties. Most importantly, brain processes take place in the brain and can be traced like any other physical processes; thoughts, on the other hand, have no spatial location, and there is nothing that research can "discover" that will show that they do. Of course, research can and has shown that certain thoughts are correlated with certain brain processes, but correlation is not yet identity.

[29]Jerome Shaffer, *The Philosophy of Mind* (Englewood Cliffs, NJ: Prentice-Hall, 1968).

4.   Eliminative Materialism

To most materialists, the identity theory seemed promising, even if its arguments proved inadequate. The real question was whether there might be some other version of the thesis—that mental states were "nothing but" brain states—that did not claim the kind of "one-to-one match" required by the identity theory. One suggestion (still popular in many quarters) is the thesis called **eliminative materialism,** which proposes to defend materialism without claiming an identity between what we call "mental states" and the workings of the brain. Rather, the argument goes, our increasing knowledge of the workings of the brain will make outmoded our "folk-psychology" talk about the mind and we will all learn to talk the language of neurology instead.

◆ on Eliminative Materialism, by Paul M. Churchland

The identity theory was called into doubt not because the prospects for a materialist account of our mental capacities were thought to be poor, but because it seemed unlikely that the arrival of an adequate materialist theory would bring with it the nice one-to-one match-ups, between the concepts of folk psychology and the concepts of theoretical neuroscience, that intertheoretic reduction requires. The reason for that doubt was the great variety of quite different physical systems that could instantiate the required functional organization. *Eliminative materialism* also doubts that the correct neuroscientific account of human capacities will produce a neat reduction of our common-sense framework, but here the doubts arise from a quite different source.

As the eliminative materialists see it, the one-to-one match-ups will not be found, and our common-sense psychological framework will not enjoy an intertheoretic reduction, *because our common-sense psychological framework is a false and radically misleading conception of the causes of human behavior and the nature of cognitive activity.* On this view, folk psychology is not just an incomplete representation of our inner natures; it is an outright *mis*representation of our internal states and activities. Consequently, we cannot expect a truly adequate neuroscientific account of our inner lives to provide theoretical categories that match up nicely with the categories of our common-sense framework. Accordingly, we must expect that the older framework will simply be eliminated, rather than be reduced, by a matured neuroscience.

HISTORICAL PARALLELS

As the identity theorist can point to historical cases of successful intertheoretic reduction, so the eliminative materialist can point to historical cases of the outright elimination of the ontology of an older theory in favor of the ontology of a new and superior theory.

· · · · · · · · · ·

It used to be thought that when a piece of wood burns, or a piece of metal rusts, a spiritlike substance called "phlogiston" was being released: briskly, in the former case, slowly in the latter. Once gone, that "noble" substance left only a base pile of ash or rust. It later came to be appreciated that both processes involve, not the loss of something, but the *gaining* of a substance taken from the atmosphere: oxygen. Phlogiston emerged, not as an incomplete description of what was going on, but as a radical misdescription. Phlogiston was therefore not suitable for reduction to or identification with some notion from within the new oxygen chemistry, and it was simply eliminated from science.

· · · · · · · · · ·

The concepts of folk psychology—belief, desire, fear, sensation, pain, joy, and so on—await a similar fate, according to the view at issue. And when neuroscience has matured to the point where the poverty of our current conceptions is apparent to everyone, the superiority of the new framework is established, we shall then be able to set about *reconceiving* our internal states and activities, within a truly adequate conceptual framework at last. Our explanations of one another's behavior will appeal to such things as our neuropharmacological states, the neural activity in specialized anatomical areas, and whatever other states are deemed relevant by the new theory. Our private introspection will also be transformed, and may be profoundly enhanced by reason of the more accurate and penetrating framework it will have to work with—just as the astronomer's perception of the night sky is much enhanced by the detailed knowledge of modern astronomical theory that he or she possesses.

The magnitude of the conceptual revolution here suggested should not be minimized: it would be enormous. And the benefits to humanity might be equally great. If each of us possessed an accurate neuroscientific understanding of (what we now conceive dimly as) the varieties and causes of mental illness, the factors involved in learning, the neural basis of emotions, intelligence, and socialization, then the sum total of human misery might be much reduced. The simple increase in mutual understanding that the new framework made possible could contribute substantially toward a more peaceful and humane society. Of course, there would be dangers as well: increased knowledge means increased power, and power can always be misused.

ARGUMENTS FOR ELIMINATIVE MATERIALISM

The arguments for eliminative materialism are diffuse and less than decisive, but they are stronger than is widely supposed. The distinguishing feature of this position is its denial that a smooth intertheoretic reduction is to be expected—even a species-specific reduction—of the framework of folk psychology to the framework of a matured neuroscience. The reason for this denial is the eliminative materialist's conviction that folk psychology is a hopelessly primitive and deeply confused conception of our internal activities. But why this low opinion of our common-sense conceptions?

There are at least three reasons. First, the eliminative materialist will point to the widespread explanatory, predictive, and manipulative failures of folk psychology. So much of what is central and familiar to us remains a complete mystery from within folk psychology. We do not know what *sleep* is, or why we have to have it, despite spending a full third of our lives in that condition. (The answer, "For rest," is mistaken. Even if people are allowed to rest continuously, their need for sleep is undiminished. Apparently, sleep serves some deeper functions, but we do not yet know what they are.) We do not understand how *learning* transforms each of us from a gaping infant to a cunning adult, or how differences in *intelligence* are grounded. We have not the slightest idea how *memory* works, or how we manage to retrieve relevant bits of information instantly from the awesome mass we have stored. We do not know what *mental illness* is, nor how to cure it.

In sum, the most central things about us remain almost entirely mysterious from within folk psychology. . . .

This argument from explanatory poverty has a further aspect. So long as one sticks to normal brains, the poverty of folk psychology is perhaps not strikingly evident. But as soon as one examines the many perplexing behavioral and cognitive deficits suffered by people with *damaged* brains, one's descriptive and explanatory resources start to claw the air. . . . As with other humble theories asked to operate successfully in unexplored extensions of their old domain (for example, Newtonian mechanics in the domain of velocities close to the velocity of light, and the classical gas law in the domain of high pressures or temperatures), the descriptive and explanatory inadequacies of folk psychology become starkly evident.

The second argument tries to draw an inductive lesson from our conceptual history. Our early folk theories of motion were profoundly confused, and were eventually displaced entirely by more sophisticated theories. Our early folk theories of the structure and activity of the heavens were wildly off the mark, and survive only as historical lessons in how wrong we can be. Our folk theories of the nature of fire, and the nature of life, were similarly cockeyed. And one could go on, since the vast majority of our past folk conceptions have been similarly exploded. All except folk psychology, which survives to this day and has only recently begun to feel pressure. But the phenomenon of conscious intelligence is surely a more complex and difficult phenomenon than any of those just listed. So far as accurate understanding is concerned, it would be a *miracle* if we had got *that* one right the very first time, when we fell down so badly on all the others. Folk psychology has survived for so very long, presumably, not because it is basically correct in its representations, but because the phenomena addressed are so surpassingly difficult that any useful handle on them, no matter how feeble, is unlikely to be displaced in a hurry. . . .

ARGUMENTS AGAINST ELIMINATIVE MATERIALISM

The initial plausibility of this rather radical view is low for almost everyone, since it denies deeply entrenched assumptions. That is at best a question-begging complaint, of course, since those assumptions are precisely what is at issue. But the following line of thought does attempt to mount a real argument.

Eliminative materialism is false, runs the argument, because one's introspection reveals directly the existence of pains, beliefs, desires, fears, and so forth. Their existence is as obvious as anything could be.

The eliminative materialist will reply that this argument makes the same mistake that an ancient or medieval person would be making if he insisted that he could just see with his own eyes that the heavens form a turning sphere, or that witches exist. The fact is, all observation occurs within some system of concepts, and our observation judgments are only as good as the conceptual framework in which they are expressed. In all three cases—the starry sphere, witches, and the familiar mental states—precisely what is challenged is the integrity of the background conceptual frameworks in which the observation judgments are expressed. To insist on the validity of one's experiences, *traditionally interpreted*, is therefore to beg the very question at issue. For in all three cases, the question is whether we should *reconceive* the nature of some familiar observational domain.

. . . .

A final criticism draws a much weaker conclusion, but makes a rather stronger case. Eliminative materialism, it has been said, is making mountains out of molehills. It exaggerates the defects in folk psychology, and underplays its real successes. Perhaps the arrival of a matured neuroscience will require the elimination of the occasional folk-psychological concept, continues the criticism, and a minor adjustment in certain folk-psychological principles may have to be endured. But the large-scale elimination forecast by the eliminative materialist is just an alarmist worry or a romantic enthusiasm.

Perhaps this complaint is correct. And perhaps it is merely complacent. Whichever, it does bring out the important point that we do not confront two simple and mutually exclusive possibilities here: pure reduction versus pure elimination. Rather, these are the end points of a smooth spectrum of possible outcomes, between which there are mixed cases of partial elimination and partial reduction. Only empirical research . . . can tell us where on that spectrum our own case will fall. Perhaps we should speak here, more liberally, of "revisionary materialism," instead of concentrating on the more radical possibility of an across-the-board elimination.[30]

Churchland's primary aim in this final section of argument is to present as at least intelligible his position that "our collective conceptual destiny lies substantially toward the revolutionary end of the spectrum."

5.　*Functionalism: The Mind and the Computer*

Despite the claims of Cartesians that "minds are non-physical," at least in the obvious sense, Churchland and other materialists based their notion of the "self" on what they felt to be scientific fact, the physical basis of minds—the brain and the central nervous system. It is the brain that makes minds possible.

On the one hand, this was a rather remarkable discovery in the history of biology. It is by no means obvious, looking at the cauliflower-like mound inside the skull, that in that space is packed billions of tiny neural networks that control our very experience, our every action, including the inner actions of our bodies of which we may not even be aware (control of metabolism and blood flow, for example). But since the introduction of computers, scientific criticisms of dualism have taken another line. Is it so obvious that minds could *only* be the product of brains? Could mental processes be based on physical processes that are not brain processes? Could, for example, mental processes be based upon a network of electronic signals in a properly designed complex of transistors and circuit boards? In other words, could mental processes be the product of a computer? Could the brain be nothing but an organic computer? Could computers—the kind that we make out of metal and minerals—have minds?

It is no coincidence that the past decade or so of computer breakthroughs has produced a revolution in the way some philosophers think about selves and minds. The philosophical position is called **functionalism,** and its basic insight is that minds are produced not so much by particular kinds of materials (for example, brains) but rather by the *relations* between parts. In another few decades, it may in fact be possible, according to the most optimistic functionalists, to build a human mind out of computer parts. But whether or not computer scientists achieve such a (frightening) miracle, less optimistic functionalists hold that the mind is, in effect, a *function* of the patterns of neurological activity in the brain.

---

[30]Paul M. Churchland, *Matter and Consciousness: A Contemporary Introduction to the Philosophy of Mind* (Cambridge, MA: MIT Press, 1988, pp. 43–49).

In computer technology (now at least in part included in our everyday language), there is a crucial distinction between "hardware" and "software." Hardware is the actual computer with its circuits. In the case of human minds, the hardware would be the brain and its neurological circuits. Software is the program that gives the computer specific instructions. (Sometimes, specific instructions can be "hard-wired," as in the case of instinct, but these are not the exciting cases that inspire most functionalists and computer scientists.) The view of the functionalists is that the mind is nothing other than an elaborate program of sorts, which is the product of a spectacularly complicated pattern embodied in the physical workings of the brain. To describe this model in more detail, MIT philosopher-psychologist Jerry Fodor explains the advantages of the functionalist philosophy.

◆**from "The Mind-Body Problem,"**
by Jerry A. Fodor[31]

Traditional philosophies of mind can be divided into two broad categories: dualist theories and materialist theories. In the dualist approach the mind is a nonphysical substance. In materialist theories the mental is not distinct from the physical; indeed, all mental states, properties, processes and operations are in principle identical with physical states, properties, processes and operations. Some materialists, known as behaviorists, maintain that all talk of mental causes can be eliminated from the language of psychology in favor of talk of environmental stimuli and behavioral responses. Other materialists, the identity theorists, contend that there are mental causes and that they are identical with neurophysiological events in the brain.

In the past 15 years a philosophy of mind called functionalism that is neither dualist nor materialist has emerged from philosophical reflection on developments in artificial intelligence, computational theory, linguistics, cybernetics and psychology. All these fields, which are collectively known as the cognitive sciences, have in common a certain level of abstraction and a concern with systems that process information. Functionalism, which seeks to provide a philosophical account of this level of abstraction, recognizes the possibility that systems as diverse as human beings, calculating machines and disembodied spirits could all have mental states. In the functionalist view the psychology of a system depends not on the stuff it is made of (living cells, metal or spiritual energy) but on how the stuff is put together. . . .

The intuition underlying functionalism is that what determines the psychological type to which a mental particular belongs is the causal role of the particular in the mental life of the organism.

[31]Jerry A. Fodor, "The Mind-Body Problem," *Scientific American*, January 1981.

Functional individuation is differentiation with respect to causal role. A headache, for example, is identified with the type of mental state that among other things causes a disposition for taking aspirin in people who believe aspirin relieves a headache, causes a desire to rid oneself of the pain one is feeling, often causes someone who speaks English to say such things as "I have a headache" and is brought on by overwork, eyestrain and tension. This list is presumably not complete. More will be known about the nature of a headache as psychological and physiological research discovers more about its causal role.

Functionalism construes the concept of causal role in such a way that a mental state can be defined by its causal relations to other mental states. In this respect functionalism is completely different from logical behaviorism. Another major difference is that functionalism is not a reductionist thesis. It does not foresee, even in principle, the elimination of mentalistic concepts from the explanatory apparatus of psychological theories.

The difference between functionalism and logical behaviorism is brought out by the fact that functionalism is fully compatible with token physicalism. The functionalist would not be disturbed if brain events turn out to be the only things with the functional properties that define mental states. Indeed, most functionalists fully expect it will turn out that way.

Since functionalism recognizes that mental particulars may be physical, it is compatible with the idea that mental causation is a species of physical causation. In other words, functionalism tolerates the materialist solution to the mind-body problem provided by the central-state identity theory. It is possible for the functionalist to assert both that mental properties are typically defined in terms of their relations and that interactions of mind and body are typically causal in however robust a notion of causality is required by psychological explanations. The logical behaviorist can endorse only the first assertion and the type physicalist only the second. As a result functionalism seems to capture the best features of the materialist alternatives to dualism. It is no wonder that functionalism has become increasingly popular. . . .

· · · · · · · · · ·

Some philosophers are suspicious of functionalism because it seems too easy. Since functionalism licenses the individuation of states by reference to their causal role, it appears to allow a trivial explanation of any observed event *E*, that is, it appears to postulate an *E*-causer. For example, what makes the valves in a machine open? Why, the operation of a valve opener. And what is a valve opener? Why, anything that has the functionally defined property of causing valves to open.

In psychology this kind of question-begging often takes the form of theories that in effect postulate homunculi with the selfsame intellectual capacities the theorist set out to explain. Such is the case when visual perception is explained by simply postulating psycho-logical mechanisms that process visual information. The behav-iorist has often charged the mentalist, sometimes justifiably, of mongering this kind of question-begging pseudo-explanation. The charge will have to be met if functionally defined mental states are to have a serious role in psychological theories.

The burden of the accusation is not untruth but triviality. There can be no doubt that it is a valve opener that open valves, and it is likely that visual perception is mediated by the processing of visual information. The charge is that such putative functional explana-tions are mere platitudes. . . . For example, for Enrico to believe Galileo was Italian apparently involves a three-way relation between Enrico, a belief and a proposition that is the content of the belief (namely the proposition that Galileo was Italian). In particular it is an essential property of Enrico's belief that it is about Galileo (and not about, say, Newton) and that it is true if, and only if, Galileo was indeed Italian. Philosophers are divided on how these consid-erations fit together, but it is widely agreed that beliefs involve semantic properties such as expressing a proposition, being true or false and being about one thing rather than another.

It is important to understand the semantic properties of beliefs because theories in the cognitive sciences are largely about the be-liefs organisms have. Theories of learning and perception, for ex-ample, are chiefly accounts of how the host of beliefs an organism has are determined by the character of its experiences and its genetic endowment. The functionalist account of mental states does not by itself provide the required insights. Mousetraps are func-tionally defined, yet mousetraps do not express propositions and they are not true or false.

There is at least one kind of thing other than a mental state that has intentional content: a symbol. Like thoughts, symbols seem to be about things. If someone says "Galileo was Italian," his utter-ance, like Enrico's belief, expresses a proposition about Galileo that is true or false depending on Galileo's homeland. This parallel be-tween the symbolic and the mental underlies the traditional quest for a unified treatment of language and mind. Cognitive science is now trying to provide such a treatment.

The basic concept is simple but striking. Assume that there are such things as mental symbols (mental representations) and that mental symbols have semantic properties. On this view having a belief involves being related to a mental symbol, and the belief in-herits its semantic properties from the mental symbol that figures in the relation. Mental processes (thinking, perceiving, learning and so on) involve causal interactions among relational states such as having a belief. The semantic properties of the words and sen-tences we utter are in turn inherited from the semantic properties of the mental states that language expresses.

Associating the semantic properties of mental states with those of mental symbols is fully compatible with the computer metaphor, because it is natural to think of the computer as a mechanism that manipulates symbols. A computation is a causal chain of computer states and the links in the chain are operations on semantically interpreted formulas in a machine code. To think of a system (such as the nervous system) as a computer is to raise questions about the nature of the code in which it computes and the semantic properties of the symbols in the code. In fact, the analogy between minds and computers actually implies the postulation of mental symbols. There is no computation without representation.

The idea that the computer will someday provide a single model of mental states and information processes has been called into question recently. It is not at all clear that the mind works like a computer, or whether instead it works on different parallel levels in a manner substantially more complicated and considerably faster than any known computer. In an analysis of the information-processing involved in vision, for instance, author David Marr suggests the need for such a complex set of analyses—not the simple analysis appropriate to a mere computing machine.

◆**from *Vision*,
by David C. Marr**

The need to understand information-processing tasks and machines has arisen only quite recently. Until people began to dream of and then to build such machines, there was no very pressing need to think deeply about them. Once people did begin to speculate about such tasks and machines, however, it soon became clear that many aspects of the world around us could benefit from an information-processing point of view. Most of the phenomena that are central to us as human beings—the mysteries of life and evolution, of perception and feeling and thought—are primarily phenomena of information processing, and if we are ever to understand them fully, our thinking about them must include this perspective.

The next point—which has to be made rather quickly to those who inhabit a world in which the local utility's billing computer is still capable of sending a final demand for $0.00—is to emphasize that saying that a job is "only" an information-processing task or that an organism is "only" an information-processing machine is not a limiting or a pejorative description. Even more importantly, I shall in no way use such a description to try to limit the kind of explanations that are necessary. Quite the contrary, in fact. One of the fascinating features of information-processing machines is that in order to understand them completely, one has to be satisfied with one's explanations at many different levels.

For example, let us look at the range of perspectives that must be satisfied before one can be said, from a human and scientific point of view, to have understood visual perception. First, and I think foremost, there is the perspective of the plain man. He knows what it is like to see, and unless the bones of one's arguments and theories roughly correspond to what this person knows to be true at first hand, one will probably be wrong (a point made with force and elegance by Austin, 1962). Second, there is the perspective of the brain scientists, the physiologists and anatomists who know a great deal about how the nervous system is built and how parts of it behave. The issues that concern them—how the cells are connected, why they respond as they do, the neuronal dogmas of Barlow (1972)—must be resolved and addressed in any full account of perception. And the same argument applies to the perspective of the experimental psychologists.

On the other hand, someone who has bought and played with a small home computer may make quite different demands. "If," he might say, "vision really is an information-processing task, then I should be able to make my computer do it, provided that it has sufficient power, memory, and some way of being connected to a home television camera." The explanation he wants is therefore a rather abstract one, telling him what to program and, if possible, a hint about the best algorithms for doing so. He doesn't want to know about rhodopsin, or the lateral geniculate nucleus, or inhibitory interneurons. He wants to know how to program vision.

The fundamental point is that in order to understand a device that performs an information-processing task, one needs many different kinds of explanations. . . . For the subject of vision, there *is* no single equation or view that explains everything. Each problem has to be addressed from several points of view—as a problem in representing information, as a computation capable of deriving that representation, and as a problem in the architecture of a computer capable of carrying out both things quickly and reliably.

If one keeps strongly in mind this necessarily rather broad aspect of the nature of explanation, one can avoid a number of pitfalls. One consequence of an emphasis on information processing might be, for example, to introduce a comparison between the human brain and a computer. In a sense, of course, the brain is a computer, but to say this without qualification is misleading, because the essence of the brain is not simply that it is a computer but that it is a computer which is in the habit of performing some rather particular computations. The term *computer* usually refers to a machine with a rather standard type of instruction set that usually runs serially but nowadays sometimes in parallel, under the control of programs that have been stored in a memory. In order to understand such a computer, one needs to understand what it is made of, how it is put together, what its instruction set is, how much memory it has and how it is accessed, and how the machine may be made to run. But this forms only a small part of understanding a computer that is performing an information-processing task.

The point bears reflection, because it is central to why most analogies between brains and computers are too superficial to be useful. Think, for example, of the international network of airline reservation computers, which performs the task of assigning flights for millions of passengers all over the world. To understand this system it is not enough to know how a modern computer works. One also has to understand a little about what aircraft are and what they do; about geography, time zones, fares, exchange rates, and connections; and something about politics, diets, and the various other aspects of human nature that happen to be relevant to this particular task.

Thus the critical point is that understanding computers is different from understanding computations. To understand a computer, one has to study that computer. To understand an information-processing task, one has to study that information-processing task. To understand fully a particular machine carrying out a particular information-processing task, one has to do both things. Neither alone will suffice.[32]

Nevertheless, like any bold new hypothesis, the functionalist-analogy analysis of the mind as a computer has crashed head-on into some of the most entrenched ideas and experiences of common sense. In defense of common sense, John Searle—one of the leading analysts of ordinary human language and the special features of human communication—attacks the notion that computers are sufficiently intelligent to threaten or to challenge human intelligence anytime soon.

◆ **from "The Myth of the Computer,"**
by John R. Searle

Our ordinary ways of talking about ourselves and other people, of justifying our behavior and explaining that of others, express a certain conception of human life that is so close to us, so much a part of common sense that we can hardly see it. It is a conception according to which each person has (or perhaps *is*) a mind; the contents of the mind—beliefs, fears, hopes, motives, desires, etc.— cause and therefore explain our actions; and the continuity of our minds is the source of our individuality and identity as persons.

In the past couple of centuries we have also become convinced that this common-sense psychology is grounded in the brain, that these mental states and events are somehow, we are not quite sure how, going on in the neurophysiological processes of the brain. So this leaves us with two levels at which we can describe and explain

[32]David C. Marr, *Vision* (New York: W. H. Freeman, 1982).

human beings: a level of common-sense psychology, which seems to work well enough in practice but which is not scientific; and a level of neurophysiology, which is certainly scientific but which even the most advanced specialists know very little about.

But couldn't there be a third possibility, a science of human beings that was not introspective common-sense psychology but was not neurophysiology either? This has been the great dream of the human sciences in the twentieth century, but so far all of the efforts have been, in varying degrees, failures. The most spectacular failure was behaviorism, but in my intellectual lifetime I have lived through exaggerated hopes placed on and disappointed by games theory, cybernetics, information theory, generative grammar, structuralism, and Freudian psychology, among others. Indeed it has become something of a scandal of twentieth-century intellectual life that we lack a science of the human mind and human behavior, that the methods of the natural sciences have produced such meager results when applied to human beings.

The latest candidate or family of candidates to fill the gap is called cognitive science, a collection of related investigations into the human mind involving psychology, philosophy, linguistics, anthropology, and artificial intelligence. Cognitive science is really the name of a family of research projects and not a theory, but many of its practitioners think that the heart of cognitive science is a theory of the mind based on artificial intelligence (AI). According to this theory minds just are computer programs of certain kinds. . . .

The theory, which is fairly widely held in cognitive science, can be summarized in three propositions.

1. *Mind as Program*   What we call minds are simply very complex digital computer programs. Mental states are simply computer states and mental processes are computational processes. Any system whatever that had the right program, with the right input and output, would have to have mental states and processes in the same literal sense that you and I do, because that is all there is to mental states and processes, that is all that you and I have. The programs in question are "self-updating" or "self-designing" "systems of representations."

2. *The Irrelevance of the Neurophysiology of the Brain*   In the study of the mind actual biological facts about actual human and animal brains are irrelevant because the mind is an "abstract sort of thing" and human brains just happen to be among the indefinitely large number of kinds of computers that can have minds. Our minds happen to be embodied in our brains, but there is no essential connection between the mind and the brain. Any other computer with the right program would also have a mind.

. . . .

3. *The Turing Test as the Criterion of the Mental*   The conclusive proof of the presence of mental states and capacities is the

ability of a system to pass the Turing test, the test devised by Alan Turing . . . : If a system can convince a competent expert that it has mental states then it really has those mental states. If, for example, a machine could "converse" with a native Chinese speaker in such a way as to convince the speaker that it understood Chinese then it would literally understand Chinese.

· · · · · · · · · ·

We might call this collection of theses "strong artificial intelligence" (strong AI).[33] These theses are certainly not obviously true and they are seldom explicitly stated and defended. . . .

Take thirst, where we actually know a little bit about how it works. Kidney secretions of renin synthesize a substance called angiotensin. This substance goes into the hypothalamus and triggers a series of neuron firings. As far as we know these neuron firings are a very large part of the cause of thirst. Now obviously there is more to be said, for example about the relations of the hypothalamic responses to the rest of the brain, about other things going on in the hypothalamus, and about the possible distinctions between the *feeling* of thirst and the *urge* to drink. Let us suppose we have filled out the story with the rest of the biochemical causal account of thirst.

Now these theses of the mind as program and the irrelevance of the brain would tell us that what matters about this story is not the specific biochemical properties of the angiotensin or the hypothalamus but only the formal computer programs that the whole sequence instantiates. Well, let's try that out as a hypothesis and see how it works. A computer can simulate the formal properties of the sequence of chemical and electrical phenomena in the production of thirst just as much as it can simulate the formal properties of anything else—we can simulate thirst just as we can simulate hurricanes, rainstorms, five-alarm fires, internal combustion engines, photosynthesis, lactation, or the flow of currency in a depressed economy. But no one in his right mind thinks that a computer simulation of a five-alarm fire will burn down the neighborhood, or that a computer simulation of an internal combustion engine will power a car or that computer simulations of lactation and photosynthesis will produce milk and sugar. To my amazement, however, I have found that a large number of people suppose that computer simulations of mental phenomena, whether at the level of brain processes or not, literally produce mental phenomena.

Again, let's try it out. Let's program our favorite PDP-10 computer with the formal program that simulates thirst. We can even program it to print out at the end "Boy, am I thirsty!" or "Won't someone please give me a drink?" etc. Now would anyone suppose that we thereby have even the slightest reason to suppose

---

[33]"Strong" to distinguish the position from "weak" or "cautious" AI, which holds that the computer is simply a very useful tool in the study of the mind, not that the appropriately programmed computer literally has a mind.

that the computer is literally thirsty? Or that any simulation of any other mental phenomena, such as understanding stories, feeling depressed, or worrying about itemized deductions, must therefore produce the real thing? The answer, alas, is that a large number of people are committed to an ideology that requires them to believe just that. So let us carry the story a step further.

The PDP-10 is powered by electricity and perhaps its electrical properties can reproduce some of the actual causal powers of the electrochemical features of the brain in producing mental states. We certainly couldn't rule out that eventuality a priori. But remember: the thesis of strong AI is that the mind is "independent of *any* particular embodiment" because the mind is just a program and the program can be run on a computer made of anything whatever provided it is stable enough and complex enough to carry the program. The actual physical computer could be an ant colony (one of their examples), a collection of beer cans, streams of toilet paper with small stones placed on the squares, men sitting on high stools with green eye shades—anything you like.

So let us imagine our thirst-simulating program running on a computer made entirely of old beer cans, millions (or billions) of old beer cans that are rigged up to levers and powered by windmills. We can imagine that the program simulates the neuron firings at the synapses by having beer cans bang into each other, thus achieving a strict correspondence between neuron firings and beer-can bangings. At the end of the sequence a beer can pops up on which is written "I am thirsty." Now, to repeat the question, does anyone suppose that this Rube Goldberg apparatus is literally thirsty in the sense in which you and I are?

· · · · · · · · · ·

I believe that everything we have learned about human and animal biology suggests that what we call "mental" phenomena are as much a part of our biological natural history as any other biological phenomena, as much a part of biology as digestion, lactation, or the secretion of bile. Much of the implausibility of the strong AI thesis derives from its resolute opposition to biology; the mind is not a concrete biological phenomenon but "an abstract sort of thing."

Digital computer programs by definition consist of sets of purely formal operations on formally specified symbols. The ideal computer does such things as print a 0 on the tape, move one square to the left, erase a 1, move back to the right, etc. It is common to describe this as "symbol manipulation" or, to use the term favored by Hofstadter and Dennett, the whole system is a "self-updating representational system"; but these terms are at least a bit misleading since as far as the computer is concerned the symbols don't *symbolize* anything or *represent* anything. They are just formal counters.

The computer attaches no meaning, interpretation, or content to the formal symbols; and qua computer it couldn't, because if we tried to give the computer an interpretation of its symbols we could only give it more uninterpreted symbols. The interpretation of the symbols is entirely up to the programmers and users of the computer. For example, on my pocket calculator if I print "3 × 3 =," the calculator will print "9" but it has no idea that "3" means 3 or that "9" means 9 or that anything means anything. We might put this point by saying that the computer has a syntax but no semantics. The computer manipulates formal symbols but attaches no meaning to them, and this simple observation will enable us to refuse the thesis of mind as program.

· · · · · · · · · ·

The details of how the brain works are immensely complicated and largely unknown, but some of the general principles of the relations between brain functioning and computer programs can be stated quite simply. First, we know that brain processes cause mental phenomena. Mental states are caused by and realized in the structure of the brain. From this it follows that any system that produced mental states would have to have powers equivalent to those of the brain. Such a system might use a different chemistry, but whatever its chemistry it would have to be able to cause what the brain causes. We know from the [previous] argument that digital computer programs by themselves are never sufficient to produce mental states. Now since brains do produce minds, and since programs by themselves can't produce minds, it follows that the way the brain does it can't be by simple instantiating a computer program. (Everything, by the way, instantiates some program or other, and brains are no exception. So in that trivial sense brains, like everything else, are digital computers.) And it also follows that if you wanted to build a machine to produce mental states, a thinking machine, you couldn't do it solely in virtue of the fact that your machine ran a certain kind of computer program. The thinking machine couldn't work solely in virtue of being a digital computer but would have to duplicate the specific causal powers of the brain.

A lot of the nonsense talked about computers nowadays stems from their relative rarity and hence mystery. As computers and robots become more common, as common as telephones, washing machines, and forklift trucks, it seems likely that this aura will disappear and people will take computers for what they are, namely useful machines.[34]

6.   Connectionism

Not all criticisms of functionalism are nonmaterialist. Recently, objections have been brought against functionalism from neurophysiologists who claim that functionalism is just too simplistic in its vision of the

---

[34] John R. Searle, "The Myth of the Computer," in the *New York Review of Books*, 1982.

brain and of computers. **Connectionists** complain that functionalism is a "top-down," "software" approach which can never be accurate in its representation of the "hardware" of either the brain or the computer. In other words, say the connectionists, a functionalist starts with behavior—either human behavior or computer behavior—and claims that understanding human consciousness is just a matter of finding the "program" for that behavior. The functionalist claims that to understand the "program" is to understand the behavior, regardless of the mechanical and physical interactions which make the program run. The connectionist, on the other hand, claims that the mechanical and physical interactions which occur in the brain determine the kinds of behavior—which kinds of software—that computers are capable of processing. Connectionists therefore advocate a "bottom-up" approach to understanding the mind. Connectionists are still materialists, but not in the simple, reductionist, way of their predecessors. They believe that consciousness—in its full color and quality—is a result of the complicated "connections" that really do go on in the brain. There is no one-to-one correspondence between neurons and thoughts or perceptions; rather, they claim, the "hardware" of the brain is an immensely complex mechanism to which the functionalists do not do justice.

E. THE PROBLEM OF CONSCIOUSNESS

Descartes claimed he knew what was going on in his mind with an immediate certainty that he could never have about what was going on in the world "outside" him. In his first "Meditation," he talks about his seeming to be sitting in front of the fire and the fact that he might be wrong (if he were in bed asleep at the time). But what he could not be wrong about is his seeming to be sitting in front of the fire. Similarly, you think you see a friend walking across the street. You are wrong, for your friend is in fact in Alaska this week. But you can still be certain that you thought that you saw him, even if you didn't. Philosophers often refer to this special kind of "immediate" certainty in the case of our own conscious experiences as **incorrigibility.** You might make a mistake in any factual claim about the world, for you might be hallucinating, or dreaming, or simply fooled by circumstances. But nothing could lead you to suspect that you might be mistaken about your own experiences. Given enough evidence against you, you might be willing to change from "but I know that I saw it" to "well, I thought I saw it." But nothing could convince you that you were wrong in thinking that you saw whatever it was. That claim, the claim about your experience, is incorrigible. Your claim about what you saw, however, is always open to further questioning.

For many years, this notion of incorrigibility served as part of the definition of "mind" and therefore, as Churchland implies, also defense against materialism. Whatever was mental could be described incorrigibly and this is very different than is the case with physical things. But doubts have begun to creep in recently. Part of the problem was Freud's introduction of the notion of the **unconscious.** According to his famous "psychoanalytic" theory, not everything mental is knowable, and therefore surely not everything "in the mind" can be described incorrigibly. In a famous passage from his "Introductory Lectures," Freud says:

◆ on the "Unconscious," by Sigmund Freud

There is no need to discuss what is to be called conscious: it is removed from all doubt. The oldest and best meaning of the word "unconscious" is the descriptive one; we call a psychical process unconscious whose existence we are obliged to assume—for some such reason as that we infer it from its effects—, but of which we know nothing. In that case we have the same relation to it as we have to a physical process in another person, except that it is in fact one of our own. If we want to be still more correct, we shall modify our assertion by saying that we call a process unconscious if we are obliged to assume that it is being activated *at the moment* though *at the moment* we know nothing about it. This qualification makes us reflect that the majority of conscious processes are conscious only for a short time; very soon they become *latent,* but can easily become conscious again. We might also say that they had become unconscious, if it were at all certain that in the condition of latency they are still something psychical. So far we should have learnt nothing new; nor should we have acquired the right to introduce the concept of an unconscious into psychology. But then comes the new observation that we were already able to make in parapraxes. In order to explain a slip of the tongue, for instance, we find ourselves obliged to assume that the intention to make a particular remark was present in the subject. We infer it with certainty from the interference with his remark which has occurred; but the intention did not put itself through and was thus unconscious. If, when we subsequently put it before the speaker, he recognizes it as one familiar to him, then it was only temporarily unconscious to him; but if he repudiates it as something foreign to him, then it was permanently unconscious. From this experience we retrospectively obtain the right also to pronounce as something unconscious what had been described as latent. A consideration of these dynamic relations permits us now to distinguish two kinds of unconscious—one which is easily, under frequently occurring circumstances, transformed into something conscious, and another with which this transformation is difficult and takes place only subject to a considerable expenditure of effort or possibly never at all. In order to escape the ambiguity as to whether we mean the one or the other unconscious, whether we are using the word in the descriptive or in the dynamic sense, we make use of a permissible and simple way out. We call the unconscious which is only latent, and thus easily becomes conscious, the "preconscious" and retain the term "unconscious" for the other. We now have three terms, "conscious," "preconscious" and "unconscious," with which we can get along in our description of mental phenomena. Once again: the preconscious is also unconscious in the purely descriptive sense, but we do not give it that name, except in talking loosely or when we have to make a defense of the existence in mental life of unconscious processes in general.[35]

Notice that Freud starts from a Cartesian position, the idea that "conscious is removed from all doubt." But then he suggests what no Cartesian can tolerate, the idea that there are ideas (experiences, intentions) in our minds that we do not and sometimes cannot know, much less know with certainty. And if we accept this notion of "the unconscious" (or even the weaker notion of "preconscious"), the traditional notion of the "incorrigibility" of the mental is seriously challenged.

The argument, however, cuts both ways. Many philosophers have rejected Freud just because his notion of "the unconscious" goes against the notion of incorrigibility. "If it isn't knowable incorrigibly," these philosophers have said, "then it can't be mental at all." And even Freud himself was forced to admit that his theory flew in the face of our normal "manner of speaking." And the debate continues. Can you be wrong about what is going on in your own mind? For a long time, it was generally agreed that you could not be. Now we aren't so sure. You are certain that you are over an old love affair, but, without too much difficulty, a friend or a psychologist convinces you that you have been thinking about it constantly. You are certain that you are angry, but on closer examination, and in retrospect, you decide that you really felt guilty. You thought that you were thinking about your professor, when suddenly you realize that in fact it was the face of your father!

Is there anything about which we could not be mistaken? What of those basic bits of data that the empiricists talked about—sensations or impressions? Could we possibly be wrong in our confidence that "right now, I am experiencing a cold feeling in my hand"? The empiricists assumed that one could not be wrong about this, for it was on the basis of such certainties that we were able to construct, through inductive reasoning, our theories about the world. Could we be wrong even about our own sensations? Consider this example (it comes from Bishop

---

[35]Sigmund Freud, *New Introductory Lectures on Psychoanalysis*, ed. and trans. James Strachey (New York: Norton, 1964).

Berkeley): A mischievous friend tells you that he is going to touch your hand with a very hot spoon. When you aren't looking, he touches you with a piece of ice. You scream and claim, with seeming certainty, that he has given you an uncomfortable sensation of heat. But you're wrong. What you felt was cold. What you seemed to feel was heat. But even your "seeming," in this case, was mistaken.

Philosophers have also pointed out that what is unique to mind as opposed to body is the fact that one and only one person can (and must) experience what is going on. I can (and must) feel only my pains, I can't experience your pains. Philosophers have referred to this as **privileged access,** sometimes as the **privacy** of mental events. The "privilege" is the fact that, whatever is going on in your mind, you are not only the first but the only one to know of it directly. The "privacy" refers to the fact that if you decide not to tell anyone or betray yourself (through your facial expressions or your behavior), no one else need ever know. If you have a wart on your thigh, you can keep it contingently "private" by choosing suitable clothing. But if you have a "dirty little secret" in your mind, you have a logical guarantee of its privacy—it is private necessarily.

"Incorrigible" means "beyond correction"; "privileged access" means "known in a special way." (These concepts must be kept separate.) Because of privileged access and the "privacy" of consciousness, our states of mind have the very peculiar status of being always knowable to ourselves (though whether or not we want to say "knowable with certainty" depends on our views about incorrigibility) and yet possibly unknowable to anyone else. That is why, as you learned in grade school, you could always fake a headache to stay home for the day but you couldn't fake a fever or a sore. As long as it was purely mental, it was also purely private. Your success depended wholly upon how good (or bad) an actor you were. But when it comes to your body, you were in no privileged position. It was the thermometer, not your opinions, that told whether you had a fever or not. And it was the doctor, not you, who decided how serious your sore really was. But when it came to your own consciousness, you were in a truly privileged and irrefutable position.

This peculiarity of the first-person position, of our relationship to our own consciousness, is one of the things that makes the notion of "self" so difficult and that makes the problem so seemingly unresolvable. It makes the way that we establish our own identity seem categorically different from how others know it. Against all forms of reductionism and materialism, philosopher Thomas Nagel has argued in an ingenious fashion that it is consciousness, or what he calls "subjectivity," that makes the problem so "intractable." If "subjectivity" can be loosely defined as "what it's like" to be something, Nagel introduces his concern about the mind-body problem with the intriguing question: "What is it like to be a bat?"

◆ "What Is It Like to Be a Bat?"
by Thomas Nagel

Consciousness is what makes the mind-body problem really intractable. Perhaps that is why current discussions of the problem give it little attention or get it obviously wrong. The recent wave of reductionist euphoria has produced several analyses of mental phenomena and mental concepts designed to explain the possibility of some variety of materialism, psychophysical identification, or reduction. But the problems dealt with are those common to this type of reduction and other types, and what makes the mind-body problem unique, and unlike the water H_2O problem . . . is ignored.

· · · · · · · · · ·

Every reductionist has his favorite analogy from modern science. It is most unlikely that any of these unrelated examples of successful reduction will shed light on the relation of mind to brain. But philosophers share the general human weakness for explanations of what is incomprehensible in terms suited for what is familiar and well understood, though entirely different. This has led to the acceptance of implausible accounts of the mental largely because they would permit familiar kinds of reduction. I shall try to explain why the usual examples do not help us to understand the relation between mind and body—why, indeed, we have at present no conception of what an explanation of the physical nature of a mental phenomenon would be. Without consciousness the mind-body problem would be much less interesting. With consciousness it seems hopeless. The most important and characteristic feature of conscious mental phenomena is very poorly understood. Most reductionist theories do not even try to explain it.

· · · · · · · · · ·

Conscious experience is a widespread phenomenon. It occurs at many levels of animal life, though we cannot be sure of its presence in the simpler organisms, and it is very difficult to say in general what provides evidence of it. (Some extremists have been prepared to deny it even of mammals other than man.) No doubt it occurs in countless forms totally unimaginable to us, on other planets in other solar systems throughout the universe. But no matter how the form may vary, the fact that an organism has conscious experience *at all* means, basically, that there is something it is like to *be* that organism. There may be further implications about the form of the experience; there may even (though I doubt it) be implications about the behavior of the organism. But fundamentally an organism has conscious mental states if and only if there is something that it is like to *be* that organism—something it is like *for* the organism.

We may call this the subjective character of experience. It is not captured by any of the familiar, recently devised reductive analyses of the mental, for all of them are logically compatible with its absence. It is not analyzable in terms of any explanatory system of functional states, or intentional states, since these could be ascribed to robots or automata that behaved like people though they experienced nothing. It is not analyzable in terms of the causal role of experiences in relation to typical human behavior—for similar reasons. I do not deny that conscious mental states and events cause behavior, nor that they may be given functional characterizations. I deny only that this kind of thing exhausts their analysis. Any reductionist program has to be based on an analysis of what is to be reduced. If the analysis leaves something out, the problem will be falsely posed. It is useless to base the defense of materialism on any analysis of mental phenomena that fails to deal explicitly with their subjective character.

· · · · · · · · · ·

While an account of the physical basis of mind must explain many things, this appears to be the most difficult. It is impossible to exclude the phenomenological features of experience from a reduction in the same way that one excludes the phenomenal features of an ordinary substance from a physical or chemical reduction of it—namely, by explaining them as effects on the minds of human observers. If physicalism is to be defended, the phenomenological features must themselves be given a physical account. But when we examine their subjective character it seems that such a result is impossible. The reason is that every subjective phenomenon is essentially connected with a single point of view, and it seems inevitable that an objective, physical theory will abandon that point of view.

Let me first try to state the issue somewhat more fully than by referring to the relation between the subjective and the objective, or between the *pour soi* and the *en soi*. This is far from easy. Facts about what it is like to be an X are very peculiar, so peculiar that some may be inclined to doubt their reality, or the significance of claims about them. To illustrate the connexion between subjectivity and a point of view, and to make evident the importance of subjective features, it will help to explore the matter in relation to an example that brings out clearly the divergence between the two types of conception, subjective and objective.

I assume we all believe that bats have experience. After all, they are mammals, and there is no more doubt that they have experience than that mice or pigeons or whales have experience. I have chosen bats instead of wasps or flounders because if one travels too far down the phylogenetic tree, people gradually shed their faith that there is experience there at all. Bats, although more closely related to us than those other species, nevertheless present a range of activity and a sensory apparatus so different from ours that the problem I want to pose is exceptionally vivid (though it certainly could be raised with other species). Even without the benefit of philosophical reflection, anyone who has spent some time in an enclosed space with an excited bat knows what it is to encounter a fundamentally *alien* form of life.

I have said that the essence of the belief that bats have experience is that there is something that it is like to be a bat. Now we know that most bats (the microchiroptera, to be precise) perceive the external world primarily by sonar, or echolocation, detecting the reflections, from objects within range, of their own rapid, subtly modulated, high-frequency shrieks. Their brains are designed to correlate the outgoing impulses with the subsequent echoes, and the information thus acquired enables bats to make precise discriminations of distance, size, shape, motion, and texture comparable to those we make by vision. But bat sonar, though clearly a form of perception, is not similar in its operation to any sense that we possess, and there is no reason to suppose that it is subjectively like anything we can experience or imagine. This appears to create difficulties for the notion of what it is like to be a bat. We must consider whether any method will permit us to extrapolate to the inner life of the bat from our own case, and if not, what alternative methods there may be for understanding the notion.

Our own experience provides the basic material for our imagination, whose range is therefore limited. It will not help to try to imagine that one has webbing on one's arms, which enables one to fly around at dusk and dawn catching insects in one's mouth; that one has very poor vision, and perceives the surrounding world by a system of reflected high-frequency sound signals; and that one spends the day hanging upside down by one's feet in an attic. Insofar as I can imagine this (which is not very far), it tells me only what it would be like for *me* to behave as a bat behaves. But that is not the question. I want to know what it is like for a *bat* to be a bat. Yet if I try to imagine this, I am restricted to the resources of my own mind, and those resources are inadequate to the task. I cannot perform it either by imagining additions to my present experience, or by imagining segments gradually subtracted from it, or by imagining some combination of additions, subtractions, and modifications.

To the extent that I could look and behave like a wasp or a bat without changing my fundamental structure, my experiences would not be anything like the experiences of those animals. On the other hand, it is doubtful that any meaning can be attached to the supposition that I should possess the internal neurophysiological constitution of a bat. Even if I could by gradual degrees be transformed into a bat, nothing in my present constitution enables me to imagine what the experiences of such a future stage of myself thus metamorphosed would be like. The best evidence would come from the experiences of bats, if we only knew what they were like.

. . . .

If anyone is inclined to deny that we can believe in the existence of facts like this whose exact nature we cannot possibly conceive, he should reflect that in contemplating the bats we are in much the same position that intelligent bats or Martians would occupy if they tried to form a conception of what it was like to be us. The structure of their own minds might make it impossible for them to succeed, but we know they would be wrong to conclude that there is not anything precise that it is like to be us: that only certain general types of mental state could be ascribed to us (perhaps perception and appetite would be concepts common to us both; perhaps not). We know they would be wrong to draw such a skeptical conclusion because we know what it is like to be us.

· · · · · · · · · ·

This brings us to the edge of a topic that requires much more discussion than I can give it here: namely, the relation between facts on the one hand and conceptual schemes or systems of representation on the other. My realism about the subjective domain in all its forms implies a belief in the existence of facts beyond the reach of human concepts. Certainly it is possible for a human being to believe that there are facts which humans never *will* possess the requisite concepts to represent or comprehend. Indeed, it would be foolish to doubt this, given the finiteness of humanity's expectations. After all, there would have been transfinite numbers even if everyone had been wiped out by the Black Death before Cantor discovered them. But one might also believe that there are facts which *could* not ever be represented or comprehended by human beings, even if the species lasted forever—simply because our structure does not permit us to operate with concepts of the requisite type. This impossibility might even be observed by other beings, but it is not clear that the existence of such beings, or the possibility of their existence, is a precondition of the significance of the hypothesis that there are humanly inaccessible facts. (After all, the nature of beings with access to humanly inaccessible facts is presumably itself a humanly inaccessible fact.) Reflection on what it is like to be a bat seems to lead us, therefore, to the conclusion that there are facts that do not consist in the truth of propositions expressible in a human language. We can be compelled to recognize the existence of such facts without being able to state or comprehend them.

I shall not pursue this subject, however. Its bearing on the topic before us (namely, the mind-body problem) is that it enables us to make a general observation about the subjective character of experience. Whatever may be the status of facts about what it is like to be a human being, or a bat, or a Martian, these appear to be facts that embody a particular point of view.

I am not adverting here to the alleged privacy of experience to its possessor. The point of view in question is not one accessible only to a single individual. Rather it is a *type*. It is often possible to take up a point of view other than one's own, so the comprehension of such facts is not limited to one's own case.

There is a sense in which phenomenological facts are perfectly objective: one person can know or say of another what the quality of the other's experience is. They are subjective, however, in the sense that even this objective ascription of experience is possible only for someone sufficiently similar to the object of ascription to be able to adopt his point of view—to understand the ascription in the first person as well as in the third, so to speak. The more different from oneself the other experiencer is, the less success one can expect with this enterprise. In our own case we occupy the relevant point of view, but we will have as much difficulty understanding our own experience properly if we approach it from another point of view as we would if we tried to understand the experience of another species without taking up *its* point of view.

This bears directly on the mind-body problem. For if the facts of experience—facts about what it is like *for* the experiencing organism—are accessible only from one point of view, then it is a mystery how the true character of experiences could be revealed in the physical operation of that organism. The latter is a domain of objective facts *par excellence*—the kind that can be observed and understood from many points of view and by individuals with differing perceptual systems. There are no comparable imaginative obstacles to the acquisition of knowledge about bat neurophysiology by human scientists, and intelligent bats or Martians might learn more about the human brain than we ever will.[36]

1.   Changing Our Minds: Holism and Consciousness

When Aristotle wrote about "the soul," he meant nothing other than "the form of the body":

◆from *De Anima,* by Aristotle

One can no more ask if the body and the soul are one than if the wax and the impression it receives are one, or speaking generally the matter of each thing and the form of which it is the matter; for admitting that the terms unity and existence are used in many senses, the paramount sense is that of actuality. We have, then, given a general definition of what the soul is: it is substance expressed as form. It is this which makes a body what it is. . . .[37]

This is not behaviorism. Aristotle is not denying the existence of anything that we normally believe in. Yet it is clearly not a dualism of the Cartesian variety, and this raises the following question: Are there ways

[36]Thomas Nagel, *Mortal Questions* (Cambridge: Cambridge University Press, 1979).
[37]Aristotle, *De Anima*, trans. W. S. Hett (Cambridge, MA: Harvard University Press, 1936).

of conceiving of ourselves without falling into the Cartesian trap of talking about minds and bodies?

We can only suggest a few possibilities here. The first, perhaps, was advanced by Ludwig Wittgenstein in his *Philosophical Investigations.* Although he is usually considered to be an unconfessed behaviorist, a more recent and perhaps more plausible interpretation is that Wittgenstein wanted to deny the very idea that human beings are a curious combination of two very different substances or kinds of entities or events. Rather, there are just people, not minds plus bodies. This Wittgensteinian view has been defended, for example, by P. F. Strawson in his essay "Persons":

◆ **"Persons,"**
by P. F. Strawson

Let us think of some of the ways in which we ordinarily talk of ourselves, of some of the things which we ordinarily ascribe to ourselves. They are of many kinds. We ascribe to ourselves *actions and intentions* (I am doing, did, shall do this); *sensations* (I am warm, in pain); *thoughts and feelings* (I think, wonder, want this, am angry, disappointed, contented); *perceptions and memories* (I see this, hear the other, remember that). We ascribe to ourselves, in two senses, position: *location* (I am on the sofa) and *attitude* (I am lying down). And of course we ascribe to ourselves not only temporary conditions, states, and situations, like most of these, but also enduring characteristics, including such physical characteristics as height, coloring, shape, and weight. That is to say, among the things we ascribe to ourselves are things of a kind that we also ascribe to material bodies to which we would not dream of ascribing others of the things that we ascribe to ourselves. Now there seems nothing needing explanation in the fact that the particular height, coloring, and physical position which we ascribe to ourselves, should be ascribed to *something or other;* for that which one calls one's body is, at least, a body, a material thing. It can be picked out from others, identified by ordinary physical criteria and described in ordinary physical terms. But it can seem, and has seemed, to need explanation that one's states of consciousness, one's thoughts and sensations, are ascribed *to the very same thing* as that to which these physical characteristics, this physical situation, is ascribed. Why are one's states of consciousness ascribed to the very same thing as certain corporeal characteristics, a certain physical situation, etc.? And once this question is raised, another question follows it, viz.: Why are one's states of consciousness ascribed to (said to be of, or to belong to) anything at all? It is not to be supposed that the answers to these questions will be independent of one another.

. . . I have in mind a very simple but, in this question, a very central, thought: viz., that it is a necessary condition of one's ascribing states of consciousness, experiences, to oneself, in the way one does, that one should also ascribe them (or be prepared to ascribe them) to others who are not oneself. This means not less than it says. It means, for example, that the ascribing phrases should be used in just the same sense when the subject is another, as when the subject is oneself. Of course the thought that this is so gives no trouble to the non-philosopher: the thought, for example, that "in pain" means the same whether one says "I am in pain" or "He is in pain." The dictionaries do not give two sets of meanings for every expression which describes a state of consciousness: a first-person meaning, and a second- and third-person meaning. But to the philosopher this thought has given trouble; indeed it has. How could the sense be the same when the method of verification was so different in the two cases—or, rather, when there *was* a method of verification in the one case (the case of others) and not, properly speaking, in the other case (the case of oneself)? Or, again, how can it be right to talk of *ascribing* in the case of oneself? For surely there can be a question of ascribing only if there is or could be a question of identifying that to which the ascription is made? And though there may be a question of identifying the one who is in pain when that one is another, how can there be such a question when that one is oneself? But this last query answers itself as soon as we remember that we speak primarily to others, for the information of others. In one sense, indeed, there is no question of my having to *tell who it is* who is in pain, when I am. In another sense I may have to *tell who it is*, i.e., to let others know who it is.

What I have just said explains, perhaps, how one may properly be said to ascribe states of consciousness to oneself, given that one ascribes them to others. But how is it that one can ascribe them to others? Well, one thing is certain; that if the things one ascribes states of consciousness to, in ascribing them to others, are thought of as a set of Cartesian egos to which *only* private experiences can, in correct logical grammar, be ascribed, *then* this question is unanswerable and this problem insoluble. If, in identifying the things to which states of consciousness are to be ascribed, private experiences are to be all one has to go on, then, just for the very same reason as that for which there is, from one's own point of view, no question of telling that a private experience is one's own, there is also no question of telling that a private experience is another's. All private experiences, all states of consciousness, will be mine, i.e., no one's. To put it briefly: one can ascribe states of consciousness to oneself only if one can ascribe them to others; one can ascribe them to others only if one can identify other subjects of experience; and one cannot identify others if one can identify them *only* as subjects of experience, possessors of states of consciousness.

It might be objected that this way with Cartesianism is too short. After all, there is no difficulty about distinguishing bodies from one another, no difficulty about identifying bodies. And does not this give us an indirect way of identifying subjects of experience, while preserving the Cartesian mode? Can we not identify such a subject as, for example, "the subject that stands to that body in the same special relation as I stand to this one"; or, in other words, "the subject of those experiences which stand in the same unique causal relation to body N as *my* experiences stand to body M"? But this suggestion is useless. It requires me to have noted that *my* experiences stand in a special relation to body M, when it is just the right to speak of *my* experiences at all that is in question. (It requires me to have noted that *my* experiences stand in a special relation to body M; but it requires me to have noted this as a condition of being able to identify other subjects of experience, i.e., as a condition of having the idea of myself as a subject of experience, i.e., as a condition of thinking of any experience as *mine*.) So long as we persist in talking, in the mode of this explanation, of experiences on the one hand, and bodies on the other, the most I may be allowed to have noted is that experiences, *all* experiences, stand in a special relation to body M, that body M is unique in just this way, that is what makes body M unique among bodies. (This "most" is, perhaps, too much—because of the presence of the word "experiences.") The proffered explanation runs: "Another subject of experience is distinguished and identified as the subject of those experiences which stand in the same unique causal relationship to body N as *my* experiences stand to body M." And the objection is: "But what is the word 'my' doing in this explanation? (It could not get on without it.)"

What we have to acknowledge, in order to begin to free ourselves from these difficulties, is the *primitiveness* of the concept of a person. What I mean by the concept of a person is the concept of a type of entity such that *both* predicates ascribing states of consciousness *and* predicates ascribing corporeal characteristics, a physical situation, etc. are equally applicable to a single individual of that single type. And what I mean by saying that this concept is primitive can be put in a number of ways. One way its to return to those two questions I asked earlier: viz., (1) why are states of consciousness ascribed to anything at all? and (2) why are they ascribed to the very same thing as certain corporeal characteristics, a certain physical situation, etc.? I remarked at the beginning that it was not to be supposed that the answers to these questions were independent of each other. And now I shall say that they are connected in this way: that a necessary condition of states of consciousness being ascribed at all is that they should be ascribed to the *very same things* as certain corporeal characteristics, a certain physical situation, etc. That is to say, states of consciousness could not be ascribed at all, *unless* they were ascribed to persons, in the sense I have claimed for this word. . . .

So, then, the word "I" never refers to this, the pure subject. But this does not mean, as the no-ownership theorist must think and as Wittgenstein, at least at one period, seemed to think, that "I" in some cases does not refer at all. It refers, because I am a person among others. And the predicates which would, *per impossibile,* belong to the pure subject if it could be referred to, belong properly to the person to which "I" does refer.

The concept of a person is logically prior to that of an individual consciousness. The concept of a person is not to be analyzed as that of an animated body or of an embodied anima. This is not to say that the concept of a pure individual consciousness might not have a logically secondary existence, if one thinks, or finds, it desirable. We speak of a dead person—a body—and in the same secondary way we might at least think of a disembodied person, retaining the logical benefit of individuality from having been a person.[38]

In this selection, Strawson makes at least two radical departures from the traditional Cartesian dualism between mind and body. To begin with, he attacks the idea that each of us is first of all a mind who "has" a body. Each of us is first of all a person, and the concept of "having a body" is no less essential than the concept of "having a mind." In other words, Strawson rejects outright Descartes' claim that he is essentially "a thinking thing," which might in fact have no body at all. We are essentially, according to Strawson, "thinking things" only if by that we mean "thinking persons." Descartes worried about how the two parts of a person can come together; Strawson says that they should never have been separated in the first place. This is one of the most famous cases in which a seemingly obvious philosophical distinction gets us into impossible trouble later on.

Second, Strawson adapts an argument from Wittgenstein that completely turns topsy-turvy Descartes' main thesis. Descartes assumed that we know for certain our own mental states and then by inference apply the same words to the mental states of other people. What Strawson now argues, following Wittgenstein, is that we can apply such "mental" words to our own thoughts, feelings, and experiences only if we can apply them at the same time to other people. In other words, there can be no self-knowledge without knowledge of others as well.

A very different kind of answer comes to us from Husserl's phenomenology. Although Husserl was not particularly concerned with the mind-body problem as such, he was obviously very interested in the nature of consciousness, since consciousness provides the subject matter of his entire life's work. What Husserl argued began with a violent attack on the spatial metaphors we use in talking about consciousness. At the beginning of the chapter, we mentioned these, suggesting that they were "just metaphors," symptoms of a problem but not a problem

[38]P. F. Strawson, "Persons," in *Minnesota Studies in the Philosophy of Science,* Vol. 2 (Minneapolis: University of Minnesota Press, 1958).

themselves. Well, Husserl shows that they are a problem, that philosophers have not used them merely as metaphors, and that it is because of their taking these metaphors literally that our problems about consciousness arise in the first place.

What Husserl attacks is the very idea of consciousness as a mysterious container, "in" which one finds ideas, thoughts, feelings, desires, etc. The same objection holds of such metaphors as "the stream of consciousness," with emotions, thoughts, and feelings floating by like so much flotsam and jetsam. Consciousness must rather be viewed in two parts (though Husserl insists these must not be thought of as a separate "dualism"): There are acts of consciousness, and there are the objects of those acts.

Simply stated, a phenomenologist would analyze my seeing a tree into (1) my act of seeing and (2) the tree as seen. So far, this looks innocent enough. But its consequences are not so innocent. First, just in passing, notice what this does to Berkeley's idealism. Berkeley's whole argument rested on his thesis that all we can experience are ideas. But this is a confusion, Husserl insists, of our act of experiencing with the objects experienced. The object experienced (the tree) is not merely my idea. Accordingly, Husserl concludes that Berkeley's idealism is "absurd." And in general, Husserl's phenomenological theory insists that philosophers have been neglectful of this crucial distinction. Many attributes of the act of experiencing do not hold of the object; for example, the object, unlike the act, is not "private." One and only one person, namely, myself, can perform my act of seeing. But any number of people can see the object of my seeing, the tree. Moreover, there can be no such thing, Husserl argues, as a conscious act without an object. You can see how this might provide a powerful argument against many traditional forms of skepticism.

Our concern here is Husserl's conception of consciousness, which he calls **intentionality.** (Accordingly, the act is often called the "intentional act," and the object is called the "intentional object.") To say that consciousness is intentional means (among other things, which are irrelevant to this chapter) that our conscious acts are always directed toward objects and that we should not, therefore, talk about conscious acts as self-contained "contents" that are mysteriously coordinated with the movements of our bodies. Rather, we can simply say that among our various acts as persons are intentional conscious acts as well as physical actions. We can look at a tree and we can kick a tree. But there is no problem of "coordination" or interaction.

This theory was never actually developed by Husserl himself, but it was worked out in great detail by one of his "existential" followers in France, Maurice Merleau-Ponty (a close friend and student of Sartre). Coming from a very different starting point, Merleau-Ponty arrives at a position surprisingly close to that of Wittgenstein. It must not be called "behaviorist," but like Wittgenstein, Merleau-Ponty does reject the traditional way of dividing up mind and body and thereby suggests a very different conception of persons in which such problematic distinctions are not allowed to arise.

Merleau-Ponty attacks dualism from the side that has so far seemed least controversial—the idea that the human body is just another "bit of matter." He introduces the notion of a "dialectic" between mind and body, by which he means that there is no ultimate distinction between them. From one point of view, he argues, it is possible to see the body as "the cause of the structure of consciousness," for example, as a physiologist interested in the workings of the brain and the sense organs. From another point of view, it is possible to see the body as a mere "object of knowledge," for example, when a medical student dissects a body in his anatomy class. But it is a mistake, Merleau-Ponty argues, to confuse either of these viewpoints with the "correct" view of the body, either as a cause of consciousness or as something wholly distinct from it. Only the *living* body can count as *my* body, except in a very special and not everyday sense, namely, the sense in which I can talk about what will happen to my body after I die.

"The body is not a self-enclosed mechanism" he argues, nor does it makes sense to treat "the soul" or consciousness as a distinct entity with some mysterious relationship with the body. "There is not a duality of substances," he writes, but only "the dialectic of living being in its biological milieu." Merleau-Ponty sometimes says the consciousness is nothing but "the meaning of one's body," all of which is to say, in extremely difficult prose, that mind and body are nothing other than a single entity, and the distinctions we make between them are always special cases. "I live my body," he says; there is no enigma of "my body" to be explained.[39]

In his difficult "dialectical" language, Merleau-Ponty defends a thesis that is strikingly similar to that defended by Wittgenstein and Strawson: One cannot treat a person as an uneasy conglomerate of mental parts and body parts but must begin with the whole person. But where Wittgenstein and Strawson proceed by attacking the mental side of Cartesian dualism, Merleau-Ponty attacks anyone who would treat the human body as "just another body." The body itself is not only alive but, in an important sense, conscious. This does not mean, as in Descartes, that it is connected with a consciousness. It is itself aware, as we often notice when we talk of "bodily awareness" or "feeling our way." The difference between the body of a living person and a corpse is not just a difference in physiology, nor is it the difference between an "inhabited" body and an "uninhabited" body. My body and myself are essentially one, and to try to separate them, as Descartes had done, is to make the

[39]Maurice Merleau-Ponty, *The Structure of Behavior*, trans. Alden L. Fisher (Boston: Beacon Press, 1963).

relationship between "me and my body" into an unnecessary mystery.

A view that is strikingly similar to the phenomenological theory was defended in this country by William James. But instead of giving consciousness the attention it receives in Husserl, he argues that there is no such thing as consciousness as an entity, only different functions of experience:

◆ from "Does Consciousness Exist?" by William James

"Thoughts" and "things" are names for two sorts of objects, which common sense will always find contrasted and will always practically oppose to each other. Philosophy, reflecting on the contrast, has varied in the past in her explanations of it, and may be expected to vary in the future. At first, "spirit and matter," "soul and body," stood for a pair of equipollent substances quite on a par in weight and interest. But one day Kant undermined the soul and brought in the transcendental ego, and ever since then the bipolar relation has been very much off its balance. The transcendental ego seems nowadays in rationalist quarters to stand for everything, in empiricist quarters for almost nothing. In the hands of . . . writers . . . the spiritual principle attenuates itself to a thoroughly ghostly condition, being only a name for the fact that the "content" of experience *is known*. It loses personal form and activity—these passing over to the content—and becomes a bare [consciousness], of which in its own right absolutely nothing can be said.

I believe that "consciousness," when once it has evaporated to this estate . . . is on the point of disappearing altogether. It is the name of a nonentity, and has no right to a place among first principles. Those who still cling to it are clinging to a mere echo, the faint rumor left behind by the disappearing "soul" upon the air of philosophy. During the past year, I have read a number of articles whose authors seemed just on the point of abandoning the notion of consciousness, and substituting for it that of an absolute experience not due to two factors. But they were not quite radical enough, not quite daring enough in their negations. For twenty years past I have mistrusted "consciousness" as an entity; for seven or eight years past I have suggested its non-existence to my students, and tried to give them its pragmatic-equivalent in realities of experience. It seems to me that the hour is ripe for it to be openly and universally discarded.

To deny plumply that "consciousness" exists seems so absurd on the face of it—for undeniably "thoughts" do exist—that I fear some readers will follow me no farther. Let me then immediately explain that I mean only to deny that the word stands for an entity, but to insist most emphatically that it does stand for a function. There is, I mean, no aboriginal stuff or quality of being, contrasted with that of which material objects are made, out of which our thoughts of them are made; but there is a function in experience which thoughts perform, and for the performance of which this quality of being is invoked. That function is *knowing.* "Consciousness" is supposed necessary to explain the fact that things not only are, but get reported, are known. Whoever blots out the notion of consciousness from his list of first principles must still provide in some way for that function's being carried on.

. . . .

My thesis is that if we start with the supposition that there is only one primal stuff or material in the world, a stuff of which everything is composed, and if we call that stuff "pure experience," then knowing can easily be explained as a particular sort of relation towards one another into which portions of pure experience may enter. The relation itself is a part of pure experience; one of its "terms" becomes the subject or bearer of the knowledge, the knower, the other becomes the object known. This will need much explanation before it can be understood. The best way to get it understood is to contrast it with the alternative view; and for that we may take the recentest alternative, that in which the evaporation of the definite soul-substance has proceeded as far as it can go without being yet complete. If neo-Kantism has expelled earlier forms of dualism, we shall have expelled all forms if we are able to expel neo-Kantism in its turn.

For the thinkers I call neo-Kantian, the word consciousness to-day does no more than signalize the fact that experience is indefeasibly dualistic in structure. It means that not subject, not object, but object-plus-subject is the minimum that can actually be. The subject-object distinction meanwhile is entirely different from that between mind and matter, from that between body and soul. Souls were detachable, had separate destinies; things could happen to them. To consciousness as such nothing can happen, for, timeless itself, it is only a witness of happenings in time, in which it plays no part. It is, in a word, but the logical correlative of "content" in an Experience of which the peculiarity is that *fact comes to light* in it, that *awareness* of *content* takes place. Consciousness as such is entirely impersonal—"self" and its activities belong to the content. To say that I am self-conscious, or conscious of putting forth volition, means only that certain contents, for which "self" and "effort of will" are the names, are not without witness as they occur.

Thus, for these belated drinkers at the Kantian spring, we should have to admit consciousness as an "epistemological" necessity, even if we had no direct evidence of its being there.

But in addition to this, we are supposed by almost every one to have an immediate consciousness of consciousness itself. When the world of outer fact ceases to be materially present, and we merely recall it in memory, or fancy it, the consciousness is believed to stand out and to be felt as a kind of impalpable inner flowing, which, once known in this sort of experience, may equally be detected in presentations of the outer world. "The moment we try to fix our attention upon consciousness and to see *what*, distinctly, it is," says a recent writer, "it seems to vanish. It seems as if we had before us a mere emptiness. When we try to introspect the sensation of blue, all we can see is the blue; the other element is as if it were diaphanous. Yet it *can* be distinguished, if we look attentively enough, and know that there is something to look for." "Consciousness," says another philosopher, "is inexplicable and hardly describable, yet all conscious experiences have this in common that what we call their content has this peculiar reference to a centre for which 'self' is the name, in virtue of which reference alone the content is subjectively given, or appears. . . . While in this way consciousness, or reference to a self, is the only thing which distinguishes a conscious content from any sort of being that might be there with no one conscious of it, yet this only ground of the distinction defies all closer explanations. The existence of consciousness, although it is the fundamental fact of psychology, can indeed be laid down as certain, can be brought out by analysis, but can neither be defined nor deduced from anything but itself."

· · · · · · · · · ·

Now my contention is exactly the reverse of this. *Experience, I believe, has no such inner duplicity; and the separation of it into consciousness and content comes, not by way of subtraction, but by way of addition*—the addition, to a given concrete piece of it, of other sets of experiences, in connection with which severally its use or function may be of two different kinds. The paint will also serve here as an illustration. In a pot in a paintshop, along with other paints, it serves in its entirety as so much saleable matter. Spread on a canvas, with other paints around it, it represents, on the contrary, a feature in a picture and performs a spiritual function. Just so, I maintain, does a given undivided portion of experience, taken in one context of associates, play the part of a knower, of a state of mind, of "consciousness"; while in a different context the same undivided bit of experience plays the part of a thing known, of an objective "content." In a word, in one group it figures as a thought, in another group as a thing. And, since it can figure in both groups simultaneously we have every right to speak of it as subjective and objective both at once. The dualism connoted by such double-barrelled terms as "experience," "phenomenon," "datum"—terms which, in philosophy at any rate, tend more and more to replace the single-barrelled terms of "thought" and "thing"—that dualism, I say, is still preserved in this account, but reinterpreted, so that, instead of being mysterious and elusive, it becomes verifiable and concrete. It is an affair of relations, it falls outside, not inside, the single experience considered, and can always be particularized and defined.

The entering wedge for this more concrete way of understanding the dualism was fashioned by Locke when he made the word "idea" stand indifferently for thing and thought, and by Berkeley when he said that what common sense means by realities is exactly what the philosopher means by ideas. Neither Locke nor Berkeley thought his truth out into perfect clearness, but it seems to me that the conception I am defending does little more than consistently carry out the "pragmatic" method which they were the first to use.

If the reader will take his own experiences, he will see what I mean. Let him begin with a perceptual experience, the "presentation," so called, of a physical object, his actual field of vision, the room he sits in, with the book he is reading as its centre; and let him for the present treat this complex object in the common-sense way as being "really" what it seems to be, namely, a collection of physical things cut out from an environing world of other physical things with which these physical things have actual or potential relations. Now at the same time it is just *those self-same things* which his mind, as we say, perceives; and the whole philosophy of perception from Democritus' time downwards has been just one long wrangle over the paradox that what is evidently one reality should be in two places at once, both in outer space and in a person's mind. "Representative" theories of perception avoid the logical paradox, but on the other hand they violate the reader's sense of life, which knows no intervening mental image but seems to see the room and the book immediately just as they physically exist.

The puzzle of how the one identical room can be in two places is at bottom just the puzzle of how one identical point can be on two lines. It can, if it be situated at their intersection; and similarly, if the "pure experience" of the room were a place of intersection of two processes, which connected it with different groups of associates respectively, it could be counted twice over, as belonging to either group, and spoken of loosely as existing in two places, although it would remain all the time a numerically single thing.

Well, the experience is a member of diverse processes that can be followed away from it along entirely different lines. The one self-identical thing has so many relations to the rest of experience that you can take it in disparate systems of association, and treat it as belonging with opposite contexts. In one of these contexts it is your "field of consciousness"; in another it is "the room in which you sit," and it enters both contexts in its wholeness, giving no pretext for being said to attach itself to consciousness by one of its parts or aspects, and to outer reality by another. What are the two processes, now, into which the room-experience simultaneously enters in this way?

One of them is the reader's personal biography, the other is the history of the house of which the room is part. The presentation, the experience, the *that* in short (for until we have decided *what* it is it must be a mere *that*) is the last term of a train of sensations, emotions, decisions, movements, classifications, expectations, etc., ending in the present, and the first term of a series of similar "inner" operations extending into the future, on the reader's part. On the other hand, the very same *that* is the *terminus ad quem* of a lot of previous physical operations, carpentering, papering, furnishing, warming, etc., and the *terminus a quo* of a lot of future ones, in which it will be concerned when undergoing the destiny of a physical room. The physical and the mental operations form curiously incompatible groups. As a room, the experience has occupied that spot and had that environment for thirty years. As your field of consciousness it may never have existed until now. As a room, attention will go on to discover endless new details in it. As your mental state merely, few new ones will emerge under attention's eye. As a room, it will take an earthquake, or a gang of men, and in any case a certain amount of time, to destroy it. As your subjective state, the closing of your eyes, or any instantaneous play of your fancy will suffice. In the real world, fire will consume it. In your mind, you can let fire play over it without effect. As an outer object, you must pay so much a month to inhabit it. As an inner content, you may occupy it for any length of time rent-free. If, in short, you follow it in the mental direction, taking it along with events of personal biography solely, all sorts of things are true of it which are false, and false of it which are true if you treat it as a real thing experienced, follow it in the physical direction, and relate it to associates in the outer world.

· · · · · · · · · ·

First of all, this will be asked: "If experience has not 'conscious' existence, if it be not partly made of 'consciousness,' of what then is it made? Matter we know, and thought we know, and conscious content we know, but neutral and simple 'pure experience' is something we know not at all. Say *what* it consists of—for it must consist of something—or be willing to give it up!"

To this challenge the reply is easy. Although for fluency's sake I myself spoke early in this article of a stuff of pure experience, I have now to say that there is no *general* stuff of which experience at large is made. There are as many stuffs as there are "natures" in the things experienced. If you ask what any one bit of pure experience is made of, the answer is always the same: "It is made of *that*, of just what appears, of space, of intensity, of flatness, brownness, heaviness, or what not. . . ." Experience is only a collective name for all these sensible natures, and save for time and space (and, if you like, for "being") there appears no universal element of which all things are made.

But a last cry of *non possumus* will probably go up from many readers. "All very pretty as a piece of ingenuity," they will say, "but our consciousness itself intuitively contradicts you. We, for our part, *know* that we are conscious. We *feel* our thought, flowing as a life within us, in absolute contrast with the objects which it so unremittingly escorts. We can not be faithless to this immediate intuition. The dualism is a fundamental *datum*: Let no man join what God has put asunder."

My reply to this is my last word, and I greatly grieve that to many it will sound materialistic. I can not help that, however, for I, too, have my intuitions and I must obey them. Let the case be what it may in others, I am as confident as I am of anything that, in myself, the stream of thinking (which I recognize emphatically as a phenomenon) is only a careless name for what, when scrutinized, reveals itself to consist chiefly of the stream of my breathing. The "I think" which Kant said must be able to accompany all my objects, is the "I breathe" which actually does accompany them. There are other internal facts besides breathing (intracephalic muscular adjustments, etc., of which I have said a word in my larger Psychology), and these increase the assets of "consciousness," so far as the latter is subject to immediate perception; but breath, which was ever the original of "spirit," breath moving outwards, between the glottis and the nostrils, is, I am persuaded, the essence out of which philosophers have constructed the entity known to them as consciousness. *That entity is fictitious, while thoughts in the concrete are fully real. But thoughts in the concrete are made of the same stuff as things are.*

I wish I might believe myself to have made that plausible in this article. In another article I shall try to make the general notion of a world composed of pure experiences still more clear.[40]

Here again, but from another perspective, the traditional Cartesian dualism is rejected. James, like Wittgenstein and Strawson, attacks the idea of separate "mental" events or "consciousness" and insists that "there is no such thing." But in saying that, he is not denying that we are conscious or that we have feeling and experiences. He is rather saying that we have to think of the overall person, and give up the idea of the mind and experience as independent and separable entities.

F. THE INDIVIDUAL AND THE COMMUNITY

So far, both our defenses and criticisms of the Cartesian model have focused on the individual. We have considered the individual and individual consciousness, asking whether or not it conforms to the Cartesian picture of the self. There is a wholly different alternative, however, which we haven't discussed yet (although Sartre's *No Exit* does touch upon it).

Even within discussions of the individual self, it becomes evident that the individual self is largely, if not entirely, a social product and a self

[40]William James, "Does Consciousness Exist?" in *Journal of Philosophy, Psychology and Scientific Methods,* September 1, 1904.

defined by society. We have all had the experience of finding ourselves in company in which we "could not be ourselves" or, even worse, in which we acted according to an identity that was wholly imposed upon us by other people. When going to school, for example, we played the role of "student," ingratiating and oppressed, long before we started to recognize that it is a role, and not a very pleasant one at that. Now we see it as a role that has been formulated solely for the advantage of other people—teachers, administrators, parents—so that we could be forced to "behave." Have you started to wonder how many other aspects of your identity have been similarly imposed upon you, not chosen at all, much less created by you? How much of your behavior has been "programmed" or "conditioned" by parents, society, television, movies, friends, and schoolmates? The suspicion deepens. And soon you start to see a split developing in your thinking about yourself: First, there is your conception of your own identity; second, there is the identity that has been imposed upon you. The two drift apart like boat and dock, and you find yourself falling between.

No wonder, then, that one of the leading psychiatrists of our times, R. D. Laing, has looked at this problem not only as the basis of much of our everyday unhappiness but as the cause of some of our most serious psychological breakdowns as well. Laing describes what he calls "ontological insecurity" as just this split between your awareness of yourself by yourself and the awareness that is imposed upon yourself as an object of other people's attention. Guilt is an example of this split; in excess (as Freud often argued) such emotions tend to be pathological. One definition of guilt is that it is a kind of self-consciousness that is caught between the need for approval and recognition by others and the feeling that you must be "yourself." Thus we tend to get the idea of a "true self" that lies concealed behind the masks that we present in public, even to our closest friends. We get the sense that our real selves are known only to ourselves, but at the same time we do not really exist except with other people.

But this is an extremely negative view of a tension that is in fact central to our whole Western notion of self, the tension between individuality and social self-identity. In most societies, Plato and Aristotle's Greece, for example, a person would always see his or her own identity in terms of the society of which one was a member. The idea of a self that was antagonistic to society would have been completely foreign to them. (Consider, for instance, Socrates' speech in the *Crito,* in our Introduction, in which he says, in effect, that he cannot serve his own interests against the state without betraying himself.) And yet our own idea of self-identity has become so individualistic that the very idea that self-identity is really social-identity flies in the face of that whole Cartesian tradition—and much of Western thinking—that begins with the autonomy of the self and self-consciousness. Nietzsche, for ex-

ample, goes so far as to suggest that self-consciousness is simply superfluous.

◆ on the Dispensability of Consciousness, by Friedrich Nietzsche

The *"Genius of the Species."*—The problem of consciousness
(or more correctly: of becoming conscious of oneself) meets us only
when we begin to perceive in what measure we could dispense with
it: and it is at the beginning of this perception that we are now
placed by physiology and zoology (which have thus required two
centuries to overtake the hint thrown out in advance by Leibniz).
For we could in fact think, feel, will and recollect, we could likewise
"act" in every sense of the term, and nevertheless nothing of it all
need necessarily "come into consciousness" (as one says metaphorically). The whole of life would be possible without its seeing itself
as it were in a mirror: as in fact even at present the far greater part
of our life still goes on without this mirroring—and even our
thinking, feeling, volitional life as well, however painful this statement may sound to an older philosopher. *What* then is *the purpose* of consciousness generally, when it is in the main *superfluous?*—Now it seems to me, if you will hear my answer and its perhaps extravagant supposition, that the subtlety and strength of consciousness are always in proportion to the *capacity for communication* of a man (or an animal), the capacity for communication
in its turn being in proportion to the *necessity for communication:*
the latter not to be understood as if precisely the individual himself who is master in the art of communicating and making known
his necessities would at the same time have to be most dependent
upon others for his necessities. It seems to me, however, to be so in
relation to whole races and successions of generations: where necessity and need have long compelled men to communicate with
their fellows and understand one another rapidly and subtly, a surplus of the power and art of communication is at last acquired, as
if it were a fortune which had gradually accumulated, and now
waited for an heir to squander it prodigally (the so-called artists
are these heirs, in like manner the orators, preachers and authors:
all of them men who come at the end of a long succession, "late-
born" always, in the best sense of the word, and as has been said,
squanderers by their very nature). Granted that this observation
is correct, I may proceed further to the conjecture that *consciousness generally has only been developed under the pressure of the
necessity for communication,*—that from the first it has been
necessary and useful only between man and man (especially between those commanding and those obeying), and has only developed in proportion to its utility. Consciousness is properly only
a connecting network between man and man,—it is only as such

that it has had to develop; the recluse and wild-beast species of men would not have needed it. The very fact that our actions, thoughts, feelings and motions come within the range of our consciousness—at least a part of them—is the result of a terrible, prolonged "must" ruling man's destiny: as the most endangered animal he *needed* help and protection; he needed his fellows, he was obliged to express his distress, he had to know how to make himself understood—and for all this he needed "consciousness" first of all: he had to "know" himself what he lacked, to "know" how he felt, and to "know" what he thought. For, to repeat it once more, man, like every living creature, thinks unceasingly, but does not know it; the thinking which is becoming *conscious of itself* is only the smallest part thereof, we may say, the most superficial part, the worst part:—for this conscious thinking alone *is done in words, that is to say, in the symbols for communication,* by means of which the origin of consciousness is revealed. In short, the development of speech and the development of consciousness (not of reason, but of reason becoming self-conscious) go hand in hand. Let it be further accepted that it is not only speech that serves as a bridge between man and man, but also looks, the pressure and the gestures; our becoming conscious of our sense impressions, our power of being able to fix them, and as it were to locate them outside of ourselves, has increased in proportion as the necessity has increased for communicating them to *others* by means of signs. The sign-inventing man is at the same time the man who is always more acutely self-conscious; it is only as a social animal that man has learned to become conscious of himself,—he is doing so still, and doing so more and more.—As is obvious, my idea is that consciousness does not properly belong to the individual existence of man, but rather to the social and gregarious nature in him; that, as follows therefrom, it is only in relation to communal and gregarious utility that it is finely developed; and that consequently each of us, in spite of the best intention of *understanding* himself as individually as possible, and of "knowing himself," will always just call into consciousness the non-individual in him, namely, his "averageness";—that our thought itself is continuously as it were *outvoted* by the character of consciousness—by the imperious "genius of the species" therein—and is translated back into the perspective of the herd. Fundamentally our actions are in comparable manner altogether personal, unique, and absolutely individual—there is no doubt about it; but as soon as we translate them into consciousness, they *do not appear so any longer. . . .* This is the proper phenomenalism and perspectivism as I understand it: the nature of *animal consciousness* involves the notion that the world of which we can become conscious is only a superficial and symbolic world, a generalised and vulgarised world;—that everything which becomes conscious *becomes* just thereby shallow, meagre, relatively stupid,—a generalisation, a symbol, a characteristic of the herd; that with the evolving of consciousness there is always combined a great, radical perversion, falsification, superficialisation and generalisation. Finally, the growing consciousness is a danger, and whoever lives among the most conscious European knows even that it is a disease. As may be conjectured, it is not the antithesis of subject and object with which I am here concerned: I leave that distinction to the epistemologists who have remained entangled in the toils of grammar (popular metaphysics). It is still less the antithesis of "thing in itself" and phenomenon, for we do not "know" enough to be entitled even to *make such a distinction*. Indeed, we have not any organ at all for *knowing*, or for "truth": we "know" (or believe, or fancy) just as much as may be of *use* in the interest of the human herd, the species; and even what is here called "usefulness" is ultimately only a belief, a fancy, and perhaps precisely the most fatal stupidity by which we shall one day be ruined.

Our response to this split between what some philosophers call the "self for itself" and the "self for others" has been varied. For some, particularly those who have been called existentialists, such as Sartre, whom we read about earlier, the response has been wholesale rebellion, the demand that we break away from "the masses" and our given social identities and create our selves. Nietzsche, for example, attacks what he calls "the herd" in the above passage and urges us to develop ourselves as unique individuals. Indeed, this is the main point of Nietzsche's entire philosophy and underlies his attack on religion and morality.

◆ "Herd Instinct," by Nietzsche

Herd-Instinct.—Wherever we meet with a morality we find a valuation and order of rank of the human impulses and activities. These valuations and orders of rank are always the expression of the needs of a community or herd: that which is in the first place to *its* advantage—and in the second place and third place—is also the authoritative standard for the worth of every individual. By morality the individual is taught to become a function of the herd, and to ascribe to himself value only as a function. As the conditions for the maintenance of one community have been very different from those of another community, there have been very different moralities; and in respect to the future essential transformations of herds and communities, states and societies, one can prophesy that there will still be very divergent moralities. Morality is the herd-instinct in the individual.[41]

---

[41] Friedrich Nietzsche, *The Joyful Wisdom*, trans. Thomas Common, in *The Complete Works of Friedrich Nietzsche*, Oscar Levy, gen. ed. (1909–11) (New York: Russell & Russell, 1964).

A similar attempt at individual rebellion was attempted even earlier by Kierkegaard, the Christian philosopher who has often been claimed as the father of existentialism. Like Nietzsche, he deplores what he sarcastically called "the public" and urges an end to collective identity and social roles in favor of renewed respect for the individual.

◆ on "The Public,"
by Søren Kierkegaard

In spite of all his exertion the subjective thinker enjoys only a meager reward. The more the collective idea comes to dominate even the ordinary consciousness, the more forbidding seems the transition to becoming a particular existing human being instead of losing oneself in the race, and saying "we," "our age," "the nineteenth century." That it is a little thing merely to be a particular existing human being is not to be denied; but for this very reason it requires considerable resignation not to make light of it. For what does a mere individual count for? Our age knows only too well how little it is, but here also lies the specific immorality of the age. Each age has its own characteristic depravity. Ours is perhaps not pleasure of indulgence or sensuality, but rather a dissolute pantheistic contempt for the individual man. In the midst of all our exultation over the achievements of the age and the nineteenth century, there sounds a note of poorly conceived contempt for the individual man; in the midst of the self-importance of the contemporary generation there is revealed a sense of despair over being human. Everything must attach itself so as to be a part of some movement; men are determined to lose themselves in the totality of things, in world-history, fascinated and deceived by a magic witchery; no one wants to be an individual human being.

In fact, so adamant is Kierkegaard on this issue that he argues that a person who "follows the crowd" and does not choose his or her own identity and live passionately as an individual cannot even be said to really exist.

◆ on Self and Passion,
by Kierkegaard

It is impossible to exist without passion, unless we understand the word "exist" in the loose sense of a so-called existence. Every Greek thinker was therefore essentially a passionate thinker. I have often reflected how one might bring a man into a state of passion. I have thought in this connection that if I could get him seated on a

horse and the horse made to take fright and gallop wildly, or better
still, for the sake of bringing the passion out, if I could take a man
who wanted to arrive at a certain place as quickly as possible, and
hence already had some passion, and could set him astride a horse
that can scarcely walk—and yet this is what existence is like if one
is to become consciously aware of it. Or if a driver were otherwise
not especially inclined toward passion, if someone hitched a team
of horses to a wagon for him, one of them a Pegasus and the other
a worn-out jade, and told him to drive—I think one might succeed.
And it is just this that it means to exist, if one is to become conscious of it. Eternity is the winged horse, infinitely fast, and time is
a worn-out jade; the existing individual is the driver. That is to
say, he is such a driver when his mode of existence is not an existence loosely so called; for then he is no driver, but a drunken peasant who lies asleep in the wagon and lets the horses take care of
themselves. To be sure, he also drives and is a driver; and so there
are perhaps many who—also exist.[42]

And in this century, borrowing from both Kierkegaard and Nietzsche, the
German existentialist Martin Heidegger has argued against collective
social identity in terms of what he (also ironically) calls *das Man,* an
extremely useful German expression that roughly translates as "they" in
"*they* say that garlic cures colds." Who are "they"? No one at all,
Heidegger says, just an anonymous no one. In extremely dense philosophical prose, he argues.[43]

◆"Dasein" and the "They," by Martin Heidegger

Dasein, as everyday Being-with-one-another, stands in *subjection*
to Others. It itself *is* not; its Being has been taken away by the Others. Dasein's everyday possibilities of Being are for the Others to
dispose of as they please. These Others, moreover, are not *definite*
Others. On the contrary, any Other can represent them. What is
decisive is just that inconspicuous domination by Others which has
already been taken over unawares from Dasein as Being-with. One
belongs to the Others oneself and enhances their power. "The
Others" whom one thus designates in order to cover up the fact of
one's belonging to them essentially oneself, are those who proxi-
mally and for the most part *"are there"* in everyday Being-with-
one-another. The "who" is not this one, not that one, not oneself,

---

[42]Søren Kierkegaard, *Concluding Unscientific Postscript,* trans. David F. Swenson and
Walter Lowrie (Princeton, NJ: Princeton University Press, 1941).
[43]For "Dasein," read "individual human being"; for "Being-with," read "being around other
people."

> not some people, and not the sum of them all. The "who" is the neuter, *the "they" [das Man].*
>
> · · · · · · · · · ·
>
> Everyone is the other, and no one is himself. The *"they,"* which supplies the answer to the question of the "who" of everyday Dasein, is the *"nobody"* to whom every Dasein has already surrendered itself in Being-among-one-other.

And against this "surrender," Heidegger urges us to "take hold of ourselves" as individuals and find our "authentic" selves.

> The Self of everyday Dasein is the *they-self,* which we distinguish from the *authentic Self*—that is, from the Self which has been taken hold of in its own way.[44]

This individualist movement is not unique to existentialism; it is in the main stream of Western thinking, from ancient Socrates through Reformation Christianity to contemporary capitalism. Socrates' rebellion was, in a very important way, an existential rebellion. He stood up for his principles against the opinions of the age. And Luther's Reformation was, among other things, very much a reassertion of the individual (individual conscience, individual actions) against the all-embracing spirit of the Catholic Church. And today, virtually every American would agree that every individual deserves at least some individual rights and respect. But individualism has always had its doubters. Individualism arises largely as a reaction against the awareness of how socially conditioned we really are. As an instrument of personal growth and as a defense against excessive socialization, individualism is extremely valuable. But when individualism becomes so powerful that personal interests eclipse the interests of everyone else and individual values begin to destroy the community, then it may be time to bring the limits of individualism into question as well. Furthermore, an excessive emphasis on individuality may lead us to forget that there are other human ways of living that are not individualistic at all. There are limits to the degree to which we can challenge the values and customs of our upbringing. Some rebellion is required for growth and change of the society as well as of the individual. But too much rebellion can be self-destructive as well as destructive to the community. For our self-identities, no matter how hard we try to think of ourselves as total individuals, are inextricably tied to the communities and values in which we were raised.

The American sociologist David Reisman looks again at individualism in the light of these considerations and defends it as follows:

[44]Martin Heidegger, *Being and Time,* trans. J. MacQuarrie and E. Robinson (New York: Harper & Row, 1962).

◆ on Individualism, by David Reisman

Social science has helped us become more aware of the extent to which individuals, great and little, are the creatures of their cultural conditioning; and so we neither blame the little nor exalt the great. But the same wisdom has sometimes led us to the fallacy that, since all men have their being in culture and as the result of the culture, they owe a debt to that culture which even a lifetime of altruism could not repay. (One might as well argue, and in fact many societies in effect do, that since we are born of parents, we must feel guilt whenever we transcend their limitations!) Sometimes the point is pushed to the virtual denial of individuality: since we arise in society, it is assumed with a ferocious determinism that we can never transcend it. All such concepts are useful correctives of an earlier solipsism. But if they are extended to hold that conformity with society is not only a necessity but also a duty, they destroy that margin of freedom which gives life its savor and its endless possibility for advance.[45]

1. *Voices of Protest*

In contemporary times, the question of how individuals are defined by or in society is a deeply political issue. It is tied to questions of how we categorize our society ethnically, sexually, racially. In our pluralist American society, we tend to believe that individual freedoms play more of a role in defining us within society than do, say, our family lineage or professional organizations. We are particularly sensitive, then, to racial or sexual stereotyping and to strict enforcement of social roles, because we feel that our identities are thereby taken out of our own control and our individuality is overlooked. This concern is similar to the concern that dualists have about materialism. We worry that if we "are" just our bodies—or similarly if we "are" just what our society makes us—then we are not the free, rational, creatures we would like to be.

Below, in a very famous passage, the Black Nationalist leader Malcolm X argues the extent to which African-Americans' self-identities are defined for them by American society in which whites are a majority.

◆ on Being "African," by Malcolm X

Right now, in this country, if you and I, 22 million African-Americans—that's what we are—Africans who are in America. You're nothing but Africans. Nothing but Africans. In fact, you'd get

---

[45] David Reisman, *Individualism Reconsidered* (New York: Doubleday, 1954).

farther calling yourself African instead of Negro. Africans don't catch hell. You're the only one catching hell. They don't have to pass civil-rights bills for Africans. An African can go anywhere he wants right now. All you've got to do is tie your head up. That's right, go anywhere you want. Just stop being a Negro. Change your name to Hoogagagooba. That'll show you how silly the white man is. You're dealing with a silly man. A friend of mine who's very dark put a turban on his head and went into a restaurant in Atlanta before they called themselves desegregated. He went into a white restaurant, he sat down, they served him, and he said, "What would happen if a Negro came in here?" And there he's sitting, black as night, but because he had his head wrapped up the waitress looked back at him and says, "Why, there wouldn't no nigger dare come in here."[46]

Malcolm X explains the moral of the story in another famous speech:

◆**from "At the Audobon,"**
by Malcolm X

You'll be surprised how fast, how easy it is for someone to steal your and my mind. You don't think so? We never like to think in terms of being dumb enough to let someone put something over on us in a very deceitful and tricky way. But you and I are living in a very deceitful and tricky society, in a very deceitful and tricky country, which has a very deceitful and tricky government. *All* of them in it aren't tricky and deceitful, but *most* of them are. And any time you have a government in which *most* of them are deceitful and tricky, you have to be on guard at all times. You have to know how they work this deceit and how they work these tricks. Otherwise you'll find yourself in a bind.

One of the best ways to safeguard yourself from being deceived is always to form the habit of looking at things for yourself, listening to things for yourself, thinking for yourself, before you try and come to any judgment. Never base your impression of someone on what someone else has said. Or upon what someone else has written. Or upon what you read about someone that somebody else wrote. Never base your judgment on things like that. Especially in this kind of country and in this kind of society which has mastered the art of very deceitfully painting people whom they don't like in an image that they know you won't like. So you end up hating your friends and loving their enemies.

An example: I was flying from Algiers to Geneva about three or

---

[46]Malcolm X, "The Ballot or the Bullet," rpt. in *Malcolm X Speaks,* ed. George Breitman (New York: Grove Press, 1965).

four weeks ago, and seated beside me on the airplane were a couple of Americans, both white, one a male and the other a female.
One was an interpreter who worked in Geneva for the United
Nations, the other was a girl who worked in one of the embassies
in some part of Algeria. We conversed for about forty or forty-five
minutes and then the lady, who had been looking at my briefcase,
said, "May I ask you a personal question?" And I said, "Yes."
Because they always do anyway. She said, "What kind of last name
do you have that begins with X?" I said, "That's it, X." So she said,
"X?" "Yes." "Well, what is your first name?" I said, "Malcolm." So
she waited for about ten minutes and then she said, "You're not
Malcolm X." And I said, "Yes, I'm Malcolm X. Why, what's the matter?" And she said, "Well, you're not what I was looking for."

What she was looking for was what the newspapers, the press,
had created. She was looking for the image that the press had created. Somebody with horns, you know, about to kill all the white
people—as if he could kill all of them, or as if he shouldn't. She
was looking for someone who was a rabble-rouser, who couldn't
even converse with people with blue eyes, you know, someone who
was irrational, and things of that sort. I take time to point this out,
because it shows how skillfully someone can take a newspaper
and build an image of someone so that before you even meet them,
you'll run. You don't even want to hear what they have to say, you
don't even know them, all you know is what the *press* has had to
say, and the press is white. And whan I say the press is white, I
mean it is *white*. And it's dangerous.

The FBI can feed information to the press to make your neighbor think you're something subversive. The FBI—they do it very
skillfully, they maneuver the press on a national scale; and the CIA
maneuvers the press on an international scale. They do all their
dirt with the press. They take the newspapers and make the newspapers blow you and me up as if all of us are criminals, all of us
are racists, all of us are drug addicts, or all of us are rioting. This
is how they do it. When you explode legitimately against the injustices that have been heaped upon you, they use the press to
make it look like you're a vandal. If you were a vandal, you have a
right to be a vandal.

They master this imagery, the image-making. They give you the
image of an extremist, and from then on anything you do is extreme. You can pull a baby out of the water and save it from
drowning—you're still an extremist, because they projected this image of you. They can create an image of you as a subversive and
you can go out and die fighting for the United States—you're still
subversive, because the press has made you a subversive. They can
paint the image of you as someone irresponsible, and you can come
up with the best program that will save the black man from the
oppression of the white man and—When I say oppression, that's
where oppression comes from, the white man. There are some op-

pressive black people, but they're only doing what the white man has taught them.[47]

Obviously, social roles have been binding to the "free individuality" of other groups, too, like women. Many contemporary feminists have analyzed how sex roles, perhaps more than anything else, falsely define us and undermine our individuality. In a now-famous article, Sherri Ortner considers the way society identifies women.

◆ **"Is Female to Male as Nature Is to Culture?"**
by Sherri Ortner[48]

Much of the creativity of anthropology derives from the tension between two sets of demands: that we explain human universals, and that we explain cultural particulars. By this canon, woman provides us with one of the more challenging problems to be dealt with. The secondary status of woman in society is one of the true universals, a pan-cultural fact. Yet within that universal fact, the specific cultural conceptions and symbolizations of woman are extraordinarily diverse and even mutually contradictory. Further, the actual treatment of women and their relative power and contribution vary enormously from culture to culture, and over different periods in the history of particular cultural traditions. Both of these points—the universal fact and the cultural variation—constitute problems to be explained.

My interest in the problem is of course more than academic: I wish to see genuine change come about, the emergence of a social and cultural order in which as much of the range of human potential is open to women as is open to men. The universality of female subordination, the fact that it exists within every type of social and economic arrangement and in societies of every degree of complexity, indicates to me that we are up against something very profound, very stubborn, something we cannot rout out simply by rearranging a few tasks and roles in the social system, or even by reordering the whole economic structure. In this paper I try to expose the underlying logic of cultural thinking that assumes the inferiority of women; I try to show the highly persuasive nature of the logic, for if it were not so persuasive, people would not keep subscribing to it. But I also try to show the social and cultural sources of that logic, to indicate wherein lies the potential for change.

· · · · · · · · · ·

---

[47]Malcolm X, "At the Audobon," *Malcolm X Speaks.*
[48]from Sherry B. Ortner, "Is Female to Male as Nature is to Culture?" reprinted in *Woman, Culture, and Society,* edited by Michelle Z. Rosaldo and Louise Lamphere, (Stanford: Stanford U. Press 1974).

THE UNIVERSALITY OF FEMALE SUBORDINATION

What do I mean when I say that everywhere, in every known culture, women are considered in some degree inferior to men? First of all, I must stress that I am talking about *cultural* evaluations; I am saying that each culture, in its own way and on its own terms, makes this evaluation. But what would constitute evidence that a particular culture considers women inferior?

Three types of data would suffice: (1) elements of cultural ideology and informants' statements that *explicitly* devalue women, according them, their roles, their tasks, their products, and their social milieux less prestige than are accorded men and the male correlates; (2) symbolic devices, such as the attribution of defilement, which may be interpreted as *implicitly* making a statement of interior valuation; and (3) social-structural arrangements that exclude women from participation in or contact with some realm in which the highest powers of the society are felt to reside. These three types of data may all of course be interrelated in any particular system, though they need not necessarily be. Further, any one of them will usually be sufficient to make the point of female inferiority in a given culture. Certainly, female exclusion from the most sacred rite or the highest political council is sufficient evidence. Certainly, explicit cultural ideology devaluing women (and their tasks, roles, products, etc.) is sufficient evidence. Symbolic indicators such as defilement are usually sufficient, although in a few cases in which, say, men and women are equally polluting to one another, a further indicator is required—and is, as far as my investigations have ascertained, always available.

On any or all of these counts, then, I would flatly assert that we find women subordinated to men in every known society.

. . . .

NATURE AND CULTURE

How are we to explain the universal devaluation of women? We could of course rest the case on biological determinism. There is something genetically inherent in the male of the species, so the biological determinists would argue, that makes them the naturally dominant sex; that "something" is lacking in females, and as a result women are not only naturally subordinate but in general quite satisfied with their position, since it affords them protection and the opportunity to maximize maternal pleasures, which to them are the most satisfying experiences of life. Without going into a detailed refutation of this position, I think it fair to say that it has failed to be established to the satisfaction of almost anyone in academic anthropology. This is to say, not that biological facts are irrelevant, or that men and women are not different, but that these facts and differences only take on significance of superior/inferior within the framework of culturally defined value systems.

If we are unwilling to rest the case on genetic determinism, it seems to me that we have only one way to proceed. We must attempt to interpret female subordination in light of other universals, factors built into the structure of the most generalized situation in which all human beings, in whatever culture, find themselves. For example, every human being has a physical body and a sense of nonphysical mind, is part of a society of other individuals and an inheritor of a cultural tradition, and must engage in some relationship, however mediated, with "nature," or the nonhuman realm, in order to survive. Every human being is born (to a mother) and ultimately dies, all are assumed to have an interest in personal survival, and society/culture has its own interest in (or at least momentum toward) continuity and survival, which transcends the lives and deaths of particular individuals. And so forth. It is in the realm of such universals of the human condition that we must seek an explanation for the universal fact of female devaluation.

I translate the problem, in other words, into the following simple question. What could there be in the generalized structure and conditions of existence, common to every culture, that would lead every culture to place a lower value upon women? Specifically, my thesis is that woman is being identified with—or, if you will, seems to be a symbol of—something that every culture devalues, something that every culture defines as being of a lower order of existence than itself. Now it seems that there is only one thing that would fit that description, and that is "nature" in the most generalized sense. Every culture, or, generically, "culture," is engaged in the process of generating and sustaining systems of meaningful forms (symbols, artifacts, etc.) by means of which humanity transcends the givens of natural existence, bends them to its purposes, controls them in its interest. We may thus broadly equate culture with the notion of human consciousness, or with the products of human consciousness (i.e., systems of thought and technology), by means of which humanity attempts to assert control over nature.

· · · · · · · · · ·

Returning now to the issue of women, their pan-cultural second-class status could be accounted for, quite simply, by postulating that women are being identified or symbolically associated with nature, as opposed to men, who are identified with culture. Since it is always culture's project to subsume and transcend nature, if women were considered part of nature, then culture would find it "natural" to subordinate, not to say oppress, them. Yet although this argument can be shown to have considerable force, it seems to oversimplify the case. The formulation I would like to defend and elaborate on in the following section, then, is that women are seen "merely" as being *closer* to nature than men. That is, culture (still equated relatively unambiguously with men) recognizes that women are active participants in its special processes, but at the same time sees them as being more rooted in, or having more direct affinity with, nature.

The revision may seem minor or even trivial, but I think it is a more accurate rendering of cultural assumptions. Further, the argument cast in these terms has several analytic advantages over the simpler formulation; I shall discuss these later. It might simply be stressed here that the revised argument would still account for the pan-cultural devaluation of women, for even if women are not equated with nature, they are nonetheless seen as representing a lower order of being, as being less transcendental of nature than men are. The next task of the paper, then, is to consider why they might be viewed in that way.

WHY IS WOMAN SEEN AS CLOSER TO NATURE?

1. Woman's physiology seen as closer to nature. This part of my argument has been anticipated, with subtlety, cogency, and a great deal of hard data, by de Beauvoir (1953). De Beauvoir reviews the physiological structure, development, and functions of the human female and concludes that "the female, to a greater extent than the male, is the prey of the species" (p. 60). She points out that many major areas and processes of the woman's body serve no apparent function for the health and stability of the individual; on the contrary, as they perform their specific organic functions, they are often sources of discomfort, pain, and danger. The breasts are irrelevant to personal health; they may be excised at any time of a woman's life. "Many of the ovarian secretions function for the benefit of the egg, promoting its maturation and adapting the uterus to its requirements; in respect to the organism as a whole, they make for disequilibrium rather than for regulation—the woman is adapted to the needs of the egg rather than to her own requirements" (p. 24). Menstruation is often uncomfortable, sometimes painful; it frequently has negative emotional correlates and in any case involves bothersome tasks of cleansing and waste disposal; and—a point that de Beauvoir does not mention—in many cultures it interrupts a woman's routine, putting her in a stigmatized state involving various restrictions on her activities and social contacts. In pregnancy many of the woman's vitamin and mineral resources are channeled into nourishing the fetus, depleting her own strength and energies. And finally, childbirth itself is painful and dangerous (pp. 24-27 *passim*). In sum, de Beauvoir concludes that the female "is more enslaved to the species than the male, her animality is more manifest" (p. 239).

While de Beauvoir's book is ideological, her survey of woman's physiological situation seems fair and accurate. It is simply a fact that proportionately more of woman's body space, for a greater percentage of her lifetime, and at some—sometimes great—cost to

her personal health, strength, and general stability, is taken up with
the natural processes surrounding the reproduction of the species.

· · · · · · · · · ·

Indeed, the fact of woman's full human consciousness, her full
involvement in and commitment to culture's project of transcendence over nature, may ironically explain another of the great puzzles of "the woman problem"—woman's nearly universal unques-
tioning acceptance of her own devaluation. For it would seem that,
as a conscious human and member of culture, she has followed out
the logic of culture's arguments and has reached culture's conclusions along with the men. As de Beauvoir puts it (p. 59):

> For she, too, is an existent, she feels the urge to surpass, and her
> project is not mere repetition but transcendence towards a dif-
> ferent future—in her heart of hearts she finds confirmation of
> the masculine pretensions. She joins the men in the festivals
> that celebrate the successes and victories of the males. Her mis-
> fortune is to have been biologically destined for the repetition
> of Life, when even in her own view Life does not carry within it-
> self its reasons for being, reasons that are more important than
> life itself.

In other words, woman's consciousness—her membership, as it
were, in culture—is evidenced in part by the very fact that she accepts her own devaluation and takes culture's point of view.

I have tried here to show one part of the logic of that view, the
part that grows directly from the physiological differences between
men and women. Because of woman's greater bodily involvement
with the natural functions surrounding reproduction, she is seen
as more a part of nature than man is. Yet in part because of her
consciousness and participation in human social dialogue, she is
recognized as a participant in culture. Thus she appears as something intermediate between culture and nature, lower on the scale
of transcendence than man.

2. *Woman's social role seen as closer to nature.* Woman's association with the domestic circle would contribute to the view of her
as closer to nature in several ways. In the first place, the sheer fact
of constant association with children plays a role in the issue; one
can easily see how infants and children might themselves be
considered part of nature. Infants are barely human and utterly
unsocialized; like animals they are unable to walk upright, they ex-
crete without control, they do not speak. Even slightly older children are clearly not yet fully under the sway of culture. They do not
yet understand social duties, responsibilities, and morals; their
vocabulary and their range of learned skills are small. One finds
implicit recognition of an association between children and nature
in many cultural practices. For example, most cultures have initiation rites for adolescents (primarily for boys; I shall return to

this point below), the point of which is to move the child ritually from a less than fully human state into full participation in society and culture; many cultures do not hold funeral rites for children who die at early ages, explicitly because they are not yet fully social beings. Thus children are likely to be categorized with nature, and woman's close association with children may compound her potential for being seen as closer to nature herself. It is ironic that the rationale for boys' initiation rites in many cultures is that the boys must be purged of the defilement accrued from being around mother and other women so much of the time, when in fact much of the woman's defilement may derive from her being around children so much of the time.

· · · · · · · · · ·

3. *Woman's psyche seen as closer to nature.* It is important to specify what we see as the dominant and universal aspects of the feminine psyche. If we postulate emotionality or irrationality, we are confronted with those traditions in various parts of the world in which women functionally are, and are seen as, more practical, pragmatic, and this-worldly than men. One relevant dimension that does seem pan-culturally applicable is that of relative concreteness vs. relative abstractness: the feminine personality tends to be involved with concrete feelings, things, and people, rather than with abstract entities; it tends toward personalism and particularism.

· · · · · · · · · ·

These differences are not innate or genetically programmed; they arise from nearly universal features of family structure, namely that "women, universally, are largely responsible for early child care and for (at least) later female socialization" (p. 43) and that "the structural situation of child rearing, reinforced by female and male role training, produces these differences, which are replicated and reproduced in the sexual sociology of adult life" (p. 44). Chodorow argues that, because mother is the early socializer of both boys and girls, both develop "personal identification" with her, i.e. diffuse identification with her general personality, behavior traits, values, and attitudes (p. 51). A son, however, must ultimately shift to a masculine role identity, which involves building an identification with the father. Since father is almost always more remote than mother (he is rarely involved in child care, and perhaps works away from home much of the day), building an identification with father involves a "positional identification," i.e. identification with father's male role as a collection of abstract elements, rather than a personal identification with father as a real individual (p. 49). Further, as the boy enters the larger social world, he finds it in fact organized around more abstract and universalistic criteria (see Rosaldo, this volume, pp. 28–29; Chodorow, p. 58), as I have indicated in the previous section; thus his earlier socialization prepares him for, and is reinforced by, the type of adult social experience he will have.

For a young girl, in contrast, the personal identification with mother, which was created in early infancy, can persist into the process of learning female role identity. Because mother is immediate and present when the daughter is learning role identity, learning to be a woman involves the continuity and development of a girl's relationship to her mother, and sustains the identification with her as an individual; it does not involve the learning of externally defined role characteristics (Chodorow, p. 51). This pattern prepares the girl for, and is fully reinforced by, her social situation in later life; she will become involved in the world of women, which is characterized by few formal role differences (Rosaldo, p. 29), and which involves again, in motherhood, "personal identification" with *her* children. And so the cycle begins anew.

· · · · · · · · · ·

THE IMPLICATIONS OF INTERMEDIACY

This intermediacy has several implications for analysis, depending upon how it is interpreted. First, of course, it answers my primary question of why woman is everywhere seen as lower than man, for even if she is not seen as nature pure and simple, she is still seen as achieving less transcendence of nature than man. Here intermediate simply means "middle status" on a hierarchy of being from culture to nature.

Second, intermediate may have the significance of "mediating," i.e. performing some sort of synthesizing or converting function between nature and culture, here seen (by culture) not as two ends of a continuum but as two radically different sorts of processes in the world. The domestic unit—and hence woman, who in virtually every case appears as its primary representative—is one of culture's crucial agencies for the conversion of nature into culture, especially with reference to the socialization of children.

· · · · · · · · · ·

Finally, woman's intermediate position may have the implication of greater symbolic ambiguity (see also Rosaldo, this volume). Shifting our image of the culture/nature relationship once again, we may envision culture in this case as a small clearing within the forest of the larger natural system. From this point of view, that which is intermediate between culture and nature is located on the continuous periphery of culture's clearing; and though it may thus appear to stand both above and below (and beside) culture, it is simply outside and around it. We can begin to understand then how a single system of cultural thought can often assign to woman completely polarized and apparently contradictory meanings, since extremes, as we say, meet. That she often represents both life and death is only the simplest example one could mention.

· · · · · · · · · ·

In short, the postulate that woman is viewed as closer to nature than man has several implications for further analysis, and can be interpreted in several different ways. If it is viewed simply as a *middle* position on a scale from culture down to nature, then it is still seen as lower than culture and thus accounts for the pan-cultural assumption that woman is lower than man in the order of things. If it is read as a *mediating* element in the culture-nature relationship, then it may account in part for the cultural tendency not merely to devalue woman but to circumscribe and restrict her functions, since culture must maintain control over its (pragmatic and symbolic) mechanisms for the conversion of nature into culture. And if it is read as an *ambiguous* status between culture and nature, it may help account for the fact that, in specific cultural ideologies and symbolizations, woman can occasionally be aligned with culture, and in any event is often assigned polarized and contradictory meanings within a single symbolic system. Middle status, mediating functions, ambiguous meaning—all are different readings, for different contextual purposes, of woman's being seen as intermediate between nature and culture.

But how would a society *without* clear social and sexual roles function? Is it even possible that we could interact with each other as entirely free individuals? Some feminists, like Ann Ferguson, believe so. She believes, however, that in order to achieve such an ideal, we must all embrace an "androgynous" sexuality.

◆On Androgyny, by Ann Ferguson

VII. ANDROGYNY AS A PROGRESSIVE IDEAL

It is the sexual division of labor in the home and at work that perpetuates complementary sex roles for men and women. In underdeveloped societies with scarce material resources such an arrangement may indeed be the most rational way to allow for the most efficient raising of children and production of goods. But this is no longer true for developed societies. In this age of advanced technology, men's relative strength compared to women's is no longer important, either in war or in the production of goods. The gun and the spinning jenny have equalized the potential role of men and women in both repression and production. And the diaphragm, the pill, and other advances in the technology of reproduction have equalized the potential power of women and men to control their bodies and to reproduce themselves. (The development of cloning would mean that men and women could reproduce without the participation of the opposite sex.)

We have seen how complementary sex roles and their extension to job segregation in wage labor make an ideal love relationship between equals impossible for men and women in our society. The questions that remain are: would the development of androgynous human beings through androgynous sex-role training be possible? If possible, would it allow for the development of equal love relationships? What other human potentials would androgyny allow to develop? And how would society have to be restructured in order to allow for androgynous human beings and equal love relationships?

There is good evidence that human babies are bisexual, and only *learn* a specific male or female identity by imitating and identifying with adult models. This evidence comes from the discovery that all human beings possess both male and female hormones (androgen and estrogen respectively), and also from concepts first developed at length by Freud. Freud argued that heterosexual identity is not achieved until the third stage of the child's sexual development. Sex identity is developed through the resolution of the Oedipus complex, in which the child has to give up a primary attachment to the mother and learn either to identify with, or love, the father. But Shulamith Firestone suggests that this process is not an inevitable one, as Freud presents it to be. Rather, it is due to the power dynamics of the patriarchal nuclear family. Note that, on this analysis, if the sexual division of labor were destroyed, the mechanism that trains boys and girls to develop heterosexual sexual identities would also be destroyed. If fathers and mothers played equal nurturant roles in child-rearing and had equal social, economic, and political power outside the home, there would be no reason for the boy to have to reject his emotional side in order to gain the power associated with the male role. Neither would the girl have to assume a female role in rejecting her assertive, independent side in order to attain power indirectly through manipulation of males. As a sexual identity, bisexuality would then be the norm rather than the exception.

If bisexuality were the norm rather than the exception for the sexual identities that children develop, androgynous sex roles would certainly be a consequence. For, as discussed above, the primary mechanism whereby complementary rather than androgynous sex roles are maintained is through heterosexual training, and through the socialization of needs for love and sexual gratification to the search for a love partner of the opposite sex. Such a partner is sought to complement one in the traits that one has repressed or not developed because in one's own sex such traits were not socially accepted.

VIII. THE ANDROGYNOUS MODEL

I believe that only androgynous people can attain the full human potential possible given our present level of material and social resources (and this only if society is radically restructured). Only such people can have ideal love relationships; and without such relationships, I maintain that none can develop to the fullest potential. Since human beings are social animals and develop through interaction and productive activity with others, such relationships are necessary.

Furthermore, recent studies have shown that the human brain has two distinct functions: one associated with analytic, logical, sequential thinking (the left brain), and the other associated with holistic, metaphorical, intuitive thought (the right brain). Only a person capable of tapping both these sides of him/herself will have developed to full potential. We might call this characteristic of the human brain "psychic bisexuality," since it has been shown that women in fact have developed skills which allow them to tap the abilities of the right side of the brain more than men, who on the contrary excel in the analytic, logical thought characteristic of the left side. The point is that men and women have the potential for using both these functions, and yet our socialization at present tends to cut off from one or the other of these parts of ourselves.

What would an androgynous personality be like? My model for the ideal androgynous person comes from the concept of human potential developed by Marx in *Economic and Philosophical Manuscripts.* Marx's idea is that human beings have a need (or a potential) for free, creative, productive activity which allows them to control their lives in a situation of cooperation with others. Both men and women need to be equally active and independent; with an equal sense of control over their lives; equal opportunity for creative, productive activity; and a sense of meaningful involvement in the community. . . .[49]

2.   "Beyond Individualism"

As we can see from the examples above, the argument for individualism is often stated as a form of mutual conflict (as in the existentialists and Reisman) which many philosophers would not accept. Why need there be a conflict? Kant, for example, while very much the champion of individual autonomy, insisted that the only individuality worth defending was the ability of the individual to participate in universal morality. The same argument is to be found in Socrates, Plato, and Aristotle. And in more recent times, this argument has found a large following among thinkers who have seen the disastrous results of overly individual thinking (what Reisman refers to as "solipsism"). The German philosopher Hegel, for example, writing in the midst of the great international movements of the early nineteenth century, argued:

[49] Ann Ferguson, "Androgyny as a Progressive Ideal for Human Development," rpt. in *Feminism and Philosophy,* ed. Mary Vetterling-Braggin, Frederick A. Elliston and Jane English (Lanham, MD: Littlefield, Adams, 1977).

◆ "Spirit" and the Individual, by Georg Hegel

> . . . at a time when the universal nature of spiritual life has be-
> come so very much emphasized and strengthened, and the mere
> individual aspect has become, as it should be, correspondingly a
> matter of indifference, when, too, that universal aspect holds, by
> the entire range of its substance, the full measure of the wealth it
> has built up, and lays claim to it all, the share in the total work of
> mind that falls to the activity of any particular individual can only
> be very small. Because this is so, the individual must all the more
> forget himself, as in fact the very nature of science implies and re-
> quires that he should; and he must, moreover, become and do
> what he can. But all the less must be demanded of him, just as he
> can expect the less from himself, and may ask the less for himself.[50]

And elsewhere, in a famous passage, he argues that individuals in history
are significant only insofar as they contribute to movements far greater
than themselves:

> . . . in contemplating history as the slaughter-bench at which the
> happiness of peoples, the wisdom of states, and the virtue of indi-
> viduals have been sacrificed, a question necessarily arises: To what
> principle, to what final purpose, have these monstrous sacrifices
> been offered?
>   . . . human agents have before them limited aims, special inter-
> ests. But they are also intelligent, thinking beings. Their purposes
> are interwoven with general and essential considerations of law, the
> good, duty, etc. For mere desire, volition in its raw and savage
> form, falls outside the scene and sphere of world history. These
> general considerations, which at the same time form norms for di-
> recting purposes and actions, have a definite content. For such
> empty abstractions as "good for its own sake" have no place in liv-
> ing actuality.
>   . . . Each individual has his position; he knows, on the whole,
> what a lawful and honorable course of conduct is. To assert in or-
> dinary private relations that it is difficult to choose the right and
> good, and to regard it as mark of an exalted morality to find diffi-
> culties and raise scruples on that score indicates an evil and
> perverse will. It indicates a will that seeks to evade obvious duties
> or, at least, a petty will that gives its mind too little to do. The
> mind, then, in idle reflection, busies itself with itself and indulges
> in moral smugness.
>
> *   . . . each individual is also the child of a people at a definite*
> *stage of its development. One cannot skip over the spirit of his*

[50]G. W. F. Hegel, *The Phenomenology of Spirit*, trans. A. N. Miller (Oxford: Oxford University Press, 1977).

people any more than one can skip over the earth. The earth is the center of gravity; a body imagined as leaving this center can only be imagined as exploding into the air. So it is with an individual. But only through his own effort can he be in harmony with his substance; he must bring the will demanded by his people to his own consciousness, to articulation. The individual does not invent his own content; he is what he is by acting out the universal as his own content.

In the course of history two factors are important. One is the preservation of a people, a state, or the well-ordered spheres of life. This is the activity of individuals participating in the common effort and helping to bring about its particular manifestations. It is the preservation of ethical life. The other important factor, however, is the decline of a state. The existence of a national spirit is broken when it has used up and exhausted itself. World history, the World Spirit, continues on its course.

. . . .

This universal is an essential phase in the development of the creating Idea, of truth striving and urging toward itself. The historical men, *world-historical individuals,* are those [*who grasp just such a higher universal, make it their own purpose, and realize this purpose in accordance with the higher law of the spirit.*][51]

In the midst of the international upheavals led by Napoleon, you can appreciate the appropriateness of such a brutal philosophy. "The slaughter-bench of history" is not a pleasant concept! And the idea that each of us is virtually insignificant in our tiny place in history also hurts our grander conceptions of ourselves. But Hegel argues that no other view of ourselves is defensible. Even the greatest among us is nothing more than an expression of the "universal," the monumental forces of society and humankind as a whole (these are what Hegel refers to as "spirit" and "the Creating Idea" and elsewhere as "the cunning of Reason").

But however appropriate in times of international warfare, Hegel's conception is bound to raise hackles among the individualists in peacetime. Consider Kierkegaard's ironic retort to Hegel's philosophy:

◆ A Retort, by Kierkegaard

Hence perhaps the many attempts to continue clinging to Hegel, even by men who have reached an insight into the questionable character of his philosophy. It is a fear that if they were to become particular existing human beings, they would vanish tracelessly, so that not even the daily press would be able to discover them,

[51] G. W. F. Hegel, *Reason in History,* trans. Robert S. Hartman (New York: Bobbs-Merrill, 1953).

still less critical journals, to say nothing at all of speculative philosophers immersed in world-history. As particular human beings they fear that they will be doomed to a more isolated and forgotten existence than that of a man in the country; for if a man lets go of Hegel he will not even be in a position to have a letter addressed to him.[52]

Karl Marx was a student of Hegel's philosophy. In his "early writings" of 1844, he too argues for a view of self as essentially social, a part of a community, a "species-being":

◆ on the Social Self, by Karl Marx

It follows from the character of this relationship [the human family] how far *man* has become, and has understood himself as, a *species-being*, a *human being*.

· · · · · · · · · ·

Activity and mind are social in their content as well as in their *origin*; they are *social* activity and social mind.

· · · · · · · · · ·

It is above all necessary to avoid postulating "society" once again as an abstraction confronting the individual. The individual *is* the *social being*. The manifestation of his life—even when it does not appear directly in the form of a communal manifestation, accomplished in association with other men—is, therefore, a manifestation, and affirmation of *social life*. Individual human life and species-life are not different things, even though the mode of existence of individual life is necessarily either a more *specific* or a more *general* mode of species-life, or that of species-life a *specific* or more *general* mode of individual life.

In his *species-consciousness* man confirms his real *social life*, and reproduces his real existence in thought; while conversely, species-life confirms itself in species-consciousness and exists for itself in its universality as a thinking being. Though man is a unique individual—and it is just his particularity which makes him an individual, a really *individual* communal being—he is equally the *whole*, the ideal whole, the subjective existence of society as thought and experienced. He exists in reality as the representation and the real mind of social existence, and as the sum of human manifestations of life.[53]

In the twentieth century, under the mixed influences of existentialism, especially as espoused by the German Martin Heidegger, and of German

[52] Kierkegaard, *Concluding Unscientific Postscript.*
[53] Karl Marx, *Early Writings*, trans. T. Bottomore (New York: McGraw-Hill, 1963).

Idealism, especially Hegel and Marx, a new philosophical school became very popular. It is called "Deconstruction," a name coined by its founder, the Frenchman Jacques Derrida. Deconstruction is the attempt to offer a social analysis and criticism which recognizes its own identification with the culture it criticizes. To "deconstruct" a theory or a belief or a tradition, then, is neither to destroy it nor to rebuild it, but rather to "reread" it, and thereby change it, see into it, add to it, *make* it our own, perhaps more plural, more disperse, action. In the following essay, "The Ends of Man," a part of his early work, Derrida argues that the school of deconstruction itself—of rereading, criticizing, and dispersing our cultural institutions and the philosophers who come from them—is itself an epitomal product of our cultural institutions. His claim is that the "unified self" is just a product of Western culture, and that it is now dying at the hands of its own creator.

> Consciousness is the truth of man to the extent that man appears to himself in consciousness in his Being-past, in his to-have-been, in his past surpassed and conserved, retained, interiorized (*erinnert*) and *relevé*. *Aufheben* is *relever,* in the sense in which *relever* can combine to relieve, to displace, to elevate, to re-place and to promote, in one and the same movement. Consciousness is the *Aufhebung* of the soul or of man, phenomenology is the *relève* of anthropology. It is *no longer,* but it is *still* a science of man. In this sense, all the structures described by the phenomenology of spirit—like everything which articulates them with the Logic—are the structures of that which has *relevé* man. In them, man remains in relief. His essence rests in *Phenomenology.* This equivocal relationship of *relief* doubtless marks the end of man, man past, but by the same token it also marks the achievement of man, the appropriation of his essence. *It is the end of finite man* [*C'est la fin de l'homme fini*]. The end of the finitude of man, the unity of the finite and the infinite, the finite as the surpassing of the self—these essential themes of Hegel's are to be recognized at the end of the Anthropology when consciousness is finally designated as the "infinite relationship to self." The *relève* or *relevance* of man is his *telos* or *eskhaton*. The unity of these two *ends* of man, the unity of his death, his completion, his accomplishment, is enveloped in the Greek thinking of *telos,* in the discourse on *telos,* which is also a discourse on *eidos,* on *ousia,* and on *alētheia*. Such a discourse, in Hegel as in the entirety of metaphysics, indissociably coordinates teleology with an eschatology, a theology, and an ontology. *The thinking of the end of man, therefore, is always already prescribed in metaphysics, in the thinking of the truth of man*. What is difficult to think today is an end of man which would not be organized by a dialectics of truth and negativity, an end of man which would not be a teleology in the first person plural. The *we,* which articulates natural and philosophical conscious-

ness with each other in the *Phenomenology of Spirit,* assures the proximity to itself of the fixed and central being for which this circular reappropriation is produced. The *we* is the unity of absolute knowledge and anthropology, of God and man, or onto-theo-teleology and humanism. *"Being"* and language—the group of languages—that the *we* governs or opens: such is the name of that which assures the transition between metaphysics and humanism via the *we.*

READING US

The "we," which in one way or another always has had to refer to itself in the language of metaphysics and in philosophical discourse, arises out of this situation. To conclude, what about this *we* in the text which better than any other has given us to read the essential, historical complicity of metaphysics and humanism in all their forms? What about this *we,* then, in Heidegger's text?

This is the most difficult question, and we will only begin to consider it. We are not going to emprison all of Heidegger's text in a closure that this text has delimited better than any other. That which links humanism and metaphysics as ontotheology became legible as such in *Sein und Zeit,* the *Letter on Humanism,* and the later texts. Referring to this acquisition, attempting to take it into account, I would like to begin to sketch out the forms of the hold which the "humanity" of man and the thinking of Being, a certain humanism and the truth of Being, maintain on one another. Naturally, it will not be a question of the falsification which, in opposition to Heidegger's most explicit warnings, consists in making this hold into a mastery or an ontic relationship in general. What will preoccupy us here will concern, rather, a more subtle, hidden, stubborn privilege, which, as in the case of Hegel or Husserl, leads us back to the position of the *we* in discourse. Once one has given up positing the *we* in the metaphysical dimension of *"we men,"* once one has given up charging the *we men* with the metaphysical determinations of the proper of man (*zōon logon ekhon,* etc.), it remains that man—and I would even say, in a sense that will become clear in a moment, the *proper of man*—the thinking of the proper of man is inseparable from the question or the truth of Being.

· · · · · · · · · ·

To conclude I would like to reassemble, under several very general rubrics, the signs which appear, in accordance with the anonymous necessity that interests me here, to mark the effects of the total trembling as concerns what I have called, for convenience, and with the necessary quotation marks or precautions, "France" or French thought.

1. *The reduction of meaning.* The attention given to system and structure, in its most original and strongest aspects, that is, those aspects which do not immediately fall back into cultural or journal-

istic gossip, or, in the best of cases, into the purest "structuralist" tradition of metaphysics—such as attention, which is rare, consists neither (a) in restoring the classical motif of the system, which can always be shown to be ordered by *telos, alētheia,* and *ousia,* all of which are values reassembled in the concepts of essence or of *meaning;* nor (b) in erasing or destroying meaning. Rather, it is a question of determining the possibility of *meaning* on the basis of a "formal" organization which in itself has no meaning, which does not mean that it is either the non-sense or the anguishing absurdity which haunt metaphysical humanism. Now, if one considers that the critique of anthropologism in the last great metaphysical systems (Hegel and Husserl, notably) was executed in the name of truth and meaning, if one considers that these "phenomenologies"—which were metaphysical systems—had as their essential motif a *reduction to meaning* (which is *literally* a Husserlian proposition), then one can conceive that the reduction *of* meaning—that is, of the signified—first takes the form of a critique of phenomenology. Moreover, if one considers that the Heideggerian destruction of metaphysical humanism is produced initially on the basis of a *hermeneutical* question on the *meaning* or the *truth* of Being, then one also conceives that the reduction of meaning operates by means of a kind of break with a thinking of Being which has all the characteristics of a *relève (Aufhebung)* of humanism.

2. *The strategic bet.* A radical trembling can only come from the *outside.* Therefore, the trembling of which I speak derives no more than any other from some spontaneous decision or philosophical thought after some internal maturation of its history. This trembling is played out in the violent relationship of the whole of the West to its other, whether a "linguistic" relationship (where very quickly the question of the limits of everything leading back to the question of the meaning of Being arises), or ethnological, economic, political, military, relationships, etc. Which does not mean, moreover, that military or economic violence is not in structural solidarity with "linguistic" violence. But the "logic" of every relation to the outside is very complex and surprising. It is precisely the force and the efficiency of the system that regularly change transgressions into "false exits." Taking into account these effects of the system, one has nothing, from the inside where "we are," but the choice between two strategies:

a. To attempt an exit and a deconstruction without changing terrain, by repeating what is implicit in the founding concepts and the original problematic, by using against the edifice the instruments or stones available in the house, that is, equally, in language. Here, one risks ceaselessly confirming, consolidating, *relifting (relever),* at an always more certain depth, that which one allegedly deconstructs. The continuous process of making explicit, moving toward an opening, risks sinking into the autism of the closure.

b. To decide to change terrain, in a discontinuous and irruptive fashion, by brutally placing oneself outside, and by affirming an absolute break and difference. Without mentioning all the other forms of *trompe-l'oeil* perspective in which such a displacement can be caught, thereby inhabiting more naively and more strictly than ever the inside one declares one has deserted, the simple practice of language ceaselessly reinstates the new terrain on the oldest ground. The effects of such a reinstatement or of such a blindness could be shown in numerous precise instances.

It goes without saying that these effects do not suffice to annul the necessity for a "change of terrain." It also goes without saying that the choice between these two forms of deconstruction cannot be simple and unique. A new writing must weave and interlace these two motifs of deconstruction. Which amounts to saying that one must speak several languages and produce several texts at once. I would like to point out especially that the style of the first deconstruction is mostly that of the Heideggerian questions, and the other is mostly the one which dominates France today. I am purposely speaking in terms of a dominant style: because there are also breaks and changes of terrain in texts of the Heideggerian type; because the "change of terrain" is far from upsetting the entire French landscape to which I am referring; because what we need, perhaps, as Nietzsche said, is a change of "style"; and if there is style, Nietzsche reminded us, it must be *plural*.[54]

Some contemporary political thinkers—especially feminist and African-American philosophers—have found deconstruction attractive. Some of the contemporary philosophical debate about individual freedoms has evolved into criticisms and defenses of the "Western philosophy" Derrida describes. If only "Western philosophy" were so univocally definable then perhaps all its mistakes and cruelties could be identified and avoided. As we've seen, however, and as Derrida admits, these very modern criticisms form an integral part of the complex, culturally interwoven philosophical debate around the world.

It is important to emphasize that none of these philosophers actually denies the individual, or individual respect or individual rights. They are, however, insisting that an individual derives his or her rights only insofar as he or she is a member of a community. This does not mean that a person cannot be eccentric, like the wierdo artist or the spaced-out rock musician, but it does mean that even their eccentricity, as well as their talents, must be viewed as social contributions. What they are denying, in other words, is what has sometimes been called "vulgar individualism," that form of self-identity that denies all social relevance and social obligations.

---

[54]Jacques Derrida, "The Ends of Man," trans. Alan Bass in *Margins of Philosophy* (Chicago: University of Chicago Press, 1982).

SUMMARY AND CONCLUSION

Self-identity is a question of essential properties: What is it about you that makes you a particular person and the same person over time? In this chapter we have reviewed a series of different answers to this question. The tradition from Descartes and Locke to Kant stresses the importance of consciousness in our conception of ourselves, i.e., the importance of our minds over our bodies. (Even Hume, who denies that there is a self, is part of this tradition.) Then there is the general question, how much is the self something that we can choose, and how much is it something that is determined for us? Does each person have just one self, one set of essential properties, or might a single "person" be several people, with several selves? Or might there really be no self at all? And how much should we conceive of ourselves as individuals, and how much as organic components of a larger community? None of these questions has any firmly agreed-upon answers, but all of us adopt one view or another, even if just for a short time, every time we attempt to define ourselves or just "be ourselves."

GLOSSARY

bad faith   Sartre's characterization of a person's refusal to accept himself or herself; this sometimes means not accepting the facts that are true about you. More often, it means accepting the facts about you as conclusive about your identity, as in the statement "Oh, I couldn't do that, I'm too shy."

behaviorism   in psychology, the radical methodological thesis that insists that only what is publicly observable can be used as subject matter or as evidence in scientific research regarding human beings. In particular, all talk of "minds" and "mental events," "desires," "purposes," "ideas," "perceptions," and "experiences" is to be given up in favor of terms that refer only to the experimental situation or the behavior of the creature (or person) in question (for example, "stimulus," "response," "reinforcements"). In philosophy and metaphysics, behaviorism is the logical thesis that there are no "covert" or "private" mental events, only patterns of behavior and psychological ways of talking about behavior as "intelligent," "deceitful," "calculating," or "inattentive." All of these must be understood not in terms of some process ("intelligence," "deceitful thinking," "calculating," or "lack of attending") going on "in the mind" but rather as ways of interpreting, predicting, and otherwise describing and evaluating behavior.

causal interactionism   the theory that mind and body causally interact; that mental events (for example, an "act of will") can cause a bodily consequence (for example, raising one's arm), and that a bodily change (for example, a puncture of the skin) can cause a mental consequence (for example, a pain). The theory sounds plausible enough on first hearing, but extremely serious objections have been raised against it.

continuity   (spatiotemporal continuity) the uninterrupted identifiability of an object over time in the same location or in a sequence of tangent locations.

criterion   test or standard.

deconstruction   initiated by Jacques Derrida, a current school of philosophical thought (especially popular among some feminist and African-American thinkers) that encourages critical reading for "cultural bias" and that rejects the idea of the "unified self."

dual aspect theory   the theory (for example, in Spinoza) that mind and body are simply different aspects (or "attributes") of one and the same substance, thus avoiding the problem of interaction between substances.

dualism   in general, the distinction between mind and body as separate substances, or very different kinds of states and events with radically different properties.

eliminative materialism   The thesis that increasing knowledge of neurology eventually will allow us to give up our "folk psychological" terminology of mental states.

empirical ego   all those characteristics of a person that can be discovered through experience and that distinguish each of us from other persons qualitatively; that which makes each of us a particular man or woman and gives us a particular "character." Compare *transcendental ego.*

epiphenomenalism   The thesis that mental events are epiphenomena, that is, side effects of various physical processes in the brain and nervous system but of little importance themselves. The model is a one-way causal model: Body states cause changes in the mind, but mental states have no effect in themselves on the body.

essence   that which is necessary for something to be what it is. The essence of a person is that without which we would not say one is *that* particular person (Fred rather than Mary, for example).

existentialism   in Sartre's terms, the philosophy that teaches that "man's existence precedes his essence." That is, people have no given self-identity, they have to choose their identities and work for them through their actions. (Neglect and omission, however, are also actions. One can be a certain type of person just by not bothering to do the appropriate activities.)

facticity   Sartre's term (borrowed from Heidegger) for the totality of facts that are true of a person at any given time.

functionalism   the view that the mind is the product of a pattern in the brain, as in a computer, rather than a product of the matter of the brain as such.

identity theory   the thesis that the mind and brain are ontologically one and the same, or, more accurately, that mental states and events are in fact certain brain and nervous system processes. The theory is usually presented as a form of materialism, but it is important to emphasize that, unlike many materialistic theories, it does not deny the existence of mental events. It denies only that they have independent existence. Mental events are nothing other than certain bodily events.

immediate   for certain and without need for argument.

incorrigibility   impossible to correct; cannot be mistaken. It has long been argued that our claims about our own mental states are incorrigible—we cannot be mistaken about them.

inference-ticket   Ryle's term for referring to the proper function of a mental state: talk, as a description of a pattern of behavior and, therefore, as an "inference-ticket" that allows us to infer what a person will do in the future. (To say "George wants an olive" is to give us an inference-ticket regarding his future behavior around olives.)

intentionality   in phenomenology, the thesis that every conscious act has an object. (The act is therefore called the "intentional act" and the object the "intentional object.") The importance of this concept is that it undercuts the metaphor of mental "contents" (as in a theater, an image explicitly used by Hume, for example). The concept was used by Husserl's teacher, Franz Brentano, who borrowed it from some medieval philosophers, before Husserl used it and made it famous.

parallelism   the thesis that mental events and bodily events parallel each other and occur in perfect coordination but do not interact.

pre-established harmony   Leibniz's view that the coordination between our ideas and the physical events of the world and our bodies was set up by God in perfect order.

privacy   the seeming inaccessibility of mental states and events to anyone other than the person who "has" them.

private language argument   Wittgenstein's argument that even if there were such "private objects" as mental states and events, it would be impossible for us to talk about them and impossible for us to identify them, even in our own case.

privileged access   the technical term used by philosophers to refer to the curious fact that a person usually (if not always) can immediately know, simply by paying attention, what is going on in his own mind, while other people can find out what is going on—if they can at all—only by watching the person's behavior, listening to what he or she says, or asking (and hoping they get a truthful answer). It is important to distinguish privileged access from incorrigibility. The first means that a person knows directly what is "in his mind" without having to observe his behavior; the second means that he knows for certain and beyond the possibility of error.

resemblance   having the same features. All people resemble each other (or at least most do) in having one and only one head; you resemble yourself five years ago in (perhaps) having the same texture hair, the same color eyes, the same fear of spiders, and the same skill at chess.

self-consciousness   being aware of oneself, whether "as others see you" (looking in a mirror or "watching yourself play a role" at a party) or just "looking into yourself" (as when you reflect on your goals in life or wonder, in a moment of philosophical perversity, whether you really exist or not). Self-consciousness requires having some concept of your "self." Accordingly, it is logically tied to questions of self-identity.

self-identity   the way you characterize yourself, either in general (as a human being, as a man or as a woman, as a creature before God or as one among many animals) or in particular (as the person who can run the fastest mile, as an all-"C" student, or as the worst-dressed slob in your class). Self-identity, on this characterization, requires self-consciousness. The self-identity of a person, in other words, is not merely the same as the identity of a "thing," for example, the identity of a human body.

transcendence   Sartre's term for a person's plan, ambitions, intentions, and hopes for the future (Do not confuse this use of the word with those introduced in Chapters 4 and 6.)

transcendental ego   the bare, logical fact of one's own self-consciousness: Descartes' "I think"; the self "behind" all of our experiences; the mental activity that unifies our various thoughts and sensations. (The term comes from Kant's *Critique of Pure Reason*.)

unconscious   Freud's famous way of referring to the fact that there are ideas, desires, memories, and experiences in our minds to which we do not have privileged access, which we may be wrong about (and, therefore, about which our claims are not incorrigible), and which may be more evident to other people than to oneself. He also distinguishes a *preconscious* ("the antechamber of consciousness"). Preconscious ideas can be made conscious simply by being attended to. (For example, you do know what the capital of California is, but you weren't conscious of it before I mentioned it; it was preconscious.) Truly unconscious ideas, however, cannot be made conscious, even when one tries to do so.

◆ *BIBLIOGRAPHY AND FURTHER READING* ◆

A recent anthology on the question of self-identity is J. Perry, *Personal Identity* (New York: Lieber-Atherton, 1975). An extended study of this traditional problem is Sidney Shoemaker, *Self-Knowledge and Self-Identity* (Ithaca, NY: Cornell University Press, 1963). Jean-Paul Sartre's existentialist view of the self is developed in his essay *Transcendence of the Ego* (New York: Noonday, 1957). Hermann Hesse's complex theory of the self is best developed in *Steppenwolf*, rev. ed., trans. Basil Creighton (New York: Holt, Rinehart and Winston, 1970), but it is most simply portrayed in *Siddhartha*, trans. H. Rosner (New York: New Directions, 1951). Further reading in Eastern conceptions of the self may begin with D. Suzuki, *Zen Buddhism*, ed. W. Barrett (New York: Doubleday, 1956) or C. Moore, ed., *The Individual in East and West* (Honolulu: East-West Center Press, 1967). A good introduction of G. W. F. Hegel's very difficult philosophy is the introduction to his lectures on the philosophy of history in his *Reason in History*, trans. R. Hartman (New York: Bobbs-Merrill, 1953).

A good short survey of the "mind-body problem" is Keith Campbell, *Body and Mind* (New York: Doubleday, Anchor, 1970); a helpful introduction to the problem and the various alternatives is J. Shaffer, *The Philosophy of Mind* (Englewood Cliffs, NJ: Prentice-Hall, 1968). A good historical discussion of the reactions against Cartesian dualism is A. Lovejoy, *The Revolt Against Dualism* (La Salle, IL: Open Court, 1955). Two more recent anthologies, with special attention to the "identity theory," are David Rosenthal, ed., *Material-*

ism and the Mind-Body Problem (Englewood Cliffs, NJ: Prentice-Hall, 1971) and C. V. Borst, ed., *The Mind-Brain Identity Theory* (New York: St. Martin's Press, 1970). A delightful presentation of the functionalist position is the collection of essays by Dan Dennett, *Brainstorms* (Newton Center, MA: Bradford Books, 1979). See also J. Margolis, *The Philosophy of Psychology* (Englewood Cliffs, NJ: Prentice-Hall, 1983), and Jay L. Garfield, *Foundations of Cognitive Science* (New York: Paragon House, 1990).

8

FREEDOM

"Two plus two equals four"—as if freedom means that!

FYODOR DOSTOYEVSKI

"The murderer had been raised in a slum. His father abandoned him when he was seven months old; he was beaten by his older siblings and constantly abused by his mother. He never had the chance to attend school; he never could get or hold a job. By the time he robbed the store, he was near starvation, addicted to hard drugs, without friends, and without help of any kind. His sister said, 'I've known since he was a child that he would do this some day.' His mother complained, 'I don't understand!' The prosecutor called it a 'cold-blooded, premeditated act.' The defense accused the whole of society, claiming that it had, through its neglect as well as its negative conditioning, made this man an inevitable killer." We know the rest of the arguments, what we don't know is their resolution. Should a man be held responsible for an act for which he has been conditioned the whole of his life? Or must we not hold out that no matter what the circumstances, he could have resisted, he could have decided not to commit the crime, and therefore he must be held responsible.

Of all the abstract problems of philosophy, the problem of **freedom** has the most obvious practical consequences. If we believe a person is free to choose his or her actions and destiny, we tend to load the person with moral responsibility, praise or blame; if we believe a person is simply a victim of the fates, a cog in a mechanical universe, or a pawn in the abstract hands of society, then our attitude toward his or her actions can be no different than our attitudes toward the movement of glaciers and the growth of flowers. "It happens that way," that's all.

A. FATALISM AND KARMA

Are we cogs in the universe? Are we pawns of the fates? People have often thought so. Our tendency to believe in fate goes back to the ancient Greeks. Most of the ancient Greeks believed that our destinies were already decided for us; no matter what our actions, the outcome was settled. Today, many people believe our actions and character are the causal result of our genes and our upbringing, and perhaps also the result of unconscious fears and desires that we may never even recognize. Then too, astrology and other theories of external determination have always been popular. (For instance, *"Virgo:* It's going to be a bad day: don't get out of bed and don't talk to anyone.") And we can see why they would be. The more our actions are the results of other forces and not our own doing, the less we need feel responsible for them, and the less we need worry about deciding what to do. It is already decided, and not by us.

Consider for example, the following news article that appeared around the nation in April 1980:[1]

> The way lawyer John Badger saw it, he was giving the judge a chance to "follow the flow into the brotherhood of man" by entertaining the notion that his client's life of crime was ordained by the stars.
>
> But Circuit Judge Ruben Costa, who said he was "inclined to believe there is a certain verity" to astrology, threw out the proposed defense at a pretrial hearing Monday for 23-year-old John Matthew Gopel, who is charged with rape, robbery and assault.
>
> Badger had planned to argue Gopel was insane by virtue of his astrological destiny.
>
> Bader said his client, born at 8:14 p.m. on Aug. 8, 1956, was literally "a born loser."
>
> "There is a force in the life of this young man that forced him to go on transmission fluid, sniff gasoline, cocaine, anything he could get his hands on," he said.
>
> Badger said he intended to present testimony from astrologers, scientists and mental health experts, as well as a bartender who would describe the effects of the full moon on human behavior.
>
> The list of defense evidence included the song "When You Wish Upon A Star," Spiderman comic books and the plays *King Lear* and *Hamlet.*

The ancient Greek tragedies, like *Oedipus the King,* depend upon **fatalism,** the view that whatever a person's actions and circumstances, however free they may seem, his or her predetermined end is inevitable.

---

[1] All names in this article have been invented to protect the individuals involved.

The story of Oedipus most famously recounted in the tragedy by Sophocles is perhaps the most stirring picture of Greek determinism. Oedipus and his wife, Iocasta, both scoffed at the prophets and made efforts to avoid their prophesied destinies.

◆**from *Oedipus the King*,
by Sophocles**

Oedipus: . . . I went to Delphi. Phoebus . . . declared
                A thing most horrible: he foretold that I
                Should mate with my own mother, and beget
                A brood that men would shudder to behold,
                And that I was to be the murderer
                Of my own father.
                                        Therefore, back to Corinth
                I never went—the stars alone have told me
                Where Corinth lies—that I might never see
                Cruel fulfillment of that oracle. [107–116]

Iocasta: Listen to me
                And you will hear the prophetic art
                Touches our human fortunes not at all.
                I soon can give you proof.—An oracle
                Once came to [my husband]. . .
                His fate it was, that he should have a son
                By me, that son would take his father's life.
                But he was killed—or so they said—by
                Strangers.
                By brigands, at a place where three ways meet.
                As for the child, it was not three days old
                When [my husband] fastened both its feet together
                And had it cast off a precipice.
                Therefore Apollo failed. . .
                So much for what prophetic voices have uttered.[2]

Unbeknown to either of them, of course, the "brigand" who killed Iocasta's husband was Oedipus himself, Iocasta's son, saved as a baby from the precipice and adopted by the man he had thought was his father, from whom he had fled. Thus, both their destinies had been fulfilled. Neither had any control over—nor even knowledge of—what happened to them, and so neither acted freely at all. Thus, the Chorus of observers declares:

     . . . I pray that I might pass my life in reverent holiness of word and deed
     For there are laws enthroned above,
     Heaven created them,
     Olympus was their father,
     And mortal men had no part in their birth. . . .

[2]From Sophocles, *Oedipus the King*, translated by H.D.F. Kitto, rpt. in: Barnet, Berman, Burto, *Types of Drama*, 3rd ed. (Boston: Little, Brown.)

How should we deal with our fate? Should we try to know our fate? Iocasta advocates that "ignorance is bliss," and tries hard throughout the play not to acknowledge her growing suspicions. If we can't do anything about our fate, she reasons, then we shouldn't even think about it. But Oedipus insists on finding out the truth, and as a whole the play seems to advocate facing the fact of our destinies.

> Iocasta: Why should we fear, seeing that man is ruled
> By chance, and there is room for no clear forethought?
> No: live at random, live as best one can.
> . . .
> Whoever thinks
> The least of this, he lives most comfortably. [80]
>
> Oedipus: Alas! you generations of men!
> Even while you live you are next to nothing!
> Has any man won for himself
> More than the shadow of happiness?
> . . .
> Time sees all, and Time, in your despite
> Disclosed and punished your unnatural marriage
>
> Creon [Oedipus' uncle/brother-in-law]:
> Seek not to have your way in all things.
> Where you had your way before,
> Your mastery broke before the end.

The anthropomorphic Greek gods were integral to the ancient Greek notion of "fate." Human choices were considered impotent to change one's fate, because human beings were thought to be at the mercy of the gods' whims. But another conception of fate, the Buddhist conception, sees human choices as tremendously important—not because they are free, but precisely the opposite. In Buddhism, all human choices are gestures of *attachment* to the physical world, each one binding its maker more and more to a difficult fate. The effects of one's choices, as we have seen in Chapter 1, are called his or her **karma,** which can only be escaped through a long-term payment of the debt which he or she has built up. Thus, there is a concept of freedom here, called *nirvana*, but it is not a freedom of the self or the individual. In fact, it is a freedom *from* the self and the individual, achieved only when there is no longer a self at all. It is our foolish attachment to this world, the Buddhist claims, which fosters the illusion that we are individuals at all. In a sense then, our fate is entirely determined; yet ironically, if we submit ourselves to fate and accept its authority, if we can stop making choices which further delude us into believing we are free, then and only then, can we ultimately become really free.

We have seen implications of the belief in karma in Buddha's *Fire Sermon* and in Nagarjuna's verses on causality. Here, we look at a section of the twenty-fourth part of the Mahāyāna (or Northern Buddhist)

Maharatnakuta Sutra, in which two disciples, Sariputra and Upali, question the Buddha on the paths to freedom and on false freedom or arrogance.

◆ The *Maharatnakuta Sutra,* on Fate

. . ."Thus, Śāriputra, these Bodhisattvas employ various skillful means to perfect sentient beings and cause them all to dwell securely in the Buddha-Dharma. Why? Because only the Tathāgata's[3] wisdom can result in liberation and ultimate nirvāṇa; there is no other vehicle that can carry one to salvation. . . . It is for this reason that the Tathāgata is called a Tathāgata. Because the Tathāgata knows thusness as it is, he is called a Tathāgata [a Thus-Come One]. Because he can do anything that sentient beings wish, he is called a Tathāgata. Because he has perfected the root of all wholesome dharmas and cut off the root of all unwholesome dharmas, he is called a Tathāgata. Because he can show sentient beings the path to liberation, he is called a Tathāgata. Because he can cause sentient beings to avoid wrong paths and remain on the right path, he is called a Tathāgata. . . . Because he can explain the true meaning of the emptiness of all dharmas, he is called a Tathāgata.

. . . .

"Śāriputra, if a Bodhisattva has committed one of the five grave offenses, a pārājika, or a saṁghāvaśeṣa; or has done harm to stūpas or monks; or has committed some other crime, he should sincerely repent in solitude day and night before the thirty-five Buddhas, saying:

. . . .

" 'May all these and other Buddhas, World-Honored Ones of all the universes, stay in the world forever. May they have compassion on me.

" 'I now repent all the transgressions which I have committed by myself, abetted others to commit, or been glad to see others commit, in my present life, in my past lives, and ever since my involvement in beginningless saṁsāra.

" 'I repent the crimes of stealing from stūpas, from monks, or from the common possessions of the Saṁgha in the four quarters—crimes which I have committed by myself, abetted others to commit, or been glad to see others commit.

" 'I repent the five grave offenses which I have committed by myself, abetted others to commit, or been glad to see others commit.

---

[3]*Tathāgata* is a name for the Buddha, meaning "A Thus-Come One." It implies the Buddha's "arrival" at perfection.

" 'I repent the ten evil deeds which I have committed by myself, abetted others to commit, or been glad to see others commit.

" 'I repent the crimes I have committed, which, whether I hide them or not, will cause me to fall to the miserable planes of existence —the planes of hell-dwellers, hungry ghosts, and animals—or cause me to be reborn in the frontiers; as a lowly, inferior being; or in a land of barbarians. May the Buddhas, the World-Honored Ones, be my witnesses and take care of me.

" 'In the presence of the Buddhas, the World-Honored Ones, I will further say: if in my present life or other lives I have planted any good roots, such as the good roots of giving, even giving only a handful of food to an animal; of keeping the discipline; of leading a pure life; of helping sentient beings; and of cultivating enlightenment and the unexcelled wisdom—then, I will gather up all these good roots, calculate them, measure them, and dedicate them to [the universal attainment of] supreme enlightenment. I will make the same dedication as that made by all the Buddhas of the present, past, and future.

· · · · · · · · · ·

"Śāriputra, what do you think? Can a small jackal roar like a lion?"

Śāriputra answered, "No, World-honored One."

"Can a donkey bear the same heavy burden borne by a large elephant?"

"No, World-Honored One."

"Can a poor, humble person be as awe-inspiring and free as a śakra or a brahmā?"

"No, World-Honored One."

"Can any small bird soar like a powerful, golden-winged garuḍa, the king of birds?"

"No, World-Honored One."

The Buddha said, "Similarly, Śāriputra, by their wisdom of renunciation, Bodhisattvas who have good roots and courage can purify their transgressions, be free of worry and remorse, and thereby see Buddhas and achieve samādhis. However, ordinary people, Śrāvakas, and Pratyekabuddhas cannot rid themselves of the hindrances caused by their transgressions.

· · · · · · · · · ·

The Buddha told Mañjuśrī, "Now you should expound the subtle meaning of the Ultimate Vinaya. Upāli will be happy to hear it."

Mañjuśrī, the Dharma Prince, said to Upāli, "All dharmas are ultimately quiescent when the mind is quiescent; this is called the Ultimate Vinaya.

"No dharma is found to have a self-entity when the mind is not defiled or attached; this is called the Vinaya of No Regret.

"All dharmas are pure by nature when the mind is not confused [by wrong views]; this is called the Supreme Vinaya.

"All dharmas are suchness itself when the mind is devoid of all views; this is called the Pure Vinaya.

"No dharma comes or goes when the mind does not discriminate; this is called the Inconceivable Vinaya.

"No dharma abides or clings when the mind ceases from moment to moment; this is called the Vinaya of the Purification of the Planes of Existence.

"All dharmas abide in emptiness when the mind is free of all signs; this is called the Vinaya of Intrinsic Transcendence.

"Dharmas have no past, present, or future, for they are inapprehensible; this is called the Vinaya of the Equality of the Three Phases of Time.

"No dharma can be established when the mind is free from discrimination; this is called the Vinaya of the Permanent Resolution of Doubt.

"Upāli, this is the Ultimate Vinaya of the dharmadhātu, by which Buddhas, World-Honored Ones, have attained Buddhahood. A good man who does not observe this well is far from keeping the pure precepts of the Tathāgata."

Thereupon, Upāli said to the Buddha, "World-Honored One, the doctrines Mañjuśrī expounds are inconceivable."

The World-Honored One told Upāli, "Mañjuśrī expounds the Dharma on the basis of inconceivable, unimpeded liberation. For this reason, whatever doctrine he preaches enables one to be free from mental forms, which is the liberation of mind. He causes the arrogant to give up their arrogance."

Upāli asked the Buddha, "What constitutes the arrogance of a Śrāvaka or a Bodhisattva?"

The Buddha replied to Upāli, "If a monk thinks he has eradicated desire, he is arrogant. If he thinks he has eradicated hatred and ignorance, he is arrogant. If he thinks that desire is different from the Dharma of Buddhas, he is arrogant. If he thinks that hatred is different from the Dharma of Buddhas, he is arrogant. If he thinks that ignorance is different from the Dharma of Buddhas, he is arrogant. If he claims to have gained something, he is arrogant. If he claims to have realized something, he is arrogant. If he claims to have attained liberation, he is arrogant. If he claims to perceive emptiness, signlessness, and wishlessness, he is also arrogant. If he claims to perceive nonarising and nonaction, he is arrogant. If he claims to perceive the existence of dharmas, he is arrogant. If he claims to perceive the impermanence of dharmas, he is arrogant. If he says, 'What is the use of practice, since all dharmas are empty?' he is also arrogant. Upāli, these constitute the arrogance of a Śrāvaka.

· · · · · · · · · ·

. . . Upāli asked the Buddha, "World-Honored One, how can a monk be free from arrogance?"

The Buddha answered Upāli, "If he is not attached to any doctrine, no matter how inconceivable it is, he is completely free from arrogance."[4]

For a contemporary view of *karma*, we turn again to a Japanese philosopher, Keiji Nishitani:

◆on Fate
by *Keiji Nishitani*

From that viewpoint [the standpoint of nihility, or openness] the world of karma is a world where each individual is determined by its ties and causal kinship within an endless world nexus, and yet each instance of individual existence and behavior, as well as each moment of their time, arises as something totally new, possessed of freedom and creativity.

Although the ebb and flow of the total nexus "since time past without beginning" is conceived as an infinite chain of causal necessity, its having no beginning implies, conversely, a *before* previous to any and all conceivable pasts. For such time to have no end means that it has an *after* that is future even to the most remote of possible futures. Any such before and after (beyond any definite before and after) lies in the present of every man and makes the present into free and creative activity.

· · · · · · · · · ·

The karmic deeds that make manifest this restless, incessant becoming always return thereby at the same time to the home-ground of karma, to the home-ground of the present. In other words, doing opens itself up on each occasion to the openness of nihility and thus preserves the dimension of ecstatic transcendence.

This means that the self is at all times itself. Even as in my karma I constantly constitute my existence as a becoming *qua* being, in the home-ground of that karma I am ever in my own home-ground: I am always myself. This is why restless, incessant becoming within time is at all times *my* existence. Karma is at all times *my* karma. And this means that it is free karma, that it implies an ecstatic transcendence to nihility.

Of course, although we call it freedom or creativity, it is not at this point true freedom or creativity. Freedom here is one with an inner necessity compelling us constantly to be doing something. It is in unison with that infinite drive and that infinite drive in turn is in unison with freedom. To be within the limitless world-nexus ceaselessly relating to something or other, and to be conditioned and determined in these relations by the world-nexus, is, seen from the other side, a self-determination. While the present karma is

[4]"The Definitive Vinaya," trans. the Buddhist Association of the U.S., from *A Treasury of Mahāyāna Sutras: Selections from the Mahāratnakota Sutra*, ed. Garma C.C. Chang (University Park: Pennsylvania State University Press, 1983).

here the free work of the self, it appears at the same time to be possessed of the character of fate. Fate arises to awareness in unison with that freedom. Here the present karma reaches awareness under its form of infinity as infinite drive, in its "willful" essence.

The self's relation with something, seen as a self-determination, is the self's exercise of free will. Of its own accord, the self accepts a thing as good or rejects it as bad. But insofar as it is determined through causal kinship within the total nexus, this free will is a fate, a causal necessity, without thereby ceasing to be free will. To accept or reject something implies a simultaneous "attachment" to it. The karma that relates to something by lusting after it is at once voluntary and compulsory. The being of the self that comes about in that karma is at once a freedom and a burden. Here spontaneity becomes a burden and a debt.

· · · · · · · · · ·

All of this indicates how deeply rooted self-centeredness is. So deeply undergound do the roots of the self extend that no karmic activity can ever reach them. The karma of the self at all times returns to its own home-ground, namely, to the self itself, but it cannot get back to the home-ground of the self as such. Karma can do no more than go back to its own home-ground in the self and there reinstate its debt-laden existence. In karma, the self is constantly oriented inward to the home-ground of the self; and yet the only thing it achieves by this is the constant reconstitution of being *qua* becoming in a time without beginning or end. To transit endlessly through time in search of the home-ground of the self is the true form of our karma, that is, of our being in time, our life.

The karma of "time past without beginning" is the true form of our life. It implies a sense of essential "despair." Karma is what Kierkegaard calls the "sickness unto death." Its despair rises to awareness from directly underfoot of the work of our present deed, word, and thought, from the fountainhead of time without beginning or end, and of being within that time, in short from our self-centeredness. We can see an awareness of that despair also underlying the confession of the Buddhist *Verse of Repentance,* which suggests that every sort of karma stemming from the body, mouth, and mind of the self is grounded in a greed, anger, and folly without beginning. . . .

Karma here comes to bear the marks of guilt and sin. In a certain sense, it takes on the character of original sin, namely, sin that is as equally elemental as the free work and existence of man. Karma is freedom determined by causal necessity within the whole infinite nexus, a freedom of spontaneity in "attachment" and, therefore, a freedom totally *bound* by fate. At the same time, having reduced the whole causal nexus to its own center, it is a freedom altogether *unbound.* In karma these two aspects of freedom and causal necessity become one. Consequently, as a freedom that derives entirely from the determining force of causal necessity, as a freedom chased out and driven away from necessity, karma binds itself in attachment to the other, while at the same time it remains an altogether unbound freedom, gathering every other into the center of the self. This freedom is in the mode of an original sin.[5]

B. PREDESTINATION

Fatalism, in its Greek or Buddhist sense, is the claim that our future is determined by a play of forces beyond our understanding. But what if these forces are understood, and in fact *created* by one, superhuman being? **Predestination** has been the view of many theologians, according to whom our every action (and every event in the universe) is known, if not also caused in advance, by God. Predestination, like fatalism, does not depend upon any particular antecedent conditions, unless we want to say that God is an antecedent condition.

All the Western theologians have had to ponder the problem of predestination and freedom, since all the Western religions' scriptures claim that God created, or caused, everything. As we saw in Chapter 6, this is of particular concern when considering evil. There, the "problem of evil" was described as the question of how evil could be caused by a good God. We now can see that the crux of the "problem of evil" is the question of freedom. It would be easy to explain much evil if human beings were free: in that case, we are the cause of evil, and not an all-good God. But if, as is stated in scripture, God created and caused everything, then surely, God creates our human actions, too. Humans sin—and so it seems we are back to the drawing board. How can an all-good God cause us or let us be free to sin?

The following lines from St. Augustine summarize the problem of freedom and one Christian solution to it. God made human beings free, because He is all-good, and free actions are better than unfree ones. However, since freedom allows us to sin, we are responsible for bringing evil into the world.

◆*On Free Choice of the Will*, **Book II,**
by St. Augustine

I.
WHY DID GOD GIVE FREEDOM OF THE WILL TO MEN,
SINCE IT IS BY THIS THAT MEN SIN?

EVODIUS. Now, if possible, explain to me why God gave man free choice of the will since if he had not received it he would not be able to sin.

---

[5] Keiji Nishitani, *Religion and Nothingness*, trans. Jan Van Bragt (Berkeley: University of California Press, 1982).

AUGUSTINE.   Are you perfectly sure that God gave to man what
you think ought not to have been given?

E.   As far as I seem to understand the discussion in the first book,
we have freedom of will, and could not sin if we were without it.

A.   I, too, remember that this was made clear to us. But I just
asked you whether you know that it was God who gave us that
which we possess, through which it is clear that we commit sin.

E.   No one else. For we are from Him, and whether we sin or
whether we do right, we earn reward or punishment from Him.

A.   I want to ask, as well: do you know this clearly, or do you believe it willingly without really knowing it, because you are
prompted by authority?

E.   I admit that at first I trusted authority on this point. But what
can be more true than that all good proceeds from God, that everything just is good, and that it is just to punish sinners and
to reward those who do right? From this it follows that through
God sinners are afflicted with unhappiness, and those who do
right endowed with happiness.

A.   I do not object, but let me ask another question: how do you
know that we are from God? You did not answer that; instead,
you explained that we merit punishment and reward from God.

E.   The answer to *that* question, too, is clear, if for no other reason than the fact that, as we have already agreed, God punished
sins. All justice is from God, and it is not the role of justice to
punish foreigners, although it is the role of goodness to bestow
benefits on them. Thus it is clear that we belong to God, since
He is not only most generous in bestowing benefits upon us, but
also most just in punishing us. Also, we can understand that
man is from God through the fact, which I proposed and you
conceded, that every good is from God. For man himself, insofar
as he is a man, is a good, because he can live rightly when he
so wills.

A.   If this is so, the question that you proposed is clearly
answered. If man is a good, and cannot act rightly unless he
wills to do so, then he must have free will, without which he cannot act rightly. We must not believe that God gave us free will
so that we might sin, just because sin is committed through free
will. It is sufficient for our question, why free will should have
been given to man, to know that without it man cannot live
rightly. That it was given for this reason can be understood from
the following: if anyone uses free will for sinning, he incurs
divine punishment. This would be unjust if free will had been
given not only that man might live rightly, but also that he might
sin. For how could a man justly incur punishment who used
free will to do the thing for which it was given? When God pun-
ishes a sinner, does He not seem to say, "Why have you not used
free will for the purpose for which I gave it to you, to act rightly?" Then too, if man did not have free choice of will, how could
there exist the good according to which it is just to condemn

evildoers and reward those who act rightly? What was not done by will would be neither evildoing nor right action. Both punishment and reward would be unjust if man did not have free will. Moreover, there must needs be justice both in punishment and in reward, since justice is one of the goods that are from God. Therefore, God must needs have given free will to man.[6]

One's opinion on the question of freedom was a crucial determinant of one's sectarian alliance in early Islam. Islam is sometimes understood in the West as a "fatalist" religion; in other words, it is thought that all Muslims believe that human beings are not free. However, the Mu'tazilites, one of the first Islamic sects, claimed that the human will is free, despite passages in scripture which would lead one to believe the contrary, such as the following:

"No misfortune befalls except by Allah's [God's] will. He guides the hearts of those who believe in him. Allah has knowledge of all things." (64:11)
"Every misfortune that befalls the earth or your own persons, is ordained before we bring it into being." (57:22–23)

Thus, Islam provides an interesting breadth of argument on the question of freedom. The Mu'tazilites claimed that human freedom is consistent with God's power, by distinguishing between two types of action, or causality. God's actions are "necessary," or law-like. They *must* happen. Human actions, however, are "intentional," they are contingent upon God's actions, which are their necessary conditions and consequences. Thus, a person is free, for instance, to hit a billiard ball with his or her pool cue. But he or she is *not* free to hit the ball and have it stay still, or to hit it in one direction and have it go in another. Only God is "free" to make necessary, physical, laws. For the Mu'tazilites, human freedom amounts to *directing* God's actions along various possible paths. We are responsible for how we direct God's creations, and so we are rightly rewarded or punished by God for our choices.

Another very important Islamic school, the Ash'arites, reacted against the Mu'tazilites in favor of a more literal interpretation of scriptural passages like the ones above. The Ash'arites, however, wound up making a distinction with regard to the question of freedom which was similar to that of the Mu'tazilites. The Ash'arites claimed that only God is free, and that all human actions are determined by God. God's "predestination" here, however, is more like an offer of a gift. God offers to human beings various actions which they can accept or acquire, or pass. Only God, therefore, can create an action, according to the Ash'arites. Human

---

[6]St. Augustine, *On Free Choice of the Will*, trans. Anna S. Benjamin and L.H. Hackstaff. (Indianapolis: Bobbs-Merrill, 1964).

beings merely acquire them, "secondhand" so to speak. When we acquire good actions, we deserve our reward. When we acquire bad ones, we deserve our punishment.

Although one may take it overall, then, that Islamic tradition does seem to believe more in God's predestination than does Christianity, the Islamic stance on the question of freedom is really a very complex one. The debate within Islam about freedom continues to this day. Here is an example from an important twentieth-century Islamic theologian, Sir Mohammad Iqbal:

◆ "The Human Ego: Its Freedom and Immortality," by Mohammad Iqbal

The life of the ego is a kind of tension caused by the ego invading the environment and the environment invading the ego. The ego does not stand outside this arena of mutual invasion. It is present in it as a directive energy and is formed and disciplined by its own experience. The Quran is clear on this directive function of the ego:
'And they ask thee of the soul. Say: the soul proceedeth from my Lord's "Amr" [Command]: but of knowledge, only a little to you is given.' (17:87.)

In order to understand the meaning of the word 'Amr', we must remember the distinction which the Quran draws between 'Amr' and 'Khalq'. Pringle-Pattison deplores that the English language possesses only one word—creation—to express the relation of God and the universe of extension on the one hand, and the relation of God and the human ego on the other. The Arabic language is, however, more fortunate in this respect. It has two words 'Khalq' and 'Amr' to express the two ways in which the creative activity of God reveals itself to us. 'Khalq' is creation; 'Amr' is direction. As the Quran says: 'To Him belong creation and direction.' The verse quoted above means that the essential nature of the soul is directive, as it proceeds from the directive energy of God; though we do not know how Divine 'Amr' functions as ego-unities. The personal pronoun used in the expression *Rabbi* ('My Lord') throws further light on the nature and behaviour of the ego. It is meant to suggest that the soul must be taken as something individual and specific, with all the variations in the range, balance, and effectiveness of its unity. 'Every man acteth after his own manner: but your Lord well knoweth who is best guided in his path'. (17:86.) Thus my real personality is not a thing, it is an act. My experience is only a series of acts, mutually referring to one another, and held together by the unity of a directive purpose. My whole reality lies in my directive attitude. You cannot perceive me like a thing in space, or a set of experiences in temporal order; you must interpret, understand,

and appreciate me in my judgements, in my will-attitudes, aims, and aspirations.

The next question is: how does the ego emerge within the spatio-temporal order? The teaching of the Quran is perfectly clear on this point:

'Now of fine clay have We created man: There We placed him, a moist germ, in a safe abode; then made We the moist germ a clot of blood: then made the clotted blood into a piece of flesh; then made the piece of flesh into bones: and We clothed the bones with flesh: *then brought forth man of yet another make.*

'Blessed, therefore, the God—the most excellent of makers.' (23:12–14.)

The 'yet another make' of man develops on the basis of physical organism—that colony of sub-egos through which a profounder Ego constantly acts on me, and thus permits me to build up a systematic unity of experience.

· · · · · · · · · ·

Does the ego then determine its own activity? If so, how is the self-determination of the ego related to the determination of the spatio-temporal order? Is personal causality a special kind of causality, or only a disguised form of the mechanism of Nature? It is claimed that the two kinds of determinism are not mutually exclusive and that the scientific method is equally applicable to human action. The human act of deliberation is understood to be a conflict of motives which are conceived, not as the ego's own present or inherited tendencies of action or inaction, but as so many external forces fighting one another, gladiator-like, on the arena of the mind. Yet the final choice is regarded as a fact determined by the *strongest* force, and not by the resultant of contending motives, like a purely physical effect. I am, however, firmly of the opinion that the controversy between the advocates of Mechanism and Freedom arises from a wrong view of intelligent action which modern psychology, unmindful of its own independence as a science, possessing a special set of facts to observe, was bound to take on account of its slavish imitation of physical sciences.

· · · · · · · · · ·

Thus the element of guidance and directive control in the ego's activity clearly shows that the ego is a free personal causality. He shares in the life and freedom of the Ultimate Ego who, by permitting the emergence of a finite ego, capable of private initiative, has limited this freedom of His own free will. This freedom of conscious behaviour follows from the view of ego-activity which the Quran takes. There are verses which are unmistakably clear on this point:

'And say: The truth is from your Lord: Let him, then, who will, believe: and let him who will, be an unbeliever.' (18:28.)

'If ye do well to your own behoof will ye do well: and if ye do evil against yourselves will ye do it.' (17:7.)

Indeed Islam recognizes a very important fact of human psychology, i.e., the rise and fall of the power to act freely, and is anxious to retain the power to act freely as a constant and undiminished factor in the life of the ego. The timing of the daily prayer which according to the Quran restores 'self-possession' to the ego by bringing it into closer touch with the ultimate source of life and freedom, is intended to save the ego from the mechanizing effects of sleep and business. Prayer in Islam is the ego's escape from mechanism to freedom.

It cannot, however, be denied that the idea of destiny runs throughout the Quran. This point is worth considering, more especially because Spengler in his *Decline of the West* seems to think that Islam amounts to a complete negation of the ego. I have already explained to you my view of 'Taqdir' (destiny) as we find it in the Quran. As Spengler himself points out, there are two ways of making the world our own. The one is intellectual; the other, for want of a better expression, we may call vital. The intellectual way consists in understanding the world as a rigid system of cause and effect. The vital is the absolute acceptance of the inevitable necessity of life, regarded as a whole which in evolving its inner richness creates serial time. This vital way of appropriating the universe is what the Quran describes as 'Iman'. Iman is not merely a passive belief in one or more propositions of a certain kind; it is living assurance begotten of a rare experience. Strong personalities alone are capable of rising to this experience and the higher 'Fatalism' implied in it. Napoleon is reported to have said—'I am a thing, not a person'. This is one way in which unitive experience expresses itself. In the history of religious experience in Islam which, according to the Prophet, consists in the 'creation of Divine attributes in man', this experience has found expression in such phrases as—'I am the creative truth' (Hallaj), 'I am Time' (Muhammad), 'I am the speaking Quran' (Ali), 'Glory to me' (Ba Yazid). In the higher Sufiism of Islam unitive experience is not the finite ego effacing its own identity by some sort of absorption into the Infinite Ego; it is rather the Infinite passing into the loving embrace of the finite. As Rumi[7] says:

'Divine knowledge is lost in the knowledge of the saint! And how is it possible for people to believe in such a thing?'

The fatalism implied in this attitude is not negation of the ego as Spengler seems to think; it is life and boundless power which recognizes no obstruction, and can make a man calmly offer his prayers when bullets are showering around him.

But is it not true, you will say, that a most degrading type of Fatalism has prevailed in the world of Islam for many centuries? This is true, and has a history behind it which requires separate treatment. It is sufficient here to indicate that the kind of Fatalism

---

[7] Jalal-al-Din Rumi was an Islamic mystic, or Sufi poet of the thirteenth century. Hallaj was a Sufi divine of the tenth century. Ali was the first Shi'ite Muslim Imam.

which the European critics of Islam sum up in the word 'Qismat' was due partly to philosophical thought, partly to political expediency, and partly to the gradually diminishing force of the life-impulse, which Islam originally imparted to its followers. Philosophy, searching for the meaning of cause as applied to God, and taking time as the essence of the relation between cause and effect, could not but reach the notion of a transcendent God, prior to the universe, and operating upon it from without. God was thus conceived as the last link in the chain of causation, and consequently the real author of all that happens in the universe. Now the practical materialism of the opportunist Omayyad rulers of Damascus needed a peg on which to hang their misdeeds at Kerbala, and to secure the fruits of Amir Muawiya's revolt against the possibilities of a popular rebellion. Mabad is reported to have said to Hasan of Basra that the Omayyads killed Muslims, and attributed their acts to the decrees of God. 'These enemies of God', replied Hasan, 'are liars.' Thus arose, in spite of open protests by Muslim divines, a morally degrading Fatalism, and the constitutional theory known as the 'accomplished fact' in order to support vested interests. This is not at all surprising. In our own times philosophers have furnished a kind of intellectual justification for the finality of the present capitalistic structure of society. Hegel's view of Reality as an infinitude of reason from which follows the essential rationality of the real, and Augustus Comte's society as an organism in which specific functions are eternally assigned to each organ, are instances in point. The same thing appears to have happened in Islam. But since Muslims have always sought the justification of their varying attitudes in the Quran, even though at the expense of its plain meaning, the fatalistic interpretation has had very far-reaching effects on Muslim peoples.[8]

A very difficult example of religious determinism comes from the African Yoruba nation. In the Yoruba version, there is a place for human freedom within a larger determinist context. Here it is described by Texas philosopher Jacqueline Trimier:

◆ on the Yoruba *Ori,* by Jackie Trimier

In Yoruba philosophy, the *ori* [or "inner head"] determines one's fate, and, contrary to most alternative cultural accounts of the soul, the Yoruba actually **chooses** his *ori*. In the creation myth *Ajala,* the "potter of heads," provides each body with a head. But before a person arrives on earth, he or she must go to the house of *Ajala* to choose a head. To make matters more complicated, *Ajala* has a

[8]Sir Mohammad Iqbal, *The Reconstruction of Religious Thought in Islam* (London: Oxford University Press, 1934).

reputation for being irresponsible and careless. As a result, *Ajala*
molds many bad heads; he sometimes forgets to fire some, mis-
shapes others, and overburns still others. Because it is said that he
owes money to many people, *Ajala* commonly hides in the ceiling
to avoid creditors and neglects some of the heads he put on the
fire, leaving them to burn. But beneath this earthy and all-too-
human depiction of the deity, certain classic concepts of fate and
freedom are evident. People choose their destinies, but it is a
choice that is fraught with dangers and uncertainties. *Ajala* molds
many bad heads and only a few good ones. When a person gets
to *Ajala*'s storehouse of heads, he or she does not know which
heads are bad or good—all people choose heads in ignorance. If a
person picks a bad head, he or she is doomed to failure in life.
Moreover, before a person reaches earth with a body, head, and
soul, rain can erode an imperfectly made head. On earth, hard
work would be useless to affect one's fortune because all of one's
energy would have been used for repairing the damaged, useless
head. Yet, if a person picks a really good head, the person is
destined to have a good, prosperous life. With hard work, he or she
will surely be successful, since little or no energy need be expended
in costly head repairs.

The concept of the *ori* or inner head carries with it a profound
belief in predestination. The life one leads depends upon the head
one chooses. One myth from *Ifa* literary corpus tells about three
friends *Oriseeku, Orileemere,* and *Afuwape* who needed heads to
travel from heaven to earth. They went to find the house of *Ajala* to
choose their heads. Before leaving heaven, they were told not to
stop at any place along with way. However, *Afuwape* did not listen;
he visited his father, and his two friends left him behind. When
the latter reached *Ajala*'s house, they did not find him because, as
usual, he was hiding in the rafters from creditors. Instead of waiting for *Ajala* to appear, the two friends picked their heads without knowing which ones were properly made; and as they de-
scended to earth, rain wore out their heads. Consequently, they
lived unsuccessful lives on earth.

Afuwape got to the home of his father, *Orunmila* (god of wisdom), who was consulting his *Ifa* (divination texts). When *Afuwape*
told his father of his plan to see *Ajala*, the *Ifa* priests consulted
for *Afuwape* and said *Orunmila* should offer money and salt as a
sacrifice and that *Afuwape* should carry part of these offerings on
his journey. *Afuwape* left his father's home and, along the way,
asked a gatekeeper for the way to *Ajala*'s house. The gatekeeper
had never used salt before and was cooking his soup over a flame
and salting it with ashes. *Afuwape* offered the gatekeeper some salt
which he liked. To return the kindness, the gatekeeper took *Afuwape* to the house of *Ajala*.

When *Afuwape* found *Ajala*'s house, *Ajala* was not at home but
one of the creditors was waiting for him. The gatekeeper had ad-
vised *Afuwape* to help *Ajala* pay part of his debt so that *Ajala*

would help him choose the best head possible. *Afuwape* paid the debt, and the creditor left. When *Ajala* came home, he was so grateful that he took *Afuwape* to his storehouse and helped him choose the best head. Consequently, *Afuwape*'s head withstood the hazards of a journey to earth, and he had a good life on earth.[9]

To Americans, the most familiar version of belief in predestination comes from that school of Protestant Christianity called Calvinism. In the following passage, the famous American Calvinist theologian, Jonathan Edwards (1703–1758), gives a defense of his belief in predestination.

◆from "Freedom of the Will," by Jonathan Edwards

WHEREIN IT IS CONSIDERED WHETHER THERE IS OR CAN BE
   ANY SUCH SORT OF FREEDOM OF WILL, AS THAT WHEREIN
   ARMINIANS[10] PLACE THE ESSENCE OF THE LIBERTY OF ALL
   MORAL AGENTS; AND WHETHER ANY SUCH THING EVER
   WAS OR CAN BE CONCEIVED OF. . . .
   First, I am to prove, that God has an absolute and certain foreknowledge of the free actions of moral agents.
   One would think, it should be wholly needless to enter on such
an argument with any that profess themselves Christians: but so it
is; God's certain foreknowledge of the free acts of moral agents,
is denied by some that pretend to believe the Scriptures to be the
word of God; and especially of late. I therefore shall consider the
evidence of such a prescience in the Most High, as fully as the
designed limits of this essay will admit of; supposing myself herein
to have to do with such as own the truth of the Bible.
   Arg I. My first argument shall be taken from God's *prediction* of
such events. Here I would, in the first place, lay down these two
things as axioms.
   (1.) If God does not foreknow, he cannot foretell such events;
that is, he cannot peremptorily and certainly foretell them. If God
has no more than an uncertain guess concerning events of this
kind, then he can declare no more than an uncertain guess. Positively to foretell, is to profess to foreknow, or to declare positive
foreknowledge.
   (2.) If God does not certainly foreknow the future volitions of
moral agents, then neither can he certainly foreknow those events
which are consequent and dependent on these volitions. The

---

[9] Jacqueline Trimier, "African Philosophy," from *World Philosophy,* ed. R.C. Solomon and K. Higgins (reprinted by permission of the editors).

[10] Jacobus Arminius (1560–1609) was a Dutch theologian who claimed that although God has foreknowledge of our actions, human beings nonetheless act freely. Edwards aims his arguments against Arminius' followers throughout.

existence of the one depending on the existence of the other; the knowledge of the existence of the one depends on the knowledge of the existence of the other; and the one cannot be more certain than the other.

Therefore, how many, how great and how extensive soever the consequences of the volitions of moral agents may be; though they should extend to an alteration of the slate of things through the universe, and should be continued in a series of successive events to all eternity, and should in the progress of things branch forth into an infinite number of series, each of them going on in an endless line or chain of events; God must be as ignorant of all these consequences, as he is of the volitions whence they take their rise: all these events, and the whole state of things depending on them, how important, extensive and vast soever, must be hid from him.

These positions being such as, I suppose, none will deny, I now proceed to observe the following things.

1. Men's moral conduct and qualities, their virtues and vices, their wickedness and good practice, things rewardable and punishable, have often been foretold by God. Pharaoh's moral conduct, in refusing to obey God's command, in letting his people go, was foretold. God says to Moses, Exod. iii. 19, "I am sure, that the king of Egypt will not let you go." Here God professes not only to guess at, but to know Pharaoh's future disobedience. In chap. vii. 4, God says, *but Pharaoh shall not hearken unto you; that I may lay mine hand upon Egypt,* &c. And chap. ix. 30, Moses says to Pharaoh, *as for thee, and thy servants, I* know *that ye will not fear the Lord.* See also chap. xi. 9. The moral conduct of Josiah, by name, in his zealously exerting himself in opposition to idolatry, in particular acts of his, was foretold above three hundred years before he was born and the prophecy sealed by a miracle, and renewed and confirmed by the words of a second prophet, as what surely would not fail, 1 Kings xiii. 1–6, 32. This prophecy was also in effect a prediction of the moral conduct of the people, in upholding their schismatical and idolatrous worship until the time, and the idolatry of those priests of the high places, which it is foretold Josiah should offer upon that altar of Bethel.—[11]

. . . .

Corol. 1. It appears from the things which have been observed, that unless God foresees the volitions of moral agents, that cannot be true which is observed by the Apostle James, Acts xv. 18, "Known unto God are all his works from the beginning of the world."

Corol. 2. It appears from what has been observed, that unless God foreknows the volitions of moral agents, all the prophecies of Scripture have no better foundation than mere conjecture; and that, in most instances, a conjecture which must have the utmost

---

[11] Here, and at other places indicated with ellipses, Edwards cites literally pages of Biblical passages in support of his claims. It is unfortunate we cannot reproduce them all here.

uncertainty; depending on an innumerable, and, as it were, infinite multitude of volitions, which are all, even to God, uncertain events: however, these prophecies are delivered as absolute predictions, and very many of them in the most positive manner, with asseverations; and some of them with the most solemn oaths.

Corol. 3. It also follows, from what has been observed, that if this notion of God's ignorance of future volitions be true, in vain did Christ say (after uttering many great and important predictions, concerning God's moral kingdom, and things depending on men's moral actions), Matthew xxiv 35, "Heaven and earth shall pass away; but my word shall not pass away."

Corol 4. From the same notion of God's ignorance, it would follow, that in vain has God Himself often spoke of the predictions of his word, as evidences of his Foreknowledge; and so as evidences of that which is his prerogative as GOD, and his peculiar glory, greatly distinguishing Him from all other beings; as in Isa. xli. 22—26, xliii. 9, 10, xliv. 8, xlv. 21, xlvi. 10, and xlviii. 14.

. . . .

SECTION XII.

God's certain Foreknowledge of the future Volitions of moral Agents, inconsistent with such a Contingence of those Volitions as is without all Necessity.

Having proved that God has a certain and infallible prescience of the act of the Will of moral agents, I come now, in the *second* place, to show the consequence; to show how it follows from hence, that these events are *necessary,* with a Necessity of connection or consequence.

The chief Arminian divines, so far as I have had opportunity to observe, deny this consequence; and affirm, that if such Foreknowledge be allowed, it is no evidence of any Necessity of the event foreknown. Now I desire, that this matter may be particularly and thoroughly inquired into. I cannot but think that, on particular and full consideration, it may be perfectly determined, whether it be indeed so or not.

In order to a proper consideration of this matter, I would observe the following things.

I. It is very evident, with regard to a thing whose existence is infallibly and indissolubly connected with something which already hath or has had existence, the existence of that thing is necessary. Here may be noted:

1. I observed before, in explaining the nature of Necessity, that in things which are past, their existence is now necessary: having already made sure of existence, it is too late for any possibility of alteration in that respect: it is now impossible that it should be otherwise than true, that that thing has existed.

2. If there be any such thing as a divine Foreknowledge of the volitions of free agents, that Foreknowledge, by the supposition, is a thing which already *has,* and long ago *had,* existence; and so, now its existence is necessary; it is now utterly impossible to be otherwise than that this Foreknowledge should be, or should have been.

3. It is also very manifest, that those things which are indissolubly connected with other things that are necessary, are themselves necessary. As that proposition whose truth is necessarily connected with another proposition, which is necessarily true, is itself necessarily true. To say otherwise, would be a contradiction: it would be in effect to say, that the connection was indissoluble, and yet was not so, but might be broken. If that, whose existence is indissolubly connected with something whose existence is now necessary, is itself not necessary, then it may *possibly not exist,* notwithstanding that indissoluble connection of its existence.—Whether the absurdity be not glaring, let the reader judge.

4. It is no less evident, that if there be a full, certain, and infallible Foreknowledge of the future existence of the volitions of moral agents, then there is a certain infallible and indissoluble connection between those events and that Foreknowledge; and that therefore, by the preceding observations, those events are necessary events; being infallibly and indissolubly connected with that whose existence already is, and so is now necessary, and cannot but have been.

To say the Foreknowledge is certain and infallible, and yet the connection of the event with that Foreknowledge is not indissoluble, but dissoluble and fallible, is very absurd. To affirm it, would be the same thing as to affirm that there is no necessary connection between a proposition's being infallibly known to be true, and its being true indeed. So that it is perfectly demonstrable, that if there be any infallible knowledge of future volitions, the event is *necessary;* or, in other words, that it is *impossible* but the event should come to pass. For if it be not impossible but that it may be otherwise, then it is not impossible but true. But how absurd is that, on the supposition that there is now an infallible knowledge (i.e. knowledge which it is impossible should fail) that it is true. There is this absurdity in it, that it is not impossible but that there now should be no truth in that proposition which is now infallibly known to be true.

II. That no future event can be certainly foreknown, whose existence is contingent, and without all necessity, may be proved thus; it is impossible for a thing to be certainly known to any intellect without *evidence.* To suppose otherwise, implies a contradiction: because, for a thing to be certainly known to any understanding, is for it to be *evident* to that understanding: and for a thing to be *evident* to any understanding, is the same thing as for that understanding to *see evidence* of it: but no understanding, created or uncreated, can *see evidence* where there is none: for that is the same thing as to see that to be which is not. And therefore, if there by any truth which is absolutely without evidence, that truth is absolutely unknowable, insomuch that it implies a contradiction to suppose that it is known.

· · · · · · · · · ·

III. To suppose the future volitions of moral agents not to be necessary events; or, which is the same thing, events which it is not impossible but that they may not come to pass; and yet to suppose that God certainly foreknows them, and knows all things, is to suppose God's knowledge to be inconsistent with itself. For to say, that God certainly, and without all conjecture, knows that a thing will infallibly be, which at the same time he knows to be so *contingent* that it may possibly not be, is to suppose his knowledge inconsistent with itself; or that one thing that he knows, is utterly inconsistent with another thing that he knows. It is the same thing as to say, he now knows a proposition to be of certain infallible truth, which he knows to be of contingent uncertain truth. If a future volition is so without all necessity, that there is nothing hinders but that it may not be, then the proposition which asserts its future existence, is so uncertain, that there is nothing hinders but that the truth of it may entirely fail. And if God knows all things, he knows this proposition to be thus uncertain. And that is inconsistent with his knowing that it is infallibly true, and so inconsistent with his infallibly knowing that it is true. If the thing be indeed contingent, God views it so, and judges it to be contingent, if he views things as they are. If the event be not necessary, then it is possible it may never be: and if it be possible it may never be, God knows it may possibly never be; and that is to know that the proposition which affirms its existence, may possibly not be true; and that is to know that the truth of it is uncertain; which surely is inconsistent with his knowing it as a certain truth. If volitions are in themselves contingent events, without all necessity, then it is no argument of perfection of knowledge in any being to determine peremptorily that they will be; but, on the contrary, an argument of ignorance and mistake, because it would argue, that he supposes that proposition to be certain, which in its own nature, and all things considered, is uncertain and contingent. To say, in such a case, that God may have ways of knowing contingent events which we cannot conceive of, is ridiculous; as much so, as to say that God may know contradictions to be true, for aught we know, or that he may know a thing to be certain, and at the same time know it not to be certain, though we cannot conceive how; because he has ways of knowing, which we cannot comprehend.[12]

---

[12]Jonathan Edwards, "Freedom of the Will," from *The Works of President Edwards, In Four Volumes,* Vol. 2 (New York: Leavitt and Allen, 1856).

C. DETERMINISM

As we have seen, the problem of freedom occurs in different contexts, from pagan fatalism to Christian predestination. The problem occurs in terms of the most abstract thesis that the universe as a whole is a single great machine or "substance" (as in Newton or Spinoza) and in very localized theories about the psychology of the human personality. At all levels, however, the problem has usually been identified with a single claim, **determinism.** We were briefly introduced to determinism in Chapter 2: Spinoza defended it in his metaphysical system; Newton gave it a convincing scientific interpretation with his physical theories. In a phrase, **determinism** can be characterized by a principle already familiar to us from Chapter 3, the "principle of universal causation." "Every event has its cause(s)." Determinism is the thesis that everything that happens in the universe is determined according to the *laws of nature.* The problem is that human actions, whatever else they might be, are also events in the physical universe. But if human action is just another law-determined natural occurrence, can it also be free? It is as if we were to start praising people (or blaming them) for obeying the law of gravity. What else could they possibly do?

Determinism as we have defined it is related, but different from fatalism and predestination. According to fatalism, despite what happens, the end is inevitable. In predestination, God's will has power over *both* human choices and natural law. According to determinism, however, an event will necessarily happen if its antecedent conditions are fulfilled. Determinism, on the other hand, need not say that any event is inevitable, it insists only that *if* certain conditions exist, *then* a certain kind of event will take place (for example, if a pot of water is heated sufficiently, then it will boil; or if a person is forced to choose between losing his life and killing an insect, then he will take the life of the insect). This "if . . . then" structure is essential to determinism. (There need be no such "ifs" or "thens" to fatalism or predestination.)

Determinism is the theory that every event in the universe, including every human action, has its natural causes; given certain antecedent conditions, then an event will take place necessarily, according to the laws of nature. But we must fill out the determinist's premise by at least one more step. It is not enough to say, "every event has its natural cause(s)," since this would leave open the possibility that although every event requires certain **antecedent conditions** in order to take place, the event might still be a matter of chance, at least to some extent, or a matter of human choice. We must say that "every event has its sufficient natural cause(s)." **Sufficient** means capable of bringing the event about by itself. Then there is no room for chance and no room for choice. And this view, which we shall call "hard" determinism ("hard" as in "hardheaded" as well as a "hard" conclusion to accept), clearly leaves no room for human freedom. Without choice, there can be no freedom, and without freedom, there is no reason to hold a person responsible for his action, no matter how virtuous or how vicious it might be. According to the hard determinist thesis, we can barely be said to be "acting" at all, for our "actions" are nothing but the result of antecedent conditions and laws of nature that leave no room for our "doing something" at all.

1. *"Hard Determinism"*

The hard determinist premise received its greatest impetus from Newton's physics and his picture of the universe as "matter in motion," determined according to the laws of motion and gravitation that he so elegantly formulated. But his followers applied these laws not only to the movements of the planets and the stars or to the ball rolling down an inclined plane. According to them, we too are "matter in motion," physical bodies that are subject to all of the laws of nature. What we "do" is just as determined by these laws as any other event in nature.

This "hardheaded" determinism has maintained a powerful hold on philosophers ever since Isaac Newton published his theories in the seventeenth century. The philosopher Pierre Simon La Place had such confidence in the Newtonian system that he claimed that if he knew the location and motion of every object in the universe, he could predict the location and motion of every object in the universe at any time in the future. (He could also *retrodict*, or look back to, every past state of the universe.) This means that if he had a proper map of the universe, including the material parts of our own bodies, he could predict everything that would ever happen, and of course, everything that we would ever do. If this is so, what possible sense could we make of our vain claims to have choices of actions, to decide what to do, or to hold ourselves and others responsible for what we have done?

La Place's confidence in the hard determinist thesis was common among the immediate successors and enthusiasts of Newton. For example, one of the philosophers of the French Enlightenment, Baron Paul Henri d'Holbach, defended the hard determinist viewpoint so uncompromisingly that he shocked even his colleagues as well as the many traditionalists.

◆**from *System of Nature*,
by Paul Henri d'Holbach**

In whatever manner man is considered, he is connected to universal nature, and submitted to the necessary and immutable laws that she imposes on all beings she contains, according to their peculiar essences or to the respective properties with which, without consulting them, she endows each particular species. Man's life is a line that nature commands him to describe upon the surface of the earth, without his ever being able to swerve from it, even for an instant. He is born without his own consent; his organization does in nowise depend upon himself; his ideas come to him involuntarily; his habits are in the power of those who cause him to contract them; he is unceasingly modified by causes, whether visible or concealed, over which he has no control, which necessarily regulate his mode or existence, give the hue to his way of thinking, and determine his manner of acting. He is good or bad, happy or miserable, wise or foolish, reasonable or irrational, without his will being for anything in these various states. Nevertheless, in spite of the shackles by which he is bound, it is pretended he is a free agent, or that independent of the causes by which he is moved, he determines his own will, and regulates his own condition.

However slender the foundation of his opinion, of which everything ought to point out to him the error, it is current at this day and passes for an incontestable truth with a great number of people, otherwise extremely enlightened; it is the basis of religion, which supposing relations between man and the unknown being she has placed above nature, has been incapable of imagining how man could merit reward or deserve punishment from this being, if he was not a free agent. Society has been believed interested in his system; because an idea has gone abroad, that if all the actions of man were to be contemplated as necessary, the right of punishing those who injure their associates would no longer exist. At length human vanity accommodated itself to a hypothesis which, unquestionably, appears to distinguish man from all other physical beings, by assigning to him the special privilege of a total independence of all other causes, but of which a very little reflection would have shown him the impossibility.

The will, as we have elsewhere said, is a modification of the brain, by which it is disposed to action, or prepared to give play to the organs. This will be necessarily determined by the qualities, good or bad, agreeable or painful, of the object or the motive that acts upon his sense, or of which the idea remains with him, and is resuscitated by his memory. In consequence, he acts necessarily, his action is the result of the impulse he receives either from the motive, from the object, or from the idea which has modified his brain, or disposed his will. When he does not act according to his impulse, it is because there comes some new cause, some new motive, some new idea, which modified his brain in a different manner, gives him a new impulse, determines his will in another way, by which the action of the former impulse is suspended: thus, the sight of an agreeable object, or its idea, determines his will to set him in action to procure it; but if a new object or a new idea more powerfully attracts him, it gives a new direction to his will, annihilates the effect of the former, and prevents the action by which it was to be procured. This is the mode in which reflection, experience, reason, necessarily arrests or suspends the action of man's will: without this he would of necessity have followed the anterior impulse which carried him toward a then desirable object. In all this he always acts according to necessary laws from which he has no means of emancipating himself.

· · · · · · · · · ·

In short, the actions of man are never free; they are always the necessary consequence of his temperament, of the received ideas, and of the notions, either true or false, which he has formed to himself of happiness; of his opinions, strengthened by example, by education, and by daily experience. So many crimes are witnessed on the earth only because every thing conspires to render man vicious and criminal; the religion he has adopted, his government, his education, the examples set before him, irresistibly drive him on to evil: under these circumstances, morality preaches virtue to him in vain. In those societies where vice is esteemed, where crime is crowned, where venality is constantly recompensed, where the most dreadful disorders are punished only in those who are too weak to enjoy the privilege of committing them with impunity, the practice of virtue is considered nothing more than a painful sacrifice of happiness. Such societies chastise, in the lower orders, those excesses which they respect in the higher ranks; and frequently have the injustice to condemn those in the penalty of death, whom public prejudices, maintained by constant example, have rendered criminal.

Man, then, is not a free agent in any one instant of his life; he is necessarily guided in each step by those advantages, whether real or fictitious, that he attaches to the objects by which his passions are roused: these passions themselves are necessary in a being who unceasingly tends towards his own happiness; their energy is necessary, since that depends on his temperament; his temperament is necessary, because it depends on the physical elements which enter into his composition; the modification of his temperament is necessary, as it is the infallible and inevitable consequence of the impulse he receives from the incessant action of moral and physical beings.[13]

2. Determinism vs. Indeterminism

Should we accept the determinist's premise? Without it, determinism cannot get to first base. Well, we have already seen the arguments traditionally advanced in earlier chapters, even by philosophers who are not themselves "hard determinists": The most general argument is that only by assuming from the outset that every event has its (sufficient natural) cause(s) can we ever understand anything. Otherwise, we

[13]Baron Paul Henri d'Holbach, *System of Nature* (London: Kearsley, 1797).

should have auto mechanics always giving us back our cars (and our bills) with the unhelpful statement that "there's no cause for our troubles." We could expect the same from doctors whenever a diagnosis gave them the least bit of trouble, and we would use it ourselves every time a problem began to get difficult.

A much stronger argument is made by Kant, who says that the basic rule of determinism, the principle of universal causation, is one of the rules by which we must interpret every experience. But even Hume, who denies that this principle can be justified either through reason or through experience, insists that it is a "natural habit" or custom that is indispensable to us and that we could not give up even if we wanted to. The consensus, then, has been that the principle itself is inescapable. Even Leibniz, who rejected the idea of causation altogether, insisted on his "Principle of Sufficient Reason," which came to the same end, that is, "every event has its sufficient reason."

The agreement of so many philosophers indicates the strength of the hard determinist position. Without the assumption that "every event has its sufficient natural cause(s)," human knowledge would seem to be without one of its most vital presuppositions. Not only scientific research but even our most ordinary, everyday beliefs would be forced to an intolerable skeptical standstill. Our every experience would be unintelligible, and our universe would appear to be nothing but a disconnected stream of incoherent happenings, from which nothing could be predicted and nothing understood. So the answer to the question, "Why should we accept the determinist's premise?" seems to be, "We cannot give it up; how could we possibly do without it?" For no matter how it is rephrased or philosophically altered (for example, by Leibniz, who eliminates the concept of "cause" from it), the assumption that every event in the universe, including our own actions, can be explained and understood, if only one knows enough about it and its antecedent conditions, is a presupposition of all human thinking that we cannot imagine doing without.

Even if the hard determinist's premise seems undeniable, it is not yet clear how we are to understand that premise. The older determinists of the Newtonian period (La Place, d'Holbach) understood the idea of a cause as a literal push or compulsion, as if one were given a shove down the stairs. On this model, our actions are no different, except in complexity, from the "actions" of billiard balls on a felt-covered table, the motion of each wholly determining the motion of the next. The exact movements of every ball, of course, are not always evident. In the opening break, for example, even the most expert player cannot predict with accuracy where each ball will go. But we can be sure that each one is absolutely determined by the movements of the other balls that make contact with it, just as with the simple predictable case of a single ball hitting another straight on.

If we view human beings as nothing more than physical bodies—bones, muscles, nerve cells, and the like—then this mechanical billiard ball model might make some sense. But a much weaker interpretation of the hard determinist premise does not require us to so radically reduce people to mere bodies. Instead of talking about actual physical pushes and compulsions, we can interpret the determinist premise in the following: To say that every event has its cause(s) is to say that if certain antecedent conditions are satisfied, then we can predict that such-and-such will occur. On the stronger mechanistic determinist interpretation, causes are actual pushes and, on such an interpretation, the notion of freedom is clearly impossible. But on the weaker interpretation, of determinism as predictability, there may yet be room for us to talk about freedom of action. For example, we may be able to predict our friend's decision, but that does not seem to mean that he was forced to make it. We may be able to predict his action, but only because, knowing him, we know what he will probably do. On the second interpretation, perhaps we can have determinism and freedom.

Many philosophers would defend determinism only as predictability on the basis of probability. We might easily be wrong. To say that every event is determined, on this view, means only that it is predictable if we know enough about antecedent conditions. But it has been objected, against the determinist, that the fact of such predictability is not sufficient to defend determinism in anything like the "hard" sense. It is one thing to say that all events, including human actions, are actually caused or compelled by physical forces. It is something quite different to say that all events including human actions, are predictable. They might be predictable, for example, only on the basis of certain statistical probabilities. "Most people in this circumstance would do that." "The odds are for it," in other words. Or, in the case of human actions, the predictability might still be due to human choices; we can predict each other's actions because we know how we would probably choose in the same circumstances. But there is no need here to talk about "causes" or compulsions. Nor, it has been argued, should we even talk any longer about "determinism," if this is all that we mean by it.

In contrast, the antideterminist thesis, called **indeterminism,** rejects both versions of determinism. Indeterminism claims that not every event has its sufficient natural cause(s). This theory at least appears to leave room for free will, for as soon as we allow that there are some events that are uncaused, human actions might be among them. And thus it would seem that we can be held properly responsible for our actions. But is the indeterminist thesis plausible?

The indeterminist argument has recently received a boost from physics, the very science that gave rise to the determinist threat in the first place. It was Newtonian physics that gave determinism its strongest claims. And you remember La Place boasting that if he knew the location and motion of every particle in the universe, he could predict every future state of the universe at any time. But it has been shown in recent physics that such knowledge is impossible. One of the most important discoveries of modern physics is the **Heisenberg Uncertainty Principle** (named after its discoverer, Werner Heisenberg), which says that we cannot know both the location and the momentum of a subatomic particle. In coming to know the one, we make it impossible for us to know the other at the same time.

From this principle, the British physicist-philosopher Sir Arthur Eddington advanced the indeterminist argument that determinism is false on physical grounds. Not every event in the universe is predictable. And furthermore, many scientists now agree, on the basis of such considerations, that the concept of "cause" does not apply to certain subatomic particles either. Therefore, the determinist premise that "every event in the universe has its sufficient natural cause" is false. Some events, namely those involving some subatomic particles, are not caused, not predictable, and therefore not determined, on any interpretation. But if not all events are determined, then perhaps human actions are not determined but free. And if they are predictable, it is not because they are caused.

The object of indeterminism is to deny the determinist position in order to make room for human freedom. But there are, unfortunately, two serious objections to this indeterminist argument. First, even if we suppose that the conclusions of modern physical ("quantum") theory are correct (a matter still in dispute among physicists), it is clear that determinism is of importance to us primarily as a theory of macroscopic bodies (that is, visible size—people, trees, cars) not subatomic particles. And no one has ever concluded that quantum theory and modern physics actually refute Newton's theories. Rather, it supplements them, puts them in their place, and qualifies them in ways that would have been unthinkable in the eighteenth century. But as for the determinism of the gravitation of the planets or the rolling of a ball down an inclined plane, the spectacular discoveries of modern particle physics don't affect them in the least. And with regard to the physical determinism of our own bodies, the case remains as before. It might be true that it is impossible to predict what a subatomic particle in our bodies might do. But it does not follow that it is impossible to predict what our bodies will do. Falling out of a plane, we still fall at exactly the same speed as a sack of potatoes. And that is all the determinist needs to continue his attack on our concept of freedom. Second, even if there should be such indeterminism, indeterminism is not the same as freedom. Suppose there should be a "gap" in the causal determinism of our decisions by the various neurological processes of our brains; that would mean, at most, that what we do is not determined at all—or is determined only randomly. Suppose all of a sudden your legs started moving and you found yourself kicking a fire hydrant; surely this is not what we mean by a "free action." Freedom means, at least, that we are free to choose what we shall do and that our decisions are effective. Indeterminisim robs us of our freedom, therefore, just as much as determinism. And the argument against determinism, in any case, is not yet sufficiently persuasive to allow the indeterminist his conclusions.

3.   The Role of Consciousness

Hard determinism is true of us as physical bodies. But, you might insist, we are not just physical bodies, we are also conscious. We can make decisions. We have a will of our own. The problem of freedom is often called "the free will problem." But we shall not use this terminology here.

The question of whether we are free or not is intimately joined to the question of who "we" are, as discussed in Chapter 7. Are we the meeting place of a body *and* a mind, or is our consciousness "just" brain processes? Whatever we are besides physical bodies, our physical bodies are still subject to all of the laws of Newtonian physics. You can see the problem. If our bodies are just cogs in the universe, what does it matter whether we are conscious or not? If you fall out of an airplane, you fall and accelerate at exactly the same rate as a sack of potatoes. The fact that you, unlike the potatoes, are aware of your falling, scared out of your mind, and wishing or praying like crazy that some miracle will save you makes not a bit of difference. But perhaps this is so with all of our actions as well? Our bodies are composed of bits of matter, various molecules undergoing chemical interactions and acted upon by the various laws of physics. No one can deny that they are subject to all the laws of physical nature. But once all the parts are determined in their various movements and activities, what is left for consciousness to do?

Suppose one insists that consciousness, unlike our physical bodies, is not part of the scheme of determinism? Consciousness, unlike our bodies, is free, free to make decisions, free to choose what to do. But if our bodies are determined in their movements, then what can consciousness do even if it is "free"? Whatever consciousness decides, it cannot have any possible effect on the movements of our bodies; in other words, it cannot affect our actions. Our "decisions," then, would be mere vanities, like fancy switches on a machine that in fact don't do anything at all. Consciousness, on this view, is nothing but a sideshow, for whatever it "decides," what we will do and what will happen are already determined by other antecedent conditions that have nothing to do with the "decision." In crude form, this was Spinoza's ethical position, and also that of some of the early Stoic philosophers. Everything is determined by the laws of nature; it is absurd to fight against nature. All that can be done is to accept the necessity of whatever happens and recognize our consciousness and our apparent freedom as a luxurious vanity. Every human action has its sufficient natural causes apart from consciousness. And so consciousness can make no difference whatsoever.

Most hard determinists, however, would probably not agree with the idea that any event, even a nonphysical event such as an act of consciousness, could be "outside" the determinism of nature. Most hard determinists would argue that our thoughts and feelings, even our decisions, are caused by the states of our brains and nervous systems. Our "decisions" are nothing but the conscious effects of complex causal antecedents—most of which we still don't understand—but are definitely part of the deterministic scheme of things. How consciousness enters this deterministic scheme is open to all of the questions that we asked in the last chapter—whether, for example, there can be causal connections between consciousness and our bodies, whether consciousness is merely an "epiphenomenon" of our brain states or identical to them, or whether we should no longer speak of "consciousness" at all. But, however those disputes are resolved, the hard determinist will insist that consciousness cannot be an exception to determinism.

If consciousness is part of the deterministic scheme of things, could we not say that what happens in consciousness, particularly our decisions, thereby causes movements of our bodies, and therefore controls our actions? This attractive compromise, however, faces an overwhelming problem. If one accepts the determinist's premise, then our decisions cannot cause our actions unless it is also true that our decisions, as part of the deterministic scheme, are caused in turn. Our decisions, therefore, are also determined, and no matter that it might seem as if we have a choice of actions, what we decide is already determined by those antecedent conditions that determine our decision.

Suppose, for example, you are deciding whether or not to go to the movies. Whether or not you go depends upon your decision. But your decision, in turn, depends upon its causal antecedents. Now suppose that we knew enough about your upbringing and tastes, your character and the workings of your brain, that we could see that your decision—let's say to go to the movies—is nothing more than the result of all of these conditions. What sense would it make, then, to say that you decided to go? Of course, it is true that you went through all of the motions of "making a decision." But the outcome of that decision, even if it was the causal result of the decision, was nevertheless nothing more than the result of conditions that preceded and had nothing to do with the decision. It is as if I gave you a choice of two alternatives, only one of which was possible anyway. That is hardly a choice. And so, if a decision enters into our actions, it must be a decision whose outcome is already determined in advance. The hard determinist thus wins in either case. If consciousness is not part of the deterministic scheme, it can have no possible effects on our actions. If it is part of the deterministic scheme of things, then it cannot be free. In either case, hard determinism is undeniable and freedom turns out to be an illusion.

4. "Soft Determinism"

The philosophers of the Newtonian tradition, those "hard" determinists who believe that determinism precludes the possibility of freedom of choice and action, have always had a powerful and simple argument on their side. But because of the urgency of our demand that we hold ourselves and each other responsible for our actions, most philosophers have not accepted "hard" determinism, even though they have accepted the determinist argument. Accordingly, many philosophers have espoused what has been called **soft determinism.** (The name comes from William James, who was not one of them.) Soft determinists, unlike the uncompromising hard determinists, believe that human freedom and determinism are compatible positions. On the one hand, they accept the determinist's argument, but, on the other, they refuse to give up the all-important demand for human freedom and responsibility. (Accordingly, they are often called *compatibilists*, and their position, **compatibilism.**)

The key to the "soft determinist" position is that an action or a decision, though fully determined, is free if it "flows from the agent's character." John Stuart Mill, for example, defends such a position in the following way:

◆ **on Causation and Necessity,**
by John Stuart Mill

The question, whether the law of causality applies in the same strict sense to human actions as to other phenomena, is the celebrated controversy concerning the freedom of the will; which, from at least as far back as the time of Pelagius, has divided both the philosophical and the religious world. The affirmative opinion is commonly called the doctrine of Necessity, as asserting human volitions and actions to be necessary and inevitable. The negative maintains that the will is not determined, like other phenomena, by antecedents, but determines itself; that our volitions are not, properly speaking, the effects of causes, or at least have no causes which they uniformly and implicitly obey.

I have already made it sufficiently apparent that the former of these opinions is that which I consider the true one; but the misleading terms in which it is often expressed, and in the indistinct manner in which it is usually apprehended, have both obstructed its reception, and perverted its influence when received. The metaphysical theory of free-will, as held by philosophers (for the practical feeling of it, common in a greater or less degree to all mankind, is in no way inconsistent with the contrary theory), was invented because the supposed alternative of admitting human actions to be *necessary* was deemed inconsistent with every one's instinctive consciousness, as well as humiliating to the pride and even degrading to the moral nature of man. Nor do I deny that the doctrine, as sometimes held, is open to these imputations; for the misapprehension in which I shall be able to show that they originate, unfortunately is not confined to the opponents of the doctrine, but is participated in by many, perhaps we might say by most, of its supporters.

Correctly conceived, the doctrine called Philosophical Necessity is simply this: that, given the motives which are present to an individual's mind, and given likewise the character and disposition of the individual, the manner in which he will act might be unerringly inferred; that if we knew the person thoroughly, and knew all the inducements which are acting upon him, we could foretell his conduct with as much certainty as we can predict any physical event. This proposition I take to be a mere interpretation of universal experience, a statement in words of what every one is internally convinced of. No one who believed that he knew thoroughly the circumstances of any case, and the characters of the different persons concerned, would hesitate to foretell how all of them would act. Whatever degree of doubt he may in fact feel, arises from the uncertainty whether he really knows the circumstances, or the character of some one or other of the persons, with the degree of accuracy required; but by no means from thinking that if he did know these things, there could be any uncertainty what the conduct would be. Nor does this full assurance conflict in the smallest degree with what is called our feeling of freedom. We do not feel ourselves the less free, because those to whom we are intimately known are well assured how we shall will to act in a particular case. We often, on the contrary, regard the doubt what our conduct will be, as a mark of ignorance of our character, and sometimes even resent it as an imputation. The religious metaphysicians who have asserted the freedom of the will, have always maintained it to be consistent with divine foreknowledge of our actions: and if with divine, then with any other foreknowledge. We may be free, and yet another may have reason to be perfectly certain what use we shall make of our freedom. It is not, therefore, the doctrine that our volitions and actions are invariable consequents of our antecedent states of mind, that is either contradicted by our consciousness, or felt to be degrading.

But the doctrine of causation, when considered as obtaining between our volitions and their antecedents, is almost universally conceived as involving more than this. Many do not believe, and very few practically feel, that there is nothing in causation but invariable, certain, and unconditional sequence. There are few to whom mere constancy of succession appears a sufficiently stringent bond of union for so peculiar a relation as that of cause and effect. Even if the reason repudiates, the imagination retains, the feeling of some more intimate connection, of some peculiar tie, or mysterious constraint exercised by the antecedent over the consequent. Now this it is which, considered as applying to the human will, conflicts with our consciousness, and revolts our feelings. We are certain that, in the case of our volitions, there is not this mysterious constraint. We know that we are not compelled, as by a magical spell, to obey any particular motive. We feel, that if we wished to prove that we have the power of resisting the motive, we could do so (that wish being, it needs scarcely be observed, a *new antecedent*); and it would be humiliating to our pride, and (what is of more importance) paralyzing to our desire of excellence, if we thought otherwise. But neither is any such mysterious compulsion now supposed, by the best philosophical authorities, to be exercised by any other cause over its effect. Those who think that causes draw their effects after them by a mystical tie, are right in believing that the relation between volitions and their antecedents is of another nature. But they should go farther, and admit that this is also true of all other effects and their antecedents. If such a tie is considered to be involved in the word Necessity, the doctrine is not true of human actions; but neither is it then true of inanimate objects. It would be more correct to say that matter is not bound by necessity, than that mind is so.

. . . .

A fatalist believes, or half believes (for nobody is a consistent fatalist), not only that whatever is about to happen will be the infallible result of the causes which produce it (which is the true necessitarian doctrine), but moreover that there is no use in struggling against it; that it will happen however we may strive to prevent it. Now, a necessitarian, believing that our actions follow from our characters, and that our characters follow from our organization, our education, and our circumstances, is apt to be, with more or less of consciousness on his part, a fatalist as to his own actions, and to believe that his nature is such, or that his education and circumstances have so moulded his character, that nothing can now prevent him from feeling and acting in a particular way, or at least that no effort of his own can hinder it. In the words of the sect which in our own day has most perseveringly inculcated and most perversely misunderstood this great doctrine, his character is formed *for* him, and not *by* him; therefore his wishing that it had been formed differently is of no use; he has no power to alter it. But this is a grand error. He has, to a certain extent, a power to alter his character. Its being, in the ultimate resort, formed for him, is not inconsistent with its being, in part formed *by* him as one of the intermediate agents. His character is formed by his circumstances (including among these his particular organization); but his own desire to mould it in a particular way, is one of those circumstances, and by no means one of the least influential. We can not, indeed, directly will to be different from what we are. But neither did those who are supposed to have formed our characters directly will that we should be what we are. Their will had no direct power except over their own actions. They made us what they did make us, by willing, not the end, but the requisite means; and we, when our habits are not too inveterate, can, by similarly willing the requisite means, make ourselves different. If they could place us under the influence of certain circumstances, we, in like manner, can place ourselves under the influence of other circumstances. We are exactly as capable of making our own character, *if we will*, as others are of making it for us.

Yes (answers the Owenite),[14] but these words, "if we will," surrender the whole point: since the will to alter our own character is given us, not by any efforts of ours, but by circumstances which we can not help, it comes to us either from external cuases, or not at all. Most true: if the Owenite stops here, he is in a position from which nothing can expel him. Our character is formed by us as well as for us; but the wish which induces us to attempt to form it is formed for us; and how? Not, in general, by our organization, nor wholly by our education, but by our experience; experience of the painful consequences of the character we previously had; or by some strong feeling of admiration or aspiration, accidentally aroused. but to think that we have no power of altering our character, and to think that we shall not use our power unless we desire to use it, are very different things, and have a very different effect on the mind. A person who does not wish to alter his character, can not be the person who is supposed to feel discouraged or paralyzed by thinking himself unable to do it. The depressing effect of the fatalist doctrine can only be felt where there *is* a wish to do what that doctrine represents as impossible. It is of no consequence what we think forms our character, when we have no desire of our own about forming it; but it is of great consequence that we should not be prevented from forming such a desire by thinking the attainment impracticable, and that if we have the desire, we should know that the work is not so irrevocably done as to be incapable of being altered.

And indeed, if we examine closely, we shall find that this feeling, of our being able to modify our own character *if we wish*, is itself the feeling of moral freedom which we are conscious of. A person feels morally free who feels that his habits or his temptations are not his masters, but he theirs; who, even in yielding to them, knows that he could resist; that were he desirous of altogether throwing them off, there would not be required for the purpose a stronger desire than he knows himself to be capable of feeling. It is of course necessary, to render our consciousness of freedom

---

[14]From Robert Owen (1771–1858), a political reformer.

complete, that we should have succeeded in making our character all we have hitherto attempted to make it; for if we have wished and not attained, we have, to that extent, not power over our own character; we are not free. Or at least, we must feel that our wish, if not strong enough to alter our character, is strong enough to conquer our character when the two are brought into conflict in any particular case of conduct. And hence it is said with truth, that none but a person of confirmed virtue is completely free.[15]

In this selection, Mill glides between the harsh alternatives of "hard determinism" and indeterminism. He begins by accepting determinism and the idea that all human actions are "necessary and inevitable," given their causes. But he then goes on to say that these causes are themselves within human control, that we can alter the causes of events and even, by taking certain steps, alter our own characters. But this is not in the least to deny determinism; nor does it deny that we are in control and have "free will" in an important sense. Human actions, following from their various causes (including "character" or personality), are as predictable as any other events. But predictability is not incompatible with freedom, for freedom means, according to Mill, nothing other than acting in accordance with one's own character, desires, and wishes. Since these are the causes of our actions, that means that Mill can defend both determinism and freedom at the same time.

David Hume is also a "soft determinist," and he too argues that the reconciliation of "liberty and necessity" is to be found in the fact that a person's actions "flow from one's character or disposition." In defending soft determinism, Hume argues that we cannot mean by a free action one that is uncaused, a matter of chance, for this flies in the face of our common assumption that every event must have a cause. Such a view of freedom is also incoherent: The free-will advocate wants to ensure that we can hold people responsible for their actions; but if people's actions were merely a matter of chance, over which they have no control, we surely would not hold them responsible. On the contrary, actions that we praise or blame are precisely those determined by the person's character.

Although Hume defends a soft determinist position, there is a sense in which Hume is not a determinist at all. Recall from Chapter 3 that Hume thinks that causality is a fiction and our penchant for seeking out causes merely a habit. Thus he can argue that just as we are never rationally justified in claiming that a particular event has a cause, so we are never fully justified in claiming that human actions have causes.

[15] John Stuart Mill, *A System of Logic*, 8th ed. (New York: Harper & Row, 1874).

◆on Causation and Character, by David Hume

But to proceed in this reconciling project with regard to the question of liberty and necessity; the most contentious question of metaphysics, the most contentious science; it will not require many words to prove, that all mankind have ever agreed in the doctrine of liberty as well as in that of necessity, and that the whole dispute, in this respect also, has been hitherto merely verbal. For what is meant by liberty, when applied to voluntary actions? We cannot surely mean that actions have so little connexion with motives, inclinations, and circumstances, that one does not follow with a certain degree of uniformity from the other, and that one affords no inference by which we can conclude the existence of the other. For these are plain and acknowledged matters of fact. By liberty, then, we can only mean *a power of acting or not acting according to the determinations of the will;* that is, if we choose to remain at rest, we may; if we choose to move, we also may. Now this hypothetical liberty is universally allowed to belong to everyone who is not a prisoner and in chains. Here then is no subject of dispute.

Whatever definition we may give of liberty, we should be careful to observe two requisite circumstances: *first,* that it be consistent with plain matter of fact; *secondly,* that it be consistent with itself. If we observe these circumstances and render our definition intelligible, I am persuaded that all mankind will be found of one opinion with regard to it.

It is universally allowed that nothing exists without a cause of its existence, and that chance, when strictly examined, is a mere negative word and means not any real power which has anywhere a being in nature. But it is pretended that some causes are necessary, some not necessary. Here then is the advantage of definitions. Let anyone *define* a cause without comprehending it, as part of the definition, a *necessary connexion* with its effect, and let him show distinctly the origin of the idea expressed by the definition, and I shall readily give up the whole controversy. But if the foregoing explication of the matter be received, this must be absolutely impracticable. Had not objects a regular conjunction with each other, we should never have entertained any notion of cause and effect; and this regular conjunction produces that inference of the understanding which is the only connexion that we can have any comprehension of. Whoever attempts a definition of cause exclusive of these circumstances will be obliged either to employ unintelligible terms or such as are synonymous to the term which he endeavours to define. And if the definition above mentioned be admitted, liberty, when opposed to necessity, not to constraint, is the same thing with chance, which is universally allowed to have no existence. . . .

All laws being founded on rewards and punishments, it is supposed as a fundamental principle, that these motives have a regular and uniform influence on the mind, and both produce the good and prevent the evil actions. We may give to this influence what name we please; but, as it is usually conjoined with the action, it must be esteemed a *cause*, and be looked upon as an instance of that necessity, which we would here establish.

The only proper object of hatred or vengeance is a person or creature, endowed with thought and consciousness; and when any criminal or injurious actions excite that passion, it is only by their relation to the person, or connexion with him. Actions are, by their very nature, temporary and perishing; and where they proceed not from some *cause* in the character and disposition of the person who performed them, they can neither redound to his honour, if good; nor infamy, if evil. The actions themselves may be blameable; they may be contrary to all the rules of morality and religion: But the person is not answerable for them; and as they proceeded from nothing in him that is durable and constant, and leave nothing of that nature behind them, it is impossible he can, upon their account, become the object of punishment or vengeance. According to the principle, therefore, which denies necessity, and consequently causes, a man is as pure and untainted, after having committed the most horrid crime, as at the first moment of his birth, nor is his character anywise concerned in his actions, since they are not derived from it, and the wickedness of the one can never be used as a proof of the depravity of the other.

Men are not blamed for such actions as they perform ignorantly and casually, whatever may be the consequences. Why? but because the principles of these actions are only momentary, and terminate in them alone. Men are less blamed for such actions as they perform hastily and unpremeditatedly than for such as proceed from deliberation. For what reason? but because a hasty temper, though a constant cause or principle in the mind, operates only by intervals, and infects not the whole character. Again, repentance wipes off every crime, if attended with a reformation of life and manners. How is this to be accounted for? but by asserting that actions render a person criminal merely as they are proofs of criminal principles in the mind; and when, by an alteration of these principles, they cease to be just proofs, they likewise cease to be criminal. But, except upon the doctrine of necessity, they never were just proofs, and consequently never were criminal.

It will be equally easy to prove, and from the same arguments, that *liberty*, according to that definition above mentioned, in which all men agree, is also essential to morality, and that no human actions, where it is wanting, are susceptible of any moral qualities, or can be the objects either of approbation or dislike. For as actions are objects of our moral sentiment, so far only as they are indications of the internal character, passions, and affections; it is impossible that they can give rise either to praise or blame, where they proceed not from these principles, but are derived altogether from external violence.[16]

In other words, Hume too suggests that not only is freedom of choice and action possible within the framework of determinism, but determinism is even necessary if we are to make sense out of the notion of freedom of choice and responsibility. His language is convoluted, but his point is plain: We can make sense of the notion of voluntary action only because there is a uniform ("necessary") connection between our motives, inclinations, circumstances, and characters and what we do. But "soft determinism" raises the same old questions yet once again. Can we be said to be responsible even for those acts that are caused by our character? Can we choose our character, as Mill suggests? Could we have done other than what we did? even if we had wanted to? Is "soft determinism" really so "soft" after all?

D. COMPULSION AND IGNORANCE

The basis of compatibilism or "soft determinism" is that we somehow carve a space within determinism for those actions that we insist on calling "free" and for which we hold ourselves and other people responsible. But this means that "free actions" must also be actions that are determined by antecedent conditions and causes. Free as well as unfree acts (like falling down the stairs) are caused according to the determinist argument. The distinction, therefore, as we saw in both Mill and Hume, depends upon whether the determining factors are within the agent or "outside" of him or her. In the latter case, we say that the act was not free but *compelled* or "done under compulsion." This distinction, of course, has important moral implications. We often say a person is *not morally responsible* for an action which he or she was *not* free *not* to do. This distinction is not a new one. Aristotle, for example, many centuries ago defined a voluntary action as one that was (1) not done under compulsion, and (2) not done from ignorance.

◆on Voluntary Action,
by Aristotle

. . . It is only voluntary feelings and actions for which praise and blame are given; those that are involuntary are condoned, and sometimes even pitied. Hence it seems to be necessary for the student of ethics to define the difference between the Voluntary and

[16]David Hume, *An Enquiry Concerning Human Understanding*, 2nd ed., ed. L.A. Selby-Bigge (Oxford: Oxford University Press, 1902).

the Involuntary; and this will also be of service to the legislator in assigning rewards and punishments.

It is then generally held that actions are involuntary when done (a) under compulsion or (b) through ignorance, and that (a) an act is compulsory when its origin is from without, being of such a nature that the agent, or person compelled, contributes nothing to it: for example, when a ship's captain is carried somewhere by stress of weather, or by people who have him in their power. But there is some doubt about actions done through fear of a worse alternative, or for some noble object—as for instance if a tyrant having a man's parents and children in his power commands him to do something base, when if he complies their lives wil be spared but if he refuses they will be put to death. It is open to question whether such actions are voluntary or involuntary. A somewhat similar case is when cargo is jettisoned in a storm; apart from circumstances, no one voluntarily throws away his property, but to save his own life and that of his shipmates any sane man would do so. Acts of this kind, then, are "mixed" or composite; but they approximate rather to the voluntary class. For at the actual time when they are done they are chosen or willed; and the end or motive of an act varies with the occasion, so that the terms "voluntary" and "involuntary" should be used with reference to the time of action; now the actual deed in the cases in question is done voluntarily, for the origin of the movement of the parts of the body instrumental to the act lies in the agent; and when the origin of an action is in oneself, it is in one's own power to do it or not. Such acts therefore are voluntary, though perhaps involuntary apart from circumstances—for no one would choose to do any such action in and for itself.

· · · · · · · · · ·

What kind of actions then are to be called "compulsory"? Used without qualification, perhaps this term applies to any case where the cause of the action lies in things outside the agent, and when the agent contributes nothing. But when actions intrinsically involuntary are yet in given circumstances deliberately chosen in preference to a given alternative, and when their origin lies in the agent, these actions are to be pronounced intrinsically involuntary but voluntary in the circumstances, and in preference to the alternative. They approximate however rather to the voluntary class, since conduct consists of particular things done, and the particular things done in the cases in question are voluntary. But it is not easy to lay down rules for deciding which of two alternatives is to be chosen, for particular cases differ widely.

To apply the term "compulsory" to acts done for the sake of pleasure or for noble objects, on the plea that these exercise constraint on us from without, is to make every action compulsory. For (1) pleasure and nobility between them supply the motives of all actions whatsoever. Also (2) to act under compulsion and invol-

untarily is painful, but actions aiming at something pleasant or noble are pleasant. And (3) it is absurd to blame external things, instead of blaming ourselves for falling an easy prey to their
attractions; or to take the credit of our noble deeds to ourselves,
while putting the blame for our disgraceful ones upon the temptations of pleasure. It appears therefore that an act is compulsory
when its origin is from outside, the person compelled contributing
nothing to it.

Everything that is done by reason of ignorance is *not* voluntary;
it is only what produces pain and repentance that is *in*voluntary.
For the man who has done something owing to ignorance, and feels
not the least vexation at his action, has not acted voluntarily, since
he did not know what he was doing, nor yet involuntarily, since
he is not pained. Of people, then, who act by reason of ignorance
he who repents is thought an involuntary agent, and the man who
does not repent may, since he is different, be called a not voluntary
agent; for, since he differs from the other, it is better that he
should have a name of his own.

Acting by reason of ignorance seems also to be different from
acting *in* ignorance; for the man who is drunk or in a rage is
thought to act as a result not of ignorance but of one of the causes
mentioned, yet not knowingly but in ignorance.

Now every wicked man is ignorant of what he ought to do and
what he ought to abstain from, and it is by reason of error of this
kind that men become unjust and in general bad; but the term 'involuntary' tends to be used not if a man is ignorant of what is to
his advantage—for it is not mistaken purpose that causes involuntary action (it leads rather to wickedness), nor ignorance of the universal (for *that* men are *blamed*), but ignorance of particulars, i.e.
of the circumstances of the action and the objects with which it
is concerned. For it is on these that both pity and pardon depend,
since the person who is ignorant of any of these acts
involuntarily.[17]

What is compulsion? According to Aristotle, an act is compulsory
"when its origin is without" such that the person who acts "contributes
nothing to it." Thus a person who is literally pushed into doing something
is compelled rather than free. But what are we to say, for example, of the
person who is neurotic, who acts compulsively or "irrationally" because
of mental illness? It might once have been said that such a person was
"possessed," as if something "external" (a demon or an evil spirit) had
"taken over" and compelled certain actions.

This, in a sense, is what Aristotle means by "ignorance." Factors
unknown to the agent influence his or her choice.

But today we talk about "compulsions" and "denial" of the facts with-

[17] Aristotle, *Nicomachean Ethics*, Bk. III, trans. H. Rackham (Cambridge, MA: Harvard
University Press, 1934).

in the person and not "external" at all. In fact, psychologists would say that the neurotic always contributes to the neurosis as well as suffers from it, and thus, according to Aristotle's criterion, such acts are not really compelled at all, but voluntary, like the acts of a drunkard.

To take a much more difficult kind of case, what are we to say of those celebrated "brain-washing" cases (as the Chinese did to UN prisoners of war during the Korean War) in which a person seemingly performs an action voluntarily, but only after he or she has been "conditioned" in a dramatic and sometimes brutal way? Sometimes even the person's "character" itself is changed. Should we hold a person responsible for such actions? (This question has been an issue in some war-crimes cases, for example.) Similarly, should we go against Aristotle, and hold a person responsible for actions performed under great stress or as the result of a violent emotion (rage or infatuation, for example)? Should we hold a person responsible for actions performed under the influence of drugs or alcohol (assuming that we might well hold them responsible for taking the drugs or drinking in the first place)? You can see that the distinction between "free" actions and acts that are "compelled" is not nearly as clear as it first seemed. We can easily distinguish between a person who breaks into a store and a person who is pushed through the front window. But in many cases where freedom is most in question, in cases of neurosis, brainwashing, great passion, and chemical "influences," the distinction between what is "external" to the person and what is within his or her character is not clear at all.

There are more serious problems with the notion of "compulsion," however. Even if we admit that some problematic examples of actions are not clearly either "free" or "compelled" (neurosis and brainwashing, great passion and drugs), we would want to insist that at least some actions are clearly free and not compelled. For example, I write a check to the American Cancer Society just because I believe that it is an important organization, and I want to make a contribution. No one has solicited me, no one has encouraged me to do it, and no one need know that I do it. Can even this act so seemingly performed "of my own free will," be counted as a "free action"? The "soft determinist" would say that this action is "free" because it flows from my generous character. But what goes into *making* my character? My education and upbringing? My social class? What about my national origin or my gender? Perhaps even my height and weight affect my choices.

Even in our "freest" acts, it can be argued that the desires and decisions, in short, our "personality" is wholly determined by forces outside of us and beyond our control. Consider the following argument, for example, by Professor John Hospers, who uses Freud and psychoanalysis as the basis for his claim that all of our acts are compelled and not free, insofar as all of our acts are brought about by a set of psychological determinants over which we have no control:

◆from "What Means This Freedom?"
by John Hospers

[Are we] in the final analysis, *responsible for any of our actions at all.* The issue may be put this way: How can anyone be responsible for his actions, since they grow out of his character, which is shaped and molded and made what it is by influences—some hereditary, but most of them stemming from early parental environment—that were not of his own making or choosing? This question, I believe, still troubles many people who would agree to all the distinctions we have just made but still have the feeling that "this isn't all." They have the uneasy suspicion that there is a more ultimate sense, a "deeper" sense, in which we are *not* responsible for our actions, since we are not responsible for the character out of which those actions spring. . . .

Let us take as an example a criminal who, let us say, strangled several persons and is himself now condemned to die in the electric chair. Jury and public alike hold him fully responsible (at least they utter the words "he is responsible"), for the murders were planned down to the minutest detail, and the defendant tells the jury exactly how he planned them. But now we find out how it all came about; we learn of parents who rejected him from babyhood, of the childhood spent in one foster home after another, where it was always plain to him that he was not wanted; of the constantly frustrated early desire for affection, the hard shell of nonchalance and bitterness that he assumed to cover the painful and humiliating fact of being unwanted, and his subsequent attempts to heal those wounds to his shattered ego through defensive aggression. . . . The poor victim is not conscious of the inner forces that exact from him this ghastly toll; he battles, he schemes, he revels in pseudo-aggression, he is miserable, but he does not know what works within him to produce these catastrophic acts of crime. His aggressive actions are the wriggling of a worm on a fisherman's hook. And if this is so, it seems difficult to say any longer, "He is responsible." Rather, we shall put him behind bars for the protection of society, but we shall no longer flatter our feeling of moral superiority by calling him personally responsible for what he did.

Let us suppose it were established that a man commits murder only if sometime during the previous week, he has eaten a certain combination of foods—say, tuna fish salad at a meal also including peas, mushroom soup, and blueberry pie. What if we were to track down the factors common to all murders committed in this country during the last twenty years and found this factor present in all of them, and only in them? The example is of course empirically absurd; but may it not be that there is *some* combination of factors that regularly leads to homicide, factors such as are described in general terms in the above quotation? (Indeed the situation in the quotation is less fortunate than in our hypothetical example, for it is easy to avoid certain foods once we have been warned about them, but the situation of the infant is thrust on him; something has already happened to him once and for all, before he knows it has happened.) When such specific factors are discovered, won't they make it clear that it is foolish and pointless, as well as immoral, to hold human beings responsible for crimes? Or, if one prefers biological to psychological factors, suppose a neurologist is called in to testify at a murder trial and produces X-ray pictures of the brain of the criminal; anyone can see, he argues, that the *cella turcica* was already calcified at the age of nineteen; it should be a flexible bone, growing, enabling the gland to grow. All the defendant's disorders might have resulted from this early calcification. Now, this particular explanation may be empirically false; but who can say that no such factors, far more complex, to be sure, exist?

When we know such things as these, we no longer feel as much tempted to say that the criminal is responsible for his crime; and we tend also (do we not?) to excuse him—not legally (we still confine him to prison) but morally; we no longer call him a monster or hold him personally responsible for what he did. Moreover, we do this in general, not merely in the case of crime: "You must excuse Grandmother for being irritable; she's really quite ill and is suffering some pain all the time." Or: "The dog always bites children after she's had a litter of pups; you can't blame her for it: she's not feeling well, and besides she naturally wants to defend them." Or: "She's nervous and jumpy, but do excuse her: she has a severe glandular disturbance." . . .

But one may still object that so far we have talked only about neurotic behavior. Isn't nonneurotic or normal or not unconsciously motivated (or whatever you want to call it) behavior still within the area of responsibility? There are reasons for answering "No" even here, for the normal person no more than neurotic one has caused his own character, which makes him what he is. Granted that neurotics are not responsible for their behavior (that part of it which we call neurotic) because it stems from undigested infantile conflicts that they had no part in bringing about, and that are external to them just as surely as if their behavior had been forced on them by a malevolent deity (which is indeed one theory on the subject); but the so-called normal person is equally the product of causes in which his volition took no part. And if, unlike the neurotic's, his behavior is changeable by rational considerations, and if he has the will power to overcome the effects of an unfortunate early environment, this again is no credit to him; he is just lucky. If energy is available to him in a form in which it can be mobilized for constructive purposes, this is no credit to him, for this too is part of his psychic legacy. Those of us who can discipline ourselves and develop habits of concentration of purpose tend to blame those who cannot, and call them lazy and weak-willed; but what we fail to see is that they literally *cannot* do what we expect; if their psyches were structured like ours, they could, but as they are burdened with a tyrannical super-ego (to use psychoanalytic jargon for the moment), and a weak defenseless ego whose energies are constantly consumed in fighting endless charges of the super-ego, they simply cannot do it, and it is irrational to expect it of them. We cannot with justification blame them for their inability, any more than we can congratulate ourselves for our ability. This lesson is hard to learn, for we constantly and naïvely assume that other people are constructed as we ourselves are.

· · · · · · · · · ·

The position, then, is this: if we *can* overcome the effects of early environment, the ability to do so is itself a product of the early environment. We did not give ourselves this ability; and if we lack it we cannot be blamed for not having it. Sometimes, to be sure, moral exhortation brings out an ability that is there but not being used, and in this lies its *occasional* utility; but very often its use is pointless, because the ability is not there. The only thing that can overcome a desire, as Spinoza said, is a stronger contrary desire; and many times there simply is no wherewithal for producing a stronger contrary desire. Those of us who do have the wherewithal are lucky.[18]

While Hospers' example of eating a tuna sandwich as a kind of physiological compulsion may seem exaggerated, we might more easily accept many physical factors as having a decisive influence on our character. Many have argued, for instance, that a person's sex or race are inescapable physical factors which compel him or her to make certain decisions. Determinist arguments of this sort have been made even among members of oppressed groups seeking tolerance. In a recent well-publicized example, a lawyer defended her client against charges of assault by claiming that her client's actions were determined by her overwhelming case of premenstrual syndrome!

A Brooklyn woman who had contended that charges against her should be dismissed because stress from the approach of her menstrual period had caused her to beat her child dropped that claim in Criminal Court yesterday.

Instead, the 25-year-old woman, Shirley Santos, pleaded guilty to a harassment charge.

Elizabeth Holtzman, the Brooklyn District Attorney, said the plea marked the end of the first known case in the United States in which "premenstrual syndrome" had been used as a defense. "The withdrawal of this defense," she said, "is a signal that PMS is a defense without merit."

[18]John Hospers, "What Means This Freedom?" in *Determinism and Freedom in the Age of Modern Science*, ed. Sidney Hook (New York: New York University Press, 1958).

Miss Santos, of 621 Rutland Road, had originally been charged with assault in the beating of her 4-year-old daughter, Quadina, last Dec. 16. In an agreement with the District Attorney's office, Miss Santos dropped the premenstrual-stress argument and pleaded to the lesser charge of harassment.

CRITICIZED BY FEMINISTS

The premenstrual-syndrome defense has been used to mitigate the sentences of at least two women in British trials, but it has drawn the fire of feminists, who say it is discriminatory and degrades women.[19]

TO THE EDITOR:

I am the attorney for Shirley Santos, whose arrest for felonious assault and endangering the welfare of a child ended in no criminal conviction, no jail, no fine and no probation (news story Nov. 4).

Your article says that Miss Santos "dropped" the claim of pre-menstrual stress syndrome (P.M.S.). She did so only with the reciprocal promise that all criminal charges would be dropped. They were. Miss Santos entered a plea of guilty to a violation (which is not a crime), that of harassment. Upon completion of her conditional discharge, the court papers will be sealed.

As to District Attorney Holtzman's assertion that the "withdrawal of this defense is a signal that P.M.S. is a defense without merit," I respectfully disagree. I wholeheartedly believe that without the P.M.S. arguments Miss Santos would still be facing criminal charges. The fact that they were all dropped is, instead, a testament to its validity.

In addition, there has been some confusion as to the nature of the defense in this case. It was never an insanity case.

My hope is that in the future women with such difficulties will be able to recognize and receive appropriate treatment for them—free of social stigma or ill-conceived fear of economic reprisals.[20]

Despite the optimism of the defense attorney, what emerges from the foregoing arguments is not an attractive conclusion. If we believe that most of our actions are physiologically compelled, then no matter how we try to wriggle free of total determinism, it seems as if we keep finding ourselves enmeshed back in "hard" determinism. We suggested that perhaps an act is free if one of its causes is a decision, but if the decision itself is caused in turn, ours is not really a decision at all. We suggested that an action is free if it "flows from a person's character" ; but then we saw that it can be argued that an act that "flows from a person's character" is no more within his or her control and no more his or her

[19]David Bird, "Defense Linked to Menstruation Dropped in Case," *New York Times*, Nov. 4, 1982.
[20]Stephanie Benson, Letter to the *New York Times*, Nov. 15, 1982.

responsiblity than any other act. We might want to say that a person's act is free if, in this case, he or she could have done otherwise, but what does this mean, given the previous arguments, except that the act would have been different if the circumstances had been different or if the person had been, in effect, another person?

For example, it is true that you could have changed the course of World War II—but *if what?* If you had been born Winston Churchill, perhaps. But that is a nonsensical "if." Does it make any more sense, however, to say that "you could have been a professional football player?" If what? If circumstances had been different? If you had been born with a different body, or raised in a different environment? But isn't this to say, for each of these "ifs," that you would be (slightly but significantly) a different person than you are? It looks as if we are trapped by the tautology that each of us is whoever he or she is. It is true of the geranium that if it had been planted in better soil, it would be larger; and if the ball had been dropped from the greater height it would have landed harder; and if you were raised differently, placed in different circumstnaces, then you might have acted other than you did. But does this have anything to do with "freedom"? Are your actions any more free than the growth of the plant or the falling of the ball? Of course, there is a difference: You think that you've made some decision. But why should what you think change the way things are determined? You might pretend to be flying after you've fallen out of the plane. But you're still falling, and whatever you think or do doesn't slow you down at all.

1.   Conditioning

Not everyone views determinism with horror. The eminent American psychologist B. F. Skinner, for example, applauds the determinist's argument as a means of controlling human behavior and changing it for the better. In his best seller *Beyond Freedom and Dignity* Skinner argues that we have made a fetish of freedom and that we should replace this with an acceptance of determinism. Behavioral scientists can and should be given the power to "engineer" human behavior in accordance with an agreed-upon set of ideals (social harmony, individual happiness, and productivity).

◆**Beyond Freedom,
by B. F. Skinner**

Perhaps the most crucial part of our democratic philosophy to be reconsidered is our attitude toward freedom—or its reciprocal, the control of human behavior. We do not oppose all forms of control because it is "human nature" to do so. The reaction is not characteristic of all men under all conditions of life. It is an attitude which has been carefully engineered, in large part by what we call the "literature" of democracy. With respect to some methods of control (for example, the threat of force), very little engineering is needed, for the techniques or their immediate consequences are objectionable. Society has suppressed these methods by branding them "wrong," "illegal," or "sinful." But to encourage these attitudes toward objectionable forms of control, it has been necessary to disguise the real nature of certain indispensable techniques, the commonest examples of which are education, moral discourse, and persuasion. The actual procedures appear harmless enough. They consist of supplying information, presenting opportunities for action, pointing out logical relationships, appealing to reason or "enlightened understanding," and so on. Through a masterful piece of misrepresentation, the illusion is fostered that these procedures do not involve the control of behavior; at most, they are simply ways of "getting someone to change his mind." But analysis not only reveals the presence of well-defined behavioral processes, it demonstrates a kind of control no less inexorable, though in some ways more acceptable, than the bully's threat of force.

Let us suppose that someone in whom we are interested is acting unwisely—he is careless in the way he deals with his friends, he drives too fast, or he holds his golf club the wrong way. We could probably help him by issuing a series of commands: don't nag, don't drive over sixty, don't hold your club that way. Much less objectionable would be "an appeal to reason." We could show him how people are affected by his treatment of them, how accident rates rise sharply at higher speeds, how a particular grip on the club alters the way the ball is struck and corrects a slice. In doing so we resort to verbal mediating devices which emphasize and support certain "contingencies of reinforcement"—that is, certain relations between behavior and its consequences—which strengthen the behavior we wish to set up. The same consequences would possibly set up the behavior without our help, and they eventually take control no matter which form of help we give. The appeal to reason has certain advantages over the authoritative command. A threat of punishment, no matter how subtle, generates emotional reactions and tendencies to escape or revolt. Perhaps the controllee merely "feels resentment" at being made to act in a given way, but even that is to be avoided. When we "appeal to reason," he "feels freer to do as he pleases." The fact is that we have exerted *less* control than in using a threat; since other conditions may contribute to the result, the effect may be delayed or, possibly in a given instance, lacking. But if we have worked a change in his behavior at all, it is because we have altered relevant environmental conditions, and the processes we have set in motion are just as real and just as inexorable, if not as comprehensive, as in the most authoritative coercion.

"Arranging an opportunity for action" is another example of disguised control. The power of the negative form has already been exposed in the analysis of censorship. Restriction of opportunity is recognized as far from harmless. As Ralph Barton Perry said in an article which appeared in the Spring, 1953, *Pacific Spectator,* "Whoever determines what alternatives shall be made known to man controls what that man shall choose *from.* He is deprived of freedom in proportion as he is denied access to *any* ideas, or is confined to any range of ideas short of totality of relevant possibilities." But there is a positive side as well. When we present a relevant state of affairs, we increase the likelihood that a given form of behavior will be emitted. To the extent that the probability of action has changed, we have made a definite contribution. The teacher of history controls a student's behavior (or, if the reader prefers, "deprives him of freedom") just as much in *presenting* historical facts as in suppressing them. Other conditions will no doubt affect the student, but the contribution made to his behavior by the presentation of material is fixed and, within its range, irresistible.

The methods of education, moral discourse, and persuasion are acceptable not because they recognize the freedom of the individual or his right to dissent, but because they make only *partial* contributions to the control of his behavior. The freedom they recognize is freedom from a more coercive form of control. The dissent which they tolerate is the possible effect of other determiners of action. Since these sanctioned methods are frequently ineffective, we have been able to convince ourselves that they do not represent control at all. When they show too much strength to permit disguise, we give them other names and suppress them as energetically as we suppress the use of force. Education grown too powerful is rejected as propaganda or "brain-washing," while really effective persuasion is decried as "undue influence," "demagoguery," "seduction," and so on.

If we are not to rely solely upon accident for the innovations which give rise to cultural evolution, we must accept the fact that some kind of control of human behavior is inevitable. We cannot use good sense in human affairs unless someone engages in the design and construction of environmental conditions which affect the behavior of men. Environmental changes have always been the condition for the improvement of cultural patterns, and we can hardly use the more effective methods of science without making changes on a grander scale. We are all controlled by the world in which we live, and part of the world has been and will be constructed by men. The question is this: Are we to be controlled by accident, by tyrants, or by ourselves in effective cultural design?

The danger of the misuse of power is possibly greater than ever. It is not allayed by disguising the facts. We cannot make wise decisions if we continue to pretend that human behavior is not controlled, or if we refuse to engage in control when valuable results might be forthcoming. Such measures weaken only ourselves, leav-

ing the strength of science to others. The first step in a defense
against tyranny is the fullest possible exposure of controlling techniques. A second step has already been taken successfully in restricting the use of physical force. Slowly, and as yet imperfectly, we
have worked out an ethical and governmental design in which the
strong man is not allowed to use the power deriving from his
strength to control his fellow men. He is restrained by a superior
force created for that purpose—the ethical pressure of the group,
or more explicit religious and governmental measures. We tend
to distrust superior forces, as we currently hesitate to relinquish
sovereignty in order to set up an international police force. But it is
only through such countercontrol that we have achieved what we
call peace—a condition in which men are not permitted to control
each other through force. In other words, control itself must be
controlled.

Science has turned up dangerous processes and materials before. To use the facts and techniques of a science of man to the
fullest extent without making some monstrous mistake will be difficult and obviously perilous. It is no time for self-deception, emotional indulgence, or the assumption of attitudes which are no
longer useful. Man is facing a difficult test. He must keep his head
now, or he must start again—a long way back.[21]

In his novel *Walden II*, Skinner gives us a prototype for his
deterministic utopia:

". . . When a particular emotion is no longer a useful part of a behavioral repertoire, we proceed to eliminate it."

"Yes, but how?"

"It's simply a matter of behavioral engineering," said Frazier.

"Behavioral engineering?"

"Each of us," Frazier began, "is engaged in a pitched battle with
the rest of mankind."

"A curious premise for a Utopia," said Castle. "Even a pessimist
like myself takes a more hopeful view than that."

"You do, you do," said Frazier. "But let's be realistic. Each of us
has interests which conflict with the interests of everybody else.
That's our original sin, and it can't be helped. Now, 'everybody else'
we call 'society.' It's a powerful opponent, and it always wins. Oh,
here and there an individual prevails for a while and gets what he
wants. Sometimes he storms the culture of a society and changes it
slightly to his own advantage. But society wins in the long run, for
it has the advantage of numbers and of age. Many prevail against
one, and men against a baby. Society attacks early, when the individual is helpless. It enslaves him almost before he has tasted
freedom. The 'ologies' will tell you how it's done. Theology calls it

[21]B.F. Skinner, "Freedom and the Control of Men," in *The American Scholar*, 1955–56.

building a conscience or developing a spirit of selflessness. Psychology calls it the growth of the super-ego.

"Considering how long society has been at it, you'd expect a better job. But the campaigns have been badly planned and the victory has never been secure. The behavior of the individual has been shaped according to revelations of 'good conduct,' never as the result of experimental study. But why not experiment? The questions are simple enough. What's the best behavior for the inidividual so far as the group is concerned? And how can the individual be induced to behave in that way? Why not explore these questions in a scientific spirit?[22]

Not every visionary has looked upon determinism with delight. More often determinism has appeared in novels as a nightmare, as the philosophical basis of societies more oppressive and authoritarian than any we have ever seen. The most famous examples are George Orwell's *1984* and Aldous Huxley's *Brave New World.* In both novels, the techniques of psychology and drugs are used to manipulate the inhabitants of entire societies and force them to conform to a single set of behavioral standards, concerning which they have no choice whatsoever. In a more recent novel, *A Clockwork Orange,* Anthony Burgess presents a nightmarish fantasy in which a young hoodlum named Alex is "reconditioned" to be "good" through a series of experiments in which his viewing of violent movies is accompanied by a drug that makes him violently ill. It works (after a fashion), but the prison chaplain summarizes the philosophical difficulties this raises:

◆ **from *A Clockwork Orange,*
by Anthony Burgess**

[The Prison Chaplain tells him:] "Very hard ethical questions are involved," he went on. "You are to be made into a good boy, 6655321. Never again will you have the desire to commit acts of violence or to offend in any way whatsoever against the State's Peace. I hope you take all that in. I hope you are absolutely clear in your own mind about that." I said:

"Oh, it will be nice to be good, sir." But I had a real horrorshow smeck at that inside, brothers. He said:

"It may not be nice to be good, little 6655321. It may be horrible to be good. And when I say that to you I realize how self-contradictory that sounds. I know I shall have many sleepless nights about this. What does God want? Does God want goodness or the choice of goodness? Is a man who chooses the bad perhaps in some way better than a man who has the good imposed upon him? Deep and hard questions, little 6655321. But all I want to say

---

[22]B.F. Skinner, *Walden II* (New York: Macmillan, 1965).

to you now is this: if at any time in the future you look back to these times and remember me, the lowest and humblest of all God's servitors, do not, I pray, think evil of me in your heart, thinking me in any way involved in what is now about to happen to you. And now, talking of praying, I realize sadly that there will be little point in praying for you. You are passing now to a region where you will be beyond the reach of the power of prayer. A terrible terrible thing to consider. And yet, in a sense, in choosing to be deprived of the ability to make an ethical choice, you have in a sense really chosen the good. So I shall like to think. So, God help us all, 6655321, I shall like to think." And he began to cry.[23]

The claims of behavioral scientists like Skinner have provoked among contemporary ethicists similar responses to those that have provoked religious determinists. The repercussions are frightening. What if, for instance, instead of associating illness and repulsion with violent movies, the scientists in *A Clockwork Orange* were to associate pleasure? Well, that is exactly what our society does, claims Catherine MacKinnon, an American feminist philosopher. MacKinnon claims that advertisers, moviemakers, pornographers, and others in the media in our society *make* men's treatment of women fundamentally violent.

◆ on Coercion of Women's Sexuality, by Catherine MacKinnon

"Representation of the world," de Beauvoir writes, "like the world itself, is the work of men; they describe it from their own point of view, which they confuse with the absolute truth." The parallel between representation and construction should be sustained: men *create* the world from their own point of view, which then *becomes* the truth to be described. This is a closed system, not anyone's confusion. *Power to create the world from one's point of view is power in its male form.* The male epistemological stance, which corresponds to the world it creates, is objectivity: the ostensibly noninvolved stance, the view from a distance and from no particular perspective, apparently transparent to its reality. It does not comprehend its own perspectivity, does not recognize what it sees as subject like itself, or that the way it apprehends its world is a form of its subjugation and presupposes it. The objectively knowable is object. Woman through male eyes is sex object, that by which man knows himself at once as man and as subject. What is objectively known corresponds to the world and can be verified by pointing to it (as science does) because the world itself is controlled from the same point of view. Combining, like any form of power, legitimation with force, male power extends beneath the representation of reality to its construction: it makes women (as it

[23] Anthony Burgess, *A Clockwork Orange*, unabridged ed. (New York: Norton, 1987).

were) and so verifies (makes true) who women "are" in its view, simultaneously confirming its way of being and its vision of truth. The eroticism that corresponds to this is "the use of things to experience self." As a coerced pornography model put it, "You do it, you do it, and you do it; then you become it." The fetish speaks feminism.

Objectification makes sexuality a material reality of women's lives, not just a psychological, attitudinal, or ideological one. It obliterates the mind/matter distinction that such a division is premised upon. Like the value of a commodity, women's sexual desirability is fetishized: it is made to appear a quality of the object itself, spontaneous and inherent, independent of the social relation which creates it, uncontrolled by the force that requires it. It helps if the object cooperates: hence, the vaginal orgasm; hence, faked orgasms altogether. Women's sexualness, like male prowess, is no less real for being mythic. It is embodied. Commodities do have value, but only because value is a social property arising from the totality of the same social relations which, unconscious of their determination, fetishize it. Women's bodies possess no less real desirability—or, probably, desire. Sartre exemplifies the problem on the epistemological level: "But if I desire a house, or a glass of water, or a woman's body, how could this body, this glass, this piece of property reside in my desire and how can my desire be anything but the consciousness of these objects as desirable?" Indeed. Objectivity is the methodological stance of which objectification is the social process. Sexual objectification is the primary process of the subjection of women. It unites act with word, construction with expression, perception with enforcement, myth with reality. Man [*expletive deleted*] woman; subject verb object.[24]

Note that MacKinnon's argument, despite its opposition to the media conditioning of sexual oppression, is thoroughly determinist. She believes that our traditions and media *cause* violence and oppression. Do we really want to believe, however, that human actions are just conditioned reflexes? One result of such a belief, claim some contemporary theorists, is our media-based, advertising-based culture. If Skinner and other determinists are right, then advertising and mass media can play a determining role in people's actions and in structuring society. In her book *Decoding Advertisements* Judith Williamson delineates how advertisements can condition behavior.

◆*Decoding Advertisements,* by Judith Williamson

A product may be connected with a way of life through being an accessory to it, but come to signify it, as in the car ad which starts,

---

[24]Catherine MacKinnon, by permission of the University of Chicago Press.

'Your way of life demands a lot of a car' and ends by making the
car signify the life-style: 'Maxi: more a way of life.'

So the product and the 'real' or human world become linked in
the ad, apparently naturally, and the product may and does 'take
over' the reality on which it was, at first, dependent for its meaning.
As product merges with the sign, its 'correlative' originally used to
translate it to us, one absorbs the other and the product becomes
the sign itself.

For example, 'Beanz means Heinz': the product has taken over
a monopoly on the empirical reality of beans, originally used
to *explain* the product, 'Heinz': i.e., the Beanz meanz Heinz slogan is a reversal of the first step in the link, which is that Heinz
means beans. Once Heinz, the brand name, was *signified* as being beans—'Heinz means beans' places beans as the anterior
reality; but now beans, all beans, are completely enclosed by
the *signifier,* Heinz. It is the old difference between 'dogs are animals' and 'animals are dogs.' To say that 'beans means Heinz' is
the equivalent of the latter; Heinz has appropriated all the meaning that was initially transferred *to* it from the exterior reality of
beans as signifiers; but the product ends up as the signifier of
reality.

· · · · · · · · · ·

(E) PRODUCT AS GENERATOR

A product may go from representing an abstract quality or feeling, to generating or *being* that feeling; it may become not only
'sign' but the actual *reference* of that sign. It is one thing for a
product to *mean* happiness, it is another for it to *be,* or create happiness. The product is always a sign within the ad: as long as you
are not in possession of it or consuming it, it remains a sign and a
potential referent; but the act of buying/consuming is what releases
the referent emotion itself. A bath oil may represent excitement;
this is all it *can* do in the advertisement, where it is inevitably a
sign, because the referent is the real thing. Yet the ad shows us the
product as generator in terms of its internal narrative, and we are
promised that the product can *create* the feeling it *represents;*
'Things happen after a Badedas bath.' (This statement has the
quality of truism—how could *nothing* happen after a Badedas
bath?—a truism which is disguised by the narrative material of the
advertisement.)

To put this more simply: a product may be connected with an
emotional referent but in two very different ways: you can go out
and buy a box of chocolates *because* you feel happy; or you can
feel happy because you have bought a box of chocolates: and these
are not the same thing. In the first case the chocolates do not
pretend to be 'more' than a sign; they mean something, but in
terms of a feeling which you had anyway. They are a *sign* for a feeling, which is the *referent.* But if the product creates the feeling, it

has become more than a sign: it enters the space of the referent, and becomes active in reality. . . .

 . . . .

Once the product precedes the feeling . . . there is a danger that it will set the bounds for the feeling and the two will become identified as the same. The result is not only speaking, but feeling in clichés. Happiness is shampooed hair, joy is a drink of champagne. There is a sort of Pavlov dog syndrome at work whereby after seeing certain products linked to certain feelings for a long time, by association the products *alone* come to create, to 'be' the feeling. 'Objective correlatives' end up by *being,* through this distortion, the very indefinable qualities they were used to *invoke:* putting everything in material and limited terms. 'Happiness is a cigar called Hamlet.' The connection of a 'thing' and an abstraction can lead them to seem the same, in real life.

 . . . .

Thus the product not only represents an emotional experience, but *becomes* that experience and *produces* it: its roles as sign and referent are collapsed together.[25]

It seems like a slippery slope: if any of our actions can really be compelled through psychological conditioning, then why not all our actions? And if our actions, good or bad, are compelled, then it doesn't seem to make sense to hold anyone responsible for his or her actions (even the people doing the conditioning). If Skinner is right, then moral education and political activity can be reduced to a repeatable scientific experiment.

The belief in determinism, even among the critics of conditioning, comes from the success of the behavioristic sciences. How can we be free, and yet our behavior be so well predicted by psychologists and marketing analysts? Feminist biologist Donna Haraway has a unique argument by which she defends human freedom and responsibility even in spite of the predictive success of the behavioral sciences. The very foundations of these sciences, she claims—the interpretation of data, the design of experiments, and likewise the subjects' behavior as observed by these scientists—are *freely chosen* from among any number of ways science might be conducted. The norms of behavioral science—its predictions and so forth—are freely engaged in by scientists and so scientists are morally responsible for their findings.

◆ **"A Political Physiology of Dominance,"**
by Donna Haraway

The concept of the body politic is not new. Elaborate organic images for human society were richly developed by the Greeks. They

---

[25] Judith Williamson, *Decoding Advertisements: Ideology and Meaning in Advertisements* (London: Marion Boyers, 1985 [1978]).

conceived the citizen, the city, and the cosmos to be built according to the same principles. To perceive the body politic as an organism, as fundamentally alive and as part of a large cosmic organism, was central for them. To see the structure of human groups as a mirror of natural forms has remained imaginatively and intellectually powerful. Throughout the early period of the Industrial Revolution, a particularly important development of the theory of the body politic linked natural and political economy on multiple levels. Adam Smith's theory of the market and of the division of labor as keystones of future capitalist economic thought, with Thomas Malthus's supposed law of the relation of population and resources, together symbolize the junction of natural forces and economic progress in the formative years of capitalist industrialism. The permeation of Darwin's evolutionary theory with this form of political economy has been a subject of considerable analysis from the nineteenth century to the present. Without question, the modern evolutionary concept of a population, as the fundamental natural group, owes much to classical ideas of the body politic, which in turn are inextricably interwoven with the social relationships of production and reproduction.

The union of the political and physiological is the focus of this essay. That union has been a major source of ancient and modern justifications of domination, especially of domination based on differences seen as natural, given, inescapable, and therefore moral. It has also been transformed by the modern biobehavioral sciences in ways we must understand if we are to work effectively for societies free from domination. The degree to which the principle of domination is deeply embedded in our natural sciences, especially in those disciplines that seek to explain social groups and behavior, must not be underestimated. In evading the importance of dominance as a part of the theory and practice of contemporary sciences, we bypass the crucial and difficult examination of the *content* as well as the social function of science. We leave this central, legitimating body of skill and knowledge to undermine our efforts, to render them utopian in the worst sense. Nor must we lightly accept the damaging distinction between pure and applied science, between use and abuse of science, and even between nature and culture. All are versions of the philosophy of science that exploits the rupture between subject and object to justify the double ideology of firm scientific objectivity and mere personal subjectivity. This antiliberation core of knowledge and practice in our sciences is an important buttress of social control.

· · · · · · · · · ·

A single experimental manipulation embodies in miniature all the layers of significance of the principle of dominance in Carpenter's seminal work on the animal body politic. In 1938 he collected about 400 rhesus monkeys in Asia and freed them on Cayo Santiago. After a period of social chaos, they organized themselves into six groups containing both sexes and ranging in size from three to

147 animals. The monkeys were allowed to range freely over the thirty-seven acre island and to divide space and other resources with little outside interference. The first major study undertaken of them was of their sexual behavior, including periodicity of estrus, homosexual, autoerotic, and "nonconformist" behavior. Carpenter's conclusions noted that intragroup dominance by males was strongly correlated with sexual activity, and so presumably with evolutionary advantage. All the sexist interpretations with which we have become monotonously familiar were present in the analysis of the study, including such renderings of animal activities as, "Homosexual females who play masculine roles attack females who play the feminine role prior to the formation of a female-female consort relation."

In harmony with the guiding notion of the ties of sex and dominance in the fundamental organization of the rhesus groups, Carpenter performed what on the surface is a very simple experiment, but one which represents the whole complex of layered explanation of the natural body politic from the physiological to the political. After watching the undisturbed group for one week as a control, he removed the "alpha male" (animal judged most dominant on the basis of priority access to food, sex, etc.), named Diablo, from his group. Carpenter then observed the remaining animals for one week, removed the number 2 male, waited another week, removed the number 3 male, waited, restored all three males to the group, and again observed the social behavior. He noted that removal of Diablo resulted in immediate restriction of the territorial range of the group on the island relative to other groups. Social order was seriously disrupted. "The group organization became more fluid and there was an increase in *intra-group conflict* and fights. . . . After a marked disruption lasting three weeks, the group was suddenly restructured when the dominant males were released." Social order was restored, and the group regained its prior favorable position relative to other groups.

Several questions immediately arise. Why did Carpenter not use as a control the removal of other than dominant males from the group to test his organizing hypothesis about the source of social order? Literally, he removed the putative head from the collective animal body. What did this field experiment, this decapitation, mean to Carpenter?

First, it must be examined on a physiological level. Carpenter relied on biological concepts for understanding social bodies. He drew from theories of embryological development that tried to explain the formation of complex whole animals from simpler starting materials of fertilized eggs. One important embryological theory used the concept of fields organized by axes of activity called dominance gradients. A field was a spatial whole formed by the complex interaction of gradients. A gradient was conceived, in this theory, to consist of an ordered series of processes from low to high levels of activity measured, for example, by differential oxygen consumption. Note that at this basic level dominance was conceived as a purely physiological property that could be objectively measured.

. . . .

From this point, it is an easy step to judgments about the amount of dominance that functions to organize social space (call that quantity leadership) and the amount that causes social disruption (call that pathological aggression). Throughout the period around World War II, similar studies of the authoritarian personality in human beings abounded; true social order must rest on a balance of dominance, interpreted as the foundation of cooperation. Competitive aggression became the chief form that organized other forms of social integration. Far from competition and cooperation being mutual opposites, the former is the precondition of the latter—on physiological grounds. If the most active (dominant) regions, the organization centers, of an organism are removed, other gradient systems compete to reestabilsh organic order: a period of fights and fluidity ensues within the body politic. The chief point is that without an organizing dominance hierarchy, social order supposedly is seen to break down into individualistic, unproductive competition. The control experiment of removing other animals than the dominant males was not done because it did not make sense within the whole complex of theory, analogies to individual organisms, and unexamined assumptions.

The authoritarian personality studies bring us to the second level of explanation of the body politic implicit in Carpenter's experiment: the psychological. The idea of a dominance hierarchy was derived in the first instance from study of "peck orders" in domestic chickens and other birds initiated by the Norwegian Thorlief Schjelderup-Ebbe as early as 1913, but not incorporated into American comparative psychology in any important way until the 1930s. Then animal sociology and psychology, as well as human branches of the disciplines, focused great attention on ideas of competition and cooperation. Society was derived from complex interactions of pairs of individuals, understood and measured by psychological techniques, which constituted the social field space. One looked for axes of dominance as organizing principles on both the physiological and psychological levels.

The third and last level implicit in Carpenter's manipulation is that of natural political economy. The group that loses its alpha male loses in the competitive struggle with other organized organic societies. The result would be reflected in less food, higher infant mortality, fewer offspring, and thus evolutionary disadvantage or even extinction. The market competition implicit in organic evolutionary theory surfaces here. The theory of the function of male dominance nicely joins the political economy aspect of the study of animal behavior and evolution (competitive, division of labor, resource allocation model) with the social integration aspect (cooperative coordination through leadership and social position) with the purely physiological understandings of reproductive and embryological phenomena. All three perspectives link functionalist equilibrium social models—established in social sciences of the period—to explicit ideological, political concerns with competition and cooperation (in labor struggles, for example). Since animal societies are seen to have in simpler form all the characteristics of human societies and cultures, one may legitimately learn from them the base of supposedly natural, integrated community for humanity. Elton Mayo—the influential Harvard, anti-labor union, industrial psychologist-sociologist of the same period—called such a community the "Garden of Industry."

The political principle of domination has been transformed here into the legitimating scientific principle of dominance as a natural property with a physical-chemical base. Manipulations, concepts, organizing principles—the entire range of tools of the science— must be seen to be penetrated by the principle of domination. Science cannot be reclaimed for liberating purposes by simply reinterpreting observations or changing terminology, a crass ideological exercise in any case, which denies a dialectical interaction with the animals in the project of self-creation through scientific labor. But the difficult process of remaking the biosocial and biobehavioral sciences for liberation has begun.[26]

E. FREEDOM IN PRACTICE

As many of the foregoing arguments show, it isn't enough just to answer the metaphysical question about the causes of human action. The demand for freedom and responsibility is not going to be satisfied by different variations of determinism, no matter how "soft" they pretend to be. If we are to understand the role of freedom in our daily lives, what we need is a breach in determinism, a conception of our actions, or at least our decisions, as truly free and not determined in any of the ways discussed previously.

The classic statement of this claim to freedom and responsiblity is to be found in the philosophy of Immanuel Kant. (I am sure that you now appreciate how truly monumental Kant's philosophy has been. We shall see more of him in the next chapter as well.) We have already seen that Kant gave an unqualified endorsement of determinism, arguing that the principle (of universal causation) upon which it is based is nothing less than a necessary rule of all human experience. And this includes human actions:

[26]Donna Haraway, "Animal Sociology and a Natural Economy of the Body Politic, Part I: A Political Physiology of Dominance." Rpt. in *The Signs Reader* (Chicago: University of Chicago Press, 1982).

Actions of men are determined in conformity with the order of Nature, by their empirical character and other causes; if we could exhaust all the appearances, there would not be found a single human action which would not be predicted with certainty.[27]

This is surely a statement of the hardest of "hard" determinism. But Kant also appreciated, as much as any philosopher ever has, the importance of unqualified freedom for human responsibility. (He called freedom, as he had called God, a "postulate" [or presupposition] of practical reason.) But how could he defend both universal determinism and human freedom? Determinism is true of every possible event and object of human knowledge, Kant says, but it does not follow that it is also applicable to human acts of will or decisions to act. Action is a wholly different matter than knowledge. The metaphysics with which Kant defends this view is far too complicated to even summarize here. But the basic principle is simple enough: Kant says that we adopt two different standpoints toward the world, one theoretical, one practical. Insofar as we want to know something, we adopt the standpoint of science and determinism. And within that standpoint, every event, including human actions, is determined, brought about by sufficient natural causes (including the states of our brains and various psychological factors). But when we are ready to do something, we switch to the practical standpoint. And the main point is this: Insofar as we are acting or deciding to act, we *must* consider our own acts of will and decisions as the sufficient causes of our actions, and we cannot continue the causal chain backward to consider whether those acts of will are themselves caused. When we act, in other words, we cannot think of ourselves except as acting freely.

Suppose that you are about to make a decision: You are finally going to give up smoking. A friend offers you a cigarette on the second day. Yes or no? Do you smoke it? Now it might very well be that, given your personality, your weakness for past habits, and any number of other psychological factors, you are clearly determined to accept and thus break your resolution. Your friend, who knows you quite well, may even know this. But you can't think of yourself in this deterministic way, for insofar as you have to make a decision, you can't simply "find out" what you will do. In other words, you can't simply predict your own behavior, no matter how much you know about the various causes and factors that allow your friend to predict your behavior. If you were to predict, "I'm going to start smoking again anyway," you would not be simply predicting; you would be, in that very act, breaking your resolution, that is, deciding to break it. So, when your own acts and decisions are concerned, you have to act as if you were totally free. This in a way denies

[27]Immanuel Kant, *The Critique of Pure Reason*, trans. Norman Kemp Smith (New York: St. Martin's Press, 1933).

determinism. It says, as you are the one that has to make the decision, determinism isn't relevant. (Kant says, "and to have to think yourself free is to *be* free.")

Kant defends both freedom and determinism, and so he undermines the distinction that philosophers had drawn between them. Kant implies that a careful reconsideration of human action from the point of view of practice may put the metaphysicians' insistence on freedom as a type of causation in a new light, and allow us to think of freedom in a new way. For Kant, freedom is a certain *type of experience*, not an "internal cause." In a similar vein, the contemporary American philosopher Harry Frankfurt rethinks the meaning of coercion (or compulsion) in terms of the experience of the agent. His claim is that coercion is not properly understood as an "external cause" of an action. Rather, the question of what counts as coercion (and similarly what counts as freedom) is bound up inseparably with the question of what it means to be a person.

◆ **"Coercion and Moral Responsibility,"
by Harry Frankfurt**

The courts may refuse to admit in evidence, on the grounds that it was coerced, a confession which the police have obtained from a prisoner by threatening to beat him. But the prisoner's accomplices, who are compromised by his confession, are less likely to agree that he was genuinely coerced into confessing. They may feel, perhaps justifiably, that he made a reprehensible choice and that he acted badly: he ought to have accepted the beating rather than to have betrayed them. Thus sometimes, though not always, the use of the term "coercion" conveys an exclusion of moral responsibility. A person who acts under coercion is for that reason regarded as not having acted freely, or of his own free will. It may be established that a person is not to be credited or blamed for what he has done, then, by showing that he was "coerced" into doing it.

A person is sometimes said to have been coerced even when he has performed no action at all. Suppose that one man applies intense pressure to another man's wrist, forcing him to drop the knife in his hand. In this case, which involves what may be called "physical coercion," the victim is not made to act; what happens is that his fingers are made to open by the pressure applied to his wrist. It may in certain situations be difficult, or even impossible, to know whether or not an action has been performed. Perhaps it will be unclear whether the man dropped the knife because his fingers were forced open or because he wished to avoid a continuation of the pressure on his wrist. Or suppose that a man is being severely tortured in order to compel him to reveal a password, and that at a certain point he utters the word. There may be no way of discovering whether he spoke the word in submission to the threat of further pain, or whether—his will having been overcome by the agony which he had already suffered—the word passed involuntarily through his lips.

I propose to consider those cases of coercion in which the victim is made to perform an action, by being provided with a certain kind of motive for doing so, but which resemble cases of physical coercion in that the victim is not to be regarded as morally responsible for what he has been coerced into doing. We might say that in instances of physical coercion the victim's body is used as an instrument, whose movements are made subject to another person's will. In those instances of coercion that concern me, on the other hand, it is the victim's will which is subjected to the will of another. How, in those cases, does coercion affect its victim's freedom? What basis does it provide for the judgment that he is not morally responsible for doing what he is made to do?

$$\cdots\cdots\cdots\cdots$$

II

But what is coercion? Coercing someone into performing a certain action cannot be, if it is to imply his freedom from moral responsibility, merely a matter of getting him to perform the action by means of a threat. A person who is coerced is *compelled* to do what he does. He has *no choice* but to do it. This is at least part of what is essential if coercion is to relieve its victim of moral responsibility—if it is to make it inappropriate either to praise him or to blame him for having done what he was coerced into doing. Now it is not necessarily true of a person who decides to avoid a penalty with which he has been threatened that he is compelled to do so or that he has no other choice. Nor is it true that a person bears no moral responsibility for what he has done just because he does it in submission to a threat. Such a person may be described as acting "under duress"; but not all duress is coercion.

It might be suggested that someone is coerced if, in addition to his acting in order to avoid a threatened penalty, two further conditions are satisfied: (1) the penalty with which he is threatened renders the action against which the threat is issued *substantially* less attractive to him than it would have been otherwise; and (2) he believes that he would be left worse off by defying the threat than by submitting to it. Adding these conditions does not, however, serve adequately to identify instances of coercion.

Suppose that P threatens to step on Q's toe unless Q sets fire to a crowded hospital, and that Q sets the fire in order to keep P off his toe. This does not satisfy the first condition, which excludes trivial threats: the penalty Q seeks to avoid by submitting to P's demand is not a substantial one. Suppose instead, then, that P threatens to break Q's thumb unless Q sets fire to the hospital, and that Q submits to this threat. Here the penalty with which P threatens Q is substantial: any course of action is rendered substantially less attractive to a person if it leads him to a broken thumb than it would if it did not involve this consequence. Thus the first condition is now satisfied. It may be, moreover, that the second condition is satisfied too. Suppose that Q thinks he will not be apprehended or punished for setting fire to the hospital, and that he does not expect to be troubled very greatly by his conscience for doing so. Then he may well believe that he would be left worse off by defying P's threat and having his thumb broken than by doing what P demands of him. Even if both conditions are satisfied in this way, however, it does not seem appropriate to describe Q as being coerced into setting the fire.

Why are we disinclined to regard Q as being coerced even when we suppose that he believes he will suffer substantially more by defying P's threat than by submitting to it? One suggestion would be that it is because we think that since Q must realize that it is better to suffer even a broken thumb than to set fire to a hospital, he cannot believe that his submission to P's threat is justifiable or reasonable. We might, accordingly, consider revising the second condition to make it require that Q believes it would be unreasonable for him to defy P's threat, or believes that he is justified in submitting to it.

Now the satisfaction of this revised condition would ensure that a person who has been coerced into performing a certain action *believes* that he cannot properly be *blamed* for having performed it. But the criterion of coercion for which we are looking must do more than this. It must ensure that a coerced person cannot properly be held *morally responsible at all* for what he has been coerced into doing. And this would not be accomplished even by strengthening (2) still further so that it required Q to believe *correctly* that he is justified in submitting to P's threat, or that it would be unreasonable for him to defy it. In fact the satisfaction of the second condition in any plausible version is neither necessary for coercion nor, even in conjunction with the satisfaction of the first condition, sufficient for it.

· · · · · · · · · ·

A person's evaluations may not only affect his judgments concerning what it is reasonable for him to do. They may also have an effect upon what he is capable of doing.

Faced with a coercive threat, the victim has no choice but to submit: he cannot prevent his desire to avoid the penalty in question from determining his response. When he decides that it is reasonable for him to submit to a threat which is not coercive, his submission is not in this way made inescapable by forces within himself which he is unable to overcome. Sometimes we speak of threats as coercive even when we have no particular evidence that their victims are incapable of defying them. This is because there are certain penalties which we do not expect anyone to be able to choose to incur. A person who surpasses this expectation thereby performs not merely rightly or wrongly but with a certain heroic quality.

We do on some occasions find it appropriate to make an adverse judgment concerning a person's submission to a threat, even though we recognize that he has genuinely been coerced and that he is therefore not properly to be held morally responsible for his submission. This is because we think that the person, although he was in fact quite unable to control a certain desire, ought to have been able to control it.

· · · · · · · · · ·

Consider the following two situations. Suppose first that a man comes to a fork in the road, that someone on a hillside adjoining the left-hand fork threatens to start an avalanche which will crush him if he goes that way, and that the man takes the fork to the right in order to satisfy a commanding desire to preserve his own life. Next, suppose that when the man comes to the fork he finds no one issuing threats but instead notices that on account of the natural conditions of things he will be crushed by an avalanche if he takes the left-hand fork, and that he is moved irresistibly by his desire to live to proceed by the fork to the right. There are interesting differences between these situations, to be sure, but there is no basis for regarding the man as acting more or less freely or of his own free will in the one case than in the other. Whether he is morally responsible for his decision or action in each case depends not on the source of the injury he is motivated to avoid but on the way in which his desire to avoid it operates within him.

We do tend, of course, to be more resentful when another person places obstacles in our way than when the environment does so. What accounts for this greater resentment is not, however, the love of liberty. It is pride; or, what is closely related to pride, a sense of injustice. Only another person can *coerce* us, or interfere with our *social* or *political* freedom, but this is no more than a matter of useful terminology. When a person chooses to act in order to acquire a benefit or in order to escape an injury, the degree to which his choice is autonomous and the degree to which he acts freely do not depend on the origin of the conditions which lead him to choose and to act as he does. A man's will may not be his own even when he is not moved by the will of another.[28]

The call for a reevaluation of freedom as a reevaluation of personhood is essential to the American civil rights advocate Dr. Martin Luther King, Jr. His stance is quite Kantian. While maintaining that freedom is integral to personhood and inalienable by law or psychological compulsion, Reverend King claims that freedom cannot be *given* by law or psychological compulsion, either. Rather, freedom is acquired only

---

[28]Harry Frankfurt, "Coercion and Moral Responsibility," from *The Importance of What We Care About* (Cambridge: Cambridge University Press, 1988).

through a restoration of personhood, which, in the case of persons so long oppressed and demeaned as African-Americans, may take a long and concerted effort on all our parts.

◆ **"The Dilemma of Negro Americans,"
by Martin Luther King, Jr.**

Negro life! Being a Negro in America means being scarred by a history of slavery and family disorganization. Negroes have grown accustomed now to hearing unfeeling and insensitive whites say: "Other immigrant groups such as the Irish, the Jews and the Italians started out with similar handicaps, and yet they made it. Why haven't the Negroes done the same?" These questioners refuse to see that the situation of other immigrant groups a hundred years ago and the situation of the Negro today cannot be usefully compared. Negroes were brought here in chains long before the Irish decided *voluntarily* to leave Ireland or the Italians thought of leaving Italy. Some Jews may have left their homes in Europe involuntarily, but they were not in chains when they arrived on these shores. Other immigrant groups came to America with language and economic handicaps, but not with the stigma of color. Above all, no other ethnic group has been a slave on American soil, and no other group has had its family structure deliberately torn apart. This is the rub.

· · · · · · · · · ·

The Negro family for three hundred years has been on the tracks of the racing locomotives of American history, dragged along mangled and crippled. Pettigrew has pointed out that American slavery is distinguished from all other forms of slavery because it consciously dehumanized the Negro. In Greece and Rome, for example, slaves preserved dignity and a measure of family life. Our institution of slavery, on the other hand, began with the break-up of families on the coasts of Africa. Because the middle passage was long and expensive, African families were torn apart in the interest of selectivity, as if the members were beasts. In the ships' holds, black captives were packed spoon fashion to live on a voyage often lasting two to six months in a space for each the size of a coffin. If water ran short, or famine threatened, or a plague broke out, whole cargoes of living and dead were thrown overboard. The sheer physical torture was sufficient to murder millions of men, women, and children. But even more incalculable was the psychological damage.

Of those families who survived the voyage, many more were ripped apart on the auction block as soon as they reached American shores. Against this ghastly background the Negro family began life in the United States. On the plantation the institution of legal marriage for slaves did not exist. The masters might direct mating, or if they did not intervene, marriage occurred without sanctions.

. . . .

The liberation from slavery in 1863, which should have initiated the birth of a stable Negro family life, meant a formal legal freedom but, as Henrietta Buckmaster put it, "With Appomattox, four million black people in the South owned their skins and nothing more." With civil war still dividing the nation, a new inferno engulfed the Negro and his family. Thrown off the plantations, penniless, homeless, still largely in the territory of their enemies and in the grip of fear, bewilderment and aimlessness, hundreds of thousands became wanderers. For security they fled to Union Army camps that were unprepared to help. One writer describes a mother carrying a child in one arm, a father holding another child, and eight other children with their hands tied to one rope held by the mother, who struggled after Sherman's army and traveled hundreds of miles to safety. All were not so fortunate. In the starvation-induced madness some Negroes killed their children to free them of their misery.

These are historical facts. If they cause the mind to reel with horror, it is still necessary to realize that this is but a tiny glimpse of the reality of the era, and it does justice neither to the enormous extent of the tragedy nor to the degree of human suffering and sorrow.

Following the Civil War, millions returned to a new form of slavery, once again imprisoned on plantations devoid of human rights and plunged into searing poverty generation after generation. Some families found their way to the North, in a movement E. Franklin Frazier aptly describes as "into the city of destruction." Illiterate, afraid and crushed by want, they were herded into the slums. The bewildering complexity of the city undermined the confidence of fathers and mothers, causing them to lose control of their children, whose bewilderment was even more acute.

. . . .

Most people are totally unware of the darkness of the cave in which the Negro is forced to live. A few individuals can break out, but the vast majority remain its prisoners. Our cities have constructed elaborate expressways and elevated skyways, and white Americans speed from suburb to inner city through vast pockets of black deprivation without ever getting a glimpse of the suffering and misery in their midst.

But while so many white Americans are unaware of conditions inside the ghetto, there are very few ghetto dwellers who are unaware of the life outside. Their television sets bombard them day by day with the opulence of the larger society. From behind the ghetto walls they see glistening towers of glass and steel springing up almost overnight. They hear jet liners speeding over their heads at six hundred miles an hour. They hear of satellites streaking through outer space and revealing details of the moon.

Then they begin to think of their own conditions. They know
that they are always given the hardest, ugliest, most menial work to
do. They look at these impressive buildings under construction
and realize that almost certainly they cannot get those well-paying
construction jobs, because building trade unions reserve them for
whites only. They know that people who built the bridges, the man-
sions and docks of the South could build modern buildings if they
were only given a chance for apprenticeship training. They realize
that it is hard, raw discrimination that shuts them out. It is not
only poverty that torments the Negro; it is the fact of poverty amid
plenty. It is a misery generated by the gulf between the affluence
he sees in the mass media and the deprivation he experiences in
his everyday life.

· · · · · · · · · ·

Here the democratic process breaks down, for the rights of the
individual voter are impossible to organize without adequate funds,
while the business community supplies the existing political machine with enough funds to organize massive campaigns and control mass media.

Here, too, the North reveals its true ambivalence on the subject
of civil rights. When, in the last session of Congress, the issue came
home to the North through a call for open housing legislation,
white Northern Congressmen who had enthusiastically supported
the 1964 and 1965 civil rights bills now joined in a mighty chorus
of anguish and dismay reminiscent of Alabama and Mississippi.
So the first piece of legislation aimed at rectifying a shocking evil in
the North went down to crushing defeat.

Nothing today more clearly indicates the residue of racism still
lodging in our society than the responses of white America to integrated housing. Here the tides of prejudice, fear and irrationality
rise to flood proportions. This is not a new backlash caused by the
Black Power movement; there had been no ominous riots in Watts
when white Californians defeated a fair housing bill in 1964. The
present resistance to open housing is based on the same premises
that came into being to rationalize slavery. It is rooted in the fear
that the alleged depravity or defective nature of the out-race will in-
filtrate the neighborhood of the in-race.[29]

Both King and Frankfurt argue a quasi-Kantian view of freedom. In
practice, they claim, actions are free to the extent that their agent is a
dignified, capable, rational human being. The ability to act freely, then,
is not *determined* by "outside" influences, but such influences—like the
economy, the society, the media, our friends and families—can and do
affect freedom. Outside influences debilitate and/or enhance an agent's
freedom and humanity.

[29]Martin Luther King, Jr., *Where Do We Go From Here? Chaos or Community?* (Boston:
Beacon Press, 1967).

F. RADICAL FREEDOM: EXISTENTIALISM

Kant's suggestion, however, has been taken up in a very different way in European philosophy, particularly by the existentialists. Like Kant, they accept (or at least do not bother to reject) determinism in science. But they insist that even if determinism is true, one must always view *him* or *herself as agent* as necessarily free. When you have to decide what to do, all the knowledge of the possible factors determining your decision are not sufficient to cause you to decide. For you cannot predict your own decision without at the same time making it.

Jean-Paul Sartre, the late French existentialist, has defended the Kantian claim for human freedom as far as it can possibly be defended. In his mammoth book *Being and Nothingness,* Sartre argued that we are, always, absolutely free. This means, as Kant had insisted, that insofar as we act (and Sartre says that we are always acting) our decisions and our actions cannot be viewed as having any causes whatsoever. We must make decisions, and no amount of information and no number of causal circumstances can ever replace our need to make them. We can, of course, refuse to make decisions, acting as if they were made for us, as if circumstances already determined them, as if the fates had already established the outcome. But even in these cases, we are making decisions, "choosing not to choose," in a classic Sartrian phrase. We are "condemned to be free," he says, in a phrase that has since become famous. Again, desires may enter into consideration, but only as "consideration." We can always act against a desire, any desire, no matter how strong, if only we are sufficiently decided that we shall do so. A starving man may yet refuse food if, for example, he is taking part in a hunger strike for a political cause to which he is dedicated. A mother may refuse to save her own life if it would be at the expense of her children. A student may miss his favorite television show if he has resolved to study for tomorrow's test. Whether trivial or grandiose, our every act is a decision, and our every decision is free. And even if we fail to live up to them or find that we "cannot" make them, we are responsible nevertheless. There is no escape from freedom or responsibility.

◆ **"Absolute Freedom,"**
by Jean-Paul Sartre

Although the considerations which are about to follow are of interest primarily to the ethicist, it may nevertheless be worthwhile after these descriptions and arguments to return to the freedom of the for-itself and try to understand what the fact of this freedom represents for human destiny.

The essential consequence of our earlier remarks is that man being condemned to be free carries the weight of the whole world on his shoulders; he is responsible for the world and for himself as a way of being. We are taking the word "responsibility" in its ordinary sense as "consciousness (of) being the incontestable author of an event or of an object." In this sense the responsibility of the for-itself is overwhelming since he is the one by whom it happens that *there is* a world; since he is also the one who makes himself be, then whatever may be the situation in which he finds himself, the for-itself must wholly assume this situation with its peculiar coefficient of adversity, even though it be insupportable. He must assume the situation with the proud consciousness of being the author of it, for the very worst disadvantages or the worst threats which can endanger my person have meaning only in and through my project; and it is on the ground of the engagement which I am that they appear. It is therefore senseless to think of complaining since nothing foreign has decided what we feel, what we live, or what we are.

Furthermore this absolute responsibility is not resignation; it is simply the logical requirement of the consequences of our freedom. What happens to me happens through me, and I can neither affect myself with it nor revolt against it nor resign myself to it. Moreover everything which happens to me is *mine*. By this we must understand first of all that I am always equal to what happens to me *qua* man, for what happens to a man through other men and through himself can be only human. The most terrible situations of war, the worst tortures do not create a non-human state of things; there is no non-human situation. It is only through fear, flight, and recourse to magical types of conduct that I shall decide on the non-human, but this decision is human, and I shall carry the entire responsibility for it. But in addition the situation is *mine* because it is the image of my free choice of myself, and everything which it presents to me is *mine* in that this represents me and symbolizes me. Is it not I who decide the coefficient of adversity in things and even their unpredictability by deciding myself?

Thus there are no *accidents* in life; a community event which suddenly bursts forth and involves me in it does not come from the outside. If I am mobilized in a war, this war is *my* war; it is in my image and I deserve it. I deserve it first because I could always get out of it by suicide or by desertion; these ultimate possibles are those which must always be present for us when there is a question of envisaging a situation. For lack of getting out of it, I have *chosen* it. This can be due to inertia, to cowardice in the face of public opinion, or because I prefer certain other values to the value of the refusal to join in the war (the good opinion of my relatives, the honor of my family, *etc.*). Any way you look at it, it is a matter of choice. This choice will be repeated later on again and again without a break until the end of the war. Therefore we must agree with the statement by J. Romains, "In war there are no innocent victims." If therefore I have preferred war to death or to dishonor, everything takes place as if I bore the entire responsibility for this war. Of course others have declared it, and one might be tempted perhaps to consider me as a simple accomplice. But this notion of complicity has only a juridical sense, and it does not hold here. For it depended on me that for me and by me this war should not exist, and I have decided that it does exist. There was no compulsion here, for the compulsion could have got no hold on a freedom. I did not have any excuse; . . . the peculiar character of human-reality is that it is without excuse. Therefore it remains for me only to lay claim to this war.

But in addition the war is *mine* because by the sole fact that it arises in a situation which I cause to be and that I can discover it there only by engaging myself for or against it, I can no longer distinguish at present the choice which I make of myself from the choice which I make of the war. To live this war is to choose myself through it and to choose it through my choice of myself. There can be no question of considering it as "four years of vacation" or as a "reprieve," as a "recess," the essential part of my responsibilities being elsewhere in my married, family, or professional life. In this war which I have chosen I choose myself from day to day, and I make it mine by making myself. If it is going to be four empty years, then it is I who bear the responsiblity for this.

Finally, . . . each person is an absolute choice of self from the standpoint of a world of knowledges and of techniques which this choice both assumes and illumines; each person is an absolute up-surge at an absolute date and is perfectly unthinkable at another date. It is therefore a waste of time to ask what I should have been if this war had not broken out, for I have chosen myself as one of the possible meanings of the epoch which imperceptibly led to war. I am not distinct from this same epoch; I could not be transported to another epoch without contradiction. Thus *I am* this war which restricts and limits and makes comprehensible the period which preceded it. In this sense we may define more precisely the responsibility of the for-itself if to the earlier quoted statement, "There are no innocent victims," we added the words, "We have the war we deserve." Thus, totally free, undistinguishable from the period for which I have chosen to be the meaning, as profoundly responsible for the war as if I had myself declared it, unable to live without integrating it in *my* situation, engaging myself in it wholly and stamping it with my seal, I must be without remorse or regrets as I am without excuse; for from the instant of my upsurge into being, I carry the weight of the world by myself alone without anything or any person being able to lighten it.

Yet this responsibility is of a very particular type. Someone will say, "I did not ask to be born." This is a naïve way of throwing greater emphasis on our facticity. I am responsible for everything, in fact, except for my very responsibility, for I am not the foundation of my being. Therefore everything takes place as if I were compelled to be responsible. I am *abandoned* in the world, not in the sense that I might remain abandoned and passive in a hostile universe like a board floating on the water, but rather in the sense that I find myself suddenly alone and without help, engaged in a world for which I bear the whole responsibility without being able, whatever I do, to tear myself away from this responsiblity for an instant. For I am responsible for my very desire of fleeing responsibilities. To make myself passive in the world, to refuse to act upon things and upon Others is still to choose myself, and suicide is one mode among others of being-in-the-world. Yet I find an absolute responsibility for the fact that my facticity (here the fact of my birth) is directly inapprehensible and even inconceivable, for this fact of my birth never appears as a brute fact but always across a projective reconstruction of my for-itself. I am ashamed of being born or I am astonished at it or I rejoice over it, or in attempting to get rid of my life I affirm that I live and I assume this life as bad. Thus in a certain sense I *choose* being born. This choice itself is integrally affected with facticity since I am not able not to choose, but this facticity in turn will appear only in so far as I surpass it toward my ends. Thus facticity is everywhere but inapprehensible; I never encounter anything except my responsibility. That is why I can not ask, "*Why* was I born?" or curse the day of my birth or declare that I did not ask to be born, for these various attitudes toward my birth—i.e., toward the *fact* that I realize a presence in the world— are absolutely nothing else but ways of assuming this birth in full responsibility and of making it *mine*. Here again I encounter only myself and my projects so that finally my abandoment—i.e., my facticity—consists simply in the fact that I am condemned to be wholly responsible for myself. I am the being which *is* in such a way that in its being its being is in question. And this "is" of my being *is* as present and inapprehensible.

Under these conditions since every event in the world can be revealed to me only as an *opportunity* (an opportunity made use of, lacked, neglected, etc.) or better yet since everything which happens to us can be considered as a *chance* (i.e., can appear to us only as a way of realizing this being which is in question in our being) and since others as transcendences-transcended are themselves only *opportunities* and *chances,* the responsibility of the for-itself extends to the entire world as a peopled-world. It is precisely thus that the for-itself apprehends itself in anguish; that is, as a being which is neither the foundation of its own being nor of the Other's being nor of the in-itselfs which form the world, but a being which is compelled to decide the meaning of being—within it and everywhere outside of it. The one who realizes in anguish his condition as *being* thrown into a responsibility which extends to his very abandonment has no longer either remorse or regret or excuse; he is no longer anything but a freedom which perfectly reveals itself and whose being resides in this very revelation. But as we pointed out . . . , most of the time we flee anguish in bad faith.[30]

Sartre's position is the culmination of a full century of existentialist thought, beginning with Søren Kierkegaard in the 1840s. Kierkegaard too argued that one is responsible for whatever one is and that self-conscious choice and commitment were the factors that made a person most human. Sartre's very strong sense of responsibility goes even so far as to ascribe an act of choice to those situations in which we seem clearly to be only victims, for example, in war. "There are no accidents in life," he argues. It is always my choice as to how I shall act in and deal with a situation. One can always complain, "I didn't ask to be born," Sartre says, but this is only one of many ways we have of trying to avoid responsibility. Given the fact that we have been born, raised in certain conditions, and so forth, it is now entirely up to us as to what we shall make of all this. Instead of looking at the events of the world as problems and intrusions, Sartre ultimately says, we should learn to look at everything as an opportunity. Here is the optimistic note to his very strong defense of human freedom.

What all of these arguments demand is the following: In one's own case, in making your decision, there can be no appeal to determinism even if determinism is true. Whatever might be theoretically determined, in practice, you must choose. And since freedom is the key to our self-esteem and our pride in ourselves, some people will demand it at any cost.

The most brilliant, if bizarre, example of this existentialist demand is formulated by the strange character in Dostoyevski's short novel *Notes from the Underground.* The argument is simple. Any prediction can be thwarted as long as you know about it. If they say, "you'll do x"; do y. Now, suppose that determinism is true. In particular, suppose that psychological determinism is true and that its basic law is this: "people always act to their own advantage." Now, what does this have to do with the predictability of a person's actions? Absolutely nothing, if you are sufficiently determined not to be predictable. Accordingly, the character in this novel is, more than anything else, spiteful. His main concern is not being predictable, in proving his freedom even if it means making himself miserable. Now you might say that his spite itself is the determinant of his behavior, and of course it is. But the very point of the argument is that causes and explanations of any kind are simply beside the point. Let the underground man know what you expect him to do, and he'll do precisely the opposite. And if you predict he'll act spiteful, he'll be as agreeable as can be—just out of spite!

---

[30] Jean-Paul Sartre, *Being and Nothingness,* trans. Hazel E. Barnes (New York: Philosophical Library, 1956).

◆ "The Most Advantageous Advantage," by Fyodor Dostoyevski

I am a sick man . . . I am a spiteful man. I am an unpleasant man. I think my liver is diseased. However, I don't know beans about my disease, and I am not sure what is bothering me. I don't treat it and never have, though I respect medicine and doctors. Besides, I am extremely superstitious, let's say sufficiently so to respect medicine. (I am educated enough not to be superstitious, but I am.) No, I refuse to treat it out of spite. You probably will not understand that. Well, but *I* understand it. . . .

. . . Why, in the first place, when in all these thousands of years has there ever been a time when man has acted only for his own advantage? What is to be done with the millions of facts that bear witness that men, *knowingly*, that is, fully understanding their real advantages, have left them in the background and have rushed headlong on another path, to risk, to chance, compelled to this course by nobody and by nothing, but, as it were, precisely because they did not want the beaten track, and stubbornly, wilfully, went off on another difficult, absurd way seeking it almost in the darkness. After all, it means that this stubbornness and wilfulness were more pleasant to them than any advantage. Advantage! What is advantage? And will you take it upon yourself to define with perfect accuracy in exactly what the advantage of man consists of? And what if it so happens that a man's advantage *sometimes* not only may, but even must, consist exactly in his desiring under certain conditions what is harmful to himself and not what is advantageous. And if so, if there can be such a condition then the whole principle becomes worthless.

. . . The fact is, gentlemen, it seems that something that is dearer to almost every man than his greatest advantages must really exist, or (not to be illogical) there is one most advantageous advantage (the very one omitted of which we spoke just now) which is more important and more advantageous than all other advantages, for which, if necessary, a man is ready to act in opposition to all laws, that is, in opposition to reason, honor, peace, prosperity—in short, in opposition to all those wonderful and useful things if only he can attain that fundamental, most advantageous advantage which is dearer to him than all.

And what is that "advantageous advantage?" Nothing other than:

One's own free unfettered choice, one's own fancy, however wild it may be, one's own fancy worked up at times to frenzy. That is the "most advantageous advantage," which is always overlooked.[31]

---

[31] Fyodor Dostoyevski, *Notes from the Underground*, in *Notes from the Underground and The Grand Inquisitor*, trans. Ralph Matlaw (New York: E. P. Dutton, 1960).

Freedom in other words, is itself what we most demand, whatever the cost, whatever the difficulties, and whatever the arguments against it. Whatever else may be true, we will refuse to see ourselves as anything but free. For it is freedom that makes us human. Dostoyevski's picture of this radical, desperate, freedom is perhaps not a very uplifting one. A similar sentiment, however, can give a very joyous image of freedom. Here is a sample from Thich Nhat Hanh, a Vietnamese Buddhist monk. It is a prayer to say when turning on the television:

◆ "Turning on the Television," by Thich Nhat Hanh

> The mind is a television
> with thousands of channels.
> I choose a world that is tranquil and calm
> so that my joy will always be fresh.

Mind is consciousness. Consciousness includes the subject which knows and the object which is known. The two aspects, subject and object, depend on each other in order to exist. As the Vietnamese meditation master, Huong Hai, said, "In seeing matter, you are at the same time seeing mind. Without the arising of the object, the subject does not arise." When our mind is conscious of something, we *are* that thing. When we contemplate a snow-covered mountain, we are that mountain. When we watch a noisy film, we are that noisy film.

Our mind is like a television set with thousands of channels, and the channel we switch on is the channel we are at that moment. When we turn on anger, we are anger. When we turn on peace and joy, we are peace and joy. We have the ability to select the channel. *We are what we choose to be.* We can select any channel of the mind. Buddha is a channel, Mara is a channel, remembering is a channel, forgetting is a channel, calm is a channel, agitation is a channel. Changing from one state of being to another is as simple as the change from a channel showing a film to a channel playing music.

There are people who cannot tolerate peace and quiet, who are afraid of facing themselves, so they turn on the television in order to be preoccupied with it for a whole evening. In contemporary culture, people rarely like to be with themselves, and they frequently seek forgetfulness—downtown at the theater or other places of amusement. People rarely like to look deeply and compassionately at themselves. Young people in America watch television more than five hours per day, and they also have all sorts of electronic games to occupy them. Where will a culture in which people do not have the chance to face themselves or form real relationships with others lead us?

There are many interesting, instructive programs on television, and we can use the TV guide to select programs which encourage mindfulness. We should decide to watch only the programs we have selected and avoid becoming a victim of the television.[32]

SUMMARY AND CONCLUSION

To say that a person's act is free is to be able to ascribe responsibility. The defense of freedom therefore becomes extremely important to us. Our confidence in the universality of scientific explanations, however, seems to imply the thesis of determinism, which holds that every event has its sufficient natural cause. Human actions, as events, thus seem to be determined and thus not free. In this chapter, we have attempted to explore the various ways in which philosophers have attempted to reconcile these two vital beliefs—that at least some human acts are free and that science can ultimately (at least in principle) explain everything.

Some philosophers have defended determinism ("hard determinism") to the exclusion of freedom. Others have defended freedom to the exclusion of determinism ("indeterminists"). Most philosophers, however, have tried to defend both theses (and so are often called "compatibilists"). They have argued that determinism does not preclude freedom if an act flows from a person's decision or character ("soft determinists"), that we can be more and less susceptible to determinists (Frankfurt, King), or that even if determinism is true, we cannot help but think of ourselves as free (Kant and the existentialists).

GLOSSARY

antecedent conditions　those circumstances, states of affairs, or events that regularly precede and can be said to cause an event. The antecedent conditions of boiling water, for example, are the application of heat to water under normal atmospheric pressure, etc. A determinist would say that the antecedent conditions of a human action would be the state of his or her nervous system, a developed character (with personality traits), certain desires and beliefs, and the circumstances (or "stimulus") in which the action takes place.

cause　that which brings something about. On the hard determinist interpretation, a cause is an antecedent condition that, together with other antecedent conditions, is sufficient to make the occurrence of some event necessary, according to the laws of nature. On a weaker interpretation, a cause may simply be an event (or condition) that regularly precedes another event, and thus can be used to predict when the latter will oc-

[32]Thich Nhat Hanh, #47, "Turning on the Television," from *Present Moment, Wonderful Moment* (Berkeley: Parallax Press, 1990).

cur. (For example, if we say "a cause of forest fires is lightning," we mean "whenever lightning strikes a sufficiently dry forest, fire will occur.") (The concept of a "cause" is also discussed in Chapters 2, 3, and 4.)

compatibilism   the thesis that both determinism (on some interpretations) and free action can be true. Determinism does not rule out free action and the possibility of free action does not require that determinism be false. They are compatible positions.

compulsion   "being forced to do something." One acts from compulsion (or is compelled to act) when he or she could not have done otherwise. Some philosophers distinguish between *external* compulsions (for example, being pushed) and *internal* compulsions (for example, a neurotic obsession).

determinism   the thesis that every event has its sufficient natural cause(s), that every event is caused by its antecedent conditions, or that every event is predictable on the basis of such conditions.

fatalism   the thesis that certain events (or perhaps all events) are going to happen inevitably, regardless of what efforts we take to prevent them.

free will   among philosophers, a somewhat antiquated expression (as in "he did it of his own free will") that means that a person is capable of making decisions that are not determined by antecedent conditions. Of course there may be antecedent considerations, such as what a person wants, what a person believes, but free will means that such considerations never determine a person's decision. At most they "enter into the decision."

freedom   the idea that a human decision or action is a person's own responsibility and that praise and blame may be appropriately ascribed. The most extreme interpretation of "freedom" is the absence of any causes or determinations. Thus an indeterminist would say that an event was free if it had no causes; a libertarian would say that a human act was free if it was only self-caused, but not determined by anything else (including a person's character). Certain determinists, however ("soft determinists"), would say that an act is free if only it is "in character" and based upon a person's desires and personality. Most generally, we say that a person's act was free whether or not it was the result of a conscious decision and whether or not certain causes may have been involved, if we would say that he or she could have done otherwise.

Heisenberg Uncertainty Principle   an important principle of recent physics that demonstrates that we cannot know both the position and the momentum of certain subatomic particles, for in our attempts to know one, we make it impossible to know the other. This principle has been used to attack the very idea of "determinism" in its classical formulations, for determinism requires just the "certainty" of possible prediction that the Heisenberg Principle rejects.

indeterminism   the thesis that at least some events in the universe are not determined, are not caused by antecedent conditions, and may not be predictable.

predestination   the thesis (usually in a theological context) that every event is destined to happen (as in fatalism) whatever efforts we make to prevent it. The usual version is that God knows and perhaps causes all things to happen, and therefore everything must happen precisely as He knows (and possibly causes) it to happen.

prediction   to say that some event will happen before it happens. Determinism normally includes the thesis that if we know enough about the antecedent conditions of an event, we can always predict that it will occur. But prediction does not require determinism. One might predict the outcome of some state of affairs on the basis of statistical probabilities without knowing any antecedent conditions and perhaps even without assuming that there are any such conditions (in quantum physics, for example). And it is also possible that a person might predict the future on the basis of lucky guesses or E.S.P., again without necessarily accepting determinism.

responsibility   answerable or accountable for some act or event presumed to be within a person's control.

retrodiction   to say, on the basis of certain present evidence, what must have happened in the past. For example, the astronomer who looks at the present course of a comet can retrodict certain facts about its history. For the determinist, retrodiction is as important to his thesis as prediction.

soft determinism   a thesis that accepts determinism but claims that certain kinds of causes, namely, a person's character, still allow us to call his or her actions "free." The soft determinist is therefore a compatibilist, for he believes in both freedom and determinism.

sufficient cause   capable of bringing something about by itself (for example, four healthy people are sufficient to push a Volkswagen up a hill).

◆ BIBLIOGRAPHY AND FURTHER READING ◆

General anthologies are Sidney Hook, ed., *Determinism and Freedom in the Age of Modern Science* (New York: Macmillan, Collier, 1961); B. Berofsky, ed., *Free Will and Determinism* (New York: Harper & Row, 1966); and H. Morris, ed., *Freedom and Responsibility* (Stanford, CA: Stanford University Press, 1961). See also D. F. Pears, ed., *Freedom and the Will* (New York: St. Martin's Press, 1963).

9

ETHICS

"From now on I'm thinking only of me."
Major Danby replied indulgently with a superior smile,
"But Yossarian, suppose everyone felt that way?"
"Then I'd certainly be a——fool to feel any
other way, wouldn't I?"

JOSEPH HELLER, CATCH 22

What should we do? And what should we not do? What acts should we praise? What acts should we condemn and blame? These are questions of **ethics,** the concern for which Socrates was willing to give up his life. The core of ethics is **morality.** Morality is a set of fundamental rules that guide our actions; for example, they may forbid us to kill each other, encourage us to help each other, tell us not to lie, command us to keep our promises.

Most of the moral rules we accept and follow are ones that we have learned and adopted from parents, friends, teachers, and our own society. At times, though, others may challenge our moral rules, demanding that we defend them. Why should we help each other? Why shouldn't we ever cheat? What reasons can we give to defend one sexual ethic rather than another? New social and technological developments may also force us to reevaluate our morality. Since minorities and women have participated more and more in public debates on moral issues, we now find ourselves constantly confronted with the injustices of discrimination on the basis of race or sex. And the development of sophisticated life-sustaining devices has forced both physicians and philosophers to question whether it is always a moral duty to preserve life whenever possible.

Whenever we try to defend or criticize a moral belief we enter the realm of ethics. Ethics is not concerned with specific moral rules but with the foundation of morality and with providing general principles that will

651

both help us evaluate the validity of a moral rule and choose between different moralities (different sets of moral rules). For example, some ethical theorists called **utilitarians** hold that any good moral rule should promote the greatest happiness for the greatest number. Other theorists, for example, Aristotle and Kant, have argued that a good moral rule helps us act in the most rational way possible.

Ethics is also concerned with whether or not to take into account others' or our own interests and desires when deciding what we ought to do. For some ethicists, morality is tied to self-interest at least in an abstract way, and they argue that morality is the best way of satisfying everyone's interests. Other philosophers retain the rigid distinction between morality and self-interest and insist that obedience to morality is good for its own sake, or equivalent to being rational, or simply required in order to make us human. Finally some authors have argued that morality is only one among many sets of principles, which we may but need not choose to obey.

In this chapter, we will begin by raising some of the perennial problems of ethics, including the nature of morality and the problem of moral relativism. Then, we will address the familiar claim that the basis of all human behavior—moral behavior included—is selfishness, or **egoism.** Finally we will examine several different ethical theories, different ways of conceiving of morals and (or) justifying moral beliefs:

• The ethics of Aristotle, who based his view of morality on the concept of "virtue" and his idea that man is by nature a social and rational animal. Aristotle argues that being virtuous—controlling our feelings and acting rationally—enables us to become fully human. In this discussion, we have the opportunity to examine a moral system that is significantly different from our own, but still sufficiently similar for us to understand it.

• The view that morality is essentially a matter of feeling; David Hume and Jean-Jacques Rousseau are its representatives.

• The monumental ethical theory of Immanuel Kant, who insisted that morality is strictly a matter of practical reason, divorced from our personal interests and desires and based solely on universal principles or laws. Thus, according to Kant, we cannot justify the morality of our actions simply by appealing to the good consequences of our actions for others or ourselves. We will also consider subsequent efforts to support or criticize Kant's view.

• The ethical theories of the utilitarians, who argued (in contrast to Kant) that moral rules are merely rules of thumb for achieving the greatest good for the greatest number of people, and who thereby tried to reconcile the interests of each individual with the interests of everyone else.

• The radical theories of Nietzsche and the existentialists, who insist that, in an important sense, we choose our moralities and that this choice cannot be justified in any of the ways argued by other modern philosophers. For Nietzsche, at least, this view also included a retrospective appreciation of the morality of the ancient Greeks, and he argued that we should inject some of their conceptions into our own. We will also look at subsequent efforts to support the idea that morality is conventional—a matter of custom in certain sorts of societies.

• The "metaethical" theories of G. E. Moore and A. J. Ayer, and the implications of these for practical ethics.

A. MORALITY

Morality gives us the rules by which we live with other people. It sets limits to our desires and our actions. It tells us what is permitted and what is not. It gives us guiding principles for making decisions. It tells us what we ought and what we ought not to do. But what is this "morality" that sounds so impersonal and "above" us? It is important to begin with an appreciation for the metaphor, which so well characterizes moral rules. Nietzsche describes it this way: "A tablet of virtues hangs over every people."

The "tablet of virtues" is morality. The prototype of morality, in this view, is those ancient codes, carved in stone, with commands that are eternal and absolute, such as the two tablets inscribed by God, in front of Moses, which we call the Ten Commandments. And they are indeed *commandments.* "Thou shalt" and "Thou shalt not" is all they say. And this is the essence of morality. It consists of commands. These commands do not appeal to individual pleasures or desires. They do not make different demands on different individuals or societies. Quite to the contrary, they are absolute rules that tell us what we must or must not do, no matter who we are, no matter what we want and regardless of whether or not our interests will be served by the command. "Thou shalt not kill" means that even if you want to, even if you have the power to, and even if you can escape all punishment, you are absolutely forbidden to kill.

The image of morality as coming "from above" is appropriate. First, because moral laws are often said, and not only in our society, to come from God. Second, because we learn these laws from our parents, who literally "stand over us" and indoctrinate us with them through their shouts, commands, examples, threats, and gestures. Finally and most importantly, morality itself is "above" any given individual or individuals, whether it is canonized in the laws of society or not. Morality is not just another aid in getting us what we want; it is entirely concerned with right and wrong. And these considerations are "above" tampering by any individual, no matter how powerful, as if they have a life of their own.

This characteristic of morality as independent of individual desires and ambitions has led many people to characterize morality simply in terms of some absolute and independent agency. Most often, this absolute and independent agency is God. St. Augustine, for example, talks about morality in this way.

> . . . Unless you turn to Him and repay the existence that He gave you, you won't be "nothing"; you will be wretched. All things owe to God, first of all, what they are insofar as they are natures. Then, those who have received a will owe to Him whatever better thing they can will to be, and whatever they ought to be. No man is ever blamed for what he has not been given, but he is justly blamed if he has not done what he should have done; and if he has received free will and sufficient power, he stands under obligation. When a man does not do what he ought, God the Creator is not at fault. It is to His glory that a man suffers justly; and by blaming a man for not doing what he should have done, you are praising what he ought to do. You are praised for seeing what you ought to do, even though you see this only through God, who is immutable Truth.[1]

And St. Thomas Aquinas: ". . . It is apparent that things prescribed by divine law are right, not only because they are put forth by law, but also because they are in accord with nature." Or "Therefore by divine law precepts had to be given, so that each man would give his neighbor his due and would abstain from doing injuries to him."[2] And in the Bible: "When thou shalt harken—to the voice of the Lord thy God, to keep all his commandments, which I command thee this day, to do that which is right in the eyes of the Lord thy God."[3]

But whether or not one believes in God, it is clear that something further is needed to help us define morality. Even assuming that there is a God, we need a way of determining what His moral commands must be. One might say that He has given these commands to various individuals, but the fact is that different people seem to have very different ideas about the morality that God has given them. Some, for example, would say that it explicitly rules out abortion and infanticide. Others would argue that God does not rule these out but makes it clear that they are, like other forms of killing (a "holy war," for example), justifiable only in certain circumstances. And in view of such disagreements, we cannot simply appeal to God but must, for reasons that we can formulate and defend, define our morality for ourselves. There is the further question, which has often been debated, but was raised originally

---

[1] St. Augustine, *On Freedom* (New York: Bobbs-Merrill, 1956).
[2] St. Thomas Aquinas, *Summa Contra Gentiles*, Bk. III (New York: Doubleday, 1955).
[3] Deuteronomy 13:18.

by Plato, in his dialogue, *Euthyphro.* Should we follow God's laws just because they are His or rather, because His laws are good? If the latter, then we have to decide what is good in order to know that God is good. If the former, then one has to decide whether or not to believe in God precisely on the basis of whether we can accept those laws. Either way, we have to decide for ourselves what laws of morality we are willing to accept.

Similar considerations hold true for that familiar appeal to conscience in determining what we ought or ought not do. Even if one believes that conscience is God-given, the same problems emerge again. Should we follow our consciences just because "conscience tells us to"? Or do we follow our conscience just because we know that what our conscience commands is good. How does one decide whether a nagging thought is or is not the prompting of God? Probably on the basis of whether what it demands is good or not. (Thus one readily attributes to conscience the nagging reminder that one shouldn't have cheated an unsuspecting child, but one does not attribute to conscience the nagging thought that one could have gotten away with shoplifting if only one had had the daring to do it.) If one believes that conscience is simply the internalization of the moral teachings of one's parents and society, then the question takes an extra dimension: Should we accept or reject what we have been taught? Since our consciences often disagree, we must still decide whose conscience and which rules of conscience one ought to obey. Identifying morality with the promptings of one's conscience is both plausible and valuable, but philosophically it only moves the question one step back: How do we know what is, and what is not, the prompting of conscience? And is it always right to follow one's conscience? But these two questions are in fact just another way of asking what is moral. What should I do?

Morality is not just obedience—whether obedience to a king, a pope, the law, or one's conscience. Morality is doing what is *right,* whether or not it is commanded by any person or law and whether or not one "feels" it in one's conscience. One way of putting this—defended later by Immanuel Kant—is to say that morality involves **autonomy,** that is, the ability to think for oneself and decide, for oneself, what is right and what is wrong, whom to obey and whom to ignore, what to do and what not to do. The danger is that this conception of morality as autonomy seems to leave us without a place to learn morality in the first place. How do we learn to judge right and wrong but from our parents, our friends, our teachers, and our society and its models? But if we try to tie morality too closely to our upbringing and our society, then it looks as if there is no room for autonomy, no way in which we could disagree with our family or society, no way to criticize the way in which we have been raised. Furthermore, tying morality to particular societies raises an additional question, and that is whether morality (or morali*ties*) might not be relative to particular societies and cultures.

B. IS MORALITY RELATIVE?

Moralities, like lifestyles, vary from culture to culture and even from person to person. But while there is nothing surprising about the fact that lifestyles vary, there is a problem in the variation of moralities. Morality, by its very nature, is supposed to be a set of universal principles, principles that do not distinguish between cultures or peoples or lifestyles. If it is morally reprehensible to kill for fun, then it is morally reprehensible in every society, in every culture, for every lifestyle, and for every person, no matter who he or she is. And this will be true even if the society or person in question does not agree with that moral principle.

Aristotle, for example, discusses at length what he calls "the wicked man," who does evil because he believes in immoral principles and therefore acts without regret, unlike the person who acts badly from momentary weakness, force of circumstances, desperation, or misinformation. But on what grounds can one society or person claim that another society's or person's principles are immoral? How could European Christians, for example, be justified in criticizing the sexual morality of Polynesians in the South Pacific? The Polynesians were a separate society, with their own mores and principles that worked quite well for them, possibly even better in certain ways than the European customs worked in Europe. Yet European missionaries felt no hesitation whatever in condemning their sexual practices as "immoral." And similarly but more seriously, what gives us the right to criticize a culture across the world that still believes in genocide as a legitimate consequence of war or in torture as a way of keeping civil order? We surely feel that we have the right to speak up in such cases, but then we too are asserting the universality of our morality, extending it even to people who might explicitly reject our principles. How can we do this? What justifies such an extension?

The problem of **relativism** has become extremely controversial since the nineteenth century, when anthropologists began telling us of exotic societies with moralities so different from ours. In a sense, relativism has always been a threat to established morality, for even the Greeks came into contact with societies that were much different from theirs. (Thus their tendency to immediately label anything non-Greek "barbarian," so that they didn't have to consider the possibility of relativism.) Kant was the most vigorous opponent of relativism, for his conception of morality was such that if a human being was to count as rational at all, he or she had to agree to at least the basic principles of a universal morality. There were people and societies that did not, but that, according to Kant, only proved that they were less than rational (and therefore less than human as well). Today we tend to be more liberal in our acceptance of different styles of life, but few people would deny that at least some moral principles hold for every society. The principle that unnecessary cruelty is wrong, for example, would be such a principle, although people might well disagree about what is "cruel" and what is "unnecessary."

Philosophers generally distinguish two theses. First, there is the factual claim that different societies have different moralities. This is called **cultural relativism.** The difficult question is whether these different moralities are only different superficially or whether they are fundamentally different. For example, Eskimos of certain tribes kill their elders by leaving them to freeze on the ice; we consider that grossly immoral (we send most of our elders to frigid "old-age homes" instead). But the question of cultural relativity is whether this difference is merely the reflection of different interpretations of some basic moral principle (such as, don't kill anyone unless it is absolutely necessary for the survival of the rest) or whether it really is a wholly different morality. This is among the most controversial anthropological questions of our time. But philosophers are interested in a somewhat different question: Assuming that two moralities really are fundamentally different, is it possible that each is as correct as the other? The philosopher who says "yes" is an **ethical relativist.** And it is ethical relativism that will occupy us here.

In the following selection, the English-American philosopher Walter Stace presents the ethical relativist position and its traditional opponent, **ethical absolutism,** the view that there is only one correct morality. Stace's own answer to the problem is more of an absolutist solution; later in the same work he says that "happiness" is a universal and absolute value, and therefore cross-cultural evaluations are possible.

◆on Ethical Relativism, by Walter Stace

There is an opinion widely current nowadays in philosophical circles which passes under the name of "ethical relativity." Exactly what this phrase means or implies is certainly far from clear. But unquestionably it stands as a label for the opinions of a group of ethical philosophers whose position is roughly on the extreme left wing among the moral theorizers of the day. And perhaps one may best understand it by placing it in contrast with the opposite kind of extreme view against which, undoubtedly, it has arisen as a protest. For among moral philosophers one may clearly distinguish a left and a right wing. Those of the left wing are the ethical relativists. They are the revolutionaries, the clever young men, the up to date. Those of the right wing we may call the ethical absolutists. They are the conservatives and the old-fashioned.

According to the absolutists there is but one eternally true and valid moral code. This moral code applies with rigid impartiality to all men. What is a duty for me must likewise be a duty for you. And this will be true whether you are an Englishman, a Chinaman, or a Hottentot. If cannibalism is an abomination in England or America, it is an abomination in central Africa, notwithstanding that the African may think otherwise. The fact that he sees nothing wrong in his cannibal practices does not make them for him morally right. They are as much contrary to morality for him as they are for us. The only difference is that he is an ignorant savage who does not know this. There is not one law for one man or race of men, another for another. There is not one moral standard for Europeans, another for Indians, another for Chinese. There is but one law, one standard, one morality, for all men. And this standard, this law, is absolute and unvarying.

Moreover, as the one moral law extends its dominion over all the corners of the earth, so too it is not limited in its application by any considerations of time or period. That which is right now was right in the centuries of Greece and Rome, nay, in the very ages of the cave man. That which is evil now was evil then. If slavery is morally wicked today, it was morally wicked among the ancient Athenians, notwithstanding that their greatest men accepted it as a necessary condition of human society. Their opinion did not make slavery a moral good for them. It only showed that they were, in spite of their otherwise noble conceptions, ignorant of what is truly right and good in this matter.

The ethical absolutist recognizes as a fact that moral customs and moral ideas differ from country to country and from age to age. This indeed seems manifest and not to be disputed. We think slavery morally wrong, the Greeks thought it morally unobjectionable. The inhabitants of New Guinea certainly have very different moral ideas from ours. But the fact that the Greeks or the inhabitants of New Guinea think something right does not make it right, even for them. Nor does the fact that we think the same things wrong make them wrong. They are *in themselves* either right or wrong. What we have to do is to discover which they are. What anyone thinks makes no difference. It is here just as it is in matters of physical science. We believe the earth to be a globe. Our ancestors may have thought it flat. This does not show that it *was* flat, and is *now* a globe. What it shows is that men having in other ages been ignorant about the shape of the earth have now learned the truth. So if the Greeks thought slavery morally legitimate, this does not indicate that it was for them and in that age morally legitimate, but rather that they were ignorant of the truth of the matter.

· · · · · · · · · ·

Now ethical absolutism was, in its central ideas, the product of Christian theology. The connection is not difficult to detect. For morality has been conceived, during the Christian dispensation, as issuing from the will of God. That indeed was its single and all-sufficient source. There would be no point, for the naïve believer in the faith, in the philosopher's questions regarding the foundations of morality and the basis of moral obligation. Even to ask such questions is a mark of incipient religious scepticism. For the true believer the author of the moral law is God. What pleases God, what God commands—that is the definition of right. What displeases God, what he forbids—that is the definition of wrong. Now there is, for the Christian monotheist, only one God ruling over the entire universe. And this God is rational, self-consistent. He does not act upon whims. Consequently his will and his commands must be the same everywhere. They will be unvarying for all peoples and in all ages. If the heathen have other moral ideas than ours—inferior ideas—that can only be because they live in ignorance of the true God. If they knew God and his commands, their ethical precepts would be the same as ours.

· · · · · · · · · ·

This explains why ethical absolutism, until very recently, was not only believed by philosophers but *taken for granted without any argument*. The ideas of philosophers, like the ideas of everyone else, are largely moulded by the civilizations in which they live. Their philosophies are largely attempts to state in abstract terms and in self-consistent language the stock of ideas which they have breathed in from the atmosphere of their social environment. This accounts for the large number of so-called "unrecognized presuppositions" with which systems of philosophy always abound. These presuppositions are simply the ideas which the authors of the systems have breathed in with the intellectual atmospheres by which they happen to be surrounded—which they have taken over therefore as a matter of course, without argument, without criticism, without even a suspicion that they might be false. . . .

We can now turn to the consideration of ethical relativity which is the proper subject of this chapter. The revolt of the relativists against absolutism is, I believe, part and parcel of the general revolutionary tendency of our times. In particular it is a result of the decay of belief in the dogmas of orthodox religion. Belief in absolutism was supported, as we have seen, by belief in Christian monotheism. And now that, in an age of widespread religious scepticism, that support is withdrawn, absolutism tends to collapse. Revolutionary movements are as a rule, at any rate in their first onset, purely negative. They attack and destroy. And ethical relativity is, in its essence, a purely negative creed. It is simply a denial of ethical absolutism. That is why the best way of explaining it is to begin by explaining ethical absolutism. If we understand that what the latter asserts the former denies, then we understand ethical relativity.

Any ethical position which denies that there is a single moral standard which is equally applicable to all men at all times may fairly be called a species of ethical relativity. There is not, the relativist asserts, merely one moral law, one code, one standard. There are many moral laws, codes, standards. What morality ordains in one place or age may be quite different from what morality ordains in another place or age. The moral code of Chinamen is quite different from that of Europeans, that of African savages quite different from both. Any morality, therefore, is relative to the age, the place, and the circumstances in which it is found. It is in no sense absolute.

This does not mean merely—as one might at first sight be inclined to suppose—that the very same kind of action which is *thought* right in one country and period may be *thought* wrong in another. This would be a mere platitude, the truth of which everyone would have to admit. Even the absolutist would admit this—would even wish to emphasize it—since he is well aware that different peoples have different sets of moral ideas, and his whole point is that some of these sets of ideas are false. What the relativist means to assert is, not this platitude, but that the very same kind of action which *is* right in one country and period may *be* wrong in another. And this, far from being a platitude, is a very startling assertion.

It is very important to grasp thoroughly the difference between the two ideas. For there is reason to think that many minds tend to find ethical relativity attractive because they fail to keep them clearly apart. It is so very obvious that moral ideas differ from country to country and from age to age. And it is so very easy, if you are mentally lazy, to suppose that to say this means the same as to say that no universal moral standard exists—or in other words that it implies ethical relativity. We fail to see that the word "standard" is used in two different senses. It is perfectly true that, in one sense, there are many variable moral standards. We speak of judging a man by the standard of his time. And this implies that different times have different standards. And this, of course, is quite true. But when the word "standard" is used in this sense it means simply the set of moral ideas current during the period in question. It means what people *think* right, whether as a matter of fact it *is* right or not. On the other hand when the absolutist asserts that there exists a single universal moral "standard," he is not using the word in this sense at all. He means by "standard" what *is* right as distinct from what people merely think right. His point is that although what people think right varies in different countries and periods, yet what actually is right is everywhere and always the same. And it follows that when the ethical relativist disputes the position of the absolutist and denies that any universal moral standard exists he too means by "standard" what actually is right. But it is exceedingly easy, if we are not careful, to slip loosely from using the word in the first sense to using it in the second sense; and to suppose that the variability of moral beliefs is the same thing as the variability of what really is moral. And unless we keep the two senses of the word "standard" distinct, we are likely to think the creed of ethical relativity much more plausible than it actually is.

The genuine relativist, then, does not merely mean that China-men may think right what Frenchmen think wrong. He means that what *is* wrong for the Frenchman may *be* right for the Chinaman. And if one enquires how, in those circumstances, one is to know what actually is right in China or in France, the answer comes quite glibly. What is right in China is the same as what people think right in China; and what is right in France is the same as what people think right in France. So that, if you want to know what is moral in any particular country or age all you have to do is to ascertain what are the moral ideas current in that age or country. Those ideas are, *for that age or country,* right. Thus what is morally right is identified with what is thought to be morally right, and the distinction which we made above between these two is sim-ply denied. To put the same thing in another way, it is denied that there can be or ought to be any distinction between the two senses of the word "standard." There is only one kind of standard of right and wrong, namely, the moral ideas current in any particular age or country.[4]

One of the things about which we feel the strongest call of conscience or morality is sex. Judgments about "what's right" and "what's wrong" seem to accompany all our beliefs about sex and sexual relationships. Sexual morality would seem to be a "natural" candidate for absolutism in morality: There are only two sexes, after all, no matter what culture one considers. Surely, one might think, there are "natural" standards for how members of the sexes should behave toward one another. There are men and women in every culture: Surely, one might think, every culture distinguishes its proper moral treatment in roughly the same way.

The American anthropologist Margaret Mead made an extensive cross-cultural study of sex distinctions and sexual morality in her famous work, *Sex and Temperament.* There she suggests that distinc-tions between the sexes themselves are culturally relative. Contrary to the absolutist view, she argues that sex distinctions are created by and dependent upon, the social mores of particular cultures.

◆*Sex and Temperament,* by Margaret Mead

The material suggests that we may say that many, if not all, of the personality traits which we have called masculine or feminine are as lightly linked to sex as are the clothing, the manners, and the form of headdress that a society at a given time period assigns

[4]Walter Stace, *The Concept of Morals* (New York: Macmillan, 1937).

to either sex when we consider the behaviour of the typical Arapesh man or woman as contrasted with the behaviour of the typical Mundugumor man or woman, the evidence is overwhelmingly in favour of the strength of social conditioning. In no other way can we account for the almost complete uniformity with which Arapesh children develop into contented, passive, secure persons, while Mundugumor children develop as characteristically into violent, aggressive, insecure persons. Only to the impact of the whole of the integrated culture upon the growing child can we lay the formation of the contrasting types. There is no other explanation of race, or diet, or selection that can be adduced to explain them. We are forced to conclude that human nature is almost unbelievably malleable, responding accurately and contrastingly to contrasting cultural conditions. The differences between individuals who are members of different cultures, like the differences between individuals within a culture, are almost entirely to be laid to differences in conditioning, especially during early childhood, and the form of this conditioning is culturally determined. Standardized personality differences between the sexes are of this order, cultural creations to which each generation, male and female, is trained to conform. There remains, however, the problem of the origin of these socially standardized differences.

While the basic importance of social conditioning is still imperfectly recognized—not only in lay thought, but even by the scientist specifically concerned with such matters—to go beyond it and consider the possible influence of variations in hereditary equipment is a hazardous matter. The following pages will read very differently to one who has made a part of his thinking a recognition of the whole amazing mechanism of cultural conditioning—who has really accepted the fact that the same infant could be developed into a full participant in any one of these three cultures—than they will read to one who still believes that the minutiae of cultural behaviour are carried in the individual germ-plasm. If it is said, therefore, that when we have grasped the full significance of the malleability of the human organism and the preponderant importance of cultural conditioning, there are still further problems to solve, it must be remembered that these problems come *after* such a comprehension of the force of conditioning; they cannot precede it. The forces that make children born among the Arapesh grow up into typical Arapesh personalities are entirely social, and any discussion of the variations which do occur must be looked at against this social background.

With this warning firmly in mind, we can ask a further question. Granting the malleability of human nature, whence arise the differences between the standardized personalities that different cultures decree for all of their members, or which one culture decrees for the members of one sex as contrasted with the members of the opposite sex? If such differences are culturally created, as this material would most strongly suggest that they are, if the new-born child can be shaped with equal ease into an unaggressive Arapesh or an aggressive Mundugumor, why do these striking contrasts occur at all? If the clues to the different personalities decreed for men and women in Tchambuli do not lie in the physical constitution of the two sexes—an assumption that we must reject both for the Tchambuli and for our own society—where can we find the clues upon which the Tchambuli, the Arapesh, the Mundugumor, have built? Cultures are manmade, they are built of human materials; they are diverse but comparable structures within which human beings can attain full human stature. Upon what have they built their diversities?

We recognize that a homogeneous culture committed in all of its gravest institutions and slight usages to a co-operative unaggressive course can bend every child to that emphasis, some to a perfect accord with it, the majority to an easy acceptance, while only a few deviants fail to receive the cultural imprint. To consider such traits as aggressiveness or passivity to be sex-linked is not possible in the light of the facts. Have such traits, then, as aggressiveness or passivity, pride or humility, objectivity or a preoccupation with personal relationships, an easy response to the needs of the young and the weak or a hostility to the young and the weak, a tendency to initiate sex-relations or merely to respond to the dictates of a situation or another person's advances—have these traits any basis in temperament at all? Are they potentialities of all human temperaments that can be developed by different kinds of social conditioning and which will not appear if the necessary conditioning is absent?[5]

C. EGOISM AND ALTRUISM

Most moral rules, whether about sexuality or otherwise, are ones that enjoin us to take into account the interests, feelings, or welfare of other people. The commands not to lie, not to kill, and not to steal, as well as the commands to keep our promises, treat others fairly, and be generous are all commands that concern our relations to other persons. (There can, of course, be moral rules that require us to take into account our own interests; for example, the prohibition of suicide or, as Kant thought, the obligation to develop our talents.)

One of the important assumptions of any morality, then, is that it is possible for us to act in the interests of other people. In addition, morality assumes that it is possible for us to do so *because* we are concerned about others' welfare or because we recognize that we ought to be. Someone who refrains from cheating, for example, simply because he or she is afraid of being caught acts purely self-interestedly; and we would not think this person is morally praiseworthy. Again, a person who visits

[5]Margaret Mead, *Sex and Temperament* (New York: Mentor, 1958 [1935]).

a dying relative in the hospital because he or she wants to ensure a substantial inheritance is not acting morally. Only if actions are motivated by a concern for others' interests do we call them truly moral actions.

There is an important theory, though, that denies that we can be motivated simply by a concern for others. This is psychological egoism. **Psychological egoism** is the thesis that everyone, in fact, acts for his or her own advantage, and the only reason why people act respectfully or kindly toward each other is that that too, for one reason or another, is to their advantage. It might be fear of punishment that makes them act "correctly." Some have "ulterior motives"; that is, they expect other things later on, perhaps a favor in return or reward in heaven after they die, or they are trying to avoid guilt or want a feeling of self-satisfaction. In popular language, the egoist position is often called **selfishness.**

One should be careful, though, to distinguish psychological egoism from ethical egoism. Psychological egoism asserts that our psychology is such that we cannot help but act in our own interests. In contrast, **ethical egoism** claims that even though we can act in others' interests because we are concerned for others, we *ought* always to act in our own interest. One of the most widely read contemporary ethical egoists is the late Ayn Rand, who wrote of "the virtue of selfishness."

It is psychological, not ethical, egoism that challenges the very possibility of any morality. One of Socrates' opponents in *The Republic* states the psychological egoist's view with brutal clarity:

◆**from *The Republic*,
by Plato**

They say that to do wrong is naturally good, to be wronged is bad, but the suffering of injury so far exceeds in badness the good of inflicting it that when men have done wrong to each other and suffered it, and have had a taste of both, those who are unable to avoid the latter and practise the former decide that it is profitable to come to an agreement with each other neither to inflict injury nor to suffer it. As a result they begin to make laws and covenants, and the law's command they call lawful and just. This, they say, is the origin and essence of justice; it stands between the best and the worst, the best being to do wrong without paying the penalty and the worst to be wronged without the power of revenge. The just then is a mean between two extremes; it is welcomed and honoured because of men's lack of the power to do wrong. The man who has that power, the real man, would not make a compact with anyone not to inflict injury or suffer it. For him that would be madness. This then, Socrates, is, according to their argument, the nature and origin of justice.

Even those who practise justice do so against their will because they lack the power to do wrong. This we could realize very clearly if we imagined ourselves granting to both the just and the unjust the freedom to do whatever they liked. We could then follow both of them and observe where their desires led them, and we would catch the just man redhanded travelling the same road as the unjust. The reason is the desire for undue gain which every organism by nature pursues as a good, but the law forcibly sidetracks him to honour equality. The freedom I just mentioned would most easily occur if these men had the power which they say the ancestor of the Lydian Gyges possessed. The story is that he was a shepherd in the service of the ruler of Lydia. There was a violent rainstorm and an earthquake which broke open the ground and created a chasm at the place where he was tending sheep. Seeing this and marvelling, he went down into it. He saw, besides many other wonders of which we are told, a hollow bronze horse. There were window-like openings in it; he climbed through them and caught sight of a corpse which seemed of more than human stature, wearing nothing but a ring of gold on its finger. This ring the shepherd put on and came out. He arrived at the usual monthly meeting which reported to the king on the state of the flocks, wearing the ring. As he was sitting among the others he happened to twist the hoop of the ring towards himself, to the inside of his hand, and as he did this he became invisible to those sitting near him and they went on talking as if he had gone. He marvelled at this and, fingering the ring, he turned the hoop outward again and became visible. Perceiving this he tested whether the ring had this power and so it happened: if he turned the hoop inwards he became invisible, but was visible when he turned it outwards. When he realized this, he at once arranged to become one of the messengers to the king. He went, committed adultery with the king's wife, attacked the king with her help, killed him, and took over the kingdom.

Now if there were two such rings, one worn by the just man, the other by the unjust, no one, as these people think, would be so incorruptible that he would stay on the path of justice or bring himself to keep away from other people's property and not touch it, when he could with impunity take whatever he wanted from the market, go into houses and have sexual relations with anyone he wanted, kill anyone, free all those he wished from prison, and do the other things which would make him like a god among men. His actions would be in no way different from those of the other and they would both follow the same path. This, some would say, is a great proof that no one is just willingly but under compulsion, so that justice is not one's private good, since wherever either thought he could do wrong with impunity he would do so. Every man believes that injustice is much more profitable to himself than justice, and any exponent of this argument will say that he is right. The man who did not wish to do wrong with that opportunity, and did not touch other people's property, would be thought by those who knew it to be very foolish and miserable. They would praise him in public, thus deceiving one another, for fear of being wronged. So much for my second topic.[6]

Both egoist positions are contrasted with what is usually called **altruism,** that is, acting for the sake of other people's interests. There are degrees of altruism. One may be altruistic because one acts morally, because he or she recognizes an obligation to other people. Or one may be altruistic in actually taking another person's interests as important or even more important than one's own interests, such as one often finds between lovers or brothers and sisters. Altruism can also be divided into two distinct theses, although these are not so often distinguished. There is *psychological altruism*, which says that people "naturally" act for each other's sakes. (We shall see this thesis defended by several important philosophers in later sections.) It has rarely been argued, however, that people are compelled to act altruistically. Thus psychological egoism is usually defended for all cases; psychological altruism, in contrast, is only defended for some cases. *Ethical altruism*, on the other hand, says that people ought to act with each other's interests in mind. This is, of course, a basic statement of morality, best summarized in the so-called **Golden Rule:** "Do unto others as you would have them do unto you." (We shall see a modern version of this ancient teaching in the philosophy of Kant.)

The most familiar and most difficult question is about psychological egoism: Is it true that people only act for their own self-interest? A famous story about Abraham Lincoln is an apt illustration of the thesis. As he was arguing the psychological egoist position with a friend, his coach was passing a mud slide where a mother pig was squealing as her piglets were drowning. Lincoln stopped the coach, saved the piglets, then moved on. His friend asked him whether that wasn't a clear case of altruism. Lincoln replied: "Why that was the very essence of selfishness. I should have had no peace of mind all day had I gone on and left that suffering old sow worrying over those piglets. I did it to get peace of mind, don't you see?"[7]

There are many actions that are based upon self-interest and are "selfish" without any question. The question is, are there any actions that are not based on self-interest? Lincoln's response is an excellent example because it would seem as if his action is not for selfish reasons at all. Yet, according to him, there was a selfish reason behind his actions: his own sense of satisfaction and "peace of mind." Could this be true of all our actions?

The arguments that are still considered to be the most powerful and definitive against psychological egoism were formulated as sermons by

[6]Plato, *The Republic*, Bk. II, trans. G. M. A. Grube (Indianapolis, IN: Hackett, 1974).
[7]Quoted in F. Sharp, *Ethics* (New York: Appleton-Century-Crofts, 1928).

an English bishop, Joseph Butler. Bishop Butler argued that such reasoning as Lincoln's turned on a number of fallacies. Butler begins by accepting the distinction between "private good and a person's own preservation and happiness" and "respect to society and the promotion of public good and the happiness of society." But then he insists that these are not, as the egoists argue, always in conflict and fighting against each other. To the contrary, they are almost always in perfect harmony.

◆Against Egoism, by Joseph Butler

From this review and comparison of the nature of man as respecting self and as respecting society, it will plainly appear that there are as real and the same kind of indications in human nature that we were made for society and to do good to our fellow creatures, as that we were intended to take care of our own life and health and private good; and that the same objections lie against one of these assertions as against the other.

First, there is a natural principle of *benevolence* in man, which is in some degree to *society* what *self-love* is to the *individual.* And if there be in mankind any disposition to friendship; if there be any such thing as compassion, for compassion is momentary love; if there be any such thing as the paternal or filial affections; if there be any affection in human nature the object and end of which is the good of another—this is itself benevolence or the love of another. Be it ever so short, be it in ever so low a degree, or ever so unhappily confined, it proves the assertion and points out what we were designed for, as really as though it were in a higher degree and more extensive. I must however remind you that though benevolence and self-love are different, though the former tends most directly to public good, and the latter to private, yet they are so perfectly coincident that the greatest satisfactions to ourselves depend upon our having benevolence in a due degree, and that self-love is one chief security of our right behavior toward society. It may be added that their mutual coinciding, so that we can scarce promote one without the other, is equally a proof that we were made for both.

· · · · · · · · · ·

Secondly, this will further appear, from observing that the *several passions and affections,* which are distinct both from benevolence and self-love, do in general contribute and lead us to *public good* as really as to *private.* It might be thought too minute and particular, and would carry us too great a length, to distinguish between and compare together the several passions or appetites distinct from benevolence, whose primary use and intention is the security and good of society; and the passions distinct from self-love, whose primary intention and design is the security and good of the individual. It is enough to the present argument that desire of esteem from others, contempt and esteem of them, love of society as distinct from affection to the good of it, indignation against successful vice—that these are public affections or passions, have an immediate respect to others, naturally lead us to regulate our behavior in such a manner as will be of service to our fellow creatures. If any or all of these may be considered likewise as private affections, as tending to private good, this does not hinder them from being public affections, too, or destroy the good influence of them upon society, and their tendency to public good. It may be added that as persons without any conviction from reason of the desirableness of life would yet of course preserve it merely from the appetite of hunger, so by acting merely from regard (suppose) to reputation, without any consideration of the good of others, men often contribute to public good. In both these instances they are plainly instruments in the hands of another, in the hands of Providence, to carry on ends, the preservation of the individual and good of society, which they themselves have not in their view or intention. The sum is, men have various appetites, passions, and particular affections, quite distinct both from self-love and from benevolence—all of these have a tendency to promote both public and private good, and may be considered as respecting others and ourselves equally and in common; but some of them seem most immediately to respect others, or tend to public good, others of them most immediately to respect self, or tend to private good; as the former are not benevolence, so the latter are not self-love; neither sort are instances of our love either to ourselves or others, but only instances of our Maker's care and love both of the individual and the species, and proofs that He intended we should be instruments of good to each other, as well as that we should be so to ourselves.

Thirdly, there is a principle of reflection in men by which they distinguish between, approve and disapprove, their own actions. We are plainly constituted such sort of creatures as to reflect upon our own nature. The mind can take a view of what passes within itself, its propensions, aversions, passions, affections, as respecting such objects and in such degrees, and of the several actions consequent thereupon. In this survey it approves of one, disapproves of another, and toward a third is affected in neither of these ways, but is quite indifferent. This principle in man by which he approves or disapproves his heart, temper, and actions, is conscience. . . . That this faculty tends to restrain men from doing mischief to each other, and leads them to do good, is too manifest to need being insisted upon. Thus a parent has the affection of love to his children; this leads him to take care of, to educate, to make due provision for them; the natural affection leads to this, but the reflection that it is his proper business, what belongs to him, that it is right and commendable so to do—this added to the affection becomes a much more settled principle and carries him on through more labor and difficulties for the sake of his children than he would undergo from that affection alone, if he thought it, and the course of action it led to, either indifferent or criminal. This indeed is impossible, to do that which is good and not to approve of it; for which reason they are frequently not considered as distinct, though they really are, for men often approve of the actions of others which they will not imitate, and likewise do that which they approve not. It cannot possibly be denied that there is this principle of reflection or conscience in human nature. Suppose a man to relieve an innocent person in great distress, suppose the same man afterwards, in the fury of anger, to do the greatest mischief to a person who had given no just cause of offense; to aggravate the injury, add the circumstances of former friendship and obligation from the injured person, let the man who is supposed to have done these two different actions coolly reflect upon them afterwards, without regard to their consequences to himself; to assert that any common man would be affected in the same way toward these different actions, that he would make no distinction between them, but approve or disapprove them equally, is too glaring a falsity to need being confuted. There is therefore this principle of reflection or conscience in mankind. . . .

If it be said that there are persons in the world who are in great measure without the natural affections toward their fellow creatures, there are likewise instances of persons without the common natural affections to themselves; but the nature of man is not to be judged of by either of these, but by what appears in the common world, in the bulk of mankind.[8]

In short, Butler argues that merely acting on one's own desires does not make an action selfish, for all actions are, in some sense, based on our desires, but at least some of those desires are desires to serve someone else's interests. Thus the "object" of desire is what makes an act selfish or unselfish, not merely the fact that one's own desire is acted upon. Nor can simply acting with some benefit to oneself make an action selfish, for even if we agreed that an act gives us some benefit (for example, peace of mind), it may still be the case that most of the benefit is for someone else. Even if peace of mind typically follows virtuous actions, that does not show that our motivation is selfish. The satisfaction that accompanies good acts is itself not the motivation of the act. Here is the answer to Lincoln. His act was, despite his philosophical claims, an altruistic one; his satisfaction was not the motive of the act but only its consequence.

[8]Bishop Joseph Butler, *Five Sermons* (New York: Bobbs-Merrill, 1950).

D. MORALITY AS VIRTUE: ARISTOTLE

Aristotle's *Ethics* (properly called *The Nicomachean Ethics*) is the best systematic guide to ancient Greek moral and ethical thinking. The significant feature of Greek ethics is its stress on being virtuous as opposed to merely following moral rules. Aristotle's concept of virtue is based on a very special conception of man as a rational being. Virtue, accordingly, is rational activity, activity in accordance with a rational principle. Having defined virtue in this way, Aristotle can then defend, for example, courage as a virtue by showing that the courageous man is more rational than the coward.

Aristotle arrives at his conception of man as an essentially rational being by asking what "the natural good for man" is. This, he argues, will be discovered by finding what all men desire "for its own sake" and not "for the sake of anything else."

◆**From *The Nicomachean Ethics*,**
by Aristotle

Every art and every kind of inquiry, and likewise every act and purpose, seems to aim at some good; and so it has been well said that the good is that at which everything aims. But a difference is observable among these aims or ends. What is aimed at is sometimes the exercise of a faculty, sometimes a certain result beyond that exercise. And where there is an end beyond that act, there the result is better than the exercise of the faculty. Now since there are many kinds of actions and many arts and sciences, it follows that there are many ends also; *e.g.* health is the end of medicine, ships of shipbuilding, victory of the art of war, and wealth of economy. But when several of these are subordinated to some one art or science,—as the making of bridles and other trappings to the art of horsemanship, and this in turn, along with all else that the soldier does, to the art of war, and so on,—then the end of the master art is always more desired than the end of the subordinate arts, since these are pursued for its sake. And this is equally true whether the end in view be the mere exercise of a faculty or something beyond that, as in the above instances.

If then in what we do there be some end which we wish for on its own account, choosing all the others as means to this, but not every end without exception as a means to something else (for so we should go on *ad infinitum*, and desire would be left void and objectless),—this evidently will be the good or the best of all things.[9]

[9]Aristotle, *The Nicomachean Ethics*, translated by F. H. Peters, 8th edition (1901). All subsequent quotations from Aristotle are from this edition.

We see here the same logical strategy that Aristotle used in Chapter 1: the idea that every act is for the sake of something else (we want to earn a dollar to buy ourselves some food, and we want that to satisfy our hunger). But since there can be no "infinite regress," there must be some ultimate end. Aristotle examines two popular conceptions of this ultimate end that is the natural good for man: pleasure and success. He rejects both because neither pleasure nor success is desired for its own sake. Rather, happiness is what all men desire for its own sake and is the natural good for man.

> . . . It seems that men not unreasonably take their notions of the good or happiness from the lives actually led, and that the masses who are the least refined suppose it to be pleasure, which is the reason why they aim at nothing higher than the life of enjoyment. For the most conspicuous kinds of life are three: this life of enjoyment, the life of the statesman, and, thirdly, the contemplative life. The mass of men show themselves utterly slavish in their preference for the life of brute beasts, but their views receive consideration because many of those in high places have the tastes of Sardanapalus. Men of refinement with a practical turn prefer honour; for I suppose we may say that honour is the aim of the statesman's life. But this seems too superficial to be the good we are seeking: for it appears to depend upon those who give rather than upon those who receive it; while we have a presentiment that the good is something that is peculiarly a man's own and can scarce be taken away from him. Moreover, these men seem to pursue honour in order that they may be assured of their own excellence,—at least, they wish to be honoured by men of sense, and by those who know them, and on the ground of their virtue or excellence. It is plain, then, that in their view, at any rate, virtue or excellence is better than honour; and perhaps we should take this to be the end of the statesman's life, rather than honour. But virtue or excellence also appears too incomplete to be what we want; for it seems that a man might have virtue and yet be asleep or be inactive all his life, and, moreover, might meet with the greatest disasters and misfortunes; and no one would maintain that such a man is happy, except for argument's sake. But we will not dwell on these matters now, for they are sufficiently discussed in the popular treatises. The third kind of life is the life of contemplation: we will treat of it further on. As for the money-making life, it is something quite contrary to nature; and wealth evidently is not the good of which we are in search, for it is merely useful as a means to something else. So we might rather take pleasure and virtue or excellence to be ends than wealth; for they are chosen on their own account. But it seems that not even they are the end, though much breath has been wasted in attempts to show that they are.
> . . . Let us return once more to the question, what this good can be of which we are in search. It seems to be different in different

kinds of action and in different arts,—one thing in medicine and another in war, and so on. What then is the good in each of these cases? Surely that for the sake of which all else is done. And that in medicine is health, in war is victory, in building is a house,—a different thing in each different case, but always, in whatever we do and in whatever we choose, the end. For it is always for the sake of the end that all else is done. If then there be one end of all that man does, this end will be the realizable good,—or these ends, if there be more than one.

By this generalization our argument is brought to the same point as before. This point we must try to explain more clearly. We see that there are many ends. But some of these are chosen only as means, as wealth, flutes, and the whole class of instruments. And so it is plain that not all ends are final. But the best of all things must, we conceive, be something final. If then there be only one final end, this will be what we are seeking,—or if there be more than one, then the most final of them. Now that which is pursued as an end in itself is more final than that which is pursued as means to something else, and that which is never chosen as means than that which is chosen both as an end in itself and as means, and that is strictly final which is always chosen as an end in itself and never as means.

Happiness seems more than anything else to answer to this description: for we always choose it for itself, and never for the sake of something else; while honour and pleasure and reason, and all virtue or excellence, we choose partly indeed for themselves (for, apart from any result, we should choose each of them), but partly also for the sake of happiness, supposing that they will help to make us happy. But no one chooses happiness for the sake of these things, or as a means to anything else at all. We seem to be led to the same conclusion when we start from the notion of self-sufficiency. The final good is thought to be self-sufficing [or all-sufficing]. In applying this term we do not regard a man as an individual leading a solitary life, but we also take account of parents, children, wife, and, in short, friends and fellow-citizens generally, since man is naturally a social being. Some limit must indeed be set to this; for if you go on to parents and descendants and friends of friends, you will never come to a stop. But this we will consider further on: for the present we will take self-sufficing to mean what by itself makes life desirable and in want of nothing. And happiness is believed to answer to this description. And further, happiness is believed to be the most desirable thing in the world, and that not merely as one among other good things: if it were merely one among other good things [so that other things could be added to it], it is plain that the addition of the least of other goods must make it more desirable; for the addition becomes a surplus of good, and of two goods the greater is always more desirable. Thus it seems that happiness is something final and self-sufficing, and is the end of all that man does.

We need some idea of what happiness is, and Aristotle here gives us his idea: Happiness is living according to rationality, the exercise of our most vital faculties.

But perhaps the reader thinks that though no one will dispute the statement that happiness is the best thing in the world, yet a still more precise definition of it is needed. This will best be gained, I think, by asking, What is the function of man? For as the goodness and the excellence of a piper or a sculptor, or the practiser of any art, and generally of those who have any function or business to do, lies in that function, so man's good would seem to lie in his function, if he has one. But can we suppose that, while a carpenter and a cobbler has a function and a business of his own, man has no business and no function assigned him by nature? Nay, surely as his several members, eye and hand and foot, plainly have each his own function, so we must suppose that man also has some function over and above all these.

What then is it? Life evidently he has in common even with the plants, but we want that which is peculiar to him. We must exclude, therefore, the life of mere nutrition and growth. Next to this comes the life of sense; but this too he plainly shares with horses and cattle and all kinds of animals. There remains then the life whereby he acts—the life of his rational nature, with its two sides or divisions, one rational as obeying reason, the other rational as having and exercising reason. But as this expression is ambiguous, we must be understood to mean thereby the life that consists in the exercise [not the mere possession] of the faculties; for this seems to be more properly entitled to the name.

The function of man, then, is exercise of his vital faculties [or soul] on one side in obedience to reason, and on the other side with reason. But what is called the function of a man of any profession and the function of a man who is good in that profession are, generically the same, *e.g.* of a harper and of a good harper; and this holds in all cases without exception, only that in the case of the latter his superior excellence at his work is added; for we say a harper's function is to harp, and a good harper's to harp well. Man's function then being, as we say, a kind of life—that is to say, exercise of his faculties and action of various kinds with reason—the good man's function is to do this well and beautifully [or nobly]. But the function of anything is done well when it is done in accordance with the proper excellence of that thing. If this be so the result is that the good of man is exercise of his faculties in accordance with excellence or virtue, or, if there be more than one, in accordance with the best and most complete virtue. But there must also be a full term of years for this exercise; for one swallow or one fine day does not make a spring, nor does one day or any small space of time make a blessed or happy man.

It is important to notice the structure of Aristotle's argument here, for we shall see it emerge often in philosophy as well as in our own thought. The argument is an argument on the basis of what is "natural" to man. The good for man is that which is "natural" to him, and that means, according to Aristotle, what is special or unique to him as well. Thus mere "nutrition and growth," that is, eating and keeping physically healthy, cannot in themselves be happiness (although it is necessary for happiness) because even plants, Aristotle says, have this "goal." Nor can happiness lie in simple experience, even exciting experiences, since even a cow has this as the "end" of its life. What is unique to man, Aristotle concludes, is his rationality, his ability to act on rational principles. But action according to rational principles, is, as we shall see, precisely what Aristotle thinks virtue is. Thus happiness turns out to be an "activity of the soul in accordance with perfect virtue." (This is the key phrase of his work.) This "perfect virtue" is also called "excellence," and thus Aristotle's ethics is often called an ethics of self-realization, the goal of which is to make each individual as perfect as possible in all ways:

> Indeed, in addition to what we have said, a man is not good at all unless he takes pleasure in noble deeds. No one would call a man just who did not take pleasure in doing justice, nor generous who took no pleasure in acts of generosity, and so on. If this be so, the manifestations of excellence will be pleasant in themselves. But they are also both good and noble, and that in the highest degree—at least, if the good man's judgment about them is right, for this is his judgment. Happiness, then, is at once the best and noblest and pleasantest thing in the world. . . .

So far, however, it sounds as if virtue and happiness are strictly individual matters. But this is not the case. Aristotle's well-known belief that man is a social animal is as important as these other principles. Thus, the principles of reason and rationality that enter into his *Ethics* will have the interests of society as well as the individual built into them. (Aristotle even says that there is no real distinction between ethics and politics and that the proper end of ethics is politics.) Virtue, accordingly, is also a social conception, and most of the virtues Aristotle discusses, for example, justice and courage, have much to do with one's role in society. Happiness in general, therefore, has its social dimensions. For example, Aristotle argues that both respect and honor are ingredients in the good life. For Aristotle, the happy person, the virtuous person, is mainly a good citizen. It is necessary to add, however, that the only people who could qualify for Aristotle's good life were Greek citizens, which meant that women, children, slaves, and anyone who did not have the good fortune to be born Greek did not even have a chance at being happy, in Aristotle's sense.[10]

Not only does happiness have a social dimension and not only are the virtues socially defined, but the good life, according to Aristotle, must be taught us by society. Accordingly, Aristotle talks a great deal about the need for "good education," and he goes so far as to say that if a person has not been brought up "properly," then no amount of philosophy will be able to make him either virtuous or happy. He also says that young people, because they are "inexperienced in the actions of life" and are "so ruled by their passions," should not try to learn moral philosophy, which depends upon maturity and rationality. On this point, however, we will ignore Aristotle's warnings. For we have seen that growing older and more "mature" is certainly no guarantee of wisdom, and the passions of youth are sometimes more virtuous than the "rationality" of established maturity.

We have already seen Aristotle's beginning: Every act has its goal (or "good"), and ultimately there is a goal (or "chief good") toward which all human acts aim, and that is generally called happiness **(eudaimonia).** But, Aristotle adds, this is not much help, for people give very different accounts of what they take to be the ingredients in happiness. Some say that it is pleasure, others say it is wealth or honor. We have seen Aristotle's arguments against these views and his conclusion that happiness must be "activity in accordance with rational principle." And that means, virtuous activity. The key to Aristotle's ethics, then, lies in his concept of **virtue.**

Aristotle distinguishes two kinds of virtues, the practical or moral virtues (courage, generosity, and so on) and the intellectual virtues (skill at mathematics and philosophy). Although Aristotle thinks the highest virtue is the intellectual virtue of philosophic contemplation, most of his discussion of virtue centers on the moral virtues. We will now take a closer look at how moral virtues are acquired, what Aristotle means by a moral virtue, and what the moral virtues are.

> Excellence, then, being of these two kinds, intellectual and moral, intellectual excellence owes its birth and growth mainly to instruction, and so requires time and experience, while moral excellence is the result of habit or custom and has accordingly in our language received a name formed by a slight change from the word for custom. From this it is plain that none of the moral excel-

---

[10]It is necessary to say something about Aristotle's special notion of *happiness*; it is not at all like our conception of "feeling happy." Aristotle's term *(eudaimonia)* means more like "living well," and it includes such matters as one's status in society and virtuous acts as well as good feelings. No matter how good you feel about yourself—even if you are in a state of ecstasy all of the time—you would not be happy in Aristotle's sense unless you had these other advantages and acted virtuously as well.

lences or virtues is implanted in us by nature; for that which is by nature cannot be altered by training. For instance, a stone naturally tends to fall downwards, and you could not train it to rise upwards, though you tried to do so by throwing it up ten thousand times, nor could you train fire to move downwards, nor accustom anything which naturally behaves in one way to behave in any other way. The virtues, then, come neither by nature nor against nature, but nature gives the capacity for acquring them, and this is developed by training.

Again, where we do things by nature we get the power first, and put this power forth in act afterwards: as we plainly see in the case of the senses; for it is not by constantly seeing and hearing that we acquire those faculties, but, on the contrary, we had the power first and then used it, instead of acquiring the power by the use. But the virtues we acquire by doing the acts, as is the case with the arts too. We learn an art by doing that which we wish to do when we have learned it; we become builders by building, and harpers by harping. And so by doing just acts we become just, and by doing acts of temperance and courage we become temperate and courageous. . . .

Again, both the moral virtues and the corresponding vices result from and are formed by the same acts; and this is the case with the arts also. It is by harping that good harpers and bad harpers alike are produced: and so with builders and the rest; by building well they will become good builders, and bad builders by building badly. Indeed, if it were not so, they would not want anybody to teach them, but would all be born either good or bad at their trades. And it is just the same with the virtues also. It is by our conduct in our intercourse with other men that we become just or unjust, and by acting in circumstances of danger, and training ourselves to feel fear or confidence, that we become courageous or cowardly. So, too, with our animal appetites and the passion of anger; for by behaving in this way or in that on the occasions with which these passions are concerned, some become temperate and gentle, and others profligate and ill-tempered. In a word, acts of any kind produce habits or characters of the same kind. Hence we ought to make sure that our acts be of a certain kind; for the resulting character varies as they vary. It makes no small difference, therefore, whether a man be trained from his youth up in this way or in that, but a great difference, or rather all the difference.

Aristotle's point here is not just that the virtues are acquired by practice, he is also arguing that virtue is a state of character. The virtuous person wants to do virtuous acts and he does them "naturally." We sometimes think that we are moral just because we believe in moral principles. But believing isn't enough, virtuous action is required. But not even virtuous action by itself is enough to make us virtuous. We sometimes think a person is virtuous because he "forces himself" to do what he is supposed to. Not according to Aristotle. The virtuous person is one who does what he is supposed to do because he wants to, because it is built into his very character. It is even essential, according to Aristotle, that the virtuous man enjoys being virtuous:

> And, further, the life of these men is in itself pleasant. For pleasure is an affection of the soul, and each man takes pleasure in that which he is said to love,—he who loves horses in horses, he who loves sight-seeing in sight-seeing, and in the same way he who loves justice in acts of justice, and generally the lover of excellence or virtue in virtuous acts or the manifestation of excellence. And while with most men there is a perpetual conflict between the several things in which they find pleasure, since these are not naturally pleasant, those who love what is noble take pleasure in that which is naturally pleasant. For the manifestations of excellence are naturally pleasant, so that they are both pleasant to them and pleasant in themselves. Their life, then, does not need pleasure to be added to it as an appendage, but contains pleasure in itself.

Here Aristotle gives us perhaps his most famous doctrine, the idea that virtues are "means between the extremes." This is often misinterpreted, however, to read, "everything in moderation." In a way, what Aristotle teaches is very different from this; he tells us that we can't do too much of a good thing, that is, if it is a virtue. One can't be too courageous (as opposed to being rash or cowardly), or too just. What he intends by "the means between the extremes" is this:

> By the absolute mean, or mean relatively to the thing itself, I understand that which is equidistant from both extremes, and this is one and the same for all. By the mean relatively to us I understand that which is neither too much nor too little for us; and this is not one and the same for all. For instance, if ten be too large and two too small, six is the mean relatively to the thing itself; for it exceeds one extreme by the same amount by which it is exceeded by the other extreme: and this is the mean in arithmetical proportion. But the mean relatively to us cannot be found in this way. If ten pounds of food is too much for a given man to eat, and two pounds too little, it does not follow that the trainer will order him six pounds: for that also may perhaps be too much for the man in question, or too little; too little for Milo, too much for the beginner. The same holds true in running and wrestling. And so we may say generally that a master in any art avoids what is too much and what is too little, and seeks for the mean and chooses it—not the absolute but the relative mean.
> If, then, every art or science perfects its work in this way, looking to the mean and bringing its work up to this standard (so that people are wont to say of a good work that nothing could be taken

from it or added to it, implying that excellence is destroyed by excess or deficiency, but secured by observing the mean; and good artists, as we say, do in fact keep their eyes fixed on this in all that they do), and if virtue, like nature, is more exact and better than any art, it follows that virtue also must aim at the mean—virtue of course meaning moral virtue or excellence; for it has to do with passions and actions, and it is these that admit of excess and deficiency and the mean. For instance, it is possible to feel fear, confidence, desire, anger, pity, and generally to be affected pleasantly and painfully, either too much or too little, in either case wrongly; but to be thus affected at the right times, and on the right occasions, and towards the right persons, and with the right object, and in the right fashion, is the mean course and the best course, and these are characteristics of virtue. And in the same way our outward acts also admit of excess and deficiency, and the mean or due amount. Virtue, then, has to deal with feelings or passions and with outward acts, in which excess is wrong and deficiency also is blamed, but the mean amount is praised and is right—both of which are characteristics of virtue. Virtue, then, is a kind of moderation inasmuch as it aims at the mean.

Again, there are many ways of going wrong (for evil is infinite in nature, to use a Pythagorean figure, while good is finite), but only one way of going right; so that the one is easy and the other hard— easy to miss the mark and hard to hit. On this account also, then, excess and deficiency are characteristic of vice, hitting the mean is characteristic of virtue.

Virtue, then, is a habit or trained faculty of choice, the characteristic of which lies in moderation or observance of the mean relatively to the persons concerned, as determined by reason, *i.e.* by the reason by which the prudent man would determine it. And it is a moderation, firstly, inasmuch as it comes in the middle or mean between two vices, one on the side of excess, the other on the side of defect; and, secondly, inasmuch as, while these vices fall short of or exceed the due measure in feeling and in action, it finds and chooses the mean, middling, or moderate amount. Regarded in its essence, therefore, or according to the definition of its nature, virtue is a moderation or middle state, but viewed in its relation to what is best and right it is the extreme of perfection.

But it is not all actions nor all passions that admit of moderation; there are some whose very names imply badness, or malevolence, shamelessness, envy, and, among acts, adultery, theft, murder. These and all other like things are blamed as being bad in themselves, and not merely in their excess or deficiency. It is impossible therefore to go right in them; they are always wrong: rightness and wrongness in such things (*e.g.* in adultery) does not depend upon whether it is the right person and occasion and manner, but the mere doing of any one of them is wrong. It would be equally absurd to look for moderation or excess or deficiency in unjust cowardly or profligate conduct; for then there would be moderation in excess or deficiency, and excess in excess, and deficiency in deficiency. The fact is that just as there can be no excess or deficiency in temperance or courage because the mean or moderate amount is, in a sense, an extreme, so in these kinds of conduct also there can be no moderation or excess or deficiency, but the acts are wrong however they be done. For, to put it generally, there cannot be moderation in excess or deficiency, nor excess or deficiency in moderation.

We see that Aristotle defines "moral virtue" as a mean both in feeling and action. Thus courage is a virtue because the courageous man feels neither too little nor too much fear. His fear is appropriate to the dangerousness of his situation. Because the courageous person feels the right amount of fear, he acts in the right way, neither plunging rashly into danger nor fleeing from it in terror. Now, finally, Aristotle gives us his examples of virtue:

> Moderation in the feelings of fear and confidence is courage: of those that exceed, he that exceeds in fearlessness has no name (as often happens), but he that exceeds in confidence is foolhardy, while he that exceeds in fear, but is deficient in confidence, is cowardly. Moderation in respect of certain pleasures and also (though to a less extent) certain pains in temperance, while excess is profligacy. But defectiveness in the matter of these pleasures is hardly ever found, and so this sort of people also have as yet received no name: let us put them down as "void of sensibility." In the matter of giving and taking money, moderation is liberality, excess and deficiency are prodigality and illiberality. But both vices exceed and fall short in giving and taking in contrary ways: the prodigal exceeds in spending, but falls short in taking; while the illiberal man exceeds in taking, but falls short in spending. . . . But, besides these, there are other dispositions in the matter of money: there is a moderation which is called magnificence (for the magnificent is not the same as the liberal man: the former deals with large sums, the latter with small), and an excess which is called bad taste or vulgarity, and a deficiency which is called meanness. . . . With respect to honour and disgrace, there is a moderation which is pride, an excess which may be called vanity, and a deficiency which is humility.
> But just as we said that liberality is related to magnificence, differing only in that it deals with small sums, so here there is a virtue related to high-mindedness, and differing only in that it is concerned with small instead of great honours. A man may have a due desire for honour, and also more or less than a due desire: he that carries this desire to excess is called ambitious, he that has not enough of it is called unambitious, but he that has the due amount

has no name. . . . In the matter of anger also we find excess and deficiency and moderation. The characters themselves hardly have recognized names, but as the moderate man is here called gentle, we will call his character gentleness; of those who go into extremes, we may take the term wrathful for him who exceeds, with wrathfulness for the vice, and wrathless for him who is deficient, with wrathlessness for his character. . . .

In the matter of truth, then, let us call him who observes the mean a true [or truthful] person, and observance of the mean truth [or truthfulness]: pretence, when it exaggerates, may be called boasting, and the person a boaster; when it understates, let the names be irony and ironical. With regard to pleasantness in amusement, he who observes the mean may be called witty, and his character wittiness; excess may be called buffoonery, and the man a buffoon; while boorish may stand for the person who is deficient, and boorishness for his character. With regard to pleasantness in the other affairs of life, he who makes himself properly pleasant may be called friendly, and his moderation friendliness; he that exceeds may be called obsequious if he have no ulterior motive, but a flatterer if he has an eye to his own advantage; he that is deficient in this respect, and always makes himself disagreeable, may be called a quarrelsome or peevish fellow.

Moreover, in mere emotions and in our conduct with regard to them, there are ways of observing the mean; for instance, shame is not a virtue, but yet the modest man is praised. For in these matters also we speak of this man as observing the mean, of that man as going beyond it (as the shamefaced man whom the least thing makes shy), while he who is deficient in the feeling, or lacks it altogether, is called shameless; but the term modest is applied to him who observes the mean. Righteous indignation, again, hits the mean between envy and malevolence. These have to do with feelings of pleasure and pain at what happens to our neighbours. A man is called righteously indignant when he feels pain at the sight of undeserved prosperity, but your envious man goes beyond him and is pained by the sight of any one in prosperity, while the malevolent man is so far from being pained that he actually exults in the misfortunes of his neighbours.

It is worth making a short list of Aristotle's moral virtues. Many of them are our own virtues also, but some of them are far more appropriate to an aristocratic, warrior society than they are to our own. In order to illustrate Aristotle's idea that virtues are the means between the extremes, I have included "the extremes" in parentheses for contrast:

Courage, particularly courage in battle (extremes: cowardice, rashness). What motivates courage, Aristotle tells us, is a sense of honor, not fear of punishment nor desire for reward, nor merely a sense of duty. The courageous man is afraid, he adds, because without fear there would be no courage. The man who feels no fear in the face of danger is rather rash.

Temperance, particularly concerning bodily pleasures, such as sex, food, and drinking (extremes: self-indulgence or piggishness, insensitivity). Notice that Aristotle does not say, along with many modern moralists, that pleasures are either "bad" or unimportant; in fact, he attacks the man who does not enjoy sex, food, and drinking as much as he attacks the man who overindulges himself. He says that such people "are not even human."

Liberality, we would say, charity (extremes: prodigality or waste, meanness or stinginess). It is worth noting that Aristotle ridicules the man who gives more than he can afford to charity as much as he chastizes the man who will not give at all.

Magnificence, in other words, how extravagantly you live (extremes: vulgarity, miserliness). Aristotle says that one ought to live "like an artist" and spend lavishly. (There is little of the ascetic in Aristotle.)

Pride (extremes: humility, vanity). It is worth noting that pride is one of the seven deadly sins in Christian morality while humility is a virtue. In Aristotle's ethics, this is reversed.

Good temper (extremes: irascibility or bad tempered, too easygoing). It is important to get angry, according to Aristotle, about the right things, but not too much (which "makes a person impossible to live with").

Friendliness (extremes: obsequious, churlish). Friendship, for Aristotle, is one of the most important ingredients in the good life, and being friendly, therefore, is an extremely important virtue. But Aristotle does not say that we should be friendly to everyone; the person who is indiscriminately friendly toward everyone is not worth being a friend with at all.

Truthfulness (extremes: lying, boasting). Especially telling the truth about oneself.

Wittiness (extremes: buffoonery, boorishness). We think of wittiness as a personal asset, but rarely as a virtue. Aristotle thinks that people who are incapable of telling a joke or who tell bad jokes are actually inferior. Fun is an important ingredient in Greek virtuousness.

Shame: Aristotle calls this a "quasi-virtue" (extreme: shamelessness). We all make mistakes and it is a sign of virtue, according to Aristotle, that the good man feels shame when he does them. Shamelessness is a sign of wickedness. Aristotle does not even talk of the other extreme, which he did not consider a problem. (We certainly would. We call it excessive guilt.)

Justice, the cardinal virtue of the Greeks. The need for lawful and fair (which does not mean equal) treatment of other men. (The sense in which justice is a mean between extremes is too complex to discuss here. Aristotle spends a full chapter explaining it.)

Finally, Aristotle gives us his view of the good life for humankind; it is the life of activity in accordance with virtue, but it is also, ideally, a life of intellectual activity, or what he calls "the life of contemplation." In other words, the happiest person is the philosopher:

> We said that happiness is not a habit or trained faculty. If it were, it would be within the reach of a man who slept all his days and lived the life of a vegetable, or of a man who met with the greatest misfortunes. As we cannot accept this conclusion, we must place happiness in some exercise of faculty, as we said before. But as the exercises of faculty are sometimes necessary (*i.e.* desirable for the sake of something else), sometimes desirable in themselves, it is evident that happiness must be placed among those that are desirable in themselves, and not among those that are desirable for the sake of something else: for happiness lacks nothing; it is sufficient in itself.
>
> Now, the exercise of faculty is desirable in itself when nothing is expected from it beyond itself. Of this nature are held to be (1) the manifestations of excellence; for to do what is noble and excellent must be counted desirable for itself: and (2) those amusements which please are more apt to be injured than to be benefited by them, through neglect of their health and fortunes. Now, most of those whom men call happy have recourse to pastimes of this sort. And on this account those who show a ready wit in such pastimes find favour with tyrants; for they make themselves pleasant in that which the tyrant wants, and what he wants is pastime. These amusements, then, are generally thought to be elements of happiness, because princes employ their leisure in them. But such persons, we may venture to say, are no criterion. For princely rank does not imply the possession of virtue or of reason, which are the sources of all excellent exercise of faculty. And if these men, never having tasted pure and refined pleasure, have recourse to the pleasures of the body, we should not on that account think these more desirable; for children also fancy that the things which they value are better than anything else. It is only natural, then, that as children differ from men in their estimate of what is valuable, so bad men should differ from good.
>
> As we have often said, therefore, that is truly valuable and pleasant which is so to the perfect man. Now, the exercise of those trained faculties which are proper to him is what each man finds most desirable; what the perfect man finds most desirable, therefore, is the exercise of virtue. Happiness, therefore, does not consist in amusement; and indeed it is absurd to suppose that the end is amusement, and that we toil and moil all our life long for the sake of amusing ourselves. We may say that we choose everything for the sake of something else, excepting only happiness; for it is the end. But to be serious and to labour for the sake of amusement seems silly and utterly childish; while to amuse ourselves in order that we

may be serious, as Anacharsis says, seems to be right; for amusement is a sort of recreation, and we need recreation because we are unable to work continuously. Recreation, then, cannot be the end; for it is taken as a means to the exercise of our faculties.

Again, the happy life is thought to be that which exhibits virtue; and such a life must be serious and cannot consist in amusement. Again, it is held that things of serious importance are better than laughable and amusing things, and that the better the organ or the man, the more important is the function; but we have already said that the function or exercise of that which is better is higher and more conducive to happiness. Again, the enjoyment of bodily pleasures is within the reach of anybody, of a slave no less than the best of men; but no one supposes that a slave can participate in happiness, seeing that he cannot participate in the proper life of man. For indeed happiness does not consist in pastimes of this sort, but in the exercise of virtue, as we have already said.

But if happiness be the exercise of virtue, it is reasonable to suppose that it will be the exercise of the highest virtue; and that will be the virtue or excellence of the best part of us. Now, that part or faculty—call it reason or what you will—which seems naturally to rule and take the lead, and to apprehend things noble and divine—whether it be itself divine, or only the divinest part of us—is the faculty the exercise of which, in its proper excellence, will be perfect happiness. . . . this consists in speculation or theorizing.

This conclusion would seem to agree both with what we have said above, and with known truths. This exercise of faculty must be the highest possible; for the reason is the highest of our faculties and of all knowable things those that reason deals with are the highest. Again, it is the most continuous; for speculation can be carried on more continuously than any kind of action whatsoever. We think too that pleasure ought to be one of the ingredients of happiness; but of all virtuous exercises it is allowed that the pleasantest is the exercise of wisdom. At least philosophy is thought to have pleasures that are admirable in purity and steadfastness; and it is reasonable to suppose that the time passes more pleasantly with those who possess, than with those who are seeking knowledge. Again, what is called self-sufficiency will be most of all found in the speculative life. The necessaries of life, indeed, are needed by the wise man as well as by the just man and the rest; but, when these have been provided in due quantity, the just man further needs persons towards whom, and along with whom, he may act justly; and so does the temperate and the courageous man and the rest; while the wise man is able to speculate even by himself, and the wiser he is the more is he able to do this. He could speculate better, we may confess, if he had others to help him, but nevertheless he is more self-sufficient than anybody else. Again, it would seem that this life alone is desired solely for its own sake; for it yields no result beyond the contemplation, but from the practical activities we get something more or less besides action.

> . . . it follows that the exercise of reason will be the complete happiness of man, *i.e.* when a complete term of days is added; for nothing incomplete can be admitted into our idea of happiness. But a life which realized this idea would be something more than human; for it would not be the expression of man's nature, but of some divine element in that nature—the exercise of which is as far superior to the exercise of the other kind of virtue, as this divine element is superior to our compound human nature. If then reason be divine as compared with man, the life which consists in the exercise of reason will also be divine in comparison with human life. Nevertheless, instead of listening to those who advise us as men and mortals not to lift our thoughts above what is human and mortal, we ought rather, as far as possible, to put off our mortality and make every effort to live in the exercise of the highest of our faculties; for though it be but a small part of us, yet in power and value it far surpasses all the rest. And indeed this part would even seem to constitute our true self, since it is the sovereign and the better part. It would be strange, then, if a man were to prefer the life of something else to the life of his true self. Again, we may apply here what we said above—for every being that is best and pleasantest which is naturally proper to it. Since, then, it is the reason that in the truest sense is the man, the life that consists in the exercise of the reason is the best and pleasantest for man—and therefore the happiest.

But it must not be thought that Aristotle's ideal philosopher does nothing but contemplate. He may also enjoy pleasure, wealth, honor, success, and power. As a man among men, he is also virtuous and chooses to act virtuously like all good men. But in addition, he has an understanding and an appreciation of reason that makes him "dearest to the Gods and presumably the happiest among men." This is surely a flattering portrait of the place of the philosopher! But if we ignore this final self-congratulation, we can see in Aristotle a powerful conception of morality, with its emphasis on virtue, excellence, and a kind of heroism (whether intellectual or moral) that is in some ways very different from our own conception of morality and the good life.

E. MORALITY AND SENTIMENT: HUME AND ROUSSEAU

Morality for Aristotle depended upon rules embedded and learned in a particular society, an elite society of the privileged males of the Greek aristocracy. Modern conceptions of morality, on the other hand, are usually thought to be universal, that is, not restricted to a particular society or a particular elite. It applies to women, men, poor people, rich people, adults, and children, even if they are only a few years old. At the same time, however, most modern conceptions of morality minimize Aristotle's emphasis on society and upbringing, preferring to place morals on some individual basis. In Kant's moral philosophy, we shall see that the key to morality is *individual autonomy*, the idea that every person can find for himself or herself, just through the use of reason, what acts are moral and what acts are not. Before Kant, the ruling conception of morality was based upon a conception of personal feelings of a special moral kind, a "natural desire" to help one's fellow man. (As in Aristotle, this philosophy insisted that morality had to be viewed as a part of nature.)

It should be clear how this conception of morality has a distinct advantage in reconciling personal interests and moral principles. Since strong moral feelings are a kind of personal interest, one can satisfy his personal feelings and the demands of morality at the same time. (Again, this lies at the heart of Bishop Butler's arguments.) There are, of course, other personal feelings—jealousy, greed, and envy—that act against these moral feelings. But at least some of our feelings are satisfied by moral action. And according to these philosophers, such moral feelings can be found in virtually all of us.

The two most famous philosophers to argue this position are David Hume and the French philosopher Jean-Jacques Rousseau. The key to both of their philosophies is the notion of **sentiment** ("feeling") and the notion of **sympathy** ("fellow feeling" or feeling pity for other people and taking their interests into account as well as our own). Hume says:

> The hypothesis which we embrace is plain. It maintains that moral-ity is determined by sentiment. It defines virtue to be *whatever mental action or quality gives to a spectator the pleasing senti-ment of approbation;* and vice the contrary.[11]

The central concern in Hume's moral philosophy distinguishes those who defend morality as a function of reason from those who say that it is rather a matter of sentiment and passion. Elsewhere Hume gives us his very strong opinion, that "reason is, and ought to be, the slave of the passions." Here is his argument:

◆On "Reason as Slave of the Passions," by David Hume

There has been a controversy started of late, much better worth examination, concerning the general foundation of *morals;* whether

---

[11]David Hume, *Enquiry Concerning the Principles of Morals* (La Salle, IL: Open Court, 1912).

they be derived from *reason* or from *sentiment;* whether we attain the knowledge of them by a chain of argument and induction or by an immediate feeling and finer internal sense; whether, like all sound judgment of truth and falsehood, they should be the same to every rational, intelligent being, or whether, like the perception of beauty and deformity, they be founded entirely on the particular fabric and constitution of the human species.

The ancient philosophers, though they often affirm that virtue is nothing but conformity to reason, yet, in general, seem to consider morals as deriving their existence from taste and sentiment. On the other hand, our modern inquirers, though they also talk much of the beauty of virtue and deformity of vice, yet have commonly endeavored to account for these distinctions by metaphysical reasonings and by deductions from the most abstract principles of the understanding. Such confusion reigned in these subjects that an opposition of the greatest consequence could prevail between one system and another, and even in the parts of almost each individual system, and yet nobody, till very lately, was ever sensible of it.

· · · · · · · · · ·

It must be acknowledged that both sides of the question are susceptible of specious arguments. Moral distinctions, it may be said, are discernible by pure *reason;* else, whence the many disputes that reign in common life, as well as in philosophy with regard to this subject, the long chain of proofs often produced on both sides, the examples cited, the authorities appealed to, the analogies employed, the fallacies detected, the inferences drawn, and the several conclusions adjusted to their proper principles? Truth is disputable, not taste: what exists in the nature of things is the standard of our judgment: what each man feels within himself is the standard of sentiment. Propositions in geometry may be proved, systems in physics may be controverted, but the harmony of verse, the tenderness of passion, the brilliancy of wit must give immediate pleasure. No man reasons concerning another's beauty, but frequently concerning the justice or injustice of his actions. In every criminal trial, the first object of the prisoner is to disprove the facts alleged and deny the actions imputed to him; the second, to prove that, even if these actions were real, they might be justified as innocent and lawful. It is confessedly by deductions of the understanding that the first point is ascertained; how can we suppose a different faculty of the mind is employed in fixing the other?

On the other hand, those who would resolve all moral determinations into *sentiments* may endeavor to show that it is impossible for reason ever to draw conclusions of this nature. To virtue, say they, it belongs to be *amiable* and vice *odious.* This forms their very nature or essence. But can reason or argumentation distribute these different epithets to any subjects and pronounce beforehand that this must produce love and that hatred? Or what other rea-

son can we ever assign for these affections but the original fabric
and formation of the human mind, which is naturally adapted to
receive them?

The end of all moral speculations is to teach us our duty, and, by
proper representations of the deformity of vice and beauty of virtue, beget correspondent habits and engage us to avoid the one and
embrace the other. But is this ever to be expected from inferences
and conclusions of the understanding, which of themselves have
no hold of the affections or set in motion the active powers of men?
They discover truths. But where the truths which they discover
are indifferent and beget no desire or aversion, they can have no
influence on conduct and behavior. What is honorable, what is fair,
what is becoming, what is noble, what is generous takes possession of the heart and animates us to embrace and maintain it.
What is intelligible, what is evident, what is probable, what is true
procures only the cool assent of the understanding and, gratifying a
speculative curiosity, puts an end to our researches.

· · · · · · · · · ·

Extinguish all the warm feelings and prepossessions in favor of
virtue, and all disgust or aversion to vice; render men totally indifferent toward these distinctions, and morality is no longer a practical study nor has any tendency to regulate our lives and actions.

These arguments on each side (and many more might be produced) are so plausible that I am apt to suspect they may, the one
as well as the other, be solid and satisfactory and that *reason* and
sentiment concur in almost all moral determinations and conclusions. The final sentence, it is probable, which pronounces characters and actions amiable or odious, praiseworthy or blamable; that
which stamps on them the mark of honor or infamy, approbation
or censure; that which renders morality an active principle and
constitutes virtue our happiness, and vice our misery—it is probable, I say, that this final sentence depends on some internal sense
of feeling which nature has made universal in the whole species.

It is worth noting here that Hume's moral philosophy, like his philosophy
of knowledge, is strictly empiricist:

. . . Men are now cured of their passion for hypotheses and systems
in natural philosophy and will hearken to no arguments but those
which are derived from experience. It is full time they should attempt a like reformation in all moral disquisitions and reject every
system of ethics, however subtle or ingenious, which is not founded
on fact and observation.

Reason, Hume argues, may be of use in deciding how we can get what we
want, but it is incapable of ever telling us what we ultimately want. Notice
the familiar argument against an infinite regress; notice also Hume's
sharp distinction between reason (which is concerned with knowledge,

truth, and falsehood) and taste or sentiment (that judges values, which ultimately depend upon pleasure and pain):

> . . . It appears evident that the ultimate ends of human actions can never, in any case, be accounted for by *reason,* but recommend themselves entirely to the sentiments and affections of mankind without any dependence on the intellectual faculties. Ask a man *why he uses exercise;* he will answer, *because he desires to keep his health.* If you then inquire *why he desires health,* he will readily reply, *because sickness is painful.* If you push your inquiries further and desire a reason *why he hates pain,* it is impossible he can ever give any. This is an ultimate end and is never referred to any other object.
>
> Perhaps to your second question, *why he desires health,* he may also reply that *it is necessary for the exercise of his calling.* If you ask *why he is anxious on that head,* he will answer, *because he desires to get money.* If you demand, *why? It is the instrument of pleasure,* says he. And beyond this, it is an absurdity to ask for a reason. It is impossible there can be a progress *in infinitum* and that one thing can always be a reason why another is desired. Something must be desirable on its own account and because of its immediate accord or agreement with human sentiment and affection.
>
> Now, as virtue is an end and is desirable on its own account, without fee or reward, merely for the immediate satisfaction which it conveys, it is requisite that there should be some sentiment which it touches—some internal taste or feeling, or whatever you please to call it, which distinguishes moral good and evil and which embraces the one and rejects the other.
>
> Thus, the distinct boundaries and offices of *reason* and of *taste* are easily ascertained. The former conveys the knowledge of truth and falsehood; the latter gives the sentiment of beauty and deformity, vice and virtue. The one discovers objects as they really stand in nature, without addition or diminution; the other has a productive faculty; and gliding or straining all natural objects with the colors borrowed from internal sentiment, raises, in a manner, a new creation. Reason, being cool and disengaged, is no motive to action and directs only the impulse received from appetite or inclination by showing us the means of attaining happiness or avoiding misery. Taste, as it gives pleasure or pain, and thereby constitutes happiness or misery, becomes a motive to action and is the first spring or impulse to desire and volition. From circumstances and relations, known or supposed, the former leads us to the discovery of the concealed and unknown. After all circumstances and relations are laid before us, the latter makes us feel from the whole a new sentiment of blame or approbation.[12]

[12]Hume, *Inquiry Concerning the Principles of Morals.*

Elsewhere Hume argues a razor-sharp distinction between facts and values. He argues with characteristic conciseness that "it is impossible to derive an 'ought' from an 'is,' " that is, any notions of value or what we *ought to do* cannot be derived from any statements of fact. One can know, as a matter of fact, that pushing this button will kill a thousand innocent children, but from that fact alone, it does not follow that I ought not push the button. What I ought to do—or ought not to do—depends on something that is not a matter of fact or reason at all, my moral feelings or sentiments. Without these sentiments, no action is either moral or immoral, praiseworthy or blameworthy, or of any value whatever. Accordingly, in one of his most shocking statements Hume says that it would not be irrational for him to prefer the death of half the world to the pricking of his little finger. This is not to say that he would prefer this, but there is *nothing in reason* to forbid it. Values are a matter of sentiment, not of reason.

A similar theory of sentiment is defended by Jean-Jacques Rousseau. Although he is often characterized as the first great "Romantic," it is worth noting that Rousseau is not nearly so antagonistic to reason as his reputation suggests. Sentiment, by his theory, is tied to a kind of "natural reason." And the key to his theory, therefore, is the concept of **conscience,** a powerful kind of moral feeling that has its own kind of divine reason. As in Hume, detached reason offers us no guidance. Notice that he too reconciles "self-love" and "moral goodness" as ultimately having the same goals:

◆**from *Emile*,**
by Jean-Jacques Rousseau

Let us lay it down as an incontrovertible rule that the first impulses of nature are always right; there is no original sin in the human heart, the how and why of the entrance of every vice can be traced. The only natural passion is self-love or selfishness taken in a wider sense. This selfishness is good in itself and in relation to ourselves; and as the child has no necessary relations to other people he is naturally indifferent to them; his self-love only becomes good or bad by the use made of it and the relations established by its means. Until the time is ripe for the appearance of reason, that guide of selfishness, the main thing is that the child shall do nothing because you are watching him or listening to him; in a word, nothing because of other people, but only what nature asks of him; then he will never do wrong.

I do not mean to say that he will never do any mischief, never hurt himself, never break a costly ornament if you leave it within his reach. He might do much damage without doing wrong, since wrong-doing depends on the harmful intention which will never be his. If once he meant to do harm, his whole education would be ruined; he would be almost hopelessly bad. . . .

The morality of our actions consists entirely in the judgments we ourselves form with regard to them. If good is good, it must be good in the depth of our heart as well as in our actions; and the first reward of justice is the consciousness that we are acting justly. If moral goodness is in accordance with our nature, man can only be healthy in mind and body when he is good. If it is not so, and if man is by nature evil, he cannot cease to be evil without corrupting his nature, and goodness in him is a crime against nature. If he is made to do harm to his fellow-creatures, as the wolf is made to devour his prey, a humane man would be as depraved a creature as a pitiful wolf; and virtue alone would cause remorse.

My young freind, let us look within, let us set aside all personal prejudices and see whither our inclinations lead us. Do we take more pleasure in the sight of the sufferings of others or their joys? Is it pleasanter to do a kind action or an unkind action, and which leaves the more delightful memory behind it? Why do you enjoy the theatre? Do you delight in the crimes you behold? Do you weep over the punishment which overtakes the criminal? They say we are indifferent to everything but self-interest; yet we find our consolation in our sufferings in the charms of friendship and humanity, and even in our pleasures we should be too lonely and miserable if we had no one to share them with us. If there is no such thing as morality in man's heart, what is the source of his rapturous admiration of noble deeds, his passionate devotion to great men? What connection is there between self-interest and this enthusiasm for virtue?

· · · · · · · · · ·

Take from our hearts this love of what is noble and you rob us of the joy of life. The mean-spirited man in whom these delicious feelings have been stifled among vile passions, who by thinking of no one but himself comes at last to love no one but himself, this man feels no raptures, his cold heart no longer throbs with joy, and his eyes no longer fill with the sweet tears of sympathy, he delights in nothing; the wretch has neither life nor feeling, he is already dead.

There are many bad men in this world, but there are few of these dead souls, alive only to self-interest, and insensible to all that is right and good. We only delight in injustice so long as it is to our own advantage; in every other case we wish the innocent to be protected. If we see some act of violence or injustice in town or country, our hearts are at once stirred to their depths by an instinctive anger and wrath, which bids us go to the help of the oppressed; but we are restrained by a stronger duty, and the law deprives us of our right to protect the innocent. On the other hand, if some deed of mercy or generosity meets our eye, what reverence and love does it inspire! Do we not say to ourselves, "I should like

to have done that myself"? What does it matter to us that two thousand years ago a man was just or unjust? and yet we take the same
interest in ancient history as if it happened yesterday. What are
the crimes of Cataline to me? I shall not be his victim. Why then
have I the same horror of his crimes as if he were living now? We
do not hate the wicked merely because of the harm they do to ourselves, but because they are wicked. Not only do we wish to be
happy ourselves, we wish others to be happy too, and if this happiness does not interfere with our own happiness, it increases it. In
conclusion, whether we will or not, we pity the unfortunate; when
we see their suffering we suffer too. Even the most depraved are
not wholly without this instinct, and it often leads them to self-
contradiction. The highwayman who robs the traveller, clothes the
nakedness of the poor; the fiercest murderer supports a fainting
man.

Men speak of the voice of remorse, the secret punishment of hidden crimes, by which such are often brought to light. Alas! who
does not know its unwelcome voice? We speak from experience and
we would gladly stifle this imperious feeling which causes us such
agony. Let us obey the call of nature; we shall see that her yoke
is easy and that when we give heed to her voice we find a joy in the
answer of a good conscience. The wicked fears and flees from her;
he delights to escape from himself; his anxious eyes look around
him for some object of diversion; without bitter satire and rude
mockery he would always be sorrowful; the scornful laugh is his
one pleasure. Not so the just man, who finds his peace within himself; there is joy not malice in his laughter, a joy which springs
from his own heart; he is as cheerful alone as in company, his satisfaction does not depend on those who approach him; it includes
them.

· · · · · · · · · ·

It is no part of my scheme to enter at present into metaphysical
discussions which neither you nor I can understand, discussions
which really lead nowhere. I have told you already that I do not
wish to philosophise with you, but to help you to consult your own
heart. If all the philosophers in the world should prove that I am
wrong, and you feel that I am right, that is all I ask.

For this purpose it is enough to lead you to distinguish between
our acquired ideas and our natural feelings; for feeling precedes
knowledge; and since we do not learn to seek what is good for us
and avoid what is bad for us, but get this desire from nature, in the
same way the love of good and the hatred of evil are as natural to
us as our self-love. The decrees of conscience are not judgments
but feelings. Although all our ideas come from without, the feelings
by which they are weighed are within us, and it is by these feelings
alone that we perceive fitness or unfitness of things in relation to
ourselves, which leads us to seek or shun these things.

To exist is to feel; our feeling is undoubtedly earlier than our intelligence, and we had feelings before we had ideas. Whatever may be the cause of our being, it has provided for our preservation by giving us feelings suited to our nature; and no one can deny that these at least are innate. These feelings, so far as the individual is concerned, are self-love, fear, pain, the dread of death, the desire for comfort. Again, if, as it is impossible to doubt, man is by nature sociable, or at least fitted to become sociable, he can only be so by means of other innate feelings, relative to his kind; for if only physical well-being were considered, men would certainly be scattered rather than brought together. But the motive power of conscience is derived from the moral system formed through this twofold relation to himself and to his fellow-men. To know good is not to love it; this knowledge is not innate in man; but as soon as his reason leads him to perceive it, his conscience impels him to love it; it is this feeling which is innate.

So I do not think, my young friend, that is is impossible to explain the immediate force of conscience as a result of our own nature, independent of reason itself. And even should it be impossible, it is necessary; for those who deny this principle, admitted and received by everybody else in the world, do not prove that there is no such thing; they are content to affirm, and when we affirm its existence we have quite as good grounds as they, while we have moreover the witness within us, the voice of conscience, which speaks on its own behalf. If the first beams of judgment dazzle us and confuse the objects we behold, let us wait till our feeble sight grows clear and strong, and in the light of reason we shall soon behold these very objects as nature has already showed them to us. Or rather let us be simpler and less pretentious; let us be content with the first feelings we experience in ourselves, since science always brings us back to these, unless it has led us astray.

Conscience! Conscience! Divine instinct, immortal voice from heaven; sure guide for a creature ignorant and finite indeed; yet intelligent and free; infallible judge of good and evil, making man like to God! In these consists the excellence of man's nature and the morality of his actions; apart from thee, I find nothing in myself to raise me above the beasts—nothing but the sad privilege of wandering from one error to another, by the help of an unbridled understanding and a reason which knows no principle.[13]

But, as we pointed out before, there is a problem with this notion of conscience and with all appeals of morality to personal feeling. What if different people disagree? Whose conscience or whose feelings should we accept? And even if we find ourselves in agreement, how do we know that our consciences or feelings are right? It is with these questions in mind that we turn to the moral philosophy of Kant.

---

[13] Jean-Jacques Rousseau, *Emile*, trans. Barbara Foxley (New York: E. P. Dutton, 1968).

F. MORALITY AND REASON: KANT

Aristotle, Hume, and Rousseau all give feeling an important place in their conceptions of morality. For Aristotle, the virtuous man wants to act virtuously and enjoys doing so. For Hume and Rousseau, sentiment defines morality. On all such accounts, our concept of *duty*—what we ought to do—is derivative, at least in part, from such feelings and from our upbringing. But what if feelings disagree? What if people are brought up to value different things? What are we to say of a person who is brought up by criminals to value what is wicked and to enjoy cruelty? And what are we to say, most importantly of all, in those familiar cases in which a person's feelings all draw him or her toward personal interests but duty calls in the opposite direction? This is the problem that Kant considered, and because of it, he rejected all attempts to base morality on feelings of any kind. Morality, he argued, must be based solely on reason and reason alone. Its central concept is the concept of **duty,** and so morality is a matter of **deontology** (from the Greek word *dein,* or "duty").

Hume had restricted the notion of reason to concern with knowledge, truth, and falsity; Kant replies that reason also has a practical side, one that is capable of telling us what to do as well as how to do it. Rousseau had said that morality must be universal, common to all men, even in a presocietal "state of nature"; Kant (who very much admired Rousseau) agrees but says that the nature of this universality cannot lie in people's feelings, which may vary from person to person and society to society, but only in reason, which by its very nature must be universal. And Aristotle had insisted that morality must be taught within society and that morals were very much a matter of public opinion and practices; but unlike most modern philosophers, Kant insisted on the independence of morality from society. What is most important, he argues, is that moraltiy be autonomous, a function of individual reason, such that every rational person is capable of finding out what is right and what is wrong for himself or herself. Where Hume and Rousseau had looked for morality in individual feeling, Kant again insists that it must be found through an examination of reason, nothing else. This is the key to Kant's moral philosophy: Morality consists solely of *rational* principles.

Since morality is based on reason, according to Kant, it does not depend on particular societies or particular circumstances; it does not depend on individual feelings or desires (Kant summarizes all such personal feelings, desires, ambitions, impulses, and emotions as **incli-nations**). The purpose of moral philosophy, therefore, is to examine our ability to reason practically and to determine from this examination the fundamental principles that lie at the basis of every morality, for every person, and in every society. In direct contrast to Aristotle, Kant begins by saying that what is ultimately good is none of those benefits and virtues that make up Greek happiness, but rather what he calls a good will. And a good will, in turn, is the will that exercises pure practical reason.

◆**from *Fundamental Principles of the Metaphysics of Morals,* by Immanuel Kant**

Nothing can possibly be conceived in the world, or even out of it, which can be called good without qualification, except a *good will.* Intelligence, wit, judgment, and other *talents* of the mind, however they may be named, or courage, resolution, perseverance, as qualities of temperament, are undoubtedly good and desirable in many respects; but these gifts of nature may also become extremely bad and mischievous if the will which is to make use of them, and which, therefore, constitutes what is called *character,* is not good. It is the same with the *gifts of fortune.* Power, riches, honor, even health, and the general well being and contentment with one's condition which is called *happiness,* inspire pride and often presumption, if there is not a good will to correct the influence of these on the mind, and with this also to rectify the whole principle of acting, and adapt it to its end. The sight of a being who is not adorned with a single feature of a pure and good will, enjoying unbroken prosperity, can never give pleasure to an impartial rational spectator. Thus a good will appears to constitute the indispensable condition even of being worthy of happiness.[14]

The argument behind this opening move is this: It makes no sense to blame or praise a person for his or her character or abilities or the consequences of his or her actions. Many factors contribute to a person's circumstances. Whether or not a person is wealthy, intelligent, courageous, witty, and so on (Aristotle's virtues) is often due to his or her upbringing and heredity rather than any personal choice. But what we *will,* that is, what we try to do, is wholly within our control. Therefore it is the only thing that is ultimately worth moral consideration. Notice that Kant is concerned with questions of morality and not questions of the good life in general. What makes us happy is not particularly his concern. He is only concerned with what makes a person morally *worthy* of being happy.

A good will is good not because of what it performs or effects, not by its aptness for the attainment of some proposed end, but

[14]Immanuel Kant, *Fundamental Principles of the Metaphysics of Morals,* trans. T. K. Abbott (New York: Longmans, Green, 1898). All subsequent quotations from Kant are from this edition.

simply by virtue of the volition—that is, it is good in itself, and considered by itelf is to be esteemed much higher than all that can be brought about by it in favor of any inclination, nay, even of the sum-total of all inclinations. Even if it should happen that, owing to special disfavor of fortune, or the niggardly provision of a step-motherly nature, this will should wholly lack power to accomplish its purpose, if with its greatest efforts it should yet achieve nothing, and there should remain only the good will (not, to be sure, a mere wish, but the summoning of all means in our power), then, like a jewel, it would still shine by its own light, as a thing which has its whole value in itself. Its usefulness or fruitlessness can neither add to nor take away anything from this value. It would be, as it were, only the setting to enable us to handle it the more conveniently in common commerce, or to attract it to the attention of those who are not yet connoisseurs, but not to recommend it to true connoisseurs, or to determine its value.

There is, however, something so strange in this idea of the absolute value of the mere will, in which no account is taken of its utility, that notwithstanding the thorough assent of even common reason to the idea, yet a suspicion must arise that it may perhaps really be the product of mere high-flown fancy, and that we may have misunderstood the purpose of nature in assigning reason as the governor of our will. Therefore we will examine this idea from this point of view.

Kant's argument here is surprisingly similar to Aristotle's argument in his *Ethics.* You remember that Aristotle argues that the good for man must be found in man's nature, in that which is unique to him. The assumption is that since man is singularly endowed with reason, then reason must have a special significance in human life. Kant's argument also begins with the observation that man, unlike other creatures, is capable of reasoning. But why should he have such a capacity? Not in order to make him happy, Kant argues, because any number of instincts would have served that end more effectively. (Remember that Kant is presupposing God as Creator here, so he believes, like Leibniz, that everything exists for some sufficient reason.)

> . . . our existence has a different and far nobler end, for which and not for happiness, reason is properly intended, and which must, therefore, be regarded as the supreme condition to which the private ends of man must, for the most part, be postponed.

This "far nobler end" and "supreme condition" is what Kant calls *duty.* "The notion of duty," he tells us, "includes that of a good will," but a good will that subjects itself to rational principles. Those rational principles are moral laws, and it is action in accordance with such laws that alone makes a man good.

It is important, however, to make a distinction, which Aristotle makes too: It is one thing to do what duty requires for some personal interest, and it is something else to do one's duty just because it is one's duty. For example, a grocer might refuse to cheat his customers (which is his duty) because it would be bad for business; then he is not acting for the sake of duty, but for personal interests. But he may refuse to cheat his customers just because he knows that he ought not to. This does count as doing his duty and thereby makes him morally worthy.

I omit here all actions which are already recognized as inconsistent with duty, although they may be useful for this or that purpose, for with these the question whether they are done *from duty* cannot arise at all, since they even conflict with it. I also set aside those actions which really conform to duty, but to which men have *no* direct *inclination,* performing them because they are impelled thereto by some other inclination. For in this case we can readily distinguish whether the action which agrees with duty is done *from duty* or from a selfish view. It is much harder to make this distinction when the action accords with duty, and the subject has besides a *direct* inclination to it. For example, it is always a matter of duty that a dealer should not overcharge an inexperienced purchaser; and wherever there is much commerce the prudent tradesman does not overcharge, but keeps a fixed price for everyone, so that a child buys of him as well as any other. Men are thus *honestly* served; but this is not enough to make us believe that the tradesman has so acted from duty and from principles of honesty; his own advantage required it; it is out of the question in this case to suppose that he might besides have a direct inclination in favor of the buyers, so that, as it were, from love he should give no advantage to one over another. Accordingly the action was done neither from duty nor from direct inclination, but merely with a selfish view.

On the other hand, it is a duty to maintain one's life; and, in addition, everyone has also a direct inclination to do so. But on this account the often anxious care which most men take for it has no intrinsic worth, and their maxim has no moral import. They preserve their life *as duty requires,* no doubt, but not *because duty requires.* On the other hand, if adversity and hopeless sorrow have completely taken away the relish for life, if the unfortunate one, strong in mind, indignant at his fate rather than desponding or dejected, wishes for death, and yet preserves his life without loving it—not from inclination or fear, but from duty—then his maxim has a moral worth.

To be beneficent when we can is a duty; and besides this, there are many minds so sympathetically constituted that, without any other motive of vanity or self-interest, they find a pleasure in spreading joy around them, and can take delight in the satisfaction of others so far as it is their own work. But I maintain that in such a case an action of this kind, however proper, however amiable it may be, has nevertheless no true moral worth, but is on a level with other inclinations, for example, the inclination to honor, which, if it is happily directed to that which is in fact of public utility and accordant with duty, and consequently honorable, deserves praise and encouragement, but not esteem. For the maxim lacks the moral import, namely, that such actions be done *from duty,* not from inclination. Put the case that the mind of that philanthropist was clouded by sorrow of his own extinguishing all sympathy with the lot of others, and that while he still has the power to benefit others in distress he is not touched by their trouble because he is absorbed with his own; and now suppose that he tears himself out of this dead insensibility and performs the action without any inclination to it, but simply from duty, then first has his action its genuine moral worth. Further still, if nature has put little sympathy in the heart of this or that man, if he, supposed to be an upright man, is by temperament cold and indifferent to the sufferings of others, perhaps because in respect of his own he is provided with the special gift of patience and fortitude and supposes, or even requires, that others should have the same—and such a man would certainly not be the meanest product of nature—but if nature had not specially framed him for a philanthropist, would he not still find in himelf a source from whence to give himself a far higher worth than that of a good-natured temperament could be? Unquestionably. It is just in this that the moral worth of the character is brought out which is incomparably the highest of all, namely, that he is beneficent, not from inclination, but from duty.

In a curious two short paragraphs, Kant tells us that we have a duty to make ourselves happy, not because we want to be happy (wants are never duties) but because it is necessary for us to do our other duties. Then, with reference to the Bible, Kant makes a famous (or infamous) distinction between two kinds of love, practical love, which is commanded as a duty, and pathological love, in other words, what we would call the *emotion* of love.

To secure one's own happiness is a duty, at least indirectly; for discontent with one's condition, under a pressure of many anxieties and amidst unsatisfied wants, might easily become a great *temptation to transgression of duty.* But here again, without looking to duty, all men have already the strongest and most intimate inclination to happiness, because it is just in this idea that all inclinations are combined in one total. But the precept of happiness is often of such a sort that it greatly interferes with some inclinations, and yet a man cannot form any definite and certain conception of the sum of satisfaction of all of them which is called happiness. It is not then to be wondered at that a single inclination, definite both as to what it promises and as to the time within which it can be gratified, is often able to overcome such a fluctuating idea, and that a gouty patient, for instance, can choose to enjoy what he likes, and to suffer what he may, since, according to his calculation, on this occasion at least, he has [only] not sacrificed the enjoyment of the present moment to a possibly mistaken expectation of a happiness which is supposed to be found in health. But even in this case, if the general desire for happiness did not influence his will, and supposing that in his particular case health was not a necessary element in this calculation, there yet remains in this, as in all other cases, this law—namely, that he should promote his happiness not from inclination but from duty, and by this would his conduct first acquire true moral worth.

It is in this manner, undoubtedly, that we are to understand those passages of Scripture also in which we are commanded to love our neighbor, even our enemy. For love, as an affection, cannot be commanded, but beneficence for duty's sake may, even though we are not impelled to it by any inclination—nay, are even repelled by a natural and unconquerable aversion. This is *practical* love, and not *pathological*—a love which is seated in the will, and not in the propensions of sense—in principles of action and not of tender sympathy; and it is this love alone which can be commanded.

Having thus defended his primary proposition that what is ultimately good is a good will acting in accordance with practical reason, in other words, from duty, Kant moves on to two corollary propositions:

The second proposition is: That an action done from duty derives its moral worth, *not from the purpose* which is to be attained by it, but from the maxim by which it is determined, and therefore does not depend on the realization of the object of the action, but merely on the *principle of volition* by which the action has taken place, without regard to any object of desire. It is clear from what precedes that the purposes which we may have in view in our actions, or their effects regarded as ends and springs of the will cannot give to actions any unconditional or moral worth. In what, then, can their worth lie if it is not to consist in the will and in reference to its expected effect? It cannot lie anywhere but in the *principle of the will* without regard to the ends which can be attained by the action. For the will stands between its *a priori* principle, which is formal, and its *a posteriori* spring which is material, as between two roads, and as it must be determined by something, it follows that it must be determined by the formal principle of volition when an action is done from duty, in which case every material principle has been withdrawn from it.

The third proposition, which is a consequence of the two preceding, I would express thus: *Duty is the necessity of acting from respect for the law.* I may have *inclination* for an object as the effect of my proposed action, but I cannot have *respect* for it just for this reason that it is an effect and not an energy of will. Similarly, I cannot have respect for inclination, whether my own or another's; I can at most, if my own, approve it; if another's, sometimes even love it, that is, look on it as favorable to my own interest. It is only what is connected with my will as a principle, by no means as an effect—what does not subserve my inclination, but overpowers it, or at least in case of choice excludes it from its calculation—in other words, simply the law of itself, which can be an object of respect, and hence a command. Now an action done from duty must wholly exclude the influence of inclination, and with it every object of the will, so that nothing remains which can determine the will except objectively the *law*, and subjectively *pure respect* for this practical law, and consequently the maxim that I should follow this law even to the thwarting of all my inclinations.

Thus the moral worth of an action does not lie in the effect expected from it, nor in any principle of action which requires to borrow its motive from this expected effect. For all these effects—agreeableness of one's condition, and even the promotion of the happiness of others—could have been also brought about by other causes, so that for this there would have been no need of the will of a rational being; whereas it is in this alone that the supreme and unconditional good can be found. The pre-eminent good which we call moral can therefore consist in nothing else than *the conception of law* in itself, *which certainly is only possible in a rational being*, in so far as this conception, and not the expected effect, determines the will. This is a good which is already preset in the person who acts accordingly, and we have not to wait for it to appear first in the result.

By what sort of law can that be the conception of which must determine the will, even without paying any regard to the effect expected from it, in order that this will may be called good absolutely and without qualification? As I have deprived the will of every impulse which could arise to it from obedience to any law, there remains nothing but the universal conformity of its actions to law in general, which alone is to serve the will as a principle. . . .

This conception of "universal conformity to law" is Kant's central notion of duty. He defines it, as we shall see, as a generalized version of the Golden Rule: "Do unto others as you would have them do unto you." The point is, decide what you ought to do by asking yourself the question, "What if everyone were to do that?" The rule, as he states it, is:

. . . I am never to act otherwise than so *that I could also will that my maxim should become a universal law*. Here, now, it is the simple conformity to law in general, without assuming any particular law applicable to certain actions, that serves the will as its principle, and must so serve it if duty is not to be a vain delusion and a chimerical notion. The common reason of men in its practical judgments perfectly coincides with this, and always has in view the principle here suggested. Let the question be, for example: May I when in distress make a promise with the intention not to keep it? I readily distinguish here between the two significations which the question may have: whether it is prudent or whether it is right to make a false promise? The former may undoubtedly often be the case. I see clearly indeed that it is not enough to extricate myself from a present difficulty by means of this subterfuge, but it must be well considered whether there may not hereafter spring from this lie much greater inconvenience than that from which I now free myself, and as, with all my supposed *cunning,* the consequences cannot be so easliy foreseen but that credit once lost may be much more injurious to me than any mischief which I seek to avoid at present, it should be considered whether it would not be more *prudent* to act herein according to a universal maxim, and to make it a habit to promise nothing except with the intention of keeping it. But it is soon clear to me that such a maxim will still only be based on the fear of consequences. Now it is a wholly different thing to be truthful from duty, and to be so from apprehension of injurious consequences. In the first case, the very notion of the action implies a law for me; in the second case, I must first look about elsewhere to see what results may be combined with it which would affect myself. For to deviate from the principle of duty is beyond all doubt wicked; but to be unfaithful to my maxim of prudence may often be very advantageous to me, although to abide by it is certainly safer. The shortest way, however, and an unerring one, to discover the answer to this question whether a lying promise is consistent with duty, is to ask myself, Should I be content that my maxim (to extricate myself from difficulty by a false promise) should hold good as a universal law, for myself as well as for others; and should I be able to say to myself, "Every one may make a deceitful promise when he finds himself in a difficulty from which he cannot otherwise extricate himself"? Then I presently become aware that, while I can will the lie, I can by no means will that lying should be a universal law. For with such a law there would be no promises at all, since it would be in vain to allege my intention in regard to my future actions to those who would not believe this allegation, or if they over-hastily did so, would pay me back in my own coin. Hence my maxim, as soon as it should be made a universal law, would necessarily destroy itself.

The impressive name Kant gives to this general formulation of his notion of duty is the **categorical imperative.** An imperative, however, is just what we called a command in our preliminary discussion of morality. It is of the form "do this!" or "don't do this!" The word that distinguishes moral commands in general is the word **ought,** and this tells us something about the term *categorical.* Some imperatives tell us to "do this!" but only in order to get or do something else. Kant calls these "hypothetical imperatives." For example, "go to law school" (if you want to be a lawyer) or "don't eat very hot curry" (unless you don't mind risking an ulcer). But imperatives with a moral *ought* in them are not tied to any such "if" or "in order to" conditions. They are simply "do this" or "don't do this," whatever the circumstances, whatever you would like or enjoy personally. For example, "don't lie" (no matter what). This is what Kant means by "categorical."

> Now all *imperatives* command either *hypothetically* or *categorically.* The former represent the practical necessity of a possible action as means to something else that is willed (or at least which one might possibly will). The categorical imperative would be that which represented an action as necessary of itself without reference to another end, that is, as objectively necessary.
>
> Since every practical law represents a possible action as good, and on this account, for a subject who is practically determinable by reason as necessary, all imperatives are formulae determining an action which is necessary according to the principle of a will good in some respects. If now the action is good only as a means *to something else,* then the imperative is *hypothetical;* if it is conceived as good *in itself* and consequently as being necessarily the principle of a will which of itself conforms to reason, then it is *categorical.*

With hypothetical imperatives, what is commanded depends upon particular circumstances. With moral or categorical imperatives, there are universal laws that tell us what to do in every circumstance. (A **maxim,** according to Kant, is a "subjective principle of action," or what we would call an *intention.* It is distinguished from an "objective principle," that is, a universal law of reason.)

> There is therefore but one categorical imperative, namely, this: *Act only on that maxim whereby thou canst at the same time will that it should become a universal law.*
>
> Now if all imperatives of duty can be deduced from this one imperative as from their principle, then, although it should remain undecided whether what is called duty is not merely a vain notion, yet at least we shall be able to show what we understand by it and what this notion means.
>
> Since the universality of the law according to which effects are produced constitutes what is properly called *nature* in the most general sense (as to form)—that is, the existence of things so far as it is determined by general laws—the imperative of duty may be expressed thus: *Act as if the maxim of thy action were to become by thy will a universal law of nature.*
>
> We will now enumerate a few duties, adopting the usual division

of them into duties to ourselves and to others, and into perfect and imperfect duties.

1. A man reduced to despair by a series of misfortunes feels wearied of life, but is still so far in possession of this reason that he can ask himself whether it would not be contrary to his duty to himself to take his own life. Now he inquires whether the maxim of his action could become a universal law of nature. His maxim is: From self-love I adopt it as a principle to shorten my life when its longer duration is likely to bring more evil than satisfaction. It is asked then simply whether this principle founded on self-love can become a universal law of nature. Now we see at once that a system of nature of which it should be a law to destroy life by means of the very feeling whose special nature it is to impel to the improvement of life would contradict itself, and therefore could not exist as a system of nature; hence that maxim cannot possibly exist as a universal law of nature, and consequently would be wholly inconsistent with the supreme principle of all duty.

2. Another finds himself forced by necessity to borrow money. He knows that he will not be able to repay it, but sees also that nothing will be lent to him unless he promises stoutly to repay it in a definite time. He desires to make this promise, but he has still so much conscience as to ask himself: Is it not unlawful and inconsistent with duty to get out of a difficulty in this way? Suppose, however, that he resolves to do so, then the maxim of his action would be expressed thus: When I think myself in want of money, I will borrow money and promise to repay it, although I know that I never can do so. Now this principle of self-love or of one's own advantage may perhaps be consistent with my whole future welfare; but the question now is, Is it right? I change then the suggestion of self-love into a universal law, and state the question thus: How would it be if my maxim were a universal law? Then I see at once that it could never hold as a universal law of nature, but would necessarily contradict itself. For supposing it to be a universal law that everyone when he thinks himself in a difficulty should be able to promise whatever he pleases, with the purpose of not keeping his promise, the promise itself would become impossible, as well as the end that one might have in view in it, since no one would consider that anything was promised to him, but would ridicule all such statements as vain pretenses.

3. A third finds in himself a talent which with the help of some culture might make him a useful man in many respects. But he finds himself in comfortable circumstances and prefers to indulge in pleasure rather than to take pains in enlarging and improving his happy natural capacities. He asks, however, whether his maxim of neglect of his natural gifts, besides agreeing with his inclination to indulgence, agrees also with what is called duty. He sees then that a system of nature could indeed subsist with such a universal law, although men (like the South Sea islanders) should let their talents rest and resolve to devote their lives merely to idleness,

amusement, and propagation of their species—in a word, to enjoyment; but he cannot possibly *will* that this should be a universal law of nature, or be implanted in us as such by a natural instinct. For, as a rational being, he necessarily wills that his faculties be developed, since they serve him, and have been given him, for all sorts of possible purposes.

4. A fourth, who is in prosperity, while he sees that others have to contend with great wretchedness and that he could help them, thinks: What concern is it of mine? Let everyone be as happy as Heaven pleases, or as he can make himself; I will take nothing from him nor even envy him, only I do not wish to contribute anything to his welfare or to his assistance in distress! Now no doubt, if such a mode of thinking were a universal law, the human race might very well subsist, and doubtless even better than in a state in which everyone talks of sympathy and good-will, or even takes care occasionally to put it into practice, but, on the other side, also cheats when he can, betrays the rights of men, or otherwise violates them. But although it is possible that a universal law of nature might exist in accordance with that maxim, it is impossible to *will* that such a principle should have the universal validity of a law of nature. For a will which resolved this would contradict itself, inasmuch as many cases might occur in which one would have need of the love and sympathy of others, and in which, by such a law of nature, sprung from his own will, he would deprive himself of all hope of the aid he desires.

These are a few of the many actual duties, or at least what we regard as such, which obviously fall into two classes on the one principle that we have laid down. We must be *able to will* that a maxim of our action should be a universal law. This is the canon of the moral appreciation of the action generally. Some actions are of such a character that their maxim cannot without contradiction be even *conceived* as a universal law of nature, far from it being possible that we should *will* that it *should* be so. In others, this intrinsic impossibility is not found, but still it is impossible to *will* that their maxim should be raised to the universality of a law of nature, since such a will would contradict itself. It is easily seen that the former violate strict or rigorous (inflexible) duty; the latter only laxer (meritorious) duty. Thus it has been completely shown by these examples how all duties depend as regards the nature of the obligation (not the object of the action) on the same principle.

Another way of describing the categorical imperative, using a term from Kant that we've already encountered, is to say that it is an a priori principle, in this case, independent of any particular circumstances. Moral principles are necessary for the same reason that certain principles of knowledge are necessary, according to Kant, that is, because they are essential to human nature. It is important, therefore, for Kant to insist that moral principles, as a priori principles of reason, hold for every human being, in fact, even more generally, for every rational creature. (There is an extremely important point hidden in this phrase; traditionally, morality has always been defended on the basis of God's will, that is, we ought to be moral because God gave us the moral laws. According to Kant, however, God does not give the laws but as a rational creature He is bound to them just as we are. Thus, in answer to the question, "Are the laws of morality good because God is good or is God good because he obeys the laws of morality?" Kant would accept the latter.)

Kant's discussion of the categorical imperative is made confusing because after he has told us that "there is but one categorical imperative," he then goes on to give us others. He calls these "alternative formulations of the categorical imperative," but their effect on most readers is to confuse them unnecessarily. In actuality, for Kant there are a great many categorical imperatives. The first one Kant gave us is merely the most general. More specific examples are "don't lie!" and "keep your promises!" Another general categorical imperative is "never use people!" There is, however, a sense in which "using people" may be perfectly innocent. For example, I "use" you in order to play tennis, since I could not play alone. In such a case, you derive as much benefit from my "using you" as I do, and we could say that you are "using me" as well. But there are cases in which we are tempted to "use" people for our own benefit without any regard to their interests. This is what Kant forbids.

> Now I say: man and generally any rational being *exists* as an end in himself, *not merely as a means* to be arbitrarily used by this or that will, but in all his actions, whether they concern himself or other rational beings, must be always regarded at the same time as an end. All objects of the inclinations have only a conditional worth; for if the inclinations and the wants founded on them did not exist, then their object would be without value. But the inclinations themselves, being sources of want, are so far from having an absolute worth for which they should be desired that, on the contrary, it must be the universal wish of every rational being to be wholly free from them. Thus the worth of any object which is *to be acquired* by our action is always conditional. Beings whose existence depends not on our will but on nature's, have nevertheless, if they are not rational beings, only a relative value as means, and are therefore called *things;* rational beings, on the contrary, are called *persons,* because their very nature points them out as ends in themselves, that is, as something which must not be used merely as means, and so far therefore restricts freedom of action (and is an object of respect). These, therefore, are not merely subjective ends whose existence has a worth *for us* as an effect of our action, but *objective ends,* that is, things whose existence is an end in itself—an end, moreover, for which no other can be substituted,

which they should subserve *merely* as means, for otherwise nothing whatever would possess *absolute worth;* but if all worth were
conditioned and therefore contingent, then there would be no
supreme practical principle of reason whatever.

If then there is a supreme practical principle or, in respect of the
human will, a categorical imperative, it must be one which, being
drawn from the conception of that which is necessarily an end for
everyone because it is *an end in itself,* constitutes an *objective*
principle of will, and can therefore serve as a universal practical
law. The foundation of this principle is: *rational nature exists as
an end in itself.* Man necessarily conceives his own existence as being so; so far then this is a *subjective* principle of human actions.
But every other rational being regards its existence similarly, just
on the same rational principle that holds for me; so that it is at the
same time an objective principle from which as a supreme practical law all laws of the will must be capable of being deduced. Accordingly the practical imperative will be as follows: *So act as to
treat humanity, whether in thine own person or in that of any
other in every case as an end withal, never as means only.* We
will now inquire whether this can be practically carried out.

To abide by the previous examples:

First, under the head of necessary duty to oneself: He who contemplates suicide should ask himself whether his action can be
consistent with the idea of humanity *as an end in itself.* If he destroys himself in order to escape from painful circumstances, he
uses a person merely as *a mean* to maintain a tolerable condition
up to the end of life. But a man is not a thing, that is to say, something which can be used merely as means, but must in all his actions be always considered as an end in himself. I cannot, therefore, dispose in any way of a man in my own person so as to muti-
late him, to damage or kill him. (It belongs to ethics proper to
define this principle more precisely, so as to avoid all misunderstanding, for example, as to the amputation of the limbs in order
to preserve myself; as to exposing my life to danger with a view to
preserve it, etc. This question is therefore omitted here.)

Secondly, as regards necessary duties, or those of strict obligation, towards others: He who is thinking of making a lying promise
to others will see at once that he would be using another man
merely as a mean, without the latter containing at the same time
the end in himself. For he whom I propose by such a promise to
use for my own purpose cannot possibly assent to my mode of acting towards him, and therefore cannot himself contain the end of
this action. This violation of the principle of humanity in other men
is more obvious if we take in examples of attacks on the freedom
and property of others. For then it is clear that he who transgres-
ses the rights of men intends to use the person of others merely as means, without considering that as rational beings they ought
always to be esteemed also as ends, that is, as beings who must be
capable of containing in themsleves the end of the very same action.

Thirdly, as regards contingent (meritorious) duties to oneself: It is not enough that the action does not violate humanity in our own person as an end in itself, it must also *harmonize with it*. Now there are in humanity capacities of greater perfection which belong to the end that nature has in view in regard to humanity in ourselves as the subject; to neglect these might perhaps be consistent with the *maintenance of* humanity as an end in itself, but not with the *advancement* of this end.

Fourthly, as regards meritorious duties towards others: The natural end which all men have is their own happiness. Now humanity might indeed subsist although no one should contribute anything to the happiness of others, provided he did not intentionally withdraw anything from it; but after all, this would only harmonize negatively, not positively, with *humanity as an end in itself*, if everyone does not also endeavor, as far as in him lies, to forward the ends of others. For the ends of any subject which is an end in himself ought as far as possible to be *my* ends also, if that conception is to have its *full* effect with me.

This principle that humanity and generally every rational nature is *an end in itself* (which is the supreme limiting condition of every man's freedom of action), is not borrowed from experience, *first*, because it is universal, applying as it does to all rational beings whatever, and experience is not capable of determining anything about them; *secondly*, because it does not present humanity as an end to men (subjectively), that is, as an object which men do of themselves actually adopt as an end; but as an objective end which must as a law constitute the supreme limiting condition of all our subjective ends, let them be what we will; it must therefore spring from pure reason.

In Kant's own terms, every human will is a will capable of acting according to universal laws of morality, not based upon any personal inclinations or interests but obeying rational principles that are categorical. Using this as a definition of morality, Kant then looks back at his predecessors:

Looking back now on all previous attempts to discover the principle of morality, we need not wonder why they all failed. It was seen that man was bound to laws by duty, but it was not observed that the laws to which he is subject are *only those of his own giving*, though at the same time they are *universal*, and that he is only bound to act in conformity with his own will—a will, however, which is designed by nature to give universal laws. For when one has conceived man only as subject to a law (no matter what), then this law required some interest, either by way of attraction or constraint, since it did not originate as a law from *his own will*, but this will was according to a law obliged by *something else* to act in a certain manner. Now by this necessary consequence all the labor spent in finding a supreme principle of *duty* was irrevocably lost. For men never elicited duty, but only a necessity of acting from a certain interest.

Any morality worthy of the name, in other words, must be a product of a person's own autonomous reason yet universal at the same time, as a product of rational will and independent of personal feeling or interest. All previous philosophy, however, has insisted upon appealing to such personal feelings and interests and thus ended up with principles that were in every case hypothetical and not, according to Kant, categorical or moral. Thus morality for Aristotle depended upon a person's being a male Greek citizen. For Kant, morality and duty are completely set apart from such personal circumstances and concerns. Morality and duty have no qualifications, and, ultimately, they need have nothing to do with the good life or with happiness. In a perfect world, perhaps, doing our duty might also bring us happiness. But this is not such a world, Kant observes, and so happiness and morality are two separate concerns, with the second always to be considered the most important. (It is at this point, however, that Kant introduces his "Postulates of Practical Reason," and God in particular, in order to give us some assurance that, at least in the [very] long run, doing our duty will bring us some reward.)

Kant's conception of morality is so strict that it is hard for most people to accept. What is most difficult to accept is the idea that morality and duty have nothing to do with our personal desires, ambitions, and feelings, which Kant called our inclinations. We can agree that at least sometimes our duties and our inclinations are in conflict. But many philosophers have felt that Kant went much too far the other way in separating them entirely. Furthermore, Kant's emphasis on the categorical imperative systematically rules out all reference to particular situations and circumstances. In response to Kant, one may ask: Isn't the right thing to do often determined only within the particular context or situation? (A very recent moral philosophy called "situation ethics" has renewed this ancient demand.) Don't we have to know the particular problems and persons involved? What is right in one situation might very well be wrong in another, just because of different personalities, for example. Some people may be extremely hurt if we tell them the "truth" about themselves. On the other hand, a little "white" lie will make them feel much better. Other people are offended at any lie, however, and prefer even hurtful truths to the "ignorant bliss" of not knowing. Must not all moral rules be tempered to the particular situation?

The Kantian response to this objection would be that there are many ways to avoid hurting people other than telling lies. One can say, "no comment." One can cough conveniently, or drop the platter in one's hand. The fact that certain deceptions are institutionalized in our society (such a "regrets" for a dinner party) does not mean that a Kantian should defend them. The question, then, becomes how one formulates an accurate description of the options in such cases. Is it ever simply the case that one has a choice—hurt someone or tell a lie?

In a more general way, it has been objected that Kant's unqualified concept of morality is much too general to help us decide what to do in any particular situation. As an example, take the categorical imperative "don't steal!" Although the imperative itself, as a categorical one, must be unqualified, in order to apply it at all, we have to understand the kinds of circumstances to which it applies. Can't we have a right to steal in certain circumstances? Or, to put the same point differently, aren't there some circumstances in which "stealing" isn't really stealing at all? But what then of the situation in which a starving man steals a loaf of bread from an extremely wealthy baker. Surely he is stealing, but wouldn't we say that under the circumstances he is justified in doing so? The Kantian reply here is to distinguish between the question whether that person is *wrong* in stealing and the question of whether (or how) he should be punished. In this case, we can presume, Kant would insist that the man did wrong, but nevertheless agree that he should not be punished.

How do we decide "under which circumstances" a moral law is to be applied? Kant's formulation of the categorical imperative only tells us that we must act in such a way that anyone in similar circumstances would act the same way. What defines these "similar" circumstances? Suppose I were to say that "anyone in these circumstances, namely, being five-foot-seven and born in Detroit in 1942, having blond hair and blue eyes, and being a graduate of C. High School, may steal." Anyone in the same circumstances can steal, but, of course, I have defined the circumstances in such a way that it is extremely unlikely that anyone but myself will ever qualify. How can we avoid such trickery? Not by any considerations within the categorical imperative itself, for by its very nature it is incapable of telling us under what circumstances a moral law applies. Another way of making the same objection is to complain that there is no way of deciding how detailed the imperative must be. For example, should we simply say, "don't steal!" or rather "don't steal unless you're starving and the other person is not!" or else, "don't steal unless you're blond and blue-eyed!" and so on? Kant's reply, to prevent such abuses, is to quite clearly leave out all mention of particular circumstances in the formulation of principles. Nevertheless we have to decide in what circumstances to apply what principles, and here the question comes up once again: how narrowly must we define the circumstances? Which circumstances are relevant to the formulation of a categorical imperative? Surely it won't be to say that *none* is relevant; at least we must know enough to know whether or not this act is an instance of stealing.

There have been other objections to Kant's severe philosophy. For example, if moral principles are categorical, then what do we do when two different moral principles conflict? The rule that tells us "don't lie!" is categorical; so is the rule that tells us "keep your promises!" Suppose that I promise not to tell anyone where you will be this weekend. Then some people wishing to kill you force me to tell. I have to say something. Either I break the promise or I lie. Kant gives us no adequate way of choosing between the promise and the lie. He has ruled out any appeal to the consequences of our actions. In Kant's argument, even if your enemies are trying to kill you, it is not morally relevant. And, most importantly, Kant has ruled out any appeal to what will make people happy, not only the person who must either lie or break a promise but everyone else who is involved as well. Kant would reply, presumably, that such cases of apparent conflict are due to a misrepresentation of the case. For example, one could respond to the intruders by playing dumb, or refusing to say anything, or trying to make them go away with force. The question of moral conflict thus becomes critical for Kant's moral philosophy. If moral principles conflict, we need a way of choosing between them. If they do not conflict, then we need a way of accounting for apparent conflicts and resolving them. But it is not clear that the Kantian theory gives us either a satisfactory criterion for getting out of moral quandaries or for explaining away some of the very painful moral conflicts in which we occasionally find ourselves.

G. UTILITARIANISM

In response to the harsh Kantian view of morality, with its neglect of happiness and the good life, a number of British philosophers, chiefly Jeremy Bentham, James Mill, and his son John Stuart Mill, developed a conception of morality that is called **utilitarianism.** It was an attempt to bring back personal inclinations and interests into moral considerations. Utilitarians wished to reconsider the consequences as well as the "will" of an action and to consider the particular circumstances of an action in an attempt to determine what is morally right. Most importantly, it was an attempt to return morality to the search for the personally satisfying life which Kant had neglected.

The basis of utilitarianism is a form of **hedonism,** the conception of the good life that says the ultimate good is pleasure and that in the final analysis we want and ought to want this pleasure. But where traditional hedonism is concerned only with one's personal pleasure, utilitarianism is concerned with pleasure in general; that is, with one's own pleasure and the pleasure of other people. In many utilitarian writings, the notions of pleasure and happiness are used interchangeably. From our earlier discussions (and especially our discussion of Aristotle), we know that we must be cautious of such an exchange. Many short-lived pleasures do not make us happy; and happiness is much more than mere pleasure. But this is a major concern for the utilitarians; their whole theory revolves around a single aim, to make the most people as happy as possible, sometimes sacrificing short-term pleasures for enduring ones. Their central principle is often summarized as "the greatest good for the greatest number."

Jeremy Bentham was motivated to formulate his utilitarian theories not so much by the strict moralism of Kant's philosophy as by the absurd complexity of the British legal system. Just as Kant sought a single principle that would simplify all morality, Bentham looked for a single principle that would simplify the law. Bentham began with the fact that people seek pleasure and avoid pain and developed the "principle of utility" on just this basis:

◆ **from . . . *The Principles of Morals and Legislation,*** **by Jeremy Bentham**

I.   Nature has placed mankind under the governance of two sovereign masters, *pain* and *pleasure.* It is for them alone to point out what we ought to do, as well as to determine what we shall do. On the one hand the standard of right and wrong, on the other the chain of causes and effects, are fastened to their throne. They govern us in all we do, in all we say, in all we think; every effort we can make to throw off our subjection, will serve but to demonstrate and confirm it. In words a man may pretend to abjure their empire: but in reality he will remain subject to it all the while. The *principle of utility* recognizes the subjection, and assumes it for the foundation of that system, the object of which is to tear the fabric of felicity by the hands of reason and of law. Systems which attempt to question it, deal in sounds instead of sense, in caprice instead of reason, the darkness instead of light.

But enough of metaphor and declamation: it is not by such means that moral science is to be improved.

II.   The principle of utility is the foundation of the present work; it will be proper therefore at the outset to give an explicit and determinate account of what is meant by it. By the principle of utility is meant that principle which approves or disapproves of every action whatsoever, according to the tendency which it appears to have to augment or diminish the happiness of the party whose interest is in question; or, what is the same thing in other words, to promote or to oppose that happiness. I say of every action whatsoever; and therefore not only of every action of a private individual, but of every measure of government.

III.   By utility is meant that property in any object, whereby it tends to produce benefit, advantage, pleasure, good, or happiness, (all this in the present case comes to the same thing) or (what comes again to the same thing) to prevent the happening of mischief, pain, evil, or unhappiness to the party whose interest is considered: if that party be the community in general, then the happiness of the community: if a particular individual, then the happiness of that individual.

IV.   The interest of the community is one of the most general expressions that can occur in the phraseology of morals: no wonder that the meaning of it is often lost. When it has a meaning, it is this. The community is a fictitious *body,* composed of the individual persons who are considered as constituting as it were its *members.* The interest of the community then is, what?—the sum of the interests of the several members who compose it.

V.   It is in vain to talk of the interest of the community, without understanding what is the interest of the individual. A thing is said to promote the interest, or to be *for* the interest, of an individual, when it tends to add to the sum total of his pleasures: or, what comes to the same thing, to diminish the sum total of his pains.

VI.   An action then may be said to be conformable to the principle of utility, or, for shortness' sake, to utility, (meaning with respect to the community at large) when the tendency it has to augment the happiness of the community is greater than any it has to diminish it.

VII.   A measure of government (which is but a particular kind of action, performed by a particular person or persons) may be said to be conformable to or dictated by the principle of utility, when in like manner the tendency which it has to augment the happiness of the community is greater than any which it has to diminish it.[15]

Morality, according to Bentham's principle of utility, means nothing other than action that tends to increase the amount of pleasure rather than diminish it.

X.   Of an action that is comfortable to the principle of utility, one may always say either that it is one that ought to be done, or at least that it is not one that ought not to be done. One may say also, that it is right it should be done; at least that it is not wrong it should be done: that it is a right action; at least that it is not a wrong action. When thus interpreted, the words *ought,* and *right* and *wrong,* and others of that stamp, have a meaning: when otherwise, they have none.

How does one defend this principle of utility? One cannot. To try to prove the principle is "as impossible as it is needless." People quite "naturally," whether they admit to it or not, act on the basis of it. This is not to say that they always act on it, but that is only because, according to Bentham,

[15]Jeremy Bentham, *An Introduction to the Principles of Morals and Legislation* (New York: Hafner, 1948). All subsequent quotations from Bentham are from this edition.

people do not always know what is best for them. That is the reason for formulating the principle in philosophy.

The heart of Bentham's theory is the formulation of a procedure for deciding, in every possible case, the value of alternative courses of action. The procedure simply involves the determination of alternative amounts of pleasures and pain, according to what has appropriately been called the **happiness calculus.**

> I.   Pleasures then, and the avoidance of pains, are the *ends* which the legislator has in view: it behoves him therefore to understand their *value*. Pleasures and pains are the *instruments* he has to work with: it behoves him therefore to understand their force, which is gain, in other words, their value.
> II.   To a person considered *by himself*, the value of a pleasure or pain considered *by itself*, will be greater or less, according to the four following circumstances.
>
> 1.   Its *intensity*.
> 2.   Its *duration*.
> 3.   Its *certainty* or *uncertainty*.
> 4.   Its *propinquity* or *remoteness*.
>
> III.   These are the circumstances which are to be considered in estimating a pleasure or a pain considered each of them by itself. But when the value of any pleasure or pain is considered for the purpose of estimating the tendency of any *act* by which it is produced, there are two other circumstances to be taken into the account; these are,
> 5.   Its *fecundity*, or the chance it has of being followed by sensations of the *same* kind: that is, pleasures, if it be a pleasure: pains, if it be a pain.
> 6.   Its *purity*, or the chance it has of *not* being followed by sensations of the *opposite* kind: that is, pains, if it be a pleasure: pleasures, if it be a pain.

· · · · · · · · · ·

Then the test itself:

> V.   To take an exact account then of the general tendency of any act by which the interests of a community are affected, proceed as follows. Begin with any one person of those whose interests seem most immediately to be affected by it: and take an account,
> 1.   Of the value of each distinguishable *pleasure* which appears to be produced by it in the *first* instance.
> 2.   Of the value of each *pain* which appears to be produced by it in the *first* instance.
> 3.   Of the value of each pleasure which appears to be produced by it *after* the first. This constitutes the *fecundity* of the first *pleasure* and the *impurity* of the first *pain*.

4.   Of the value of each *pain* which appears to be produced by it after the first. This constitutes the *fecundity* of the first *pain,* and the *impurity* of the first pleasure.

5.   Sum up all the values of all the *pleasures* on the one side, and those of all the pains on the other. The balance, if it be on the side of pleasure, will give the *good* tendency of the act upon the whole, with respect to the interests of that *individual* person; if on the side of pain, the *bad* tendency of it upon the whole.

6.   Take an account of the *number* of persons whose interests appear to be concerned; and repeat the above process with respect to each. *Sum up* the numbers expressive of the degrees of *good* tendency, which the act has, with respect to each individual, in regard to whom the tendency of it is *good* upon the whole: do this again with respect to each individual, in regard to whom the tendency of it is *bad* upon the whole. Take the balance; which, if on the side of *pleasure,* will give the general *good tendency* of the act, with respect to the total number of community of individuals concerned; if on the side of pain the general *evil tendency,* with respect to the same community.

Let us take an example. Bentham himself discusses the problem of lust (Prop. XXX), which he says is always bad. Why? "Because if the effects of the motive are not bad, then we do not call it lust." Lust, in other words, is sexual desire that is so excessive that it brings about more pain than pleasure. Suppose you are sexually attracted to another person. How do you decide (assuming that there is already mutual agreement) whether to follow through or not? First, you estimate the amount of pleasure each person will gain. An important question is whether the pleasure of only these two people should be estimated or the pleasure of others besides. If it is a question of adultery, then the interests of at least a third person should be considered. But assuming that no such direct complications are involved, even the indirect interests of the rest of society must be considered. (If you and your potential lover are sufficiently young, should the happiness of your parents enter into your decision?) Then, after you have considered its initial pleasure, estimate the initial pain. (In this case, we may presume it will be slight.) Then ask about the longer term pleasures and pains for each person involved. If a sexual relationship will leave you feeling happy about yourself and the other person, then the subsequent pleasure will be considerable. If either person will feel regrets, or degraded, or embarrassed, or if sex will spoil a good friendship, or if a sexual relationship will set up expectations that one or both of you is unwilling to fulfill, then the amount of subsequent pain may be overwhelming. Then add up the pleasures and pains for each person, match the total amount of pleasure against the total pain, and if the balance is positive, go ahead. If the balance is negative, don't do it.

Suppose, for example, you each expect a great deal of initial pleasure, and one of you expects nothing but good feelings afterward while the other expects only mild regrets. No one else need even know, and so the balance, clearly, is very positive. But suppose neither of you expects to enjoy it all that much, and the subsequent hassles will be a prolonged and troublesome bother, then, very likely the balance will be negative. We don't often make this kind of decision in this way, we simply do what we want to do at the time. And this is precisely what Bentham says we shouldn't do. He argues that it is because we so often act on the basis of impulses without rational calculations that we end up unhappy. In other words, the fact that we are usually irrational is not an argument against Bentham's principles. Their purpose is precisely to make us rational, to help us get what we really want.

There are problems with Bentham's theory. All that is considered, according to his "happiness calculus," is solely the amount of pleasure and pain. But some of you, in response to our preceding example, might well say, "It doesn't matter how much pleasure and how little pain two people will gain if they get into a sexual relationship. Under certain circumstances (if it is adultery, or simply if they are not married) such behavior is wrong! Mere happiness is not enough!" And here we see the beginning of a swing back toward Kant. To see why such a move is necessary, let us examine the following objection to Bentham.

Suppose a great many people would get a great deal of pleasure out of seeing some innocent person tortured and slaughtered like a beast. Of course the victim would suffer a great deal of pain, but by increasing the size of the crowd we could eventually obtain an amount of pleasure on the part of everyone else that more than balanced the suffering of the victim. Bentham's calculus has no way of rejecting such a gruesome outcome. A less horrible example is this: If a person gets great pleasure from some activity and no pain, there are no other considerations that apply to him or her (assuming that his or her actions do not affect others). Are we then to say that a life of sloth and self-indulgence, if it satisfies everyone and gives them a lot of pleasure and no pain, is to be preferred to any other life of any kind? Does Bentham give us any reason to try for anything "better" than being happy pigs? This was the problem that bothered Bentham's godson, John Stuart Mill.

Mill's version of utilitarianism added an important qualification to Bentham's purely quantitative calculus. He said that it is not only the quantity of pleasure that counts, but the quality as well. Needless to say, this makes the calculations much more complicated. In fact, it makes them impossible, for there cannot be precise calculations of quality, even though there can be precise calculations of quantity. Mill's now-famous example is the following: If a pig can live a completely satisfied life, while a morally concerned and thoughtful individual like Socrates cannot ever be so satisfied, is the life of the pig therefore preferable? Mill's answer is this:

It is better to be a human being dissatisfied than a pig satisfied; better to be Socrates dissatisfied than a fool satisfied.

On what grounds can he say this? Aren't the pig and the fool happier?

If the fool, or the pig, are of a different opinion, it is because they only know their own side of the question. The other party [Socrates] knows both sides.[16]

Some problems emerge from this theory. How are we to evaluate different "qualities" of pleasure, even if we have tried them all? But first let us look to Mill's revision of utilitarianism, as summarized in his popular pamphlet, appropriately called *Utilitarianism*. (It was Mill, not Bentham, who invented this term.) It begins with a general consideration of morality, and of Kant's moral philosophy in particular.

◆ from *Utilitarianism*, by John Stuart Mill

Our moral faculty, according to all those of its interpreters who are entitled to the name of thinkers, supplies us only with the general principles of moral judgments; it is a branch of our reason, not of our sensitive faculty; and must be looked to for the abstract doctrines of morality, not for perception of it in the concrete. The intuitive, no less than what may be termed the inductive, school of ethics insists on the necessity of general laws. They both agree that the morality of an individual action is not a question of direct perception, but of the application of a law to an individual case. They recognize also, to a great extent, the same moral laws but differ as to their evidence and the source from which they derive their authority. According to the one opinion, the principles of morals are evident *a priori*, requiring nothing to command assent except that the meaning of the terms be understood. According to the other doctrine, right and wrong, as well as truth and falsehood, are questions of observation and experience. But both hold equally that morality must be deduced from principles; and the intuitive school affirm as strongly as the inductive that there is a science of morals. Yet they seldom attempt to make out a list of the *a priori* principles which are to serve as the premises of the science; still more rarely do they make any effort to reduce those various principles to one first principle, or common ground of obligation. They either assume the ordinary precepts of morals as of *a priori* authority, or they lay down as the common groundwork of those maxims, some generality much less obviously authoritative than the maxims themselves, and which has never succeeded in gaining

[16]John Stuart Mill, *Utilitarianism* (New York: Bobbs-Merrill, 1957).

popular acceptance. Yet to support their pretensions there ought either to be some one fundamental principle or law at the root of all morality, or, if there be several, there should be a determinate order of precedence among them; and the one principle, or the rule for deciding between the various principles when they conflict, ought to be self-evident.

To inquire how far the the bad effects of this deficiency have been mitigated in practice, or to what extent the moral beliefs of mankind have been vitiated or made uncertain by the absence of any distinct recognition of an ultimate standard, would imply a complete survey and criticism of past and present ethical doctrine. It would, however, be easy to show that whatever steadiness or consistency these moral beliefs have attained has been mainly due to the tacit influence of a standard not recognized. Although the nonexistence of an acknowledged first principle has made ethics not so much a guide as a consecration of men's actual sentiments, still, as men's sentiments, both in favor and of aversion, are greatly influenced by what they suppose to be the effect of things upon their happiness, the principle of utility, or, as Bentham latterly called it, the greatest happiness principle, has had a large share in forming the moral doctrines even of those who most scornfully eject its authority. Nor is there any school of thought which refuses to admit that the influence of actions on happiness is a most material and even predominant consideration in many of the details, of morals, however unwilling to acknowledge it as the fundamental principle of morality and the source of moral obligation. I might go much further and say that to all those *a priori* moralists who deem it necessary to argue at all, utilitarian arguments are indispensable. It is not my present purpose to criticize these thinkers; but I cannot help referring, for illustration, to a systematic treatise by one of the most illustrious of them, the *Metaphysics of Ethics* by Kant. This remarkable man, whose system of thought will long remain one of the landmarks in the history of philosophical speculation, does, in the treatise in question, lay down a universal first principle as the origin and ground of moral obligation; it is this: "So act that the rule on which thou actest would admit of being adopted as a law by all rational beings." But when he begins to deduce from this precept any of the actual duties of morality, he fails, almost grotesquely, to show that there would be any contradiction, and logical (not to say physical) impossibility, in the adoption by all rational beings of the most outrageously immoral rules of conduct. All he knows is that the *consequences* of their universal adoption would be such as no one would choose to incur.

Then Mill gets down to the business of redefining utilitarianism. Like Bentham, he insists that the principle of utility cannot be proven as such, for it is the ultimate end in terms of which everything else is justified. But there is, Mill tells us, a "larger sense of the word 'proof' ":

On the present occasion, I shall, without further discussion of the other theories, attempt to contribute something towards the understanding and appreciation of the "utilitarian" or "happiness" theory, and towards such proof as it is susceptible of. It is evident that this cannot be proof in the ordinary and popular meaning of the term. Questions of ultimate ends are not amenable to direct proof. Whatever can be proved to be good must be so by being shown to be a means to something admitted to be good without proof. The medical art is proved to be good by its conducing to health; but how is it possible to prove that health is good? The art of music is good, for the reason, among others, that it produces pleasure; but what proof is it possible to give that pleasure is good? If, then, it is asserted that there is a comprehensive formula, including all things which are in themselves good, and that whatever else is good is not so as an end but as a means, the formula may be accepted or rejected, but is not a subject of what is commonly understood by proof. We are not, however, to infer that its acceptance or rejection must depend on blind impulse, or arbitrary choice. There is a larger meaning of the word "proof," in which this question is as amenable to it as any other of the disputed questions of philosophy. The subject is within the cognizance of the rational faculty; and neither does that faculty deal with it solely in the way of intuition. Considerations may be presented capable of determining the intellect either to give or withhold its assent to the doctrine; and this is equivalent to proof.

WHAT UTILITARIANISM IS

A passing remark is all that needs be given to the ignorant blunder of supposing that those who stand up for utility as the test of right and wrong use the term in that restricted and merely colloquial sense in which utility is opposed to pleasure. An apology is due to the philosophical opponents of utilitarianism, for even the momentary appearance of confounding them with anyone capable of so absurd a misconception; which is the more extraordinary, inasmuch as the contrary accusation, of referring everything to pleasure, and that, too, in its grossest form, is another of the common charges against utilitarianism: and, as has been pointedly remarked by an able writer, the same sort of persons, and often the very same persons, denounce the theory "as impracticably dry when the word 'utility' precedes the word 'pleasure,' and as too practicably voluptuous when the word 'pleasure' precedes the word 'utility.'" Those who know anything about the matter are aware that every writer, from Epicurus to Bentham, who maintained the theory of utility, meant by it, not something to be contradistinguished from pleasure, but pleasure itself, together with exemption from pain; and instead of opposing the useful to the agreeable to the ornamental, have always declared that the useful means these, among other things. Yet the common herd, including the herd of

writers, not only in newspapers and periodicals, but in books of
weight and pretension, are perpetually falling into this shallow mistake. Having caught up the word "utilitarian," while knowing
nothing whatever about it but its sound, they habitually express by
it the rejection or the neglect of pleasure in some of its forms: of
beauty, of ornament, or of amusement. Nor is the term thus ignorantly misapplied solely in disparagement, but occasionally in compliment, as though it implied superiority to frivolity and the mere
pleasures of the moment. And this perverted use is the only one in
which the word is popularly known, and the one from which the
new generation are acquiring their sole notion of its meaning.
Those who introduced the word, but who had for many years dis-
continued it as a distinctive apellation, may well feel themselves
called upon to resume it if by doing so they can hope to contribute
anything towards rescuing it from this utter degradation.

The creed which accepts as the foundation of morals "utility" or
the "greatest happiness principle" holds that actions are right in
proportion as they tend to promote happiness, wrong as they tend
to produce the reverse of happiness. By happiness is intended pleasure, and the absence of pain; by unhappiness, pain, and the privation of pleasure. To give a clear view of the moral standard set
up by the theory, much more requires to be said; in particular,
what things it includes in the ideas of pain and pleasure; and to
what extent this is left an open question. But three supplementary
explanations do not affect the theory of life on which this theory
of morality is grounded—namely, that pleasure and freedom from
pain are the only things desirable as ends, and that all desirable
things (which are as numerous in the utilitarian as in any other
scheme) are desirable either for the pleasure inherent in themselves, or as means to the promotion of pleasure and the preven-
tion of pain.

Now such a theory of life excites in many minds, and among
them in some of the most estimable in feeling and purpose, inveterate dislike. To suppose that life has (as they express it) no higher
end than pleasure—no better and nobler object of desire and pursuit—they designate as utterly mean and groveling; as a doctrine
worthy only of swine, to whom the followers of Epicurus were, at a
very early period, contemptuously likened; and modern holders
of the doctrine are occasionally made the subject of equally polite
comparisons by its German, French, and English assailants.

When thus attacked, the Epicureans have always answered that
it is not they, but their accusers, who represent human nature in a
degrading light, since the accusation supposes human beings to
be capable of no pleasures except those of which swine are capable.
If this supposition were true, the charge could not be gainsaid, but
would then be no longer an imputation; for if the sources of pleasure were precisely the same to human beings and to swine, the
rule of life which is good enough for the one would be good enough
for the other. The comparison of the Epicurean life to that of

beasts is felt as degrading, precisely because a beast's pleasures do not satisfy a human being's conception of happiness. Human beings have faculties more elevated than the animal appetites and, when once made conscious of them, do not regard anything as happiness which does not include their gratification. I do not, indeed, consider the Epicureans to have been by any means faultless in drawing out their scheme of consequences from the utilitarian principle. To do this in any sufficient manner, many Stoic, as well as Christian, elements require to be included. But there is no known Epicurean theory of life which does not assign to the pleasures of the intellect, of the feelings and imagination, and of the moral sentiments, a much higher value of pleasures than to those of mere sensation. It must be admitted, however, that utilitarian writers in general have placed the superiority of mental over bodily pleasures chiefly in the greater permanency, safety, uncostliness, etc., of the former—that is, in their circumstantial advantages rather than in their intrinsic nature. And on all these points utilitarians have fully proved their case; but they might have taken the other and, as it may be called, higher ground with entire consistency. It is quite compatible with the principle of utility to recognize the fact that some kinds of pleasure are more desirable and more valuable than others. It would be absurd that, while, in estimating all other things, quality is considered as well as quantity, the estimation of pleasures should be supposed to depend on quantity alone.

If I am asked what I mean by difference of quality in pleasures, or what makes one pleasure more valuable than another, merely as a pleasure, except its being greater in amount, there is but one possible answer. Of two pleasures, if there be one to which all or almost all who have experience of both give a decided preference, irrespective of a feeling of moral obligation to prefer it, that is the more desirable pleasure. If one of the two is, by those who are competently acquainted with both, placed so far above the other that they prefer it, even though knowing it to be attended with a greater amount of discontent, and would not resign it for any quantity of the other pleasure which their nature is capable of, we are justified in ascribing to the preferred enjoyment a superiority in quality so far outweighing quantity as to render it, in comparison, of small account.

Now it is an unquestionable fact that those who are equally acquainted with and equally capable of appreciating and enjoying both, do give a most marked preference to the manner of existence which employs their higher faculties. Few human creatures would consent to be changed into any of the lower animals for a promise of the fullest allowance of a beast's pleasures; no intelligent human being would consent to be a fool, no instructed person would be an ignoramus, no person of feeling and conscience would be selfish and base, even though they should be persuaded that the fool, the dunce, or the rascal is better satisfied with his lot than they are with theirs. They would not resign what they possess more than he for the most complete satisfaction of all the desires which they have in common with him. If they ever fancy they would, it is only in cases of unhappiness so extreme that to escape from it they would exchange their lot for almost any other, however undesirable in their own eyes. A being of higher faculties requires more to make him happy, is capable probably of more acute suffering, and certainly accessible to it at more points, than one of an inferior type; but in spite of these liabilities, he can never really wish to sink into what he feels to be a lower grade of existence. We may give what explanation we please of this unwillingness; we may attribute it to pride, a name which is given indiscriminately to some of the most and to some of the least estimable feelings of which mankind are capable: we may refer it to the love of liberty and personal independence, an appeal to which was with the Stoics one of the most effective means for the inculcation of it; to the love of power or to the love of excitement, both of which do really enter into and contribute to it; but its most appropriate appellation is a sense of dignity, which all human beings possess in one form or other, and in some, though by no means in exact, proportion to their higher faculties, and which is so essential a part of the happiness of those in whom it is strong that nothing which conflicts with it could be otherwise than momentarily an object of desire to them. Whoever supposes that this preference takes place at a sacrifice of happiness—that the superior being, in anything like equal circumstances, is not happier than the inferior—confounds the two very different ideas of happiness and content. It is indisputable that the being whose capacities of enjoyment are low has the greatest chance of having them fully satisfied; and a highly endowed being will always feel that any happiness which he can look for, as the world is constituted, is imperfect. But he can learn to bear its imperfections, if they are at all bearable; and they will not make him envy the being who is indeed unconscious of the imperfections, but only because he feels not at all the good which those imperfections qualify. It is better to be a human being dissatisfied than a pig satisfied; better to be Socrates dissatisfied than a fool satisfied. And if the fool, or the pig, are of a different opinion, it is because they only know their own side of the question. The other party to the comparison knows both sides.

It may be objected that many who are capable of the higher pleasures occasionally, under the influence of temptation, postpone them to the lower. But this is quite compatible with a full appreciation of the intrinsic superiority of the higher. Men often, from infirmity of character, make their election for the nearer good, though they know it to be the less valuable; and this no less when the choice is between two bodily pleasures than when it is between bodily and mental. They pursue sensual indulgences to the injury of health, though perfectly aware that health is the greater good. It may be further objected that many who begin with youthful enthusiasm for everything noble, as they advance in years, sink into indolence and selfishness. But I do not believe that those who undergo this very common change voluntarily choose the lower description of pleasures in preference to the higher. I believe that, before they devote themselves exclusively to the one, they have already become incapable of the other. Capacity for the nobler feelings is in most natures a very tender plant, easily killed, not only by hostile influences, but by mere want of sustenance; and in the majority of young persons it speedily dies away if the occupations to which their position in life has devoted them, and the society into which it has thrown them, are not favorable to keeping that higher capacity in exercise. Men lose their high aspirations as they lose their intellectual tastes, because they have no time or opportunity for indulging them; and they addict themselves to inferior pleasures, not because they deliberately prefer them, but because they are either the only ones to which they have access, or the only ones which they are any longer capable of enjoying. It may be questioned whether any one who has remained equally susceptible to both classes of pleasures, ever knowingly and calmly preferred the lower, though many, in all ages, have broken down in an ineffectual attempt to combine both.

I have dwelt on this point, as being a necessary part of a perfectly just conception of utility or happiness considered as the directive rule of human conduct. But it is by no means an indispensable condition to the acceptance of the utilitarian standard; for that standard is not the agent's own greatest happiness, but the greatest amount of happiness altogether; and if it may possibly be doubted whether a noble character is always the happier for its nobleness, there can be no doubt that it makes other people happier, and that the world in general is immensely a gainer by it. Utilitarianism, therefore, could only attain its end by the general cultivation of nobleness of character, even if each individual were only benefited by the nobleness of others, and his own, so far as happiness is concerned, were a sheer deduction from the benefit. But the bare enunciation of such an absurdity as this last renders refutation superfluous.

According to the greatest happiness principle, as above explained, the ultimate end, with reference to and for the sake of which all other things are desirable—whether we are considering our own good or that of other people—is an existence exempt as far as possble from pain, and as rich as possible in enjoyments, both in point of quantity and quality; the test of quality and the rule for measuring it against quantity being the preference felt by those who, in their opportunities of experience, to which must be added their habits of self-consciousness and self-observation, are best furnished with the means of comparison. This, being, according to the utilitarian opinion, the end of human action, is necessarily also the standard of morality, which may accordingly be defined "the rules and precepts for human conduct," by the observance of which an existence such as has been described might be, to the greatest extent possible, secured to all mankind; and not to them only, but, so far as the nature of things admits, to the whole sentient creation.[17]

H. MORALITY AND DEVELOPMENT

In the 1960s, the psychologist Lawrence Kohlberg offered an interesting series of experiments in support of a new theory of human moral development. His interviews with children of different ages indicated that as people grow up, they make and justify their moral choices using more and more intellectually sophisticated reasoning. Kohlberg claimed that every person undergoes a development of moral cognition or moral thinking in the same way, proceeding through stages from less to more logically sophicated. Eventually, he claimed, people who are very highly developed morally make moral choices and justify them according to an abstract moral "principle," essentially like Kant's "categorical imperative." Basically, Kohlberg gave empirical evidence for a Kantian moral theory.

In the early 1980s, however, Carol Gilligan, a Harvard psychologist, made strong criticisms of Kohlberg's method, and disputed his interpretation of his results. Gilligan reviewed Kohlberg's interviews and found that some of his conclusions—particularly the conclusion that women do not develop as high a level of moral reasoning as do men— were not based on an objective and careful reading of the subject's responses to the interviews. Gilligan's interesting critique of Kohlberg's findings wound up suggesting a whole new moral theory. Gilligan claimed that none of the extant moral theories captured adequately the advanced and complicated reasoning that women tend to apply to their moral decisions. She claimed that there is a "feminine" way of reasoning morally, in which the "good" is conceptualized, not in terms of principle, but in terms of personal responsibility and relatedness to others.

◆**from *In a Different Voice*,
by Carol Gilligan**

Since the imagery of relationships shapes the narrative of human development, the inclusion of women, by changing that imagery, implies a change in the entire account.

The shift in imagery that creates the problem in interpreting women's development is elucidated by the moral judgments of two eleven-year-old children, a boy and a girl, who see, in the same

[17]Mill, *Utilitarianism.*

dilemma, two very different moral problems. While current theory brightly illuminates the line and the logic of the boy's thought, it casts scant light on that of the girl. The choice of a girl whose moral judgments elude existing categories of developmental assessment is meant to highlight the issue of interpretation rather than to exemplify sex differences per se. Adding a new line of interpretation, based on the imagery of the girl's thought, makes it possible not only to see development where previously development was not discerned but also to consider differences in the understanding of relationships without scaling these differences from better to worse.

The two children were in the same sixth-grade class at school and were participants in the rights and responsibilities study, designed to explore different conceptions of morality and self. The sample selected for this study was chosen to focus the variables of gender and age while maximizing developmental potential by holding constant, at a high level, the factors of intelligence, education, and social class that have been associated with moral development, at least as measured by existing scales. The two children in question, Amy and Jake, were both bright and articulate and, at least in their eleven-year-aspirations, resisted easy categories of sex-role stereotyping, since Amy aspired to become a scientist while Jake preferred English to math. Yet their moral judgments seem initially to confirm familiar notions about differences between the sexes, suggesting that the edge girls have on moral development during the early school years gives way at puberty with the ascendance of formal logical thought in boys.

The dilemma that these eleven-year-olds were asked to resolve was one in the series devised by Kohlberg to measure moral development in adolescence by presenting a conflict between moral norms and exploring the logic of its resolution. In this particular dilemma, a man named Heinz considers whether or not to steal a drug which he cannot afford to buy in order to save the life of his wife. In the standard format of Kohlberg's interviewing procedure, the description of the dilemma itself—Heinz's predicament, the wife's disease, the druggist's refusal to lower his price—is followed by the question, "Should Heinz steal the drug?" The reasons for and against stealing are then explored through a series of questions that vary and extend the parameters of the dilemma in a way designed to reveal the underlying structure of moral thought.

Jake, at eleven, is clear from the outset that Heinz should steal the drug. Constructing the dilemma, as Kohlberg did, as a conflict between the values of property and life, he discerns the logical priority of life and uses that logic to justify his choice:

> For one thing, a human life is worth more than money, and if the druggist only makes $1,000, he is still going to live, but if Heinz doesn't steal the drug, his wife is going to die. *(Why is life worth more than money?)* Because the druggist can get a thousand dollars later from rich people with cancer, but Heinz can't get his

wife again. *(Why not?)* Because people are all different and so you couldn't get Heinz's wife again.

Asked whether Heinz should steal the drug if he does not love his wife, Jake replies that he should, saying that not only is there "a difference between hating and killing," but also, if Heinz were caught, "the judge would probably think it was the right thing to do." Asked about the fact that, in stealing, Heinz would be breaking the law, he says that "the laws have mistakes, and you can't go writing up a law for everything that you can imagine."

Thus, while taking the law into account and recognizing its function in maintaining social order (the judge, Jake says, "should give Heinz the lightest possible sentence"), he also sees the law as man-made and therefore subject to error and change. Yet his judgment that Heinz should steal the drug, like his view of the law as having mistakes, rests on the assumption of agreement, a societal consensus around moral values that allows one to know and expect others to recognize what is "the right thing to do."

Fascinated by the power of logic, this eleven-year-old boy locates truth in math, which, he says, is "the only thing that is totally logical." Considering the moral dilemma to be "sort of like a math problem with humans," he sets it up as an equation and proceeds to work out the solution. Since his solution is rationally derived, he assumes that anyone following reason would arrive at the same conclusion and thus that a judge would also consider stealing to be the right thing for Heinz to do. Yet he is also aware of the limits of logic. Asked whether there is a right answer to moral problems, Jake replies that "there can only be right and wrong in judgment," since the parameters of action are variable and complex. Illustrating how actions undertaken with the best of intentions can eventuate in the most disastrous of consequences, he says, "like if you give an old lady your seat on the trolley, if you are in a trolley crash and that seat goes through the window, it might be that reason that the old lady dies."

. . . .

. . . While this boy's judgments at eleven are scored as conventional on Kohlberg's scale, a mixture of stages three and four, his ability to bring deductive logic to bear on the solution of moral dilemmas, to differentiate morality from law, and to see how laws can be considered to have mistakes points toward the principled conception of justice that Kohlberg equates with moral maturity.

In contrast, Amy's response to the dilemma conveys a very different impression, an image of development stunted by a failure of logic, an inability to think for herself.

. . . .

. . . Seeing in the dilemma not a math problem with humans but a narrative of relationships that extends over time, Amy envisions the wife's continuing need for her husband and the husband's continuing concern for his wife and seeks to respond to the druggst's need in a way that would sustain rather than sever connection. Just as she ties the wife's survival to the preservation of relationships, so she considers the value of the wife's life in a context of relationships, saying that it would be wrong to let her die because, "if she died, it hurts a lot of people and it hurts her." Since Amy's moral judgment is grounded in the belief that, "if somebody has something that would keep somebody alive, then it's not right not to give it to them," she considers the problem in the dilemma to arise not from the druggist's assertion of rights but from his failure of response.

· · · · · · · · · ·

Her world is a world of relationships and psychological truths where an awareness of the connection between people gives rise to a recognition of responsibility for one another, a perception of the need for response. Seen in this light, her understanding of morality as arising from the recognition of relationship, her belief in communication as the mode of conflict resolution, and her conviction that the solution to the dilemma will follow from its compelling representation seem far from naive or cognitively immature. Instead, Amy's judgments contain the insights central to an ethic of care, just as Jake's judgments reflect the logic of the justice approach. Her incipient awareness of the "method of truth," the central tenet of nonviolent conflict resolution, and her belief in the restorative activity of care, lead her to see the actors in the dilemma arrayed not as opponents in a contest of rights but as members of a network of relationships on whose continuation they all depend. Consequently her solution to the dilemma lies in activating the network by communication, securing the inclusion of the wife by strengthening rather than severing connections.

But the different logic of Amy's response calls attention to the interpretation of the interview itself. Conceived as an interrogation, it appears instead as a dialogue, which takes on moral dimensions of its own, pertaining to the interviewer's uses of power and to the manifestations of respect. With this shift in the conception of the interview, it immediately becomes clear that the interviewer's problem in understanding Amy's response stems from the fact that Amy is answering a different question from the one the interviewer thought had been posed. Amy is considering not *whether* Heinz should act in this situation ("*should* Heinz steal the drug?") but rather *how* Heinz should act in response to his awareness of his wife's need ("Should Heinz *steal* the drug?"). The interviewer takes the mode of action for granted, presuming it to be a matter of fact; Amy assumes the necessity for action and considers what form it should take. In the interviewer's failure to imagine a response not dreamt of in Kohlberg's moral philosophy lies the failure to hear Amy's question and to see the logic in her response, to discern that what appears, from one perspective, to be an evasion of the dilemma signifies in other terms a recognition of the problem and a search for a more adequate solution.

· · · · · · · · ·

This shift in perspective toward increasingly differentiated, comprehensive, and reflective forms of thought appears in women's responses to both actual and hypothetical dilemmas. But just as the conventions that shape women's moral judgment differ from those that apply to men, so also women's definition of the moral domain diverges from that derived from studies of men. Women's construction of the moral problem as a problem of care and responsibility in relationships rather than as one of rights and rules ties the development of their moral thinking to changes in their understanding of responsibility and relationships, just as the conception of morality as justice ties development to the logic of equality and reciprocity. Thus the logic underlying an ethic of care is a psychological logic of relationships, which contrasts with the formal logic of fairness that informs the justice approach.

• • • • • • • • • •

The transition from the first to the second perspective, the shift from selfishness to responsibility, is a move toward social participation. Whereas from the first perspective, morality is a matter of sanctions imposed by a society of which one is more subject than citizen, from the second perspective, moral judgment relies on shared norms and expectations. The woman at this point validates her claim to social membership through the adoption of societal values. Consensual judgment about goodness becomes the overriding concern as survival is now seen to depend on acceptance by others.

Here the conventional feminine voice emerges with great clarity, defining the self and proclaiming its worth on the basis of the ability to care for and protect others. The woman now constructs a world perfused with the assumptions about feminine goodness that are reflected in the stereotypes of the Broverman et al. studies (1972), where all the attributes considered desirable for women presume an other—the recipient of the "tact, gentleness and easy expression of feeling" which allow the woman to respond sensitively while evoking in return the care that meets her "very strong need for security". . . . The strength of this position lies in its capacity for caring; the limitation of this position lies in the restriction it imposes on direct expression.[18]

I. THE CREATION OF MORALITY: NIETZSCHE AND EXISTENTIALISM

The single term *morality* must not mislead us. We have been discussing not simply different theories of morality (ethics) but different conceptions of morality, and that means different moralities, even if they should have many principles in common. The problem of relativism, in other

[18]Carol Gilligan, *In a Different Voice* (Cambridge, MA: Harvard University Press, 1982).

words, is not confined to the comparison of exotically different cultures. It faces us in a far more urgent form in our own conceptions of morality. We might agree that killing without extreme provocation is wrong. But why do we believe that it is wrong? One person claims that it is wrong because the Ten Commandments (and therefore God) forbid it. Another says it is wrong because it is a mark of insensitivity and therefore a flaw in character. Another says it is wrong because it violates peoples' rights, while still another says it increases the amount of pain in the world without equally adding to happiness. They all agree that killing is wrong, but the different reasons point to different circumstances in which each would kill. The first, if God commanded him or her to. The second, if the killing could be seen as a sign of strength and heroism. The third, if he or she found a way to take away people's right to live or found another right that was overriding. The fourth, as a utilitarian, would only have to find a circumstance in which the death of one person was more than balanced by the increased welfare of the others (as in a criminal execution).

From the three great moral philosophies we have studied, four such conceptions emerge. They all agree on many principles, but the reasons differ widely, and some of the principles do also. But most dramatic is the difference between Aristotle's ancient Greek morality and Kant's modern morality of duty. Kant's morality may be taken as a fair representation of the modern Judeo-Christian morality in its strictest form: the emphasis on moral principle and laws, the emphasis on reason and individual autonomy, the emphasis on good intentions ("a good will") and doing one's duty. There are small differences that we have already pointed out: the Greek emphasis on pride as a virtue in contrast to the Christian condemnation of pride as a "deadly sin" (or at least a personality flaw) and its emphasis on humility. One of Aristotle's first virtues was courage in battle, while most modern moralities consider that as a special case, not as a matter of being an everyday "good person" at all. This difference might well be attributed to the different political climates of the two societies. But that is not enough. As we shall see, the differences are much deeper than that.

There are crucial differences between ancient and modern moral perspectives; the most striking is the difference in the scope of their applicability. In Aristotle's moral philosophy, only a small elite is thought to be capable of true happiness (*eudaimonia*) through virtuous action and contemplation. Other people (women, slaves, noncitizens) may live comfortably enough and do their duties and chores efficiently, but they cannot be called "happy." The elite, however, are characterized by their excellence, by their individual achievements, including wealth, power, honor, intelligence, wit, and all of those rewards that come with an aristocratic upbringing, the best of education and a life that is guaranteed in basic comforts from birth. In Kant's conception of morality, by contrast, all people who are rational (that is, everyone except morons, very young children, and popular musicians) are to be judged by the same moral standards, the standards of duty. There are no elites. And since the judgments of moral worth are made solely on the basis of good intentions, no "external" advantages are relevant to a person's goodness or badness. In fact, it is possible that a perfectly "good" person would, with only the best intentions, cause chaos and unhappiness around him wherever he goes. And the harder he tries to make amends, the more he fouls them up. Dostoyevski wrote one of his greatest novels, *The Idiot,* about just this—a perfectly good man, with all the right intentions, causes suffering and even death every time he tries to do good. Yet the point is, he is, by this modern conception, still the perfectly good man. Aristotle would find this laughable. How could we call a man virtuous just because of his intentions? How can a perfect failure be an example of ideal goodness?

In Aristotle's morality, the only people who operate on the basis of duty are those who are incapable of being truly good and truly happy. Duty is a morality for women and servants. For the elite, it is rather a question of personal excellence—in battle, in games, in business, in love, in debate, and in all things, especially philosophy. And where Kant's morality mostly consists (like the Ten Commandments) of "thou shalt not . . ." Aristotle's morality appropriately consists of personal desires and ambitions, not commands to achieve, and certainly not negative commands. The key element of Kant's philosophy, duty, is treated minimally in Aristotle, where the emphasis is on personal growth and achievement. But, on the other side, the image of the well-rounded, successful man, excellent in all things and the envy of his fellow men, plays only a secondary role in Kant's philosophy (for example, in his *Doctrine of Virtue,* the second part of the *Metaphysics of Morals*). For him, what is important is the person who does what he or she is supposed to do. For Aristotle, the ideal is to strive for personal excellence, and doing what a person is supposed to do is simply taken for granted along the way.

Now notice that both moralities have many of the same results. Aristotle's morality will praise many and condemn most of the same acts as Kant's morality: Killing needlessly and stealing are wrong; telling the truth and keeping promises are right. But their conceptions of morality, and consequently, their conceptions of people are distinctively different. And as we appreciate the nature of this difference, we will be in a position to understand one of the most dramatic moral revolutions of modern times, initiated by Friedrich Nietzsche. Nietzsche called himself an **immoralist,** and he attacked morality as viciously as he attacked Christianity. But though he has often been interpreted as saying that we should give up morality and feel free to kill, steal, and commit crimes of all kinds, his moral philosophy does not in fact say that at all. What he did was to attack modern morality, as summarized by Kant and Christianity, and urge us to return to ancient Greek morality as summarized by Aristotle. He also attacked utilitarianism, which he considered "vulgar." Like a great many philosophers of the nineteenth century (particularly German philosophers: Fichte, Hegel, Marx), Nietzsche saw in the ancient Greeks a sense of personal harmony and a sense of excellence that had been lost in the modern world. Nietzsche, like Aristotle, saw the concept of duty as fit for servants and slaves, but such a morality was wholly inadequate to motivate us to personal excellence and achievement. And Nietzsche, like Aristotle, was an unabashed elitist. Only a few people were capable of this "higher" morality. For the rest, the "slave morality" of duty would have to suffice. But for those few, nothing was more important than to give up the "thou shalt not . . ." of Judeo-Christian morality and seek out one's own virtues and abilities. This does not mean that such a person need ever violate the laws of morality although it must be said that Nietzsche's belligerent style and often war-like terminology certainly suggests that his master morality will include a good amount of cruelty and immorality. But it is clear that Nietzsche does not consider obedience to laws as the most important thing in life. Nor does this mean that Nietzsche is (as he is often thought to be) an ethical egoist. To say that a person should develop his or her own virtues and become excellent in as many ways as possible is not at all to say that one must act only in one's own interests. As in Aristotle, the excellence of the individual is part of and contributes to the excellence of mankind as a whole.

Nietzsche takes his central project as a philosopher to be what he calls "the creation of values." In this he is rightly listed as one of the existentialist philosophers, or at least as one of their most important predecessors. The phrase is perhaps misleading, however. What Nietzsche is doing is not inventing new values so much as reasserting very old ones. Furthermore, Nietzsche, like Aristotle, takes ethics to be based solely upon human nature, and so it is not a question of "creating values" so much as finding them in oneself. But where such a philosophy for Aristotle was in agreement with most of the thinking of his times, Nietzsche's thought was a radical disruption of the usual Kantian style of thinking of the modern period and so takes on the tone of violent destructiveness rather than—as in Aristotle—the self-satisfied tones of a gentleman. And since Nietzsche, unlike Aristotle, did not believe that every human "nature" was the same, he taught that different individuals would most assuredly find and follow different values, different conceptions of excellence and thus have different moralities. For this reason, students who read Nietzsche looking for concrete moral advice, a set of principles to act on, are always disappointed. His central teaching is rather "follow yourself, don't follow me." Consequently, he can't—and won't—try to tell you how to live. But he does tell you to live and to give up the servile views that we have held of ourselves for many centuries.

Nietzsche's moral philosophy is largely critical, and most of his efforts have gone into the rejection of Kant's conception of morality in order to make room for individual self-achieving as found in Aristotle. His argument, however, is not a refutation in the usual sense. Instead, he undermines morality by showing that the motivation behind it is decrepit and weak. The central categories of Nietzsche's philosophy are strength and weakness, and he considers the Greek tradition of personal excellence a source of strength, the modern conception of morality a facade for weakness. Accordingly, he calls the first a "master morality," the second, a "slave morality" or, with reference to modern mass movements, a "herd instinct." The excerpts that follow, therefore, are illustrative of Nietzsche's general attack on morality. But never forget that his purpose is not merely destructive but, in his eyes, creative, and the point is to get us to look to ourselves for values and to excel, each in our own ways (the phrase "will to power" refers to just this effort to excel as individuals).

◆on "Master and Slave Morality," by Friedrich Nietzsche

What does your conscience say? "You should become him who you are."

Herd-Instinct.—Wherever we meet with a morality we find a valuation and order of rank of the human impulses and activities. These valuations and orders of rank are always the expression of the needs of a community or herd: that which is in the first place to *its* advantage—and in the second place and third place—is also the authoritative standard for the worth of every individual. By morality the individual is taught to become a function of the herd, and to ascribe to himself value only as a function. As the conditions for the maintenance of one community have been very different from those of another community, there have been very different moralities; and in respect to the future essential transformations of herd and communities, states and societies, one can prophesy that there will still be very divergent moralities. Morality is the herd-instinct in the individual.[19]

Apart from the value of such assertions as "there is a categorical imperative in us," one can always ask: What does such an assertion indicate about him who makes it? There are systems of morals which are meant to justify their author in the eyes of other people;

[19]Friedrich Nietzsche, The *Joyful Wisdom*, trans. Thomas Common, in *The Complete Works of Friedrich Nietzsche*, Oscar Levy, gen. ed. (1909–11) (New York: Russell & Russell, 1964).

other systems of morals are meant to tranquillise him, and make
him self-satisfied; with other systems he wants to crucify and humble himself; with others he wishes to take revenge; with others to
conceal himself; with others to glorify himself and gain superiority
and distinction;—this system of morals helps its author to forget,
that system makes him, or something of him, forgotten; many a
moralist would like to exercise power and creative arbitrariness
over mankind; many another, perhaps, Kant especially, gives us to
understand by his morals that "what is estimable in me, is that I
know how to obey—and with you it *shall* not be otherwise than
with me!" In short, systems of morals are only a *sign-language of
the emotions.* . . .

In a tour through the many finer and coarser moralities which
have hitherto prevailed or still prevail on the earth, I found certain
traits recurring regularly together and connected with one another,
until finally two primary types revealed themselves to me, and a
radical distinction was brought to light. There is *master-morality*
and *slave-morality;*—I would at once add, however, that in all
higher and mixed civilisations, there are also attempts at the reconciliation of the two moralities; but one finds still oftener the confusion and mutual misunderstanding of them, indeed sometimes
their close juxtaposition—even in the same man, within one soul.
The distinctions of moral values have either originated in a ruling
caste, pleasantly conscious of being different from the ruled—or
among the ruled class, the slaves and dependents of all sorts. In
the first case, when it is the rulers who determine the conception
"good," it is the exalted, proud disposition which is regarded as the
distinguishing feature, and that which determines the order of
rank. The noble type of man separates from himself the beings in
whom the opposite of this exalted, proud disposition displays itself:
he despises them. Let it at once be noted that in this first kind of
morality the antithesis "good" and "bad" means practically the
same as "noble" and "despicable";—the antithesis "good" and
"evil" is of a different origin. The cowardly, the timid, the insignificant, and those thinking merely of narrow utility are despised;
moreover, also, the distrustful, with their constrained glances, the
self-abasing, the dog-like kind of men who let themselves be
abused, the mendicant flatterers, and above all the liars:—it is a
fundamental belief of all aristocrats that the common people are
untruthful. "We truthful ones"—the nobility in ancient Greece
called themselves. It is obvious that everywhere the designations
of moral value were at first applied to *men,* and were only deriva-
tively and at a later period applied to *actions;* it is a gross mistake,
therefore, when historians of morals start questions like, "Why
have sympathetic actions been praised?" The noble type of man
regards *himself* as a determiner of values; he does not require to
be approved of; he passes the judgment: "What is injurious to me
is injurious in itself"; he knows that it is he himself only who
confers honour on things; he is a *creator of values.* He honours

whatever he recognises in himself: such morality is self-glorifi-
cation. In the foreground there is the feeling of plenitude, of power,
which seeks to overflow, the happiness of high tension, the
consciousness of a wealth which would fain give and bestow:—
the noble man also helps the unfortunate, but not—or scarcely—
out of pity, but rather from an impulse generated by the super-
abundance of power. The noble man honours in himself the powerful one, him also who has power over himself, who knows how to
speak and how to keep silence, who takes pleasure in subjecting
himself to severity and hardness, and has reverence for all that is
severe and hard. "Wotan placed a hard heart in my breast," says an
old Scandinavian Saga: it is thus rightly expressed from the soul
of a proud Viking. Such a type of man is even proud of *not* being
made for sympathy; the hero of the Saga therefore adds warningly;
"He who has not a hard heart when young, will never have one."
The noble and brave who think thus are the furthest removed from
the morality which sees precisely in sympathy, or in acting for the
good of others, or in *désintéressement,* the characteristic of the
moral; faith in oneself, pride in oneself, a radical enmity and irony
towards "selflessness," belong as definitely to noble morality, as
do a careless scorn and precaution in presence of sympathy and
the "warm heart."—It is the powerful who *know* how to honour, it
is their art, their domain for invention. The profound reverence
for age and for tradition—all law rests on this double reverence,—
the belief and prejudice in favour of ancestors and unfavourable
to newcomers, is typical in the morality of the powerful; and if,
reversely, men of "modern ideas" believe almost instinctively in
"progress" and the "future," and are more and more lacking in
respect for old age, the ignoble origin of these "ideas" has compla-
cently betrayed itself thereby. A morality of the ruling class, however, is more especially foreign and irritating to present-day taste in
the sternness of its principle that one has duties only to one's
equals; that one may act towards beings of a lower rank, towards
all that is foreign, just as seems good to one, or "as the heart
desires," and in any case "beyond good and evil": it is here that
sympathy and similar sentiments can have a place. The ability and
obligation to exercise prolonged gratitude and prolonged revenge—
both only within the circle of equals,—artfulness in retaliation,
raffinement of the idea in friendship, a certain necessity to have
enemies (as outlets for the emotions of envy, quarrelsomeness,
arrogance—in fact, in order to be a good *friend*): all these are typical characteristics of the noble morality, which, as has been pointed
out, is not the morality of "modern ideas," and is therefore at
present difficult to realise, and also to unearth and disclose.—It is
otherwise with the second type of morality, *slave-morality.* Supposing that the abused, the oppressed, the suffering, the unemanci-
pated, the weary, and those uncertain of themselves, should mora-
lise, what will be the common element in their moral estimates?
Probably a pessimistic suspicion with regard to the entire situa-

tion of man will find expression, perhaps a condemnation of man, together with his situation. The slave has an unfavourable eye for the virtues of the powerful; he has a scepticism and distrust, a *refinement* of distrust of everything "good" that is there honoured—he would fain persuade himself that the very happiness there is not genuine. On the other hand, *those* qualities which serve to alleviate the existence of sufferers are brought into prominence and flooded with light; it is here that sympathy, the kind, helping hand, the warm heart, patience, diligence, humility, and friendliness attain to honour for here these are the most useful qualities, and almost the only means of supporting the burden of existence. Slave-morality is essentially the morality of utility. Here is the seat of the origin of the famous antithesis "good" and "evil":—power and dangerousness are assumed to reside in the evil, a certain dreadfulness, subtlety, and strength, which do not admit of being despised. According to slave-morality, therefore, the "evil" man arouses fear; according to master-morality, it is precisely the "good" man who arouses fear and seeks to arouse it, while the bad man is regarded as the despicable being. The contrast attains its maximum when, in accordance with the logical consequences of slave-morality, a shade of depreciation—it may be slight and well-intentioned—at last attaches itself to the "good" man of this morality; because, according to the servile mode of thought, the good man must in any case be the *safe* man: he is good-natured, easily deceived, perhaps a little stupid, *un bonhomme.* Everywhere that slave-morality gains the ascendency, language shows a tendency to approximate the significations of the words "good" and "stupid."—At last fundamental difference: the desire for *freedom,* the instinct for happiness and the refinements of the feeling of liberty belong as necessarily to slave-morals and morality, as artifice and enthusiasm in reverence and devotion are the regular symptoms of an aristocratic mode of thinking and estimating.—Hence we can understand without further detail why love *as a passion*—it is our European specialty—must absolutely be of noble origin. . . .

And on the philosopher:

. . . The philosophical workers, after the excellent pattern of Kant and Hegel, have to fix and formalise some great existing body of valuations—that is to say, former *determinations of value,* creations of value, which have become prevalent, and are for a time called "truths"—whether in the domain of the *logical,* the *political* (moral), or the *artistic.* It is for these investigators to make whatever has happened and been esteemed hitherto, conspicuous, conceivable, intelligible, and manageable, to shortern everything long, even "time" itself, and to *subjugate* the entire past: an immense and wonderful task, in the carrying out of which all refined pride, all tenacious will, can surely find satisfaction. *The real philoso-*

phers, however, are commanders and law-givers; they say: "Thus *shall* it be!" They determine first the Whither and the Why of mankind, and thereby set aside the previous labour of all philosophical workers and all subjugators of the past—they grasp at the future with a creative hand, and whatever is and was, becomes for them thereby a means, an instrument, and a hammer. Their "knowing" is *creating*, their creating is a law-giving, their will to truth is—*Will to Power.*—Are there at present such philosophers? Have there ever been such philosophers? *Must* there not be such philosophers some day? . . .[20]

Nietzsche is often viewed as the most extreme of the antimoralists, those who attack the traditional duty-bound Kantian-Christian conception of morality. In fact, he is but one among many philosophers who have rejected that morality in exchange for a more personal and individual set of principles. And given his emphasis on human "nature," we can say that even Nietzsche is much more traditional than is usually supposed (though it is the Aristotelian, not the Kantian tradition). In the past few decades, however, morality has become far more personalized than even Nietzsche suggested. In Anglo-American philosophy, largely in the wake of logical positivism, ethics has been reduced to a matter of emotions, prescriptions, and attitudes rather than principles and rational laws. (Ironically, Nietzsche has always been in extreme disfavor among such philosophers while Kant has been considered with extreme favor.)

The attack on the absolute moral principles of reason, which are the same for everyone, has been one of the most vigorous philosophical movements of the twentieth century, so much so that many philosophers, religious leaders, and moralists have become alarmed at the destruction of uniform moral codes and have attempted to reassert the old moral laws in new ways. The problem is one of relativism. Is there a single moral code? Or are there possibly as many moralities as there are people? There are intermediary suggestions, such as relativizing morals to particular groups or societies, but the question is still the same: "Is there ultimately any way of defending one moral code against any other?"

The most extreme relativist position of all has emerged from Nietzsche's existentialist successors, particularly Jean-Paul Sartre. In Sartre's philosophy, not only the idea of a uniform morality but the idea of a human nature upon which this morality might be based is completely rejected. Not because different people might have different "natures," as in Nietzsche, but because for Sartre our values are quite literally a question of creation, of personal commitment. In answer to any question about morality, the only ultimate answer is "because I choose to accept

[20]Friedrich Nietzsche, *Beyond Good and Evil*, trans. Helen Zimmern, in *The Complete Works of Friedrich Nietzsche*, Oscar Levy, gen. ed. (1909–11) (New York: Russell & Russell, 1964).

these values." But what is most fascinating about Sartre's conception of morality as choice is that he does not therefore abandon general principles as Nietzsche does. Quite the contrary, he adopts an almost Kantian stance about the need to choose principles for all mankind, not just oneself. The difference is that Sartre, unlike Kant, makes no claims about the singular correctness of these principles. All he can say is "this is what I choose mankind to be." Thus Sartre's moral philosophy is a curious mixture of the most radical relativism and the most traditional moralizing.

◆**from "Existentialism,"
by Jean-Paul Sartre**

Man is nothing else but that which he makes of himself. That is the first principle of existentialism. And this is what people call its "subjectivity," using the word as a reproach against us. But what do we mean to say by this, but that man is of a greater dignity than a stone or a table? For we mean to say that man primarily exists— that man is, before all else, something which propels itself towards a future and is aware that it is doing so. Man is, indeed, a project which possesses a subjective life, instead of being a kind of moss, or a fungus or a cauliflower. Before that projection of the self nothing exists; not even in the heaven of intelligence: man will only attain existence when he is what he purposes to be. Not, however, what he may wish to be. For what we usually understand by wishing or willing is a conscious decision taken—much more often than not—after we have made ourselves what we are. I may wish to join a party, to write a book or to marry—but in such a case what is usually called my will is probably a manifestation of a prior and more spontaneous decision. If, however, it is true that existence is prior to essence, man is responsible for what he is. Thus, the first effect of existentialism is that it puts every man in possession of himself as he is, and places the entire responsibility for his existence squarely upon his own shoulders. And, when we say that man is responsible for himself, we do not mean that he is responsible only for his own individuality, but that he is responsible for all men. The word "subjectivism" is to be understood in two senses, and our adversaries play upon only one of them. Subjectivism means, on the one hand, the freedom of the individual subject and, on the other, that man cannot pass beyond human subjectivity. It is the latter which is the deeper meaning of existentialism. When we say that man chooses himself, we do mean that every one of us must choose himself; but by that we also mean that in choosing for himself he chooses for all men. For in effect, of all the actions a man may take in order to create himself as he wills to be, there is not one which is not creative, at the same time, of an image of man such as he believes he ought to be. To choose between this or that is at the same time to affirm the value of that which is chosen; for we are unable ever to choose the worse. What we choose is always the better and nothing can be better for us unless it is better for all. If, moreover, existence precedes essence and we will to exist at the same time as we fashion our image, that image is valid for all and for the entire epoch in which we find ourselves. Our responsibility is thus much greater than we had supposed, for it concerns mankind as a whole. If I am a worker, for instance, I may choose to join a Christian rather than a Communist trade union. And if, by that membership, I choose to signify that resignation is, after all, the attitude that best becomes a man, that man's kingdom is not upon this earth, I do not commit myself alone to that view. Resignation is my will for everyone, and my action is, in consequence, a commitment on behalf of all mankind. Or if, to take a more personal case, I decide to marry and to have children, even though this decision proceeds simply from my situation, from my passion or my desire, I am thereby committing not only myself, but humanity as a whole, to the practice of monogamy. I am thus responsible for myself and for all men, and I am creating a certain image of man as I would have him to be. In fashioning myself I fashion man.

· · · · · · · · · ·

... Who can prove that I am the proper person to impose, by my own choice, my conception of man upon mankind? I shall never find any proof whatever; there will be no sign to convince me of it.

· · · · · · · · · ·

If I regard a certain course of action as good, it is only I who choose to say that it is good and not bad. . . . nevertheless I also am obliged at every instant to perform actions which are examples. Everything happens to every man as though the whole human race had its eyes fixed upon what he is doing and regulated its conduct accordingly.

· · · · · · · · · ·

As an example by which you may the better understand this state of abandonment, I will refer to the case of a pupil of mine, who sought me out in the following circumstances. His father was quarrelling with his mother and was also inclined to be a "collaborator"; his elder brother had been killed in the German offensive of 1940 and this young man, with a sentiment somewhat primitive but generous, burned to avenge him. His mother was living alone with him, deeply afflicted by the semi-treason of his father and by the death of her eldest son, and her only consolation was in this young man. But he, at this momemt, had the choice between going to England to join the Free French Forces or of staying near his mother, and helping her to live. He fully realized that this

woman lived only for him and that his disappearance—or perhaps
his death—would plunge her into despair. He also realized that,
concretely and in fact, every action he performed on his mother's
behalf would be sure of effect in the sense of aiding her to live,
whereas anything he did in order to go and fight would be an ambiguous action which might vanish like water into sand and serve
no purpose. For instance, to set out for England he would have
to wait indefinitely in a Spanish camp on the way through Spain;
or, on arriving in England or in Algiers he might be put into an
office to fill up forms. Consequently, he found himself confronted
by two very different modes of action; the one concrete, immediate,
but directed towards only one individual; and the other an action
addressed to an end infinitely greater, a national collectivity, but for
that very reason ambiguous—and it might be frustrated on the
way. At the same time, he was hesitating between two kinds of
morality; on the one side the morality of sympathy, of personal devotion and, on the other side, a morality of wider scope but of
more debatable validity. He had to choose between those two. What
could help him to choose? Could the Christian doctrine? No.
Christian doctrine says: Act with charity, love your neighbour, deny
yourself for others, choose the way which is hardest, and so forth.
But which is the harder road? To whom does one owe the more
brotherly love, the patriot or the mother? Which is the more useful
aim, the general one of fighting in and for the whole community,
or the precise aim of helping one particular person to live? Who
can give an answer to that *a priori*? No one. Nor is it given in any
ethical scripture. The Kantian ethic says, Never regard another as a
means, but always as an end. Very well; if I remain with my
mother, I shall be regarding her as the end and not as a means:
but by the same token I am in danger of treating as means those
who are fighting on my behalf; and the converse is also true, that if
I go to the aid of the combatants I shall be treating them as the
end at the risk of treating my mother as a means.

If values are uncertain, if they are still too abstract to determine
the particular, concrete case under consideration, nothing remains
but to trust in our instincts. That is what this young man tried to
do; and when I saw him he sad, "In the end, it is feeling that
counts; the direction in which it is really pushing me is the one I
ought to choose. If I feel that I love my mother enough to sacrifice
everything else for her—my will to be avenged, all my longings for
action and adventure—then I stay with her. If, on the contrary, I
feel that my love for her is not enough, I go." But how does one
estimate the strength of a feeling? The value of his feeling for his
mother was determined precisely by the fact that he was standing
by her. I may say that I love a certain friend enough to sacrifice
such or such a sum of money for him, but I cannot prove that unless I have done it. I may say, "I love my mother enough to remain
with her," if actually I have remained with her. I can only estimate

the strength of this affection if I have performed an action by which it is defined and ratified. But if I then appeal to this affection to justify my action, I find myself drawn into a vicious circle. . . .

In other words, feeling is formed by the deeds that one does; therefore I cannot consult it as a guide to action. And that is to say that I can neither seek within myself for an authentic impulse to action, nor can I expect, from some ethic, formulae that will enable me to act. You may say that the youth did, at least, go to a professor to ask for advice. But if you seek counsel—from a priest, for example—you have selected that priest; and at bottom you already knew, more or less, what he would advise. In other words, to choose an adviser is nevertheless to commit oneself by that choice. If you are a Christian, you will say, Consult a priest; but there are collaborationists, priests who are resisters and priests who wait for the tide to turn: which will you choose? Had this young man chosen a priest of the resistance, or one of the collaboration, he would have decided beforehand the kind of advice he was to receive. Similarly, in coming to me, he knew what advice I should give him, and I had but one reply to make. You are free, therefore choose— that is to say, invent. No rule of general morality can show you what you ought to do.

To say that it does not matter what you choose is not correct. In one sense choice is possible, but what is not possible is not to choose. I can always choose but I must know that if I do not choose, that is still a choice. This although it may appear merely formal, is of great importance as a limit to fantasy and caprice. For, when I confront a real situation—for example, that I am a sexual being, able to have relations with a being of the other sex and able to have children—I am obliged to choose my attitude to it, and in every respect I bear the responsibility of the choice which, in committing myself, also commits the whole of humanity. . . . Man finds himself in an organized situation in which he is himself involved: his choice involves mankind in its entirety, and he cannot avoid choosing. Either he must remain single, or he must marry without having children, or he must marry and have children. In any case, and whichever he may choose, it is impossible for him, in respect of this situation, not to take complete responsibility. Doubtless he chooses without reference to any pre-established values, but it is unjust to tax him with caprice. Rather let us say that the moral choice is comparable to the construction of a work of art.

· · · · · · · · · ·

No one can tell what the painting of tomorrow will be like; one cannot judge a painting until it is done. What has that to do with morality: We are in the same creative situation. We never speak of a work of art as irresponsible; when we are discussing a canvas by Picasso, we understand very well that the composition became what it is at the time when he was painting it, and that his works are part and parcel of his entire life.

It is the same upon the plane of morality. There is this in common between art and morality, that in both we have to do with creation and invention. We cannot decide *a priori* what it is that should be done. I think it was made sufficiently clear to you in the case of that student who came to see me, that to whatever ethical system he might appeal, the Kantian or any other, he could find no sort of guidance whatever; he was obliged to invent the law for himself. Certainly we cannot say that this man, in choosing to remain with his mother—that is, in taking sentiment, personal devotion and concrete charity as his moral foundations—would be making an irresponsible choice, nor could we do so if he preferred the sacrifice of going away to England. Man makes himself; he is not found ready-made; he makes himself by the choice of his morality, and he cannot but choose a morality, such is the pressure of circumstances upon him.[21]

Sartre says that "man makes himself." He believes this to be true both individually and collectively. It is through my actions that I commit myself to values, not through principles I accept a priori or rules that are imposed upon me by God or society. If you accept the voice of some authority, you have chosen to accept that authority rather than some other. If you appeal for advice or help, you have chosen to seek that kind of advice rather than some other kind. If you refuse to choose between alternatives, then you are responsible for neglecting both or all the alternatives, for "copping-out." In any case, you must do something, even if what you do is "doing nothing" (that is, not taking one of the important alternatives before you).

Here is Sartre's reply to his predecessors. We are no longer in the position of Aristotle, in which morality appears to us as a given, as "natural," and without alternatives of the most irresolvable kind. We can no longer trust our "sentiments," as Hume did, for we now find ourselves torn with conflicting sentiments of every kind. We can no longer accept the a priori moralizing of Kant, for we now see that the circumstances in which we must act are never so simple that they will allow for a simple "categorical" imperative. And even "the greatest good for the greatest number" no longer provides a guide for our actions, for we no longer pretend that we can calculate the consequences of our actions with any such accuracy. And besides, who is to say what "the greatest good" or, for that matter, "the greatest number" is today? Against all of this, Sartre argues that there is simply our choice of actions and values, together with their consequences, whatever they are. There is no justification for these, and no "right" or "wrong." But this does not mean that we need not choose or that it is all "arbitrary." To the contrary, the upshot of Sartre's thesis is precisely that we are always choosing and that morality is

[21] Jean-Paul Sartre, *Existentialism As a Humanism*, trans. Philip Mairet (New York: Philosophical Library, 1949).

nothing other than our commitments, at least for the present, to those values we choose to follow through our actions.

J. ETHICS UNNATURALIZED: METAETHICS AND ITS CONSEQUENCES

Each of the theories we have examined, from Aristotle to the existentialists and the pragmatists, is an attempt to say what is good and right, as opposed to what is bad and wrong. In some cases, this moral advice is specific and straightforward, as in Aristotle's list of the virtues. In other cases, it is not specific at all, as in Hume and Rousseau's celebration of sympathy, Nietzsche's enthusiasm about strength and creativity, and Sartre's exhortation of responsibility. Both Kant and Mill present us with a conception of morality in which abstract principles are to be used to figure out specific actions. All of these theories, in other words, are *normative* theories of ethics. They present us with *norms* or standards and ideals of good (and bad) behavior. They tell us, specifically or abstractly, what we are to do.

But in addition to this central normative concern, there is also a second level of analysis in each of the above theories. It is the more abstract analysis of what the key terms of ethics *mean*—words such as "good" and "ought" and "right," for example. And with this analysis of the meaning of ethical terms, each philosopher also makes a statement about the nature of the justification of ethical statements. Aristotle justifies such statements by reference to the *telos* of being human; Kant justifies them by appeal to reason; Mill to the principle of utility and, ultimately, individual well-being. One might formulate each author's views by way of a definition of "good," such as: for Mill, "good" means conducive to the general happiness, or, for Nietzsche, "good" means expressing the strength of the strongest, or, for Kant, "good" means in accordance with the principles of practical reason. Such analyses of the meaning and justification of ethical terms, as opposed to the actual presentation of a normative ethics telling us what to do, is called **metaethics.** Metaethical theories do not tell us what to do but rather tell us about the nature of ethics and ethical statements. What are they? How are they to be justified? Can they be ultimately justified?

What is common to all of the theories we have examined so far is that, in addition to being normative theories, they have also assumed a position which metaethicists call **naturalism.** Ethical naturalism is the view that ethical statements are based on facts—facts about human nature, facts about what makes us happy, facts about human feelings such as sympathy, facts about human faculties such as practical reason. Sometimes, the naturalism in an ethical theory is quite straightforward, as in John Stuart Mill's equation of goodness and pleasure and as in Aristotle's appeal of all ethical questions to human nature or *telos.* Sometimes, the naturalism is paradoxical; for example, Hume explicitly denies that ethics is based on facts in his sharp separation of "is" and "ought," but then he goes ahead and develops an ethical system in which morals are firmly (if not rationally) based on natural human sentiments, in particular our sympathy or "fellow-feeling." Sometimes, the ethical naturalism of an author can be convoluted indeed; Kant's ethics seems clearly to distinguish between questions of fact and nature (such as, "what makes us happy?" and "what feelings are natural?") and questions of morals, which are always questions of reason and will. But on what ground does he make such a distinction? On the basis of the *fact* that we have a faculty of reason.

Nevertheless, it is clear that Kant, even more than Hume, adamantly insists on a distinction between the facts of nature and the nature of morality, between any concern for the empirically verifiable state of affairs in which an action is performed and the rational, normative considerations which govern the goodness of that action. Indeed, despite the rationality of Kant's ethics, he insists that moral principles are not matters of *knowledge.* Thus he anticipates the position of a great many metaethicists in this century—**nonnaturalism** and **noncognitivism.** The nonnnaturalist believes that ethical statements are not based on empirically verifiable facts. The noncognitivist further believes that the truth of ethical statements cannot be known at all; indeed, ethical statements are neither true nor false.

Nonnaturalism can be traced as far back as Plato, to Socrates' view that the Form of the Good is something distinct from all factual questions about happiness, pleasure, and power. In modern times, the father of nonnaturalism is David Hume, who argued the unbreachable logical gap between "is" and "ought." In this century, the patriarch of nonnaturalism is the Cambridge philosopher G. E. Moore, who pursued Hume's distinction with a tough-minded argument and the name of a new kind of logical fallacy—the **naturalistic fallacy.** The argument is what Moore called "the open question argument." It picks up with Hume's distinction and asks, "Well, you've told me that Phaedo is housebroken, obedient, playful with children and threatening to strangers, but—the question is still open—is Phaedo a *good* dog?" In other words, no matter how many facts are accumulated in an ethical matter, it is still always an "open question" whether the thing or act in question is good or not. The fallacy—the naturalistic fallacy—is ignoring just this logical gap and arguing, wrongly, that a thing or an action is good *because* such and such facts are true of it.

◆on the "Open Question Argument," by G. E. Moore

. . . What, then, is good? How is good to be defined? Now, it may be thought that this is a verbal question. A definition does indeed often mean the expressing of one word's meaning in other words. But this is not the sort of definition I am asking for. . . . My business is solely with that object or idea, which I hold, rightly or wrongly, that the word is generally used to stand for. What I want to discover is the nature of that object or idea, and about this I am extremely anxious to arrive at an agreement.

But, if we understand the question in this sense, my answer to it may seem a very disappointing one. If I am asked "What is good?" my answer is that good is good, and that is the end of the matter. Or if I am asked "How is good to be defined?" my answer is that it cannot be defined, and that is all I have to say about it. But disappointing as these answers may appear, they are of the very last importance. To readers who are familiar with philosophic terminology, I can express their importance by saying that they amount to this: That propositions about the good are all of them synthetic and never analytic; and that is plainly no trivial matter. And the same thing may be expressed more popularly, by saying that, if I am right, then nobody can foist upon us such an axiom as that "Pleasure is the only good" or that "The good is the desired" on the pretence that this is "the very meaning of the word."

Let us, then, consider this position. My point is that "good" is a simple notion, just as "yellow" is a simple notion; that, just as you cannot, by any manner of means, explain to any one who does not already know it, what yellow is, so you cannot explain what good is. Definitions of the kind that I was asking for, definitions which describe the real nature of the object or notion denoted by a word, and which do not merely tell us what the word is used to mean, are only possible when the object or notion in question is something complex. You can give a definition of a horse, because a horse has many different properties and qualities, all of which you can enumerate. But when you have enumerated them all, when you have reduced a horse to his simplest terms, then you can no longer define those terms. They are simply something which you think of or perceive, and to any one who cannot think of or perceive them, you can never, by any definition, make their nature known. It may perhaps be objected to this that we are able to describe to others, objects which they have never seen or thought of. We can, for instance, make a man understand what a chimaera is, although he has never heard of one or seen one. You can tell him that it is an animal with a lioness's head and body, with a goat's head growing from the middle of its back, and with a snake in place of a tail. But here the object which you are describing is a complex object; it is entirely composed of parts, with which we are all perfectly familiar—a snake, a goat, a lioness; and we know, too, the manner to which those parts are to be put together, because we know what is meant by the middle of a lioness's back, and where her tail is wont to grow. And so it is with all objects, not previously known, which we are able to define: they are all complex; all composed of parts, which may themselves, in the first instance, be capable of similar definition, but which must in the end be reducible to simplest parts, which can no longer be defined. But yellow and good, we say, are not complex: they are notions of that simple kind, out of which definitions are composed and with which the power of further defining ceases.

· · · · · · · · · ·

"Good," then, if we mean by it that quality which we assert to belong to a thing, when we say that the thing is good, is incapable of any definition, in the most important sense of that word. The most important sense of "definition" is that in which a definition states what are the parts which invariably compose a certain whole; and in this sense "good" has no definition because it is simple and has no parts. It is one of those innumerable objects of thought which are themselves incapable of definition, because they are the ultimate terms by reference to which whatever *is* capable of definition must be defined. That there must be an indefinite number of such terms is obvious, on reflection; since we cannot define anything except by an analysis, which, when carried so far as it will go, refers us to something, which is simply different from anything else, and which by that ultimate difference explains the peculiarity of the whole which we are defining: for every whole contains some parts which are common to other wholes also. There is, therefore, no intrinsic difficulty in the contention that "good" denotes a simple and indefinable quality. . . . Ethics aims at discovering what are those other properties belonging to all things which are good. But far too many philosophers have thought that when they named those other properties they were actually defining good; that these properties, in fact, were simply not "other," but absolutely and entirely the same with goodness. This view I propose to call the "naturalistic fallacy" and of it I shall now endeavour to dispose.

Let us consider what it is such philosophers say. And first it is to be noticed that they do not agree among themselves. They not only say that they are right as to what good is, but they endeavour to prove that other people who say that it is something else, are wrong. One, for instance, will affirm that good is pleasure, another, perhaps, that good is that which is desired; and each of these will argue eagerly to prove that the other is wrong. But how is that possible? One of them says that good is nothing but the object of desire, and at the same time tries to prove that it is not pleasure. But from his first assertion, that good just means the object of desire, one of two things must follow as regards his proof:

(1) He may be trying to prove that the object of desire is not pleasure. But, if this be all, where is his Ethics? The position he is

maintaining is merely a psychological one. Desire is something which occurs in our minds, and pleasure is something else which so occurs; and our would-be ethical philosopher is merely holding that the latter is not the object of the former. But what has that to do with the question in dispute? His opponent held the ethical proposition that pleasure was the good, and although he should prove a million times over the psychological proposition that pleasure is not the object of desire, he is no nearer proving his opponent to be wrong. The position is like this. One man says a triangle is a circle: another replies "A triangle is a straight line, and I will prove to you that I am right: *for*" (this is the only argument) "a straight line is not a circle." "That is quite true," the other may reply, "but nevertheless a triangle is a circle, and you have said nothing whatever to prove the contrary. What is proved is that one of us is wrong, for we agree that a triangle cannot be both a straight line and a circle: but which is wrong, there can be no earthly means of proving, since you define triangle as straight line and I define it as circle."—Well, that is one alternative which any naturalistic Ethics has to face; if good is *defined* as something else, it is then impossible either to prove that any other definition is wrong or even to deny such definition.

(2)   The other alternative will scarcely be more welcome. It is that the discussion is after all a verbal one. When A says "Good means pleasant" and B says "Good means desired," they may merely wish to assert that most people have used the word for what is pleasant and for what is desired respectively. And this is quite an interesting subject for discussion: only it is not a whit more an ethical discussion than the last was. Nor do I think that any exponent of naturalistic Ethics would be willing to allow that this was all he meant. They are all so anxious to persuade us that what they call the good is what we really ought to do. "Do, pray, act so, because the word 'good' is generally used to denote actions of this nature": such, on this view, would be the substance of their teaching. And in so far as they tell us how we ought to act, their teaching is truly ethical, as they mean it to be. But how perfectly absurd is the reason they would give for it! "You are to do this, because most people use a certain word to denote conduct such as this." "You are to say the thing which is not, because most people call it lying." That is an argument just as good!—My dear sirs, what we want to know from you as ethical teachers, is not how people use a word; it is not even, what kind of actions they approve, which the use of this word "good" may certainly imply: what we want to know is simply what *is* good. We may indeed agree that what most people do think good, is actually so; we shall at all events be glad to know their opinions: but when we say their opinions about what *is* good, we do mean what we say; we do not care whether they call that thing which they mean "horse" or "table" or "chair"; "gut" or "bon" or "αʹγαʹτʹοο"; we want to know what it is that they so

call. When they say "Pleasure is good," we cannot believe that they merely mean "Pleasure is pleasure" and nothing more than that. . . .

My objections to Naturalism are then, in the first place, that it offers no reason at all, far less any valid reason, for any ethical principle whatever; and in this it already fails to satisfy the requirements of Ethics, as a scientific study. But in the second place I contend that, though it gives a reason for no ethical principle, it is a *cause* of the acceptance of false principles—it deludes the mind into accepting ethical principles, which are false; and in this it is contrary to every aim of Ethics. It is easy to see that if we start with a definition of right conduct as conduct conducive to general happiness; then, knowing that right conduct is universally conduct conducive to the good, we very easily arrive at the result that the good is general happiness. If, on the other hand, we once recognize that we must start our Ethics without a definition, we shall be much more apt to look about us, before we adopt any ethical principle whatever; and the more we look about us, the less likely are we to adopt a false one. . . .

Our first conclusion as to the subject-matter of Ethics is, then, that there is a simple, indefinable, unanalysable object of thought by reference to which it must be defined. By what name we call this unique object is a matter of indifference, so long as we clearly recognise what it is and that it does differ from other objects. The words which are commonly taken as the signs of ethical judgments all do refer to it; and they are expressions of ethical judgments solely because they do so refer.[22]

Moore rejects naturalism, but he still insists that ethical statements refer to something—namely, an indefinable nonnatural property of goodness. Accordingly, although one cannot prove that something is good through an argument based on the facts, one can still "see that it is so," and that is a justification of sorts. But other philosophers, following Moore, reject even this kind of justification, insisting that there is *no* property referred to by ethical statements and therefore no grounds for knowing whether such a statement is true or false. These are the *noncognitivists,* who maintain the Humean-Kantian distinction between "is" and "ought" with such fervor that ethics threatens to disappear as a rational discipline. Indeed some of the leading noncognitivists—who call themselves **emotivists**—have argued that there can be no justification of ethical statements. At most, we can encourage and persuade one another to accept certain ethical positions, but the positions themselves are merely matters of emotion or attitude, not questions of belief that can be rationally challenged or rationally justified.

[22] G. E. Moore, *Principia Ethica* (Cambridge: Cambridge University Press, 1st ed. 1903).

◆**on "Emotivism,"**
by A. J. Ayer

. . . It is our business to give an account of "judgements of value" which is both satisfactory in itself and consistent with our general empiricist principles. We shall set ourselves to show that in so far as statements of value are significant, they are ordinary "scientific" statements; and that in so far as they are not scientific, they are not in the literal sense significant, but are simply expressions of emotion which can be neither true nor false. . . .

The ordinary system of ethics, as elaborated in the works of ethical philosophers, is very far from being a homogeneous whole. Not only is it apt to contain pieces of metaphysics, and analyses of non-ethical concepts: its actual ethical contents are themselves of very different kinds. We may divide them, indeed, into four main classes. There are, first of all, propositions which express definitions of ethical terms, or judgements about the legitimacy or possibility of certain definitions. Secondly, there are propositions describing the phenomena of moral experience and their causes. Thirdly, there are exhortations to moral virtue. And, lastly, there are actual ethical judgements. It is unfortunately the case that the distinction between these four classes, plain as it is, is commonly ignored by ethical philosophers; with the result that it is often very difficult to tell from their works what it is that they are seeking to discover or prove.

In fact, it is easy to see that only the first of our four classes, namely that which comprises the propositions relating to the definitions of ethical terms, can be said to constitute ethical philosophy. The propositions which describe the phenomena of moral experience, and their causes, must be assigned to the science of psychology, or sociology. The exhortations to moral virtue are not propositions at all, but ejaculations or commands which are designed to provoke the reader to action of a certain sort. Accordingly, they do not belong to any branch of philosophy or science. As for the expressions of ethical judgements, we have not yet determined how they should be classified. But inasmuch as they are certainly neither definitions nor comments upon definitions, nor quotations, we may say decisively that they do not belong to ethical philosophy. A strictly philosophical treatise on ethics should therefore make no ethical pronouncements. But it should, by giving an analysis of ethical terms, show what is the category to which all such pronouncements belong. And this is what we are now about to do.

A question which is often discussed by ethical philosophers is whether it is possible to find definitions which would reduce all ethical terms to one or two fundamental terms. But this question, though it undeniably belongs to ethical philosophy, is not relevant to our present enquiry. We are not now concerned to discover which term, within the sphere of ethical terms, is to be taken as fundamental; whether, for example, "good" can be defined in terms of "right" or "right" in terms of "good," or both in terms of "value." What we are interested in is the possibility of reducing the whole sphere of ethical terms to non-ethical terms. We are enquiring whether statements of ethical value can be translated into statements of empirical fact.

That they can be so translated is the contention of those ethical philosophers who are commonly called subjectivists, and of those who are known as utilitarians. For the utilitarian defines the rightness of actions, and the goodness of ends, in terms of the pleasure, or happiness, or satisfaction, to which they give rise; the subjectivist, in terms of the feelings of approval which a certain person, or group of people, has towards them. Each of these types of definition makes moral judgements into a sub-class of psychological or sociological judgements; and for this reason they are very attractive to us. For, if either was correct, it would follow that ethical assertions were not generically different from the factual assertions which are ordinarily contrasted with them; and the account which we have already given of empirical hypotheses would apply to them also.

Nevertheless we shall not adopt either a subjectivist or a utilitarian analysis of ethical terms. We reject the subjectivist view that to call an action right, or a thing good, is to say that it is generally approved of, because it is not self-contradictory to assert that some actions which are generally approved of are not right, or that some things which are generally approved of are not good. And we reject the alternative subjectivist view that a man who asserts that a certain action is right, or that a certain thing is good, is saying that he himself approves of it, on the ground that a man who confessed that he sometimes approved of what was bad or wrong would not be contradicting himself. And a similar argument is fatal to utilitarianism. We cannot agree that to call an action right is to say that all of the actions possible in the circumstances it would cause, or be likely to cause, the greatest happiness, of the greatest balance of pleasure over pain, or the greatest balance of satisfied over unsatisfied desire, because we find that it is not self-contradictory to say that it is sometimes wrong to perform the action which would actually or probably cause the greatest happiness, or the greatest balance of pleasure over pain, or of satisfied over unsatisfied desire. And since it is not self-contradictory to say that some pleasant things are not good, or that some bad things are desired, it cannot be the case that the sentence "x is good" is equivalent to "x is pleasant," or "x is desired." And to every other variant of utilitarianism with which I am acquainted the same objection can be made. And therefore we should, I think, conclude that the validity of ethical judgements is not determined by the felicific tendencies of actions, any more than by the nature of people's feelings; but that it must be regarded as "absolute" or "intrinsic," and not empirically calculable. . . .

In admitting that normative ethical concepts are irreducible to empirical concepts, we seem to be leaving the way clear for the "absolutist" view of ethics—that is, the view that statements of value are not controlled by observation, ordinary empirical propositions are but only by a mysterious "intellectual intuition." A feature of this theory, which is seldom recognized by its advocates, is that it makes statements of value unverifiable. For it is notorious that what seems intuitively certain to one person may seem doubtful, or even false, to another. So that unless it is possible to provide some criterion by which one may decide between conflicting intuitions, a mere appeal to intuition is worthless as a test of a proposition's validity. But in the case of moral judgements, no such criterion can be given. Some moralists claim to settle the matter by saying that they "know" that their own moral judgements are correct. But such an assertion is of purely psychological interest and has not the slightest tendency to prove the validity of any moral judgement. For dissentient moralists may equally well "know" that their ethical views are correct. And, as far as subjective certainty goes, there will be nothing to choose between them. When such differences of opinion arise in connection with an ordinary empirical proposition, one may attempt to resolve them by referring to, or actually carrying out, some relevant empirical test. But with regard to ethical statements, there is, on the "absolutist" or "intuitionist" theory, no relevant empirical test. We are therefore justified in saying that on this theory ethical statements are held to be unverifiable. . . .

Considering the use which we have made of the principle that a synthetic proposition is significant only if it is empirically verifiable, it is clear that the acceptance of an "absolutist" theory of ethics would undermine the whole of our main argument. And as we have already rejected the "naturalistic" theories which are commonly supposed to provide the only alternative to "absolutism" in ethics, we seem to have reached a difficult position. We shall meet the difficulty by showing that the correct treatment of ethical statements is afforded by a third theory, which is wholly compatible with our radical empiricism.

We begin by admitting that the fundamental ethical concepts are unanalysable, inasmuch as there is no criterion by which one can test the validity of the judgements in which they occur. So far we are in agreement with the absolutists. But, unlike the absolutists, we are able to give an explanation of this fact about ethical concepts. We say that the reason why they are unanalysable is that they are mere pseudo-concepts. The presence of an ethical symbol in a proposition adds nothing to its factual content. Thus if I say to someone, "You acted wrongly in stealing that money," I am not stating anything more than if I had simply said, "You stole that money." In adding that this action is wrong I am not making any further statement about it. I am simply evincing my moral disapproval of it. It is as if I had said, "You stole that money," in a peculiar tone of horror, or written it with the addition of some special exclamation marks. The tone, or the exclamation marks, adds nothing to the literal meaning of the sentence. It merely serves to show that the expression of it is attended by certain feelings in the speaker.

If now I generalise my previous statement and say, "Stealing money is wrong," I produce a sentence which has no factual meaning—that is, expresses no proposition which can be either true or false. It is as if I had written "Stealing money!!"—where the shape and thickness of the exclamation marks show, by a suitable convention, that a special sort of moral disapproval is the feeling which is being expressed. It is clear that there is nothing said here which can be true or false. Another man may disagree with me about the wrongness of stealing, in the sense that he may not have the same feelings about stealing as I have, and he may quarrel with me on account of my moral sentiments. But he cannot, strictly speaking, contradict me. For in saying that a certain type of action is right or wrong, I am not making any factual statement, not even a statement about my own state of mind. I am merely expressing certain moral sentiments. And the man who is ostensibly contradicting me is merely expressing his moral sentiments. So that there is plainly no sense in asking which of us is in the right. For neither of us is asserting a genuine proposition.

What we have just been saying about the symbol "wrong" applies to all normative ethical symbols. Sometimes they occur in sentences which record ordinary empirical facts besides expressing ethical feeling about those facts: sometimes they occur in sentences which simply express ethical feeling about a certain type of action, or situation, without making any statement of fact. But in every case in which one would commonly be said to be making an ethical judgement, the function of the relevant ethical word is purely "emotive." It is used to express feeling about certain objects, but not to make any assertion about them.[23]

The problems with emotivism are rather obvious, but their exploration quickly takes us deep into the nature of ethics. What happens, in the emotivist theory, to questions of justification, for surely we do justify our actions and appeal to principles? Why should a statement be unjustifiable just because it is based on emotion, for are not emotions—at least sometimes—justifiable? (One can have a right to be jealous, and one can be angry with good reason.) And does emotivism mean that any ethical opinion is as warranted as any other, if only it is the sincere expression of a felt attitude or emotion? (But then, why should sincerity be important either?) Today, almost every ethicist agrees that emotivism is an inadequate and extreme theory. But if one accepts the distinction between "is" and "ought" in any of its versions and consequently accepts Moore's "open question argument," what alternatives to emotivism are

[23]A. J. Ayer, *Language, Truth and Logic* (New York: Dover, 1936).

there? In fact, as you can imagine, ethicists have suggested a great many more plausible metaethical theories, but these must be the substance of another course.

The rise of emotivism in ethics does suggest, however, that something has gone very wrong, not only in metaethical theory, but in the realm of normative ethics as well. Could it be, for example, that the rise of emotivism reflects a society in which—unlike the society of Aristotle or even Kant—no one knows with any confidence what is to be done, what is good or right, whether some values are really better than others? This is the argument of moral philosopher Alasdair MacIntyre, who combines normative ethics, metaethics and sociology to arrive at a diagnosis of what has gone wrong in contemporary ethical theory. (What he ultimately advocates is a return to the ethics of Aristotle.)

◆from *After Virtue,* by Alasdair MacIntyre

Imagine that the natural sciences were to suffer the effects of a catastrophe. A series of environmental disasters are blamed by the general public on the scientists. Widespread riots occur, laboratories are burnt down, physicists are lynched, books and instruments are destroyed. Finally a Know-Nothing political movement takes power and successfully abolishes science teaching in schools and universities, imprisoning and executing the remaining scientists. Later still there is a reaction against this destructive movement and enlightened people seek to revive science, although they have largely forgotten what it was. But all that they possess are fragments: a knowledge of experiments detached from any knowledge of the theoretical context which gave them significance; parts of theories unrelated either to the other bits and pieces of theory which they possess or to experiment; instruments whose use has been forgotten; half-chapters from books, single pages from articles, not always fully legible because torn and charred. None the less all these fragments are reembodied in a set of practices which go under the revived names of physics, chemistry and biology. Adults argue with each other about the respective merits of relativity theory, evolutionary theory and phlogiston theory, although they possess only a very partial knowledge of each. Children learn by heart the surviving portions of the periodic table and recite as incantations some of the theorems of Euclid. Nobody, or almost nobody, realises that what they are doing is not natural science in any proper sense at all. For everything that they do and say conforms to certain canons of consistency and coherence and those contexts which would be needed to make sense of what they are doing have been lost, perhaps irretrievably.

In such a culture men would use expressions such as "neutrino," "mass," "specific gravity," "atomic weight" in systematic and often interrelated ways which would resemble in lesser or greater degrees the ways in which such expressions had been used in earlier times before scientific knowledge had been so largely lost. But many of the beliefs presupposed by the use of these expressions would have been lost and there would appear to be an element of arbitrariness and even of choice in their application which would appear very surprising to us. What would appear to be rival and competing premises for which no further argument could be given would abound. Subjectivist theories of science would appear and would be criticised by those who held that the notion of truth embodied in what they took to be science was incompatible with subjectivism.

· · · · · · · · · ·

What is the point of constructing this imaginary world inhabited by fictitious pseudo-scientists and real, genuine philosophy? The hypothesis which I wish to advance is that in the actual world which we inhabit the language of morality is in the same state of grave disorder as the language of natural science in the imaginary world which I described. What we possess, if this view is true, are the fragments of a conceptual scheme, parts which now lack those contexts from which their significance derived. We possess indeed simulacra of morality, we continue to use many of the key expressions. But we have—very largely, if not entirely—lost our comprehension, both theoretical and practical, of morality.

· · · · · · · · · ·

[ON EMOTIVISM AND MORAL DECLINE]

It is, I take it, no accident that the acutest of the modern founders of emotivism . . . were pupils of Moore; it is not implausible to suppose that they did in fact confuse moral utterance at Cambridge (and in other places with a similar inheritance) after 1903 with moral utterance as such, and that they therefore presented what was in essentials a correct account of the former as though it were an account of the latter. Moore's followers had behaved as if their disagreements over what is good were being settled by an appeal to an objective and impersonal criterion; but in fact the stronger and psychologically more adroit will was prevailing. It is unsurprising that emotivists sharply distinguished between factual, including perceptual, disagreement and what Stevenson called "disagreement in attitude." But if the claims of emotivism, understood as claims about the use of moral utterance at Cambridge after 1903 and its heirs and successors in London and elsewhere rather than about the meaning of moral expressions at all times and places, seem remarkably cogent, it turns out to be for reasons which at first sight seem to undermine emotivism's universal claims and with them emotivism's apparent threat to my original thesis.

What makes emotivism convincing as a thesis about a certain

kind of moral utterance at Cambridge after 1903 are certain features specific to that historical episode. Those whose evaluative utterances embodied Moore's interpretations of those utterances could not have been doing what they took themselves to be doing because of the falsity of Moore's thesis. But nothing whatsoever seems to follow about moral utterance in general. Emotivism on this account turns out to be an empirical thesis, or rather a preliminary sketch of an empirical thesis, presumably to be filled out later by psychological and sociological and historical observations, about those who continue to use moral and other evaluative expressions, as if they were governed by objective and impersonal criteria, when all grasp of any such criterion has been lost. We should therefore expect emotivist types of theory to arise in a specific local circumstance as a response to types of theory and practice which share certain key features of Moore's intuitionism. Emotivism thus understood turns out to be, as a cogent theory of use rather than a false theory of meaning, connected with one specific stage in moral development or decline, a stage which our own culture entered early in the present century.

   • • • • • • • • • •

 The scheme of moral decline which these remarks presuppose would, as I suggested earlier, be one which required the discrimination of three distinct stages; a first at which evaluative and more especially moral theory and practice embody genuine objective and impersonal standards which provide rational justification for particular policies, actions and judgments and which themselves in turn are susceptible of rational justification; a second stage at which there are unsuccessful attempts to maintain the objectivity and impersonality of moral judgments, but during which the project of providing rational justifications both by means of and for the standards continuously breaks down; and a third stage at which theories of an emotivist kind secure wide implicit acceptance because of a general implicit recognition in practice, though not in explicit theory, that claims to objectivity and impersonality cannot be made good. . . . What I have suggested to be the case by and large about our own culture—that in moral argument the apparent assertion of principles functions as a mask for expressions of personal preference—is what emotivism takes to be universally the case.

   • • • • • • • • • •

[THE SOCIAL CONTEXT OF EMOTIVISM]

 A moral philosophy—and emotivism is no exception—characteristically presupposes a sociology. For every moral philosophy offers explicitly or implicitly at least a partial conceptual analysis of the relationship of an agent to his or her reasons, motives, intentions and actions, and in so doing generally presupposes some claim that these concepts are embodied or at least can be in the real social world. Even Kant, who sometimes seems to restrict moral agency to the inner realm of the noumenal, implies otherwise in his writings on law, history and politics. Thus it would generally be a decisive refutation of a moral philosophy to show that moral agency on its own account of the matter could never be socially embodied; and it also follows that we have not yet fully understood the claims of any moral philosophy until we have spelled out what its social embodiment would be. Some moral philosophers in the past, perhaps most, have understood this spelling out as itself one part of the task of moral philosophy. So, it scarcely needs to be said, Plato and Aristotle, so indeed also Hume and Adam Smith; but at least since Moore the dominant narrow conception of moral philosophy has ensured that the moral philosophers could ignore this task; as notably do the philosophical proponents of emotivism. We therefore must perform it for them.

What is the key to the social content of emotivism? It is the fact that emotivism entails the obliteration of any genuine distinction between manipulative and non-manipulative social relations. Consider the contrast between, for example, Kantian ethics and emotivism on this point. For Kant . . . the difference between a human relationship uninformed by morality and one so informed is precisely the difference between one in which each person treats the other primarily as a means to his or her ends and one in which each treats the other as an end. To treat someone else as an end is to offer them what I take to be good reasons for acting in one way rather than another, but to leave it to them to evaluate those reasons. It is to be unwilling to influence another except by reasons which that other he or she judges to be good. It is to appeal to impersonal criteria of the validity of which each rational agent must be his or her own judge. By contrast, to treat someone else as a means is to seek to make him or her an instrument of my purposes by adducing whatever influences or considerations will in fact be effective in this or that occasion. The generalisations of the sociology and psychology of persuasion are what I shall need to guide me, not the standards of a normative rationality.

If emotivism is true, this distinction is illusory. For evaluative utterance can in the end have no point or use by the expression of my own feelings or attitudes and the transformation of the feelings and attitudes of others. I cannot genuinely appeal to impersonal criteria, for there are no impersonal criteria. I may think that I so appeal and others may think that I so appeal, but these thoughts will always be mistakes. The sole reality of distinctively moral discourse is the attempt of one will to align the attitudes, feelings, preferences and choices of another with its own. Others are always means, never ends.

What then would the social world *look* like, if seen with emotivist eyes? And what would the social world *be* like, if the truth of emotivism came to be widely presupposed? The general form of the answer to these questions is now clear, but the social detail depends in part on the nature of particular social contexts; it will make a difference in what milieu and in the service of what particular and specific interests the distinction between manipulative and non-manipulative social relationships has been obliterated. William Gass has suggested that it was a principle concern of Henry James to examine the consequences of the obliteration of this distinction in the lives of a particular kind of rich European in *The Portrait of a Lady* . . . that the novel turns out to be an investigation, in Gass's words, "of what it means to be a consumer of persons, and of what it means to be a person consumed." The metaphor of consumption acquires its appropriateness from the milieu; James is concerned with rich aesthetes whose interest is to fend off the kind of boredom that is so characteristic of modern leisure by contriving behaviour in others that will be responsive to their wishes, that will feed their stated appetites. Those wishes may or may not be benevolent, but the distinction between characters who entertain themselves by willing the good of others and those who pursue the fulfillment of their desires without a concern for any good but their own . . . is not as important to James as the distinction between a whole milieu in which the manipulative mode of moral instrumentalism has triumphed and one, such as the New England of *The Europeans*, of which this was not true . . . The unifying preoccupation of that tradition is the condition of those who see in the social world nothing but a meeting place for individual wills each with its own set of attitudes and preferences and who understand that world solely as an arena for the achievement of their own satisfaction, who interpret reality as a series of opportunities for their enjoyment and for whom the last enemy is boredom.

Another social context is that provided by the life of organisations, of those bureaucratic structures which, whether in the form of private corporations or of government agencies, define the working tasks of so many of our contemporaries. One sharp contrast with the lives of the aesthetic rich secures immediate attention. The rich aesthete with a plethora of means searches restlessly for ends on which he may employ them; but the organisation is characteristically engaged in a competitive struggle for scarce resources to put to the service of its predetermined ends. It is therefore a central responsibility of managers to direct and redirect their organisations' available resources, both human and non-human, as effectively as possible toward those ends. Every bureaucratic organisation embodies some explicit or implicit definition of costs and benefits from which the criteria of effectiveness are derived. Bureaucratic rationality is the rationality of matching means to ends economically and efficiently.

· · · · · · · · · ·

[CONCLUSION]

It is always dangerous to draw too precise parallels between one historical period and another; and among the most misleading of such parallels are those which have been drawn between our own age in Europe and North America and the epoch in which the Roman empire declined into the Dark Ages. None the less certain parallels there are. A crucial turning point in that earlier history occurred when men and women of good will turned aside from the task of shoring up the Roman *imperium* and ceased to identify the continuation of civility and moral community with the maintenance of that *imperium*. What they set themselves to achieve instead— often not recognising fully what they were doing—was the construction of new forms of community within which the moral life could be sustained so that both morality and civility might survive the coming ages of barbarism and darkness. If my account of our moral condition is correct, we ought also to conclude that for some time now we too have reached that turning point. What matters at this stage is the construction of local forms of community within which civility and the intellectual and moral life can be sustained through the new dark ages which are already upon us. And if the tradition of the virtues was able to survive the horrors of the last dark ages, we are not entirely without ground for hope. This time however the barbarians are not waiting beyond the frontiers; they have already been governing us for quite some time. . . .[24]

SUMMARY AND CONCLUSION

In this chapter, we have reviewed a half dozen or so theories of morality. (1) Aristotle takes the key to morality to be the concept of "virtue," which he argues to be activity in accordance with rational principles. He bases this argument on a concept of what is "natural" for man, but his discussion is clearly limited to a small class of Greek male citizens, whom he views as the ideal specimens of humanity. (2) Hume and Rousseau both argue that morality must be based on certain kinds of feelings or "sentiments." "Reason is and ought to be the slave of the passions," Hume argues, and Rousseau similarly argues that man is "naturally" good. (3) Kant insists that morality is strictly a matter of rational principle divorced from all personal interests and desires ("inclinations"). This includes a rejection of Hume and Rousseau, who base morality on feelings (which are inclinations in Kant's sense). This also includes a rejection of Aristotle. Although both philosophers use the notion of a "rational principle," Kant intends his notion to apply to every human being, and therefore every person has the same duties and obligations. (4) The utilitarians, Bentham and Mill, reject Kant's divorce between morality and personal interest and argue that morality is our guide to the satisfaction of the greatest number of interests of the greatest number of people. (5) Nietzsche rejects both Kant and the utilitarians, preferring a return to the elitism and "virtue" orientation of Aristotle's

[24]Alasdair MacIntyre, *After Virtue* (Notre Dame, IN: University of Notre Dame Press, 1981).

ethics. He argues that we create our values and live with them according to our personal needs. Following him, the existentialists, particularly Jean-Paul Sartre, argue that all values are chosen by us; there is no "true" morality, only those values to which we have voluntarily committed ourselves. (6) American pragmatism rejects the sharp boundaries between "is" and "ought," and (7) shifting to the "metaethical" level of analysis, contemporary English and American ethicists have suggested that the whole idea of justification by reference to happiness or reason may be mistaken, with some disturbing consequences.

GLOSSARY

a priori   in moral philosophy, independent of particular circumstances. In Kant's philosophy, moral laws are said to be a priori in this sense.

altruism   the thesis that one ought to act for the sake of the interests of others.

autonomy   independence. Moral autonomy is the ability of every rational person to reach his or her own moral conclusions about what is right and what is wrong. (This does not mean that they will therefore come to different conclusions.)

categorical imperative   in Kant's philosophy, a moral law, a command that is unqualified and not dependent on any conditions or qualifications. In particular, that rule that tells us to act in such a way that we would want everyone else to act the same way.

commitment   to form a binding obligation voluntarily. In Sartre's moral philosophy, a commitment is a freely chosen adoption of a moral principle or project which one thereby vows to defend and practice, even in the absence of any other reasons for doing so. And since, according to Sartre, there are never conclusive reasons for adopting any particular moral position, one must always defend his or her position through commitment and nothing else.

conscience   a sense or feeling about what is right and wrong, usually without argument. (It is like intuition in matters of knowledge.) In Christian moral theory, it is a moral sense instilled in us by God. In Freudian psychology, it is the internalization of the moral lessons given us as children by our parents and teachers.

contemplation (the life of)   according to Aristotle (and other philosophers), the happiest life, the life of thought and philosophy.

cultural relativism   the descriptive anthropological thesis that different societies have different moralities. It is important to stress that these moralities must be fundamentally different, not only different in details. Some societies consider an act as stealing while others do not, but a society that does not have a conception of private property might be fundamentally different from one that does.

deontology   ethics based on duty (Gk: *dein*). Kant's ethic is deontological in that it stresses obedience to principle rather than attention to consequences (including happiness).

duty   what one is morally bound to do.

egoism   the thesis that people act for their own interests. *Psychological egoism* is merely the thesis that they in fact act in their own interests; *ethical egoism* is the thesis that people ought to act in their own interests.

emotivism   the view that ethical statements are simply an expression of feeling or attitude and therefore not justifiable or knowable as true or false.

ethics   a system of general moral principles and a conception of morality and its foundation. Or, the study of moral principles.

ethical absolutism   the thesis that there is one and only one correct morality.

ethical egoism   the thesis that people ought to act in their own interests.

ethical relativism   the thesis that different moralities should be considered equally correct even if they directly contradict each other. A morality is "correct," by this thesis, merely if it is correct according to the particular society that accepts it.

eudaimonia   Aristotle's word for "happiness," or, more literally, "living well."

existentialism   the modern movement in philosophy that puts great emphasis on individual choice and the voluntary acceptance of all values.

Golden Rule   "Do unto others as you would have them do unto you."

happiness   the achievement of the good life. In Aristotle, the name we all agree to give to the good life, whatever it is. Happiness, in this sense, must not be confused with pleasure, which is but one (among many) concerns and conceptions of the good life.

happiness calculus (also *felicity calculus*)   Bentham's technique for quantifying and adding up pleasures and pains as a way of deciding what to do.

hedonism   the conception of the good life that takes pleasure to be the ultimate good. Hedonism is the premise of most forms of utilitarianism. It is often the premise—though sometimes a consequence—of ethical egoism. (These two are not the same: hedonism refers to the *end;* egoism refers to *whose* ends.)

hypothetical imperative   in Kant, a command that is conditional, depending upon particular aims or inclinations. For example, "if you want to be a doctor, then go to medical school." According to Kant, all other philosophers (Aristotle, Hume, Rousseau) took morality to be a hypothetical imperative. He does not.

immoralist   a person who rejects the ultimate claims of morality. An immoralist need not actually break the rules of morality; he does not consider them absolute rules and claims that other considerations (even personal considerations) may override them.

imperative   a command.

inclination   Kant's term for all personal considerations: desires, feelings, emotions, attitudes, moods, etc.

law   an objective rule that is binding on individuals whether they personally accept it or not. Contrasted with *maxim*.

master morality   in Nietzsche, a morality that takes personal self-realization as primary, so-called because it was the morality of the "masters" in the slave states of the ancient world (including Greece).

maxim   in Kant, a personal rule or intention. Contrasted with *law*.

mean (between the extremes)   in Aristotle, the middle course, not too much, not too little. Courage, for example, is a mean because a person with courage is neither too timid to fight nor so lacking in fear that he or she is rash or reckless in the face of danger.

metaethics   the study of ethical language and the nature of justification of ethical statements.

morality   in general, the rules for right action and prohibitions against wrong acts. Sometimes morality is that single set of absolute rules and prohibitions that are valid for all men at all times and all societies. More loosely, a morality can be any set of ultimate principles, and there might be any number of moralities in different societies.

naturalism   the view that ethical statements are ultimately based on facts (about human nature, happiness, reason, feeling).

naturalistic fallacy   according to Moore, inferring on "ought" statement from factual premises.

noncognitivism   the view that ethical statements are neither true nor false and so cannot be *known* to be true or false.

nonnaturalism   the view that ethical statements are not ultimately based on facts.

obligation   bound by duty. For example, "you have an obligation to keep your promises."

ought   the term most often used to express moral duty or obligation. Sometimes "should" is used, but this is ambiguously between "ought" and merely "preferable." Sometimes "must" or "have to" is used, but this is ambiguously between "ought to" and "forced to." In Hume's ethics (and in many others as well) "ought" is contrasted with "is" as the hallmark of value (esp. moral) judgment.

principle of utility   in Bentham, the principle that one ought to do what gives the greatest pleasure to the greatest number of people.

psychological egoism   the thesis that people always act for their own self-interest, even when it seems as if they are acting for other people's benefit (for example, in giving to charity, the egoist would say, the person is simply making himself or herself feel self-righteous).

rationality   acting in the best possible way; according to reason. Sometimes, rationality means simply doing what is best under the circumstances, without insisting that there is only one rational way of acting. In other words, rationality is considered relative to particular interests and circumstances. In Kant's philosophy, however, rationality refers to that faculty that allows us to act in the correct way, without reference to particular interests and circumstances.

relativism   the thesis that morals are relative to particular societies, particular interests, particular circumstances, or particular individuals. (See *cultural relativism, ethical relativism.*)

selfishness   acting in one's own interest to the exclusion of others' interests. The word has a nasty connotation and so should be separated from the more neutral claims of the psychological egoist. To say that a person is acting selfishly is to condemn him or her and say that the action is blameworthy. It is possible to act for one's own interests, however, and not be selfish, for one may also act for the benefit of others. A selfish act is to the exclusion of other people's interests; an act may be both in one's own interests and in the interests of others, however.

sentiment   feeling, emotion; particularly moral feelings (as in Hume, Rousseau).

slave morality   in Nietzsche's moral philosophy, a morality that takes duties and obligations as primary, so called because it was the morality of the slaves who were not allowed to aspire any higher than mere efficiency and personal comfort.

sympathy   fellow feeling; felt concern for other people's welfare. In the ethics of Hume and Rousseau, the necessary and univeral sentiment without which morals—and society—would be impossible.

utilitarianism   the moral philosophy that says that we should act in such ways as to make the greatest number of people as happy as possible.

virtue   moral excellence. In Aristotle's philosophy, a state of character according to which we enjoy doing what is right. In Kant, willing what is right (whether or not we enjoy it, in fact, especially if we don't enjoy it).

will   the power of mind that allows us to choose our own actions, or, at least, what we shall try to do. In Kant, a good will is the only thing that is good "without qualification," in other words, acting for the right reasons and good intentions.

will to power   in Nietzsche's philosophy, the thesis that every act is ultimately aimed at superiority, sometimes over other people, but, more importantly, superiority according to one's own standards. In other words, it is what Aristotle meant by excellence. (Nietzsche has often been interpreted, however, to mean political power.)

◆ *BIBLIOGRAPHY AND FURTHER READING* ◆

A comprehensive but brief history of ethics is A. MacIntyre, *A Short History of Ethics* (New York: Macmillan, 1966). A general schematic discussion of the problems of ethics is W. Fankena, *Ethics* (Englewood Cliffs, NJ: Prentice-Hall, 1963). A much more detailed survey of the problems and the recent history of ethics is Richard R. Brandt, *Ethical Theory,* (Englewood Cliffs, NJ: Prentice-Hall, 1959). Also available is a companion anthology, Richard R. Brandt, *Value and Obligation* (New York: Harcourt Brace Jovanovich, 1961). The classic arguments against egoism are in J. Butler, *Fifteen Sermons Upon Human Nature* (London: Macmillan, 1900). A more modern and technical set of arguments is in T. Nagel, *The Possibility of Altruism* (New York: Oxford University Press, 1970). Textbooks that include various discussions of ethical options are R. N. Beck and J. B. Orr, *Ethical Choice* (New York: Free Press, 1970) and John Hospers, *Human Conduct* (New York: Harcourt Brace Jovanovich, 1962). Aristotle's *Nicomachean Ethics* is translated by W. D. Ross (Oxford: Oxford University Press, 1925). Ross also has a good summary of the arguments in his *Aristotle* (New York: Meridian, 1959). Some excellent articles on Aristotle's ethics are collected in J. Walsh and H. Shapiro, eds., *Aristotle's Ethics* (Belmont, CA: Wadsworth, 1967) and J. Moravscik, ed., *Aristotle* (New York: Doubleday, Anchor, 1966). David Hume's moral philosophy is most accessible in his *Enquiry Concerning the Principles of Morals* (La Salle, IL: Open Court, 1912). Jean-Jacques Rousseau's moral theories are to be found in his second discourse "On the Origins of Inequality" in *The Social Contract* (New York: Dutton, 1950) and in *Emile* (New York: Dutton,

1970). The best summary of Immanuel Kant's moral philosophy is his own *Foundations of the Metaphysics of Morals,* available in various translations, the most helpful, because of the commentary, being *Groundwork of the Metaphysics of Morals,* trans H. J. Paton (New York: Harper & Row, 1957). See also Immanuel Kant, *Lectures in Ethics,* trans. L. Infield (New York: Harper & Row, 1963). John Stuart Mill's utilitarianism is well summarized in his pamphlet *Utilitarianism* (New York: Dutton, 1910). A good summary of Friedrich Nietzsche's ethics is in Walter Kaufmann, *Nietzsche* (Princeton, NJ: Princeton University Press, 1950). A good summary of existentialist ethics is M. Warnock, *Existentialist Ethics* (New York: St. Martin's Press, 1967). For a concise history of twentieth-century metaethics, see M. Warnock, *Ethics Since 1900* (London: Oxford University Press, 1974). MacIntyre's *After Virtue* is published by the University of Notre Dame Press (2nd ed. 1984).

10

JUSTICE AND THE STATE

Man is by nature an animal designed for living in states.

ARISTOTLE

"Man is a social animal," wrote Aristotle. Therefore, he is a political animal as well. We live with other people, not just our friends and families but thousands and millions of others, most of whom we will never meet and many of whom we come across in only the most casual way—passing them as we cross the street or buying a ticket at the movie theater. Yet we have to be concerned about them, and they about us, for there is a sense in which we are all clearly dependent upon each other. For example, we depend on them not to attack us without reason or steal our possessions. Of course, our confidence varies from person to person and from city to city. But it is clear that, in general, we have duties toward people we never know, for example, the duty not to contaminate their water or air supplies, or place their lives in danger. And they have similar duties to us. We also claim certain rights for ourselves: for example, the right not to be attacked as we walk down the street, the right to speak our mind about politically controversial issues without being thrown in jail, the right to believe in this religion or that religion or no religion without having our jobs, our homes, or our freedom taken from us.

Political and social philosophy is the study of people in societies with particular attention to the abstract claims they have on each other in the form of "rights," "duties," and "privileges," and their demands for "justice," "equality," and "freedom." (It is important to distinguish this sense of *political* freedom from the causal or metaphysical freedom that we discussed earlier. These can be and are almost always discussed independently of each other). At least ideally, politics is continuous with morality. Our political duties and obligations, for example, are often the same as our moral duties and obligations. Our claims to certain "moral rights" are often claims to political rights as well, and political rights—

particularly those very general and absolute rights which we call human rights (for example, the right not to be tortured or degraded, the right not to be exploited by powerful institutions or persons)—are typically defended on the basis of moral principles. The virtues of government are ideally the virtues of individuals: Government should be just, temperate, courageous, honest, humane, considerate, and reasonable.

Plato and Aristole, for example, portrayed their visions of the ideal state in precisely these terms. (Both Plato and Aristotle, unlike most modern philosophers, actually had the opportunity to set up such governments; both failed, but for reasons that were hardly their fault.) This is not to say that all politics or all politicians are moral; we know much better than that. But it is to say that our politics are constrained and determined by our sense of morality. Morality is concerned more with relations between particular people while politics is concerned more with large and impersonal groups. But the difference is one of degree. In ancient Greece, Plato and Aristotle lived in relatively small "city-states" (each called a *polis*), with fewer citizens than even most American towns. It was much easier for them to treat morality and politics together. But even today, we still speak hopefully of "the human family" and "international brotherhood," which is to reassert our enduring belief that politics—even at the international level—ought to be based on inter-personal moral principles.

The key to a successful society is cooperation. With few exceptions, it is in everyone's interest that society work smoothly, without vast bureaucratic confusion, without corruption, without general chaos, without exploitation of the weaker members of society, and without forcing anyone to feel that he or she is justified in stealing, cheating, murdering, or "getting even" with society as a whole. But the smooth working of society as a whole, even though it generally benefits everyone, is not the only concern. Societies of ants and bees work more "smoothly" than any human society, but they are not to be envied or imitated. Even if it is agreed that the smooth working of society is generally in everyone's interest, what we may call the public interest, individual interests deserve and sometimes demand recognition even in opposition to this broader public interest. A person who is critical of the government may very well disrupt the smooth operations of that government. He or she may even, at least for a short time, interfere with the public interest. But most of us would agree that such a person has a right to speak his or her mind and that he or she has a right to be heard as well.

Or, to take a very different example, scientists or artists might feel the need to act in ways that are very unpopular or antisocial in order to do their work with the intensity they require. Despite the fact that they might annoy us, we would say that they have a right to live that way. Or, to take still a different example, people who have sexual preferences and desires that are not approved of by most people around them—perhaps they just enjoy an occasional obscene movie—can claim to have rights as well, so long as they don't force their preferences on other people or otherwise interfere with other people's lives. But you can see that with this last set of examples we have entered an area of continuing controversy. Do people have rights to enjoy things that are disapproved of by the rest of society? Should governments dictate morals (for example, by passing laws against the things that most people or at least some powerful people consider "immoral")? And the very existence of such controversies shows very clearly how different we are from ants and bees. In their societies, species preservation and instinct dictate all; in our societies, there must always be a balance between the public interest on the one hand and individual rights and interests on the other. Ideally, these will agree as much as possible. In fact, they often do not agree. And political and social philosophy makes this disagreement its primary concern.

If people do not cooperate, the success of society requires that some authority have the power to bring individual interests into line with the public interest. This authority is generally called the state. The state passes laws and enforces them; its purpose is to protect the public interest. But is it only this? We would probably say *no*. Its purpose is also to protect individual rights, for example, against powerful corporations and against strongly mobilized pressure groups that try to interfere with individual lives. In general, we might say that the function of the state is to protect justice. But there has been disagreement ever since ancient times about what that means and how much the primary emphasis should be placed on the public interest and how much on individual rights and interests.

Our concept of the state and the extent of its power and **authority** depends very much on our conception of human nature and of people's willingness to cooperate without being forced to do so. At one extreme are those who place such strong emphasis on the smooth workings of society that they are willing to sacrifice most individual rights and interests; they are generally called *authoritarians,* and their confidence in willing individual cooperation is very slight compared to their confidence in a strong authoritarian state. ("He makes the trains run on time" was often said of the fascist Italian dictator Benito Mussolini.) At the other extreme are people with so much confidence in individual cooperation and so little confidence in the state that they argue that the state should be eliminated altogether. They are called **anarchists.** Between these extremes are those positions that are more moderate, for example, people who have some confidence both in individual cooperation and in the possibility of a reasonably just state, but don't have complete confidence in either. Democrats and Republicans, for example, both believe in a government that is at least partially run by the people themselves but with sufficient power to enforce its laws over individual interests whenever necessary. All these people believe in varying solutions to the same central problem: the problem of a balance between the public interest and the need for cooperation on the one hand and individual rights and interests on the other—in other words, the problem of **justice.**

A. THE PROBLEM OF JUSTICE

When we think of justice, we first tend to think of criminal cases and of punishment. Justice, in this sense, is catching the criminal and "making him pay for his crime." The oldest sense of the word *justice,* therefore, is what philosophers call **retributive justice,** or simply, "getting even." Retribution for a crime is making the criminal suffer or pay an amount appropriate to the severity of the crime. In ancient traditions, the key phrase was "an eye for an eye, a tooth for a tooth." If a criminal caused a person to be blind, he was in turn blinded. We now view this as brutal and less than civilized. But is it so clear that we have in fact given up this retributive sense of justice? Do we punish our criminals (that is, demand retribution), or do we sincerely attempt to reform them? Or is the purpose of prison simply to keep them off the street? Should we ever punish people for crimes, or should we simply protect ourselves against their doing the same thing again? If a man commits an atrocious murder, is it enough that we guarantee that he won't do another one? Or does he deserve punishment even if we know that he won't do it again?

But retributive justice and the problems of punishment are really only a small piece of a much larger concern. Justice is not just "getting even" for crimes and offenses. It concerns the running of society as a whole in day-to-day civil matters as well as the more dramatic criminal concerns. Given the relative scarcity of wealth and goods, how should they be distributed? Should everyone receive exactly the same amount? Should the person who works hard at an unpleasant job receive no more than the person who refuses to work at all and prefers to watch TV all day and just amuse himself or herself? Should the person who uses his wealth to the benefit of others receive no more than the person who "throws away" his or her money on gambling, drinking, and debauchery? If a class of people has historically been deprived of its adequate share because of the color of their skin, their religious beliefs, or their sex or age, should that class now be given more than its share in compensation, or is this too an injustice against other people?

Not only are wealth and goods at issue here, however. Distribution of privileges and power are equally important. Who will vote? Will everyone's vote count exactly the same? Should the opinions of an illiterate who does not even know the name of his political leaders have as much say in the government as the political scientist or economist who has studied these matters for years? Should everyone be allowed to drive? Or to drink? Should everone receive exactly the same treatment before the law? Or are there concerns that would indicate that some people (for example, congressmen or foreign diplomats) should receive special privileges?

Enjoyment of society's cultural gifts is also at issue. Should everyone receive the same education? What if that turns out to be "impractical" (since job training is much more efficient than "liberal arts")? But doesn't that mean that some—the workers and career persons who are trained to do a job—are deprived of the education necessary to enjoy great books, music, poetry, philosophy, intellectual debate, or proficiency in foreign languages, which give considerable enjoyment to those who have been taught to appreciate them?

There are also questions of status. Should there be social classes? What if it could be proved that such divisions make a society run more smoothly? How minimal should distinctions in status be? And this in turn leads to the more general question: Shouldn't all members of society be able to expect equal treatment and respect not only by the law but in every conceivable social situation? All of these are the concerns of justice. But what is just? Who decides? And how?

Theories of justice, in one sense, are as old as human society. The ancient codes of the Hebrews, the Persians, and the Babylonians were theories of justice in the sense that they tried, in their various ways, to develop rules to cover fair dealing and distribution of goods, the punishment of criminals, and the settling of disputes. A fully developed theory of justice, however, should go beyond this and try to analyze the nature of justice itself. The first great theories of justice to try to do this were those of Plato and Aristotle. In *The Republic*, Plato argues that justice in the state is precisely the same as justice in the individual, that is, a harmony between the various parts for the good of the whole. In other words, cooperation among all for the sake of a successful society is the key to justice. But this means that the interests of the individual take a clearly secondary role to the interests of society. In ancient Greece, this may have been only rarely true for the wealthy and powerful, but for the majority of people—especially the slaves—this secondary role was the norm. Because their docile submission was seen as necessary to the overall success of society, their individual interests and rights were extremely minimal. They expected to be rewarded and satisfied only insofar as their efforts benefited their betters, and then they expected their betters to reap far more reward from their labor than they themselves. In Plato's universe, everyone has his or her "place," and justice means that they act and are treated accordingly:

◆from *The Republic,* by Plato

I think that justice is the very thing, or some form of the thing which, when we were beginning to found our city, we said had to be established throughout. We stated, and often repeated, if you re-member, that everyone must pursue one occupation of those in the city, that for which his nature best fitted him.

Yes, we kept saying that.

Further, we have heard many people say, and have often said ourselves, that justice is to perform one's own task, and not to meddle with that of others.

We have said that.

This then, my friend, I said, when it happens, is in some way justice, to do one's own job. And do you know what I take to be a proof of this?

No, tell me.

I think what is left over of those things we have been investigat-ing, after moderation and courage and wisdom have been found, was that which made it possible for those three qualities to appear in the city and to continue as long as it was present. We also said that what remained after we found the other three was justice.

It had to be.

And surely, I said, if we had to decide which of the four will make the city good by its presence, it would be hard to judge whether it is a common belief among the rulers and the ruled, or the preservation among the soldiers of a law-inspired belief as to the nature of what is, and what is not, to be feared, or the knowl-edge and guardianship of the rulers, or whether it is, above all, the presence of this fourth in child and woman, slave and free, arti-san, ruler and subject, namely that each man, a unity in himself, performed his own task and was not meddling with that of others.

How could this not be hard to judge?

It seems then that the capacity for each in the city to perform his own task rivals wisdom, moderation, and courage as a source of excellence for the city.

It certainly does.

You would then describe justice as a rival to them for excellence in the city?

Most certainly.

Look at it this way and see whether you agree: you will order your rulers to act as judges in the courts of the city?

Surely.

And will their exclusive aim in delivering judgement not be that no citizen should have what belongs to another or be deprived of what is his own?

That would be their aim.

That being just?

Yes.

In some way then possession of one's own and the performance of one's own task could be agreed to be justice.

That is so.

Consider then whether you agree with me in this: if a carpenter attempts to do the work of a cobbler, or a cobbler that of a carpenter, and they exchange their tools and the esteem that goes with the job, or the same man tries to do both, and all the other exchanges are made, do you think that this does any great harm to the city?

No.

But I think that when one who is by nature a worker or some other kind of moneymaker is puffed up by wealth, or by the mob, or by his own strength, or some other such thing, and attempts to enter the warrior class, or one of the soldiers tries to enter the group of counselors and guardians, though he is unworthy of it, and these exchange their tools and the public esteem, or when the same man tries to perform all these jobs together, then I think you will agree that these exchanges and this meddling bring the city to ruin.

They certainly do.

The meddling and exchange between the three established orders does very great harm to the city and would most correctly be called wickedness.

Very definitely.

And you would call the greatest wickedness worked against one's own city injustice?

Of course.

That then is injustice. And let us repeat that the doing of one's own job by the moneymaking, auxiliary, and guardian groups, when each group is performing its own task in the city, is the opposite, it is justice and makes the city just.

I agree with you that this is so.[1]

Plato's rigid hierarchy of social classes and insistence on the inequality of people offends our sense of universal equality, but it is important to see that equality (or, more properly, **egalitarianism,** the view that all men and women are equal just by virtue of their being human) is a position that must be argued and is not a "natural" state of affairs or a belief that has always been accepted by everyone. The same is true of Aristotle's theory of justice.

In his *Politics*, he gives an unabashed defense of slavery, not only on the grounds that slaves are efficient and good for society as a whole, but because those who are slaves are "naturally" meant to be slaves and would be unhappy and unable to cope if they were granted freedom and made citizens. (This is not just an ancient argument, however, I am sure you have heard similar arguments about other groups of people in your

[1] Plato, *The Republic*, Bk. VI, trans. G. M. A. Grube (Indianapolis, IN: Hackett, 1974).

own lifetime.)   For Aristotle as for Plato, different people have different roles, and to treat unequals equally is as unjust, according to them, as it is to treat equals unequally. They would consider the view that morons and children and foreigners deserve the same respect and treatment as citizens ridiculous. So too would they find the contemporary argument that we should treat men and women as equals.* But despite these opinions, Plato and Aristotle laid the foundations of much of our own conceptions of justice. The idea that equals must be treated as equals is the foundation of our sense of justice just as much as theirs. The difference is that we are taught to believe that everybody is an equal. Similarly, the theory of what is called **distributive justice,** the fair distribution of wealth and goods among the members of society, is a current international as well as national concern that owes much to Aristotle's original formulations. The idea that individuals are due certain rewards for their labor is also Aristotle's idea. But despite his aristocratic opinions and his harsh elitism, Aristotle saw quite clearly that the members of society who depended most upon an adequate theory of justice were the poorer and less powerful members. It was for them that the just society was most vital (since the powerful and wealthy had a much better chance of taking care of themselves). And it was Aristotle who made the vital distinction, with which we began this section, between that restricted concern for justice that rights certain wrongs (in crimes, in bad business deals, and in public misfortunes) and the general concern of justice for a well-balanced and reasonable society.

◆**from *The Nicomachean Ethics,*
by Aristotle**

Let us take as a starting-point, then, the various meanings of "an unjust man." Both the lawless man and the greedy and unfair man are thought to be unjust, so that evidently both the law-abiding and the fair man will be just. The just, then, is the lawful and the fair, the unjust the unlawful and the unfair.

Since the lawless man was seen to be unjust and the law-abiding man just, evidently all lawful acts are in a sense just acts; for the acts laid down by the legislative art are lawful, and each of these, we say, is just. Now the laws in their enactments on all subjects aim at the common advantage either of all or of the best or of those who hold power, or something of the sort; so that in one sense we call those acts just that tend to produce and preserve happiness and its components for the political society. And the law bids us do both the acts of a brave man (*e.g.* not to desert our post nor take to flight nor throw away our arms), and those of a temperate man

*Plato did venture that women as well as men ought to be rulers.

(*e.g.* not to commit adultery nor to gratify one's lust), and those of a good-tempered man (*e.g.* not to strike another nor to speak evil), and similarly with regard to the other virtues and forms of wickedness, commanding some acts and forbidding others; and the rightly-framed law does this rightly, and the hastily conceived one less well.

This form of justice, then, is complete virtue, but not absolutely, but in relation to our neighbour. And therefore justice is often thought to be the greatest of virtues, and "neither evening nor morning star" is so wonderful; and proverbially "in justice is every virtue comprehended." And it is complete virtue in its fullest sense, because it is the actual exercise of complete virtue. It is complete because he who possesses it can exercise his virtue not only in himself but towards his neighbour also; for many men can exercise virtue in their own affairs, but not in their relations to their neighbour.

· · · · · · · · · ·

But at all events what we are investigating is the justice which is a *part* of virtue; for there is a justice of this kind, as we maintain. Similarly it is with injustice in the particular sense that we are concerned.

That there is such a thing is indicated by the fact that while the man who exhibits in action the other forms of wickedness acts wrongly indeed, but not graspingly (*e.g.* the man who throws away his shield through cowardice or speaks harshly through bad temper or fails to help a friend with money through meanness), when a man acts graspingly he often exhibits none of these vices—no, nor all together, but certainly wickedness of some kind (for we blame him) and injustice. There is, then, another kind of injustice which is a part of injustice in the wide sense, and a use of the word "unjust" which answers to a part of what is unjust in the wide sense of "contrary to the law." Again, if one man commits adultery for the sake of gain and makes money by it, while another does so at the bidding of appetite though he loses money and is penalized for it, the latter would be held to be self-indulgent rather than grasping, but the former is unjust, but not self-indulgent; evidently, therefore, he is unjust by reason of his making gain by his act. Again, all other unjust acts are ascribed invariably to some particular kind of wickedness, for example adultery to self-indulgence, the desertion of a comrade in battle to cowardice, physical violence to anger; but if a man makes gain, his action is ascribed to no form of wickedness but injustice. Evidently, therefore, there is apart from injustice in the wide sense another, "particular," injustice which shares the name and nature of the first, because its definition falls within the same genus; for the significance of both consists in a relation to one's neighbour, but the one is concerned with honour or money or safety—or that which includes all these, if we had a single name for it—and its motive is the pleasure that arises from gain; while the other is concerned with all the objects with which the good man is concerned.

It is clear, then, that there is more than one kind of justice, and that there is one which is distinct from virtue entire; we must try to grasp its genus and differentia.

• • • • • • • • • •

Of particular justice and that which is just in the corresponding sense, (A) one kind is that which is manifested in distributions of honour or money or the other things that fall to be divided among those who have a share in the constitution (for in these it is possible for one man to have a share either unequal or equal to that of another), and (B) one is that which plays a rectifying part in transactions between man and man. Of this there are two divisions; of transactions (1) some are voluntary and (2) others involuntary— voluntary such transactions as sale, purchase, loan for consumption, pledging, loan for use, depositing, letting (they are called voluntary because the origin of these transactions is voluntary), while of the involuntary (a) some are clandestine, such as theft, adultery, posioning, procuring, enticement of slaves, assassination, false witness, and (b) others are violent, such as assault, imprisonment, murder, robbery with violence, mutilation, abuse, insult.

• • • • • • • • • •

(A) We have shown that both the unjust man and the unjust act are unfair or unequal; now it is clear that there is also an intermediate between the two unequals involved in either case. And this is the equal; for in any kind of action in which there is a more and a less there is also what is equal. If, then, the unjust is unequal, the just is equal, as all men suppose it to be, even apart from argument. And since the equal is intermediate, the just will be an intermediate. Now equality implies at least two things. The just, then, must be both intermediate and equal and relative (*i.e.* for certain persons). And *qua* intermediate it must be between certain things (which are respectively greater and less); *qua* equal, it involves *two* things; *qua* just, it is for certain people. The just, therefore, involves at least four terms; for the persons for whom it is in fact just are two, and the things in which it is manifested, the objects distributed, are two. And the same equality will exist between the persons and between the things concerned; for as the latter—the things concerned—are related, so are the former; if they are not equal, they will not have what is equal, but this is the origin of quarrels and complaints—when either equals have and are awarded unequal shares, or unequals equal shares. Further, this is plain from the fact that awards should be "according to merit"; for all men argee that what is just in distribution must be according to merit in some sense, though they do not all specify the same sort of merit, but democrats identify it with the status of freeman, supporters of oligarchy with wealth (or with noble birth), and supporters of aristocracy with excellence.

    This, then, is what the just is—the proportional; the unjust is
what violates the proportion. Hence one term becomes too great,
the other too small, as indeed happens in practice, for the man
who acts unjustly has too much, and the man who is unjustly
treated too little, of what is good. In the case of evil the reverse is
true; for the lesser evil is reckoned a good in comparison with the
greater evil, since the lesser evil is rather to be chosen than the
greater, and what is worthy of choice is good, and what is worthier
of choice a greater good.
    This, then, is one species of the just.
                    . . . .

(B) The remaining one is the rectificatory, which arises in connexion with transactions both voluntary and involuntary. This form
of the just has a different specific character from the former. For
the justice which distributes common possessions is always in accordance with the kind of proportion mentioned above (for in the
case also in which the distribution is made from the common
funds of a partnership it will be according to the same ratio which
the funds put into the business by the partners bear to one
another); and the injustice opposed to this kind of justice is that
which violates the proportion. But the justice in transactions
between man and man is a sort of equality indeed, and the injustice a sort of inequality; not according to that kind of proportion,
however, but according to arithmetical proportion. For it makes no
difference whether a good man has defrauded a bad man or a bad
man a good one, nor whether it is a good or a bad man that has
committed adultery; the law looks only to the distinctive character
of the injury, and treats the parties as equal, if one is in the wrong
and the other is being wronged, and if one inflicted injury and the
other has received it. Therefore, this kind of injustice being an
inequality, the judge tries to equalize it; for in the case also in
which one has received and the other has inflicted a wound, or one
has slain and the other been slain, the suffering and the action
have been unequally distributed; but the judge tries to equalize
things by means of the penalty, taking away from the gain of the as-
sailant. For the term "gain" is applied generally to such cases, even
if it be not a term appropriate to certain cases, for example to the
person who inflicts a wound—and "loss" to the sufferer; at all
events when the suffering has been estimated, the one is called loss
and the other gain. Therefore the equal is intermediate between
the greater and the less, but the gain and the loss are respectively
greater and less in contrary ways; more of the good and less of the
evil are gain, and the contrary is loss; intermediate between them
is, as we saw, the equal, which we say is just; therefore corrective
justice will be the intermediate between loss and gain. This is why,
when people dispute, they take refuge in the judge; and to go to
the judge is to go to justice; for the nature of the judge is to be a
sort of animate justice; and they seek the judge as an intermediate;

> and in some states they call judges mediators, on the assumption
> that if they get what is intermediate they will get what is just. The
> just, then, is an intermediate, since the judge is so. The judge
> restores equality. . . .[2]

In contrast to the Greeks, the premise of most modern theories of
justice has been the equality of everyone with everyone else. No one is
"better" than anyone else, whatever his or her talents, achievements,
wealth, family, or intelligence. This view rules out slavery on principle,
whatever the benefits to society as a whole and whatever the alleged
benefits to the slaves. Slavery is inequality and is thus to be condemned.
But this egalitarian principle has its problems too. It is obvious that, as
a matter of fact, all people are not equally endowed with intelligence or
talent, good looks or abilities. Is it therefore to the good of all that
everyone should be treated equally? One person is a doctor, capable of
saving many lives; another is a chronic profligate and drunkard. If they
were to commit exactly the same crime, would it be to the public interest
to give them equal jail terms? Obviously not. But would it be just to give
them different terms? It doesn't appear so. One problem that recent
theorists have tried to answer is connected with cases in which the public
interest seems at odds with the demands for equal treatment. A similar
problem gives rise to one of the "paradoxes of democracy," which we
mentioned before. Does it make sense to treat the opinions of an ignorant
person whose only knowledge of current events comes from fifteen
minutes (at best) of television news a day in the way that we treat the
opinions of a skilled political veteran? But the ballots we vote on make
no such distinction. And it is obvious that our society, despite its
egalitarian principles, treats people who are cleverer at business or
power-brokering much better than everyone else. Is this an example of
systematic injustice? Or are there cases, even for us, in which inequality
can still be justified as justice?

The theory of justice has been one of the central concerns of British
philosophy for several centuries. Thomas Hobbes developed a theory
that began with equality as a "natural fact" and took justice to be that
which "assured peace and security to all" enforced by the government.
There is no justice in "the state of nature," Hobbes argued; justice like
law comes into existence only with society, through a "social compact" in
which everyone agrees to abide by certain rules and to cooperate rather
than compete—all for their mutual benefit. Several years later, John
Locke and then David Hume argued a similar theory of justice; again,
equality was the premise, and mutual agreement the basis of government
authority. For both philosophers, the ultimate criterion of justice was

[2]Aristotle, *Nicomachean Ethics*, trans. W. D. Ross (Oxford: Oxford University Press,
1925).

utility, the public interest, and therefore the satisfaction of the interests of at least most citizens. This would have been rejected by Plato and Aristotle.

Hume exemplifies this modern view—that justice is to be characterized not just in terms of the structure of the overall society and everyone's "place" in it, but by the interests and well-being of each and every individual. But what about an instance, Hume asks, in which a particular act of justice clearly is contrary to the public interests, such as the case in which an obviously guilty criminal is released for technical reasons or a disgusting pornographer is allowed to publish and sell his or her wares under the protection of "free speech"? Hume replies that there is a need to distinguish between the utility of a single act and the utility of an overall system; that although a specific act of justice might go against the public interest, the system of justice necessarily will be in the public interest. This means that a single unjust act is to be challenged not as an isolated occurrence but as an example of a general set of rules and practices.

◆ on "Justice and Utility," by David Hume

To make this more evident, consider, that though the rules of justice are established merely by interest, their connection with interest is somewhat singular, and is different from what may be observed on other occasions. A single act of justice is frequently contrary to *public interest;* and were it to stand alone, without being followed by other acts, may, in itself, be very prejudicial to society. When a man of merit, of a beneficent disposition, restores a great fortune to a miser, or a seditious bigot, he has acted justly and laudably, but the public is a real sufferer. Nor is every single act of justice, considered apart, more conducive to private interest, than to public; and it is easily conceived how a man may impoverish himself by a single instance of integrity, and have reason to wish that with regard to that single act, the laws of justice were for a moment suspended in the universe. But however single acts of justice may be contrary, either to public or private interest, it is certain, that the whole plan or scheme is highly conducive, or indeed absolutely requisite, both to the support of society, and the well-being of every individual.[3]

The most explicitly "utilitarian" statement of justice as utility is found, however, in John Stuart Mill's influential pamphlet, *Utilitarianism.*

[3]David Hume, *Enquiry Concerning the Principles of Morals* (La Salle, IL: Open Court, 1912).

◆from *Utilitarianism,*
by John Stuart Mill

In the case of this, as of our other moral sentiments, there is no necessary connexion between the question of its origin and that of its binding force. That a feeling is bestowed on us by nature does not necessarily legitimate all its promptings. The feeling of justice might be a peculiar instinct, and might yet require, like our other instincts, to be controlled and enlightened by a higher reason. If we have intellectual instincts leading us to judge in a particular way, as well as animal instincts that prompt us to act in a particular way, there is no necessity that the former should be more infallible in their sphere than the latter in theirs; it may as well happen that wrong judgments are occasionally suggested by those, as wrong actions by these.

· · · · · · · · · ·

In the first place, it is mostly considered unjust to deprive any-one of his personal liberty, his property, or any other thing which belongs to him by law. Here, therefore, is one instance of the application of the terms "just" and "unjust" in a perfectly definite sense, namely, that it is just to respect, unjust to violate, the *legal rights* of anyone. But this judgment admits of several exceptions, arising from the other forms in which the notions of justice and injustice present themselves. For example, the person who suffers the deprivation may (as the phrase is) have forfeited the rights which he is so deprived of—a case to which we shall return presently. . . .

Secondly, the legal rights of which he is deprived may be rights which *ought* not to have belonged to him; in other words, the law which confers on him these rights may be a bad law. When it is so or when (which is the same thing for our purpose) it is supposed to be so, opinions will differ as to the justice or injustice of infring-ing it. Some maintain that no law, however bad, ought to be dis-obeyed by an individual citizen; that his opposition to it, if shown at all, should only be shown in endeavoring to get it altered by competent authority. This opinion (which condemns many of the most illustrious benefactors of mankind, and would often protect pernicious institutions against the only weapons which, in the state of things existing at the time, have any chance of succeeding against them) is defended by those who hold it on grounds of expediency, principally on that of the importance to the common interest of mankind, of maintaining inviolate the sentiment of submission to law. Other persons, again, hold the directly contrary opinion that any law, judged to be bad, may blamelessly be disobeyed, even though it be not judged to be unjust but only inexpedient, while others would confine the license of disobedience to the case of un-just laws; but, again, some say that all laws which are inexpedient are unjust, since every law imposes some restriction on the natural liberty of mankind, which restriction is an injustice unless legitimated by tending to their good. Among these diversities of opinion it seems to be universally admitted that there may be unjust laws, and that law, consequently, is not the ultimate criterion of justice, but may give to one person a benefit, or impose on another an evil, which justice condemns. When, however, a law is thought to be unjust, it seems always to be regarded as being so in the same way in which a breach of law is unjust, namely, by infringing some-body's right, which, as it cannot in this case be a legal right, receives a different appellation and is called a moral right. We may say, therefore, that a second case of injustice consists in taking or withholding from any person that to which he has a *moral right.*

Thirdly, it is universally considered just that each person should obtain that (whether good or evil) which he *deserves,* and unjust that he should obtain a good or be made to undergo an evil which he does not deserve. This is, perhaps, the clearest and most emphatic form in which the idea of justice is conceived by the general mind. As it involves the notion of desert, the question arises what constitutes desert? Speaking in a general way, a person is understood to deserve good if he does right, evil if he does wrong; and in a more particular sense, to deserve good from those to whom he does or has done good, and evil from those to whom he does or has done evil. The precept of returning good for evil has never been regarded as a case of the fulfillment of justice, but as one in which the claims of justice are waived, in obedience to other considerations.

Fourthly, it is confessedly unjust to *break faith* with anyone: to violate an engagement, either express or implied, or disappoint expectations raised by our own conduct, at least if we have raised those expectations knowingly and voluntarily. Like the other obligations of justice already spoken of, this one is not regarded as absolute, but as capable of being overruled by a stronger obligation of justice on the other side, or by such conduct on the part of the person concerned as is deemed to absolve us from our obligation to him and to constitute a *forfeiture* of the benefit which he has been led to expect.

Fifthly, it is, by universal admission, inconsistent with justice to be *partial*—to show favor or preference to one person over another in matters to which favor and preference do not properly apply. Impartiality, however, does not seem to be regarded as a duty in itself, but rather as instrumental to some other duty; for it is admitted that favor and preference are not always censurable, and, indeed, the cases in which they are condemned are rather the exception than the rule. A person would be more likely to be blamed than applauded for giving his family or friends no superiority in good offices over strangers when he could do so without violating any other duty; and no one thinks it unjust to seek one person in preference to another as a friend, connection, or companion. Impartiality where rights are concerned is of course obligatory, but this is involved in the more general obligation of giving to everyone his right. A tribunal, for example, must be impartial because it is bound to award, without regard to any other consideration, a disputed object to the one of two parties who has the right to it. There are other cases in which impartiality means being solely influenced by desert, as with those who, in the capacity of judges, preceptors, or parents, administer reward and punishment as such. There are cases, again, in which it means being solely influenced by consideration for the public interest, as in making a selection among candidates for a government employment. Impartiality, in short, as an obligation of justice, may be said to mean being exlusively influenced by the considerations which it is supposed ought to influence the particular case in hand, and resisting solicitation of any motives which prompt to conduct different from what those considerations would dictate.

Nearly allied to the idea of impartiality is that of *equality,* which often enters as a component part both into the conception of justice and into the practice of it, and, in the eyes of many persons, constitutes its essence. But in this, still more than in any other case, the notion of justice varies in different persons, and always conforms in its variations to their notion of utility. Each person maintains that equality is the dictate of justice, except where he thinks that expediency requires inequality. The justice of giving equal protection to the rights of all is maintained by those who support the most outrageous inequality in the rights themselves. Even in slave countries it is theoretically admitted that the rights of the slave, such as they are, ought to be as sacred as those of the master, and that a tribunal which fails to enforce them with equal strictness is wanting in justice; while, at the same time, institutions which leave to the slave scarcely any rights to enforce are not deemed unjust because they are not deemed inexpedient. Those who think that utility requires distinctions of rank do not consider it unjust that riches and social privileges should be unequally dispensed; but those who think this inequality inexpedient think it unjust also. Whoever thinks that government is necessary sees no injustice in as much inequality as is constituted by giving to the magistrate powers not granted to other people. Even among those who hold leveling doctrines, there are differences of opinion about expediency. Some communists consider it unjust that the produce of the labor of the community should be shared on any other principle than that of exact equality; others think it just that those should receive most whose wants are greatest; while others hold that those who work harder, or who produce more, or whose services are more valuable to the community, may justly claim a larger quota in the division of the produce. And the sense of natural justice may be plausibly appealed to in behalf of every one of these opinions.

Mill then goes on to define a **right:**

When we call anything a person's right, we mean that he has a valid claim on society to protect him in the possession of it, either by the force of law or by that of education and opinion. If he has what we consider a sufficient claim, on whatever account, to have something guaranteed to him by society, we say that he has a right to it.

To have a right, then, is, I conceive, to have something which society ought to defend me in the possession of. If the objector goes on to ask why it ought, I can give him no other reason than general utility. If that expression does not seem to convey a sufficient feeling of the strength of the obligation, nor to account for the peculiar energy of the feeling, it is because there goes to the composition of the sentiment, not a rational only but also an animal element— the thirst for retaliation; and this thirst derives its intensity, as well as its moral justification, from the extraordinarily important and impressive kind of utility which is concerned. The interest involved is that of security, to everyone's feelings the most vital of all interests. All other earthly benefits are needed by one person, not needed by another; and many of them can, if necessary, be cheerfully foregone or replaced by something else; but security no human being can possibly do without; on it we depend for all our immunity from evil and for the whole value of all and every good, beyond the passing moment, since nothing but the gratification of the instant could be of any worth to us if we could be deprived of everything the next instant by whoever was momentarily stronger than ourselves. Now this most indispensable of all necessaries, after physical nutriment, cannot be had unless the machinery for providing it is kept unintermittedly in active play. Our notion, therefore, of the claim we have on our fellow creatures to join in making safe for us the very groundwork of our existence gathers feelings around it so much more intense than those concerned in any of the more common cases of utility that the difference in degree (as is often the case in psychology) becomes a real difference in kind. The claim assumes that character of absoluteness, that apparent infinity and incommensurability with all other considerations which constitute the distinction between the feeling of right and wrong and that of ordinary expediency and inexpediency. The feelings concerned are so powerful, and we count so positively on finding a responsive feeling in others (all being alike interested) that *ought* and *should* grow into *must,* and recognized indispensability becomes a moral necessity, analogous to physical, and often not inferior to it in binding force.[4]

Mill's utilitarian theory of justice is a logical extension of his ethical theories: What is good and desirable is what is best for the greatest number of people. But although it might at first seem as if the greatest happiness of the greatest number leaves no room for such abstract concerns

[4]John Stuart Mill, *Utilitarianism* (New York: Bobbs-Merrill, 1957).

as "justice," Mill argues that, to the contrary, only utility can give that abstract sense of justice some concrete basis in human life.

The problem with the utilitarian theory of justice is identical to the problem we saw with the utilitarian theory of morals. Could there not be a case in which the public interest and general utility would be served only at the clearly unjust expense of a single unfortunate individual? Suppose we lived in a society that ran extremely well, such that we had few if any complaints about our government and the way it was run, when a single muckraking journalist started turning the peace upside down with his insistence that something was very wrong in the government. We might easily suppose that, at least in the short run, the public confusion and trauma would be much more harmful to the public interest than the slight correction that would result from public exposure. Should the government forcefully silence the journalist? We would say no. He has a right to his inquiries and a right to speak his mind. Or suppose that the most efficient way to solve a series of on-going crimes was to torture a recently captured suspect and hold him without evidence? Here again public interest and justice are at odds. Or more generally, should the government have the authority to throw people in jail just because it has reason (even good reason) to believe that they will create a public disturbance or commit certain crimes? Public interest says yes; justice says no.

This is the problem with utilitarian theories of justice in general: although we may well agree that justice *ought* to serve the public interest and every individual's interests as well, the utilitarian view is always in an awkward position when it must choose to serve the public interest at the intolerable expense and injustice of a small number of individuals or even a single individual. Consider the extreme example of an entire city that would prosper if it would sacrifice the life of one innocent child. Arguably, utilitariansim would seem to defend the sacrifice; justice, however, says that such a sacrifice is inexcusable.

It is because of increased sensitivity to the unacceptability of such scenarios that a very different conception of justice has once again begun to dominate—a set of views that recognizes the desirability of serving every individual's interests while having a primary concern for justice, not in terms of utility but in terms of *rights*. Thus, public interest is important but respect for every individual's rights is even more important. This view dates back (at least) to Kant, who defended the notions of "duty" and "obligation" as morally basic to any concern for utility. In its modern conception, this view is most ably defended by Harvard philosopher John Rawls in his profound work entitled *Theory of Justice*. For nearly six hundred pages, Rawls essentially defends two principles in order of priority. The first (and more fundamental) principle asserts that we all have basic rights and equal rights, in particular with reference to our personal freedom. The second principle (which assumes the first) asserts that although we cannot expect everyone in society to enjoy equal wealth, equal health, and equal opportunities, we can and should insist that all inequalities are to every individual's advantage. For example, it should not be such that society allows that "the rich get richer and the poor get poorer." Rawls' actual statement from *Theory of Justice* is as follows:

> First: each person is to have an equal right to the most extensive basic liberty compatible with a similar liberty for others.
> Second: social and economic inequalities are to be arranged so that they are both (a) reasonably expected to be to everyone's advantage, and (b) attached to positions and offices open to all.

Rawls' justification for establishing the rationality and necessity of these "liberal" principles derives from his view that all of us (or our ancestors) might be in "the original position"—like Hobbes' "State of Nature"—and "unencumbered" by any of our particular traits or interests. In such a situation, what would be rational for us to choose by way of the principles according to which society would be run? Because we do not know, in the essential sense, who we will be in that society, it does us no good to adopt principles that benefit the persons we are now. For example, in a society composed entirely of purple people and green people (remembering that in the original position we do not know which we will be), it would only be rational, Rawls argues, to enact a law that would treat all people equally, whether purple or green. It is much like (but much more complicated and uncertain than) the childhood example involving one of us being asked to cut a pie into sections, giving everyone else first choice. The only rational decision—even if you suspect that the other children are dullards, is to divide the pie equally. So too, the aim of Rawls' dual principles is to cut for all of us—if not equal pieces of the social pie, at least pieces that are as equal as possible.

The following selection is from one of Rawls' early essays.

◆from "Justice as Fairness," by John Rawls

It might seem at first sight that the concepts of justice and fairness are the same, and that there is no reason to distinguish them, or to say that one is more fundamental than the other. I think that this impression is mistaken. In this paper I wish to show that the fundamental idea in the concept of justice is fairness; and I wish to offer an analysis of the concept of justice from this point of view. To bring out the force of this claim, and the analysis based upon it, I shall then argue that it is this aspect of justice for which utilitarianism, in its classical form, is unable to account, but which is expressed, even if misleadingly, by the idea of the social contract.

· · · · · · · · · ·

Throughout I consider justice only as a virtue of social institutions, or what I shall call practices.[5] The principles of justice are regarded as formulating restrictions as to how practices may define positions and offices, and assign thereto powers and liabilities, rights and duties. Justice as a virtue of particular actions or of persons I do not take up at all. It is important to distinguish these various subjects of justice, since the meaning of the concept varies according to whether it is applied to practices, particular actions, or persons. These meanings are, indeed, connected, but they are not identical. I shall confine my discussion to the sense of justice as applied to practices, since this sense is the basic one. Once it is understood, the other senses should go quite easily.

The conception of justice which I want to develop may be stated in the form of two principles as follows: first, each person participating in a practice, or affected by it, has an equal right to the most extensive liberty compatible with a like liberty for all; and second, inequalities are arbitrary unless it is reasonable to expect that they will work out for everyone's advantage, and provided the positions and offices to which they attach, or from which they may be gained, are open to all. These principles express justice as a complex of three ideas: liberty, equality, and reward for services contributing to the common good.

The term "person" is to be construed variously depending on the circumstances. On some occasions it will mean human individuals, but in others it may refer to nations, provinces, business firms, churches, teams, and so on. The principles of justice apply in all these instances, although there is a certain logical priority to the case of human individuals. As I shall use the term "person," it will be ambiguous in the manner indicated.

The first principle holds, of course, only if other things are equal: that is, while there must always be a justification for departing from the initial position of equal liberty (which is defined by the pattern of rights and duties, powers and liabilities, established by a practice), and the burden or proof is placed on him who would depart from it, nevertheless, there can be, and often there is, a justification for doing so. Now, that similar particular cases, as defined by a practice, should be treated similarly as they arise, is part of the very concept of a practice; it is involved in the notion of an activity in accordance with rules. The first principle expresses an analogous conception, but as applied to the structure of

---

[5]I use the word "practice" throughout as a sort of technical term meaning any form of activity specified by a system of rules which defines offices, roles, moves, penalties, defences, and so on, and which gives the activity its structure. As examples one may think of games and rituals, trials and parliaments, markets and systems or property. I have attempted a partial analysis of the notion of a practice in a paper, "Two Concepts of Rules," *Philosophical Review,* 64 (1955), pp. 3–32 [Rawls' note].

practices themselves. It holds, for example, that there is a presumption against the distinctions and classifications made by legal systems and other practices to the extent that they infringe on the original and equal liberty of the persons participating in them. The second principle defines how this presumption may be rebutted.

It might be argued at this point that justice requires only an equal liberty. If, however, a greater liberty were possible for all without loss or conflict, then it would be irrational to settle on a lesser liberty. There is no reason for circumscribing rights unless their exercise would be incompatible, or would render the practice defining them less effective. Therefore no serious distortion of the concept of justice is likely to follow from including within it the concept of the greatest equal liberty.

The second principle defines what sorts of inequalities are permissible; it specifies how the presumption laid down by the first principle may be put aside. Now by inequalities it is best to understand not *any* differences between offices and positions, but differences in the benefits and burdens attached to them either directly or indirectly, such as prestige and wealth, or liability to taxation and compulsory services. Players in a game do not protest against there being different positions, such as batter, pitcher, catcher, and the like, nor to there being various privileges and powers as specified by the rules; nor do the citizens of a country object to there being the different offices of government such as president, senator, governor, judge, and so on, each with their special rights and duties. It is not differences in the resulting distribution established by a practice, or made possible by it, of the things men strive to attain or avoid. Thus they may complain about the pattern of honors and rewards set up by a practice (*e.g.* the privileges and salaries of government officials) or they may object to the distribution of power and wealth which results from the various ways in which men avail themselves of the opportunities allowed by it (*e.g.* the concentration of wealth which may develop in a free price system allowing large entrepreneurial or speculative gains).

It should be noted that the second principle holds that an inequality is allowed only if there is reason to believe that the practice with the inequality, or resulting from it, will work for the advantage of *every* party engaging in it. Here it is important to stress that *every* party must gain from the inequality. Since the principle applies to practices, it implies that the representative man in every office or position defined by a practice, when he views it as a going concern, must find it reasonable to prefer his condition and prospects with the inequality to what they would be under the practice without it. The principle excludes, therefore, the justification of inequalities on the grounds that the disadvantages of those in one position are outweighed by the greater advantages of those in another position. This rather simple restriction is the main modification I wish to make in the utilitarian principle as usually understood. When coupled with the notion of a practice, it is a restriction of consequence, and one which some utilitarians, for example Hume and Mill, have used in their discussions of justice without realizing apparently its significance, or at least without calling attention to it. Why it is a significant modification of principle, changing one's conception of justice entirely, the whole of my argument will show.

Further, it is also necessary that the various offices to which special benefits or burdens attach are open to all. It may be, for example, to the common advantage, as just defined, to attach special benefits to certain offices. Perhaps by doing so the requisite talent can be attracted to them and encouraged to give its best efforts. But any offices having special benefits must be won in a fair competition in which contestants are judged on their merits. If some offices were not open, those excluded would normally be justified in feeling unjustly treated, even if they benefited from the greater efforts of those who were allowed to compete for them. Now if one can assume that offices are open, it is necessary only to consider the design of practices themselves and how they jointly, as a system, work together. It will be a mistake to focus attention on the varying relative positions of particular persons, who may be known to us by their proper names, and to require that each such change, as a once for all transaction viewed in isolation, must be in itself just. It is the system of practices which is to be judged, and judged from a general point of view: unless one is prepared to criticize it from the standpoint of a representative man holding some particular office, one has no complaint against it.[6]

Rawls, like Hume in particular, ties the concept of "justice" to the concept of "equality." The main theme of his work is an attempt to develop this connection and to state precisely the kind of "equality" that is most important for justice. Against the conservative suggestion that people are equal in legal rights and "opportunities" alone, without any right to material goods and social services, he argues that a just society will consider the welfare of the worst-off members of society as an obligation. Here he differs with Mill and the utilitarians, who would say that such help is a matter of utility; for Rawls, it is more like a Kantian duty. Moreover, Rawls clearly distinguishes himself from socialists as well, who would argue that all property should be shared; he says only that it is obligatory to help out the worst-off members of society, but nowhere does he suggest that all people therefore ought to have equal wealth and property. Justice, in other words, does not equate fair distribution with equal distribution. Equality becomes a far more complex notion, therefore, than simple egalitarianism often takes it to be.

Is equality the primary concern of justice? Even Rawls admits that a society in which everyone had exactly equal shares of social goods is

[6]John Rawls, "Justice as Fairness," in *The Philosophical Review* 67 (April 1958).

impossible. But why is it impossible? We can all imagine a situation—
and some radical thinkers even propose it—in which all material goods
(at least) would be collected and cataloged by the state, then redistributed
to every citizen in precisely equal shares. Most of us, including Rawls,
find this suggestion intolerable. Yet why, if it realizes the equality that
justice demands? Something stops us, and it is not simply the idea that
we might lose our own goods, for many of us would in fact benefit from
such a redistribution scheme. What bothers us initially is the very idea
of anyone, including (perhaps especially) the government, intruding into
our lives and exerting such power. However, we also sense that such a
scheme for redistributing the wealth violates something very basic to
justice—namely, the rights we have to our possessions. Rawls, of course,
gives rights top priority in his theory; but they are rights having to do with
liberty in general, not rights having to do with possession as such. We all
feel, with whatever reservations, that we have a right to what we earn and
that we have a right to keep what we already possess. We resent that the
government takes from us a substantial percentage of our earnings to use
in ways not directly (or perhaps even indirectly) under our control. And
we believe we have the right, for instance, to the modest sum that grand-
father left us in his will (presumably the residue of earlier taxation), even
though we did not earn it in any sense. Thus many philosophers have
become increasingly aware of another kind of right that is not treated
adequately by such liberal theories of Rawls'—in fact, a right that goes
against the modest scheme of redistribution (for example, through
taxation) encouraged by his principles. This other kind of right, known
as **entitlement,** gives rise to a very different kind of theory of justice.

The popular name for this alternative theory is *libertarianism*, and
it has recently become a powerful force in American politics. The basic
idea, an "entitlement theory," puts the right to private property first
and foremost, and couples with it a deep skepticism as to the wisdom
or fairness of government. The original entitlement theory was developed by John Locke, who argued that the right to private property
was so basic that it preceded any social conventions or laws and existed
quite independent of any government or state. What gave a person the
right to a piece of property, Locke argued, was that he had "mixed his
labor with it," in other words, worked with it and improved it and so
had the right to it. In today's terms—where what is at stake consists
mainly of salaries and what we can buy with them (Locke was thinking
mainly of land)—we would say that a person has the basic right to
keep what he or she earns. Very recently, Locke's theory has been
updated considerably and argued forcefully by John Rawls' younger
Harvard colleague, Robert Nozick. In *Anarchy, State and Utopia*,
Nozick argues for the entitlement theory and against any attempt to
set "patterns" of fair distribution, for the en-forcement of any such
pattern must result in the violation of people's rights.

◆from *Anarchy, State and Utopia* by Robert Nozick

Individuals have rights, and there are things no person or group may do to them (without violating their rights). So strong and far-reaching are these rights that they raise the question of what, if anything, the state and its officials may do. How much room do individual rights leave for the state? . . . Our main conclusions about the state are that a minimal state, limited to the narrow functions of protection against force, theft, fraud, enforcement of contracts, and so on, is justified; that any more extensive state will violate persons' rights not be forced to do certain things, and is unjustified; and that the minimal state is inspiring as well as right. Two noteworthy implications are that the state may not use its coercive apparatus for the purpose of getting some citizens to aid others, or in order to prohibit activities to people for their *own* good or protection.

. . . .

THE ENTITLEMENT THEORY

The subject of justice in holdings consists of three major topics. The first is the *original acquisition of holdings,* the appropriation of unheld things. This includes the issues of how unheld things may come to be held, the process, or processes, by which unheld things may come to be held, the things that may come to be held by these processes, the extent of what comes to be held by a particular process, and so on. We shall refer to the complicated truth about this topic, which we shall not formulate here, as the principle of justice in acquisition. The second topic concerns the *transfer of holdings* from one person to another. By what processes may a person transfer holdings to another? How may a person acquire a holding from another who holds it? Under this topic come general descriptions of voluntary exchange, and gift and (on the other hand) fraud, as well as reference to particular conventional details fixed upon in a given society. The complicated truth about this subject (with placeholders for conventional details) we shall call the principle of justice in transfer. (And we shall suppose it also includes principles governing how a person may divest himself of a holding, passing it into an unheld state.)

If the world were wholly just, the following inductive definition would exhaustively cover the subject of justice in holdings.

1. A person who acquires a holding in accordance with the principle of justice in acquisition is entitled to that holding.
2. A person who acquires a holding in accordance with the principle of justice in transfer, from someone else entitled to the holding, is entitled to the holding.
3. No one is entitled to a holding except by (repeated) applications of 1 and 2.

The complete principle of distributive justice would say simply that a distribution is just if everyone is entitled to the holdings they possess under the distribution.

A distribution is just if it arises from another just distribution by legitimate means. The legitimate means of moving from one distribution to another are specified by the principle of justice in transfer. The legitimate first "moves" are specified by the principle of justice in acquisition. Whatever arises from a just situation by just steps is itself just. The means of change specified by the principle of justice in transfer preserve justice. As correct rules of inference are truth-preserving, and any conclusion deduced via repeated application of such rules from only true premises is itself true, so the means of transition from one situation to another specified by the principle of justice in transfer are justice-preserving, and any situation actually arising from repeated transitions in accordance with the principle from a just situation is itself just. The parallel between justice-preserving transformations and truth-preserving transformations illuminates where it fails as well as where it holds. That a conclusion could have been deduced by truth-preserving means from premises that are true suffices to show its truth. That from a just situation a situation *could* have arisen via justice-preserving means does *not* suffice to show its justice. The fact that a thief's victims voluntarily *could* have presented him with gifts does not entitle the thief to his ill-gotten gains. Justice in holdings is historical; it depends upon what actually has happened. We shall return to this point later.

Not all actual situations are generated in accordance with the two principles of justice in holdings: the principle of justice in acquisition and the principle of justice in transfer. Some people steal from others, or defraud them, or enslave them, seizing their product and preventing them from living as they choose, or forcibly exclude others from competing in exchanges. None of these are permissible modes of transition from one situation to another. And some persons acquire holdings by means not sanctioned by the principle of justice in acquisition. The existence of past injustice (previous violations of the first two principles of justice in holdings) raises the third major topic under justice in holdings: the rectification of injustice in holdings. If past injustice has shaped present holdings in various ways, some identifiable and some not, what now, if anything, ought to be done to rectify these injustices? What obligations do the performers of injustice have toward those whose position is worse than it would have been had the injustice not been done? Or, than it would have been had compensation been paid promptly? How, if at all, do things change if the beneficiaries and those made worse off are not the direct parties in the act of injustice, but, for example, their descendants? Is an injustice done to someone whose holding was itself based upon an unrectified injustice? How far back must one go in wiping clean the historical slate of injustices? What may victims of injustice permissibly do in order to rectify the injustices being done to them, including the many injustices done by persons acting through their government? I do not know of a thorough or theoretically sophisticated treatment of such issues. Idealizing greatly, let us suppose theoretical investigations will produce a principle of rectification. This principle uses historical information about previous situations and injustices done in them (as defined by the first two principles of justice and rights against interference), and information about the actual course of events that flowed from these injustices, until the present, and it yields a description (or descriptions) of holdings in the society. The principle of rectification presumably will make use of its best estimate of subjunctive information about what would have occurred (or a probability distribution over what might have occurred, using the expected value) if the injustice had not taken place. If the actual description of holdings turns out not to be one of the descriptions yielded by the principle, then one of the descriptions yielded must be realized.[7]

The general outlines of the theory of justice in holdings are that the holdings of a person are just if he is entitled to them by the principles of justice in acquisition and transfer, or by the principle of rectification of injustice (as specified by the first two principles). If each person's holdings are just, then the total set (distribution) of holdings is just. To turn these general outlines into a specific theory we would have to specify the details of each of the three principles of justice in holdings: the principle of acquisition of holdings, the principle of transfer of holdings, and the principle of rectification of violations of the first two principles. I shall not attempt that task here. (Locke's principle of justice in acquisition is discussed below.)

HISTORICAL PRINCIPLES AND END-RESULT PRINCIPLES

The general outlines of the entitlement theory illuminate the nature and defects of other conceptions of distributive justice. The entitlement theory of justice in distribution is *historical;* whether a distribution is just depends upon how it came about. In contrast, *current time-slice principles* of justice hold that the justice of a distribution is determined by how things are distributed (who has what) as judged by some *structural* principle(s) of just distribution. A utilitarian who judges between any two distributions by seeing which has the greater sum of utility and, if the sums tie, applies some fixed equality criterion to choose the more equal distribution, would hold a current time-slice principle of justice. As would someone who had a fixed schedule of trade-offs between the sum of

---

[7] If the principle of rectification of violations of the first two principles yields more than one description of holdings, then some choice must be made as to which of these is to be realized. Perhaps the sort of considerations about distributive justice and equality that I argue against play a legitimate role in *this* subsidiary choice. Similarly, there may be room for such considerations in deciding which otherwise arbitrary features a statute will embody, when such features are unavoidable because other considerations do not specify a precise line; yet a line must be drawn.

happiness and equality. According to a current time-slice principle, all that needs to be looked at, in judging the justice of a distribution, is who ends up with what; in comparing any two distributions one need look only at the matrix presenting the distributions. No further information need be fed into a principle of justice. It is a consequence of such principles of justice that any two structurally identical distributions are equally just. (Two distributions are structurally identical if they present the same profile, but perhaps have different persons occupying the particular slots. My having ten and your having five, and my having five and your having ten are structurally identical distributions.) Welfare economics is the theory of current time-slice principles of justice. The subject is conceived as operating on matrices representing only current information about distribution. This, as well as some of the usual conditions (for example, the choice of distribution is invariant under relabeling of columns), guarantees that welfare economics will be a current time-slice theory, with all of its inadequacies.

Most persons do not accept current time-slice principles as constituting the whole story about distributive shares. They think it relevant in assessing the justice of a situation to consider not only the distribution it embodies, but also how that distribution came about. If some persons are in prison for murder or war crimes, we do not say that to assess the justice of the distribution in the society we must look only at what this person has, and that person has, and that person has, . . . at the current time. We think it relevant to ask whether someone did something so that he *deserved* to be punished, deserved to have a lower share. Most will agree to the relevance of further information with regard to punishments and penalties. Consider also desired things. One traditional socialist view is that workers are entitled to the product and full fruits of their labor; they have earned it; a distribution is unjust if it does not give the workers what they are entitled to. Such entitlements are based upon some past history. No socialist holding this view would find it comforting to be told that because the actual distribution *A* happens to coincide structurally with the one he desires *D*, *A* therefore is no less just than *D*; it differs only in that the "parasitic" owners of capital receive under *A* what the workers are entitled to under *D*, and the workers receive under *A* what the owners are entitled to under *D*, namely very little. This socialist rightly, in my view, holds onto the notions of earning, producing, entitlement, desert, and so forth, and he rejects current time-slice principles that look only to the structure of the resulting set of holdings. (The set of holdings resulting from what? Isn't it implausible that how holdings are produced and come to exist has no effect at all on who should hold what?) His mistake lies in his view of what entitlements arise out of what sorts of productive processes.

We construe the position we discuss too narrowly by speaking of *current* time-slice principles. Nothing is changed if structural principles operate upon a time sequence of current time-slice profiles and, for example, give someone more now to counterbalance the less he has had earlier. A utilitarian or an egalitarian or any mixture of the two over time will inherit the difficulties of his more myopic comrades. He is not helped by the fact that *some* of the information others consider relevant in assessing a distribution is reflected, unrecoverably, in past matrices. Henceforth, we shall refer to such unhistorical principles of distributive justice, including the current time-slice principles, as *end-result principles* or *end-state principles.*

In contrast to end-result principles of justice, *historical principles* of justice hold that past circumstances or actions of people can create differential entitlements or differential deserts to things. An injustice can be worked by moving from one distribution to another structurally identical one, for the second, in profile the same, may violate people's entitlements or deserts; it may not fit the actual history.[8]

B. THE LEGITIMACY OF THE STATE

The entitlement theory calls into question whether government ought to have the power to take away people's property, not to mention their lives. But when people do not cooperate willingly with the government and act for the public interest, they are often forced to relinquish their property. How does government get the power and the authority to take people's property or threaten their lives? Ought the government to have such power?

The authority with the power to define the public interest and to enforce its definition is what philosophers call the **state.**[9] But it must not be thought that the state or its instrument—the government—is merely a bookkeeping and organizational institution. Ideally, in a well-functioning society in which most people act in the public interest, it may be not much more than this, and then as minimally as necessary. But since people do not always act in the public interest, the role of the state is necessarily that of *legislator,* making laws and rules that tell people how to act (and how not to act), and that of *enforcer,* applying enough force through threat of punishment to make sure that people obey those laws and rules. Then too it is the state that may have to step in when the rights of an individual are threatened, and pass laws to protect those rights and punish those who violate them.

Ideally, the function of the state is to keep the balance between the public interest and individual rights, in other words, to preserve justice.

---

[8]Robert Nozick, *Anarchy, State and Utopia* (Cambridge, MA: Harvard University Press, 1974).

[9]This is a general term for any highest authority in a society; it includes federal government as well as "states" in a more restricted sense, for example, Alabama and Massachusetts. Thus the sovereign cities of the ancient Greeks were called "city-states."

Some theorists would add that the function of the state is to make life for its citizens such that the public interest and individual rights and interests almost always coincide. Others would hope that the state would serve this function so well that it would no longer be needed, except perhaps as a bureau of records and an occasional enforcer of contracts. Some people think that the state is an end in itself, a matter of pride and a rallying point for its citizens, something like a football team in a small town. Still others would say that the only proper state is virtually no state at all.

We have been talking about the state as the center of power and authority, and many people would simply define "politics" in terms of "power." But "power" alone is not enough to characterize the state; we must add that it is legitimate power. **Legitimacy** means that this power must be justified. A person or organization might have tremendous power and rule a society with an iron hand. But rulers might be gangsters who rule by force alone. Or they might be invaders from another country who rule without popular consent. Or they might be citizens who, because of powerful positions in the government or the army, acquire this power in illegal or unacceptable ways. The idea of the state, therefore, is not simply that it is the center of power; it is the center of legitimate power or, in other words, *authority*. When philosophers and political scientists use the term *authority*, they almost always mean "legitimate authority." And sometimes, when they say that "the state has the power to do such and such," they mean "that the state has the legitimate power to do such and such." Legitimate authority (or simply, authority) has the legal power to make laws. Crude military or political power is only the ability to force people to do what one wants; it is not therefore legitimate. A central question of political philosophy, accordingly, is "what makes a state's power legitimate?" In other words, "what gives a state its authority?"

It is necessary to distinguish three different levels on which the question of legitimacy and authority must be raised. First, there is the question of the legitimacy of the state itself. On what authority did the English, for example, rule over the American colonies and consider them a part of the British Empire? Conversely, what authority did the American colonists claim when they declared themselves independent of England and set themselves up as a separate state? Much recent history involves the creation, recreation, and realignment of various states. If we look at maps of Europe for the past fifty years, for example, we will see that states go into and out of existence, sometimes several times. The question of the legitimacy of the state itself, therefore, is one of the main causes of the wars and political battles of our times (and earlier times as well).

Second, there is the question of the legitimacy of a certain form of government. In some Asian and Latin American countries, for example, there are frequent changes between military dictatorships and republics or democracies. In the recent history of Spain, as another example, there have been changes from a monarchy to a republic to a dictatorship back to a monarchy trying to establish democratic processes. The geographical boundaries of the state in all these instances remain the same, the population also remains pretty much the same (making allowances for casualties and refugees), but the form of government changes radically. It is possible that the same people or party, however, will remain in power even though the form of government changes. (For example, the president of a democracy may become the dictator in a dictatorship.)

This brings us to our third level of legitimacy: Particular governments must be shown to be legitimate within the framework of the form of government in a state. The form of government confers legitimacy. For example, a democracy confers legitimacy through elections, a monarchy confers legitimacy on a new king or queen through birth. In our own state, the form of government has remained constant for the past two hundred years, but the particular governments have changed quite frequently, from one party to the other, and sometimes new parties are created and succeed in getting elected. A particular government (whether Republican or Democratic, for example) is made legitimate by the election laws created by our form of government. Usually these laws make it clear which particular government (that is, which party) is the legitimate government at a particular time. In a close election, however, this may be in hot dispute, and in such instances the distinction between the form of government and particular governments is thrown into sharp contrast.

1.   Five Theories of Legitimacy

The legitimacy of a particular government, a form of government, or a state means that its power is justified. But what justifies this power? We might say that what justifies a particular government, form of government, or state is the willingness of its citizens to obey its laws, the recognition of it by other governments and states whom it in turn recognizes, and in general the widespread belief in its legitimacy by virtue of which the people or party in power are accepted as such. But this extremely loose definition encounters many problems, particularly in dictatorships where people are forced to accept governments, in powerful military states that can force recognition from other states, and powerful governments that are able to force their citizens to obey them, whether the citizens really want to or not. Moreover, the crucial belief in a government, form of government, or state may be based on many different kinds of justifications. It is necessary, therefore, to mention at least five different kinds of justifications for this belief, each of which might be called a theory of legitimacy.

DIVINE RIGHT TO RULE THEORY   Since ancient times it has been argued that kings, queens, pharaohs, princes, and emperors have been given their authority directly by God or gods. Until modern times this was a difficult theory to refute and a dangerous one to argue against. But even in ancient times, for example, in Greece, it was maintained that this divine right had to be supported by justice and a modicum of wisdom and, at least to a small extent, the acceptance of the people ruled. But since the people who were ruled were more often than not forced to accept the authority of the divinely appointed ruler, this last qualification was mostly nominal. Kings sometimes enjoyed the support of the people, but it is debatable whether they actually needed it.

MIGHT-MAKES-RIGHT THEORY   This theory holds that power itself makes a government legitimate. In a sense, therefore, this theory rejects the very idea of legitimacy, since according to it any government or state that has power has legitimate power and therefore the distinction between legitimate and illegitimate power disappears. For obvious reasons, this theory is usually favored more by those who are already in power than by those who are not in power. But it is rare that a government or state that has power will publicly state the might-makes-right theory. Usually it will invoke one of the other theories in its defense.

UTILITARIAN THEORY   Just as utilitarianism in moral theory defends that action that will promote the greatest good for the greatest number, utilitarianism in political theory defends the government or state that will promote the greatest good for the greatest number of its citizens. Jeremy Bentham's classic treatise, for example, is called *An Introduction to the Principles of Morals and Legislation.* And Mill's pamphlet, *Utilitarianism,* is partly devoted to the political problem of justice. According to the utilitarian theory, a government is legitimate so long as it provides the most services and best protection for its citizens in general. Or to characterize this theory slightly differently, the utilitarian theory says that a government is justified insofar as it furthers the public interest. (Thus it might also be called "public interest theory.")

JUSTICE THEORY   One possible problem with the utilitarian theory, as we have seen in other contexts in this chapter, is that it may promote the best interests of most of the people at the expense of a small minority. Neither the divine right nor might-makes-right theories include any mention of justice at all, and so it is important that the demand that governments and states be just be made independently of these others. Plato and Aristotle, for example, used a justice theory to defend their conceptions of the state. But the fact that Plato's and Aristotle's conception of the state was so different from ours (and so unjust in some respects) points to an important qualification of this kind of theory. What the theory amounts to depends wholly on the concept of justice one defends. If justice means equality, then the legitimate state will maximize equality; if justice means "everyone in his or her proper place" (as in Plato and Aristotle), then the state will be legitimate if the various parts of the state are "in harmony" and working together smoothly.

CONSENT OF THE GOVERNED THEORY   This theory is the one that most people accept today. It is assumed, however, that the consent of the governed will also ensure the public interest and justice for everyone as well. Consent of the governed theory is based on the idea that the people who are ruled should have some say in how they are ruled and perhaps even have a choice in who rules them. These two ideas are not equivalent, although they usually go together in our society. People might have a say in government policies without being able to choose the government, as in most monarchies, for example. Even Plato accepted this theory to some degree. In *The Republic*, he argues (through Socrates), "in our state, if anywhere, the governors and the governed will share the same conviction on the question who ought to rule. Don't you think so?"[10]

The most powerful modern versions of the consent of the governed theory are summed up in the phrase, "social contract." According to the theory of the social contract, governments and states are legitimate only because the citizens agree to be ruled by them.

2.   *The Social Contract*

The single most influential defense of the legitimacy of the state in modern times has been called the "social contract theory." The **social contract** is an agreement among people to share certain interests and make certain compromises for the good of them all. It is a "consent of the governed theory." In one form or another, it existed even in ancient times. For example, read Socrates' argument in the *Crito,* in which he says that by staying in Athens he had implicitly agreed to abide by its laws, even when those laws unfairly condemned him to death. What is most important in understanding the nature of this social contract is that, as in Socrates' argument, there need not have been any actual, physical contract or even oral agreement in order to talk about it. We are bound by social contract, in other words, even if we never signed or saw such a contract. Moreover, it may not be the case that there was ever such a contract, even in past history. It happens, however, that Americans are among the few people in the world whose state was actually formed explicitly by such a contract, namely, our *Constitution.* But the actual existence of such a piece of paper is not necessary to a discussion about a social contract. Simply to live in a society, according to these philoso-

[10]Plato, *The Republic,* trans. Francis M. Cornford (Oxford: Oxford University Press, 1941).

phers, is to have agreed, at least implicitly, to such an agreement. (Thus, living in a society you are expected to obey its laws; "ignorance is no excuse," and you cannot get out of an arrest by saying "I don't really live here," much less "I don't recognize your right to arrest me.")

Two very different pictures of the original social contract are presented to us by the English philosopher Thomas Hobbes and the French philosopher Jean-Jacques Rousseau. Both begin by considering man in "the state of nature," without laws and without society, before men and women came together to accept the social contract. Hobbes bases his conception of the social contract, however, on an extremely unfavorable conception of human nature. He attacks the idealistic political philosophies of Plato and Aristotle for being unrealistic and assuming wrongly that people are naturally capable of virtue and wisdom. Like Machiavelli, whom he follows with praise, he considers himself a "realist." As with most realists, this meant seeing the nasty side of things. So, according to his theory of human nature, natural man is a selfish beast, fighting for his own interests against everyone else. Human life is a "war of all against all" and a person's life, consequently, is "nasty, brutish and short." He dismisses reason and appeals to human passions, particularly the passion for self-preservation. The social contract, therefore, is mainly an agreement of equally selfish and self-seeking persons not to commit mutual murder.

◆ **from *Leviathan*,**
by Thomas Hobbes

OF THE NATURAL CONDITION OF MANKIND AS
CONCERNING THEIR FELICITY, AND MISERY

Men by nature equal. Nature hath made men so equal, in the faculties of the body, and mind; as that though there be found one man sometimes manifestly stronger in body, or of quicker mind than another; yet when all is reckoned together, the difference between man, and man, is not so considerable, as that one man can thereupon claim to himself any benefit, to which another may not pretend, as well as he. For as to the strength of body, the weakest has strength enough to kill the strongest, either by secret machination or by confederacy with others, that are in the same danger with himself.

· · · · · · · · · ·

For such is the nature of men, that howsoever they may acknowledge many others to be more witty, or more eloquent, or more learned; yet they will hardly believe there be many so wise as themselves; for they see their own wit at hand, and other men's at a distance. But this proveth rather that men are in that point equal, than unequal. For there is not ordinarily a greater sign of the equal distribution of any thing, than that every man is contented with his share.

From equality proceeds diffidence. From this equality of ability, ariseth equality of hope in the attaining of our ends. And therefore if any two men desire the same thing, which nevertheless they cannot both enjoy, they become enemies; and in the way to their end, which is principally their own conservation, and sometimes their delectation only, endeavour to destroy, or subdue one another. And from hence it comes to pass, that where an invader hath no more to fear, than another man's single power; if one plant, sow, build, or possess a convenient seat, others may probably be expected to come prepared with forces united, to dispossess, and deprive him, not only of the fruit of his labour, but also of his life, or liberty. And the invader again is in the like danger of another.

From diffidence war. And from this diffidence of one another, there is no way for any man to secure himself, so reasonable, as anticipation; that is, by force, or wiles, to master the persons of all men he can, so long, till he see no other power great enough to endanger him: and this is no more than his own conservation requireth, and is generally allowed. Also because there be some, that taking pleasure in contemplating their own power in the acts of conquest, which they pursue farther than their security requires; if others, that otherwise would be glad to be at ease within modest bounds, should not by invasion increase their power, they would not be able, long time, by standing only on their defence, to subsist. And by consequence, such augmentation of dominion over men being necessary to a man's conservation, it ought to be allowed him.

Again, men have no pleasure, but on the contrary a great deal of grief, in keeping company, where there is no power able to over-awe them all. For every man looketh that his companion should value him, at the same rate he sets upon himself: and upon all signs of contempt, or undervaluing, naturally endeavors, as far as he dares (which amongst them that have no common power to keep them in quiet, is far enough to make them destroy each other), to extort a greater value from his contemners, by damage; and from others, by the example.

So that in the nature of man, we find three principal causes of quarrel. First, competition; secondly, diffidence; thirdly, glory.

The first, maketh men invade for gain; the second, for safety; and the third, for reputation. The first use violence, to make themselves masters of other men's persons, wives, children, and cattle; the second, to defend them; the third, for trifles, as a word, a smile, a different opinion, and any other sign of undervalue, either direct in their persons, or by reflection in their kindred, their friends, their nation, their profession, or their name.

Out of civil states, there is always war of every one against every one. Hereby it is manifest, that during the time men live without a common power to keep them all in awe, they are in that condition which is called war; and such a war, as is of every man, against every man. For war, consisteth not in battle only, or the act of fighting, but in a tract of time, wherein the will to contend by battle is sufficiently known. . . .

The incommodities of such a war. Whatsoever therefore is consequent to a time of war, where every man is enemy to every man; the same is consequent to the time, wherein men live without other security, than what their own strength, and their own invention shall furnish them withal. In such condition, there is no place for industry; because the fruit thereof is uncertain: and consequently no culture of the earth; no navigation, nor use of the commodities that may be imported by sea; no commodious building; no instruments of moving, and removing, such things as require much force; no knowledge of the face of the earth; no account of time; no arts; no letters; no society; and which is worst of all, continual fear, and danger of violent death; and the life of man, solitary, poor, nasty, brutish, and short.

It may seem strange to some man, that has not well weighed these things; that nature should thus dissociate, and render men apt to invade, and destroy one another: and he may therefore, not trusting to this inference, made from the passions, desire perhaps to have the same confirmed by experience. Let him therefore consider with himself, when taking a journey, he arms himself, and seeks to go well accompanied; when going to sleep, he locks his doors; when even in his house he locks his chests; and this when he knows there be laws, and public officers, armed to revenge all injuries shall be done him; what opinion he has of his fellow-subjects, when he rides armed; of his fellow citizens, when he locks his doors; and of his children, and servants, when he locks his chests. Does he not there as much accuse mankind by his actions, as I do by my words? But neither of us accuse men's nature in it. The desires, and other passions of man, are in themselves no sin. No more are the actions, that proceed from those passions, till they know a law that forbids them: which till laws be made they cannot know: nor can any law be made, till they have agreed upon the person that shall make it.

It may peradventure be thought, there was never such a time, nor condition of war as this; and I believe it was never generally so, over all the world: but there are many places, where they live so now. For the savage people in many places of America, except the government of small families, the concord whereof dependeth on natural lust, have no government at all; and live at this day in that brutish manner, as I said before. Howsoever, it may be perceived what manner of life there would be, where there were no common power to fear, by the manner of life, which men that have formerly lived under a peaceful government, use to degenerate into, in a civil war.

OF THE FIRST AND SECOND NATURAL LAWS, AND OF CONTRACTS

Right of nature what. The right of nature, which writers commonly call *jus naturale,* is the liberty each man hath, to use his own power, as he will himself, for the preservation of his own nature; that is to say, of his own life; and consequently, of doing any thing, which in his own judgment, and reason, he shall conceive to be the aptest means thereunto.

Liberty what. By liberty, is understood, according to the proper signification of the word, the absence of external impediments: which impediments, may oft take away part of a man's power to do what he would; but cannot hinder him from using the power left him, according as his judgment, and reason shall dictate to him.

A law of nature what. A law of nature, *lex naturalis,* is a precept or general rule, found out by reason, by which a man is forbidden to do that, which is destructive of his life, or taketh away the means of preserving the same; and to omit that, by which he thinketh it may be best preserved.

Difference of right and law. For though they that speak of this subject, use to confound *jus,* and *lex, right* and *law:* yet they ought to be distinguished; because right, consisteth in liberty to do, or to forbear: whereas law, determineth, and bindeth to one of them: so that law, and right, differ as much, as obligation, and liberty; which in one and the same matter are inconsistent.

Naturally every man has right to every thing. And because the condition of man, as hath been declared in the precedent chapter, is a condition of war of every one against every one; in which case every one is governed by his own reason; and there is nothing he can make use of, that may not be a help unto him, in preserving his life against his enemies; it followeth, that in such a condition, every man has a right to every thing; even to one another's body. And therefore, as long as this natural right of every man to every thing endureth, there can be no security to any man, how strong or wise soever he be, of living out the time, which nature ordinarily alloweth men to live.

The fundamental law of nature. And consequently it is a precept, or general rule of reason, *that every man, ought to endeavour peace, as far as he has hope of obtaining it; and when he cannot obtain it, that he may seek, and use, all helps, and advantages of war.*

· · · · · · · · · ·

The second law of nature. From this fundamental law of nature, by which men are commanded to endeavour peace, is derived this second law; *that a man be willing, when others are so too, as far-forth, as for peace, and defence of himself he shall think it necessary, to lay down this right to all things; and be contented with so much liberty against other men, as he would allow other men against himself.* For as long as every man holdeth this right, of doing any thing he liketh; so long are all men in the condition of war. But if other men will not lay down their right, as well as he; then there is no reason for any one, to divest himself of his: for that were to expose himself to prey, which no man is bound to, rather than to dispose himself to peace. This is that law of the Gospel; *whatsoever you require that others should do to you, that do ye to them.*

. . . .

What it is to lay down a right. To *lay down* man's *right* to any thing, is to *divest* himself of the *liberty,* of hindering another of the benefit of his own right to the same. For he that renounceth, or passeth away his right, giveth not to any other man a right which he had not before; because there is nothing to which every man had not right by nature: but only standeth out of his way, that he may enjoy his own original right, without hindrance from him; not without hindrance from another. So that the effect which re-doundeth to one man, by another man's defect of right, is but so much diminution of impediments to the use of his own right ori-ginal.

. . . .

Not all rights are alienable. Whensoever a man transferreth his right, or renounceth it; it is either in consideration of some right reciprocally transferred to himself; or for some other good he hopeth for thereby. For it is a voluntary act: and of the voluntary acts of every man, the object is some *good to himself.* And there-fore there be some rights, which no man can be understood by any words, or other signs, to have abandoned, or transferred. As first a man cannot lay down the right of resisting them, that assault him by force, to take away his life; because he cannot be understood to aim thereby, at any good to himself. The same may be said of wounds, and chains, and imprisonment; both because there is no benefit consequent to such patience; as there is to the patience of suffering another to be wounded, or imprisoned: as also because a man cannot tell, when he seeth men proceed against him by vio-lence, whether they intend his death or not. And lastly the motive, and end for which this renouncing, and transferring of right is introduced, is nothing else but the security of a man's person, in his life, and in the means of so preserving life, as not to be weary of it. And therefore if a man by words, or other signs, seem to despoil himself of the end, for which those signs were intended; he is not to be understood as if he meant it, or that it was his will; but that he was ignorant of how such words and actions were to be inter-preted.

Contract what. The mutual transferring of right, is that which men call CONTRACT.

. . . .

Covenants of mutual trust, when invalid. If a covenant be made, wherein neither of the parties perform presently, but trust one another; in the condition of mere nature, which is a condition of war of every man against every man, upon any reasonable suspicion, it is void: but if there be a common power set over them both, with right and force sufficient to compel performance, it is not void. For he that performeth first, has no assurance the other will perform after; because the bonds of words are too weak to bridle men's ambition, avarice, anger, and other passions, without the fear of some coercive power; which in the condition of mere nature, where all men are equal, and judges of the justness of their own fears, cannot possibly be supposed. And therefore he which performeth first, does but betray himself to his enemy; contrary to the right, he can never abandon, of defending his life, and means of living.

But in a civil estate, where there is a power set up to constrain those that would otherwise violate their faith, that fear is no more reasonable; and for that cause, he which by the covenant is to perform first, is obliged so to do.

The cause of fear, which maketh such a covenant invalid, must be always something arising after the covenant made; as some new fact, or other sign of the will not to perform: else it cannot make the covenant void. For that which could not hinder a man from promising, ought not to be admitted as a hindrance of performing. **Right to the end, containeth right to the means.** He that transferreth any right, transferreth the means of enjoying it, as far as lieth in his power. As he that selleth land, is understood to transfer the herbage, and whatsoever grows upon it: nor can he that sells a mill turn away the stream that drives it. And they that give to a man the right of government in sovereignty, are understood to give him the right of levying money to maintain soldiers; and of appointing magistrates for the administration of justice.[11]

Hobbes begins his argument with the perhaps surprising observation that people are basically equal in nature. He is not talking here about legal equality or equal rights (for there are no laws and no legal rights) but rather equality in abilities, talents, and power. This seems strange because the problem of equality usually pays attention to the great differences between people. Instead Hobbes points out our similarities. In particular, he points out that almost everyone is strong and smart enough to kill or inflict grievous injury on others. Even a puny moron can, with a knife or a handgun, kill the strongest and smartest person on earth. Accordingly, the basis of the social contract (or "covenant") according to Hobbes is our mutual protection. Everyone agrees not to kill other people and in return is guaranteed that he or she won't be killed. Although it is a cynical view of human nature, it also continues to be one of the most powerful arguments for strong governments. (Hobbes himself was a conservative monarchist.)

[11] Thomas Hobbes, *Leviathan* (New York: Hafner, 1926).

Rousseau, quite to the contrary, had an extremely optimistic view of human nature, as we saw in the preceding chapter. He believed that people were "naturally good," and it was only the corruptions of society that made them selfish and destructive. Rousseau does not take the social contract, therefore, to be simply a doctrine of protection between mutually brutish individuals. The function of the state is rather to allow people to develop the "natural goodness" that they had in the absence of any state at all. This is not to say (although Rousseau is often interpreted this way) that he was nostalgic and wanted to "go back to the state of nature." That is impossible. (It is not even clear that Rousseau believed that there ever was a "state of nature" as such; his example, like Hobbes' example, is a way of giving a picture of "human nature," whether or not it is historically accurate.) We are already in society, that is a given fact. So Rousseau's aim is to develop a conception of the state that will allow us to live as morally as possible. This is important, for Rousseau, unlike most social contract theorists, is not at all a utilitarian; it is not happiness that is most important but goodness. (Hobbes, by way of contrast, took utility, pleasure and well-being, in addition to self-preservation, to be the purpose of the social contract.)

Rousseau's ambition, therefore, is not to "get us back to nature" but rather to revise our conception of the state. His "revision," however, is one of the most radical documents in modern history and has rightly been said to be one of the causes of both the American and French revolutions. The main thesis is one that Rousseau inherits from Locke: The state has legitimate power only so long as it serves the people it governs. The revolutionary corollary is that when a state ceases to serve its citizens, the citizens have a right to overthrow that government. This was a radical claim, again reminiscent of Locke. Even Rousseau was not comfortable with it. (Locke had made his statement *after* the English Revolution.) He called revolution "the most horrible alternative," to be avoided wherever possible. But subsequent French history took his theories quite literally and demonstrated too the "horror" that may follow too radical and abrupt a change in the authority that citizens accept as legitimate.

In earlier works, Rousseau had argued his famous thesis that "natural man" is "naturally good" and that contemporary society has corrupted him (and her). He went on to say that competition and the artificiality of our lust for private property are responsible for this corruption, and he even included marriage and romantic love as forms of this "lust for private property." In the state of nature, he suggests, people mated when they felt like it, with whomever they felt like, and duels fought between rivals were unheard of. Rousseau does not suggest that we return to that prehistoric custom, but he does use it as a wedge to pry open even the most sacred of our modern civil institutions. All of these, he argues, must be reexamined, and the tool for that reexamination is the social contract.

The key to his most famous book, appropriately called *The Social Contract,* is that man must regain his freedom within society. This does not mean, however, that a person can do whatever he or she would like to do. Quite the contrary, to be a citizen, according to Rousseau, is to want and do what is good for the society as well. To be free is precisely to want to do what is good for the society as well. And in one of the most problematic statements of the social contract, Rousseau says that a person who does not so act for the good of the society may have to "be forced to be free." Here is the basis for a strange paradox. On the one hand, Rousseau has properly been regarded as the father of the most liberal and revolutionary political theories of our time. (Marx, for example, claims a great debt to Rousseau). His political philosophy stresses individual freedom and rights above all, even above the state itself. But another side to Rousseau emerges in this paradoxical phrase; his stress on the state as an entity in itself ("the sovereign," presumably the king, but essentially any government) and the sub-servience of the individual to the state has also caused him to be labeled an authoritarian and the forerunner of totalitarian and fascist governments.

This paradox is not easily resolved, but we can at least explain how it comes about. Rousseau believes that the state is subject to and receives its legitimacy from the people it governs. But that does not mean that individual people need have any real power in determining the form or functions of government. Rousseau is not a democrat. What he says instead is that the state is subject to what he calls the general will, which is not simply a collection of individuals but something more. For example, we talk about "the spirit of the revolution" or "the discontent of the working class," but this spirit or discontent is not simply the product of each individual person. A poll of workers or revolutionaries would not show it either way. The revolution may have spirit even though some participants do not; indeed, they may even dislike the whole idea. And here is the source of the paradox: Legitimacy is given to the state by the general will, not by every individual person. And the person who does not agree with the general will, therefore, may very well find himself or herself forced into compliance with the state (as Rousseau says, "forced to be free"). How much force, however, is a matter about which Rousseau is not very clear; nor have his many followers agreed on that crucial point either. On one extreme, Rousseau's authoritarian followers have insisted that all dissent from the general will must be stifled; on the other extreme, Rousseau's most libertarian and anarchist followers have insisted that the rights of the individual to be free from government intevention and to live according to his or her own "natural goodness" outweigh any claims that the state may have. What follows are a few selections from *The Social Contract,* beginning with one of Rousseau's best-known slogans.

◆from *The Social Contract,* by Jean-Jacques Rousseau

Man is born free; and everywhere he is in chains. One thinks himself the master of others, and still remains a greater slave than they. How did this change come about? I do not know. What can make it legitimate? That question I think I can answer.

If I took into account only force, and the effects derived from it, I should say: "As long as a people is compelled to obey, and obeys, it does well; as soon as it can shake off the yoke, and shakes it off, it does still better; for, regaining its liberty by the same right as took it away, either it is justified in resuming it, or there was no justification for those who took it away." But the social order is a sacred right which is the basis of all other rights. Nevertheless, this right does not come from nature, and must therefore be founded on conventions. Before coming to that, I have to prove what I have just asserted.

THE FIRST SOCIETIES

The most ancient of all societies, and the only one that is natural, is the family: and even so the children remain attached to the father only so long as they need him for their preservation. As soon as this need ceases, the natural bond is dissolved. The children, released from the obedience they owed to the father, and the father, released from the care he owed his children, return equally to independence. If they remain united, they continue so no longer naturally, but voluntarily; and the family itself is then maintained only by convention.

This common liberty results from the nature of man. His first law is to provide for his own preservation, his first cares are those which he owes to himself; and, as soon as he reaches years of discretion, he is the sole judge of the proper means of preserving himself, and consequently becomes his own master.

The family then may be called the first model of political societies; the ruler corresponds to the father, and the people to the children; and all, being born free and equal, alienate their liberty only for their own advantage. The whole difference is that, in the family, the love of the father for his children repays him for the care he takes of them, while, in the State, the pleasure of commanding takes the place of the love which the chief cannot have for the peoples under him.

· · · · · · · · · ·

THE SOCIAL COMPACT

I suppose men to have reached the point at which the obstacles in the way of their preservation in the state of nature show their power of resistance to be greater than the resources at the disposal of each individual for his maintenance in that state. That primitive condition can then subsist no longer; and the human race would perish unless it changed its manner of existence.

But, as men cannot engender new forces, but only unite and direct existing ones, they have no other means of preserving themselves than the formation, by aggregation, of a sum of forces great enough to overcome the resistance. These they have to bring into play by means of a single motive power, and cause to act in concert.

This sum of forces can arise only where several persons come together: but, as the force and liberty of each man are the chief instruments of his self-preservation, how can he pledge them without harming his own interests, and neglecting the care he owes to himself? This difficulty, in its bearing on my present subject, may be stated in the following terms:

"The problem is to find a form of association which will defend and protect with the whole common force the person and goods of each associate, and in which each, while uniting himself with all, may still obey himself alone, and remain as free as before." This is the fundamental problem of which the *Social Contract* provides the solution.

The clauses of this contract are so determined by the nature of the act that the slightest modification would make them vain and ineffective; so that, although they have perhaps never been formally set forth, they are everywhere the same and everywhere tacitly admitted and recognized, until, on the violation of the social compact, each regains his original rights and resumes his natural liberty, while losing the conventional liberty in favour of which he renounced it.

These clauses, properly understood, may be reduced to one—the total alienation of each associate, together with all his rights, to the whole community; for, in the first place, as each gives himself absolutely, the conditions are the same for all; and, this being so, no one has any interest in making them burdensome to others.

Moreover, the alienation being without reserve, the union is as perfect as it can be, and no associate has anything more to demand: for, if the individuals retained certain rights, as there would be no common superior to decide between them and the public, each, being on one point his own judge, would ask to be so on all; the state of nature would thus continue, and the association would necessarily become inoperative or tyrannical.

Finally, each man, in giving himself to all, gives himself to nobody; and as there is no associate over which he does not acquire the same right as he yields others over himself, he gains an equivalent for everything he loses, and an increase of force for the preservation of what he has.

If then we discard from the social compact what is not of its essence, we shall find that it reduces itself to the following terms:

"*Each of us puts his person and all his power in common un-*

der the supreme direction of the general will, and, in our corporate capacity, we receive each member as an indivisible part of the whole."

At once, in place of the individual personality of each contracting party, this act of association creates a moral and collective body, composed of as many members as the assembly contains voters, and receiving from this act its unity, its common identity, its life, and its will. This public person, so formed by the union of all other persons, formerly took the name of *city*, and now takes that of *Republic* or *body politic*; it is called by its members *State* when passive, *Sovereign* when active, and *Power* when compared with others like itself. Those who are associated in it take collectively the name of *people*, and severally are called *citizens*, as sharing in the sovereign power, and *subjects*, as being under the laws of the State. But these terms are often confused and taken one for another: it is enough to know how to distinguish them when they are being used with precision.

THE SOVEREIGN

This formula shows us that the act of association comprises a mutual undertaking between the public and the individuals, and that each individual, in making a contract, as we may say, with himself, is bound in a double capacity; as a member of the Sovereign he is bound to the individuals, and as a member of the State to the Sovereign. But the maxim of civil right, that no one is bound by undertakings made to himself, does not apply in this case; for there is a great difference between incurring an obligation to yourself and incurring one to a whole of which you form a part.

Attention must further be called to the fact that public deliberation, while competent to bind all the subjects to the Sovereign, because of the two different capacities in which each of them may be regarded, cannot, for the opposite reason, bind that Sovereign to itself; and that it is consequently against the nature of the body politic for the Sovereign to impose on itself a law which it cannot infringe. Being able to regard itself in only one capacity, it is in the position of an individual who makes a contract with himself; and this makes it clear that there neither is nor can be any kind of fundamental law binding on the body of the people—not even the social contract itself. This does not mean that the body politic cannot enter into undertakings with others, provided the contract is not infringed by them; for in relation to what is external to it, it becomes a simple being, an individual.

But the body politic or the Sovereign, drawing its being wholly from the sanctity of the contract, can never bind itself, even to an outsider, to do anything derogatory to the original act, for instance, to alienate any part of itself, or to submit to another Sovereign. Violation of the act by which it exists would be self-annihilation; and that which is itself nothing can create nothing.

As soon as this multitude is so united in one body, it is impossible to offend against one of the members without attacking the body, and still more to offend against the body without the members resenting it. Duty and interest therefore equally oblige the two contracting parties to give each other help; and the same men should seek to combine, in their double capacity, all the advantages dependent upon that capacity.

Again, the Sovereign, being formed wholly of the individuals who compose it, neither has nor can have any interest contrary to theirs; and consequently the sovereign power need give no guarantee to its subjects, because it is impossible for the body to wish to hurt all its members. We shall also see later on that it cannot hurt any in particular. The Sovereign, merely by virtue of what it is, is always what it should be.

This, however, is not the case with the relation of the subjects to the Sovereign, which, despite the common interest, would have no security that they would fulfil their undertakings unless it found means to assure itself of their fidelity.

In fact, each individual, as a man, may have a particular will contrary or dissimilar to the general will which he has as a citizen. His particular interest may speak to him quite differently from the common interest: his absolute and naturally independent existence may make him look upon what he owes to the common cause as a gratuitous contribution, the loss of which will do less harm to others than the payment of it is burdensome to himself; and, regarding the moral person which constitutes the State as a *persona ficta,* because not a man, he may wish to enjoy the rights of citizenship without being ready to fulfil the duties of a subject. The continuance of such an injustice could not but prove the undoing of the body politic.

In order then that the social compact may not be an empty formula, it tacitly includes the undertaking, which alone can give force to the rest, that whoever refuses to obey the general will shall be compelled to do so by the whole body. This means nothing less than that he will be forced to be free; for this is the condition which, by giving each citizen to his country, secures him against all personal dependence. In this lies the key to the working of the political machine; this alone legitimizes civil undertakings, which, without it, would be absurd, tyrannical, and liable to the most frightful abuses.

THE CIVIL STATE

The passage from the state of nature to the civil state produces a very remarkable change in man, by substituting justice for instinct in his conduct, and giving his actions the morality they had formerly lacked. Then only, when the voice of duty takes the place of physical impulses and right of appetite, does man, who so far had considered only himself, find that he is forced to act on different-principles, and to consult his reason before listening to his inclinations. Although, in this state, he deprives himself of some advantages which he got from nature, he gains in return others so great, his faculties are so stimulated and developed, his ideas so extended, his feelings so ennobled, and his whole soul so uplifted, that, did not the abuses of this new condition often degrade him below that which he left, he would be bound to bless continually the happy moment which took him from it for ever, and, instead of a stupid and unimaginative animal, made him an intelligent being and a man.

Let us draw up the whole account in terms easily commensurable. What man loses by the social contract is his natural liberty and an unlimited right to everything he tries to get and succeeds in getting; what he gains is civil liberty and the proprietorship of all he possesses. If we are to avoid mistake in weighing one against the other, we must clearly distinguish natural liberty, which is bounded only by the strength of the individual, from civil liberty, which is limited by the general will; and possession, which is merely the effect of force or the right of the first occupier, from property, which can be founded only on a positive title.

We might, over and above all this, add, to what man acquires in the civil state, moral liberty, which alone makes him truly master of himself; for the mere impulse of appetite is slavery, while obedience to a law which we prescribe to ourselves is liberty.[12]

Although Rousseau shares with Hobbes a belief in the social contract theory, the differences between them could not be more striking. Where Hobbes begins with a brutal view of human nature forced into agreement by fear of mutual violence, Rousseau begins by saying that "man is born free." For Rousseau, the social contract is not an instrument of mutual protection but a means of improving people and bringing out what is best in them. His central theme is not antagonism but humanity's "natural goodness." With unmistakable clarity, Rousseau rejects all might-makes-right theories and insists that legitimacy must always be a matter of the consent of the governed. "The general will" is not a general compromise but the creation of a new power, the power of the people, which for Rousseau is the ultimate voice of authority.

The most famous example of social contract theory at work is in our own Declaration of Independence. In that document, social contract theory combined with a theory of "natural" ("unalienable") rights provided an epoch-making announcement of the right of a people to overthrow an established government:

[12] Jean-Jacques Rousseau, *The Social Contract and Discourses*, trans. G. D. H. Cole (New York: Everyman's Library Edition, E. P. Dutton, 1947).

◆**from The Declaration of Independence,
by Thomas Jefferson et al.**

We hold these Truths to be self-evident, that all Men are created equal, that they are endowed by their Creator with certain unalienable Rights, that among these are Life, Liberty, and the pursuit of Happiness—That to secure these rights, Governments are instituted among Men, deriving their just Powers from the Consent of the Governed, that whenever any Form of Government becomes destructive of these Ends, it is the Right of the People to alter or to abolish it, and to institute new Government, laying its Foundation on such Principles, and organizing its Powers in such Form, as to them shall seem most likely to effect their Safety and Happiness. Prudence, indeed, will indicate that Governments long established should not be changed for light and transient causes; and accordingly all Experience hath shewn, that Mankind are more disposed to suffer, while Evils are sufferable, than to right themselves by abolishing the Forms to which they are accustomed. But when a long Train of Abuses and Usurpations, pursuing invariably the same Object, evinces a Design to reduce them under absolute Despotism, it is their Right, it is their Duty, to throw off such Government, and to provide new Guards for their future Security.

C. INDIVIDUAL RIGHTS AND FREEDOM

If our concern were only the smooth workings of society, almost any government would do—the stronger the better, the more authoritarian the more efficient. But efficiency is only one of several concerns and probably not the most important. You might argue that the public interest could be served by such a government, but it is clear that justice and individual rights could not. The importance of the social contract theory (and consent-of-the governed theories in general) is precisely its clear emphasis on justice and rights, even when these go against the general public interest. However, the social contract theory by itself is not entirely clear about the status of individual rights. Those rights concerning freedom are of particular concern here. How much personal freedom does the social contract guarantee us? Thus any discussion of justice and the state must include some special concern for the status of basic freedoms and "unalienable rights" (that is, rights that no one and no government may take away), such as freedom to speak one's political opinions without harassment, freedom to worship (or not worship) without being penalized or punished, freedom to defend oneself against attack ("the right to bear arms" is a controversial case), and the freedom to pursue one's own interests (where these do not interfere with the rights of others). In addition, we can add the right not to be imprisoned without reason, or accused without a fair trial, or punished unduly for a crime committed. Our best-known list of such freedoms and rights is the American Bill of Rights, appended to the main body of the Constitution as a kind of contractual guarantee of personal rights.

1. The Proper Extent of the State

But even if the importance of such rights is indisputable, the precise formulation and extent of those rights are highly debatable. We speak of "unalienable rights," but should such rights be left unrestricted, for example, even in wartime? It is clear, to mention the most common example, that freedom of speech does not extend so far as the right to falsely yell "fire" in a crowded theater. Freedom of speech, therefore, like other rights, is limited by considerations of public welfare and utility. But how limited? Is mere annoyance to the government sufficient? or general boredom among the populace? Similarly, we can go back to the difficult examples we raised in earlier sections. Are the rights against imprisonment and harsh punishment always valid against overwhelming public interest? For example, are they valid in the case of a criminal who has committed crimes repeatedly? Or, to take a difficult example, is "free enterprise" an "unalienable" right in our society? Or is free enterprise rather a theory (and a debatable one) that suggests that public interest and justice will best be served by open competition and a free market? But that theory evolved before modern monopolies developed and before it was obvious that "free" markets could be manipulated so as not to be either free or in the public interest at all. Is that "freedom" still a right? Or should it also be tempered by other concerns?

One of the most important basic rights is the presumed right to own private property. John Locke, writing just after the English ("Glorious") Revolution of 1688, listed three basic rights that would become the main ingredients of both the American Declaration of Independence and a still-prominent political philosophy called liberalism. Foremost among them were "life, liberty, and the right to own private property." (The original draft of the American Declaration included just these three, but Jefferson replaced the last with the less commital "pursuit of happiness.") For Locke, private property is the bulwark of freedom and the basis of other human rights. One's own body is private property in the most basic sense; no one else has the authority to violate or use it without permission. Most contemporary societies recognize this right to one's own body as fundamental. But then Locke adds that the right to own property that one has helped cultivate with his or her body ("hath mixed his labour with it") is also basic to freedom and human dignity. The Protestant work ethic emerges very powerfully in this view, in which work and rights are treated together, the first being our way of earning the second:

◆**from *The Second Treatise on Government,*
by John Locke**

Though the earth and all inferior creatures be common to all
men, yet every man has a *property* in his own *person*. This nobody
has any right to but himself. The *labour* of his body and the *work*
of his hands, we may say, are properly his. Whatsoever, then, he re-
moves out of the state that nature hath provided and left it in, he
hath mixed his labour with it, and joined to it something that is his
own, and thereby makes it his property. It being by him removed
from the common state nature placed it in, it hath by this labour
something annexed to it that excludes the common right of other
men. For his labour being the unquestionable property of the
labourer, no man but he can have a right to what that is once
joined to, at least where there is enough, and as good left in common for others.

He that is nourished by the acorns he picked up under an oak,
or the apples he gathered from the trees in the wood, has certainly
appropriated them to himself. Nobody can deny but the nourishment is his. I ask, then, when did they begin to be his? when he di-
gested? or when he ate? or when he boiled? or when he brought
them home? or when he picked them up? And 'tis plain, if the first
gaterhing made them not his, nothing else could. That labour put
a distinction between them and common. That added something to
them more than Nature, the common mother of all, had done, and
so they became his private right. And will any one say he had not
right to those acorns or apples he thus appropriated because he
had not the consent of all mankind to make them his? Was it a
robbery thus to assume to himself what belonged to all in common? If such a consent as that was necessary, man had starved,
notwithstanding the plenty God had given him. We see in com-
mons, which remain so by compact, that 'tis the taking any part of
what is common, and removing it out of the state Nature leaves it
in, which begins the property, without which the common is of no
use. And the taking of this or that part does not depend on the
express consent of all the commoners. Thus, the grass my horse
has bit, the turfs my servant has cut, and the ore I have digged in
any place, where I have a right to them in common with others, become my property without the assignation or consent of any body.
The labour that was mine, removing them out of that common
state they were in, hath fixed my property in them.

And thus, I think, it is very easy to conceive, without any difficulty, how labour could at first begin a title of property in the common things of nature, and how the spending it upon our uses
bounded it; so that there could then be no reason of quarrelling
about title, nor any doubt about the largeness of possession it gave.
Right and conveniency went together. For as a man had a right to
all he could employ his labour upon, so he had no temptation to labour for more than he could make use of. This left no room for

controversy about the title, nor for encroachment on the right of others. What portion a man carved to himself was easily seen; and it was useless as well as dishonest to carve himself too much, or take more than he needed.[13]

It is important to point out that discussions of rights should never be set apart from discussions of political duties and obligations. As the several versions of the social contract make clear, these are always part of one and the same agreement—certain rights in return for certain obligations. To discuss freedom of speech, for example, without also discussing the obligation to be well informed and logically coherent, is to provide a dangerously one-sided view of the problem. One way of developing this idea of an exchange of rights and obligations has been to distinguish two different senses of "freedom": a *negative* freedom from interference and a *positive* freedom to realize one's own potential and find one's place in society. Freedom from interference may be necessary for a person to enjoy life and contribute to the welfare of those around him or her, but a person also needs positive goods—health and education, for example. Thus freedom takes on a double meaning, freedom *from* interference but freedom *to* participate in society too. And since positive freedom also includes a person's being able to take on responsibilities, some philosophers have pointed out a paradox in the idea of being "free to perform obligations."

The idea that one is "free to perform obligations" may sound odd to us because we are so used to talking exclusively about freedom from constraints and the demands made by authority. But one of the themes that has recurred since the ancient Greeks is that all rights and "freedoms from" must be coupled with duties and obligations and the freedom to perform them. In Rousseau, for example, the citizen's obligations to the state are just as important as the state's obligations to its citizens. Many philosophers are concerned that simple freedom from constraint leaves people without direction or morality and can easily degenerate into chaos and anarchy. Thus these philosophers stress the necessity of laws and guidelines as an essential part of freedom. This is why they call it "positive" freedom since it necessarily includes "positive," goods (health and education) as well as a set of roles, duties, obligations, and constraints. This notion can be abused easily, however, for "positive freedom" can be made compatible with the most authoritarian state. (The Soviet Union, for example, often used the term *freedom* in this "positive" sense.) But despite possible abuses, it is important to see that there is more to freedom than simple freedom from interference. Whenever someone demands freedom, it is important to ask not only "from what?" but also "for what?"

---

[13]John Locke, *The Second Treatise on Government* (New York: Hafner, 1956).

It is also worth distinguishing several different kinds of rights. We can distinguish between "negative" and "positive" rights as well as freedoms; one has a right not to be interfered with, and one has rights *to* certain goods that society can provide. We have mostly been discussing negative rights (the right to be left alone, the right not to be arrested without good reason). But there are positive rights that are equally important, although they are often more controversial in this society, for example, the right to a minimal income regardless of the work one performs, the right to adequate health care regardless of one's ability to pay for it. Many rights are clearly localized to a particular state or a particular community, as, for example, the right of university regents to free football game tickets and lunches at taxpayers' expense. These rights exist by convention only, and cannot be generalized from one community to another.

Then, more generally, there are **civil rights,** rights that are guaranteed in a particular state. One example can be the right to equal treatment despite differences in skin color or sex or religion, as required by various state and federal laws. These are clearly much more important than the conventional rights, and they have a clearly moral basis. For that reason, even though they are defined by reference to a particular state and society, they are often generalized to other societies as well. Insofar as they are generalized in this way, they become *moral* rights or **human rights,** extendable to all people, in any society, regardless of the laws and customs of the society in which they live. Some apparent human rights have been hotly debated: for example, whether the U.S. government has the moral authority to interfere with the harsh abuses of human rights in, say, China or Castro's Cuba. If the right in question is harsh punishment for a seemingly minor crime, it might be argued that their system of punishment is simply more severe than ours, and we should not apply our values. If the right in question is the ability of citizens to speak out against the government without threat of imprisonment or worse, a strong argument has been made that the U.S. government does indeed have that moral authority (whether or not it wishes to risk the consequences is another matter). But if the right in question is one of those basic human rights against torture or debasement or pointless murder, then it can be argued that everyone has a moral obligation to defend such rights. Human rights are those that transcend all social and national boundaries; they demand that people deserve certain treatment just because they are human, regardless of all else.

A right is a kind of demand, the demand that one is owed something by society and the state, usually a certain sort of consideration or treatment. But most of the rights we have been discussing are in fact rights to freedom or to liberty, that is, the right to be left alone and not interfered with. A belief in individual freedom forms the basis of the liberal political philosophy, which is defined most of all by a commitment to the right of each individual to be free to do whatever he or she wishes as long as it doesn't interfere with similar rights of others. The classic statement of this position is another pamphlet by John Stuart Mill, *On Liberty* (1859). In it, he defends the rights of individuals and minorities against the tyranny of democratic majorities, for Mill sees that liberty can be as endangered in a democracy as it can in an authoritarian state. Mill goes on to offer a "very simple principle," that individual liberty is to be considered inviolable except when other people are threatened with harm.

◆from *On Liberty,* by John Stuart Mill

The object of this Essay is to assert one very simple principle, as entitled to govern absolutely the dealings of society with the individual in the way of compulsion and control, whether the means used be physical force in the form of legal penalties, or the moral coercion of public opinion. That principle is, that the sole end for which mankind are warranted, individually or collectively, in interfering with the liberty of action of any of their number, is self-protection. That the only purpose for which power can be rightfully exercised over any member of a civilised community, against his will, is to prevent harm to others. His own good, either physical or moral, is not a sufficient warrant. He cannot rightfully be compelled to do or forbear because it will be better for him to do so, because it will make him happier, because, in the opinions of others, to do so would be wise, or even right. These are good reasons for remonstrating with him, or reasoning with him, or persuading him, or entreating him, but not for compelling him, or visiting him with any evil in case he do otherwise. To justify that, the conduct from which it is desired to deter him must be calculated to produce evil to some one else. The only part of the conduct of any one, for which he is amenable to society, is that which concerns others. In the part which merely concerns himself, his independence is, of right, absolute. Over himself, over his own body and mind, the individual is sovereign.

It is, perhaps, hardly necessary to say that this doctrine is meant to apply only to human beings in the maturity of their faculties. We are not speaking of children, or of young persons below the age which the law may fix as that of manhood or womanhood. Those who are still in a state to require being taken care of by others, must be protected against their own actions as well as against external injury. For the same reason, we may leave out of consideration those backward states of society in which the race itself may be considered as in its nonage. The early difficulties in the way of spontaneous progress are so great, that there is seldom any choice of means for overcoming them; and a ruler full of the spirit of improvement is warranted in the use of any expedients that will attain an end, perhaps otherwise unattainable. Despotism is a legitimate mode of government in dealing with barbarians, provided the end be their improvement,[14] and the means justified by actually affecting that end. Liberty, as a principle, has no application to any state of things anterior to the time when mankind have become capable of being improved by free and equal discussion.

It is proper to state that I forego any advantage which could be derived to my argument from the idea of abstract right, as a thing independent of utility. I regard utility as the ultimate appeal on all ethical questions; but it must be utility in the largest sense, grounded on the permanent interests of a man as a progressive being. Those interests, I contend, authorise the subjection of individual spontaneity to external control, only in respect to those actions of each, which concern the interest of other people. If any one does an act hurtful to others, there is a *prima facie* case for punishing him, by law, or, where legal penalties are not safely applicable, by general disapprobation. There are also many positive acts for the benefit of others, which he may rightfully be compelled to perform; such as to give evidence in a court of justice; to bear his fair share in the common defence, or in any other joint work necessary to the interest of the society of which he enjoys the protection; and to perform certain acts of individual beneficence, such as saving a fellow creature's life, or interposing to protect the defenceless against ill-usage, things which whenever it is obviously a man's duty to do, he may rightfully be made responsible to society for not doing. A person may cause evil to others not only by his actions but by his inaction, and in either case he is justly accountable to them for the injury. The latter case, it is true, requires a much more cautious exercise of compulsion than the former. To make any one answerable for doing evil to others is the rule; to make him answerable for not preventing evil is, comparatively speaking, the exception. Yet there are many cases clear enough and grave enough to justify that exception. In all things which regard the external relations of the individual, he is *de jure* amenable to those whose interests are concerned, and, if need be, to society as their protector. There are often good reasons for not holding him to the responsibility; but these reasons must arise from the special expediencies of the case: either because it is a kind of case in which he is on the whole likely to act better, when left to his own discretion, than when controlled in any way in which society have it in their power to control him; or because the attempt to exercise control would produce other evils, greater than those which it would prevent. When such reasons as these preclude the enforcement of responsibility, the conscience of the agent himself should step into the vacant judgment seat, and protect those interests of

[14]Notice the political implications for this qualification, however, in "underdeveloped" countries and colonies. The principle of *paternalism*—that one ought to take care of those who cannot take care of themselves—is easily abused, and therefore always dangerous.

others which have no external protection; judging himself all the more rigidly, because the case does not admit of his being made accountable to the judgment of his fellow creatures.

But there is a sphere of action in which society, as distinguished from the individual, has, if any, only an indirect interest; comprehending all that portion of a person's life and conduct which affects only himself, or if it also affects others, only with their free, voluntary, and undeceived consent and participation. When I say only himself, I mean directly, and in the first instance; for whatever affects himself, may affect others through himself; and the objection which may be grounded on this contingency, will receive consideration in the sequel. This, then, is the appropriate region of human liberty. It comprises, first, the inward domain of consciousness; demanding liberty of conscience in the most comprehensive sense; liberty of thought and feeling; absolute freedom of opinion and sentiment on all subjects, practical or speculative, scientific, moral, or theological. The liberty of expressing and publishing opinions may seem to fall under a different principle, since it belongs to that part of the conduct of an individual which concerns other people; but, being almost of as much importance as the liberty of thought itself, and resting in great part on the same reasons, is practically inseparable from it. Secondly, the principle requires liberty of tastes and pursuits; of framing the plan of our life to suit our own character; of doing as we like, subject to such consequences as may follow: without impediment from our fellow creatures, so long as what we do does not harm them, even though they should think our conduct foolish, perverse, or wrong. Thirdly, from this liberty of each individual, follows the liberty, within the same limits, of combination among individuals; freedom to unite, for any purpose not involving harm to others: the persons combining being supposed to be of full age, and not forced or deceived.

No society in which these liberties are not, on the whole, respected, is free, whatever may be its form of government; and none is completely free in which they do not exist absolute and unqualified. The only freedom which deserves the name, is that of pursuing our own good in our own way, so long as we do not attempt to deprive others of theirs, or impede their efforts to obtain it. Each is the proper guardian of his own health, whether bodily, *or* mental and spiritual. Mankind are greater gainers by suffering each other to live as seems good to themselves, than by compelling each to live as seems good to the rest.[15]

Mill's main concern in this essay is the extent to which government and public interest have authority over individuals and individual actions. If an action harms other people or presents a public menace, then government does have the authority to prevent it or punish a person for doing it. But if an action is not harmful to others, the government has no

[15]John Stuart Mill, *On Liberty* (London: Longmans, 1859).

such authority. In the question of freedom of speech, for example, this means that governments have no authority to censor some comment or publication unless it clearly harms other people, not merely annoys or personally offends them. Mill is particularly concerned with protecting individuals against "the tyranny of the majority." The public interest is authoritative to "a limit," but that limit does not include interfering with personal affairs or opinions.

2.   Obligations to the State

Governments are made up of people, and people make mistakes. No matter what theory of individual rights you adopt, you can imagine a government, acting entirely within its legitimate role, making such a mistake. Sometimes, for instance, innocent people are convicted of crimes. Sometimes a bad law stays on the books of an otherwise good government. Sometimes police fail to enforce good laws that are on the books. Sometimes, different members of government interpret the laws differently and consequently disagree about how particular cases ought to be handled. Or sometimes members of the government just wrongfully overstep its bounds. In all these cases, a legitimate state is responsible for injustices against citizens.

We also talk about the *obligations* of the citizen to the government. Obligations accompany rights. For instance, Hobbes claimed, as have others after him, that the state, in order to be legitimate, owes its citizens protection in times of danger. Well, doesn't the citizen who lives in such a state and is protected by his government *owe* the state his service in the military? Or, consider that our American Constitution bestows to each citizen a right to a fair trial. But if the accused is entitled to "trial by jury," are not all citizens therefore *obliged* to serve on such juries and to obey the courts?

This is part of what is at issue in Plato's *Crito*, at which we looked in the introductory chapter. There, Socrates claims that he owes the state his obedience to the law—which in his case, since he was sentenced to death in court, meant he owed the state his life. This was because, he said, he had accepted the rights and privileges of the state all his life. Indeed, Socrates claimed, he *did* owe the state his life.

What follows are four modern views about citizens' obligations to the state. In the first, the famous nineteenth-century abolitionist and former slave Frederick Douglass defends his friend's decision to buy back his freedom from his old master (i.e., to obey a bad law) rather than ignore the bad law and run away. His decision is similar to Socrates' and for some similar reasons. But Douglass continues where Socrates left off, citing utilitarian reasons for this decision as well, and claiming in addition that particular human intentions are relevant to the judgment of a law. Buying someone *into* slavery, he claims, is qualitatively different from buying someone *out of* slavery.

◆ "In Defense of Purchasing Freedom," by Frederick Douglass

22, St. Ann's Square, Manchester,
December 22, 1846

Dear Friend:

Your letter of the 12th December reached me at this place, yesterday. Please accept my heartfelt thanks for it. I am sorry that you deemed it necessary to assure me, that it would be the last letter of advice you would ever write me. It looked as if you were about to cast me off for ever! I do not, however, think you meant to convey any such meaning; and if you did, I am sure you will see cause to change your mind, and to receive me again into the fold of those, whom it should ever be your pleasure to advise and instruct.

The subject of your letter is one of deep importance, and upon which, I have thought and felt much; and, being the party of all others most deeply concerned, it is natural to suppose I have an opinion, and ought to be able to give it on all fitting occasions. I deem this a fitting occasion, and shall act accordingly.

You have given me your opinion: I am glad you have done so. You have given it to me direct, in your own emphatic way. You never speak insipidly, smoothly, or mincingly; you have strictly adhered to your custom, in the letter before me. I now take great pleasure in giving you my opinion, as plainly and unreservedly as you have given yours, and I trust with equal good feeling and purity of motive. I take it, that nearly all that can be said against my position is contained in your letter; for if any man in the wide world would be likely to find valid objections to such a transaction as the one under consideration, I regard you as that man. I must, however, tell you, that I have read your letter over, and over again, and have sought in vain to find anything like what I can regard a valid reason *against the purchase of my body, or against my receiving the manumission papers, if they are ever presented to me.*

Let me, in the first place, state the facts and circumstances of the transaction which you so strongly condemn. It is your right to do so, and God forbid that I should ever cherish the slightest desire to restrain you in the exercise of that right. I say to you at once, and in all the fulness of sincerity, speak out; speak freely; keep nothing back; let me know your whole mind. "Hew to the line, though the chips fly in my face." Tell me, and tell me plainly, when you think I am deviating from the strict line of duty and principle; and when I become unwilling to hear, I shall have attained a character which I now despise, and from which I would hope to be preserved. But to the facts.

I am in England, my family are in the United States. My sphere of usefulness is in the United States; my public and domestic duties are there; and there it seems my duty to go. But I am *legally* the property of Thomas Auld, and if I go to the United States, (no matter to what part, for there is no City of Refuge there, no spot sacred to freedom there,) Thomas Auld, *aided by the American Government*, can seize, bind and fetter, and drag me from my family, feed his cruel revenge upon me, and doom me to unending slavery. In view of this simple statement of facts, a few friends, desirous of seeing me released from the terrible liability, and to relieve my wife and children from the painful trepidation, consequent upon the liability, and to place me on an equal footing of safety with all other anti-slavery lecturers in the United States, and to enhance my usefulness by enlarging the field of my labors in the United States, have nobly and generously paid Hugh Auld, the agent of Thomas Auld, £150—in consideration of which, Hugh Auld (acting as his agent) and the Government of the United States agree, that I shall be free from all further liability.

These, dear friend, are the facts of the whole transaction. The principle here acted on by my friends, and that upon which I shall act in receiving the manumission papers, I deem quite defensible.

First, *as to those who acted as my friends, and their actions.* The actuating motive was, to secure me from a liability full of horrible forebodings to myself and family. With this object, I will do you the justice to say, I believe you fully unite, although some parts of your letters would seem to justify a different belief.

Then, as to the measure adopted to secure this result. Does it violate a fundamental principle, or does it not? This is the question, and to my mind the only question of importance, involved in the discussion. I believe that, on our part, no just or holy principle has been violated.

Before entering upon the argument in support of this view, I will take the liberty (and I know you will pardon it) to say, I think you should have pointed out some principle violated in the transaction, before you proceeded to exhort me to repentance. You have given me any amount of indignation against "Auld" and the United States, in all which I cordially unite, and felt refreshed by reading; but it has no bearing whatever upon the conduct of myself, or friends, in the matter under consideration. It does not prove that I have done wrong, nor does it demonstrate what is right, or the proper course to be pursued. Now that the matter has reached its present point, before entering upon the argument, let me say one other word; it is this—I do not think you have acted quite consistently with your character for promptness, in delaying your advice till the transaction was completed. You knew of the movement at its conception, and have known it through its progress, and have never, to my knowledge, uttered one syllable against it, in conversa-

tion or letter, till now that the deed is done. I regret this, not because I think your earlier advice would have altered the result, but
because it would have left me more free than I can now be, since
the thing is done. Of course, you will not think hard of my alluding
to this circumstance. Now, then, to the main question.

The principle which you appear to regard as violated by the
transaction in question, may be stated as follows:—*Every man has
a natural and inalienable right to himself.* The inference from
this is, *"that man cannot hold property in man"—and as man
cannot hold property in man, neither can Hugh Auld nor the
United States have any right of property in me—and having no
right of property in me, they have no right to sell me—and,
having no right to sell me, no one has a right to buy me.* I think I
have now stated the principle, and the inference from the principle, distinctly and fairly. Now, the question upon which the whole
controversy turns is, simply, this: does the transaction, which you
condemn, really violate this principle? I own that, to a superficial
observer, it would seem to do so. But I think I am prepared to
show, that, so far from being a violation of that principle, it is truly
a noble vindication of it. Before going further, let me state here,
briefly, what sort of a purchase would have been a violation of this
principle, which, in common with yourself, I reverence, and am
anxious to preserve inviolate.

1st. It would have been a violation of that principle, had those
who purchased me done so, *to make me a slave, instead of a freeman.* And,

2ndly. It would have been a violation of that principle, had those
who purchased me done so with a view to compensate the
slaveholder, for what he and they regarded as his rightful property.

In neither of these ways was my purchase effected. My liberation
was, in their estimation, of more value than £150; the happiness
and repose of my family were, in their judgment, more than paltry
gold. The £150 was paid to the remorseless plunderer, not because
he had any just claim to it, but to induce him to give up his legal
claim to something which they deemed of more value than money.
It was not to compensate the slaveholder, but to release me from
his power; not to establish my *natural right* to freedom, but to release me from all legal liabilities to slavery. And all this, you and
I, and the slaveholders, and all who know anything of the transaction, very well understand. The very letter to Hugh Auld, proposing
terms of purchase, informed him that those who gave, *denied his
right to it.* The error of those, who condemn this transaction,
consists in their confounding the crime of buying men *into slavery,*
with the meritorious act of buying men out of slavery, and the
purchase of legal freedom with abstract right and natural freedom.
They say, "If you BUY, you recognize the right to sell. If you receive,
you recognize the right of the giver to give." And this has a show
of truth, as well as of logic. But a few plain cases will show its entire fallacy.

There is now, in this country, a heavy duty on corn. The government of this country has imposed it; and though I regard it a most unjust and wicked imposition, no man of common sense will charge me with endorsing or recognizing the right of this government to impose this duty, simply because, to prevent myself and family from starving, I buy and eat this corn.

Take another case:—I have had dealings with a man. I have owed him one hundred dollars, and have paid it; I have lost the receipt. He comes upon me the second time for the money. I know, and he knows, he has no right to it; but he is a villain, and has me in his power. The law is with him, and against me. I must pay or be dragged to jail. I choose to pay the bill a second time. To say I sanctioned his right to rob me, because I preferred to pay rather than go to jail, is to utter an absurdity, to which no sane man would give heed. And yet the principle of action, in each of these cases, is the same. The man might indeed say, the claim is unjust—and declare, I will rot in jail, before I will pay it. But this would not, certainly, be demanded by any principle of truth, justice, or humanity; and however much we might be disposed to respect his daring, but little diference could be paid to his wisdom. The fact is, we act upon this principle every day of our lives, and we have an undoubted right to do so. When I came to this country from the United States, I came in the *second* cabin. And why? Not because my natural right to come in the *first* cabin was not as good as that of any other man, but because a wicked and cruel prejudice decided, that the second cabin was the place for me. By coming over in the second, did I sanction or justify this wicked proscription? Not at all. It was the best I could do. I acted from necessity.

One other case, and I have done with this view of the subject. I think you will agree with me, that the case I am now about to put is pertinent, though you may not readily pardon me for making yourself the agent of my illustration. The case respects the passport system on the continent of Europe. That system you utterly condemn. You look upon it as an unjust and wicked interference, a bold and infamous violation of the *natural* and *sacred* right of locomotion. You hold, (and so do I,) that the image of our common God ought to be a passport all over the habitable world. But bloody and tyrannical governments have ordained otherwise; they usurp authority over you, and decide for you, on what conditions you shall travel. They say, you shall have a passport, or you shall be put in prison. Now, the question is, have they a right to prescribe any such terms? and do you, by complying with these terms, sanction their interference? I think you will answer, no; submission to injustice, and sanction of injustice, are different things; and he is a poor reasoner who confounds the two, and makes them one and the same thing. Now, then, for the parallel, and the application of the passport system to my own case.

I wish to go to the United States. I have a natural right to go there, and be free. My natural right is as good as that of Hugh Auld, or James K. Polk; but that plundering government says, I shall not return to the United States in safety—it says, I must allow Hugh Auld to rob me, or my friends, of £150, or be hurled into the infernal jaws of slavery. I must have a "bit of paper, signed and sealed," or my liberty must be taken from me, and I must be torn from my family and friends. The government of Austria said to you, "Dare to come upon my soil, without a passport, declaring you to be an American citizen, (which you say you are not,) you shall at once be arrested, and thrown into prison." What said you to that Govern ment? Did you say that the threat was a villainous one, and an infamous invasion of your right of locomotion? Did you say, "I will come upon your soil; I will go where I please! I dare and defy your government!" Did you say, "I will spurn your passports; I would not stain my hand, and degrade myself, by touching your miserable parchment. You have no right to give it, and I have no right to take it. I trample your laws, and will put your constitutions under my feet! I will not recognize them!" Was this your course? No! dear friend, it was not. Your practice was wiser than your theory. You took the passport, submitted to be examined while travelling, and availed yourself of all the advantages of your "passport"—or, in other words, escaped all the evils which you ought to have done, without it, and would have done, but for the tyrannical usurpation in Europe.

I will not dwell longer upon this view of the subject; and I dismiss it, feeling quite satisfied of the entire correctness of the reasoning, and the principle attempted to be maintained. As to the expediency of the measures, different opinions may well prevail; but in regard to the principle, I feel it difficult to conceive of two opinions. I am free to say, that, had I possessed one hundred and fifty pounds, I would have seen Hugh Auld *kicking,* before I would have given it to him. I would have waited till the emergency came, and only given up the money when nothing else would do. But my friends thought it best to provide against the contingency; they acted on their own responsibility, and I am not disturbed about the result. But, having acted on a true principle, I *do not feel free to disavow their proceedings.*

In conclusion, let me say, I anticipate no such change in my position as you predict. I shall be Frederick Douglass still, and once a slave still. I shall neither be made to forget nor cease to feel the wrongs of my enslaved fellow-countrymen. My knowledge of slavery will be the same, and my hatred of it will be the same. By the way, I have never made my own person and suffering the theme of public discourse, but have always based my appeal upon the wrongs of the three millions now in chains; and these shall still be the burthen of my speeches. You intimate that I may reject the papers, and allow them to remain in the hands of those friends who have effected the purchase, and thus avail myself of the security afforded to them, without sharing any part of the responsibility of the transaction. My objection to this is one of honor. I do not think it would be very honorable on my part, to remain silent during the whole transaction, and giving it more than my silent approval; and then, when the thing is completed, and I am safe, attempt to play the *hero,* by throwing off all responsibility in the matter. It might be said, and said with great propriety, "Mr. Douglass, your indignation is very good, and has but one fault, and that is, *it comes too late!"* It would be a show of bravery when the danger is over. From every view I have been able to take of the subject, I am persuaded to receive the papers, if presented,—not, however, as a proof of my right to be free, for *that is self-evident,* but as a proof that my friends have been legally robbed of £150, in order to secure that which is the birth-right of every man. And I will hold up those papers before the world, in proof of the plundering character of the American government. It shall be the brand of infamy, stamping the nation, in whose name the deed was done, as a great aggregation of hypocrites, thieves and liars,—and their condemnation is just. They declare that all men are created equal, and have a natural and inalienable right to liberty, while they rob me of £150, as a condition of my enjoying this natural and inalienable right. It will be their condemnation, in their own hand-writing, and may be held up to the world as a means of humbling that haughty republic into repentance.

I agree with you, that the contest which I have to wage is against the government of the United States. But the representative of that government is the slaveholder, *Thomas Auld.* He is commander-in-chief of the army and navy. The whole civil and naval force of the nation are at his disposal. He may command all these to his assistance, and bring them all to bear upon me, until I am made entirely subject to his will, or submit to be robbed myself, or allow my friends to be robbed, of seven hundred and fifty dollars. And rather than be subject to his will, I have submitted to be robbed, or allowed my friends to be robbed, of the seven hundred and fifty dollars.

Sincerely yours,
Frederick Douglass[16]

The great American essayist, Henry David Thoreau, did not agree with Socrates or with Douglass. In his famous essay "Civil Disobedience" he defended his decision not to pay his taxes. He claimed that for a person to obey the laws of government which behaved unjustly was the same as his or her behaving unjustly him or herself. While "lesser men"—degraded, immoral, unthinking pawns of government—might go along year after year, casting their impotent and thoughtless vote, no man of moral character would do so, claimed Thoreau. Being such a man himself, he

[16]Frederick Douglass, *Selected Writings,* ed. Michael Meyer (New York: Modern Library, 1984).

absolved himself of any obligations toward his country other than to "do what he believed right."

◆ "Civil Disobedience," by Henry David Thoreau

RESISTANCE TO CIVIL GOVERNMENT[17]

I heartily accept the motto,—"That government is best which governs least;" and I should like to see it acted up to more rapidly and systematically. Carried out, it finally amounts to this, which also I believe,—"That government is best which governs not at all;" and when men are prepared for it, that will be the kind of government which they will have. Government is at best but an expedient; but most governments are usually, and all governments are sometimes, inexpedient. The objections which have been brought against a standing army, and they are many and weighty, and deserve to prevail, may also at least be brought against a standing government. The standing army is only an arm of the standing government. The government itself, which is only the mode which the people have chosen to execute their will, is equally liable to be abused and perverted before the people can act through it. Witness the present Mexican war, the work of comparatively a few individuals using the standing government as their tool; for, in the outset, the people would not have consented to this measure.

This American government,—what is it but a tradition, though a recent one, endeavoring to transmit itself unimpaired to posterity, but each instant losing some of its integrity? It has not the vitality and force of a single living man; for a single man can bend it to his will. It is a sort of wooden gun to the people themselves; and, if ever they should use it in earnest as a real one against each other, it will surely split. But it is not the less necessary for this; for the people must have some complicated machinery or other, and hear its din, to satisfy that idea of government which they have. Governments show thus how successfully men can be imposed on, even impose on themselves, for their own advantage. It is excellent, we must all allow; yet this government never of itself furthered any enterprise, but by the alacrity with which it got out of its way. *It* does not keep the country free. *It* does not settle the West. *It* does not educate. The character inherent in the American people has done all that has been accomplished; and it would have done somewhat more, if the government had not sometimes got in its way. For government is an expedient by which men would fain succeed in letting one another alone; and, as has been said, when it is most expedient, the governed are most let alone by it. Trade and

[17]Henry David Thoreau, "Resistance to Civil Government," 1849, rpt. in the *Norton Anthology of American Literature* (New York: Norton, 1990).

commerce, if they were not made of India rubber, would never manage to bounce over the obstacles which legislators are continually putting in their way; and, if one were to judge these men wholly by the effects of their actions, and not partly by their intentions, they would deserve to be classed and punished with those mischievous persons who put obstructions on the railroads.

But, to speak practically and as a citizen, unlike those who call themselves no-government men, I ask for, not at once no government, but *at once* a better government. Let every man make known what kind of government would command his respect, and that will be one step toward obtaining it.

After all, the practical reason why, when the power is once in the hands of the people, a majority are permitted, and for a long period continue, to rule, is not becauase they are most likely to be in the right, nor because this seems fairest to the minority, but because they are physically the strongest. But a government in which the majority rule in all cases cannot be based on justice, even as far as men understand it. Can there not be a government in which majorities do not virtually decide right and wrong, but conscience?— in which majorities decide only those questions to which the rule of expediency is applicable? Must the citizen ever for a moment, or in the least degree, resign his conscience to the legislator? Why has every man a conscience, then? I think that we should be men first, and subjects afterward. It is not desirable to cultivate a respect for the law, so much as for the right. The only obligation which I have a right to assume, is to do at any time what I think right. It is truly enough said, that a corporation has no conscience; but a corporation of conscientious men is a corporation *with* a conscience. Law never made men a whit more just; and, by means of their respect for it, even the well-disposed are daily made the agents of injustice. A common and natural result of an undue respect for law is, that you may see a file of soldiers, colonel, captain, corporal, privates, powder-monkeys and all, marching in admirable order over hill and dale to the wars, against their wills, aye, against their common sense and consciences, which makes it very steep marching indeed, and produces a palpitation of the heart. They have no doubt that it is a damnable business in which they are concerned; they are all peaceably inclined. Now, what are they? Men at all? or small moveable forts and magazines, at the service of some unscrupulous man in power?

· · · · · · · · · ·

All voting is a sort of gaming, like chequers or backgammon, with a slight moral tinge to it, a playing with right and wrong, with moral questions; and betting naturally accompanies it. The character of the voters is not staked. I cast my vote, perchance, as I think right; but I am not vitally concerned that that right should prevail. I am willing to leave it to the majority. Its obligation, therefore, never exceeds that of expediency. Even voting *for the right* is *doing* nothing for it. It is only expressing to men feebly your desire that it should prevail. A wise man will not leave the right to the mercy of chance, nor wish it to prevail through the power of the majority. There is but little virtue in the action of masses of men. When the majority shall at length vote for the abolition of slavery, it will be because they are indifferent to slavery, or because there is but little slavery left to be abolished by their vote. *They* will then be the only slaves. Only *his* vote can hasten the abolition of slavery who asserts his own freedom by his vote.

. . . .

Under a government which imprisons any unjustly, the true place for a just man is also a prison. The proper place to-day, the only place which Massachusetts has provided for her freer and less desponding spirits, is in her prisons, to be put out and locked out of the State by her own act, as they have already put themselves out by their principles. It is there that the fugitive slave, and the Mexican prisoner on parole, and the Indian come to plead the wrongs of his race, should find them; on that separate, but more free and honorable ground, where the State places those who are not *with* her but *against* her,—the only house in a slave-state in which a free man can abide with honor. If any think that their influence would be lost there, and their voices no longer afflict the ear of the State, that they would not be as an enemy within its walls, they do not know by how much truth is stronger than error, nor how much more eloquently and effectively he can combat in-justice who has experienced a little in his own person. Cast your whole vote, not a strip of paper merely, but your whole influence. A minority is powerless while it conforms to the majority; it is not even a minority then; but it is irrestible when it clogs by its whole weight. If the alternative is to keep all just men in prison, or give up war and slavery, the State will not hesitate which to choose. If a thousand men were not to pay their tax-bills this year, that would not be a violent and bloody measure, as it would be to pay them, and enable the State to commit violence and shed innocent blood. This is, in fact, the definition of a peaceable revolution, if any such is possible. If the tax-gatherer, or any other public officer, asks me, as one has done, "But what shall I do?" my answer is, "If you re-ally wish to do any thing, resign your office." When the subject has refused allegiance, and the officer has resigned his office, then the revolution is accomplished. But even suppose blood should flow. Is there not a sort of blood shed when the conscience is wounded? Through this wound a man's real manhood and immortality flow out, and he bleeds to an everlasting death. I see this blood flow-ing now.

. . . .

I have paid no poll-tax for six years. I was put into a jail once on this account, for one night; and, as I stood considering the walls of solid stone, two or three feet thick, the door of wood and iron, a foot thick, and the iron grating which strained the light, I could not help being struck with the foolishness of that institution which treated me as if I were mere flesh and blood and bones, to be locked up. I wondered that it should have concluded at length that this was the best use it could put me to, and had never thought to avail itself of my services in some way. I saw that, if there was a wall of stone between me and my townsmen, there was a still more difficult one to climb or break through, before they could get to be as free as I was. I did not for a moment feel confined, and the walls seemed a great waste of stone and mortar. I felt as if I alone of all my townsmen had paid my tax. They plainly did not know how to treat me, but behaved like persons who are underbred. In every threat and in every compliment there was a blunder; for they thought that my chief desire was to stand the other side of that stone wall. I could not but smile to see how industriously they locked the door on my meditations, which followed them out again without let or hinderance, and *they* were really all that was dangerous. As they could not reach me, they had resolved to punish my body; just as boys, if they cannot come at some person against whom they have a spite, will abuse his dog. I saw that the State was half-witted, that it was timid as a lone woman with her silver spoons, and that it did not know its friends from its foes, and I lost all my remaining respect for it, and pitied it.

Thus the State never intentionally confronts a man's sense, intellectual or moral, but only his body, his senses. It is not armed with superior wit or honesty, but with superior physical strength. I was not born to be forced. I will breathe after my own fashion. Let us see who is the strongest. What force has a multitude? They only can force me who obey a higher law than I. They force me to become like themselves. I do not hear of *men* being *forced* to live this way or that by masses of men. What sort of life were that to live? When I meet a government which says to me, "Your money or your life," why should I be in haste to give it my money? It may be in a great strait, and not know what to do: I cannot help that. It must help itself; do as I do. It is not worth the while to snivel about it. I am not responsible for the successful working of the machinery of society. I am not the son of the engineer. I perceive that, when an acorn and a chestnut fall side by side, the one does not remain inert to make way for the other, but both obey their own laws, and spring and grow and flourish as best they can, till one, perchance, overshadows and destroys the other. If a plant cannot live according to its nature, it dies; and so a man.

A little more than a hundred years later, in 1963, Martin Luther King, Jr., used similar reasoning in his decision to participate in the civil rights protests in Birmingham, Alabama. King was famous for his advocacy of nonviolent protest; nonetheless, King did believe in protest. In fact, he claims in the following famous "Letter from Birmingham Jail" that *dis*obeying the law was his moral—and Christian—obligation.

◆ "Letter from Birmingham Jail," by the Rev. Martin Luther King, Jr.

. . . I think I should indicate why I am here in Birmingham, since you have been influenced by the view which argues against "outsiders coming in." I have the honor of serving as president of the Southern Christian Leadership Conference, an organization operating in every southern state, with headquarters in Atlanta, Georgia. We have some eighty-five affiliated organizations across the South, and one of them is the Alabama Christian Movement for Human Rights. Frequently we share staff, educational and financial resources with our affiliates. Several months ago the affiliate here in Birmingham asked us to be on call to engage in a nonviolent direct-action program if such were deemed necessary. We readily consented, and when the hour came we lived up to our promise. So I, along with several members of my staff, am here because I was invited here. I am here because I have organizational ties here.

But more basically, I am in Birmingham because injustice is here. Just as the prophets of the eighth century B.C. left their villages and carried their "thus saith the Lord" far beyond the boundaries of their home towns, and just as the Apostle Paul left his village of Tarsus and carried the gospel of Jesus Christ to the far corners of the Greco-Roman world, so am I compelled to carry the gospel of freedom beyond my own home town. Like Paul, I must constantly respond to the Macedonian call for aid.

Moreover, I am cognizant of the interrelatedness of all communities and states. I cannot sit idly by in Atlanta and not be concerned about what happens in Birmingham. Injustice anywhere is a threat to justice everywhere. We are caught in an inescapable network of mutuality, tied in a single garment of destiny. Whatever affects one directly, affects all indirectly. Never again can we afford to live with the narrow, provincial "outside agitator" idea. Anyone who lives inside the United States can never be considered an outsider anywhere within its bounds.

You deplore the demonstrations taking place in Birmingham. But your statement, I am sorry to say, fails to express a similar concern for the conditions that brought about the demonstration. I am sure that none of you would want to rest content with the superficial kind of social analysis that deals merely with effects and does not grapple with underlying causes. It is unfortunate that demonstrations are taking place in Birmingham, but it is even more unfortunate that the city's white power structure left the Negro community with no alternative.

In any nonviolent campaign there are four basic steps: collection of the facts to determine whether injustices exist; negotiation; self-purification; and direct action. We have gone through all these steps in Birmingham. There can be no gainsaying the fact that racial injustice engulfs this community. Birmingham is probably the most thoroughly segregated city in the United States. Its ugly record of brutality is widely known. Negroes have experienced grossly unjust treatment in the courts. There have been more un-solved bombings of Negro homes and churches in Birmingham than in any other city in the nation. These are the hard, brutal facts of the case. On the basis of these conditions, Negro leaders sought to negotiate with the city fathers. But the latter consistently refused to engage in good-faith negotiation.

Then, last September, came the opportunity to talk with leaders of Birmingham's economic community. In the course of the negoti-ations, certain promises were made by the merchants—for exam-ple, to remove the stores' humiliating racial signs. On the basis of these promises, the Reverend Fred Shuttlesworth and the lead-ers of the Alabama Christian Movement for Human Rights agreed to a moratorium on all demonstrations. As the weeks and months went by, we realized that we were the victims of a broken prom-ise. A few signs, briefly removed, returned; the others remained.

As in so many past experiences, our hopes had been blasted, and the shadow of deep disappointment settled upon us. We had no alternative except to prepare for direct action, whereby we would present our very bodies as a means of laying our case before the conscience of the local and the national community. Mindful of the difficulties involved, we decided to undertake a process of self-purification. We began a series of workshops on nonviolence, and we repeatedly asked ourselves: "Are you able to accept blows without retaliating?" "Are you able to endure the ordeal of jail?" We decided to schedule our direct-action program for the Easter sea-son, realizing that except for Christmas, this is the main shopping period of the year. Knowing that a strong economic-withdrawal pro-gram would be the by-product of direct action, we felt that this would be the best time to bring pressure to bear on the merchants for the needed change.

Then it occurred to us that Birmingham's mayoralty election was coming up in March, and we speedily decided to postpone action until after election day. When we discovered that the Commissioner of Public Safety, Eugene "Bull" Connor, had piled up enough votes to be in the run-off, we decided again to postpone action until the day after the run-off so that the demonstrations could not be used to cloud the issues. Like many others, we waited to see Mr. Connor defeated, and to this end we endured postponement after postpone-ment. Having aided in this community need, we felt that our direct-action program could be delayed no longer.

You may well ask: "Why direct action? Why sit-ins, marches and so forth? Isn't negotiation a better path?" You are quite right in calling for negotiation. Indeed, this is the very purpose of direct action. Nonviolent direct action seeks to create such a crisis and foster such a tension that a community which has constantly refused to negotiate is forced to confront the issue. It seeks so to dramatize the issue that it can no longer be ignored. My citing the creation of tension as part of the work of the nonviolent-resister may sound rather shocking. But I must confess that I am not afraid of the word "tension." I have earnestly opposed violent tension, but there is a type of constructive, nonviolent tension which is necessary for growth. Just as Socrates felt that it was necessary to create a tension in the mind so that individuals could rise from the bondage of myths and half-truths to the unfettered realm of creative analysis and objective appraisal, so must we see the need for nonviolent gadflies to create the kind of tension in society that will help men rise from the dark depths of prejudice and racism to the majestic heights of understanding and brotherhood.

The purpose of our direct-action program is to create a situation so crisis-packed that it will inevitably open the door to negotiation. I therefore concur with you in your call for negotiation. Too long has our beloved Southland been bogged down in a tragic effort to live in monologue rather than dialogue.

· · · · · · · · · ·

We know through painful experience that freedom is never voluntarily given by the oppressor; it must be demanded by the oppressed. Frankly, I have yet to engage in a direct-action campaign that was "well timed" in the view of those who have not suffered unduly from the disease of segregation. For years now I have heard the word "Wait!" It rings in the ear of every Negro with piercing familiarity. This "Wait" has almost always meant "Never." We must come to see, with one of our distinguished jurists, that "justice too long delayed is justice denied."

You express a great deal of anxiety over our willingness to break laws. This is certainly a legitimate concern. Since we so diligently urge people to obey the Supreme Court's decision of 1954 outlawing segregation in the public schools, at first glance it may seem rather paradoxical for us consciously to break laws. One may well ask: "How can you advocate breaking some laws and obeying others?" The answer lies in the fact that there are two types of laws: just and unjust. I would be the first to advocate obeying just laws. One has not only a legal but a moral responsibility to obey just laws. Conversely, one has a moral responsibility to disobey unjust laws. I would agree with St. Augustine that "an unjust law is no law at all."

Now, what is the difference between the two? How does one determine whether a law is just or unjust? A just law is a man-made code that squares with the moral law or the law of God. An unjust law is a code that is out of harmony with the moral law. To put it in the terms of St. Thomas Aquinas: An unjust law is a human law

that is not rooted in eternal law and natural law. Any law that up-
lifts human personality is just. Any law that degrades human
personality is unjust. All segregation statutes are unjust because
segregation distorts the soul and damages the personality. It gives
the segregator a false sense of superiority and the segregated a false
sense of inferiority. Segregation, to use the terminology of the
Jewish philosopher Martin Buber, substitutes an "I-it" relationship
for an "I-thou" relationship and ends up relegating persons to the
status of things. Hence segregation is not only politically, economically and sociologically unsound, it is morally wrong and sinful.
Paul Tillich has said that sin is separation. Is not segregation an existential expression of man's tragic separation, his awful estrange-
ment, his terrible sinfulness? Thus it is that I can urge men to obey
the 1954 decision of the Supreme Court, for it is morally right;
and I can urge them to disobey segregation ordinances, for they are
morally wrong.

Let us consider a more concrete example of just and unjust laws.
An unjust law is a code that a numerical or power majority group
compels a minority group to obey but does not make binding on itself. This is *difference* made legal. By the same token, a just law
is a code that a majority compels a minority to follow and that it is
willing to follow itself. This is *sameness* made legal.

Let me give another explanation. A law is unjust if it is inflicted
on a minority that, as a result of being denied the right to vote, had
no part in enacting or devising the law. Who can say that the leg-
islature of Alabama which set up that state's segregation laws was
democratically elected? Throughout Alabama all sorts of devious
methods are used to prevent Negroes from becoming registered
voters, and there are some counties in which, even though Negroes
constitute a majority of the population, not a single Negro is registered. Can any law enacted under such circumstances be considered democratically structured?

Sometimes a law is just on its face and unjust in its application.
For instance, I have been arrested on a charge of parading without
a permit. Now, there is nothing wrong in having an ordinance
which requires a permit for a parade. But such an ordinance becomes unjust when it is used to maintain segregation and to deny
citizens the First-Amendment privilege of peaceful assembly and
protest.

· · · · · · · · · ·

Oppressed people cannot remain oppressed forever. The yearning for freedom eventually manifests itself, and that is what has
happened to the American Negro. Something within has reminded
him of his birthright of freedom, and something without has reminded him that it can be gained. Consciously or unconsciously, he
has been caught up by the *Zeitgeist*, and with his black brothers
of Africa and his brown and yellow brothers of Asia, South America
and the Caribbean, the United States Negro is moving with a sense

of great urgency toward the promised land of racial justice. If one recognizes this vital urge that has engulfed the Negro community, one should readily understand why public demonstrations are taking place. The Negro has many pent-up resentments and latent frustrations, and he must release them. So let him march; let him make prayer pilgrimages to the city hall; let him go on freedom rides—and try to understand why he must do so. If his repressed emotions are not released in nonviolent ways, they will seek expression through violence; this is not a threat but a fact of history. So I have not said to my people: "Get rid of your discontent." Rather, I have tried to say that this normal and healthy discontent can be channeled into the creative outlet of nonviolent direct action. And now this approach is being termed extremist.

But though I was initially disappointed at being categorized as an extremist, as I continued to think about the matter I gradually gained a measure of satisfaction from the label. Was not Jesus an extremist for love: "Love your enemies, bless them that curse you, do good to them that hate you, and pray for them which despitefully use you, and persecute you." Was not Amos an extremist for justice: "Let justice roll down like waters and righteousness like an ever-flowing stream." Was not Paul an extremist for the Christian gospel: "I bear in my body the marks of the Lord Jesus." Was not Martin Luther an extremist: "Here I stand; I cannot do otherwise, so help me God." And John Bunyan: "I will stay in jail to the end of my days before I make a butchery of my conscience." And Abraham Lincoln: "This nation cannot survive half slave and half free." And Thomas Jefferson: "We hold these truths to be self-evident, that all men are created equal . . ." So the question is not whether we will be extremists, but what kind of extremists we will be. Will we be extremists for hate or for love? Will we be extremists for the preservation of injustice or for the extension of justice? In that dramatic scene on Calvary's hill three men were crucified. We must never forget that all three were crucified for the same crime—the crime of extremism. Two were extremists for immorality, and thus fell below their environment. The other, Jesus Christ, was an extremist for love, truth, and goodness, and therefore rose above his environment. Perhaps the South, the nation and the world are in dire need of creative extremists.[18]

Malcolm X, a contemporary of King, believed in taking a far more aggressive stand against unjust government. He was one of the leaders of the "Black Nationalist" movement, which pursued not just justice, but an independent and separate state, for black people of all nations. Malcolm X's famous phrase "by any means necessary," indicated his rejection of King's (or Thoreau's) nonviolence and "civility" of disobedience. Rather, Malcolm X argued, building on Thomas Hobbes, that those

[18]Martin Luther King, Jr. "Letter from Birmingham Jail," rpt. as Chapter 5 of *Why We Can't Wait* (New York: New American Library, 1988 [reprint]).

mistreated by an unjust government have the right and the obligation to
overthrow it. The following very strong words come from one of Malcolm
X's most famous speeches, "The Ballot or the Bullet."

◆ "The Ballot or the Bullet," by Malcolm X

. . . anti-white, but it does mean we're anti-exploitation, anti-degrad-
ation, we're anti-oppression. And if the white man doesn't want us
to be anti-him, let him stop oppressing and exploiting and degrading us. Whether we are Christians or Muslims or nationalists or agnostics or atheists, we must first learn to forget our differences. If
we have differences, let us differ in the closet; when we come out in
front, let us not have anything to argue about until we get finished
arguing with the man. If the late President Kennedy could get together with Khrushchev and exchange some wheat, we certainly
have more in common with each other than Kennedy and Khrushchev had with each other.

If we don't do something real soon, I think you'll have to agree
that we're going to be forced either to use the ballot or the bullet.
It's one or the other in 1964. It isn't that time is running out—time
has run out! 1964 threatens to be the most explosive year America has ever witnessed. The most explosive year. Why? It's also a
political year. It's the year when all of the white politicians will be
back in the so-called Negro community jiving you and me for some
votes. The year when all of the white political crooks will be right
back in your and my community with their false promises, building
up our hopes for a letdown, with their trickery and their treachery, with their false promises which they don't intend to keep. As
they nourish these dissatisfactions, it can only lead to one thing, an
explosion; and now we have the type of black man on the scene in
American today—I'm sorry, Brother Lomax—who just doesn't
intend to turn the other cheek any longer.

Don't let anybody tell you anything about the odds are against
you. If they draft you, they send you to Korea and make you face
800 million Chinese. If you can be brave over there, you can be
brave right here. These odds aren't as great as those odds. And if
you fight here, you will at least know what you're fighting for.

· · · · · · · · · ·

Well, I am one who doesn't believe in deluding myself. I'm not
going to sit at your table and watch you eat, with nothing on my
plate, and call myself a diner. Sitting at the table doesn't make you
a diner, unless you eat some of what's on that plate. Being here
in America doesn't make you an American. Being born here in
America doesn't make you an American. Why, if birth made you
American, you wouldn't need any legislation, you wouldn't need any
amendments to the Constitution, you wouldn't be faced with civil-

rights filibustering in Washington, D.C., right now. They don't have to pass civil-rights legislation to make a Polack an American.

No, I'm not an American. I'm one of the 22 million black people who are the victims of Americanism. One of the 22 million black people who are the victims of democracy, nothing but disguised hypocrisy. So, I'm not standing here speaking to you as an American, or a patriot, or a flag-saluter, or a flag-waver—no, not I. I'm speaking as a victim of this American system. And I see America through the eyes of the victim. I don't see any American dream; I see an American nightmare.

These 22 million victims are waking up. Their eyes are coming open. They're beginning to see what they used to only look at. They're becoming politically mature. They are realizing that there are new political trends from coast to coast. As they see these new political trends, it's possible for them to see that every time there's an election the races are so close that they have to have a recount. They had to recount in Massachusetts to see who was going to be governor, it was so close. It was the same way in Rhode Island, in Minnesota, and in many other parts of the country. And the same with Kennedy and Nixon when they ran for president. It was so close they had to count all over again. Well, what does this mean? It means that when white people are evenly divided, and black people have a bloc of votes of their own, it is left up to them to determine who's going to sit in the White House and who's going to be in the dog house.

. . . .

So it's time in 1964 to wake up. And when you see them coming up with that kind of conspiracy, let them know your eyes are open. And let them know you got something else that's wide open too. It's got to be the ballot or the bullet. The ballot or the bullet. If you're afraid to use an expression like that, you should get on out of the country, you should get back in the cotton patch, you should get back in the alley. They get all the Negro vote, and after they get it, the Negro gets nothing in return. All they did when they got to Washington was give a few big Negroes big jobs. Those big Negroes didn't need big jobs, they already had jobs. That's camouflage, that's trickery, that's treachery, window-dressing. I'm not trying to knock out the Democrats for the Republicans, we'll get to them in a minute. But it is true—you put the Democrats first and the Democrats put you last.

Look at it the way it is. What alibis do they use, since they control Congress and the Senate? What alibi do they use when you and I ask, "Well, when are you going to keep your promise?" They blame the Dixiecrats. What is a Dixiecrat? A Democrat. A Dixiecrat is nothing but a Democrat in disguise. The titular head of the Democrats is also the head of the Dixiecrats, because the Dixiecrats are a part of the Democratic Party. The Democrats have never kicked the Dixiecrats out of the party. The Dixiecrats bolted themselves once, but the Democrats didn't put them out. Imagine, these low-down Southern segregationists put the Northern Democrats down. But the Northern Democrats have never put the Dixiecrats down. No, look at that thing the way it is. They have got a con game going on, a political con game, and you and I are in the middle. It's time for you and me to wake up and start looking at it like it is, and trying to understand it like it is; and then we can deal with it like it is.

· · · · · · · · · ·

How can you thank a man for giving you what's already yours? How then can you thank him for giving you only part of what's already yours? You haven't even made progress, if what's being given to you, you should have had already. That's not progress. And I love my Brother Lomax, the way he pointed out we're right back where we were in 1954. We're not even as far up as we were in 1954. We're behind where we were in 1954. There's more segregation now than there was in 1954. There's more social animosity, more racial hatred, more racial violence today in 1964, than there was in 1954. Where is the progress?

· · · · · · · · · ·

I might stop right here to point out one thing. Whenever you're going after something that belongs to you, anyone who's depriving you of the right to have it is a criminal. Understand that. Whenever you are going after something that is yours, you are within your legal rights to lay claim to it. And anyone who puts forth any effort to deprive you of that which is yours, is breaking the law, is a criminal. And this was pointed out by the Supreme Court decision. It outlawed segregation. Which means segregation is against the law. Which means a segregationist is breaking the law. A segregationist is a criminal. You can't label him as anything other than that. And when you demonstrate against segregation, the law is on your side. The Supreme Court is on your side.

Now, who is it that opposes you in carrying out the law? The police department itself. With police dogs and clubs. Whenever you demonstrate against segregation, whether it is segregated education, segregated housing, or anything else, the law is on your side, and anyone who stands in the way is not the law any longer. They are breaking the law, they are not representatives of the law. Any time you demonstrate against segregation and a man has the audacity to put a police dog on you, kill that dog, kill him, I'm telling you, kill that dog. I say it, if they put me in jail tomorrow, kill—that—dog. Then you'll put a stop to it. Now, if these white people in here don't want to see that kind of action, get down and tell the mayor to tell the police department to pull the dogs in. That's all you have to do. If you don't do it, someone else will.

If you don't take this kind of stand, your little children will grow up and look at you and think "shame." If you don't take an uncompromising stand—I don't mean go out and get violent; but at the same time you should never be nonviolent unless you run into some nonviolence. I'm nonviolent with those who are nonviolent with me. But when you drop that violence on me, then you've made me go insane, and I'm not responsible for what I do. And that's the way every Negro should get. Any time you know you're within the law, within your legal rights, within your moral rights, in accord with justice, then die for what you believe in. But don't die alone. Let your dying be reciprocal. This is what is meant by equality. What's good for the goose is good for the gander.

. . . .

Let the world know how bloody his hands are. Let the world know the hypocrisy that's practiced over here. Let it be the ballot or the bullet. Let him know that it must be the ballot or the bullet.[19]

D. A DIFFERENT SENSE OF FREEDOM

From a liberal perspective, this English emphasis on rights and liberty seems indisputable. But what happens when the "natural right" to private property is abused, when people take more than they can use personally and use their excess possession merely as a means to manipulate other people? And it is all well and good to defend the rights of freedom of speech and religion, but what if many people in the society find themselves far more concerned just with the exigencies of existence—putting food on the table, surviving a dangerous job, and not having enough protection under the law to prevent them from being grossly exploited and underpaid for unrewarding and painful labor? There is an obvious sense in which people in such conditions are not all "free," even if they are guaranteed freedom of speech and religion. Freedom from government persecution is not necessarily freedom from economic exploitation. And it is the latter freedom that concerns Karl Marx and his frequent coauthor Friedrich Engels.

It is worth mentioning that Locke wrote his two treatises on government before the industrial revolution; Marx wrote when that revolution was at its peak, transforming cities like Manchester, England, into virtual slave-farms of underpaid, overworked laborers. With this in mind, the freedoms of speech and religion protected by well-to-do and comfortable liberals seemed not nearly so important as the basic freedom to a decent life. So Marx turned from political liberties to economic necessities and turned his attention from the right to private property to the abuse of private property.

Although Marx insists on "the abolition of private property" as the

---

[19]Malcolm X, "The Ballot or the Bullet," rpt. in *Malcolm X Speaks* (New York: Grove Press, 1965).

central theme of communism, he still retains the idea that a man or woman has the right to the products of his or her labor. What he rejects is the ownership of property that one has not personally produced and that serves only as a means of getting richer at the expense of other people, who are thereby forced to work without enjoying the products of their labor. This is what Marx means by his very important notion of **alienation.** A person is alienated if he or she is no longer working for himself or herself but only for the benefit of another person. Even though a person might get paid for this labor, that does not make it less alienated. Factory workers may be well paid, but they are alienated insofar as their work is meaningless to them, and the profits of their work do not go to them but to someone else. Thus, despite their obvious differences, Marx and Locke agree to this extent: A person has a right to something "if he has mixed his labour with it." Both philosophers agree on the importance of human productivity and creativity to the good life, and the person's right to his or her own creation is therefore essential to any adequate society.

Marx was a *historical materialist,* which means that he placed new emphasis on the economic modes of production of goods and saw history and politics (and all other human enterprises) as conditioned by economic relations. Accordingly, the key to human freedom and the lack of freedom was also economic. In the following passage from his early writings (of 1844), Marx summarizes his notion of alienation as the unnatural separation of a person from the object he or she creates, resulting in separation ("alienation") from other people and ultimately from oneself. Quite the contrary of the "natural" identity the worker should feel with what he or she has made, the object produced is "set against him [or her] as an alien and hostile force." Instead of pride or enjoyment, the worker feels only resentment against those who have made the labor meaningless; and the pay received for this only makes it clearer how personally irrelevant it is.

◆**from "Alienated Labor,"**
by Karl Marx

We shall begin from a *contemporary* economic fact. The worker becomes poorer the more wealth he produces and the more his production increases in power and extent. The worker becomes an ever cheaper commodity the more goods he creates. The *devaluation* of the human world increases in direct relation with the *increase in value* of the world of things. Labor does not only create goods; it also produces itself and the worker as a *commodity,* and indeed in the same proportion as it produces goods.

This fact simply implies that the object produced by labor, its product, now stands opposed to it as an *alien being,* as a *power independent* of the producer. The product of labor is labor which has been embodied in an object and turned into a physical thing; this product is an *objectification* of labor. The performance of work is at the same time its objectification. The performance of work appears in the sphere of political economy as a *vitiation* of the worker, objectification as a *loss* and as *servitude to the object,* and appropriation as *alienation.*

So much does the performance of work appear as vitiation that the worker is vitiated to the point of starvation. So much does objectification appear as loss of the object that the worker is deprived of the most essential things not only of life but also of work. Labor itself becomes an object which he can acquire only by the greatest effort and with unpredictable interruptions. So much does the appropriation of the object appear as alienation that the more objects the worker produces the fewer he can possess and the more he falls under the domination of his product, of capital.

All these consequences follow from the fact that the worker is related to the *product of his labor* as to an *alien* object. For it is clear on this presupposition that the more the worker expends himself in work the more powerful becomes the world of objects which he creates in face of himself, the poorer he becomes in his inner life, and the less he belongs to himself. The life which he has given to the object sets itself against him as an alien and hostile force.[20]

Marx introduces the new concept of freedom from alienation, which requires a return to the "natural" state in which people and their labor are one. (In this notion of return to the natural state, Marx is heavily influenced by Rousseau.) It is important to emphasize that nowhere does Marx suggest or desire that people should someday be free of work. According to him, work makes us human. Instead he argues that we should make ourselves free of alienated work. This does not mean that he denies other freedoms—freedom of speech, for example—but he does argue that such freedoms are meaningless in the face of the cruel economic necessities that rule most people's lives. Men and women, desperate for a job and forced to undertake meaningless tasks for forty hours a week, need more than just the freedom to speak out. They require freedom from the economic exploitation that keeps them in such desperate circumstances. They must have, in general, freedom from material need. Marx makes a great deal of what he considers humanity's crucial difference from the animals: their ability to work and produce, thereby freeing themselves from the needs of nature.

Marx is a very modern theorist. He no longer argues on the basis of endless human requirements for food and shelter but sees that in the modern world the means of producing enough food and shelter for

[20]Karl Marx, *Early Writings,* trans. T. Bottomore (New York: McGraw-Hill, 1964).

everyone are already at hand. What is needed is simply a more equitable form of distribution. This means no private property except for those products a person uses directly. There can be factories but no "owners," as opposed to the laborers. There might be "corporations" but only if they are nothing more than a coalition of the workers, who share in the benefits of their own work.

But this Marxist vision, in which there are no owners except the workers and in which everyone is a worker and no one is alienated from his work, is not going to come about without enormous upheaval. Marx's "classless society" requires a thoroughgoing revolution—not so much a political revolution as an economic one. This is the key to Marx's concept of freedom. It proposes freedom from want and freedom from economic exploitation, not political freedom in terms of rights and the freedom from government interference that we have mainly discussed so far. The revolution he envisions, in which the various economic classes of society will continue to war against each other until all such classes disappear, may therefore be called a battle for freedom just as much as the traditional battles for freedom of speech and self-government. It is a revolution that he sees as inevitable, one in the making since ancient times, and in which "Workers of the world unite; you have nothing to lose but your chains" will become the rallying cry around which the human world will experience its greatest upheaval ever. Marxists continue to argue that the collapse of Soviet-imposed communism does not refute Marx's claims.

The excerpt that follows, from the *Communist Manifesto* of 1848, is the most popular statement of Marx's theory. Marx wrote it with his friend and long-time collaborator, Friedrich Engels. In it, they explain human history in terms of historical materialism, define the two social classes they see at war with each other, the *bourgeoisie* or ownership class and the *proletariat* or working class, and suggest the course that history now has to take. They are not just predicting and theorizing, however, but are also advocating the revolution they describe in no uncertain terms.

◆from the *Communist Manifesto,* by Karl Marx and Friedrich Engels

BOURGEOIS AND PROLETARIANS

The history of all hitherto existing society is the history of class struggles.

Freeman and slave, patrician and plebeian, lord and serf, guildmaster and journeyman, in a word, oppressor and oppressed, stood in constant opposition to one another, carried on an uninterrupted, now hidden, now open fight, a fight that each time ended, either in a revolutionary re-constitution of society at large, or in the common ruin of the contending classes.

In the earlier epochs of history, we find almost everywhere a complicated arrangement of society into various orders, a manifold gradation of social rank. In ancient Rome we have patricians, knights, plebeians, slaves; in the middle ages, feudal lords, vassals, guild-masters, journeymen, apprentices, serfs; in almost all of these classes, again, subordinate gradations.

The modern bourgeois society that has sprouted from the ruins of feudal society, has not done away with class antagonisms. It has but established new classes, new conditions of oppression, new forms of struggle in place of the old ones.

Our epoch, the epoch of the bourgeoisie, possesses, however, this distinctive feature; it has simplified the class antagonisms. Society as a whole is more and more splitting up into two great hostile camps, into two great classes directly facing each other: Bourgeoisie and Proletariat.

THE RISE OF THE BOURGEOISIE

From the serfs of the Middle Ages sprang the chartered burghers of the earliest towns. From these burgesses the first elements of the bourgeoisie were developed.

The discovery of America, the rounding of the Cape, opened up fresh ground for the rising bourgeoisie. The East-Indian and Chinese markets, the colonization of America, trade with the colonies, the increase in the means of exchange and in commodities generally, gave to commerce, to navigation, to industry, an impulse never before known, and thereby, to the revolutionary element in the tottering feudal society, a rapid development.

The feudal system of industry, under which industrial production was monopolized by closed guilds, now no longer sufficed for the growing wants of the new markets. The manufacturing system took its place. The guild-masters were pushed on one side by the manufacturing middle-class; division of labor between the different corporate guilds vanished in the face of division of labor in each single workshop.

Meantime the markets kept ever growing, the demand, ever rising. Even manufacture no longer sufficed. Thereupon, steam and machinery revolutionzied industrial production. The place of manufacture was taken by the giant, Modern Industry, the place of the industrial middle-class by industrial millionaires, the leaders of whole industrial armies, the modern bourgeois.

Modern industry has established the world-market, for which the discovery of America paved the way. This market has given an immense development to commerce, to navigation, to communication by land. This development has, in its turn, reacted on the extension of industry; and in proportion as industry, commerce, navigation, railways extended, in the same proportion the bourgeoisie developed, increased its capital, and pushed into the background every class handed down from the Middle Ages.

We see, therefore, how the modern bourgeoisie is itself the product of a long course of development, of a series of revolutions in the modes of production and of exchange.

Each step in the development of the bourgeoisie was accompanied by a corresponding political advance of that class. An oppressed class under the sway of the feudal nobility, an armed and self-governing association in the mediaeval commune, here independent urban republic (as in Italy and Germany), there taxable "third estate" of the monarchy (as in France), afterwards, in the period of manufacture proper, serving either the semifeudal or the absolute monarchy as a counterpoise against the nobility, and, in fact, cornerstone of the great monarchies in general, the bourgeoisie has at last, since the establishment of Modern Industry and of the world-market, conquered for itself, in the modern representative State, exclusive political sway. *The executive of the modern State is but a committee for managing the common affairs of the whole bourgeoisie.*

REVOLUTIONARY ROLE OF THE BOURGEOISIE

The bourgeoisie, historically, has played a most revolutionary part.

The bourgeoisie, wherever it has got the upper hand, has put an end to all feudal, patriarchal, idyllic relations. It has pitilessly torn asunder the motley feudal ties that bound man to his "natural superiors," and has left remaining no other nexus between man and man than naked self-interest, callous "cash payment." It has drowned the most heavenly ecstasies of religious fervor, of chivalrous enthusiasm, of philistine sentimentalism, in the icy water of egotistical calculation. It has resolved personal worth into exchange value, and in place of the numberless indefeasible chartered freedoms, has set up that single, unconscionable freedom—Free Trade. In one word, for exploitation, veiled by religious and political illusions, it has substituted naked, shameless, direct, brutal exploitation.

The bourgeoisie has stripped of its halo every occupation hitherto honored and looked up to with reverent awe. It has converted the physician, the lawyer, the priest, the poet, the man of science, into its paid wage-laborers.

The bourgeoisie has torn away from the family its sentimental veil, and has reduced the family relation to a mere money relation.

The bourgeoisie has disclosed how it came to pass that the brutal display of vigor in the Middle Ages, which Reactionists so much admire, found its fitting complement in the most slothful indolence. It has been the first to show what man's activity can bring about. It has accomplished wonders far surpassing Egyptian pyramids,

Roman aqueducts, and Gothic cathedrals; it has conducted expeditions that put in the shade all former Exoduses of nations and crusades.

The bourgeoisie cannot exist without constantly revolutionizing the instruments of production, and thereby the relations of production, and with them the whole relations to society. Conservation of the old modes of production in unaltered form, was, on the contrary, the first condition of existence for all earlier industrial classes. Constant revolutionizing of production, uninterrupted disturbance of all social conditions, everlasting uncertainty and agitation distinguish the bourgeois epoch from all earlier ones. All fixed, fast-frozen relations, with their train of ancient and venerable prejudices and opinions, are swept away, all new-formed ones become antiquated before they can ossify. All that is solid melts into air, all that is holy is profaned, and man is at last compelled to face, with sober senses, his real conditions of life, and his relations with his kind.

The need of a constantly expanding market for its products chases the bourgeoisie over the whole surface of the globe. It must nestle everywhere, settle everywhere, establish connections everywhere.

The bourgeoisie has through its exploitation of the world-market given a cosmopolitan character to production and consumption in every country. To the great chagrin of Reactionists, it has drawn from under the feet of industry the national ground on which it stood. All old-established national industries have been destroyed or are daily being destroyed. They are dislodged by new industries, whose introduction becomes a life and death question for all civilized nations, by industries that no longer work up indigenous raw material, but raw material drawn from the remotest zones; industries whose products are consumed, not only at home, but in every quarter of the globe. In place of the old wants, satisfied by the productions of the country, we find new wants, requiring for their satisfaction the products of distant lands and climes. In place of the old local and national seclusion and self-sufficiency, we have intercourse in every direction, universal interdependence of nations. And as in material, so also in intellectual production. The intellectual creations of individual nations become common property. National one-sidedness and narrow-mindedness become more and more impossible, and from the numerous national and local literatures there arises a world-literature.

The bourgeoisie, by the rapid improvement of all instruments of production, by the immensely facilitated means of communications, draws all, even the most barbarian, nations into civilization. The cheap prices of its commodities are the heavy artillery with which it batters down all Chinese walls, with which it forces the barbarians' intensely obstinate hatred of foreigners to capitulate. It compels all nations, on pain of extinction, to adopt the bourgeois mode of production; it compels them to introduce what it calls civilization into their midst, i.e., to become bourgeois themselves. In a word, it creates a world after its own image.

The bourgeoisie has subjected the country to the rule of the towns. It has created enormous cities, has greatly increased the urban population as compared with the rural, and has thus rescued a considerable part of the population from the idiocy of rural life. Just as it has made the country dependent on the towns, so it has made barbarian and semibarbarian countries dependent on the civilized ones, nations of peasants on nations of bourgeois, the East on the West.

The bourgeoisie keeps more and more doing away with the scattered state of the population, of the means of production, and of property. It has agglomerated population, centralized means of production, and has concentrated property in a few hands. The necessary consequence of this was political centralization. Independent, or but loosely connected provinces, with separate interests, laws, governments, and systems of taxation, became lumped together in one nation, with one government, one code of laws, one national class-interest, one frontier and one customs-tariff.

The bourgeoisie, during its rule of scarce one hundred years, has created more massive and more colossal productive forces than have all preceding generations together. Subjection of Nature's forces to man, machinery, application of chemistry to industry and agriculture, steam-navigation, railways, electric telegraphs, clearing of whole continents for cultivation, canalization of rivers, whole populations conjured out of the ground—what earlier century had even a presentiment that such productive forces slumbered in the lap of social labor?

THE REVOLT OF PRODUCTIVE FORCES AGAINST PROPERTY RELATIONS

We see then: the means of production and of exchange on whose foundation the bourgeoisie built itself up, were generated in feudal society. At a certain stage in the development of these means of production and of exchange, the conditions under which feudal society produced and exchanged, the feudal organization of agriculture and manufacturing industry, in one word, the feudal relations of property became no longer compatible with the already developed productive forces; they became so many fetters. They had to burst asunder; they were burst asunder.

Into their places stepped free competition, accompanied by a social and political constitution adapted to it, and by the economical and political sway of the bourgeois class.

A similar movement is going on before our own eyes. *Modern bourgeois society with its relations of production, of exchange and of property, a society that has conjured up such gigantic means of production and of exchange, is like the sorcerer, who is no longer able to control the powers of the nether world whom he has called up by his spells.* For many a decade past the history of industry and commerce is but the history of the revolt of modern productive forces against modern conditions of production, against the property relations that are the conditions for the existence of the bourgeoisie and of its rule. It is enough to mention the commercial crises that by their periodical return put on its trial, each time more threateningly, the existence of the entire bourgeois society. In these crises a great part not only of the existing products, but also of the previously created productive forces, are periodically destroyed. In these crises there breaks out an epidemic that, in all earlier epochs, would have seemed an absurdity—the epidemic of over-production. Society suddenly finds itself put back into a state of momentary barbarism; it appears as if a famine, a universal war of devastation had cut off the supply of every means of subsistence; industry and commerce seem to be destroyed; and why? Because there is too much civilization, too much means of subsistence, too much industry, too much commerce. The productive forces at the disposal of society no longer tend to further the development of the conditions of bourgeois property; on the contrary, they have become too powerful for these conditions, by which they are fettered, and so soon as they overcome these fetters, they bring disorder into the whole of bourgeois society, endanger the existence of bourgeois property. The conditions of bourgeois society are too narrow to comprise the wealth created by them. And how does the bourgeoisie get over these crises? On the one hand by enforced destruction of a mass of productive forces; on the other, by the conquest of new markets, and by the more thorough exploitation of the old ones. That is to say, by paving the way for more extensive and more destructive crises, and by diminishing the means whereby crises are prevented. The weapons with which the bourgeoisie felled feudalism to the ground are now turned against the bourgeoisie itself.

But not only has the bourgeoisie forged the weapons that bring death to itself; it has also called into existence the men who are to wield those weapons—the modern working-class—the proletarians.

THE STRUGGLE AND VICTORY OF THE PROLETARIAT

The proletariat goes through various stages of development. With its birth begins its struggle with the bourgeoisie. At first the contest is carried on by individual laborers, then by the workpeople of a factory, then by the operatives of one trade, in one locality, against the individual bourgeois who directly exploits them. They direct their attacks not against the bourgeois conditions of production, but against the instruments of production themselves; they destroy imported wares that compete with their labor, they smash to pieces machinery, they set factories ablaze, they seek to restore by force the vanished status of the workman of the Middle Ages.

At this stage the laborers still form an incoherent mass scattered over the whole country, and broken up by their mutual competition. If anywhere they unite to form more compact bodies, this is not yet the consequence of their own active union, but of the union of the bourgeoisie, which class, in order to attain its own political ends, is compelled to set the whole proletariat in motion, and is moreover, yet, for a time, able to do so. At this stage, therefore, the proletarians do not fight their enemies, but the enemies of their enemies, the remnants of absolute monarchy, the landowners, the non-industrial bourgeois, the petty bourgeoisie. Thus the whole historical movement is concentrated in the hands of the bourgeoisie; every victory so obtained is a victory for the bourgeoisie.

But with the development of industry the proletariat not only increases in number, it becomes concentrated in greater masses, its strength grows, and it feels that strength more. The various interests and conditions of life within the ranks of the proletariat are more and more equalized, in proportion as machinery obliterates all distinctions of labor, and nearly everywhere reduces wages to the same low level. The growing competition among the bourgeois, and the resulting commercial crises, make the wages of the workers ever more fluctuating. The unceasing improvement of machinery, ever more rapidly developing, makes their livelihood more and more precarious; the collisions between individual workmen and individual bourgeois take more and more the character of collisions between two classes. Thereupon the workers begin to form combinations (Trades' Unions) against the bourgeois; they club together in order to keep up the rate of wages; they found permanent associations in order to make provision beforehand for these occasional revolts. Here and there the contest breaks out into riots.

Now and then the workers are victorious, but only for a time. The real fruit of their battle lies, not in the immediate result, but in the ever-expanding union of the workers. This union is helped on by the improved means of communication that are created by modern industry, and that place the workers of different localities in contact with one another. It was just this contact that was needed to centralize the numerous local struggles, all of the same character, into one national struggle between classes. But every class struggle is a political struggle. And that union, to attain which the burghers of the Middle Ages, with their miserable highways, required centuries, the modern proletarians, thanks to railways, achieve in a few years.

This organization of the proletarians into a class, and consequently into a political party, is continually being upset again by the competition between the workers themselves. But it ever rises up again, stronger, firmer, mightier. It compels legislative recognition of particular interest of the workers, by taking advantage of the divisions among the bourgeoisie itself. Thus the ten-hour bill in England was carried.

Altogether collisions between the classes of the old society further, in many ways, the course of development of the proletariat.
The bourgeoisie finds itself involved in a constant battle. At first
with the aristocracy; later on, with those portions of the bourgeoisie itself, whose interests have become antagonistic to the progress
of industry; at all times, with the bourgeoisie of foreign countries.
In all these battles it sees itself compelled to appeal to the proletariat, to ask for its help, and thus, to drag it into the political arena.
The bourgeoisie itself, therefore, supplies the proletariat with its
own elements of political and general education, in other words, it
furnishes the proletariat with weapons for fighting the bourgeoisie.

Further, as we have already seen, entire sections of the ruling
classes are, by the advance of industry, precipitated into the proletariat, or are at least threatened in their conditions of existence.
These also supply the proletariat with fresh elements of enlightenment and progress.

Finally, in times when the class-struggle nears the decisive hour,
the process of dissolution going on within the ruling class, in fact,
within the whole range of old society, assumes such a violent,
glaring character, that a small section of the ruling class cuts itself
adrift, and joins the revolutionary class, the class that holds the
future in its hands. Just as, therefore, at an earlier period, a section of the nobility went over to the bourgeoisie, so now a portion
of the bourgeoisie goes over to the proletariat, and in particular,
a portion of the bourgeois ideologists, who have raised themselves
to the level of comprehending theoretically the historical movements as a whole.

PROPERTY AND FREEDOM

All property relations in the past have continually been subject to
historical change consequent upon the change in historical conditions.

The French Revolution, for example, abolished feudal property in
favor of bourgeois property.

The distinguishing feature of Communism is not the abolition of
property generally, but the abolition of bourgeois property. But
modern bourgeois private property is the final and most complete
expression of the system of producing and appropriating products,
that is based on class antagonism, on the exploitation of the many
by the few.

In this sense, the theory of the Communists may be summed up
in the single sentence: Abolition of private property. . . .

You are horrifed at our intending to do away with private property. But in your existing society, private property is already done
away with for nine-tenths of the population; its existence for the
few is solely due to its nonexistence in the hands of those nine-
tenths. You reproach us, therefore, with intending to do away with
a form of property, the necessary condition for whose existence is

the nonexistence of any property for the immense majority of society.

In a word, you reproach us with intending to do away with your property. Precisely so; that is just what we intend.

From the moment when labor can no longer be converted into capital, money, or rent, into a social power capable of being monopolized, *i.e.*, from the moment when individual property can no longer be transformed into bourgeois property, into capital, from that moment, you say, individuality vanishes.

You must, therefore, confess that by "individual" you mean no other person than the bourgeois, than the middle-class owner of property. This person must, indeed, be swept out of the way, and made impossible.

Communism deprives no man of the power to appropriate the products of society; all that it does is to deprive him of the power to subjugate the labor of others by means of such appropriation. . . .

And then Marx's final optimism:

When, in the course of development, class distinctions have disappeared, and all production has been concentrated in the hands of a vast association of the whole nation, the public power will lose its political character. Political power, properly so called, is merely the organized power of one class for oppressing another. If the proletariat during its contest with the bourgeoisie is compelled, by the force of circumstances, to organize itself as a class; if, by means of a revolution, it makes itself the ruling class, and, as such sweeps away by force the old conditions of production, then it will, along with these conditions, have swept away the conditions for the existence of class antagonisms, and of classes generally, and will thereby have abolished its own supremacy as a class.

In place of the old bourgeois society, with its classes and class antagonisms, we shall have an association, in which the free development of each is the condition for the free development of all.[21]

E. THE ABSOLUTE STATE: FASCISM

We think of "fascism" as a nasty word. People of very different political persuasions accuse their opponents of fascism if they consider their policies oppressive. But this is a new meaning of the word. *Fascism* once was the proud name of a political theory, the theory of the absolute state. In the 1920s, Benito Mussolini swept into power in Italy with enormous popularity, a popularity he retained until his disastrous alliance with

---

[21]Karl Marx and Friedrich Engels, *The Communist Manifesto*, trans. Samuel Moore (Chicago: Regnery, 1969).

Adolf Hitler (also a Fascist) in the Second World War. For Mussolini, and for most of his followers, *Fascism* had an almost religious significance: the state was raised to an almost divine status. The state was like a god, the source of laws and duties not unlike those discussed in the Bible. The individual existed only to serve and identify with the state. According to Fascism, if some people were brutally repressed, it was only for the good of the general will and the state. (Rousseau's notion of "the general will" often enters into Fascist theory.) If Fascism had to use force to protect the government, that force, so it was argued, was ultimately for the good of its people. And if Fascism so often meant war, what better way to bring the citizens together into a virtual family? This identification of the state with the family plays a central part in the almost religious language of Fascism. What follows is an extract from one of Mussolini's most often-quoted speeches:

◆ **on Fascism,**
by Benito Mussolini

Fascism is a religious conception in which man is seen in his immanent relationship with a superior law and with an objective Will that transcends the particular individual and raises him to conscious membership of a spiritual society. Whoever has seen in the religious politics of the Fascist regime nothing but mere opportunism has not understood that Fascism besides being a system of government is also, and above all, a system of thought.

Fascism is a historical conception, in which man is what he is only in so far as he works with the spiritual process in which he finds himself, in the family or social group, in the nation and in the history in which all nations collaborate. From this follows the great value of tradition, in memories, in language, in customs, in the standards of social life. Outside history man is nothing. Consequently, Fascism is opposed to all the individualistic abstractions of a materialistic nature like those of the eighteenth century; and it is opposed to all Jacobin utopias and innovations. It does not consider that "happiness" is possible upon earth, as it appeared to be in the desire of the economic literature of the eighteenth century, and hence it rejects all teleological theories according to which mankind would reach a definitive stabilized condition at a certain period in history. This implies putting oneself outside history and life, which is a continual change and coming to be. Politically, Fascism wishes to be a realistic doctrine; practically, it aspires to solve only the problems which arise historically of themselves and that of themselves find or suggest their own solution. To act among men, as to act in the natural world, it is necessary to enter into the process of reality and to master the already operating forces.

Against individualism, the Fascist conception is for the State;

and it is for the individual in so far as he coincides with the State, which is the conscience and universal will of man in his historical existence. It is opposed to classical Liberalism, which arose from the necessity of reacting against absolutism, and which brought its historical purpose to an end when the State was transformed into the conscience and will of the people. Liberalism denied the State in the interests of the particular individual; Fascism reaffirms the State as the true reality of the individual. And if liberty is to be the attribute of the real man, and not of that abstract puppet envisaged by individualistic Liberalism, Fascism is for liberty. And for the only liberty which can be a real thing, the liberty of the State and of the individual within the State. Therefore, for the Fascist, everything is in the State, and nothing human or spiritual exists, much less has value, outside the State. In this sense Fascism is totalitarian, and the Fascist State, the synthesis and unity of all values, interprets, develops and gives strength to the whole life of the people.

· · · · · · · · · ·

This higher personality is truly the nation in so far as it is the State. It is not the nation that generates the State, as according to the old naturalistic concept which served as the basis of the political theories of the national States of the nineteenth century. Rather the nation is created by the State, which gives to the people, conscious of its own moral unity, a will and therefore an effective existence. The right of a nation to independence derives not from a literary and ideal consciousness of its own being, still less from a more or less unconscious and inert acceptance of a *de facto* situation, but from an active consciousness, from a political will in action and ready to demonstrate its own rights: that is to say, from a state already coming into being. The State, in fact, as the universal ethical will, is the creator of right.[22]

In the other political theories we have discussed, the state and its interests are always balanced against the interests of the public and the individual citizen. This is the main point of most social contract theories, of consent of the governed theories, of utilitarian and justice theories, and the main goal of Marx's theory as well (although Marx is more concerned with economic power than just political power). In Fascism, by contrast, the balance tips towards the interests of the state. This is not to say that the purpose of Fascism is not also to serve the public interest and the individual citizen, but in terms of priorities, the state comes first. In social contract theories (including democratic theories), a state that does not serve the public interest can be legitimately overthrown; in Fascist theory, the state has absolute legitimacy whether or not it

---

[22]Benito Mussolini, *The Doctrine of Fascism*, trans. I. S. Munro (Rome: Encyclopedie Italiano, 1934).

succeeds in satisfying its citizens, and this is part of its religious significance.

In view of the Fascist doctrine of the absolute state, it is in the interest of the state, but not its obligation, to have its citizens support it as enthusiastically as possible. This means that the Fascist state will try to get the approval of its people perhaps just as fervently as a democratic state but primarily in order to enhance its own power. About four hundred years before the advent of modern Fascism, one of Mussolini's countrymen, Niccolò Machiavelli, wrote a short treatise designed to instruct the leaders of absolute states on the art of keeping their power, including the art of winning and keeping public support. In *The Prince* (1513), Machiavelli writes a "how to" book for rulers, telling them the best ways of winning wars, tricking their enemies, and, in general, keeping power. (Machiavelli himself was not a Fascist; he also wrote the *Discourses*, which deals in part with how to establish a republic. But *The Prince* has always served as the classic book for Fascist theories.) The following is a representative excerpt from *The Prince*. Notice that its concern throughout is "how to stay in power," not how to be just or fair or even good. Justice or compassion are but means of keeping power, and that is the key to modern Fascism as well.

◆**from *The Prince*, by Niccolò Machiavelli**

OF CRUELTY AND CLEMENCY, AND WHETHER IT IS
BETTER TO BE LOVED THAN FEARED

Coming down now to the other aforementioned qualities, I say that every prince ought to desire the reputation of being merciful, and not cruel; at the same time, he should be careful not to misuse that mercy. Cesare Borgia was reputed cruel, yet by his cruelty he reunited the Romagna to his states, and restored that province to order, peace, and loyalty; and if we carefully examine his course, we shall find it to have been really much more merciful than the course of the people of Florence, who, to escape the reputation of cruelty, allowed Pistoia to be destroyed. A prince, therefore, should not mind the ill repute of cruelty, when he can thereby keep his subjects united and loyal; for a few displays of severity will really be more merciful than to allow, by an excess of clemency, disorders to occur, which are apt to result in rapine and murder; for these injure a whole community, while the executions ordered by the prince fall only upon a few individuals. And, above all others, the new prince will find it almost impossible to avoid the reputation of cruelty because new states are generally exposed to many dangers. It was on this account that Virgil made Dido to excuse the severity of her government, because it was still new, saying,—

> My cruel fate,
> And doubts attending an unsettled state,
> Force me to guard my coasts from foreign foes.[23]

A prince, however, should be slow to believe and to act; nor should he be too easily alarmed by his own fears, and should proceed moderately and with prudence and humanity, so that an excess of confidence may not make him incautious, nor too much mistrust make him intolerant. This, then, gives rise to the question "whether it be better to be beloved than feared, or to be feared than beloved." It will naturally be answered that it would be desirable to be both the one and the other; but as it is difficult to be both at the same time, it is much more safe to be feared than to be loved, when you have to choose between the two. For it may be said of men in general that they are ungrateful and fickle, dissemblers, avoiders of danger, and greedy of gain. So long as you shower benefits upon them, they are all yours; they offer you their blood, their substance, their lives, and their children, provided the necessity for it is far off; but when it is near at hand, then they revolt. And the prince who relies upon their words, without having otherwise provided for his security, is ruined; for friendships that are won by rewards, and not by greatness and nobility of soul, although deserved, yet are not real, and cannot be depended upon in time of adversity.

Besides, men have less hesitation in offending one who makes himself beloved than one who makes himself feared; for love holds by a bond of obligation which, as mankind is bad, is broken on every occasion whenever it is for the interest of the obliged party to break it. But fear holds by the apprehension of punishment, which never leaves men. A prince, however, should make himself feared in such a manner that, if he has not won the affections of his people, he shall at least not incur their hatred; for the being feared, and not hated, can go very well together, if the prince abstains from taking the substance of his subjects, and leaves them their women. And if you should be obliged to inflict capital punishment upon any one, then be sure to do so only when there is manifest cause and proper justification for it; and, above all things, abstain from taking people's property, for men will sooner forget the death of their fathers than the loss of their patrimony. Besides, there will never be any lack of reasons for taking people's property; and a prince who once begins to live by rapine will ever find excuses for seizing other people's property. On the other hand, reasons for taking life are not so easily found, and are more readily exhausted. But when a prince is at the head of his army, with a multitude of soliders under his command, then it is above all things necessary for him to disregard the reputation of cruelty; for without such

---

[23]Translated from the Latin original by John Dryden.

severity an army cannot be kept together, nor disposed for any successful feat of arms.

Among the many admirable qualities of Hannibal, it is related of him that, having an immense army composed of a very great variety of races of men, which he led to war in foreign countries, no quarrels ever occurred among them, nor were there ever any dissensions between them and their chief, either in his good or in his adverse fortunes; which can only be accounted for by his extreme cruelty. This, together with his boundless courage, made him ever venerated and terrible in the eyes of his soldiers; and without that extreme severity all his other virtues would not have sufficed to produce that result.

Inconsiderate writers have, on the one hand, admired his great deeds, and, on the other, condemned the principal cause of the same. And the proof that his other virtues would not have sufficed him may be seen from the case of Scipio, who was one of the most remarkable men, not only of his own time, but in all History. His armies revolted in Spain solely in consequence of his extreme clemency, which allowed his soldiers more license than comports with proper military discipline. This fact was censured in the Roman Senate by Fabius Maximus, who called Scipio the corrupter of the Roman soldiers. The tribe of the Locrians having been wantonly destroyed by one of the lieutenants of Scipio, he neither punished him for that nor for this insolence,—simply because of his own easy nature; so that, when somebody wished to excuse Scipio in the Senate, he said, "that there were many men who knew better how to avoid errors themselves than to punish them in others." This easy nature of Scipio's would in time have dimmed his fame and glory if he had persevered in it under the Empire, but living as he did under the government of the Senate, this dangerous quality of his was not only covered up, but actually redounded to his honor.

To come back now to the question whether it be better to be beloved than feared, I conclude that, as men love of their own free will, but are inspired with fear by the will of the prince, a wise prince should always rely upon himself, and not upon the will of others; but, above all, should he always strive to avoid being hated, as I have already said above.[24]

F. THE ALTERNATIVE TO GOVERNMENT: ANARCHISM

We have all known and heard about bad governments. Sometimes it is a single corrupt politician that is bad, other times it is the political

---

[24] Niccolò Machiavelli, *The Prince*, trans. Christian E. Detmold (New York: Airmont, 1965).

system itself. But those political (or perhaps "antipolitical") philosophers who call themselves "anarchists" would say that it is the very nature of government that is "bad," insofar as every government has and exercises unjustified power over its citizens. No one and no institution, including governments, has the right to interfere with our lives, according to the anarchist. Of course we must agree not to kill each other (as the social contract insists), but we don't need a government in order to enforce such agreements. Proper upbringing and mutual respect alone will be sufficient.

Sometimes anarchists are also tied to theories of revolution insofar as they believe that economic inequality and desperation force most people to commit crimes and destroy social harmony. But in a society where people had no unsatisfied needs, they argue, there would be no need for violence or robbery either. It is essential to anarchism to have an optimistic, Rousseauian view of human nature as "naturally good." It is impossible to accept a Hobbesian "mutual-murder" view and still have faith in people's ability to live together without governments. Anarchists often suggest breaking mass societies into smaller units, such as communes and local communities in which mutual personal relationships make the need for impersonal government unnecessary. In such communities, there may be those who are in charge of certain tasks, but this is a matter of efficiency and administration, not of power. There may be rules but not laws, for the very idea of enforcement of laws presupposes a government in power and is antithetical to the anarchist ideal.

"Anarchism" has often been used as a nasty word pointing to total chaos. Politicians in power often refer to the alternative to their rule as "anarchy and chaos," as if anarchy must always be sheer confusion. Although the word originally meant simply "without a leader," it perhaps has taken on the meaning of chaos because of those anarchists in history who have attacked their governments in a wild and destructive fashion. The word now conjures up images of "bomb-throwing anarchists" and widespread rape and murder. But this is not essential to anarchism as a political theory. (Sometimes the word *anarchism* is used to refer to the theory; *anarchy* is used to point to political confusion and chaos.) Many anarchists would argue that it is only because governments treat us like children that we can no longer conceive what it would be like without them. But if we are to take the notion of individual freedom and rights seriously, according to the anarchist, then we will have to conclude that the only good government is no government, for any government is by its very existence a threat to individual freedom and an infringement of individual rights.

The anarchist position is here represented by Benjamin R. Tucker, an American who believed in the social contract theory but argued that the only logical conclusion to a social contract would be no state at all:

◆"For Anarchism," by Benjamin R. Tucker

Presumably the honor which you have done me in inviting me to address you to-day upon "The Relation of the State to the Individual" is due principally to the fact that circumstances have combined to make me somewhat conspicuous as an exponent of the theory of Modern Anarchism—a theory which is coming to be more and more regarded as one of the few that are tenable as a basis of political and social life. In its name, then, I shall speak to you in discussing this question, which either underlies or closely touches almost every practical problem that confronts this generation. The future of the tariff, of taxation, of finance, of property, of woman, of marriage, of the family, of the suffrage, of education, of invention, of literature, of science, of the arts, of personal habits, of private character, of ethics, of religion, will be determined by the conclusion at which mankind shall arrive as to whether and how far the individual owes allegiance to the State.

Anarchism, in dealing with this subject, has found it necessary, first of all, to define its terms. Popular conceptions of the terminology of politics are incompatible with the rigorous exactness required in scientific investigation. . . . Take the term "State," for instance, with which we are especially concerned to-day. It is a word that is on every lip. But how many of those who use it have any idea of what they mean by it? And, of the few who have, how various are their conceptions! We designate by the term "State" institutions that embody absolutism in its extreme form and institutions that temper it with more or less liberality. We apply the word alike to institutions that do nothing but aggress and to institutions that, besides aggressing, to some extent protect and defend. But which is the State's essential function, aggression or defence, few seem to know or care. . . . Brought fact to face with these diverse views, the Anarchists, whose mission in the world is the abolition of aggression and all the evils that result therefrom, perceived that, to be understood, they must attach some definite and avowed significance to the terms which they are obliged to employ, and especially in the words "State" and "government." Seeking, then, the elements common to all the institutions to which the name "State" has been applied, they have found them two in number: first, aggression; second, the assumption of sole authority over a given area and all within it, exercised generally for the double purpose of more complete oppression of its subjects and extension of its boundaries. That this second element is common to all States, I think, will not be denied,—at least, I am not aware that any State has ever tolerated a rival State within its borders; and it seems plain that any State which should do so would thereby cease to be a State and to be considered as such by any. The exercise of authority over the same area by two States is a contradiction. That the first element, aggression, has been and is common to all States will probably be less generally admitted. Nevertheless, I shall not attempt to reenforce here the conclusion of Spencer, which is gaining wider acceptance daily,—that the State had its origin in aggression, and has continued as an aggressive institution from its birth. Defence was an afterthought, prompted by necessity; and its introduction as a State function, though effected doubtless with a view to the strengthening of the State, was really and in principle the initiation of the State's destruction. Its growth in importance is but an evidence of the tendency of progress toward the abolition of the State. Taking this view of the matter, the Anarchists contend that defence is not an essential of the State, but that aggression is. Now what is aggression? Aggression is simply another name for government. Aggression, invasion, government, are interconvertible terms. The essence of government is control, or the attempt to control. He who attempts to control another is a governor, an aggressor, an invader; and the nature of such invasion is not changed, whether it is made by one man upon another man, after the manner of the ordinary criminal, or by one man upon all other men, after the manner of an absolute monarch, or by all other men upon one man, after the manner of a modern democracy. On the other hand, he who resists another's attempt to control is not an aggressor, an invader, a governor, but simply a defender, a protector; and the nature of such resistance is not changed whether it be offered by one man to another man, as when one repels a criminal's onslaught, or by one man to all other men, as when one declines to obey an oppressive law, or by all other men to come to one man, as when a subject people rises against a despot, or as when the members of a community voluntarily unite to restrain a criminal. This distinction between invasion and resistance, between government and defence, is vital. Without it there can be no valid philosophy of politics. Upon this distinction and the other considerations just outlined, the Anarchists frame the desired definitions. This, then, is the Anarchistic definition of government: the subjection of the non-invasive individual to an external will. And this is the Anarchistic definition of the State: the embodiment of the principle of invasion in an individual, or a band of individuals, assuming to act as representatives or masters of the entire people within a given area. As to the meaning of the remaining term in the subject under discussion, the word "individual," I think there is little difficulty. Putting aside the subtleties in which certain metaphysicians have indulged, one may use this word without danger of being misunderstood. Whether the definitions thus arrived at prove generally acceptable or not is a matter of minor consequence. I submit that they are reached scientifically, and serve the purpose of a clear conveyance of thought. The Anarchists, having by their adoption taken due care to be explicit, are entitled to have their ideas judged in the light of these definitions.

Now comes the question proper: What relations should exist between the State and the individual? The general method of determining these is to apply some theory of ethics involving a basis of moral obligation. In this method the Anarchists have no confidence. The idea of moral obligation, of inherent rights and duties, they totally discard. They look upon all obligations, not as moral, but as social, and even then not really as obligations except as these have been consciously and voluntarily assumed. If a man makes an agreement with men, the latter may combine to hold him to his agreement; but, in the absence of such agreement, no man, so far as the Anarchists are aware, has made any agreement with God or with any other power of any order whatsoever. The Anarchists are not only utilitarians, but egoists in the farthest and fullest sense. So far as inherent right is concerned, might is its only measure. . . .

If this, then, were a question of right, it would be, according to the Anarchists, purely a question of strength. But, fortunately, it is not a question of right: it is a question of expediency, of knowledge, of science—the science of living together, the science of society. The history of humanity has been largely one long and gradual discovery of the fact that the individual is the gainer by society exactly in proportion as society is free, and of the law that the condition of a permanent and harmonious society is the greatest amount of individual liberty compatible with equality of liberty. The average man of each new generation has said to himself more clearly and consciously than his predecessor: "My neighbor is not my enemy, but my friend, and I am his, if we would but mutually recognize the fact. We help each other to a better, fuller, happier living; and this service might be greatly increased if we would cease to restrict, hamper, and oppress each other. Why can we not agree to let each live his own life, neither of us transgressing the limit that separates our individualities?" It is by this reasoning that mankind is approaching the real social contract, which is not, as Rousseau thought, the origin of society, but rather the outcome of a long social experience, the fruit of its follies and disasters. It is obvious that this contract, this social law, developed to its perfection, excludes all aggression, all violation of equality of liberty, all invasion of every kind. Considering this contract in connection with the Anarchistic definition of the State as the embodiment of the principle of invasion, we see that the State is antagonistic to society; and, society being essential to individual life and development, the conclusion leaps to the eyes that the relation of the State to the individual and of the individual to the State must be one of hostility, enduring till the State shall perish.

"But," it will be asked of the Anarchists at this point in the argument, "what shall be done with those individuals who undoubtedly will persist in violating the social law of invading their neighbors?" The Anarchists answer that the abolition of the State will leave in existence a defensive association, resting no longer on a compulsory but on a voluntary basis, which will restrain invaders by any means that may prove necessary. "But that is what we have now," is the rejoinder. "You really want, then, only a change of name?" Not so fast, please. Can it be soberly pretended for a moment that the State, even as it exists here in America, is purely a defensive institution? Surely not, save by those who see of the State only its most palpable manifestations,—the policeman on the street-corner. And one would not have to watch him very closely to see the error of this claim. Why, the very first act of the State, the compulsory assessment and collection of taxes, is itself an aggression, a violation of equal liberty, and, as such, vitiates every subsequent act, even those acts which would be purely defensive if paid for out of a treasury filled by voluntary contributions. How is it possible to sanction, under the law of equal liberty, the confiscation of a man's earnings to pay for protection which he has not sought and does not desire? And if this is an outrage, what name shall we give to such confiscation when the victim is given, instead of bread, a stone, instead of protection, oppression? To force a man to pay for the violation of his own liberty is indeed an addition of insult to injury. But that is exactly what the State is doing. Read the "Congressional Record"; follow the proceedings of the State legislatures; examine our statute-books; test each act separately by the law of equal liberty,—you will find that a good nine-tenths of existing legislation serves, not to enforce that fundamental social law, but either to prescribe the individual's personal habits, or, worse still, to create and sustain commercial, industrial, financial, and proprietary monopolies which deprive labor of a large part of the reward that it would receive in a perfectly free market. "To be governed," says Proudhon, "is to be watched, inspected, spied, directed, law-ridden, regulated, penned up, indoctrinated, preached at, checked, appraised, sized, censured, commanded, by beings who have neither title nor knowledge nor virtue. To be governed is to have every operation, every transaction, every movement noted, registered, counted, rated, stamped, measured, numbered, assessed, licensed, refused, authorized, indorsed, admonished, prevented, reformed, redressed, corrected. To be governed is, under pretext of public utility and in the name of the general interest, to be laid under contribution, drilled, fleeced, exploited, monopolized, extorted from, exhausted, hoaxed, robbed; then, upon the slightest resistance, at the first word of complaint, to be repressed, fined, vilified, annoyed, hunted down, pulled about, beaten, disarmed, bound, imprisoned, shot, mitrailleused, judged, condemned, banished, sacrificed, sold, betrayed, and, to crown all, ridiculed, derided, outraged, dishonored." And I am sure I do not need to point out to you the existing laws that correspond to and justify nearly every count in Proudhon's long indictment. How thoughtless, then, to assert that the existing political order is of a purely defensive character instead of the aggressive State which the Anarchists aim to abolish![25]

[25]Benjamin R. Tucker, *Instead of a Book* (New York: Benjamin R. Tucker, 1893).

SUMMARY AND CONCLUSION

In some areas of philosophy, the question arises, "What does this have to do with everyday life?" In political philosophy, as in moral philosophy, the connection between philosophy and "everyday life" is obvious. It is no coincidence that the major revolutions of the eighteenth and nineteenth centuries came soon after a flurry of philosophical radicalism. And we know that much of the world is divided and ruled according to rival political philosophies at the present time.

What is always at issue is the concept of justice. The ideas that people are equal and should be treated equally, that people have natural or human rights that no one and no government can take away from them, that people should equally share the material goods of society—these have all been the subject of constant debate, and sometimes wars and revolutions, for most of modern times. Then too, the nature of the state itself has been part of that debate as well as the stage on which the debate has been carried out. How much should the state serve the people and how much the people serve the state? What constitutes a good state? And when, if ever, do people have the right to overthrow the state, or a particular government, or a particular law? We cannot even begin to give adequate answers to these complex questions in the context of a general introduction to philosophy; but neither can we avoid asking them in the world as it is today.

GLOSSARY

alienation   in Marx, the unnatural separation of a person from the products he or she makes, from other people, or from oneself.

anarchism   the view that no government has the legitimate authority to coerce people and that the public interest and individual rights can only be served without a state of any kind.

authority   that which controls; usually, that which has the right to control. (For example, the government has the authority to tax your income.)

civil rights   those rights that are determined by a particular state and its laws; constitutional rights, for example, are civil rights in this sense, guaranteed by the law of the land.

democracy   that form of government in which policies or at least the makers of policy are chosen by popular mandate.

distributive justice   the ideal of everyone receiving his or her fair share. For example, concerns over ownership of land, just wages, and fair prices are all matters of distributive justice.

egalitarianism   the view that all people are equal in rights and respect.

entitlement   a right; for instance, a right to own property.

equality   in political philosophy, the nondiscriminatory treatment of every person, regardless of sex, race, religion, physical or mental abilities, wealth, social status, etc.

fascism　the view that the best government is the strongest, and that the government has the right—and perhaps the duty—to control the lives of every citizen for the sake of the most efficient society.

freedom　see liberty

government　the instrument of authority; that body that rules, passes and enforces laws, etc.

human rights　those rights that are considered to be universal, "unalienable," and common to every person regardless of where or when he or she lives. For example, freedom from torture and degradation would be a human right.

justice　in the general sense, the virtues of an ideal society. In the more particular sense, the balance of public interest and individual rights, the fair sharing of the available goods of society, the proper punishment of criminals, and the fair restitution of victims of crime and misfortune within society.

legitimacy　the right to have authority; sanctioned power (for example, through the grace of God, or by means of legal succession, or by appeal to justice, or to the general consent of the people governed).

liberty (political freedom)　the ability to act without restraint or threat of punishment. For example, the ability to travel between states without a passport, the ability to speak one's opinions without prosecution, the ability to work for or choose one's own profession or career. This ability, however, is not mere physical or mental ability; one might have the liberty to travel or to try to become a doctor without having the means to do so. It is also important to distinguish this political sense of liberty or freedom from the metaphysical or causal sense discussed previously. Whether our acts are really free in that sense must be distinguished from the question whether we are constrained or free to act in this political sense. The first refers to the causes of human behavior; the second refers only to the existence of legislation and political forces constraining our behavior.

retributive justice　"getting even," "an eye for an eye. . . ."

rights　demands that a member of society is entitled to make upon his or her society. Everyone, for example, has a right to police protection. Some people, by virtue of their position, have special rights; for example, congressmen have the right to send mail to their constitutents without paying postage.

social contract　an agreement, tacit or explicit, that all members of society shall abide by the laws of the state in order to maximize the public interest and ensure cooperation among themselves. It is important that such a contract need never have actually been signed in history; what is important is that every member of a society, by choosing to remain in that society, implicitly makes such an agreement.

society　a group of people with common historical and cultural ties; usually, but not always, members of the same state and ruled by the same government.

sovereign   independent. A sovereign state is one that is subject to the laws of no other state. A sovereign is a person (for example, a king) who is not subject or answerable to the commands of anyone else. A people are sovereign when their wishes are ultimate in the same way and not subject to commands by anyone else or any government. (To say that a people is sovereign is not to say that the will of any individual or group is sovereign within it.)

state   the center of authority in a society, for example, the largest political unit in a society. Usually a state is a nation, for example, America, Germany, etc. Usually, but not always, coextensive with a society, and usually, but not always, distinguished by a single form of government and a single government (for example, the American federal government).

unalienable rights   those rights that no one and no government can take away, for example, the right of a person to protect his or her own life. In other words, *human rights.*

◆ *BIBLIOGRAPHY AND FURTHER READING* ◆

Plato, *The Republic,* trans. Francis M. Cornford (Oxford: Oxford University Press, 1941), is still standard reading for the basics and some thought-provoking alternatives in political philosophy. See also Aristotle, *Politics,* in *The Basic Works of Aristotle,* ed. R. McKeon (New York: Random House, 1941). Our own national documents, the Declaration of Independence and the Constitution, are always important reading. John Stuart Mill, *On Liberty,* ed. C. Shields (New York: Bobbs-Merrill, 1956), has long been the classic defense of liberalism. Michael Oakeshott, *Rationalism in Politics* (New York: Basic Books, 1962) is an important challenge to liberal philosophy. See also Robert Nisbet, *Conservatism: Dream and Reality* (Minneapolis: University of Minnesota Press, 1986). Karl Marx's *Communist Manifesto,* trans. S. Moore (Chicago: Regnery, 1969) and his *Early Writings,* trans. T. Bottomore (New York: McGraw-Hill, 1963), are essential reading for beginning students in political philosophy. Niccolò Machiavelli, *The Prince,* trans. C. Detmold (New York: Airmont, 1965), and Jean-Jacques Rousseau, *The Social Contract* (New York: Dutton, 1950) are both important and rewarding reading. For more general discussions of the philosophy of politics, see F. Olafson, ed., *Justice and Social Policy* (Englewood Cliffs, NJ; Prentice-Hall, 1961); G. Sabine, *A History of Political Theory,* 3rd ed. (New York: Holt, Rinehart and Winston, 1961); and P. Laslett and W.G. Runciman, eds. *Philosophy, Politics and Society* (Oxford: Blackwell, 1964). See also *Selected Writings of Frederick Douglass,* M. Myer, ed. (New York: Random House, 1984), *The Autobiography of Malcolm X,* coauthored with Alex Haley (New York: Ballantine, 1987), and Martin Luther King, Jr., *A Testament of Hope,* James M. Washington, ed. (New York: Harper & Row, 1986).

Chapter

11

Beauty

A thing of beauty is a joy forever.

John Keats

Philosophy is not just the study of the True and the Good but also of the Beautiful.[1] The study of philosophy would surely be incomplete if it included only the subjects of knowledge and reality, and ignored the very real fulfillment from what is unreal—stories, paintings, and artificially produced sounds—whose sole purpose seems to be that we enjoy them for what they are. And our sense of value would be truncated indeed if the study of philosophy included only moral values, and ignored all matters artistic, giving no importance to what we term "aesthetic experience"—especially the experience of beauty.

What is art? What is its purpose, its role in human life? What is good art; what is bad art? And what, despite the endeavor, isn't art at all? How do we tell the difference? Is it true, as David Hume argued two centuries ago, that "there is no disputing over tastes"—that in matters of art there is only your opinion and another's opinion, and no standard for choosing between them?

These are the compelling questions faced by the philosophical study of **aesthetics,** and they remain as difficult and intractable as the eternal questions faced by metaphysics, ethics, and epistemology. Moreover, art, unlike philosophy, is clearly an important achievement in virtually every society. But what art means in different societies—or, indeed, whether it is even conceived of as "art"—differs considerably from culture to culture.

---

[1] I am most grateful to Kathleen Higgins for her extensive help in the preparation of this chapter.

A. PLATO AND THE TRANSCENDENCE OF BEAUTY

When we experience a work of art that is remarkably beautiful and moving, we sometimes say that it is "heavenly" or "out of this world." Indeed, we often think of beauty as a form of perfection not to be expected in our imperfect lives. Consequently, any rare glimpse of (more or less) perfect beauty contrasts sharply with the mundane experiences of daily life. It is as if we are permitted a fleeting view of another world—an eternal world, a perfect world. Taken literally, this is Plato's conception of the nature of the beautiful. Beauty exists in a world apart from us, is unchanging, and manifests itself only in rare and fleeting instances.

Of course, beauty exists outside of art and works of art. Plato, perhaps paradoxically, distrusted the beauty that could be found in art, even the spectacular art of the recent Golden Age of Athens. But he appreciated other forms of beauty, for example, beauty found in people such as Socrates (who was not at all physically beautiful—in fact, he was said to be quite ugly). Given that beautiful people were manifestations of a heavenly or "transcendent" ideal of beauty, to experience true beauty was profoundly more wonderful than any mere earthly experience. In Shakespeare's *Romeo and Juliet*, Romeo thinks of Juilet and muses, "Beauty too rich for use, for earth too dear. . . ." Romeo has experienced the Platonic vision. He believes that he has encountered in his beloved a transcendent beauty more wondrous than any other beauty on earth.

Although Romeo thinks that his experience is unique, as members of Shakespeare's audience we accept Romeo's reaction as a universal kind of experience—in fact, an experience described by Plato two thousand years before Romeo's literary birth. Plato also connects love and the vision of the beautiful, especially in his dialogue *The Symposium*. Plato, like Romeo, speaks of beauty that is too wondrous for this world; unlike Romeo, Plato presents the concept as more than an expression of his own emotions. In fact, Plato takes a philosophical approach to the idea of beauty: he is not concerned primarily with his own experience, but with the role of beauty and love in the larger scheme of reality.

Plato conceived of Beauty as a transcendent Form. His Forms (Chapter 1) are the ideal entities that comprise the transcendent "World of Being." The things that exist in our material "world of becoming" are real to a lesser degree than the Forms, and are real only because they participate in the Forms. In other words, the true being of any thing in this world is the ideal Form that shapes its structure. Insight into true reality occurs when we recognize the ideal Form behind the imperfect appearance of things in this world. And just as there are Forms for the "True" and the "Good" and for "Justice," there is an ideal Form of Beauty. We recognize the manifestation of this ideal Form of Beauty when we experience and fall in love with things and persons that are beautiful.

We come to know the Form of Beauty through the beautiful beings and things of this world. For example, when we recognize the beauty of another human being, we catch a glimpse of the transcendent Beauty in which that person participates. This is what happens when we fall in love. Our normal behavior and attitudes are disrupted completely when we fall in love because we are recognizing something that exists on another plane of reality. Of all the Forms, the Form of Beauty attracts us most naturally. Thus, the experience of falling in love is one of life's most momentous.

Love, then, paves the way toward insight into the Form of Beauty. And if we come to recognize that it is the Form of Beauty that we experience and love in another, our response to beauty becomes the initial step toward insight into the realm of Forms in general. But such insight is, as we have seen, a matter of "recollection." And because first experiences with beauty involve an encounter with an order of reality entirely different from the one to which we are accustomed, we are often confused by the first experience we have with love. We tend to think, like Romeo, that the beauty we encounter is uniquely characteristic of the beloved person (or, in the case of art, of the beautiful work of art). We do not realize initially that the beauty of our beloved is identical to the beauty of every other beautiful person or thing. And it is only when we recognize that beauty in all its earthly manifestations is identical that we gain genuine insight into the Form of Beauty.

In Plato's *Symposium*, Socrates describes the stages involved in gaining insight into the Form of Beauty. Socrates tells the audience that a woman named Diotima taught him the mysteries of love. According to Diotima, true love begins with love of one person but reaches a higher level of development when the lover comes to love all that is beautiful. Ultimately, in loving all that is beautiful, the lover comes to realize that he or she loves only one thing, absolute Beauty itself. Socrates recounts what Diotima told him:

◆**from *The Symposium*,
by Plato**

. . . he who would proceed aright in this matter should begin in youth to visit beautiful forms; and first, if he be guided by his instructor aright, to love one such form only—out of that he should create fair thoughts; and soon he will of himself perceive that the beauty of one form is akin to the beauty of another; and then if beauty of form in general is his pursuit, how foolish would he be not to recognize that the beauty in every form is one and the same! And when he perceives this he will abate his violent love of the one, which he will despise and deem a small thing, and will become a lover of all beautiful forms; in the next stage he will consider that the beauty of the mind is more honourable than the beauty of the outward form. So that if a virtuous soul have but a little comeliness, he will be content to love and tend him, and will search out and bring to the birth thoughts which may improve the young, until he is compelled to contemplate and see the beauty of institutions and laws, and to understand that the beauty of them all is of one family, and that personal beauty is a trifle; and after laws and institutions he will go on to the sciences, that he may see their beauty, being not like a servant in love with the beauty of one youth or man or institution, himself a slave mean and narrow-minded, but drawing towards and contemplating the vast sea of beauty, he will create many fair and noble thoughts and notions in boundless love of wisdom; until on that shore he grows and waxes strong, and at last the vision is revealed to him of a single science, which is the science of beauty everywhere. To this I will proceed; please to give me your very best attention:

"He who has been instructed thus far in the things of love, and who has learned to see the beautiful in due order and succession, when he comes toward the end will suddenly perceive a nature of wondrous beauty (and this, Socrates, is the final cause of all our former toils—a nature which in the first place is everlasting, not growing and decaying, or waxing and waning; secondly, not fair in one point of view and foul in another, or at one time or in one relation or at one place fair, at another time or in another relation or at another place foul, as if fair to some and foul to others, or in the likeness of a face or hands or any other part of the bodily frame, or in any form of speech or knowledge, or existing in any other being, as for example, in an animal, or in heaven, or in earth, or in any other place; but beauty absolute, separate, simple, and everlasting, which without diminution and without increase, or any change, is imparted to the ever-growing and perishing beauties of all other things. He who from these ascending under the influence of true love, begins to perceive that beauty, is not far from the end. And the true order of going, or being led by another, to the things of love, is to begin from the beauties of earth and mount upwards for the sake of that other beauty, using these as steps only, and from one going on to two, and from two to all fair forms, and from fair forms to fair practices, and from fair practices to fair notions, until from fair notions he arrives at the notion of absolute beauty, and at last knows what the essence of beauty is. This, my dear Socrates . . . is that life above all others which man should live, in the contemplation of beauty absolute; a beauty which if you once beheld, you would see not to be after the measure of gold, and garments, and fair boys and youths, whose presence now entrances you; and you and many a one would be content to live seeing them only and conversing with them without meat or drink, if that were possible— you only want to look at them and to be with them. But what if man had eyes to see the true beauty—the divine beauty, I mean, pure and clear and unalloyed, not clogged with the pollutions of mortality and all the colours and vanities of human life—thither looking, and holding converse with the true beauty simple and divine? Remember how in that communion only, beholding beauty with the eye of the mind, he will be enabled to bring forth, not images of beauty, but realities (for he has hold not of an image but of a reality), and bringing forth and nourishing true virtue to become the friend of God and be immortal, if mortal man may. Would that be an ignoble life?"[2]

The beauty of a particular person, according to Diotima's doctrine, is our starting point for discovering absolute Beauty. Our ultimate goal in loving the beauty of another is not to win that person's love, but for our soul to see the eternal Form of Beauty, and to contemplate Beauty continuously. Plato's vision of what love should lead us toward is thus very different from Romeo's vision of what he wants. Romeo believes he loves Juliet, a particular woman. But Plato's Socrates would say that what Romeo really loves is Beauty itself, the Beauty he sees shining through Juliet.

Even Plato seems to have mixed feelings about the impersonal vision of love that Diotima describes. For in continuing the *Symposium,* Plato follows Socrates' speech with a speech by a drunken Alcibiades, who waxes eloquent on his particular and passionate love for Socrates. Some commentators have suggested that Plato means to imply that Socrates' story of love is too abstract, and that it must be balanced by recognition of the importance of the particular person who is loved. So too, we should ask whether a work of art is beautiful in itself or beautiful as a representation of abstract Beauty. If our spiritual development is furthered when we recognize that beauty is the same wherever we recognize it, it might seem that Plato would do better to emphasize our love of beauty in various nonhuman things. Even if we recoil from the idea that the uniqueness of the individual one loves is not important ultimately, we might well see some point to the idea that various beautiful objects in the world have something important in common. Why, then, does Plato not focus his attention on beautiful objects? And, in particular, why does Plato not suggest that works of Art guide us toward insight into Beauty itself?

The Form of Beauty is unambivalently wondrous for Plato—works of art are not. In fact, Plato is extremely suspicious of art. At times Plato criticizes artists for not knowing what they are doing; at other times he insists that what artists are doing is dangerous to the audience of their works. Plato emphasizes the beauty of human beings in his account of Beauty because he thinks that love of another is the primary way that

[2]Plato, *The Symposium,* trans. Benjamin Jowett (Oxford: Oxford University Press, 1892).

most people gain insight into a higher spiritual realm. Yet, by contrast, Plato thinks that works of art tend to impress us with the wrong thing entirely: with the appearances of this world and with unenlightened talent. Beauty is one thing; art is something very different.

Plato's suspicion of art is complicated, however. For despite harsh judgments about the damage art can do, it is clear that Plato both admires some art and links it to a higher spiritual dimension. One of the clearest indications of Plato's ambivalence toward art is his treatment of poetry in his dialogue entitled *The Ion.* In *The Ion,* Socrates discusses poetic talent with Ion, a poetic interpreter by profession. Ion observes that he moves audiences tremendously whenever he interprets Homer, but that his art seems quite feeble when he attempts to interpret any other poet. Socrates convinces Ion that his ability is not appropriately called an "art" at all; for if he performed with an art, he would know the rules to apply to *all* poetic material. Art, according to Socrates, is a kind of knowledge that can be applied by one who knows it to all appropriate materials. But Ion does not possess this kind of knowledge. Instead, Ion performs Homer well because he is divinely inspired.

◆ from *The Ion,* by Plato

SOCRATES: I do see, Ion, and I'm going to announce to you what I think that is. As I said earlier, that's not a subject you've mastered—speaking well about Homer; it's a divine power that moves you, as a "Magnetic" stone moves iron rings. (That's what Euripides called it; most people call it "Heraclean.") This stone not only pulls those rings, if they're iron, it also puts power *in* the rings, so that they in turn can do just what the stone does—pull other rings—so that there's sometimes a very long chain of iron pieces and rings hanging from one another. And the power in all of them depends on this stone. In the same way, the Muse makes some people inspired herself, and then through those who are inspired a chain of other enthusiasts is suspended. You know, none of the epic poets, if they're good, are masters of their subject; they are inspired, possessed, and that is how they utter all those beautiful poems. The same goes for lyric poets if they're good: just as the Corybantes are not in their right minds when they dance, lyric poets, too, are not in their right minds when they make those beautiful lyrics, but as soon as they sail into harmony and rhythm they are possessed by Bacchic frenzy. Just as Bacchus worshippers when they are possessed draw honey and milk from rivers, but not when they are in their right minds—the soul of a lyric poet does this too, as they say themselves. For of course poets tell us that they gather songs at honey-flowing springs, from glades and gardens of the Muses, and that they bear songs to us as bees carry honey, flying like bees. And what they say is true. For a poet is an airy thing, winged and holy, and he is not able to make poetry until he becomes inspired and goes out of his mind and his intellect is no longer in him. As long as a human being has his intellect in his possession he will always lack the power to make poetry or sing prophecy. Therefore because it's not by mastery that they make poems or say many lovely things about their subjects (as you do about Homer)—but because it's by a divine gift—each poet is able to compose beautifully only that for which the Muse has aroused him: one can do dithyrambs, another encomia, one can do dance songs, another, epics, and yet another, iambics; and each of them is worthless for the other types of poetry. You see, it's not mastery that enables them to speak those verses, but a divine power, since if they knew how to speak beautifully on one type of poetry by mastering the subject, they could do so for all the others also. That's why the god takes their intellect away from them when he uses them as his servants, as he does prophets and godly diviners, so that we who hear should know that *they* are not the ones who speak those verses that are of such high value, for their intellect is not in them: the god himself is the one who speaks, and he gives voice through them to us. The best evidence for this account is Tynnichus from Chalcis, who never made a poem anyone would think worth mentioning, *except* for the praise-song everyone sings, almost the most beautiful lyric-poem there is, and simply, as he says himself, "an invention of the Muses." In this more than anything, then, I think, the god is showing us, so that we should be in no doubt about it, that these beautiful poems are not human, not even *from* human beings, but are divine and from gods; that poets are nothing but representatives of the gods, possessed by whoever possesses them. To show *that,* the god deliberately sang the most beautiful lyric poem through the most worthless poet. Don't you think I'm right, Ion?[3]

The poet and his interpreters are in touch with the divine. Divine intervention by the Muses transports the poet from his ordinary state and empowers him to utter "his oracles." Plato suggests in this passage that poets do speak the truth about higher reality when they are possessed by the gods. And through the image of the magnet, Plato suggests that such truths or insights are communicated through the poet to the interpreter to the audience. Thus, what is communicated to the audience is of divine origin and presumably of value for spiritual insight. Nevertheless, although the poetry generated by divine possession is favorably cast in *The Ion,* the powers of the poet are not. Socrates, while acknowledging Ion's divine possession, discounts Ion the poet. Ion is a mere vessel employed by the gods; his soul has not regained knowledge of the Forms. Were Ion performing with knowledge—if Ion himself had

[3]Plato, *The Ion,* trans. Paul Woodruff (Indianapolis, IN: Hackett, 1983).

insight—his ability would not be limited to Homer's poetry. But Ion does not possess knowledge nor control the art he claims to practice. Divine possession, not Ion himself, controls Ion's performance. Ion the poet operates in ignorance and has no control over his talent whatever.

Plato's ambivalence toward art is even more evident in *The Republic.* There Socrates discourses on the ignorance of artists, arguing at length for censorship of poetry—which might seem surprising in light of Socrates' suggestion in *The Ion* that the poet is divinely inspired. In order to understand Socrates' harsh stance in *The Republic,* we must understand the concerns that motivate the Socrates of this dialogue.

In *The Republic,* Socrates and some of his disciples are concerned with the qualities that make a good state. Socrates' comments on the dangers of art arise in connection with this concern. Plato's suspicion of art revealed in this context derives from his beliefs about art's powers to distract citizens from their proper roles in the good state. As Plato understands it, the good state is one in which individuals serve their own particular function, and in this manner promote the good of the whole. Ideally, citizens of the good state perform these functions in harmony with each other.

For harmony to exist in the external social order, the souls of the citizens must be in a state of harmony. An individual soul attains a state of harmony when each element of that soul performs its proper function, unimpeded by any other element. The state of harmony is achieved when reason—one of the three components of the soul—rules over the remaining components, the appetites and the spirited element. Ruling over the remaining two elements is reason's appropriate function, and the functions of the remaining elements are coordinated properly only when reason plays this role. Similarly, on the political level, the elements of the state can operate in coordination with one another only when the state is ruled in accordance with reason.

This vision of the good state and of the citizens who comprise it makes art problematic for two reasons: the first concerns reason's function, the second concerns art's capacity to arouse passion. Reason, in Plato's view, is the faculty that discerns true realities behind appearances. Our reliance on reason to rule our soul involves willingness to forego attention to appearances and to turn our attention to the deeper truths that appearances obscure. The arts, however, direct attention to appearances. For this reason, Socrates in *The Republic* disparages all imitative art as being a distraction from divine insight. Imitative art copies the appearance of material things, which themselves are appearances that disguise the true reality of the Forms. Consequently, this kind of art is "thrice removed from the truth." Socrates considers art's distance from truth with his disciples:

◆from *The Republic,* by Plato

. . . but I do not mind saying to you, that all poetical imitations are ruinous to the understanding of the hearers, and that the knowledge of their true nature is the only antidote to them.

Explain the purport of your remark.

Well, I will tell you, although I have always from my earliest youth had an awe and love of Homer, which even now makes the words falter on my lips, for he is the great captain and teacher of the whole of that charming tragic company; but a man is not to be reverenced more than the truth, and therefore I will speak out.

Very good, he said.

Listen to me then, or rather, answer me.

Put your question.

Can you tell me what imitation is? for I really do not know.

A likely thing, then, that I should know.

Why not? for the duller eye may often see a thing sooner than the keener.

Very true, he said; but in your presence, even if I had any faint notion, I could not muster courage to utter it. Will you enquire yourself?

Well then, shall we begin the enquiry in our usual manner: Whenever a number of individuals have a common name, we assume them to have also a corresponding idea or form:—do you understand me?

I do.

Let us take any common instance; there are beds and tables in the world—plenty of them, are there not?

Yes.

But there are only two ideas or forms of them—one the idea of a bed, the other of a table.

True.

And the maker of either of them makes a bed or he makes a table for our use, in accordance with the idea—that is our way of speaking in this and similar instances—but no artificer makes the ideas themselves: how could he?

Impossible.

And there is another artist,—I should like to know what you would say of him.

Who is he?

One who is the maker of all the works of all other workmen.

What an extraordinary man!

Wait a little, and there will be more reason for your saying so. For this is he who is able to make not only vessels of every kind, but plants and animals, himself and all other things—the earth and heaven, and the things which are in heaven or under the earth; he makes the gods also.

He must be a wizard and no mistake.

Oh! you are incredulous, are you? Do you mean that there is no such maker or creator, or that in one sense there might be a maker of all these things but in another not? Do you see that there is a way in which you could make them all yourself?

What way?

An easy way enough; or rather, there are many ways in which the feat might be quickly and easily accomplished, none quicker than that of turning a mirror round and round—you would soon enough make the sun and the heavens, and the earth and yourself, and other animals and plants, and all the other things of which we were just now speaking, in the mirror.

Yes, he said; but they would be appearances only.

Very good, I said, you are coming to the point now. And the painter too is, as I conceive, just such another—a creator of appearances, is he not?

Of course.

But then I suppose you will say that what he creates is untrue. And yet there is a sense in which the painter also creates a bed?

Yes, he said, but not a real bed.

And what of the maker of the bed? were you not saying that he too makes, not the idea which, according to our view, is the essence of the bed, but only a particular bed?

Yes, I did.

Then if he does not make that which exists he cannot make true existence, but only some semblance of existence; and if any one were to say that the work of the maker of the bed, or of any other workman, has real existence, he could hardly be supposed to be speaking the truth.

At any rate, he replied, philosophers would say that he was not speaking the truth.

No wonder, then, that his work too is an indistinct expression of truth.

No wonder.

Suppose now that by the light of the examples just offered we enquire who this imitator is?

If you please.

Well then, here are three beds: one existing in nature, which is made by God, as I think that we may say—for no one else can be the maker?

No.

There is another which is the work of the carpenter?

Yes.

And the work of the painter is a third?

Yes.

Beds, then, are of three kinds, and there are three artists who superintend them: God, the maker of the bed, and the painter?

Yes, there are three of them.

God, whether from choice or from necessity, made one bed in nature and one only; two or more such ideal beds neither ever have been nor ever will be made by God.

Why is that?

Because even if He had made but two, a third would still appear behind them which both of them would have for their idea, and that would be the ideal bed and not the two others.

Very true, he said.

God knew this, and He desired to be the real maker of a real bed, not a particular maker of a particular bed; and therefore He created a bed which is essentially and by nature one only.

So we believe.

Shall we, then, speak of Him as the natural author or maker of the bed?

Yes, he replied; inasmuch as by the natural process of creation He is the author of this and of all other things.

And what shall we say of the carpenter—is not he also the maker of the bed?

Yes.

But would you call the painter a creator and maker?

Certainly not.

Yet if he is not the maker, what is he in relation to the bed?

I think, he said, that we may fairly designate him as the imitator of that which the others make.

Good, I said; then you call him who is third in the descent from nature an imitator?

Certainly, he said.

And the tragic poet is an imitator, and therefore, like all other imitators, he is thrice removed from the king and from the truth?

That appears to be so.[4]

Thus, Plato contends, the imitative arts endanger their audience's ability to attend to true reality, for the arts direct attention to appearances and away from realities. In addition, art, especially poetry, has the dangerous potential to arouse passion. Nevertheless, Plato does not view passion as undesirable in itself; in fact, as we have seen, he believes that passion for beauty is the first developmental stage toward insight into the Forms. But when passion is not limited and controlled properly, Plato believes that passion can inspire the person who experiences it to disregard reason. And the consequences are disastrous, both to the person's inner harmony and to his or her respect for the rule of reason in the state.

Passion, in Plato's opinion, also can distract citizens from attending to their functions in the community. In particular, poetry can endanger the

---

[4]Plato, *The Republic*, trans. Benjamin Jowett (Indianapolis, IN: Hackett, 1974). All subsequent quotations from Plato's *The Republic* are from this edition unless otherwise noted.

state in this way, especially when it depicts characters who are unsuitable role models. Even Homer's depictions of the gods often present the gods engaged in unworthy behavior that could inspire the impressionable to socially undesirable aims and lifestyles. Plato concludes that poetry should be strictly censored, convinced as he is that poetry has the power to harm even the state's best citizens.

Hear and judge: The best of us, as I conceive, when we listen to a passage of Homer, or one of the tragedians in which he represents some pitiful hero who is drawling out his sorrows in a long oration, or weeping, and smiting his breast—the best of us, you know, delight in giving way to sympathy, and are in raptures at the excellence of the poet who stirs our feelings most.

Yes, of course I know.

But when any sorrow of our own happens to us, then you may observe that we pride ourselves on the opposite quality—we would fain be quiet and patient; this is the manly part, and the other which delighted us in the recitation is now deemed to be the part of a woman.

Very true, he said.

Now can we be right in praising and admiring another who is doing that which any one of us would abominate and be ashamed of in his own person?

No, he said, that is certainly not reasonable.

Nay, I said, quite reasonable from one point of view.

What point of view?

If you consider, I said, that when in misfortune we feel a natural hunger and desire to relieve our sorrow by weeping and lamentation, and that this feeling which is kept under control in our own calamities is satisfied and delighted by the poets;—the better nature in each of us, not having been sufficiently trained by reason or habit, allows the sympathetic element to break loose because the sorrow is another's; and the spectator fancies that there can be no disgrace to himself in praising and pitying any one who comes telling him what a good man he is, and making a fuss about his troubles; he thinks that the pleasure is a gain, and why should he be supercilious and lose this and the poem too? Few persons ever reflect, as I should imagine, that from the evil of other men something of evil is communicated to themselves. And so the feeling of sorrow which has gathered strength at the sight of the misfortunes of others is with difficulty repressed in our own.

How very true!

And does not the same hold also of the ridiculous? There are jests which you would be ashamed to make yourself, and yet on the comic stage, or indeed in private, when you hear them, you are greatly amused by them, and are not at all disgusted at their unseemliness;—the case of pity is repeated;—there is a principle in human nature which is disposed to raise a laugh, and this which you once restrained by reason, because you were afraid of being thought a buffoon, is now let out again; and having stimulated the risible faculty at the theatre, you are betrayed unconsciously to yourself into playing the comic poet at home.

Quite true, he said.

And the same may be said of lust and anger and all the other affections, of desire and pain and pleasure, which are held to be inseparable from every action—in all of them poetry feeds and waters the passions instead of drying them up; she lets them rule, although they ought to be controlled, if mankind are ever to increase in happiness and virtue.

I cannot deny it.

Therefore, Glaucon, I said, whenever you meet with any of the eulogists of Homer declaring that he has been the educator of Hellas, and that he is profitable for education and for the ordering of human things, and that you should take him up again and again and get to know him and regulate your whole life according to him, we may love and honour those who say these things—they are excellent people, as far as their lights extend; and we are ready to acknowledge that Homer is the greatest of poets and first of tragedy writers; but we must remain firm in our conviction that hymns to the gods and praises of famous men are the only poetry which ought to be admitted into our State. For if you go beyond this and allow the honeyed muse to enter, either in epic or lyric verse, not law and the reason of mankind, which by common consent have ever been deemed best, but pleasure and pain will be the rulers in our State.

That is most true, he said.

And now since we have reverted to the subject of poetry, let this our defence serve to show the reasonableness of our former judgment in sending away out of our State an art having the tendencies which we have described; for reason constrained us. But that she may not impute to us any harshness or want of politeness, let us tell her that there is an ancient quarrel between philosophy and poetry; of which there are many proofs, such as the saying of "the yelping hound howling at her lord," or of one "mighty in the vain talk of fools," and "the mob of sages circumventing Zeus," and the "subtle thinkers who are beggars after all"; and there are innumerable other signs of ancient enmity between them.

Despite this lengthy indictment of poetry, Plato's conclusions are again mixed. Already, in the next sentence of the dialogue, Socrates suggests the possibility of a conciliation between truth, the good state, and poetry.

. . . Notwithstanding this, let us assure our sweet friend and the sister arts of imitation, that if she will only prove her title to exist in a well-ordered State we shall be delighted to receive her—we are very conscious of her charms; but we may not on that account betray the truth. I dare say, Glaucon, that you are as much charmed by her as I am, especially when she appears in Homer?

Yes, indeed, I am greatly charmed.

Shall I propose, then, that she be allowed to return from exile, but upon this condition only—that she make a defence of herself in lyrical or some other metre?

Certainly.

And we may further grant to those of her defenders who are lovers of poetry and yet not poets the permission to speak in prose on her behalf: let them show not only that she is pleasant but also useful to States and to human life, and we will listen in a kindly spirit; for if this can be proved we shall surely be the gainers—I mean, if there is a use in poetry as well as a delight?

Certainly, he said, we shall be the gainers.

If her defence fails, then, my dear friend, like other persons who are enamoured of something, but put a restraint upon themselves when they think their desires are opposed to their interests, so too must we after the manner of lovers give her up, though not without a struggle. We too are inspired by that love of poetry which the education of noble States has implanted in us, and therefore we would have her appear at her best and truest; but so long as she is unable to make good her defence, this argument of ours shall be a charm to us, which we will repeat to ourselves while we listen to her strains; that we may not fall away into the childish love of her which captivates the many. At all events we are well aware that poetry being such as we have described is not to be regarded seriously as attaining to the truth; and he who listens to her, fearing for the safety of the city which is within him, should be on his guard against her seductions and make our words his law.

Yes, he said, I quite agree with you.

Yes, I said, my dear Glaucon, for great is the issue at stake, greater than appears, whether a man is to be good or bad. And what will any one be profited if under the influence of honour or money or power, aye, or under the excitement of poetry, he neglect justice and virtue?

B. ARISTOTLE AND THE SELF-SUFFICIENCY OF ART

The metaphysical differences between Plato and Aristotle are apparent in their respective aesthetics. Plato links beauty to the transcendent, and judges art harshly when art fails to illuminate transcendent truth. By contrast, Aristotle focuses instead on the observable characteristics of art as a phenomenon in this world. Aristotle, concerned with art as a mode of Becoming, is interested in how artworks come about and in the process of intelligence that guides their formation. Beauty is, for

Aristotle, an eminent feature of things in this world, which can be studied through examination of the structure of beautiful things.

Because Aristotle is concerned with art as a phenomenon in this world, he does not emphasize the same things that Plato emphasizes. Although Aristotle describes poetic talent as a gift (in *The Poetics*), he does not describe artistic creation as an intervention of the divine. Instead, Aristotle sees art as the product of human intentions, and he believes that some account can be given of the specific elements that comprise a good work of art. Artworks are products of "art" in the exact sense that Socrates denied art to Ion. Art is the capacity to make, involving a true course of reasoning. In other words, art is a kind of rational knowledge that a proficient artist knows how to employ in case after case.

Aristotle also differs from Plato in his account of art's desirable function. Plato sees art as valuable only insofar as it can serve an extra-artistic function. Aristotle, by contrast, believes that the arts are valuable in themselves. Although Aristotle, like Plato, discusses the role of art (especially music) in education, he does not believe that the arts have primarily a functional purpose. Instead, according to Aristotle, the arts are self-sufficient activities that contribute dignity to life and that give us a sense of the joy to be found in contemplation for its own sake. In addition, the arts also provide innocent amusement and relaxation from toil. However, the primary purpose of art is not to complement some extra-artistic purpose, but simply to give us something to cherish and contemplate in our leisure. For example, Aristotle sees imitative art as an innocent pleasure. He observes that we learn through imitating, and that we take great pleasure in learning (which includes, in this case, grasping what is being imitated). Aristotle also points out that we take a natural delight in imitations of all sorts. Imitative art, far from being inherently pernicious, springs from a natural human aptitude.

Aristotle's most important discussion of art occurs in *The Poetics;* in particular, his theory of tragedy has been tremendously influential. Proceeding from his definition of tragedy, consider Aristotle's succinct analysis.

◆**from *The Poetics*,
by Aristotle**

. . . A tragedy then, is the imitation of an action that is serious and also, as having magnitude, complete in itself; in language with pleasurable accessories, each kind brought in separately in the parts of the work; in a dramatic, not in a narrative form; with incidents arousing pity and fear, wherewith to accomplish its catharsis of such emotions. Here by "language with pleasurable acces-

sories" I mean that with rhythm and harmony or song superadded;
and by "the kinds separately" I mean that some portions are
worked out with verse only, and others in turn with song.

Aristotle, beginning with a discussion of plot and focusing on the
magnitude of the tragic work, proceeds to analyze the elements of
tragedy.

> . . . We have laid it down that a tragedy is an imitation of an ac-
> tion that is complete in itself, as a whole of some magnitude; for a
> whole may be of no magnitude to speak of. Now a whole is that
> which has beginning, middle, and end. A beginning is that which is
> not itself necessarily after anything else, and which has naturally
> something else after it; an end is that which is naturally after some-
> thing itself, either as its necessary or usual consequent, and with
> nothing else after it; and a middle, that which is by nature after one
> thing and has also another after it. A well-constructed Plot, there-
> fore, cannot either begin or end at any one point one likes; begin-
> ning and end in it must be of the forms just described. Again: to be
> beautiful, a living creature, and every whole made up of parts, must
> not only present a certain order in its arrangement of parts, but
> also be of a certain definite magnitude. Beauty is a matter of size
> and order, and therefore impossible either (1) in a very minute
> creature, since our perception becomes indistinct as it approaches
> instantaneity; or (2) in a creature of vast size—one, say, 1,000
> miles long—as in that case, instead of the object being seen all at
> once, the unity and wholeness of it is lost to the beholder. Just in
> the same way, then, as a beautiful whole made up of parts, or a
> beautiful living creature, must be of some size, but a size to be
> taken in by the eye, so a story or Plot must be of some length, but
> of a length to be taken in by the memory. As for the limit of its
> length, so far as that is relative to public performances and specta-
> tors, it does not fall within the theory of poetry. If they had to
> perform a hundred tragedies, they would be timed by water-clocks,
> as they are said to have been at one period. The limit, however,
> set by the actual nature of the thing is this: the longer the story,
> consistently with its being comprehensible as a whole, the finer
> it is by reason of its magnitude. As a rough general formula, "a
> length which allows of the hero passing by a series of probable or
> necessary stages from misfortune to happiness, or from happiness
> to misfortune," may suffice as a limit for the magnitude of the
> story.[5]

Aristotle may appear to be stating the obvious. In fact, his precepts on
magnitude establish one of the most significant principles of traditional

---

[5]Aristotle, *The Poetics*, from *The Works of Aristotle*, ed. W. D. Ross (Oxford: Clarendon
Press, 1908). The subsequent quotation from Aristotle's *The Poetics* is from this edition.

Western aesthetics—the principle of **closure.** According to the principle of closure, an artwork should have clear, well-defined limits and should not "begin or end at any point one likes." Instead, it should present something that is complete in itself.

In comparing a tragedy to a living creature, Aristotle also proposes a model that dominates the traditional Western understanding of the artwork—the model of Organic Life. The composition of an artwork should resemble that of a living organism. Each of the elements should serve the "life" of the work as a whole, and the functions of the elements should operate in harmony. The observer should get the impression that every element in the work is exactly as it should be, and that no elements should distract from the Unified Effect of the work as a whole. Closely related to this idea is the notion of Aesthetic Necessity, the idea that the composition of the work should be so perfectly structured and the elements so perfectly coordinated in serving the effect of the whole that any change would be a change for the worse. Aristotle makes this point as well. ". . . [I]n poetry the story, as an imitation of action, must represent one action, a complete whole, with its several incidents so closely connected that the transposal or withdrawal of any one of them will disjoin and dislocate the whole."

Aristotle goes on to suggest appropriate techniques for unifying the tragedy. Simply tracing the events in one person's life does not unify a play, for many unrelated incidents transpire in a single individual's life. Instead, the unity of a tragedy should come from presenting the play as a single action. Aristotle believes that to accomplish this the playwright should limit the material to the events of one twenty-four hour period.

Aristotle again departs from Plato in his further comments on the material employed in tragedy. Far from thinking that an "ancient quarrel" exists between poetry and philosophy, Aristotle argues that poetry is itself philosophical.

> From what we have said it will be seen that the poet's function is to describe, not the thing that has happened, but a kind of thing that might happen, i.e. what is possible as being probable or necessary. The distinction between historian and poet is not in the one writing prose and the other verse—you might put the work of Herodotus into verse, and it would still be a species of history; it consists really in this, that the one describes the thing that has been, and the other a kind of thing that might be. Hence poetry is something more philosophic and of graver import than history, since its statements are of the nature rather of universals, whereas those of history are singulars. By a universal statement I mean one as to what such or such a kind of man will probably or necessarily say or do—which is the aim of poetry, though it affixes proper names to the characters; by a singular statement, one as to what, say, Alcibiades did or had done to him.

Aristotle analyzed each of the elements indicated in his definition of tragedy, treating some at greater length than others. Other than Aristotle's comments on plot, his most influential remarks probably are those dealing with the effects of tragedy on the audience. And yet, these remarks are terse and ambiguous. The definition of tragedy states that the incidents portrayed should arouse "pity and fear" in order to effect a catharsis of these emotions. And later on Aristotle states that although pity and fear can be aroused by the spectacle of the play, the more artistic method is to arouse them "by the very structure and incidents of the play." So desirable is it that the incidents provoke these emotions that Aristotle insists, "The Plot . . . should be so framed that, even without seeing the things take place, he who simply hears the account of them shall be filled with horror and pity at the incidents."

Elsewhere, in *The Rhetoric,* Aristotle elaborates on what these peculiarly tragic emotions involve. Fear arises from a mental picture of destructive or painful evil that we believe might befall us in the future. And we experience pity when such an evil befalls someone who does not deserve it, and when we recognize that the same thing might befall us or someone close to us. The tragic emotions of pity and fear are aroused, therefore, only when we feel some identification with the tragic hero's circumstances. In essence, we must identify with the tragic hero's vulnerability.

The tragedy aims to inspire pity and fear in its audience, but at the same time it aims to transform its audience by means of **catharsis.** Although the precise meaning of "catharsis" has been debated since Aristotle suggested this idea, presumably he means that the tragic emotions are either purged or purified. The burden of our sense of vulnerability is lightened as a result of our sympathetic co-suffering with the tragic hero. Perhaps Aristotle believes that we master our feelings of insecurity and vulnerability by expressing them vicariously through the play.

As one who is concerned primarily with the phenomena and mechanisms of this world, Aristotle admires verisimilitude in tragic depiction. He claims that characters should be lifelike and consistent with themselves, and that the poet should persuade the audience that the events portrayed are necessary or probable. Nonetheless, Aristotle is not a radical realist; the tragedy should, in his view, resemble life but also ennoble it. The tragic hero should be somewhat idealized, and even the impossible can be presented successfully as long as it appears to be the probable outcome of events. Again, Aristotle departs from Plato with respect to appearances. Tragedy can make good use of appearances to achieve a tragic effect, as Aristotle sees it. And while the ultimate aim of tragedy, and all poetry, is to reveal universal truths about human beings, these truths might be conveyed more forcefully by means of the idealized or the imaginary than by means of the unvarnished truth.

C. THE DISPUTE
ABOUT TASTES

Both Plato and Aristotle profoundly affected later Western thought about beauty and art. Plato's suspicion of art—reinforced by Christian suspicion of sensual enjoyment—lingered in theoretical treatments of the subject for many centuries, and colors popular Western thinking about art to this day. On the other hand, Aristotle's principles and models for successful art remain paradigmatic through recent times, and even departures from his general theories often rework Aristotelian models.

From the early Christian period through the medieval period, art was judged primarily on its ability to reveal truth in some fashion. Plotinus (ca. A.D. 204–270), a neo-Platonic philosopher, argued that art can provoke insight into the Forms more effectively than nature can. To recognize beauty in anything is, in his view, already to be attuned to true reality. Thus, beautiful art should be seen not as a distraction but as a vehicle to transcendent truth. And in this capacity art can be more valuable than beautiful nature, for art—enlightened by human insight—can be designed with the explicit intention of illuminating the underlying reality to its audience.

Influenced by such neo-Platonic ideas, St. Augustine attempted to establish the legitimacy of art for Christians. In Augustine's view the artistic beholder can gain insight into the divine mind by contemplating beauty. For underlying both God's creation in general, and all beautiful art and nature, is numerical proportion and harmony. Thus, it is appropriate for the Christian to contemplate such beauty. For by means of the senses, beauty reveals something of God's nature to the mind. The arts, therefore, can bring us closer to God. And because the arts reflect the harmonious structure that underlies God's creative power, the arts can be used to symbolize the transcendent. The idea that art can be used to symbolize levels of reality that are not themselves sensuous dominated the medieval perspective on art as well.

David Hume, while adopting an extreme subjectivist stance toward aesthetic judgments, proposed another explanation of the fact that some aesthetic judgments are better than others. Hume is especially influential in the history of aesthetics, for it is Hume, in particular, whom Kant set out to refute in his aesthetic theory. Consider Hume's analysis of the problem that among different aesthetic observers there are extreme divergences of taste.

◆from "Of the Standard of Taste," by David Hume

It is natural for us to seek a *Standard of Taste*; a rule, by which the various sentiments of men may be reconciled; at least, a decision, afforded, confirming one sentiment, and condemning another.

There is a species of philosophy, which cuts off all hopes of success in such an attempt, and represents the impossibility of ever attaining any standard of taste. The difference, it is said, is very wide between judgment and sentiment. All sentiment is right; because sentiment has a reference to nothing beyond itself, and is always real, wherever a man is conscious of it. But all determinations of the understanding are not right; because they have a reference to something beyond themselves, to wit, real matter of fact; and are not always comformable to that standard. Among a thousand different opinions which different men may entertain of the same subject, there is one, and but one, that is just and true; and the only difficulty is to fix and ascertain it. On the contrary, a thousand different sentiments, excited by the same object, are all right: Because no sentiment represents what is really in the object. It only marks a certain conformity or relation between the object and the organs or faculties of the mind; and if that conformity did not really exist, the sentiment could never possibly have being. Beauty is no quality in things themselves: It exists merely in the mind which contemplates them; and each mind perceives a different beauty. One person may even perceive deformity, where another is sensible of beauty; and every individual ought to acquiesce in his own sentiment, without pretending to regulate those of others. To seek the real beauty, or real deformity, is as fruitless an enquiry, as to pretend to ascertain the real sweet or real bitter. According to the disposition of the organs, the same object may be both sweet and bitter; and the proverb has justly determined it to be fruitless to dispute concerning tastes. It is very natural, and even quite necessary, to extend this axiom to mental, as well as bodily taste; and thus common sense, which is so often at variance with philosophy, especially with the skeptical kind, is found, in one instance at least, to agree in pronouncing the same decision.

But though this axiom, by passing into a proverb, seems to have attained the sanction of common sense; there is certainly a species of common sense which opposes it, at least serves to modify and restrain it. Whoever would assert an equality of genius and elegance between OGILBY and MILTON, or BUNYAN and ADDISON, would be thought to defend no less an extravagance, than if he had maintained a mole-hill to be as high as TENERIFFE, or a pond as extensive as the ocean. Though there may be found persons, who give the preference to the former authors; no one pays attention to such a taste; and we pronounce without scruple the sentiment of these pretended critics to be absurd and ridiculous. The principle of the natural equality of tastes is then totally forgot, and while we

> admit it on some occasions, where the objects seem near an equal-
> ity, it appears an extravagant paradox, or rather a palpable absur-
> dity, where objects so disproportioned are compared together.[6]

Although Hume believes it a reasonable principle of common sense that
some aesthetic judgments are simply faulty, he refuses to conclude that
any a priori rules can ground the validity of some judgments against their
rivals.

> It is evident that none of the rules of composition are fixed by
> reasonings *a priori*, or can be esteemed abstract conclusions of the
> understanding, from comparing those habitudes and relations of
> ideas, which are eternal and immutable. Their foundation is the
> same with that of all the practical sciences, experience; nor are they
> any thing but general observations, concerning what has been uni-
> versally found to please in all countries and in all ages. Many of the
> beauties of poetry and even of eloquence are founded on falsehood
> and fiction, on hyperboles, metaphors, and an abuse or perversion
> of terms from their natural meaning. To check the sallies of the
> imagination, and to reduce every expression to geometrical truth
> and exactness, would be the most contrary to the laws of criticism;
> because it would produce a work, which, by universal experience,
> has been found the most insipid and disagreeable. But though
> poetry can never submit to exact truth, it must be confined by rules
> of art, discovered to the author either by genius or observation. If
> some negligent or irregular writers have pleased, they have not
> pleased by their transgressions of rule or order, but in spite of
> these transgressions: They have possessed other beauties, which
> were conformable to just criticism; and the force of these beauties
> has been able to overpower censure, and give the mind a satis-
> faction superior to the disgust arising from the blemishes.

How then can we criticize any taste as deplorable? Hume argues that
we judge beauty much as we judge morality: we judge by means of a
peculiarly aesthetic sentiment. Although each of us judges subjectively,
the sentiment by which we judge is a natural and human one. Thus, we
can expect considerable agreement among those whose sensibilities have
been nurtured properly. Agreement about what is beautiful indicates
that the aesthetic sentiment, which beauty naturally arouses, in the human soul has been aroused in various observers by a particular object.

However, Hume realizes that this account does not yet explain the
considerable disagreement that we observe among those who pass aesthetic judgments. Hume goes on to explain that many contingencies
interfere with the arousal of aesthetic sentiment by appropriate objects.

[6]David Hume, "Of the Standard of Taste," from *Essays, Moral, Political and Literary*, ed.
T. H. Green (London: Longmans, Green and Co., 1882). All subsequent quotations of
Hume's "Of the Standard of Taste" are from this edition unless otherwise noted.

But though all the general rules of art are founded only on experience and on the observation of the common sentiments of human nature, we must not imagine, that, on every occasion, the feelings of men will be conformable to these rules. Those finer emotions of the mind are of a very tender and delicate nature, and require the concurrence of many favourable circumstances to make them play with facility and exactness, according to their general and established principles. The least exterior hindrance to such small springs, or the least internal disorder, disturbs their motion, and confounds the operation of the whole machine. When we would make an experiment of this nature, and would try the force of any beauty or deformity, we must choose with care a proper time and place, and bring the fancy to a suitable situation and disposition. A perfect serenity of mind, a recollection of thought, a due attention to the object; if any of these circumstances be wanting, our experiment will be fallacious, and we shall be unable to judge of the catholic and universal beauty. The relation, which nature has placed between the form and the sentiment will at least be more obscure; and it will require greater accuracy to trace and discern it. We shall be able to ascertain its influence not so much from the operation of each particular beauty, as from the durable admiration, which attends those works, that have survived all the caprices of mode and fashion, all the mistakes of ignorance and envy.

Rather surprisingly, we find Hume suggesting that if we really want to know whether or not a thing can appropriately be called beautiful, we should consult the experience of others. Durable admiration is a good indication of the aesthetic quality of an artwork, whereas our personal judgments of a work might well be distorted by our condition of mind or our prejudices. Hume rests his claim to the validity of particular aesthetic judgments, then, on the collective experience of generations, not on the particular experience of an individual on a particular occasion. He does not, therefore, believe that everyone has equally valid tastes.

Hume does, however, believe that the criterion for calling something beautiful is ultimately a subjective one. A thing is appropriately called beautiful if and only if it provokes aesthetic sentiment in appropriately disposed competent judges. What matters, then, is not so much the character of the object as the state of mind occasioned in the observer. Of course, the characteristics of the aesthetic object are relevant to whether or not it occasions aesthetic sentiment in the observer. Hume even indicates some of the objective characteristics commonly observed in artworks that have inspired durable admiration. But the test of an object's beauty is the experience it provokes in an observer. In this respect, as we are about to see, Hume resembles Kant. In general, modern Western aesthetics have turned their attention from the characteristics of the object to consideration of the state of mind that beauty and art occasion.

D. KANT: DISPUTES ABOUT TASTE RESOLVED

In his aesthetic work, Kant's primary concern is essentially the same as Hume's. He is interested in how our subjective aesthetic judgments are valid and in how we can claim that some such judgments are better than others. In the *Critique of Judgment,* Kant's explicit task is to establish aesthetic judgment on an **intersubjective** basis. However, although the problems that concern Kant resemble those that interest Hume, here as elsewhere Kant takes Hume as his target. Specifically, Kant sets out to refute Hume's idea that our disputes over taste can only be resolved empirically, and that such resolution is only a matter of consulting the empirical judgments of many aesthetic observers over time.

Kant wonders how it is that the judgment of the beautiful carries with it an expectation that others besides the subject will agree with the judgment. This is perplexing because a judgment that a thing is beautiful means that it provokes aesthetic pleasure within us. We cannot legitimately convince others of the correctness of our aesthetic judgments by providing them with conceptual arguments; argument is beside the point of whether we experience such pleasure or not.

But where does this universality of aesthetic experience come from if not from compelling argument? It comes from our capacity to contemplate suitable objects with our mental faculties in the extraordinary but intrinsically satisfying mode of operation that Kant describes as "free play." The faculties that are involved in free play are the very faculties that Kant takes to be essential to the possibility of human cognition: imagination and understanding.

In his *Critique of Pure Reason,* Kant characterizes the respective roles of **imagination** and **understanding** for ordinary knowledge. Imagination gathers together the stuff of our experience into definite images or representations. On the basis of these representations, understanding forms definite concepts.

Consider a concrete example. In approaching a flower from the standpoint of cognition, the representation of the flower that the imagination presents to the understanding is "understood" by means of a definite concept (e.g., a petunia). Once the understanding has determined the appropriate concept with which to designate the represented object, the process of cognition is complete.

In aesthetic experience, the same two faculties (imagination and understanding) again operate together. However, the end result is not a determinate concept. Instead, the two faculties interact in free play. In this case, again, the imagination forms a representation of the object. But unlike the case of cognition, the representation generated by imagination is not enshrined cognitively by a definite concept. Indeed, in aesthetic experience, we feel that no definite concept could define adequately what we observe. Thus, the two faculties do not neatly finish their work in aesthetic experience. Instead, they "play" by mutually enlivening one another.

When we view the petunia aesthetically, our minds are not statically contemplative, but actively so. We leap from focusing on one aspect of the flower's form to focusing on another. And in the midst of all this we find our understanding sufficiently engaged that often we do seek words to communicate the features of what we notice: "Isn't the way that petal curves interesting? It almost seems flirtatious." Such comments do not *explain* our enjoyment—in this case, of the flower's form. Yet they do reveal that our understanding in its own peculiar way is at work while our imagination is reworking its presentation.

The understanding's shifting emphasis, too, seems to encourage imagination to further reformulation of the image that it impresses on the mind. Imagination may present us with a differently focused representation of the petunia in light of the understanding's sensuous description "flirtatious." Because no conceptual classification confines the imagination, it can attend to more and more features of the object. It thus enhances our experience of the object's particularity as opposed to its generically classifiable features.

Against Hume, Kant argues that the convergence of our judgments about beauty are not merely empirical accidents but the necessary consequence of the very mental faculties we possess. Kant's defense of this claim depends again on the fact that the faculties employed in aesthetic experience are the very ones employed in cognition. Insofar as we can communicate with others—something that we assume in the case of all human beings and something that depends on our common ability to form concepts—we assume their reliance on the same processes of cognition as those we employ. In making this assumption, we assess that their cognitive faculties do function harmoniously.

But to the extent that we have presupposed this, we have presupposed in every human being the active capacity for aesthetic experience. For aesthetic experience depends only on the active, harmonious free play of the cognitive faculties. As Kant says later in the *Critique of Judgment*, the pleasure accompanying aesthetic experience is a satisfaction taken simply in the "harmonious (subjectively purposive) activity of the two cognitive powers in their freedom." Kant feels justified therefore in calling taste a kind of "common sense," for this "sense" is a responsive, harmonious condition of the cognitive faculties that can be activated in any aware human being.

Kant describes a judgment that a thing is beautiful as a necessary judgment. He does not mean that everyone empirically agrees that a thing is beautiful. Kant means that when we claim an object is beautiful, we mean it is an example of the sort of thing that can be contemplated aesthetically by any mentally healthy human being. If someone disagrees with our particular judgment that a thing is beautiful, we might discuss the disagreement as a consequence of his or her being preoccupied with practical concerns or by a private mood. But if someone never agreed with anyone that anything were beautiful, we would be right to believe that the person lacked something basic to a human being.

Kant makes two other important points about the nature of the beautiful: aesthetic experience of a beautiful object, he tells us, involves a stance of disinterestedness. The basic idea is that our enjoyment of the beautiful does not provoke any personal interest on our part. However, our enjoyment of the sensuously pleasing provokes an interest in sensuously appropriating the object. Our enjoyment of a T-bone steak, for example, essentially involves our experience of desire to eat it. Appreciation of the beautiful, by contrast, inspires no desire with respect to the object. Instead, we are content simply to contemplate the object.

Kant's other point is that an aesthetic judgment of a beautiful object involves contemplation of mere form. Kant has been described as a Formalist because he believes aesthetic contemplation considers form alone. Even in the case of art, Kant contends that consideration of the content is irrelevant and even distracting from aesthetic contemplation. The sensuous satisfaction we might take in the materials of art are also, in Kant's view, irrelevant to aesthetic satisfaction. Kant goes so far in defending this claim that he insists that in painting it is the delineation only, not the colors (which might please or displease us on a purely sensuous level), that we consider when we are judging the work aesthetically. Kant also argues against the view that our emotional response to art has anything to do with the aesthetic satisfaction we take in it.

When we contemplate a beautiful object aesthetically, Kant tells us, we observe what he calls **purposiveness without a purpose.** The object, in other words, forms an organic unity that coheres as if toward a definite *telos,* or purpose. Kant accepts the Aristotelian model of the beautiful object as akin to a living organism. But although the elements of the beautiful object seem to function together toward a unifying purpose, we do not, in contemplating, discover what it is. If we did discover a definite purpose, it would provide the key to a conceptual account of the arrangement of elements in a beautiful object. A botanical account of the parts of a flower would be a conceptual explanation of the function of each element with respect to a definite end (the continued life of the flower). But no such definite, objectively identifiable end accounts for the aesthetic form of an object. We recognize only that the parts cohere without being able to explain why.

Although primarily we associate the concept of aesthetic beauty with art, the history of the subject often looks elsewhere. Plato took as his example of beauty the beautiful *person;* Kant's analysis of the beautiful focused primarily on *nature* rather than art. Kant, however, does consider art at some length. He considers art essentially to be representational, and therefore believes that concepts mediate our appreciation of art. In other words, our impression of the kind of thing being represented is crucial to our judgment of whether or not it is well portrayed.

Nevertheless, while Kant believes that both artist and observer are constrained by their conceptions of the things being represented by art, he does not believe that concepts dictate recipes for art. Great art is a product of genius, not conceptual construction. Artistic genius is a natural faculty for producing "aesthetic ideas." These ideas are not conceptual and well defined in nature; instead they are generative, occasioning imaginative thought, but no particular thought. They are intuitive, and they guide the activity of the artist. Great artistic talent, on Kant's model, is thus a bit like poetic inspiration on Plato's. The artist can neither explain the origin of his or her ideas nor give a knowledgeable account of why his or her masterpiece takes the precise form that it does.

In tying artistic creation to genius, to some extent Kant sides with the empiricists. But Kant does not believe that unbridled genius is itself artistically desirable. If the ideas of the genius are not subjected to controlled forms, there is danger that the artistic product will be unintelligible to the artist's audience. Thus, Kant insists that *taste* must govern genius if works of art are to remain purposive. (Taste is the faculty of judging that a thing is beautiful.) Thus, in order for a genius to create artworks of value, the genius must examine and shape his productions from a critical posture.

Kant concludes his account of the beautiful with the suggestion that to us beauty symbolizes morality. By stimulating the free play of our faculties of imagination and understanding, beauty naturally reminds us of another situation in which we are free: our legislation of the moral law as free and rational agents. In the case of the moral law, another mental faculty, that of reason, freely determines the morally ideal. And insofar as we behave in accordance with this moral ideal, we are free from determination by inclination. We are not constrained by the moral law; we are constrained by inclinations that naturally overtake us. When we resist natural inclinations and guide our lives only by our own rational faculties, we are truly free. Our sense of freedom in aesthetic experience naturally reminds us of our moral freedom; and in Kant's own view, this is beauty's highest accomplishment.

E. AFTER KANT: ART, SOCIETY, AND SELF-AWARENESS

Friedrich Schiller (1759–1805), who was influenced strongly by Kantian aesthetics, further developed the idea that beauty symbolizes morality. Schiller, in his *Letters on the Aesthetic Education of Man*, argued against the view of some of his contemporaries that concern for beauty is a distraction from the more serious, political concerns of life. To the contrary, Schiller contends, beauty first makes us capable of becoming good citizens.

In early life, Schiller argues, we conceive of the external world as an adversary that we must force to give us what we want. But when we begin to experience beauty, we learn that our interests and the external world can coincide harmoniously. This experience provides our first step toward personal and political maturity. For only when we have come to believe that the external world sometimes will cooperate with us are we willing to cooperate with the external world.

Beauty intimates to us the possibility of social harmony, for it allows us to conceive of peaceful coexistence with others that does not involve constraint on anyone's part. Schiller believes that this intuition of a world of cooperation and mutual freedom among ourselves and others is indispensable for any lasting political solution to the tensions among human beings. Thus, Schiller believes that it is our political responsibility to make beauty central in the education of our young.

Much later in the nineteenth century, Count Lev Nikolayevich Tolstoy (1828–1910) similarly argued that the value of art lay in its social/ political function. But the function that Tolstoy had in mind was quite different from that of Schiller. Art serves its purpose, in Tolstoy's view, when art sincerely communicates emotion and thereby promotes feelings of community among people. Tolstoy, however, believed that most of the art of his culture did not serve its proper function. The art of the socially elite aimed only to give pleasure to its audience. By contrast, the art of the common people had the appropriate aim of sincere communication of feeling. Thus, Tolstoy's theory of art's purpose was not simply idealistic, but also quite critical of contemporary artistic practice.

1.   G. W. F. Hegel

Nineteenth-century aesthetics did not, however, focus exclusively on the social/political function that art might serve. Rather, the most powerful theories of beauty emphasized the capacity of art to make human beings understand themselves. Foremost among such theorists was G. W. F. Hegel. Although Hegel did not believe that self-consciousness is a purely personal matter, he did believe that art is a vehicle which human beings have employed to become conscious of a shared spirit. Art, as Hegel understood it, is born of an attempt by human beings to humanize the materials that they find around them. In giving creative form to such materials, they make them less alien from themselves. Moreover, because the forms that human beings use to give shape to these materials stem from the human mind, artworks embody the ideas of the mind in an external form. In this way art makes the ideas of the mind present to those who make it. Observing art, human beings can come to know themselves.

Artworks are under obligation to a sensuous medium. Yet ultimately they are addressed, not to the senses, but to the mind. So art's primary function is a spiritual one. However, because art involves a sensuous medium, tensions can exist between the medium and the spiritual idea that shapes it. For Hegel, the human spirit is always historically located, and its expressions reveal their historical context. Art, as an expression of the human spirit, has a history. Some of the developments of that history can be understood in terms of gradual human progress in learning to shape the materials of the world in accordance with the mind. Hegel describes three basic stages in art's development, which he distinguishes on the basis of their artworks' physical form to adequately embody the ideal spiritual content behind it.

◆**from *The Philosophy of Fine Art*,
by G. W. F. Hegel**

We have here to consider *three* relations of the Idea to its external process of configuration.

(a) First, the origin of artistic creation proceeds from the Idea when, being itself still involved in defective definition and obscurity, or in vicious and untrue determinacy, it becomes embodied in the shapes of art. As indeterminate it does not as yet possess in itself that individuality which the Ideal demands. Its abstract character and onesidedness leaves its objective presentment still defective and contingent. Consequently this first type of art is rather a mere search after plastic configuration than a power of genuine representation. The Idea has not as yet found the formative principle within itself, and therefore still continues to be the mere effort and strain to find it. We may in general terms describe this form as the *symbolic* type of art. The abstract Idea possesses in it its external shape outside itself in the purely material substance of Nature, from which the shaping process proceeds, and to which in its expression it is entirely yoked. Natural objects are thus in the first instance left just as they are, while, at the same time the substantive Idea is imposed upon them as their significance, so that their function is henceforth to express the same, and they claim to be interpreted, as though the Idea itself was present in them. A rationale of this is to be found in the fact that the external objects of reality do essentially possess an aspect in which they are qualified to express a universal import. But as a completely adequate coalescence is not yet possible, all that can be the outcome of such a relation is an *abstract attribute,* as when a lion is understood to symbolize strength.

On the other hand this abstractness of the relation makes present to consciousness no less markedly how the Idea stands relatively to natural phenomena as an alien; and albeit it expatiates in all these shapes, having no other means of expression among all that is real, and seeks after itself in their unrest and defects of genuine proportion, yet for all that it finds them inadequate to meet its needs. It consequently exaggerates natural shapes and the phenomena of Nature in every degree of indefinite and limitless extension; it flounders about in them like a drunkard, and seethes and ferments, doing violence to their truth with the distorted growth of unnatural shapes, and strives vainly by the contrast, hugeness, and splendour of the forms accepted to exalt the phenomena to the plane of the Idea. For the Idea is here still more or less indeterminate, and unadaptable, while the objects of Nature are wholly definite in their shape.

. . . .

(b) In the *second* type of art, which we propose to call *"Classical,"* the twofold defect of symbolic art is annulled. Now the symbolic configuration is imperfect, because, first, the Idea here only enters into consciousness in *abstract* determinacy or indeterminateness: and, secondly, by reason of the fact that the coalescence of import with embodiment can only throughout remain defective, and in its turn also wholly abstract. The classical art-type solves both these difficulties. It is, in fact, the free and adequate embodiment of the Idea in the shape which, according to its notional concept, is uniquely appropriate to the Idea itself. . . . Such a configuration, which the Idea essentially possesses as spiritual, and indeed as individually determinate spirituality, when it must perforce appear as a temporal phenomenon, is the *human form.* Personification and anthropomorphism have frequently been abused as a degradation of the spiritual. But art, in so far as its function is to bring to vision the spiritual in sensuous guise, must advance to such anthropomorphism, inasmuch as Spirit is only adequately presented to perception in its bodily presence. The transmigration of souls is in this respect an abstract conception, and physiology ought to make it one of its fundamental principles, that life has necessarily, in the course of its evolution, to proceed to the human form, for the reason that it is alone the visible phenomenon adequate to the expression of intelligence.

The human bodily form, then, is employed in the classical type of art not as purely sensuous existence, but exclusively as the existence and natural shape appropriate to mind. It has therefore to be relieved of all the defective excrescences which adhere to it in its purely physical aspect, and from the contingent finiteness of its phenomenal appearance. The external shape must in this way be purified in order to express in itself the content adequate for such a purpose; and, furthermore, along with this, that the coalescence of import and embodiment may be complete, the spirituality which constitutes the content must be of such a character that it is completely able to express itself in the natural form of man, without projecting beyond the limits of such expression within the sensuous and purely physical sphere of existence. Under such a condition Spirit is at the same time defined as particular, the spirit or mind of man, not as simply absolute and eternal. In this latter case it is only capable of asserting and expressing itself as intellectual being.

Out of this latter distinction arises, in its turn, the defect which brings about the dissolution of the classical type of art, and makes the demand for a third and higher form, namely the *romantic* type.

(c) The romantic type of art annuls the completed union of the Idea and its reality, and occurs, if on a higher plane, to the difference and opposition of both sides, which remained unovercome in symbolic art. The classical type of art no doubt attained the highest excellence of which the sensuous embodiment of art is capable. The defect, such as it is, is due to the defect which obtains in art itself throughout, the limitations of its entire province, that is to say. The limitation consists in this, that art in general and, agreeably to its fundamental idea, accepts for its object Spirit, the notion of which is infinite concrete universality, under the guise of sensuously concrete form. In the classical type it sets up the perfected coalescence of spiritual and sensuous existence as adequate conformation of both. As a matter of fact, however, in this fusion mind itself is not represented agreeably to its *true notional concept*. Mind is the infinite subjectivity of the Idea, which as absolute inwardness, is not capable of freely expanding in its entire independence, so long as it remains within the mould of the bodily shape, fused therein as in the existence wholly congenial to it.

To escape from such a condition the romantic type of art once more cancels that inseparable unity of the classical type, by securing a content which passes beyond the classical stage and its mode of expression. . . . [I]n this third stage the object of art consists in the free and concrete presence of spiritual activity, whose vocation it is to appear as such a presence or activity for the inner world of conscious intelligence. In consonance with such an object art cannot merely work for sensuous perception. It must deliver itself to the inward life, which coalesces with its object simply as though this were none other than itself, in other words, to the intimacy of soul, to the heart, the emotional life, which as the medium of Spirit itself essentially strives after freedom, and seeks and possesses its reconciliation only in the inner chamber of spirit. It is this inward or ideal world which constitutes the content of the romantic sphere: it will therefore necessarily discover its representation as such inner idea or feeling, and in the show or appearance of the same. The world of the soul and intelligence celebrates its triumph over the external world, and, actually in the medium of that outer world, makes that victory to appear, by reason of which the sensuous appearance sinks into worthlessness.

On the other hand, this type of art, like every other, needs an external vehicle of expression. As already stated, the spiritual content has here withdrawn from the external world and its immediate unity into its own world. The sensuous externality of form is consequently accepted and represented, as in the symbolic type, as unessential and transient; furthermore the subjective finite spirit and volition is treated in a similar way; a treatment which even includes the idiosyncracies or caprice of individuals, character, action, or the particular features of incident and plot. The aspect of external existence is committed to contingency and handed over to the adventurous action of imagination, whose caprice is just as able to reflect the facts given *as* they are, as it can change the shapes of the external world into a medley of its own invention and distort them to mere caricature. For this external element has no longer its notion and significance in its own essential province, as in classical art. It is now discovered in the emotional realm, and this is manifested in the medium of that realm itself rather than in the external and *its* form of reality, and is able to secure or to recover again the condition of reconciliation with itself in every accident, in all the chance circumstance that falls into independent shape, in all misfortune and sorrow, nay, in crime itself.

Hence it comes about that the characteristics of symbolic art, its indifference, incompatibility and severance of Idea from configurative expression, are here reproduced once more, if with essential difference. And this difference consists in the fact that in romantic art the Idea, whose defectiveness, in the case of the symbol, brought with it the defect of external form, has to display itself as Spirit and in the medium of soul-life as essentially self-complete. And it is to complete fundamentally this higher perfection that it withdraws itself from the external element. It can, in short, seek and consummate its true reality and manifestation nowhere but in its own domain.

This we may take to be in general terms the character of the symbolic, classical, and romantic types of art, which in fact constitute the three relations of the Idea to its embodiment in the realm of human art. They consist in the aspiration after the attainment and transcendency of the Ideal, viewed as the true concrete notion of beauty.[7]

In the Romantic stage of art's development, Hegel concludes, the ideal content is too completely spiritualized to be fully embodied by any physical form whatsoever. Thus, the significant spiritual concerns of the Romantic age eventually turn away from art as a primary vehicle of expression. Hegel concludes,

---

[7]G. W. F. Hegel, *The Philosophy of Fine Art*, trans. B. Bosanquet (London: Routledge and Kegan-Paul, 1905).

... [I]t certainly is the case that Art is no longer able to discover the satisfaction of spiritual wants, which previous epochs and nations have sought for in it and exclusively found in it, a satisfaction which, at least on the religious side, was associated with art in the most intimate way. The fair days of Greek art, as also the golden time of the later middle ages, are over. . . . [A]rt is and remains for us, on the side of its highest possibilities, a thing of the past.[8]

Reflective thought, in Hegel's view, has replaced art as the vehicle for humanity's most significant spiritual contents and as the means by which humanity comes to know itself. Although art remains a source of enjoyment to modern human beings, it is no longer central to the pursuit of their central spiritual concerns.

2. *Arthur Schopenhauer*

Arthur Schopenhauer (1788–1860) does not share Hegel's sense of "the end of art." Schopenhauer, like Hegel, sees art as a medium through which human beings can gain insight into themselves. But Schopenhauer considers this self-awareness to be a private experience that any individual, at any historical period, might have, and of no less value now than for the ancients.

Schopenhauer's theory of art is bound intimately to his metaphysical theory. Accepting Kant's distinction between the noumenal and the phenomenal world, Schopenhauer is unwilling to accept Kant's view that we cannot come to know the noumenal reality behind phenomena. On the contrary, Schopenhauer argues, we know the noumenal world directly. The fundamental, noumenal reality is a turbulent, chaotic **Will;** and we directly experience this Will in our individual wills.

This fate may seem happier than that proposed by Kant when he denies us any knowledge of the thing-in-itself. But for Schopenhauer, this is not a happy fate at all. The Will, the ultimate reality, is a turbulent cauldron of struggle within itself. The phenomenal world, which is the Will's manifestation, is accordingly a vale of struggle and turbulence. The various phenomena struggle among themselves, and even a single being's individual will struggles within itself. Desire, which each of us experiences as the basic manifestation of our nature, is our immediate experience of the dissatisfaction and the internal tension of the will.

From the standpoint of our ordinary outlook on things, we are unaware of our true situation as regards our desires. We believe that we will be content once we gain what we want, although all of our experience shows us differently. And we do not consider those who obstruct us as being in the same position that we are, motivated by blind desire and

---

[8]Hegel, *Introduction to Aesthetics*, trans. B. Bosanquet (London: Routledge and Kegan-Paul, 1905).

incapable of doing otherwise. However, occasionally ethical insight indicates the fallacy of this usual way of thinking. When ethical insight overtakes us, we recognize that we are all in the same situation, and that we cannot violate another being's will without violating ourselves. Schopenhauer interprets this kind of insight as a recognition that we are all one thing, namely, the Will. However, most of us do not change our lives as a result of such insight, but instead continue blindly through our lives, swinging like a pendulum between desire and (when we occasionally are satisfied) boredom.

The only way out of such misery is to renounce desire. Schopenhauer, one of the first Germans to become interested in Buddhism, adopted the Buddhist beliefs that desire causes suffering and that suffering ceases only with cessation of desire. Schopenhauer realized that the ascetic life that he proposed as the means to this end would not attract many of his readers. Indeed, if one considers his biography, it seems not to have greatly attracted Schopenhauer himself.

What did attract Schopenhauer was beauty. He believed that for both himself and most others, beauty alone provides a respite from what he calls "the penal servitude of willing." In the aesthetic experience we comport ourselves without motive or desire toward the object that we contemplate. We cease to be our ordinary willing selves and become instead "pure will-less subjects of knowledge." What we come to know in experience of the beautiful is the universal essence of the thing that we behold. Schopenhauer believes that we contemplate the Platonic Form of the beautiful thing, although he interprets the Forms as various hierarchical levels through which the Will manifests itself. When we contemplate aesthetically, both the beholder and the object become universal. The beholder ceases to be his or her private self with personal, willful motives, and the object beheld becomes its universal essence. In aesthetic experience we leave willing behind.

In the case of art, as in the case of beautiful nature, the observer contemplates the eternal Forms behind phenomena. The aim of art is to communicate knowledge of the Forms. Artistic talent, or genius, is an unusually developed ability to contemplate the universal in phenomena. Because the talented artist has this ability, he or she is able to present objects of the world in a manner that makes the universal present to the audience. (The exception to this rule is music. Music does not represent phenomenal things in a universal light. Instead it portrays the movements of the will directly. Music, alone among the arts, bypasses the Platonic Forms and portrays the deeper reality that Schopenhauer believes is behind them.)

In the case both of beautiful art and beautiful nature, we expand our awareness of our own nature. Schopenhauer believes that the Platonic Forms are more real than the phenomenal things of our world; he thinks that our ordinary sense of ourselves as private, separate individualities is illusory. The Platonic Forms are themselves aspects of the Will. Thus, to the extent that aesthetic experience illuminates them, it illuminates our fundamental nature, which is the Will itself. Schopenhauer suggests that aesthetic experience is akin to ethical insight, and that frequent aesthetic experience is potentially good for our ethical orientation. Unfortunately, however, any insight we might gain from aesthetic experience is, for most of us, transient. As soon as aesthetic contemplation is over, most of us are immediately back in the willful fray.

3.   *Friedrich Nietzsche*

Nietzsche believed that aesthetic experience not only gives us insight into our true nature but also that it justifies life. Nietzsche postulates two aesthetic principles, the **Dionysian** and the **Apollonian.** Each of these principles guides a particular kind of aesthetic experience. Dionysian principle fashions art that is frenzied and chaotic; Dionysian experience communicates to the beholder a sense of our fundamental union with the dynamic reality of life. Apollonian principle depicts phenomena through beautiful, idealizing images; Apollonian experience communicates to the beholder a sense that the things of the world are clearly delineated and orderly. The paradigmatic Dionysian art is music; the paradigmatic Apollonian art is sculpture.

Thus, the Dionysian and the Apollonian principles each reveal something important about one's nature as a human being. The Dionysian principle reminds the individual of his participation in the dynamic flux of life. The Apollonian principle reinforces the individual's usual sense that he or she, like everything else, is separate and self-contained. Although Nietzsche concurs with Schopenhauer that this perspective is ultimately an illusion, he believes that it is a necessary illusion. We must, Nietzsche believes, behave as independent agents and believe that the world is relatively stable in order to accomplish the practical tasks essential to our sustained existence. Thus, both Apollonian and Dionysian perspectives remind us of something important about ourselves in relation to the world.

The Apollonian and Dionysian principles also remind us that life is worth living despite the suffering that it involves. Discussing the religion of the ancient Greeks, Nietzsche observes that the pantheon of gods and goddesses was invented by the Greeks under the sway of the Apollonian principle, for the gods and goddesses amounted to beautiful, idealizing images for aspects of human life. The gods, Nietzsche contends, justified human life by living it.

The Dionysian principle, too, had a role in the theodicy of the ancient Greeks. Nietzsche believes that the ancient Greeks used tragedy to reconcile the Apollonian and Dionysian modes of self-understanding. The subject matter of tragedy was explicitly the suffering of an individual, the tragic hero. In identifying with the tragic hero, the audience adopted the Apollonian perspective, which takes seriously the individual character of existence. Prior to the tragic catastrophe that befalls him, the tragic hero is preoccupied with individual pursuits.

The tragic catastrophe reveals the inherent fragility of individual existence and individual pursuits. From the Apollonian standpoint, the tragic hero has lost virtually everything. The audience is reminded of an important aspect of individual life—that it is inherently vulnerable.

At this point, however, the Dionysian principle reminds the audience that a human being's individual character is not the only aspect of his being. For even when he has suffered terribly as an individual, the tragic hero comes to recognize that he is still a part of the larger flux of being. This was what happened when the tragic hero made peace with the larger world order. The larger, Dionysian flux is so powerful and enthralling that this recognition is deeply joyous and sustaining.

Thus, when the Apollonian illusion that life is orderly and safe for the individual is destroyed, the tragic hero experiences the Dionysian insight that life is wonderful and joyous anyway. The ultimate purpose of tragedy was a spiritual one. It recalled its audience to an understanding of both Apollonian and Dionysian aspects of their lives, and it revealed the Dionysian truth that suffering is no argument against life's meaning.

By positing two aesthetic principles, Nietzsche challenged the traditional assumption that art had a single aim. Nietzsche's Apollonian principle embodied many traditional values, such as the aspiration for beautiful form and the desirability of closure. But his Dionysian principle made values of dynamism and chaos. Although the values of the Apollonian principle were compatible with disinterested contemplation, the Dionysian principle promoted interested participation. Nietzsche suggests with his duality that aesthetic experience can take more than one form, and that the various forms it can take might all be valuable to its audience's understanding of itself and its world.

F. ART AND REALITY IN THE TWENTIETH CENTURY

The twentieth century has produced many additional challenges to traditional aesthetics both from artistic and theoretical corners. Artists of various media deliberately have shirked such time-honored aesthetic values as closure and organic unity. Visual artists no longer necessarily aspire toward representation. And a large percentage of modern composers resist traditional tonal harmony as an organizing feature of their works. Meanwhile, philosopher Arthur Danto agrees with Hegel that the "death of art" is upon us. Reflective thought, Danto contends, has become both the formative agent and the aim of most modern art. Art is no longer a definitively spiritual activity.

Other twentieth-century challenges to the traditional conception of art have been radical reconsiderations of the tradition's assessment of art's relation to reality. José Ortega y Gasset attributes the unpopularity of the twentieth century to its predominant concern to "dehumanize" art. Ortega y Gasset sees this aspiration as a radical abandonment of the idea that art should illuminate reality. Art, in his view, inspires sentiments unrelated to those of everyday reality, and dehumanized art exists only for its own sake.

◆from *The Dehumanization of Art,* by José Ortega y Gasset

Far from going more or less clumsily toward reality, the artist is seen going against it. He is brazenly set on deforming reality, shattering its human aspect, dehumanizing it. With the things represented on traditional paintings we could have imaginary intercourse. Many a young Englishman has fallen in love with Gioconda. With the objects of modern pictures no intercourse is possible. By divesting them of their aspect of "lived" reality the artist has blown up the bridges and burned the ships that could have taken us back to our daily world. He leaves us locked up in an abstruse universe, surrounded by objects with which human dealings are inconceivable, and thus compels us to improvise other forms of intercourse completely distinct from our ordinary ways with things. We must invent unheard-of gestures to fit those singular figures. This new way of life which presupposes the annulment of spontaneous life is precisely what we call understanding and enjoyment of art. Not that this life lacks sentiments and passions, but those sentiments and passions evidently belong to a flora other than that which covers the hills and dales of primary and human life. What those ultra-objects[9] evoke in our inner artist are secondary passions, specifically aesthetic sentiments.

It may be said that, to achieve this result, it would be simpler to dismiss human forms—man, house, mountain—altogether and to construct entirely original figures. But, in the first place, this is not feasible.[10] Even in the most abstract ornamental line a stubborn reminiscence lurks of certain "natural" forms. Secondly—and this is the crucial point—the art of which we speak is inhuman not only because it contains no things human, but also because it is an explicit act of dehumanization. In his escape from the human world

---

[9]"Ultraism" is one of the most appropriate names that have been coined to denote the new sensibility.

[10]An attempt has been made in this extreme sense—in certain works by Picasso—but it has failed signally.

the young artist cares less for the *"terminus ad quem,"* the star-tling fauna at which he arrives, than for the *"terminus a quo,"* the human aspect which he destroys. The question is not to paint something altogether different from a man, a house, a mountain, but to paint a man who resembles a man as little as possible; a house that preserves of a house exactly what is needed to reveal the metamorphosis; a cone miraculously emerging—as the snake from his slough—from what used to be a mountain. For the modern artist, aesthetic pleasure derives from such a triumph over human matter. That is why he has to drive home the victory by present-ing in each case the strangled victim.[11]

John Dewey, by contrast, argues that art's distance from reality in the twentieth century is an illusion, largely created by our tendency to insist on a radical dichotomy between the aesthetic and the rest of our lives. If most of the twentieth-century art audience does not discover illumina-tion of the everyday in art, this is because they fail to recognize the germ of the aesthetic in the everyday.

In everyday experience we encounter tensions that aim at equilibrium and their ultimate resolutions. The basic rhythm of organic existence results from an organism's falling out of step with its environment and the restoration of equilibrium between the two. Art is thus built on the same pattern as the necessary rhythm of organic life. Our natural delight in artistic resolution of tensions is rooted in the satisfaction we feel when our own being, after being in tension with the environment, has reached a new and more highly developed state of adjustment than it has ever attained before. This fundamentally biological satisfaction, according to Dewey, is itself a kind of aesthetic delight.

Dewey contends that the kind of significance we give to meaningful experiences in our lives also is an aesthetic significance. When we de-scribe a situation in our past as "an experience," we are describing it as something unified. The tensions involved in the situation have run their course to completion and, as a result, the experience exhibits a kind of closure. As we recall "an experience" of this sort, we sense that the elements that compose it are integrated by a kind of pervasive emotion that Dewey describes as an "aesthetic quality." An aesthetic quality is a particular, unrepeatable feeling that we associate with the experience as a whole. Thus, the traditional aesthetic principles of closure and organic unity characterize the experiences that we designate as particularly significant in our lives.

As Dewey sees it, experiences of this sort are the primary unit of life. When we consider what makes our lives meaningful and significant, such experiences come to mind. We find an experience that we designate "an

[11] José Ortega y Gasset, *The Dehumanization of Art and Other Essays* (Princeton, NJ: Princeton University Press, 1948).

experience" intrinsically satisfying, even if the contents of the experience were less than comfortable at the time.

Observing the kinship between the experiences of life that are most meaningful to us and aesthetic experiences we have in connection with art, Dewey argues that aesthetic experience presents a challenge to philosophy. Our aim throughout life—the aim that philosophy desirably helps us reach—is to reconstruct our everyday experiences so that they become more determinate, harmonious, and meaningful. Art develops and accentuates what is characteristically valuable in the everyday. Art presents tensions that build to a culmination and resolution; aesthetic qualities that unify the effect of an artwork's materials dominate our experience of art. Therefore, if philosophy is to illuminate experience in general, it should examine art—which reveals experience in its integrity.

◆ **from *Art as Experience*,
by John Dewey**

THE CHALLENGE TO PHILOSOPHY

Esthetic experience is imaginative. This fact, in connection with a false idea of the nature of imagination, has obscured the larger fact that all *conscious* experience has of necessity some degree of imaginative quality. For while the roots of every experience are found in the interaction of a live creature with its environment, that experience becomes conscious, a matter of perception, only when meanings enter it that are derived from prior experiences. Imagination is the only gateway through which these meanings can find their way into a present interaction; or rather, as we have just seen, the conscious adjustment of the new and the old *is* imagination. Interaction of a living being with an environment is found in vegetative and animal life. But the experience enacted is human and conscious only as that which is given here and now is extended by meanings and values drawn from what is absent in fact and present only imaginatively.[12]

There is always a gap between the here and now of direct interaction and the past interactions whose funded result constitutes the meanings with which we grasp and understand what is now occurring. Because of this gap, all conscious perception involves a risk; it is a venture into the unknown, for as it assimilates the present to the past it also brings about some reconstruction of that past. When past and present fit exactly into one another, when there is only recurrence, complete uniformity, the resulting experience is routine and mechanical; it does not come to consciousness

[12]"Mind denotes a whole system of meanings as they are embodied in the workings of organic life. . . . Mind is a constant luminosity; consciousness is intermittent, a series of flashes of different intensities."

in perception. The inertia of habit overrides adaptation of the meaning of the here and now with that of experiences, without which there is no consciousness, the imaginative phase of experience.

Mind, that is the body of organized meanings by means of which events of the present have significance for us, does not always enter into the activities and undergoings that are going on here and now. Sometimes it is baffled and arrested. Then the stream of meanings aroused into activity by the present contact remain aloof. Then it forms the matter of reverie, of dream; ideas are floating, not anchored to any existence as its property, its possession of meanings. Emotions that are equally loose and floating cling to these ideas. The pleasure they afford is the reason why they are entertained and are allowed to occupy the scene; they are attached to existence only in a way that, as long as sanity abides, is felt to be only fanciful and unreal.

In every work of art, however, these meanings are actually embodied in a material which thereby becomes the medium for their expression. This fact constitutes the peculiarity of all experience that is definitely esthetic. Its imaginative quality dominates, because meanings and values that are wider and deeper than the particular here and now in which they are anchored are realized by way of *expressions* although not by way of an object that is physically efficacious in relation to other objects. Not even a useful object is produced except by the intervention of imagination. Some existent material was perceived in the light of relations and possibilities not hitherto realized when the steam engine was invented. But when the imagined possibilities were embodied in a new assemblage of natural materials, the steam engine took its place in nature as an object that has the same physical effects as those belonging to any other physical object. Steam did the physical work and produced the consequences that attend any expanding gas under definite physical conditions. The sole difference is that the conditions under which it operates have been arranged by human contrivance.

The work of art, however, unlike the machine, is not only the outcome of imagination, but operates imaginatively rather than in the realm of physical existences. What it does is to concentrate and enlarge an immediate experience. The formed matter of esthetic experience directly *expresses*, in other words, the meanings that are imaginatively evoked; it does not, like the material brought into new relations in a machine, merely provide *means* by which purposes over and beyond the existence of the object may be executed. And yet the meanings imaginatively summoned, assembled, and integrated are embodied in material existence that here and now interacts with the self. The work of art is thus a challenge to the performance of a like act of evocation and organization, through imagination, on the part of the one who experiences it. It is not just a stimulus to and means of an overt course of action.

This fact constitutes the uniqueness of esthetic experience, and this uniqueness is in turn a challenge to thought. It is particularly a challenge to that systematic thought called philosophy. For esthetic experience is experience in its integrity. Had not the term "pure" been so often abused in philosophic literature, had it not been so often employed to suggest that there is something alloyed, impure, in the very nature of experience and to denote something beyond experience, we might say that esthetic experience is pure experience. For it is experience freed from the forces that impede and confuse its development as experience; freed, that is, from factors that subordinate an experience as it is directly had to something beyond itself. To esthetic experience, then, the philosopher must go to understand what experience is.

For this reason, while the theory of esthetics put forth by a philosopher is incidentally a test of the capacity of its author to have the experience that is the subject-matter of his analysis, it is also much more than that. It is a test of the capacity of the system he puts forth to grasp the nature of experience itself. There is no test that so surely reveals the one-sidedness of a philosophy as its treatment of art and esthetic experience. Imaginative vision is the power that unifies all the constituents of the matter of a work of art, making a whole out of them in all their variety. Yet all the elements of our being that are displayed in special emphases and partial realizations in other experiences are merged in esthetic experience. And they are so completely merged in the immediate wholeness of the experience that each is submerged:—it does not present itself in consciousness as a distinct element.[13]

G. ART IN THE ESSENCE OF CULTURE: AFRICA

The category of "art" is in fact a relatively recent European invention. Cultures have been producing art for many thousands of years, of course, from the cave paintings in Lascaux, France, to the rich production of sculptures, paintings, weavings, and utensils in virtually every one of the world's cultures, whether urban and aesthetically sophisticated or a peasant culture in which aesthetics must serve daily necessity. But the idea of art as a separate and particularly precious realm, the "art for art's sake" of the late nineteenth century, is relatively rare. In most societies, art serves the purpose of religion, or social ritual and identification, or practical utility. But that raises a difficult philosophical question. The very concept of aesthetics, as practiced in the West since Plato, seems to presuppose the impractical place of art. Thus Plato criticizes at least some art as "nothing but an imitation of an imita-

---

[13]John Dewey, *Art as Experience* (New York: G. P. Putnam, 1934).

tion." The idea of taste as "subjective" is also a recent notion, dependent on art conceived to "please" rather than to serve.

In many societies, however, art plays a central role in the very identity of a culture without, nevertheless, calling attention to itself as art. African art, for example, serves many social and religious functions, and the notion of "pure art" or "art for art's sake," familiar only from the odd behavior of tourist collectors of "native art," has no place in that culture. But then, how should we think of art in such a society? Are our interpretations dependent on the native intentions and interpretations? And if they do not see their own beautiful creations as art, is it right for us to consider them so? In the following essay, American philosopher and art critic Arthur Danto considers the difficult question of "art versus artifact," and the cross-cultural question, what is art?

◆ **"Artifact and Art,"**
by Arthur C. Danto

Whatever they may mean, and however they may be perceived and responded to by their contemporaries, works of art are dense with latent properties that will be revealed and appreciated only later, through modes of consciousness contemporaries cannot have imagined. Because of the limits of historical or cultural imagination, whole arrays of artistic qualities may be invisible until released, as if by the transformative kiss in the fairy tale, through which the radiant prince is released from the frogdom in which he had been cast by a spell.

Because of the dilating substance of individual artworks in the backward illuminations of present art, the belief that art itself must lack a stable identity becomes irresistible, that anything can be a work of art even though it may not have had that exalted status when it was first made, and that the boundaries of art are themselves philosophically indeterminate. One chief purpose of the present essay is to resist this belief. It does not follow from the facts with which I began, namely that works of art have latencies that become actual when released by other, later works of art, that art itself, as a concept and category, has a corresponding openness. It is one thing to say that what a work of art is, is a function of what other works of art show it to be. It is quite another thing to say that whether something is a work of art at all is a function of what other things are works of art. The population of artworks is a mutually self-enriching system of objects, any given member of which is considerably richer because of the existence of other artworks than it would have been if it alone existed (it is an independently interesting question whether there could be only one artwork in the world). But something must already be an artwork to benefit from this enrichment. The boundary between art and the rest of reality is, on the other hand, philosophically inflexible. It is of course possible to *discover* something to be a work of art, even a great work of art, which before then was regarded as having occupied a vastly less exalted, vastly more dubious status.

I take Picasso to have been just such a discoverer when he underwent, in May or June of 1907, an epiphany among the dusty display cases in the ethnographic museum in the Palais du Trocadero. There, amidst the emblems of imperial conquest or scientific curiosity, admist what must have been taken as palpable evidence of the artistic superiority of European civilization and therein palpable justificatory grounds for cultural intervention, Picasso perceived absolute masterpieces of sculptural art, on a level of achievement attained only at their best by the acknowledged masterpieces of the Western sculptural tradition. "We have the habit of thinking that the power to create expressive plastic form is one of the greatest of human achievements," Roger Fry wrote in 1920 of an exhibition at the Chelsea Book Club of what he termed "Negro sculpture." "It seems unfair," he continued, "to be forced to admit that certain nameless savages have possessed this power not only in a higher degree than we at this moment, but than we as a nation have ever possessed it."

Picasso's discovery was possible only because painting and sculpture in his own tradition had undergone changes of a kind that made the values of African sculpture visible, at least to someone who had participated in effecting those changes. In this respect, I suppose, his relationship to art from an alien culture is of a piece with the relationship in which the Carracci stood at the end of the sixteenth century to Correggio at its beginning. Certain internal developments in Italian art, due in part to external developments in religious beliefs and institutions which mandated changes in artistic representation, made it possible to see, in work from which the Carracci were separated by decades, models to follow in Correggio, an artist who had been regarded as backward and provincial by his own contemporaries. Picasso's own breakthroughs, his powerful redefinition of the whole purpose of painting, like a great political revolution, raised those dispossessed African objects into the regions of high art from their erstwhile captivity in the precincts of ethnographic study. If Picasso had something of great moment to tell the world, so, against all probability, had they. In liberating himself from his own representational traditions, Picasso liberated the art of Africa from those same traditions, in the light of which they could not be seen for what they were. In the process, he restructured the way we were to see all of art by restructuring the way we saw *that* art.

One can discover only what is *already there* but has remained up until then unknown or misrecognized. My point then is that Picasso discovered, through the distortions induced by incorrect and misapplied artistic theories as much as by cultural prejudice, the fact—known or not—that the master carvers of Africa were artists and that artistic greatness was possible for them, not simply within their own traditions, but against the highest artistic standards anywhere.

A good philosophical procedure for drawing lines consists in imagining things on opposite sides of them that have in common as many properties as possible, for at least it will be plain that what divides them cannot be located in what they share. In drawing the distinction between artworks and mere things, for example, the history of contemporary art has been extremely fertile in generating things so outwardly similar that no perceptual criterion seems relevant to that task. . . . We might make the matter even more complicated by enlisting the current strategy of "appropriation," so that the contemporary artist "appropriates" the Primitive artifact and displays it as a work of art. Putting an object forward in an act of display does not help solve the problem, since often the identical object can be displayed either as a work of art or an artifact, though admittedly there are conventions of display which in practice remove or reduce the ambiguity.

I want to approach this question by a more detailed imaginary example. I shall invent a plausible anthropology for a pair of African tribes occupying distant regions of the same vaguely bounded area, but separated by some geographical feature that has enabled them to evolve in different ways, even though the differences may not be obvious to field investigators who are immediately if superficially impressed by the great resemblances between Tribe A and Tribe B, to be known respectively as the Pot People and the Basket Folk.

Both tribes are known for their baskets and their pots. The baskets are tightly woven and of an extreme simplicity of design. The pots have a certain squat elegance, and their smooth sides strike out from the base in a daring curve, and then curve back sharply, as if in emulation of the trajectory of a marvelous bird, to form the wide mouth, a perfect circle. The pots have a pattern of solid semicircles, like a necklace, circling their necks. Perhaps the tribes were part of a single nation in time past memory, for the pots and the baskets of one look exactly like the pots and baskets of the other. There are differences, even deep differences, but they are not of a kind that meets the eye. It is these I mean now to describe.

The Basket Folk—that is the name they give themselves and I shall respect their name—stand in a special relationship to their baskets, which are for them objects of great meaning and possessed of special powers, evidence for which resides in the fact that even years after they have been shaped, baskets left in the soft rain of the mountain slope where these people are found give off the odor of fresh grasses, as if they carried the memory of their beginnings—as if when touched by water the grasses return to their youth and strength, as the Basket Folk themselves hope to do after death. The baskets show, by profound analogy, that we carry our youth within ourselves as an eternal essence. The Wise Persons of this tribe tell us that the world itself is a basket, woven of grass and air and water by her whom I shall respect them by calling God, who is a Basketmaker. The basketmakers of the tribe imitate God in her creativity, much as painters and sculptors imitate God in His creativity, according to Giorgio Vasari. These works embody the principles of the universe itself, and each basket gives occasion for reflection at how the unlikely strands of the universe hold together by forces the Basket Folk regard as magic, and evidence of powers they can at most imitate (if they have a philosophy of art it is: art is imitation). Men, women, and animals are built upon the principles of the basket, a weave of grass and wind that unravels at death, but only momentarily. A man's wealth is in his baskets, and basketmakers are, appropriately, greatly respected. They are almost like priests.

The Basket Folk's potmakers, on the other hand, are artisans like any other. Pots are useful and necessary, every household has four or five, but however admired they may be by missionaries and ethnographers, the Basket Folk attach no further importance to them: they are of a piece with fishnets and arrow heads, textiles of bark and flax, or the armatures of wood that give shape to their dwellings. If they had the words, they would describe baskets as artworks, and their pots as artifacts. The baskets in any case belong to what Hegel has called Absolute Spirit: a realm of being which is that of art, religion, and philosophy. The pots are merely part of what, with his genius for phrase, he spoke of as The Prose of the World.

This philosophical allocation is precisely reversed in the worldview of their neighboring tribe, whose own practice I follow in calling them the Pot People. There is an ethic of craftsmanship that governs the manufacture of their baskets, whose meaning is their use as items of domestic life, whose essence is defined by daily function. The pots, by contrast, are thick with significations, for in them are stored the seeds, reserved from last year's harvest, to be used in the agricultural year to come. So the pots have a use, though this is quite transcended by their meaning. The Wise Persons among the Pot People say that God is a potmaker. . . . Indeed this people can hardly look upon pots without feeling themselves symbolically present at the beginning of the world order. Predictably, they hold that human beings, and most especially womenfolk, are pots, for they carry in their inner emptiness the seeds of the next generation. The semi-circles, incidentally, are half-moons, referring to the turning of the seasons, though the same semi-circles, in the Basket Folk culture, have no meaning to speak of—they simply say pots do not look right if they lack these—and specialists conjecture that some meaning has been lost. Basket aestheticians shrug their shoulders when queried about these marks, saying only that pots have always been made that way though admittedly they would carry water or store seeds quite as effectively without them. Pot people are by no means certain that the half-moons are irrelevant to the deep function of pots, which is, of course, to insure continuity, nourishment, well-being, and life. Lying at the cross point of art, philosophy, and religion, the pots of the Pot People belong to Absolute Spirit. Their baskets, tightly woven to insure sustained utility, are drab components in the Prose of the World.

It has at times struck anthropologists as curious that neither of these tribes, for all their evolved cosmology and artisan skill, should have among their cultural objects anything that seems to represent the human form. Their art accordingly seems truly primitive and merely symbolic. This observation would strike members of either tribe as perplexing and false. For the Basket Folk, human beings really are baskets; as for the Pot People they are pots. Missionaries reason patiently with their backward subjects, saying that anyone can see that there is no greater resemblance between a person and a pot than there is between a pot and a basket—we, made in the image of God, do not look like these mere things at all. And perhaps the anthropologist may point back and forth between the image of a Basket person and a basket—or a Pot person and a pot—the anthropologist feels that it hardly needs stating that they do not look alike, certainly not in the way a son looks like his father or two villagers resemble one another. For the Basket and the Pot persons, such considerations have no weight whatever. Anyone can see there is not this resemblance. Their point is that people really are, appearances notwithstanding, baskets (or pots), that like baskets (or pots) we are woven (or shaped) in mysterious ways, and, that for reasons no less mysterious, we become unravelled (or sharded). Of course the resemblances do not meet the eye, which is why we need Wise Persons to enable us to see and admire the deep harmonies and correspondences in the universe that move us to wonder.

. . . Let us imagine now a museum of fine arts in the capital of the country which financed their expeditions and field trips. It faces, across a park, a museum of natural history, much as the *Kunsthistorisches Museum* faces the *Naturhistorisches Museum* across the Mariatheresianplatz in Vienna—or The Metropolitan Museum of Art and the American Museum of Natural History stand on opposite sides of Central Park in New York. The Fine Arts Museum has a wing for anthropological art. The wing for Primitive art reflects the revolution in artistic perception ushered in by Picasso's discoveries at the Palais du Trocadero. It was realized that objects of the greatest artistic significance had been housed all these years in the anthropological wing of the Natural History Museum because of misapplied theories of art, very much like the theories that initially blinded critics to the merit of Impressionist and certainly of Post-Impressionist painting—theories which, if true, would in fact have ruled Picasso's work out as art, and explained it as the daubing of a madman or a charlatan trying to pull something over on us. All of that has changed, and everyone today is disposed to regard Primitive art as art of often the greatest degree of achievement. Collectors have donated some marvelous examples to the Fine Arts Museum, and enthusiasts and philanthropists have in fact built the wing, whose curators nevertheless look with envy across the park to the anthropological wing of the Natural History Museum, to which collectors had donated specimens and to which bales and boxes of Primitive carvings and assemblages were brought back for scientific purposes, and incidentally to enable citizens to see how really backward our black brothers really are, how considerable the distance is between them and us, as anyone with eyes to see with can see immediately and convincingly, by visiting the galleries of Renaissance painting and sculpture in the Museum of Fine Arts.

The curators of the Natural History Museum recognize the anomaly, but in the manner of their kind they are not in the least anxious to rectify it by giving their collections over to the Primitive Wing in exchange for certain of the Fine Art Museum's collections whose claim to art remains under contest—wrought iron work from medieval Spain, swords or halberds from Nuremburg, and certain other things, of unquestioned craft, which may forever be but high-class artifacts. With the objects gathered from the Basket Folk and the Pot People, there is no such problem. The baskets of the former and the pots of the latter are housed, as they should be, in the Primitive Wing of the Fine Arts Museum. The pots of the former and the baskets of the latter are properly displayed among the artifacts of the two tribes in the Museum of Natural History, possessed of no artistic significance—but that is not to say that they are without scientific meaning.

Philosophers have tended to address the problem of Other Cultures on the model of constructing a lexicon, and seeing the degree to which cross-cultural synonymy can be achieved through term-by-term pairings with our own language. This reveals the usual philosophical prejudices in semantical theory, that meaning is a matter of reference and that words mean what they refer to. If we cannot fix reference, we cannot fix meaning, and if meaning escapes us the Other Culture—or the Other Mind for that matter—is an impenetrable mystery. But this is really not the way to get into the minds the cultures shape. It is again through a system of philosophical thought that we must construct the questionnaires that are to take us into the other culture, and through which the contours of a concept will gradually reveal themselves and a map of the mind can be made. It is in this way, rather than by seeking references for the terms of their language, that we find out which are the artworks. The reference-class of *tekne* will give us a pool of artworks and artifacts, leading us to suppose that the Greeks drew no distinction between hammers or fishnets and statues and epics. But in any case, the criteria through which perception allows us to pick things out will not greatly help in identifying works of art when, as in the case of the two tribes we considered, the artifact of one might look exactly like the artwork of another. What makes the one an artwork is the fact that, just as a human action gives embodiment to a thought, the artwork embodies something we could not conceptualize without the material object which conveys its soul.

My sense is that the philosophical structure of African artworks is the same as the philosophical structure of artworks in any culture. If a human being is a compound in relationships of spirit and body that keep philosophers tossing sleeplessly in their beds, an artwork is a compound of thought and matter. The material thing makes the thought. What makes the artworks of Africa different from those of Greece are the hidden things they embody or make objective, giving them a presence in the lives of men and women. The works have a power artifacts could not possibly have because of the spiritual content they embody. An artifact is shaped by its function, but the shape of an artwork is given by its content. The forms of African art are powerful because the ideas they express are ideas about power or perhaps what they express are the powers themselves.[14]

H. THE OTHER HALF OF THE PICTURE: FEMINIST AESTHETICS AND WOMEN ARTISTS

Just as philosophy has been historically dominated by men, the most celebrated arts have been dominated by male artists as well. Of course, many of the crafts and "minor arts," including such practical arts as weaving, everyday clothes design, potmaking, and decorating have been the primary province of women, but often these arts become dominated by men as they become more prestigious. Witness cooking in France and more recently in America, where many of the best-known chefs are men. But in the most prestigious "fine arts," sculpture and painting, the Western tradition is overwhelmingly dominated by male artists. Even today, according to a major art publication in America, 80 to 90 percent of the art works shown will be by men, and only a small percentage by women.

Feminists have argued, in aesthetics as in other branches of philosophy, that there are considerable differences between the way men and women experience art, and so too, considerable differences between male and female artists. In the following selections, two prominent feminists discuss these differences. Marilyn French first answers the question, "Is there a peculiarly feminist aesthetic?" Then Linda Nochlin, an art historian, suggests a very different, "institutional" answer to the

[14]Reproduced by kind permission of the author.

question, "Why have there been no great women artists in the rich history of Western art?"

◆ "Is There a Feminist Aesthetic?"
by Marilyn French

It is questionable whether the terms and issues of traditional aesthetics are applicable to feminist art. Some critics claim traditional aesthetic principles are universal, and that art is "above" sex, or at least, that sex is irrelevant to it. There is an art which is specifically feminist: that much is clear. Some, by virtue of its feminism, would deny it the title *art,* arguing that its political interest violates aesthetic standards. An aesthetics like Susanne Langer's, which defines what art creates and is indeed universal, fits feminist art as well as any other (Langer 1953). But most aesthetics are more prescriptive, and therefore more political: feminism has taught us that all critical approaches imply political standards, however tacitly. Before we can evaluate feminist art by any aesthetic principles, we need a definition of the art. In what follows, I will discuss the characteristics of feminist art as I understand them. For the sake of brevity, I will limit myself to the art I know best, literature; but the principles have parallels in the other arts.

The clearest proof of the existence of a feminist aesthetics is the distaste or rage feminists feel on encountering works that violate it. Sometimes a negative response seems to refer to subject matter— for example, I loathe lingering loving descriptions of mutilations of female bodies; yet when a writer like Andrea Dworkin treats such a theme, I feel it to be not offensive, but only unpleasant—it falls within the boundaries of "taste." So it is less subject-matter (content) than treatment (style) that is at issue. . . . Perhaps all a prescriptive aesthetic can be is a set of principles describing a particular style, a taste.

There are two fundamental, related principles that mark a work of art as feminist: 1.) it approaches reality from a feminist perspective; and 2.) it endorses female experience. Each principle has several ramifications, so is more complicated than it sounds.

In a work with a feminist perspective, the narrational point of view, the point of view lying behind the characters and events, penetrates, demystifies, or challenges patriarchal ideologies. So much has been written about patriarchy in the last two decades that one tends to assume readers understand the term; yet I have met highly educated people who do not understand the feminist use of the term, so I'll explain it briefly. Patriarchy is a way of thinking, a set of assumptions that has been translated into various structures or ideologies. The assumptions are, first: males are superior to females. Their superiority may be granted by a deity or by nature, but it is absolute in conferring on men authority over women.

Second: males have individual destinies; they are promised domination, a surrogate godhead, transcendence over the natural world through power in heroism, sainthood, or some form of transcendent paternity—founding a dynasty, an institution, a religion, or a state, or creating an enduring work of art or technology. Third: the form taken by patriarchy is hierarchy, a structure designed to maintain and transmit power from spiritual father to spiritual son. This form absolutely excludes females unless they "make themselves male" (the requirement Jesus places on women entering "the Life" in the gnostic Gospel of Thomas) (1977). Women control biological transmission, the ability to bring forth young passed from mother to daughter. Having this power, they must be excluded from institutional power—which was modeled on the biological sort—if they are not to overwhelm men. Females have only a "natural" destiny; interchangeable parts of nature's cycles, they are maids (in both senses), who become mothers, and finally widows (or hags), in which avatar they are expendable.

Finally, domination is divine, so to pursue it is noble, heroic, glorious. The material to be dominated is, essentially, nature—all women; the body and emotions; "bestial" men; and natural processes, the flux and transitoriness of time, material decay, life itself. Patriarchal works focus on individual males who pursue glory; lonely, self-made and self-defeating, men are isolated from community and exiled forever from the "female" fate of happiness.

Since almost all modern worlds are patriarchal, feminist literature necessarily depicts patriarchy. But it does not underwrite its standards. Feminist literature may show patriarchal attitudes destroying a character or a world, but the narrative does not approve the destruction. When, in *The Faerie Queene,* Guyon destroys the luscious female world called The Bower of Bliss, Spenser, who has used his highest imaginative skills to create the Bower, judiciously approves its ruin. This is true also of Vergil in *The Aeneid.* The poet sighs about the tears of things *(lacrimae rerum),* regretting that beauty and feeling (Dido and sexual love for instance) are destroyed in the pursuit of glory, yet approves Aeneas's desertion of Dido, and his slaughter of those who oppose his domination. Aeneas's destiny is to found Rome; it overrides humanitarian or emotional concerns. Clearly, despite their feelings, both poets uphold patriarchy.

It is less clear where Tolstoy stands in *Anna Karenina,* or Austen in *Pride and Prejudice.* Both authors accept the patriarchal societies in which they live. Yet the pity Tolstoy lavishes on Anna, and the acute irony with which Austen pricks upper-class pretention and the unctuous ambition of the middle-classes, subvert patriarchal standards. This sympathy is not in the eye of the reader; it is built-in. Tolstoy's novel induces readers to feel the world lessened by Anna's death, rather than to feel that it was necessary, like Dido's, to a greater purpose. Austen's heroines maintain self-respect and integrity (wholeness) even as they triumph within a patriarchal structure. Many works of the past three centuries stretch patriarchal standards in this way; they are not feminist, but do not wholly support patriarchy either.

The feminist perspective is partly a reversal of patriarchal views. Feminism sees women as at least equal to men, humanly if not politically or economically; it considers transcendence illusory or factitious and pursuit of power a fatally doomed enterprise, since it cannot ever be satisfied, and usually or always involves the destruction of vital qualities and even life itself. Domination is not divine but lethal to dominator and dominated. It harms the dominator by cutting him off from trust and mutuality, the foundations of friendship and love, the two primary values; it harms the dominated by forcing them into dependency, which precludes truth in relationships. Domination creates false forms of friendship (society) and love (conventional marriage) which mask power relations. And feminist art focuses on people as wholes; the human is made up of body and emotion as well as mind and spirit; she is also part of a community, connected to others; and—on the broadest level—to nature in both positive and negative aspects.

The second principle is equally complicated. To endorse women's experience, feminist art must present it honestly, wholly. This is difficult because literature, like all art, is made up of conventions which are particularly marked in the area of gender. Just as it would be startling to observe a painting of a male nude reclining seductively à la Maja, or Olympe, or of a clothed female Picasso contemplating a naked male with emphatic genitals, literary shifts in presentation of gender startle, distracting attention from *what* is being shown to *the fact* that it is shown. A work's political impact obliterates its other features. This means that either considerable time—decades or even centuries—must elapse before readers can concentrate on what is being shown, or the work will be forgotten without this ever happening. And conventions governing female characters in literature are extraordinarily powerful and tenacious.

One convention holds women's work trivial, insignificant, uninteresting. Indeed, even men's work was considered an inappropriate subject for literature until recently. Yet work fills our lives; domestic work *is* most women's entire life and takes up considerable time even for women who also work outside the home. What such work means to one's sense of self, of the larger world; how it affects a woman's relation to her children, mates, lovers, friends; its pleasures, pains, the personal and political consequences of endless work for which one is not paid: these experiences remain relatively unexplored because of convention.

Conventionally, women's stories had happy endings, usually marriage to a prince and living happily ever after—unless the heroine is guilty of a sexual transgression, in which case she is required to die. This convention has stretched to allow sexual women to survive, but readers still complain when a "good" woman does not live happily ever after. The assumption behind this convention seems to be that the world is ruled by a male bar of justice. All female characters come up before this bar, and males being just, grant the good ones happiness—a female, not a male condition (male heroes almost never live happily ever after). If the author does not grant a virtuous female character eternal felicity, either she doesn't deserve it or the male bar is not just. Since in a patriarchal world the latter is unthinkable, her virtue must be deceptive. So male critics pore over Shakespeare's Cordelia searching for the hidden flaw that explains her fate and alter Edith Wharton's perception of her heroines (who *are* flawed), making them responsible for their own unhappiness.

If the definition of a "good" woman no longer involves chastity, heroines are still required to be sweet, vulnerable, *likeable*. Readers do not expect sweetness or honesty of male protagonists: they don't even have to be likeable: consider the heroes of *Under the Volcano, Notes from Underground, Look Back in Anger*. Authoritative, angry, rebellious heroines make most readers impatient; they tend to blame the character for not finding a way to be happy. I think about Andrea Dworkin's *Ice and Fire*, which could not at first find an American publisher, or my own *The Bleeding Heart*, which female and male reviewers (if not readers) uniformly condemned. Actual women, we ourselves, may walk around in a constant state of rage and yet reject heroines like us. The most lethal combination is authority and sexuality; it is almost impossible to depict a woman with both except as a villain.

· · · · · · · · · ·

These principles may sound limiting, as if feminist work could deal only and always with the middle ground, the mundane, the probable, eschewing flights of fancy, excessive characters, extremes of good and evil. This is not at all the case, although precisely that middle ground needs examination. Consider that for the 2500+ years of its existence, Western philosophy has looked at life strictly from a male perspective, and strictly as if men were constituted only of intellect, ambition, and political concern; as if they never had to deal with upset stomachs, irritation at their children, emotional dependency, hunger, or distress at growing bald. As Nietzsche pointed out, philosophy has ignored and dismissed the life of the body and the emotions, and—I would add—social involvement with women and children. It has been able to show men transcending only by pretending that the mundane does not exist and that other people do not matter.[15]

◆ **"Why Are There No Great Women Artists?"**
by Linda Nochlin

"Why are there no great women artists?" This question tolls reproachfully in the background of discussions of the so-called

[15]Marilyn French, "Is There a Feminist Aesthetic?" in *Hypatia* 5 no. 2 (Summer 1990).

woman problem, causing men to shake their heads regretfully and women to grind their teeth in frustration. Like so many other questions involved in the red-hot feminist controversy, it falsifies the nature of the issue at the same time that it insidiously supplies its own answer: "There are no great women artists because women are incapable of greatness." The assumptions lying behind such a question are varied in range and sophistication, running anywhere from "scientifically" proven demonstrations of the inability of human beings with wombs rather than penises to create anything significant, to relatively open-minded wonderment that women, despite so many years of near-equality—and after all, a lot of men have had their disadvantages too—have still not achieved anything of major significance in the visual arts.

The feminist's first reaction is to swallow the bait, hook, line and sinker and to attempt to answer the question as it is put: that is, to dig up examples of worthy or insufficiently appreciated women artists throughout history; to rehabilitate rather modest, if interesting and productive careers; to rediscover forgotten flower painters or David-followers and make out a case for them; to demonstrate that Berthe Morisot was really less dependent upon Manet than one had been led to think—in other words, to engage in activity not too different from that of the average scholar, man or woman, making out a case for the importance of his own neglected or minor master. Whether undertaken from a feminist point of view, such attempts, like the ambitious article on women artists which appeared in the 1858 *Westminster Review,* or more recent scholarly studies and reevaluations of individual woman artists like Angelica Kauffmann or Artemisia Gentileschi, are certainly well worth the effort, adding to our knowledge both of women's achievement and of art history generally; and a great deal still remains to be done in this area. Unfortunately, such efforts, if written from an uncritically feminist viewpoint, do nothing to question the assumptions lying behind the question "Why are there no great women artists?"; on the contrary, by attempting to answer it and by doing so inadequately, they merely reinforce its negative implications.

At the same time that champions of women's equality may feel called upon to falsify the testimony of their own judgment by scraping up neglected female artistic geniuses or puffing up the endeavors of genuinely excellent but decidedly minor women painters and sculptors into major contributions, they may resort to the easily refuted ploy of accusing the questioner of using "male" standards as the criterion of greatness or excellence. This attempt to answer the question involves shifting the ground slightly; by asserting, as many contemporary feminists do, that there is actually a different kind of greatness for women's art than for men's, one tacitly assumes the existence of a distinctive and recognizable feminine style, differing in both its formal and its expressive qualities from that of male artists and positing the unique character of women's situation and experience.

This, on the surface of it, seems reasonable enough: in general, women's experience and situation in society, and hence as artists, is different from men's; certainly, the art produced by a group of consciously united and purposefully articulate women intent on bodying forth a group consciousness of feminine experience might be stylistically identifiable as feminist, if not feminine art. Unfortunately, this remains within the realm of possibility; so far, it has not occurred. While the Danube School, Caravaggio's followers, the painters gathered around Gauguin at Pont Aven, the Blue Rider, or the Cubists may be recognized by certain clearly defined stylistic or expressive qualities, no such common qualities of femininity would seem to link the styles of women artists generally, any more than such qualities can be said to link all women writers. . . . In every instance women artists and writers would seem to be closer to other artists and writers of their own period and outlook than they are to each other.

· · · · · · · · · ·

The problem here lies not so much with the feminists' concept of what femininity is, but rather with their misconception of what art is: with the naive idea that art is the direct, personal expression of individual emotional experience, a translation of personal life into visual terms. Art is almost never that, great art certainly never. The making of art involves a self-consistent language of form, more or less dependent upon, or free from, given temporally defined conventions, schemata, or systems of notation, which have to be learned or worked out, either through teaching, apprenticeship, or a long period of individual experimentation. The language of art is, more materially, embodied in paint and line on canvas or paper, in stone or clay or plastic or metal—it is neither a sob story nor a hoarse, confidential whisper. The fact of the matter is that there have been no great women artists, as far as we know—although there have been many interesting and good ones who have not been sufficiently investigated or appreciated—or any great Lithuanian jazz pianists, or Eskimo tennis players, no matter how much we might wish there had been. That this should be the case is regrettable, but no amount of manipulating the historical or critical evidence will alter the situation; neither will accusations of male-chauvinist distortions of history and obfuscation of actual achievements of women artists (or black physicists or Lithuanian jazz musicians). The fact is that there *are* no women equivalents for Michelangelo or Rembrandt, Delacroix or Cézanne, Picasso or Matisse, or even, in very recent times, for de Kooning or Warhol, any more than there are any black American equivalents for the same. If there actually were large numbers of "hidden" great women artists, or if there really should be different standards for women's art as opposed to men's—and logically, one cannot have it both ways—then what would feminists be fighting for? If women have in fact achieved the same status as men in the arts, then the status quo is fine as it is.

But in actuality things as they are and as they have been in the arts, as in a hundred other areas, are stultifying, oppressive and discouraging to all who did not have the good fortune to be born white, preferably middle-class or above, males. The fault lies not in our stars, our hormones, our menstrual cycles, or our empty internal spaces, but in our institutions and our education—education understood to include everything that happens to us from the moment we enter, head first, into this world of meaningful symbols, signs, and signals. The miracle is, in fact, that given the overwhelming odds against women, so many have managed to achieve so much in bailiwicks of masculine prerogative like science, politics, or the arts. In some areas, indeed, women have achieved equality. While there may have been no great women composers, there have been great women singers; if no female Shakespeares, there have been Rachels, Bernhardts and Duses, to name only a few great women stage performers. Where there is a need there is a way, institutionally speaking: once the public and the authors themselves demanded more realism and range than boys in drag or piping castrati could offer, a way was found to include women in the institutional structure of the performing arts, even if in some cases they might have to do a little whoring on the side to keep their careers in order. In fact, in some of the performing arts like the ballet, women have exercised a virtual monopoly on greatness, though, it is true, they generally had to serve themselves up to Grand Dukes or aspiring bankers as an added professional obligation. . . .

Now the women problem, like all human problems, so-called (and the very idea of calling anything to do with human beings a problem is, of course, a fairly recent one), and unlike mathematical or scientific ones, is not amenable to solution at all, since what human problems involve is an actual reinterpretation of the nature of the situation, or even a radical alteration of stance or program of action *on the part of the problems themselves,* recourses unavailable to mathematical symbols, molecules, or microbes. In other words, the "objects" involved in the solution to human problems are at the same time *subjects,* capable of turning on that other group of human beings who has decided that their fellows are problem-objects to be solved, and capable of refusing both the solution, and, at the same time, the status of being problematic at all. Thus, women and their situation in the arts, as in other realms of endeavor, are not a problem to be viewed through the eyes of the dominant male power elite, at whose will or whose whim their demands may possibly some day be answered, at masculine convenience, of course. Women must conceive of themselves as potentially—if not actually—equal subjects, willing to look the facts of their situation as an institutional and objective problem not merely as a personal and subjective one, full in the face, without self-pity or copouts. Yet at the same time, they must view their situation with that high degree of emotional and intellectual commitment necessary to create a world in which truly equal achievement will be not only made possible, but actively encouraged by social institutions.

It is certainly not realistic to hope, as some feminists optimistically do, that a majority of men in the arts or in any other field will soon see that it is actually in their own self-interest to grant complete equality to women or to maintain that men themselves will soon realize that they are diminished by denying themselves access to traditionally feminine realms and emotional reactions. After all, there are few areas that are really denied to men, if the level of operations demanded be transcendent, responsible, or rewarding enough: men who have a need for feminine involvement with babies or children can certainly fulfill their needs adequately, and gain status and a sense of achievement to boot, in the field of pediatrics or child psychology, with a female nurse to do the more routine work; those who feel the urge for creativity at the stove may gain fame as master chefs or restaurateurs; and of course, men who yearn to fulfill themselves through what are often termed feminine artistic interests can easily find themselves as painters or sculptors, rather than as volunteer museum aides or as part-time ceramicists, as their presumably more aesthetically oriented female counterparts so often end up. As far as scholarship is concerned, how many men would really be willing to exchange their roles as teachers and researchers for that of unpaid, part-time research assistants and typists as well as full-time nannies and domestic workers?

It is only the extraordinarily enlightened or altruistic man who can really want to grant—the term itself is revealing—equality to women, and he will certainly not offer to switch places with one under present circumstances; on the contrary, he realizes that true equality for women will certainly involve considerable sacrifice of comfort, convenience, not to speak of ego-support and "natural" prerogatives, even down to the assumption that "he" is the subject of every sentence unless otherwise stated. Such sacrifices are not made lightly. It is unlikely that the French aristocracy in the eighteenth century would willingly have changed places with the Third Estate, or even granted its members a shred more privilege than they already had, unless forced to do so by the French Revolution; the working classes did not convince their capitalist employers that it would actually be to the latters' advantage to grant them a living wage and a modicum of security until after a long and bloody struggle when unions could reinforce such modest demands; certainly, the slaveowners of the South were willing to go to war to preserve their way of life with its still viable social and economic advantages, conferred by the possession of black slaves. While some of the more enlightened slaveowners may have granted freedom to their slaves, certainly none of them in their right minds could have ever suggested in anything but a spirit of black humor that he might prefer the carefree, irresponsible, watermelon-eating, spiritual-singing life of the darky to his own burdensome superiority. "I've got plenty of nothin' " is the tag-line of bad faith, coined by the uneasy conscience that would metamorphose the powerless victim into the lucky devil. It is through such bad faith that the holders of power can avoid the sacrifices that a truly egalitarian society would demand of all holders of privilege. It is no wonder that those who have such privilege inevitably hold on to it, and hold tight, no matter how marginal the advantage involved, until compelled to bow to superior power of one sort or another.

Thus, the question of women's equality—in art as in any other realm—devolves not upon the relative benevolence or ill-will of individual men, or the self-confidence or abjectness of individual women, but rather on the very nature of our institutional structures themselves and the view of reality that they impose on the human beings who are part of them. As John Stuart Mill pointed out more than a century ago: "Everything which is usual appears natural. The subjection of women to men being a universal custom, any departure from it quite naturally appears unnatural." Most men, despite lip service to equality, are reluctant to give up this natural order of things in which their advantages so far outweigh their disadvantages; for women the case is further complicated by the fact that, as Mill astutely pointed out, theirs is the only oppressed group or caste whose masters demand not only submission, but unqualified affection as well; thus, women are often weakened by the internalized demands of the male-dominated society itself, as well as by a plethora of material goods and comforts: the middle-class woman has a great deal more to lose than her chains.[16]

SUMMARY AND CONCLUSION

Philosophy includes the study of the Beautiful as well as the metaphysical, epistemological, and ethical concerns for the True and the Good. The experience of the beautiful usually is referred to as "aesthetics" and, typically, it is bound up with the study of art and artworks. But Plato took as his example the beautiful person and distrusted art; Kant took as his paradigm the beauty of nature and its ultimate significance, the inspiration to be moral. Foremost among the concerns that have dominated aesthetics since ancient times are the questions of how one can justify an aesthetic judgment and what is the place of art in society. Plato gave the first question a powerful answer, suggesting that our sense of beauty is in fact the recognition of a transcendent Form of Beauty. But he answered the second question with considerable suspicion, and ever since art has seemed at least to some philosophers to be more of a distraction than an important addition to social life.

[16]Linda Nochlin, "Why Are There No Great Women Artists?" in *Woman in Sexist Society,* ed. Vivian Gornick and Barbara K. Moran (New York: Basic Books, 1971).

Aristotle countered that art plays a vital role in everyday life, both as innocent entertainment and as a model of a kind of perfection. Christian thought often sided with Plato on this question, but modern thought tended to move back toward Aristotle. David Hume raised the serious challenge as to whether there could be any "objective" decision about the quality of art; Immanuel Kant answered Hume by saying that it is the very nature of our mental faculties that explains taste and our sense of beauty. Hegel, Schopenhauer, and Nietzsche defended the view that art provides a means of self-awareness, and therein lies its importance. The twentieth century has raised new questions as art has become more abstract and less representational—which José Ortega y Gasset calls "dehumanization" but John Dewey defends as a fundamental human experience. Finally, a new awareness of non-Western art and of gender in Western art has aroused contemporary sensibilities and created new challenges.

GLOSSARY

aesthetics   the study of beauty and the experience of the beautiful.
Apollonian   (Nietzsche)   the rational principle in art, Form.
catharsis   (Aristotle)   the purging (or purifying) of emotion through art.
closure   coming to a satisfactory end or conclusion, self-contained.
Dionysian   (Nietzsche)   the irrational principle in art, energy, willfulness.
free play   (Kant) the interplay between the imagination and the understanding that produces the sense of beauty.
imagination   (Kant)   that mental faculty responsible for the production (and reproduction) of representations.
intersubjective   experience shared by different subjects.
purposiveness without a purpose   (Kant)   the idea that the elements of a beautiful object seem to cohere as if toward a purpose, but we can find no definite purpose. For example, a sunset seems to us a unified aesthetic phenomenon, but there obviously is no "purpose" to a sunset.
understanding   (Kant)   the faculty that provides determinate concepts to experience.
will   (Schopenhauer)   the ultimate irrational force, which art allows us to escape (temporarily).

◆ *BIBLIOGRAPHY AND FURTHER READING* ◆

Plato, *Symposium,* trans. Paul Woodruff and Alexander Nehamas (soon to be published) (Indianapolis, IN: Hackett). Plato, *The Republic,* trans. G. M. A. Grube (Indianapolis, IN: Hackett, 1974). Plato, *The Ion,* trans. Paul Woodruff (Indianapolis, IN: Hackett, 1983). Aristotle, *Poetics,* trans. W. D. Ross (Oxford: Clarendon Press, 1946). Immanuel Kant, *Critique of Judgment,* trans. W. Pluhar (Indianapolis, IN: Hackett, 1987). David Hume, "Of the Standard of Taste" in *Essays on Morality, Politics and Literature,* ed. T. H. Green (London: Longmans, 1882). G. W. F. Hegel, *Art, Religion, Philosophy,* ed. J.

Glenn Gray (New York: Harper & Row, 1970). G. W. F. Hegel, *Aesthetics: Lectures on Fine Arts,* trans. T. M. Knox (2 vols.) (New York: Oxford University Press, 1975). Friedrich Nietzsche, *The Birth of Tragedy,* trans. Walter Kaufmann (New York: Random House, 1967). José Ortega y Gasset, *The Dehumanization of Art and Other Essays* (Princeton: Princeton University Press, 1948). Arthur Schopenhauer, *The World As Will and Idea,* trans. E. F. J. Payne (2 vols.) (New York: Dover, 1958). Leo Tolstoy, *What Is Art?* trans. Louise and Aylmer Maude (New York: Oxford University Press, 1930). Two general anthologies are A. Hofstadter and R. Kuhns, eds., *Philosophies of Art and Beauty* (Chicago: Chicago University Press, 1964), and R. Stern and E. Robinson, eds., *Changing Concepts of Art* (New York: Haven, 1983). For a recent treatment of the philosophy of art, see Arthur Danto, *Transfiguration of the Commonplace* (Cambridge, MA: Harvard University Press, 1981).

BRIEF BIOGRAPHIES

Anaximander (611–547? B.C.) Pre-Socratic philosopher who taught that reality is ultimately composed of an indeterminate something that we can never know directly through experience.

Anaximenes (6th century B.C.) Pre-Socratic philosopher who taught that the basic element of reality was air and that all things in the universe are different forms of air.

Anselm, Saint (1033–1109) Archbishop of Canterbury and author of the ontological argument for God's existence. He was one of the main defenders of the intellect and "understanding" against the then current anti-intellectualism of the Church. He is best known for his *Monologion* and *Proslogion*, in which the ontological argument is developed.

Aquinas, Saint Thomas (1225–1274) Architect of the most comprehensive theological structure of the Roman Catholic Church, the *Summa Theologica*, which has long been recognized as the "official" statement of orthodox Christian beliefs by many theologians. Aquinas drew many of his arguments from Aristotle, as can be seen in his "five ways" of demonstrating the existence of God.

Aristippus (435?–356? B.C.) One of the Cynics and a student of Socrates, who taught that the good life consists solely of immediate pleasures.

Aristotle (384–322 B.C.) One of the greatest Western philosophers. Aristotle was born in northern Greece (Stagira). His father was the physician to Philip, king of Macedonia, and he himself was to become the tutor to Philip's son, Alexander the Great. For eighteen years Aristotle was a student in Plato's academy in Athens, where he learned and parted from Plato's views. After Plato's death, he turned to the study of biology, and many of his theories ruled Western science until the Renaissance. He was with Alexander until 335 B.C., when he returned to Athens to set up his own school, the Lyceum. After Alexander's death, the anti-Macedonian sentiment in Athens forced Aristotle to flee (commenting that the Athenians would not sin twice against philosophy). In addition to his biological studies, Aristotle virtually created the sciences of logic and linguistics, developed extravagant theories in physics and astronomy, and made significant contributions to metaphysics, ethics, politics, and aesthetics. His *Metaphysics* is still a basic text on the subject, and *Nicomachean Ethics* codified ancient Greek morality. This latter work stresses individual virtue and excellence for a small elite of Greek citizens. The best life of all, according to Aristotle, is the life of contemplation, that is, the life of a philosopher, for it is the most self-contained and the "closest to the gods." But such contemplation must be together with the pleasures of life, honor, wealth, and virtuous action.

Augustine, Saint (354–430) The main figure in the development of medieval Christian thought from its roots in classical Greece and Rome. Augustine was born in North Africa and lived during the decline of the Roman Empire. After exploring various pagan beliefs, he was converted to Christianity and became Bishop of Hippo in North Africa. He is best known for his theological treatise *The City of God* and for his very personal *Confessions.*

Austin, John Langshaw (1911–1960) Oxford "ordinary-language" philosopher who had enormous influence on the development of "therapeutic" philosophy through attention to the details and nuances of everyday speech.

Ayer, Alfred J. (1910–   ) Oxford philosopher who became the major British defender of the powerful philosophical movement called logical positivism (logical empiricism). His *Language, Truth and Logic* (1936) was England's (and soon America's) first introduction to the very important work that had been developed in Austria by Rudolf Carnap, Hans Reichenbach, Moritz Schlick, C. G. Hempel, and Otto Neurath (the "Vienna Circle"). The main thesis of *Language, Truth and Logic,* and of logical positivism in general, is, in an updated version of Hume, that all knowledge can be divided only into matters of empirical fact and matters of language and logic and that all other claims are "meaningless," including the concepts of metaphysics, religion, ethics, and aesthetics.

Baumgarten, Alexander Gottlieb (1714–1762) German aesthetician, influential in the years immediately preceding Immanuel Kant.

Bayle, Pierre (1647–1706) Enlightenment philosopher and teacher. His *Historical and Critical Dictionary* (1697) influenced Voltaire and much of the Enlightenment.

Bentham, Jeremy (1748–1832) A leader in the legal reform movement in England and the founding father of that ethical position called utilitarianism. His *principle of utility,* which says that one should act to produce the greatest good for the greatest number of people, was the central theme of utilitarianism and slowly worked its way into the confusion of rules and statutes that constituted the English legal system of his day. His best-known work is his *Introduction to the Principles of Morals and Legislation* (1789).

Berkeley, Bishop George (1685–1753) Wrote virtually all the works that made him famous before he turned twenty-eight. He was born, raised, and educated in Ireland, and as a student he immersed himself in the writings of the important philosophers of the time, particularly Locke, Newton, and some of the French metaphysicians. In later life, Berkeley became an educational missionary, visiting America and Bermuda, and then a bishop, eventually moving to Oxford. Unlike Locke and Hume, whose interests spread across the whole of philosophy, science, and human affairs, Berkeley restricted himself to a single problem—perception—and his entire philosophy is aptly summarized in his famous phrase "to be is to be perceived" *(esse est percipi).* His arguments for this position are most thoroughly outlined in his *Treatise Concerning the Principles of Human Knowledge* (1710).

Blanshard, Brand (1892–) Contemporary idealist and main American defender of the coherence theory of truth, still working at Yale University.

Bradley, Francis Herbert (1846–1924) The best-known and perhaps the most brilliant of the "British idealists" working at the turn of the century. He is best known for his work *Appearance and Reality* (1893), in which he argues a very strong version of the coherence theory of truth.

Buddha (6th century B.C.) The "Awakened One"; a name for the founder of the Buddhist religion; the ancient Indian prince, Siddharta Gautama, after his enlightenment.

Butler, Bishop Joseph (1692–1752) Powerful English clergyman who formulated what are still recognized as the standard arguments against psychological egoism in his *Fifteen Sermons* (1726).

Churchland, Paul (1942–) American philosopher at the University of California, San Diego; specialist in cognitive science and the interplay between philosophy, computer science, and neurology.

Confucius (6th–5th century B.C.) Ancient Chinese sage and founder of the Confucian religion. His doctrine sought "gentlemanly conduct," which was to be achieved through adherence to ritual.

Cynics (4th century B.C.) Group of post-Socratic philosophers who taught that the good life was a life of complete autonomy. Therefore they minimized the social values of success, wealth, and honor and focused their attention on what makes a person wholly self-sufficient. For Diogenes, this consisted of the simplest life possible, based upon simple pleasures and simple virtues. For Aristippus, this consisted of a life of immediate pleasure.

Davidson, Donald (1917–) Contemporary American philosopher who has become one of the leading philosophers of language in the world. One of his continuing efforts is to generalize Alfred Tarski's semantic theory of truth as a general theory of truth for natural languages.

Democritus (5th century B.C.) Pre-Socratic philosopher who taught that reality is divisible into small "atoms," which combine to make up all things but which themselves are eternal and indivisible.

Derrida, Jacques (1930–) French philosopher and founder of the school of "deconstruction." He teaches at the Ecole Normal Superior in France, but is occasionally a visiting lecturer at American universities. He has taught at Yale, Cornell, and the University of California at Irvine.

Descartes, René (1596–1650) French philosopher who is usually considered the "father of modern philosophy." He was raised in the French aristocracy and educated at the excellent Jesuit College of La Flèche. He became skilled in the classics, law, and medicine; however, he decided that they fell far short of proper knowledge, and so he turned to modern science and mathematics. His first book was a defense of Copernicus, which he prudently did not publish. He discovered, while still a young man, the connections between algebra and geometry (which we now call "analytic geometry") and used this discovery as a model for the rest of his career. Basing the principles of philosophy and theology on a similar mathematical basis, he was able to develop a method in philosophy that could be carried through according to individual reason and no longer depended upon appeal to authorities whose insights and methods were questionable. In *Discourse on Method* (1637), he set out these basic principles, which he had already used in *Meditations on First Philosophy* (not published until 1641), to reexamine the foundations of philosophy. He sought a basic premise from which, as in a geometrical proof, he could deduce all those principles that could be known with certainty.

Dewey, John (1859–1952) American pragmatist and social critic, reformer. Author of a great many influential books on education as well as the central topics of philosophy.

Diogenes (412?–323? B.C.) Cynic philosopher who lived an extremely simple life. Offered anything he wanted by Alexander the Great, he replied, "Get out of my light."

Douglass, Frederick (1818–1895) American abolitionist and freed slave; he became one of this country's greatest speakers and writers about freedom.

Edwards, Jonathan (1703–1758) American philosopher and Calvinist theologian. President at the time of his death of what is now Princeton University.

Epicurus (342?–270 B.C.) Greek philosopher who argued that the good life was pleasure, but not just the immediate pleasure talked about by Aristippus. Some pleasures last longer than others; some have a lower price than others. Accordingly, he taught self-control and avoidance of violent pleasures, which often caused more pain than ultimate pleasure. Ultimately what was most pleasurable, according to Epicurus, was a life of peace and quiet. Today we use the word "Epicurean" to describe someone who often indulges in pleasures, particularly sophisticated pleasures (gourmet food, for example).

Fichte, Johann Gottlieb (1762–1814) German philosopher, student of Immanuel Kant, who turned Kant's "transcendental" philosophy into a practically oriented and relativistic "ethical idealism." He taught that "the kind of philosophy a man chooses depends upon the kind of man he is." One of the first German nationalists.

Fodor, Jerry (1935–) Professor of psychology, linguistics, and philosophy at MIT. One of the leading voices in the current discussion of "functionalism" in minds and computers.

Frankfurt, Harry American moral philosopher, currently teaching at Princeton University.

Frege, Gottlob (1848–1925) Brilliant logician whose work on the foundations of arithmetic inspired Bertrand Russell and Alfred North Whitehead and turned the current of logical thinking from the Mill-like empiricism that was then reigning (in Germany as well as England) to a hardheaded mathematical discipline. He is often said to have been the pioneer and innovator of modern mathematical logic. Most important, perhaps, is his *Foundations of Arithmetic* (1884).

Gadamer, Hans-Georg (1900–) Leading German promoter of hermeneutics.

Ghazali, Mohammad Al (1058–1111) Islamic philosopher and theologian, known especially for his criticisms of Aristotelianism and Avicenna. His most famous work was called *The Incoherence of the Philosophers.*

Gilligan, Carol (1936–) American developmental psychologist, best known for her work *In a Different Voice,* which proposed a theory of feminine moral development. She teaches education at Harvard University.

Goodman, Nelson (1906–) Contemporary American pragmatist who, together with W. V. O. Quine, has made pragmatism once again a dominant force in philosophy.

Hanh, Thich Nhat Vietnamese Buddhist monk, peace activist, and writer. He currently lives in France and occasionally teaches in the United States.

Hegel, Georg Wilhelm Friedrich (1770–1831) German philosopher who, during the age of Napoleon, wrote his *Phenomenology of Spirit* (1807), which was the single most powerful influence in European philosophy—after Kant's works—for the next hundred years. He argued that there were many different views of the world, that none of them should be thought to be wholly correct or incorrect in exclusion of the others, but that these various views could still be compared and evaluated according to a "dialectic," in which some views are shown to be more developed, more inclusive, and more adequate than others.

Heidegger, Martin (1889–1976) German phenomenologist and student of Edmund Husserl, whose rebellion against his teacher began the "existential" movement in phenomenology. His best-known work is *Being and Time* (1927). Although focusing on metaphysics and phenomenology, this work is also one of the first existentialist studies of "human nature."

Held, Virginia American philosopher, specializing in feminist epistemology. She currently teaches at the City University of New York Graduate Center.

Hempel, Carl Gustav (1905–) Contemporary American philosopher of science and mathematics, member of the "Vienna Circle," and one of the continuing most powerful voices of the empiricist tradition. A good collection of his essays is *Aspects of Scientific Explanation* (1965).

Heraclitus (5th century B.C.) Pre-Socratic philosopher who taught that the basic element of reality was fire and that all things are in constant flux but yet are unified by an underlying logic or *logos*.

Hobbes, Thomas (1588–1679) The author of *Leviathan* (1651) and one of England's first great modern philosophers. He is generally credited with the formulation of the theory of the "social contract" for the establishment of governments and society, and he was one of the first philosophers to base his theory of government on a conception of man prior to his "civilization," in what he called "the state of nature." This was, according to Hobbes, "solitary, poor, nasty, brutish, and short." Therefore people were motivated to become part of society for their mutual protection. Hobbes also defended a materialist conception of the universe. Even the human mind, he argued, was nothing more than "matter in motion."

d'Holbach, Baron Paul Henri (1723–1789) French philosopher and one of the leaders of the Enlightenment. An ardent materialist and atheist, he represented the most radical fringe of the brilliant free-thinkers of prerevolutionary France.

Hospers, John (1918–) Professor of philosophy at the University of Southern California, articulate follower of Ayn Rand, and one-time Libertarian candidate for President of the United States.

Hume, David (1711–1776) Often admired as the outstanding genius of British philosophy. Born in Scotland (Edinburgh), where he spent much of his life, he often traveled to London and Paris. After a vacation in France, he wrote the *Treatise of Human Nature* (1739). He achieved notoriety as well as literary fame in his lifetime, was involved in scandals and proscribed by the Church. He was refused professorships at the leading universities for his "heresies." Yet he was, by all accounts, an utterly delightful man who never lost his sense of humor. He was "the life of the party" in London,

Edinburgh, and Paris, and he has long set the standard of the ideal thinker for British philosophers. Hume's *Enquiry Concerning the Principles of Morals* (1751) created as much of a stir in the intellectual world as his *Enquiry Concerning Human Understanding* (1748). Like the latter book, the book on morality was a rewriting of his youthful *Treatise,* which never received the attention it deserved. Hume's thesis in moral philosophy was as skeptical and shocking as his thesis in epistemology: There is no knowledge of right and wrong and no rational defense of moral principles. These are based upon sentiment or feeling and, as such, cannot be defended by argument.

Husserl, Edmund (1859–1938) German-Czech philosopher and mathematician who was the founder of phenomenology, a modern form of rational intuitionism. With Gottlob Frege, he fought against the empiricist view of necessary truth defended by John Stuart Mill and developed an alternative view in which matters of necessity were not matters of ordinary experience but rather of a special kind of intuition. His best-known works are *Ideas* (Vol. 1) (1913) and *Cartesian Meditations* (1931).

Irigaray, Luce French feminist philosopher. Her work incorporates literary criticism, feminism, and philosophy. Her best known works are *Speculum of the Other Woman* and *The Sex Which Is Not One.*

James, William (1842–1910) Perhaps the greatest American philosopher (and psychologist) to this day. He developed the particularly American philosophy of pragmatism from the brilliant but obscure formulations of his colleague at Harvard, Charles Sanders Peirce, into a popular and still very powerful intellectual force. James was born in New York City and graduated from Harvard with a medical degree, but he decided to teach (at Harvard) rather than to practice medicine. His best-known work in philosophy, besides his work called *Pragmatism: A New Name for Some Old Ways of Thinking* (1907), is *The Varieties of Religious Experience* (1902). He also established himself as one of the fathers of modern psychology with his *Principles of Psychology* (1890).

Kant, Immanuel (1724–1804) German philosopher, probably the greatest philosopher since Plato and Aristotle, who lived his entire life in a small town in East Prussia (Königsburg). He was a professor at the university there for over thirty years; he never married, and his neighbors said that his habits were so regular that they could set their watches by him. (A later German poet said, "It is hard to write about Kant's life, for he had no life.") Yet, from a safe distance, he was one of the most persistent defenders of the French Revolution and, in philosophy, created no less a revolution himself. His philosophical system, embodied in three huge volumes called *Critique of Pure Reason* (1781), *Critique of Practical Reason* (1788), and *Critique of Judgment* (1790), changed the thinking of philosophers as much as the revolution changed France. His central thesis was the defense of what he called "synthetic *a priori*" judgments (and their moral and religious equivalents) by showing their necessity for all human experience. In this way, he escaped from Hume's skepticism and avoided the dead-end intuitionism of his rational predecessors.

Keller, Evelyn Fox An American scientist and philosopher, Keller writes about the consequences of feminism on the philosophy of science.

Kierkegaard, Søren (1813–1855) Danish philosopher and theologian who is generally recognized as the father of existentialism and the founder of many varieties of contemporary religious irrationalism. Kierkegaard dedicated himself to religious writing after a short and not altogether successful attempt at the wild life and a brief engagement, which he broke off in order to devote himself to his work. The basic tenet of Kierkegaard's philosophy was the need for each individual to choose his own way of life. Christianity, as one of the possible choices, could not be considered anything other than just such a choice, a passionate choice, which had nothing to do with doctrines, churches, social groups, and ceremonies.

King, Martin Luther, Jr. (1929–1968) American Baptist minister, civil rights leader, and Nobel Prize Laureate. He was assassinated in 1968.

Leibniz, Gottfried Wilhelm von (1646–1716) Leibniz has been called "the last of the universal geniuses." He was one of the inventors of the calculus, the father of modern formal linguistics, the inventor of a primitive computer, a military strategist (who may have influenced Napoleon), a physicist who in his own time was thought to be the rival of Newton, and most of all a great philosopher. He grew up in Leipzig but traveled considerably (to Paris and Amsterdam and all over Germany). He spoke personally with most of the great philosophers of his time and debated with them constantly. His metaphysics is a curious combination of traditional theology and a radical alternative to the physical doctrines of Newton, to whose philosophy he had once been attracted but which he had given up as "absurd." His short *Monadology* (1714) is a summary of his mature metaphysical theories.

Lloyd, Genevieve Feminist philosopher, currently at the University of New South Wales in Australia.

Locke, John (1632–1704) Spent his early life in the English countryside, including many years at Oxford where he taught philosophy and the classics until he earned a medical degree and turned to medicine. Much of Locke's mature life, however, was spent in politics, and he joined a more or less revolutionary group that was fighting for the overthrow of the government. He was forced to flee England in 1683, and he lived in Holland until the Glorious Revolution of 1688. For his part in the struggle, he received a government position, although he spent most of his time writing his two *Treatises on Government* (1689) to justify the revolution and its political principles and defending his *Essay Concerning Human Understanding* (1690), which he had written while in exile. He is generally credited as not only the founder of British empiricism but the father of modern political liberalism as well.

Logical positivism (from roughly 1929 until the Nazis proscribed it in 1938) A powerful school of philosophy that originated in Vienna with a group of scientists and philosophers of anti-Nazi, liberal, antimetaphysical, and scientific persuasion—the "Vienna Circle." Against the horrendous mythologies and superstitions propagandized by the Nazis, using the old metaphysics as a tool, these philosophers used the clarity of science to dispel nonsense and to defend common sense. Accordingly, the group was broken by the Nazis, and most of its members, except for Moritz Schlick, who was shot by an insane student, left for America, England, and Holland. The main thrust of logical positivism is its total rejection of metaphysics in favor of a strong emphasis on science and verifiability through experience. The method of the logical positivists, accordingly, is strongly empiricist (they actually called themselves "logical empiricists") and has much in common with the method of Hume, according to which all knowledge is to be defended either as a matter of empirical fact to be verified (that is, confirmed) through experience or as a matter of logic and language to be demonstrated through analysis. Arithmetic and geometry, for the logical positivists, consist of analytic truths.

Mackinnon, Catherine American professor of law, known particularly for her writings on philosophy of law and feminism.

Malcolm X (1925–1965) Outspoken leader of the black nationalist movement in this country. He was assassinated in 1965, upon his return from a trip to the Middle East.

Marcuse, Herbert Twentieth-century philosopher of the "Frankfurt School," which sought inter-disciplinary Marxist social criticism. He emigrated to America during WWII, and taught during his later years at the University of California at LaJolla.

Marx, Karl (1818–1883) German philosopher and social theorist who formulated the philosophical basis for one of the most cataclysmic political ideologies of the twentieth century. He received a doctorate in philosophy but could not teach in Germany because of his radical views. He spent most of his life abroad, in Paris, Brussels, and London, developing his theories and writing for various journals and newspapers (including the *New York Herald Tribune*). His savage attacks on established beliefs and advocacy of revolution were constant throughout his life and forced him into exile. As a young man he wrote a devastating critique of G. W. F. Hegel, whom he had studied and followed as a young student, and whose concept of "dialectic" he used in developing a powerful social-political philosophy of class conflict and economic determination.

Mead, Margaret (1901–1978) American anthropologist and author. Her two most famous works are *Coming of Age in Samoa* and *Sex and Temperament in Three Primitive Societies*.

Merleau-Ponty, Maurice (1908–1961) French "existentialist," the most serious of the existential phenomenologists who followed Husserl in France. His most important work is the *Phenomenology of Perception* (1945). He is also well known for his political writings and his art criticism. In his early *Structure of Behavior* (1942), he argued that the human body cannot be considered merely another "fragment of matter," in other words, merely a body, but must be viewed as the center of our experience.

Michaels, Meredith (1950–   ) American philosopher, Mount Holyoke College.

Mill, John Stuart (1806–1873) Son of James Mill, also a philosopher, and one of the documented geniuses of modern history. His intellectual feats by the age of ten would have been to the credit of most scholars at the age of sixty. He pushed himself so hard, however, that he suffered a nervous breakdown in 1826, at the age of twenty, and turned his attention from the "hard" sciences to poetry and political reform. He is best known for his moral and political writings, particularly *On Liberty* (1859) and *Utilitarianism* (1861). His logic and epistemology are the best to be found in the British empiricist tradition of the nineteenth century. His views on mathematics, for example, became one of those positions that every writer on the subject had either to accept or to fight forcefully.

Nagarjuna (2nd century A.D.) Late ancient Indian skeptic, he claimed that knowledge of causation and substance was impossible.

Nagel, Thomas (1937–   ) American philosopher at New York University, and a broadranging thinker who has written on a spectrum of topics from sex and death to political philosophy and racism in South Africa. He is the author of *Mortal Questions* and *The View from Nowhere.*

Nietzsche, Friedrich (1844–1900) German philosopher who declared himself the archenemy of traditional morality and Christianity and spent much of his life writing polemics against them. His most sustained and vicious attack (partly included in the text) is in one of his last books, *Antichrist* (1888). Although generally known as an immoralist (a name he chose for himself), Nietzsche's moral philosophy is actually an attack on one conception of morality in order to replace it with another. The morality he attacked was the morality of traditional Christianity as defined by Kant. The morality he sought to defend was the ancient morality of personal excellence, as defined by Aristotle. He referred to the first as "slave morality," suggesting that it was suitable only for the weak and servile, and to the latter as "master morality," suggesting that it was the morality of the strong and independent few.

Nishitani, Keiji (1900–   ) Japanese philosopher, a representative of the "Kyoto School," founded by Kitaro Nishida (1870–1945). Their work was devoted to incorporating Western thought, especially existentialism, with Buddhism.

Nozick, Robert (1938–   ) American philosopher at Harvard University; author of an influential book on political philosophy, *Anarchy, State and Utopia* and *Philosophical Explanations.*

Oakeshott, Michael (1901–1990) British conservative political philosopher; his works include *A Guide to the Classics* (1936), *Rationalism in Politics, and Other Essays* (1962), and *On Human Conduct* (1975).

Ortega y Gasset, José (1883–1955) Spanish philosopher and author of the controversial book *The Revolt of the Masses.* He also wrote widely on metaphysics and aesthetics, and published a book on the subject of romantic love.

Ortner, Sherry American anthropologist, best known for her work in cross-cultural gender distinctions.

Parmenides (5th century B.C.) Pre-Socratic philosopher who taught that reality was eternal and unchanging and that therefore we could not know it as such.

Pascal, Blaise (1623–1662) French scientist and philosopher with mildly mystical tendencies. He stressed confidence in the "heart" rather than in reason, and many of his best-known writings are concerned with the problems of religious faith. However, he was also one of the inventors of the computer and a famous mathematician. His best-known work is *Pensées* ("Thoughts") (1669).

Plato (427–347 B.C.) Plato was born into a family of wealth and political power. But in Athens he fell under the influence of Socrates and turned his talents to philosophy. He combined his heritage with his interests in his famous conception of the "philosopher-king," the ideal wise ruler, who certainly did not exist in Athens. He was disillusioned by Socrates' death and devoted his life to continuing his work. Plato set up the Academy for this purpose and spent the rest of his life teaching there. He first set down his reminiscences of Socrates' life and death, and, using the dialogue form, with Socrates as his mouthpiece, he extended Socrates' thought into entirely new areas, notably, metaphysics and the theory of knowledge. Plato incorporated a theory of morality into his metaphysics and politics, particularly in *The Republic*. Like all Greeks, he saw ethics as part of politics and the good life for the individual in terms of the strength and harmony of the society. In *The Republic*, accordingly, Socrates argues against the various views of selfishness and hedonism that would interfere with such a conception. Virtue, he argues, is the harmony of the individual soul as well as the harmony of the individual within the society. It is still difficult, since we have nothing from Socrates himself, to know how much is original Plato and how much is transcribed Socrates.

Pythagoras (6th–5th century B.C.) The religious mystic who believed that numbers were the essence of all things. One of the Pre-Socratics.

Quine, Willard Van Orman (1908–   ) Contemporary American pragmatist whose early attacks on logical positivism and its basic tenets have been responsible for several of the dominant concerns of recent American philosophy. His attack on Immanuel Kant's distinction between "analytic" and "synthetic" sentences, for example, along with the more traditional distinction between necessity and contingency, have thrown the entire philosophical enterprise into considerable turmoil. According to Quine, there are no indubitably "necessary" statements or beliefs, just those that happen, at a particular point in our knowledge and interests, to hold a relatively protected place in the overall system of our beliefs for ostensibly practical reasons. He is the author of *Word and Object* (1960) and many other works in logic and the philosophy of language.

Rawls, John (1921–   ) Author of *A Theory of Justice* (1971) and professor of philosophy at Harvard University.

Rorty, Richard American philosopher, currently teaching at the University of Virginia, Charlottesville.

Rousseau, Jean-Jacques (1712–1778) Stormy Enlightenment philosopher who fought with most of his peers (including David Hume) and developed a dramatic conception of "natural morality," which he contrasted to what he saw as the fraud and hypocrisy of contemporary civilized man. He formulated a picture of man in "the state of nature," before civilization, in which his "natural goodness" was not yet "corrupted" by society. The key to this idea was his conception of moral sentiment, which was innate in all people and not learned from society. His writings were condemned, and he spent much of his life running from the police. He died in total poverty, but only a few years after his death his political ideas became the central ideology of the French Revolution.

Rushd, Ibn (Averroes) (1126–1198) Spanish Islamic theologian, generally considered to be the last Islamic Aristotelian.

Russell, Bertrand (1872–1970) One of the greatest philosophers of our century. As a young man, he wrote, with Alfred North Whitehead, a book called *Principia Mathematica* (1903), which set the stage for modern logic and foundations of mathematics and gave logic a central role as a philosophical tool. He wrote an enormous number of philosophical books on virtually every topic, including several notorious polemics in favor of what was branded "free love" and atheism. He was a persistent and harsh critic of religion in general and Christianity in particular, as a source of what he called superstition and legitimized murder. Russell was a committed pacifist during World War I and wrote at least one of his most famous books while sitting in prison for his antiwar activities. Like his famous predecessor, David Hume (with whom he has much in common), Russell was too controversial for most universities, and a famous court case prevented him from teaching at the City College of New York. He won the Nobel prize in 1950.

Ryle, Gilbert (1900–1978) Oxford "ordinary-language" philosopher whose book *The Concept of Mind* (1949) set the stage for several decades of debate over his quasi-behavioristic resolution of the mind–body problem. His main thesis is that the distinction between mind and body rests on what he calls a "category mistake," that is, wrongly believing something to be one kind of thing when it is really another. In particular, it has been thought that mental events were events on a par with, but wholly different from, bodily events. Instead, Ryle argues, to talk about mind is to talk about behavioral dispositions and abilities. (To say that a person *wants* to do something is to say that he *would* do that if given the opportunity.)

Sadra, Mulla (Sadr al-Din Shirazi) (157?–1641) Persian Islamic Shiite theologian, best known for his integration of mysticism and Aristotelianism.

Sartre, Jean-Paul (1905–1980) Contemporary French philosopher who began as a literary writer and a phenomenologist, in the style of Edmund Husserl, but who converted that austere philosophy to his own radical ends. He is generally regarded as the main proponent of the philosophy of "existentialism." Sartre's existentialism is a moral philosophy as well as a philosophy of freedom. It denies that there is any such thing as "human nature" and therefore insists that "man makes himself." That is, through our various choices and moral commitments we define what we want humanity to be. According to Sartre, we do not simply find moral principles upon which we should act, but rather we *choose* those moral principles *through our acting.* Thus Sarte's moral philosophy places most of its emphasis on action and minimizes the importance of moral deliberation and all that sort of moralizing in which we simply talk about what is good rather than actually doing it. For Sartre, it is action that is ultimately good, rather than simply a "good will" as in Kant. In his novels and plays, Sartre's characters are always torn by alternative identities, suffering just because they cannot make up their minds. In his greatest work, *Being and Nothingness* (1943), Sartre argues that everyone "is who he is not, and is not who he is," by which he means (in a paradoxical phrase) that our identity is never simply the totality of facts ("facticity") that are true of us; we always identify ourselves with our plans and intentions for the future (our "transcendence") as well. And this means that so long as we are alive, we have no fixed "identity" at all.

Schiller, Friedrich (1759–1805) German playwright and philosopher. Schiller followed Kant in philosophy and Goethe in literature, combining the influence of the two in his *Letters on the Aesthetic Education of Mankind.*

Schopenhauer, Arthur (1788–1860) German philosopher; famous pessimist and man of letters. His main work, *The World as Will and Idea,* was an elaboration on Kant's philosophy. Yet instead of Kant's rationality, irrationality of the will became the centerpiece of Schopenhauer's philosophy. The book was first published in 1819, but did not become popular and earn its author the fame he much desired until the second half of the nineteenth century.

Searle, John (1932–   ) American philosopher at the University of California, Berkeley; the best-known proponent of "speech–act theory" in the philosophy of language and the author of many controversial books and articles, including a now-raging attack on the ambitions of cognitive science and computer models of the mind.

Shaffer, Jerome (1929–   ) American philosopher, presently teaching at the University of Connecticut. One of the best-known critics of the now influential "identity theory" of mind and body.

Shaftsbury, Earl of (1671–1713) Scottish "moral sentiment" theorist; defended and studied the role of such emotions as sympathy and compassion in moral life.

Smart, J. J. C. (1920–   ) Australian philosopher late of the Australian National University in Canberra. Classic defender of the mind–body "identity theory."

Socrates (470–399 B.C.) Athenian philosopher with a gift for rhetoric and debating. He had a notoriously poor marriage, had several children, and lived in poverty most of his life. Socrates began his studies in the physical sciences but soon turned to the study of human nature, morality, and politics. He became famous debating with the many "sophists" who wandered about giving practical training in argument and persuasion (the ancient equivalent of law school). Socrates found their general skepticism intolerable and urged a return to the absolute ideals of wisdom, virtue, justice, and the good life. In his philosophy, he approached these questions as matters of finding the exact definitions of these concepts in order to clarify our pursuit of them. In doing so, he developed a brilliant technique of dialogue or "dialectic" in which he would discover these definitions by constant debating, forcing his opponents or students to advance varying theories, which he in turn would knock down. In the process, the correct definition would slowly emerge. In his not always tactful search for truth, however, Socrates made many enemies, who eventually had him condemned to death, a cruel and unfair verdict he accepted with dignity.

Spinoza, Benedictus de (1632–1677) Spinoza was born Baruch ben Michael, the son of Jewish refugees from the Spanish Inquisition. He was born and grew up in Amsterdam, a relative haven of toleration in a world still dangerous because of religious hatreds. He studied to be a rabbi, making himself familiar with Christian theology as well. He was always a recluse and was later ostracized by his fellow Jews for his heretical beliefs, wandering about the country making a living by grinding lenses. His best-known book is *Ethics* (1677); it is a radical reinterpretation of God as identical to the universe (pantheism) and a protracted argument concerning the uselessness of human struggle in the face of a thoroughly determined universe.

Stoics (4th century B.C., with revisions until the 1st century A.D.) An ancient movement in philosophy that taught self-control and minimized passion, with a willingness to endure whatever fate has in store. Some believers were Zeno of Citium in Greece (not the same as Zeno of the paradoxes), Seneca, and Marcus Aurelius in Rome.

Strawson, Peter Frederick (1919–) Contemporary Oxford philosopher whose book *Individuals* (1959) was responsible for reintroducing systematic metaphysics into current British philosophy. He called his metaphysics "descriptive," however, by which he meant to insist that it was only to be construed as an analysis and description of "our conceptual framework," not of "reality-in-itself." In the third chapter of that book, Strawson argues the thesis that the distinction between mind and body can be made only after we have recognized the primary category of "persons." Persons are not conglomerates of minds and bodies, and we can talk of minds and bodies only because we first have a way of specifying the different attributes of a person.

Swoyer, Chris (1949–) American philosopher, Oklahoma University.

Tao Te Ching Poets (including Lao Tsu) (5th century B.C.) Ancient Chinese mystics whose doctrine was that the "Tao" or "Way" was the ineffable underpinning of existence.

Tarski, Alfred (1902–) American logician who formulated the still controversial "semantic theory of truth" in 1944.

Thales (6th century B.C.) The first known Greek philosopher, who taught that all things were ultimately composed of water.

Thoreau, Henry David (1817–1862) American essayist, naturalist, and philosopher; a champion of individualism. His most famous work was *Walden*.

Tillich, Paul (1886–1965) German-born philosopher who spent many of his later years teaching in the United States. He is among the best known of those modern theologians who, like the Romantics of the last century, place the emphasis on emotion and "concern" rather than on reason in religion. In Tillich's theology, God is no longer the transcendent judge of the scriptures but simply the symbol of our "ultimate concern." He is the author of *Systematic Theology* (1953–63), *The Dynamics of Faith* (1957), and *The Courage to Be* (1952).

The Upanishads (800–500 B.C.) The ancient Indian "secret doctrines" which form part of the Veda, in turn part of the scripture of Hinduism and Buddhism.

Watson, John (1878–1958) American psychologist generally recognized as the founder of behaviorism. He attacked the notion of "consciousness" as a remnant of the age-old religious belief in the "soul" and urged that we give up what he called such "magical" nonsense in favor of a purely scientific view, which allows us to talk sensibly only about observables, in other words, human behavior rather than the human "mind." He is the author of *Behaviorism* (1924).

Whitehead, Alfred North (1861–1947) Famous logician who, together with Bertrand Russell, established the basis of modern logic and who late in life turned to metaphysics. In place of the concept of substance, however, he argued for a concept of process, a universe in constant evolutionary change.

Williamson, Judith (1954–   ) British philosopher of film and popular culture; her most recent book is *Consuming Passions.*

Wittgenstein, Ludwig (1889–1951) Austrian-born philosopher who became the single most powerful influence on twentieth-century "analytic" philosophy. He entered philosophy as an engineer, studied with Bertrand Russell, and wrote the book *Tractatus Logico-Philosophicus* (1922), which inspired logical positivism. Giving up philosophy for a number of years and changing his mind about his arguments in the *Tractatus,* he returned to philosophy at Cambridge and developed that "therapeutic" brand of philosophy that became known as "ordinary-language" philosophy. In his later works, culminating in his *Philosophical Investigations* (1953, published posthumously), Wittgenstein initiated a devastating attack on Cartesian dualism and the problems it carried with it. His so-called "private language argument," in fact culled from a series of aphorisms, argues that even if there were such "private" occurrences as mental events, we should have no way of talking about them and no way of knowing about them, even in our own case. But although he is often described as a "behaviorist," Wittgenstein is better described as one of those philosophers who was groping for an entirely new conception of a "person" or at least attempting to reject all the old ones.

Zarathustra (Zoroaster) (6th century B.C.) Ancient Persian reformer and prophet of the first monotheistic religion, Zoroastrianism.

Zeno of Elea (5th century B.C.) Pre-Socratic philosopher and student of Parmenides who taught that motion was unreal and developed a series of brilliant paradoxes in order to prove it.

INDEX

931

PERMISSIONS and ACKNOWLEDGMENTS

American Mathematical Monthly For the excerpt from "On the Nature of Mathematical Truth," by C. G. Hempel, from *American Mathematical Monthly*, LII, 1945. Reprinted by permission of The Mathematical Association of America.

Airmont Publishing Company For excerpt from *The Prince*, by Niccolo Machiavelli, translated by Christian E. Detmold. Reprinted by permission of the publisher.

Bantam Books, Inc. For the excerpt from *The Clouds*, by Aristophanes, in *The Complete Plays of Aristophanes*, edited by Moses Hadas, copyright © 1962 by Bantam Books, Inc. Reprinted by permission of Bantam Books, Inc. For the excerpts from *The Brothers Karamazov*, by Fyodor Dostoyevski, translated by Andrew R. MacAndrew. English language translation copyright © 1970 by Bantam Books, Inc. Reprinted by permission of Bantam Books, a division of Bantam, Doubleday, Dell Publishing Group, Inc.

Basic Books, Inc. For the excerpts from *Anarchy, State, and Utopia*, by Robert Nozick. Copyright © 1974 by Basic Books, Inc. Reprinted by permission of publisher.

The Bobbs-Merrill Company, Inc. For the excerpts from *Proglomena to Any Future Metaphysics*, by Immanuel Kant, edited by Lewis White Beck. Copyright © 1950 by The Liberal Arts Press, Inc. Reprinted by permission of the publisher. For the excerpts from *Reason in History*, by G. W. F. Hegel, translated by Robert S. Hartman. Copyright © 1953 by The Liberal Arts Press, Inc. Reprinted by permission of the publisher. For the excerpts from the *Critique of Practical Reason and Other Writings on Moral Philosophy*, by Immanuel Kant, translated by Lewis White Beck. Copyright © 1949 by University of Chicago Press. Reprinted by permission of The Bobbs-Merrill Company, Inc. For the excerpt from *On Free Choice of the Will*, by St. Augustine, translated by Anna S. Benjamin and L. H. Hackstaff. Reprinted by permission of The Bobbs-Merrill Company, Inc. For the excerpt from

excerpt from Paul Woodruff's translation of *Ion*, by Plato. Reprinted by permission of the publisher.

Haigh and Hochland Ltd. For the excerpt "Husserl's Syllabus for the Paris Lectures on 'Introduction to Transcendental Phenomenology,'" *Journal of the British Society for Phenomenology* 7 (1976). Reprinted in F. Elliston and M. McCormick, eds., *Husserl: Shorter Works.* University of Notre Dame Press. Reprinted by permission of Haigh and Hochland Ltd.

Hamish Hamilton Ltd. For the excerpt from *No Exit and Other Plays*, by Jean-Paul Sartre, translated by Stuart Gilbert. Copyright 1961 by Stuart Gilbert. Reprinted by permission of Alfred A. Knopf, Inc. and Hamish Hamilton Ltd.

HarperCollins Publishers For the excerpts from "The Dilemma of Negro Americans," from *Where Do We Go From Here? Chaos or Community*, by Martin Luther King, Jr. Reprinted by permission of HarperCollins Publishers. For the excerpts from "Why Are There No Great Women Artists," from *Women, Art and Power and Other Essays*, by Linda Nochlin. Reprinted by permission of HarperCollins Publishers.

Harvard University Press For the excerpts from *Metaphysics*, by Aristotle, translated by Hugh Tredennick. Copyright © 1935 by Harvard University Press. Reproduced by permission of the publisher. For the excerpt from *De Anima*, by Aristotle, translated by Hett. Copyright 1936 by Harvard University Press. Reprinted by permission of the publisher. For the excerpt from *In a Different Voice*, by Carol Gilligan, Cambridge, Mass.: Harvard University Press. Copyright © 1982 by Carol Gilligan. Reprinted by permission of publisher.

Virginia Held For excerpt from "Feminism and Epistemology: Recent Work on the Connection Between Gender and Knowledge," in *Philosophy and Public Affairs* 14 (1985). Reprinted by permission of the author.

Hutchinson Publishing Group Ltd. For the excerpts from *The Concept of Mind*, by Gilbert Ryle.

Kluwer Academic Publishers For the excerpts from *The 1929 Paris Lectures*, by Edmund Husserl. Reprinted by permission of the publisher.

Les Editions Nagel Paris For excerpts from *Existentialism as a Humanism*, by Jean-Paul Sartre, translated by P. Mairet, N. Y. Philosophical Library, 1949. Reproduced by permission of Les Editions Nagel Paris.

Macmillan Publishing Co., Inc. For excerpts from *Ideas*, by Edmund Husserl, translated by W. R. Boyce-Gibson. Reprinted by permission of the publisher.

McGraw-Hill, Inc. For excerpts from "Marx's Critique of Hegel's Philosophy of Right," from *Karl Marx: Early Writings (1963)*. Reproduced with the permission of the publisher.

Metaphilosophy For excerpts from "The Man of Reason," by Genevieve Lloyd, in *Metaphilosophy*, No. 10, January 1979. Reprinted by permission of the publisher.

The MIT Press For the excerpts from *Matter and Consciousness*, by Paul M. Churchland. Copyright © 1988 by The MIT Press. Reprinted by permission of the publisher.

New York University Press For excerpt from *Determinism and Freedom in the Age of Modern Science*, edited by Sidney Hook. © 1958 by New York University. Reprinted by permission of New York University Press.

W. W. Norton & Company Inc. For the excerpt from *The Future of an Illusion*, by Sigmund Freud, translated from the German and edited by James Strachey. Copyright © 1961 by James Strachey. Reprinted by permission of the publisher. For the excerpt from *New Introductory Lectures on Psychoanalysis*, by Sigmund Freud, translated and edited by James Strachey. Copyright © by James Strachey, 1964, 1965. Reprinted by permission of the publisher.

Open Court Publishing Company For the excerpt from *New Essays Concerning Human Understanding*, by Gottfried Leibniz, translated by A. G. Langley. Reprinted by permission of publisher.

Oxford University Press For the excerpts from *Inquiries into Truth and Interpretation*, by Donald Davidson. Copyright © 1984 by Donald Davidson. Reprinted by permission of the publisher. For the excerpts from *The Phenomenology of Spirit*, by Georg Hegel, translated by A. V. Miller. Copyright © 1977 Oxford University Press. Reprinted by permission of the publisher. For the excerpt from *The Reconstruction of Thought*, by Sir Mohammad Iqbal. Copyright © 1934 by Oxford University Press. Reprinted by permission of the publisher.

Parallax Press Excerpt from *Present Moment, Wonderful Moment*, by Thich Nhat Hanh, Parallax Press, Berkeley, California, 1990.

Penguin Books Ltd. For the excerpts from St. Augustine, *Confessions*, pp. 136–149, translated by R. S. Pine-Coffin (Penguin Classics, 1961). Copyright © 1961 R. S. Pine-Coffin. Reprinted by permission of Penguin Books Ltd. For the excerpt from *Steppenwolf*, by Hermann Hesse, translated by Basil Creighton. Reprinted by permission of the publisher.

Penn State University Press For the excerpt from *A Treasury of Mahayana Sutras,* edited by Garma C. C. Chana (University Park: The Pennsylvania State University Press, 1983). Copyright by Penn State University. Reproduced by permission of the publisher.

Philosophical Review For the excerpt from "Sensations and Brain Processes," by J. J. C. Smart, in *Philosophical Review,* 68 (1959), pp. 141–156. Reprinted by permission of the author.

Philosophy and Phenomenological Research For the excerpts from "The Semantic Theory of Truth," by Alfred Tarski, in *Philosophy and Phenomenological Research,* Vol. IV, No. 3 (March 1944). Reprinted by permission of the publisher.

Prentice Hall, Inc. For the excerpt from *Philosophy of Mind,* by Jerome A. Shaffer. Copyright © 1968 by Prentice Hall, Inc. Reprinted by permission of Prentice Hall, Inc., Englewood Cliffs, New Jersey.

Princeton University Press For the excerpt from *The Wisdom of the Throne: An Introduction to the Philosophy of Mulla Sadra,* by Mulla Sadra, translated by James Morris Winston. Copyright © 1981 by Princeton University Press. Reprinted by permission of the publisher. For the excerpts from *Philosophical Fragments,* by Søren Kierkegaard, translated by David Swenson. Copyright © 1936, 1962 by Princeton University Press. Reprinted by permission of the publisher. For the excerpts from *The Dehumanization of Art,* by Jose Ortega y Gasset. Copyright © 1948 by Princeton University Press. Reprinted by permission of the publisher.

Rowman and Littlefield For the excerpt from *Feminism and Philosophy* (edited by Mary Vetterling-Braggin, Fredrick A. Elliston, and Jane English), "Androgyny as an Ideal for Human Development," by Ann Ferguson, Rowman & Littlefield Publishers, Inc., 1977, Lanham, Maryland. Reprinted by permission of the publisher.

Scientific American For the excerpts from the "The Mind-Body Problem," by Jerry Fodor. Copyright © 1981 by Scientific American, Inc. All rights reserved. Reprinted by permission of *Scientific American.*

Charlotte Sheedy Literary Agency For excerpt from "Is There a Feminist Aesthetic?" by Marilyn French, in *Hypatia.* Copyright © 1990 by Marilyn French. Reprinted by permission of the Charlotte Sheedy Literary Agency, Inc.

B. F. Skinner For the excerpt from "Freedom and the Control of Men," by B.F. Skinner, in *The American Scholar,* 1955–56. Reprinted by permission of the author.